THE ENGLISH AND SCOTTISH
POPULAR BALLADS

THE
ENGLISH AND SCOTTISH
POPULAR BALLADS

EDITED BY

FRANCIS JAMES CHILD

IN FIVE VOLUMES

VOLUME IV

NEW YORK
DOVER PUBLICATIONS, INC.

This Dover edition, first published in 1965, is an unabridged and unaltered republication of the work originally published by Houghton, Mifflin and Company, as follows:

Vol. I—Part I, 1882; Part II, 1884
Vol. II—Part III, 1885; Part IV, 1886
Vol. III—Part V, 1888; Part VI, 1889
Vol. IV—Part VII, 1890; Part VIII, 1892
Vol. V—Part IX, 1894; Part X, 1898.

This edition also contains as an appendix to Part X an essay by Walter Morris Hart entitled "Professor Child and the Ballad," reprinted *in toto* from Vol. XXI, No. 4, 1906 [New Series Vol. XIV, No. 4] of the *Publications of the Modern Language Association of America*.

International Standard Book Number: 0-486-21412-5
Library of Congress Catalog Card Number: 65-24347

Manufactured in the United States of America

Dover Publications, Inc.
180 Varick Street
New York, N.Y. 10014

ADVERTISEMENT TO PART VII

NUMBERS 189–225

I WOULD acknowledge with particular gratitude the liberality of the HON. MRS MAX-WELL-SCOTT in allowing the examination and use of the rich store of ballads accumulated at Abbotsford by her immortal ancestor; and also that of LORD ROSEBERY in sending to Edinburgh for inspection the collection of rare Scottish broadsides formed by the late David Laing, and permitting me to print several articles.

The REV. S. BARING-GOULD has done me the great favor of furnishing me with copies of traditional ballads and songs taken down by him in the West of England.

I am much indebted to the REV. W. FORBES-LEITH for his good offices, and to MR MAC-MATH, as I have been all along, for help of every description.

F. J. C.

OCTOBER, 1890.

ADVERTISEMENT TO PART VIII

NUMBERS 226–265

———

A CONSIDERABLE portion of this eighth number is devoted to texts from Abbotsford. Many of these were used by Sir WALTER SCOTT in the compilation of the Minstrelsy of the Scottish Border; many, again, not less important than the others, did not find a place in that collection. They are now printed either absolutely for the first time, or for the first time without variation from the form in which they were written. All of them, and others which were obtained in season for the Seventh Part, were transcribed with the most conscientious and vigilant care by Mr MACMATH, who has also identified the handwriting, has searched the numerous volumes of letters addressed to Sir WALTER SCOTT for information relating to the contributors and for dates, and has examined the humbler editions of printed ballads in the Abbotsford library; this without remitting other help.

Very cordial thanks are offered, for texts or information, or for both, to the Rev. S. BARING-GOULD, the Rev. W. FORBES-LEITH, Mr ANDREW LANG, Dr GEORGE BIRKBECK HILL, Mr P. Z. ROUND, Dr F. J. FURNIVALL, Mr JAMES BARCLAY MURDOCH, Dr GIUSEPPE PITRÈ, of Palermo, Mr WILLIAM WALKER, of Aberdeen, Mr DAVID MACRITCHIE, of Edinburgh, Mr JAMES GIBB, of Joppa, Mr JAMES RAINE, of York, Rev. WILLIAM LESLIE CHRISTIE, of London, Mrs MARY THOMSON, of Fochabers, and Mr GEORGE M. RICHARDSON, late of Harvard College; for notes on Slavic popular literature, to Mr JOHN KARŁOWICZ, of Warsaw, and Professor WILHELM WOLLNER; and for miscellaneous notes, to my colleague, Professor G. L. KITTREDGE.

So far as can be foreseen, one part more will bring this book to a close; it is therefore timely to say again that I shall be glad of any kind of assistance that will make it less imperfect, whether in the way of supplying omissions or of correcting errors, great or small.

F. J. C.

FEBRUARY, 1892.

CONTENTS OF VOLUME IV

HOBIE NOBLE

a. Caw's Poetical Museum, p. 193.   b. 'Hobie Noble,' Percy Papers.

SCOTT'S MINSTRELSY, I, 164, 1802, II, 90, 1833. The source is not mentioned, but was undoubtedly Caw's Museum, though there are variations of text, attributable to the editor. A copy in the Campbell MSS, I, 230, is again from the Museum, with several corrections, two of which are also found in Scott. Caw received the ballad, says Sir Walter, from John Elliot of Reidheugh. b seems to have been sent Percy (with 'Dick o the Cow') by Roger Halt, in 1775.

Hobie Noble, though banished from Bewcastle for his irregularities, will always command the hearty liking of those who live too late to suffer from them, on account of his gallant bearing in the rescue of Jock o the Side. See especially No 187, A, of which Hobie is the hero. All that we know of him is so much as we are told in that ballad and in this. He attached himself, after his expulsion from England, to the laird of Mangerton, who gives him the praise ' Thy coat is blue, thou has been true.'

Sim o the Mains, an Armstrong of the Whithaugh branch (the most important after that of Mangerton), undertakes to betray Hobie to the English land-sergeant. A tryst is set at Kershope-foot, the junction of that stream with the Liddel; and Hobie, who lives a little way up the Liddel, rides eagerly down the water to keep it. He meets five men, who ask him to join them in a raid into England. Hobie dares not go by day; the land-sergeant is at feud with him on account of a brother's death, in which Hobie must have had a hand, and ' the great earl of Whitfield' has suffered from his depredations;* but he will be their guide if they will wait till night. He takes them to the Foulbogshiel, where they alight, and word is sent by Sim to the land-sergeant at Askerton, his adversary's residence; the land-sergeant orders the men of the neighborhood to meet him at daybreak. Hobie has a bad dream, wakes his comrades in alarm, and sets out to guide them across the Waste; but the sergeant's force come before him, and Sim behind; his sword breaks; he is bound with his own bow-string and taken to Carlisle. As he goes up the quarter called the Rickergate, the wives say one to the other, That's the man that loosed Jock o the Side! They offer him bread and beer, and urge him to confess stealing "my lord's" horses; he swears a great oath that he never had beast of my lord's. He is to die the next day, and says his farewell to Mangerton; he would rather be called 'Hobie Noble' and be hanged in Carlisle, than be called 'Traitor Mains' and eat and drink.

Mr R. B. Armstrong informs me that he has found no notice of Hobie Noble except that Hobbe Noble, with eight others, "lived within the Nyxons, near to Bewcastle."

1569. " Lancy Armistrang of Quhithauch obliged him . . . for Sym Armistrang of the Mains and the rest of the Armistrangis of

---

* The brother is Peter o Whitfield. ' Jock o the Side,' **A**, begins, ' Peeter a Whifeild *he* hath slaine, and John a Side he is tane.' ' The great Earl of Whitfield,' 10³, seemed to Scott a corruption, and he suggested ' the great Ralph ' Whitfield; but Surtees gave him information (which has not transpired) that led him to think that the reading 'Earl' might be right. Whitfield, in Northumberland, is a few miles southwest of Hexham, and about twenty-five, in a straight line, from Kershope, or the border.

his gang. Syme of the Mains was lodged in Wester Wemys." (Register of the Privy Council of Scotland.)

4. The Mains was a place a very little to the east of Castleton, on the opposite, or north, side of the Liddel. 13–17. Askerton is in the Waste of Bewcastle, "about seventeen miles" northeast of Carlisle. "Willeva and Spear-Edom [otherwise Spade-Adam] are small districts in Bewcastle dale, through which also the Hartlie-burn takes its course. Conscowthart-Green and Rodric-haugh and the Foulbogshiel are the names of places in the same wilds, through which the Scottish plunderers generally made their raids upon England." (Scott.)

Sim o the Mains fled into England from the resentment of his chief, but was himself executed at Carlisle about two months after Hobie's death. "Such is at least the tradition of Liddesdale," says Scott. This is of course, notwithstanding the precision of the interval of two months, what Lord Bacon calls "an imagination as one would"; an appendage of a later generation, in the interest of poetical justice.

---

1 FOUL fa the breast first treason bred in!
   That Liddisdale may safely say,
For in it there was baith meat and drink,
   And corn unto our geldings gay.
      Fala la diddle, etc.

2 We were stout-hearted men and true,
   As England it did often say;
But now we may turn our backs and fly,
   Since brave Noble is seld away.

3 Now Hobie he was an English man,
   And born into Bewcastle dale,
But his misdeeds they were sae great,
   They banishd him to Liddisdale.

4 At Kershope-foot the tryst was set,
   Kershope of the lily lee;
And there was traitour Sim o the Mains,
   With him a private companie.

5 Then Hobie has graithd his body weel,
   I wat it was wi baith good iron and steel;
And he has pulld out his fringed grey,
   And there, brave Noble, he rade him weel.

6 Then Hobie is down the water gane,
   Een as fast as he may drie;
Tho they shoud a' brusten and broken their
      hearts,
   Frae that tryst Noble he would not be.

7 'Weel may ye be, my feiries five!
   And aye, what is your wills wi me?'
Then they cryd a' wi ae consent,
   Thou 'rt welcome here, brave Noble, to me.

8 Wilt thou with us in England ride?
   And thy safe-warrand we will be,
If we get a horse worth a hundred punds,
   Upon his back that thou shalt be.

9 'I dare not with you into England ride,
   The land-sergeant has me at feid;
I know not what evil may betide
   For Peter of Whitfield his brother's
      dead.

10 'And Anton Shiel, he loves not me,
   For I gat twa drifts of his sheep;
The great Earl of Whitfield loves me not,
   For nae gear frae me he eer coud
      keep.

11 'But will ye stay till the day gae down,
   Until the night come oer the grund,
And I 'll be a guide worth ony twa
   That may in Liddisdale be fund.

12 'Tho dark the night as pick and tar,
   I 'll guide ye oer yon hills fu hie,
And bring ye a' in safety back,
   If you 'll be true and follow me.'

13 He 's guided them oer moss and muir,
   Oer hill and houp, and mony ae down,
Til they came to the Foulbogshiel,
   And there brave Noble he lighted down.

14 Then word is gane to the land-sergeant,
   In Askirton where that he lay:
'The deer that ye hae hunted lang
   Is seen into the Waste this day.'

15 'Then Hobie Noble is that deer;
  I wat he carries the style fu hie!
Aft has he beat your slough-hounds back,
  And set yourselves at little ee.

16 'Gar warn the bows of Hartlie-burn,
  See they shaft their arrows on the wa!
Warn Willeva and Spear Edom,
  And see the morn they meet me a'.

17 'Gar meet me on the Rodrie-haugh,
  And see it be by break o day;
And we will on to Conscowthart Green,
  For there, I think, w'll get our prey.'

18 Then Hobie Noble has dreamd a dream,
  In the Foulbogshiel where that he lay;
He thought his horse was neath him shot,
  And he himself got hard away.

19 The cocks could crow, and the day could dàwn,
  And I wat so even down fell the rain;
If Hobie had no wakend at that time,
  In the Foulbogshiel he had been tane or
    slain.

20 'Get up, get up, my feiries five —
  For I wat here makes a fu ill day —
And the warst clock of this companie
  I hope shall cross the Waste this day.'

21 Now Hobie thought the gates were clear,
  But, ever alas! it was not sae;
They were beset wi cruel men and keen,
  That away brave Noble could not gae.

22 'Yet follow me, my feiries five,
  And see of me ye keep good ray,
And the worst clock of this companie
  I hope shall cross the Waste this day.'

23 There was heaps of men now Hobie before,
  And other heaps was him behind,
That had he been as wight as Wallace was
  Away brave Noble he could not win.

24 Then Hobie he had but a laddies sword,
  But he did more than a laddies deed;
In the midst of Conscouthart Green,
  He brake it oer Jers a Wigham's head.

25 Now they have tane brave Hobie Noble,
  Wi his ain bowstring they band him sae;

And I wat his heart was neer sae sair
  As when his ain five band him on the brae.

26 They have tane him [on] for West Carlisle;
  They askd him if he knew the way;
Whateer he thought, yet little he said;
  He knew the way as well as they.

27 They hae tane him up the Ricker-gate;
  The wives they cast their windows wide,
And ilka wife to anither can say,
  That's the man loosd Jock o the Side!

28 'Fy on ye, women! why ca ye me man?
  For it's nae man that I'm usd like;
I'm but like a forfoughen hound,
  Has been fighting in a dirty syke.'

29 Then they hae tane him up thro Carlisle
    town,
  And set him by the chimney-fire;
They gave brave Noble a wheat loaf to eat,
  And that was little his desire.

30 Then they gave him a wheat loaf to eat
  And after that a can o beer;
Then they cried a', wi ae consent,
  Eat, brave Noble, and make good cheer!

31 Confess my lord's horse, Hobie, they say,
  And the morn in Carlisle thou's no die;
'How shall I confess them?' Hobie says,
  'For I never saw them with mine eye.'

32 Then Hobie has sworn a fu great aith,
  By the day that he was gotten or born,
He never had onything o my lord's
  That either eat him grass or corn.

33 'Now fare thee weel, sweet Mangerton!
  For I think again I'll neer thee see;
I wad betray nae lad alive,
  For a' the goud in Christentie.

34 'And fare thee well now, Liddisdale,
  Baith the hie land and the law!
Keep ye weel frae traitor Mains!
  For goud and gear he'll sell ye a'.

35 'I'd rather be ca'd Hobie Noble,
  In Carlisle, where he suffers for his faut,
Before I were ca'd traitor Mains,
  That eats and drinks of meal and maut.'

a. 9[4]. brother is dead: *cf.* b. (Dead *is* death.)

10[2]. For twa drifts of his sheep I gat: *corrected in Scott and in the Campbell MS.*

15[4]. lee, b lye: *corrected to* fee *in Campbell MS.* (ee = awe.)

16[2]. shaft *is corrected to* sharp *in Scott and the Campbell MS.*

24[4]. Jersawigham's: *cf.* b.

b. *There is a burden after the first, second, and fourth line, variously given; as,* Fa (La, Ta) la didle, Ta la la didle, *etc., after the first and second;* Fala didle, lal didle, Tal didle, tal diddle, *after the fourth.*

2[1,2] *wanting.* 2[3,4]. 1[5,6] *in the MS.*

2[3]. flee. 2[4]. he is. 3[1]. Then *for* Now.

5[2]. both with. 5[3]. out a.

6[3]. If they should all have bursen.

6[4]. From. 7[4]. here *wanting.* 8[1]. Will.

8[2]. we shall. 8[3]. pound. 8[4]. shall.

9[1]. in. 9[4]. brother's dead (*death*).

10[2]. For twa drifts of his sheep I gott.

10[3]. not me. 10[4]. me that he can keep.

11[3]. worth other three. 11[4] *wanting.*

12[1,2] *written as* 11[4]: The pick and tar was never so dark but I'le guide you over yon hillies high.

12[3,4] *wanting.* 15[1]. he was that. 15[3]. slooth.

15[4]. little lye. 16[2]. shaft. 16[3]. Gar warn.

17[1]. me the morn.

17[2]. see that it be by the.

17[3]. Corscowthart. 17[4]. ow? 18[3]. beneath.

19[1]. cra: da. 19[3]. not. 19[4]. either tane.

21[1]. But H.: gates they had been. 21[3]. set.

21[4]. Noble he.

23[1]. lumps *for* heaps (heaps *in* 23[2]).

24[3]. Corscothart. 24[4]. Jers a wighams.

25[1]. They have tane now H. N.

25[2]. bow-strings.

25[3]. his heart was never so wae.

26[1]. on for. 27[2]. cuist. 27[3]. Then every.

27[4]. John of. 28[3]. for fouchald.

29[3]. brave *wanting:* for to. 30[1] *wanting.*

32[3]. had nothing. 33[1]. now *for* sweet.

33[4]. Crisenty. 34[3]. And keep.

35[1]. cald now.

35[4]. That eat and drank him a of.

190

JAMIE TELFER OF THE FAIR DODHEAD

Minstrelsy of the Scottish Border, I, 80, 1802; II, 3, 1833.

SCOTT, by whom this ballad was first published, and to whom alone it seems to be known, gives us no information how he came by it. He says, "There is another ballad, under the same title as the following, in which nearly the same incidents are narrated, with little difference except that the honor of rescuing the cattle is attributed to the Liddesdale Elliots, headed by a chief, there called Martin Elliot of the Preakin Tower, whose son, Simon, is said to have fallen in the action. It is very possible that both the Teviotdale Scotts and the Elliots were engaged in the affair, and that each claimed the honor of the victory." Ed. 1833, II. 3.

Scott has suggested that an article in the list of attempts upon England, fouled by the commissioners at Berwick in the year 1587, may relate to the subject of the ballad.

October, 1582.*

| Thomas Musgrave, deputy of Bewcastle, and the tenants, against | Walter Scott, Laird of Buckluth, and his complices; for | 200 kine and oxen, 300 gait and sheep. |

Bewcastle, of which Thomas Musgrave at the above date was deputy and captain, was, says Percy, a great rendezvous of thieves and moss-troopers down to the last century. " It

* Nicolson and Burn, History of Westmorland and Cumberland, p. xxxi.

is handed down by report," he remarks, "that there was formerly an Order of Council that no inhabitant of Bewcastle should be returned on a jury." That the deputy of the warden, an officer of the peace, should be exhibited as making a raid, not in the way of retaliation, but simply for plunder, is too much out of rule even for Bewcastle, and does not speak favorably for the antiquity of the ballad.

Taking the story as it stands, the Captain of Bewcastle, who is looking for a prey, is taken by a guide to the Fair Dodhead, which he pillages of kye and everything valuable. Jamie Telfer, whose threat of revenge the Captain treats with derision, runs ten miles afoot to the Elliots of Stobs Hall, to whom he says he has paid mail, st. 11, and asks help. Gib Elliot denies the mail, and tells him to go to the Scotts at Branksome where he has paid it. Telfer keeps on to Coultart Cleugh, and there makes his case known to a brother-in-law, who gives him a mount "to take the fray" to Catslockhill. There William's Wat, who had often eaten of the Dodhead basket, gives him his company and that of two sons, and they take the fray to Branksome. Buccleuch collects a body of men of his name, and sends them out under the command of Willie Scott, who overtakes the marauders, and asks the Captain if he will let Telfer's kye go back. This he will not do for love or for fear. The Scotts set on them; Willie is killed, but two and thirty of the raiders' saddles are emptied, and the Captain is badly wounded and made prisoner. Nor is that all, for the Scotts ride to the Captain's house and loose his cattle, and when they come to the Fair Dodhead, for ten milk kye Jamie Telfer has three and thirty.

Walter Scott of Harden and Walter Scott of Goldielands, and, according to Scott of Satchells, Scott of Commonside, st. 26, were engaged with Buccleuch in the rescue of Kinmont Willie. So was Will Elliot of Gorrombye, st. 27[4].

The ballad was retouched for the Border Minstrelsy, nobody can say how much. The 36th stanza is in Hardyknute style. St. 12 is not only found elsewhere (cf. 'Young Beichan,' E 6), but could not be more inappropriately brought in than here ; Scott, however, is not responsible for that.

Scott makes the following notes on the localities :

2. Hardhaughswire is the pass from Liddesdale to the head of Teviotdale. Borthwick water is a stream which falls into the Teviot three miles above Hawick. 3. The Dodhead was in Selkirkshire, near Singlee, where there are still the vestiges of an old tower. 7. Stobs Hall: upon Slitterick. 10. Branksome Ha, the ancient family-seat of the lairds of Buccleuch, near Hawick. 13. The Coultart Cleugh is nearly opposite to Carlinrig, on the road between Hawick and Mosspaul. 26. The estates mentioned in this verse belonged to families of the name of Scott residing upon the waters of Borthwick and Teviot, near the castle of their chief. 27. The pursuers seem to have taken the road through the hills of Liddesdale in order to collect forces and intercept the forayers at the passage of the Liddel on their return to Bewcastle. 29. The Frostylee is a brook which joins the Teviot near Mosspaul. 33, 38. The Ritterford and Kershopeford are noted fords on the river Liddel. 36. The Dinlay is a mountain in Liddesdale. 44. Stanegirthside: a house belonging to the Foresters, situated on the English side of the Liddel.

---

1 It fell about the Martinmas tyde,
   Whan our Border steeds get corn and hay,
  The Captain of Bewcastle hath bound him to ryde,
   And he 's ower to Tividale to drive a prey.

2 The first ae guide that they met wi,
   It was high up in Hardhaughswire ;
  The second guide that they met wi,
   It was laigh down in Borthwick water.

3 'What tidings, what tidings, my trusty guide?'
    'Nae tidings, nae tidings, I hae to thee;
But gin ye 'll gae to the Fair Dodhead,
    Mony a cow's cauf I 'll let thee see.'

4 And when they cam to the Fair Dodhead,
    Right hastily they clam the peel;
They loosed the kye out, ane and a',
    And ranshakled the house right weel.

5 Now Jamie Telfer's heart was sair,
    The tear aye rowing in his ee;
He pled wi the Captain to hae his gear,
    Or else revenged he wad be.

6 The Captain turned him round and leugh;
    Said, Man, there 's naething in thy house
But ae auld sword without a sheath,
    That hardly now wad fell a mouse.

7 The sun was na up, but the moon was down,
    It was the gryming of a new-fa'n snaw;
Jamie Telfer has run ten myles a-foot,
    Between the Dodhead and the Stobs's Ha.

8 And when he cam to the fair tower-yate,
    He shouted loud, and cried weel hie,
Till out bespak auld Gibby Elliot,
    'Whae 's this that brings the fray to me?'

9 'It 's I, Jamie Telfer o the Fair Dodhead,
    And a harried man I think I be;
There 's naething left at the Fair Dodhead
    But a waefu wife and bairnies three.'

10 'Gae seek your succour at Branksome Ha,
    For succour ye 'se get nane frae me;
Gae seek your succour where ye paid black-
        mail,
    For, man, ye neer paid money to me.'

11 Jamie has turned him round about,
    I wat the tear blinded his ee:
'I 'll neer pay mail to Elliot again,
    And the Fair Dodhead I 'll never see.

12 'My hounds may a' rin masterless,
    My hawks may fly frae tree to tree,
My lord may grip my vassal-lands,
    For there again maun I never be!'

13 He has turned him to the Tiviot-side,
    Een as fast as he could drie,

Till he cam to the Coultart Cleugh,
    And there he shouted baith loud and hie.

14 Then up bespak him auld Jock Grieve:
    'Whae 's this that brings the fray to me?'
'It 's I, Jamie Telfer o the Fair Dodhead,
    A harried man I trew I be.

15 'There 's naething left in the Fair Dodhead
    But a greeting wife and bairnies three,
And sax poor ca's stand in the sta,
    A' routing loud for their minnie.'

16 'Alack a wae!' quo auld Jock Grieve,
    'Alack, my heart is sair for thee!
For I was married on the elder sister,
    And you on the youngest of a' the three.'

17 Then he has taen out a bonny black,
    Was right weel fed wi corn and hay,
And he 's set Jamie Telfer on his back,
    To the Catslockhill to tak the fray.

18 And whan he cam to the Catslockhill,
    He shouted loud and cried weel hie,
Till out and spak him William's Wat,
    'O whae 's this brings the fray to me?'

19 'It 's I, Jamie Telfer o the Fair Dodhead,
    A harried man I think I be;
The Captain o Bewcastle has driven my
        gear;
    For God's sake, rise and succour me!'

20 'Alas for wae!' quo William's Wat,
    'Alack, for thee my heart is sair!
I never cam bye the Fair Dodhead
    That ever I fand thy basket bare.'

21 He 's set his twa sons on coal-black steeds,
    Himsel upon a freckled gray,
And they are on wi Jamie Telfer,
    To Branksome Ha to tak the fray.

22 And when they cam to Branksome Ha,
    They shouted a' baith loud and hie,
Till up and spak him auld Buccleuch,
    Said, Whae 's this brings the fray to me?

23 'It 's I, Jamie Telfer o the Fair Dodhead,
    And a harried man I think I be;
There 's nought left in the Fair Dodhead
    But a greeting wife and bairnies three.'

24 'Alack for wae!' quo the gude auld lord,
　　'And ever my heart is wae for thee!
But fye, gar cry on Willie, my son,
　　And see that he cum to me speedilie.

25 'Gar warn the water, braid and wide!
　　Gar warn it sune and hastilie!
They that winna ride for Telfer's kye,
　　Let them never look in the face o me!

26 'Warn Wat o Harden and his sons,
　　Wi them will Borthwick water ride;
Warn Gaudilands, and Allanhaugh,
　　And Gilmanscleugh, and Commonside.

27 'Ride by the gate at Priesthaughswire,
　　And warn the Currors o the Lee;
As ye cum down the Hermitage Slack,
　　Warn doughty Willie o Gorrinberry.'

28 The Scotts they rade, the Scotts they ran,
　　Sae starkly and sae steadilie,
And aye the ower-word o the thrang
　　Was, Rise for Branksome readilie!

29 The gear was driven the Frostylee up,
　　Frae the Frostylee unto the plain,
Whan Willie has lookd his men before,
　　And saw the kye right fast driving.

30 'Whae drives thir kye,' can Willie say,
　　'To make an outspeckle o me?'
'It's I, the Captain o Bewcastle, Willie;
　　I winna layne my name for thee.'

31 'O will ye let Telfer's kye gae back?
　　Or will ye do aught for regard o me?
Or, by the faith of my body,' quo Willie Scott,
　　'I'se ware my dame's cauf's skin on thee.'

32 'I winna let the kye gae back,
　　Neither for thy love nor yet thy fear;
But I will drive Jamie Telfer's kye
　　In spite of every Scott that's here.'

33 'Set on them, lads!' quo Willie than;
　　'Fye, lads, set on them cruellie!
For ere they win to the Ritterford,
　　Mony a toom saddle there sall be!'

34 Then till't they gaed, wi heart and hand;
　　The blows fell thick as bickering hail;

And mony a horse ran masterless,
　　And mony a comely cheek was pale.

35 But Willie was stricken ower the head,
　　And through the knapscap the sword has gane;
And Harden grat for very rage,
　　Whan Willie on the grund lay slane.

36 But he's taen aff his gude steel cap,
　　And thrice he's waved it in the air;
The Dinlay snaw was neer mair white
　　Nor the lyart locks of Harden's hair.

37 'Revenge! revenge!' auld Wat can cry;
　　'Fye, lads, lay on them cruellie!
We'll neer see Tiviot side again,
　　Or Willie's death revenged sall be.'

38 O mony a horse ran masterless,
　　The splintered lances flew on hie;
But or they wan to the Kershope ford,
　　The Scotts had gotten the victory.

39 John o Brigham there was slane,
　　And John o Barlow, as I hear say,
And thirty mae o the Captain's men
　　Lay bleeding on the grund that day.

40 The Captain was run through the thick of the thigh,
　　And broken was his right leg-bane;
If he had lived this hundred years,
　　He had never been loved by woman again.

41 'Hae back the kye!' the Captain said;
　　'Dear kye, I trow, to some they be;
For gin I suld live a hundred years
　　There will neer fair lady smile on me.'

42 Then word is gane to the Captain's bride,
　　Even in the bower where that she lay,
That her lord was prisoner in enemy's land,
　　Since into Tividale he had led the way.

43 'I wad lourd have had a winding-sheet,
　　And helped to put it ower his head,
Ere he had been disgraced by the border Scot,
　　Whan he ower Liddel his men did lead!'

44 There was a wild gallant amang us a',
　　His name was Watty wi the Wudspurs,

Cried, On for his house in Stanegirthside,
If ony man will ride with us!

45 When they cam to the Stanegirthside,
They dang wi trees and burst the door;
They loosed out a' the Captain's kye,
And set them forth our lads before.

46 There was an auld wyfe ayont the fire,
A wee bit o the Captain's kin:
'Whae dar loose out the Captain's kye,
Or answer to him and his men?'

47 'It's I, Watty Wudspurs, loose the kye,
I winna layne my name frae thee;

And I will loose out the Captain's kye
In scorn of a' his men and he.'

48 Whan they cam to the Fair Dodhead,
They were a wellcum sight to see,
For instead of his ain ten milk-kye,
Jamie Telfer has gotten thirty and three.

49 And he has paid the rescue-shot,
Baith wi gowd and white monie,
And at the burial o Willie Scott
I wat was mony a weeping ee.

28¹, 32⁴, 38⁴. Scots, Scot. *In the last edition,*
Scotts, Scott.
29⁴. drivand *in the later edition.*
31⁴. cauf *in the later edition.*
37¹. gan *in the later edition.*

40. "The Editor has used some freedom with
the original. The account of the Captain's
disaster (teste læva vulnerata) is rather too
naive for literal publication."

191

HUGHIE GRAME

A. 'The Life and Death of Sir Hugh of the Grime.'
a. Roxburghe Ballads, II, 294. b. Douce Ballads,
II, 204 b. c. Rawlinson Ballads, 566, fol. 9. d.
Pills to purge Melancholy, VI, 289, 17. e. Roxburghe Ballads, III, 344.

B. 'Hughie Graham,' Johnson's Museum, No 303, p.
312; Cromek, Reliques of Robert Burns, 4th ed.,
1817, p. 287; Cromek, Select Scottish Songs, 1810,
II, 151.

C. 'Hughie the Græme,' Scott's Minstrelsy, 1803, III,
85; 1833, III, 107.

D. 'Sir Hugh in the Grime's Downfall,' Roxburghe
Ballads, III, 456, edited by J. F. Ebsworth for The
Ballad Society, VI, 598.

E. 'Sir Hugh the Græme,' Buchan's MSS, I, 53;
Dixon, Scottish Traditional Versions of Ancient
Ballads, p. 73, Percy Society, vol. xvii.

F. Macmath MS., p. 79, two stanzas.

G. 'Hughie Grame,' Harris MS., fol. 27 b, one stanza.

THERE is a copy of the broadside among the
Pepys ballads, II, 148, No 130, printed, like
a, b, c, for P. Brooksby, with the variation,
"at the Golden Ball, near the Bear Tavern,
in Pye Corner." The ballad was given in
Ritson's Ancient Songs, 1790, p. 192, from
A a, collated with another copy "in the hands
of John Baynes, Esq." In a note, p. 332,

Ritson says: "In the editor's collection is a
somewhat different ballad upon the same
subject, intitled 'Sir Hugh in the Grimes
downfall, or a new song made on Sir Hugh
in the Grime, who was hangd for stealing the
Bishop's mare.' It begins, 'Good Lord John
is a hunting gone.'" This last was evidently
the late and corrupt copy **D**. Of **C** Scott

says: "The present edition was procured for me by my friend Mr W. Laidlaw, in Blackhouse, and has been long current in Selkirkshire. Mr Ritson's copy has occasionally been resorted to for better readings." B is partially rewritten by Cunningham, Songs of Scotland, I, 327. The copy in R. H. Evans's Old Ballads, 1810, I, 367, is A; that in The Ballads and Songs of Ayrshire, First Series, p. 47, is of course B; Aytoun, ed. of 1859, II, 128, reprints C; Maidment, 1868, II, 140, A, II, 145, C.

"According to tradition," says Stenhouse, "Robert Aldridge, Bishop of Carlisle, about the year 1560, seduced the wife of Hugh Graham, one of those bold and predatory chiefs who so long inhabited what was called the debateable land on the English and Scottish border. Graham, being unable to bring so powerful a prelate to justice, in revenge made an excursion into Cumberland, and carried off, *inter alia*, a fine mare belonging to the bishop; but being closely pursued by Sir John Scroope, warden of Carlisle, with a party on horseback, was apprehended near Solway Moss, and carried to Carlisle, where he was tried and convicted of felony. Great intercessions were made to save his life, but the bishop, it is said, being determined to remove the chief obstacle to his guilty passions, remained inexorable, and poor Graham fell a victim to his own indiscretion and his wife's infidelity. Anthony Wood observes that there were many changes in this prelate's time, both in church and state, but that he retained his office and preferments during them all." Musical Museum, 1853, IV, 297.

The pretended tradition is plainly extracted from the ballad, the bishop's name and the date being supplied from without. The *inter alia* is introduced, and the mare qualified as a fine one, to mitigate the ridiculousness of making Hugh Graham steal a mare to retaliate the wrong done him by the bishop. As Allan Cunningham remarks, "tradition, in all the varieties of her legends, never invented such an unnecessary and superfluous reason as this. By habit and by nature thieves, the Græmes never waited for anything like a pretence to steal." In passing, it may be observed that Hugh is quite arbitrarily elevated to the rank of a predatory chief.

Scott suggested in 1803, Minstrelsy, I, 86 f., that Hugh Graham may have been one of more than four hundred borderers against whom complaints were exhibited to the lord bishop of Carlisle for incursions, murders, burnings, mutilations, and spoils committed by the English of Cumberland and Westmoreland upon Scots "presently after the queen's departure;" that is, after Mary Stuart's going to France, which was in 1548. Nearly a third of the names given in a partial list are Grames, but there is no Hugh among them.* The bishop of Carlisle at the time was Robert Aldridge, who held the see from 1537 till his death in 1555.† Lord Scroope (Screw) is the English warden of the West Marches in A, C, D. A Lord Scroope had that office in 1542, but Lord Wharton, Lord Dacre, and others during the last years of Bishop Aldridge's life, say from 1548 to 1555. Henry Lord Scroope of Bolton was appointed to the place in 1563, retained it thirty years, and was succeeded by his son, Thomas.‡ Considering how long the Scroopes held the wardenship, and that the ballad is not so old as the middle of the sixteenth century, the fact that

---

[I have received, too late for present use, three traditional copies of 'Hughie Grame' from Abbotsford, two of which are varieties of B, the third the original of C. C 2-5, 16, were taken from Ritson, not without changes. One of the varieties of B has E 15 in a form very near to No 169, B b, c.]

* I do not know whether the document cited is extant or accessible, or whether it was examined by Mr T. J. Carlyle for his paper on the Debateable Land; he mentions no Hugh Grame, p. 13 f.

Though Grames are numerous (in 1592 they were considered the greatest surname on the west border of England, R. B. Armstrong), I have found only one Hugh out of the ballad. Hugh's Francie, that is Hugh's son Francie, is in the list of the Grames transported to Ireland in 1607. Nicolson and Burn, History of Westmorland and Cumberland, I, cxx.

† Nicolson and Burn, I, lxxxi, II, 279 f. As for Bishop Aldridge's character, his being a trimmer does not make him a "limmer." Ecclesiastics are not infrequently accused in ballads, but no man is to lose his reputation without better evidence than that.

‡ Nicolson and Burn, I, x, xiii, xcii.

a Lord Scroope was not warden in the precise year when the complaints were addressed to the bishop of Carlisle would be of no consequence if Scott's conjecture were well supported.

The story is the same in A–D, and in E also till we near the end, though there are variations in the names. The scene is at Carlisle in A, C, D; at Stirling in B, E. Lord Home, who appears as intercessor for Hugh Graham in C, exercises the authority of the Scottish warden and arrests Hugh in E. Lord Home was warden of the *east* marches of Scotland from 1550, and I know not how much earlier, to 1564. The Lord Boles of A may possibly represent Sir Robert Bowes, who was warden of the *east* marches of England in 1550 and earlier. The Whitefoords of B are adopted into the ballad from the region in which that version circulated, they being "an ancient family in Renfrewshire and Lanarkshire, and latterly in Ayrshire." *

The high jump which Hugh makes in A 18, C 12, D 4 (fourteen, or even eighteen, feet, with his hands tied on his back), is presumably an effort at escape, though, for all that is said, it might be a leap in the air. In E 16–19, the prisoner jumps an eighteen-foot wall (tied as before), is defended by four brothers against ten pursuers, and sent over sea: which is certainly a modern perversion.

A is strangely corrupted in several places, 2^2, 11^4, 13^2. Screw is plainly for Scroope. Garlard, sometimes printed Garland, is an obscuration of Cárlisle. The extravagance in 16^3, it is to be hoped, is a corruption also. Stanzas 3, 8 of B are obviously, as Cromek says, the work of Burns, and the same is true of $10^{3,4}$. But Burns has left some nonsense in 11, 12: 'my sword that's bent in the middle clear,' ' my sword that's bent in the middle brown.' We have more of this meaningless phraseology in E 10, 11, 12, where swords are pointed ' wi the metal clear,' ' brown,' ' fine.' Stanza 15 of E is borrowed from ' Johnie Armstrong.'

A

a. Roxburghe Ballads, II, 294. b. Douce Ballads, II, 204 b. c. Rawlinson Ballads, 566, fol. 9. All printed for P. Brooksby: 1672–95(?). d. Pills to purge Melancholy, VI, 289, 17. e. Roxburghe Ballads, III, 344.

1 As it befell upon one time,
    About mid-summer of the year,
Every man was taxt of his crime,
    For stealing the good Lord Bishop's mare.

2 The good Lord Screw he sadled a horse,
    And rid after this same scrime;
Before he did get over the moss,
    There was he aware of Sir Hugh of the
        Grime.

3 ' Turn, O turn, thou false traytor,
    Turn, and yield thyself unto me;
Thou hast stolen the Lord Bishops mare,
    And now thou thinkest away to flee.'

4 ' No, soft, Lord Screw, that may not be!
    Here is a broad sword by my side,

And if that thou canst conquer me,
    The victory will soon be try'd.'

5 ' I ner was afraid of a traytor bold,
    Although thy name be Hugh in the Grime;
I 'le make thee repent thy speeches foul,
    If day and life but give me time.'

6 ' Then do thy worst, good Lord Screw,
    And deal your blows as fast as you can;
It will be try'd between me and you
    Which of us two shall be the best man.'

7 Thus as they dealt their blows so free,
    And both so bloody at that time,
Over the moss ten yeomen they see,
    Come for to take Sir Hugh in the Grime.

8 Sir Hugh set his back against a tree,
    And then the men encompast him round;
His mickle sword from his hand did flee,
    And then they brought Sir Hugh to the
        ground.

* Ballads and Songs of Ayrshire, 1st Series, p. 50.

9 Sir Hugh of the Grime now taken is
    And brought back to Garland town ;
[Then cry'd] the good wives all in Garland
        town,
    'Sir Hugh in the Grime, thou 'st ner gang
        down.'

10 The good Lord Bishop is come to the town,
    And on the bench is set so high ;
And every man was taxt to his crime,
    At length he called Sir Hugh in the Grime.

11 'Here am I, thou false bishop,
    Thy humours all to fulfill ;
I do not think my fact so great
    But thou mayst put it into thy own will.'

12 The quest of jury-men was calld,
    The best that was in Garland town ;
Eleven of them spoke all in a breast,
    'Sir Hugh in the Grime, thou 'st ner gang
        down.'

13 Then another questry-men was calld,
    The best that was in Rumary ;
Twelve of them spoke all in a breast,
    'Sir Hugh in the Grime, thou'st now guilty.'

14 Then came down my good Lord Boles,
    Falling down upon his knee :
'Five hundred pieces of gold would I give,
    To grant Sir Hugh in the Grime to me.'

15 'Peace, peace, my good Lord Boles,
    And of your speeches set them by !
If there be eleven Grimes all of a name,
    Then by my own honour they all should
        dye.'

16 Then came down my good Lady Ward,
    Falling low upon her knee :

'Five hundred measures of gold I 'le give,
    To grant Sir Hugh of the Grime to me.'

17 'Peace, peace, my good Lady Ward,
    None of your proffers shall him buy !
For if there be twelve Grimes all of a name,
    By my own honour they all should dye.'

18 Sir Hugh of the Grime's condemnd to dye,
    And of his friends he had no lack ;
Fourteen foot he leapt in his ward,
    His hands bound fast upon his back.

19 Then he lookt over his left shoulder,
    To see whom he could see or spy ;
Then was he aware of his father dear,
    Came tearing his hair most pittifully.

20 'Peace, peace, my father dear,
    And of your speeches set them by !
Though they have bereavd me of my life,
    They cannot bereave me of heaven so high.'

21 He lookt over his right shoulder,
    To see whom he could see or spye ;
There was he aware of his mother dear,
    Came tearing her hair most pittifully.

22 'Pray have me remembred to Peggy, my
        wife ;
    As she and I walkt over the moor,
She was the cause of [the loss of] my life,
    And with the old bishop she plaid the
        whore.

23 'Here, Johnny Armstrong, take thou my
        sword,
    That is made of the mettle so fine,
And when thou comst to the border-side,
    Remember the death of Sir Hugh of the
        Grime.'

B

Johnson's Museum, No 303, p. 312, contributed by Burns ;
Cromek, Reliques of Robert Burns, 4th ed., 1817, p. 287 ;
Cromek, Select Scottish Songs, etc., 1810, II, 151. From
oral tradition in Ayrshire.

1 OUR lords are to the mountains gane,
    A hunting o the fallow deer,
And they hae gripet Hughie Graham,
    For stealing o the bishop's mare.

2 And they hae tied him hand and foot,
    And led him up thro Stirling town ;
The lads and lasses met him there,
    Cried, Hughie Graham, thou art a loun !

3 'O lowse my right hand free,' he says,
    'And put my braid sword in the same,
He 's no in Stirling town this day
    Daur tell the tale to Hughie Graham.'

4 Up then bespake the brave Whitefoord,
  As he sat by the bishop's knee :
'Five hundred white stots I 'll gie you,
  If ye 'll let Hughie Graham gae free.'

5 'O haud your tongue,' the bishop says,
  'And wi your pleading let me be !
For tho ten Grahams were in his coat,
  Hughie Graham this day shall die.'

6 Up then bespake the fair Whitefoord,
  As she sat by the bishop's knee :
'Five hundred white pence I 'll gee you,
  If ye 'll gie Hughie Graham to me.'

7 'O haud your tongue now, lady fair,
  And wi your pleading let it be !
Altho ten Grahams were in his coat,
  It 's for my honour he maun die.'

8 They 've taen him to the gallows-knowe,
  He looked to the gallows-tree,
Yet never colour left his cheek,
  Nor ever did he blink his ee.

9 At length he looked round about,
  To see whatever he could spy,

And there he saw his auld father,
  And he was weeping bitterly.

10 'O haud your tongue, my father dear,
  And wi your weeping let it be !
Thy weeping 's sairer on my heart
  Than a' that they can do to me.

11 'And ye may gie my brother John
  My sword that 's bent in the middle clear,
And let him come at twelve o'clock,
  And see me pay the bishop's mare.

12 'And ye may gie my brother James
  My sword that 's bent in the middle brown,
And bid him come at four o'clock,
  And see his brother Hugh cut down.

13 'Remember me to Maggy my wife,
  The niest time ye gang oer the moor ;
Tell her, she staw the bishop's mare,
  Tell her, she was the bishop's whore.

14 'And ye may tell my kith and kin
  I never did disgrace their blood,
And when they meet the bishop's cloak,
  To mak it shorter by the hood.'

C

Scott's Minstrelsy, 1803, III, 85, 1833, III, 107, procured by W. Laidlaw in Blackhouse, and long current in Selkirkshire ; with readings from Ritson's copy.

1 GUDE Lord Scroope 's to the hunting gane,
  He has ridden oer moss and muir,
And he has grippet Hughie the Græme,
  For stealing o the bishop's mare.

2 'Now, good Lord Scroope, this may not
    be !
Here hangs a broad sword by my side,
  And if that thou canst conquer me,
The matter it may soon be tryed.'

3 'I neer was afraid of a traitor thief ;
  Although thy name be Hughie the Græme,
I 'll make thee repent thee of thy deeds,
  If God but grant me life and time.'

4 'Then do your worst now, good Lord Scroope,
  And deal your blows as hard as you can ;

It shall be tried, within an hour,
  Which of us two is the better man.'

5 But as they were dealing their blows so free,
  And both so bloody at the time,
Over the moss came ten yeomen so tall,
  All for to take brave Hughie the Græme.

6 Then they hae grippit Hughie the Græme,
  And brought him up through Carlisle town ;
The lasses and lads stood on the walls,
  Crying, Hughie the Græme, thou 'se neer
    gae down !

7 Then they hae chosen a jury of men,
  The best that were in Carlisle town,
And twelve of them cried out at once,
  Hughie the Græme, thou must gae down !

8 Then up bespak him gude Lord Hume,
  As he sat by the judge's knee :
'Twenty white owsen, my gude lord,
  If you 'll grant Hughie the Græme to me.'

9 'O no, O no, my gude Lord Hume,
    Forsooth and sae it mauna be;
For were there but three Græmes of the name,
    They suld be hanged a' for me.'

10 'T was up and spake the gude Lady Hume,
    As she sat by the judge's knee:
'A peck of white pennies, my good lord judge,
    If you 'll grant Hughie the Græme to me.'

11 'O no, O no, my gude Lady Hume,
    Forsooth and so it mustna be;
Were he but the one Græme of the name,
    He suld be hanged high for me.'

12 'If I be guilty,' said Hughie the Græme,
    'Of me my friends shall hae small talk;'
And he has loupd fifteen feet and three,
    Though his hands they were tied behind his
    back.

13 He looked over his left shoulder,
    And for to see what he might see;
There was he aware of his auld father,
    Came tearing his hair most piteouslie.

14 'O hald your tongue, my father,' he says,
    'And see that ye dinna weep for me!
For they may ravish me o my life,
    But they canna banish me fro heaven hie.

15 'Fare ye weel, fair Maggie, my wife!
    The last time we came ower the muir
'T was thou bereft me of my life,
    And wi the bishop thou playd the whore.

16 'Here, Johnnie Armstrang, take thou my
    sword,
    That is made o the metal sae fine,
And when thou comest to the English side
    Remember the death of Hughie the Græme.'

D

Roxburghe Ballads, III, 456; edited for the Ballad Society by J. W. Ebsworth, VI, 598.

1 GOOD Lord John is a hunting gone,
    Over the hills and dales so far,
For to take Sir Hugh in the Grime,
    For stealing of the bishop's mare.
      He derry derry down

2 Hugh in the Grime was taken then
    And carried to Carlisle town;
The merry women came out amain,
    Saying, The name of Grime shall never go
    down!

3 O then a jury of women was brought,
    Of the best that could be found;
Eleven of them spoke all at once,
    Saying, The name of Grime shall never go
    down!

4 And then a jury of men was brought,
    More the pity for to be!
Eleven of them spoke all at once,
    Saying, Hugh in the Grime, you are
    guilty.

5 Hugh in the Grime was cast to be hangd,
    Many of his friends did for him lack;

For fifteen foot in the prisin he did jump,
    With his hands tyed fast behind his back.

6 Then bespoke our good Lady Ward,
    As she set on the bench so high:
'A peck of white pennys I 'll give to my lord,
    If he 'll grant Hugh Grime to me.

7 'And if it be not full enough,
    I 'll stroke it up with my silver fan;
And if it be not full enough,
    I 'll heap it up with my own hand.'

8 'Hold your tongue now, Lady Ward,
    And of your talkitive let it be!
There is never a Grime came in this court
    That at thy bidding shall saved be.'

9 Then bespoke our good Lady Moor,
    As she sat on the bench so high:
'A yoke of fat oxen I 'll give to my lord,
    If he 'll grant Hugh Grime to me.'

10 'Hold your tongue now, good Lady Moor,
    And of your talkitive let it be!
There is never a Grime came to this court
    That at thy bidding shall saved be.'

11 Sir Hugh in the Grime lookd out of the door,
    With his hand out of the bar;

There he spy'd his father dear,
 Tearing of his golden hair.

12 'Hold your tongue, good father dear,
  And of your weeping let it be!
 For if they bereave me of my life,
  They cannot bereave me of the heavens
   so high.'

13 Sir Hugh in the Grime lookd out at the
   door,
  Oh, what a sorry heart had he!

There [he] spy'd his mother dear,
 Weeping and wailing 'Oh, woe is me!'

14 'Hold your tongue now, mother dear,
  And of your weeping let it be!
 For if they bereave me of my life,
  They cannot bereave me of heaven's fee.

15 'I'll leave my sword to Johnny Armstrong
  That is made of mettal so fine,
 That when he comes to the border-side
  He may think of Hugh in the Grime.'

E

Buchan's MSS, I, 53.

1 LORD HOME he is a hunting gane,
  Through the woods and valleys clear,
 And he has taen Sir Hugh the Græme,
  For stealing o the bishop's mare.

2 They hae taen Sir Hugh the Græme,
  Led him down thro Strieveling town;
 Fifeteen o them cried a' at ance,
  'Sir Hugh the Græme he must go down!'

3 They hae causd a court to sit,
  Mang a' their best nobilitie;
 Fifeteen o them cried a' at ance,
  'Sir Hugh the Græme he now must die!'

4 Out it speaks the lady Black,
  And o her will she was right free:
 'A thousand pounds, my lord, I'll gie,
  If Hugh the Græme set free to me.'

5 'Hold your tongue, ye Lady Black,
  And ye'll let a' your pleadings be!
 Though ye woud gie me thousands ten,
  It's for my honour he must die.'

6 Then out it speaks her Lady Bruce,
  And o her will she was right free:
 'A hundred steeds, my lord, I'll gie,
  If ye'll gie Hugh the Græme to me.'

7 'O hold your tongue, ye Lady Bruce,
  And ye'll let a' your pleadings be!
 Though a' the Græmes were in this court,
  It's for my honour he must die.'

8 He looked over his shoulder,
  It was to see what he coud see,
 And there he saw his auld father,
  Weeping and wailing bitterlie.

9 'O hold your tongue, my old father,
  And ye'll let a' your mourning be!
 Though they bereave me o my life,
  They canno had the heavens frae me.

10 'Ye'll gie my brother John the sword
  That's pointed wi the metal clear,
 And bid him come at eight o'clock,
  And see me pay the bishop's mare.

11 'And, brother James, take here the sword
  That's pointed wi the metal brown;
 Come up the morn at eight o'clock,
  And see your brother putten down.

12 'And, brother Allan, take this sword
  That's pointed wi the metal fine;
 Come up the morn at eight o'clock,
  And see the death o Hugh the Græme.

13 'Ye'll tell this news to Maggy my wife,
  Niest time ye gang to Strievling town,
 She is the cause I lose my life,
  She wi the bishop playd the loon.'

14 Again he ower his shoulder lookd,
  It was to see what he could see,
 And there he saw his little son,
  Was screaming by his nourice knee.

15 Then out it spake the little son,
  'Since 'tis the morn that he must die,

If that I live to be a man,
My father's death revengd shall be.'

16 'If I must die,' Sir Hugh replied,
'My friends o me they will think lack;'
He leapd a wa eighteen feet high,
Wi his hands bound behind his back.

17 Lord Home then raised ten armed men,
And after him they did pursue;

But he has trudged ower the plain
As fast as ony bird that flew.

18 He looked ower his left shoulder,
It was to see what he coud see;
His brother John was at his back,
And a' the rest o his brothers three.

19 Some they wound, and some they slew,
They fought sae fierce and valiantly;
They made his enemies for to yield,
And sent Sir Hugh out ower the sea.

———•———

F

Macmath MS., p. 79. "Received by me 20th August
and 7th September, 1887, from my aunt, Miss Jane Webster, who derived it from her mother, Janet Spark, Kirkcudbrightshire."

1 'Ye may tell to my wife Maggie,
When that she comes to the fair,

She was the cause of all my ruin,
It was her that stole the bishop's mare.

2 'Ye may tell to my wife Maggie,
When that she comes to the town,
She was the cause of all my ruin,
It was her that stole the bishop's gown.'

———•———

G

Harris MS., fol. 27 b.

Dukes an lords a huntin gane,
Over hills an vallies clear;

There the 've bound him Hughie Grame,
For stealin o the bishop's mare.

———•———

A. a. Printed for P. Brooksby, at the Golden-Ball,
in West-smith-field, neer the Hospital-gate.
12^2. Garland. 13^1. another.
22^3. the causer of my life.
b. To a pleasant new northern tune.
Printed for P. Brooksby at the Golden-Ball,
in Westsmithfield.
3^3. Lords. 9^3. Then cry'd *wanting*.
9^4. never. 10^4. of the. 12^2. Garlard.
13^1. other. 21^3. ware.
22^3. the causer of my life. 22^4. plays.
23^3. borders.
c. Printed for P. Brooksby [*torn off*] West-
smith-field.
2^4. he *wanting*. 5^3. of thy.
9^3. Then cry'd *wanting*. 10^4. of the.
11^3. thy fact. 12^2. Garlard. 13^1. other.
21^3. ware. 22^3. the causer of my life.
22^4. plays. 23^3. borders.
d. 2^2. the same serime. 8^1. again.

8^2. compact. $9^{2,3}$, 12^2. Garland.
9^3. Then cry'd. 10^1. the *wanting*.
11^4. it *wanting*. 13^1. other. 14^3. will I.
17^4. they *wanting*. 22^3. cause of the loss.
e. *No imprint*.
2^2. rid *wanting*: the same. 2^3. he could.
5^2. my *for* thy. 7^1. as *wanting*.
8^2. compact. $9^{2,3}$. Garland.
9^3. Then cry'd. 10^1. to town.
10^4. calld to. 11^2. for to. 13^1. other.
14^3. will I. 18^4. With his. 19^4. come.
22^3. of the loss of.
B. 8^4. blin' *in Johnson's Museum*: blink *in Cromek*.
D.   Sir Hugh in the Grime's Downfall, or, A New
Song made on Sir Hugh in the Grime, who
was hangd for stealing the Bishop's Mare.
London: Printed and sold by L. How.
(About 1770?)
5^2. did leet: *cf.* A 18^2. 10^4. biding. 14^1. tonge.

192

THE LOCHMABEN HARPER

A. a. 'The Blind Harper of Lochmaben,' Glenriddell MSS, XI, 42, 1791. **b.** 'The Blind Harper,' Johnson's Museum, No 579, 1803. **c.** 'The Lochmaben Harper,' Minstrelsy of the Scottish Border, 1802, I, 65 ; 1833, I, 422.

B. 'Lochmaben Harper,' Glenriddell MSS, XI, 39.

C. 'The Auld Harper,' The Edinburgh Topographical, Traditional, and Antiquarian Magazine, 1849, p. 58.

D. Macmath MS, p. 35.

E. 'The Jolly Harper,' Buchan's MSS, I, 35; Dixon, Scottish Traditional Versions of Ancient Ballads, Percy Society, vol. xvii, p. 37.

THE Stationers' Registers, 22 July, 1564–22 July, 1565, Arber, I, 260, have an entry of a fee from Owyn Rogers for license to print " a ballett intituled The Blende Harper, etc."; and again, the following year, Arber, I, 294, of a fee from Lucas Haryson for license to print " a ballet intituled The Blynde Harpers, with the Answere." Nothing further is known of this ballet.

Boyd, the translator of Dante, had a recollection of a ballad of a Scotch minstrel who stole a horse from one of the Henries of England : Ritson, Scotish Song, I, xxxvi, note 25, 1794.

Printed in Scott's Minstrelsy, 1802 (**A c**), and the next year in the Musical Museum (**A b**), as communicated by Burns. Burns's copy differs very slightly from **A a**, however he came by it. Scott had access to the Glenriddell collection, and his ballad (of which he gives no account) was made by changing **A a** to his taste, substituting one stanza of his own in place of 18, and the last two of **B**, with alterations, for the last of **A a**. To reduce improbabilities, Scott put the Lord Warden for King Henry.

C was pointed out to me, and transcribed from the short-lived periodical in which it was printed, by Mr James Barclay Murdoch, to whom I have been from the beginning indebted for the most essential help.

Of **D** Mr Macmath writes : This version was copied by me in fac-simile from the original manuscript in the handwriting of the late Rev. George Murray, of Troquhain, minister of Balmaclellan, in the Stewartry of Kirkcudbright, and was in possession of his son, the Rev. George Murray, to whose kindness I was indebted for the loan of it. The late Mr Murray took down the ballad from the singing of Sarah Rae, a poor weak-minded woman of his parish. Sarah Rae was the last person known to Mr Murray — and he was a keen observer of such matters — to use the distaff. The present Mr George Murray wrote to me on 12th January, 1883 : " I may add that I have heard her sing the ballad myself, to a very simple but particularly plaintive lilt — more like a rapid chant than an ordinary song — which rings in my ear yet, although I only heard it once, when a lad." *

A-C. A harper of Lochmaben (blind, **A, B**) who means to steal the Wanton Brown, a horse of King Henry's, consults with his wife before setting about the business, and gets a few valuable hints; among them, to leave his mare's foal at home. He goes up to England, and has the good luck, so common in ballads,

---

* See also a paper by Dr Arthur Mitchell in the Proceedings of the Society of Antiquaries of Scotland, XII, 260, June 11, 1877. Dr Mitchell was with Mr Murray when he visited Sarah Rae, and he supplies the date 1866. The last stanza of the ballad and the burden are cited in this paper.

of finding King Henry at his gate. The king wants to hear some of his harping, and, as the harper makes a difficulty about the stabling of his mare, orders the beast to be put into his own stable. The harper harps all his hearers asleep; then makes his way softly to the stable, slips a halter over the Wanton's nose and ties him to the mare's tail, and turns the mare out. She goes straight to Lochmaben, to her foal, neighs at the harper's house, and is let in by the servant-lass, who exclaims at the braw foal that the mare has got. In the morning they find in England that both the Wanton Brown and the mare have been stolen. The harper breaks out into 'allaces:' he has lost a foal in Scotland and had his mare stolen in England! The king quiets him with a promise of a better mare and pay for his foal to boot.

In D, E, the harper steals the horse on a wager, which, however, is passed over lightly in D. The wager in E is with two knights of Stirling, five ploughs of land with one and five thousand pounds with the other, and "John" has to go all the way to London to win it. The knights pay their loss and then restore the Wanton Brown to Henry! — so great an improvement upon the dealings of the Scots with English horseflesh as to compel one to assign this particular version of the story to the nineteenth, if not the twentieth, century.*

The twelve armed men in armor bright that guard the stable night and day in E 23 remind us of popular tales; as of the Grimms' 'Master Thief.'

A b is loosely translated by Knortz, Schottische Balladen, No 16, p. 58.

<hr>

A

a. Glenriddell MS. XI, 42, 1791; "from a MS. collection of Mr Henderson." b. Johnson's Museum, No 579, VI, 598, 1803, communicated by Burns. c. Scott's Minstrelsy, 1802, I, 65.

1 HEARD ye eer of the silly blind harper,
  That long livd in Lochmaben town,
How he wad gang to fair England,
  To steal King Henry's Wanton Brown?
    Sing, Faden dilly and faden dilly
    Sing, Faden dilly and deedle dan

2 But first he gaed to his gude wife,
  Wi a' the speed that he coud thole;
'This wark,' quo he, 'will never work
  Without a mare that has a foal.'

3 Quo she, Thou has a gude gray mare,
  That'al rin oer hills baith law and hie;
Gae tak the gray mare in thy hand,
  And leave the foal at hame wi me.

4 'And tak a halter in thy hose,
  And o thy purpose dinna fail;
But wap it oer the Wanton's nose,
  And tie her to the gray mare's tail.

5 'Syne ca her out at yon back geate,
  Oer moss and muir and ilka dale;
For she 'll neer let the Wanton bite
  Till she come hame to her ain foal.'

6 So he is up to England gane,
  Even as fast as he can hie,
Till he came to King Henry's geate;
  And wha was there but King Henry?

7 'Come in,' quo he, 'thou silly blind harper,
  And of thy harping let me hear;'
'O, by my sooth,' quo the silly blind harper,
  'I 'd rather hae stabling for my mare.'

8 The king he looks oer his left shoulder,
  And says unto his stable-groom,

* The innocent comments of certain editors must not be lost. "The whole incident surely implies a very early and primitive system of manners, not to speak of the circumstance of the court being held at Carlisle, which never was the case in any late period of English history." (Chambers's Scottish Ballads, p. 306.) "In our version [E] the scene of the theft is laid at London, but Carlisle, we are inclined to think, is the true reading. The great distance between Scotland and London, and the nature of the roads in times of old, would render the event an improbable, if not altogether an impossible, one to have occurred; and we can easily imagine, when the court was at Carlisle, that such a good practical joke was planned and carried into execution by some waggish courtiers." (Dixon, p. 93 f.)

Gae tak the silly poor harper's mare,
   And tie her side my Wanton Brown.

9 And ay he harpit, and ay he carpit,
   Till a' the lords had fitted the floor;
  They thought the music was sae sweet,
   And they forgot the stable-door.

10 And ay he harpit, and ay he carpit,
   Till a' the nobles were sound asleep;
  Than quietly he took aff his shoon,
   And safly down the stair did creep.

11 Syne to the stable-door he hies,
   Wi tread as light as light coud be,
  And when he opned and gaed in,
   There he fand thirty gude steads and three.

12 He took the halter frae his hose,
   And of his purpose did na fail;
  He slipt it oer the Wanton's nose,
   And tied it to his gray mare's tail.

13 He ca'd her out at yon back geate,
   Oer moss and muir and ilka dale,
  And she loot neer the Wanton bite,
   But held her still gaun at her tail.

14 The gray mare was right swift o fit,
   And did na fail to find the way,
  For she was at Lochmaben geate
   Fu lang three hours ere 't was day.

15 When she came to the harper's door,
   There she gave mony a nicher and sneer;

'Rise,' quo the wife, 'thou lazey lass,
   Let in thy master and his mare.'

16 Then up she rose, pat on her claes,
   And lookit out through the lock-hole;
  'O, by my sooth,' then quoth the lass,
   'Our mare has gotten a braw big foal!'

17 'Come had thy peace, thou foolish lass,
   The moon's but glancing in thy eye;
  I'll wad my hail fee against a groat,
   It's bigger than eer our foal will be.'

18 The neighbours too that heard the noise
   Cried to the wife to put hir in;
  'By my sooth,' then quo the wife,
   'She's better than ever he rade on.'

19 But on the morn, at fair day light,
   When they had ended a' thier chear,
  King Henry's Wanton Brown was stawn,
   And eke the poor old harper's mare.

20 'Allace! allace!' says the silly blind harper,
   'Allace, allace, that I came here!
  In Scotland I've tint a braw cowte-foal,
   In England they've stawn my gude gray
     mare.'

21 'Come had thy tongue, thou silly blind harper,
   And of thy allacing let me be;
  For thou shalt get a better mare,
   And weel paid shall thy cowte-foal be.'

———◆———

B

Glenriddell MSS, XI, 39, 1791; "from Dr Clapperton, of
Lochmaben."

1 HARD ye tell of the silly blind harper?
   Long he lived in Lochmaben town;
  He's away to fair Carlisle,
   To steal King Henry's Wanton Brown.
     Sing, Fadle didle dodle didle
     Sing, Fadle didle fadle doo

2 He has mounted his auld gray mare,
   And ridden oer both hills and mire,

Till he came to fair Carlisle town,
   And askd for stabling to his mare.

3 'Harp on, harp on, thou silly blind harper,
   'Some of thy harping let us hear;'
  'By my sooth,' says the silly blind harper,
   'I would rather hae stabling to my mare.'

4 The king looked oer his left shoulder
   And called to his stable-groom:
  'Gae stable up the harper's mare,
   And just beyond the Wanton Brown.'

5 Ay he carped, and ay he harped,
　　Till a' the lords gaed thro the floor;
　But and the musick was sae sweet
　　The groom forgot the key o the stable-door.

6 Ay he harped, and ay he carped,
　　Till a' the lords fell fast asleep,
　And, like a fause deceiver as he was,
　　He quickly down the stair did creep.

7 He pulld a colt-halter out o his hoe,
　　On purpose as I shall to you tell;
　He sliped it oer the Wanton's nose,
　　And tyed it to his gray mare's tail.

8 'My blessing light upon my wife!
　　I think she be a daily flower;
　She told me to ken my ain gray mare
　　When eer I felt her by the ewer.'

9 'Harp on, harp on, thou silly blind harper,
　　Some of thy harping let us hear:'
　'Oh and alas!' says the silly blind harper,
　　'Oh and alas that eer I came here!

10 'For in Scotland I lost a good brown foal,
　　And in England a good gray mare,

·　·　·　·　·　·　·　·

11 'Harp on, harp on, thou silly blind harper,
　　Some of thy harping let us hear,
　And thy brown foal shall be well payed,
　　And thou's hae a far better gray mare.'

12 Ay he harped, and ay he carped,
　　And some of his harping he let them hear,
　And his brown foal it was well payed,
　　And he got a better gray mare.

13 His mare 's away to Lochmaben,
　　Wi mony a nicker and mony a sneer;
　His wife cry'd, Rise up, you lazy lass,
　　Let in your master and his mare.

14 The lazy lass was loth to rise;
　　She looked through a little hole;
　'By my troth,' crys the lazy lass,
　　'Our mare has brought a bonie foal.'

15 'Rise up, rise up, thou lazy lass,
　　And, een as the sun it shines sae clear,
　I 'll wager my life against a groat
　　The foal was better than ever the mare.'

———◆———

C

The Edinburgh Topographical, Traditional, and Antiquarian Magazine, 1849, p. 58; communicated by W. G. "from the recitation of a friend, who learned it many years ago from her grandfather," a farmer in Wigtonshire, who died in 1813, at the age of ninety-four.

1 IT 's hae ye heard tell o the auld harper
　　That lang lived in Lochmaben town,
　How he maun awa to England fair,
　　To steal King Henry's Wanton Brown?
　　　Faw aiden diden an diden an diden
　　　Faw aiden diden faw aiden dee

2 Out then bespak his gude auld wife,
　　I wat she spak out very wiselie;
　'Ye 'll ride the mear to England fair,
　　But the foal ye 'll leave at hame wi me.

3 'Ye 'll hide your halter in o your hose,
　　And o your purpose ye 'll no fail;

　　Ye 'll cast a hook on the Wanton's nose,
　　　And tie him to the gray mear's tail.

4 'Ye 'll lead them awa by a back yett,
　　And hound them out at a wee hole;
　The mear she 'll neer [let] the Wanton bait
　　Till hame at Lochmaben town wi her foal.'

5 Awa then rade the auld harper,
　　I wat he rade right merrilie,
　Until he cam to England fair,
　　Where wonned the gude King Henerie.

6 'Light down, light down, ye auld harper,
　　And some o your harping let me hear;
　'O williwa!' quo the auld harper,
　　Will I get stabling for my mear?'

*　　*　　*　　*　　*

7 And aye he harped and he carped,
　　Till a' the lordlings fell asleep;
　Syne bundled his fiddles upon his back,
　　And down the stairs fu fast did creep.

8 He's taen the halter out o his hose,
　　And o his purpose he didna fail;
　He's cast a hook on the Wanton's nose,
　　And tied him to the gray mear's tale.

9 He's led them awa by the back yett,
　　And hounded them out at a wee hole;
　The mear she neer let the Wanton bait
　　Till hame at Lochmaben town wi her foal.

10 And when they cam to the house-end,
　　Wi mony a nicker but an a neigh,
　They waukend the auld wife out o her sleep;
　　She was a-dreaming she was fouie.

11 'Rise up, rise up, my servant-lass,
　　Let in your master and his mear;'
　'It's by my sooth,' the wee lassie goud say,
　　'I'm in a sleeping drowsy air.'

12 Wi mony a gaunt she turned her round,
　　And keekit through at a wee hole;

'It's by my sooth!' the wee lassie goud say,
　'Our mear has gotten a braw brown foal!'

13 'Lie still, lie still, ye lazy lass,
　　It's but the moon shines in your ee;'
　'Na, by my sooth,' the lassie goud say,
　　'And he's bigger than ony o his degree.'

14 Then lightly rose the gude auld wife,
　　I wat the first up in a' the town;
　She took the grit oats intil her lap
　　And fodderd King Henry's Wanton Brown.

15 King Henry's groom rase in the morn,
　　And he was of a sorry cheer:
　'King Henry's Wanton Brown's awa,
　　And sae is the silly auld harper's mear!'

16 Up then rase the auld harper,
　　And loudly he did curse and swear:
　'In Scotland they but steald my foal,
　　In England ye hae steald my mear!'

17 'It's haud your tongue," King Henry did say,
　　'Ye'll hae nae cause to curse or swear;
　Here's thirty guineas for your foal,
　　And three times thirty for your mear.'

————◆————

D

Taken down by the Rev George Murray from the singing of Sarah Rae, a weak-minded woman of Balmaclellan, Kirkcudbright, 1866.   Communicated by Mr Macmath.

1 THERE was a poor silly harper-man,
　　And he lived in Lochmaben toon,
　And he has wagered wi lairds and lords,
　　And mony a guinea against a croon.
　　　Tum tid iddly
　　　Dodaly diddely
　　　Tidaly diddaly
　　　Dodaly dan

2 And he has wagered wi lairds and lords,
　　And mony a guinea against a croon,
　That into England he would go,
　　And steal King Henerie's Wanton Broun.

3 Out spak the silly poor harper's wife,
　　And O but she spak wililie:

'If into England you do go,
　Leave the wee-wee foal wi me.'

4 The harper he got on to ride,
　　And O but he rode richt highlie!
　The very first man that he did meet,
　　They said it was King Henerie.

5 'Licht doon, licht doon, ye silly poor harper,
　　And o your harping let me hear;'
　'And by my sooth,' quoth the silly poor harper,
　　'I'd rather hae stabling for my mear.'

6 O he lookit ower his left shoulder,
　　And saw ane of the stable-grooms:
　'Go take the sillie poor harper's mear,
　　And stable her by my Wanton Brown.'

7 And aye he harpit, and aye he carpit,
　　Till a' the nobles fell on the floor,
　And aye he harpit, and aye he carpit,
　　Till they forgot the key of the stable-door.

8 And aye he harpit, and aye he carpit,
   Till a' the nobles fell fast asleep;
   He has taen his harp upon his back,
   And doon the stair did softly creep.

9 He has taen a halter frae his hose,
   And o his purpose did not fail;
   He coost a wap on Wanton's nose,
   And tyed her to his ain mear's tail.

10 He ca'd her through at the bye-yett,
   Through mony a syre and mony a hole;
   She never loot Wanton licht till she
   Was at Lochmaben, at her foal.

11 And she came oer Lochmaben heights,
   Wi mony a nicker and mony a sneeze,
   And waukend the silly poor harper's wife,
   As she was a sleeping at her ease.

12 'Rise up, rise up, ye servant-lass,
   Let in the maister and the mear;'
   'By my sooth,' quoth the servant-lass,
   'I think my maister be na here.'

13 Up then rose the servant-lass,
   And lookit through a wee, wee hole;

'By my sooth,' quoth the servant-lass,
'Our mear has gotten a waly foal.'

14 'Ye clatter, ye clatter, ye servant-lass,
   It is the moon shines in your ee;'
   'By my sooth,' quoth the servant-lass,
   'It 's mair than ever her ain will be.'

15 It 's whan the stable-groom awoke,
   Put a' the nobles in a fear;
   King Henerie's Wanton Brown was stown,
   And Oh! the silly poor harper's mear.

16 Out then spak the silly poor harper,
   Says, Oh, this loss I douna thole!
   In England fair a guid grey mear,
   In fair Scotland a guid cout-foal.

17 'Haud your tongue, ye sillie poor harper,
   And wi your carping let me be;
   Here 's ten pounds for your auld gray mear,
   And a weel paid foal it 's be to thee!'

18 And O the silly poor harper's wife,
   She 's aye first up in Lochmaben toun;
   She 's stealing the corn and stealing the hay,
   And wappin it oer to Wanton Broun.

E

Buchan's MSS, I, 35; Dixon, Scottish Traditional Versions of Ancient Ballads, p. 37, Percy Society, vol. xvii.

1 THERE was a jolly harper-man,
   That harped aye frae toun to toun;
   A wager he made, with two knights he laid
   To steal King Henry's Wanton Brown.

2 Sir Roger he wagered five ploughs o land,
   Sir Charles wagered five thousand pound,
   And John he 's taen the deed in hand,
   To steal King Henry's Wanton Brown.

3 He 's taen his harp into his hand,
   And he gaed harping thro the toun,
   And as the king in his palace sat,
   His ear was touched wi the soun.

4 'Come in, come in, ye harper-man,
   Some o your harping let me hear;'

'Indeed, my liege, and by your grace,
I 'd rather hae stabling to my mare.'

5 'Ye 'll gang to yon outer court,
   That stands a little below the toun;
   Ye 'll find a stable snug and neat,
   Where stands my stately Wanton Brown.'

6 He 's down him to the outer court,
   That stood a little below the toun;
   There found a stable snug and neat,
   For stately stood the Wanton Brown.

7 Then he has fixd a good strong cord
   Unto his grey mare's bridle-rein,
   And tied it unto that steed's tail,
   Syne shut the stable-door behin.

8 Then he harped on, an he carped on,
   Till all were fast asleep;

Then down thro bower and ha he 's gone,
  Even on his hands and feet.

9 He 's to yon stable snug and neat,
    That lay a little below the toun;
  For there he placed his ain grey mare,
    Alang wi Henry's Wanton Brown.

10 ' Ye 'll do you down thro mire an moss,
    Thro mony bog an lairy hole;
  But never miss your Wanton slack;
    Ye 'll gang to Mayblane, to your foal.'

11 As soon's the door he had unshut,
    The mare gaed prancing frae the town,
  An at her bridle-rein was tied
    Henry's stately Wanton Brown.

12 Then she did rin thro mire an moss,
    Thro mony bog an miery hole;
  But never missed her Wanton slack
    Till she reachd Mayblane, to her foal.

13 When the king awaked from sleep
    He to the harper-man did say,
  O waken ye, waken ye, jolly John,
    We 've fairly slept till it is day.

14 ' Win up, win up, ye harper-man,
    Some mair o harping ye 'll gie me: '
  He said, My liege, wi a' my heart,
    But first my gude grey mare maun see.

15 Then forth he ran, and in he came,
    Dropping mony a feigned tear:
  ' Some rogue[s] hae broke the outer court,
    An stown awa my gude grey mare.'

16 ' Then by my sooth,' the king replied,
    ' If there 's been rogues into the toun,
  I fear, as well as your grey mare,
    Awa is my stately Wanton Brown.'

17 ' My loss is great,' the harper said,
    ' My loss is twice as great, I fear;
  In Scotland I lost a gude grey steed,
    An here I 've lost a gude grey mare.'

18 ' Come on, come on, ye harper-man,
    Some o your music lat me hear;

Well paid ye 'se be, John, for the same,
    An likewise for your gude grey mare.'

19 When that John his money received,
    Then he went harping frae the toun,
  But little did King Henry ken
    He 'd stown awa his Wanton Brown.

20 The knights then lay ower castle-wa,
    An they beheld baith dale an down,
  An saw the jolly harper-man
    Come harping on to Striveling toun.

21 Then, ' By my sooth,' Sir Roger said,
    ' Are ye returned back to toun?
  I doubt my lad ye hae ill sped
    Of stealing o the Wanton Brown.'

22 ' I hae been into fair England,
    An even into Lunan toun,
  An in King Henry's outer court,
    An stown awa the Wanton Brown.'

23 ' Ye lie, ye lie,' Sir Charles he said,
    ' An aye sae loud 's I hear ye lie;
  Twall armed men, in armour bright,
    They guard the stable night and day.'

24 ' But I did harp them all asleep,
    An managed my business cunninglie;
  If ye make light o what I say,
    Come to my stable an ye 'll see.

25 ' My music pleasd the king sae well
    Mair o my harping he wishd to hear;
  An for the same he paid me well,
    And also for my gude grey mare.'

26 Then he drew out a gude lang purse,
    Well stored wi gowd an white monie,
  An in a short time after this
    The Wanton Brown he lat them see.

27 Sir Roger produced his ploughs o land,
    Sir Charles produced his thousand pounds,
  Then back to Henry, the English king,
    Restored the stately Wanton Brown.

A. a. "I have here given another copy of this Border Ballad, which I took from a MS. collection of Mr Henderson. It varies a little from the former [A], which I had from Dr Clapperton of Lochmaben."

4^4, 13^4, 18^4. *The Wanton Brown is a mare: so* b, *and* D, 9^4. *But the Brown is a stallion in* C, 3^4, 8^4, 13^4, *and is so made to be in* A c, 13^4, 17^3: *rightly, I should suppose.* 8^2. say. 12^4. to *wanting.*

b. *The third and fourth lines are repeated as burden.*

1^1. O heard ye of a silly harper. 1^2. Livd long. 1^3. he did. 8^1. he *wanting*. 9^2. lords gaed through. 9^4. That they forgat. 14^4. ere it. 15^2. gae. 16^1. raise. 17^1. then (*misprint*) *for* those. 17^3. gainst. 21^3. shall.

c. *No burden.* 1^1. O heard ye na o. 1^2. How lang he lived. 1^3. And how. 1^4. steal the Lord Warden's. 2^2. the haste. 2^3. will neer gae weel. 3^1. hast. 3^2. That can baith lance oer laigh. 3^3. Sae set thee on the gray mare's back. 4, 5, *wanting*. 6^2. And even: he may drie. 6^3. And when he cam to Carlisle gate. 6^4. O whae: but the Warden, he. 7^1. into my hall, thou. 7^4. I wad. 8^1. The Warden lookd ower. 8^2. said. 8^3. silly blind. 8^4. beside. 9^1. Then aye. 9^2. the lordlings footed. 9^3. But an the. 9^4. The groom had nae mind o. 10^2. were fast. 11^1 hied. 11^4. gude *wanting*. 12^1. took a cowt halter. 12^2. he did. 13^1. He turned them loose at the castle gate. 13^2. muir and moss. 13^3. neer let: bait. 13^4. But kept him a-galloping hame to her foal. 14^1. The mare she was: foot. 14^2. She didna. 14^4. A lang: before the day. 15^3. Rise up. 16^1. cloathes. 16^2. keekit through at the. 16^3. then cried. 16^4. braw brown. 17^1. haud thy tongue, thou silly wench. 17^2. morn's: in your ee. 17^3. He 's.

18. Now all this while, in merry Carlisle,
The harper harped to hie and law,

And the fiend thing dought they do but listen
him to,
Untill that the day began to daw.

19^3. Behold the Wanton Brown was gane. 19^4. poor blind. 20^1. quo the cunning auld. 20^2. And ever allace. 20^3. I lost a. 21, 22, *alteration of* B 11, 12:

Come cease thy allacing, thou silly blind harper,
And again of thy harping let us hear;
And weel payd sall thy cowt-foal be,
And thou sall have a far better mare.

Then aye he harped, and aye he carped,
Sae sweet were the harpings he let them hear!
He was paid for the foal he had never lost,
And three times ower for the gude gray mare.

B. 1^2. in a Bell town: *see* 13^1.
5. *The burden is here:* Sing, Fadle fidle, etc.

C. "The following is an oral version of a ballad which appears in the first volume of the 'Minstrelsy.' I have written it down from the recitation of a friend who learned it many years ago from her grandfather, a Mr John Macreddie, farmer, Little Laight parish of Inch, Wigtonshire. He died in 1813, at the age of ninety-four, and is supposed to have acquired the song from tradition in his youth. On comparison, it will be found to differ in several respects from Sir Walter's version. 11 Hill Street, Anderston, Glasgow. W. G."

D. 3^2, 4^2, 6^1, 18^1, oh. 10^1, at, 16^1, then, *added by Mr Murray in pencil above the line, as if on reading over what he had written down.*
18^4. *Dr Mitchell gives:* An waps. "The owerword," *he adds*, "was something like the following:"

Hey tum tidly
Doodlem didly
Hey tum tidly
Doodley dan.

E. 2^2. *The reading is perhaps* pounds.
$7^{2,3}$. *Absurdity could be avoided by exchanging* grey mare *and* steed.
24^2. by *for* my.

193

THE DEATH OF PARCY REED

A. 'A song of Parcy Reed and the Three False Halls,' the late Robert White's papers.

B. 'The Death of Parcy Reed,' Richardson's Border-

er's Table Book, 1846, VII, 361; J. H. Dixon, Ancient Poems, Ballads and Songs of the Peasantry of England, p. 99, Percy Society, vol. xvii, 1846.

OF B, which purports to have been taken down from an old woman's singing by James Telfer, Mr Robert White, from whom I received A, said in a letter to Mr J. H. Dixon: "Parcy Reed, as you suspect, is not genuine, for it bears marks of our friend's improvements. I have a copy of the original somewhere, but may not be able to find it." And again, Telfer himself, "in a letter to the late Robert Storey, the Northumbrian poet," wrote, "I will send Mr Dixon the real verses, but it is but a droll of a ballad." (J. H. Dixon, in Notes and Queries, Fourth Series, I, 108, V, 520.)

Comparison will show that almost the whole of A is preserved in B, and in fairly good form. B has also some stanzas not found in A which may be accepted as traditional. Telfer may have added a dozen of his own, and has retouched others.

Mr White, after remarking that there is no historical evidence to show when the event on which the ballad was founded occurred, informs us that almost every circumstance in the narrative has been transmitted to the present century by local tradition.

"Percival, or Parcy, Reed," in the words of Mr White, "was proprietor of Troughend, an elevated tract of land lying on the west side and nearly in the centre of Redesdale, Northumberland. The remains of the old tower may still be seen, a little to the west of the present mansion, commanding a beautiful and most extensive view of nearly the whole valley. Here he resided, and being a keen hunter and brave soldier, he possessed much

influence, and was appointed warden or keeper of the district. His office was to suppress and order the apprehension of thieves and other breakers of the law; in the execution of which he incurred the displeasure of a family of brothers of the name of Hall, who were owners of Girsonsfield, a farm about two miles east from Troughend. He also drew upon himself the hostility of a band of moss-troopers, Crosier by name, some of whom he had been successful in bringing to justice. The former were, however, artful enough to conceal their resentment, and under the appearance of friendship calmly awaited an opportunity to be avenged. Some time afterwards, they solicited his attendance on a hunting expedition to the head of Redesdale, and unfortunately he agreed to accompany them. His wife had some strange dreams anent his safety on the night before his departure, and at breakfast, on the following morning, the loaf of bread from which he was supplied chanced to be turned with the bottom upwards, an omen which is still accounted most unfavorable all over the north of England. Considering these presages undeserving of notice, Reed set out in company with the Halls, and, after enjoying a good day's sport, the party withdrew to a solitary hut in Bating-hope, a lonely glen stretching westward from the Whitelee, whose little stream forms one of the chief sources of Reedwater. The whole of this arrangement had been previously planned by the Halls and Crosiers, and when the latter came down, late in the evening, to execute their purpose of vengeance, they found

Parcy Reed altogether a defenceless man. His companions not only deserted him, but had previously driven his sword so firmly in its scabbard that it could not be drawn, and had also moistened the powder with which the very long gun he carried with him was charged, so as to render both useless when he came to rely upon them for protection. Accordingly the Crosiers instantly put him to death; and so far did they carry out their sanguinary measures, even against his lifeless body, that tradition says the fragments thereof had to be collected together and conveyed in pillow-slips home to Troughend. Public indignation was speedily aroused against the murderers; the very name of Crosier was abhorred throughout Redesdale, and the abettors were both driven from their residence and designated as the fause-hearted Ha's, an appellation which yet remains in force against them." (Richardson's Borderer's Table Book, VII, 361.)

The farm of Girsonsfield, according to the ballad, A 3, 18, belonged to the Halls. But that place has been the property of others, says Mr White, " ever since the reign of Elizabeth ; " whence he concludes that the story is not to be dated later than the sixteenth century.

Parcy Reed is famed to have had a favorite dog named Keeldar, and, though a " peerless archer," to have killed him by an unlucky shot while hunting. Sir Walter Scott has celebrated this mishap and its consequence in ' The Death of Keeldar' (Table Book, as above, p. 240) ; and he alludes to the treacherous murder of Reed (with which he became acquainted through Robert Roxby's ' Lay of the Reedwater Minstrel,' 1809) in Rokeby, written in 1812, Canto I, xx.

A

The late Robert White's papers ; " Woodburn, December 1, 1829, Thomas Hedley, Bridge End, Corsonside Parish."

1 THE Liddesdale Crosiers hae ridden a race,
    And they had far better staid at hame,
For they have lost a gallant gay,
    Young Whinton Crosier it was his name.

2 For Parcy Reed he has him taen,
    And he's delivered him to law,
But auld Crosier has made answer
    That he'll gar the house of the Troughend fa.

3 So as it happened on a day
    That Parcy Reed is a hunting gane,
And the three false Halls of Girsonsfield
    They all along with him are gane.

4 They hunted up and they hunted down,
    They hunted all Reedwater round,
Till weariness has on him seized ;
    At the Batinghope he's fallen asleep.

5 O some they stole his powder-horn,
    And some put water in his lang gun:

' O waken, waken, Parcy Reed !
    For we do doubt thou sleeps too sound.

6 ' O waken, O waken, Parcy Reed !
    For we do doubt thou sleeps too long ;
For yonder 's the five Crosiers coming,
    They 're coming by the Hingin Stane.

7 ' If they be five men, we are four,
    If ye will all stand true to me ;
Now every one of you may take one,
    And two of them ye may leave to me.'

8 ' We will not stay, nor we dare not stay,
    O Parcy Reed, for to fight with thee ;
For thou wilt find, O Parcy Reed,
    That they will slay both us and thee.'

9 ' O stay, O stay, O Tommy Hall,
    O stay, O man, and fight with me !
If we see the Troughend again,
    My good black mare I will give thee.'

10 ' I will not stay, nor I dare not stay,
    O Parcy Reed, to fight for thee ;
For thou wilt find, O Parcy Reed,
    That they will slay both me and thee.'

11 'O stay, O stay, O Johnnie Hall,
　　O stay, O man, and fight for me!
　If I see the Troughend again,
　　Five yoke of oxen I will give thee.'

12 'I will not stay, nor I dare not stay,
　　O Parcy Reed, for to fight with thee;
　For thou wilt find, O Parcy Reed,
　　That they will slay both me and thee.'

13 'O stay, O stay, O Willie Hall,
　　O stay, O man, and fight for me!
　If we see the Troughend again,
　　The half of my land I will give thee.'

14 'I will not stay, nor I dare not stay,
　　O Parcy Reed, for to fight with thee;
　For thou wilt find, O Parcy Reed,
　　That they will slay both me and thee.'

15 'Now foul fa ye, ye traitors all,
　　That ever ye should in England won!
　You have left me in a fair field standin,
　　And in my hand an uncharged gun.

16 'O fare thee well, my wedded wife!
　　O fare you well, my children five!
　And fare thee well, my daughter Jane,
　　That I love best that 's born alive!

17 'O fare thee well, my brother Tom!
　　And fare you well his children five!
　If you had been with me this day,
　　I surely had been man alive.

18 'Farewell all friends! as for my foes,
　　To distant lands may they be tane,
　And the three false Halls of Girsonsfield,
　　They 'll never be trusted nor trowed again.'

———◆———

B

Richardsons' Borderers' Table Book, VII, 361, 1846; "taken down by James Telfer, of Saughtree, Liddesdale, from the chanting of an old woman named Kitty Hall, a native of Northumberland."

1 GOD send the land deliverance
　　Frae every reaving, riding Scot;
　We 'll sune hae neither cow nor ewe,
　　We 'll sune hae neither staig nor stot.

2 The outlaws come frae Liddesdale,
　　They herry Redesdale far and near;
　The rich man's gelding it maun gang,
　　They canna pass the puir man's mear.

3 Sure it were weel, had ilka thief
　　Around his neck a halter strang;
　And curses heavy may they light
　　On traitors vile oursels amang.

4 Now Parcy Reed has Crosier taen,
　　He has delivered him to the law;
　But Crosier says he 'll do waur than that,
　　He 'll make the tower o Troughend fa.

5 And Crosier says he will do waur,
　　He will do waur if waur can be;
　He 'll make the bairns a' fatherless,
　　And then, the land it may lie lee.

6 'To the hunting, ho!' cried Parcy Reed,
　　'The morning sun is on the dew;
　The cauler breeze frae off the fells
　　Will lead the dogs to the quarry true.

7 'To the hunting, ho!' cried Parcy Reed,
　　And to the hunting he has gane;
　And the three fause Ha's o Girsonsfield
　　Alang wi him he has them taen.

8 They hunted high, they hunted low,
　　By heathery hill and birken shaw;
　They raised a buck on Rooken Edge,
　　And blew the mort at fair Ealylawe.

9 They hunted high, they hunted low,
　　They made the echoes ring amain;
　With music sweet o horn and hound,
　　They merry made fair Redesdale glen.

10 They hunted high, they hunted low,
　　They hunted up, they hunted down,
　Until the day was past the prime,
　　And it grew late in the afternoon.

11 They hunted high in Batinghope,
　　When as the sun was sinking low;
　Says Parcy then, Ca off the dogs,
　　We 'll bait our steeds and homeward go.

12 They lighted high in Batinghope,
    Atween the brown and benty ground;
  They had but rested a little while
    Till Parcy Reed was sleeping sound.

13 There's nane may lean on a rotten staff,
    But him that risks to get a fa;
  There's nane may in a traitor trust,
    And traitors black were every Ha.

14 They've stown the bridle off his steed,
    And they've put water in his lang gun;
  They've fixed his sword within the sheath
    That out again it winna come.

15 'Awaken ye, waken ye, Parcy Reed,
    Or by your enemies be taen;
  For yonder are the five Crosiers
    A-coming owre the Hingin-stane.'

16 'If they be five, and we be four,
    Sae that ye stand alang wi me,
  Then every man ye will take one,
    And only leave but two to me:
  We will them meet as brave men ought,
    And make them either fight or flee.'

17 'We mayna stand, we canna stand,
    We daurna stand alang wi thee;
  The Crosiers haud thee at a feud,
    And they wad kill baith thee and we.'

18 'O turn thee, turn thee, Johnie Ha,
    O turn thee, man, and fight wi me;
  When ye come to Troughend again,
    My gude black naig I will gie thee;
  He cost full twenty pound o gowd,
    Atween my brother John and me.'

19 'I mayna turn, I canna turn,
    I daurna turn and fight wi thee;
  The Crosiers haud thee at a feud,
    And they wad kill baith thee and me'

20 'O turn thee, turn thee, Willie Ha,
    O turn thee, man, and fight wi me;
  When ye come to Troughend again,
    A yoke o owsen I'll gie thee.'

21 'I mayna turn, I canna turn,
    I daurna turn and fight wi thee;
  The Crosiers haud thee at a feud,
    And they wad kill baith thee and me.'

22 'O turn thee, turn thee, Tommy Ha,
    O turn now, man, and fight wi me;
  If ever we come to Troughend again,
    My daughter Jean I'll gie to thee.'

23 'I mayna turn, I canna turn,
    I daurna turn and fight wi thee;
  The Crosiers haud thee at a feud,
    And they wad kill baith thee and me.'

24 'O shame upon ye, traitors a'!
    I wish your hames ye may never see;
  Ye've stown the bridle off my naig,
    And I can neither fight nor flee.

25 'Ye've stown the bridle off my naig,
    And ye've put water i my lang gun;
  Ye've fixed my sword within the sheath
    That out again it winna come.'

26 He had but time to cross himsel,
    A prayer he hadna time to say,
  Till round him came the Crosiers keen,
    All riding graithed and in array.

27 'Weel met, weel met, now, Parcy Reed,
    Thou art the very man we sought;
  Owre lang hae we been in your debt,
    Now will we pay you as we ought.

28 'We'll pay thee at the nearest tree,
    Where we shall hang thee like a hound;'
  Brave Parcy raisd his fankit sword,
    And felld the foremost to the ground.

29 Alake, and wae for Parcy Reed,
    Alake, he was an unarmed man;
  Four weapons pierced him all at once,
    As they assailed him there and than.

30 They fell upon him all at once,
    They mangled him most cruellie;
  The slightest wound might caused his deid,
    And they hae gien him thirty-three;
  They hacket off his hands and feet,
    And left him lying on the lee.

31 'Now, Parcy Reed, we've paid our debt,
    Ye canna weel dispute the tale,'
  The Crosiers said, and off they rade;
    They rade the airt o Liddesdale.

32 It was the hour o gloaming gray,
        When herds come in frae fauld and pen ;
    A herd he saw a huntsman lie,
        Says he, Can this be Laird Troughen ?

33 'There 's some will ca me Parcy Reed,
        And some will ca me Laird Troughen ;
    It 's little matter what they ca me,
        My faes hae made me ill to ken.

34 'There 's some will ca me Parcy Reed,
        And speak my praise in tower and town ;
    It 's little matter what they do now,
        My life-blood rudds the heather brown.

35 'There 's some will ca me Parcy Reed,
        And a' my virtues say and sing ;
    I would much rather have just now
        A draught o water frae the spring.'

36 The herd flung aff his clouted shoon
        And to the nearest fountain ran ;
    He made his bonnet serve a cup,
        And wan the blessing o the dying man.

37 'Now, honest herd, ye maun do mair,
        Ye maun do mair, as I you tell ;
    Ye maun bear tidings to Troughend,
        And bear likewise my last farewell.

38 'A farewell to my wedded wife,
        A farewell to my brother John,
    Wha sits into the Troughend tower
        Wi heart as black as any stone.

39 'A farewell to my daughter Jean,
        A farewell to my young sons five ;
    Had they been at their father's hand,
        I had this night been man alive.

40 'A farewell to my followers a',
        And a' my neighbours gude at need ;
    Bid them think how the treacherous Ha's
        Betrayed the life o Parcy Reed.

41 'The laird o Clennel bears my bow,
        The laird o Brandon bears my brand ;
    Wheneer they ride i the Border-side,
        They 'll mind the fate o the laird Trough-
            end.'

———◆———

A. 10^1, 12^1, 14^1, or *for* nor ; *cf.* 8^1.
    12^2. "O Parcy Reed, etc. (same as stanza 8,
    save at end, thee and me)." *The same
    abridgment and remark at* 10^2, 14^2, *but the*

last words are there given as me *and* thee.
Uniformity is to be expected.
16^1. fare thou: *cf.* 16^3, 17^1.

———————

194

THE LAIRD OF WARISTON

A. 'The Laird of Waristoun,' Jamieson's Popular Ballads, I, 109.

B. 'Laird of Wariestoun,' Kinloch MSS, VII, 217 ; Kinloch's Ancient Scottish Ballads, p. 49.

C. 'Death of Lord Warriston,' Buchan's Ballads of the North of Scotland, I, 56.

———◆———

BIRRELL'S DIARY, under the date of July 2, 1600, has the following entry : "John Kinland [Kincaid] of Waristone murderit be hes awin wyff and servant-man, and the nurische being also upone the conspiracy. The said gentilwoman being apprehendit, scho was tane to the Girth Crosse upon the 5 day of Julii, and her heid struck fra her bodie at the Cannagait fit; quha diet verie patiently. Her nurische was brunt at the same tyme, at 4 houres in the morneing, the 5 of Julii." P. 49.

Both husband and wife belonged to houses of some note. The wife, Jean Livingston, was a daughter of John Livingston of Dunipace, "and related to many of the first families in Scotland."

Nothing seems to have been done to keep the murder from divulging. Warriston being only about a mile from Edinburgh, information very soon reached the authorities of justice, and those who were found in the house, the mistress, the nurse, and two female servants, were arrested. The crime was committed on Tuesday morning, not long after midnight. On Thursday such trial as there was took place, and it may have occupied three hours, probably less. At three o'clock on Saturday morning sentence was executed. This had been burning (*i. e.* after strangling), both for the principal and her accomplice, the nurse; but for the well-born woman, no doubt through the influence of her kindred, it was commuted to beheading. The servant-man who did the handiwork fled, but the penalty for undue devotion to his former master's daughter overtook him within four years. He was broken on a cart-wheel with a plough-coulter.

The judicial records in the case of Jean Livingston are lost, but the process of the murder and the provocation are known from a register of the trial of Robert Weir, the actual perpetrator, and partly also from Jean Livingston's own relation. Jean Livingston, having conceived a deadly hatred and malice against her husband, John Kincaid, "for the alleged biting of her in the arm and striking her divers times," sent word by her nurse, Janet Murdo, to Robert Weir, formerly servant to her father, to come to Wariston to speak with her concerning the murdering of him. The nurse, who, we may safely suppose, had been the witness of Kincaid's brutal behavior, was no unwilling agent. "She helped me too well in mine evil purpose," says her mistress; "for when I told her what I was minded to do, she consented to the doing of it, and . . . when I

sent her to seek the man who would do it, she said, I shall go and seek him, and if I get him not, I shall seek another; and if I get none, I shall do it myself." This the nurse confessed. The other two women knew nothing of the deed before it was done; "and that which they knew," says the mistress again, "they durst not tell for fear, for I had compelled them to dissemble." Robert Weir, having given consent, was put in a cellar, where he stayed till midnight, about which time he came up and went to Kincaid's chamber. Kincaid, who had waked with the "din," and was leaning over the side of his bed, was knocked to the floor by a blow in the neck, kicked in the belly, and then throttled. "As soon as that man gripped him and began his evil turn," says the wife, "so soon as my husband cried so fearfully, I leapt outover my bed and went to the hall, where I sat all the time till that unhappy man came to me and reported that mine husband was dead." She desired Weir, she says, to take her away with him, for she feared trial, albeit flesh and blood made her think that her father's interest at court would have saved her (this may have been an after-thought). But Weir refused, saying, You shall tarry still, and if this matter come not to light, you shall say he died in the gallery, and I shall return to my master's service. But if it be known, I shall fly and take the crime on me, and none dare pursue you.

A benevolent minister, who visited Jean Livingston in prison about ten o'clock on Thursday, the third day after the murder, found her "raging in a senseless fury, disdainfully taunting every word of grace that was spoken to her, impatiently tearing her hair, sometimes running up and down the house like one possessed, sometimes throwing herself on the bed and sprawling, refusing all comfort by word, and, when the book of God was brought to her, flinging it upon the walls, twice or thrice, most unreverently." His warnings of wrath to come and his exhortations to seek mercy through repentance were treated as "trittle, trattle," and she stubbornly refused to pray for herself, or to take part in his prayer, or to say so much as God help me. He told her that she was promising herself impunity, but within a few hours, when she should have the sentence of death pronounced against her, the pride of her heart would be broken. The trial and sentence followed hard upon this, and when the minister returned, some time in the afternoon, he found a visible and apparent grace beginning in her. He remained with her till after midnight, and when he left her, Jean Livingston could say that she felt in her heart a free remission of all her sins. This worthy man came to the prison again early the next morning, and found God's grace wonderfully augmented in her. She was full of joy and courage. Those that stood about her said they never saw her so amiable or well-favored. The glory of God was shining both without and within her.

To follow no further this astounding chapter in psychology, this bairn of twenty-one years,[*] with whom the Lord began to work in mercy upon Thursday at two hours in the afternoon, gave up her soul to him in peace upon the Saturday following at three hours in the morning. "When she came to the scaffold and was carried up upon it, she looked up to the Maiden with two longsome looks," but her serenity was not disturbed. She made a confession at each of the four corners of the scaffold, took "good night" cheerfully of all her friends, kissing them, and then, "as a constant saint of God, humbled herself on her knees and offered her neck to the axe." [†]

It may be gathered from Weir's indictment that it was the ill treatment which she had received from her husband that incited the wife to the murder. Two of the ballads, A 4, B 2, make the same representation. An epitaph on Jean Livingston gives us to understand that both parties were very young, and were married aganst their will (invita invito subjuncta puella puello) : whence perpetual disagreements (nihil in thalamo nisi rixæ, jurgia, lites).

In A, B, the strangling is done by the nurse and her lady, Man's Enemy personally knotting the tether in A; in C it is done by the nurse alone. In B 8 the great Dunipace, in his anger at hearing what his daughter has done, cries out for her to be put in a barrel of pikes [‡] and rolled down some lea. In C the father, mother, and brother come to see Jean, and would fain give everything to borrow her. This is a by much too flattering account of the behavior of her relatives, who were principally anxious to have her got out of the world with as little éclat as might be. None of them came near her in prison, though Wariston's brother did. C makes Wariston's mortal offence not the throwing a plate at her face (A) or striking her on the mouth (B), but the taxing her with a bairn by another man. [§] The unfriendly relations of the pair must have been notorious. In the prison the wife "purged herself very sincerely from many scandalous things she had been bruited with. Not that she would excuse herself that she was a sinner in the highest rank, but that she might clear herself from these false reports that her house was charged with:" Memorial, p. XXVII.

Wolff, Halle der Völker, II, 161; Grundtvig, III, 700, No 178, A–D, Prior, II, 160, Arwidsson, II, 62, No 80, and Grundtvig, ib. p. 698; Hoffmann, Niederländische Volkslieder, 1856, p. 19, No 3, Le Jeune, p. 87, No 3, Prior, II, 238; Pidal, Asturian Romances, p. 163, No 36; Grimms, K.-u. H. märchen, Nos 13, 89, 135; Asbjørnsen og Moe, p. 464. Sharpe, in his preface to the Memorial, p. v, gives B 8 in this form, "partly from tradition:"

Up spak the laird o Dunypace,
    Sat at the king's right knee;
' Gar nail her in a tar-barrel
    And hurl her in the sea.'

§ The day before the execution Lady Wariston desired to see her infant son. The minister feared lest the sight of him should make her wae to leave him, but she assured that the contrair should be seen, took the child in her arms, kissed him, blessed him, and recommended him to the Lord's care, and sent him away again without taking of any sorrow. Memorial, p. IX.

---

* So the Memorial referred to in the next note, p. VI. Sharpe, in his preface, p. iv, says nineteen. B 9 is of course quite wrong as to the duration of her married life.

† A Memorial of the Conversion of Jean Livingston, Lady Waristoun, etc., printed from the manuscript by C. K. Sharpe, Edinburgh, 1827. An Epitaphium Janetæ Livingstoune is subjoined. The record of Weir's trial is given in the preface: see also Pitcairn's Criminal Trials, II, 445 ff. The Memorial is powerfully interesting, but, in Sharpe's words, would have been a mischievous present to the world, whatever one may think of the change of heart in this "dear saint of God," as she is therein repeatedly called. It may be noted that Jean Livingston, when it was supposed her last hour had come, called for a drink and drank to all her friends. Memorial, p. XIII: cf. "Mary Hamilton."

‡ Rolling in a spiked barrel is well known as a popular form of punishment. For some examples later than Regulus, see Grundtvig, II, 174, No 58; Grundtvig, II, 547, No 101, A–D, Prior, I, 349, Afzelius, No 3 (two copies),

A

Jamieson's Popular Ballads, I, 109, as taken down by Sir Walter Scott from the recitation of his mother.

1 Down by yon garden green
 Sae merrily as she gaes;
She has twa weel-made feet,
 And she trips upon her taes.

2 She has twa weel-made feet,
 Far better is her hand;
She's as jimp in the middle
 As ony willow-wand.

3 'Gif ye will do my bidding,
 At my bidding for to be,
It's I will make you lady
 Of a' the lands you see.'

*   *   *   *   *   *

4 He spak a word in jest;
 Her answer wasna good;
He threw a plate at her face,
 Made it a' gush out o blood.

5 She wasna frae her chamber
 A step but barely three,
When up and at her richt hand
 There stood Man's Enemy.

6 'Gif ye will do my bidding,
 At my bidding for to be,
I'll learn you a wile
 Avenged for to be.'

7 The Foul Thief knotted the tether,
 She lifted his head on hie,
The nourice drew the knot
 That gard lord Waristoun die.

8 Then word is gane to Leith,
 Also to Edinburgh town,
That the lady had killd the laird,
 The laird o Waristoun.

*   *   *   *   *   *

9 'Tak aff, tak aff my hood,
 But lat my petticoat be;
Put my mantle oer my head,
 For the fire I downa see.

10 'Now, a' ye gentle maids,
 Tak warning now by me,
And never marry ane
 But wha pleases your ee.

11 'For he married me for love,
 But I married him for fee;
And sae brak out the feud
 That gard my dearie die.'

B

Kinloch MSS, VII, 217; from the recitation of Jenny Watson.

1 It was at dinner as they sat,
 And whan they drank the wine,
How happy war the laird and lady
 Of bonnie Wariston!

2 The lady spak but ae word,
 The matter to conclude;
The laird strak her on the mouth,
 Till she spat out o blude.

3 She did not know the way
 Her mind to satisfy,
Till evil cam into [her] head
 All by the Enemy.

*   *   *   *   *   *

4 'At evening when ye sit,
 And whan ye drink the wine,
See that ye fill the glass weill up
 To the laird o Wariston.'

5 So at table whan they sat,
 And whan they drank the wine,
She made the glass aft gae round
 To the laird o Wariston.

6 The nurice she knet the knot,
 And O she knet it sicker!
The lady did gie it a twig,
 Till it began to wicker.

7 But word 's gane doun to Leith,
    And up to Embro toun,
That the lady she has slain the laird,
    The laird o Waristoun.

8 Word has gane to her father, the grit Dunipace,
    And an angry man was he;
Cries, Gar mak a barrel o pikes,
    And row her down some lea!

9 She said, Wae be to ye, Wariston,
    I wish ye may sink for sin!

For I have been your wife
    These nine years, running ten;
And I never loved ye sae well
    As now whan ye 're lying slain.

10 'But tak aff this gowd brocade,
    And let my petticoat stay,
And tie a handkerchief round my face,
    That the people may not see.'

C

Buchan's Ballads of the North of Scotland, I, 56.

1 'My mother was an ill woman,
    In fifteen years she married me;
I hadna wit to guide a man,
    Alas! ill counsel guided me.

2 'O Warriston, O Warriston,
    I wish that ye may sink for sin!
I was but bare fifteen years auld,
    Whan first I enterd your yates within.

3 'I hadna been a month married,
    Till my gude lord went to the sea;
I bare a bairn ere he came hame,
    And set it on the nourice knee.

4 'But it fell ance upon a day,
    That my gude lord returnd from sea;
Then I did dress in the best array,
    As blythe as ony bird on tree.

5 'I took my young son in my arms,
    Likewise my nourice me forebye,
And I went down to yon shore-side,
    My gude lord's vessel I might spy.

6 'My lord he stood upon the deck,
    I wyte he haild me courteouslie:
Ye are thrice welcome, my lady gay,
    Whae 's aught that bairn on your knee?'

7 She turnd her right and round about,
    Says, 'Why take ye sic dreads o me?
Alas! I was too young married,
    To love another man but thee.'

8 'Now hold your tongue, my lady gay,
    Nae mair falsehoods ye 'll tell to me;
This bonny bairn is not mine,
    You 've loved another while I was on sea.'

9 In discontent then hame she went,
    And aye the tear did blin her ee;
Says, Of this wretch I 'll be revenged
    For these harsh words he 's said to me.

10 She 's counselld wi her father's steward
    What way she coud revenged be;
Bad was the counsel then he gave,
    It was to gar her gude lord dee.

11 The nourice took the deed in hand,
    I wat she was well paid her fee;
She kiest the knot, and the loop she ran,
    Which soon did gar this young lord dee.

12 His brother lay in a room hard by,
    Alas! that night he slept too soun;
But then he wakend wi a cry,
    'I fear my brother 's putten down.

13 'O get me coal and candle light,
    And get me some gude companie;'
But before the light was brought,
    Warriston he was gart dee.

14 They 've taen the lady and fause nourice,
    In prison strong they hae them boun;
The nourice she was hard o heart,
    But the bonny lady fell in swoon.

15 In it came her brother dear,
    And aye a sorry man was he:

'I woud gie a' the lands I heir,
O bonny Jean, to borrow thee.'

16 'O borrow me, brother, borrow me?
O borrowd shall I never be;
For I gart kill my ain gude lord,
And life is nae pleasure to me.'

17 In it came her mother dear,
I wyte a sorry woman was she:
'I woud gie my white monie and gowd,
O bonny Jean, to borrow thee.'

18 'Borrow me, mother, borrow me?
O borrowd shall I never be;
For I gart kill my ain gude lord,
And life's now nae pleasure to me.'

19 Then in it came her father dear,
I wyte a sorry man was he;
Says, 'Ohon, alas! my bonny Jean,
If I had you at hame wi me!

20 'Seven daughters I hae left at hame,
As fair women as fair can be;
But I would gie them ane by ane,
O bonny Jean, to borrow thee.'

21 'O borrow me, father, borrow me?
O borrowd shall I never be;
I that is worthy o the death,
It is but right that I shoud dee.'

22 Then out it speaks the king himsell,
And aye as he steps in the fleer;

Says, 'I grant you your life, lady,
Because you are of tender year.'

23 'A boon, a boon, my liege the king,
The boon I ask, ye'll grant to me;'
'Ask on, ask on, my bonny Jean,
Whateer ye ask it's granted be.'

24 ''Cause take me out at night, at night,
Lat not the sun upon me shine,
And take me to yon heading-hill,
Strike aff this dowie head o mine.

25 'Ye'll take me out at night, at night,
When there are nane to gaze and see,
And hae me to yon heading-hill,
And ye'll gar head me speedilie.'

26 They've taen her out at nine at night,
Loot not the sun upon her shine,
And had her to yon heading-hill,
And headed her baith neat and fine.

27 Then out it speaks the king himsell,
I wyte a sorry man was he:
'I've travelld east, I've travelld west,
And sailed far beyond the sea,
But I never saw a woman's face
I was sae sorry to see dee.

28 'But Warriston was sair to blame,
For slighting o his lady so;
He had the wyte o his ain death,
And bonny lady's overthrow.'

———◆———

B.   4. *The MS indicates that this is the nurse's
speech.*
5¹. whan *struck out, as* written *over.*
8. has *struck out,* 's *substituted.*
10². stay *struck out,* be *substituted.*
10⁸. *Originally* handkerchief; hand *struck
out.*

*Kinloch has made several changes in print-
ing:*
7¹. has gane. 8³. Fy! gar. 8⁴. some brae.
9³. gud wife. *He gives as in* 5¹; be *in* 10²;
handkerchief *in* 10⁸.

C. 6⁴. Whase. *Perhaps,* Wha's *rather than*
Whae's.

195

LORD MAXWELL'S LAST GOODNIGHT

A. 'Lord Maxwell's Last Goodnight,' communicated to Percy by G. Paton, 1778.

B. 'Lord Maxwell's Goodnight,' Glenriddell MSS, XI, 18, 1791, Scott's Minstrelsy, I, 194, 1802; II, 133, 1833.

———◆———

FIRST published in the Minstrelsy of the Scottish Border, "from a copy in Glenriddell's MS., with some slight variations from tradition." I understand this to mean, not that the variations were derived from tradition, but that the text of the Minstrelsy departs somewhat from that of the manuscript.

A and B agree entirely as to matter. The order of the stanzas, not being governed by an explicit story, might be expected to vary with every reciter.

In the year 1585, John, Lord Maxwell, having incurred the enmity of the king's favorite, the Earl of Arran, was denounced rebel, on such charges as were always at hand, and a commission was given to the Laird of Johnstone to pursue and take him. A hired force, by the aid of which this was expected to be done, was badly routed by the Maxwells in a sharp fight. Johnstone made a raid on Maxwell's lands; Maxwell burnt Johnstone's house. Finally, in one of their skirmishes, Johnstone was captured: "the grief of this overthrow gave Johnstone, shortly after he was liberated, his death."

After some years of feud, the two chiefs, "by the industry of certain wise gentlemen of the Johnstones," surprised all Scotland by making a treaty of peace. On April 1, 1592, they entered into a bond to forget and forgive all rancor and malice of the past, and to live in amity, themselves and their friends, in all time coming. A little more than a year after, a party of Johnstones, relying, no doubt, on the forbearance of their new ally, then warden of the West Marches, "rode a stealing" in the lands of Lord Sanquhar and of the knights of Drumlanrig, Lag, and Closeburn, carried off a large booty, and killed eighteen men who endeavored to retrieve their property. (See No 184, 'The Lads of Wamphray.') The injured gentlemen made complaint to Maxwell as warden, and also procured a commission directing him to proceed against the Johnstones. Maxwell was in an awkward plight. To induce him to take action, several of the sufferers engaged to enter into a bond of manrent, or homage, to Maxwell, by which they should be obliged to service and he to protection. "Maxwell, thinking this to be a good occasion for bringing all Nithsdale to depend upon him, embraced the offer." But this bond, through negligence, came to the hands of Johnstone, who, seeing what turn matters would take, made a league with Scotts, Eliots, and others, and in a battle at Dryfe Sands, by superior strategy, defeated Maxwell, though the warden had much larger numbers. This was in December, 1593. "The Lord Maxwell, a tall man and heavy in armor, was in the chase overtaken and stricken from his horse. The report went that he called to Johnstone and desired to be taken as he had sometime taken his father, but was unmercifully used, and the hand that he reached forth cut off. But of this," says Spotiswood, "I can affirm nothing. There always the Lord Maxwell fell, having received many wounds." Drumlanrig, Closeburn, and other of the Nithsdale lairds of Maxwell's faction, barely escaped with their lives.

Sir James Johnstone soon made his peace with the king, whose warden had been slain while acting under royal authority. The heir of the slain warden, John, the ninth Lord Maxwell, is said to have been only eight years old at the time of his father's death.* If this was so, he became very early of age for all purposes of offence. The two clans kept up a bloody and destructive private war. Both chiefs were imprisoned and proclaimed rebel or traitor; Maxwell twice, first in 1601, as favoring popery, and again in 1607, for his extravagant turbulence; and in each case he made his own escape, the second time by the use of violence. At length, influenced perhaps by a conviction that his defiance of the law had gone too far for his safety, Maxwell seemed to be seriously disposed to reconcile himself with his inveterate enemy.† Sir James Johnstone, as it happened, had already asked Sir Robert Maxwell, who was his brother-in-law and cousin to Lord Maxwell, to speak to his kinsman with that view. Sir Robert had no wish to meddle, for his cousin, he said, was a dangerous man to have to do with. Lord John, however, spontaneously sent for Sir Robert, and said to him, You see my estate and the danger I stand in. I would crave your counsel as a man that tenders my weal. The result of much conference and writing (in which Sir Robert Maxwell, evidently feeling imperfect confidence in his cousin, acted with great caution) was that Lord Maxwell proposed a tryst with Sir James Johnstone, each of them to be accompanied by one person only, and no others to be present except Sir Robert, and faithfully promised, with his hands between Sir Robert's hands, that neither he nor the man he should bring with him should do any wrong, "whether they agreed or not." Johnstone accepted the terms and

made corresponding promises. The meeting came off the 6th of April, 1608. Johnstone brought Willie Johnstone with him, and Maxwell Charlie Maxwell, a man that Sir Robert strongly disapproved, but his chief undertook to be answerable for him. Sir Robert required the same guaranty on the part of Johnstone for his follower, and these men were ordered to keep away from one another. The two principals and their mediator between them rode off, with their backs to their men, and began their parley. Looking round, Sir Robert saw that Charlie Maxwell had left his appointed place and gone to Willie Johnstone, at whom, after some words between them, he fired a pistol. Sir Robert cried to Lord Maxwell, Fie, make not yourself a traitor and me both! Lord Maxwell replied, I am blameless. Sir James Johnstone slipped away to see to his follower's safety. Lord Maxwell followed Sir James, shot him in the back, and rode off. ‡

Lord Maxwell fled the country, but was tried in his absence and sentenced to death, with forfeiture of his estates. He came back to Scotland after four years, was basely betrayed into the power of the government by a kinsman, and was beheaded at Edinburgh May 21, 1613. §

"Thus was finally ended," remarks Sir Walter Scott, "by a salutary example of severity, the 'foul debate' betwixt the Maxwells and Johnstones, in the course of which each family lost two chieftains: one dying of a broken heart, one in the field of battle, one by assassination, and one by the sword of the executioner."

A 1, 2, and *passim*. The very affectionate relations of Lord Maxwell and his 'lady and

* Fraser, The Book of Carlaverock, I, 300. "John, ninth Lord Maxwell, was born about the year 1586." He was married in 1601, and imprisoned for his papistical propensity in the same year. Either the date is too late, or Maxwell was one of those avenging children who mature so very fast: see 'Jellon Grame,' II, 303, 513.

† Some sort of "agreement" had been made in 1605, as we see by the "Summons" referred to further on, and Lord Maxwell mentions this agreement in a conversation with Sir Robert Maxwell. Pitcairn's Trials, III, 36, 44.

‡ In the indictment ("Summons, etc., against John, Lord Maxwell"), it is said that Johnstone was shot through the shoulder with two poisoned bullets. If there was evidence as to this aggravating circumstance, it has not been made

accessible. In his "Offers of Submission," etc., by which Lord Maxwell hoped to avoid the extreme penalty of the law, he makes oath on his salvation and damnation that the unhappy slaughter was nowise committed upon forethought felony or set purpose; and on the scaffold, while declaring that he had justly deserved his death and asking forgiveness of the Johnstone family, he protested that his act had been without dishonor or infamy; meaning, of course, perfidy.

§ Spotiswood's History, ed. 1655, pp. 338 f., 400 f., 504 f.; Historie of King James the Sext, pp. 209 f., 297-99; Moysie's Memoirs, p. 109 f.; Pitcairn's Criminal Trials, III, 31-40, 43-47, 51-53; Fraser, The Book of Carlaverock, 1873, pp. 300 f., 314, 321; Taylor, The Great Historic Families of Scotland, 1887, II, 10, 14-25.

only joy,' are a fiction of the ballad-maker. His wife was daughter of the first Marquis of Hamilton. Maxwell instituted a process of divorce against her, and she died while this was pending, before he fled the country in 1608. By his treatment of his wife he made her brother, the second marquis, and the Hamiltons generally, his enemies.*

5, 6. Carlaverock castle had from far back belonged to the Maxwells, and is theirs still. They had a house, or castle, at Dumfries, and the custody of the "houses" of Lochmaben, Langholm, and Thrieve.

9, 10. Douglas of Drumlanrig, Kirkpatrick of Closeburn, and Grierson of Lag fled in the *sauve qui peut* of Dryfe Sands, and the partisans of Lord Maxwell, who there lost his life, would naturally describe them as deserting their chief. They (or two of them) had entered into a "band" with Maxwell, as aforesaid. The ballad-maker seems to intimate that they were in a band with each other, or with somebody, to betray Maxwell.

11, and B 1. 'Robin in the Orchet,' 'Robert of Oarchyardtoan,' is properly Sir Robert Maxwell of Orchardton, Lord John's cousin, but it is evident, from the conjunction of mother and sisters, that the person here intended is his brother Robert, to whom, some years after the execution and forfeiture of Lord John, the estates were restored.

14. Maxwell's wife, as said above, was no longer living. The "offers" which he made, to save his life, contain a proposal that he should marry the slain Sir James Johnstone's daughter, without any dowry.

"Goodnight" is to be taken loosely as a farewell. Other cases are 'John Armstrong's last Goodnight,' and the well-known beautiful fragment (?) of two stanzas called 'Armstrong's Goodnight;' again, Essex's last Goodnight, to the tune of The King's last Goodnight, Chappell, Roxburghe Ballads, I, 570, and Popular Music, p. 174. The Earl of Derby sings a Goodnight (though the name is not used) in 'Flodden Field,' No 168, III, 356, stanzas 36–58. Justice Shallow sang those tunes that he heard the carmen whistle, and sware they were his Fancies, or his Goodnights: Second Part of Henry IV, III, 2. Lord Byron, in the preface to Childe Harold's Pilgrimage, says "the good-night in the beginning of the first canto was suggested by Lord Maxwell's Goodnight in the Border Minstrelsy."

A

Communicated to Percy by G. Paton, Edinburgh, December 4, 1778.

1 'GOOD lord of the land, will you stay thane
    About my faither's house,
And walk into these gardines green,
    In my arms I 'll the embraice.

2 'Ten thousand times I 'll kiss thy face;
    Make sport, and let 's be mery:'
'I thank you, lady, fore your kindness;
    Trust me, I may not stay with the.

3 'For I have kil'd the laird Johnston;
    I vallow not the feed;
My wiked heart did still incline;
    He was my faither's dead.

4 'Both night and day I did proced,
    And a' on him revainged to be;
But now have I gotten what I long sowght,
    Trust me, I may not stay with the.

5 'Adue, Dumfriese, that proper place!
    Fair well, Carlaurike faire!

* In a petition presented to the Privy Council by Robert Maxwell in behalf of his brother, the 'sometime' Lord Maxwell, by his attorney, craves "forgiveness of his offence done to the Marquis of Hamilton [his wife's brother] and his friends." Pitcairn, III, 52. Whether this was penitence or policy, it shows that great offence had been taken. Some verses inserted by Scott in his edition of the ballad, in which his lady urges Maxwell to go with her to her brother's stately tower, where "Hamiltons and Douglas baith shall rise to succour thee," are quite misplaced.

Adue the castle of the Trive,
    And all my buldings there!

6 'Adue, Lochmaben gaits so faire,
    And the Langhm shank, where birks bobs
        bony!
Adue, my leady and only joy!
    Trust me, I may not stay with the.

7 'Adue, fair Eskdale, up and doun,
    Wher my poor frends do duell!
The bangisters will beat them doun,
    And will them sore compell.

8 'I'll reveinge the cause mysell,
    Again when I come over the sea;
Adue, my leady and only joy!
    Fore, trust me, I may not stay with the.

9 'Adue, Dumlanark! fals was ay,
    And Closburn! in a band;
The laird of the Lag from my faither fled
    When the Jhohnstones struek of his hand.

10 'They wer three brethren in a band;
    I pray they may never be merry;
Adue, my leady and only joy!
    Trust me, I may not stay with the.

11 'Adue, madam my mother dear,
    But and my sister[s] two!
Fair well, Robin in the Orchet!
    Fore the my heart is wo.

12 'Adue, the lillie, and fair well, rose,
    And the primros, spreads fair and bony!
Adue, my leady and only joy!
    Fore, trust me, I may not stay with the.'

13 He took out a good gold ring,
    Where at hang sygnets three:
'Take thou that, my own kind thing,
    And ay have mind of me.

14 'Do not mary another lord
    Agan or I come over the sea;
Adue, my leady and only joy!
    For, trust me, I may not stay with the.'

15 The wind was fair, and the ship was clare,
    And the good lord went away;
The most part of his frends was there,
    Giving him a fair convoy.

16 They drank the wine, they did not spare,
    Presentting in that good lord's sight;
Now he is over the floods so gray;
    Lord Maxwell has te'n his last good-night.

———◆———

B

Glenriddell MSS, XI, 18.   1791.

1 'ADIEW, madam my mother dear,
    But and my sisters two!
Adiew, fair Robert of Oarchyardtoan!
    For thee my heart is woe.

2 'Adiew, the lilly and the rose,
    The primrose, sweet to see!
Adiew, my lady and only joy!
    For I manna stay with thee.

3 'Tho I have killed the laird Johnston,
    What care I for his feed?
My noble mind dis still incline;
    He was my father's dead.

4 'Both night and day I laboured oft
    Of him revenged to be,

And now I've got what I long sought;
    But I manna stay with thee.

5 'Adiew, Drumlanrig! false was ay,
    And Cloesburn! in a band,
Where the laird of Lagg fra my father fled
    When the Johnston struck off his hand.

6 'They were three brethren in a band;
    Joy may they never see!
But now I've got what I long sought,
    And I maunna stay with thee.

7 'Adiew, Dumfries, my proper place,
    But and Carlaverock fair,
Adiew, the castle of the Thrieve,
    And all my buildings there!

8 'Adiew, Lochmaben's gates so fair,
    The Langholm shank, where birks they be!

Adiew, my lady and only joy!
　　And, trust me, I maunna stay with thee.

9 'Adiew, fair Eskdale, up and down,
　　Where my poor friends do dwell!
　The bangisters will ding them down,
　　And will them sore compel.

10 'But I'll revenge that feed mysell
　　When I come ou'r the sea;
　Adiew, my lady and only joy!
　　For I maunna stay with thee.'

11 'Lord of the land, will you go then
　　Unto my father's place,
　And walk into their gardens green,
　　And I will you embrace.

12 'Ten thousand times I'll kiss your face,
　　And sport, and make you merry;'
　'I thank thee, my lady, for thy kindness,
　　But, trust me, I maunna stay with thee.'

13 Then he took off a great gold ring,
　　Where at hang signets three:
　'Hae, take thee that, my ain dear thing,
　　And still hae mind of me.

14 'But if thow marry another lord
　　Ere I come ou'r the sea —
　Adiew, my lady and only joy!
　　For I maunna stay with thee.'

15 The wind was fair, the ship was close,
　　That good lord went away,
　And most part of his friends were there,
　　To give him a fair convay.

16 They drank thair wine, they did not spare,
　　Even in the good lord's sight;
　Now he is oer the floods so gray,
　　And Lord Maxwell has taen his good-
　　night.

A.　1². faither's place?　*So* B.
　4². And a' to be revainged on him.　*Cf.* B.
　5². Fair well the Lanrike faires. (?)
　9⁴. struet. (?)
　13¹,². He took out a good gold ring [where it
　　　hang, *partly erased.*]
　　　Where it hang signets three.
B.　*Written in stanzas of eight lines.*
　4¹. labourod.
　The variations of the Minstrelsy, being edito-
　rial, do not require to be recorded, but some
　of them have a certain interest.
　1². sisters three.　1⁴. My heart is wae for thee.

3³. mind their wrath disdains.
6³,⁴. Their treacherous art and cowardly heart
　　　Has twin'd my love and me.

11 Lord of the land, that ladye said,
　　O wad ye go wi me
　Unto my brother's stately tower,
　　Where safest ye may be!

12¹,². There Hamiltons and Douglas baith
　　　Shall rise to succour thee.
14³. His life is but a three days' lease.
15¹. was clear, *as in* A.

196

THE FIRE OF FRENDRAUGHT

A. a. 'The Fire of Frendraught,' Motherwell's Minstrelsy, p. 161, 1827. **b.** 'Burning of Frendraught,' Maidment's North Countrie Garland, p. 4, 1824.

B. 'The Burning of Frendraught,' Kinloch MSS, V, 399.

C. 'The Fire of Frendraught,' from a note-book of Dr Joseph Robertson's.

D. Ritson's Scotish Songs, II, 35, 1794.

E. Kinloch MSS, VI, 27, one stanza.

A a was communicated to Motherwell by Charles Kirkpatrick Sharpe. (Corrections have here been adopted from Motherwell's Errata: see also the Musical Museum, 1853, IV, 322*.) **A b**, says Motherwell, has the "disadvantage of containing a very considerable number of slight verbal and literal inaccuracies." The implication is, or should be, that these variations are of editorial origin. Some of the readings of **b** are in themselves better than those of **a**. **b** is repeated in Buchan's Gleanings, p. 165. The copy in Maidment's Scotish Ballads, 1868, I, 267, is **a** with a reading or two from **b**, arbitrary alterations, and some misprints.

Dr Joseph Robertson has, in one of his notebooks, "Adversaria," p. 63, the two following stanzas, given him by a gentleman of Buchan as belonging to 'The Burning of Frendraught House."

'Will ye play at the cards, Lord John?
  Will ye drink at the wine?
Or will ye [gang] to a weel made bed,
  And sleep till it be time?'

'I 'll no play at the cards, ladie,
  I 'll no drink at the wine;
But I 'll gang to a weel made bed,
  An sleep till it be time.'

Undoubtedly these stanzas may have occurred in a version of this ballad, but they are a commonplace, and sometimes an intrusive one. See II, 109, 'Fair Janet,' F 4, 5; 154,

'Young Hunting,' K 8, 9; 164, 'Clerk Saunders,' F, 5, 6; 409, 'Willie o Douglas Dale,' B 20.

The modern, and extremely vapid, ballad of 'Frennet Hall' appeared originally (I suppose) in Herd's Scottish Songs, 1776, I, 142, and was afterwards received into Ritson's Scotish Songs, II, 31, The Musical Museum, No 286, etc.

James Crichton of Frendraught and William Gordon of Rothiemay (a neighboring estate *) had a fierce quarrel about fishing-rights pertaining to lands which Gordon had sold to Crichton. A legal decision was rendered in favor of Frendraught, who, however, pursued his adversary with excessive vigor and procured him to be outlawed. After this, Rothiemay would hear to no terms of peace, and collected a party of loose fellows with the intent to waste Frendraught's lands. Frendraught obtained a commission to arrest Rothiemay, and on the first day of the year 1630 set out to put this in force, accompanied, among others, by his uncle (George Gordon) James Leslie, son of the laird of Pitcaple, and John Meldrum, who was married to young Leslie's aunt. Rothiemay, hearing of Frendraught's coming, rode out to meet him, and there was a fight, in which Rothiemay and George Gordon were mortally

* Frendraught is in the parish of Forgue, Aberdeenshire, Rothiemay in Banffshire; they lie on opposite sides of the Deveron.

wounded, and Meldrum badly. The feud waxed hot, and Frendraught's lands were in danger of being burned and ravaged by Highlanders, with whom John Gordon of Rothiemay, son to the slain laird, had combined for the purpose. But in the end, by the strenuous exertions of the Marquis of Huntly and others, a settlement was effected. The laird of Rothiemay and the children of George Gordon were "to remit their father's slaughter mutually," and in satisfaction thereof the laird of Frendraught was to pay a certain sum of money to young Rothiemay and to George Gordon's children : " which both, Frendraught obeyed and performed willingly, and so, all parties having shaken hands, they were heartily reconciled."

This broil was no sooner settled than another sprouted, a side-shoot from the same stem. Meldrum, who had been with Frendraught in the affray with Rothiemay, and had been wounded, was dissatisfied with such requital as he received, and, getting nothing more by his bickering and threats, helped himself one night to two of Frendraught's best horses. Summoned to court for the theft, he " turned rebel " and did not appear. Frendraught obtained a commission to arrest him, and went to look for him at Pitcaple, a place belonging to John Leslie, Meldrum's brother-in-law. He did not find Meldrum, but fell in with James Leslie, Pitcaple's son, who had also been of Frendraught's party at the encounter on New Year's day. There was talk about Meldrum's behavior, in which Frendraught comported himself forbearingly ; but James Leslie and Robert Crichton, a kinsman of Frendraught, had hot words, which ended in Leslie's getting a dangerous shot in the arm. Hereupon the larger part of the surname of Leslie rose in arms against the Crichtons. Frendraught, grieved for what had happened to James Leslie, betook himself to the Marquis of Huntly, and entreated him to make peace. The marquis sent for the Leslies, and did his best to recon-

cile them, but Pitcaple would listen to nothing until he knew whether his son James was to live or die. Huntly, fearing for Frendraught's safety, kept him two days at the Bog of Gight, and then, hearing that the Leslies were lying in wait, sent his own son, Viscount Melgum, and the young laird of Rothiemay, to protect him on the way home. Arrived there, the laird and his lady begged these young gentlemen to remain overnight, " and did their best, with all demonstration of love and kindness, to entertain them, thinking themselves happy now to have purchased such friends who had formerly been their foes." At about two in the morning the tower of Frendraught house, in which these guests lay, took fire, and they with four of their servants were burnt to death. This occurred on the eighth (ninth) of October.

So far Sir Robert Gordon, uncle of the lady of Frendraught and cousin of the Marquis of Huntly, who was perfectly acquainted with all the parties and circumstances. He goes on to say, with entire fairness : " The rumor of this unhappy accident did speedily spread itself throughout the whole kingdom, every man bewailing it, and constructing it diversly as their affections led them ; some laying an aspersion upon Frendraught, as if he had wilfully destroyed his guests, who had come thither to defend him against his enemies ; which carried no appearance of truth ; for, besides the improbability of the matter, he did lose therein a great quantity of silver, both coined and uncoined, and likewise all his writs and evidents were therein burnt." *

The monstrous wickedness of this act would not, in the light of the history of those times, afford an argument that would of itself avail to clear Frendraught ; but what words could describe his recklessness and folly ! Supposing him willing to set fire to his own house, and sacrifice his silver and securities, for the gratification of burning young Rothiemay with the rest, he knew very well what consequences he had to expect. He had been glad to com-

* A Genealogical History of the Earldom of Sutherland, 1813, pp. 412, 416 ff. Sir Robert Gordon's book stops before the (inconclusive) legal and judicial proceedings were finished. He seems to share the suspicion of the "most part," that the Leslies and Meldrum set the fire.

pound his feud with the Rothiemays by the payment of money (some say the considerable sum of 50,000 merks). He had been alarmed, and with good reason, at the prospect of a feud with the Leslies. But what were these to a feud with the Marquis of Huntly, which would bring down upon him, and did bring down upon him, not only the reprisals of the Gordons, but spoliation from all the brigands of the country? *

'Lewed people demen gladly to the badder ende,'

says Chaucer, and so it was with ballad-makers, and sometimes even with clerks; John Spalding, for instance, the other contemporary authority upon this subject, who gives a lively and detailed account of the burning of the tower, as follows.†

"The viscount was laid in a bed in the Old Tower, going off the hall, and standing upon a vault, wherein there was a round hole, devised of old, just under Aboyne's ‡ bed. Robert Gordon, born in Sutherland, his servitor, and English Will, his page, was both laid beside him in the same chamber. The laird of Rothiemay, with some servants beside him, was laid in an upper chamber just above Aboyne's chamber; and in another room above that chamber was laid George Chalmer of Noth, and George Gordon, another of the viscount's servants; with whom also was laid

Captain Rollok, then in Frendraught's own company. Thus all being at rest, about midnight that dolorous tower took fire in so sudden and furious manner, yea, and in a clap, that this noble viscount, the laird of Rothiemay, English Will, Colin Ivat, another of Aboyne's servitors, and other two, being six in number, were cruelly burnt and tormented to the death, but help or relief; the laird of Frendraught, his lady and whole household looking on, without moving or stirring to deliver them from the fury of this fearful fire, as was reported. Robert Gordon, called Sutherland Robert, being in the viscount's chamber, escaped this fire with his life. George Chalmer and Captain Rollok, being in the third room, escaped also this fire, and, as was said, Aboyne might have saved himself also if he had gone out of doors, which he would not do, but suddenly ran up stairs to Rothiemay's chamber, and wakened him to rise, and as he is wakening him, the timber passage and lofting of the chamber hastily takes fire, so that none of them could win down stairs again; so they turned to a window looking to the close, where they piteously cried help, help, many times, for God's cause! the laird and the lady, with their servants, all seeing and hearing this woeful crying, but made no help nor manner of helping; § which they perceiving, they cried oftentimes mercy

* See Spalding, Memorialls of the Trubles in Scotland and in England, 1624–1645, Spalding Club, I, 45–51, 420–23, 430–35, and the continuator of Sir Robert Gordon, p. 474 f. Frendraught is generally represented to have been utterly ruined in his estate, but that is probably an exaggeration. His sufferings are thus depicted in the Charges against the Marquis of Huntly and others anent the disorders in the North (Spalding, I, 420): "Forasmuch as the Lords of Secret Council are informed that great numbers of sorners and broken men of the clan Gregor, clan Lachlan (etc.), as also divers of the name of Gordon . . . have this long time, and now lately very grievously, infested his Majesty's loyal subjects in the north parts, especially the laird of Frendraught and his tenants, by frequent slaughters, herships, and barbarous cruelties committed upon them, and by a late treasonable fireraising within the said laird of Frendraught his bounds, whereby not only is all the gentleman's lands laid waste, his whole goods and bestial spoiled, slain and maigled, some of his servants killed and cruelly demeaned, but also the whole tenants of his lands and domestics of his house have left his service, and himself, with the hazard of his life, has been forced to steal away under night and have his refuge to his Majesty's Council, etc." It was reported

that Frendraught obtained a decree against the marquis for 200,000 merks (Scots) for scathe, and another for 100,000 pounds (or merks) for spoliation of tithes, but that he recovered the money does not appear. (Spalding, I, 71, 115.) In 1636, through the exertions of Sir Robert Gordon, Huntly and Frendraught were brought to submit all differences on either side, "and particularly a great action of law prosecuted by Frendraught against the marquis," to the arbitrament of friends. Huntly died before a decision was reached, but "the Laird of Frendraught retired himself home to his own lands, and there lived peaceably." (Genealogical History of Sutherland, p. 479.)

† Memorials, I, 17 ff., and the Appendix, p. 381 ff.

‡ So John Gordon, Viscount Melgum, the second son of the Marquis of Huntly, was indifferently called, though the title of Viscount Aboyne belonged to his elder brother, George, and was not conferred upon him until after John's death. Sir Robert Gordon says that the Marquis of Huntly "ordained" for Melgum the lands of Aboyne, and others. Melgum was married to Sophia Hay, daughter of the Earl of Errol, as appears also in the ballad.

§ What manner of helping Frendraught could have given Spalding does not "condescend upon." The way down

at God's hands for their sins, syne clasped in other arms, and cheerfully suffered this cruel martyrdom. Thus died this noble viscount, of singular expectation, Rothiemay, a brave youth, and the rest, by this doleful fire never enough to be deplored, to the great grief and sorrow of their kin, friends, parents, and whole country people, especially to the noble marquis, who for his goodwill got this reward."

Spalding tells us that it was reported that, the morning after the fire, Lady Frendraught, riding on a small nag, and with no attendants but a boy to lead her horse, came weeping to the Bog, desiring to speak with the marquis, but was refused. The Huntly-Gordons, the Earl of Errol (brother of Viscountess Melgum), and many other friends held a council, and after serious consideration came to the conclusion that the fire "could not come by chance, sloth, or accident, but was plotted and devised of set purpose;" Frendraught, his lady, his friends and servants, one or other, knowing thereof. The marquis, however, was resolved not to revenge himself "by way of deed," but to invoke the laws. Frendraught, as far as we can see, desired a legal inquiry no less than Huntly. He addressed himself to the Lord Chancellor and to the Privy Council, and offered to undergo any form of trial, and, delays occurring, he repeated to the Council his wish to have "that hidden mystery brought to a clear light." Examinations and prosecutions, extended to the middle of the year 1634, failed to fix the

guilt of the fire on him or anybody, although John Meldrum, on the strength of some threats which he had uttered, was wrongfully convicted of the act and was executed.*

A. The date is the eighteenth of October, new style for the eighth. When Gordon and Rothiemay (having convoyed Frendraught safely home) are on the point of returning, Lady Frendraught urges them to stay, in token of good feeling between Huntly and her husband. Lord John is quite disposed to comply, but Rothiemay says that his horse has been tampered with since their coming, and he fears that he is fey. After the regular evening-mass of ballads (which would have suited Lady Frendraught, a concealed Catholic, but not her husband), Lord John and Rothiemay are laid in one chamber, an arrangement which would have allowed both to escape, as Robert Gordon did, who slept in his master's room. Lord John wakes with the smoke and heat, and rouses Rothiemay. The doors and windows are fastened. Rothiemay goes to the 'wire-window,' and finds the stanchions too strong to be dealt with. He sees Lady Frendraught below, and cries to her for mercy; her husband killed the father, and now she is burning the son. Lady Frendraught is sorry that she must burn Lord John in order to burn Rothiemay, but there is no help; the keys are cast in the deep draw-well.† [Robert] Gordon, who has escaped though the keys were in the well, calls to his master to jump from the window; he will catch him in his arms. His

---

stairs was barred by fire, the windows were barred with iron. ["But the stairs or monty being in fire, and the windows grated with strong bars of iron, there was no moyen to escape:" Blakhal's Narration, Spalding Club, p. 125.] Ladders and crowbars occur to us, but a tower with walls ten feet thick was not expected to burn, the servants had not been drilled in managing fires, people smoked from their beds at two in the morning are not apt to have their wits about them, and the combustion was rapid.

* All the documents will be found in the Appendix to Spalding. Dr John Hill Burton, in Narratives from Criminal Trials in Scotland, 1852, I, 202 ff., leans hard against Frendraught. "With pretty abundant materials, it is impossible, even at the present day, entirely to clear up the mystery, but we can see by what machinations inquiry was baffled." "It will be seen that no evidence against him was received, that it was considered an offence to accuse him." "Frendraught, though he had with a high hand averted even the pretence of inquiry on the part of the government, did

not go unpunished, *whether he was guilty or not*." Dr Burton speaks with more reserve in his History of Scotland, VI, 209; little more is insisted on than a wish of the Court to foster the Crichtons as a balance to the power of the house of Huntly. It is clear that Frendraught had all the consideration and help from the government which he could claim. Mr Charles Rampini, who has discussed the affair in The Scottish Review, X, 143 ff., 1887, concludes favorably to Frendraught's innocence of the fire.

† "Many years ago, when the well was cleared out, this tradition was corroborated by their finding the keys: at least, such was the report of the country." (Finlay, I, xxi, citing a correspondent.) Of course we should have had to believe everything against Lady Frendraught, even that she had been so simple as to throw them in, if keys had been found in the well; but the land-steward of the proprietor of the estate informed the late Mr Norval Clyne that the draw-well was searched, and no keys were found.

master answers that no fire shall part him and Rothiemay, and besides, the window is fast. He throws his finger-rings down, to be given to his lady. When the servant goes home to his mistress, she reproaches him for coming back alive and leaving his master dead. She tears off the clothes which her maid puts on her, exclaiming that she won a sore heart the day she was married, and that that day has returned (which is not easy to understand: see Appendix).

B. This fragment represents Lady Frendraught as being very importunate with Lord John: she presses him three times over to stay, and promises him a morning-gift of lands if he will comply; by a perversion of tradition, Strathbogie, which had been in his family three hundred years, and which, further on, he offers to give her if she will let him out. Finding that he cannot escape (perhaps stanza 7 should come later), Lord John takes out his psalm-book and sings three verses, with 'God end our misery' at each verse's end. In 9 he sees his elder brother, Lord George, from the window, and asks what news he has, but a defect conceals from us the point of this passage. Stanza 16 seems to belong to Lord John's wife.

C. When the gentlemen are in their saddles, ready to ride away, Lady Frendraught, on her bare knees, begs them to remain, and promises them a firlot of red gold if they will. When everybody has gone to bed, the doors

are locked and the windows shut. The reek begins to rise and the joists to crack; Lord John betakes himself to the window, and finds the stanchions too strong to break. He goes back and wakens Rothiemay, and proposes to him to praise the Lord in the fifty-third psalm, * for there is treason about them. He calls to Lady Frendraught, walking on the green, for mercy; she replies that the keys are in the well, and the doors were locked yesterday. He reproaches her for burning her own flesh. George Chalmers (who really escaped, though lodged in the third story) is described as leaping the ditches and coming, from without, to Rothiemay's help, and Colin Irving (the Colin Ivat of Spalding, who was burnt) as doing the same in behalf of Lord John, to whom he calls to jump into his arms. Lord John is burning, and there is little more left of him than his spirit; but he throws down a purse of gold for the poor and his rings for his wife. Lady Rothiemay comes in the morning to cry vengeance on Frendraught, who has betrayed the gay Gordons, killed her lord, and burnt her son. †

D. " ' There are some intermediate particulars,' Mr Boyd says, 'respecting the lady's lodging her victims in a turret or flanker which did not communicate with the castle.' 'This,' adds he, 'I only have from tradition, as I never heard any other stanzas besides the foregoing.' The author of the original, we may perceive, either through ignorance or

---

* This is, of course, the style of the kirk. The fifty-third psalm of the Vulgate would not have been out of place for Lord John, who was a Catholic; but no doubt Lord John is taken for a Presbyterian in the ballad, and the 'three' is for rhyme. Father Blakhal maintains that Frendraught burnt his tower, not to rid himself of Rothiemay, but out of theological malice to Melgum "for his zeal in defending and protecting the poor Catholics against the tyranny of our puritanical bishops and ministers." " As he [Melgum] was dying for the defence of the poor Catholics, God did bestow upon him the grace to augment the number at the last hour of his life, persuading the Baron of Rothiemay to abjure the heresy of Calvin, and make the profession of the Catholic faith openly, to the hearing of the traitor and all who were with him in the court. They two being at a window, and whilst their legs were burning, they did sing together *Te Deum*; which ended, they did tell at the window that their legs being consumed even to their knees, etc. . . . And so this noble martyr finished this mortal life, at the

age of four and twenty years." A Brief Narration, etc., p. 124 f.

Blakhal, who is far from being a cautious writer, also tells us that "the traitor," Frendraught, "with his men, in arms, walked all the night in the court," to kill Gordon and Rothiemay, if they should escape from the fire. There is a passage of the same purport in one of Arthur Johnston's two poems on the burning of Frendraught, " Querela Sophiæ Hayæ," etc. :

Cur vigil insuetis noctem traduxit in armis,
  Cætera cum somno turba sepulta foret ?

The other piece ends with a ferocious demand for the use of torture to discover the guilty party. (Delitiæ Poetarum Scotorum, Amsterdam, 1637, pp. 585, 587 ; or, A. I. Poemata Omnia, Middelburg, 1642, pp. 329, 331.)

† Stanza 21 recalls the verses in Hume of Godscroft :

Edinburgh castle, towne, and tower,
  God grant thou sink for sinne ! etc.

design, had deviated from the fact in supposing Lady Frennet's husband to have been slain
by Lord John's father." Ritson, p. 36.

It may be noted that three of the most
tragical of the Scottish historical ballads are
associated with the name of Gordon: the
Burning of Towie, as we might call 'Captain

Car,' No 178, through Adam Gordon, uncle
of the first marquis of Huntly; the Burning
of Donibristle, known as 'The Bonny Earl
of Murray,' No 181, of which the responsibility
is put upon the marquis (then earl) himself;
and the Burning of Frendraught, in which his
son perished.

A

a. Motherwell's Minstrelsy, p. 161, from a MS. of Charles
Kirkpatrick Sharpe. b. Maidment's North Countrie Garland, p. 4; "long preserved by tradition in Aberdeenshire,
and procured from an intelligent individual resident in that
part of Scotland."

1 THE eighteenth of October,
    A dismal tale to hear
How good Lord John and Rothiemay
    Was both burnt in the fire.

2 When steeds was saddled and well bridled,
    And ready for to ride,
Then out it came her false Frendraught,
    Inviting them to bide.

3 Said, 'Stay this night untill we sup,
    The morn untill we dine;
'T will be a token of good greement
    'Twixt your good lord and mine.'

4 'We 'll turn again,' said good Lord John;
    'But no,' said Rothiemay,
'My steed 's trapand, my bridle 's broken,
    I fear the day I 'm fey.'

5 When mass was sung, and bells was rung,
    And all men bound for bed,
Then good Lord John and Rothiemay
    In one chamber was laid.

6 They had not long cast off their cloaths,
    And were but now asleep,
When the weary smoke began to rise,
    Likewise the scorching heat.

7 'O waken, waken, Rothiemay!
    O waken, brother dear!
And turn you to our Saviour;
    There is strong treason here.'

8 When they were dressed in their cloaths,
    And ready for to boun,
The doors and windows was all secur'd,
    The roof-tree burning down.

9 He did him to the wire-window,
    As fast as we could gang;
Says, Wae to the hands put in the stancheons!
    For out we 'll never win.

10 When he stood at the wire-window,
    Most doleful to be seen,
He did espy her Lady Frendraught,
    Who stood upon the green.

11 Cried, Mercy, mercy, Lady Frendraught!
    Will ye not sink with sin?
For first your husband killed my father,
    And now you burn his son.

12 O then out spoke her Lady Frendraught,
    And loudly did she cry;
'It were great pity for good Lord John,
    But none for Rothiemay;
But the keys are casten in the deep draw-well,
    Ye cannot get away.'

13 While he stood in this dreadful plight,
    Most piteous to be seen,
There called out his servant Gordon,
    As he had frantic been:

14 'O loup, O loup, my dear master!
    O loup and come to me!
I 'll catch you in my arms two,
    One foot I will not flee.

15 'O loup, O loup, my dear master!
    O loup and come away!
I 'll catch you in my arms two,
    But Rothiemay may lie.'

16 'The fish shall never swim in the flood,
Nor corn grow through the clay,
Nor the fiercest fire that ever was kindled
Twin me and Rothiemay.

17 'But I cannot loup, I cannot come,
I cannot win to thee;
My head 's fast in the wire-window,
My feet burning from me.

18 'My eyes are seething in my head,
My flesh roasting also,
My bowels are boiling with my blood;
Is not that a woeful woe?

19 'Take here the rings from my white fingers,
That are so long and small,
And give them to my lady fair,
Where she sits in her hall.

20 'So I cannot loup, I cannot come,
I cannot loup to thee;
My earthly part is all consumed,
My spirit but speaks to thee.'

21 Wringing her hands, tearing her hair,
His lady she was seen,

And thus addressed his servant Gordon,
Where he stood on the green.

22 'O wae be to you, George Gordon!
An ill death may you die!
So safe and sound as you stand there,
And my lord bereaved from me.'

23 'I bad him loup, I bad him come,
I bad him loup to me;
I 'd catch him in my arms two,
A foot I should not flee.   &c.

24 'He threw me the rings from his white fingers,
Which were so long and small,
To give to you, his lady fair,
Where you sat in your hall.'   &c.

25 Sophia Hay, Sophia Hay,
O bonny Sophia was her name,
Her waiting maid put on her cloaths,
But I wot she tore them off again.

26 And aft she cried, Ohon! alas! alas!
A sair heart 's ill to win;
I wan a sair heart when I married him,
And the day it 's well returnd again.

B

Kinloch MSS, V, 399, in the handwriting of John Hill Burton.

*   *   *   *   *   *   *

1 'YE 'LL stay this night wi me, Lord John,
Ye 'll stay this night wi me,
For there is appearence of good greement
Betwixt Frendraught and thee.'

2 'How can I bide, or how shall I bide,
Or how can I bide wi thee,
Sin my lady is in the lands of Air,
And I long till I her see?'

3 'Oh stay this night wi me, Lord John,
Oh stay this night wi me,
And bonny ['s] be the morning-gift
That I will to you gie.

4 'I 'll gie you a Strathboggie lands,
And the laigh lands o Strathray,
.   .   .   .
.   .   .   .

5 'Ye 'll stay this night wi me, Lord John,
Ye 'll stay this night wi me,
And I 'll lay you in a bed of down,
And Rothiemay you wi.'

6 When mass was sung, and bells were rung,
And a' men bun to bed,
Gude Lord John and Rothiemay
In one chamber were laid.

*   *   *   *   *   *   *

7 Out hes he taen his little psalm-buik,
And verses sang he three,
And aye at every verse's end,
'God end our misery!'

8 The doors were shut, the keys were thrown
    Into a vault of stone,

   .   .   .   .   .   .

    .   .

9 He is dune him to the weir-window,
    The stauncheons were oer strong;
There he saw him Lord George Gordon
    Come haisling to the town.

10 'What news, what news now, George Gordon?
    Whats news hae you to me?

   .   .   .   .   .   .

    .   .   .   .   .

11 He 's dune him to the weir-window,
    The stauncheons were oer strang;
And there he saw the Lady Frendraught,
    Was walking on the green.

12 'Open yer doors now, Lady Frendraught,
    Ye 'll open yer doors to me;
And bonny 's be the mornin-gift
    That I shall to you gie.

13 'I 'll gie you a' Straboggie lands,
    And the laigh lands o Strathbrae,

   .   .   .   .

14 'Now there 's the rings frae my fingers,
    And the broach frae my breast-bone;
Ye 'll gae that to my gude ladye

    .   .   .   .

*   *   *   *   *   *   *

15 'How can I loup, or how shall I loup?
    How can I loup to thee?
When the blood is boiling in my body,
    And my feet burnin frae me?'

*   *   *   *   *   *   *

16 'If I was swift as any swallow,
    And then had wings to fly,
I could fly on to fause Frendraught
    And cry vengeance till I die.'

C

From a note-book of Dr Joseph Robertson: " procured in the parish of Forgue by A. Scott; communicated to me by Mr John Stuart, Aberdeen, 11 October, 1832."

1 IT was in October the woe began —
    It lasts for now and aye, —
The burning o the bonny house o fause Frend-
    raught,
    Lord John and Rothiemay.

2 When they were in their saddles set,
    And ready to ride away,
The lady sat down on her bare knees,
    Beseeching them to stay.

3 'Ye 's hae a firlot o the gude red gowd,
    Well straiket wi a wan;
And if that winna please you well,
    I 'll heap it wi my han.'

4 Then out it spake the gude Lord John,
    And said to Rothiemay,
'It is a woman that we 're come o,
    And a woman we 'll obey.'

5 When a' man was well drunken,
    And a' man bound for bed,
The doors were lockd, the windows shut,
    And the keys were casten by.

6 When a' man was well drunken,
    And a' man bound for sleep,
The dowy reek began to rise,
    And the joists began to crack.

7 He 's deen him to the wire-window,
    And ruefu strack and dang;
But they would neither bow nor brack,
    The staunchions were so strang.

8 He 's deen him back and back again,
    And back to Rothiemay;
Says, Waken, waken, brother dear!
    Waken, Rothiemay!

9 'Come let us praise the Lord our God,
    The fiftieth psalm and three;
For the reek and smoke are us about,
    And there 's fause treason tee.

10 'O mercy, mercy, Lady Frendraught!
   As ye walk on the green:'
   'The keys are in the deep draw-well,
   The doors were lockt the streen.'

11 'O woe be to you, Lady Frendraught!
   An ill death may you die!
   For think na ye this a sad torment
   Your own flesh for to burn?'

12 George Chalmers was a bonny boy;
   He leapt the stanks so deep,
   And he is on to Rothiemay,
   His master for to help.

13 Colin Irving was a bonny boy,
   And leapt the stanks so deep:
   'Come down, come down, my master dear!
   In my arms I'll thee kep.'

14 'Come down? come down? how can I come?
   How can I come to thee?
   My flesh is burning me about,
   And yet my spirit speaks to thee.'

15 He's taen a purse o the gude red gowd,
   And threw it oer the wa:
   'It's ye'll deal that among the poor,
   Bid them pray for our souls a'.'

16 He's taen the rings off his fingers,
   And threw them oer the wa;
   Says, Ye'll gie that to my lady dear,
   From me she'll na get more.

17 'Bid her make her bed well to the length,
   But no more to the breadth,
   For the day will never dawn
   That I'll sleep by her side.'

18 Ladie Rothiemay came on the morn,
   She kneeled it roun and roun:
   'Restore your lodgers, fause Frendraught,
   That ye burnd here the streen.

19 'O were I like yon turtle-dove,
   Had I wings for to flie,
   I'd fly about fause Frendraught
   Crying vengeance till I die.

20 'Frendraught fause, all thro the ha's,
   Both back and every side;
   For ye've betrayd the gay Gordons,
   And lands wherein they ride.

21 'Frendraught fause, all thro the ha's;
   I wish you'd sink for sin;
   For first you killd my own good lord,
   And now you've burnd my son.

22 'I caredna sae muckle for my good lord
   I saw him in battle slain,
   But a' is for my own son dear,
   The heir o a' my lan.

23 'I caredna sae muckle for my good lord
   I saw him laid in clay,
   But a' is for my own son dear,
   The heir o Rothiemay.'

D

Ritson's Scotish Songs, 1794, II, 35; remembered by the
Rev. Mr Boyd, translator of Dante, and communicated to
the editor by J. C. Walker.

1 THE reek it rose, and the flame it flew,
   And oh! the fire augmented high,
   Until it came to Lord John's chamber-window,
   And to the bed where Lord John lay.

2 'O help me, help me, Lady Frennet!
   I never ettled harm to thee;
   And if my father slew thy lord,
   Forget the deed and rescue me.'

3 He looked east, he looked west,
   To see if any help was nigh;
   At length his little page he saw,
   Who to his lord aloud did cry:

4 'Loup doun, loup doun, my master dear!
   What though the window's dreigh and hie?
   I'll catch you in my arms twa,
   And never a foot from you I'll flee.'

5 'How can I loup, you little page?
   How can I leave this window hie?
   Do you not see the blazing low,
   And my twa legs burnt to my knee?'

E

Kinloch MSS, VI, 27, in the handwriting of Joseph
Robertson when a youth.

Now wake, now wake you, Rothiemay!
    I dread you sleep oer soun;
The bed is burnin us about
    And the curtain 's faain down.

A. a. 23, 24. *The &c. at the end denote that the
    servant repeated the substance of 15–18
    and of 20, which, however, was not writ-
    ten out.*

b. 1¹. day of. 1⁴. Were. 2¹, 5¹, 5⁴, 8³. were.
2³. out there came the. 6². but new.
6³. the *wanting*. 7³. to your. 8¹. dressed wi.
9¹. did flee to. 10¹. While he.
10³, 12¹. the *for* her. 11¹. Cried *wanting*.
12⁵. The keys were casten. 12⁶. win away.
13³. Then called. 15⁴. may lay.
17¹. But *wanting*. 18¹. are southering.
19². Which are. 20¹. So *wanting*.

20⁴. but *wanting*. 21². fair *for* she.
21³. Calling unto his. 22⁴. lord burned.
23². come to. 23⁴. would not: *no &c.*
24⁴. sit: *no &c.* 25². O *wanting*.
25⁴. I wat *wanting*. 26¹. *One* alas *wanting*.
26². heart 's easy wan.
26⁴. And, well *wanting*.
Some readings of b *are preferable, as in
6², 18¹, 21³, 22⁴; others also, which may
be editorial improvements.*

B. 16. "This is another stanza which I after-
    wards received."

C. 4¹. *A small stroke between* out *and* it.

APPENDIX

A 26 And aft she cried, ' Ohon ! alas ! alas !
    A sair heart 's ill to win ;
I wan a sair heart when I married him,
    And the day it 's well returned again.'

My friend the late Mr Norval Clyne thought
that this obscure stanza might perhaps be cleared
up by the following verses, communicated to him in
1873 by the Rev. George Sutherland, Episcopal
clergyman at Tillymorgan, Aberdeenshire.

YOUNG TOLQUHON

WORD has come to Young Tolquhon,
    In his chamber where he lay,
That Sophia Hay, his first fair love,
    Was wedded and away.

'Sophia Hay, Sophia Hay,
    My love, Sophia Hay,

I wish her anes as sair a heart
    As she 's gien me the day.

'She thinks she has done me great wrang,
    But I don't think it so ;
I hope to live in quietness
    When she shall live in woe.

'She 'll live a discontented life
    Since she is gone from me ;
Ower seen, ower seen, a wood o green
    Will shortly cover me.

'When I am dead and in my grave,
    Cause write upon me so :
"Here lies a lad who died for love,
    And who can blame my woe." '

Mr Sutherland wrote : This fragment I took
down from the recitation of my mother, twenty or
twenty-five years ago. She was born in 1790, and
her great-grandmother was a servant of the last
Forbes of Tolquhon. She had a tradition that
Sophia Hay was one of the Errol family, and mar-

ried Lord John Gordon, who was burned at Frendraught. Mr Clyne remarked: The Young Tolquhon at the time of this marriage, about 1628, was Alexander Forbes, eldest son of William Forbes of Tolquhon. Alexander is recorded to have died without issue, and the following additional particulars, singularly suggestive of a determination on the unfortunate lover's part to renounce the world, have been communicated to me by Dr John Stuart. In 1631 William Forbes granted a charter of the lands of Tolquhon to his second son Walter and his heirs male, and in 1632 another deed of the same sort to Walter, with the express consent of Alexander, his elder brother. In 1641 Alexander is supposed to have been dead, as Walter is then styled "of Tolquhon." The lady's somewhat enigmatical exclamation,

> 'I wan a sair heart when I married him,
> And the day it 's well returned again,'

may have its explanation in the words of Young Tolquhon,

> 'I wish her anes as sair a heart
> As she 's gien me the day.'

Mr Clyne did not fail to observe that Father Blakhal has recorded of Lady Melgum that he had often heard her say that she had never loved anybody but her husband, and never would love another (Narration, p. 92). This testimony, if not decisive, may be considered not less cogent as to the matter of fact than anything in 'Young Tolquhon' to the contrary. But it may be that stanza 24 became attached to the Frendraught ballad in consequence of the coexistence of this or some similar ballad of Young Tolquhon.

197

JAMES GRANT

Motherwelll's MS., p. 470, communicated apparently by Buchan; 'The Gordons and the Grants,' Buchan's Ballads of the North of Scotland, II, 220.

THERE was an implacable feud between the Grants of Ballindalloch and the Grants of Carron, "for divers ages," Sir Robert Gordon says, certainly for ninety years after 1550. This fragment has to do with the later stage of their enmity. In 1628, John Grant of Ballindalloch killed John Grant of Carron. James Grant of Carron, uncle of the slain man, burnt all the corn, barns, and byres of Ballindalloch young and old, and took to the hills (1630). The Ballindallochs complained to Murray, the lieutenant, and he, "to gar ane devil ding another," set the Clanchattan upon James Grant. They laid siege to a house where he was with a party of his men; he made his way out, was pursued, and was taken after receiving eleven arrow-wounds. When he was well enough to travel, he was sent to Edinburgh, and, as everybody supposed, to his death; but after a confinement of more than a year he broke ward (October, 1632). Large sums were offered for him, alive or dead; but James Grant was hard to keep and hard to catch, and in November, 1633, he began to kythe again in the north. A gang of the forbidden name of McGregor, who had been brought into the country by Ballindalloch to act against James Grant, beset him in a small house in Carron where he was visiting his wife, having only his son and one other man with him; but he defended himself with the spirit of another Cloudesly, shot the captain, and got off to the bog with his men.[*]

* Gordon's History of Sutherland, p. 414; Spalding's Memorials, I, 11, 21–23, 29 f., 43 f.

"The year of God one thousand six hundred thirty-six, some of the Marquis of Huntly's followers and servants did invade the rebel James Grant and some of his associates, hard by Strathbogy. They burnt the house wherein he was, but, the night being dark and windy, he and his brother, Robert Grant, escaped." *

This last escapade of James Grant may perhaps be the one to which this fragment has reference, though Ballindalloch was not personally engaged in the assault on the house, and I know of no Douglas having sheltered Grant of Carron. One almost wonders that this mettlesome and shifty outlaw was not celebrated in a string of ballads.

Early in 1639, James Grant got his peace from the king; later in the year, he joined the "barons" at Aberdeen with five hundred men, and in 1640, we are told, "he purchased his remission orderly and went home to his own country peaceably (against all men's expectation, being such a blood-shedder and cruel oppressor) after he had escaped so many dangers." †

———◆———

1 'AWAY with you, away with you, James de
    Grant!
  And, Douglas, ye 'll be slain;
  For Baddindalloch 's at your gates,
    With many brave Highland men.'

2 'Baddindalloch has no feud at me,
    And I have none at him;
  Cast up my gates baith broad and wide,
    Let Baddindalloch in.'

3 'James de Grant has made a vaunt,
    And leaped the castle-wa;
  But, if he comes this way again,
    He 'll no win sae well awa.

4 'Take him, take him, brave Gordons,
    O take him, fine fellows a'!
  If he wins but ae mile to the Highland hills,
    He 'll defy you Gordons a'.'

———◆———

As printed by Buchan:
1[8], 2[1.4]. Balnadallach. 1[4]. man. 2[4] come in.

3[4]. nae won. 4[8]. on the Highland hill.

* Gordon's History, pp. 481, 460; Spalding, with details, I, 70.

† Spalding, I, 141, 188, 244.

198

BONNY JOHN SETON

A. 'Bonny John Seton,' Maidment's North Countrie Garland, p. 15 ; Buchan's Gleanings, p. 161 ; Maidment's Scotish Ballads and Songs, Historical and Traditionary, I, 280.

B. 'The Death of John Seton,' Buchan's Ballads of the North of Scotland, II, 136.

BUCHAN had another copy, sent him in manuscript by a young lady in Aberdeen, in which the Earl Marischal was made prominent : Ballads, II, 321. Aytoun, I, 139, had a copy which had been annotated by C. K. Sharpe, and from this he seems to have derived a few variations. The New Deeside Guide [1832], p. 5 (nominally by James Brown, but written by Dr Joseph Robertson), gives **A**, with a few trifling improvements which seem to be editorial.

A, B, 1–8. The ballad is accurate as to the date, not commonly a good sign for such things. On Tuesday, the eighteenth of June, 1639, Montrose began an attack on the bridge of Dee, which had been fortified and manned by the royalists of Aberdeen to stop his advance on the city. The bridge was bravely defended that day and part of the next by Lieutenant - Colonel Johnston (not Middleton ; Middleton was of the assailants). The young Lord of Aboyne, just made the king's lieutenant in the north, had a small body of horse on the north side of the river. Montrose's cavalry were sent up the south side as if to cross (though there was no ford), and Aboyne's were moved along the opposite bank to resist a passage. This exposed the latter to Montrose's cannon, and the Covenanters let fly some shot at them, one of which killed "a gallant gentleman, John Seton of Pitmeddin, most part of his body above the

saddle being carried away." Johnston's leg was crushed by stones brought down from one of the turrets of the bridge by a cannon-shot, and he had to be carried off. The loss of their commander and the disappearance of Aboyne's horse discouraged the now small party who were holding the bridge, and they abandoned it. Aboyne rode off, and left Aberdeen to to shift for itself.*

A 9–12, B 9–13. The spoiling of John Seton by order of Sir William Forbes of Craigievar is not noticed by Gordon and Spalding, though other matters of not greater proportion are.

A 13–15. The reference is to the affair called the Raid of Stonehaven, June 15, three days before that of the Bridge of Dee. Aboyne's Highlanders, a thousand or more, were totally unused to artillery, and a few shots from Montrose's cannon lighting among them so frightened them that "they did run off, all in a confusion, never looking behind them, till they were got into a moss." †

B 14–17. " When Montrose entered Aberdeen," says James Gordon, " the Earl Marischal and Lord Muchall pressed him to burn the town, and urged him with the Committee of Estates' warrant for that effect. He answered that it were best to advise a night upon it, since Aberdeen was the London of the north, and would prejudice themselves by want of it. So it was taken to consideration

* Gordon, History of Scots Affairs, II, 276–80 ; Spalding, Memorials, I, 209–11. Seton is called a bold, or brave, *baron*, in **A** 2, **B** 3, not in the mediæval way, but as one of the gentlemen of the king's party. The Gordons and their associates "at this time were called the Barons, and their actings, by way of derision, the Barons' Reign." Gordon, p. 261. "Northern," **B** 1³, should be southern, as in **A**.

† Gordon, II, 274 ; Spalding, I, 208 ; Napier's Montrose and the Covenanters, I, 284 f. The Hieland men, says Baillie, " avowed that they could not abide *the musket's mother*, and so fled in troops at the first volley." Letters, ed. Laing, I, 221.

for that night, and next day the Earl Marischal and Lord Muchall came protesting he
would spare it. He answered he was desir-
ous so to do, but durst not except they would
be his warrant. Whereupon they drew up a
paper, signed with both their hands, declaring that they had hindered it, and promising
to interpose with the Committee of Estates
for him. Yet the next year, when he was
made prisoner and accused, this was objected
to Montrose, that he had not burned Aberdeen, as he had orders from the Committee of
Estates. Then he produced Marischal and
Muchall's paper, which hardly satisfied the
exasperated committee." *

A

Maidment's North Countrie Garland, p. 15.

1 UPON the eighteenth day of June,
    A dreary day to see,
The southern lords did pitch their camp
    Just at the bridge of Dee.

2 Bonny John Seton of Pitmeddin,
    A bold baron was he,
He made his testament ere he went out,
    The wiser man was he.

3 He left his land to his young son,
    His lady her dowry,
A thousand crowns to his daughter Jean,
    Yet on the nurse's knee.

4 Then out came his lady fair,
    A tear into her ee;
Says, Stay at home, my own good lord,
    O stay at home with me!

5 He looked over his left shoulder,
    Cried, Souldiers, follow me!
O then she looked in his face,
    An angry woman was she:
'God send me back my steed again,
    But neer let me see thee!'

6 His name was Major Middleton
    That manned the bridge of Dee,
His name was Colonel Henderson
    That let the cannons flee.

7 His name was Major Middleton
    That manned the bridge of Dee,
And his name was Colonel Henderson
    That dung Pitmeddin in three.

8 Some rode on the black and grey,
    And some rode on the brown,
But the bonny John Seton
    Lay gasping on the ground.

9 Then bye there comes a false Forbes,
    Was riding from Driminere;
Says, Here there lies a proud Seton;
    This day they ride the rear.

10 Cragievar said to his men,
    'You may play on your shield;
For the proudest Seton in all the lan
    This day lies on the field.'

11 'O spoil him! spoil him!' cried Cragievar,
    'Him spoiled let me see;
For on my word,' said Cragievar,
    'He had no good will at me.'

12 They took from him his armour clear,
    His sword, likewise his shield;
Yea, they have left him naked there,
    Upon the open field.

13 The Highland men, they're clever men
    At handling sword and shield,
But yet they are too naked men
    To stay in battle field.

14 The Highland men are clever men
    At handling sword or gun,
But yet they are too naked men
    To bear the cannon's rung.

15 For a cannon's roar in a summer night
    Is like thunder in the air;
There's not a man in Highland dress
    Can face the cannon's fire.

* History of Scots Affairs, II, 281, note: see also what is
added to that note.

B

Buchan's Ballads of the North of Scotland, II, 136.

1 IT fell about the month of June,
   On Tuesday, timouslie,
  The northern lords hae pitchd their camps
   Beyond the brig o Dee.

2 They ca'ed him Major Middleton
   That mand the brig o Dee;
  They ca'ed him Colonel Henderson
   That gard the cannons flee.

3 Bonny John Seton o Pitmedden,
   A brave baron was he;
  He made his tesment ere he gaed,
   And the wiser man was he.

4 He left his lands unto his heir,
   His ladie her dowrie;
  Ten thousand crowns to Lady Jane,
   Sat on the nourice knee.

5 Then out it speaks his lady gay,
   'O stay my lord wi me;
  For word is come, the cause is won
   Beyond the brig o Dee.'

6 He turned him right and round about,
   And a light laugh gae he;
  Says, I wouldna for my lands sae broad
   I stayed this night wi thee.

7 He's taen his sword then by his side,
   His buckler by his knee,
  And laid his leg in oer his horse,
   Said, Sodgers, follow me!

8 So he rade on, and further on,
   Till to the third mile corse;
  The Covenanters' cannon balls
   Dang him aff o his horse.

9 Up then rides him Cragievar,
   Said, Wha's this lying here?
  It surely is the Lord o Aboyne,
   For Huntly was not here.

10 Then out it speaks a fause Forbes,
   Lived up in Druminner;
  'My lord, this is a proud Seton,
   The rest will ride the thinner.'

11 'Spulyie him, spulyie him,' said Craigievar,
   'O spulyie him, presentlie;
  For I could lay my lugs in pawn
   He had nae gude will at me.'

12 They 've taen the shoes frae aff his feet,
   The garters frae his knee,
  Likewise the gloves upon his hands;
   They 've left him not a flee.

13 His fingers they were sae sair swelld
   The rings would not come aff;
  They cutted the grips out o his ears,
   Took out the gowd signots.

14 Then they rade on, and further on,
   Till they came to the Crabestane,
  And Craigievar, he had a mind
   To burn a' Aberdeen.

15 Out it speaks the gallant Montrose,
   Grace on his fair body!
  'We winna burn the bonny burgh,
   We 'll even laet it be.'

16 Then out it speaks the gallant Montrose,
   'Your purpose I will break;
  We winna burn the bonny burgh,
   We 'll never build its make.

17 'I see the women and their children
   Climbing the craigs sae hie;
  We 'll sleep this night in the bonny burgh,
   And even lat it be.'

B. 11^{1,2}. Spulzie.
  *Readings in Aytoun which may have been
   derived from Sharpe:*
A. 4^2. The tear stood in.
  8^3. But bonny John Seton o Pitmeddin.

B. 8^3. And there the Covenanters' shot.
  8^4. It dang him frae his.
  10^2. Was riding frae D.
  10^3. This is the proudest Seton of a'.
  14^3. And wha sae ready as Craigievar.

15¹. Then up and spake the gude.
16². As he rade owre the field.
16³. Why should we burn the bonny.
16⁴. When its like we couldna build.

Readings in The New Deeside Guide :

A. 1³. lords their pallions pitched.
2². A baron bold. 3¹. To his.
4¹. and came. 5⁵. your steed.
11⁴. He bore : to me. 15⁴. cannon's rair.

199

THE BONNIE HOUSE O AIRLIE

A. a. Sharpe's Ballad Book, p. 59, No 20. b. 'The Bonnie House o Airly,' Finlay's Ballads, II, 25. c. Skene MS., pp. 28, 54. d. 'The Bonny House of Airly,' Campbell MSS, II, 113. e. 'The Bonny House of Airly,' an Aberdeen stall-copy, without date. f. 'The Bonny House o Airly,' another Aberdeen stall-copy, without date. g. Hogg's Jacobite Relics, II, 152. h. Kinloch MSS, VI, 5, one stanza.

B. Kinloch MSS, V, 273.

C. a. 'The Bonny House of Airley,' Kinloch MSS, V, 205. b. 'Young Airly,' Cromek's Remains of Nithsdale and Galloway Song, p. 226. c. 'The Bonny House o Airlie,' Smith's Scottish Minstrel, II, 2. d. 'The Bonny House o Airlie,' Christie's Traditional Ballad Airs, II, 276, 296.

D. Kinloch MSS, V, 106 ; Kinloch MSS, VII, 207 ; Kinloch's Ancient Scottish Ballads, p. 104.

THE earliest copy of this ballad hitherto found is a broadside of about 1790 (a hundred and fifty years later than the event celebrated), which Finlay combined with two others, derived from recitation, for his edition (A b). C b, c, d, are not purely traditional texts, and A g has borrowed some stanzas from C b. C b is transcribed into the Campbell MSS, I, 184. Aytoun's edition, 1859, II, 270, is compounded from A a, A b, with half a dozen words changed, and it is not quite clear how the editor means to be understood when he says, " the following, I have reason to believe, is the original."

One summer day, Argyle, who has a quarrel with Airlie, sets out to plunder the castle of that name. The lord of the place is at the time with the king. Argyle (something in the style of Captain Car) summons Lady Ogilvie to come down and kiss him ; else he will not leave a standing stone in Airlie. This she will not do, for all his threat. Argyle demands of the lady where her dowry is

(as if it were tied up in a handkerchief). She gives no precise information : it is east and west, up and down the water-side. Sharp search is made, and the dowry is found in a plum-tree (balm-tree, cherry-tree, palm-tree, A a, b, d, e, g). Argyle lays or leads the lady down somewhere while the plundering goes forward. She tells him that no Campbell durst have taken in hand such a thing if her lord had been at home. She has born seven (ten) sons, and is expecting another ; but had she as many more (a hundred more), she would give them all to King Charles.

In A d 7 Lady Ogilvie asks the favor of Argyle that he will take her to a high hill-top that she may *not* see the burning of Airlie ; the passage is of course corrupt. In A g 7 she more sensibly asks that her face may not be turned that way. In C a 5, 6, b 5, 6, the rational request is made that she may be taken to some dark dowey glen * to avoid the sight ; but Argyle leads her " down to the top of the town," and bids her look at the plundering, a ; sets her upon a bonnie knowe-tap, and

* " 'The deep, deep den' referred to in the ballad is the Den of Airlie, celebrated for its fine scenery and romantic beauty. It extends about a mile below the junction of the

Isla and the Melgum." Christie, Traditional Ballad Airs, II, 296.

bids her look at Airlie fa'ing, b. D 7, 8, goes a step further. The lady asks that she may be thrown over the castle-wall rather than see the plundering; Argyle lifts her up 'sae rarely' and throws her over, and she never saw it.

In C a 8 Argyle would have Lord Airlie informed that one kiss from his lady would have saved all the plundering. In D 5 he tells Lady Ogilvie that if she had surrendered on the first demand there would have been no plundering; and this assurance he repeats to 'Captain' Ogilvie, whom he meets on his way home.

A b 2, D 1, 2, represent Argyle to be acting under the orders of Montrose, or in concert with him.

A piece in five or six stanzas which appears, with variations, in Cromek's Remains, p. 195, Hogg's Jacobite Relics, II, 151, Cunningham's Songs of Scotland, III, 218, under the caption of 'Young Airly' (the title of C b also in Cromek), moves forward the burning of Airlie to "the 45;" not very strangely (if there is anything traditional in these verses), when we consider the prominence of the younger Lord Ogilvie and his wife among the supporters of Charles Edward. (The first three of Cromek's stanzas are transcribed into Campbell MSS, I, 187.) No doubt the Charlie and Prince Charlie of some versions of our ballad were understood by the reciters to be the Young Chevalier.

The Committee of Estates, June 12, 1640, gave commission to the Earl of Argyle to rise in arms against certain people, among whom was the Earl of Airlie, as enemies to religion and unnatural to their country, and to pursue them with fire and sword until they should be brought to their duty or else utterly subdued and rooted out. The Earl of Airlie had gone to England, fearing lest he should be pressed to subscribe the Covenant, and had left his house to the keeping of his eldest son, Lord Ogilvie. Montrose, who had signed the commission as one of the Committee, but was not inclined to so strenuous proceedings, invested Airlie, forced a surrender, and put a garrison in the place to hold it for the "public." Argyle did not interpret his commission in this mild way. He took Airlie in hand in the beginning of July, and caused both this house and that of Forthar, belonging to Lord Ogilvie, to be pillaged, burned, and demolished. Thereafter he fell upon the lands both of the proprietor and his tenantry, and carried off or destroyed "their whole goods, gear, corns, cattle, horse, nolt, sheep," and left nothing but bare bounds.

According to one writer, Lady Ogilvie was residing at Forthar, and, being big with child, asked leave of Argyle to stay till she was brought to bed; but this was not allowed, and she was put out, though she knew not whither to go. By another account, Argyle accused Montrose of having suffered the lady to escape.*

The ballad puts Lady Airlie in command of the house or castle, but none of the family were there at the time it was sacked. She is called Lady Margaret in A b 4, but her name was Elizabeth. The earl, James, is called the great Sir John in C a 9. A 10 and the like elsewhere are applicable to the younger Lady Ogilvie in respect to the unborn child. Chambers says that Lady Airlie had three children and Lady Ogilvie but one, and "the poet must be wrong." "The poet," besides being inaccurate, does not tell the same story in all the versions, and this inconsistency is again observable in 'Geordie,' A 9, B 18, C 8, etc.

'Gleyd Argyle' is "generally described as of mean stature, with red hair and squinting eyes." † His morals appear to some disadvantage again in 'Geordie,' I a 23.

---

* Spalding's Memorials, ed. 1850, I, 290–2; Gordon's History of Scots Affairs, III, 164 f.; also, II, 234; Gardiner, History of England, 1603–1642, ed., 1884, IX, 167 f. Both Spalding and Gordon say that Montrose besieged Airlie but did not succeed in taking it. Argyle, continues Spalding, "raises an army of about 5,000 men and marches towards Airlie; but the Lord Ogilvie, hearing of his coming with such irresistible forces, resolves to fly and leave the house manless, and so for their own safety they wisely fled. But Argyle most cruelly and inhumanly enters the house of Airlie," etc. A letter of Argyle's to one Dugald Campbell (dated July, 1640) would seem to show that he was not there in person during the razing and burning. "You need not let know," says Argyle, "that ye have directions from me to fire it." Notes and Queries, Fifth Series, IX, 364; reprinted by Gardiner.

† Napier, Montrose and the Covenanters, 1838, I, 129.

A

a. Sharpe's Ballad Book, p. 59, No 20, 1823. b. Finlay's Ballads, II, 25, 1808, from two recited copies and "one printed about twenty years ago on a single sheet." c. Skene MS., pp. 28, 54, from recitation in the north of Scotland, 1802-3. d. Campbell MSS, II, 113, probably from a stall-copy. e, f. Aberdeen stall copies, "printed for the book-sellers." g. Hogg's Jacobite Relics, II, 152, No 76, "Cromek and a street ballad collated, 1821." h. Kinloch MSS, VI, 5, one stanza, taken down from an old woman's recitation by J. Robertson.

1 It fell on a day, and a bonny simmer day,
 When green grew aits and barley,
That there fell out a great dispute
 Between Argyll and Airlie.

2 Argyll has raised an hunder men,
 An hunder harnessd rarely,
And he 's awa by the back of Dunkell,
 To plunder the castle of Airlie.

3 Lady Ogilvie looks oer her bower-window,
 And oh, but she looks weary !
And there she spy'd the great Argyll,
 Come to plunder the bonny house of Airlie.

4 'Come down, come down, my Lady Ogilvie,
 Come down, and kiss me fairly :'
'O I winna kiss the fause Argyll,
 If he should na leave a standing stane in
  Airlie.'

5 He hath taken her by the left shoulder,
 Says, Dame where lies thy dowry ?
'O it 's east and west yon wan water side,
 And it 's down by the banks of the Airlie.'

6 They hae sought it up, they hae sought it down,
 They hae sought it maist severely,
Till they fand it in the fair plumb-tree
 That shines on the bowling-green of Airlie.

7 He hath taken her by the middle sae small,
 And O but she grat sairly !
And laid her down by the bonny burn-side,
 Till they plundered the castle of Airlie.

8 'Gif my gude lord war here this night,
 As he is with King Charlie,
Neither you, nor ony ither Scottish lord,
 Durst avow to the plundering of Airlie.

9 'Gif my gude lord war now at hame,
 As he is with his king,
There durst nae a Campbell in a' Argyll
 Set fit on Airlie green.

10 'Ten bonny sons I have born unto him,
 The eleventh neer saw his daddy ;
But though I had an hundred mair,
 I 'd gie them a' to King Charlie.'

B

Kinloch MSS, V, 273.

1 It fell on a day, a clear summer day,
 When the corn grew green and bonny,
That there was a combat did fall out
 'Tween Argyle and the bonny house of Airly.

2 Argyle he did raise five hundred men,
 Five hundred men, so many,
And he did place them by Dunkeld,
 Bade them shoot at the bonny house of Airly.

3 The lady looked over her own castle-wa,
 And oh, but she looked weary !
And there she espied the gleyed Argyle,
 Come to plunder the bonny house of Airly.

4 'Come down the stair now, Madam Ogilvie,
 And let me kiss thee kindly ;
Or I vow and I swear, by the sword that I
  wear,
 That I winna leave a standing stone at
  Airly.'

5 'O how can I come down the stair,
 And how can I kiss thee kindly,
Since you vow and you swear, by the sword
  that you wear,
 That you winna leave a standing stone on
  Airly ?'

6 'Come down the stair then, Madam Ogilvie,
 And let me see thy dowry ;'
'O 't is east and it is west, and 't is down by
  yon burn-side,
 And it stands at the planting sae bonny.'

7 'But if my brave lord had been at hame this
    day,
  As he is wi Prince Charlie,
There durst na a Campbell in all Scotland
  Set a foot on the bowling-green of Airly

8 'O I hae born him seven, seven sons,
  And an eighth neer saw his daddy,
And tho I were to bear him as many more,
  They should a' carry arms for Prince
    Charlie.'

C

a. Kinloch MSS, V, 205, recited by John Rae. b. Cromek's Remains of Nithsdale and Galloway Song, p. 226, 1810. c. Smith's Scottish Minstrel, II, 2. d. Christie's Traditional Ballad Airs, II, 276, "from the recitation of a relative."

1 IT fell on a day, on a bonny summer day,
  When the corn grew green and yellow,
That there fell out a great dispute
  Between Argyle and Airley.

2 The great Argyle raised five hundred men,
  Five hundred men and many,
And he has led them down by the bonny
    Dunkeld,
Bade them shoot at the bonny house of
    Airley.

3 The lady was looking oer her castle-wa,
  And O but she looked weary!
And there she spied the great Argyle,
  Came to plunder the bonny house of Airley.

4 'Come down stairs now, Madam,' he says,
  'Now come down and kiss me fairly;'
'I'll neither come down nor kiss you,' she says,
  'Tho you should na leave a standing stane
    in Airley.'

5 'I ask but one favour of you, Argyle,
  And I hope you'll grant me fairly

To tak me to some dark dowey glen,
  That I may na see the plundering of Airley.'

6 He has taen her by the left shoulder,
  And O but she looked weary!
And he has led her down to the top of the town,
  Bade her look at the plundering of Airley.

7 'Fire on, fire on, my merry men all,
  And see that ye fire clearly;
For I vow and I swear by the broad sword I
    wear
That I winna leave a standing stane in Airley.'

8 'You may tell it to your lord,' he says,
  'You may tell it to Lord Airley,
That one kiss o his gay lady
  Wad hae sav'd all the plundering of Airley.'

9 'If the great Sir John had been but at hame,
  As he is this night wi Prince Charlie,
Neither Argyle nor no Scottish lord
  Durst hae plundered the bonny house of
    Airley.

10 'Seven, seven sons hae I born unto him,
  And the eight neer saw his dady,
And altho I were to have a hundred more,
  The should a' draw their sword for Prince
    Charlie.'

D

Kinloch MSS, V, 106, in the handwriting of James Beattie, and from the recitation of Elizabeth Beattie.

1 O GLEYD Argyll has written to Montrose
  To see gin the fields they were fairly,
And to see whether he should stay at hame,
  'Or come to plunder bonnie Airly.

2 Then great Montrose has written to Argyll
  And that the fields they were fairly,
And not to keep his men at hame,
  But to come and plunder bonnie Airly.

3 The lady was looking oer her castle-wa,
  She was carrying her courage sae rarely,

And there she spied him gleyd Arguill,
  Was coming for to plunder bonnie Airly.

4 'Wae be to ye, gleyd Argyll!
  And are ye there sae rarely?
Ye might hae kept your men at hame,
  And not come to plunder bonnie Airly.'

5 'And wae be to ye, Lady Ogilvie!
  And are ye there sae rarely?
Gin ye had bowed when first I bade,
  I never wad hae plunderd bonnie Airly.'

6 'But gin my guid lord had been at hame,
  As he is wi Prince Charlie,
There durst not a rebel on a' Scotch ground
  Set a foot on the bonnie green of Airly.

7 'But ye 'll tak me by the milk-white hand,
  And ye 'll lift me up sae rarely,
And ye 'll throw me outoure my [ain] castle-
    wa,
  Let me neuer see the plundering of Airly.'

8 He 's taen her by the milk-white hand,
  And he 's lifted her up sae rarely,
And he 's thrown her outoure her ain castle-wa,
  And she neuer saw the plundering of Airly.

9 Now gleyd Argyll he has gane hame,
  Awa frae the plundering of Airly,
And there he has met him Captain Ogilvie,
  Coming over the mountains sae rarely.

10 'O wae be to ye, gleyd Argyll!
  And are you there sae rarely?
Ye might hae kept your men at hame,
  And no gane to plunder bonnie Airly.'

11 'O wae be to ye, Captain Ogilvie!
  And are you there sae rarely?
Gin ye wad hae bowed when first I bade,
  I neer wad hae plunderd bonnie Airly.'

12 'But gin I had my lady gay,
  Bot and my sister Mary,
One fig I wad na gie for ye a',
  Nor yet for the plundering of Airly.'

———·———

A. b. 1². When the corn grew green and yellow.
  2¹,². The Duke o Montrose has written to Ar-
    gyle To come in the morning early.
  2³. An lead in his men by.
  2⁴. the bonnie house o Airly.
  3¹. The lady lookd oer her window sae hie.
  4¹. down Lady Margaret he says.
  4²,³ (cf. f.).

'Or before the morning clear day light,
  I 'll no leave a standing stane in Airly.'

'I wadna kiss thee, great Argyle,
  I wadna kiss thee fairly,
I wadna kiss thee, great Argyle,
  Gin you shoudna leave a standing stane in
    Airly.'

5¹. by the middle sae sma.
5². Says, Lady, where is your drury?
5³,⁴. It 's up and down by the bonnie burn-side,
  Amang the planting of Airly.
6². They sought it late and early.
6³. And found: bonnie balm-tree.

7¹. by the left shoulder.
7³. And led: to yon green bank.
8¹ (10¹). lord had been at hame.
8² (10²). As this night he is wi C.
8³ (10³). There durst na a Campbell in a' the
    west.
8⁴ (10⁴). Hae plundered the bonnie house.
9. Wanting.
10¹ (9¹). O it 's I hae seven braw sons, she says.
10² (9²). And the youngest.
10³ (9³). had as mony mae.
10⁴ (9⁴). to Charlie.
c. 1–5¹ are repeated at p. 54, with some differ-
    ences.
  1¹. fell about a [the] Lammass time.
  1². corn [the corn] grew green and yellow.
  2¹. has gathered three hunder.
  2². Three hunder men and mair O.
  2³. is on to.   2⁴. the bonnie house o A.
  3¹. The lady lookit oure the castle-wa.
  3². she was sorry.
  3³. Whan she saw gleyd Argyle an his [300]
    men.
  4¹. Come down the stair, Lady Airly [he says].

4². An it 's ye maun kiss [An kiss me fairly].
4³. I wad na kiss ye, gleyd Argyll.
4⁴. Atho [Tho] ye leave na.
5¹. Come down the stair, Lady Airly, he says.
5². An tell whar. 5³. Up and down the bonnie.
5⁴. And by the bonnie bowling-green o.
6. *Wanting.* 7¹. took : the milk-white hand.
7². And led her fairly.
7³. Up an down the bonnie water-side.
7⁴. the bonnie house o Airly.
8¹. But an : were at hame (= 9¹).
8². awa wi Charley.
8³. The best Campbell in a' your kin.
8⁴. Durst na plunder the b. h. o. A.
9. *Wanting.*
10¹ (7¹). Seven sons have I born, she says.
10² (7²). The eight : its.
10³ (7³). Altho : as many mare.
10⁴ (7⁴). a' to fight for Charley.
d. 1². When corn grew green. 2¹. has hired.
2². A hundred men and mairly. 2³. to the.
2⁴. the b. h. of A.
3¹. The lady lookit over her window.
3². lookit waely. 3³. she saw. 3⁴. Coming.
4³. I wadna kiss the great. 4⁴. Tho you.
5¹. by the milk-white hand.
5². Lady, where 's your.
5³. It 's up and down yon bonny burn-side.
5⁴. It shines in the bowling-green of A.
6². sought it late and early.
6³. They 've found : the bonny cherry-tree.
6⁴. That grows in.
Between 6 and 7 :

There is ae favour I ask of thee,
  I beg but ye 'll grant it fairly :
That ye will take me to yon high hill-top,
  That I maunna see the burning of Airly.

7¹. by the left shoulder. 7². lookit queerly.
7³. he 's led. 7⁴. the b. h. of A.
Between 7 and 8 :

He 's taen her by the milk-white hand,
  He 's led her right and fairly ;
He 's led her to yon high hill-top,
  Till they 've burned the bonny house of Airly.

8². away wi Prince Charlie.
8³. The great Argyle and a' his men.
8⁴. Wadna hae plunderd the b. h. of A.
9. *Wanting.*
10³. And if I had a hundred men.

10⁴. to Prince.
e. 1². When the corn grew green and yellow.
2². A hundred men and mairly.
2³. he has gone to.
2⁴. the bonny house of Airly.
3¹. The lady looked over her window.
3². looked. 3⁴. Coming.
4¹. down, madam, he says.
4³. thee, great Argyle. 4⁴. If you.
5¹. by the middle so small.
5². Says, Lady, where is your.
5³. It is up and down the bonny burn-side.
5⁴. Among the plantings of A.
6². They sought it late and early.
6³. And found it in the bonny palm-tree.
7¹. by the left shoulder.
7². she looked weary.
7³. down on the green bank.
7⁴. he plundered the b. h. of A.
8¹. O if my lord was at home : this night
  wanting.
8². As this night he 's wi Charlie.
8³·⁴. Great Argyle and all his men Durst not
  plunder the b. h. of A.
9. *Wanting.*
10¹. 'Tis ten : unto him *wanting.*
10³. But though. 10⁴. to Charlie.
f. 1². When the clans were a' wi Charlie.
2¹. has called a hundred o his men.
2². To come in the morning early.
2³. And they hae gane down by.
2⁴. plunder the b. h. of A.
3¹. L. O. looked frae her window sae hie.
3². she grat sairly.
3³. To see Argyle and a' his men.
4¹. down, Lady Ogilvie, he cried.
4³·⁴. Or ere the morning's clear daylight I 'll
  no leave a standing.
After 4 :

I wadna come doon, great Argyle, she cried,
  I wadna kiss thee fairly,
I wadna come doon, false Argyle, she cried,
  Though you shouldna leave a standing stane
    in Airly.

5–7. *Wanting.*

8. But were my ain guid lord at hame,
  As he is noo wi Charlie,
The base Argyle and a his men
  Durstna enter the bonny house o Airly.

9. *Wanting.*

10^1. O I hae seven bonny sons, she said.

10^2. And the youngest has neer seen.

10^3. had ane as mony mae.

10^4. They 'd a' be followers o Charlie.

After 10 this spurious stanza:

Then Argyle and his men attacked the bonny
    ha,
    And O but they plundered it fairly!
In spite o the tears the lady let fa,
    They burnt doon the bonny house o Airly.

g. 1^2. When the flowers were blooming rarely.

2^2. An hundred men and mairly.

2^4. the b. h. of A.

3^1. The lady lookd oer her w.

3^2. she sighd sairly.

4^3. No, I winna kiss thee.

4^4. Though ye.

5^1. by the middle sae sma.

5^2. Says *wanting:* Lady where is your.

$5^{3,4}$. It 's up and down by the bonny burn-side,
    Amang the plantings o Airly.

6^2. it late and early.

6^3. under the bonny palm-tree.

6^4. That stands i.   *After 6 (cf. A d, C 5):*

A favour I ask of thee, Argyle,
    If ye will grant it fairly;
O dinna turn me wi my face
    To see the destruction of Airly!

*The remainder of g is taken from C b, with
two or three slight variations.*

h. 8. An my gude lord had been at hame,
    As he 's awa wi Charlie,
There durstna a gleyd duke in a' Argyle
    Set a coal to the bonnie house o Airlie.

B. 5^1, 8^1. Oh.

C. b. *No reliance can be placed upon the genuine-
    ness of this copy, and a particular collation
    is not required.*

$1^{1,2}$. It fell in about the Martinmas time, An
    the leaves were fa'ing early.

4. *Two stanzas, much as in A b, f.*

5. But take me by the milk-white hand,
    An lead me down right hoolie,

An set me in a dowie, dowie glen,
    That I mauna see the fall o Airly.

6. He has taen her by the shouther-blade
    An thurst her down afore him,
Syne set her upon a bonnie knowe-tap,
    Bad her look at Airly fa'ing.

*Here follows a stanza (6) not found elsewhere,
no doubt Cunningham's:*

Haste! bring to me a cup o gude wine,
    As red as ony cherrie;
I 'll tauk the cup, an sip it up;
    Here 's a health to bonnie Prince Charlie!

7, 8. *Wanting: found only in* a.

9. *Nearly* e, f, 8.

10^1. I hae born me eleven braw sons.

*A concluding stanza may be assigned to Cun-
ningham.*

Were my gude lord but here this day,
    As he 's awa wi Charlie,
The dearest blude o a' thy kin
    Wad sloken the lowe o Airly.

*Another copy is said in the editor's preface to
begin thus:*

The great Argyle raised ten thousand men,
    Eer the sun was waukening early,
And he marched them down by the back o
    Dunkel,
    Bade them fire on the bonnie house o Airlie.

c. *Made over from a copy resembling B, C a.*

4. *Two stanzas here, as in* B: *kisses are
    dropped for propriety.*

5, 6. *The last half of these is substantially
    preserved in* c 7, 8.

d. *A blending, perhaps not accidental, of vari-
    ous copies; mainly of A g, C b, C c.*

1, 2. *Nearly* A g 1, 2.   3. *Nearly* c 3.

$4^{1,2}$. *Nearly* A g $4^{1,2}$.

$4^{3,4}$. *Nearly* c $4^{3,4}$.

5. *Nearly a compound of* A b (Finlay) 5 and
    c 5: *cf.* B 5.

6. *Cf.* b 4 (5 above), c 7.   7. *Nearly* c 8.

8. b 6 *altered.   The stanza cited by Christie
    at p. 296 is the spurious conclusion of* c.

200

THE GYPSY LADDIE

A. 'Johny Faa, the Gypsy Laddie,' Ramsay's Tea-Table Miscellany, vol. iv, 1740. Here from the edition of 1763, p. 427.

B. a. The Edinburgh Magazine and Literary Miscellany (vol. lxxx of the Scots Magazine), November, 1817, p. 309. **b.** A fragment recited by Miss Fanny Walker, of Mount Pleasant, near Newburgh-on-Tay.

C. 'Davie Faw,' Motherwell's MS., p. 381 ; 'Gypsie Davy,' Motherwell's Minstrelsy, 1827, p. 360.

D. 'The Egyptian Laddy,' Kinloch MSS, V, 331.

E. 'The Gypsie Laddie,' Mactaggart's Scottish Gallovidian Encyclopedia, 1824, p. 284.

F. 'Johnny Faa, the Gypsey Laddie,' The Songs of England and Scotland [P. Cunningham], London, 1835, II, 346.

G. a. 'The Gypsie Loddy,' a broadside, Roxburghe Ballads, III, 685. **b.** A recent stall-copy, Catnach, 2 Monmouth Court, Seven Dials.

H. 'The Gipsy Laddie,' Shropshire Folk-Lore, edited by Charlotte Sophia Burne, p. 550.

I. Communicated by Miss Margaret Reburn, as sung in County Meath, Ireland, about 1860.

J. a. 'The Gipsey Davy,' from Stockbridge, Massachusetts. **b.** From a lady born in Maine.

K. 'Lord Garrick,' **a, b,** communicated by ladies of New York.

———◆———

THE English ballad, though derived from the Scottish, may perhaps have been printed earlier. A conjectural date of 1720 is given, with hesitation, to **G a,** in the catalogue of the British Museum.

The Scottish ballad appears to have been first printed in the fourth volume of the Tea-Table Miscellany, 1740, but no copy of that edition has been recovered. From the Tea-Table Miscellany it was repeated, with variations, some traditional, some arbitrary, in : Herd's Ancient and Modern Scots Songs, 1769, 'Gypsie Laddie,' p. 88, ed. 1776, II, 54; The Fond Mother's Garland, not dated, but earlier than 1776; Pinkerton's Select Scotish Ballads, 1783, I, 67; Johnson's Museum, 'Johny Faa, or, The Gypsie Laddie,' No 181, p. 189; Ritson's Scotish Songs, 1794, II, 176; and in this century, Cromek's Select Scotish Songs, 1810, II, 15; Cunningham's Songs of Scotland, 1825, II, 175. A transcript in the Campbell MSS, 'The Gypsies,' I, 16, is from Pinkerton.

"The people in Ayrshire begin this song,

'The gypsies cam to my lord Cassilis' yett.'

They have a great many more stanzas . . . than I ever yet saw in any printed.'' Burns, in Cromek's Reliques, 1809, p. 161. (So Sharpe, in the Musical Museum, 1853, IV, 217, but perhaps repeating Burns.) B, from Galloway, has eight more stanzas than **A**, and **E**, also from Galloway, fourteen more, but quite eight of the last are entirely untraditional,* and the hand of the editor is frequently to be recognized elsewhere.

Finlay, Scottish Ballads, 1808, II, 39, inserted two stanzas after **A** 2, the first of which is nearly the same as 5, and the second as **B** 3, **C** 3. The variations of his text, and others in his notes, are given under **A**. Kinloch MSS, V, 299; Chambers, Scottish Ballads, 1829, p. 143; Aytoun, 1859, I, 187, repeat Finlay, with a few slight changes. The Ballads and Songs of Ayrshire, I, 9, follows Chambers.

The copy in Smith's Scotish Minstrel, III, 90, is derived from **B a,** but has readings of

---

* In 18–21 the lady makes her lord not only forgive the abettors of Jockie Faa, whom he was about to hang, but present ten guineas to Jockie, whom he was minded to burn.

other texts, and is of no authority. That in Maidment's Scotish Ballads and Songs, 1868, II, 185, is B a with changes. Ten stanzas in a manuscript of Scottish songs and ballads, copied 1840 or 1850 by a granddaughter of Lord Woodhouselee, p. 46, are from B a. This may be true also of B b, which, however, has not Cassilis in 1¹.

C is from a little further north, from Renfrewshire; D from Aberdeenshire. F is from the north of England, and resembles C. The final stanza of G a is cited by Ritson, Scotish Songs, II, 177, 1794. 'The Rare Ballad of Johnnie Faa and the Countess o Cassilis,' Sheldon's Minstrelsy of the English Border, p. 326, which the editor had " heard sung repeatedly by Willie Faa," and of which he "endeavored to preserve as much as recollection would allow," has the eleven stanzas of the English broadside, and twelve more of which Sheldon must have been unable to recollect anything. H–K are all varieties of the broadside.

The Rev. S. Baring-Gould has most obligingly sent me a ballad, taken down by him from the singing of an illiterate hedger in North Devon, in which ' The Gypsy Laddie,' recomposed (mostly with middle rhyme in the third verse, as in A 1, 8), forms the sequel to a story of an earl marrying a very reluctant gypsy maid. When the vagrant who has been made a lady against nature hears some of her tribe singing at the castle-gate, the passion for a roving life returns, and she deserts her noble partner, who pursues her, and, not being able to induce her to return to him, smites her " lily-white " throat with his sword. This little romance, retouched and repaired, is printed as No 50 of Songs and Ballads of the West, now publishing by Baring-Gould and Sheppard. Mr Baring-Gould has also given me a defective copy of the second part of ' The Gipsy Countess ' (exhibiting many variations), which he obtained from an old shoemaker of Tiverton.

Among the Percy papers there is a set of ballads made over by the Bishop, which may have been intended for the contemplated extension of his Reliques. ' The Gipsie Laddie,' in eighteen stanzas, and not quite finished, is one of these. After seven stanzas of A, not much altered, the husband ineffectually pursues the lady, who adopts the gipsy trade, with her reid cheek stained wi yallow. Seven years pass, during which the laird has taken another wife. At Yule a wretched carline begs charity at his gate, who, upon questioning, reveals that she had been a lady gay, with a comely marrow, but had proved false and ruined herself.

A. Gypsies sing so sweetly at our lord's gate as to entice his lady to come down; as soon as she shows herself, they cast the glamour on her (so B–F, G b). She gives herself over to the chief gipsy, Johny Faa by name, without reserve of any description. Her lord, upon returning and finding her gone, sets out to recover her, and captures and hangs fifteen gypsies. (It is extremely likely that this version has lost several stanzas.)

Our lord, unnamed in A, is Lord Cassilis in B, C, F (so Burns, and Johnson's Museum). Cassilis has become Cassle, Castle in E, G, Corsefield * in D, Cashan in Irish I, Garrick † in American K. The Gypsy Laddie is again Johnie, Jockie, Faa in B, D, E; but Gipsy Davy in C (where Lady Cassilis is twice called Jeanie Faw), and in American I a b; and seems to be called both Johnnie Faw and Gypsie Geordie in F. The lady gives the gypsies the good wheat bread B, E (beer and wine, Finlay); they give her (sweetmeats, C) ginger, nutmeg, or both, and she gives them the ring (rings) off her finger (fingers), B, C, E, G, I, (and Finlay).

B a has a full story from this point on. The gypsy asks the lady to go with him, and swears that her lord shall never come near her. The lady changes her silk mantle for a

---

* " Corse field may very possibly be Corse, the ancient seat of the Forbeses of Craigievar, from the close vicinity of which the reciter of this ballad came." Burton, in Kinloch MSS, V, 334.

† Recalling Carrick, of which Maybole is the capital.

" The family of Cassilis, in early times, had been so powerful that the head of it was generally termed the King of Carrick : " Sharpe. But Garrick may have come in in some other way.

plaid, and is ready to travel the world over with the gypsy, B a 5, A 3, C 4, D 3, E 4, F 4, (B a 6 is spurious). They wander high and low till they come to an old barn, and by this time she is weary. The lady begins to find out what she has undertaken: last night she lay with her lord in a well-made bed, now she must lie in an old barn, B a 7, 8, A 4, C 6, D 7, F 5 (reeky kill E 8, on a straw bed H 7, in the ash-corner I 6). The gypsy bids her hold her peace, her lord shall never come near her. They wander high and low till they come to a wan water, and by this time she is weary. Oft has she ridden that wan water with her lord ; now she must set in her white feet and wade, B a 11, C 5, D 5, 6, E 7, (and carry the gipsie laddie, B a 11, badly ; follow, B b). The lord comes home, is told that his lady is gone off with the gypsy, and immediately sets out to bring her back (so all). He finds her at the wan water, B a 14 ; in Abbey Dale, drinking wi Gipsey Davy, C 10 ; near Strabogie, drinking wi Gypsie Geordie, F 10 ;* by the riverside, J a 4 ; at the Misty Mount, K 5, 6. He asks her tenderly if she will go home, B a 15, E 15, F 12, he will shut her up so securely that no man shall come near, B a 15, E 15 ; he expostulates with her, more or less reproachfully, C 11, F 11, G 9, H 5, J 5. She will not go home ; as she has brewed, so will she drink, B a 16, G 10 ; she cares not for houses or lands or babes (baby) G 10, H 6, J 6. But she swears to him that she is as free of the gypsies as when her mother bare her, B a 17, E 16.

Fifteen gypsies are hanged, or lose their lives, A 10, B 18, D 14 ; sixteen, all sons of one mother, C 12, 13 ; seven, F 13, G 11, (cf. I 1).†

D 8–11 is ridiculously perverted in the interest of morals: compare B a 17, E 16. 'I swear that my hand shall never go near thee,' D 8, is transferred to the husband in I 5: 'A hand I 'll neer lay on you' (in the way of correction).

In G 4 the lady, in place of exchanging her

silk mantle for a plaidie, pulls off her high-heeled shoes, of Spanish leather, and puts on Highland brogues. In I 7 gypsies take off her high-heeled shoes, and she puts on Lowland brogues. The high-heeled shoes, to be sure, are not adapted to following the Gypsy Laddie, but light may perhaps be derived from C 12, where the gypsies 'drink her stockings and her shoon.' In K these high-heeled shoes of Spanish leather are wrongly transferred to Lord Garrick in the copy as delivered, but have been restored to the lady.

It is not said (except in the spurious portions of E) that the lady was carried back by her husband, but this may perhaps be inferred from his hanging the gypsies. In D and K we are left uncertain as to her disposition, which is elsewhere, for the most part, to stick to the gypsy. J, a copy of very slight authority, makes the lord marry again within six months of his wife's elopement.

The earliest edition of the ballad styles the gypsy Johny Faa, but gives no clew to the fair lady. Johnny Faa was a prominent and frequent name among the gypsies. Johnnë Faw's right and title as lord and earl of Little Egypt were recognized by James V in a document under the Privy Seal, February 15, 1540, and we learn from this paper that, even before this date, letters had been issued to the king's officers, enjoining them to assist Johnnë Faw "in execution of justice upon his company and folks, conform to the laws of Egypt, and in punishing of all them that rebels against him." But in the next year, by an act of the Lords of Council, June 6, Egyptians are ordered to quit the realm within thirty days on pain of death, notwithstanding any other letters or privileges granted them by the king, his grace having discharged the same. The gypsies were expelled from Scotland by act of Parliament in 1609. Johnnë, *alias* Willie, Faa, with three others of the name, remaining notwithstanding, were sentenced to be hanged, 1611, July 31. In 1615, January 25, a man was delated for harboring of Egyp-

---

* F 7, if it belongs to the countess, gives her an unlady-like taste for brandy.

† "There is indeed a stanza of no merit, which, in some

copies, concludes the ballad, and states that eight of the gypsies were hanged at Carlisle, and the rest at the Border :" Finlay, II. 43.

tians, "specially of Johnnë Fall, a notorious Egyptian and chieftain of that unhappy sort of people." In 1616, July 24, Johnnë Faa, Egyptian, his son, and two others were condemned to be hanged for contemptuous repairing to the country and abiding therein. Finally, in 1624, January 24, Captain Johnnë Faa and seven others were sentenced to be hanged for the same offence, and on the following 29th Helen Faa, relict of the late Captain Johnnë Faa, with ten other women, was sentenced to be drowned, but execution was stayed. Eight men were executed, but the rest, "being either children and of less-age and women with child or giving suck to children," were, after imprisonment, banished the country under pain of death, to be inflicted without further process should they be found within the kingdom after a day fixed.* The execution of the notorious Egyptian and chieftain Johnny Faa must have made a considerable impression, and it is presumable that this ballad may have arisen not long after. Whether this were so or not, Johnny Faa acquired popular fame, and became a personage to whom any adventure might plausibly be imputed. It is said that he has even been foisted into 'The Douglas Tragedy' ('Earl Brand'), and Scott had a copy of 'Captain Car' in which, as in F, G, of that ballad, the scene was transferred to Ayrshire, and the incendiary was called Johnny Faa.†

Toward the end of the last century we begin to hear that the people in Ayrshire make the wife of the Earl of Cassilis the heroine of the ballad. This name, under the instruction of Burns, was adopted into the copy in Johnson's Museum (which, as to the rest, is Ramsay's), and in the index to the second volume of the Museum, 1788, we read, "neighboring tradition strongly vouches for the truth of this story." After this we get the tradition in full, of course with considerable variety in the details, and sometimes with criticism, sometimes without. ‡

The main points in the traditional story are that John, sixth earl of Cassilis, married, for his first wife, Lady Jean Hamilton, whose affections were preëngaged to one Sir John Faa, of Dunbar. Several years after, when Lady Cassilis had become the mother of two children, § Sir John Faa took the opportunity of the earl's absence from home (while Lord Cassilis was attending the Westminster Assembly, say some) to present himself at the castle, accompanied by a band of gypsies and himself disguised as a gypsy, and induced his old love to elope with him. But the earl returned in the nick of time, went in pursuit, captured the whole party, or all but one,‖ who is supposed to tell the story, and hanged them on the dule tree, "a most umbrageous plane, which yet flourishes upon a mound in front of the castle gate." The fugitive wife was banished from board and bed, and confined for life in a tower at Maybole, built for the purpose. "Eight heads carved in stone below one of the turrets are said to be the effigies of so many of the gypsies." ¶ The ford by which the lady and her lover crossed the River Doon is still called The Gypsies' Steps.

* Pitcairn's Criminal Trials, III, 201, 307 f., 397–9, 559–62, 592–94; Acts of the Parliament of Scotland, IV, 440.

† Sharpe's Ballad Book, ed. Laing, 1880, pp. 142, 154. I have unluckily lost my voucher for Johnny Faa's figuring in 'The Douglas Tragedy.'

‡ Finlay, II, 35; The Scots Magazine, LXXX, 306, and the Musical Museum, 1853, IV, *217, Sharpe; Chambers, Scottish Ballads, p. 143; The New Statistical Account of Scotland, V, 497; Paterson, The Ballads and Songs of Ayrshire, I, 10; Maidment, Scotish Ballads and Songs, 1868, II, 179.

§ She had four children according to the Historical Account of the Noble Family of Kennedy, Edinburgh, 1849, p. 44.

‖ 'We were a' put down but ane' first appears in Herd, 1769.

¶ These eight heads would correspond very neatly to the number of gypsies executed in 1624. But in the circumstantial account given by Chambers we are told that the house belonging to the family at Maybole was fitted for the countess's reception "by the addition of a fine projecting stair-case, upon which were carved heads representing those of her lover and his band. . . . The effigies of the gypsies are very minute, being subservient to the decoration of a fine triple window at the top of the stair-case, and stuck upon the tops and bottoms of a series of little pilasters which adorn that part of the building. The head of Johnie Faa himself is distinct from the rest, larger, and more lachrymose in the expression of the features. *Some windows in the upper flat of Cassilis Castle are similarly adorned; but regarding them tradition is silent.*"

Several accounts put the abduction at the time when the Earl of Cassilis was attending the Assembly of Divines at Westminster. This was in September, 1643. It is now known that Lady Cassilis died in December, 1642. What is much more important, it is known from two letters written by the earl immediately after her death that nothing could have occurred of a nature to alienate his affection, for in the one he speaks of her as a " dear friend " and " beloved yoke-fellow," and in the other as his " dear bed-fellow." *

" Seldom, when stripped of extraneous matter, has tradition been better supported than it has been in the case of Johnie Faa and the Countess of Cassilis:" Maidment, Scotish Ballads, 1868, II, 184. In a sense not intended, this is quite true ; most of the traditions which have grown out of ballads have as slight a foundation as this. The connection of the ballad with the Cassilis family (as Mr Macmath has suggested to me) may possibly have arisen from the first line of some copy reading, ' The gypsies came to the castle-gate.' As F 1³ has perverted Earl of Cassilis to Earl of Castle, so Castle may have been corrupted into Cassilis.†

Knortz, Schottische Balladen, p. 28, translates freely eight stanzas from Aytoun.

A

Ramsay's Tea-Table Miscellany, vol. iv, 1740. Here from the London edition of 1763, p. 427.

1 THE gypsies came to our good lord's gate,
    And wow but they sang sweetly !
  They sang sae sweet and sae very compleat
    That down came the fair lady.

2 And she came tripping down the stair,
    And a' her maids before her ;
  As soon as they saw her well-far'd face,
    They coost the glamer oer her.

3 ' Gae tak frae me this gay mantile,
    And bring to me a plaidie ;
  For if kith and kin and a' had sworn,
    I 'll follow the gypsie laddie.

4 ' Yestreen I lay in a well-made bed,
    And my good lord beside me ;

This night I 'll ly in a tenant's barn,
    Whatever shall betide me.'

5 ' Come to your bed,' says Johny Faa,
    ' Oh come to your bed, my deary ;
  For I vow and I swear, by the hilt of my
      sword,
    That your lord shall nae mair come near ye.'

6 ' I 'll go to bed to my Johny Faa,
    I 'll go to bed to my deary ;
  For I vow and I swear, by what past yestreen,
    That my lord shall nae mair come near me.

7 ' I 'll mak a hap to my Johnny Faa,
    And I 'll mak a hap to my deary ;
  And he 's get a' the coat gaes round,
    And my lord shall nae mair come near
      me.'

8 And when our lord came hame at een,
    And speir'd for his fair lady,

---

* Sharp, in Johnson's Museum, 1853, IV, 218*; Paterson, in Ballads and Songs of Ayrshire, I, 13. It is also clear from these letters that the countess was a sober and religious woman. Some minor difficulties which attend the supposition of this lady's absconding with Johnny Faa, or any gypsy, are barely worth mentioning. At the time when Johnny Faa was put down, in 1624, the countess was seventeen years old, and yet she is made the mother of two children. If we shift the elopement to the other end of her life, there was then (so severe had been the measures taken with these limmers) perhaps not a gypsy left in Scotland. See Aytoun, 1859, I, 186.

† John, seventh earl of Cassilis, son of the sixth earl by a second wife, married for his second wife, some time before 1700, Mary Foix (a name also spelt Faux): Crawford's Peerage, 1716, p. 76, corrected by the Decreets of the Lords of Council and Session, vol. 145, div. 2. May this explain the Faws coming to be associated in the popular mind with a countess of Cassilis ? (A suggestion of Mr Macmath's.) The lady is even called Jeanie Faw in C 7, 11, first by the gypsy, then by her husband. The seventh earl had two children by Mary Foix.

The tane she cry'd, and the other reply'd,
  'She's away with the gypsie laddie.'

9 'Gae saddle to me the black, black steed,
  Gae saddle and make him ready;
Before that I either eat or sleep,
  I'll gae seek my fair lady.'

10 And we were fifteen well-made men,
  Altho we were nae bonny;
And we were a' put down for ane,
  A fair young wanton lady.

B

a. The Edinburgh Magazine and Literary Miscellany,
being a new series of the Scots Magazine (vol. lxxx of the
entire work), November, 1817, p. 309, communicated by
Charles Kirkpatrick Sharpe, as taken down from the recitation of a peasant in Galloway. b. A fragment recited by
Miss Fanny Walker, of Mount Pleasant, near Newburgh-on-
Tay, as communicated by Mr Alexander Laing, 1873.

1 The gypsies they came to my lord Cassilis' yett,
  And O but they sang bonnie!
They sang sae sweet and sae complete
  That down came our fair ladie.

2 She came tripping down the stairs,
  And all her maids before her;
As soon as they saw her weel-far'd face,
  They coost their glamourie owre her.

3 She gave to them the good wheat bread,
  And they gave her the ginger;
But she gave them a far better thing,
  The gold ring off her finger.

4 'Will ye go with me, my hinny and my heart?
  Will ye go with me, my dearie?
And I will swear, by the staff of my spear,
  That your lord shall nae mair come near
    thee.'

5 'Sae take from me my silk mantel,
  And bring to me a plaidie,
For I will travel the world owre
  Along with the gypsie laddie.

6 'I could sail the seas with my Jockie Faa,
  I could sail the seas with my dearie;
I could sail the seas with my Jockie Faa,
  And with pleasure could drown with my
    dearie.

7 They wandred high, they wandred low,
  They wandred late and early,

Untill they came to an old tenant's-barn,
  And by this time she was weary.

8 'Last night I lay in a weel-made bed,
  And my noble lord beside me,
And now I must ly in an old tenant's-barn,
  And the black crew glowring owre me.'

9 'O hold your tongue, my hinny and my heart,
  O hold your tongue, my dearie,
For I will swear, by the moon and the stars,
  That thy lord shall nae mair come near
    thee.'

10 They wandred high, they wandred low,
  They wandred late and early,
Untill they came to that wan water,
  And by this time she was wearie.

11 'Aften have I rode that wan water,
  And my lord Cassilis beside me,
And now I must set in my white feet and
    wade,
  And carry the gypsie laddie.'

12 By and by came home this noble lord,
  And asking for his ladie,
The one did cry, the other did reply,
  'She is gone with the gypsie laddie.'

13 'Go saddle to me the black,' he says,
  'The brown rides never so speedie,
And I will neither eat nor drink
  Till I bring home my ladie.'

14 He wandred high, he wandred low,
  He wandred late and early,
Untill he came to that wan water,
  And there he spied his ladie.

15 'O wilt thou go home, my hinny and my heart,
  O wilt thou go home, my dearie?

And I 'll close thee in a close room,
  Where no man shall come near thee."

16 'I will not go home, my hinny and my heart,
  I will not go home, my dearie ;
  If I have brewn good beer, I will drink of the
    same,
  And my lord shall nae mair come near me.

17 'But I will swear, by the moon and the stars,
  And the sun that shines so clearly,
  That I am as free of the gypsie gang
  As the hour my mother did bear me.'

18 They were fifteen valiant men,
  Black, but very bonny,
  And they lost all their lives for one,
  The Earl of Cassillis' ladie.

C

Motherwell's MS., p. 381, from the recitation of Agnes
Lyle, Kilbarchan, 27 July, 1825.

1 THERE cam singers to Earl Cassillis' gates,
  And oh, but they sang bonnie !
  They sang sae sweet and sae complete,
  Till down cam the earl's lady.

2 She cam tripping down the stair,
  And all her maids before her ;
  As soon as they saw her weel-faurd face,
  They coost their glamourye owre her.

3 They gave her o the gude sweetmeats,
  The nutmeg and the ginger,
  And she gied them a far better thing,
  Ten gold rings aff her finger.

4 'Tak from me my silken cloak,
  And bring me down my plaidie ;
  For it is gude eneuch,' she said,
  'To follow a Gipsy Davy.

5 'Yestreen I rode this water deep,
  And my gude lord beside me ;
  But this nicht I maun set in my pretty fit and
    wade,
  A wheen blackguards wading wi me.

6 'Yestreen I lay in a fine feather-bed,
  And my gude lord beyond me ;
  But this nicht I maun lye in some cauld ten-
    ant's-barn,
  A wheen blackguards waiting on me.'

7 'Come to thy bed, my bonny Jeanie Faw,
  Come to thy bed, my dearie,

For I do swear, by the top o my spear,
  Thy gude lord 'll nae mair come near thee.'

8 When her good lord cam hame at nicht,
  It was asking for his fair ladye ;
  One spak slow, and another whisperd out,
  'She 's awa wi Gipsey Davy !'

9 'Come saddle to me my horse,' he said,
  'Come saddle and mak him readie !
  For I 'll neither sleep, eat, nor drink
  Till I find out my lady.'

10 They socht her up, they socht her doun,
  They socht her thro nations many,
  Till at length they found her out in Abbey
    dale,
  Drinking wi Gipsey Davy.

11 'Rise, oh rise, my bonnie Jeanie Faw,
  Oh rise, and do not tarry !
  Is this the thing ye promised to me
  When at first I did thee marry ?'

12 They drank her cloak, so did they her goun,
  They drank her stockings and her shoon,
  And they drank the coat that was nigh to her
    smock,
  And they pawned her pearled apron.

13 They were sixteen clever men,
  Suppose they were na bonny ;
  They are a' to be hangd on ae tree,
  For the stealing o Earl Cassillis' lady.

14 'We are sixteen clever men,
  One woman was a' our mother ;
  We are a' to be hanged on ae day,
  For the stealing of a wanton lady.'

D

Kinloch MSS, V, 331, in the handwriting of John Hill Burton; from a reciter who came from the vicinity of Craigievar.

1 THERE came Gyptians to Corse Field yeats,
  Black, tho they warna bonny;
 They danced so neat and they danced so fine,
  Till down came the bonny lady.

2 She came trippin down the stair,
  And her nine maidens afore her;
 But up and starts him Johny Fa,
  And he cast the glamour oer her.

3 'Ye 'll take frae me this gay mantle,
  And ye 'll gie to me a plaidie;
 For I shall follow Johny Fa,
  Lat weel or woe betide me.'

4 They 've taen frae her her fine mantle,
  And they 've gaen to her a plaidie,
 And she 's awa wi Johny Fa,
  Whatever may betide her.

5 When they came to a wan water,
  I wite it wasna bonny,
  . . . . . .
   . . . . . .

6 'Yestreen I wade this wan water,
  And my good lord was wi me;
 The night I man cast aff my shoes and wide,
  And the black bands widen wi me.

7 'Yestreen I lay in a well made bed,
  And my good lord lay wi me;
 The night I maun ly in a tenant's barn,
  And the black bands lyin wi me.'

8 'Come to yer bed,' says Johnie Fa,
  'Come to yer bed, my dearie,
 And I shall swer, by the coat that I wear,
  That my hand it shall never go near thee.'

9 'I will never come to yer bed,
  I will never be yer dearie;
 For I think I hear his horse's foot
  That was once called my dearie.'

10 'Come to yer bed,' says Johny Fa,
  'Come to yer bed, my dearie,
 And I shall swear, by the coat that I wear,
  That my hand it shall never go oer thee.'

11 'I will niver come to yer bed,
  I will niver be yer dearie;
 For I think I hear his bridle ring
  That was once called my dearie.'

   * * * * * *

12 When that good lord came hame at night,
  He called for his lady;
 The one maid said, and the other replied,
  'She 's aff wi the Gyptian laddy.'

13 'Ye 'll saddle to me the good black steed,
  Tho the brown it was never so bonny;
 Before that ever I eat or drink,
  I shall have back my lady.'

   * * * * * *

14 'Yestreen we were fifteen good armed men;
  Tho black, we werena bonny;
 The night we a' ly slain for one,
  It 's the Laird o Corse Field's lady.'

E

The Scottish Gallovidian Encyclopedia, by John Mactaggart, 1824, p. 284.

1 THE gypsies they came to Lord Cassle's yet,
  And O but they sang ready!
 They sang sae sweet and sae complete
  That down came the lord's fair lady.

2 O she came tripping down the stair,
  Wi a' her maids afore her,
 And as soon as they saw her weelfared face
  They cuist their glaumry owre her.

3 She gaed to them the gude white bread,
  And they gaed to her the ginger,
 Then she gaed to them a far brawer thing,
  The gowd rings af her finger.

4 Quo she to her maids, There's my gay mantle,
   And bring to me my plaidy,
 And tell my lord whan he comes hame
   I'm awa wi a gypsie laddie.

5 For her lord he had to the hounting gane,
   Awa in the wild green wuddie,
 And Jockie Faw, the gypsie king,
   Saw him there wi his cheeks sae ruddy.

6 On they mounted, and af they rade,
   Ilk gypsie had a cuddy,
 And whan through the stincher they did prance
   They made the water muddy.

7 Quo she, Aft times this water I hae rade,
   Wi many a lord and lady,
 But never afore did I it wade
   To follow a gypsie laddie.

8 'Aft hae I lain in a saft feather-bed,
   Wi my gude lord aside me,
 But now I maun sleep in an auld reeky kilt,
   Alang wi a gypsie laddie.'

9 Sae whan that the yirl he came hame,
   His servants a' stood ready;
 Some took his horse, and some drew his boots,
   But gane was his fair lady.

10 And whan he came ben to the parlour-door,
   He asked for his fair lady,
 But some denied, and ithers some replied,
   'She's awa wi a gypsie laddie.'

11 'Then saddle,' quoth he, 'my gude black naig,
   For the brown is never sae speedy;
 As I will neither eat nor drink
   Till I see my fair lady.

12 'I met wi a cheel as I rade hame,
   And thae queer stories said he;
 Sir, I saw this day a fairy queen
   Fu pack wi a gypsie laddie.

13 'I hae been east, and I hae been west,
   And in the lang town o Kircadie,
 But the bonniest lass that ever I saw
   Was following a gypsie laddie.'

14 Sae his lordship has rade owre hills and dales,
   And owre mony a wild hie mountain,
 Until that he heard his ain lady say,
   'Now my lord will be hame frae the hounting.'

15 'Than will you come hame, my hinnie and my
     love?'
   Quoth he to his charming dearie,
 'And I'll keep ye aye in a braw close room,
   Where the gypsies will never can steer ye.'

16 Said she, 'I can swear by the sun and the
     stars,
   And the moon whilk shines sae clearie,
 That I am as chaste for the gypsie Jockie
     Faw
   As the day my minnie did bear me.'

17 'Gif ye wad swear by the sun,' said he,
   'And the moon, till ye wad deave me,
 Ay and tho ye wad take a far bigger aith,
   My dear, I wadna believe ye.

18 'I'll tak ye hame, and the gypsies I'll hang,
   Ay, I'll make them girn in a wuddie,
 And afterwards I'll burn Jockie Faw,
   Wha fashed himself wi my fair lady.

19 Quoth the gypsies, We're fifteen weel-made men,
   Tho the maist o us be ill bred ay,
 Yet it wad be a pity we should a' hang for ane,
   Wha fashed himself wi your fair lady.

20 Quoth the lady, My lord, forgive them a',
   For they nae ill eer did ye,
 And gie ten guineas to the chief, Jockie Faw,
   For he is a worthy laddie.

21 The lord he hearkened to his fair dame,
   And O the gypsies war glad ay!
 They danced round and round their merry Jockie
     Faw,
   And roosed the gypsie laddie.

22 Sae the lord rade hame wi his charming spouse,
   Owre the hills and the haughs sae whunnie,
 And the gypsies slade down by yon bonny burn-
     side,
   To beek themsells there sae sunnie.

F

The Songs of England and Scotland [by P. Cunning-ham], London, 1835, II, 346, taken down, as current in the north of England, from the recitation of John Martin, the painter.

1 THE gypsies came to the Earl o Cassilis' gate,
    And O but they sang bonnie !
They sang sae sweet and sae complete
    That down cam our fair ladie.

2 And she cam tripping down the stair,
    Wi her twa maids before her;
As soon as they saw her weel-far'd face,
    They coost their glamer oer her.

3 'O come wi me,' says Johnnie Faw,
    'O come wi me, my dearie,
For I vow and swear, by the hilt of my sword,
    Your lord shall nae mair come near ye.'

4 'Here, tak frae me this gay mantile,
    And gie to me a plaidie;
Tho kith and kin and a' had sworn,
    I 'll follow the gypsie laddie.

5 'Yestreen I lay in a weel-made bed,
    And my gude lord beside me;
This night I 'll lie in a tenant's barn,
    Whatever shall betide me.

6 'Last night I lay in a weel-made bed,
    Wi silken hangings round me;
But now I 'll lie in a farmer's barn,
    Wi the gypsies all around me.

7 'The first ale-house that we come at,
    We 'll hae a pot o brandie;
The next ale-house that we came at,
    We 'll drink to gypsie Geordie.'

8 Now when our lord cam home at een,
    He speir'd for his fair lady;
The ane she cried, [the] tither replied,
    'She 's awa wi the gypsie laddie.'

9 'Gae saddle me the gude black steed;
    The bay was neer sae bonnie;
For I will neither eat nor sleep
    Till I be wi my lady.'

10 Then he rode east, and he rode west,
    And he rode near Strabogie,
And there he found his ain dear wife,
    Drinking wi gypsie Geordie.

11 'And what made you leave your houses and
      land?
    Or what made you leave your money?
Or what made you leave your ain wedded lord,
    To follow the gypsie laddie?

12 'Then come thee hame, my ain dear wife,
    Then come thee hame, my hinnie,
And I do swear, by the hilt of my sword,
    The gypsies nae mair shall come near thee.'

13 Then we were seven weel-made men,
    But lack! we were nae bonnie,
And we were a' put down for ane,
    For the Earl o Cassilis' ladie.

G

a. A broadside in the Roxburghe Ballads, III, 685, entered in the catalogue, doubtfully, as of Newcastle upon Tyne, 1720. b. A recent stall-copy, Catnach, 2 Monmouth Court, Seven Dials.

1 THERE was seven gypsies all in a gang,
    They were brisk and bonny; O
They rode till they came to the Earl of Cas-
    tle's house,
    And there they sang most sweetly. O

2 The Earl of Castle's lady came down,
    With the waiting-maid beside her;

As soon as her fair face they saw,
    They called their grandmother over.

3 They gave to her a nutmeg brown,
    And a race of the best ginger;
She gave to them a far better thing,
    'Twas the ring from off her finger.

4 She pulld off her high-heeld shoes,
    They was made of Spanish leather;
She put on her highland brog[u]es,
    To follow the gypsey loddy.

5 At night when my good lord came home,
   Enquiring for his lady,
The waiting-maid made this reply,
   ' She 's following the gypsey loddy.'

6 ' Come saddle me my milk-white steed,
   Come saddle it so bonny,
As I may go seek my own wedded wife,
   That 's following the gypsey loddy.

7 ' Have you been east? have you been west?
   Or have you been brisk and bonny?
Or have you seen a gay lady,
   A following the gypsey loddy?'

8 He rode all that summer's night,
   And part of the next morning;

At length he spy'd his own wedded wife,
   She was cold, wet, and weary.

9 ' Why did you leave your houses and land?
   Or why did you leave your money?
Or why did you leave your good wedded lord,
   To follow the gypsey loddy?'

10 'O what care I for houses and land?
   Or what care I for money?
So as I have brewd, so will I return;
   So fare you well, my honey!'

11 There was seven gypsies in a gang,
   And they was brisk and bonny,
And they 're to be hanged all on a row,
   For the Earl of Castle's lady.

H

Shropshire Lolk-Lore, edited by Charlotte Sophia Burne, p. 550, as sung May 23, 1885, by gypsy children.

1 THERE came a gang o gipsies by,
   And they was singing so merry, O
Till they gained the heart o my lady gay,
   . . . .

2 As soon as the lord he did come in,
   Enquired for his lady, O
And some o the sarvants did-a reply,
   ' Her 's away wi the gipsy laddie.' O

3 ' O saddle me the bay, and saddle me the grey,
   Till I go and sarch for my lady;'
And some o the sarvants did-a reply,
   ' Her 's away wi the gipsy laddie.'

4 And he rode on, and he rode off,
   Till he came to the gipsies' tentie,
And there he saw his lady gay,
   By the side o the gipsy laddie.

5 ' Did n't I leave you houses and land?
   And did n't I leave you money?
Did n't I leave you three pretty babes
   As ever was in yonder green island?'

6 ' What care I for houses and land?
   And what care I for money?
What do I care for three pretty babes?'
   . . . . .

7 ' The tother night you was on a feather bed,
   Now you 're on a straw one,'
   . . . . .
   . . . . .

I

From Miss Margaret Reburn, " as sung in County Meath, Ireland, about 1860."

1 THERE come seven gypsies on a day,
   Oh, but they sang bonny! O
And they sang so sweet, and they sang so clear,
   Down cam the earl's ladie. O

2 They gave to her the nutmeg,
   And they gave to her the ginger;
But she gave to them a far better thing,
   The seven gold rings off her fingers.

3 When the earl he did come home,
   Enquiring for his ladie,

One of the servants made this reply,
  'She 's awa with the gypsie lad[d]ie.'

4 'Come saddle for me the brown,' he said,
  ' For the black was neer so speedy,
And I will travel night and day
  Till I find out my ladie.

5 'Will you come home, my dear ? ' he said,
  ' Oh will you come home, my honey ?
And, by the point of my broad sword,
  A hand I 'll neer lay on you.'

6 ' Last night I lay on a good feather-bed,
  And my own wedded lord beside me,

And tonight I 'll lie in the ash-corner,
  With the gypsies all around me.

7 'They took off my high-heeled shoes,
  That were made of Spanish leather,
And I have put on coarse Lowland brogues,
  To trip it oer the heather.'

8 'The Earl of Cashan is lying sick ;
  Not one hair I 'm sorry ;
I 'd rather have a kiss from his fair lady's lips
  Than all his gold and his money.'

J

a. Written down by Newton Pepoun, as learned from a boy with whom he went to school in Stockbridge, Massachusetts, about 1845. b. From the singing of Mrs Farmer, born in Maine, as learned by her daughter, about 1840.

1 THERE was a gip came oer the land,
  He sung so sweet and gaily ;
He sung with glee, neath the wild wood tree,
  He charmed the great lord's lady.
    Ring a ding a ding go ding go da,
    Ring a ding a ding go da dy,
    Ring a ding a ding go ding go da,
    She 's gone with the gipsey Davy.

2 The lord he came home late that night ;
  Enquiring for his lady,
'She 's gone, she 's gone,' said his old servant-man,
  'She 's gone with the gipsey Davy.'

3 'Go saddle me my best black mare;
  The grey is neer so speedy ;

For I 'll ride all night, and I 'll ride all day,
  Till I overtake my lady.'

4 Riding by the river-side,
  The grass was wet and dewy ;
Seated with her gipsey lad,
  It 's there he spied his lady.

5 ' Would you forsake your house and home?
  Would you forsake your baby?
Would you forsake your own true love,
  And go with the gipsey Davy ?'

6 'Yes, I 'll forsake my house and home,
  Yes, I 'll forsake my baby;
What care I for my true love?
  I love the gipsey Davy.'

7 The great lord he rode home that night,
  He took good care of his baby,
And ere six months had passed away
  He married another lady.

K

a. From Mrs Helena Titus Brown of New York. b. From Miss Emma A. Clinch of New York. Derived, 1820, or a little later, a directly, b indirectly, from the singing of Miss Phœbe Wood, Huntington, Long Island, and perhaps learned from English soldiers there stationed during the Revolutionary war.

*   *   *   *   *   *   *

1 ' Go bring me down my high-heeled shoes,
  Made of the Spanish leather,
And I 'll take off my low-heeled shoes,
  And away we 'll go together.'
    Lumpy dumpy linky dinky day
    Lumpy dumpy linky dinky daddy

2 They brought her down her high-heeled shoes,
  Made of the Spanish leather,
And she took off her low-heeled shoes,
  And away they went together.

3 And when Lord Garrick he got there,
  Inquiring for his lady,
Then up steps his best friend :
  'She's gone with a gipsy laddie.'

4 'Go saddle me my bonny brown,
  For the grey is not so speedy,
And away we'll go to the Misty Mount,
  And overtake my lady.'

5 They saddled him his bonny brown,
  For the grey was not so speedy,
And away they went to the Misty Mount,
  And overtook his lady.

6 And when Lord Garrick he got there,
  'T was in the morning early,
And there he found his lady fair,
  And she was wet and weary.

7 'And it's fare you well, my dearest dear,
  And it's fare you well for ever,
And if you don't go with me now,
  Don't let me see you never.'

--- ◆ ---

A. *Variations of Finlay,* II, 39 ff.
  Inserted after 2 :

'O come with me,' says Johnie Faw,
  'O come with me, my dearie ;
For I vow and I swear, by the hilt of my
    sword,
  That your lord shall nae mair come near ye.'

Then she gied them the beer and the wine,
  And they gied her the ginger ;
But she gied them a far better thing,
  The goud ring aff her finger.

4². Wi my. 4³. But this.
6³. For I vow and I swear, by the fan in my
    hand.
7². And *wanting.*
9². *Otherwise :* The brown was neer sae ready.
10³. but ane. 10⁴. For a.
Herd has in 10³,⁴ but ane, For. *Pinkerton
follows Herd, with changes of his own in* 1,
10, *and the omission of* 7. *The copy in
Johnson's Museum is Herd's, with changes :
in* 10³,⁴, *are* a' *put down for* ane, The Earl of
Cassilis' lady. *Ritson follows Ramsay, except that in* 6² *he has* And I'll, *found in
Herd ; perhaps also in some edition of the
Tea-Table Miscellany.*

B. a. "Some lines have been omitted on account
  of their indelicacy :" p. 308 b. *The reference is no doubt to a stanza corresponding
  to* A 7, *or perhaps to a passage like* 5-7.

b. *Only* 1, 2, 5, 10-13, *are preserved.*
  1¹. gipsies cam to oor ha-door.
  1⁴. doon stairs cam oor gay leddie.
  2². afore.
  2³. An whan they. 2⁴. cuist the glamour.
  5¹. my gay mantle. 5². me my.
  5³. For I maun leave my guid lord at hame.
  5⁴. An follow the.
  10¹. They travelld east, they travelld wast.
  10². They travelld. 10³. to the.
  10⁴. By that time she. 11¹. I crost this.
  11². An my guid man. 11³. Noo I maun put.
  11⁴. An follow.
  12¹. Whan her guid lord cam hame at nicht.
  12². He spierd for his gay.
  12³. The tane she cried an the ither replied.
  12⁴. She's aff. 13¹. the brown, he said.
  13². The black neer rides. 13³. For I.
  13⁴. Till I've brought back.

C. 4¹. *Originally* plaid *was written for* cloak ; *evidently by accidental anticipation.*
  5³. fit *altered perhaps from* fut ; *printed* fit.
    *Motherwell has made several verbal
    changes in printing, and has inserted three
    stanzas to fill out the ballad. After* 3,

'Come with me, my bonnie Jeanie Faw,
  O come with me, my dearie ;
For I do swear, by the head o my spear,
  Thy gude lord 'll nae mair come near thee.'

After 7,
  'I'll go to bed,' the lady she said,
  'I'll go to bed to my dearie ;

For I do swear, by the fan in my hand,
　　That my lord shall nae mair come near me.

'I 'll mak a hap,' the lady she said,
　'I 'll mak a hap to my dearie,
And he 's get a' this petticoat gaes round,
　And my lord shall nae mair come near me.'

E. 12, 13. *After 9 of* A, *says Finlay, some copies insert :*

And he 's rode east, and he 's rode west,
　Till he came near Kirkaldy;
There he met a packman-lad,
　And speir'd for his fair lady.

'O cam ye east? or cam ye west?
　Or cam ye through Kirkaldy?
O saw na ye a bonny lass,
　Following the gypsie laddie?'

'I cam na east, I cam na west,
　Nor cam I through Kirkaldy;
But the bonniest lass that eer I saw
　Was following the gypsie laddie!'

　See also G 7.
G. a. 4³. br oges.
　b. *In stanzas of eight lines.*
　1¹. There were. 2². With her. 2³. fair *wanting.*
　2⁴. They cast the glamer over her.
　3². Which was of the belinger.
　3⁴. 'T was *wanting.* 4². They were.
　4³. brogues. 4⁴. laddy, *and always.*
　6¹. me *wanting.* 6³. That I may go and seek.
　6⁴. Who 's. 7⁴. Following a.
　8¹. all the summer. 8³. espied.
　8⁴. and wet. 9¹. O why.
　9³. your own. 10¹. lands. 10³. will I remain.
　11¹. There were. 11². They were.
　11³. all in.
H. 2¹. the lawyer did.

J. b. 1. The gypsy came tripping over the lea,
　　The gypsy he sang boldly;
　　He ·sang till he made the merry woods
　　　ring,
　　And he charmed the heart of the lady.

Order : 1, 5, 6, 2, 3.

2 (*as* 4). The lord came home that self-same
　　night,
　　Inquired for his lady ;
　The merry maid made him this reply,
　　'She 's gone with the gypsy Davy.'

3 (*as* 5). 'O bring me out the blackest steed;
　　The brown one 's not so speedy;
　I 'll ride all day, and I 'll ride all night,
　　Till I overtake my lady.'

4 (*as* 7). He rode along by the river-side,
　　The water was black and rily,

　　·　·　·　·　·　·　·
·　·　·　·　·　·　·

5 (*as* 2). 5¹,². Will you.
5³. Will you forsake your own wedded lord.
6·(*as* 3). 6². And I 'll.
6³. I will forsake my own wedded lord.
6⁴. And go with the gypsy Davy. 7. *Wanting.*
b 6. I lay last night. *The rest wanting.*
b 8. *Puts the question whether she will go back.*
b 9. I lay last night. *The rest wanting.*

K. a. *The order as delivered was* 3, 1, 2, *etc., and
　the* high-heeled shoes *were attributed to Lord
　Garrick. Him, his, he* in 2 *have been
　changed* to her, her, she. *But a further
　change should be made for sense, in* 1, 2 :
　*the lady should take off her high-heeled
　shoes and put on her low-heeled shoes ; see*
　G 4, I 8.
　Burden given also :
　　Lal dee dumpy dinky diddle dah day
　b. *Burden :* Rump a dump a dink a dink a day
　　　　Rump a dump a dink a dink a dady.
　Or,　　Rink a dink a dink a dink a day
　　　　Rink a dink a dink a dink a day dee.
　Order as in a.
　1¹. fetch me. 1³. And take away.
　2¹. fetched him down his.
　2³. And they took away his.
　3¹. got home. 3⁴. with the.
　4¹. Go fetch me out. 4³. And we 'll away to.
　4⁴. To *for* And. 5¹. They fetched him out.
　5⁴. To overtake my. 6³. lady bright.
　7³. you won't.

201

BESSY BELL AND MARY GRAY

a. Sharpe's Ballad Book, 1823, p. 62.   **b.** Lyle's Ancient Ballads and Songs, 1827, p. 160, "collated from the singing of two aged persons, one of them a native of Perthshire."   **c.** Scott's Minstrelsy, 1833, I, 45, two stanzas.

A SQUIB on the birth of the Chevalier St George, beginning

> Bessy Bell and Mary Grey,
> Those famous bonny lasses,

shows that this little ballad, or song, was very well known in the last years of the seventeenth century.* The first stanza was made by Ramsay the beginning of a song of his own, and stands thus in Ramsay's Poems, Edinburgh, 1721, p. 80 : †

> O Bessy Bell and Mary Gray,
> They are twa bonny lasses;
> They biggd a bower on yon Burn-brae,
> And theekd it oer wi rashes.

Cunningham, Songs of Scotland, III, 60, gives, as recited to him by Sir Walter Scott, four stanzas which are simply a with 'Lyndoch brae' substituted in the third for Sharpe's 'Stronach haugh.' 'Dranoch haugh,' nearly as in b, is, as will presently appear, the right reading. Sharpe's third stanza, with the absurd variation of *royal* kin, occurs in a letter of his of the date November 25, 1811 (Letters, ed. Allardyce, I, 504), and is printed in the Musical Museum, IV, *203, ed. 1853.

In the course of a series of letters concerning the ballad in The Scotsman (newspaper), August 30 to September 8, 1886, several verses are cited with trivial variations from the texts here given.

'Bessy Bell' was made into this nursery-song in England (Halliwell's Nursery Rhymes of England, 1874, p. 246, No 484) :

> Bessy Bell and Mary Gray,
> They were two bonny lasses;
> They built their house upon the lea,
> And covered it with rashes.

> Bessy kept the garden-gate,
> And Mary kept the pantry;
> Bessy always had to wait,
> While Mary lived in plenty.

The most important document relating to Bessy Bell and Mary Gray is a letter written June 21, 1781, by Major Barry, then proprietor of Lednock, and printed in the Transactions of the Society of the Antiquaries of Scotland, II, 108, 1822.‡

"When I came first to Lednock," says Major Barry, "I was shewn in a part of my ground (called the Dranoch-haugh) an heap of stones almost covered with briers, thorns and fern, which they assured me was the burial place of Bessie Bell and Mary Gray.

"The tradition of the country relating to these ladys is, that Mary Gray's father was laird of Lednock and Bessie Bell's of Kinvaid, a place in this neighbourhood; that they were both very handsome, and an intimate friendship subsisted between them; that while Miss Bell was on a visit to Miss Gray, the plague

---

* I have seen this piece only in Elizabeth Cochrane's Song-Book, MS., p. 38, and in Buchan's MSS, I, 220. Its contents agree with what is alleged in W. Fuller's "Brief Discovery of the True Mother of the pretended Prince of Wales, known by the name of Mary Grey," London, 1696, pp. 5 f, 11, 17 f, and it was probably composed not long after.

† Afterwards inserted in the first volume of The Tea-Table Miscellany (p. 66 of A New Miscellany of Scots Sangs, London, 1727, p. 68 of T. T. M., Dublin, 1729), from which source it may have been adopted by Sharpe.

‡ Here from the original, Communications to the Society of Antiquaries of Scotland, vol. i, from a copy furnished by Mr Macmath.

broke out, in the year 1666; in order to avoid which they built themselves a bower about three quarters of a mile west from Lednock House, in a very retired and romantic place called Burn-braes, on the side of Brauchie-burn. Here they lived for some time; but the plague raging with great fury, they caught the infection, it is said, from a young gentle-man who was in love with them both. He used to bring them their provision. They died in this bower, and were buried in the Dranoch-haugh, at the foot of a brae of the same name, and near to the bank of the river Almond. The burial-place lies about half a mile west from the present house of Lednock.*

"I have removed all the rubbish from this little spot of classic ground, inclosed it with a wall, planted it round with flowering shrubs, made up the grave double, and fixed a stone in the wall, on which is engraved the names of Bessie Bell and Mary [Gray]."

The estate passed by purchase to Thomas Graham, afterwards Lord Lynedoch, who re-placed the wall, which had become dilapi-dated in the course of half a century, with a stone parapet and iron railing, and covered the grave with a slab inscribed, "They lived, they loved, they died." This slab is now hidden under a cairn of stones raised by successive pilgrims.

Major Barry's date of 1666 should be put back twenty years. Perth and the neighbor-hood (Lednock is seven miles distant) were fearfully ravaged by the plague in 1645 and a year or two following. Three thousand people are said to have perished. Scotland escaped the pestilence of 1665–6. †

The young gentleman who is said to have brought food to Bessy and Mary is sometimes described as the lover of both, sometimes as the lover of one of the pair. Pennant says that the ballad was "composed by a lover deeply stricken with the charms of both." In the course of tradition, the lover is said to have perished with the young women, which we might expect to happen if he brought the contagion to the bower. But this lover, who ought to have had his place in the song, appears only in tradition, and his reality may be called in question. It is not rational that the young women should seclude themselves to avoid the pest and then take the risk of the visits of a person from the seat of the in-fection. ‡ To be sure it may be doubted, notwithstanding the tenor of the ballad, whether the retirement of these young ladies was voluntary, or at least whether they had not taken the plague before they removed to their bower. In that case the risk would have been for the lover, and would have been no more than he might naturally assume. §

---

1 O Bessie Bell and Mary Gray,
    They war twa bonnie lasses;

They bigget a bower on yon burn-brae,
    And theekit it oer wi rashes.

* The most of this account, and in nearly the same words, was given in an earlier letter from Major Barry to James Cant, who printed (Perth, 1774) an edition of 'The Muses Threnodie, by Mr H. Adamson, 1638' (p. 19). The principal items of the story are repeated from Cant by Pen-nant, Tour in Scotland, 1772, Part II, London, 1776, p. 112. Pennant cites Cant's book as the Gabions of Perth. "It seems," says Mr Macmath, who has extracted for me the passage in Cant, "that Adamson's work was sometimes known as Gall's Gabions, the latter being a coined word."

† An "old manuscript volume" cited in The New Statis-tical Account of Scotland, X, 37; Chambers, Domestic Annals of Scotland, 1858, II, 167.

‡ The remark is made in The Scotsman, September 11, 1886.

§ In the manuscript cited in The New Statistical Account of Scotland, p. 37, we are told that, to prevent the spread of infection, "it was thought proper to put those out of the town at some distance who were sick. Accordingly, they went out and builded huts for themselves in different places around the town, particularly in the South Inch [etc.] and the grounds near the river Almond, at the mouth thereof, in all which places there are as yet the remains of their huts which they lodged in." So, when this same pestilence was raging in the parish of Monivaird, the gentlemen "caused many huts to be built, and ordered all who perceived that they were infected immediately to repair into them:" Por-teous, History of the Parishes of Monivaird and Strowan, MS., Communications to the Society of Antiquaries of Scotland, vol. i, printed in the Transactions, II, 72, 1822.

2 They theekit it oer wi rashes green,
   They theekit it oer wi heather;
But the pest cam frae the burrows-town,
   And slew them baith thegither.

3 They thought to lye in Methven kirk-yard,
   Amang their noble kin;

But they maun lye in Stronach haugh,
   To biek forenent the sin.

4 And Bessy Bell and Mary Gray,
   They war twa bonnie lasses;
They biggit a bower on yon burn-brae,
   And theekit it oer wi rashes.

———•———

a. *In eight-line stanzas.*
b. 1³. house *for* bower.   2¹. wi birk and brume.
   2³. Till the: frae the neibrin.
   2⁴. An streekit.   3¹. They were na buried in.
   3². Amang the rest o their kin.
   3³. they were buried by Dornoch-haugh.
   3⁴. On the bent before.   4¹. Sing *for* And.

4³. Wha *for* They.   4⁴. wi thrashes.
c. 1¹. O *wanting.*   2. *Wanting.*
   3¹. They wadna rest in Methvin kirk.
   3². gentle kin.
   3³. But they wad lie in Lednoch braes.
   3⁴. beek against.
4. *Wanting.*

———————

202

THE BATTLE OF PHILIPHAUGH

Minstrelsy of the Scottish Border, III, 153, 1803, II, 166, 1833 · "preserved by tradition in Selkirkshire."

———•———

AFTER six brilliant victories, at Tippermuir, Aberdeen, Inverlochy, Auldearn, Alford, Kilsyth, gained in less than a year, September 1, 1644–August 15, 1645, Montrose was surprised by David Leslie at Philiphaugh, September 13 following, and his army cut to pieces or dispersed. This army, consisting of only five hundred Irish foot and twelve hundred Scottish horse, the last all gentry, was lying at Philiphaugh, a meadow on the west side of the Ettrick, and at Selkirk, on and above the opposite bank. Leslie came down from the north with four thousand cavalry and some infantry, was less than four miles from Selkirk the night of the twelfth, and on the morrow, favored by a heavy mist, had advanced to about half a

mile's distance before his approach was reported. A hundred and fifty of Montrose's horse received and repulsed two charges of greatly superior numbers; the rest stood off and presently took to flight. The foot remained firm. Two thousand of Leslie's horse crossed the river and got into Montrose's rear, and made resistance vain. Montrose and a few friends hewed their way through the enemy.*

1. Harehead wood is at the western end of the plain of Philiphaugh.

2, 3. Leslie had come up from Berwick along the eastern coast as far as Tranent, and then suddenly turned south. His numbers are put too low, and Montrose's, in 10, about nine times too high.

4. The Shaw burn is a small stream that

* This is Wishart's account. Another, by Covenanters, makes Montrose to have been more on the alert, and has nothing of the two thousand horse sent to take him in the rear. The royalists are admitted to have maintained their ground with great resolution for almost an hour. The numbers are as given by Gardiner, History of the Great Civil War, II, 335 f.

flows into the Ettrick from the south, a little north of the town.

5. Lingly burn falls into the Ettrick from the north, a little above the Shaw burn.

The 'aged father,' 6, to accept a tradition reported by Sir Walter Scott, was one " Brydone, ancestor to several families in the parish of Ettrick." This is probably the personage elsewhere called Will, upon whose advice Leslie (according to tradition again) "sent a strong body of horse over a dip in the bank that separated his advanced guard from the river Ettrick, and still known as " Will's Nick," with instructions to follow their guide up Netley burn, wheel to the left round Linglee hill, and then fall upon the flank of Montrose's army at Philiphaugh." * It does not appear that Leslie adopted that portion of the aged father's recommendation which is conveyed in stanzas 11, 12, notwithstanding the venerable man's unusual experience, which, as Scott points out, extended from Solway Moss, 1542, to Dunbar, where, in 1650, five years after Philiphaugh, Leslie was defeated by Cromwell.

Other pieces of popular verse relating, in part or wholly, to Montrose are 'The Gallant Grahams,' Roxburghe collection, III, 380, Douce, III, 39 back, Ebsworth, Roxburghe Ballads, VI, 587, Scott's Minstrelsy, III, 371, 1803, II, 183, 1833; 'The Haughs o Cromdale,' Ritson's Scotish Songs, 1794, II, 40, Johnson's Museum, No 488, Maidment's Scotish Ballads and Songs, 1868, I, 299, Hogg's Jacobite Relics, I, 157 ff; 'The Battle of Alford,' Laing's Thistle of Scotland, p. 68.

---

1 On Philiphaugh a fray began,
    At Hairheadwood it ended ;
The Scots outoer the Græmes they ran,
    Sae merrily they bended.

2 Sir David frae the Border came,
    Wi heart an hand came he ;
Wi him three thousand bonny Scots,
    To bear him company.

3 Wi him three thousand valiant men,
    A noble sight to see !
A cloud o mist them weel conceald,
    As close as eer might be.

4 When they came to the Shaw burn,
    Said he, Sae weel we frame,
I think it is convenient
    That we should sing a psalm.

5 When they came to the Lingly burn,
    As daylight did appear,
They spy'd an aged father,
    And he did draw them near.

6 'Come hither, aged father,'
    Sir David he did cry,
'And tell me where Montrose lies,
    With all his great army.'

7 'But first you must come tell to me,
    If friends or foes you be ;
I fear you are Montrose's men,
    Come frae the north country.'

8 'No, we are nane o Montrose's men,
    Nor eer intend to be ;
I am Sir David Lesly,
    That's speaking unto thee.'

9 "If you 're Sir David Lesly,
    As I think weel ye be,
I am sorry ye hae brought so few
    Into your company.

10 'There's fifteen thousand armed men
    Encamped on yon lee ;
Ye 'll never be a bite to them,
    For aught that I can see.

11 'But halve your men in equal parts,
    Your purpose to fulfill ;
Let ae half keep the water-side,
    The rest gae round the hill.

12 'Your nether party fire must,
    Then beat a flying drum ;
And then they 'll think the day 's their ain,
    And frae the trench they 'll come.

* T. Craig-Brown, History of Selkirkshire, 1886, I, 188.

13 'Then, those that are behind them maun
    Gie shot, baith grit and sma ;
    And so, between your armies twa,
    Ye may make them to fa.'

14 'O were ye ever a soldier ?'
    Sir David Lesly said ;
    'O yes ; I was at Solway Flow,
    Where we were all betrayd.

15 'Again I was at curst Dunbar,
    And was a prisner taen,
    And many weary night and day
    In prison I hae lien.'

16 'If ye will lead these men aright,
    Rewarded shall ye be ;
    But, if that ye a traitor prove,
    I 'll hang thee on a tree.'

17 'Sir, I will not a traitor prove ;
    Montrose has plunderd me ;

    I 'll do my best to banish him
    Away frae this country.'

18 He halvd his men in equal parts,
    His purpose to fulfill ;
    The one part kept the water-side,
    The other gaed round the hill.

19 The nether party fired brisk,
    Then turnd and seemd to rin ;
    And then they a' came frae the trench,
    And cry'd, The day 's our ain !

20 The rest then ran into the trench,
    And loosd their cannons a' :
    And thus, between his armies twa,
    He made them fast to fa.

21 Now let us a' for Lesly pray,
    And his brave company,
    For they hae vanquishd great Montrose,
    Our cruel enemy.

4⁴. *Var.* That we should take a dram : *Scott.*
Probably a jocose suggestion.

203

THE BARON OF BRACKLEY

A. a. 'The Baronne of Braikley,' [Alexander Laing's] Scarce Ancient Ballads, 1822, p. 9. b. 'The Baron of Braikley,' Buchan's Gleanings, 1825, p. 68. c. 'The Barrone of Brackley,' The New Deeside Guide, by James Brown (pseudonym for Joseph Robertson), Aberdeen, [1832*], p. 46.

B. 'The Baron of Brackley,' Kinloch MSS, V, 379; in the handwriting of John Hill Burton.

C. a. 'The Baron of Braikly,' Jamieson-Brown MS., Appendix, p. viii. b. 'The Baron of Brackley,' Jamieson's Popular Ballads, 1806, I, 102.

D. 'The Baron of Breachell,' Skene MS., p. 110.

FIRST printed by Jamieson (C b) in 1806, who says : "For the copy of the ballad here given I am indebted to Mrs Brown. I have also collated it with another, less perfect, but not materially different, so far as it goes, with which I was favored by the editor of the Bor-

* Not 1829, as put in the reprint of 1869. "Written hurriedly, in supply of the press, in April and May, 1832. J. R." : Dr J. Robertson's interleaved copy of the undated

first edition. A c is reprinted (with some errors) in The Great North of Scotland Railway, A Guide, by W. Ferguson, 1881, p. 163.

der Minstrelsy, who took it down from the recitation of two ladies, great-grandchildren of Farquharson of Inverey; so that the ballad, and the notices that accompany it, are given upon the authority of a Gordon [Anne Gordon, Mrs Brown] and a Farquharson." * A c is also a compounded copy: see the notes.

The text in The Thistle of Scotland, p. 46, is C b. That which is cited in part in the Fourth Report on Historical Manuscripts, 1874, p. 534, is A c. The ballad is rewritten by Allan Cunningham, Songs of Scotland, II, 208.

A. Inverey comes before day to Brackley's gate, and calls to him to open and have his blood spilled. Brackley asks over the wall whether the people below are gentlemen or hired gallows-birds; if gentlemen, they may come in and eat and drink; in the other case, they may go on to the Lowlands and steal cattle. His wife urges him to get up; the men are nothing but hired gallows-birds. Brackley will go out to meet Inverey (both know it is he, 12, 19), but these same gallows-birds will prove themselves men. His wife derisively calls on her maids to bring their distaffs; if Brackley is not man enough to protect his cattle, she will drive off the robbers with her women. Brackley says he will go out, but he shall never come in. He arms and sallies forth, attended by his brother William, his uncle, and his cousin; but presently bids his brother turn back because he is a bridegroom. William refuses, and in turn, but equally to no effect, urges Brackley to turn back for his wife's and his son's sake. The Gordons are but four against four hundred of Inverey's, and are all killed. Brackley's wife, so far from tearing her hair, braids it, welcomes Inverey, and makes him a feast. The son, on the nurse's knee, vows to be revenged if he lives to be a man. (Cf. ' Johnie Armstrong,' III, 367, where this should have been noted.)

The other versions agree with A a in the material points. Inverey's numbers are diminished. In B 10, C 11, Brackley has only his brother with him, meaning, perhaps, when he leaves his house. The fight was not simply at the gates, but was extended over a considerable distance (A 33, B 11), and other men joined the Gordons in the course of it. In B 12 we learn that the miller's four sons (D 10, the miller and his three sons) were killed with the Gordons (and William Gordon's wife, or bride, in A 25, is ' bonnie Jean, the maid o the mill'). In B 15, D 12, Craigevar comes up with a party, and might have saved Brackley's life had he been there an hour sooner. In A a, b, C, D, Brackley's wife is Peggy (Peggy Dann, wrongly, D 14, 15); in B 19 (wrongly) Catharine Fraser. D makes Catharine the wife of Gordon of Glenmuick (Alexander Gordon, A a 35), who rives her hair, as Brackley's wife does not (14, 15, 18, 19). In C, Peggy Gordon, besides feasting Inverey, keeps him till morning, and then shows him a road by which he may go safely home. C b adds, for poetical justice, that Inverey at once let this haggard down the wind.

This affray occurred in September, 1666. The account of it given by the Gordons (the son of the murdered laird and the Marquis of Huntly) was that John Gordon of Brackley, having poinded cattle belonging to John Farquharson of Inverey, or his followers, Inverey " convoked his people, to revenge himself on Brackley for putting the law in execution; that he came to the house of Brackley, and required the laird to restore his cattle which had been poinded; and that, although the laird gave a fair answer, yet the Farquharsons, with the view of drawing him out of his house, drove away not only the poinded cattle but also Brackley's own cattle, and when the latter was thus forced to come out of his house, the Farquharsons fell on him and murdered him and his brother."

A memorandum for John Farquharson of

* Jamieson writes to the Scots Magazine, October, 1803, p. 699: " The Baron of Braikly begins,

O Inverey cam down Dee-side
Whistling and playing;

He 's landed at Braikly's yates
At the day dawing.

Of this I have got a compleat copy, and the story is very interesting; but I have got a fragment of it from another quarter, which, so far as it goes, is superior." Etc.

Inverey and others, 24 January, 1677, "sets forth that John Gordon of Brackley, having bought from the sheriff of Aberdeen the fines exigible from Inverey and others for killing of black-fish, the said Brackley made friendly arrangements with others, but declined to settle with Inverey ; whereupon the latter, being on his way to the market at Tullich,* sent Mr John Ferguson, minister at Glenmuick, John McHardy of Crathie, a notary, and Duncan Erskine, portioner of Invergelder, to the laird of Brackley, with the view of representing to him that Inverey and his tenants were willing to settle their fines on the same terms as their neighbors. These proposals were received by Brackley with contempt, and during the time of the communing he gathered his friends and attacked Inverey, and having 'loused severall shotts' against Inverey's party, the return shots of the latter were in self-defence. The result was that the laird of Brackley, with his brother William and their cousin James Gordon in Cults, were killed on the one side, and on the other Robert McWilliam in Inverey, John McKenzie, sometime there, and Malcom Gordon the elder." The convocation of Inverey's friends is accounted for in the same document by the fact that Inverey was captain of the watch for the time; that he and his ancestors had been used to go to the market with men to guard it; and that it is the custom of the country for people who are going to the market to join any numerous company that may be going the same way, either for their own security or out of " kindness for the persons with whom they go," and also the custom of that mountainous country to go with arms, especially at markets. (Abstract, by Dr. John Stuart, of a MS. of Col. James Farquharson of Invercauld, Historical MSS Commission, Fourth Report, p. 534).

Another account, agreeing in all important points with the last, is given in a history of the family of Macintosh.† It will be borne in mind that Inverey belonged to this clan, and that acts of his would therefore be put in a favorable light. Brackley had seized the horses of some of Inverey's people on account of fines alleged to be due by them for taking salmon in the Dee out of season. Inverey represented to Brackley that the sufferers by this proceeding were men who had incurred no penalty, and offered, if the horses should be restored, to deliver the guilty parties for punishment. Brackley would not return the horses on these terms, and Inverey then proposed that the matter in dispute should be left to friends. While Brackley was considering what to do, Alexander Gordon of Aberfeldy came to offer his services, with a body of armed men, and Brackley, now feeling himself strong, rejected the suggestion of a peaceful solution, and set out to attack Inverey. When a collision was impending, Inverey at first drew back, begging Brackley to desist from violence, which only made Brackley and Aberfeldy the keener. Two of Inverey's followers were slain ; and then Inverey and his men, in self-defence, turned on their assailants, and killed Gordon of Brackley, his brother William, and James Gordon of Cults.

The Gordons, this account further says, began a prosecution of Inverey and his party before the Court of Justiciary. Inverey had recourse to Macintosh, his chief, who exerted himself so effectually in behalf of his kinsman that when the case was called no plaintiff appeared. Nevertheless Dr John Stuart (Historical MSS, as above) produces a warrant " for apprehending John Farquharson of Inverey and others his followers, who had been outlawed for not compearing to answer at their trial, and had subsequently continued for many years in their outlawry, associating with themselves a company of thieves, murderers, and sorners ; therefore empowering

---

* A market was established here in 1661 by an act in favor of William Farquharson of Inverey, his heirs, etc. This William had a brother and a son John. William Farquharson of Inverey younger, as "a person of known trust and approven ability," is appointed to keep a guard "this summer for the sherifdom of Kincardine" against cattle-driving Highlanders, July of the same year. Thomson's Acts, VII, 18, 1, 286: pointed out to me by Mr Macmath.

† Macfarlane's Genealogical Collections, MS., in the Advocates' Library, I, 299 f ; already cited by Jamieson, Ballads, I, 108.

James Innes, Serjeant, and Corporal Radnoch, commanding a party of troops at Kincardine O'Neill, to apprehend the said John Farquharson and his accomplices." From this warrant Dr Stuart considers that we may infer that Inverey was the aggressor in the affray with Brackley. But there is nothing to identify the case, and the date of the warrant is February 12, 1685, nearly twenty years from the affair which we are occupied with, during which space, unless he were of an unusually peaceable habit, Inverey might have had several broils on his hands.

Gordon of Brackley, as reported by Mrs Brown, from what she may have heard in her girlhood, a hundred years after his tragical end, was "a man universally esteemed."* "Farquharson of Inverey," says Jamieson, without giving his authority, "a renowned freebooter on Deeside, was his relation, and in habits of friendly intercourse with him. Farquharson was fierce, daring, and active, exhibiting all the worst characteristics of a freebooter, with nothing of that blunt and partially just and manly generosity which were then not uncommonly met with among that description of men. The common people supposed him (as they did Dundee, and others of the same cast who were remarkable for their fortunate intrepidity and miraculous escapes) to be a warlock, and proof against steel and lead. He is said to have been buried on the north side of a hill, which the sun could never shine upon, etc." All which, as far as appears, is merely the tradition of Jamieson's day, and will be taken at different values by different readers.

The 'Peggy' of A a, b, C, D was Margaret Burnet, daughter of Sir Thomas Burnet of Leys, and own cousin of Gilbert Burnet, Bishop of Salisbury.† This lady married Gordon of Brackley against her friends' wishes, or without their consent, and so probably made a love-match. After Brackley's death she married one James Leslie, Doctor of Medicine,‡ a fact which will suffice to offset the unconfirmed scandal of the ballad.

It is now to be noted that a baron of Brackley had been murdered by caterans towards the end of the preceding century. "The Clanchattan, who, of all that faction, most eagerly endeavored to revenge the Earl of Murray his death, assembling their forces under Angus Donald Williamson his conduct, entered Strathdee and Glenmuick, where they invaded the Earl of Huntly his lands, and killed four of the surname of Gordon, Henry Gordon of the Knock, Alexander Gordon of Teldow, Thomas Gordon of Blaircharrish, and the old baron of Breaghly, whose death and manner thereof was so much the more lamented because he was very aged, and much given to hospitality, and slain under trust. He was killed by them in his own house after he had made them good cheer, without suspecting or expecting any such reckoning for his kindly entertainment; which happened the first day of November, 1592. In revenge whereof the Earl of Huntly assembled some of his forces and made an expedition into Pettie," etc. (See No 183, III, 456.) So writes Sir Robert Gordon, before 1630.§

Upon comparing Sir Robert Gordon's description of the old baron of Brackley who was murdered in 1592 with what is said of the baron in the ballad (A), there is a likeness for which there is no historical authority in the instance of the baron of 1666. The

---

* See a little further on.

† Gilmour's Decisions, 1701, p. 43. (Macmath.)

‡ Col. H. W. Lumsden's Memorials of the Families of Lumsdaine, etc., p. 59.

§ History of the Earldom of Sutherland, p. 217 f. To the same effect, Johnstone, Historia Rerum Britannicarum, Amsterdam, 1655, p. 160 f, under the year 1591, and Spotiswood, p. 390, of the editions of 1655, 1666, 1668, under the year 1592. "The History of the Feuds," etc., p. 67, ed. 1764, merely repeats Sir Robert Gordon. William Gordon's History of the Family of Gordon, cites Sir Robert Gordon and Johnstone, and calls Gordon of Brackley Alexander.

Still another "Gordon, Baron of Brackley in Deeside," is said to have been murdered by the country people about him in or near 1540: The Genealogy of the Grants, in Macfarlane's Genealogical Collections, I, 168, and An Account of the Rise and Offspring of the Name of Grant, printed for Sir Archibald Grant, Bart., of Monymusk, 1876, p. 30 ff, where the date is put (perhaps through a misprint) before 1480. A horrible revenge was said to have been taken by the Earl of Huntly and James Grant: see the well-known story of the orphans fed at a trough, in Scott's Tales of a Grandfather, chap. xxxix.

ballad intimates the hospitality which is emphasized by Sir Robert Gordon, and also the baron's unconsciousness of his having any foe to dread. ("An honest aged man," says Spotiswood, "against whom they could pretend no quarrel.") Other details are not pertinent to the elder baron, but belong demonstrably to the Brackley who had a quarrel with Farquharson.

Of the two, the older Brackley would have a better chance of being celebrated in a ballad. He was an aged and innocent man, slain while dispensing habitual hospitality, "slain under trust." The younger Brackley treated Inverey's people harshly, there was an encounter, Brackley was killed, and others on both sides. His friends may have mourned for him, but there was no call for the feeling expressed in the ballad; that would be more naturally excited by the death of the kindly old man, 'who basely was slain.' On the whole it may be surmised that two occurrences, or even two ballads, have been blended, and some slight items of corroborative evidence may favor this conclusion.

'The Gordons may mourn him and bann Inverey,' says B 14. It appears that the Earl of Aboyne sided with Inverey, though the Marquis of Huntly supported the laird of Brackley's son; * whereas all the Gordons would have mourned the older baron, and none would have maintained the caterans who slew him.

In the affray with the Farquharsons in 1666 there were killed, of the Gordons, besides Brackley, his brother William and his cousin James Gordon of Cults. The Gordons killed by the Clanchattan in 1592 were Brackley, Henry Gordon of the Knock, an Alexander Gordon (also a Thomas). According to A 34, 35, the Gordons killed were Brackley and his brother William, his cousin James of the

Knox [Knocks, Knock], and his uncle Alexander Gordon; according to B 12, 13, there were killed, besides Brackley, "Harry Gordon and Harry of the Knock" (one and the same person), Brackley's brother, as we see from 10; in D 10, the killed are Brackley, and Sandy Gordon o the Knock, called Peter in 21. A Gordon of the Knock is named as killed in A, B, D, and it is Henry Gordon in B; an Alexander Gordon is named in A, B. A William Gordon and a James (of the Knocks, not of the Cults) are named in A. On the whole, the names sort much better with the earlier story.

In B 15 we are told that if Craigievar had come up an hour sooner, Brackley had not been slain. Upon this Dr Joseph Robertson (who assigned the ballad to 1592) has observed, Kinloch MSS, VI, 24, that Craigievar passed to a branch of the family of Forbes in 1625; so that Craigievar would have done nothing to save Brackley in 1666, the Gordons and the Forbeses having long been at feud. To make sense of this stanza we must suppose an earlier date than 1625.

The fourth edition of Spotiswood's history, printed in 1677 (about forty years after the author's death), calls Brackley of 1592 *John* Gordon. Further, there is this anonymous marginal note, not found in the preceding editions: "I have read in a MS. called the Acts of the Gordons, that Glenmuick, Glentaner, Strathdee and Birs were spoiled, and Brachlie, with his son-in-law, slain, by Mackondoquy [that is Maconochie, *alias* Campbell] of Inner-Aw." †

Brackley, on the Muick, is in close vicinity to the village of Ballater, on the Dee, some forty miles westward from Aberdeen.

Translated by Knortz, Lieder u. Romanzen Alt-Englands, p. 156, after Allingham.

* See the Memorandum for Farquharson in "Fourth Report," as above, p. 534.

† Pointed out to me by Mr. Macmath, who, in making this and other communications relating to the Gordons of Brackley, suggested and urged the hypothesis of a mixture of two events in this ballad.

A

a. Scarce Ancient Ballads [Alexander Laing], Aberdeen, 1822, p. 9. b. Buchan's Gleanings, p. 68. c. The New Deeside Guide, by James Brown (*i. e.* Joseph Robertson), Aberdeen [1832], p. 46.

1 Inverey cam doun Deeside, whistlin and playin,
　He was at brave Braikley's yett ere it was
　　dawin.

2 He rappit fu loudly an wi a great roar,
　Cried, Cum doun, cum doun, Braikley, and
　　open the door.

3 'Are ye sleepin, Baronne, or are ye wakin?
　Ther's sharpe swords at your yett, will gar
　　your blood spin.

4 'Open the yett, Braikley, and lat us within,
　Till we on the green turf gar your bluid rin.'

5 Out spak the brave baronne, owre the castell-
　　wa:
　'Are ye cum to spulyie and plunder mi ha?

6 'But gin ye be gentlemen, licht and cum in:
　Gin ye drink o my wine, ye'll nae gar my
　　bluid spin.

7 'Gin ye be hir'd widifus, ye may gang by,
　Ye may gang to the lawlands and steal their fat
　　ky.

8 'Ther spulyie like rievers o wyld kettrin clan,
　Who plunder unsparing baith houses and lan.

9 'Gin ye be gentlemen, licht an cum [in],
　Ther's meat an drink i my ha for every man.

10 'Gin ye be hir'd widifus, ye may gang by,
　Gang doun to the lawlands, and steal horse and
　　ky.'

11 Up spak his ladie, at his bak where she lay,
　'Get up, get up, Braikley, and be not afraid;
　The 'r but young hir'd widifus wi belted plaids.'

12 'Cum kiss me, mi Peggy, I 'le nae langer stay,
　For I will go out and meet Inverey.

13 'But haud your tongue, Peggy, and mak nae
　　sic din,
　For yon same hir'd widifus will prove them-
　　selves men.'

14 She called on her marys, they cam to her
　　hand;
　Cries, Bring me your rocks, lassies, we will
　　them command.

15 'Get up, get up, Braikley, and turn bak your
　　ky,
　Or me an mi women will them defy.

16 'Cum forth then, mi maidens, and show them
　　some play;
　We'll ficht them, and shortly the cowards will
　　fly.

17 'Gin I had a husband, whereas I hae nane,
　He woud nae ly i his bed and see his ky taen.

18 'Ther's four-and-twenty milk-whit calves, twal
　　o them ky,
　In the woods o Glentanner, it's ther thei a' ly.

19 'Ther's goat i the Etnach, and sheep o the
　　brae,
　An a' will be plunderd by young Inverey.'

20 'Now haud your tongue, Peggy, and gie me a
　　gun,
　Ye'll see me gae furth, but I'll never cum in.

21 'Call mi brother William, mi unkl also,
　Mi cousin James Gordon; we'll mount and
　　we'll go.'

22 When Braikley was ready and stood i the
　　closs,
　He was the bravest baronne that eer mounted
　　horse.

23 Whan all wer assembld o the castell green,
　No man like brave Braikley was ther to be seen.

24 .　　.　　.　　.　　.　　.
　'Turn bak, brother William, ye are a bride-
　　groom;

25 'Wi bonnie Jean Gordon, the maid o the mill;
　O sichin and sobbin she'll soon get her fill.'

26 'I'm no coward, brother, 't is kend I'm a man;
　I'll ficht i your quarral as lang 's I can stand.

27 'I'll ficht, my dear brother, wi heart and gude
　　will,
　And so will young Harry that lives at the mill.

28 'But turn, mi dear brother, and nae langer
      stay :
      What 'll cum o your ladie, gin Braikley thei
      slay ?

29 'What 'll cum o your ladie and bonnie young
      son ?
      O what 'll cum o them when Braikley is
      gone ? '

30 'I never will turn : do you think I will fly ?
      But here I will ficht, and here I will die.'

31 'Strik dogs,' crys Inverey, 'and ficht till ye 're
      slayn,
      For we are four hundered, ye are but four
      men.

32 'Strik, strik, ye proud boaster, your honour is
      gone,
      Your lands we will plunder, your castell we 'll
      burn.'

33 At the head o the Etnach the battel began,
      At Little Auchoilzie thei killd the first man.

34 First thei killd ane, and soon they killd twa,
      Thei killd gallant Braikley, the flour o them a'.

35 Thei killd William Gordon, and James o the
      Knox,
      And brave Alexander, the flour o Glenmuick.

36 What sichin and moaning was heard i the glen,
      For the Baronne o Braikley, who basely was
      slayn !

37 'Cam ye bi the castell, and was ye in there ?
      Saw ye pretty Peggy tearing her hair ? '

38 'Yes, I cam by Braikley, and I gaed in there,
      And there [saw] his ladie braiding her hair.

39 'She was rantin, and dancin, and singin for
      joy,
      And vowin that nicht she woud feest Inverey.

40 'She eat wi him, drank wi him, welcomd him
      in,
      Was kind to the man that had slayn her bar-
      onne.'

41 Up spake the son on the nourice's knee,
      'Gin I live to be a man, revenged I 'll be.'

42 Ther 's dool i the kitchin, and mirth i the ha,
      The Baronne o Braikley is dead and awa.

B

Kinloch MSS, V, 379, in the handwriting of John Hill
Burton.

1 'Baron of Brackley, are ye in there ?
      The 're sharp swords at yer yetts, winna ye
      spear.'

2 'If they be gentlemen, lat them cum in ;
      But if they be reavers, we 'll gar them be
      taen.'

3 'It is na gentlemen, nor yet pretty lads,
      But a curn hir'd widdifus, wears belted
      plaids.'

4 She called on her women and bade them come
      in :
      'Tack a' yer rocks, lasses, and we 'll them
      coman.

5 'We 'll fecht them, we 'll slight them, we 'll do
      what we can,
      And I vow we will shoot them altho we shod
      bang.

6 'Rise up, John,' she said, 'and turn in yer
      kye,
      For they 'll hae them to the Hielands, and you
      they 'l defie.'

7 'Had your still, Catharine, and still yer young
      son,
      For ye 'll get me out, but I 'll never cum in.'

8 'If I had a man, as I hae na nane,
      He wudna lye in his bed and see his kye tane.'

9 'Ye 'll cum kiss me, my Peggy, and bring me
      my gun,
      For I 'm gaing out, but I 'll never cum in.'

10 There was twenty wi Invery, twenty and
      ten ;
   There was nane wi the baron but his brother
      and him.

11 At the head of Reneeten the battle began ;
   Ere they wan Auchoilzie, they killed mony a
      man.

12 They killed Harry Gordon and Harry of the
      Knock,
   The mullertd's four sons up at Glenmuick.

13 They killed Harry Gordon and Harry of the
      Knock,
   And they made the brave baron like kail to a
      pot.

14 First they killed ane, and then they killed
      twa,
   Then they killed the brave baron, the flower o
      them a'.

15 Then up came Craigievar, and a party wi him ;
   If he had come an hour sooner, Brackley had
      not been slain.

16 'Came ye by Brackley? and was ye in there?
   Or say ye his lady, was making great care?'

17 'I came by Brackley, and I was in there,
   But I saw his lady no makin great care.

18 'For she eat wi them, drank wi them, welcomed
      them in ;
   She drank to the villain that killed her guid
      man.

19 'Woe to ye, Kate Fraser! sorry may yer heart
      be,
   To see yer brave baron's blood cum to yer
      knee.'

20 There is dule in the kitchen, and mirth i the ha,
   But the Baron o B[r]ackley is dead and awa.

———•———

C

a. Jamieson-Brown MS., Appendix, p. viii, as transcribed
for Jamieson by Rev. Andrew Brown, and sent him by Mrs
Brown in a letter of June 18, 1801.   b. Jamieson's Popular
Ballads, I, 102 ; Mrs. Brown's copy combined with an imperfect one taken down by Sir W. Scott " from the recitation
of two ladies, great-grandchildren of Farquharson of Inverey."

1 O Inverey came down Dee side, whistling and
      playing ;
   He 's landed at Braikly's yates at the day daw-
      ing.

2 Says, Baron of Braikly, are ye within ?
   There 's sharp swords at the yate will gar your
      blood spin.

3 The lady raise up, to the window she went ;
   She heard her kye lowing oer hill and oer
      bent.

4 'O rise up, John,' she says, 'turn back your
      kye ;
   They 're oer the hills rinning, they 're skipping
      away.'

5 'Come to your bed, Peggie, and let the kye
      rin,
   For were I to gang out, I would never get in.'

6 Then she 's cry'd on her women, they quickly
      came ben :
   'Take up your rocks, lassies, and fight a' like
      men.

7 'Though I 'm but a woman, to head you I 'll
      try,
   Nor let these vile Highland-men steal a' our
      kye.'

8 Then up gat the baron, and cry'd for his
      graith ;
   Says, Lady, I 'll gang, tho to leave you I 'm
      laith.

9 'Come, kiss me, my Peggie, nor think I 'm to
      blame ;
   For I may well gang out, but I 'll never win in.'

10 When the Baron of Braikly rade through the
      close,
   A gallanter baron neer mounted a horse.

11 Tho there came wi Inverey thirty and three,
    There was nane wi bonny Braikly but his
    brother and he.

12 Twa gallanter Gordons did never sword draw;
    But against four and thirty, wae's me, what
    was twa?

13 Wi swords and wi daggers they did him sur-
    round,
    And they've pierc'd bonny Braikly wi mony
    a wound.

14 Frae the head of the Dee to the banks of the
    Spey,
    The Gordons may mourn him, and bann In-
    verey.

15 'O came ye by Braikly, and was ye in there?
    Or saw ye his Peggy dear riving her hair?'

16 'O I came by Braikly, and I was in there,
    But I saw not his Peggy dear riving her hair.'

17 'O fye on ye, lady! how could ye do sae?
    You opend your yate to the faus Inverey.'

18 She eat wi him, drank wi him, welcomd him
    in;
    She welcomd the villain that slew her baron.

19 She kept him till morning, syne bad him be
    gane,
    And showd him the road that he woud na be
    tane.

20 'Thro Birss and Aboyne,' she says, 'lyin in a
    tour,
    Oer the hills of Glentanor you'll skip in an
    hour.'

21 There is grief in the kitchen, and mirth in the
    ha,
    But the Baron of Braikly is dead and awa.

———————

D

Skene MS., p. 110; north of Scotland, 1802–3.

1 'Baron o Breachell, are ye within?
    The sharp souerd is at yer gate, Breachell,
    we'll gar yer blood spin.'

2 'Thei'r at yer gate, Breachel, thei'r neither
    men nor lads,
    But fifty heard widifas, wi belted plaids.'

3 'O if I had a man,' she says, 'as it looks I had
    nane,
    He widna sit in the house and see my kye tane.

4 'But lasses tak down yer rocks, and we will
    defend
    .   .   .   .

5 'O kiss me, dear Peggy, and gee me down my
    gun,
    I may well ga out, but I ll never come in.'

6 Out spak his brither, says, Gee me yer hand;
    I'll fight in yer cause sae lang as I may stand.

7 Whan the Baron o Breachell came to the closs,
    A braver baron neir red upon horse.

8 .   .   .   .
    I think the silly heard widifas are grown
    fighten men.

9 First they killed ane, and syen they killed twa,
    And the Baron o Breachell is dead and awa.

10 They killed Sandy Gordon, Sandy Gordon o
    the Knock,
    The miller and his three sons, that lived at
    Glenmuick.

11 First they killed ane, and seyn they killed twa,
    And the Baron o Breachell is dead and awa.

12 Up came Crigevar and a' his fighten men:
    'Had I come an hour soonur, he sudna been
    slain.'

13 For first they killed ane, and seyn they killed
    twa,
    And the Baron o Breachell is dead and awa.

14 'O came ye by Breachell, lads? was ye in
        their?
    Saw ye Peggy Dann riving her hair?'

15 'We cam by Breachell, lads, we was in there,
    And saw Peggie Dann cairling her hair.

16 'She eat wi them, drank wi them, bad them
        come in
    To her house an bours that had slain her baron.

17 'Come in, gentlemen, eat and drink wi me;
    Tho ye ha slain my baron, I ha na a wite at ye.'

18 'O was [ye] at Glenmuik, lads? was ye in
        theire?
    Saw ye Cathrin Gordon rivin her hair?'

19 'We was at Glenmuik, lads, we was in
        there,
    We saw Cathrin Gordon rivin her hair.

20 'Wi the tear in her eye, seven bairns at her
        foot,
    The eighth on her knee . . .

21 They killed Peter Gordon, Peter Gordon of
        the Knock,
    The miller and his three sons, that lived at
        Glenmuik.

22 First they killed ane, and syn they killed
        twa,
    And the Baron of Breachell is dead and
        awa.

———◆———

A. *No division of stanzas. Both copies are prob-
    ably from stall-prints or broadsides.* b *dif-
    fers frequently from* a *in spelling.*
  a. $5^2, 8^1$. spulzie. 6^1. gentlmen.
     $11^3, 25^1, 40^1$. we *for* wi.
     22^1. thee. 30^1. I will never.
  b. 11^1. laid. 11^3. young *wanting.*
     13^2. prove to be men. 15^2. For me.
     16^1. ply. 19^1. Ther are goats.
     20^2. never return. 22^1. thee.
     25^2. seen (*phonetic*). 26^1. it's kent.
     30^1. I never will: ye. 30^2. No, here.
     34^1. an syne. 36^1. was heard. 38^2. ther said.
  c. *This copy is to the extent of about two thirds
     taken from* a; *half a dozen stanzas are
     from Jamieson's text,* C b; *half a dozen
     more agree, nearly or entirely, with* B,
     *and may have been derived from Dr. J. H.
     Burton, or directly from some traditional
     source. The order has been regulated by
     the editor, who has also made a slight ver-
     bal change now and then.*
     $1-3 = $ a $1-3$. $4-8 = 5-9$. $9 = 11^{1, 2}$, *near-
     ly* (c 9^2, *and* face Inverey). $11^2 = 13^2$.
     $12-14 = 18, 19, 17$. $15 = 15$, *nearly:
     cf.* B 6^1. $17^1 = 16^2$. $18 = 20$, *nearly.*
     $19 = 21$. $22 = 31$, *with different num-
     bers.* $23 = 33$: Reneatan *for* Etnach, *cf.*
     B 11^1. $24 = 35$. $25 = 34$. $29 = 38$.
     $30 = 39$. $31^1 = 40^1$. $32^2 = 40^2$, B 18^2.
     $35 = 41$. $36 = 42$. $37 = 36$.

From C b. $20 = 12$. $21 = 13$, *nearly.* $26
    = 16$. $33, 34 = 23, 24$, *nearly.* $38 = 17$.
10 (*nearly* B 6: *cf.* c 15^1).

    Get up, get up Brackley, and turn back your
        kye,
    Or they'll hae them to the Highlands, and
        you they'll defy.

16 (*nearly* B 4: *cf.* a 14):

    She called on her maidens, and bade them
        come in:
    Tak a' your rocks, lasses, we will them com-
        man.

27 (*nearly* B 15: *cf.* D 12). Had he come
    one hour, *etc.*
$28 = $ B 16. $31^2 = $ B 18^2 (a 40^2). She
    drank to the villain that killed her barrone.
$32 = $ B 19, *nearly.* Wae to you, Kate Fra-
    ser, sad may your heart be.
B. 11^1. Keneeten *perhaps*: b. Reneatan.
   12^1. They *for* The.
C. a. *Not divided, but roughly marked off into
      stanzas of four verses.*
   6^2. frocks *for* rocks.
  b. 1^1. Down Dee side came Inverey.
     1^2. lighted at Brackley yates.
     2^1. O are. 4^1. rise up, ye baron, and.

4². For the lads o Drumwharran are driving
  them bye.

5. 'How can I rise, lady, or turn them again?
  Whareer I have ae man, I wat they hae
  ten.'

6. 'Then rise up, my lasses, tak rocks in your
  hand,
  And turn back the kye; I hae you at command.

7. 'Gin I had a husband, as I hae nane,
  He wadna lye in his bower, see his kye
  tane.'

8¹. got.
After 8:

  Come kiss me then, Peggy, and gie me my
    speir;
  I ay was for peace, tho I never feard weir.

9¹. me then, Peggy.   9². I weel may gae out.
10¹. When Brakley was busked and rade oer
  the closs.
10². neer lap to a.
After 10:

  When Brackley was mounted and rade oer
    the green,
  He was as bald a baron as ever was seen.

12². what is.   15¹. by Brackley yates, was.
16¹. by Brackley yates, I.
16². And I saw his Peggy a-making good
  cheer.
After 16:

  The lady she feasted them, carried them
    ben;
  She laughd wi the men that her baron had
    slain.

17¹. on you: could you.   17². yates.
19². shoudna.
" Poetical justice requires that I should subjoin
  the concluding stanza of the fragment, which
  could not be introduced into the text; as the
  reader cannot be displeased to learn that
  the unworthy spouse of the amiable, affectionate, and spirited baron of Brackley was
  treated by her unprincipled gallant as she
  deserved, and might have expected:

  Inverey spak a word, he spak it wrang;
  'My wife and my bairns will be thinking
    lang.'

  'O wae fa ye, Inverey! ill mat ye die!
  First to kill Brackley, and then to slight me.'

D. *Title,* 1¹, *etc.* Breachell. *Perhaps miscopied
  by Skene from* Breachlie; *and so* Crigeran,
  12¹, *for* Crigevar.
  17². at thee.

204

JAMIE DOUGLAS

A. 'Lord Douglas,' or, 'The Laird of Blackwood,' Kinloch MSS, I, 93.

B. 'Jamie Douglas,' Kinloch MSS, V, 387.

C. 'Lady Douglas and Blackwood,' Kinloch MSS, V, 207, I, 103.

D. 'Jamie Douglas,' Kinloch MSS, I, 107.

E. 'The Laird o Blackwood,' Kinloch MSS, VII, 127; Kinloch's Ancient Scottish Ballads, p. 58.

F. 'Jamie Douglas,' Motherwell's MS., p. 507.

G. 'Lord Jamie Douglas,' Motherwell's MS., p. 345.

H. 'Jamie Douglas,' Motherwell's MS., p. 297.

I. 'Jamie Douglas,' Motherwell's MS., p. 500.

J. 'Jamie Douglas,' Motherwell's MS., p. 299.

K. 'Jamie Douglas,' Motherwell's MS., p. 302.

L. 'Jamie Douglas,' Finlay's Scottish Ballads, II, 4.

M. Herd's MSS, I, 54 ; Herd's Scottish Songs, 1776, I, 144.

O. 'Lord Jamie Douglas,' Motherwell's Minstrelsy, Appendix, p. v, the last three stanzas.

N. 'Jamie Douglas,' Motherwell's Minstrelsy, Appendix, p. xvii, IX, one stanza.

THIS ballad first appeared in print in the second edition of Herd's Scottish Songs, 1776, but only as a fragment of five stanzas. Pinkerton repeats three stanzas from Herd, very slightly "polished by the editor," Tragic Ballads, 1781, pp. 83, 119. A stall-copy, says Motherwell, was printed in 1798, under the title of 'Fair Orange Green.' A and C were used by Aytoun for the copy given in his second edition, 1859, I, 133, and D for Part Fourth of Chambers's compilation, Scottish Ballads, p. 157. The "traditionary version," in thirty-four stanzas, given in the Appendix to Motherwell's Minstrelsy, p. v (see his Introduction, p. lxiii, note 5), is made up, all but the fifth stanza and the three last, from F–J and O : see note to N.

Lady Barbara Erskine, eldest daughter of John, Earl of Mar, was married to James, second Marquis of Douglas, near the end of the year 1670. The marriage did not prove to be happy, and the parties were formally separated in 1681. They had had one child, James, Earl of Angus, and he having been killed in battle in the Netherlands in 1692, the Marquis of Douglas married again, and had two sons and a daughter. The second of the sons was Archibald, the third marquis, and first and only duke of Douglas.

In an affectionate letter of December, 1676 (succeeding several others to which no answer had been returned), the Marchioness of Douglas writes to her husband: "I am not such a stranger to myself to pretend to the exactness of obedience and duty that my humor or frowardness may not have offended you, and all I can say is, that hereafter I shall so study yours and what may please you that I shall endeavor a conformity to your good will so near as I can. This only I must (most) complain of, that you should retain those in your service or company who takes the liberty of talking so much to the prejudice of your honor and mine. Sure I am I never give the least occasion for it, neither do I think, my dear, that you really believe it. If religion and virtue were not ties strong enough, sense of your honor and mine own, and of that noble family of yours and our posterity, could not but prevail against such base thoughts, and God, who knows my heart, knows my innocence and the malice of those who wounds us both by such base calumnies." In February, 1677, the marchioness (not for the first time, as it appears) invokes the interposition of the Privy Council in her domestic affairs, and applies for an "aliment" on which she may live apart from her husband, whom she charges with shunning her company and treating her with contempt. The marquis in his reply alleges that his wife had not treated him with due respect, but seems to be averse to a separation. Four years after, a separation was mutually agreed to, and in the contract to this effect the ground is expressed to be "great animosities, mistakes and differences betwixt the said marquis and his lady, which have risen to a great height, so as neither of them are satisfied longer to continue together." *

The blame of the alienation of Douglas from his wife is imputed by tradition to William Lawrie, the marquis's principal chamberlain or factor, who was appointed to that place in 1670, the year of the marriage. Lawrie married Marion Weir, of the family of Blackwood, then a widow. He is often styled the laird of Blackwood, a title which belonged to his son by this marriage, his own proper designation being, after that event, the Tutor of Blackwood. "The belief that Blackwood was the chief cause of this unhappy quarrel was current at the time among the Douglas tenantry, with whom he was very unpopular, and it is corroborated by letters and other documents in the Douglas charter-chest. The marchioness, indeed, evinces temper, but the marquis appears to have been morose and

peevish, and incapable of managing his own affairs. In this matter he consulted, and was advised by, Blackwood at every step, sending him copies of the letters he wrote to his wife, and subscribing whatever document Blackwood thought fit to prepare. Members of the family and dependents alike characterized Lawrie as hypocritical and double-dealing; but on the other hand, it is only fair to mention that on two occasions, Charles, Earl of Mar, wrote to Blackwood thanking him for his kindness to his sister, and assuring him of his esteem." †

John, Earl of Mar, the father of Lady Barbara Erskine, died in 1668, before his daughter's marriage, and it would have been her brother Charles, the next earl, who took her home. He was colonel of a regiment of foot at the time of the separation, whence, probably, the drums, trumpets, and soldiers in the ballad. Barbara Douglas died in 1690, two years before the marquis's second marriage.

The reciter of A, who got her information from an old dey at Douglas castle, as far back as 1770, told Kinloch that the ballad was a great favorite with Archibald, Duke of Douglas, who lived till 1761. "The Duke used often to get the old dey to sing it to him while he wheeled round the room in a gilded chair . . . and muttered anathemas against Lourie, saying, O that Blackwood must have been a damned soul!" ‡

The story of the ballad is very simple. A lady, daughter of the Earl of Mar, B, I, married to Lord James Douglas, Marquis of Douglas, D, lives happily with him until Blackwood (Blacklaywood, Blackly) makes

---

* Fraser, The Douglas Book, Edinburgh, 1885, II, 277 f, 449 f. The contract, being a mutual paper, may not express to the full the supposed grievances of either party.

† The Douglas Book, II, 450 f. "Lawrie is mentioned by Lord Fountainhall as 'late chamberlain to the Marquis of Douglas, and repute a bad instrument between him and his lady in their differences.' Decisions, I, 196."

What should prompt Lawrie to malice against the marchioness is unknown. Kinloch, Ancient Scottish Ballads, p. 58, accepting the story of the old woman from whom he obtained E, says: "The Laird of Blackwood and the Marquis of —— were rivals in the affection of a lovely and amiable young lady, who, preferring the latter, became his wife. Blackwood . . . vowed revenge," etc. Chambers, who repeats this account, Scottish Ballads, p. 150, re-

marks that Lawrie seems to have been considerably advanced in life at the time. Lawrie's son made a "retour of services" in 1650, and may be supposed then to have been of age. The Marquis of Douglas was in his twenty-fourth year when he married, in 1670, and probably Lady Barbara Erskine was not older. Maidment is surprised that Lawrie, "a man of uncertain lineage," should have succeeded with the widow Marion Weir. What is to be thought of his aspiring, at the age of sixty, or more, to "the affection of a lovely and amiable young lady" of the family of Mar, one of the most ancient in Scotland?

‡ Kinloch MSS, I, 95 f. For one or two points see Maidment's Scotish Ballads and Songs, 1868, II, 262 ff., the preface to the ballad there called 'Lady Barbara Erskine's Lament.'

her husband believe that she has trespassed (with one Lockhart, **A**). Her protestations of innocence and the blandishments with which she seeks to win back her lord's affections are fruitless. Her father sends for her and takes her home. He offers to get a bill of divorce and make a better match for her, but she will listen to no such proposal.

The lady is daughter of the Earl of York, **D**; her brother is the Duke of York (a somewhat favorite personage in ballads), **B**; her mother is daughter of the Duke of York, **G**, and her father is the Lord of Murray. Her husband is the Earl of March, **I** (and **F**?). Had she foreseen the event of the marriage with Douglas, she would have staid at Lord Torchard's gates (Argyle's, Athol's, Lord Orgul's) and have been his lady, **G**, **H**, **I**, **L**, or in fair Orange green and have been his (Orange's?) **K**. (Orange gate appears in **D**, also, and so it may be Orange wine, and not orange, that Jamie Douglas is invited to drink in **I** 5.) A handsome nurse makes trouble in **F** 6, but nowhere else. It is not Blackwood that whispers mischief into the husband's ear in **J** 4, but a small bird; a black bird, fause bird, in two of Finlay's three copies, a blackie in the other, **L**. In **E** 7 the lady will not wash her face, comb her hair, or have fire or light in her bower: cf. Nos 69, 92, II, 156, 317. In **I** 15, when the lady had returned to her father's and the tenants came to see her, she could not speak, and "the buttons off her clothes did flee;" "an affecting image of overpowering grief," says Chambers. See also 'Andrew Lammie.'

D 10–15, **N**, are palpable and vulgar tags

to a complete story. James Douglas comes to his father-in-law's house with his three children, and sends a soldier to the gate to bid his lady come down; he has hanged false Blackwood, and she is to come home: **N**. In **D** the hanging of Blackwood is not mentioned; Douglas calls for wine to drink to his gay lady, she takes a cup in her hand, but her heart breaks.*

A–M have all from one stanza to four of a beautiful song, known from the first quarter of the eighteenth century, and printed fifty years earlier than any copy of the ballad.† This song is the lament of an unmarried woman for a lover who has proved false, and, as we find by the last stanza, has left her with an unborn babe. **A**, **C** have this last stanza, although the lady in these copies has born three children (as she has in every version except the fragmentary **E**).‡

WALY, WALY, GIN LOVE BE BONY.

a. Ramsay's Tea-Table Miscellany, the second volume, published before 1727; here from the Dublin edition of 1729, p. 176. b. Thomson's Orpheus Caledonius, second edition, 1733, I, 71; four stanzas in the first edition, 1725, No 34. §

1 O WALY, waly up the bank!
    And waly, waly, down the brae!
  And waly, waly yon burn-side,
    Where I and my love wont to gae!

2 I leand my back unto an aik,
    I thought it was a trusty tree;
  But first it bowd, and syne it brak,
    Sae my true-love did lightly me.

3 O waly, waly! but love be bony
    A little time, while it is new;

* "Matthew Crawford, weaver, Howwood, sings 'Jamie Douglas' with the conclusion in which the lady dies after her return and reconciliation with her lord." Motherwell's Note-Book, p. 56.

"I was informed by A. Lile that she has heard a longer set of the ballad in which, while Lady Douglas is continuing her lament, she observes a troop of gentlemen coming to her father's, and she expresses a wish that these should be sent by her lord to bring her home. They happen to be sent for that purpose, and she accompanies them. On her meeting, however, with her lord, and while putting a cup of wine to her lips, her heart breaks, and she drops down dead at his feet." Motherwell, note to G, MS., p. 347.

Lawrie came near losing his head in 1683 for political reasons, but he survived the revolution of 1688, "got all

the proceedings against him annulled, and a complete rehabilitation." Wodrow, II, 295; Maidment, 1868, II, 268.

† All but **E** have b 4: **E** has a 4. All but **A**, **D**, **E**, **L**, **M** have 1. **A**, **C**, **E** have 10; **J** has 2, 3; **A** has 8; **F** has 9.

‡ It must be said, however, that stanza 8, 'When we came in by Glasgow town,' etc., hardly suits the song (as it is in **A** 2). It may have been taken up from this ballad (which must date from the last quarter of the seventeenth century), or from some other.

§ a is followed in Percy's Reliques, 1765, III, 144, Herd, Ancient and Modern Scots Songs, 1769, p. 196; b, in the Musical Museum, p. 166, No 158; with slight variations in each copy.

But when 't is auld, it waxeth cauld,
    And fades away like morning dew.

4 O wherefore shoud I busk my head?
    Or wherfore shoud I kame my hair?
  For my true-love has me forsook,
    And says he 'll never love me mair.

5 Now Arthur-Seat shall be my bed,
    The sheets shall neer be fyl'd by me;
  Saint Anton's well shall be my drink,
    Since my true-love has forsaken me.

6 Martinmas wind, when wilt thou blaw,
    And shake the green leaves off the tree?
  O gentle death, when wilt thou come?
    For of my life I am weary.

7 'T is not the frost that freezes fell,
    Nor blawing snaw's inclemency;
  'T is not sic cauld that makes me cry,
    But my love's heart grown cauld to me.

8 When we came in by Glasgow town,
    We were a comely sight to see;
  My love was cled in the black velvet,
    And I my sell in cramasie.

9 But had I wist, before I kissd,
    That love had been sae ill to win,
  I'd lockd my heart in a case of gold,
    And pin'd it with a silver pin.

10 Oh, oh, if my young babe were born,
    And set upon the nurse's knee,
  And I my sell were dead and gane!
    For a maid again I 'll never be.

A stanza closely resembling the third of this song occurs in a Yule medley in Wood's MSS, about 1620.*

  Hey trollie lollie, love is jolly
    A qhyll qhill it is new;
  Qhen it is old, it grows full cold,
    Woe worth the love untrew!

The Orpheus Caledonius has for the fourth stanza this, which is found (with variations) in A-M, excepting the imperfect copy E:

  When cockle-shells turn siller bells,
    And mussles grows on evry tree,
  When frost and snaw shall warm us a',
    Then shall my love prove true to me.
                    Ed. 1725.

Several stanzas occur in a song with the title 'Arthur's Seat shall be my bed,' etc., which is thought to have been printed as early as the Tea-Table Miscellany, or even considerably earlier. This song is given in an appendix.

Aytoun's ballad, 1859, I, 135, is loosely translated by Knortz, Schottische Balladen, p. 59.

A

Kinloch MSS, I, 93; from the recitation of Mary Barr, Lesmahago, Lanarkshire, May, 1827, and learned by her about sixty years before from an old dey at Douglas Castle.

1 I wAs a lady of high renown
    As lived in the north countrie;
  I was a lady of high renown
    Whan Earl Douglas loved me.

2 Whan we came through Glasgow toun,
    We war a comely sight to see;
  My gude lord in velvet green,
    And I mysel in cramasie.

3 Whan we cam to Douglas toun,
    We war a fine sight to behold;
  My gude lord in cramasie,
    And I myself in shining gold.

* Scottish Psalter, 1566, Wood's MSS, Bassus, Laing's MSS, University of Edinburgh, MS. Books, 483, III, p. 209. The medley is by a different and later hand: Laing in the Musical Museum, 1853, I, xxviii f., IV, 440*. It is printed in the second edition of Forbes's Cantus, Aberdeen, 1666.

There was a much older stave, or proverb, to the same purport, as we see by Chaucer's Clerk's Tale, vv. 855, 57.

  But sooth is seyd, algate I fynde it trewe,
  Loue is noght old as whan that it is newe.

4 Whan that my auld son was born,
  And set upon the nurse's knee,
I was as happy a woman as eer was born,
  And my gude lord he loved me.

5 But oh, an my young son was born,
  And set upon the nurse's knee,
And I mysel war dead and gane,
  For a maid again I 'll never be!

6 There cam a man into this house,
  And Jamie Lockhart was his name,
And it was told to my gude lord
  That I was in the bed wi him.

7 There cam anither to this house,
  And a bad friend he was to me ;
He put Jamie's shoon below my bed-stock,
  And bade my gude lord come and see.

8 O wae be unto thee, Blackwood,
  And ae an ill death may ye dee !
For ye was the first and the foremost man
  That parted my gude lord and me.

9 Whan my gude lord cam in my room,
  This grit falsehood for to see,
He turnd about, and, wi a gloom,
  He straucht did tak farewell o me.

10 'O fare thee well, my once lovely maid !
   O fare thee well, once dear to me !

O fare thee well, my once lovely maid !
For wi me again ye sall never be.'

11 'Sit doun, sit doun, Jamie Douglas,
   Sit thee doun and dine wi me,
And Ill set thee on a chair of gold,
   And a silver towel on thy knee.'

12 'Whan cockle-shells turn silver bells,
   And mussels they bud on a tree,
Whan frost and snaw turns fire to burn,
   Then I 'll sit down and dine wi thee.'

13 O wae be unto thee, Blackwood,
   And ae an ill death may ye dee !
Ye war the first and the foremost man
   That parted my gude lord and me.

14 Whan my father he heard word
   That my gude lord had forsaken me,
He sent fifty o his brisk dragoons
   To fesh me hame to my ain countrie.

15 That morning before I did go,
   My bonny palace for to leave,
I went into my gude lord's room,
   But alas ! he wad na speak to me.

16 'Fare thee well, Jamie Douglas !
   Fare thee well, my ever dear to me !
Fare thee well, Jamie Douglas !
   Be kind to the three babes I 've born to thee.'

———•———

B

Kinloch MSS, V, 387, in the handwriting of John Hill
Burton when a youth.

1 WALY, waly up the bank !
  And waly, waly down the brae !
And waly, waly to yon burn-side,
  Where me and my love wunt to gae !

2 As I lay sick, and very sick,
  And sick was I, and like to die,
And Blacklaywood put in my love's ears
  That he staid in bower too lang wi me.

3 As I lay sick, and very sick,
  And sick was I, and like to die,

And walking into my garden green,
  I heard my good lord lichtlie me.

4 Now woe betide ye, Blacklaywood !
  I 'm sure an ill death you must die ;
Ye 'll part me and my ain good lord,
  And his face again I 'll never see.

5 'Come down stairs now, Jamie Douglas,
  Come down stairs and drink wine wi me ;
I 'll set thee into a chair of gold,
  And not one farthing shall it cost thee.'

6 'When cockle-shells turn silver bells,
  And muscles grow on every tree,
When frost and snaw turn fiery baas,
  I 'll come down the stair and drink wine wi
    thee.'

7 'What's needs me value you, Jamie Douglas,
   More than you do value me?
The Earl of Mar is my father,
   The Duke of York is my brother gay.

8 'But when my father gets word o this,
   I trow a sorry man he'll be;
He'll send four score o his soldiers brave
   To tak me hame to mine ain countrie.'

9 As I lay owre my castell-wa,
   I beheld my father comin for me,
Wi trumpets sounding on every side;
   But they werena music at a' for me.

10 'And fare ye weel now, Jamie Douglas!
    And fare ye weel, my children three!
And fare ye weel, my own good lord!
   For my face again ye shall never see.

11 'And fare ye weel now, Jamie Douglas!
    And fare ye weel, my children three!

And fare ye weel now, Jamie Douglas!
   But my youngest son shall gae wi me.'

12 'What ails ye at yer youngest son,
    Sits smilin at the nurse's knee?
I'm sure he never knew any harm,
   Except it was from his nurse or thee.'

13 . . . .
   . . . .
And when I was into my coaches set,
   He made his trumpets a' to soun.

14 I've heard it said, and it's oft times seen,
   The hawk that flies far frae her nest;
And a' the world shall plainly see
   It's Jamie Douglas that I love best.

15 Ive heard it said, and [it's] oft times seen,
   The hawk that flies from tree to tree;
And a' the world shall plainly see
   It's for Jamie Douglas I maun die.

—◆—

O

Kinloch MSS, V, 207, I, 103; from John Rae, Lesmahago.

1 O WALLY, wally up yon bank!
   And wally down yon brae!
And wally, wally up yon burn-side,
   Where me and my lord wont to gae!

2 I leand me on yon saugh sae sweet,
   I leand me on yon saugh sae sour,
And my gude lord has forsaken me,
   And he swears he'll never loe me more.

3 There came a young man to this town,
   And Jamie Lockhart was his name;
Fause Blackwood lilted in my lord's ear
   That I was in the bed wi him.

4 'Come up, come up, Jamie Douglas,
   Come up, come up and dine wi me,
And I'll set thee in a chair of gold,
   And use you kindly on my knee.'

5 'When cockle-shells turn silver bells,
   And mussels hing on every tree,

When frost and snow turn fire-brands,
   Then I'll come up and dine wi thee.'

6 When my father and mother they got
      word
   That my good lord had forsaken me,
They sent fourscore of soldiers brave
   To bring me hame to my ain countrie.

7 That day that I was forc'd to go,
   My pretty palace for to leave,
I went to the chamber were my lord lay,
   But alas! he wad na speak to me.

8 'O fare ye weel, Jamie Douglas!
   And fare ye weel, my children three!
I hope your father will prove mair kind
   To you than he has been to me.

9 'You take every one to be like yoursel,
   You take every one that comes unto thee;
But I could swear by the heavens high
   That I never knew anither man but thee.

10 'O foul fa ye, fause Blackwood,
   And an ill death now may ye die!

For ye was the first occasioner
   Of parting my gude lord and me.'

11 Whan we gaed in by Edinburgh town,
   My father and mither they met me,
Wi trumpets sounding on every side;
   But alas! they could na cherish me.

12 'Hold your tongue, daughter,' my father said,
   'And with your weeping let me be;
And we 'll get out a bill of divorce,
   And I 'll get a far better lord to thee.'

13 'O hold your tongue, father,' she says,
   'And with your talking let me be;
I wad na gie a kiss o my ain lord's lips
   For a' the men in the west country.'

14 Oh an I had my baby born,
   And set upon the nurse's knee,
And I myself were dead and gone!
   For a maid again I will never be.

D

Kinloch MSS, I, 107: "West-Country version."

1 I FELL sick, and very, very sick,
   Sick I was, and like to dee;
A friend o mine cam frae the west,
   A friend o mine came me to see,
And the black told it to my gude lord
   He was oure lang in the chamber wi me.

*   *   *   *   *   *

2 'Come doun the stair, Jamie Douglas,
   Come doun and drink wine wi me;
I 'll set ye on a chair of gold,
   And not ae farthing will it cost thee.'

3 'Whan cockle-shells turn siller bells,
   And fishes flee frae tree to tree,
Whan frost and snaw turn fire-beams,
   I 'll come doun and drink wine wi thee.'

*   *   *   *   *   *

4 'What ails ye at your young son James,
   That sits upo the nurse's knee?
I 'm sure he never did ye no harm,
   If it war na for the nurse or me.

5 'What care I for you, Jamie Douglas?
   Not a small pin I value thee;
For my father he is the Earl of York,
   And of that my mither 's the gay ladie;
They will send fourscore of his soldiers bold
   For to tak me hame to my ain countrie.'

*   *   *   *   *   *

6 Whan I was set in my coach and six,
   Taking fareweel o my babies three,
'I beg your father's grace to be kind,
   For your face again I 'll never see.'

*   *   *   *   *   *

7 As I was walking up London streets,
   My father was coming to meet me,
Wi trumpets sounding on every side;
   But that was na music at a' for me.

8 'Hold your tongue, my dochter dear,
   And of your weeping let abee;
A bill o divorcement I 'll send to him,
   A far better match I 'll get for thee.'

9 'Hold your tongue, my father dear,
   And with your folly let abee;
There 'll never man sleep in my twa arms,
   Sin my gude lord has forsaken me.'

*   *   *   *   *   *

10 As I was sitting at my bouer-window,
   What a blythe sicht did I see!
I saw four score of his soldiers bold,
   And I wishd that they were coming for me.

11 Out bespeaks the foremost man,
   And what a weel-spoken man was he!
'If the Marquis o Douglas's lady be within,
   You 'll bid her come doun and speak to
     me.'

12 It's out bespak my auld father then,
    I wat an angry man was he;
  'Ye may gang back the road ye cam,
    For her face again ye'll never see.'

13 'Hold your tongue, my father dear,
    And with your folly let abee;
  For I'll ga back, and I'll ne'er return;
    Do ye think I love you as weel as he?'

14 As I cam in by the Orange gate,
    What a blythe sicht did I see!
  I saw Jamie Douglas coming me to meet,
    And at his foot war his babies three.

15 'Ga fetch, ga fetch a bottle of wine,
    That I may drink to my gay ladie;'
  She took the cup into her hand,
    But her bonnie heart it broke in three.

E

Kinloch MSS, VII, 127; 24 April, 1826, from the recitation of Jenny Watson, Lanark, aged 73, who had it from her grandmother.

1 I LAY sick, and very sick,
    And I was bad, and like to dee;

    . . . .
  A friend o mine cam to visit me,
  And Blackwood whisperd in my lord's ear
    That he was oure lang in chamber wi me.

2 'O what need I dress up my head,
    Nor what need I caim doun my hair,
  Whan my gude lord has forsaken me,
    And says he will na love me mair!

3 'But oh, an my young babe was born,
    And set upon some nourice knee,
  And I mysel war dead and gane!
    For a maid again I'll never be.'

4 'Na mair o this, my dochter dear,
    And of your mourning let abee;

For a bill of divorce I'll gar write for him,
  A mair better lord I'll get for thee.'

5 'Na mair o this, my father dear,
    And of your folly let abee;
  For I wad na gie ae look o my lord's face
  For aw the lords in the haill cuntree.

6 'But I'll cast aff my robes o red,
    And I'll put on my robes o blue,
  And I will travel to some other land,
    To see gin my love will on me rue.

7 'There shall na wash come on my face,
    There shall na kaim come on my hair;
  There shall neither coal nor candle-licht
    Be seen intil my bouer na mair.

8 'O wae be to thee, Blackwood,
    And an ill death may ye dee!
  For ye've been the haill occasion
    Of parting my lord and me.'

F

Motherwell's MS, p. 507; from the recitation of old Mrs Brown, residing at Linsart, parish of Lochwinnoch, September, 1826.

1 WALY, waly up yon bank!
    And waly, waly up yon brae!
  And waly, waly by yon river-side,
    Where me and my love were wont to gae!

2 My mither tauld me when I was young
    That young men's love was ill to trow;

But to her I would give nae ear,
  And alas! my ain wand dings me now.

3 But gin I had wist or I had kisst
    That young man's love was sae ill to win,
  I would hae lockt my heart wi a key o gowd,
    And pinnd it wi a sillar pin.

4 When lairds and lords cam to this toun,
    And gentlemen o a high degree,
  I took my auld son in my arms,
    And went to my chamber pleasantly.

5 But when gentlemen come thro this toun,
    And gentlemen o a high degree,
  I must sit alane in the dark,
    And the babie on the nurse's knee.

6 I had a nurse, and she was fair,
    She was a dearly nurse to me;
  She took my gay lord frae my side,
    And used him in her company.

7 Awa! awa, thou false Blackwood!
    Ay and an ill death may thou die!
  Thou wast the first occasioner
    Of parting my gay lord and me.

8 When I was sick, and very sick,
    Sick I was, and like to die,
  I drew me near to my stair-head,
    And I heard my own lord lichtly me.

9 'Come doun, come doun, thou Earl of March,
    Come doun, come doun and dine with
        me;
  I'll set thee on a chair of gowd,
    And treat thee kindly on my knee!'

10 'When cockle-shells grow sillar bells,
    And mussells grow on every tree,
  When frost and snaw turns fiery ba's,
    Then I'll come doun and dine with thee.'

11 When my father and mother got word
    That my gay lord had forsaken me,
  They sent three score of soldiers bold
    To bring me to my own countrie.

12 When I in my coach was set,
    My tenants all was with me tane;
  They set them doun upon their knees,
    And they begd me to come back again.

13 Fare ye weel, Jamie Douglas!
    And fare ye weel, my babies three!
  I wish your father may be kind
    To these three faces that I do see.

14 When we cam in by Edinbro toun,
    My father and mother they met me;
  The cymbals sounded on every side,
    But alace! the gave no comfort to me.

15 'Hold your tongue, my daughter dear,
    And of your weeping let abee,
  And I'll give him a bill of divorce,
    And I'll get as good a lord to thee.'

16 'Hold your tongue, my father dear,
    And of your scoffing let me bee;
  I would rather hae a kiss of my own lord's
        mouth
    As all the lords in the north countrie.'

G

Motherwell's MS., p. 345.

1 O WALY, waly up the bank!
    And waly, waly down the brae!
  And waly by yon river side,
    Where me and my lord was wont to gae!

2 An I had wit what I wit now,
    Before I came over the river Tay,
  I would hae staid at Lord Torchard's yetts,
    And I micht hae been his own lady gay.

3 When I lay sick, and was very sick,
    A friend of mine came me to see;
  When our Blacklywood told it in my lord's
        ears
    That he staid too long in chamber with me.

4 Woe be to thee, thou Blacklywood!
    I wish an ill death may thou die;
  For thou's been the first and occasion last
    That put strife between my good lord and
        me.

5 When my father he heard of this,
    His heart was like for to break in three;
  He sent fourscore of his soldiers brave
    For to take me home to mine own countree.

6 In the morning when I arose,
    My bonnie palace for to see,
  I came unto my lord's room-door,
    But he would not speak one word to me.

7 'Come down the stair, my lord Jamie Douglas,
    Come down and speak one word with me;

I 'll set thee in a chair of gold,
  And the never a penny it will cost thee.'

8 'When cockle-shells grow silver bells,
  And grass grows over the highest tree,
When frost and snaw turns fiery bombs,
  Then will I come down and drink wine with
    thee.'

9 O what need I care for Jamie Douglas
  More than he needs to care for me ?
For the Lord of Murray 's my father dear,
  And the Duke of York's daughter my
    mother be.

10 Thou thocht that I was just like thyself,
  And took every one that I did see ;
But I can swear by the heavens above
  That I never knew a man but thee.

11 But fare thee weel, my lord Jamie Douglas !
  And fare you weel, my sma childer three !
God grant your father grace to be kind
  Till I see you all in my own countrie.

12 Quickly, quickly then rose he up,
  And quickly, quickly came he down ;
When I was in my coaches set,
  He made his trumpets all to sound.

13 As we came in by Edinburgh town,
  My loving father came to meet me,
With trumpets sounding on every side ;
  But it was not comfort at all to me.

14 'O hold your tongue, my daughter dear,
  And of your weeping pray let abee ;
A bill of divorcement I 'll to him send,
  And a better lord I will chose for thee.'

15 'Hold your tongue, my father dear,
  And of your flattery pray let abee ;
I 'll never lye in another man's arms,
  Since my Jamie Douglas has forsaken me.'

16 It 's often said in a foreign land
  That the hawk she flies far from her nest ;
It 's often said, and it 's very true,
  He 's far from me this day that I luve best.

———————

H

Motherwell's MS, p. 297 ; from the recitation of Mrs
Traill of Paisley.

1 O WALY, waly up the bank !
  And waly, waly doun the brae !
And waly, waly by yon burn-side,
  Whare me and my luve was wont to gae !

2 If I had kent what I ken now,
  I wud neer hae crossed the waters o Tay ;
For an I had staid at Argyle's yetts,
  I might hae been his lady gay.

3 When I lay sick, and very sick,
  And very sick, just like to die,
A gentleman, a friend of mine own,
  A gentleman came me to see ;
But Blackliewoods sounded in my luve's ears
  He was too long in chamer with me.

4 O woe be to thee, Blackliewoods,
  But an an ill death may you die !

Thou 's been the first and occasion last
  That eer put ill twixt my luve and me.

5 'Come down the stairs now, Jamie Douglas,
  Come down the stairs and drink wine wi
    me ;
I 'll set thee in a chair of gold,
  And it 's not one penny it will cost thee.'

6 'When cockle-shells grow silver bells,
  And gowd grows oer yon lily lea,
When frost and snaw grows fiery bombs,
  I will come down and drink wine wi thee.'

7 'What ails you at our youngest son,
  That sits upon the nurse's knee ?
I 'm sure he 's never done any harm
  And it 's not to his ain nurse and me.'

8 My loving father got word of this,
  But and an angry man was he ;
He sent three score of his soldiers brave
  To take me to my own countrie.

    *   *   *   *   *   *   *

9 'O fare ye weel now, Jamie Douglas!
    And fare ye weel, my children three!
God grant your father may prove kind
    Till I see you in my own countrie.'

10 When she was set into her coach

11 'Cheer up your heart, my loving daughter,
    Cheer up your heart, let your weeping bee!
A bill of divorce I will write to him,
    And a far better lord I'll provide for thee.'

12 It's very true, and it's often said,
    The hawk she's flown and she's left her
        nest;
But a' the warld may plainly see
    They're far awa that I luve best.

I

Motherwell's MS., p. 500; from Mrs Notman.

1 'O WALY, waly up yon bank!
    And waly, waly down yon brae!
And waly, waly by yon burn-bank,
    Where me and my lord wont to gae!

2 'A gentleman of good account,
    A friend of mine, came to visit me,
And Blackly whispered in my lord's ears
    He was too long in chamber with me.

3 'When my father came to hear 't,
    I wot an angry man was he;
He sent five score of his soldiers bright
    To take me safe to my own countrie.

4 'Up in the mornin when I arose,
    My bonnie palace for to lea,
And when I came to my lord's door,
    The neer a word he would speak to me.

5 'Come down, come down, O Jamie Douglas,
    And drink the Orange wine with me;
I'll set thee in a chair of gold,
    That neer a penny it cost thee.'

6 'When sea and sand turns foreign land,
    And mussels grow on every tree,
When cockle-shells turn silver bells,
    I'll drink the Orange wine with thee.'

7 'Wae be to you, Blackly,' she said,
    'Aye and an ill death may you die!
You are the first, and I hope the last,
    That eer made my lord lichtly me.'

8 'Fare ye weel then, Jamie Douglas!
    I value you as little as you do me;
The Earl of Mar is my father dear,
    And I soon will see my own countrie.

9 'Ye thought that I was like yoursell,
    And loving each ane I did see;
But here I swear, by the day I die,
    I never loved a man but thee.

10 'Fare ye weel, my servants all!
    And you, my bonny children three!
God grant your father grace to be kind
    Till I see you safe in my own countrie.'

11 'As I came into Edinburgh toune,
    With trumpets sounding my father met me;
But no mirth nor musick sounds in my ear,
    Since the Earl of March has forsaken me.'

12 'O hold your tongue, my daughter dear,
    And of your weeping let abee;
I'll send a bill of divorce to the Earl of March,
    And get a better lord for thee.'

13 'Hold your tongue, my father dear,
    And of your folly let abee;
No other lord shall lye in my arms,
    Since the Earl of March has forsaken me.

14 'An I had known what I know now,
    I'd never crossed the water o Tay,
But stayed still at Atholl's gates;
    He would have made me his lady gay.'

15 When she came to her father's lands,
    The tenants a' came her to see;

Never a word she could speak to them,
But the buttons off her clothes did flee.

16 'The linnet is a bonnie bird,
And aften flees far frae its nest;

So all the warld may plainly see
They 're far awa that I luve best.'

J

Motherwell's MS., p. 299; from the recitation of Rebecca
Dunse, a native of Galloway, 4 May, 1825. "A song of her
mother's, an old woman."

1 O WALY, waly up yon bank!
And waly, waly doun yon brae!
And waly, waly by yon burn-side,
Where me and my luve used to gae!

2 Oh Johnie, Johnie, but love is bonnie
A little while, when it is new;
But when love grows aulder, it grows mair
caulder,
And it fades awa like the mornin dew.

3 I leaned my back against an aik,
I thocht it was a trusty tree;
But first [it] bowed, and syne it brak,
And sae did my fause luve to me.

4 Once I lay sick, and very sick,
And a friend of mine cam to visit me,
But the small bird whispered in my love's ears
That he was ower lang in the room wi me.

5 'It 's come down stairs, my Jamie Douglas,
Come down stairs, luve, and dine wi me;
I 'll set you on a chair of gold,
And court ye kindly on my knee.'

6 'When cockle-shells grow silver bells,
And gold it grows on every tree,
When frost and snaw turns fiery balls,
Then, love, I 'll come down and dine wi
thee.'

7 If I had known what I know now,
That love it was sae ill to win,
I should neer hae wet my cherry cheek
For onie man or woman's son."

8 When my father he cam to know
That my first luve had sae slighted me,
He sent four score of his soldiers bright
To guard me home to my own countrie.

9 Slowly, slowly rose I up,
And slowly, slowly I came down,
And when he saw me sit in my coach,
He made his drums and trumpets sound.

10 It 's fare ye weel, my pretty palace!
And fare ye weel, my children three!
And I hope your father will get mair grace,
And love you better than he 's done to me.

11 When we came near to bonnie Edinburgh
toun,
My father cam for to meet me;
He made his drums and trumpets sound,
But they were no comfort at all to me.

12 'It 's hold your tongue, my daughter dear,
And of your weeping pray let be;
For a bill of divorcement I 'll send to him,
And a better husband I 'll you supply.'

13 'O hold your tongue, my father dear,
And of your folly pray now let be;
For there 's neer a lord shall enter my bower,
Since my first love has so slighted me.'

K

Motherwell's MS., p. 302 ; from Jean Nicol.

1 O WALY, waly up the bank !
   And waly, waly doun the brae !
   And waly by yon river-side,
   Where me and my love were wont to gae !

2. A gentleman, a friend of mine,
   Came to the toun me for to see,
   .   .   .   .
   .   .   .   .

3 'Come doun the stair, Jamie Douglas,
   Come doun the stair and drink wine wi
   me ;
   For a chair of gold I will set thee in,
   And not one farthing it will cost thee.'

4 'When cockle-shells grow siller bells,
   And mussels grow on ilka tree,
   When frost and snaw turns out fire-bombs,
   Then I 'll come doun and drink wine wi
   thee.'

5 But when her father heard of this,
   O but an angry man was he !
   And he sent four score of his ain regiment
   To bring her hame to her ain countrie.

6 O when she was set in her coach and six,
   And the saut tear was in her ee,
   Saying, Fare you weel, my bonnie palace !
   And fare ye weel, my children three !

7 O when I came into Edinburgh toun,
   My loving father for to see,
   The trumpets were sounding on every side,
   But they were not music at all for me.

8 'O hold your tongue, my daughter dear,
   And of your folly I pray let be ;
   For a bill of divorcement I 'll send him,
   And a better lord I 'll provide for thee.'

9 'O hold your tongue, my father dear,
   And of your folly I pray let be ;
   For if I had stayed in fair Orange Green,
   I might have been his gay ladye.'

———————

L

Finlay's Scottish Ballads, II, 1, a collation of three
copies, one of which was **M**.

1 WHEN I fell sick, an very sick,
   An very sick, just like to die,
   A gentleman of good account
   He cam on purpose to visit me ;
   But his blackie whispered in my lord's ear
   He was owre lang in the room wi me.

2 'Gae, little page, an tell your lord,
   Gin he will come and dine wi me
   I 'll set him on a chair of gold
   And serve him on my bended knee.'

3 The little page gaed up the stair :
   'Lord Douglas, dine wi your ladie ;
   She 'll set ye on a chair of gold,
   And serve you on her bended knee.'

4 'When cockle-shells turn silver bells,
   When wine drieps red frae ilka tree,
   When frost and snaw will warm us a',
   Then I 'll cum down an dine wi thee."

5 But whan my father gat word o this,
   O what an angry man was he !
   He sent fourscore o his archers bauld
   To bring me safe to his countrie.

6 When I rose up then in the morn,
   My goodly palace for to lea,
   I knocked at my lord's chamber-door,
   But neer a word wad he speak to me.

7 But slowly, slowly, rose he up,
   And slowly, slowly, cam he down,
   And when he saw me set on my horse,
   He caused his drums and trumpets soun.

8 'Now fare ye weel, my goodly palace !
   And fare ye weel, my children three !
   God grant your father grace to love you
   Far more than ever he loved me.'

9 He thocht that I was like himsel,
   That had a woman in every hall ;
   But I could swear, by the heavens clear,
   I never loved man but himsel.

10 As on to Embro town we cam,
  My guid father he welcomed me ;
He caused his minstrels meet to sound,
  It was nae music at a' to me.

11 'Now haud your tongue, my daughter dear,
  Leave off your weeping, let it be ;
For Jamie's divorcement I 'll send over ;
  Far better lord I 'll provide for thee.'

12 'O haud your tongue, my father dear,
  And of such talking let me be ;
For never a man shall come to my arms,
  Since my lord has sae slighted me.'

13 O an I had neer crossed the Tweed,
  Nor yet been owre the river Dee,
I might hae staid at Lord Orgul's gate,
  Where I wad hae been a gay ladie.

14 The ladies they will cum to town,
  And they will cum and visit me ;
But I 'll set me down now in the dark,
  For ochanie ! who 'll comfort me ?

15 An wae betide ye, black Fastness,
  Ay, and an ill deid may ye die !
Ye was the first and foremost man
  Wha parted my true lord and me.

M

Herd's MSS, I, 54.

1 EARL DOUGLAS, than wham never knight
  Had valour moe ne courtesie,
Yet he 's now blamet be a' the land
  For lightlying o his gay lady.

2 'Go, little page, and tell your lord,
  Gin he will cum and dine wi me,
I 'll set him on a seat of gold,
  I 'll serve him on my bended knee.'

3 The little page gaed up the stair :
  'Lord Douglas, dyne wi your lady ;
She 'll set ye on a seat of gold,
  And serve ye on her bended knee.'

4 'When cockle-shells turn siller bells,
  When mussels grow on ilka tree,
When frost and snow sall warm us a',
  Then I sall dyne wi my ladie.'

5 'Now wae betide ye, black Fastness,
  Ay and an ill dead met ye die !
Ye was the first and the foremost man
  Wha parted my true lord and me.'

N

Motherwell's Minstrelsy, Appendix, p. v, the last three stanzas.

1 SHE looked out at her father's window,
  To take a view of the countrie ;
Who did she see but Jamie Douglas,
  And along with him her children three !

2 There came a soldier to the gate,
  And he did knock right hastilie :
'If Lady Douglas be within,
  Bid her come down and speak to me.'

3 'O come away, my lady fair,
  Come away now alang with me,
For I have hanged fause Blackwood,
  At the very place where he told the lie.'

O

Motherwell's Minstrelsy, Appendix, p. xvii, IX.

'O come down stairs, Jamie Douglas,
  O come down stairs and speak to me,
And I 'll set thee in a fine chair of gowd,
  And I 'll kindly daut thee upon my knee.

———◆———

Variations of Waly, Waly, *etc.*

a. *Put among* 'Auld Sangs brushd up' *in Ramsay's* "Contents," *p.* 329. *Printed in eight-line stanzas.*

  4. *Burns had heard this stanza* "*in the west country*" *thus* (*Cromek's Reliques*, 1817, p. 245):

    O wherefore need I busk my head?
      Or wherefore need I kame my hair?
    Sin my fause luve has me forsook,
      And says he 'll never luve me mair.

  7^3. my cry: me *in the London edition of* 1733.

b. 1^1. up yon bank. 1^2. down yon brea. 1^3. And waly by yon river's side. 1^4. Where my love and I was wont to gae. 2, 3 are 3, 2. 2^4. And sae did my fause love to me. 3^1. Waly, waly, gin love be bonny. 3^2. little while when. 3^3. it's: waxes. 3^4. wears away like. 4. *Already given.* 6^1. O Martinmas. 6^4. And take a life that wearies me.

B. 3^3. walking. 6^1. bells turn silver shells.

C. *These variations in the second copy* (I, 103) *are Kinloch's:*

  4^3. on a. 9^2. to thee. 12^2. let abee. 12^4. for thee. 13^1. father, I said. 13^3. ae kiss. 14^4. I 'll.

F. 5^1. *For* gentlemen *Motherwell queries*, lairds and lords? 9^1. Earl of Marquis; March *queried by Motherwell. It is* March *in* I.

I. 5^2, 6^4. Orange, *not* orange, *in the* MS. 6^1. *Motherwell queries* far in *for* foreign.

J. 2^1. nonnie, **nonny** *is written in pencil by Motherwell between* 1 *and* 2; *no doubt as a conjectural emendation of* Johnie, Johnie.

L. 2, 3, 4, 15 *are* M 2–5, *with slight changes.* 1^5. "*One copy here bears* black-bird *and another* a fause bird." (*Finlay.*) 13^3. Lord Orgul. "*This name is differently given by reciters.*" (*Finlay.*) 15^1. Fastness *as a proper name, but evidently meant for* faustness, falseness, *as Motherwell has observed.*

M. Quham, quhen, quha *are printed* wham, when, wha; zet, ze, zour, *are printed* yet, ye, your.

N. Motherwell's ballad is "traditionary" to the extent that it is substantially made up from traditionary material. The text of the recited copies is not always strictly adhered to. The fifth stanza happens not to occur in the texts used, but may have come in in some other recitation obtained by Motherwell, or may simply have been adopted from Ramsay. The three last stanzas (N) are from some recitation not preserved in Motherwell's relics. Neglecting unimportant divergencies, the constituent parts are as follows:

$1 = $ H $1^{1\text{-}3}$, G 1^4. 2, 3 $=$ J 2, 3. 4 $=$ F 2. (5 $=$ Ramsay 4.) 6 $=$ F 3. 7 $=$ I 14. 8 – 10 $=$ F 4 – 6. 11 $=$ F $7^{1,2,4}$, H 4^3. 12 $=$ H 3 (*see* E $1^{4,5}$, L 1^4). 13 $=$ F 8. 14 $=$ I $5^{1\text{-}3}$, O^4. 15 $=$ I 6. 16 $=$ H 7. 17 $=$ J 7. 18 $=$ F 11^2, I $3^{1,3,4}$. 19, 20 $=$ I 4, 8. 21 $=$ I 9 (*see* L 9^3). 22 $=$ J 9. 23 $=$ F 12. 24 $=$ J 10. 25 $=$ I 10. 26 $=$ I $7^{1\text{-}3}$, G 4^4. 27 $=$ G 13, I $11^{3,4}$. 28 $=$ F 15, G 14. 29 $=$ F 16. 30, 31 $=$ I 15, 16. (32 *resembles* D $10^{1,2}$, $14^{3,4}$; 33, D 11.)

APPENDIX

———

ARTHUR'S SEAT SHALL BE MY BED, ETC., OR, LOVE IN DESPAIR

A NEW song much in request, sung with its own proper tune.

Laing, Broadsides Ballads, No. 61, not dated but considered to have been printed towards the end of the seventeenth or the beginning of the eighteenth century, and probably at Edinburgh.

1 COME lay me soft, and draw me near,
    And lay thy white hand over me,
  For I am starving in the cold,
    And thou art bound to cover me.

2 O cover me in my distress,
    And help me in my miserie,
  For I do wake when I should sleep,
    All for the love of my dearie.

3 My rents they are but very small
  For to maintain my love withall,
  But with my labour and my pain
  I will maintain my love with them.

4 O Arthur's Seat shall be my bed,
    And the sheets shall never be fil'd for me,
  St Anthony's well shall be my drink,
    Since my true-love 's forsaken me.

5 Should I be bound, that may go free?
  Should I love them that loves not me?

I 'le rather travel into Spain,
Where I 'le get love for love again.

6 And I 'le cast off my robs of black,
    And will put on the robs of blue,
  And I will to some other land
    Till I see my love will on me rue.

7 It 's not the cold that makes me cry,
    Nor is 't the weet that wearies me,
  Nor is 't the frost that freezes fell ;
    But I love a lad, and I dare not tell.

8 O faith is gone and truth is past,
    And my true-love 's forsaken me;
  If all be true that I hear say,
    I 'le mourn until the day I die.

9 Oh, if I had nere been born
    Than to have dy'd when I was young !
  Then I had never wet my cheeks
    For the love of any woman's son.

10 Oh, oh, if my young babe were born,
    And set upon the nurse's knee,
   And I my self were dead and gone !
    For a maid again I 'le never be.

11 Martinmas wind, when wilt thou blow,
    And blow the green leafs off the tree
   O gentle Death, when wilt thou come !
    For of my life I am wearie.

1¹. darw.

———

205

LOUDON HILL, OR, DRUMCLOG

'The Battle of Loudoun Hill,' Minstrelsy of the Scottish Border, III, 188, 1803; II, 206, 1833.

———

THE " gospel-lads," otherwise self-styled the true Presbyterian party, had in 1679, May 29 (observed both as the king's birthday and the anniversary of the Restoration), begun their testimony against the iniquity of the times by publishing a Declaration, putting out loyal bonfires, and burning all acts of Parliament obnoxious to Covenanters, in retaliation for the burning of the Covenant at London seventeen years before. They had intended to do this at Glasgow, but as Claverhouse had established himself there, the demonstration was made at Rutherglen, a little place two miles off. On the 31st Claverhouse

laid hands on three of the rioters and an outlawed minister. The Covenanters had appointed a great meeting, an armed conventicle, for the next day, Sunday, June 1, at
Loudon Hill, on the borders of the shires
of Ayr and Lanark. Not so many came
as were expected, for Claverhouse had been
heard of, but there were at least two hundred and fifty armed men; and these numbers were subsequently increased.* It was
resolved to rescue the prisoners taken the
day before, if the Lord should enable them,
and in prosecution of this object they moved
on to Drumclog, a swampy farm two miles
east of Loudon Hill. The chief of command
was Robert Hamilton, and with him were associated John Balfour of Kinloch, called Burly,
Hackston of Rathillet, and others. What
ensued is told in a frank letter of Claverhouse, written the night of the same Sunday.

The prisoners were to be conveyed to Glasgow. "I thought," says Claverhouse, "that
we might make a little tour, to see if we could
fall upon a conventicle; which we did, little to
our advantage. For, when we came in sight
of them, we found them drawn up in battle,
upon a most advantageous ground, to which
there was no coming but through mosses and
lakes. They were not preaching, and had
got away all their women and children. They
consisted of four battalions of foot, and all
well armed with fusils and pitchforks, and
three squadrons of horse. We sent, both, parties to skirmish, they of foot and we of dragoons; they run for it, and sent down a bat-
talion of foot against them (the dragoons).
We sent threescore of dragoons, who made

them run again shamefully. But in the end
(they perceiving that we had the better of
them in skirmish), they resolved a general
engagement, and immediately advanced with
their foot, the horse following. They came
through the loch, and the greatest body of all
made up against my troop. We kept our fire
till they were within ten pace of us. They
received our fire and advanced to shock. The
first they gave us brought down the cornet,
Mr Crafford, and Captain Bleith. Besides
that, with a pitchfork, they made such an
opening in my sorrel horse's belly that his guts
hung out half an ell, and yet he carried me off
a mile; which so discouraged our men that
they sustained not the shock, but fell into disorder. Their horse took the occasion of this,
and pursued us so hotly that we got no time
to rally. I saved the standards, but lost on
the place about eight or ten men, besides
wounded. But the dragoons lost many more.
They are not come easily off on the other
side, for I saw several of them fall before we
came to the shock. I made the best retreat
the confusion of our people would suffer." †

The cornet killed was Robert Graham, the
"nephew" of Claverhouse, of whom so much
is made in "Old Mortality." There is no evidence beyond the name to show that he was a
near kinsman of his captain. The Covenanters thought they had killed Claverhouse himself, because of the name Graham being
wrought into the cornet's shirt, and treated
the body with much brutality. In 'Bothwell
Bridge,' st. 12, Claverhouse is represented as
refusing quarter to the Covenanters in revenge
for 'his cornet's death.' ‡

* " Public worship was begun by Mr Douglas, when the
accounts came to them that Claverhouse and his men were
coming upon them, and had Mr King and others their
friends prisoners. Upon this, finding evil was determined
against them, all who had arms drew out from the rest of
the meeting, and resolved to go and meet the soldiers and
prevent their dismissing the meeting, and, if possible, relieve
Mr King and the other prisoners." Wodrow's History,
1722, II, 46.

   † (Postscript: " My lord, I am so wearied and so sleepy
that I have written this very confusedly.") See Russell, in
the Appendix to C. K. Sharpe's edition of Kirkton's Secret
and True History of the Church of Scotland, p. 438 ff.; Napier's Memorials and Letters of John Graham of Claverhouse, II, 219–223. There is a good account of the affair
in Mowbray Morris's " Claverhouse," ch. iv.

‡ Napier interprets the cornet to be Mr Crafford (Crawford), who, in the preceding February, was a corporal in the
troop: Memorials, II, 191. But Creichton, in his Memoirs,
mentions "the loss of Cornet Robert Graham" at Drumclog. Russell speaks of a Graham killed at Drumclog, and,
like Creichton, tells a story of the disfigurement of his face
(which he attributes to the cornet's own dog). Lawrie of
Blackwood, Lord Jamie Douglas's Iago, was indicted and
tried, Nov. 24, 1682–Feb. 7, 1683, for (among other things)
countenancing John Aulston, who "in the late rebellion"
murdered Cornet Graham: Wodrow, II, 293, 295. Guild,
in his Bellum Bothuellianum, cited by Scott, has "signifer,
trajectus globulo, Græmus."

   Napier will know only of a William Graham as cornet to
Claverhouse, "and certainly not killed at Drumclog."
William Graham is referred to in a dispatch of Claver-

1 You 'l marvel when I tell ye o
    Our noble Burly and his train,
  When last he marchd up through the land,
    Wi sax-and-twenty westland men.

2 Than they I neer o braver heard,
    For they had a' baith wit and skill ;
  They proved right well, as I heard tell,
    As they cam up oer Loudoun Hill.

3 Weel prosper a' the gospel-lads
    That are into the west countrie
  Ay wicked Claverse to demean,
    And ay an ill dead may he die !

4 For he 's drawn up i battle rank,
    An that baith soon an hastilie ;
  But they wha live till simmer come,
    Some bludie days for this will see.

5 But up spak cruel Claverse then,
    Wi hastie wit an wicked skill,
  ' Gae fire on yon westlan men ;
    I think it is my sovreign's will.'

6 But up bespake his cornet then,
    ' It 's be wi nae consent o me ;
  I ken I 'll neer come back again,
    An mony mae as weel as me.

7 ' There is not ane of a' yon men
    But wha is worthy other three ;
  There is na ane amang them a'
    That in his cause will stap to die.

8 ' An as for Burly, him I knaw ;
    He 's a man of honour, birth, an fame ;
  Gie him a sword into his hand,
    He 'll fight thysel an other ten.'

9 But up spake wicked Claverse then —
    I wat his heart it raise fu hie —
  And he has cry'd, that a' might hear,
    ' Man, ye hae sair deceived me.

10 ' I never kend the like afore,
    Na, never since I came frae hame,
  That you sae cowardly here suld prove,
    An yet come of a noble Græme.'

11 But up bespake his cornet then,
    ' Since that it is your honour's will,
  Mysel shall be the foremost man
    That shall gie fire on Loudoun Hill.

12 ' At your command I 'll lead them on,
    But yet wi nae consent o me ;
  For weel I ken I 'll neer return,
    And mony mae as weel as me.'

13 Then up he drew in battle rank —
    I wat he had a bonny train —
  But the first time that bullets flew
    Ay he lost twenty o his men.

14 Then back he came the way he gaed,
    I wat right soon an suddenly ;
  He gave command amang his men,
    And sent them back, and bade them flee.

15 Then up came Burly, bauld an stout,
    Wi 's little train o westland men,
  Wha mair than either aince or twice
    In Edinburgh confind had been.

16 They hae been up to London sent,
    An yet they 're a' come safely down ;
  Sax troop o horsemen they hae beat,
    And chased them into Glasgow town.

house's, March (?) 1679, as commanding a small garrison :
Napier II, 201. A Cornet Graham in Claverhouse's troop
captured a rebel in March, 1682 : R. Law's Memorials, ed.
Sharpe, p. 222. A William Graham was " cornet to Claver-
house," January 3, 1684 : Wodrow, II, 338. (See " Clavers,
The Despot's Champion, by a Southern," London, 1889,

p. 48 f., a careful and impartial book, to which I owe a
couple of points that I had not myself noticed.)
    C. K. Sharpe calls Robert Graham Claverhouse's cousin,
Napier, I, 271, but probably would not wish the title to be
taken strictly.

206

BOTHWELL BRIDGE

Minstrelsy of the Scottish Border, III, 209, 1803; II, 226, 1833.   From recitation.

———•———

THE report of the success of the Covenant-ers at Drumclog brought four or five thousand malcontents into the rising, many of whom, however, were not radicals of the Hamilton type, but moderate Presbyterians.   After not a little moving up and down, they established their camp on the nineteenth of June at Ham-ilton, on the south side of the Clyde, near the point where the river is crossed by Bothwell Bridge.   They were deficient in arms and am-munition and in officers of military expe-rience.   " But," as a historian of their own party says, " the greatest loss was their want of order and harmony among themselves; neither had they any person in whom they heartily centred, nor could they agree upon the grounds of their appearance."   Both be-fore and after their final encampment at Ham-ilton, they were principally occupied with de-bating what testimony they should make against Popery, Prelacy, Erastianism, and the Indulgence, and whether their declaration should contain an acknowledgment of the king's authority.   Dissension ran high, " and enemies had it to observe and remark that ministers preached and prayed against one another."

The king named the Duke of Monmouth to command his army in Scotland.   Both the instructions which were given him and the duke's own temper were favorable to an accommodation.   The royal forces were at Bothwell Muir on the twenty-second of June, and their advanced guards within a quarter of a mile of the bridge.   The duke marched his army to an eminence opposite the main body of the enemy, who lay on the moor (st. 10).   The bridge was held by Hackston of Rathillet and other resolute men.   It was very defensible, being only twelve feet wide and rising from each end to the middle, where there was a gate, and it was also obstructed with stones.   Early in the morning a deputa-tion was sent by the rebels to the duke to lay before him their demands.   He heard them patiently, and expressed his willingness to do all that he could for them with the king, but would engage himself to nothing until they laid down their arms.   He gave them an hour to make up their mind.   The officers of the insurgents were unable to come to an agree-ment.   Hamilton, who assumed the general command, was against any pacific arrange-ment, and no answer was returned.   In the interim four field-pieces had been planted against the bridge.   The defenders main-tained themselves under the fire of these and of the musketeers and dragoons until their own powder was exhausted, and then unwil-lingly withdrew to the main body, by Hamil-ton's order.   The bridge was cleared of ob-structions, and the royal army crossed and advanced in order of battle against the rebels on the moor.   The first fire made the Cove-nanters' horse wheel about, and their retreat threw the nearest foot into disorder; in con-sequence of which the whole army fell into confusion.   Twelve hundred surrendered with-out resistance, the rest fled, and several hun-dred were killed in the pursuit.*

1–9. William Gordon of Earlston, a hot Covenanter, while on his way to Hamilton on the twenty-second to join the insurgents, fell in with some dragoons who were pursuing his already routed copartisans, and, resisting their attempt to make him prisoner, was

* Wodrow's History, 1722, II, 54–67; Creichton's Me-moirs; Russell, in Sharpe's ed. of Kirkton, p. 447 ff.

killed. His son Alexander, a man of more temperate views, was at Bothwell Bridge,* and escaped. Although Earlston in st. 4 is represented as bidding farewell to his father, the grotesque narrative with which the ballad begins can be understood only of the father; sts. 7, 8 make this certain.

9. It seems to be meant, as grammar would require, that it is the 'Lennox lad,' and a Covenanter, that sets up 'the flag of red set about with blue.' In "Old Mortality," Sir Walter Scott makes the Covenanters plant "the scarlet and blue colors of the Scottish covenant" on the keep of Tillietudlem. Whether he had other authority than this ballad for the scarlet, I have not been able to ascertain. All the flags of the covenant may not have been alike, but all would probably have a ground of blue, which is known to have been the Covenanters' color. One flag, which belonged to a Covenanter who figured at Drumclog and Bothwell Bridge, has fortunately been preserved. It is of blue silk, with three inscriptions, one of which is, "No Quarters to yᵉ Active Enimies of yᵉ Covenant," first painted in some light color, afterwards repainted in a dull red. (Napier, I, xliv).

The last half of the stanza must be spoken by Monmouth, and the tone of it is more chivalrous than the circumstances call for.

12–15. For Claverhouse's cornet, see the preceding ballad. Captain John Graham, for that was all he then was, was not conspicuous at Bothwell Bridge. He commanded the horse on the right, and Captain Stuart the dragoons on the left, when the advance was made on the Covenanters. He was as capable of insubordination as Robert Hamilton was of Erastianism, and it is nearly as unnecessary, at this day, to vindicate him from the charge of cruelty as from that of procuring Monmouth's execution six years in advance of the fates.†

'Earlistoun,' Chambers, Twelve Romantic Scottish Ballads, p. 26, is this piece with the battle omitted, or stanzas 1–6, 7¹,², 8³,⁴, 16.

Scott observes: "There is said to be another song upon this battle, once very popular, but I have not been able to recover it."

There is a stall-ballad of Bothwell Brigg, not traditional, a very good ballad of its sort, with a touching story and a kindly moral, which may or may not be later than Sir Walter Scott's day. It is of John Carr and his wife Janet and a non-covenanting lady, who carries off John, badly wounded, from the field (where he had fought better than most of his party), and nurses him in her lord's castle till he is well enough to be visited by his wife.

Translated by Talvj, Charakteristik, p. 581.

---

1 'O BILLIE, billie, bonny billie,
    Will ye go to the wood wi me?
  We'll ca our horse hame masterless,
    An gar them trow slain men are we.'

2 'O no, O no!' says Earlstoun,
    'For that's the thing that mauna be;
  For I am sworn to Bothwell Hill,
    Where I maun either gae or die.'

3 So Earlstoun rose in the morning,
    An mounted by the break o day,
  An he has joind our Scottish lads,
    As they were marching out the way.

4 'Now, farewell, father! and farewell, mother!
    An fare ye weel, my sisters three!

* Russell, as above, p. 464; Wodrow, II, 86.

An fare ye well, my Earlstoun!
    For thee again I'll never see.'

5 So they're awa to Bothwell Hill,
    An waly, they rode bonnily!
  When the Duke o Monmouth saw them comin,
    He went to view their company.

6 'Ye're welcome, lads,' then Monmouth said,
    'Ye're welcome, brave Scots lads, to me;
  And sae are you, brave Earlstoun,
    The foremost o your company.

7 'But yield your weapons ane an a',
    O yield your weapons, lads, to me;
  For, gin ye'll yield your weapons up,
    Ye'se a' gae hame to your country.'

† But see "Clavers, the Despot's Champion," p. 72 ff.

8 Out then spak a Lennox lad,
   And waly, but he spoke bonnily!
'I winna yield my weapons up,
   To you nor nae man that I see.'

9 Then he set up the flag o red,
   A' set about wi bonny blue:
'Since ye 'll no cease, and be at peace,
   See that ye stand by ither true.'

10 They stelld their cannons on the height,
   And showrd their shot down in the how,
An beat our Scots lads even down;
   Thick they lay slain on every know.

11 As eer you saw the rain down fa,
   Or yet the arrow frae the bow,
Sae our Scottish lads fell even down,
   An they lay slain on every know.

12 'O hold your hand,' then Monmouth cry'd,
   'Gie quarters to yon men for me;'

But wicked Claverhouse swore an oath
   His cornet's death revengd sud be.

13 'O hold your hand,' then Monmouth cry'd,
   'If ony thing you 'll do for me;
Hold up your hand, you cursed Græme,
   Else a rebel to our king ye 'll be.'

14 Then wicked Claverhouse turnd about —
   I wot an angry man was he —
And he has lifted up his hat,
   And cry'd, God bless his Majesty!

15 Than he 's awa to London town,
   Ay een as fast as he can dree;
Fause witnesses he has wi him taen,
   An taen Monmouth's head frae his body.

16 Alang the brae beyond the brig,
   Mony brave man lies cauld and still;
But lang we 'll mind, and sair we 'll rue,
   The bloody battle of Bothwell Hill.

207

LORD DELAMERE

A. 'The Long-armed Duke,' first printed, about 1843, in a periodical called the Story Teller; afterwards in Notes and Queries, First Series, V, 243, 1852.

B. 'Devonshire's Noble Duel with Lord Danby, in the year 1687,' Llewellynn Jewitt's Ballads and Songs of Derbyshire, p. 55, 1867.

C. Llewellynn Jewitt's Ballads and Songs of Derbyshire, p. 57, two stanzas.

D. 'Lord Delaware,' Thomas Lyle's Ancient Ballads and Songs, chiefly from tradition, manuscripts, and scarce works, etc., London, 1827, p. 125. 'Lord Delamare,' Motherwell's MS., p. 539.   Dixon, Ancient Poems, Ballads and Songs of the Peasantry of England, p. 80, Percy Society, vol. xvii, 1846; the same, ed. Robert Bell, 1857, p. 66.

OF D the editor says: "An imperfect copy . . . was noted down by us from the singing of a gentleman in this city [Glasgow], which has necessarily been remodelled and smoothed down to the present measure, without any other liberties, however, having been taken with the original narrative, which is here carefully preserved as it was committed to us." The air, says Lyle, was "beautiful, and peculiar to the ballad."

E. Leigh, Ballads and Legends of Cheshire, p. 203, repeats A.

Mr E. Peacock had an imperfect manuscript copy with the title 'Lord Delamere,' beginning

I wonder very much that our sovereign king
So many large taxes upon this land should bring.
   Notes and Queries, First Series, II, 104, 1851.

Dr Rimbault remembered hearing a version

sung at a village in Staffordshire, about 1842, in which Hereford was substituted for Devonshire: Notes and Queries, First Series, V, 348, 1852.

Lord Delamere, upon occasion of the imposition of some new taxes, begs a boon of the king, in the Parliament House; it is that he may have all the poor men in the land down to Cheshire and hang them, since it would be better for them to be hanged than to be starved. A French (Dutch) lord says that Delamere ought to be stabbed for publicly affronting the king. The Duke of Devonshire offers himself to fight for Delamere, and a stage is set up for a duel to the utterance. Devonshire's sword bends at the first thrust and then breaks. An English lord who is standing by (Willoughby, B) gives him another, and advises him to play low, for there is treachery. Devonshire drops on his knee and gives his antagonist his death-wound. The king orders the dead man to be taken away, but Devonshire insists on first examining the body. He finds that the French lord had been wearing armor, and the king's armor, while he himself was fighting bare. He reproaches the king with the purpose of taking his life, and tells him that he shall not have his armor back until he wins it.

According to the title of B, the duel was between Devonshire and Lord Danby, and in 1687. The other party is, however, called a Dutch lord in the ballad. The king is James. Delamere is said to be under age (he was thirty-five in 1687).

In D, Delamere is changed to Delaware, of Lincolnshire; the Duke of Devonshire is called a Welsh lord, and fights a Dutch lord in defence of *young* Delaware. When Devonshire's sword breaks, he springs from the stage, borrows another from a soldier in the ring, and leaps back to the stage.

It is scarcely necessary to say that the duel is on a par for historical verity with that in ' Johnie Scot ' (No 99). If there was to be a duel, Devonshire (Earl, he was not created Duke till 1694, the last year of Delamere's

life) was well chosen for the nonce. He had fought with Lord Mohun, in 1676, and was credited with challenging Count Königsmark, in 1682. What is true in the ballad is that Delamere was a strenuous and uncompromising advocate of constitutional government, and that he and Devonshire were political and personal friends. Both were particularly active in bringing in the Prince of Orange; and so was Lord Danby, with whom, according to the title of B, Devonshire was fighting the duel the year before the revolution.

It has been suggested,* and it is barely conceivable, that the ballad may have grown out of a perverted report of the affair of the Earl of Devonshire with Colonel Colepepper.

" On Sunday the 24th of April, 1687, the said earl, meeting on Colonel Culpepper in the drawing-room in Whitehall (who had formerly affronted the said earl in the king's palace, for which he had not received any satisfaction), he spake to the said colonel to go with him into the next room, who went with him accordingly; and when they were there, the said earl required of him to go down stairs, that he might have satisfaction for the affront done him, as aforesaid; which the colonel refusing to do, the said earl struck him with his stick, as is supposed."† For this, Devonshire was summoned to the King's Bench and required to give sureties to the amount of £30,000 that he would appear to stand trial. Delamere was surety for £5,000. Devonshire was in the end fined £30,000, and Delamere made a strong plea, apparently in the House of Lords, against the legality of the proceedings of the court.

There is the slightest possible similitude here to the facts of the ballad. It is merely that one party stands up for the other; but Delamere appears as the champion of Devonshire, not Devonshire of Delamere. If Devonshire had testified for Delamere when the latter was tried for high treason in 1686, there would be something to go upon. A more plausible explanation is desirable.

---

* In Notes and Queries, First Series, V, 249.
† The Works of the late L. Delamer, 1694, The Case of

William, Earl of Devonshire, p. 563; which is the plea referred to further on.

A

Taken down from recitation in Derbyshire, and first printed, about 1843, in a periodical called The Story Teller; afterwards in Notes and Queries, First Series, V, 243, by C. W. G.

1 GOOD people, give attention, a story you shall
    hear,
  It is of the king and my lord Delamere;
  The quarrel it arose in the Parliament House,
  Concerning some taxations going to be put in
    force.
        Ri toora loora la.

2 Says my lord Delamere to his Majesty soon,
  'If it please you, my liege, of you I'll soon beg
    a boon.'
  'Then what is your boon? let me it under-
    stand:'
  'It's to have all the poor men you have in your
    land.

3 'And I'll take them to Cheshire, and there I
    will sow
  Both hempseed and flaxseed, and [hang] them
    all in a row.
  Why, they'd better be hanged, and stopped
    soon their breath,
  If it please you, my liege, than to starve them
    to death.'

4 Then up starts a French lord, as we do
    hear,
  Saying, 'Thou art a proud Jack,' to my lord
    Delamere;
  'Thou oughtest to be stabbed' — then he
    turnd him about —
  'For affronting the king in the Parliament
    House.'

5 Then up starts his grace, the Duke of Devon-
    shire,
  Saying, I'll fight in defence of my lord
    Delamere.
  Then a stage was erected, to battle they went,
  To kill or to be killed was our noble duke's
    intent.

6 The very first push, as we do understand,
  The duke's sword he bended it back into his
    hand.
  He waited a while, but nothing he spoke,
  Till on the king's armour his rapier he broke.

7 An English lord, who by that stage did stand,
  Threw Devonshire another, and he got it in his
    hand:
  'Play low for your life, brave Devonshire,'
    said he,
  'Play low for your life, or a dead man you
    will be.'

8 Devonshire dropped on his knee, and gave him
    his death-wound;
  O then that French lord fell dead upon the
    ground.
  The king called his guards, and he unto them
    did say,
  'Bring Devonshire down, and take the dead
    man away.'

9 'No, if it please you, my liege, no! I've slain
    him like a man;
  I'm resolved to see what clothing he's got on.
  Oh, fie upon your treachery, your treachery!'
    said he,
  'Oh, king, 't was your intention to have took
    my life away.

10 'For he fought in your armour, whilst I have
    fought in bare;
  The same thou shalt win, king, before thou
    does it wear.'
  Then they all turned back to the Parliament
    House,
  And the nobles made obesiance with their
    hands to their mouths.

11 'God bless all the nobles we have in our land,
  And send the Church of England may flourish
    still and stand;
  For I've injured no king, no kingdom, nor no
    crown,
  But I wish that every honest man might enjoy
    his own.'

B

Llewellynn Jewitt, Ballads and Songs of Derbyshire, 1867, p. 55, from a broad-sheet.

1 GOOD people give attention to a story you shall
    hear :
  Between the king and my lord Delamere,
  A quarrel arose in the Parliament House,
  Concerning the taxes to be put in force.
    With my fal de ral de ra.

2 I wonder, I wonder that James, our good king,
  So many hard taxes upon the poor should bring ;
  So many hard taxes, as I have heard them say
  Makes many a good farmer to break and run
    away.

3 Such a rout has been in the parliament, as I hear,
  Betwixt a Dutch lord and my lord Delamere.
  He said to the king, as he sat on the throne,
  ' If it please you, my liege, to grant me a boon.'

4 ' O what is thy boon ? Come, let me understand.'
  ' 'T is to give me all the poor you have in the
    land ;
  I 'll take them down to Cheshire, and there I
    will sow
  Both hemp-seed and flax-seed, and hang them
    in a row.

5 ' It 's better, my liege, they should die a
    shorter death
  Than for your Majesty to starve them on earth.'
  With that up starts a Dutch lord, as we hear,
  And he says, ' Thou proud Jack,' to my lord
    Delamere,

6 ' Thou ought to be stabbed,' and he turned
    him about,
  ' For affronting the king in the Parliament
    House.'
  Then up got a brave duke, the Duke of Devon-
    shire,
  Who said, I will fight for my lord Delamere.

7 ' He is under age, as I 'll make it appear,
  So I 'll stand in defence of my lord Delamere.'

A stage then was built, and to battle they went,
To kill or be killed it was their intent.

8 The very first blow, as we understand,
  Devonshire's rapier went back to his hand ;
  Then he mused awhile, but not a word spoke,
  When against the king's armour his rapier he
    broke.

9 O then he stept backward, and backward stept
    he,
  And then stept forward my lord Willoughby ;
  He gave him a rapier, and thus he did say ;
  Play low, Devonshire, there 's treachery, I
    see.

10 He knelt on his knee, and he gave him the
    wound,
  With that the Dutch lord fell dead on the
    ground :
  The king calld his soldiers, and thus he did
    say :
  Call Devonshire down, take the dead man
    away.

11 He answered, My liege, I 've killed him like a
    man,
  And it is my intent to see what clothing he 's
    got on.
  O treachery ! O treachery ! as I well may say,
  It was your intent, O king, to take my life
    away.

12 ' He fought in your armour, while I fought him
    bare,
  And thou, king, shalt win it before thou dost it
    wear ;
  I neither do curse king, parliament, or throne,
  But I wish every honest man may enjoy his
    own.

13 ' The rich men do flourish with silver and gold,
  While poor men are starving with hunger and
    cold ;
  And if they hold on as they have begun,
  They 'll make little England pay dear for a
    king.'

C

Llewellynn Jewitt's Ballads and Songs of Derbyshire, p. 57. "Another version, which I have in MS., has, besides many minor variations, these verses."

1 O THE Duchess of Devonshire was standing hard by ;
Upon her dear husband she cast her lovely eye :
'Oh, fie upon treachery ! there 's been treachery I say,
It was your full intent to have taen my duke's life away.'

2 Then away to the parliament these votes all went again,
And there they acted like just and honest men.
I neither curse my king, nor kingdom, crown or throne,
But I wish every honest man to enjoy but what is his own.

D

T. Lyle's Ancient Ballads and Songs, p. 135, 1827, as "noted down from the singing of a gentleman," and then "remodelled and smoothed down" by the editor.

1 IN the Parliament House a great rout has been there,
Betwixt our good king and the lord Delaware :
Says Lord Delaware to his Majesty full soon,
'Will it please you, my liege, to grant me a boon ?'

2 'What 's your boon?' says the king, 'now let me understand.'
'It 's, give me all the poor men we 've starving in this land,
And without delay I 'll hie me to Lincolnshire,
To sow hemp-seed and flax-seed, and hang them all there.

3 'For with hempen cord it 's better to stop each poor man's breath
Than with famine you should see your subjects starve to death.'
Up starts a Dutch lord, who to Delaware did say,
Thou deservest to be stabbd ! then he turnd himself away.

4 'Thou deservest to be stabbd, and the dogs have thine ears,
For insulting our king, in this parliament of peers.'
Up sprang a Welsh lord, the brave Duke of Devonshire :
'In young Delaware's defence, I 'll fight this Dutch lord, my sire.

5 'For he is in the right, and I 'll make it so appear ;
Him I dare to single combat, for insulting Delaware.'
A stage was soon erected, and to combat they went ;
For to kill or to be killd, it was either's full intent.

6 But the very first flourish, when the heralds gave command,
The sword of brave Devonshire bent backward on his hand.
In suspense he paused a while, scannd his foe before he strake,
Then against the king's armour his bent sword he brake.

7 Then he sprang from the stage to a soldier in the ring,
Saying, Lend your sword, that to an end this tragedy we bring.
Though he 's fighting me in armour, while I am fighting bare,
Even more than this I 'd venture for young Lord Delaware.

8 Leaping back on the stage, sword to buckler now resounds,
Till he left the Dutch lord a bleeding in his wounds.
This seeing, cries the king to his guards without delay,
Call Devonshire down ! take the dead man away !

9 'No,' says brave Devonshire, 'I've fought
      him as a man;
   Since he's dead, I will keep the trophies I
      have won.
   For he fought me in your armour, while I
      fought him bare,
   And the same you must win back, my liege,
      if ever you them wear.

10 'God bless the Church of England! may it
      prosper on each hand,
   And also every poor man now starving in this
      land.
   And while I pray success may crown our king
      upon his throne,
   I'll wish that every poor man may long enjoy
      his own.'

A. 4¹. Dutch *for* French, *according to some re-
      citers.*
   8². Oh.
B. 4¹, 9¹. Oh.
C. 1¹. Oh.
D. *Printed by Lyle in stanzas of eight short lines.
   The copy in Motherwell's MS. is not in Motherwell's handwriting. It may have been
   written down from recollection of Lyle, or
   may have been arbitrarily altered.*

The variations are as follows:
1². Delamare, *and always.* 2¹. pray let.
2². now *for* we've. 2⁴. with flax seed.
3¹. the poor men's. 4². or *for* our.
5¹. it *wanting.* 6². in his. 6³. the stroke.
6⁴. broke. 7¹. The sprang.
8². he laid. 8³. to the.
9⁴. must won: my liege *wanting.*
10¹. bliss. 10³. the king.

208

LORD DERWENTWATER

A. 'Lord Dunwaters,' Motherwell's MS., p. 331; 'Lord Derwentwater,' Motherwell's Minstrelsy, p. 349.

B. 'Lord Derwentwater,' Notes and Queries, First Series, XII, 492.

C. Bell's Rhymes of Northern Bards, 1812, p. 225, three stanzas.

D. 'Lord Derntwater,' Kinloch MSS, I, 323.

E. 'Lord Derwentwater,' Notes and Queries, Fourth Series, XI, 499.

F. 'Lord Arnwaters,' Buchan's MSS, II, 478.

G. 'Lord Dunwaters,' Motherwell's MS., p. 126.

H. 'Lord Derwentwater's Death,' Shropshire Folk-Lore, edited by Charlotte Sophia Burne, p. 537.

I. The Gentleman's Magazine, vol. xcv, 1825, Part First, p. 489.

THREE stanzas of this ballad were printed in 1812 (C). I followed in 1825, a full copy, which would have been a very good one had it been given as taken down, and not restored "to something like poetical propriety." * The editor of the "old song" observes that it was

---

* Such poetical propriety as 'The second, more alarming still,' 3²; 'The words that passd, alas! presaged' 18³.

But really the text was not very much altered. Some verses, here dropped, were added "to give a finish."

one of the most popular in the north of England for a long period after the event which it records, and a glance at what is here brought together will show that the ballad was at least equally popular in Scotland. I is repeated in Richardson's Borderer's Table-Book, VI, 291, and in Harland and Wilkinson's Ballads and Songs of Lancashire, 1882, p. 265. Mr J. H. Dixon, in Notes and Queries, 4th Series, XI, 389, says that the ballad "originally appeared in the Town and Country Magazine."

'Lord Derwentwater's Goodnight,' Hogg's Jacobite Relics, II, 30, 268, was both communicated and composed by Robert Surtees. 'Derwentwater,' Cromek's Remains of Nithsdale and Galloway Song, 1810, p. 127, is from the pen of Allan Cunningham. It is repeated in Hogg's Jacobite Relics, 1821, II, 28, and in Cunningham's Songs of Scotland, 1825, III, 192, etc. ; also in Kinloch MSS, V, 413, with two lines to fill out an eighth stanza. (Translated by Loève-Veimars, p. 375.) 'Young Ratcliffe,' Sheldon's Minstrelsy of the English Border, p. 400, is another ballad of the same class.

James Ratcliffe, Earl of Derwentwater, being suspected or known to be engaged in concerting a rising in the north of England in behalf of the Pretender, a warrant was issued by the Secretary of State for his apprehension, towards the end of September, 1715. Hereupon he took arms, and he was one of the fifteen hundred English and Scots who were forced to an inglorious surrender at Preston, November 14. The more distinguished prisoners were conveyed to London, where they had a boisterous reception from the mob. Derwentwater was committed to the Tower, December 9 ; was impeached of high treason, and pleaded guilty, in January; was sentenced to death, February 9, at Westminster Hall, and was executed February 24 (1716). In a paper which he read from the scaffold he stated that he had regarded his plea of guilty as a formality consequent upon his "having submitted to mercy," and declared that he had never had "any other but King James the Third for his rightful and lawful sovereign."

Derwentwater had not attained the age of twenty-seven at the time of his death. We may believe that the character given of him by the renegade Patten was not overcharged : "The sweetness of his temper and disposition, in which he had few equals, had so secured him the affection of all his tenants, neighbors, and dependants that multitudes would have lived and died with him. The truth is, he was a man formed by nature to be generally beloved, for he was of so universal a beneficence that he seemed to live for others. As he lived among his own people, there he spent his estate, and continually did offices of kindness and good neighborhood to everybody, as opportunity offered. He kept a house of generous hospitality and noble entertainment, which few in that country do, and none come up to. He was very charitable to poor and distressed families on all occasions, whether known to him or not, and whether Papist or Protestant. His fate will be sensibly felt by a great many who had no kindness for the cause he died in."

The king's letter, which, in the ballad, summons Derwentwater to London (to answer for his head, D 3), suggests the Secretary of State's warrant of arrest, which his lordship, unhappily for himself, evaded. But very probably the ballad-maker supposed Derwentwater to have gone home after his less than six weeks in arms. As he is setting forth to obey the mandate, his wife calls to him from child-bed to make his will. This business does not delay him long: one third of his estate is to be his wife's, and the rest to go to his children. (He had a son not two years old at the date of his execution, and a daughter who must have been born, at the earliest, not much before the rising. His very large estates first passed to the crown, and were afterwards bestowed on Greenwich hospital.) Bad omens attend his departure. As he mounts his horse, his ring drops from his finger, or breaks, and his nose begins to bleed, B 5, D 6, E 8, F 9, H 7, I 10; presently his horse stumbles, A 8, E 9, F 10, I 11; it begins to rain, H 8. When he comes to London, to Westminster Hall, B 6, F 11, to

Whitehall, **D** 7, rides up Westminster Street, in sight of the White Hall, **I** 12, the lords and knights, the lords and ladies, a mob, **H** 9, call him "traitor." How can that be, he answers, with surprise or indignation, except for keeping five hundred men (five thousand, seven thousand, eight score), to fight for King Jamie? **A** 10, **D** 8, **E** 11, **F** 12, **H** 10, **I** 13. A man with an ax claims his life, which he ungrudgingly resigns, **B** 8, **D** 9, 10, **E** 12, 13, **F** 13, 14, **H** 11, 12, **I** 14, 15, directing that a good sum of money which he has in his pockets shall be given to the poor, **A** 12, **D** 11, **E** 14, **F** 15, **I** 17.

In **A** 2, **D** 12, Derwentwater seems to be taken for a Scot.

Ellis, Brand's Antiquities, 1813, II, 261, note, remarks that he had heard in Northumberland that when the Earl of Derwentwater was beheaded, the stream (the Divelswater) that runs past his seat at Dilston Hall flowed with blood.*

The Northern Lights (perhaps the red-colored ones) were peculiarly vivid on the night of February 16, 1716, and were long called Lord Derwentwater's Lights in the north of England, where, it is said, many of the people know (or knew) them by no other name. It was even a popular belief that the aurora borealis was first seen on that night: Notes and Queries, Third Series, IX, 154, 268; Gibson, Dilston Hall, p. 111.

The omen of nose-bleed occurs in the ballad of 'The Mother's Malison,' No 216, **C**; both nose-bleed and horse-stumbling, as omens, in Webster's Dutchess of Malfi, Act II, Scene 2, Dyce, 1859, p. 70, cited, with other cases, in Ellis's ed. of Brand's Antiquities, II, 497.

'Brig. Macintosh's Farewell to the Highlands,' or 'Macintosh was a Soldier Brave,' is one half a Derwentwater ballad: see Harland's Ballads and Songs of Lancashire, 1865, p. 75, Ritson's Northumberland Garland, p. 85, Hogg's Jacobite Relics, II, 102, etc.

A

Motherwell's MS., p. 331, July 19, 1825, "from the recitation of Agnes Lile, Kilbarchan, a woman verging on fifty;" learned from her father, who died fourteen years before, at the age of eighty.

1 Our king has wrote a lang letter,
    And sealed it owre with gold;
He sent it to my lord Dunwaters,
    To read it if he could.

2 He has not sent it with a boy, with a boy,
    Nor with anie Scotch lord;
But he's sent it with the noblest knight
    Eer Scotland could afford.

3 The very first line that my lord did read,
    He gave a smirkling smile;
Before he had the half o't read,
    The tears from his eyes did fall.

4 'Come saddle to me my horse,' he said,
    'Come saddle to me with speed;

* See W. S. Gibson, Dilston Hall, etc., 1850, p. 54.

For I must away to fair London town,
    For me was neer more need.'

5 Out and spoke his lady gay,
    In child-bed where she lay:
'I would have you make your will, my lord
        Dunwaters,
    Before you go away.'

6 'I leave to you, my eldest son,
    My houses and my land;
I leave to you, my second son,
    Ten thousand pounds in hand.

7 'I leave to you, my lady gay —
    You are my wedded wife —
I leave to you, the third of my estate;
    That 'll keep you in a lady's life.'

8 They had not rode a mile but one,
    Till his horse fell owre a stane:
'It's warning gude eneuch,' my lord Dunwaters said,
    'Alive I'll neer come hame.'

9 When they came into fair London town,
  Into the courtiers' hall,
The lords and knichts in fair London town
  Did him a traitor call.

10 'A traitor! a traitor!' says my lord,
   'A traitor! how can that be,
An it was na for the keeping of five thousand
   men
   To fight for King Jamie?'

11 'O all you lords and knichts in fair London
     town,
   Come out and see me die;
O all you lords and knichts into fair London
     town,
   Be kind to my ladie.

12 'There's fifty pounds in my richt pocket,
   Divide it to the poor;
There's other fifty pounds in my left pocket,
   Divide it from door to door.'

B

Notes and Queries, First Series, XII, 492, 1855; learned
some forty five years before from an old gentleman, who,
about 1773, got it by heart from an old washerwoman singing at her tub.

1 THE king he wrote a love-letter,
  And he sealed it up with gold,
And he sent it to Lord Derwentwater,
  For to read it if he could.

2 The first two lines that he did read,
  They made him for to smile;
But the next two lines he looked upon
  Made the tears from his eyes to fall.

3 'Oh,' then cried out his lady fair,
  As she in child-bed lay,
'Make your will, make your will, Lord Der-
  wentwater,
  Before that you go away.'

4 'Then here's for thee, my lady fair,
  .   .   .   .
A thousand pounds of beaten gold,
  To lead you a lady's life.'

5 .   .   .   .
  .   .   .   his milk-white steed,
The ring dropt from his little finger,
  And his nose it began to bleed.

6 He rode, and he rode, and he rode along,
  Till he came to Westminster Hall,
Where all the lords of England's court
  A traitor did him call.

7 'Oh, why am I a traitor?' said he;
  'Indeed, I am no such thing;
I have fought the battles valiantly
  Of James, our noble king.'

8 O then stood up an old gray-headed man,
  With a pole-axe in his hand:
''T is your head, 't is your head, Lord Der-
  wentwater,
  'T is your head that I demand.'

9 .   .   .   .
  His eyes with weeping sore,
He laid his head upon the block,
  And words spake never more.

C

Bell's Rhymes of Northern Bards, 1812, p. 225.

1 THE king has written a broad letter,
  And seald it up with gold,
And sent it to the lord of Derwentwater,
  To read it if he would.

2 He sent it with no boy, no boy,
  Nor yet with eer a slave,
But he sent it with as good a knight
  As eer a king could have.

3 When he read the three first lines,
  He then began to smile;
And when he read the three next lines
  The tears began to sile.

D

Kinloch MSS, I, 323.

1 THE king has written a braid letter,
  And seald it up wi gowd,
And sent it to Lord Derntwater,
  To read it if he coud.

2 The first lines o 't that he read,
  A blythe, blythe man was he ;
But ere he had it half read through,
  The tear blinded his ee.

3 ' Go saddle to me my milk-white horse,
  Go saddle it with speed ;
For I maun ride to Lun[n]on town,
  To answer for my head.'

4 ' Your will, your will, my lord Derntwater,
  Your will before ye go ;
For you will leave three dochters fair,
  And a wife to wail and woe.'

5 ' My will, my will, my lady Derntwater ?
  Ye are my wedded wife ;
Be kind, be kind to my dochters dear,
  If I should lose my life.'

6 He set his ae fit on the grund,
  The tither on the steed ;
The ring upon his finger burst,
  And his nose began to bleed.

7 He rode till he cam to Lunnon town,
  To a place they ca Whiteha ;
And a' the lords o merry England
  A traitor him gan ca.

8 ' A traitor ! a traitor ! O what means this ?
  A traitor ! what mean ye ? '
' It 's a' for the keeping o five hundred men
  To fecht for bonny Jamie.'

9 Then up started a gray-headed man,
  Wi a braid axe in his hand :
' Your life, your life, my lord Derntwater,
  Your life 's at my command.'

10 ' My life, my life, ye old gray-headed man,
  My life I 'll freely gie ;
But before ye tak my life awa
  Let me speak twa words or three.

11 ' I 've fifty pounds in ae pocket,
  Go deal it frae door to door ;
I 've fifty five i the other pocket,
  Go gie it to the poor.

12 ' The velvet coat that I hae on,
  Ye may tak it for your fee ;
And a' ye lords o merry Scotland
  Be kind to my ladie ! '

E

Communicated to Notes and Queries, Fourth Series, XI, 499, 1873, by Mr J. P. Morris, as taken down by him from the recitation of a woman nearly seventy years of age, at Ulverston, North Lancashire.

1 THE king wrote a letter to my lord Derwent-
      water,
  And he sealed it with gold ;
He sent it to my Lord Derwentwater,
  To read it if he could.

2 He sent it by no boy,
  He sent it by no slave,
But he sent it by as true a knight
  As heart could wish or have.

3 The very first line that he looked upon
  Made him for to laugh and to smile ;
The very next line that he looked upon,
  The tears from his eyes did fall.

4 He called to his stable-boy
  To saddle his bonny grey steed,
' That I unto loving London
  May ride away with speed.'

5 His wife heard him say so,
  In childbed as she lay ;
Says she, ' My lord Derwentwater,
  Make thy will before thou goest away.'

6 ' It 's to my little son I give
  My houses and my land,

And to my little daughter
    Ten thousand pounds in hand.

7 'And unto thee, my lady gay,
    Who is my wedded wife,
The third part of my estate thou shalt have,
    To maintain thee through thy life.'

8 He set his foot in the level stirrup,
    And mounted his bonny grey steed;
The gold rings from his fingers did break,
    And his nose began for to bleed.

9 He had not ridden past a mile or two,
    When his horse stumbled over a stone;
'These are tokens enough,' said my lord Der-
    wentwater,
    'That I shall never return.'

10 He rode and he rode till he came to merry
    London,
    And near to that famous hall;
The lords and knights of merry London,
    They did him a traitor call.

11 'A traitor! a traitor! a traitor!' he cried,
    'A traitor! how can that be,
Unless it's for keeping five hundred men
    For to fight for King Jamie?'

12 It's up yon steps there stands a good old man,
    With a broad axe in his hand;
Says he, 'Now, my lord Derwentwater,
    Thy life's at my command.'

13 'My life, my life, thou good old man,
    My life I'll give to thee,
And the green coat of velvet on my back
    Thou mayst take it for thy fee.

14 'There's fifty pounds and five in my right
    pocket,
    Give that unto the poor;
There's twenty pounds and five in my left
    pocket,
    Deal that from door to door.'

15 Then he laid his head on the fatal block,
    *   *   *   *   *   *

F

Buchan's MSS, II, 478.

1 THE king has written a broad letter,
    And seald it with his hand,
And sent it on to Lord Arnwaters,
    To read and understand.

2 Now he has sent it by no boy,
    No boy, nor yet a slave,
But one of England's fairest knights,
    The one that he would have.

3 When first he on the letter lookd,
    Then he began to smile;
But ere he read it to an end,
    The tears did trickling fall.

4 He calld upon his saddle-groom
    To saddle his milk-white steed,
'For I unto London must go,
    For me there is much need.'

5 Out then speaks his gay lady,
    In child-bed where she lay:

'Make your will, make your will, my knight,
    For fear ye rue the day.'

6 'I'll leave unto my eldest son
    My houses and my lands;
I'll leave unto my youngest son
    Full forty thousand pounds.

7 'I'll leave unto my gay lady,
    And to my loving wife,
The second part of my estate,
    To maintain a lady's life.'

8 He kissd her on the pillow soft,
    In child-bed where she lay,
And bade farewell, neer to return,
    Unto his lady gay.

9 He put his foot in the stirup,
    His nose began to bleed;
The ring from's finger burst in two
    When he mounted on his steed.

10 He had not rode a mile or two
    Till his horse stumbled down;

'A token good,' said Lord Arnwaters,
'I 'll never reach London town.'

11 But when into Westminster Hall,
Amongst the nobles all,
'A traitor, a traitor, Lord Arnwaters,
A traitor,' they did him call.

12 'A traitor? a traitor how call ye me?
And a traitor how can I be
For keeping seven thousand valiant men
To fight for brave Jamie?'

13 Up then came a brave old man,
With a broad ax in his hand:
'Your life, your life, Lord Arnwaters,
Your life 's at my command.'

14 'My life, my life, my brave old man,
My life I 'll give to thee,
And the coat of green that 's on my back
You shall have for your fee.

15 'There 's fifty pounds in one pocket,
Pray deal 't among the poor;
There 's fifty and four in the other pocket,
Pray deal 't from door to door.

16 'There 's one thing more I have to say,
This day before I die;
To beg the lords and nobles all
To be kind to my lady.'

———•———

G

Motherwell's MS., p. 126, from the recitation of Mrs
Trail, Paisley, July 9, 1825: a song of her mother's.

1 THE king has wrote a long letter,
And sealed it with his han,
And he has sent it to my lord Dunwaters,
To read it if he can.

2 The very first line he lookit upon,
It made him to lauch and to smile;
The very next line he lookit upon,
The tear from his eye did fall.

3 'As for you, my auldest son,
My houses and my land;
And as for you, my youngest son,
Ten thousand pound in hand.

4 'As for you, my gay lady,
You being my wedded wife,
The third of my estate I will leave to you,
For to keep you in a lady's life.'

*   *   *   *   *

———•———

H

Shropshire Folk-Lore, edited by Charlotte Sophia Burne,
p. 537; as recited in 1881 by Mrs Dudley, of Much Wen-
lock.

1 THE king he wrote a letter,
And sealëd it with gold,
And sent it to Lor Derwentwater,
To read it if he could.

2 The first three lines he looked upon,
They made him to smile;
And the next three lines he looked upon
Made tears fall from his eyes.

3 O then bespoke his gay lady,
As she on a sick-bed lay:
'Make your will, my lord,
Before you go away.'

4 'O there is for my eldest son
My houses and my land,
And there is for my youngest son
Ten thousand pounds in hand.

5 'There is for you, my gay lady,
My true and lawful wife,
The third part of my whole estate,
To maintain you a lady's life.'

6 Then he called to his stable-groom
    To bring him his gray steed ;
For he must to London go,
    The king had sent indeed.

7 When he put his foot in the stirrup,
    To mount his grey steed,
His gold ring from his finger burst,
    And his nose began to bleed.

8 He had not gone but half a mile
    When it began to rain ;
' Now this is a token,' his lordship said,
    ' That I shall not return again.'

9 When he unto London came,
    A mob did at him rise,
And they callëd him a traitor,
    Made the tears fall from his eyes.

10 ' A traitor, a traitor !' his lordship said,
   .   .   .   .   .   .
Is it for keeping eight score men
    To fight for pretty Jimmee ? '

11 O then bespoke a grave man,
    With a broad axe in his hand :
' Hold your tongue, Lord Derwentwater,
    Your life lies at my command.'

12 ' My life, my life,' his lordship said,
    ' My life I will give to thee,
And the black velvet coat upon my back,
    Take it for thy fee.'

13 Then he laid his head upon the block,
    He did such courage show,
And asked the executioner
    To cut it off at one blow.

I

The Gentleman's Magazine, 1825, vol. xcv, Part First, p. 489, taken down by G. H., apparently in Westmoreland, from the dictation of an old person who had learned it from her father ; restored " to something like poetical propriety " by the assistance of " a poetical friend."

1 KING GEORGE he did a letter write,
    And sealed it up with gold,
And sent it to Lord Derwentwater,
    To read it if he could.

2 He sent his letter by no post,
    He sent it by no page,
But sent it by a gallant knight
    As eer did combat wage.

3 The first line that my lord lookd on
    Struck him with strong surprise;
The second, more alarming still,
    Made tears fall from his eyes.

4 He called up his stable-groom,
    Saying, Saddle me well my steed,
For I must up to London go,
    Of me there seems great need.

5 His lady, hearing what he said,
    As she in child-bed lay,
Cry'd, My dear lord, pray make your will
    Before you go away.

6 ' I 'll leave to thee, my eldest son,
    My houses and my land ;
I 'll leave to thee, my younger son,
    Ten thousand pounds in hand.

7 ' I 'll leave to thee, my lady gay,
    My lawful married wife,
A third part of my whole estate,
    To keep thee a lady's life.'

8 He knelt him down by her bed-side,
    And kissed her lips so sweet ;
The words that passd, alas ! presaged
    They never more should meet.

9 Again he calld his stable-groom,
    Saying, Bring me out my steed,
For I must up to London go,
    With instant haste and speed.

10 He took the reins into his hand,
    Which shook with fear and dread ;
The rings from off his fingers dropt,
    His nose gushd out and bled.

11 He had but ridden miles two or three
    When stumbling fell his steed;
' Ill omens these,' Derwentwater said,
    ' That I for James must bleed.'

12 As he rode up Westminster street,
    In sight of the White Hall,

The lords and ladies of London town
    A traitor they did him call.

13 ' A traitor !' Lord Derwentwater said,
    ' A traitor how can I be,
Unless for keeping five hundred men
    Fighting for King Jemmy ? '

14 Then started forth a grave old man,
    With a broad-mouthd axe in hand :
' Thy head, thy head, Lord Derwentwater,
    Thy head 's at my command.'

15 ' My head, my head, thou grave old man,
    My head I will give thee ;
Here 's a coat of velvet on my back
    Will surely pay thy fee.

16 ' But give me leave,' Derwentwater said,
    ' To speak words two or three ;
Ye lords and ladies of London town,
    Be kind to my lady.

17 ' Here 's a purse of fifty sterling pounds,
    Pray give it to the poor;
Here 's one of forty-five beside
    You may dole from door to door.'

18 He laid his head upon the block,
    The axe was sharp and strong,
  .   .   .   .   .

A. 2^4. Ere. 7^3. the 3rd.
    *Motherwell has made a few changes in his
    printed copy.*
  12. *This stanza is given in Notes and Que-
    ries, First Series, I, 318, by a scholar of
    Christ's Hospital, who informs us that
    the ballad was there current about 1785–
    1800 :*

    There 's fifty pounds in my right pocket,
      To be given to the poor ;

    There 's fifty pounds in my left pocket,
      To be given from door to door.

E. 1^2. And sealëd it with gold *in Mr J. P. Mor-
    ris's communication to Notes and Queries,
    the same volume, p. 333.*
F. 2^1. by and by : *cf.* E 2.
    2^2. No one, no not a slave : *cf.* E 2.
I. 18. *The remainder of four stanzas appended
    by G. H. is omitted.*

209

GEORDIE

A. 'Geordie,' Johnson's Musical Museum, No 346,
p. 357, 1792.

B. " Scotch Ballads, Materials for Border Minstrelsy,"
Abbotsford, 1802.

C. a. 'The Laird of Geight, or Gae.' b. 'The Laird
of Geight.' " Scotch Ballads, Materials for Border
Minstrelsy," Abbotsford, 1813–15.

D. 'The Laird of Gigh, or Gae,' " Scotch Ballads, Materials for Border Minstrelsy," Abbotsford, 1813–15.

E. a. Kinloch MSS, V, 130. b. 'Geordie,' Kinloch's
Ancient Scottish Ballads, p. 192.

F. 'Geordie Lukely,' Motherwell's MS., p. 367.

G. 'Geordie,' 'Geordie Lukelie,' Motherwell's Note-
Book, p. 17, p. 10.

H. 'Will ye go to the Hielans, Geordie ?' Christie,
Traditional Ballad Airs, II, 44.

I. a. 'Gight's Lady,' Buchan's MSS, II, 143. b. 'Laird
(Lord ?) of Gight,' Kinloch MSS, VI, 1.

J. 'Gight's Lady,' Buchan's Ballads of the North of
Scotland, I, 133.

K. Motherwell's MS., p. 400, two stanzas.

L. 'Geordie,' Cunningham's Songs of Scotland, II, 186, two stanzas.

M. 'Geordie,' 'Geordie Lukely,' Motherwell's Note-Book, p. 2, one stanza.

N. 'Geordie,' Motherwell's Note-Book, p. 20, one stanza.

" OF this," says Motherwell, "many variations exist among reciters," and his remark is borne out by what is here given.

The copy in Cunningham's Songs of Scotland, II, 186, is **A** retouched, with st. 5 dropped and two stanzas (**L**) inserted from recitation. The texts of Christie, I, 52, 84, are **J** abridged and **E** b. Of **J** Christie says that he heard in 1848 a version sung by a native of Buchan, Aberdeenshire, who had it through her grandmother and great-grandmother, which differed only in being more condensed and wanting the catastrophe, and in having Badenoch's lady for Bignet's, and Keith-Hall and Gartly for Black Riggs and Kincraigie.

Geordie Gordon, **A**, of Gight (Gigh), **B** b, **C**, **D**, **I**, of the Bog o Gight, **H**, is in prison, on a charge endangering his life. He sends a message to his wife to come to Edinburgh. She rides thither with the utmost haste, and finds Geordie in extremity. She is told that his life may be redeemed by the payment of a large sum of money. She raises a contribution on the spot, pays the ransom, and rides off with her husband.

Kinloch and others incline to take Geordie to be George Gordon, fourth earl of Huntly, who incurred the Queen Regent's displeasure for failing to execute a commission against a Highland robber in 1554. Huntly was committed to Edinburgh Castle, and some of his many enemies urged that he should be banished to France, others that he should be put to death. The Earl of Cassilis, though a foe to Huntly, resisted these measures on grounds of patriotism, and proposed that he should be deprived of certain honors and offices and fined. A fine was exacted, and the places which had been taken from him were restored.* With regard to this hypothesis, it may at least be said that, if it should be accepted, the ballad would be quite as faithful to history as many others.

A–E are the purer forms of the ballad; F–J are corrupted by admixture.

Geordie is Geordie Lukely of Stirling in **F**. In **G**, he is the Earl of Cassilis, 'of Hye,' as if some singer of the Gordons had turned the tables on Huntly's enemy. In **H**, Geordie lives at the Bog o Gight, and should be the Earl, or Marquis, of Huntly; but writers of peerages will consult st. 17.

There has been a battle in the North in A–E. Sir Charles Hay† has been killed, and Geordie is in custody for this, **A**, **B**. Geordie has killed a man and is to die, **C**; the man is his wife's brother, **D**. In **E**, Geordie is a rebel.

F begins with two stanzas from a vulgar last-dying-speech, of which more by and by: otherwise the story is not essentially injured, though the style is lowered. Geordie (in the first two stanzas) has done many an ill deed, but no murder or slaughter; he has stolen fifteen of the king's horse and sold them in Bohemia. Earl Cassilis, likewise, in **G**, could not keep his hand off horses; he has stolen three geldings out of a park and sold them to Balleny (Balveny). Huntly, if it be he, in **H**, has only made free with the king's deer. In **I**, **J**, Geordie has had an intrigue with Bignet's (Pilbagnet's, Badenoch's) lady, for which the husband has thrown him into prison, and he is to die. But he owns to more than this in **J**. Beginning with an acknowledgment of one of the king's best steeds stolen

---

* Buchanan, Rer. Scot. Hist., fol. 186; Lesley, History of Scotland, p. 251 f.

† In **J**, which cannot be relied on for smaller points, we read that Charles Hay has been hanged, for reasons not given: st. 20.

and sold in 'Bevany,' upon being pressed, he confesses to a woman abused and five orphan babes killed for their money.

Geordie points his message to his wife in C 2, D 4, by begging her to sew him or bring him his linen shirt (shirts), a good side shirt, which will be the last he shall need, and a lang side sark is equally prominent in the lady's thoughts in I 8.

The lady stops for nothing in her ride to Edinburgh. She will not, and does not, eat or drink all the way, A 4, 5. When she comes to the water-side, finding no boat ready, she swims the Queen's Ferry, B 7, C 5, D 9, J 13, L 1; or pays a boatman prodigally to take her over, H 9, I 9, J 14.

When the lady gaes oer the pier of Leith, comes to Edinburgh, to the West Port, the Canongate, the Parliament Close, the tolbooth-stair, the prison-door, she deals out crowns and ducatoons, makes the handfus o red gold fly, among the numerous poor, and bids them pray for Geordie. She has the prudence, in G 5, to do the same among the nobles many at the tolbooth-gate, that they may plead for Geordie.

The block and axe are in sight, and Geordie, in chains, is coming down the stair, A; the napkin is laid over his face, and the gallows is making ready, B (so F, but put further on), his head is to go, C; the rest of the nobles sit (stand) hat on head, but hat in hand stands Geordie, D, E, H, I, J, L.

The lady makes a plea for her husband's life. She is the mother of many children (the tale ranges from six to eleven) and is going with yet another, B, C, K, N. She would bear them all over again for the life of Geordie, C, D, or see them all streekit before her eyes, B; and for his life she will part with all that she owns, A 10, B 11, 16, D 14.

The king in A is moved by neither of these appeals. The number of her children is so

far from affecting him that he orders the heading-man to make haste. But the Gordons collect and pass the word to be ready. There would have been bloody bouks upon the green.*

The lady is told that by paying a good round sum, 5,000 (500) pounds, 10,000 (1000) crowns, she can redeem Geordie's life. An aged lord prompts the king to offer these terms in A; in the other versions, they are proposed directly; by the king himself, F, G, I; by the queen, B, I; by the good Argyle, D; by an English lord, H. The bystanders contribute handsomely; she pays the ransom down, and wins the life of Geordie, A–D, G–J.

In E, which is a mere fragment, there is no fine or collection: a bold baron says, such true lovers shall not be parted, and she gets her Geordie forthwith. In F, no contribution is required, because the lady, after scattering the red gold among the poor, is still in a condition to produce the five thousand pound from her own pocket. For this she receives a 'remit,' with which she hies to the gallows and stops the impending execution. In I b, which is defective, the money collected is to pay the jailer's fee. After the discharge has been secured (in two or three copies earlier), Lord Corstorph, B a, the Laird o Logie, B b, an Irish lord, C, H, an English lord, D, the gleid Argyle, I, Lord Montague, J, expresses a wish that Geordie's head were off, because he might have succeeded to the lady. The lady checks this aspiration, sometimes in very abusive language.

The pair now ride off together, and when she is set in her saddle, no bird in bush or on briar ever sang so sweet as she, B, C, E, F, H, I. If we were to trust some of those who recite her story, the lady who has shown so much spirit and devotion was not one of those who blush to find good deeds fame. 'Gar print me ballants that I am a worthy lady,'

---

* This intimation is repeated in G 10, with the ludicrous variation of bloody 'breeks.' In B, an English lord, whose competency and interest in the matter are alike difficult to comprehend, declares that he will have Geordie hanged, will have Geordie's head, before the morrow. A Scottish lord rejoins that he will cast off his coat and fight, will fight in blood up to the knees; and the king adds, there will be bloody heads among us all, before that happens. Who the parties to the fight are to be, unless it is the English lord against Scotland, is not evident. B is inflated with superfluous verses.

B 30 makes her say; 'Hae me to some writer's house, that I may write down Gight's lament and how I borrowed Geordie,' I a 25; 'Call for one of the best clerks, that he may write all this I've done for Geordie,' J 36. What she really did say is perhaps faithfully given in D 18: 'Where is there a writer's house, that I may write to the north that I have won the life of Geordie?'

I and J are probably from stall-prints, and it has not been thought necessary to notice some things which may have been put into these to eke them out to a convenient length. J has an entirely spurious supplement. When the pair are riding away, and even as the wife is protesting her affection, Geordie turns round and says, A finger of Bignet's lady's hand is worth a' your fair body. A dispute ensues, and Geordie pulls out a dagger and stabs his lady; he then takes to flight, and never is found. Another set, mentioned by Motherwell, makes Geordie drown his deliverer in the sea, in a fit of jealousy (Minstrelsy, p. lxxvi, 46).

There is an English broadside ballad, on the death of "George Stoole" which seemed to Motherwell "evidently imitated from the Scottish song." This was printed by H. Gosson, whose time is put at 1607–41.* This ballad was to be sung "to a delicate Scottish tune;" Georgy comes in as a rhyme at the end of stanzas not seldom; Georgy writes to his lady, bewailing his folly; he never stole no oxe nor cow, nor ever murdered any, but fifty horse he did receive of a merchant's man of Gory, for which he was condemned to die, and did die. These are the data for determining the question of imitation.

There is a later 'Georgy' ballad, of the same general cast, on the life and death of "George of Oxford," a professed and confessed highwayman, a broadside printed in the last quarter of the seventeenth century. In this, Lady Gray hastens to Newcastle to beg Georgy's life of the judge, and offers gold and land to save him, after the fashion of Lady Ward in 'Hughie Graham;' to no purpose, as in 'Hughie Graham.' This Georgy owns and boasts himself a thief, but with limitations much the same as those which are made a point of by the other; he never stole horse, mare, or cloven-foot, with one exception — the king's white steeds, which he sold to Bohemia.

Both of these ballads are given in an appendix.

Whether the writers of these English ballads knew of the Scottish 'Geordie,' I would not undertake to affirm or deny; it is clear that some far-back reciter of the Scottish ballad had knowledge of the later English broadside. The English ballads, however, are mere "goodnights." The Scottish ballads have a proper story, with a beginning, middle, and end, and (save one late copy), a good end, and they are most certainly original and substantially independent of the English. The Scottish Geordie is no thief, nor even a Johnie Armstrong. There are certain passages in certain versions which give that impression, it is true, but these are incongruous with the story, and have been adopted from some copy of the broadside, the later rather than the earlier. These are, the first two stanzas of F, utterly out of place, where we have the king's horses stolen and sold in Bohemia, almost exactly as in the ballad of 'George of Oxford,' 15; G 7, where the Earl of Cassilis is made to steal geldings and sell them in Balleny; and J 23, in which the Laird of Gight steals one of the king's steeds (precisely as in 'George of Oxford') and sells it in Bevany. That is to say, we have the very familiar case of the introduction (generally accidental and often infelicitous) of a portion of one ballad into another; which, if accidental in the present instance, would easily be accounted for by a George being

---

* It seems to have been familiar in Aberdeen as early as 1627. Joseph Haslewood made an entry in his copy of Ritson's Scotish Song of a manuscript Lute-Book (presented in 1781 to Dr Charles Burney by Dr Skene of Marischal College) which contained airs noted and collected by Robert Gordon, "at Aberdein, in the yeare of our Lord 1627." Among some ninety titles of tunes mentioned, there occur 'Ther wer three ravns' and 'God be with the, Geordie.' (W. Macmath.)

the hero in each. Further; the burden of E, embodied in the ballad in two versions, I 27, J 35, has a general resemblance to that of 'George Stoole,' and could hardly have been original with the Scottish ballad. There was probably a 'Geordie Luklie,' a Scottish variety of one of the English broadsides.

G is translated by Gerhard, p. 56; A, in part, by Knortz, Schottische Balladen, p. 101.

A

Johnson's Museum, No 346, p. 357, 1792; communicated by Robert Burns.

1 THERE was a battle in the north,
And nobles there was many,
And they hae killd Sir Charlie Hay,
And they laid the wyte on Geordie.

2 O he has written a lang letter,
He sent it to his lady:
'Ye maun cum up to Enbrugh town,
To see what word 's o Geordie.'

3 When first she lookd the letter on,
She was baith red and rosy;
But she had na read a word but twa
Till she wallowt like a lily.

4 'Gar get to me my gude grey steed,
My menyie a' gae wi me,
For I shall neither eat nor drink
Till Enbrugh town shall see me.'

5 And she has mountit her gude grey steed,
Her menyie a' gaed wi her,
And she did neither eat nor drink
Till Enbrugh town did see her.

6 And first appeard the fatal block,
And syne the aix to head him,
And Geordie cumin down the stair,
And bands o airn upon him.

7 But tho he was chaind in fetters strang,
O airn and steel sae heavy,
There was na ane in a' the court
Sae bra a man as Geordie.

8 O she 's down on her bended knee,
I wat she 's pale and weary:
'O pardon, pardon, noble king,
And gie me back my dearie!

9 'I hae born seven sons to my Geordie dear,
The seventh neer saw his daddie;
O pardon, pardon, noble king,
Pity a waefu lady!'

10 'Gar bid the headin-man mak haste,'
Our king reply'd fu lordly:
'O noble king, tak a' that 's mine,
But gie me back my Geordie!'

11 The Gordons cam, and the Gordons ran,
And they were stark and steady,
And ay the word amang them a'
Was, Gordons, keep you ready!

12 An aged lord at the king's right hand
Says, Noble king, but hear me;
Gar her tell down five thousand pound,
And gie her back her dearie.

13 Some gae her marks, some gae her crowns,
Some gae her dollars many,
And she 's telld down five thousand pound,
And she 's gotten again her dearie.

14 She blinkit blythe in her Geordie's face,
Says, Dear I 've bought thee, Geordie;
But there sud been bluidy bouks on the green
Or I had tint my laddie.

15 He claspit her by the middle sma,
And he kist her lips sae rosy:
'The fairest flower o woman-kind
Is my sweet, bonie lady!'

B

a. " Scotch Ballads, Materials for Border Minstrelsy," No 13, Abbotsford.   Sent to Scott by William Laidlaw, September 11, 1802 (Letters, vol. i, No 73), as written down by Laidlaw from the recitation of Mr Bartram of Biggar.   b. Variations received by Laidlaw from J. Scott.

1 'THERE was a battle i the north
   Amang our nobles many,
And they have killed Sir Charles Hay,
   And they 've taen thrae me my Geordie.'

2 'O where 'll I gett a wi bit boy,
   A bonnie boy that 's ready,
That will gae in to my biggin
   With a letter to my ladie?'

3 Then up and startit a wi bit boy,
   An a bonnie boy was ready :
'It 's I 'll gae in to your biggin
   Wi a letter to your ladie.'

4 When the day was fair an the way was clear,
   An the wi bit boy was ready,
An he 's gane in to his biggin,
   Wi a letter to his ladie.

5 When she lookd the letter on,
   She was no a wearit ladie ;
But when she lookit the other side,
   She mourned for her Geordie.

6 'Gar sadle to me the black,' she says,
   'For the brown rade neer sey bonnie,
An I 'll gae down to Enbro town,
   An see my true-love Geordie.'

7 When she cam to the water-side,
   The cobles war na ready ;
She 's turnd her horse's head about,
   An in by the Queen's Ferry.

8 When she cam to the West Port,
   There war poor folks many ;
She dealt crowns an the ducatdowns,
   And bade them pray for Geordie.

9 When she cam to the Parliament Closs,
   There amang our nobles many,
Cravats an caps war standing there,
   But low, low lay her Geordie.

10 When she gaed up the tolbooth-stairs,
   Amang our nobles manie,

The napkin 's tyed oer Geordie's face,
   And the gallows makin ready.

11 'O wad ye hae his lands or rents?
   Or wad ye hae his monie ?
Take a', a' frae him but his sark alone,
   Leave me my true-love Geordie.'

12 The captain pu'd her on his knee,
   An ca'd her heart an honey :
'An ye wad wait se'en years for me,
   Ye wad never jump for Geordie.'

13 'O hold your tongue, you foolish man,
   Your speech it 's a' but folly ;
For an ye wad wait till the day ye die,
   I wad neer take John for Geordie.'

14 'T was up an spak the Lord Corstarph,
   The ill gae wi his body !
'O Geordie's neck it war on a block,
   Gif I had his fair ladie !'

15 'O haud yer tongue, ye foolish man,
   Yer speech is a' but folly ;
For if Geordie's neck war on a block,
   Ye sould neer enjoy his ladie.

16 'It 's I hae se'en weel gawn mills,
   I wait they a' gang daily ;
I 'll gie them a' an amang ye a'
   For the sparin o my Geordie.

17 'I hae ele'en bairns i the wast,
   I wait the're a' to Geordie ;
I 'd see them a' streekit afore mine eyes
   Afore I lose my Geordie.

18 'I hae ele'en bairns i the wast,
   The twalt bears up my body ;
The youngest 's on his nurse's knee,
   An he never saw his dadie.

19 'I hae se'en uncles in the north,
   They gang baith proud an lordly ;
I 'd see them a' tread down afore my eyes
   Afore I lose my Geordie.'

20 Then out an spak an English lord,
   The ill gae wi his bodie !
'It 's I gard hang Sir Francie Grey,
   An I 'll soon gar hang your Geordie.'

21 It 's out an spak than a Scottish lord,
    May the weel gae wi his body !
    'It 's I 'k cast of my coat an feght
      Afore ye lose your Geordie.'

22 It 's out then spak an English lord,
    May the ill gae wi his bodie !
    'Before the morn at ten o'clock,
      I 's hae the head o Geordie.'

23 Out then spak the Scottish lord,
    May the weel gae wi his body !
    'I 'll fight i bluid up to the knees
      Afore ye lose your Geordie.'

24 But out an spak the royal king,
    May the weel gae wi his body !
    'There 's be bluidie heads amang us a'
      Afore ye lose your Geordie.'

25 'T was up than spak the royal queen,
    'May the weel gae wi his body !
    Tell down, tell down five hunder pound,
      An ye 's get wi you yer Geordie.'

26 Some gae her gold, some gae her crowns,
    Some gae her ducats many,
    An she 's telld down five hundred pound,
      An she 's taen away her Geordie.

27 An ay she praisd the powers above,
    An a' the royal family,
    An ay she blessed the royal queen,
      For sparin o her Geordie.

28 . . . .
    . . . .
    Nae bird sang sweeter in the bush
      Than she did wi her Geordie.

29 'It 's wo be to my Lord Costorph,
    It 's wo be to him daily !
    For if Geordie's neck had been on the block
      He had neer enjoyd his ladie.

30 'Gar print me ballants weel,' she said,
    'Gar print me ballants many,
    Gar print me ballants weel,' she said,
      'That I am a worthy ladie.'

C

a. "Scotch Ballads, Materials for Border Minstrelsy," Abbotsford, No 38, MS. of Thomas Wilkie, 1813–15, p. 16 ; taken down from the singing of Miss Christy Robertson, Dunse. b. "Scotch Ballads," etc., No 108, in a lady's hand, and perhaps obtained directly from Miss Robertson.

1 THERE was a battle in the north,
    Among the nobles many ;
    The Laird of Geight he 's killd a man,
      And there 's nane to die but Geordie.

*   *   *   *   *   *   *

2 'What news? what news, my bonny boy ?
    What news hae ye frae Geordie ? '
    'He bids ye sew his linen shirts,
      For he 's sure he 'll no need many.'

3 'Go saddle the black, go saddle the brown,
    Go saddle to me the bonny ;
    For I will neither eat nor drink
      Until I see my Geordie.'

4 They 've saddled the black, they 've saddled
      the brown,
    They 've saddled her the bonny,
    And she is away to Edinborough town,
      Straight away to see her Geordie.

5 When she came to the sea-side,
    The boats they were nae ready ;
    She turned her horse's head about,
      And swimd at the Queen's Ferry.

6 And when she came to the prison-door,
    There poor folks they stood many ;
    She dealt the red guineas them among,
      And bade them pray weel for Geordie.

7 And when she came into the hall,
    Amang the nobles many,
    The napkin 's tied on Geordie's face,
      And the head 's to gae frae Geordie.

8 'I have born ten bonny sons,
    And the eleventh neer sa his dadie,

And I will bear them all oer again
   For the life o bonny Geordie.

9 'I have born the Laird of Gight,
   And the Laird of bonny Pernonnie;
  And I will gie them all to thee
   For the life of my bonny Geordie.'

10 Up then spoke [a kind-hearted man],
   Wha said, He's done good to many;
  If ye'll tell down ten hundred crowns
   Away ye shall hae yer Geordie.

11 Some telld shillings, and some telld crowns,
   But she telld the red guineas many,
  Till they've telld down ten hundred crowns,
   And away she's got her Geordie.

12 [It's up then spoke an Irish lord,
   And O but he spoke bauldly!]
  'I wish his head had been on the block,
   That I might hae got his fair lady.'

13 She turned about . . . .
   And O but she spoke boldly!
  'A pox upon your nasty face!
   Will ye eer be compared to my Geor-
   die?'

14 She set him on a milk-white steed,
   Herself upon another;
  The thrush on the briar neer sang so clear
   As she sang behind her Geordie.

D

"Scotch Ballads, Materials for Border Minstrelsy," No 64, MS. of Thomas Wilkie, 1813–15, p. 50, Abbotsford. "I took this down from the recitation of Janet Scott, Bowden, who sung it to a beautiful plaintive old air."

1 THERE was a battle i the north
   Among the nobles many,
  The Laird of Gigh he's killd a man,
   The brother of his lady.

2 'Where will I get a man or boy,
   That will win both goud and money,
  That will run into the north,
   And fetch to me my lady?'

3 Up then spake a bonny boy,
   He was both blythe and merry;
  'O I will run into the north,
   And fetch to you your lady.'

4 'You may tell her to sew me a gude side shirt,
   She'll no need to sew me mony;
  Tell her to bring me a gude side shirt,
   It will be the last of any.'

5 He has written a broad letter,
   And he's seald it sad and sorry;
  He's gaen it to that bonny boy,
   To take to his fair lady.

6 Away the bonny boy he's gaen,
   He was both blythe and merrie;

He's to that fair lady gane,
   And taen her word frae Geordie.

7 When she looked the letter on,
   She was both sad and sorrie:
  'O I'll away to fair Edinburgh town
   Myself and see my Geordie.

8 'Gar saddle to me the black,' she says,
   'The brown was neer sae bonny;
  And I'll straight to Edinburgh
   Myself and see my Geordie.'

9 When she came to that wan water,
   The boats was not yet ready;
  She wheeld her horse's head around,
   And swimd at the Queen's Ferry.

10 When she came to the Parliament Close,
   Amang the poor folks many,
  She dealt the crowns with duckatoons,
   And bade them pray for Geordy.

11 When she came to the Parliament House,
   Among the nobles many,
  The rest sat all wi hat on head,
   But hat in hand sat Geordie.

12 Up bespake an English lord,
   And he spake blythe and merrie;
  'Was Geordie's head upon the block,
   I am sure I would have his lady.'

13 Up bespake that lady fair,
   And O but she was sorrie!
'If Geordie's head were on the block,
   There's never a man gain his lady.

14 'I have land into the north,
   And I have white rigs many,
And I could gie them a' to you
   To save the life of Geordie.

15 'I have seven children in the north,
   And they seem very bonnie,
And I could bear them a' over again
   For to win the life o Geordie.'

16 Up bespake the gude Argyle;
   He has befriended many;
'If ye'll tell down ten hundred crowns,
   Ye's win the life o Geordie.'

17 Some gaed her shillings, and some her crowns,
   And some gaed her guineas many,
And she's telld down ten hundred crowns,
   And she's wone the life o Geordie.

18 When she came down through Edinborough,
   And Geordie in her hand, O,
'Where will I get a writer's [house],
   A writer's house so ready,
That I may write into the north
   I have wone the life o Geordie'?

E

a. Kinloch MSS, V, 130; in the handwriting of James Beattie. b. Kinloch's Ancient Scottish Ballads, p. 192.

1 THERE was a battle in the north,
   And rebels there were many,
And they were a' brought before the king,
   And taken was my Geordie.
      My Geordie O, O my Geordie O,
         O the love I bear to Geordie!
      For the very ground I walk upon
         Bears witness I love Geordie.

2 As she went up the tolbooth-stair,
   The cripples there stood many,
And she dealt the red gold them among,
   For to pray for her love Geordie.

3 And when she came unto the hall
   The nobles there stood many,
And every one stood hat on head,
   But hat in hand stood Geordie.

4 O up bespoke a baron bold,
   And O but he spoke bonnie!
'Such lovers true shall not parted be,'
   And she's got her true-love Geordie.

5 When she was mounted on her high horse,
   And on behind her Geordie,
Nae bird on the brier eer sang sae clear
   As the young knight and his lady.
      O my Geordie O, O my Geordie O,
         O the love I bear to Geordie!
      The very stars in the firmament
         Bear tokens I love Geordie.

F

Motherwell's MS., p. 367; from the recitation of Agnes Lyle, Kilbarchan.

1 'GEORDIE Lukely is my name,
   And many a one doth ken me; O
Many an ill deed I hae done,
   But now death will owrecome me. O

2 'I neither murdered nor yet have I slain,
   I never murdered any;

But I stole fyfteen o the king's bay horse,
   And I sold them in Bohemia.

3 'Where would I get a pretty little boy,
   That would fain win gold and money,
That would carry this letter to Stirling town,
   And give it to my lady?'

4 'Here am I, a pretty little boy,
   That wud fain win gold and money;

I 'll carry your letter to Stirling town,
  And give it to your lady.'

5 As he came in by Stirling town
  He was baith weet and weary ;
  The cloth was spread, and supper set,
  And the ladies dancing merry.

6 When she read the first of it,
  She was baith glad and cheery ;
  But before she had the half o 't read,
  She was baith sad and sorry.

7 'Come saddle to me the bonnie dapple gray,
  Come saddle to me the wee poney ;
  For I 'll awa to the king mysell,
  And plead for my ain love Geordie.'

8 She gaed up the Cannogate,
  Amang the puir folk monie ;
  She made the handfus o red gold fly,
  And bade them pray for Geordie,
  And aye she wrang her lily-white hands,
  Saying, I am a wearyd lady !

9 Up and spoke the king himsell,
  And oh, but he spok bonnie !
  'It 's ye may see by her countenance
  That she is Geordie's lady.'

10 Up and spoke a bold bluidy wretch,
  And oh, but he spoke boldly !
  'Tho [thou] should pay ten thousand pounds,
  Thou 'll never get thy own love Geordie.

11 'For I had but ae brother to mysell,
  I loved him best of any ;

They cutted his head from his fair bodie,
  And so will they thy love Geordie.'

12 Up and spoke the king again,
  And oh, but he spak bonnie !
  'If thou 'll pay me five thousand pound,
  I 'll gie thee hame thy love Geordie.'

13 She put her hand in her pocket,
  She freely paid the money,
  And she 's awa to the Gallows Wynd,
  To get her nain love Geordie.

14 As she came up the Gallows Wynd,
  The people was standing many ;
  The psalms was sung, and the bells was
    rung,
  And silks and cords hung bonnie.

15 The napkin was tyed on Geordie's face,
  And the hangman was just readie :
  'Hold your hand, you bluidy wretch !
  O hold it from my Geordie !
  For I 've got a remit from the king,
  That I 'll get my ain love Geordie.'

16 When he heard his lady's voice,
  He was baith blythe and merry :
  'There 's many ladies in this place ;
  Have not I a worthy ladie ?'

17 She mounted him on the bonnie dapple
    grey,
  Herself on the wee poney,
  And she rode home on his right hand,
  All for the pride o Geordie.

—————◆—————

G

Motherwell's Note-Book, p. 17, p. 10; from Mrs Rule,
Paisley, August 16, 1825. Apparently learned from a blind
aunt, pp. 1, 3.

1 THE weather it is clear, and the wind blaws
    fair,
  And yonder a boy rins bonnie,
  And he is awa to the gates of Hye,
  With a letter to my dear ladie.

2 The first line that she lookit on,
  She was baith red and rosy ;

She droppit down, and she dropt in a swoon,
  Crys, Och and alace for Geordie !

3 'Gar saddle to me the black, black horse ;
  The brown is twice as bonnie ;
  But I will neither eat nor drink
  Till I relieve my Geordie.'

4 When she cam to the canny Cannygate,
  Amang the puir folk many,
  She made the dollars flee amang them a',
  And she bade them plead for Geordie.

5 When she came to the tolbooth-gate,
   Amang the nobles many,
She made the red gold flee amang them a',
   And she bade them plead for Geordie.

6 Out and spoke the king himsell,
   'Wha's aught this weary lady?'
Out and spoke a pretty little page,
   'She's the Earl o Cassilis lady.'

7 'Has he killed? or has he slain?
   Or has he ravishd any?'
'He stole three geldings out o yon park,
   And sold them to Balleny.'

8 'Pleading is idle,' said the king,
   'Pleading is idle with any;
But pay you down five hundred pund.
   And tak you hame your Geordie.'

9 Some gave marks, and som gave crowns,
   Some gave dollars many;
She's paid down the five hundred pund,
   And she's relieved her Geordie.

10 The lady smiled in Geordie's face:
   'Geordie, I have bocht thee;
But down in yon green there had been bluidy
     breeks
   Or I had parted wi thee.'

H

Christie's Traditional Ballad Airs, II, 44; "long favorite in the counties of Aberdeen and Banff."

1 'WILL ye go to the Hielans, my bonny lad?
   Will ye go to the Hielans, Geordie?
Though ye tak the high road and I tak the
    low,
   I will be in the Hielans afore ye.'

2 He hadna been in the high Hielans
   A month but barely twa, O,
Till he was laid in prison strong,
   For hunting the king's deer and rae, O.

3 'O where will I get a bonny, bonny boy,
   That will run my errand cannie,
And gae quickly on to the bonny Bog o Gight,
   Wi a letter to my lady?'

4 'O here am I, a bonny, bonny boy,
   That will run your errand cannie,
And will gae on to the bonny Bog o Gight,
   Wi a letter to your lady.'

5 When she did get this broad letter,
   A licht, licht laugh gae she, O;
But before she read it to an end
   The saut tear was in her ee, O.

6 'O has he robbd? or has he stown?
   Or has he killëd ony?
Or what is the ill that he has done,
   That he's gaun to be hangd sae shortly?'

7 'He hasna robbd, he hasna stown,
   He hasna killëd ony;
But he has hunted the king's deer and rae,
   And he will be hangëd shortly.'

8 'Come saddle to me the bonny brown steed,
   For the black never rade sae bonny,
And I will gae on to Edinboro town
   To borrow the life o my Geordie.'

9 The first water-side that she cam to,
   The boatman wasna ready;
She gae anither skipper half-a-crown,
   To boat her oer the ferry.

10 When she cam on to Edinboro town,
   The poor stood thick and mony;
She dealt them money roun and roun,
   Bade them pray for the life o her Geordie.

11 When she gaed up the tolbooth-stair,
   She saw there nobles mony,
And ilka noble stood hat on head,
   But hat in hand stood Geordie.

12 Then out it spak an English lord,
   And vow, but he spake bonny!
'If ye pay down ten thousand crouns,
   Ye'll get the life o your Geordie.'

13 Some gae her marks, some gae her crouns,
   Some gae her guineas rarely,
Till she paid down ten thousand crouns,
   And she got the life o her Geordie.

14 Then out it spak an Irish lord,
      O wae befa his body!
   'It's a pity the knicht didna lose his head,
      That I micht hae gotten his lady.'

15 But out it spak the lady hersel,
      And vow, but she spak bonny!
   'The pock-marks are on your Irish face,
      You could not compare wi my Geordie!'

16 When she was in the saddle set,
      And on ahint her Geordie,

The bird on the bush neer sang sae sweet,
   As she sung to her love Geordie.

17 'First I was mistress o bonny Auchindown,
      And I was lady o a' Carnie,
   But now I have come to the bonny Bog o Gight,
      The wife o my true-love Geordie.

18 'If I were in the high Hielans,
      I would hear the white kye lowing;
   But I'd rather be on the bonny banks o Spey,
      To see the fish-boaties rowing.'

—————•—————

I

a. Buchan's MSS, II, 143. b. Kinloch MSS, VI, 1, in the handwriting of Joseph Robertson.

1 'I CHOOSED my love at the bonny yates of
      Gight,
   Where the birks an the flowers spring bony,
   But pleasures I had never one,
      But crosses very mony.

2 'First I was mistress of Pitfan
      And madam of Kincraigie,
   And now my name is bonny Lady Anne,
      And I am Gight's own lady.

3 'He does not use me as his wife,
      Nor cherish me as his lady,
   But day by day he saddles the grey,
      And rides off to Bignet's lady.'

4 Bignet he got word of this,
      That Gight lay wi his lady;
   He swore a vow, and kept it true,
      To be revengd on's body.

5 'Where will I get a bonny boy
      Will run my errand shortly,
   That woud run on to the bonny yates o Gight
      Wi a letter to my lady?'

6 Gight has written a broad letter,
      And seald it soon and ready,
   And sent it on to Gight's own yates,
      For to acquaint his lady.

7 The first of it she looked on,
      O dear! she smiled bonny;

But as she read it till an end
   The tears were thick an mony.

8 'Come saddle to me the black,' she says,
      'Come saddle him soon and shortly,
   Ere I ride down to Edinburgh town,
      Wi a lang side sark to Geordy.'

9 When she came to the boat of Leith,
      I wad she did na tarry;
   She gave the boatman a guinea o gold
      To boat her oer the ferry.

10 As she gaed oer the pier of Leith,
      Among the peerls many,
   She dealt the crowns and dukedoons,
      Bade them a' pray for Geordy.

11 As she gaed up the tolbooth-stair,
      Among the nobles many,
   Every one sat hat on head,
      But hat in hand stood Geordy.

12 'Has he brunt? or has he slain?
      Or has he robbèd any?
   Or has he done any other crime,
      That gars you head my Geordy?'

13 'He hasna brunt, he hasna slain,
      He hasna robbed any;
   But he has done another crime,
      For which he will pay dearly.'

14 In it comes him First Lord Judge,
      Says, George, I'm sorry for you;
   You must prepare yourself for death,
      For there'll be nae mercy for you.

15 In it comes him Second Lord Judge,
    Says, George I 'm sorry for you;
    You must prepare yourself for death,
        For there 'll be nae mercy for you.

16 Out it speaks Gight's lady herself,
    And vow, but she spake wordy!
    'Is there not a lord among you all
        Can plead a word for Geordy?'

17 Out it speaks the first Lord Judge:
    'What lady 's that amang you
    That speaks to us so boldly here,
        And bids us plead for Geordy?'

18 Out then spake a friend, her own,
    And says, It 's Gight's own lady,
    Who is come to plead her own lord's
        cause,
    To which she 's true and steady.

19 The queen, looking oer her shott-window,
    Says, Ann, I 'm sorry for you;
    If ye 'll tell down ten thousand crowns,
        Ye shall get home your Geordy.

20 She 's taen the hat out of his hand,
    And dear! it set her bonny;
    She 's beggd the red gold them among,
        And a' to borrow Geordy.

21 She turnd her right and round about
    Among the nobles many;
    Some gave her dollars, some her crowns,
        And some gave guineas many.

22 She spread her mantle on the floor,
    O dear! she spread it bonny,
    And she told down that noble sum;
        Says, Put on your hat, my Geordy.

23 But out it speaks him gleid Argyle,
    Says, Woe be to your body!
    I wish that Gight had lost his head,
        I should enjoyd his lady.

24 She looked oer her left shoulder,
    A proud look and a saucy;
    Says, Woe be to you, gleid Argyle!
        Ye 'll neer be like my Geordy.

25 'You 'll hae me to some writer's house,
    And that baith seen and shortly,
    That I may write down Gight's lament,
        And how I borrowed Geordy.'

26 When she was in her saddle set,
    And aye behind her Geordy,
    Birds neer sang blyther in the bush
        Than she behind her Geordy.

27 'O bonny George, but I love thee well,
    And O sae dear as I love thee!
    The sun and moon and firmament above
        Bear witness how I love thee!'

28 'O bonny Ann, but I love thee well,
    And O but sae dear as I love thee!
    The birds in the air, that fly together pair and
        pair,
    Bear witness, Ann, that I love thee!'

J

Buchan's Ballads of the North of Scotland, I, 133.

1 'FIRST I was lady o Black Riggs,
    And then into Kincraigie;
    Now I am the Lady o Gight,
        And my love he 's ca'd Geordie.

2 'I was the mistress o Pitfan,
    And madam o Kincraigie;
    But now my name is Lady Anne,
        And I am Gight's own lady.

3 'We courted in the woods o Gight,
    Where birks and flowrs spring bonny;
    But pleasures I had never one,
        But sorrows thick and mony.

4 'He never ownd me as his wife,
    Nor honourd me as his lady,
    But day by day he saddles the grey,
        And rides to Bignet's lady.'

5 When Bignet he got word of that,
    That Gight lay wi his lady,
    He 's casten him in prison strong,
        To ly till lords were ready.

6 'Where will I get a little wee boy,
    That is baith true and steady,
That will run on to bonny Gight,
    And bring to me my lady?'

7 'O here am I, a little wee boy,
    That is baith true and steady,
That will run to the yates o Gight,
    And bring to you your lady.'

8 'Ye 'll bid her saddle the grey, the grey,
    The brown rode neer so smartly;
Ye 'll bid her come to Edinbro town,
    A' for the life of Geordie.'

9 The night was fair, the moon was clear,
    And he rode by Bevany,
And stopped at the yates o Gight,
    Where leaves were thick and mony.

10 The lady lookd oer castle-wa,
    And dear, but she was sorry!
'Here comes a page frae Edinbro town;
    A' is nae well wi Geordie.

11 'What news, what news, my little boy?
    Come tell me soon and shortly;'
'Bad news, bad news, my lady,' he said,
    'They 're going to hang your Geordie.'

12 'Ye 'll saddle to me the grey, the grey,
    The brown rade neer so smartly;
And I 'll awa to Edinbro town,
    Borrow the life o Geordie.'

13 When she came near to Edinbro town,
    I wyte she didna tarry,
But she has mounted her grey steed,
    And ridden the Queen's Ferry.

14 When she came to the boat of Leith,
    I wat she didna tarry;
She gae the boatman a guinea o gowd
    To boat her ower the ferry.

15 When she came to the pier o Leith,
    The poor they were sae many;
She dealt the gowd right liberallie,
    And bade them pray for Geordie.

16 When she gaed up the tolbooth-stair,
    The nobles there were many:

And ilka ane stood hat on head,
    But hat in hand stood Geordie.

17 She gae a blink out-ower them a',
    And three blinks to her Geordie;
But when she saw his een fast bound,
    A swoon fell in this lady.

18 'Whom has he robbd? What has he stole?
    Or has he killed ony?
Or what 's the crime that he has done,
    His foes they are sae mony?'

19 'He hasna brunt, he hasna slain,
    He hasna robbed ony;
But he has done another crime,
    For which he will pay dearly.'

20 Then out it speaks Lord Montague,
    O wae be to his body!
'The day we hangd young Charles Hay,
    The morn we 'll head your Geordie.'

21 Then out it speaks the king himsell,
    Vow, but he spake bonny!
'Come here, young Gight, confess your sins,
    Let 's hear if they be mony.

22 'Come here, young Gight, confess your sins,
    See ye be true and steady;
And if your sins they be but sma,
    Then ye 'se win wi your lady.'

23 'Nane have I robbd, nought have I stown,
    Nor have I killed ony;
But ane o the king's best brave steeds,
    I sold him in Bevany.'

24 Then out it speaks the king again,
    Dear, but he spake bonny!
'That crime 's nae great; for your lady's sake,
    Put on your hat now, Geordie.'

25 Then out it speaks Lord Montague,
    O wae be to his body!
'There 's guilt appears in Gight's ain face,
    Ye 'll cross-examine Geordie.'

26 'Now since it all I must confess,
    My crimes' baith great and mony:
A woman abused, five orphan babes,
    I killd them for their money.'

27 Out it speaks the king again,
    And dear, but he was sorry!
'Your confession brings confusion,
    Take aff your hat now, Geordie.'

28 Then out it speaks the lady hersell,
    Vow, but she was sorry!
'Now all my life I'll wear the black,
    Mourn for the death o Geordie.'

29 Lord Huntly then he did speak out,
    O fair mot fa his body!
'I there will fight doublet alane
    Or ony thing ails Geordie.'

30 Then out it speaks the king again,
    Vow, but he spake bonny!
'If ye'll tell down ten thousand crowns,
    Ye'll buy the life o Geordie.'

31 She spread her mantle on the ground,
    Dear, but she spread it bonny!
Some gae her crowns, some ducadoons,
    And some gae dollars mony:
Then she tauld down ten thousand crowns,
    'Put on your hat, my Geordie.'

32 Then out it speaks Lord Montague,
    Wae be to his body!
'I wisht that Gight wanted the head;
    I might enjoyd his lady.'

33 Out it speaks the lady hersell,
    'Ye need neer wish my body;
O ill befa your wizzend snout!
    Woud ye compare wi Geordie?'

34 When she was in her saddle set,
    Riding the leys sae bonny,

The fiddle and fleet playd neer sae sweet
    As she behind her Geordie.

35 'O Geordie, Geordie, I love you well,
    Nae jealousie coud move me;
The birds in air, that fly in pairs,
    Can witness how I love you.

36 'Ye'll call for one, the best o clerks,
    Ye'll call him soon and shortly,
As he may write what I indite,
    A' this I've done for Geordie.'

37 He turned him right and round about,
    And high, high looked Geordie:
'A finger o Bignet's lady's hand
    Is worth a' your fair body.'

38 'My lands may a' be masterless,
    My babes may want their mother;
But I've made a vow, will keep it true,
    I'll be bound to no other.'

39 These words they causd a great dispute,
    And proud and fierce grew Geordie;
A sharp dagger he pulled out,
    And pierced the heart o's lady.

40 The lady's dead, and Gight he's fled,
    And left his lands behind him;
Altho they searched south and north,
    There were nane there coud find him.

41 Now a' that lived into Black Riggs,
    And likewise in Kincraigie,
For seven years were clad in black,
    To mourn for Gight's own lady.

———•———

K

Motherwell's MS., p. 370, as sung by Agnes Lyle's father.

1 'I HAVE eleven babes into the north,
    And the twelfth is in my body, O
And the youngest o them's in the nurse's arms,
    He neer yet saw his daddy.' O

2 Some gied her ducks, some gied her drakes,
    And some gied her crowns monie,
And she's paid him down five thousand pound,
    And she's gotten hame her Geordie.

L

Cunningham's Songs of Scotland, II, 186, 188 ; "from the recitation of Mrs Cunningham."

1 AND soon she came to the water broad,
    Nor boat nor barge was ready ;
  She turned her horse's head to the flood,
    And swam through at Queensferry.

2 But when she to the presence came,
    'Mang earls high and lordlie,
  There hat on head sat every man,
    While hat in hand stood Geordie.

M

Motherwell's Note-Book, pp. 2, 1; from Miss Brown, sister of Dr James Brown, of Glasgow.

WHEN he came out at the tolbooth-stair,
    He was baith red and rosy ;
  But gin he cam to the gallows-fit,
    He was wallourt like the lily.

N

Motherwell's Note-Book, p. 20.

I HAVE nine children in the west,
    The tenth ane 's in my bodie ;
  The eldest o them she never knew a man,
    And she knows not wha 's her daddy.

A. 4[2], 5[2]. menzie.
B. a. 8[3], 9[3], 19[2], 21[3]. & *for* an.
    13[2]. for *struck out before* Your.
    14[3]. O *has been altered from* If, *and is not very distinct.*
    25[2]. wi her?
    25[3]. Tell down, tell tell down.

    26. *Or,* She 's put her hand to her pocket,
        She 's pulld out ducats many,
        An she 's telld down, etc.

    27[1]. *Var.* she blessd.
    28[3,4]. *No indication that this is an imperfect stanza. The last line is nearly bound in, and not easy to read.*
    30[3]. Gar print, etc.
  b. *Variations written on the margin of* a.
    1[3]. The Laird of Gigh has killd a man.
    2[3]. That will gae rin to the yates of Gigh.
    7[1]. Burntisland sands *for* the water-side.
    8[1]. the water-yate.
    8[3]. dealt the red gold them amang.

    14. 'T was up than spak a gentleman,
        Was ca'd the Laird of Logie,
        War Gighie's head but on the blo[ck],
        If I had his fair ladie !'

    21[1]. the gude Argyle *for* a Scottish lord.
    21[2]. He 's been a friend to many.
C. a. "This song was taken down from a Miss Christy Robertson, Dunse, who sung it to a very pretty old tune. Being an old maid herself, she did not let it want any of the original plainture which I suppose the original air would have."
    The MS. of Thomas Wilkie is inscribed, at the beginning, Gattonside, 4th Sept., 1813 ; *at the end,* Bowden, 2d Sept., 1815.
    6[3]. goud *written over* guineas.
    8[1,2]. *Var.* six *for* ten, seventh *for* eleventh.
    10[1]. a kind-hearted man, *wanting in* b, *has evidently been supplied.*
    12[1,2]. *Supplied : originally only* A man spoke loud.
    12[3]. Geordie's *written over* his ; were *over* had been.
  b. 2[3]. shirt.   4[2]. And they saddled to her.
    6[3]. red goud. 7[1]. When she. 9[1]. Geight.
    10[1]. a kind-hearted man *wanting.*
    12[1,2]. A man spoke loud.
    13[4]. my *wanting.*
    14[2]. And herself.
D. 2[2]. goud and money *substituted for* hose and shoon *struck out.*
    9[2]. they *struck out before* was.

18³⁻⁶. *Written in two lines.*

E. b. *No account is given of the variations of the printed copy from the manuscript, but it is presumed that the larger ones were traditional.*

1³. And monie ane got broken heads.

2¹. she gaed.   2⁴. To pray.   3¹. into.

3³. And ilka ane.

After 3:

> Up bespak a Norlan lord,
> I wat he spak na bonnie;
> 'If ye 'll stay here a little while,
> Ye 'll see Geordie hangit shortly.'

4¹. Then up bespak.

4³,⁴. If ye 'll pay doun five hundred crowns,
Ye 'se get your true-love Geordie.

After 4:

> Some lent her guineas, some lent her crowns,
> Some lent her shillings monie,
> And she 's paid doun five hundred crowns,
> And she 's gotten her bonnie love Geordie.

5¹. hie steed.   5². ahint.

Burden, first line: My Geordie O, my Geordie O.

F. "Sung to a tune something similar to 'My Nannie O.'"

10³. 10000.   12³. 5000.

G. 8³, 9³. 500.

10³. breeks *is a corruption, for* bouks, A 14³.

I. a. 10³. crowns like duke o Downs: *cf.* b 21³, G 31³.

12⁴. gars your.

b. 1¹. I was courted a wife in the bonny woods of Fife.

1². and flowers.

1³. And pleasures I 've had never nane.

1⁴. I 've had mony.

2¹. was lady of bonny Pitfauns.   2². Then.

2³. is Lady.

2⁴. I 'm even.   3¹. He never owns me.

3². Nor loves me.   3³. But every day.

3⁴. rides to Pilbagnet's.

4¹. Pilbagnet he 's.

4². has lien wi.

4³. And he 's put him in prison strang.

4⁴. *Wanting.*

5³. That will rin on to Ythan side.

5⁴. Wi letters.

6. Now here am I, a bonny boy,
   Will rin your errand shortly,

That will rin on to Ythan side
   Wi letters to your ladye.

7¹. But when she looked the letter on.

7³. But ere: to an.   7⁴. tears fell.

8¹. Ye 'll saddle: said.

8². Tho the brown should ride never so bonny.

8³. I 'll go on to.

8⁴. To see how they 're using my.

9. As she rode down by the pier of Leith,
   The poor met her never so mony,
   And she dealt the red gold right liberally,
   And bade them pray well for her Geordie.

10. As she rode down by Edinbro town,
    The poor met her never so mony,
    And she dealt the red gold right liberallie,
    And bade them pray weel for her Geordie.

After 10:

> The king looked ower his castle-wa,
> And he spak seen and shortly;
> 'Now who is this,' said our liege the king,
> 'Deals the red gold sae largely?'

> Then up bespak a bonny boy,
> Was richt nigh to her Geordie;
> 'I 'll wager my life and a' my lan
> That it is Gicht's own ladye.'

11¹. Then she went down the toolbooth-stair.

11². all the nobles so.

11³. And every one had his hat on.

12–20. *Wanting.*

21. Then she went down the toolbooth-stair,
    Among all the nobles so many;
    Some gave her guineas, some gave her crowns,
    Some gave her dukedoons many,
    And she has paid down the jailor's fee,
    And now she enjoys her Geordie.

22–26. *Wanting.*

27. 'O bonnie George, I love you weel!
    O dear George, as I love you!
    The sun and the moon, go together roun and roun,
    Bear witness, dear George, how I love you!'

28. 'O bonnie Anne, I love you weel!
      Oh dear Anne, how I love you!
    The birds of the air, fly together pair and
          pair,
        Bear witness, dear Anne, how I love
          you!'

J. 13⁴. the queen's berry.
  26². crimes. *I suppose* crimes is *to be meant.*

K. "Of the preceding ballad [F], Agnes Lile says
      she has heard her father sing a different set,
      all of which she forgets except this, that
      there was nothing said of 'a bold bluidy
      wretch,' and in place of what is given to him
      in this version [F 10, 11], there were the
      two following stanzas." *Motherwell's MS.,*
      p. 370 f.
   2³. 5000.

APPENDIX

"A lamentable new ditty, made upon the death
of a worthy gentleman named George Stoole, dwell-
ing sometime on Gate-side Moore, and sometime
at New-Castle in Northumberland: with his peni-
tent end. To a delicate Scottish tune." Roxburghe
Collection, I, 186, 187. Roxburghe Ballads, ed.
W. Chappell, I, 576.   Previously printed by [Rit-
son], Northumberland Garland, Newcastle, 1793,
p. 33 (p. 43 of Haslewood's reprint, London, 1809),
and in Bell's Rhymes of Northern Bards, p. 162.

1 COME, you lusty northerne lads,
    That are so blith and bonny,
  Prepare your hearts to be full sad,
    To hear the end of Georgey.
      Heigh-ho, heigh-ho, my bon[n]y love,
      Heigh-ho, heigh-ho, my bonny!
      Heigh-ho, heigh-ho, my owne deare love,
        And God be with my Georgie!

2 When Georgie to his triall came,
    A thousand hearts were sorry;
  A thousand lasses wept full sore,
    And all for love of Georgy.

3 Some did say he would escape,
    Some at his fall did glory;
  But these were clownes and fickle friends,
    And none that lovëd Georgy.

4 Might friends have satisfide the law,
    Then Georgie would find many;
  Yet bravely did he plead for life,
    If mercy might be any.

5 But when this doughty carle was cast,
    He was full sad and sorry;
  Yet boldly did he take his death,
    So patiently dyde Georgie.

6 As Georgie went up to the gate,
    He tooke his leave of many;

He tooke his leave of his lard's wife,
  Whom he lovd best of any.

7 With thousand sighs and heavy lookes,
    Away from thence he parted
  Where he so often blith had beene,
    Though now so heavy-hearted.

8 He writ a letter with his owne hand,
    He thought he writ it bravely;
  He sent to New-castle towne,
    To his belovëd lady.

9 Wherein he did at large bewaile
    The occasion of his folly,
  Bequeathing life unto the law,
    His soule to heaven holy.

10 'Why, lady, leave to weepe for me!
     Let not my ending grieve ye!
   Prove constant to the man you love,
     For I cannot releeve ye.

11 'Out upon the, Withrington!
     And fie upon the, Phœnix!
   Thou hast put downe the doughty one
     That stole the sheepe from Anix.

12 'And fie on all such cruell carles
     Whose crueltie's so fickle
   To cast away a gentleman,
     In hatred, for so little!

13 'I would I were on yonder hill,
     Where I have beene full merry,
   My sword and buckeler by my side,
     To fight till I be weary.

14 'They well should know, that tooke me first,
     Though hopes be now forsaken,
   Had I but freedome, armes, and health,
     I'de dye ere I'de be taken.

15 'But law condemns me to my grave,
     They have me in their power;
   Ther's none but Christ that can mee save
     At this my dying houre.'

16 He calld his dearest love to him,
 When as his heart was sorry,
 And speaking thus, with manly heart,
  'Deare sweeting, pray for Georgie.'

17 He gave to her a piece of gold,
 And bade her give 't her barnes,
 And oft he kist her rosie lips,
  And laid him into her armes.

18 And comming to the place of death,
 He never changëd colour ;
 The more they thought he would looke pale,
  The more his veines were fuller.

19 And with a cheerefull countenance,
 Being at that time entreated
 For to confesse his former life,
  These words he straight repeated.

20 'I never stole no oxe nor cow,
 Nor never murdered any ;
 But fifty horse I did receive
  Of a merchant's man of Gory.

21 'For which I am condemnd to dye,
 Though guiltlesse I stand dying ;
 Deare gracious God, my soule receive !
  For now my life is flying.'

22 The man of death a part did act
 Which grieves mee tell the story ;
 God comfort all are comfortlesse,
  And did[e] so well as Georgie!
  Heigh-ho, heigh-ho, my bonny love,
  Heigh-ho, heigh[-ho], my bonny,
  Heigh-ho, heigh-ho, mine own true love,
   Sweet Christ receive my Georgie!

 1. *Burden to st.* 1 : honny *in the second line.*
 10³. the ney. 14². whoops. 14⁴. dye are.

"The Life and Death of George of Oxford. To a pleasant tune, called Poor Georgy." Roxburghe Collection, IV, 53, Pepys, II, 150, Jersey, I, 86, Huth, I, 150, according to Mr J. W. Ebsworth, Roxburghe Ballads, VII, 70, 1890. It was printed for P. Brooksby, whose time Mr Ebsworth gives as between 1671 and 1692.

1 As I went over London Bridge,
 All in a misty morning,
 There did I see one weep and mourn,
  Lamenting for her Georgy.
  His time it is past, his life it will not last,
   Alack and alas, there is no remédy!
  Which makes the heart within me ready to
   burst in three,
  To think on the death of poor Georgy.

2 'George of Oxford is my name,
 And few there 's but have known me ;
 Many a mad prank have I playd,
  But now they 've overthrown me.'

3 O then bespake the Lady Gray ;
 'I 'le haste me in the morning,
 And to the judge I 'le make my way,
  To save the life of Georgy.

4 'Go saddle me my milk-white steed,
 Go saddle me my bonny,
 That I may to New-Castle speed,
  To save the life of Georgy.'

5 But when she came the judge before,
 Full low her knee she bended ;
 For Georgy's life she did implore,
  That she might be befriended.

6 'O rise, O rise, fair Lady Gray,
 Your suit cannot be granted ;
 Content your self as well you may,
  For Georgy must be hanged.'

7 She wept, she waild, she [w]rung her hands,
 And ceasëd not her mourning ;
 She offerd gold, she offerd lands,
  To save the life of Georgy.

8 'I have travelld through the land,
 And met with many a man, sir,
 But, knight or lord, I bid him stand ;
  He durst not make an answer.

9 'The Brittain bold that durst deny
 His money for to tender,
 Though he were stout as valiant Guy,
  I forced him to surrender.

10 'But when the money I had got,
 And made him cry *peccavi*,
 To bear his charge and pay his shot,
  A mark or noble gave I.

11 'The ladies, when they had me seen,
 Would ner have been affrighted ;
 To take a dance upon the green
  With Georgy they delighted.

12 'When I had ended this our wake,
 And fairly them bespoken,
 Their rings and jewels would I take,
  To keep them for a token.'

13 The hue-and-cry for George is set,
 A proper handsome fellow,
 With diamond eyes as black as jet,
  And locks like gold so yellow.

14 Long it was, with all their art,
    Ere they could apprehend him,
    But at the last his valiant heart
    No longer could defend him.

15 'I ner stole horse nor mare in my life,
    Nor cloven foot, or any,
    But once, sir, of the king's white steeds,
    And I sold them to Bohemia.'

16 Georgy he went up the hill,
    And after followed many;
    Georgy was hanged in silken string,
    The like was never any.

The burden (here given with only the first stanza) is from time to time varied.
    3^1, 6^1. Oh. *After* 7. George's Confession.

210

BONNIE JAMES CAMPBELL

A. Herd's MSS, I, 40, II, 184.

B. Finlay's Scottish Ballads, 1808, I, xxxiii.

C. 'Bonnie George Campbell,' Smith's Scotish Minstrel, V, 42.

D. Cunningham's Songs of Scotland, III, 2.

A WAS copied by Sir Walter Scott (with slight variations) into a MS. at Abbotsford, 'Scottish Songs,' fol. 68 (1795–1806). The first half is printed from notes of Scott in Laing's edition of Sharpe's Ballad Book, pp. 143, 156 f, and to these two stanzas, nearly as here printed, there are added in the second case, p. 157, the following verses, which are evidently modern, with the exception of the last:

His hawk and his hounds they are wandered and gane,
His lady sits dowie and weary her lane,
His bairns wi greetin hae blinded their een,
His croft is unshorn, and his meadow grows green.

Scott subjoins, "I never heard more of this." He was familiar with Herd's MSS.

C, like many things in the Scotish Minstrel, has passed through editorial hands, whence the 'never return' of st. 4, and 'A plume in his helmet, a sword at his knee,' st. 5. This copy furnished the starting point for Allan Cunningham, III, 1, who, however, substitutes Finlay's 'wife' for the Minstrel's 'bryde,' and presents her with three bairns.

Motherwell made up his 'Bonnie George Campbell' (Minstrelsy, p. 44) from **B, C, D**. In a manuscript copied out by a granddaughter of Lord Woodhouselee (1840–50), **D** is combined with Cunningham's ballad.

Motherwell says that this ballad "is probably a lament for one of the adherents of the house of Argyle who fell in the battle of Glenlivet, stricken on Thursday, the third day of October, 1594." Sir Robert Gordon observes that Argyle lost in this battle his two cousins, Archibald and James Campbell: Genealogical History of Sutherland, p. 229. Maidment, Scotish Ballads, 1868, I, 240, chooses to think that "there can be little doubt" that the ballad refers to the murder of Sir John Campbell of Calder by one of his own surname, in 1591, and alters the title accordingly to 'Bonnie John Campbell.' Motherwell has at least a name to favor his supposition. But Campbells enow were killed, in battle or feud, before and after 1590, to forbid a guess as to an individual James or George grounded upon the slight data afforded by the ballad.

Motherwell's ballad is translated by Wolff, Halle der Völker, I, 79, Hausschatz, p. 225.

A

Herd's MSS, I, 40, II, 184.

1 O it's up in the Highlands,
    and along the sweet Tay,
Did bonie James Campbell
    ride monie a day.

2 Sadled and bridled,
    and bonie rode he;
Hame came horse, hame came sadle,
    but neer hame cam he.

3 And doun cam his sweet sisters,
    greeting sae sair,
And down cam his bonie wife,
    tearing her hair.

4 'My house is unbigged,
    my barn's unbeen,
My corn's unshorn,
    my meadow grows green.'

*   *   *   *   *

B

Finlay's Scottish Ballads, 1808, I, xxxiii.

1 Saddled and briddled
    and booted rade he;
Toom hame cam the saddle,
    but never cam he.

2 Down cam his auld mither,
    greetin fu sair,

And down cam his bonny wife,
    wringin her hair.

3 Saddled and briddled
    and booted rade he;
Toom hame cam the saddle,
    but never cam he.

C

Smith's Scotish Minstrel, V, 42.

1 Hie upon Hielands,
    and laigh upon Tay,
Bonnie George Campbell
    rode out on a day.

2 He saddled, he bridled,
    and gallant rode he,
And hame cam his guid horse,
    but never cam he.

3 Out cam his mother dear,
    greeting fu sair,
And out cam his bonnie bryde,
    riving her hair.

4 'The meadow lies green,
    the corn is unshorn,
But bonnie George Campbell
    will never return.'

5 Saddled and bridled
    and booted rode he,
A plume in his helmet,
    a sword at his knee.

6 But toom cam his saddle,
    all bloody to see,
Oh, hame cam his guid horse,
    but never cam he!

D

Cunningham's Songs of Scotland, III, 2, communicated by Mr Yellowlees.

1 High upon Highlands,
    and low upon Tay,

Bonnie George Campbell
    rode out on a day.

2 'My meadow lies green,
    and my corn is unshorn,
My barn is to build,
    and my babe is unborn.

A *is written, and* C *printed, in stanzas of four long lines.*
A. 1¹. *Sharpe,* 143, O *wanting.*
    1². *Scottish Songs and Sharpe, and wanting.*

2². *Scottish Songs,* and gallant, *as in* C.
2⁴. *Sharpe,* but hame cam na he.
4⁴. *Scottish Songs,* meadows grow green.

211

BEWICK AND GRAHAM

a. 'The Song of Bewick and Grahame,' a stall-copy, in octavo, British Museum, 11621. e. 1. (4.) **b.** 'A Remarkable and Memorable Song of Sir Robert Bewick and the Laird Graham,' broadside, Roxburghe Ballads, III, 624. **c.** 'A Remarkable and Memorable Song of Sir Robert Bewick and the Laird Graham,' broadside, Percy papers. **d.** 'Bewick and Graham's Garland,' M. Angus and Son, Newcastle, Bell Ballads, Abbotsford Library, P. 5, vol. i, No 60. **e.** Broadside, in "A Jolly Book of Garlands collected by John Bell in Newcastle," No 29, Abbotsford Library, E. 1. **f.** 'Bewick and Graham,' chapbook, Newcastle, W. Fordyce. **g.** "Scotch Ballads, Materials for Border Minstrelsy," No 145, Abbotsford. **h.** 'Chirstie Græme,' the same, No 89.

No copy of this ballad earlier than the last century is known to me. The Museum Catalogue gives a conjectural date of 1740 to a and of 1720 to b, and, conjecturally again, assigns both to Newcastle. c, d, e are also without date. c may be as old as b; d, e are at least not old, and f is of this century. The ballad was given under the title 'Græme and Bewick,' in Scott's Minstrelsy, 1803, III, 93, "from the recitation of a gentleman" who remembered it but imperfectly. In a succeeding edition, III, 66, 1833, deficiencies were partly supplied and some different readings adopted "from a copy obtained by the recitation of an ostler in Carlisle." The first copy (entitled 'Chirstie Græme') was sent Scott by William Laidlaw, January 3, 1803 (Letters, vol. i, No 78), as taken down by him from the singing of Mr Walter Grieve, in Craik, on Borthwick Water. It is preserved in "Scotch Ballads, Materials for Border Minstrelsy," No 89, Abbotsford (h); and in the same volume, No 145, is what is shown by internal evidence to be the ostler's copy (g). Both copies were indisputably derived from print, though h may have passed through several mouths. g agrees with b–f closely as to minute points of phraseology which it is difficult to believe that a reciter would have retained. It looks more like an immediate, though faulty, transcript from print. Of many deviations, though most may be chargeable to a bad copyist, or, if one pleases, a bad memory, others indicate an original which differed in some particulars from b–f; and the same may perhaps be true of h, which is, however, of only very trifling value.*

'The Brothers-in-Arms,' Maidment, Scotish Ballads and Songs, 1868, II, 150, is Scott's later copy.

Old Graham and old Bewick are drinking together at Carlisle. Graham proposes the health of their respective sons. Bewick demurs. Young Graham is no peer for young Bewick, who is good at both books and arms, whereas Graham is no scholar. Old Graham goes home mortified and angry, repeats to his son Christy what Bewick had said, and bids him, as he would have his blessing, prove that he can at least hold his own in a fight with young Bewick. Christy is 'faith and troth,' or sworn-brother, to young Bewick, and begs his father to forbear. The father insists; Christy may make his choice, to fight with young Bewick or with himself. Christy, upon reflection, concludes that it would be a less crime to kill his sworn-brother than to kill his father, but swears that, should it be his lot to kill his friend, he will never come home alive. He arms himself and goes to seek his comrade. Bewick, who has been teaching his five scholars their fence, and apparently also their psalms, is walking in his father's close, with his sword under his arm, and sees a man in armor riding towards him. Recognizing Graham, he welcomes him affectionately. Graham informs him that he has come to fight with him, rehearses the scene with old Graham, and puts by all his friend's remonstrances and the suggestion that the fathers may be reconciled through arbitrators. Forced to fight, Bewick vows, as Graham had done, that, if it be his fortune to kill his brother, he will never go home alive. Graham throws off

his armor that he may have no advantage; they fight two hours with no result, and then Graham gives Bewick one of those 'ackward' strokes which have determined several duels in foregoing ballads. The wound is deadly; Bewick intreats Graham to fly the country; Graham swears that his vow shall be kept, leaps on his sword and is the first to die. Old Bewick comes up and is disposed to congratulate his son on his victory. Young Bewick begs him to make one grave for both, and to lay young Graham on the sunny side, for he had been the better man. The two fathers indulge in exclamations of grief.

I am persuaded that there was an older and better copy of this ballad than those which are extant. The story is so well composed, proportion is so well kept, on the whole, that it is reasonable to suppose that certain passages (as stanzas 3, 4, 50) may have suffered some injury. There are also phrases which are not up to the mark of the general style, as the hack-rhymester lines at 7^3, 19^2. But it is a fine-spirited ballad as it stands, and very infectious.

"The ballad is remarkable," observes Sir Walter Scott, "as containing probably the very latest allusion to the institution of brotherhood in arms." And he goes on to say: "The quarrel of the two old chieftains over their wine is highly in character. Two generations have not elapsed [1803] since the custom of drinking deep and taking deadly revenge for slight offences produced very tragical events on the border; to which the custom of going armed to festive meetings contributed not a little."

Scott's later edition is translated by Loève-Veimars, p. 323; by Rosa Warrens, Schottische Volkslieder der Vorzeit, p. 99, No 22.

---

* Somebody, perhaps J., the editor of The Common-Place Book of Ancient and Modern Ballad, etc., Edinburgh, 1824, attempted an improvement of the later edition of Scott's ballad. The recension was used by Loève-Veimars for his translation, and is given in his Popular Ballads and Songs from Tradition, Manuscripts, and Scarce Editions, Paris, 1825, p. 71. This copy, with variations, is found in the Campbell MSS, I, 348. The alterations are mostly trivial.

1 OLD Grahame [he] is to Carlisle gone,
    Where Sir *Robert* Bewick there met he;
  In arms to the wine they are gone,
    And drank till they were both merry.

2 Old Grahame he took up the cup,
    And said, 'Brother Bewick, here's to thee;
  And here's to our two sons at home,
    For they live best in our country.'

3 'Nay, were thy son as good as mine,
    And of some books he could but read,
  With sword and buckler by his side,
    To see how he could save his head,

4 'They might have calld two bold breth-
      ren
    Where ever they did go or ride;
  They might [have] been calld two bold
      brethren,
    They might have crackd the Border-side.

5 'Thy son is bad, and is but a lad,
    And bully to my son cannot be;
  For my son Bewick can both write and read,
    And sure I am that cannot he.'

6 'I put him to school, but he would not learn,
    I bought him books, but he would not read;
  But my blessing he's never have
    Till I see how his hand can save his head.'

7 Old Grahame called for an account,
    And he askd what was for to pay;
  There he paid a crown, so it went round,
    Which was all for good wine and hay.

8 Old Grahame is into the stable gone,
    Where stood thirty good steeds and three;
  He's taken his own steed by the head,
    And home rode he right wantonly.

9 When he came home, there did he espy,
    A loving sight to spy or see,
  There did he espy his own three sons,
    Young Christy Grahame, the foremost was
      he.

10 There did he espy his own three sons,
    Young Christy Grahame, the foremost was
      he:
  'Where have you been all day, father,
    That no counsel you would take by me?'

11 'Nay, I have been in Carlisle town,
    Where Sir Robert Bewick there met me;
  He said thou was bad, and calld thee a lad,
    And a baffled man by thou I be.

12 'He said thou was bad, and calld thee a lad,
    And bully to his son cannot be;
  For his son Bewick can both write and read,
    And sure I am that cannot thee.

13 'I put thee to school, but thou would not learn,
    I bought thee books, but thou would not read;
  But my blessing thou's never have
    Till I see with Bewick thou can save thy
      head.'

14 'Oh, pray forbear, my father dear;
    That ever such a thing should be!
  Shall I venture my body in field to fight
    With a man that's faith and troth to me?'

15 'What's that thou sayst, thou limmer loon?
    Or how dare thou stand to speak to me?
  If thou do not end this quarrel soon,
    Here is my glove thou shalt fight me.'

16 Christy stoopd low unto the ground,
    Unto the ground, as you'll understand:
  'O father, put on your glove again,
    The wind hath blown it from your hand.'

17 'What's that thou sayst, thou limmer loon?
    Or how dare thou stand to speak to me?
  If thou do not end this quarrel soon,
    Here is my hand thou shalt fight me.'

18 Christy Grahame is to his chamber gone,
    And for to study, as well might be,
  Whether to fight with his father dear,
    Or with his bully Bewick he.

19 'If it be [my] fortune my bully to kill,
    As you shall boldly understand,
  In every town that I ride through,
    They'll say, There rides a brotherless man!

20 'Nay, for to kill my bully dear,
    I think it will be a deadly sin;
  And for to kill my father dear,
    The blessing of heaven I neer shall win.

21 'O give me your blessing, father,' he said,
    'And pray well for me for to thrive;

If it be my fortune my bully to kill,
   I swear I 'll neer come home alive.'

22 He put on his back a good plate-jack,
   And on his head a cap of steel,
   With sword and buckler by his side ;
   O gin he did not become them well !

23 'O fare thee well, my father dear !
   And fare thee well, thou Carlisle town !
   If it be my fortune my bully to kill,
   I swear I 'll neer eat bread again.'

24 Now we 'll leave talking of Christy Grahame,
   And talk of him again belive ;
   But we will talk of bonny Bewick,
   Where he was teaching his scholars five.

25 Now when he had learnd them well to fence,
   To handle their swords without any doubt,
   He 's taken his own sword under his arm,
   And walkd his father's close about.

26 He lookd between him and the sun,
   To see what farleys he coud see ;
   There he spy'd a man with armour on,
   As he came riding over the lee.

27 'I wonder much what man yon be
   That so boldly this way does come ;
   I think it is my nighest friend,
   I think it is my bully Grahame.

28 'O welcome, O welcome, bully Grahame !
   O man, thou art my dear, welcome !
   O man, thou art my dear, welcome !
   For I love thee best in Christendom.'

29 'Away, away, O bully Bewick,
   And of thy bullyship let me be !
   The day is come I never thought on ;
   Bully, I 'm come here to fight with thee.'

30 'O no ! not so, O bully Grahame !
   That eer such a word should spoken be !
   I was thy master, thou was my scholar :
   So well as I have learnëd thee.'

31 'My father he was in Carlisle town,
   Where thy father Bewick there met he ;
   He said I was bad, and he calld me a lad,
   And a baffled man by thou I be.'

32 'Away, away, O bully Grahame,
   And of all that talk, man, let us be !
   We 'll take three men of either side
   To see if we can our fathers agree.'

33 'Away, away, O bully Bewick,
   And of thy bullyship let me be !
   But if thou be a man, as I trow thou art,
   Come over this ditch and fight with me.'

34 'O no ! not so, my bully Grahame !
   That eer such a word should spoken be !
   Shall I venture my body in field to fight
   With a man that 's faith and troth to me ?'

35 'Away, away, O bully Bewick,
   And of all that care, man, let us be !
   If thou be a man, as I trow thou art,
   Come over this ditch and fight with me.'

36 'Now, if it be my fortune thee, Grahame, to
      kill,
   As God's will 's, man, it all must be ;
   But if it be my fortune thee, Grahame, to kill,
   'T is home again I 'll never gae.'

37 'Thou art of my mind then, bully Bewick,
   And sworn-brethren will we be ;
   If thou be a man, as I trow thou art,
   Come over this ditch and fight with me.'

38 He flang his cloak from [off] his shoulders,
   His psalm-book out of his hand flang he,
   He clapd his hand upon the hedge,
   And oer lap he right wantonly.

39 When Grahame did see his bully come,
   The salt tear stood long in his eye :
   'Now needs must I say that thou art a man,
   That dare venture thy body to fight with me.

40 'Now I have a harness on my back ;
   I know that thou hath none on thine ;
   But as little as thou hath on thy back,
   Sure as little shall there be on mine.'

41 He flang his jack from off his back,
   His steel cap from his head flang he ;
   He 's taken his sword into his hand,
   He 's tyed his horse unto a tree.

42 Now they fell to it with two broa[d swords],
   For two long hours fought Bewick [and he] ;

Much sweat was to be seen on them both,
    But never a drop of blood to see.

43 Now Grahame gave Bewick an ackward stroke,
    An ackward stroke surely struck he ;
He struck him now under the left breast,
    Then down to the ground as dead fell he.

44 'Arise, arise, O bully Bewick,
    Arise, and speak three words to me !
Whether this be thy deadly wound,
    Or God and good surgeons will mend thee.'

45 'O horse, O horse, O bully Grahame,
    And pray do get thee far from me !
Thy sword is sharp, it hath wounded my heart,
    And so no further can I gae.

46 'O horse, O horse, O bully Grahame,
    And get thee far from me with speed !
And get thee out of this country quite !
    That none may know who 's done the deed.'

47 'O if this be true, my bully dear,
    The words that thou dost tell to me,
The vow I made, and the vow I 'll keep ;
    I swear I 'll be the first that die.

48 Then he stuck his sword in a moody-hill,
    Where he lap thirty good foot and three ;
First he bequeathed his soul to God,
    And upon his own sword-point lap he.

49 Now Grahame he was the first that died,
    And then came Robin Bewick to see ;
'Arise, arise, O son !' he said,
    'For I see thou 's won the victory.

50 'Arise, arise, O son !' he said,
    ' For I see thou 's won the victory :'
'[Father, co]uld ye not drunk your wine at
      home,
    [And le]tten me and my brother be ?

51 'Nay, dig a grave both low and wide,
    And in it us two pray bury ;
But bury my bully Grahame on the sun-side,
    For I 'm sure he 's won the victory.'

52 Now we 'll leave talking of these two brethren,
    In Carlisle town where they lie slain,
And talk of these two good old men,
    Where they were making a pitiful moan.

53 With that bespoke now Robin Bewick :
    ' O man, was I not much to blame ?
I have lost one of the liveliest lads
    That ever was bred unto my name.'

54 With that bespoke my good lord Grahame :
    ' O man, I have lost the better block ;
I have lost my comfort and my joy,
    I have lost my key, I have lost my lock.

55 'Had I gone through all Ladderdale,
    And forty horse had set on me,
Had Christy Grahame been at my back,
    So well as he woud guarded me.'

56 I have no more of my song to sing,
    But two or three words to you I 'll name ;
But 't will be talk'd in Carlisle town
    That these two [old] men were all the blame.

---

a. The Song of Bewick and Grahame : containing an account how the Lord Grahame met with Sir Robert Bewick in the town of Carlisle, and, going to the tavern, a dispute happened betwixt them which of their sons was the better man ; how Grahame rode away in a passion, and, meeting with his son, persuaded him to go and fight young Bewick, which he did accordingly ; and how it prov'd both their deaths.

Licensd and enterd according to order.

2⁴. love. b—g *have* live ; h, like us.
11⁴. thou. *Cf.* 31⁴. 13⁴. you can.
18². might he.
25¹, 36¹, 40¹, 42¹, 43¹, 49¹. Nay *for* Now.
37¹. art in mind then.
    b, c, e, f. art then of my mind.
40²⁴. of *for* on. 41⁸. spear *for* sword :
    so b—f, *but* g, k, sword.
42¹⁺², 50³⁺⁴. *The top corner is torn off : cf.* b—f.
b—f. A remarkable and memorable Song [f,
    Remarkable and memorable History] of

Sir Robert Bewick and the Laird Graham, giving an account of Laird Graham's meeting with Sir Robert Bewick in the town of Carlisle, and, they going to a tavern, a dispute happened betwixt them which of their sons was the best man. How Graham rode home in a passion, and caused his son to fight young Bewick, which proved their deaths.

1¹. b, c, d, e. he is. f. he has.

1⁴. b. drink. 2¹. d. he *wanting*.

2⁴. live best. 3⁴. b. safe. 4². do go.

4³. might have. 5¹. he is. 5³,⁴. *Wanting*

6⁴. how he can. 7¹. he calld.

7². what there was to.

7⁴. b, d, e, f. good *wanting*. 8¹. is to.

9¹. came there he did. 9³. d. spy.

10¹,². *Wanting.* 10⁴. you 'll take. 11¹. been at.

11³,⁴. d. *Wanting.*

11³. f. wast. b. calld thou. e. he called.

11⁴. b. a *wanting*. b, c, e, f. by thee.

12¹. d, f. wast. e. he called.

12⁴. b, c, d, e. cannot be.

13¹. b, d, f. wouldst.

13². b, d, e, f. wouldst. 13³. e. blessings.

13⁴. d, e. see if with. b, d, e, f. thou canst.

14³. d. in a.

15¹. d. you say, you. e. thou says.

15². d, e, f. dare you. 16¹. d, e. Christy he.

17². dare you. f. Or *wanting*. 17³. If you.

18². might be. c. for no study, *wrongly*.

19¹. be my. 19³. d. town as.

20¹. my brother. 20². it were.

20⁴. d. blessings. 21². me then to.

21⁴. b, d, e, f. I shall. b—f. never.

22¹. good old. b, d, e, f. jacket. c. jack.

22⁴. weel. 23¹. b. O fare the *torn away*.

d. weel. 23². b. And fa *torn away*.

23⁴. c, d, e. I 'll swear.

24¹. leave off. d, e, f. we leave.

24². b, c, f. of them.

25¹. b, d, e, f. Now, c. Nay.

b—f. learned: well *wanting*.

25³. own *wanting*.

26¹. b, c. between them.

26³. b, c, d, e. espy'd. f. And espied.

27². doth. 27³. b. is *wanting*.

28¹. my bully.

29³. b, c, e, f. come that I neer. d. come neer.

29⁴. b, c, d, e. come hither. 30¹. d. my bully.

30³. b, d, e, f. and thou wast. c. and thou was.

30⁴. b, c, d. as *wanting*. b. have *wanting*.

31³. d, e, f. he *wanting*. 31⁴. d. a *wanting*. f. by you.

32². all *wanting*.

32³. on either. b, c. make.

33³, 35³, 37³. b, c, e. I true.

33³. d. thou be. 34³. d. in a.

34⁴. b. truth. 35¹. thou *for* O.

35². all that *wanting*.

36¹. b, c, d, e. Nay. f. Now.

36². will. b, c. almost.

36³. f. But *wanting*. 36⁴. d. I'd.

37¹. b, c, e, f. art then of my mind. d. then *wanting*.

37². d, e, f. we will.

38¹. from off. d. flung. b. shoulder.

38². b, c, d, e. book from off (d, from) his shoulders.

39². tears. 39³. that *wanting*. 40¹. Nay.

40². none on. f. hast. 40³. c, d, f. hast.

40⁴. be on. f. Sure *wanting*. 41¹. jacket.

41². b, c, d, e. from off. f. cap of steel.

41³. his spear. 42¹. b, d, e, f. Now. c. Nay. b—f. broad swords.

42². and he. 43¹. b, d, e, f. Now. c. Nay.

43³. f. now *wanting*.

44³. d, e. Were this to be.

45³. b, c, f. it is. d. has wounded.

46⁴. That not one. 47¹. Oh. 47². b, d, e. doth.

47⁴. d, e, f. first to.

48¹. b, c. struck. b—f. mould hill.

48². b, c, d, e. Then he leapd. f. And he leapt. b—f. feet.

48⁴. sword leapd he.

49¹. b, d, e, f. Now. c. Nay.

49². then Robert (d, e, f, Sir Robert) Bewick came. c. see *wanting*.

50¹,². d, f. *Wanting.*

50³. b, c, d, e. Father, could you not drink. f. could not you drink.

50⁴. And letten : my bully. 51¹. f. Now.

52¹. leave of, off : these bold. 52². they were.

53¹. b. c, d, e. Robert. b. Berwick.

54¹. d, e, f. laird. 55¹. Lauderdale.

55². d. horses set. 55⁴. well he would have.

56². b, d, e, f. to you *wanting*. f. I will.

56³. f. But *wanting*. 56⁴. b, c. two old.

Readings found only in f *which have an editorial character.*

6³. he shall.

12⁴. And sure I cannot say that of thee.

13³. thou shalt.

13⁴. Till with Bewick thou canst.

22⁴. And O he did become.

29[4]. Bully *wanting:* I'm hither come to fight
  with thee.

38[2]. psalm-book from his pouch.

44[3]. Is this to be thy deadly wound.

53[1]. And now up spake Sir Robert Bewick.

54[1]. With that up spake my good laird.

g. (*Only partially collated.*) 1[2]. he is.

2[2]. Billy Bewick.

2[4]. leave (= live).   5[2]. billy, *and always.*

5[3,4]. *Wanting.*

6[4]. see with Bewick he can.   *Cf.* 13[4].

7[4]. good wine, *as in* a, c.

10[1,2]. *Wanting.*   10[4]. you will take.

12[4]. cannot be.   13[1,2]. would.   13[3]. thou shall.

14[2]. should spoken be.   *Cf.* 30[2].

20[1]. my brother.

20[2]. think that were.   22[1]. good ould jack.

24[1]. leave of.

25[1], 36[1], 40[1], 42[1], 43[1], 44[1]. Nay.

25[1]. had teacht.   28[1]. my billey.   30[1]. my billy.

30[4]. have teacht.   31[4]. by thou.

35[1]. thou *for* O.   36[2]. will.   36[3]. Nay *for* But.

37[1]. then *wanting.*   38[1]. from of his back.

38[2]. book from his shoulders.   39[2]. tear.

39[4]. in feald to fight.   40[4]. Sure *wanting.*

41[1]. jacket from.

41[3]. sword *for* spear: *much better.*

48[1]. mould hill.   48[2]. feet.   48[4]. lept.

50[4]. my billy.   51[3]. sunney side.

52[1]. leave of: thease bould.   52[2]. they were.

53[4]. was born.   55[4]. well he would a.

56[4]. two old.

h. 2[4]. like us best.   5[2]. billie, *and always.*

41[3]. he stuck his sword into the grund.

48[1]. moudie hill.   51[3]. on the sunny side.

The Common Place Book of Ancient and Modern Ballad, etc., p. 292, *gives* 18 *thus:*

Then Christie Graham's to his chamber gane,
  And his thoughts within him made him sick,
Whether he suld fight wi his auld father,
  Or wi his billie, learnd Bewick.

212

THE DUKE OF ATHOLE'S NURSE

A. Cromek's Select Scotish Songs, 1810, II, 196.

B. Skene MS., p. 10.

C. 'Duke of Athole's Gates,' Kinloch MSS, I, 335.

D. 'Duke of Athole's Nurse,' Kinloch MSS, I, 337.

E. a. 'Duke o Athole's Nourice,' Kinloch MSS, VII, 171. b. 'The Duke of Athol's Nourice,' Kinloch's Ancient Scottish Ballads, p. 127.

F. 'The Duke of Athole's Nurse.' a. Buchan's Ballads of the North of Scotland, II, 23. b. Christie's Traditional Ballad Airs, I, 80.

M, N of No 214 have stanzas belonging here. M 1, 3 = A 3, 5; N 4, 6, 7 = A 2, 4, 5. A 1[1,2], 2 nearly, are found in No 213, 'Sir James the Rose,' 4[1,2], 5, where also there is a treacherous leman.

B. The 'new-come darling' of the Duke of Athole offers the duke's nurse a ring if she will carry a word to her leman. This leman had previously been the nurse's lover, and comes to tell her that another has now possession of his heart. The nurse plans revenge, but dissimulates; she tells the faithless fellow to go for the night to an ale-house, and she will meet him there in the morning. But instead of the nurse he sees a band of men, her seven brothers (nine brothers, F), coming towards the house, and easily divines that they are come to slay him. He appeals to the landlady to save him; she dresses him in woman's clothes and sets him to her baking. The seven brothers ask the landlady if she had a lodger last night; they are come to pay his reckoning. A lodger had been there, but he did not stay till morning. They search the house and stab the beds, often passing the sham baking-maid without detecting the disguise.

C–F have nothing about the 'new-come darling,' but begin at once with the nurse, who longs for her lover, and would give her half-year's fee to see him. He appears, and avows to her that another woman has gained his heart.

———

A

Cromek's Select Scotish Songs, 1810, II, 196, 194; sent, with other fragments, by Robert Burns to William Tytler, August, 1790; stanzas 2–6.

* * * * * * *

1 'WHERE shall I gang, my ain true love?
  Where shall I gang to hide me?
For weel ye ken i yere father's bowr
  It wad be death to find me.'

2 'O go you to yon tavern-house,
  An there count owre your lawin,
An, if I be a woman true,
  I 'll meet you in the dawin.'

3 O he 's gone to yon tavern-house,
  An ay he counted his lawin,
An ay he drank to her guid health
  Was to meet him in the dawin.

4 O he 's gone to yon tavern-house,
  An counted owre his lawin,
When in there cam three armed men,
  To meet him in the dawin.

5 'O woe be unto woman's wit!
  It has beguiled many;
She promised to come hersel,
  But she sent three men to slay me.'

———

B

Skene MS., p. 10; taken down in the north of Scotland, 1802–3.

1 'YE are the Duke of Athol's nurse,
  And I 'm the new-come darling;
I 'll gie you my gay gold rings
  To get ae word of my leman.'

2 'I am the Duke of Athol's nurse,
  And ye 're the new-come darling;
Keep well your gay gold rings,
  Ye sall get twa words o your leman.'

3 He leand oure his saddle-bow,
  It was not for to kiss her:
'Anither woman has my heart,
  And I but come here to see ye.'

4 'If anither woman has your heart,
  O dear, but I am sorry!
Ye hie you down to yon ale house,
  And stay untill 't be dawing,

And if I be a woman true
  I 'll meet you in the dawing.'

5 He did him down to yon ale-house,
  And drank untill 't was dawing;
He drank the bonnie lassie's health
  That was to clear his lawing.

6 He lookit out of a shot-window,
  To see if she was coming,
And there he seed her seven brithers,
  So fast as they were running!

7 He went up and down the house,
  Says, 'Landlady, can you save me?
For yonder comes her seven brithers,
  And they are coming to slay me.'

8 So quick she minded her on a wile
  How she might protect him!
She dressd him in a suit of woman's attire
  And set him to her baking.

9 'Had you a quarterer here last night,
   Or staid he to the dawing?
Shew us the room the squire lay in,
   We are come to clear his lawing.'

10 'I had a quarterer here last night,
   But he staid not to the dawing;

He called for a pint, and paid as he went,
   You have nothing to do with his lawing.'

11 They searchd the house baith up and down,
   The curtains they spaird not to rive em,
And twenty times they passd
   The squire at his baking.

C

Kinloch MSS, I, 335.

1 As I went down by the Duke of Athole's gates,
   Where the bells of the court were ringing,
And there I heard a fair maid say,
   O if I had but ae sight o my Johnie!

2 'O here is your Johnie just by your side;
   What have ye to say to your Johnie?
O here is my hand, but anither has my heart,
   So ye 'll never get more o your Johnie.'

3 'O ye may go down to yon ale-house,
   And there do sit till the dawing;
And call for the wine that is very, very fine,
   And I 'll come and clear up your lawing.'

4 So he 's gane down to yon ale-house,
   And he has sat till the dawing;
And he 's calld for the wine that 's very, very
      fine,
   But she neer cam to clear up his lawing.

5 Lang or the dawing he oure the window looks,
   To see if his true-love was coming,
And there he spied twelve weel armd boys,
   Coming over the plainstanes running.

6 'O landlady, landlady, what shall I do?
   For my life it 's not worth a farthing!'

'O young man,' said she, 'tak counsel by me,
   And I will be your undertaking.

7 'I will clothe you in my own body-clothes
   And I 'll send you like a girl to the baking:'
And loudly, loudly they rapped at the door,
   And loudly, loudly they rappëd.

8 'O had you any strangers here late last night?
   Or were they lang gane or the dawing?
O had you any strangers here late last night?
   We are now come to clear up his lawing.'

9 'O I had a stranger here late last night,
   But he was lang gane or the dawing;
He called for a pint, and he paid it as he went,
   And ye 've no more to do with his lawing.'

10 'O show me the room that your stranger lay in,
   If he was lang gane or the dawing:'
She showed them the room that her stranger
      lay in,
   But he was lang gane or the dawing.

11 O they stabbed the feather-bed all round and
      round,
   And the curtains they neer stood to tear
      them;
And they gade as they cam, and left a' things
      undone,
   And left the young squire by his baking.

D

Kinloch MSS, I, 337.

1 As I cam in by the Duke of Athole's gate,
   I heard a fair maid singing,
Wi a bonny baby on her knee,
   And the bells o the court were ringing.

2 'O it 's I am the Duke of Athole's nurse,
   And the place does well become me;
But I would gie a' my half-year's fee
   Just for a sight o my Johnie.

*   *   *   *   *   *   *

3 'If ye 'll gae down to yon ale-house,
   And stop till it be dawing,
   And ca for a pint o the very, very best,
   And I 'll come and clear up your lawing.'

4 O he 's gane down to yon ale-house,
   And stopt till it was dawing;
   He ca'd for a pint o the very, very best,
   But she cam na to clear up his lawing.

5 He looked out at the chamber-window,
   To see if she was coming;
   And there he spied ten armed men,
   Across the plain coming running.

6 'O landlady, landlady, what shall I do?
   For my life is not worth a farthing;
   I paid you a guinea for my lodging last
      night,
   But I fear I 'll never see sun shining.'

7 'If ye will be advised by me,
   I 'll be your undertaking;
   I 'll dress you up in my ain body-clothes
   And set you to the baking.'

8 So loudly at the door they rapt,
   So loudly are they calling,
   'O had you a stranger here last night,
   Or is he within your dwalling?'

9 'O I had a stranger here last night,
   But he wos gane or dawing;
   He ca'd for a pint, and he paid it or he went,
   And I hae nae mair to do wi his lawing.'

10 They stabd the feather-beds round and round,
   The curtains they spared na to tear them;
   But they went as they came, and left a' things
      undone,
   And the young man busy baking.

E

a. Kinloch MSS, VII, 171; from the recitation of Mrs
Charles, Torry.   b. Kinloch's Ancient Scottish Ballads,
p. 127.

1 'I AM the Duke o Athole's nurse,
   My part does weill become me,
   And I wad gie aw my half-year's fee
   For ae sicht o my Johnie.'

2 'Keep weill, keep weill your half-year's fee,
   For ye 'll soon get a sicht o your Johnie;
   But anither woman has my heart,
   And I 'm sorry for to leave ye.'

3 'Ye 'll dow ye doun to yon changehouse,
   And ye 'll drink till the day be dawin;
   At ilka pint's end ye 'll drink my health out,
   And I 'll come and pay for the lawin.'

4 Ay he ranted and he sang,
   And drank till the day was dawin,

And ay he drank the bonnie lassy's health
   That was coming to pay the lawin.

5 He spared na the sack, tho it was dear,
   The wine nor the sugar-candy,

   .   .   .   .

   .   .   .   .

6 He 's dune him to the shot-window,
   To see an she was coming,
   And there he spied twelve armed men,
   That oure the plain cam rinning.

7 He 's dune him doun to the landlady,
   To see gin she wad protect him;
   She 's buskit him up into women's claiths
   And set him till a baking.

8 Sae loudly as they rappit at the yett,
   Sae loudly as they callit,
   'Had ye onie strangers here last nicht,
   That drank till the day was dawin?'

   *   *   *   *   *   *   *

F

a. Buchan's Ballads of the North of Scotland, II, 23.
b. Christie's Traditional Ballad Airs, I, 80.

1 As I gaed in yon greenwood-side,
  I heard a fair maid singing;
Her voice was sweet, she sang sae complete
  That all the woods were ringing.

2 'O I'm the Duke o Athole's nurse,
  My post is well becoming;
But I woud gie a' my half-year's fee
  For ae sight o my leman.'

3 'Ye say, ye're the Duke o Athole's nurse,
  Your post is well becoming;
Keep well, keep well your half-year's fee,
  Ye 'se hae twa sights o your leman.'

4 He leand him ower his saddle-bow
  And cannilie kissd his dearie:
'Ohon and alake! anither has my heart,
  And I darena mair come near thee.'

5 'Ohon and alake! if anither hae your heart,
  These words hae fairly undone me;
But let us set a time, tryst to meet again,
  Then in gude friends you will twine me.

6 'Ye will do you down to yon tavern-house
  And drink till the day be dawing,
And, as sure as I ance had a love for you,
  I'll come there and clear your lawing.

7 'Ye'll spare not the wine, altho it be fine,
  Nae Malago, tho it be rarely,
But ye'll aye drink the bonnie lassie's health
  That's to clear your lawing fairly.'

8 Then he's done him down to yon tavern-house
  And drank till day was dawing,
And aye he drank the bonny lassie's health
  That was coming to clear his lawing.

9 And aye as he birled, and aye as he drank,
  The gude beer and the brandy,
He spar'd not the wine, altho it was fine,
  The sack nor the sugar candy.

10 'It's a wonder to me,' the knight he did say,
  'My bonnie lassie's sae delaying;

She promisd, as sure as she loved me ance,
  She woud be here by the dawing.'

11 He's done him to a shott-window,
  A little before the dawing,
And there he spied her nine brothers bauld,
  Were coming to betray him.

12 'Where shall I rin? where shall I gang?
  Or where shall I gang hide me?
She that was to meet me in friendship this
      day
  Has sent nine men to slay me!'

13 He's gane to the landlady o the house,
  Says, 'O can you supply me?
For she that was to meet me in friendship this
      day
  Has sent nine men to slay me.'

14 She gae him a suit o her ain female claise
  And set him to the baking;
The bird never sang mair sweet on the bush
  Nor the knight sung at the baking.

15 As they came in at the ha-door,
  Sae loudly as they rappit!
And when they came upon the floor,
  Sae loudly as they chappit!

16 'O had ye a stranger here last night,
  Who drank till the day was dawing?
Come show us the chamber where he lyes in,
  We'll shortly clear his lawing.'

17 'I had nae stranger here last night
  That drank till the day was dawing;
But ane that took a pint, and paid it ere he
      went,
  And there's naething to clear o his law-
      ing.'

18 A lad amang the rest, being o a merry mood,
  To the young knight fell a-talking;
The wife took her foot and gae him a kick,
  Says, Be busy, ye jilt, at your baking.

19 They stabbed the house baith but and ben,
  The curtains they spared nae riving,
And for a' that they did search and ca,
  For a kiss o the knight they were striv-
      ing.

E. **a.** 1¹. nurse *altered to* nurice.

    3³. drink the bonnie out, *originally.*

    4¹. drank *struck out for* sang.

    7². and *struck out before* gin.

    8². callit *changed in pencil to* were calling.

  b. *The printed copy seems to have been made up from* **a** *and Kinloch's other versions.*

    1. *Preceded by these two lines, taken from* **D** :

> As I cam in by Athol's yetts,
>   I heard a fair maid singing.

    1². And I wat it weel does set me.

    3². ye 'll *omitted.*   3³. drink the lass' health.

    3⁴. That 's coming to pay the. (*This stanza occurs in Motherwell's Note-Book, p. 46, where it is credited to a MS.*)

After 3 :

> He hied him doun to yon change-house,
>   And he drank till the day was dawing,
> And at ilka pint's end he drank the lass'
>   health
> That was coming to pay for his lawing.

    4¹. and aye.

    6². see gin she war.

  6³. There he saw the duke and a' his merry men.

  6⁴. the hill.   7¹. doun *omitted.*

  7³. She buskit : woman's.

  8². they war calling.

  8³. Had ye a young man here yestreen.

After 8 :

> 'He drank but ae pint, and he paid it or he
>   went,
> And ye 've na mair to do wi the lawing.'
> They searchit the house a' round and round,
>   And they spared na the curtains to tear
>   them,
>
> While the landlady stood upo the stair-head,
>   Crying, 'Maid, be busy at your baking !'
> They gaed as they cam, and left a' undone,
>   And left the bonnie maid at her baking.

F. **b.** "*Some alterations made from the way it was sung*" *by the editor's maternal grandfather.*

    4². And kindly said, My dearie.

    6³. as you ance had a love for me.

    11⁴. That were.

    12². Where shall I gang to hide me.

    14⁴. Than the.

213

SIR JAMES THE ROSE

'Sir James the Rose.' **a.** From a stall-tract of about 1780, Abbotsford library. **b.** Motherwell's Minstrelsy, p. 321. **c.** Sir James the Rose's Garland, one of a volume of the like from Heber's library. **d.** Motherwell's MS., p. 281 ; from the recitation of Mrs Gentles, of Paisley. **e.** Herd's MSS, I, 82. **f.** The same, II, 42. **g.** 'Sir James the Rose,' Pinkerton's Scottish Tragic Ballads, 1781, p. 61.

---

b, says Motherwell, "is given as it occurs in early stall-prints, and as it is to be obtained from the recitations of elderly people." Most of the variations are derived from **d**. **c** may have been printed earlier than **a**, but is astonishingly faulty. **d**, well remembered from print, is what Motherwell meant by "the recitations of elderly people." **e** was obtained by Herd, probably from recitation, as early as 1776, but must have been learned from print. **f** is **e** with a few missing lines supplied. **g**, says Pinkerton, "is given from a modern edition in one sheet 12mo," but was beyond question considerably manipulated by the editor. All the important variations are certainly his work.

The copy in Buchan's Gleanings, p. 9, is g. Whitelaw, in his Book of Scotish Ballads, p. 39, has combined b and g.

Half a dozen lines preserved by Burns, Cromek's Select Scotish Songs, II, 196 (see the preface to No 212), seem to belong to this ballad.

'Sir James the Ross, A Historical Ballad' (sometimes called 'The Buchanshire Tragedy'), was composed by the youthful Michael Bruce († 1767) upon the story of the popular ballad, and has perhaps enjoyed more favor with "the general" than the original.* 'Elfrida and Sir James of Perth,' Caw's Poetical Museum, 1784, p. 290 (probably taken, as most of the pieces are by the collector said to be, from some periodical publication), looks more like an imitation of Bruce's ballad than of its prototype. It is in fact a stark plagiarism.

Sir James the Rose has killed a squire, and men are out to take him. A nurse at the house of Marr is his leman, and he resorts to her in the hope that she may befriend him. She advises him to go to an ale-house for the night, promising to meet him there in the morning; he says he will do so, but, perhaps from distrust, which proves to be well grounded, prefers to wrap himself in his plaid and sleep under the sky. The party sent out to take him question the nurse, who at first makes a deceptive answer, then gives them a direction to his hiding-place. They find James the Rose asleep and take away his arms; he wakes and begs for mercy, and is told that he shall have such as he has given. He appeals to his servant to stay by him till death, and then to take his body to Loch Largan (Loughargan), for which service the man shall have his clothes and valuables. The avengers cut out his heart and take it to his leman at the house of Marr; she raves over her treachery, and is 'born away' bodily, to be seen no more.

e, f, it may be by accident, lack the vulgar passage 18, 19, which may be a later addition, for nothing is said of a man being in attendance when Sir James goes to his lair. The leader of the band that takes Sir James the Rose is Sir James the Graham, Sir James Graham, in c, e, f; a simple error, evidently. No motive is furnished in a-f for the woman's betraying her leman. g makes her offer information on condition of getting a proper reward, and she is promised Sir James's purse and brechan, but in the end is tendered his bleeding heart and his bleeding tartan, whatever that may be other than his brechan. This must be one of Pinkerton's improvements. The moral tag, st. 24, is dropped, or wanting, in c, e, f, g.

The topography of traditional ballads frequently presents difficulties, both because it is liable to be changed, wholly, or, what is more embarrassing, partially, to suit a locality to which a ballad has been transported, and again because unfamiliar names, when not exchanged, are exposed to corruption. Some of the places, also, have not a dignity which entitles them to notice in gazetteers. The first point, in the case before us, would be to settle the whereabouts of the House of Marr, in the vicinity of which the scene is laid. This I am unable to do. There is a Ballechin in Logierait Parish, Perthshire. There is said to be a Baleichan in Forfarshire.† It is not easy to see why the heir of either of these places (Buleighan and the rest may stand for either) should wish to have his body taken to Loch Largon in Invernesshire, if Loch Largon means Loch Laggan, as seems likely.‡

Translated by Knortz, Schottische Balladen, p. 79, after Aytoun.

---

* 'Sir James the Ross' was first printed in The Weekly Magazine, or, Edinburgh Amusement, IX, 371, in 1770 (Grosart, Works of Michael Bruce, p. 257, the ballad at p. 197), and in the same year in "Poems on Several Occasions, by Michael Bruce" (p. 30), with differences, which are attributed to Logan, the editor.

† "The older ballad, entitled 'The Young Heir of Baleichan,' or Baleighan, . . . is claimed for this parish [Crimond, Aberdeenshire]; while the same ballad is said to be founded on a traditionary tale of Baleichan in Forfarshire." Smith, A New History of Aberdeenshire, 1875, p. 429.

‡ Pinkerton reads Loch Lagan. He also reads 'the Hichts of Lundie,' in 10⁴, for 'the gates of London.' Lundie is in Forfarshire. I suppose both readings to be Pinkerton's emendations.

1 O HEARD ye of Sir James the Rose,
   The young heir of Buleighen?
For he has killd a gallant squire,
   An 's friends are out to take him.

2 Now he 's gone to the House of Marr,
   Where the nourrice was his leman;
To see his dear he did repair,
   Thinking she would befriend him.

3 'Where are you going, Sir James?' she says,
   'Or where now are you riding?'
'O I am bound to a foreign land,
   For now I 'm under hiding.

4 'Where shall I go? Where shall I run?
   Where shall I go to hide me?
For I have killd a gallant squire,
   And they 're seeking to slay me.'

5 'O go ye down to yon ale-house,
   And I 'll pay there your lawing;
And, if I be a woman true,
   I 'll meet you in the dawing.'

6 'I 'll not go down to yon ale-house,
   For you to pay my lawing;
There 's forty shillings for one supper,
   I 'll stay in 't till the dawing.'

7 He 's turnd him right and round about
   And rowd him in his brechan,
And he has gone to take a sleep,
   In the lowlands of Buleighen.

8 He was not well gone out of sight,
   Nor was he past Milstrethen,
Till four and twenty belted knights
   Came riding oer the Leathen.

9 'O have you seen Sir James the Rose,
   The young heir of Buleighen?
For he has killd a gallant squire,
   And we 're sent out to take him.'

10 'O I have seen Sir James,' she says,
   'For he past here on Monday;
If the steed be swift that he rides on,
   He 's past the gates of London.'

11 But as they were going away,
   Then she calld out behind them;
'If you do seek Sir James,' she says,
   'I 'll tell you where you 'll find him.

12 'You 'll seek the bank above the mill,
   In the lowlands of Buleighen,
And there you 'll find Sir James the Rose,
   Lying sleeping in his brechan.

13 'You must not wake him out of sleep,
   Nor yet must you affright him,
Till you run a dart quite thro his heart,
   And thro the body pierce him.'

14 They sought the bank above the mill,
   In the lowlands of Buleighan,
And there they found Sir James the Rose,
   A sleeping in his brechan.

15 Then out bespoke Sir John the Græme,
   Who had the charge a keeping;
'It 's neer be said, dear gentlemen,
   We 'll kill him when he 's sleeping.'

16 They seizd his broadsword and his targe,
   And closely him surrounded;
But when he wak'd out of his sleep,
   His senses were confounded.

17 'O pardon, pardon, gentlemen!
   Have mercy now upon me!'
'Such as you gave, such you shall have,
   And so we 'll fall upon thee.'

18 'Donald my man, wait me upon,
   And I 'll give you my brechan,
And, if you stay here till I die,
   You 'll get my trews of tartan.

19 'There is fifty pounds in my pocket,
   Besides my trews and brechan;
You 'll get my watch and diamond ring;
   And take me to Loch Largon.'

20 Now they have taken out his heart
   And stuck it on a spear,
Then took it to the House of Marr,
   And gave it to his dear.

21 But when she saw his bleeding heart
   She was like one distracted;
She smote her breast, and wrung her hands,
   Crying, 'What now have I acted!

22 'Sir James the Rose, now for thy sake
   O but my heart 's a breaking!
Curst be the day I did thee betray,
   Thou brave knight of Buleighen.'

23 Then up she rose, and forth she goes,
    All in that fatal hour,
  And bodily was born away,
    And never was seen more.

24 But where she went was never kend,
    And so, to end the matter,
  A traitor's end, you may depend,
    Can be expect'd no better.

———•———

a. *From* "A collection of Popular Ballads and Tales," *in six volumes*, "formed by me," *says Sir W. Scott*, "when a boy, from the baskets of the travelling pedlars. . . . It contains most of the pieces that were popular about thirty years since." ("1810.") *Vol. IV, No 21. In stanzas of eight lines.*

b. 1^2. Buleighan, *and always*. 2^3. To seek (d). 5^2. there pay. 5^3. maiden true (d). 11^1. As they rode on, man after man. 11^2. she cried. 11^3. James the Rose. 12^1. Seek ye the bank abune. 13^3. you drive (d). 13^4. through his (d). 14^1. abune (d). 14^4. Lying sleeping (d). 15^1. Up then spake (d). 15^3. It shall (d). 15^4. We killed: when a (d). 16^3. And (d). 17^4. we fall (d). 20^1. they 've taen out his bleeding heart (d). 21^3. wrung her hands and tore her hair (d). 21^4. Oh, what have I. 22^1. It's for your sake, Sir J. the R. (d). 22^2. That my poor heart's (d). 23^3. She bodily. 24^4. Can never be no.

c. 1^1. Did you hear. 1^2. That young. $1^2, 7^4, 9^2$. Belichan. 1^3. For *wanting*. 1^4. Who was sent out. 2^1. Now *wanting*. 2^2. nurse she was his layman. 3^2. where are you a. 3^3. I am going to some land. 3^4. For I am. 4^1. Where must : I turn. 4^2. I run. $4^3, 9^3$. esquire. 4^4. And my friends are out to take me. 5^1. Go you. 5^2. There you 'll stay till the dawning. 5^4. I 'll come and pay your lawing. 6^1. down *wanting*. 6^2. To stay unto the dawning. 6^3. Now if you be a woman true. 6^4. [D] o (?) come and pay the lawning. 7^1. himself quite round. 7^3. he is. 8^1. not quite out. 8^2. *Wanting*. 8^4. ore Beligham. 9^1. did you see. 9^2. That. 9^3. For *wanting*.

9^4. Who was sent. 10^1. Oh yes, I seed S. J. the R. 10^2. He passed by here. 10^3. His steed was : rid. 10^4. And past. 11^1. Just as. 11^2. They thought no more upon him. 11^3. Oh if you want S. J. the R. 12^2. And the : Belighan. 12^3. And *wanting*. 13 *as* 14. 13^1. him from his. 13^2. you *wanting*. 13^3. But in his breast must run a dart. 14 *as* 13. 14^2. And lowlands. 14^4. Lying sleeping. 15^1. up bespoke Sir James the Graham. 15^2. charge in. 15^3. Let it neer : gentleman. 15^4. We killd a man a sleeping. 16^1. They have taken from him his sword and target. 16^3. wakened out of sleep. 16^4. was. 17^1. O *wanting*. 17^2. And now have mercy on. 17^3. Which as. 17^4. And so shall fall upon you. 18^2. Until I be a dead man. 18^3. You 'll get my hose, likewise my shoes. 18^4. Likewise my Highland brichan. $19^{1,2}$. *Wanting*. $19^{3,4}$ *with* $20^{1,2}$: $20^{3,4}$ *with* $21^{1,2}$: $21^{3,4}$ *with* $22^{3,4}$: $22^{1,2}$ *wanting*. 19^3. You shall have my. 19^4. If you 'll carry me to Loughargan. 20^1. tane out his bleeding heart. 20^2. And fetched it on a spear man. 20^3. And locked it to the Marr. 20^4. A present to. 21^2. She ran. 21^3. She wrung her hands and smote her breast. 21^4. Oh what have I done, what have I acted. 22^3. day I you betrayd. 22^4. of Brichan. 23^1. Then *wanting*. 23^2. And in. 23^3. Her body by. 23^4. never was heard tell of : more *wanting*. 24. *Wanting*.

d. 1^2. Buleichan, *and always*. 1^4. And his.

2¹. Now *wanting*. 2³. To seek.

3. *Wanting*.

4⁴. They 're seeking for to. 5². there I 'll pay.

5⁸. a maiden. 6¹. no gae.

6⁸. thirty shillings for your.

6⁴. And stay until the. 8¹. He had.

8². And past the Mill strethan.

10¹. S. J. the Rose. 11¹. But *wanting*.

11². She cried out. 11⁸. S. J. the Rose.

12¹. Search the. 13⁸. you drive.

13⁴. through his. 14¹. They searched : abune.

14⁴. Lying sleeping. 15¹. Up then spoke.

15⁸. It shall. 15⁴. We killed him when a.

16⁸. And. 17⁴. we fall.

19¹. There is *wanting*.

20¹. They 've taen out his bleeding.

20⁸. And they 've gone to. 20⁴. And gien.

21¹. But *wanting*.

21⁸. She wrung her hands and tore her hair.

21⁴. Crying, Now what.

22¹. It 's for your sake, S. J. the R.

22². That my poor heart 's.

23¹. Then *wanting*. 23². And in.

23⁸. Bodily : She *prefixed later*. 24¹. kent.

24⁴. Cannot expect no.

e, f. e. Another song of Sir James the Ross ; *this following Bruce's ballad, which has the title* (*p.* 73) Sir James the Rose or de Ross. f. Another song of Sir James de Ross.

1¹. O did ye na ken Sir.

1². e. Ballachen, *and always.* f. 1², 7⁴, 9², Ballachen ; 12², Ballichan ; 14², Ballichin ; 22⁴, Ballichen.

1⁴. e. And they seeking. f. And they 're seeking.

2¹. He 's hy'd him : Moor.

2²⁻⁴, 3. e. *Wanting.*

3². f. O where away are.

3⁸. f. to some. 4¹. O where.

4². O whither shall I hide me.

4⁴. to kill. 5¹. e. gan ye. f. gang you.

5². I will pay your. 5⁸. And gin there be.

6¹. gang. 6⁸. shillings in my purse.

6⁴. We 'l stake it in the. 7¹. He turnd.

7⁸. is gone. 8². Mill Strechin. 8⁸. Ere.

8⁴. the Rechin. 9¹. O saw ye.

10¹. O yes, I saw S. J. the R.

10⁸. And gif : swift he : on *wanting.*

10⁴. He 's near.

11¹. They were not well gane out o sight.

11². Ere she. 11⁸. O gin ye seek S. J. the R.

11⁴. ye where to.

12¹. Ye 'll search the bush aboon the know.

13¹. him from his sleep.

13². Neither man you

14¹. the bush aboon the know.

14⁴. Lying sleeping.

15¹. O then spake up Sir James Graham.

15⁸. Let it not be. 15⁴. We killd : while.

16¹. They 've tane his broadsword from his side.

16². him they have *for* closely him.

16⁸. o *for* of his.

17². O pardon me, I pray ye.

17⁸. ye gae, such shall ye hae.

17⁴. There is no pardon for ye.

18, 19. *Wanting.*

20¹. they 've tane out his bleeding heart.

20². f. stickt it.

20⁸. Then carried. e. Mure. f. Moor.

20⁴. And shewd. 21¹. But *wanting.*

21². She rav'd.

21⁸. And cried, Alake, a weel (well) a day.

21⁴. Alas what have. 22². My heart it is a.

22⁸. Wae to the day I thee betrayd.

22⁴. Thou bold. 23². In that unhappy hour.

23⁴. neer was heard of more. 24. *Wanting.*

g. 1². Buleighan, *and always.*

1⁴. Whase friends. 2¹. has gane.

2². Whar nane might seek to find him.

2⁴. Weining. 3¹. said.

3². O whar awa are ye. 3⁸. I maun be bound.

3⁴. And now. 4². I rin to lay.

4⁴. And his friends seek. 5¹. yon laigh.

5². I sall pay there.

5⁸. And as I am your leman trew.

5⁴. at the. 6. *Wanting.* 7¹. He turnd.

7². And laid him doun to. 8⁸. Whan.

9⁴. sent to. 10¹. Yea, I : said.

10². He past by here. 10⁸. Gin.

10⁴. the Hichts of Lundie.

11¹. as wi speid they rade awa.

11². She leudly cryd.

11⁸. Gin ye 'll gie me a worthy meid.

11⁴. whar to.

12. 'O tell, fair maid, and, on our band,
    Ye 'se get his purse and brechan : '
  ' He 's in the bank aboon the mill,
    In the lawlands o Buleighan.'

13, 14. *Wanting.* 15¹. out and spak.

15⁸. said, my stalwart feres.

15⁴. We killd him whan a.

16⁸,⁴. O pardon, mercy, gentlemen !
    He then fou loudly sounded.

17³,⁴–19.
  'Sic as ye gae sic ye sall hae,
    Nae grace we shaw to thee can.'
  'Donald my man, wait till I fa,
    And ye shall hae my brechan;
  Ye 'll get my purse, thouch fou o gowd,
    To tak me to Loch Lagan.'

20¹. Syne they tuke out his bleeding heart.
20². And set.   20⁴. And shawd.

21. We cold nae gie Sir James's purse,
      We cold nae gie his brechan,
    But ye sall ha his bleeding heart,
      Bot and his bleeding tartan.

22¹. O for.   22². My heart is now.
22³. day I wrocht thy wae.   22⁴. brave heir.
23²,³. And in that hour o tein, She wanderd
      to the dowie glen.
23⁴. never mair was sein.   24. *Wanting.*

214

THE BRAES O YARROW

A. 'The Braes of Yarrow,' communicated to Percy by Dr Robertson, Principal of Edinburgh.

B. 'The Braes o Yarrow,' Murison MS., p. 105.

C. 'The Dowie Downs o Yarrow,' Motherwell's MS., p. 334 ; Motherwell's Minstrelsy, p. 252.

D. 'The Bonny Braes of Yarrow,' communicated to Percy by Robert Lambe, of Norham, 1768.

E. a. 'The Dowy Houms o Yarrow,' "Scotch Ballads, Materials for Border Minstrelsy," Abbotsford. **b.** 'The Dowie Dens of Yarrow,' Scott's Minstrelsy III, 72, 1803, III, 143, 1833.

F. 'The Dowie Dens o Yarrow,' "Scotch Ballads, Materials for Border Minstrelsy," Abbotsford.

G. 'The Dowie Dens of Yarrow,' "Scotch Ballads, Materials for Border Minstrelsy," Abbotsford.

H. 'The Dowie Dens of Yarrow,' Campbell MSS, II, 55.

I. 'Braes of Yarrow,' Buchan's MSS, II, 161; Buchan's Ballads of the North of Scotland, II, 203 ; Dixon, Scottish Traditional Versions of Ancient Ballads, p. 68, Percy Society, vol. xvii.

J. 'The Dowie Glens of Yarrow,' "Scotch Ballads, Materials for Border Minstrelsy," Abbotsford.

K. 'The Dowie Den in Yarrow,' Campbell MSS, I, 8.

L. 'The Dowie Dens,' Blackwood's Magazine, CXLVII, 741, June, 1890.

M. 'Dowie Banks of Yarrow,' "Scotch Ballads, Materials for Border Minstrelsy," Abbotsford.

N. 'The Yetts of Gowrie,' "Scotch Ballads, Materials for Border Minstrelsy," Abbotsford.

O. Herd's MSS, I, 35, II, 181; Herd's Ancient and Modern Scottish Songs, 1776, I, 145; four stanzas.

P. Cromek's Select Scotish Songs, 1810, II, 196 ; two stanzas.

FIRST published in Minstrelsy of the Scottish Border, 1803 (E b). Scott remarks that he "found it easy to collect a variety of copies, but very difficult indeed to select from them such a collated edition as might in any degree suit the taste of 'these more light and giddy-paced times.'" The copy principally used was E a. St. 12 of Scott, which suited the taste of the last century, but does not suit with a popular ballad, is from O, and also st. 13, and there are traces of F, G, M, but 5–7 have lines which do not occur in any version that I have seen.

A had been somewhat edited before it was communicated to Percy ; the places were, however, indicated by commas. Several copies besides **O**, already referred to, have slight passages that never came from the unsophisticated people; as **J** 2, in which a page "runs with sorrow," for rhyme and without reason, **L** 2³, and **L** 12³˒⁴, which is manifestly taken from Logan's Braes of Yarrow.* **N** has been interpolated with artificial nonsense,† and is an almost worthless copy; the last stanza may defy competition for silliness.

M 1, 3, and **N** 4, 6, 7, belong to 'The Duke of Athole's Nurse.' So also does one half of a fragment sent by Burns in a letter to William Tytler, Cromek's Select Scotish Songs, 1810, II, 194–8, which, however, has two stanzas of this ballad (**P**) and two of 'Rare Willie's drowned in Yarrow,' No 215.

The fragment in Ritson's Scotish Songs, 1794, I, lxvii, is **O**.

Herd's MSS, I, 36, II, 182, have the following couplets, evidently from a piece treating the story of this ballad:

O when I look east my heart is sair,
But when I look west it 's mair and mair,
For there I see the braes of Yarrow,
And there I lost for ay my marrow.

The groups A–I and J–P are distinguished by the circumstance, of no importance to the story, that the hero and heroine in the former are man and wife, in the other unmarried lovers. In all the versions (leaving out of account the fragments **O, P**) the family of the woman are at variance with the man. Her brothers think him an unfit match for their sister, **A** 8, **B** 2.‡ In **C** 2 the brothers have taken offence because their sister was not regarded as his equal by her husband, which is perhaps too much of a refinement for ballads,

and may be a perversion. She was worth stealing in **C** as in **B**. The dispute in two or three copies appears to take the form who is the flower, or rose, of Yarrow, that is the best man, **C** 8, 9, 17, **B** 1, 12, **D** 1,. 14; but this matter is muddled, cf. **C** 2, 3, **D** 2. We hear nothing about the unequal match in **D–I**, but in **J–L** a young lady displeases her father by refusing nine gentlemen in favor of a servant-lad.

Men who are drinking together fall out and set a combat for the next day, **B–F, H, I**. It is three lords that drink and quarrel in **B–D** (ten (?) in **I**). The lady fears that her three brothers will slay her husband, **B** 5, **C** 5. The lord in **D** 2 seems not to be one of the three in **D** 1, and we are probably to understand that three brothers get into a brawl with a man who has surreptitiously married their sister. Only one brother is spoken of in **A** (6), from whom treachery is looked for, **E** 2.

In **I–L** the father makes the servant-lad fight with the nine high-born suitors.

The wife tries to keep her husband at home, **A–E, I**; but he is confident that all will go well, and that he shall come back to her early, **A, B, C, I**. She kisses (washes) and combs him, and helps to arm him, **B, C, E, F, G, I**; so **J, K**.§ He finds nine armed men awaiting him on the braes or houms of Yarrow, **A, E–G, I–M**, ten **B, D**.‖ They ask if he has come to hawk, hunt (drink), or fight; he replies that he has come to fight, **C, E, I**; cf. **A** 5, 6. Five (four) he slays and four (five) he wounds, **A, B, D, E, I, J, K**; in **F** he kills all the nine; in **L** he gets no further than the seventh; in **G** he kills all but one.

These nine, after the way of ballads, should

---

* Logan has a page, and the page may have come from some previously corrupted version of the popular ballad which **J** may follow. The first half of the stanza corresponding to **L** 12 in Logan is from the popular ballad.

† Sometimes also with sensible prose, as 7², 'But I find she has deceived me;' 12³, 'I dreamed my luive had lost his life.'

The loose, though limited, rhyme in this ballad, in 'The Bonnie House of Airlie,' etc., does not favor exact recollection, and furnishes a temptation to invention: hence the sparrow in **B** 6, the arrow in **D** 7, the narrow in **I** 12, and, I fear, the harrow in **L** 9, which of itself is good, while all the others are bad.

‡ It must be noted, however, that in 'Ye think me an un-

meet marrow,' **A** 8², Ye is an editorial reading. I may remark that I have included **M–P** in the second group simply because the hero in these is called love or true-love. The husband, however, has both titles in **A**.

§ 'Wi a *thrusty* rapier,' **J**, which I feel compelled to understand as the commonplace 'trusty;' but, guided by 'a rusted rapier,' **K**, we ought perhaps to read 'rusty.' In **L** the lady kisses and combs the swain, and sets him on her milk-white steed. — Since I suppose lover to have been substituted for husband in the course of tradition, I shall not be so precise as to distinguish the two when this would be inconvenient.

‖ Nine is the number also in **H**, as we see from st. 5, compared with **E**, 5, 11.

be the lady's brothers, and such they are in A 7, 8. Three of them, but only three, should be the lady's brothers according to B 1–5, C 1–5. Three brethren are charged by the husband with a message to his lady in D 8, and these might be his brothers-in-law. The message is sent in E 9 by a good-brother, or wife's brother, John, who clearly was not in the fight in E, though the husband says he is going to meet this brother John in A 6. This brother-in-law of E is probably intended by brother in I 8.

After the hero has successfully disposed of his nine or ten antagonists (he takes them 'man for man'), he is stabbed from behind in a cowardly way, A, B, C, E, I, L, N, by somebody. The tradition is much blurred here; it is a squire out of the bush, a cowardly man, a fause lord. An Englishman shoots him with an arrow out of a bush in D. But other reports are distinct. The lady's father runs him through (not from behind) in J, K. Her brother springs from a bush behind and runs him through, L. Her brother John comes behind him and slays him, N. Up and rose her brother James and slew him, M. In E " that stubborn knight" comes behind him and runs his body through, and that (a) "stubborn lord" is the author of his death in G, F. Taking E 2, 8, 9 together, the stubborn knight, at least in E, may be interpreted as good-brother John, whose treachery is feared in E 2, who is prominent in A 6, and who is expressly said to slay his sister's true-love in N. On the whole, the preponderance of tradition is to the effect that the hero was treacherously slain by his wife's (love's) brother.

Word of her husband's death is sent or carried to the wife by her brother, brother John, A, E, L, N; her or his three brothers, D 8; her or his brother, I 8; his man John, C 12, by mistake; her father (?), J, K; her sister Anne, F, G, H. The wife has had a dream that she, her lord or true-love and she, had been pulling green heather (birk) in Yarrow, A, C–F, I–M, O.* The dream is explained to signify her lord's death, and she is enjoined to fetch him home. In A, the dream occurs before the fight and is double, of pulling green heather and of her love coming headless home; in B, the lady dreams that her lord was sleeping sound in Yarrow, and in the highly vitiated N that ' he had lost his life.'

The wife hurries to Yarrow; † up a high, high hill and down into the valley, where she sees nine (ten) dead men, E, F, G, M (nine well-armed men, wrongly, H).‡ She sees her true-love lying slain, finds him sleeping sound, in Yarrow, A, B, J, K. She kisses him and combs his hair, A, E, F, G, I, L, M; she drinks the blood that runs from him, E 12, F 11, G 7, M 9. §

Her hair is five quarters long; she twists it round his hand and draws him home, C; ties it round his middle and carries him home, D. She takes three lachters of her hair, ties them tight round his middle and carries him home, B. *His* hair is five quarters long ! she ties it to her horse's mane and trails him home, K.‖ The carrying strikes one as unpractical, the trailing as barbarous. In L, after the lover is slain, the surviving lords and her brother trail him by the heels to Yarrow water and throw him into a whirlpool. The lady, searching for him, sees him ' deeply drowned.' His hair,

* It will be remembered that green is an unlucky color: see II, 181 f.

† She tears the ribbons from her head in D 11, I 12, when she hears the tidings: but this belongs to the bride in the ballad which succeeds, No 215.

‡ Ten in F, to include the lord with his nine foemen. But why only nine in E, G, M? Is it not because one of the brothers had not been mortally wounded, the brother who is said to kill the husband (lover) in L, M, N, and who may reasonably be supposed to do this in E, F, G? Such a matter would not be left in obscurity in the original ballad.

§ This is disagreeable, assuredly, and unnatural too. It is 'drank,' probably, that is softened to 'wiped' in A 14. Scott, to avoid unpleasantness, reads ' She kissd them (his wounds) till her lips grew red ;' which would not take long.

This is all nicely arranged in L: ' She laid him on her milk-white steed, and bore him home from Yarrow; she washed his wounds in yon well-strand, and dried him wi the hollan.' The washing and drying are done in J on the spot, where there might have been water, but no hollan.

‖ The reciters of A and J, whether they gave what they had received, or tried to avoid the material difficulties about the hair, graze upon absurdity. Her hair was three quarters long, she tied it round ' her ' (for his ?) white hause-bane — and died, A 15. His hair was three quarters long, she 's wrapt it round her middle — and brought it home, J 16. The hair comes in again in the next two ballads, and causes difficulty. Wonderful things are done with hair in ballads and tales: see I, 40 b, and the note at 486 b.

which we must suppose to float, is five quarters long; she twines it round her hand and draws him out. Raising no petty questions, it appears enough to say that this is the only version of fourteen in which the drowning occurs, and that the drowning of the lover is the characteristic of No 215, the next following ballad, which has otherwise been partly confused with this.*

The lady's father urges her to restrain her grief; he will wed her with as good a lord as she has lost, or a better; she rejects his suggestions. Her heart breaks, B, I; she dies in her father's arms, D, F–H, J–L, being at the time big with child, B, D, F–H, J.

The lady tells her father to wed his sons, B 12; his seven sons, J 18. So 'Clerk Saunders' (of which this may be a reminiscence, for we do not hear of seven sons in this ballad), No 69, G 28; cf. A 26, E 19.

She bids him take home his ousen and his kye, E 15, F 12, G 8, H 9. This I conceive to be an interpolation by a reciter who followed the tradition cited from Hogg further on.

The message to the mother to come take up her son in I 8 may possibly be a reminiscence from 'Johnie Cock,' No 114. It occurs in no other copy, and comes in awkwardly.

'The Braes of Yarrow' ('Busk ye, busk ye, my bony, bony bride'), written by William Hamilton of Bangour "in imitation of the ancient Scottish manner,' was suggested by this ballad.†

'The Dowy Dens,' Evans's Old Ballads, 1810, III, 342, has the same foundation. 'The Haughs o Yarrow,' a modern piece in Buchan's Ballads of the North of Scotland, II, 211, repeats with a slight change the third

stanza of O, and has further on half a stanza from 'Willie's rare,' No 215.

James Hogg, in sending E a to Sir Walter Scott, wrote as follows: "Tradition placeth the event on which this song is founded very early. That the song hath been written near the time of the transaction appears quite evident, although, like others, by frequent singing the language is become adapted to an age not so far distant. The bard does not at all relate particulars, but only mentions some striking features of a tragical event which everybody knew. This is observable in many of the productions of early times; at least the secondary bards seem to have regarded their songs as purely temporary.

"The hero of the ballad is said to have been of the name of Scott, and is called a knight of great bravery. He lived in Ettrick, some say at Oakwood, others Kirkhope; but was treacherously slain by his brother-in-law, as related in the ballad, who had him at ill will because his father had parted with the half of all his goods and gear to his sister on her marriage with such a respectable man. The name of the murderer is said to be Annand, a name I believe merely conjectural from the name of the place where they are said both to be buried, which at this day is called Annan's Treat, a low muir lying to the west of Yarrow church, where two huge tall stones are erected, below which the least child that can walk the road will tell you the two lords are buried that were slain in a duel."

Sir Walter Scott, in the revised edition of his Minstrelsy, expressed a conviction that this ballad referred to a duel fought between John Scott of Tushielaw and his brother-in-

---

* L 19 is also found only in that copy. It seems to me, but only because L does not strike me as being of an original cast — rather a ballad improved by reciters, — to be an adaptation of No 215, A 2.

† James Chalmers, in Archæologia Scotica, III, 261, says that Hamilton's ballad was contributed to the second volume of the Tea Table Miscellany in 1724. It is not in the Dublin edition of 1729. It is at p. 242 of the London edition of 1733; in Thomson's Orpheus Caledonius, II, 34, of the same year; at p. 46 of the first edition of [Hamilton's] Poems on Several Occasions, Glasgow, 1748. The author died in 1754. The copy in the second edition of Hamilton's Poems, 1760, p. 67, says Chalmers, is somewhat altered.
In Hamilton's ballad it is a lover, and not a husband, who

is slain, and he is thrown into the Yarrow. It is a question whether Hamilton's ballad did not affect tradition in the case of J, K, L, particularly L. The editorial Douglas in A 11 is from Hamilton 24. 'Wi her tears she bathed his wounds,' I 13³, looks like Hamilton 9¹. The 'dule and sorrow' of O 4² is a recurring phrase in Hamilton, and 'slain the comeliest swain.' O 4³, is in Hamilton 6³.
In Hamilton's ballad the slayer of the lover endeavors to induce the lady to marry him, as is done in the Icelandic ballad spoken of under No 89, II, 297 f.
A song by Ramsay, T. T. M., Dublin, 1729, p. 139, has nearly the same first four lines as Hamilton's ballad, and these have been thought to be traditional.

law Walter Scott of Thirlestane, in which the latter was slain.* Contemporary entries in the records of the Presbytery of Selkirk show that John Scott, son to Walter of Tushielaw, killed Walter Scott, brother of Sir Robert of Thirlestane, in 1609. The slain Walter Scott was not, however, the brother-in-law of John of Tushielaw, for his wife was a daughter of Sir Patrick Porteous. A violent feud ensued, as might be expected, between the Scotts of Thirlestane and of Tushielaw. Seven years later, in 1616, a Walter Scott of Tushielaw made "an informal and inordinat marriage with Grizel Scott of Thirlestane without consent of her father." The record of the elopement is three months after followed by an entry of a summons to Simeon Scott of Bonytoun (an adherent of Thirlestane) and three other Scotts "to compear in Melrose to hear themselves excommunicat for the horrible slaughter of Walter Scott" [of Tushielaw]. Disregarding the so-called duel, we have a Walter Scott of Tushielaw carrying off a wife from the Scotts of Thirlestane, with which family he was at feud; and a Walter Scott of Tushielaw horribly slaughtered by Scotts of Thirlestane. These facts correspond rather closely with the incidents of the ballad. We do not know, to be sure, that the two Walter Scotts of Tushielaw were the same person. There were Walter Scotts many; but tradition is capable of confounding the two or the three connected with this series of events. On the other hand, there is nothing in the ballad to connect it preferably with the Scotts; the facts are such as are likely to

have occurred often in history, and a similar story is found in other ballads.

In the Scandinavian ballad 'Herr Helmer,' Helmer has married a lady whose family are at feud with him for the unatoned slaughter of her uncle; he meets her seven brothers, who will now hear of no satisfaction; there is a fight; Helmer kills six, but spares the seventh, who treacherously kills him: Afzelius, ed. Bergström, I, 264, Arwidsson, I, 155 (etc., see II, 170 of this collection, note ‡). Other forms make the last of the brothers willing to accept an arrangement: 'Herr Helmer Blau,' Danske Viser, IV, 251, No 209, 'Herr Hjælm,' Grundtvig, Danske Folkeminder, 1861, p. 81. 'Jomfruen i Skoven,' Danske Viser, III, 99, No 123, has also several features of our ballad. The hero, on parting from a lady with whom he has passed the night in a wood, is warned by her to avoid her seven brothers. This he is too brave to do, and he meets them. They ask him where are his hawk and his hound. He tries, unsuccessfully, to induce them to give him their sister for wife; they fight; he kills all the seven brothers, and is slain himself, in some way not explained. (These ballads are translated in Prior, III, 371, 230.)

The next ballad has been partially confused with this.

E b, Scott's ballad, is translated by Doenniges, p. 237; by Loève-Veimars, p. 347. Knortz, Lieder und Romanzen Alt-Englands, p. 92, translates Allingham's ballad.

A

Communicated to Percy by Dr William Robertson, Principal of Edinburgh.

1 'I DREAMED a dreary dream this night,
    That fills my heart wi sorrow;
I dreamed I was pouing the heather green
    Upon the braes of Yarrow.

2 'O true-luve mine, stay still and dine,
    As ye ha done before, O;'
'O I'll be hame by hours nine,
    And frae the braes of Yarrow.'

3 I dreamed a dreary dream this night,
    That fills my heart wi sorrow;

* Minstrelsy, 1833, III, 144. For a criticism of Sir Walter Scott's remarks and a correction of some errors, with much new information, see Mr T. Craig-Brown's

History of Selkirkshire, Edinburgh, 1886, I, 14–16, 311–15, of which work grateful use is here made.

I dreamed my luve came headless hame,
 O frae the braes of Yarrow !

4 'O true-luve mine, stay still and dine,
 As ye ha done before, O ; '
'O I 'll be hame by hours nine,
 And frae the braes of Yarrow.'

5 'O are ye going to hawke,' she says,
 'As ye ha done before, O ?
Or are ye going to weild your brand,
 Upon the braes of Yarrow ? '

6 'O I am not going to hawke,' he says,
 'As I have done before, O,
But for to meet your brother Jhon,
 Upon the braes of Yarrow.'

7 As he gade down yon dowy den,
 Sorrow went him before, O ;
Nine well-wight men lay waiting him,
 Upon the braes of Yarrow.

8 'I have your sister to my wife,
 'Ye' think me an unmeet marrow ;
But yet one foot will I never flee
 Now frae the braes of Yarrow.'

9 'Than' four he killd and five did wound,
 That was an unmeet marrow !
'And he had weel nigh wan the day
 Upon the braes of Yarrow.'

10 'Bot' a cowardly 'loon' came him behind,
 Our Lady lend him sorrow !
And wi a rappier pierced his heart,
 And laid him low on Yarrow.

11 'Now Douglas' to his sister 's gane,
 Wi meikle dule and sorrow :
'Gae to your luve, sister,' he says,
 'He 's sleeping sound on Yarrow.'

12 As she went down yon dowy den,
 Sorrow went her before, O ;
She saw her true-love lying slain
 Upon the braes of Yarrow.

13 'She swoond thrice upon his breist
 That was her dearest marrow ;
Said, Ever alace and wae the day
 Thou wentst frae me to Yarrow ! '

14 She kist his mouth, she kaimed his hair,
 As she had done before, O ;
She 'wiped' the blood that trickled doun
 Upon the braes of Yarrow.

15 Her hair it was three quarters lang,
 It hang baith side and yellow ;
She tied it round 'her' white hause-bane,
 'And tint her life on Yarrow.'

B

Murison MS., p. 105 ; Old Deer, Aberdeenshire.

1 THREE lords sat drinking at the wine
 I the bonny braes o Yarrow,
An there cam a dispute them between,
 Who was the Flower o Yarrow.

2 'I 'm wedded to your sister dear,
 Ye coont nae me your marrow ;
I stole her fae her father's back,
 An made her the Flower o Yarrow.'

3 'Will ye try hearts, or will ye try hans,
 I the bonnie braes o Yarrow ?

Or will ye try the weel airmt sword,
 I the bonnie braes o Yarrow ? '

4 'I winna try hearts, I winna try hans,
 I the bonnie braes o Yarrow,
But I will try the weel airmt sword,
 I the bonnie braes o Yarrow.'

5 'Ye 'll stay at home, my own good lord,
 Ye 'll stay at home tomorrow ;
My brethren three they will slay thee,
 I the bonnie braes o Yarrow. '

6 'Bonnie, bonnie shines the sun,
 An early sings the sparrow ;

Before the clock it will strike nine
    An I 'll be home tomorrow.'

7 She 's kissed his mouth, an combed his hair,
    As she had done before, O ;
  She 's dressed him in his noble bow,
    An he 's awa to Yarrow.

8 As he gaed up yon high, high hill,
    An doon the dens o Yarrow,
  An there he spied ten weel airmt men
    I the bonnie braes o Yarrow.

9 It 's five he wounded, an five he slew,
    I the bonnie braes o Yarrow ;
  There cam a squire out o the bush,
    An pierced his body thorough.

10 'I dreamed a dream now sin the streen,
    God keep us a' fae sorrow !
  That my good lord was sleepin soun
    I the bonnie braes o Yarrow.'

11 'O hold your tongue, my daughter dear,
    An tak it not in sorrow ;

I 'll wed you wi as good a lord
    As you 've lost this day in Yarrow.'

12 'O haud your tongue, my father dear,
    An wed your sons wi sorrow ;
  For a fairer flower neer sprang in May nor June
    Nor I 've lost this day in Yarrow.'

13 Fast did she gang, fast did she rin,
    Until she cam to Yarrow,
  An there she fan her own good lord,
    He was sleepin soun in Yarrow.

14 She 's taen three lachters o her hair,
    That hung doon her side sae bonny,
  An she 's tied them roon his middle tight,
    An she 's carried him hame frae Yarrow.

15 This lady being big wi child,
    She was fu o grief an sorrow ;
  Her heart did break, and then she died,
    She did not live till morrow.

———•———

C

Motherwell's MS., pp. 334, 331, from the recitation of Agnes Lile, Kilbarchan, July 19, 1825; learned from her father, who died fourteen years earlier, at the age of eighty.

1 THERE were three lords birling at the wine
    On the dowie downs o Yarrow ;
  They made a compact them between
    They would go fight tomorrow.

2 'Thou took our sister to be thy bride,
    And thou neer thocht her thy marrow ;
  Thou stealed her frae her daddie's back,
    When she was the rose o Yarrow.'

3 'Yes, I took your sister to be my bride,
    And I made her my marrow ;
  I stealed her frae her daddie's back,
    And she 's still the rose o Yarrow.'

4 He is hame to his lady gane,
    As he had dune before ! O ;
  Says, Madam, I must go and fight
    On the dowie downs o Yarrow.

5 'Stay at hame, my lord,' she said,
    'For that will cause much sorrow ;
  For my brethren three they will slay thee,
    On the dowie downs o Yarrow.'

6 'Hold your tongue, my lady fair,
    For what needs a' this sorrow ?
  For I 'll be hame gin the clock strikes nine,
    From the dowie downs o Yarrow.'

7 She wush his face, she kamed his hair,
    As she had dune before, O ;
  She dressed him up in his armour clear,
    Sent him furth to fight on Yarrow.

8 'Come you here to hawk or hound,
    Or drink the wine that 's so clear, O ?
  Or come you here to eat in your words,
    That you 're not the rose o Yarrow ?'

9 'I came not here to hawk or hound,
    Nor to drink the wine that 's so clear, O ;
  Nor I came not here to eat in my words,
    For I 'm still the rose o Yarrow.'

10 Then they a' begoud to fight,
    I wad they focht richt sore, O,
    Till a cowardly man came behind his back,
    And pierced his body thorough.

11 'Gae hame, gae hame, it 's my man John,
    As ye have done before, O,
    And tell it to my gay lady
    That I soundly sleep on Yarrow.'

12 His man John he has gane hame,
    As he had dune before, O,
    And told it to his gay lady,
    That he soundly slept on Yarrow.

13 'I dreamd a dream now since the streen,
    God keep us a' frae sorrow!
    That my lord and I was pu'ing the heather
        green
    From the dowie downs o Yarrow.'

14 Sometimes she rade, sometimes she gaed,
    As she had dune before, O,
    And aye between she fell in a soune,
    Lang or she cam to Yarrow.

15 Her hair it was five quarters lang,
    'T was like the gold for yellow;
    She twisted it round his milk-white hand,
    And she 's drawn him hame from Yarrow.

16 Out and spak her father dear,
    Says, What needs a' this sorrow?
    For I 'll get you a far better lord
    Than ever died on Yarrow.

17 'O hold your tongue, father,' she said,
    'For ye 've bred a' my sorrow;
    For that rose 'll neer spring sae sweet in
        May
    As that rose I lost on Yarrow.'

———◆———

D

Communicated to Percy by Robert Lambe, Norham, April
16, 1768.

1 THERE were three lords drinking of wine
    On the bonny braes of Yarrow;
    There fell a combat them between,
    Wha was the rose of Yarrow.

2 Up then spak a noble lord,
    And I wot it was bot sorrow:
    'I have as fair a flower,' he said,
    'As ever sprang on Yarrow.'

3 Then he went hame to his ain house,
    For to sleep or the morrow,
    But the first sound the trumpet gae
    Was, Mount and haste to Yarrow.

4 'Oh stay at hame,' his lady said,
    'Oh stay untill the morrow,
    And I will mount upon a steed,
    And ride with you to Yarrow.'

5 'Oh hawd your tongue, my dear,' said he,
    'And talk not of the morrow;
    This day I have to fight again,
    In the dowy deans of Yarrow.'

6 As he went up yon high, high hill,
    Down the dowy deans of Yarrow,
    There he spy'd ten weel armd men,
    There was nane o them his marrow.

7 Five he wounded and five he slew,
    In the dowy deans of Yarrow,
    But an English-man out of a bush
    Shot at him a lang sharp arrow.

8 'Ye may gang hame, my brethren three,
    Ye may gang hame with sorrow,
    And say this to my fair lady,
    I am sleeping sound on Yarrow.'

9 'Sister, sister, I dreamt a dream —
    You read a dream to gude, O!
    That I was puing the heather green
    On the bonny braes of Yarrow.'

10 'Sister, sister, I 'll read your dream,
    But alas! it 's unto sorrow;
    Your good lord is sleeping sound,
    He is lying dead on Yarrow.'

11 She as pu'd the ribbons of her head,
    And I wot it was wi sorrow,
    And she 's gane up yon high, high hill,
    Down the dowy deans of Yarrow.

12 Her hair it was five quarters lang,
    The colour of it was yellow;
    She as ty'd it round his middle jimp,
    And she as carried him frae Yarrow.

13 'O hawd your tongue!' her father says,
    'What needs a' this grief and sorrow?
    I 'll wed you on as fair a flower
    As ever sprang on Yarrow.'

14 'No, hawd your tongue, my father dear,
    I 'm fow of grief and sorrow;
    For a fairer flower ne[v]er sprang
    Than I 've lost this day on Yarrow.'

15 This lady being big wi bairn,
    And fow of grief and sorrow,
    She as died within her father's arms,
    And she died lang or the morrow.

E

a. In the handwriting of James Hogg, the Ettrick Shepherd, about 1801; now in a volume with the title "Scotch Ballads, Materials for Border Minstrelsy," No 136, Abbotsford. b. Scott's Minstrelsy, III, 72, 1803, III, 143, 1833.

1 LATE at een, drinkin the wine,
    Or early in a mornin,
    The set a combat them between,
    To fight it in the dawnin.

2 'O stay at hame, my noble lord!
    O stay at hame, my marrow!
    My cruel brother will you betray,
    On the dowy houms o Yarrow.'

3 'O fare ye weel, my lady gaye!
    O fare ye weel, my Sarah!
    For I maun gae, tho I neer return
    Frae the dowy banks o Yarrow.'

4 She kissd his cheek, she kaimd his hair,
    As she had done before, O;
    She belted on his noble brand,
    An he 's awa to Yarrow.

5 O he 's gane up yon high, high hill —
    I wat he gaed wi sorrow —
    An in a den spied nine armd men,
    I the dowy houms o Yarrow.

6 'O ir ye come to drink the wine,
    As ye hae doon before, O?
    Or ir ye come to wield the brand,
    On the bonny banks o Yarrow?'

7 'I im no come to drink the wine,
    As I hae don before, O,
    But I im come to wield the brand,
    On the dowy houms o Yarrow.'

8 Four he hurt, an five he slew,
    On the dowy houms o Yarrow,
    Till that stubborn knight came him behind,
    An ran his body thorrow.

9 'Gae hame, gae hame, good-brother John,
    An tell your sister Sarah
    To come an lift her noble lord,
    Who 's sleepin sound on Yarrow.'

10 'Yestreen I dreamd a dolefu dream;
    I kend there wad be sorrow;
    I dreamd I pu'd the heather green,
    On the dowy banks o Yarrow.'

11 She gaed up yon high, high hill —
    I wat she gaed wi sorrow —
    An in a den spy'd nine dead men,
    On the dowy houms o Yarrow.

12 She kissd his cheek, she kaimd his hair,
    As oft she did before, O;
    She drank the red blood frae him ran,
    On the dowy houms o Yarrow.

13 'O haud your tongue, my douchter dear,
    For what needs a' this sorrow?
    I 'll wed you on a better lord
    Than him you lost on Yarrow.'

14 'O haud your tongue, my father dear,
    An dinna grieve your Sarah;
    A better lord was never born
    Than him I lost on Yarrow.

15 'Tak hame your ousen, tak hame your kye,
    For they hae bred our sorrow;
    I wiss that they had a' gane mad
    Whan they cam first to Yarrow.'

F

"From Nelly Laidlaw." In the handwriting of William
Laidlaw, "Scotch Ballads, Materials for Border Minstrelsy,"
No 20 a, Abbotsford.

1 LATE in the eenin, drinkin the wine,
      Or early in the mornin,
   The set a combat them between,
      To fight it out i the dawnin.

2 She 's kissd his lips, an she 's caimd his hair,
      As she did ay afore, O,
   She 's belted him in his noble brown,
      Afore he gaed to Yarrow.

3 Then he 's away oer yon high hill —
      A wait he 's gane wi sorrow —
   An in a den he spied nine armd men,
      On the dowie banks o Yarrow.

4 'If I see ye a', ye 'r nine for ane,
      But ane 's [un]equal marrow;
   Yet as lang 's I 'm able wield my brand,
      I 'll fight an bear ye marrow.

5 'There are twa swords into my sheath,
      The 're ane and equal marrow;
   Now wale the best, I 'll take the warst,
      An, man for man, I 'll try ye.'

6 He has slain a' the nine men,
      A ane an equal marrow,
   But up there startit a stuborn lord,
      That gard him sleep on Yarrow.

*   *   *   *   *   *   *

7 'Gae hame, gae hame, my sister Anne,
      An tell yer sister Sarah
   That she may gang an seek her lord,
      He 's lyin sleepin on Yarrow.'

8 'I dreamd a dream now sin yestreen,
      I thought it wad be sorrow;
   I thought I was pouin the hether green
      On the dowie banks o Yarrow.'

9 Then she 's away oer yon high hill —
      I wat she 's gane wi sorrow —
   And in a den she 's spy'd ten slain men,
      On the dowie banks o Yarrow.

10 'My love was a' clad oer last night
      Wi the finest o the tartan,
   But now he 's a' clad oer wi red,
      An he 's red bluid to the garten.'

11 She 's kissd his lips, she 's caimd his hair,
      As she had done before, O;
   She drank the red bluid that frae him ran,
      On the dowie banks o Yarrow.

12 'Tak hame your ousen, father, and yer
         kye,
      For they 've bred muckle sorrow;
   I wiss that they had a' gaen mad
      Afore they came to Yarrow.'

13 'O haud yer tongue, my daughter dear,
      For this breeds ay but sorrow;
   I 'll wed you to a better lord
      Than him you lost on Yarrow.'

14 'O haud yer tongue, my father dear,
      For ye but breed mair sorrow;
   A better rose will never spring
      Than him I 've lost on Yarrow.'

15 This lady being big wi child,
      An fu o lamentation,
   She died within her father's arms,
      Amang this stuborn nation.

———◆———

G

"Carterhaugh, June 15, 1802." "Scotch Ballads, Materials for Border Minstrelsy," No 135, Abbotsford.

*   *   *   *   *   *   *

1 SHE kissd his mouth and she combd his hair,
      As she had done before, O,
   She belted him in his noble broun,
      Before he went to Yarrow.

2 O he 's gone up yon high, [high] hill —
      I wat it was with sorrow —
   In a den he spied nine weal armd men,
      On the bonny banks of Yarrow.

3 'I see that you are nine for one,
    Which are of an unequal marrow;
As lang 's I 'm able to wield my bran,
    I 'll fight and be your marrow.'

4 O he has killed them a' but one,
    Which bred to him great sorrow;
For up and rose that stubborn lord,
    Made him sleep sound in Yarrow.

5 'Rise up, rise up, my daughter Ann,
    Go tell your sister Sarah
She may rise up go lift her lord;
    He 's sleeping sound in Yarrow.'

6 She 's gone up yon high, high hill —
    I wat it was with sorrow —
And in a den she spied nine slain men,
    On the dowie banks o Yarrow.

7 O she kissed his mouth, and she combd his
        hair,
    As she had done before, O;

She drank the bleed that from him ran,
    On the dowie banks o Yarrow.

8 'Take hame your oxen, tak hame your kye,
    They 've bred to me great sorrow;
I wish they had all now gone mad
    First when they came to Yarrow.'

9 'O hold your tongue now, daughter dear,
    These words to me 's great sorrow;
I 'll wed you on a better lord
    Than you have lost on Yarrow.'

10 'O hold your tongue now, father dear,
    These words to me 's great sorrow;
A brighter O shall there never spread
    Than I have lost in Yarrow.'

11 This lady being big with child,
    And full of lamentation,
She died unto her father's arms,
    Among the stubborn nation.

———◆———

H

Campbell MSS, II, 55.

1 'T was late at evening drinking wine,
    And early in the morning,
He set a combat them among,
    And he fought it in the morning.

*   *   *   *   *   *

2 'I have two swords by my side,
    They cost me both gold and money;
Take ye the best, I 'll take the worst,
    Come man for man, I 'll try ye.'

3 He has foughten them all round,
    His equal man and marrow,
While up bespake the stubborn lord,
    'He 's made them sleep in Yarrow.'

4 He says, Go home, my daughter Ann,
    And tell your sister Sarah
To come and lift her stubborn lord;
    The lad 's made him sleep in Yarrow.

5 As she gaed up yon high, high hill,
    I wot she gaed right sorrow,

And in a den spied nine well armd men,
    In the dowie dens of Yarrow.

6 'My love was dressd in the finest robes,
    And of the finest tartan,
And now he 's a' clad oer wi red,
    He 's bloody to the gartan!'

7 'O hold yer tongue, daughter!' he says,
    'That would breed but sorrow;
Ye shall be wed to a finer lord
    Than the one you 've lost in Yarrow.'

8 'Hold your tongue, father!' she says,
    'For that will breed but sorrow;
A finer lord can neer be born
    Than the one I 've lost in Yarrow.

9 'Take hame yer ox, and take hame yer kye,
    You 've bred me muckle sorrow;
I wish they 'd a' gane mad that day,
    That day they came to Yarrow.'

10 This woman being big wi child,
    And full of lamentation,
She died into her father's arms,
    Among that stubborn nation.

I

Buchan's MSS, II, 161.

1 TEN lords sat drinking at the wine
    Intill a morning early;
  There fell a combat them among,
    It must be fought, nae parley.

2 'O stay at hame, my ain gude lord!
    O stay, my ain dear marrow!'
  'Sweetest min, I will be thine,
    An dine wi you tomorrow.'

3 She kissd his lips, an combed his hair,
    As she had done before O,
  Gied him a brand down by his side,
    An he is on to Yarrow.

4 As he gaed oer yon dowey knowe,
    As he had dane before O,
  Nine armed men lay in a den,
    Upo the braes o Yarrow.

5 'O came ye here to hunt or hawk,
    As ye hae dane before O?
  Or came ye here to wiel your brand,
    Upo the braes o Yarrow?'

6 'I came nae here to hunt nor hawk,
    As I hae done before O;
  But I came here to wiel my brand,
    Upo the braes o Yarrow.'

7 Four he hurt, an five he slew,
    Till down it fell himsell O;
  There stood a fause lord him behin,
    Who thrust his body thorrow.

8 'Gae hame, gae hame, my brother John,
    An tell your sister sorrow;
  Your mither woud come take up her son,
    Aff o the braes o Yarrow.'

9 As he gaed oer yon high, high hill,
    As he had dane before O,
  There he met his sister dear,
    Came rinnin fast to Yarrow.

10 'I dreamd a dream last night,' she says,
    'I wish it binna sorrow;
  I dreamd I was puing the heather green
    Upo the braes o Yarrow.'

11 'I'll read your dream, sister,' he says,
    'I'll read it into sorrow;
  Ye're bidden gae take up your luve,
    He's sleeping sound on Yarrow.'

12 She's torn the ribbons frae her head —
    They were baith thick an narrow —
  She's kilted up her green claithing,
    An she's awa to Yarrow.

13 She's taen him in her arms twa,
    An gaen him kisses thorough,
  An wi her tears she bath'd his wounds,
    Upo the braes o Yarrow.

14 Her father, looking oer the castle-wa,
    Beheld his daughter's sorrow;
  'O had your tongue, daughter,' he says,
    'An lat be a' your sorrow!
  I'll wed you wi a better lord
    Than he that died on Yarrow.'

15 'O had your tongue, father,' she says,
    'An lat be till tomorrow!
  A better lord there coudna be
    Than he that died on Yarrow.'

16 She kissd his lips, an combd his hair,
    As she had done before O,
  An wi a crack her head did brack,
    Upo the braes o Yarrow.

J

Taken down from the singing of Marion Miller, in Threepwood, in the parish of Melrose. In Thomas Wilkie's handwriting, "' Scotch Ballads, Materials for Border Minstrelsy," No 107, Abbotsford. Another copy in Thomas Wilkie's MS., 1813–15, p. 57, No 67 of "Scotch Ballads," etc.

1 IN Thoro town there lives a maid,
  I am sure she has no marrow;
For she has forsaken both lords and knights,
  And loved a servant-lad in Galla.

2 Evening and morning her page he ran,
  Her page he ran wi sorrow,
With letters bound, just frae the town,
  To the servant-lad in Galla.

3 Her father he got word of that,
  And he 's bred all her sorrow;
He sent him forth to fight wi nine,
  In the dowie glens of Yarrow.

4 She washd his face, she combd his hair,
  She thought he had no marrow;
Wi a thrusty rapier by his side,
  She sent him forth to Yarrow.

5 She 's taen fareweel of him that day,
  As she had done before, O,
And she 's comd back to her bonny bower,
  But her love 's away to Yarrow.

6 He wanderd up, he wandred down,
  His heart was full of sorrow;
There he spied nine gentlemen,
  Watering their steeds in Yarrow.

7 'O come away, young man,' they said,
  'I 'm sure ye 'r no our marrow;
Ye 'r welcome here, young man,' they said,
  'For the bonny lass o Thorro.'

8 'Nine against one, weel do ye ken,
  That 's no an equal marrow;
Yet for my love's sake I 'll venture my life,
  In the dowie glens of Yarrow.'

9 Five was wounded, and four was slain,
  Amongst them a' he had no marrow;
He 's mounted on his horse again,
  Cries, I have won the bonny lass of Thorro!

10 Up then spake her father dear —
  And he 's bred all her sororw —
And wi a broad sword ran him through,
  In the dowie glens of Yarrow.

11 'I have dreamd a dream, father,
  I doubt I have dreamd for sorrow;
I dreamd I was pouing the heather green
  Wi my true love in Yarrow.'

12 'O I will read your dream, daughter,
  Although it be for your sorrow;
Go, and ye 'll find your love lying sound,
  In a heather-bush in Yarrow.'

13 She 's calld on her maidens then —
  Her heart was full of sorrow —
And she 's away wi her maidens twa,
  To the dowie glens o Yarrow.

14 She wandered up, she wandred down,
  In the dowie glens of Yarrow,
And there she spied her love lying sound,
  In a heather-bush in Yarrow.

15 She 's washd him in the clear well-strand,
  She 's dry'd him wi the holland,
And aye she sighd, and said, Alass!
  For my love I had him chosen.

16 His hair it was three quarters long,
  Three quarters long and yellow;
And she 's rapt it round her middle small,
  And brought it home to Thorro.

17 'O hold your tongue, my daughter dear,
  And talk no more of sorrow;
I 'll soon wed you on a better match
  Than your servant-lad in Galla.'

18 'O you may wed a' your seven sons,
  I wish you may wed them in sorrow:
O you may wed a' your seven sons,
  For you 'll neer wed the bonny lass of
    Thoro.'

19 This lady being big wi child,
  And her heart was full wi sorrow,
She died between her father's arms,
  In the bonny house of Thorro.

K

Campbell MS., I, 8; "communicated by Janet Ormstone, Innerleithen, who sung it to a beautiful old air."

1 THERE lived a lady in the south,
  She thought she had not her marrow;
And she was courted by nine gentlemen,
  In the dowie dens in Yarrow.

2 All their offers they proved in vain,
  She thought that they were not her marrow;
She has forsaken a' the nine,
  Loved a servant-lad on Galla.

3 Up bespoke her father dear,
  Who bred them a' this sorrow;
You must go far, far to fight the nine,
  In the dowie den in Yarrow.'

4 She washd his face, she combd his hair,
  Her heart being full of sorrow,
With a rusted rapier down by his side,
  To fight his foes in Yarrow.

5 He 's ridden east, he 's ridden west,
  He 's ridden into Yarrow,
And there he espied all the nine,
  Watering their steeds in Yarrow.

6 'Ye 'r welcome, welcome, young man,' they
    said,
  'But I think ye are not our marrow;'
'But I 'll fight ye all out, one by one,
  In the dowie dens o Yarrow.'

7 Four he has wounded, five he has slain,
  He left them a' sound in Yarrow;
He turned him round with rejoyfull looks,
  Says, I wone the lady of Thoro.

8 Up then spoke her father dear,
  Who bred them a' this sorrow;
He 's taen out a broadsword and run him
    through,
  In the dowie dens o Yarrow.

9 'I dreamed a dream last night,' she says,
  'I fear it is for sorrow;
I dreamd I was pulling the heather green
  With my true love in Yarrow.'

10 'I 'll read your dream now, daughter dear,
  I fear it is for sorrow;
You will find your true-love lying sound,
  In a heather bush in Yarrow.'

11 She 's ridden east, she 's ridden west,
  She 's ridden into Yarrow;
There she found her true lover sound,
  In a heather bush in Yarrow.

12 His hair it was five quarters lang,
  It was baith lang and yellow;
She 's tied it to her horse's mane,
  She 's trailed him home from Yarrow.

13 'O woe be to you, father dear!
  You 've bred me all this sorrow;'
So she died between her father's arms,
  In the dowie dens o Yarrow.

———◆———

L

Blackwood's Magazine, CXLVII, 741, June, 1890; communicated by Professor John Veitch, as received from William Welsh, a Peeblesshire cottar and poet, born 1799, whose mother used to recite the ballad, and whose grandmother had a copy in her father's handwriting.

1 AT Dryhope lived a lady fair,
  The fairest flower in Yarrow,
And she refused nine noble men
  For a servan lad in Gala.

2 Her father said that he should fight
  The nine lords all to-morrow,

And he that should the victor be
  Would get the Rose of Yarrow.

3 Quoth he, You 're nine, an I 'm but ane,
  And in that there 's no much marrow;
Yet I shall fecht ye, man for man,
  In the dowie dens o Yarrow.

4 She kissed his lips, and combed his hair,
  As oft she 'd done before, O,
An set him on her milk-white steed,
  Which bore him on to Yarrow.

215. THE BRAES O YARROW

5 When he got oer yon high, high hill,
    An down the dens o Yarrow,
There did he see the nine lords all,
    But there was not one his marrow.

6 'Now here ye 're nine, an I 'm but ane,
    But yet I am not sorrow;
For here I 'll fecht ye, man for man,
    For my true love in Yarrow.'

7 Then he wheeld round, and fought so fierce
    Till the seventh fell in Yarrow,
When her brother sprang from a bush behind,
    And ran his body thorough.

8 He never spoke more words than these,
    An they were words o sorrow;
'Ye may tell my true love, if ye please,
    That I 'm sleepin sound in Yarrow.'

9 They 've taen the young man by the heels
    And trailed him like a harrow,
And then they flung the comely youth
    In a whirlpool o Yarrow.

10 The lady said, I dreamed yestreen —
    I fear it bodes some sorrow —
That I was pu'in the heather green
    On the scroggy braes o Yarrow.'

11 Her brother said, I 'll read your dream,
    But it should cause nae sorrow;
Ye may go seek your lover hame,
    For he 's sleepin sound in Yarrow.

12 Then she rode oer yon gloomy height,
    An her heart was fu o sorrow,
But only saw the clud o night,
    Or heard the roar o Yarrow.

13 But she wandered east, so did she wast,
    And searched the forest thorough,
Until she spied her ain true love,
    Lyin deeply drowned in Yarrow.

14 His hair it was five quarters lang,
    Its colour was the yellow;
She twined it round her lily hand,
    And drew him out o Yarrow.

15 She kissed his lips, and combed his head,
    As oft she 'd done before, O;
She laid him oer her milk-white steed,
    An bore him home from Yarrow.

16 She washed his wounds in yon well-strand,
    And dried him wi the hollan,
And aye she sighed, and said, Alas!
    For my love I had him chosen.

17 'Go hold your tongue,' her father said,
    'There 's little cause for sorrow;
I 'll wed ye on a better lad
    Than ye hae lost in Yarrow.'

18 'Haud your ain tongue, my faither dear,
    I canna help my sorrow;
A fairer flower neer sprang in May
    Than I hae lost in Yarrow.

19 'I meant to make my bed fu wide,
    But you may make it narrow;
For now I 've nane to be my guide
    But a deid man drowned in Yarrow.'

20 An aye she screighed, and cried Alas!
    Till her heart did break wi sorrow,
An sank into her faither's arms,
    Mang the dowie dens o Yarrow.

M

In the handwriting of James Hogg, the Ettrick Shepherd
(later than **E** a). "Scotch Ballads, Materials for Border
Minstrelsy," No 11 a, Abbotsford.

1 O AY he sat, and ay he drank,
    An ay he counted the laying,
An ay he drank to the lass'es health
    Was to meet him in the dawning.

2 Up he gaes on yon high, high hill,
    An a wat he gaes wi sorrow,
An in a den he spy'd nine well armd men,
    On the dowie banks of Yarrow.

3 'Oh woe be to young women's wit!
    For the 've bred to me meikle sorrow;
She promisd for to meet me here,
    An she 's sent nine men to slay me.

4 'But there is two swords in my scabba[rd],
  They cost me gold and money;
  Tak ye the best, and I 'll tak the wa[rst],
  An come man for man, I 'll not fly yo[u].'

5 Ay he stood, an ay he fought,
  Till it was near the dawning,
  Then up an rose her brother James,
  An has slain him in the dawning.

6 'O the last night I dreamd a dream,
  God keep us a' frae sorrow!
  I dreamd I was powing the heather green
  In the dowie banks of Yarrow.'

7 Up she gaes on yon high, high hill,
  An a wat she gaes with sorrow,
  An in a den she spy'd nine slain men,
  In the dowie banks of Yarrow.

8 'O the last time I saw my love
  He was a' clad oer in tartan;
  But now he 's a' clad oer in red,
  An he 's a' blood to the gartin.'

9 She kist his mouth, an she 's combd his hair,
  As she had done before, O,
  She drank the blood that from him ran,
  In the dowie banks of Yarrow.

10 'O hold your tongue now, daughter,' he says,
   'An breed to me no more sorrow;
   For I 'll wed you on a better match
   Than you have lost on Yarrow.'

11 'Hold your tongue now, father,' she says,
   'An breed to me no more sorrow;
   For a better rose will never spring
   Than I have lost on Yarrow.'

N

Communicated to Scott by Mrs Christiana Greenwood, London, May 27, 1806 (Letters, I, No 189); presumably learned by her at Longnewton, near Jedburgh. " Scotch Ballads, Materials for Border Minstrelsy," No 84, Abbotsford.

1 THE cock did craw, and the day did daw,
  And the moon shone fair and clearly;
  Sir James gade out o his castle-yett,
  To meet fair Anne, his dearie.

2 'O come down, come down, my true-love Anne,
  And speak but ae word to me!
  But ae kiss o your bonny mouth
  Wad yield much comfort to me.'

3 'O how can I come down?' she says,
  'Or how can I win to thee?
  When there is nane that I can trust
  Wad safe convey me to thee.

4 'But gang doun, gang doun, to yon hostess'
    house,
  And there take on yere lawing,
  And, as I 'm a woman kind and true,
  I 'll meet you at the dawing.'

5 Then he gade thro the good green-wood,
  And oer the moor sae eerie,

And lang he stayd, and sair he sighd,
But he never mair saw his dearie.

6 And ay he sat, and lang he drank,
  And ay he counted his lawing,
  Till fifteen men did him surround,
  To slay him or the dawing.

7 'O she promisd ance to meet me this night,
  But I find she has deceived me;
  She promisd ance to meet me this night,
  And she 's sent fifteen to slay me!

8 'There are twa swords in my scabard,
  They cost me gowd and money;
  Take ye the best, and gie me the warst,
  And man for man I 'll try ye.'

9 Then they fought on, and on they fought,
  Till maist o them were fallen,
  When her brother John cam him behind,
  And slew him at the dawing.

10 Then he 's away to his sister Anne,
   To the chamber where 's she 's lying:
   'Come doun, come doun, my sister Anne,
   And take up your true-love Jamie!

11 'Come doun, come doun now, sister Anne!
   For he 's sleeping in yon logie;

Sound, sound he sleeps, nae mair to wake,
  And nae mair need ye be vogie.'

12 'I dreamd a drearie dream yestreen,
    Gin it be true, it will prove my sorrow;
  I dreamd my luive had lost his life,
    Within the yetts o Gowrie.

13 'O wae betide ye, lassies o Gowrie
    For ye hae sleepit soundly;
  Gin ye had keepit your yetts shut,
    Ye might hae sav'd the life o my Jamie.

14 'Yestreen my luive had a suit o claise
    Were o the finest tartan;

But lang or ere the day did daw
  They war a' red bluid to the garten.

15 'Yestreen my luive had a suit o claise
    Were o the apple reamin;
  But lang or ere the day did daw
    The red bluid had them streamin.'

16 In yon fair ha, where the winds did blaw,
    When the moon shone fair and clearly,
  She's thrawn her green skirt oer her head,
    And ay she cried out mercy.

O

Herd's MSS, I, 35, II, 181.

1 'I DREAMD a dreary dream last night,
    God keep us a' frae sorrow!
  I dreamd I pu'd the birk sae green
    Wi my true luve on Yarrow.'

2 'I'll read your dream, my sister dear,
    I'll tell you a' your sorrow;
  You pu'd the birk wi your true luve,
    He's killd, he's killd on Yarrow!'

3 'O gentle wind, that blaweth south
    To where my love repaireth,
  Convey a kiss from his dear mouth,
    And tell me how he fareth!

4 'But oer yon glen run armed men,
    Have wrought me dule and sorrow;
  They've slain, they've slain the comliest swain,
    He bleeding lies on Yarrow.'

P

Cromek's Select Scotish Songs, 1810, II, 196, the seventh and tenth stanzas; sent by Burns to William Tytler in 1790.

1 'GET up, get up now, sister Ann,
    I fear we've wrought you sorrow;
  Get up, ye'll find your true love slain,
    Among the banks of Yarrow.'

2 'I made my love a suit of clothes,
    I clad him all in tartan,
  But ere the morning sun arose,
    He was a' bluid to the gartan.'

A. *The words in ' ' are so distinguished in the MS., and are of course emendations. 'Than,' 9[1], is obviously an insertion; 'Now Douglas,' 11[1], is entirely unauthorized, and, as before said, is taken from Hamilton's ballad; 'wiped,' 14[3], is probably substi-* tuted for *drank, cf.* 12[3], *etc.; and* 'her,' 15[3], *is very likely to have been* his.
B. 12[1]. *Var.* O father dear, I pray forbear.
C. 7[1]. He. 7[3]. SHe, *originally* He. 9[1,3]. a *in* came *is not closed; possibly* cume.

A few changes were, as usual, made by Moth-erwell in printing.

D. 1[4]. Wha *is blotted.*

E. b. *A minute collation of a copy constructed by Scott would be useless and deceptive, and therefore only the larger variations will be noted.*

1[2]. And ere they paid the lawing.

5[1]. As he gaed up the Tennies bank.

6[1,2]. O come ye here to part your land,
The bonnie forest thorough.

7[1,2]. I come not here to part my land,
And neither to beg nor borrow.

After 7:
If I see all, ye 're nine to ane, (*Cf.* F 4[1].)
And that 's an unequal marrow; (*Cf.* G 3[2].)
Yet will I fight while lasts my brand,
(*Cf.* F 4[8], G 3[8].)
On the bonny banks of Yarrow. (*Cf.* E a 6[4].)

10[4]. Wi my true love, on Yarrow. (*Cf.* O 1[4].)
After 10, *two stanzas which are nearly* O 3, 4.
11[8]. ten slain men. (*Cf.* F 9[8].)
12[2,8]. She searchd his wounds all thorough;
She kissd them till her lips grew red.
13[2]. For a' this breeds but sorrow. (*Cf.* F 13[2].)
14[2]. Ye mind me but of sorrow.
14[8,4]. A fairer rose did never bloom
Than now lies croppd on Yarrow.
(*Cf.* M 11[8,4].)
Scott gives in a note, III, 79, 1803, "the last stanza, as (*since?*) it occurs in most copies." (*Cf.* F, G, H.)

That lady, being big with child,
And full of consternation,
She swooned in her father's arms,
Amidst that stubborn nation.

F. 2[8]. browns, *and so again* G 1[8]. *A derivation from* bruny, *mail-coat, is scarcely to be thought of. Apparently a corruption of* brand, (*cf.* E 4[8]); *but* brand *occurs in* F 4[8], G 3[8].

G. 1[2]. before him. 1[8]. and his noble brouns.
10[8]. shalt.

H. 3, 4. *The* stubborn lord *in* 3[8] *is the wife's father, and the race, or family, is* stubborn *according to* 10. *Stubborn folk think opposers* stubborn, *no doubt; still the epithet is unlikely in* 4[8]. Lad *I suppose to refer*

to the man who in the other versions stabs from behind.

5[8]. dern *for* den. *The* nine men *must be* dead, *as in* E 11, F 9, G 6. *The* well armd *belongs to an earlier (lost) stanza, corresponding to* E 5, F 3, G 2.

I. *Variations in Buchan's printed copy:*
1[1]. Ten lords. The lords *in my copy of the MS., but, as Dixon has also* Ten, *I presume* The *'to be an error. Otherwise I should have read* Th[re]e, *as in* B, C, D.
4[2]. As aft he 'd.
7[4]. thrust him thro body and mell, O.
8[8]. mother to. 14[4]. ower his.

J. *The first copy seems to be the earlier, and that which was transcribed into the MS. to have been slightly edited, but the variations are few, mostly spellings. The first copy has no title. The title of the second is altered from* The Braes of Yarrow *to* The Dowie Glens of Yarrow. *At the end of the second is this note:* This song I took down from Marion Miller in Threepwood, in the Parish of Melrose. The air was plaintive and extremely wild. I consider this song more valuable on account that Mern had never sung it to any but myself for fifteen years, and she had almost said, or rather promised, that she would never sing it to another.
Thoro, 1[1], *etc., is spelt* Thorough, Thorrough, *in the first copy,* Thorough, Thorrough, Thorro, Thoro, *in the second; but in the latter* ugh *is struck out wherever it occurs.*
4[8]. thrusty, *in both; i. e.,* trusty.
11[8]. the (birks) heather green, *in both.*
First. 5[2], 17[1], 18[1]. oh, Oh.
Second. 5[2]. What she had neer done before, O.
6[2], 19[2]. was filled wi.
9[1]. Five he. 9[2]. nae. 9[8]. steed.
12[2]. to your.
18[2]. wi *for* in.

K. 3[8]. far far *should probably be* forth, *as in* J; *possibly* forth for.

L. 12[8,4], 13[1,2]. *Compare Logan's* Braes of Yarrow.

They sought him east, they sought him west,
They sought him all the forest thorough;
They only saw the cloud of night
They only heard the roar of Yarrow.

O. " A fragment, to the tune of Leaderhaughs and Yarrow."

215

RARE WILLIE DROWNED IN YARROW, OR, THE WATER O GAMRIE

A. 'Willy 's rare and Willy 's fair,' Thomson's Orpheus Caledonius, II, 110, 1733.

B. a. Cromek's Select Scotish Songs, 1810, II, 196.
b. Stenhouse, Musical Museum, 1853, IV, 464.

C. 'The Dowie Dens o Yarrow,' Gibb MS., p. 37.

D. Skene MS., p. 47.

E. 'Willie 's drowned in Gamery,' Buchan's Ballads of the North of Scotland, I, 245.

F. 'The Water o Gamery,' Buchan's MSS., II, 159. Dixon, Scottish Traditional Versions of Ancient Ballads, p. 66, Percy Society, vol. xvii.

G. 'The Water o Ganrie,' Motherwell's MS., p. 637.

H. 'The Water o Gemrie,' Campbell MSS, II, 78.

A WAS inserted in the fourth volume of The Tea-Table Miscellany, and stands in the edition of 1763 at p. 321, 'Rare Willie drowned in Yarrow,' It is given in Herd's Ancient and Modern Scots Songs, 1769, p. 197 (with two or three trifling changes); in Johnson's Museum, p. 542, No 525. F is epitomized in Christie's Traditional Ballad Airs, I, 66, "with some changes from the way the editor has heard it sung."

The fragment in Cromek's Select Scotish Songs, 1810, II, 196, sent by Burns in a letter to William Tytler, 1790, belongs, as already said, mostly with 'The Duke of Athole's Nurse,' but has two stanzas of 'Willie drowned in Yarrow' (B).

'The Braes of Yarrow,' Ritson's Scotish Song, I, 154, composed upon the story of this ballad by the Rev. John Logan (1748–88), has two of the original lines (nearly):

They sought him east, they sought him west,
They sought him all the forest thorough.

Willie is drowned in Yarrow according to the older (southern) tradition, A; also B, C. In the northern copies, D, E, F, with which G, H, agree, the scene is transferred to Gamrie, on the coast of the Moray Frith, where, as Christie remarks, "there is no water that Willie could have been drowned in but the sea, on his way along the sands to the old kirk." * In the ballad which follows this, a western variety of the same story, Willie is drowned in the Clyde.

C 2, 3, 5, 6, belong to the preceding ballad, and 4 is common to that and this.

A 2 would come in better at the end of the story (as it does in C, a copy of slight authority), if it might properly find a place anywhere in the ballad. But this stanza suits only a woman who has been for some time living with her husband. A woman on her wedding-day could have no call to make her bed broad in her mother's house, whether yestreen or the morrow. I therefore conclude that A 2 does not belong to this ballad.†

* Buchan's note to E is, for a wonder, to the purpose. With his usual simplicity, he informs us that "the unfortunate hero of this ballad was a factor to the laird of Kinmundy." He then goes on to say: "As the young woman to whom he was to be united in connubial wedlock resided in Gamery, a small fishing-town on the east coast of the Murray Frith, the marriage was to be solemnized in the church of that parish; to which he was on his way when overtaken by some of the breakers which overflow a part of the road he had to pass, and dash with impetuous fury against the lofty and adamantine rocks with which it is skirted." I, 315.

† Professor Veitch has remarked on the incongruousness of this stanza in Blackwood's Magazine, June, 1890, p. 739 ff. Something like it, but adjusted to the circumstances of a maid, occurs in the ballad which he there prints as the "Original Ballad of the Dowie Dens." See No 214, p. 174, L 19.

D–H. Rare Willie has promised to marry Meggie, E (also A, C, D). His mother would give her the wale of all her other sons, but not Willie; she will have him only; D, E (cf. G 1). The bridegroom, with a large company, is mounted to ride for the bride; he tells his friends to go forward, he has forgotten to ask his mother's blessing; D, E, F, H. He receives the blessing, D, F, H; her blessing goes not with him, G; he gets her heavy curse, E; even in F his mother, after giving her blessing, says that he will never see his wedding. (The mother's curse is the characteristic feature of the next following ballad.) The bridal party come to the river, or burn, of Gamrie; all the others pass the stream safely, but Willie is washed from his saddle, D–H. The rest ride on to the kirk of Gamrie. The bride asks where is the man who was to marry her, and is told that Willie is drowned. She tears the ribbons from her hair and runs to the river, plunges in, and finds Willie in the deepest pot, the middle, the deepest weil. She will make her bed with him in Gamrie; both mothers shall be alike sorry; D–G.

In H, Willie's horse comes home with an empty saddle. His mother is sure that her son is dead; her daughter tries in vain to persuade her that all is well; Meggie takes her lover's body from the river and lays it on the grass; she will sleep with him in the same grave at Gamrie.

In A, B, the drowned body is found in the cleft of a rock, the clifting or clintin of a craig; in C 4 neath a buss of brume, that stanza belonging, as most of the copy does, to the preceding ballad; cf. J 14, K 11 of No 214. The bride ties three links of her hair, which is three quarters long, round Willie's waist, and draws him out of the water, B 2, C 5; for the hair, cf. No 214, where also it is not advantageously used. The bride's tearing the ribbons from her head, D 12, E 15, F 8, G 7, H 14, is found also in No 214, D 11, I 12, but is inappropriate there. A brother, brother John, whether the man's or the woman's, tells the bad news in No 214, A 11, E 9, I 8, L 11, N 9, 10, as here D 11, E 14, F 7, G 6, H 13.

'Annan Water,' a ballad in which a lover is drowned on his way to visit his mistress, is given in an appendix.

A

Thomson's Orpheus Caledonius, II, 110, 1733.

1 'WILLY 's rare, and Willy 's fair,
    And Willy 's wondrous bony,
    And Willy heght to marry me,
    Gin eer he marryd ony.

2 'Yestreen I made my bed fu brade,
    The night I 'll make it narrow,
    For a' the live-long winter's night
    I lie twin'd of my marrow.

3 'O came you by yon water-side?
    Pu'd you the rose or lilly?
    Or came you by yon meadow green?
    Or saw you my sweet Willy?'

4 She sought him east, she sought him west,
    She sought him brade and narrow;
    Sine, in the clifting of a craig,
    She found him drownd in Yarrow.

B

a. Cromek's Select Scotish Songs, 1810, II, 196; eighth and ninth stanzas of a fragment sent William Tytler by Burns in 1790. b. Stenhouse's edition of the Musical Museum, 1853, IV, 464.

1 SHE sought him east, she sought him west,
    She sought him braid and narrow,

Till in the clintin of a craig
    She found him drownd in Yarrow.

2 She 's taen three links of her yellow hair,
    That hung down lang and yellow,
    And she 's tied it about sweet Willie's waist,
    An drawn him out o Yarrow.

C

Gibb MS., No 7, p. 37; from recitation. "Traced to Eppie Fraser, daughter of a tramp, and unable to read, *circa* 1840."

1 'WILLIE 's fair, an Willie 's rare,
  An Willie 's wondrous bonny,
  An Willie 's promised to marry me,
  If eer he marry ony.'

2 'O sister dear, I 've dreamed a dream,
  I 'm afraid it 's unco sorrow ;
  I dreamed I was pu'in the heather green,
  In the dowie dens o Yarrow.'

3 'O sister dear, I 'll read your dream,
  I 'm afraid it will be sorrow ;

Ye 'll get a letter ere it 's een
  Your lover 's drowned in Yarrow.'

4 She socht him up, she socht him doun,
  In mickle dule an sorrow ;
  She found him neath a buss o brume,
  In the dowie dens o Yarrow.

5 Her hair it was three quarters lang,
  Its colour it was yallow ;
  She tied it to his middle sma,
  An pu'ed him oot o Yarrow.

6 'My bed it was made wide yestreen,
  The nicht it sall be narrow ;
  There 's neer a man lie by my side
  Since Willie 's drowned in Yarrow.'

D

Skene MS., p. 47; taken down from recitation in the north of Scotland, 1802–3.

1 'WILLIE 's fair, and Willie 's rare,
  An he is wondrous bonnie,
  An Willie has promist to marry me,
  Gin ever he marry ony.'

2 'Ye 's get Jammie, or ye 's [get] Johnnie,
  Or ye 's get bonny Peter ;
  Ye 's get the wale o a' my sons,
  But leave me Willie the writer.'

3 'I winna hae Jamie, I winna hae Johnie,
  I winna hae bonny Peter ;
  I winna hae ony o a' your sons,
  An I get na Willie the writer.'

4 .   .   .   .
  .   .   .   .
  There was threescore and ten brisk young men
  Was boun to briddal-stool wi him :

5 'Ride on, ride on, my merry men a',
  I forgot something behind me ;
  I forgat my mither's blessing,
  To hae to bride-stool wi me.'

6 'God's blessin an mine gae wi ye, Willie,
  God's blessing an mine gae wi ye ;

For ye 're nae ane hour but bare nineteen,
  Fan ye 're gauin to meet your Meggie.'

7 They rode on, and farther on,
  Till they came to the water of Gamrie,
  An they a' wan safe through,
  Unless it was sweet Willie.

8 The first ae step that Willie's horse steppit,
  He steppit to the bridle ;
  The next ae step that Willie's horse steppit,
  Toom grew Willie's saddle.

9 They rod on, an farther on,
  Till they came to the kirk of Gamrie.
  .   .   .   .   .   .
  .   .   .   .   .   .

10 Out spak the bonny bride,
  .   .   .   .   .   .
  'Whar is the man that's to gie me his han
  This day at the kirk of Gamrie ? '

11 Out spak his brother John,
  An O bat he was sorrie !
  'It fears me much, my bonny bride,
  He sleeps oure soun in Gamerie.'

12 The ribbons that were on her hair —
  An they were thick and monny —
  She rive them a', let them down fa,
  An is on[to] the water o Gamerie.

13 She sought it up, she sought it down,
  She sought it braid and narrow;
  An in the deepest pot o Gamerie,
  There she got sweet Willie.

14 She has kissd his comely mouth,
  As she had done before [O] :
  'Baith our mithers sall be alike sorry,
  For we's baith sleep in Gamery.'

E

Buchan's Ballads of the North of Scotland, I, 245.

1 'O WILLIE is fair, and Willie is rare,
  And Willie is wondrous bonny,
  And Willie says he'll marry me,
  Gin ever he marry ony.'

2 'O ye'se get James, or ye'se get George,
  Or ye's get bonny Johnnie;
  Ye'se get the flower o a' my sons,
  Gin ye'll forsake my Willie.'

3 'O what care I for James or George,
  Or yet for bonny Peter?
  I dinna value their love a leek,
  An I getna Willie the writer.

4 'O Willie has a bonny hand,
  And dear but it is bonny!'
  'He has nae mair for a' his land;
  What woud ye do wi Willie?'

5 'O Willie has a bonny face,
  And dear but it is bonny!'
  'But Willie has nae other grace;
  What woud ye do wi Willie?'

6 'Willie's fair, and Willie's rare,
  And Willie's wondrous bonny;
  There's nane wi him that can compare,
  I love him best of ony.'

7 On Wednesday, that fatal day,
  The people were convening;
  Besides all this, threescore and ten,
  To gang to the bride-steel wi him.

8 'Ride on, ride on, my merry men a',
  I've forgot something behind me;
  I've forgot to get my mother's blessing,
  To gae to the bride-steel wi me.'

9 'Your Peggy she's but bare fifteen,
  And ye are scarcely twenty;
  The water o Gamery is wide and braid;
  My heavy curse gang wi thee!'

10 Then they rode on, and further on,
  Till they came on to Gamery;
  The wind was loud, the stream was proud,
  And wi the stream gaed Willie.

11 Then they rode on, and further on,
  Till they came to the kirk o Gamery;
  And every one on high horse sat,
  But Willie's horse rade toomly.

12 When they were settled at that place,
  The people fell a mourning,
  And a council held amo them a',
  But sair, sair wept Kinmundy.

13 Then out it speaks the bride hersell,
  Says, What means a' this mourning?
  Where is the man amo them a'
  That shoud gie me fair wedding?

14 Then out it speaks his brother John,
  Says, Meg, I'll tell you plainly;
  The stream was strong, the clerk rade wrong,
  And Willie's drownd in Gamery.

15 She put her hand up to her head,
  Where were the ribbons many;
  She rave them a', let them down fa',
  And straightway ran to Gamery.

16 She sought it up, she sought it down,
  Till she was wet and weary;
  And in the middle part o it,
  There she got her deary.

17 Then she stroakd back his yellow hair,
  And kissd his mou sae comely:
  'My mother's heart's be as wae as thine!
  We'se baith asleep in the water o Gamery.'

F

Buchan MSS, II, 159.

1 WHAN Willie was in his saddle set,
    And all his merry men wi him,
'Stay still, stay still, my merry men all,
    I 've forgot something behind me.

2 'Gie me God's blessing an yours, mither,
    To hae me on to Gamery;
Gie me God's blessing an yours, mither,
    To gae to the bride-stool wi me.'

3 'I 'll gie ye God's blessing an mine, Willie,
    To hae you on to Gamery;
Ye 's hae God's blessing an mine, Willie,
    To gae to the bride-stool wi you.

4 .   .   .   .   .   .
    .   .   .   .   .   .
'But Gamery it is wide and deep,
    An ye 'll never see your wedding;'

5 Some rede back, an some rede fore,
    An some rede on to Gamery;
The bonniest knight's saddle among them all
    Stood teem in the Water o Gamery.

6 Out it spake the bride hersell,
    Says, What makes all this riding?
Where is the knight amongst you all
    Aught me this day for wedding?

7 Out it spake the bridegroom's brother,
    Says, Margaret, I 'll tell you plainly;
The knight ye should hae been wedded on
    Is drownd in the Water o Gamery.

8 She 's torn the ribbons aff her head —
    They were baith thick an mony —
She kilted up her green claithing,
    And she has passed the Gamery.

9 She 's plunged in, so did she down,
    That was baith black an jumly,
And in the middle o that water
    She found her ain sweet Willie.

10 She 's taen him in her arms twa
    And gied him kisses many:
'My mother 's be as wae as thine!
    We 'll baith lie in the Water o Gamery.'

———————————

G

Motherwell's MS., p. 637; from the recitation of the wife
of James Baird, forester at Dalrymple.

1 'O STAY at hame, my ain son Willie,
    And let your bride tak Johnie!
O stay at hame, my ain son Willie!
    For my blessing gaes not wi thee.'

2 'I canna stay, nor I winna stay,
    And let my bride tak Johnie;
I canna stay, nor I winna stay,
    Though your blessing gaes na wi me.

3 'I have a steed in my stable
    That cost me monie a pennie,
And on that steed I winna dread
    To ride the water o Genrie.'

4 The firsten step that Willie stept,
    He steppit to the bellie;
The wind blew loud, the stream ran proud,
    And awa wi it gaed Willie.

5 And when the bride gaed to the kirk,
    Into the kirk o Ganrie,
She cuist her ee among them a',
    But she sawna her love Willie.

6 Out and spak her auld brither,
    Saying, Peggie, I will tell thee;
The man ye should been married till
    Lyes in the water o Genrie.

7 She tore the ribbons aff her head,
    That were baith rich and manie,
And she has kiltit up her coat,
    And ran to the water o Ganrie.

8 She 's sought him up, sae did she doun,
    Thro a' the water o Ganrie;
In the deepest weil in a' the burn,
    Oh, there she fand her Willie!

9 She has taen him in her arms twa,
    Sae fondly as she kisst him!
Said, 'My mither sall be wae as thine,'
    And she 's lain doun aside him.

H

Campbell MSS, II, 78.

1 THEY were saddled a', they were briddled a',
   Bridegroom and a' was ready;
'Stop,' says he, 'my nobles a',
   For I 've left something behind me.

2 'It is your blessing, mother dear,
   To bound [to] the bride-styl with me:'
'God's blessing now, my son,' says she,
   'And mine and a' gang wi ye!

3 'For ye are scarce nineteen years of age
   When ye met in wi bonny Maggie,
And I 'm sure, my dear, she 'll welcome you
   This day in the kirk o Gemrie.'

4 It 's they have ridden up, it 's they have ridden
     down,
   And joy was in their gallant company;
It 's they have ridden up, and they have ridden
     down,
   Till they came to the water o Gemrie.

5 When they came to the water, it was flooded;
   In the middle Sweet William he fell;
The spray brook over his horse's mane,
   And the wind sang his funeral knell.

6 'O much is the pity!   O much is the pity!'
   Cried that joyful company;
'O much is the pity!   O much is the pity!'
   But alas! now are woeful and wae.

7 Hame and hame came his stead,
   And ran to its ain stable;
They 've gien it corn and hay to eat,
   As much as it was able.

8 His mother she was a waefu woman,
   As dung as woman could be;
'My son,' says she, 'is either hurt or slain,
   Or drowned in the waters of Gemrie.'

9 It 's up and spak her daughter Ann:
   'What needs be a' this mourning?
He 's lighted at yon bonny kirk-style,
   And his steed has run away from him.'

10 'O had yer tongue, my daughter Ann,
   Nor scold na me about mourning;
Hadna my son there men enew
   To hae taken his steed from him?'

11 They 've ridden up, they 've ridden down,
   Till they came to the kirk o Gemrie;
There they saw his winsome bride,
   Alone at the kirk-style standing.

12 'Where away is the man,' says she,
   'That promised me fair wedding?
This day he vowd to meet me here,
   But O he 's lang o coming!'

13 Up and spak his brother John,
   Says, 'Meg, I 'll tell ye plainly;
The stream was strang, and we rade wrang,
   And he 's drownd in the water o Gemrie.'

14 She 's torn the ribons frae her hair,
   That were baith thick and many;
She 's torn them a', lettin them fa',
   And she 's away to the waters o Gemrie.

15 She ['s] sought him up, she 's sought him down,
   Until that she 's gotten his body,
And she 's laid it on the green, green grass,
   And flung her mantle oer him.

16 'O Willie was red, but O now he 's white!
   And Willie was wondrous bonny,
And Willie he said he 'd marry me,
   Gin ere he married oney.

17 'He was red, he was white, he was my delight,
   And aye, aye I thought him bonny;
But now since Willie has dy'd for me,
   I will sleep wi him in the same grave at
     Gemrie.'

———·———

B. b. "The editor has often heard the following
   additional stanza [*the second*], though it is
   omitted by Thomson."
   2¹. links o her gowden locks.

2³. She 's tied them about.
D. *Not divided into stanzas in the MS.*
E. *Variations in Christie*, I, 66:
   2¹⁻³. ye 'll.   6¹. O Willie 's.

7³. And there were mair than threescore and
ten.
14⁴. at Gamery.   15². Where she had ribbons.
15⁸. And tore them a' and let.

15⁴. And syne she ran.   16⁴. 'T was there.
17¹. She straiked back.   17⁴. We 'll baith sleep.
G.   6¹. *Originally* But out.
H.   2². bound the bridgestyle.

APPENDIX

ANNAN WATER

Minstrelsy of the Scottish Border, 1833, III, 282; 1802,
II, 138.

THE first edition lacks stanzas 5, 6, 8, 9. Two
of these were inserted "from another copy of the
ballad in which the conclusion proves fortunate."

"The ballad," says Scott, "is given from tradition," for which a more precise expression would perhaps be "oral repetition." It is asserted in the
Minstrelsy to be "the original words of the tune of
'Allan Water,' by which name the song is mentioned
in Ramsay's Tea-Table Miscellany" ('Allan Water,
or, My love Annie 's very bonny,' T. T. M., vol. i,
p. 105, of the Dublin edition of 1729). This asser-
tion is not justified by any reasons, nor does it seem
pertinent, if the Allan was originally the river of
the ballad, to add, as the editor does, that "the
Annan and the Frith of Solway, into which it falls,
are the frequent scenes of tragical accidents."

A song which may pass for the original Allan
Water until an earlier is produced is among the
Laing broadsides (now in the possession of Lord
Rosebery), No 59. There is no date or place, but it
is thought to have been printed toward the end of
the seventeenth century, or the beginning of the
eighteenth, and probably at Edinburgh.

The title is: 'Allan Water, or, A Lover in Captivity.*   A new song, sung with a pleasant new
air.' There are three eight-line stanzas, and it begins:

> Allan Water 's wide and deep,
>   and my dear Anny 's very bonny;
> Wide 's the straith that lyes above 't,
>   if 't were mine, I 'de give it all for Anny.

Allan Cunningham says of the ballad, Songs of

Scotland, II, 102: "I have heard it sung on the
banks of the Annan. Like all traditional verses,
there are many variations." And he cites as "from
an old fragment" these couplets:

> O Annan water's wading deep, [*i. e.* wide and]
> Yet I am loth to weet my feet;
> But if ye 'll consent to marry me,
> I 'll hire a horse to carry thee.†

It is my conviction that 'Anna Water,' in Ramsay's language, is one of the "Scots poems wrote
by the ingenious before" 1800.

"By the Gatehope Slack," says Sir Walter
Scott, "is perhaps meant the Gate Slack, a pass
in Annandale."

1 'ANNAN water 's wading deep,
       And my love Annie 's wondrous bonny,
   And I am laith she suld weet her feet,
       Because I love her best of ony.

2 'Gar saddle me the bonny black,
       Gar saddle sune, and make him ready,
   For I will down the Gatehope-Slack,
       And all to see my bonny ladye.'

3 He has loupen on the bonny black,
       He stirrd him wi the spur right sairly;
   But, or he wan the Gatehope-Slack,
       I think the steed was wae and weary.

4 He has loupen on the bonny grey,
       He rade the right gate and the ready ;
   I trow he would neither stint nor stay,
       For he was seeking his bonny ladye.

5 O he has ridden oer field and fell,
       Through muir and moss, and mony a mire ;
   His spurs o steel were sair to bide,
       And frae her fore-feet flew the fire.

6 'Now, bonny grey, now play your part!
       Gin ye be the steed that wins my deary,

---

* Mr Macmath informs me that in "A Collection of Old
Ballads, etc., printed at Edinburgh between the years 1660
and 1720," No 7228 of the catalogue issued by John Stevenson, Edinburgh, 1827, there is this item: "Be valiant still,

etc., a new song much in request; also Logan Water, or, A
Lover in Captivity."

† "Hire a horse," in an "old fragment"? — Cunningham
gives the first two stanzas of the ballad, with variations in
the first, in his edition of Burns, 1834, V, 107.

Wi corn and hay ye 'se be fed for aye,
    And never spur sall make you wearie.'

7 The grey was a mare, and a right good mare,
    But when she wan the Annan water
  She couldna hae ridden a furlong mair
    Had a thousand merks been wadded at her.

8 'O boatman, boatman, put off your boat!
    Put off your boat for gowden money!
  I cross the drumly stream the night,
    Or never mair I see my honey.'

9 'O I was sworn sae late yestreen,
    And not by ae aith, but by many;
  And for a' the gowd in fair Scotland
    I dare na take ye through to Annie.'

10 The ride was stey, and the bottom deep,
    Frae bank to brae the water pouring,
  And the bonny grey mare did sweat for fear,
    For she heard the water-kelpy roaring.

11 O he has poud aff his dapperpy coat,
    The silver buttons glanced bonny;
  The waistcoat bursted aff his breast,
    He was sae full of melancholy.

12 He has taen the ford at that stream tail;
    I wot he swam both strong and steady;
  But the stream was broad, and his strength did
      fail,
    And he never saw his bonny ladye!

13 'O wae betide the frush saugh wand!
    And wae betide the bush of brier!
  It brake into my true-love's hand,
    When his strength did fail, and his limbs did tire.

14 'And wae betide ye, Annan Water,
    This night that ye are a drumlie river!
  For over thee I 'll build a bridge,
    That ye never more true love may sever.'

216

THE MOTHER'S MALISON, OR, CLYDE'S WATER

A. 'Clyde's Water,' Skene MS., p. 50.

B. 'Willie and May Margaret,' Jamieson's Popular Ballads, 1806, I, 135.

C. 'The Drowned Lovers,' Buchan's Ballads of the North of Scotland, I, 140; 'Willie and Margaret,' Motherwell's MS., p. 611; printed in part in Motherwell's Minstrelsy, Appendix, p. iii.

STANZAS 1, 5, 6, 7, 16, of B were printed by Jamieson (under the title of Sweet Willie and May Margaret) in the Scots Magazine, October, 1803, p. 700, in the hope of obtaining a complete copy.

In notes to B are here given some various readings and supplementary verses which were entered by Motherwell in a copy of his Minstrelsy, without indication of their origin.* Motherwell made a few changes in transcribing C into his MS., and others in the verses which he printed in the appendix to his Minstrelsy.

* This volume came in 1836 into the hands of Motherwell's friend, Mr P. A. Ramsay. The entries have been communicated to me by Mr Macmath.

The copy of this ballad in Nimmo's Songs and Ballads of Clydesdale, p. 134, was compounded from B and C.

Willie orders his horse and his man to be fed, for he means to be that very night with his love Margaret. His mother would have him stay with her: he shall have the best bed in the house and the best hen in the roost, A; the best cock in the roost and the best sheep in the flock, B; a sour wind is blowing and the night will be dark, C. He cares for none of these, and will go. My malison drown thee in Clyde! says his mother. Clyde is roaring fearfully, but he wins through. Arrived at Margaret's bower, he tirls at the pin and calls to her to open. A voice asks, Who is there? It is her lover, his boots full of Clyde's water. An answer comes, as if from Margaret, that she has no lovers without and none within, and she will not open, A, C; her mother is fast asleep, and she dares make no din, B. Then he begs for some shelter for the night; but is told that one chamber is full of corn, another full of hay, and the third full of gentlemen, who will not go till morning. Farewell, then; he has won his mother's malison by coming. Clyde's water is half up over the brae, B, and sweeps him off his horse, C. Margaret wakens from a dreary dream that her love had been 'staring' (standing?) at the foot of her bed, A; had been at the gates, and nobody would let him in, C. Her mother informs her that her lover had really been at the gates but half an hour before. Margaret instantly gets up and goes after Willie, crying to him against the loud wind. She does not stop for the river. No more was ever seen of Willie but his hat, no more of Margaret but her comb and her snood, A, which might end well so, but has lost a few lines. C ends like the preceding ballad: Margaret finds Willie in the deepest pot in Clyde; they shall sleep together in its bed.

C 20, 21 absurdly represents Willie's brother as standing on the river-bank and expostulating with him; this in the dead of night.[*]

The passage in two of the copies, A 10–16, C 11–15, 22–25, in which the mother, pretending to be her daughter, repels the lover, and the daughter, who has dreamed that her lover had come and had been refused admittance, is told by her mother that this had actually happened, and sets off in pursuit of her lover, seems to have been adopted from 'The Lass of Roch Royal,' No 76. Parts are exchanged, as happens not infrequently with ballads; in the 'Lass of Roch Royal,' the lass is turned away by her lover's mother, pretending to speak in his person. There is verbal correspondence, particularly in A 16; cf. No 76,

D 26, 27, E 22, 23. In D 19 of No 76 the professed Love Gregor tells Annie that he has another love, as the professed Meggie in A 11 (inconsistently with what precedes) tells Willie.

The three steps into the water, C 26–28, occur also in 'Child Waters,' No 63, B 7–9, C 6–8, I 3, 4, 6. Nose-bleed, C 1, is a bad omen; see No 208.

Verses A 8[1,2], C 10[1,2],

> Make me your wrack as I come back,
> But spare me as I go,

are found in a broadside 'Tragedy of Hero and Leander,' Roxburghe Ballads, III, 152, etc., of the date, it is thought, of about 1650; Ebsworth's Roxburghe Ballads, VI, 558, Collier's Book of Roxburghe Ballads, 1847, p. 227. The conceit does not overwell suit a popular ballad. The original is Martial's Parcite dum propero, mergite cum redeo, otherwise, Mergite me, fluctus, cum rediturus ero, Epigr. lib., 25 b, and lib. xiv, 181.

A very popular Italian ballad has some of the traits of 'The Mother's Malison,' parts being exchanged and the girl drowned. A girl is asked in marriage; her mother objects, in most of the copies on the ground of her daughter's youth; she goes off with her lover; the mother wishes that she may drown in the sea; arrived at the seashore her horse becomes restive, and the girl is drowned (or she goes down in mid-sea): 'Maledizione della Madre,' Nigra, Canti popolari del Piemonte, p. 151, No 23 A–F; 'La Maledizione materna,' 'Marcoaldi, p. 170, No 15; 'La Maledetta,' Ferraro, C. p. monferrini, p. 35, No 27; 'Buonasera, vedovella,' Ferraro, C. p. del Basso Monferrato, p. 16, No 7; 'La Figlia disobbediente,' Bolza, C. p. comasche, No 55; 'Amor di Fratello,' Bernoni, C. p. veneziani, Puntata 9, No 4; Righi, C. p. veronesi, p. 30, No 93; Wolf, Volkslieder aus Venetien, No 92 (a fragment). In 'Marinai,' Ferraro, C. p. di Ferrara, etc., p. 59, No 9, the suitor is a sailor, and the girl goes down in his ship, and so in 'Il marinaro e la sua amorosa,' No 94, Wolf, but in this last she is still told to stick to her horse. A fragment in Marie Aycard's Bal-

---

[*] The cane in 18[1] of this copy is a touch of "realism" which we have had in a late copy of Tam Lin; see J 16, III, 505.

lades et ch. p. de la Provence, p. xix, repeated in Arbaud, II, 166, makes it probable that the Italian ballad was known in the south of France. (All the above are cited by Count Nigra.)

A mother's curse upon her son, who is riding to fetch his bride, results in his breaking his neck, in a Bohemian ballad already spoken of under 'Clerk Colvil,' No 42; see I, 368 (where a translation by Wenzig, Slawische Volkslieder, p. 47, might have been noted).

A mother refuses to give her daughter in marriage because the girl is under age; the daughter is forcibly carried off; the mother wishes that she may not live a year, which comes to pass: 'Der Mutter Fluch,' Meinert, p. 246.

B is translated by Grundtvig, Engelske og skotshe Folkeviser, p. 64, No 10, and (with use of C), by Wolff, Halle der Völker, I, 26, Hausschatz, p. 203; Aytoun's ballad (with use of C) by Rosa Warrens, Schottische Volkslieder, p. 152, No 35; Allingham's ballad by Knortz, L. u. R. Alt-Englands, p. 123.

A

Skene MS., p. 50; taken down from recitation in the north of Scotland, 1802–3.

1 'YE gie corn unto my horse,
    An meat unto my man,
  For I will gae to my true-love's gates
    This night, gin that I can.'

2 'O stay at hame this ae night, Willie,
    This ae bare night wi me;
  The best bed in a' my house
    Sall be well made to thee.'

3 'I carena for your beds, mither,
    I carena ae pin,
  For I 'll gae to my love's gates
    This night, gin I can win.'

4 'O stay, my son Willie, this night,
    This ae night wi me;
  The best hen in a' my roost
    Sall be well made ready for thee.'

5 'I carena for your hens, mither,
    I carena ae pin;
  I sall gae to my love's gates
    This night, gin I can win.'

6 'Gin ye winna stay, my son Willie,
    This ae bare night wi me,
  Gin Clyde's water be deep and fu o flood,
    My malisen drown ye!'

7 He rode up yon high hill,
    An down yon dowie glen;
  The roaring of Clyde's water
    Wad hae fleyt ten thousand men.

8 'O spare me, Clyde's water,
    O spare me as I gae!
  Mak me your wrack as I come back,
    But spare me as I gae!'

9 He rade in, and farther in,
    Till he came to the chin;
  And he rade in, and farther in,
    Till he came to dry lan.

10 An whan he came to his love's gates,
    He tirled at the pin:
  'Open your gates, Meggie,
    Open your gates to me,
  For my beets are fu o Clyde's water,
    And the rain rains oure my chin.'

11 'I hae nae lovers therout,' she says,
    'I hae nae love within;
  My true-love is in my arms twa,
    An nane will I lat in.'

12 'Open your gates, Meggie, this ae night,
    Open your gates to me;
  For Clyde's water is fu o flood,
    An my mither's malison 'll drown me.'

13 'Ane o my chamers is fu o corn,' she says,
    'An ane is fu o hay;

Anither is fu o gentlemen,
    An they winna move till day.'

14 Out waked her May Meggie,
    Out o her drousy dream:
'I dreamed a dream sin the yestreen,
    God read a' dreams to guid!
That my true-love Willie
    Was staring at my bed-feet.'

15 'Now lay ye still, my ae dochter,
    An keep my back fra the call,
For it's na the space of hafe an hour
    Sen he gad fra yer hall.'

16 'An hey, Willie, an hoa, Willie,
    Winne ye turn agen?'
But ay the louder that she crayed
    He rod agenst the wind.

17 He rod up yon high hill,
    An doun yon douey den;
The roring that was in Clid[e]'s water
    Wad ha flayed ten thousand men.

18 He road in, an farder in,
    Till he came to the chine;
An he road in, an farder in,
    Bat neuer mare was seen.

*   *   *   *   *   *

19 Ther was na mare seen of that guid lord
    Bat his hat frae his head;
Ther was na mare seen of that lady
    Bat her comb an her sneed.

20 Ther waders went up an doun
    Eadying Claid's water
Hav don us wrang

———◆———

B

Jamieson's Popular Ballads, I, 135; from Mrs Brown's
recitation, apparently in 1800.

1 'GIE corn to my horse, mither,
    Gie meat unto my man,
For I maun gang to Margaret's bower
    Before the nicht comes on.'

2 'O stay at hame now, my son Willie,
    The wind blaws cald and sour;
The nicht will be baith mirk and late
    Before ye reach her bower.'

3 'O tho the nicht were ever sae dark,
    Or the wind blew never sae cald,
I will be in my Margaret's bower
    Before twa hours be tald.'

4 'O gin ye gang to May Margaret,
    Without the leave of me,
Clyde's water's wide and deep enough,
    My malison drown thee!'

5 He mounted on his coal-black steed,
    And fast he rade awa,
But ere he came to Clyde's water
    Fu loud the wind did blaw.

6 As he rode oer yon hich, hich hill,
    And down yon dowie den,
There was a roar in Clyde's water
    Wad feard a hunder men.

7 His heart was warm, his pride was up;
    Sweet Willie kentna fear;
But yet his mither's malison
    Ay sounded in his ear.

8 O he has swam through Clyde's water,
    Tho it was wide and deep,
And he came to May Margaret's door,
    When a' were fast asleep.

9 O he's gane round and round about,
    And tirled at the pin;
But doors were steekd, and windows barrd,
    And nane wad let him in.

10 'O open the door to me, Margaret!
    O open and lat me in!
For my boots are full o Clyde's water
    And frozen to the brim.'

11 'I darena open the door to you,
    Nor darena lat you in,
For my mither she is fast asleep,
    And I darena mak nae din.'

12 'O gin ye winna open the door,
      Nor yet be kind to me,
    Now tell me o some out-chamber
      Where I this nicht may be.'

13 'Ye canna win in this nicht, Willie,
      Nor here ye canna be;
    For I 've nae chambers out nor in,
      Nae ane but barely three.

14 'The tane o them is fu o corn,
      The tither is fu o hay;
    The tither is fu o merry young men;
      They winna remove till day.'

15 'O fare ye weel, then, May Margaret,
      Sin better manna be;
    I 've win my mither's malison,
      Coming this nicht to thee.'

16 He 's mounted on his coal-black steed,
      O but his heart was wae!
    But, ere he came to Clyde's water,
      'T was half up oer the brae.

*   *   *   *   *   *

17 . . . .
    . . . . . .
    . . . he plunged in,
    But never raise again.

———◆———

O

Buchan's Ballads of the North of Scotland, I, 140.

1 WILLIE stands in his stable-door,
      And clapping at his steed,
    And looking oer his white fingers
      His nose began to bleed.

2 'Gie corn to my horse, mother,
      And meat to my young man,
    And I 'll awa to Maggie's bower;
      I 'll win ere she lie down.'

3 'O bide this night wi me, Willie,
      O bide this night wi me;
    The best an cock o a' the reest
      At your supper shall be.'

4 'A' your cocks, and a' your reests,
      I value not a prin,
    For I 'll awa to Meggie's bower;
      I 'll win ere she lie down.'

5 'Stay this night wi me, Willie,
      O stay this night wi me;
    The best an sheep in a' the flock
      At your supper shall be.'

6 'A' your sheep, and a' your flocks,
      I value not a prin,
    For I 'll awa' to Meggie's bower;
      I 'll win ere she lie down.'

7 'O an ye gang to Meggie's bower,
      Sae sair against my will,
    The deepest pot in Clyde's water,
      My malison ye 's feel.'

8 'The guid steed that I ride upon
      Cost me thrice thretty pound;
    And I 'll put trust in his swift feet
      To hae me safe to land.'

9 As he rade ower yon high, high hill,
      And down yon dowie den,
    The noise that was in Clyde's water
      Woud feard five huner men.

10 'O roaring Clyde, ye roar ower loud,
      Your streams seem wondrous strang;
    Make me your wreck as I come back,
      But spare me as I gang!'

11 Then he is on to Maggie's bower,
      And tirled at the pin;
    'O sleep ye, wake ye, Meggie,' he said,
      'Ye 'll open, lat me come in.'

12 'O wha is this at my bower-door,
      That calls me by my name?'
    'It is your first love, sweet Willie,
      This night newly come hame.'

13 'I hae few lovers thereout, thereout,
      As few hae I therein;

The best an love that ever I had
    Was here just late yestreen.'

14 'The warstan stable in a' your stables,
    For my puir steed to stand!
The warstan bower in a' your bowers,
    For me to lie therein!
My boots are fu o Clyde's water,
    I 'm shivering at the chin.'

15 'My barns are fu o corn, Willie,
    My stables are fu o hay;
My bowers are fu o gentlemen,
    They 'll nae remove till day.'

16 'O fare ye well, my fause Meggie,
    O farewell, and adieu!
I 've gotten my mither's malison
    This night coming to you.'

17 As he rode ower yon high, high hill,
    And down yon dowie den,
The rushing that was in Clyde's water
    Took Willie's cane frae him.

18 He leand him ower his saddle-bow,
    To catch his cane again;
The rushing that was in Clyde's water
    Took Willie's hat frae him.

19 He leand him ower his saddle-bow,
    To catch his hat thro force;
The rushing that was in Clyde's water
    Took Willie frae his horse.

20 His brither stood upo the bank,
    Says, Fye, man, will ye drown?
Ye 'll turn ye to your high horse head
    And learn how to sowm.

21 'How can I turn to my horse head
    And learn how to sowm?

I 've gotten my mither's malison,
    It 's here that I maun drown.'

22 The very hour this young man sank
    Into the pot sae deep,
Up it wakend his love Meggie
    Out o her drowsy sleep.

23 'Come here, come here, my mither dear,
    And read this dreary dream;
I dreamd my love was at our gates,
    And nane wad let him in.'

24 'Lye still, lye still now, my Meggie,
    Lye still and tak your rest;
Sin your true-love was at your yates,
    It 's but twa quarters past.'

25 Nimbly, nimbly raise she up,
    And nimbly pat she on,
And the higher that the lady cried,
    The louder blew the win.

26 The first an step that she steppd in,
    She stepped to the queet;
'Ohon, alas!' said that lady,
    'This water 's wondrous deep.'

27 The next an step that she wade in,
    She wadit to the knee;
Says she, 'I coud wide farther in,
    If I my love coud see.'

28 The next an step that she wade in,
    She wadit to the chin;
The deepest pot in Clyde's water
    She got sweet Willie in.

29 'You 've had a cruel mither, Willie,
    And I have had anither;
But we shall sleep in Clyde's water
    Like sister an like brither.'

———◆———

A. *Not divided into stanzas in the MS.; sometimes not into verses.*

  15³. For *is written after* call *in the preceding line.*

  16³. But ay *is written after* agen *in the preceding line.*

  16⁴. He *is written after* crayed *in the preceding line.*

18². Till *is written after* in *in the preceding line.*

19. Ther was na mare seen of that guid lord bat his hat frae his head ther was na mare seen of that lady bat her comb an her sneed.

20[1]. Doun *stands at the beginning of the next line.*

A 14–16 *might perhaps be better put after the drowning, as in* C.

B. *Readings inserted by Motherwell in a copy of his Minstrelsy.*

4[3,4]. My malison and deidly curse
    Shall bear ye companie.

After 7:

> He swam high, and he swam low,
>   And he swam to and fro,
> Until he gript a hazel-bush,
>   That brung him to the brow.

9[4]. *Var.* But his mother answered him.

10. O rise, O rise, May Marget, h[e says],
        (*cut away by the binder*)
    O rise and let me in,
    For the very steed that I came on
    Does tremble at every limb.

11[3]. mither and father's baith awauk.

12. O hae ye neer a stable, he says,
        Or hae ye neer a barn,
    Or hae ye neer a wild-guse house,
        Where I might rest till morn?

14[1]. My barn is.   14[2]. My stable is.

14[3]. The house is fu o wild, wild gees.

14[4]. They canna be moved.

15[4]. Rides in my companie.

16[1]. his milk-white.

16[2]. And who could ride like him.

16[4]. 'T was far outowre the brim.

After 16:

> He swam high, and he swam low,
>   And he swam to and fro,
> But he neer could spy the hazel-bush
>   That would bring him to the brow.

Comment: The mother was a witch; made responses for Margaret; met him in a green habit on his return home. He inquired for the ford; she directed him to the deepest linn. When he got into the water, two hounds seized on his horse, and left him to struggle with the current.

Willie's mother had transferred herself to Margaret's house according to the variation in 9[4]; so she is the witch.

All this is very paltry. The mother's curse was enough to drown Willie without her bestirring herself further.

217

THE BROOM OF COWDENKNOWS

A. 'The Laird of Knotington,' Percy papers, 1768.

B. 'Bonny May.' a. Herd's Ancient and Modern Scots Songs, 1769, p. 308 ; 1776, I, 98. b. Johnson's Museum, No 110, p. 113.

C. 'Laird o Ochiltree,' Kinloch MSS, VII, 143 ; Kinloch's Ancient Scottish Ballads, p. 160.

D. 'The Laird o Ochiltree Wa's,' Motherwell's MS., p. 517.

E. Motherwell's MS., p. 175.

F. 'Bonny May,' Gibb MS., p. 9.

G. 'The Broom of Cowdenknows,' Scott's Minstrelsy, III, 280, 1803 ; III, 37, 1833.

H. 'The Maid o the Cowdenknows,' Kinloch MSS, I, 137.

I. 'Laird o Lochnie,' Kinloch MSS, VII, 153 ; Kinloch's Ancient Scottish Ballads, p. 167.

J. Kinloch MSS, VI, 11.

K. 'Maiden o the Cowdenknowes,' Dr Joseph Robertson's Journal of Excursions, No 6.

L. 'The Broom of the Cowden Knowes,' Buchan's MSS, II, 178.

M. 'Broom o the Cowdenknowes,' Buchan's Ballads of the North of Scotland, I, 172.

N. 'The Laird of Lochinvar,' Kinloch MSS, I, 145.

THIS ballad was widely diffused in Scotland. "It would be useless," says Motherwell, "to enumerate the titles of the different versions which are common among reciters." "Each district has its own version," says Kinloch. So it must have done no little mischief in its day. The earliest known copies, A, B, are of the second half of the last century.

There is an English "ditty" (not a traditional ballad) of a northern lass who got harm while milking her father's ewes, which was printed in the first half of the seventeenth century. It is here given in an appendix. This ditty is "to a pleasant Scotch tune called The broom of Cowden Knowes," and the burden is:

> With, O the broome, the bonny broome,
> The broome of Cowden Knowes!
> Fain would I be in the North Countrey,
> To milk my dadyes ewes.

The tune was remarkably popular, and the burden is found, variously modified, in connection with several songs: see Chappell's Popular Music, pp. 458–461, 613, 783. 'The Broom of Cowdenknows,' a "new" song, in the Tea-Table Miscellany, p. 22, Dublin, 1729, has the burden not greatly changed; also G, L, M, of this ballad.

There is very little story to the English ditty. A maid is beguiled by a shepherd-boy while milking her father's ewes; the consequences are what might be expected; her mother puts her out of doors, and she ranges the world; a young man who hears her complaint offers to marry her, and go to the North Country with her to milk her father's ewes. The Scottish ballad could not have been developed from a story of this description. On the other hand, it is scarcely to be believed that the author of the English ditty, if he had known the Scottish ballad, would have dropped all the interesting particulars. It is possible that he may have just heard about it, but much more likely that he knew only the burden and built his very slight tale on that. It may be observed that his maid, though she

haunts Liddesdale, and should have belonged to Cowdenknowes, was born in Danby Forest, Yorkshire.

Two passages which do not occur in A may have been later additions: D 9, 10, F 5, 6, G 13, 14, M 19, 20, in which the laird, returning to his men, is told that he has tarried long, and answers that, east or west, he has never seen so bonny a lass as was in the ewe-buchts; and H 12–15, J 2–5, L 5–8, where the laird tries to pass himself off for one of his men, and the maid for one of her mother's servants (found in part, also, in G 9, 10, I 5, M 12–14). "The maid of a place, such as the maid of the Cowdenknows," as Dr Joseph Robertson remarks, "means the eldest daughter of the tenant or proprietor, who is generally called by the name of his farm." *

It is obvious that the maid would keep her counsel when she came back to her father. She puts him off with a riddle, C 9, D 13, E 11, F 9, G 18, H 20, J 6, L 14, M 23, N 7, which it is the height of absurdity to make her explain, as is done in A 11, B 4, C 10, D 14, E 12; and so of the exclamation against the shepherd if uttered in the father's presence, as in F 8, H 19, I 11, L 13, N 8.

H 10, 11 (cf. D 6), where the maid asks the man's name, is a familiar commonplace: see No 39, I, 340 a; No 50, I, 444, 446; No 110, II, 458 ff. (especially p. 473, H 3, 4); No 111, II, 478 f.

M has many spurious stanzas of its own; as 3–5, 25, 30–32, 35. N is quite perverted from 9 to 28. It is impossible that 9–14 should follow upon 8, and stanzas 15–27 have not a genuine word in them.

Cunningham has rewritten the ballad, Songs of Scotland, II, 113. He says that through Dumfriesshire and Galloway the hero is always Lord Lochinvar, and cites this stanza, which he had heard sung:

> For I do guess, by your golden-rimmed hat,
> And by the silken string,
> That ye are the lord of the Lochinvar,
> Who beguiles all our young women.

---

* The attempt to lessen the disproportion of the match seems to me a decidedly modern trait. In H 27, 28, this goes so far that the maid has twenty ploughs and three against the laird's thirty and three. In M 3–5, the maid's father was once a landed laird, but gambles away his estate, and then both father and mother take to drinking!

'Malfred og Sadelmand,' Kristensen, I, 258, No 99, is an independent ballad, but has some of the traits of this: the maid, who is treated with great violence, asks the knight's name, as in **H, D**; he comes back to marry her, after she has borne twins.

Cowdenknowes is on the east bank of Leader, near Earlston, and some four or five miles from Melrose. Auchentrone, in **B b 11**, Stenhouse conjectures to be a corruption of Auchentroich, an estate in the county of Stirling, and Oakland Hills, in **G**, to be Ochil Hills, in the same county: Musical Museum, IV, 112.

B is translated by Knortz, Schottische Balladen, p. 92, No 29.

----◆----

A

Percy papers; communicated to Percy by R. Lambe, of Norham, August 17, 1768, and dated May, 1768.

1 THERE was a troop of merry gentlemen
   Was riding atween twa knows,
And they heard the voice of a bonny lass,
   In a bught milking her ews.

2 There 's ane o them lighted frae off his steed,
   And has ty'd him to a tree,
And he 's gane away to yon ew-bught,
   To hear what it might be.

3 'O pity me, fair maid,' he said,
   'Take pity upon me;
O pity me, and my milk-white steed
   That 's trembling at yon tree.'

4 'As for your steed, he shall not want
   The best of corn and hay;
But as to you yoursel, kind sir,
   I 've naething for to say.'

5 He 's taen her by the milk-white hand,
   And by the green gown-sleeve,
And he as led her into the ew-bught,
   Of her friends he speerd nae leave.

6 He as put his hand in his pocket,
   And given her guineas three:
'If I dinna come back in half a year,
   Then luke nae mair for me.

7 'Now show to me the king's hie street,
   Now show to me the way;
Now show to me the king's hie street,
   And the fair water of Tay.'

8 She showd to him the king's hie street,
   She showd to him the way;
She showd him the way that he was to go,
   By the fair water of Tay.

9 When she came hame, her father said,
   'Come, tell to me right plain;
I doubt you 've met some in the way,
   You have not been your lain.'

10 'The night it is baith mist and mirk,
   You may gan out and see;
The night is mirk and misty too,
   There 's nae body been wi me.

11 'There was a tod came to your flock,
   The like I neer did see;
When he spake, he lifted his hat,
   He had a bonny twinkling eee.'

12 When fifteen weeks were past and gane,
   Full fifteen weeks and three,
Then she began to think it lang
   For the man wi the twinkling eee.

13 It fell out on a certain day,
   When she cawd out her father's ky,
There was a troop of gentlemen
   Came merrily riding by.

14 'Weel may ye sigh and sob,' says ane,
   'Weel may you sigh and see;
Weel may you sigh, and say, fair maid,
   Wha 's gotten this bairn wi thee?'

15 She turned her sel then quickly about,
   And thinking meikle shame,

'O no, kind sir, it is na sae,
    For it has a dad at hame.'

16 'O hawd your tongue, my bonny lass,
    Sae loud as I hear you lee!
  For dinna you mind that summer night
    I was in the bught wi thee?'

17 He lighted off his milk-white steed,
    And set this fair maid on;

'Now caw out your ky, good father,' he said,
    'She 'll neer caw them out again.

18 'I am the laird of Knottington,
    I 've fifty plows and three;
  I 've gotten now the bonniest lass
    That is in the hale country.'

———◆———

B

a. Herd's Ancient and Modern Scots Songs, 1769, p. 308.
b. Johnson's Museum, No 110, p. 113.

1 It was on an evning sae saft and sae clear
    A bonny lass was milking the kye,
  And by came a troup of gentlemen,
    And rode the bonny lassie by.

2 Then one of them said unto her,
    'Bonny lass, prythee shew me the way:'
  'O if I do sae, it may breed me wae,
    For langer I dare nae stay.'

*   *   *   *   *   *   *

3 But dark and misty was the night
    Before the bonny lass came hame:
  'Now where hae you been, my ae doughter?
    I am sure you was nae your lane.'

4 'O father, a tod has come oer your lamb,
    A gentleman of high degree,
  And ay whan he spake he lifted his hat,
    And bonny, bonny blinkit his ee.'

5 Or eer six months were past and gane,
    Six months but and other three,
  The lassie begud for to fret and to frown,
    And think lang for his blinkin ee.

6 'O wae be to my father's shepherd,
    An ill death may he die!
  He bigged the bughts sae far frae hame,
    And trysted a gentleman to me!'

7 It fell upon another fair evening
    The bonny lassie was milking her ky,
  And by came the troup of gentlemen,
    And rode the bonny lassie by.

8 Then one of them stopt, and said to her,
    'Whae 's aught that baby ye are wi?'
  The lassie began for to blush, and think,
    To a father as good as ye.

9 'O had your tongue, my bonny may,
    Sae loud I hear you lie!
  O dinnae you mind the misty night
    I was in the bught with thee?'

10 Now he 's come aff his milk-white steed,
    And he has taen her hame:
  'Now let your father bring hame the ky,
    You neer mair shall ca them agen.

11 'I am a lord of castles and towers,
    With fifty ploughs of land and three,
  And I have gotten the bonniest lass
    That is in this countrie.'

———◆———

C

Kinloch MSS, VII, 143, from the recitation of Jenny
Watson, 24 April, 1826; Clydesdale.

1 It was on a day whan a lovely may
    Was cawing out her father's kye,

    And she spied a troop o' gentlemen,
      As they war passing bye.

2 'O show me the way, my pretty maid,
    O show me the way,' said he;

'My steed has just now rode wrong,
  And the way I canna see.'

3 'O haud you on the same way,' she said,
  'O haud ye on 't again,
For, if ye haud on the king's hieway,
  Rank rievers will do ye na harm.'

4 He took her by the milk-white hand,
  And by the gerss-green sleeve,
And he has taiglet wi the fair may,
  And of her he askd na leave.

5 Whan ance he got her gudwill,
  Of her he craved na mair,
But he poud out a ribbon frae his pouch,
  And snooded up the may's hair.

6 He put his hand into his pouch,
  And gave her guineas three:
'If I come na back in twenty weeks,
  Ye need na look mair for me.'

7 But whan the may did gang hame,
  Her father did her blame;
'Whare hae ye been now, dame?' he said
  'For ye've na been your lane.'

8 'The nicht is misty and mirk, father,
  Ye may come to the door and see;
The nicht is misty and mirk, father,
  And there's na body wi me.

9 'But there cam a tod to your flock, father,
  The like o him I never saw;
Or he had tane the lambie that he had,
  I wad rather he had tane them aw.

10 'But he seemd to be a gentleman,
  Or a man of some pious degree;
For whanever he spak, he lifted up his hat,
  And he had [a] bonnie twinkling ee.'

11 Whan twenty weeks were come and gane,
  Twenty weeks and three,
The lassie began to grow thick in the waist,
  And thoucht lang for his twinkling ee.

12 It fell upon a day whan bonnie may
  Was cawing out the kye,
She spied the same troop o gentlemen,
  As they war passing bye.

13 'O well may you save, my pretty may,
  Weill may you save and see!
Weill may ye save, my lovely may!
  Go ye wi child to me?'

14 But the may she turnd her back to him,
  She begoud to think meikle shame;
'Na, na, na, na, kind sir,' she said,
  'I've a gudeman o my ain.'

15 'Sae loud as I hear ye lie, fair may,
  Sae loud as I hear ye lee!
Dinna ye mind o yon misty nicht
  Whan I was in the bucht wi thee?'

16 He lichted aff his hie, hie horse,
  And he set the bonnie may on:
'Now caw out your kye, gud father,
  Ye maun caw them out your lone.

17 'For lang will ye caw them out,
  And weary will ye be,
Or ye get your dochter again
  .   .   .   .   .   .

18 He was the laird o Ochiltree,
  Of therty ploughs and three,
And he has stown awa the loveliest may
  In aw the south cuntree.

D

Motherwell's MS., p. 517; from the singing of Mrs Storie, of Lochwinnoch.

1 O BONNIE May is to the yowe-buchts gane,
  For to milk her daddie's yowes,
And ay she sang, and her voice it rang
  Out-ower the tap o the knows, knows, knowes,
  Out-owr the tap o the knowes.

2 Ther cam a troop o gentilmen,
  As they were rydand by,
And ane o them he lichtit doun,
  For to see May milkand her kye.

3 'Milk on, milk on, my bonnie lass,
  Milk on, milk on,' said he,
'For out o the buchts I winna gang
  Till ye shaw me owr the lee.'

4 'Ryde on, ryde on, ye rank rydars,
    Your steeds are stout and strang,
  For out o the yowe-buchts I winna gae,
    For fear that ye do me some wrang.'

5 He took her by the milk-white hand,
    And by the green gown-sleive,
  And thare he took his will o her,
    Bot o her he askit nae leive.

6 But whan he gat his will o her
    He loot her up again,
  And a' this bonny maid said or did
    Was, Kind sir, tell me your name.

7 He pou't out a sillar kame,
    Sayand, Kame your yellow hair;
  And, gin I be na back in three quarters o a
      year,
    It 's o me ye 'll see nae mair.

8 He pu't out a silken purse
    And he gied her guineas thrie,
  Saying, Gin I may na be back in three quar-
      ters o a year,
    It will pay the nourice fee.

9 He put his fut into the stirrup
    And rade after his men,
  And a' that his men said or did
    Was, Kind maister, ye 've taiglit lang.

10 'I hae rade east, I hae rade wast,
    And I hae rade owr the knowes,
  But the bonniest lassie that I ever saw
    Was in the yowe-buchts, milkand her yowes.'

11 She put the pail upon her heid,
    And she 's gane merrilie hame,
  And a' that her faither said or did
    Was, Kind dochter, ye 've taiglit lang.

12 'Oh, wae be to your men, faither,
    And an·ill deth may they die!
  For they cawit a' the yowes out-owre the
      knowes,
    And they left naebody wi me.

13 'There cam a tod unto the bucht,
    The like I never saw,
  An, afore that he took the ane that he took,
    I wad leifar he had tane ither twa.

14 'There cam a tod unto the bucht,
    The like I never did see,
  And, ay as he spak, he liftit his hat,
    And he had a bonnie twinkland ee.'

15 It was on a day, and it was a fine simmer day,
    She was cawing out her faither's kye,
  There cam a troup o gentilmen,
    And they rade ways the lass near by.

16 'Wha has dune to you this ill, my dear?
    Wha has dune to you this wrang?'
  And she had na a word to say for hersell
    But, 'Kind sir, I hae a man o my ain.'

17 'Ye lie, ye lie, bonnie May,' he says,
    'Aloud I hear ye lie!
  For dinna ye mind yon bonnie simmer nicht
    Whan ye war in the yowe-buchts wi me?

18 'Licht doun, licht doun, my foremaist man,
    Licht doun and let her on,
  For monie a time she cawit her faither's
      kye,
    But she 'll neir caw them again.

19 'For I am the laird o Ochiltree Wawis,
    I hae threttie pleuchs and thrie,
  And I hae tane awa the bonniest lass
    That is in a' the north countrie.'

— ◆ —

E

Motherwell's Manuscript, p. 175; "from the recitation
of Mrs Thomson, Kilbarchan, a native of Dumbartonshire,
where she learned it."

1 THERE was a may, and a bonnie may,
    In the bught, milking the ewes,
  And by came a troop of gentlemen,
    And they rode by and by.

2 'O I 'll give thee my milk-white steed,
    It cost me three hundred pound,
  If ye 'll go to yon sheep-bught,
    And bring yon fair maid doun.'

3 'Your steed ye canna want, master,
    But pay to ane a fee;
  Fifty pound of good red gold,
    To be paid down to me.'

4 'Come shew me the way, pretty may,' he
    said,
  'For our steeds are quite gone wrong;
Will you do to me such a courtesy
    As to shew us the near-hand way?'

5 'O go ye doun to yon meadow,
    Where the people are mowing the hay;
Go ye doun to yon meadow,
    And they'll shew you the near-hand way.'

6 But he's taen her by the milk-white hand,
    And by the grass-green sleeve;
He's bowed her body to the ground,
    Of her kin he asked no leave.

7 When he lifted her up again
    He's gien her guineas three:
'If I be na back gin three quarters o a year,
    Ye need neer think mair on me.'

*   *   *   *   *   *

8 'O where hast thou been, bonnie may,' he
    said,
  'O where hast thou been sae lang?
O where hast thou been, bonnie may?' he
    said,
  'Thou hast na been sae lang thy lane.'

9 'O come to the door and see, father,
    O come to the door and see,
And see such a weety and a windy night;
    There were nobody wi me.

10 'But wae be to your herd, father,
    And an ill death may he die!
For he left the ewes strayed owre the knowes,
    And he left naebody wi me.

11 'But there came a tod to your bught, father,
    The like o him I neer saw;

For or he had taen the bonnie lamb he took,
    Ye had as weel hae gien them a'.

12 'There came a tod to your bught, father,
    The like o him I neer did see;
For aye when he spak he lifted up his hat,
    And he had a bonnie twinkling ee.'

13 But when twenty weeks were come and gane,
    Aye, twenty weeks and three,
This lassie began to spit and to spew,
    And to lang for the twinkling ee.

14 It fell on a day, and a bonnie summer day,
    She was ca'ing out her father's kye,
And by came a troop of gentlemen,
    And they rode by and by.

15 'O wha got the bairn wi thee, bonnie may?
    O wha got the bairn wi thee?'

  .   .   .   .
  .   .   .   .

16 She turned hersell right round about,
    She began to blush and think shame,
And never a word this bonnie lassie spok
    But 'I have a good-man at hame.'

17 'Thou lie, thou lie, my bonnie may,
    Sae loud I hear thee lie!
Do ye mind o the weety and windy night
    When I was in the ewe-bught wi thee?

18 'Light off, light off, the gentlest of my men,
    And set her on behind,
And ca out your kye, good father, yoursell,
    For she'll never ca them out again.'

19 He was the laird o twenty plough o land,
    Aye, twenty plough and three,
And he's taen awa the bonniest lass
    Was in a' the south countrie.

—◆—

F

Gibb MS., p. 9. "From recitation; traced to Mary Jack, Lochlee, Forfarshire, died 1881, aged 94."

1 BONNY MAY has to the ewe-bughts gane,
    To milk her father's ewes,
An aye as she milked her bonny voice rang
    Far out amang the knowes.

*   *   *   *   *   *

2 'Milk on, milk on, my bonny, bonny may,
    Milk on, milk on,' said he;
'Milk on, milk on, my bonny, bonny may;
    Will ye shew me out-ower the lea?'

3 'Ride on, ride on, stout rider,' she said,
    'Yere steed's baith stout and strang;

For out o the ewe-bught I daurna come,
　　For fear ye do me wrang.'

4 But he 's tane her by the milk-white hand,
　　An by the green gown-sleeve,
　An he 's laid her low on the dewy grass,
　　An at nae ane spiered he leave.

5 Then he 's mounted on his milk-white steed,
　　An ridden after his men,
　An a' that his men they said to him
　　Was, Dear master, ye 've tarried lang.

6 'I 've ridden east, an I 've ridden wast,
　　An I 've ridden amang the knowes,
　But the bonniest lassie eer I saw
　　Was milkin her daddie's yowes.'

7 She 's taen the milk-pail on her heid,
　　An she 's gane langin hame,
　An a her father said to her
　　Was, Daughter, ye 've tarried lang.

8 'Oh, wae be to your shepherds! father,
　　For they take nae care o the sheep;
　For they 've bygit the ewe - bught far frae
　　hame,
　　An they 've trysted a man to me.

9 'There came a tod unto the bucht,
　　An a waefu tod was he,
　An, or ever he had tane that ae ewe-lamb,
　　I had rather he had tane ither three.'

10 But it fell on a day, an a bonny summer day,
　　She was ca'in out her father's kye,
　An bye came a troop o gentlemen,
　　Cam ridin swiftly bye.

11 Out an spoke the foremost ane,
　　Says, Lassie hae ye got a man?
　She turned herself saucy round about,
　　Says, Yes, I 've ane at hame.

12 'Ye lee, ye lee, ye my bonny may,
　　Sae loud as I hear ye lee!
　For dinna ye mind that misty nicht
　　Ye were in the ewe-bughts wi me?'

13 He ordered ane o his men to get down;
　　Says, Lift her up behind me;
　Your father may ca in the kye when he likes,
　　They sall neer be ca'ed in by thee.

14 'For I 'm the laird o Athole swaird,
　　Wi fifty ploughs an three,
　An I hae gotten the bonniest lass
　　In a' the north countrie.'

———•———

G

Scott's Minstrelsy, III, 280, 1803; from Ettrick Forest.

1 O THE broom, and the bonny, bonny broom,
　　And the broom of the Cowdenknows!
　And aye sae sweet as the lassie sang,
　　I the bought, milking the ewes.

2 The hills were high on ilka side,
　　An the bought i the lirk o the hill,
　And aye, as she sang, her voice it rang
　　Out-oer the head o yon hill.

3 There was a troop o gentlemen
　　Came riding merrilie by,
　And one o them has rode out o the way,
　　To the bought to the bonny may.

4 'Weel may ye save an see, bonny lass,
　　An weel may ye save an see!'
　'An sae wi you, ye weel-bred knight,
　　And what 's your will wi me?'

5 'The night is misty and mirk, fair may,
　　And I have ridden astray,
　And will ye be so kind, fair may,
　　As come out and point my way?'

6 'Ride out, ride out, ye ramp rider!
　　Your steed 's baith stout and strang;
　For out of the bought I dare na come,
　　For fear at ye do me wrang.'

7 'O winna ye pity me, bonny lass?
　　O winna ye pity me?
　An winna ye pity my poor steed,
　　Stands trembling at yon tree?'

8 'I wadna pity your poor steed,
   Tho it were tied to a thorn;
For if ye wad gain my love the night
   Ye wad slight me ere the morn.

9 'For I ken you by your weel-busked hat,
   And your merrie twinkling ee,
That ye 're the laird o the Oakland hills,
   An ye may weel seem for to be.'

10 'But I am not the laird o the Oakland hills,
   Ye 're far mistaen o me;
But I 'm ane o the men about his house,
   An right aft in his companie.'

11 He 's taen her by the middle jimp,
   And by the grass-green sleeve,
He 's lifted her over the fauld-dyke,
   And speerd at her sma leave.

12 O he 's taen out a purse o gowd,
   And streekd her yellow hair:
'Now take ye that, my bonnie may,
   Of me till you hear mair.'

13 O he 's leapt on his berry-brown steed,
   An soon he 's oertaen his men;
And ane and a' cried out to him,
   O master, ye 've tarryd lang!

14 'O I hae been east, and I hae been west,
   An I hae been far oer the knows,
But the bonniest lass that ever I saw
   Is i the bought, milkin the ewes.'

15 She set the cog upon her head,
   An she 's gane singing hame:
'O where hae ye been, my ae daughter?
   Ye hae na been your lane.'

16 'O nae body was wi me, father,
   O nae body has been wi me;
The night is misty and mirk, father,
   Ye may gang to the door and see.

17 'But wae be to your ewe-herd, father,
   And an ill deed may he die!

He bug the bought at the back o the know
   And a tod has frighted me.

18 'There came a tod to the bought-door,
   The like I never saw;
And ere he had taken the lamb he did
   I had lourd he had taen them a'.'

19 O whan fifteen weeks was come and gane,
   Fifteen weeks and three,
That lassie began to look thin and pale,
   An to long for his merry-twinkling ee.

20 It fell on a day, on a het simmer day,
   She was ca'ing out her father's kye,
By came a troop o gentlemen,
   A' merrilie riding bye.

21 'Weel may ye save an see, bonny may!
   Weel may ye save and see!
Weel I wat ye be a very bonny may,
   But whae 's aught that babe ye are wi?'

22 Never a word could that lassie say,
   For never a ane could she blame,
An never a word could the lassie say,
   But, I have a good man at hame.

23 'Ye lied, ye lied, my very bonny may,
   Sae loud as I hear you lie!
For dinna ye mind that misty night
   I was i the bought wi thee?

24 'I ken you by your middle sae jimp,
   An your merry-twinkling ee,
That ye 're the bonny lass i the Cowdenknow,
   An ye may weel seem for to be.'

25 Than he 's leapd off his berry-brown steed,
   An he 's set that fair may on:
'Caw out your kye, gude father, yoursel,
   For she 's never caw them out again.

26 'I am the laird of the Oakland hills,
   I hae thirty plows and three,
An I hae gotten the bonniest lass
   That 's in a' the south country.'

H

Kinloch MSS, I, 137; from Mrs Boutchart.

1 THERE was a may, a maiden sae gay,
    Went out wi her milking-pail;
Lang she foucht or her ewes wad bucht,
    And syne she a milking fell.

2 And ay as she sang the rocks they rang,
    Her voice gaed loud and shill;
Ye wad hae heard the voice o the maid
    On the tap o the ither hill.

3 And ay she sang, and the rocks they rang,
    Her voice gaed loud and hie;
Till by there cam a troop o gentlemen,
    A riding up that way.

4 'Weel may ye sing, ye bonnie may,
    Weel and weel may ye sing!
The nicht is misty, weet, and mirk,
    And we hae ridden wrang.'

5 'Haud by the gate ye cam, kind sir,
    Haud by the gate ye cam;
But tak tent o the rank river,
    For our streams are unco strang.'

6 'Can ye na pity me, fair may,
    Canna ye pity me?
Canna ye pity my puir steed,
    Stands trembling at yon tree?'

7 'What pity wad ye hae, kind sir?
    What wad ye hae frae me?
If he has neither corn nor hay,
    He has gerss at libertie.'

8 'Can ye na pity me, fair may,
    Can ye na pity me?
Can ye na pity a gentle knicht
    That's deeing for love o thee?'

9 He's tane her by the milk-white hand,
    And by the gerss-green sleeve;
He's laid her laigh at the bucht-end,
    At her kin speird na leave.

10 'After ye hae tane your will o me,
    Your will as ye hae tane,
Be as gude a gentle knicht
    As tell to me your name.'

11 'Some do ca me Jack,' says he,
    'And some do ca me John;
But whan I'm in the king's hie court
    Duke William is my name.

12 'But I ken by your weel-faurd face,
    And by your blinking ee,
That ye are the Maid o the Cowdenknows,
    And seem very weel to be.'

13 'I am na the maid o the Cowdenknows,
    Nor does not think to be;
But I am ane o her best maids,
    That's aft in her companie.

14 'But I ken by your black, black hat,
    And by your gay gowd ring,
That ye are the Laird o Rochna hills,
    Wha beguiles a' our women.'

15 'I am na the Laird o Rochna hills,
    Nor does na think to be;
But I am ane o his best men,
    That's aft in his companie.'

16 He's put his hand in his pocket
    And tane out guineas three;
Says, Tak ye that, my bonnie may;
    It'll pay the nourice fee.

17 She's tane her cog upon her head,
    And fast, fast gaed she hame:
'Whare hae ye been, my dear dochter?
    Ye hae na been your lane.

18 'The nicht is misty, weet, and mirk;
    Ye may look out and see;
The ewes war skippin oure the knowes,
    They wad na bucht in for me.

19 'But wae be to your shepherd, father,
    An ill death may he dee!
He bigget the buchts sae far frae the toun,
    And he trysted a man to me.

20 'There cam a tod amang the flock,
    The like o him I neer did see;
Afore he had tane the lamb that he took,
    I'd rather he'd tane ither three.'

21 Whan twenty weeks war past and gane,
    Twenty weeks and three,

The lassie begoud to spit and spue,
  And thought lang for 's blinkin ee.

22 'T was on a day, and a day near bye,
  She was ca'ing out the kye,
That by cam a troop o merry gentlemen,
  Cam riding bye that way.

23 'Wha 's gien ye the scorn, bonnie may?
  O wha 's done ye the wrang?'
'Na body, na body, kind sir,' she said,
  'My baby's father 's at hame.'

24 'Ye lee, ye lee, fause may,' he said,
  'Sae loud as I hear ye lee!
Dinna ye mind o the mirk misty nicht
  I buchted the ewes wi thee?'

25 'Weel may I mind yon mirk misty nicht,
  Weel may I mind,' says she;
'For ay whan ye spak ye lifted up your hat,
  Ye had a merry blinkin ee.'

26 He 's turned him round and richt about,
  And tane the lassie on;
'Ca out your ky, auld father,' he said,
  'She sall neer ca them again.

27 'For I am the Laird o Rochna hills,
  O thirty plows and three;
And I hae gotten the bonniest lass
  O a' the west countrie.'

28 'And I 'm the Maid o the Cowdenknows,
  O twenty plows and three;
And I hae gotten the bonniest lad
  In a' the north countrie.'

I

Kinloch MSS, VII, 153; from the recitation of Miss M. Kinnear, August 23, 1826, a North Country version.

1 THE lassie sang sae loud, sae loud,
  The lassie sang sae shill;
The lassie sang, and the greenwud rang,
  At the farther side o yon hill.

2 Bye there cam a troop o merry gentlemen,
  They aw rode merry bye;
The very first and the foremaist
  Was the first that spak to the may.

3 'This is a mark and misty nicht,
  And I have ridden wrang;
If ye wad be sae gude and kind
  As to show me the way to gang.'

4 'If ye binna the laird o Lochnie's lands,
  Nor nane o his degree,
I 'll show ye a nearer road that will keep you
  frae
The glen-waters and the raging sea.'

5 'I 'm na the laird o Lochnie's lands,
  Nor nane o his degree;
But I am as brave a knicht,
  And ride aft in his company.

6 'Have ye na pity on me, pretty maid?
  Have ye na pity on me?
Have ye na pity on my puir steed,
  That stands trembling by yon tree?'

7 'What pity wad ye hae, kind sir?
  What pity wad ye hae frae me?
Though your steed has neither corn nor hay,
  It has gerss at its liberty.'

8 He has trysted the pretty maid
  Till they cam to the brume,
And at the end o yon ew-buchts
  It 's there they baith sat doun.

9 Till up she raise, took up her milk-pails,
  And away gaed she hame;
Up bespak her auld father,
  'It 's whare hae ye been sae lang?'

10 'This is a mark and a misty nicht,
  Ye may gang to the door and see;
The ewes hae taen a skipping out-oure the
  knows,
They winna bucht in for me.

11 'I may curse my father's shepherd;
  Some ill death mat he dee!
He has buchted the ewes sae far frae the toun,
  And has trysted the young men to me.'

J

Kinloch MSS, VI, 11; in the handwriting of Dr Joseph Robertson, and given him by his mother, Christian Leslie.

1 IT was a dark and a misty night,

. . . .

And by came a troop o gentlemen,
Said, Lassie, shew me the way.

2 'Oh well ken I by your silk mantle,
And by your grass-green sleeve,
That you are the maid of the Cowdenknows,
And may well seem to be.'

3 'I 'm nae the maid of the Cowdenknows,
Nor ever think to be ;
I am but ane of her hirewomen,
Rides aft in her companie.

4 'Oh well do I ken by your milk-white steed,
And by your merry winking ee,
That you are the laird of Lochinvar,
And may well seem to be.'

5 'I 'm nae the laird of Lochinvar,
Nor may well seem to be ;
But I am one of his merry young men,
And am oft in his companie.'

*   *   *   *   *   *

6 'The tod was among your sheep, father,
You may look forth and see ;
And before he had taen the lamb he 's taen
I had rather he had taen three.'

7 When twenty weeks were come and gane,
Twenty weeks and three,
The lassie she turned pale and wan

. . . .

8 . . . .

And was caain out her father's kye,
When by came a troop of gentlemen,
Were riding along the way.

9 'Fair may it fa thee, weel-fa'rt may !
Wha 's aught the bairn ye 're wi ?'
'O I hae a husband o my ain,
To father my bairn te.'

10 'You lie, you lie, you well-far'd may,
Sae loud 's I hear you lie !
Do you mind the dark and misty night
I was in the bught wi thee ?'

11 'Oh well do I ken by your milk-white steed,
And by your merry winkin ee,
That you are the laird of Lochinvar,
That was in the bught wi me.'

K

Joseph Robertson's Journal of Excursions, No 6 ; "taken down from a man in the parish of Leochel, 12 February, 1829."

*   *   *   *   *   *

1 THERE was four and twenty gentlemen,
As they were ridin by,
And aff there loups the head o them,
Cums in to this fair may.

2 'It 's a mark and a mark and a misty night,
And we canna know the way ;
And ye wad be as gude to us
As shew us on the way.'

3 'Ye 'll get a boy for meat,' she says,
'Ye 'll get a boy for fee,

. . . .

That will shew you the right way.'

4 'We 'll get a boy for meat,' he says,
'We 'll get a boy for fee,
But we do not know where to seek
That bonny boy out.'

*   *   *   *   *   *

5 'It 's foul befa my auld father's men,
An ill death mat they die !
They 've biggit the ewe bucht sae far frae the
town
They 've tristed the men to me.'

L

Buchan's MSS, II, 178.

O THE broom, the bonny, bonny broom,
  The broom grows oer the burn !
Aye when I mind on 's bonny yellow hair,
  I aye hae cause to mourn.

1 There was a bonny, a well-fared may,
  In the fauld milking her kye,
When by came a troop of merry gentlemen,
  And sae merrily they rode by.
    O the broom, etc.

2 The maid she sang till the hills they rang,
  And a little more forebye,
Till in came ane of these gentlemen
  To the bught o the bonny may.

3 'Well mat ye sing, fair maid,' he says,
  'In the fauld, milking your kye;
The night is misty, weet and dark,
  And I've gane out o my way.'

4 'Keep on the way ye ken, kind sir,
  Keep on the way ye ken;
But I pray ye take care o Clyde's water,
  For the stream runs proud and fair.'

5 'I ken you by your lamar beads,
  And by your blinking ee,
That your mother has some other maid
  To send to the ewes than thee.'

6 'I ken you by your powderd locks,
  And by your gay gold ring,
That ye are the laird o Rock-rock lays,
  That beguiles all young women.'

7 'I'm not the laird o the Rock-rock lays,
  Nor ever hopes to be;
But I am one o the finest knights
  That's in his companie.

8 'Are ye the maid o the Cowden Knowes?
  I think you seem to be;'
'No, I'm not the maid o the Cowden Knowes,
  Nor ever hopes to be;
But I am one o her mother's maids,
  And oft in her companie.'

9 He's taen her by the milk-white hand,
  And by her grass-green sleeve,

He's set her down upon the ground
  Of her kin spierd nae leave.

10 He's gien her a silver comb,
  To comb her yellow hair;
He bade her keep it for his sake,
  For fear she never got mair.

11 He pat his hand in his pocket,
  He's gien her guineas three;
Says, Take ye that, fair maid, he says,
  'T will pay the nourice's fee.

12 She's taen her milk-pail on her head,
  And she gaed singing hame,
And a' that her auld father did say,
  'Daughter, ye've tarried lang.'

13 'Woe be to your shepherd, father,
  And an ill death mat he die!
He's biggit the bught sae far frae the town,
  And trystit a man to me.

14 'There came a tod into the bught,
  The like o 'm I neer did see:
Before he'd taen the lamb he's taen,
  I'd rather he'd taen other three.'

15 Or eer six months were past and gane,
  Six months but other three,
The lassie begud for to fret and frown,
  And lang for his blinking ee.

16 It fell upon another day,
  When ca'ing out her father's kye,
That by came the troop o gentlemen,
  Sae merrily riding by.

17 Then ane of them stopt, and said to her,
  'Wha's aught that bairn ye're wi?'
The lassie began for to blush, and think,
  To a father as good as ye.

18 She turnd her right and round about
  And thought nae little shame;
Then a' to him that she did say,
  'I've a father to my bairn at hame.'

19 'Ye lie, ye lie, ye well-fared may,
  Sae loud's I hear ye lie!
For dinna ye mind yon misty night
  I was in the bught wi thee?

20 'I gave you a silver comb,
  To comb your yellow hair;
  I bade you keep it for my sake,
  For fear ye 'd never get mair.

21 'I pat my hand in my pocket,
  I gae you guineas three;
  I bade you keep them for my sake,
  And pay the nourice's fee.'

22 He 's lappen aff his berry-brown steed
  And put that fair maid on;

'Ca hame your kye, auld father,' he says,
  'She shall never mair return.

23 'I am the laird o the Rock-rock lays,
  Hae thirty ploughs and three,
  And this day will wed the fairest maid
  That eer my eyes did see.'

O the broom, the bonny, bonny broom,
  The broom grows oer the burn!
Aye when she minds on his yellow hair,
  She shall neer hae cause to mourn.

M

Buchan's Ballads of the North of Scotland, I, 172.

1 'T was on a misty day, a fair maiden gay
  Went out to the Cowdenknowes;
Lang, lang she thought ere her ewes woud
    bught,
  Wi her pail for to milk the ewes.
    O the broom, the bonny, bonny broom,
    The broom o the Cowdenknowes!
  And aye sae sweet as the lassie sang,
    In the ewe-bught, milking her ewes.

2 And aye as she sang the greenwoods rang,
  Her voice was sae loud and shrill;
They heard the voice o this well-far'd maid
  At the other side o the hill.

3 'My mother she is an ill woman,
  And an ill woman is she;
Or than she might have got some other maid
  To milk her ewes without me.

4 'My father was ance a landed laird,
  As mony mair have been;
But he held on the gambling trade
  Till a 's free lands were dune.

5 'My father drank the brandy and beer,
  My mother the wine sae red;
Gars me, poor girl, gang maiden lang,
  For the lack o tocher guid.'

6 There was a troop o merry gentlemen
  Came riding alang the way,
And one o them drew the ewe-bughts unto,
  At the voice o this lovely may.

7 'O well may you sing, my well-far'd maid,
  And well may you sing, I say,
For this is a mirk and a misty night,
  And I 've ridden out o my way.'

8 'Ride on, ride on, young man,' she said,
  'Ride on the way ye ken;
But keep frae the streams o the Rock-river,
  For they run proud and vain.

9 'Ye winna want boys for meat, kind sir,
  And ye winna want men for fee;
It sets not us that are young women
  To show young men the way.'

10 'O winna ye pity me, fair maid?
  O winna ye pity me?
O winna ye pity my poor steed,
  Stands trembling at yon tree?'

11 'Ride on, ride on, ye rank rider,
  Your steed 's baith stout and strang;
For out o the ewe-bught I winna come,
  For fear that ye do me wrang.

12 'For well ken I by your high-colld hat,
  And by your gay gowd ring,
That ye are the Earl o Rock-rivers,
  That beguiles a' our young women.'

13 'O I 'm not the Earl o the Rock-rivers,
  Nor ever thinks to be;
But I am ane o his finest knights,
  Rides aft in his companie.

14 'I know you well by your lamar beads,
  And by your merry winking ee,

That ye are the maid o the Cowdenknowes,
    And may very well seem to be.'

15 He 's taen her by the milk-white hand,
    And by the grass-green sleeve,
He 's laid her down by the ewe-bught-wa,
    At her he spiered nae leave.

16 When he had got his wills o her,
    And his wills he had taen,
He lifted her up by the middle sae sma,
    Says, Fair maid, rise up again.

17 Then he has taen out a siller kaim,
    Kaimd down her yellow hair;
Says, Fair maid, take that, keep it for my sake,
    Case frae me ye never get mair.

18 Then he put his hand in his pocket,
    And gien her guineas three;
Says, Take that, fair maiden, till I return,
    'T will pay the nurse's fee.

19 Then he lap on his milk-white steed,
    And he rade after his men,
And a' that they did say to him,
    ' Dear master, ye 've tarried lang.'

20 ' I 've ridden east, I 've ridden west,
    And over the Cowdenknowes,
But the bonniest lass that eer I did see,
    Was i the ewe-bught, milking her ewes.'

21 She 's taen her milk-pail on her head,
    And she gaed singing hame;
But a' that her auld father did say,
    ' Daughter, ye 've tarried lang.'
      ' O the broom, the bonny, bonny broom,
        The broom o the Cowdenknowes!
      Aye sae sair 's I may rue the day,
        In the ewe-bughts, milking my ewes.

22 ' O this is a mirk and a misty night,
    O father, as ye may see;
The ewes they ran skipping over the knowes,
    And they woudna bught in for me.

23 .   .   .   .
    .   .   .   .   .   .
    ' Before that he 'd taen the lamb that he took,
    I rather he 'd taen other three.'

24 When twenty weeks were come and gane,
    And twenty weeks and three,

The lassie's colour grew pale and wan,
    And she longed this knight to see.

25 Says, ' Wae to the fox came amo our flock!
    I wish he had taen them a'
Before that he 'd taen frae me what he took;
    It 's occasiond my downfa.'

26 It fell ance upon a time
    She was ca'ing hame her kye,
There came a troop o merry gentlemen,
    And they wyled the bonny lassie by.

27 But one o them spake as he rode past,
    Says, Who owes the bairn ye are wi?
A little she spake, but thought wi hersell,
    ' Perhaps to ane as gude as thee.'

28 O then she did blush as he did pass by,
    And dear! but she thought shame,
And all that she did say to him,
    ' Sir, I have a husband at hame.'

29 ' Ye lie, ye lie, ye well-far'd maid,
    Sae loud as I hear you lie!
For dinna ye mind yon misty night,
    Ye were in the bught wi me?
      ' O the broom, the bonny, bonny broom,
        The broom o the Cowdenknowes!
      Aye say sweet as I heard you sing,
        In the ewe-bughts, milking your ewes.'

30 ' O well do I mind, kind sir,' she said,
    ' As ye rode over the hill;
Ye took frae me my maidenhead,
    Fell sair against my will.
      ' O the broom, the bonny, bonny broom,
        The broom o the Cowdenknowes!
      And aye sae sair as I rue the day
        I met you, milking my ewes.

31 ' And aye as ye spake, ye lifted your hat,
    Ye had a merry winking ee;
I ken you well to be the man,
    Then kind sir, O pity me!'

32 ' Win up, win up, fair maiden,' he said,
    ' Nae langer here ye 'll stay;
This night ye 'se be my wedded wife,
    Without any more delay.'

33 He lighted aff his milk-white steed
    And set the lassie on;

'Ca in your kye, auld man,' he did say,
    'She 'll neer ca them in again.

34 'I am the Earl o the Rock-rivers,
       Hae fifty ploughs and three,
   And am sure I 've chosen the fairest maid
       That ever my eyes did see.'

35 Then he stript her o the robes o grey,
       Donned her in the robes o green,
   And when she came to her lord's ha
       They took her to be some queen.
           O the broom, the bonny, bonny broom,
               The broom o the Cowdenknowes!
           And aye sae sweet as the bonny lassie sang,
               That ever she milked the ewes.

N

Kinloch MSS, I, 145; from Mary Barr.

1 O THERE war a troop o merry gentlemen
       Cam riding oure the knowes,
   And they hear the voice o a bonny lass,
       In the buchts, milking the yowes.

2 'O save thee, O save thee, my bonnie may!
       O saved may ye be!
   My steed he has riden wrang,
       Fain wad I ken the way.'

3 She has tane the steed by the bridle-reins,
       Has led him till the way,
   And he has tane out three gowd rings,
       Gien them to that bonnie may.

4 And he has tane her by the milk-white hand
       And by the gerss-green sleeve,
   And he laid her doun on the side o yon hill,
       At her daddie speird na leave.

5 Now she has hame to her father gane,
       Her father did her blame:
   'O whare hae ye been, my ae dochter?
       For ye hae na been your lane.'

6 'O the nicht is mirk, and very, very wet,
       Ye may gang to the door and see;
   O there 's nabody been wi me, father,
       There 's nabody been wi me.

7 'But there cam a tod to your bucht, father,
       The like o him I neer saw;
   Afore you 'd gien him the lamb that he took,
       Ye 'd rather hae gien them a'.

8 'O wae be to my father's sheep-hird,
       An ill death may he dee!

For bigging the bucht sae nar the road,
    Let the Lochinvar to me!'

9 She 's tane her pig and her cog in her hand,
       And she 's gane to milk the kye;
   But ere she was aware, the Laird o Lochinvar
       Cam riding in the way.

10 'O save thee, O save thee, my bonnie may!
       I wish ye may be sound;
   O save thee, O save thee, my bonnie may!
       What maks thy belly sae round?'

11 O she has turnd hersel round about,
       And she within her thoucht shame:
   'O it 's nabody's wills wi me, kind sir,
       For I hae a gudeman o my ain.'

12 'Ye lee, ye lee, my bonnie may,
       Weel do I ken ye lee!
   For dinna ye mind o the three gowd rings
       I gied ye o the new moneye?'

13 'O weel do I mind thee, kind sir,
       O weel do I mind thee;
   For ae whan ye spak ye lifted up your hat,
       And ye had a bonnie twinklin ee.'

14 'O ye need na toil yoursel, my dear,
       Neither to card nor to spin;
   For there 's ten pieces I gie unto thee;
       Keep them for your lying in.'

15 Now she has hame to her father gane,
       As fast as she could hie;
   And she was na weel crownd wi joy
       Till her auld son gat she.

16 But she 'll na tell the daddie o it
       Till father nor to mither,
   And she 'll na tell the daddie o it
       To sister nor to brither.

17 And word is to the Lochinvar,
  And word is to him gane,
That sic a tenant's dochter
  Has born a bastard son:

18 And she 'll na tell the daddie o it
  To father nor to mither,
And she 'll na tell the daddie o it
  Till sister nor to brither.

19 'O weel do I ken the reason o that,
  And the reason weel do I ken;
O weel ken I the reason o that;
  It 's to some o her father's men.

20 'But I will awa to Littlejohn's house,
  Shule them out o the door;
For there 's na tenant on a' my land
  Shall harbour an arrant hure.'

21 Then out and spak the house-keeper,
  'Ye 'd better lat her abee;
For an onie harm befa this may,
  A' the wyte will be on me.'

22 O he has turnd himsel round about,
  Within himsel thoucht he
'Better do I loe her little finger
  Than a' thy haill bodie.

23 'Gae saddle to me my six coach-mares,
  Put a' their harness on,

And I will awa to Littlejohn's house
  For reports o this bastard son.'

24 Now whan he cam to Littlejohn's house,
  Littlejohn was at the door:
'Ye rascal, ye rogue, ye impudent dog,
  Will ye harbour an arrant hure!'

25 'O pardon me, my sovereign liege,
  O pardon me, I pray;
Oh that the nicht that she was born
  She 'd deed the very neist day!'

26 But he is in to his bonnie lassie gane,
  And has bolted the door behind,
And there he has kissd his bonnie lassie sweet,
  It 's over and over again.

27 'Ye did weel, ye did weel, my bonnie may,
  To keep the secret twixt me and thee;
For I am the laird o the Ochilberry swair,
  The lady o 't I 'll mak thee.

28 'Come doun, come doun, now gentlemen a',
  And set this fair lady on;
Mither, ye may milk the ewes as ye will,
  For she 'll neer milk them again.

29 'For I am the laird o the Ochilberry swair,
  O thirty plows and three,
And I hae gotten the bonniest may
  That 's in a' the south countrie.'

B. a. 6 *should probably come before* 5. 9². Whare.
  b. 2². lassie shew.
    5¹. But when twenty weeks were.
    5². O twenty weeks and three.
    5⁸. lassie began to grow pale and wan.
    6¹. father's herd. 6⁴. And wadna bide wi me.
    9². loud 's.

  11. He was the laird of Auchentrone,
      With fifty ploughs and three,
    And he has gotten the bonniest lass
      In a' the south countrie.

C. 3⁸. if he.
  Kinloch has made changes in his printed copy.
D. 1. Oh.
    1⁸. *Changed later to* ay as she sang, her.
    2⁴. *Burden:* To see.
    3⁴. *Changed to* out owr.

5⁴. axit *in the burden.* 6¹. But quhan.
7⁴. neer *inserted later after* ye 'll.
Burden: It 's ye 'll see me.
8¹. purse-string *originally.* 8³. in 3.
8⁴. It will; t *seems to be crossed out.* I *in the burden.*
9¹. fit *originally, altered to* fut, *or* fot.
13⁸. *Originally,* An afore the ane he took.
15¹. *Changed to* and a bonnie simmer day.
16¹·². Quha. 17². *Changed to* Sae loud 's.
The first stanza is given by Motherwell, Minstrelsy, Appendix, xvii, X, under the title 'Ochiltree Walls,' *with the variation,* O May, bonnie May.
E. 2¹. Oh.
I. *Kinloch has made changes in his printed copy.*
J. 11⁴. thee *for* me.
L. 4⁴. fair. vain? *Cf.* M, 8⁴.

APPENDIX

THE LOVELY NORTHERNE LASSE

a. Roxburghe Ballads, I, 190, in the Ballad Society's reprint, ed. W. Chappell, I, 587. b. Rawlinson Ballads, 566, fol. 205.

a WAS printed at London for F. Coules, who, according to Mr Chappell, flourished during the last five years of James First's reign and throughout that of Charles First: dated by Mr Bullen, 1640. b was printed for F. Coles, T. Vere, and J. Wright, 1655–80 (Chappell). There is another copy in the Euing collection, No 166, printed for Francis Coles in the Old Bayly, who may be the same person as the printer of a; and a fourth in the Douce collection, II, 137, verso, without printer's name. A copy differing from a by only three words is given by R. H. Evans, Old Ballads, 1810, I, 88.

Burton, in the fifth edition of his Anatomy of Melancholy, Oxford, 1638, p. 536, says: " The very rusticks and hog-rubbers . . . have their ballads, country tunes, O the broome, the bonny, bonny broome," etc. (Chappell). This remark is not found in the fourth edition, Oxford, 1632, p. 544. Concerning the air, see Chappell's Popular Music, pp. 458–61, 613, 783.

THE LOVELY NORTHERNE LASSE.

Who in this ditty, here complaining, shewes
What harme she got, milking her dadyes ewes.

To a pleasant Scotch tune, called The broom of Cowden Knowes.

1   THROUGH Liddersdale as lately I went,
      I musing on did passe ;
    I heard a maid was discontent,
      she sighd, and said, Alas !
    All maids that ever deceived was
      beare a part of these my woes,
    For once I was a bonny lasse,
      when I milkt my dadyes ewes.
    With, O the broome, the bonny broome,
      the broome of Cowdon Knowes !
    Faine would I be in the North Countrey,
      to milke my dadyes ewes.

2   'My love into the fields did come,
      when my dady was at home ;
    Sugred words he gave me there,
      praisd me for such a one.
    His honey breath and lips so soft,
      and his alluring eye
    And tempting tong, hath woo'd me oft,
      now forces me to cry,
    All maids, &c.

3   'He joyed me with his pretty chat,
      so well discourse could he,
    Talking of this thing and of that,
      which greatly likëd me.
    I was so greatly taken with his speech,
      and with his comely making ;
    He usëd all the meanes could be
      to inchant me with his speaking.

4   'In Danby Forest I was borne ;
      my beauty did excell ;
    My parents dearely lovëd me
      till my belly began to swell.
    I might have beene a prince's peere
      when I came over the knoes,
    Till the shepherds boy beguilëd me,
      milking my dadyes ewes.

5   'When once I felt my belly swell,
      no longer might I abide ;
    My mother put me out of doores,
      and bangd me backe and side.
    Then did I range the world so wide,
      wandering about the knoes,
    Cursing the boy that helpëd me
      to fold my dadyes ewes.

6   'Who would have thought a boy so young
      would have usd a maiden so
    As to allure her with his tongue,
      and then from her to goe ?
    Which hath also procured my woe,
      to credit his faire shewes,
    Which now too late repent I doe,
      the milking of the ewes.

7   'I often since have wisht that I
      had never seen his face ;
    I needed not thus mournefully
      have sighed, and said Alas !
    I might have matchëd with the best,
      as all the country knowes,
    Had I escaped the shepherds boy
      helpt me to fold my ewes.

8   'All maidens faire, then have a care
      when you a milking goe ;
    Trust not to young men's tempting tongues,
      that will deceive you so.
    Them you shall finde to be unkinde
      and glory in your woes ;
    For the shepheards boy beguilëd mee
      folding my dadyes ewes.'

9   'If you your virgin honours keepe,
      esteeming of them deare,
    You need not then to waile and weepe,
      or your parents anger feare.

As I have said, of them beware
  would glory in your woes ;
You then may sing with merry cheere,
  milking your dadyes ewes.'

10 A young man, hearing her complaint,
  did pity this her case,
Saying to her, Sweet beautious saint,
  I grieve so faire a face
Should sorrow so; then, sweeting, know,
  to ease thee of thy woes,
Ile goe with thee to the North Country,
  to milke thy dadyes ewes.

11 'Leander like, I will remaine
  still constant to thee ever,
As Piramus, or Troyalus,
  till death our lives shall sever.
Let me be hated evermore,
  of all men that me knowes,
If false to thee, sweet heart, I bee,
  milking thy dadyes ewes.'

12 Then modestly she did reply,
  'Might I so happy bee

Of you to finde a husband kinde,
  and for to marrie me,
Then to you I would during life
  continue constant still,
And be a true, obedient wife,
  observing of your will.
With, O the broome, the bonny broome,
  the broome of Cowden Knoes!
Faine would I be in the North Country,
  milking my dadyes ewes.

13 Thus, with a gentle soft imbrace,
  he tooke her in his armes,
And with a kisse he smiling said,
  'Ile shield thee from all harmes,
And instantly will marry thee,
  to ease thee of thy woes,
And goe with thee to the North Country,
  to milke thy dadyes ewes.'
With, O the broome, the bonny broome,
  the broome of Cowden Knoes!
Faine would I be in the North Country,
  to milke my dadyes ewes.

a. *After* 7 : The Second Part.
b. *Title :* in the ditty.
  2^1. field. 2^2. from home. 5^6. amongst *for* about.
  6^8. So to. 6^5. hath alas.   7. *Wanting.*

8^5. Then. 9^1. virgins.
10^5. I know. 13^8. my *for* thy.
13^9. With O the broom, &c.

218

THE FALSE LOVER WON BACK

A. 'The Fause Lover,' Buchan's MSS, I, 114; Buchan's Ballads of the North of Scotland, I, 268.

B. 'The place where my love Johnny dwells,' Christie's Traditional Ballad Airs, I, 144.

A YOUNG man is deserting one maid for another. The object of his new fancy lives at a distance, and he is on his way to her. He is followed by his old love from stage to stage; he repelling her, and she tenderly remonstrating. His heart gradually softens; he buys her gifts from town to town, and though each time he bids her go back, he ends with buying her a wedding gown (ring) and marrying her.

Two pretty stanzas in A, 4, 5, seem not to belong to this story. The inconstant youth would have been only too glad to have the faithful maid look to other men, and gives her all liberty to do so. These two stanzas are first found in Herd's MSS, I, 53, and in

Herd's Ancient and Modern Scottish Songs, 1776, II, 6, as follows:

> False luve, and hae ye played me this,
>   In the simmer, mid the flowers?
> I sall repay ye back agen,
>   In the winter, mid the showers.
>
> Bot again, dear luve, and again, dear luve,
>   Will ye not turn again?
> As ye look to ither women,
>   Sall I to ither men.

In a manuscript at Abbotsford, entitled Scottish Songs, 1795 (containing pieces dated up to 1806), fol. 69, they stand thus:

> False luve, and hae ye played me this,
>   In simmer amang the flowers?

> I shall repay you back agen
>   In winter amang the showers.
>
> Unless again, again, dear luve,
>   But if ye turn agen,
> As ye look other women to,
>   Sall I to other men.

Scott has put these verses, a little varied, into Davie Gellatley's mouth, in the ninth chapter of 'Waverley.' The first, with a change, occurs also in 'The Gardener,' No 219, A 7, B 15, C 3.

A is translated by Rosa Warrens, Schottische Volkslieder, p. 141, No 32; by Gerhard, p. 114.

A

Buchan's MSS, I, 114.

1 A FAIR maid sat in her bower-door,
    Wringing her lily hands,
  And by it came a sprightly youth,
    Fast tripping oer the strands.

2 'Where gang ye, young John,' she says,
    'Sae early in the day?
  It gars me think, by your fast trip,
    Your journey's far away.'

3 He turnd about wi surly look,
    And said, What's that to thee?
  I'm gaen to see a lovely maid,
    Mair fairer far than ye.

4 'Now hae ye playd me this, fause love,
    In simmer, mid the flowers?
  I shall repay ye back again,
    In winter, mid the showers.

5 'But again, dear love, and again, dear love,
    Will ye not turn again?
  For as ye look to other women,
    I shall to other men.'

6 'Make your choice of whom you please,
    For I my choice will have;

I've chosen a maid more fair than thee,
    I never will deceive.'

7 But she's kilt up her claithing fine,
    And after him gaed she;
  But aye he said, Ye'll turn again,
    Nae farder gae wi me.

8 'But again, dear love, and again, dear love,
    Will ye never love me again?
  Alas for loving you sae well,
    And you nae me again!'

9 The first an town that they came till,
    He bought her brooch and ring;
  And aye he bade her turn again,
    And gang nae farder wi him.

10 'But again, dear love, and again, dear love,
    Will ye never love me again?
  Alas for loving you sae well,
    And you nae me again!'

11 The next an town that they came till,
    He bought her muff and gloves;
  But aye he bade her turn again,
    And choose some other loves.

12 'But again, dear love, and again, dear love,
    Will ye never love me again?

Alas for loving you sae well,
And you nae me again!'

13 The next an town that they came till,
His heart it grew mair fain,
And he was as deep in love wi her
As she was ower again.

14 The next an town that they came till,
He bought her wedding gown,
And made her lady of ha's and bowers,
Into sweet Berwick town.

B

Christie's Traditional Ballad Airs, I, 144; from the recitation of a woman born in Buchan.

1 THE sun shines high on yonder hill,
And low on yonder town;
In the place where my love Johnny dwells,
The sun gaes never down.

2 'O when will ye be back, bonny lad,
O when will ye be hame?'
'When heather-hills are nine times brunt,
And a' grown green again.'

3 'O that 's ower lang awa, bonny lad,
O that 's ower lang frae hame;
For I 'll be dead and in my grave
Ere ye come back again.'

4 He put his foot into the stirrup
And said he maun go ride,
But she kilted up her green claithing
And said she woudna bide.

5 The firsten town that they came to,
He bought her hose and sheen,

And bade her rue and return again,
And gang nae farther wi him.

6 'Ye likena me at a', bonny lad,
Ye likena me at a';'
'It 's sair for you likes me sae weel
And me nae you at a'.'

7 The nexten town that they came to,
He bought her a braw new gown,
And bade her rue and return again,
And gang nae farther wi him.

8 The nexten town that they came to,
He bought her a wedding ring,
And bade her dry her rosy cheeks,
And he would tak her wi him.

9 'O wae be to your bonny face,
And your twa blinkin een!
And wae be to your rosy cheeks!
They 've stown this heart o mine.

10 'There 's comfort for the comfortless,
There 's honey for the bee;
There's comfort for the comfortless,
There 's nane but you for me.'

A. 9^1. first and: come. 11^1, 13^1. next and.
Variations in Buchan's Ballads of the North
of Scotland, I, 268.

5^4. Shall I. 6^1. your choose. 7^3. turn back.
7^4. gang. 11, 12. *Omitted*. 13^3. as *wanting*.
14^4. In bonny Berwick.

212

219

THE GARDENER

A. Kinloch MSS, V, 47. 'The Gardener,' Kinloch MSS, VII, 19; Kinloch's Ancient Scottish Ballads, p. 74.

B. 'The Gardener Lad,' Buchan's Ballads of the North of Scotland, II, 187.

C. Fragment communicated by Dr Thomas Davidson.

———•———

A GARDENER will apparel a maid from head to foot with flowers, if she will be his bride. He gets a wintry answer: the snow shall be his shirt, the wind his hat, the rain his coat.

B 1–6 is mere jargon, foisted into this pretty ballad as a preface.

A 7, B 15, C 3, is found, substantially, in the preceding ballad, and perhaps belonged originally to neither.

Freely translated from **A** and **B** by Rosa Warrens, Schottische Volkslieder, p. 134, No 30.

———•———

A

Kinloch MSS, V, 47, in the handwriting of James Beattie; from the recitation of his aunt, Miss Elizabeth Beattie.

1 THE gardener stands in his bower-door,
    With a primrose in his hand,
And by there came a leal maiden,
    As jimp 's a willow wand.
    And by, etc.

2 'O lady, can you fancy me,
    For to be my bride,
You 'll get a' the flowers in my garden,
    To be to you a weed.

3 'The lily white shall be your smock;
    Becomes your body neat;
And your head shall be deckd with jelly-
        flower,
    And the primrose in your breast.

4 'Your gown shall be o the sweet-william,
    Your coat o camovine,
And your apron o the salads neat,
    That taste baith sweet and fine.

5 'Your stockings shall be o the broad kail-blade,
    That is baith broad and long;
And narrow, narrow at the coot,
    And broad, broad at the brawn.

6 'Your gloves shall be the marygold,
    All glittering to your hand,
Well spread oer wi the blue blaewort,
    That grows in corn-land.'

7 'O fare you well, young man,' she says,
    'Farewell, and I bid adieu;
Since you 've provided a weed for me,
    Among the summer flowers,
Then I 'll provide another for you,
    Among the winter showers.

8 'The new-fallen snow to be your smock;
    Becomes your body neat;
And your head shall be deckd with the eastern
        wind,
    And the cold rain on your breast.'

B

Buchan's Ballads of the North of Scotland, II, 187

1 ALL ye young men, I pray draw near,
    I 'll let you hear my mind
Concerning those who fickle are,
    And inconstant as the wind.

2 A pretty maid who late livd here,
    And sweethearts many had,
The gardener-lad he viewd them all,
    Just as they came and gaed.

3 The gardener-lad he viewd them all,
    But swore he had no skill:
'If I were to go as oft to her,
    Ye surely would me kill.

4 'I 'm sure she 's not a proper maid,
    I 'm sure she is not tall;'
Another young man standing by,
    He said, Slight none at all.

5 'For we 're all come of woman,' he said,
    'If ye woud call to mind,
And to all women for her sake
    Ye surely should be kind.'

6 'The summer hours and warm showers
    Make the trees yield in the ground,
And kindly words will woman win,
    And this maid I 'll surround.'

7 The maid then stood in her bower-door,
    As straight as ony wand,
When by it came the gardener-lad,
    With his hat in his hand.

8 'Will ye live on fruit,' he said?
    'Or will ye marry me?
And amongst the flowers in my garden
    I 'll shape a weed for thee.'

9 'I will live on fruit,' she says,
    'But I 'll never marry thee;
For I can live without mankind,
    And without mankind I 'll die.'

10 'Ye shall not live without mankind,
    If ye 'll accept of me;
For among the flowers in my garden
    I 'll shape a weed for thee.

11 'The lily white to be your smock;
    Becomes your body best;
And the jelly-flower to be your quill,
    And the red rose in your breast.

12 'Your gown shall be o the pingo white,
    Your petticoat cammovine,
Your apron o the seel o downs;
    Come smile, sweet heart o mine!

13 'Your shoes shall be o the gude rue red —
    Never did I garden ill —
Your stockings o the mary mild;
    Come smile, sweet heart, your fill!

14 'Your gloves shall be o the green clover,
    Comes lockerin to your hand,
Well dropped oer wi blue blavers,
    That grow among white land.'

15 'Young man, ye 've shap'd a weed for me,
    In summer among your flowers;
Now I will shape another for you,
    Among the winter showers.

16 'The snow so white shall be your shirt;
    It becomes your body best;
The cold bleak wind to be your coat,
    And the cold wind in your breast.

17 'The steed that you shall ride upon
    Shall be o the weather snell,
Well bridled wi the northern wind,
    And cold sharp showers o hail.

18 'The hat you on your head shall wear
    Shall be o the weather gray,
And aye when you come into my sight
    I 'll wish you were away.'

C

Communicated from memory by Dr Thomas Davidson as learned in Old Deer, Aberdeenshire.

1 BURD ELLEN stands in her bower-door,
  As straucht 's a hollan wand,
And by it comes the gairdner-lad,
  Wi a red rose in his hand.

2 Says, I have shapen a weed for thee
  Amang my simmer flowers;

. . . .

* * * * * * *

3 'Gin ye hae shapen a weed for me,
  Amang your simmer flowers,
It 's I 'll repay ye back again,
  Amang the winter showers.

4 'The steed that ye sall ride upon
  Sall be o the frost sae snell,
And I 'll saddle him wi the norlan winds,
  And some sharp showers o hail.'

* * * * * *

A. *Kinloch has made changes in MSS, VII, 19, which appear in his printed copy.*
C. 2. "He goes on to describe his weed, promising to array her in flowers more gorgeously than Solomon in all his glory."
4. "She continues, after the same style."

220

THE BONNY LASS OF ANGLESEY

A. 'The Bonny Lass of Anglesey,' Herd's MSS, I, 148; Herd's Ancient and Modern Scottish Songs, 1776, II, 231.

B. 'The Bonny Lass o Englessie's Dance,' Buchan's Ballads of the North of Scotland, II, 63.

THIS little ballad might perhaps rightfully have come in earlier, if I had known what to make of it. There is a resemblance, remarkable as far as it goes, to 'Little Kirstin's Dance,' Grundtvig, V, 118, No 263. Here the dance is for a match; the lass asks what she is to have if she wins, and is promised fifteen (five) ploughs and a mill, and her choice of the king's knights for a husband. In the Danish ballad (A), a king's son, to induce Little Kirstin to dance before him, promises a succession of gifts, none of which avail until he plights his honor and troth. The remainder of the story is like the conclusion of 'Gil Brenton,' No 5: see especially I, 66. (Danish A is translated by Prior, III, 89, No 112.)

Kirstin tires out fifteen knights in Danish A 12, B 10, D 14 (in C 7 eleven); and a Kirstin tires out fifteen partners again in Grundtvig, No 126, F 32, No 245, A 16. In Norwegian versions of No 263, given by Grundtvig in an appendix, numbers are not specified; Kirstin in Norwegian A 6, D 18, tires out all the king's knights.

Buchan quite frightens one by what he says of his version, II, 314: "It is altogether a political piece, and I do not wish to interfere much with it."

A

Herd's MSS, I, 148.

1 OUR king he has a secret to tell,
    And ay well keepit it must be:
The English lords are coming down
    To dance and win the victory.

2 Our king has cry'd a noble cry,
    And ay well keepit it must be:
'Gar saddle ye, and bring to me
    The bonny lass of Anglesey.'

3 Up she starts, as white as the milk,
    Between him and his company:
What is the thing I hae to ask,
    If I sould win the victory?'

4 'Fifteen ploughs but and a mill
    I gie thee till the day thou die,
And the fairest knight in a' my court
    To chuse thy husband for to be.'

5 She's taen the fifteen lord[s] by the hand,
    Saying, 'Will ye come dance with me?'
But on the morn at ten o'clock
    They gave it oer most shamefully.

6 Up then rais the fifteenth lord —
    I wat an angry man was he —
Laid by frae him his belt and sword,
    And to the floor gaed manfully.

7 He said, 'My feet shall be my dead
    Before she win the victory;'
But before 't was ten o'clock at night
    He gaed it oer as shamefully.

———

B

Buchan's Ballads of the North of Scotland, II, 63.

1 WORD has gane thro a' this land,
    And O well noticed it maun be!
The English lords are coming down
    To dance and gain the victorie.

2 The king has made a noble cry,
    And well attended it maun be:
'Come saddle ye, and bring to me
    The bonny lass o Englessie.'

3 She started up, a' dress'd in white,
    Between him and his companie;
Said, What will ye gie, my royal liege,
    If I will dance this dance for thee?

4 'Five good ploughs but and a mill
    I'll give you till the day ye die;
The bravest knight in all my court,
    I'll give, your husband for to be.'

5 She's taen the first lord by the hand,
    Says, 'Ye'll rise up and dance wi me;'
But she made a' these lords fifteen
    To gie it up right shamefullie.

6 Then out it speaks a younger lord,
    Says, 'Fye for shame! how can this be?'
He loosd his brand frae aff his side,
    Likewise his buckler frae his knee.

7 He sware his feet should be his dead
    Before he lost the victorie;
He danc'd full fast, but tired at last,
    And gae it up as shamefullie.

———

A. 1², 2². we'll keep it must and be.

221

KATHARINE JAFFRAY

A. a. 'Katharine Jaffray,' Herd's MSS, I, 61, II, 56.
b. The Aldine edition of Burns, 1839, III, 181, four stanzas.

B. 'The Laird of Laminton,' Herd's MSS, I, 164, II, 58.

C. 'Katherine Jaffarie,' "Scotch Ballads, Materials for Border Minstrelsy," No 30, Abbotsford.

D. 'The Laird of Laminton,' "Scotch Ballads, Materials for Border Minstrelsy," No 3, Abbotsford.

E. 'Cathrine Jaffray,' Skene MS., p. 81.

F. 'Catherine Janferry,' Kinloch MSS, V, 315.

G. 'Catharine Jaffery,' Maidment's North Countrie Garland, 1824, p. 34.

H. Kinloch MSS, V, 313.

I. Motherwell's MS., p. 327.

J. 'Catherine Johnson,' Motherwell's MS., p. 75 ; 'Catherine Johnstone,' Motherwell's Minstrelsy, 1827, p. 225.

K. 'Loch-in-var,' Buchan's Gleanings, 1825, p. 74.

L. Macmath MS., p. 72, two stanzas.

———◆———

THE ballad was first published by Sir Walter Scott, under the title 'The Laird of Laminton,' in the first edition of the Minstrelsy, 1802, I, 216. This copy was fashioned by the editor from two in Herd's MSS, A, B. In later editions of the Minstrelsy (III, 122, 1833), the ballad was given, with the title Katharine Janfarie, "in a more perfect state, from several recited copies." Twelve stanzas out of twenty-one, however, are repeated from the first edition. Much the larger part of what is not in Herd is taken from **C**; the name Lochinvar is adopted from `D`.* A few peculiar readings may be from copies now not known, or may be the editor's.

The ballad in Christie, II, 16, is Scott's later copy, with the omission of the 16th stanza. That in Nimmo's Songs and Ballads of Clydesdale, p. 141, is J, from Motherwell's Minstrelsy.

A Scots laird wooes a Scots maid and wins her favor. An English laird or lord, very liberal as to gowd and gear, comes to court the same lass, gains the consent of her friends (who had at least made no opposition to the earlier suit), and sets the wedding-day. The first lover comes to the wedding, backed by a strong body of armed men, whom he keeps out of sight. He is asked why he has come ; it is for a sight of the bride or a word with her, or to take a glass of wine with her or the bridegroom, and this had he will go away. Getting near the bride on this pretence, he swings her on to his horse and is off. A bloody fight follows, but the bride is not retrieved. Englishmen may take warning by this not to seek wives in Scotland ; it will always end in their being tricked and balked.

The attitude of the young woman to her first lover is not distinctly brought out in several copies. That she had jilted him in favor of a wealthier Englishman would probably

---

* Of **D**, W. Laidlaw writes as follows, September 11, 1802: "I had the surprise of a visit from my crack-brained acquaintance Mr Bartram of Biggar, the other day. He brought me a copy of the 'Laird of Laminton,' which has greatly disappointed my expectations. It is composed of those you have and some nonsense. But it overturns the tradition of this country, for it makes the wedding and battle to have been at Lauchinwar." Letters addressed to Sir Walter Scott, I, No 73, Abbotsford.

For the particulars of the compilation of the copies in the Minstrelsy, see the notes to **B, C**.

not lessen the Scot's pleasure in carrying her off. In E 18, she does not go willingly; she greets and wrings her hands, and says it 's foul play.* In F 2, G 2, the first lover openly charges her with changing and foul play, and such is the implication in E 13. In B 14, the bride, seeing the bloodshed, exclaims, Wae 's me for foul play! and her lover replies, Wae to your wilful will for causing so much good blood to be spilt! from which we must infer a fault on her part. I 2 has the ambiguous line 'and his love drew away,' which cannot be interpreted to mean that the first lover was inconstant without flying in the face of all the other copies. D, J, K, unequivocally represent the lass as faithful to her first love. The bridegroom, in these versions, arranges the match with the family, and does not mention the matter to the lass until the wedding-day: so in C, H.† She sends word to her lover that if he will come for her she will go with him, D; writes 'to let him understand,' J, K, and not to pay him the cold compliment of an invitation to see her wed the man that has supplanted him, as in B 3, E 5, F 5, I 3.

In E 7–9, while the first lover is drinking with his comrades they incite him to carry off the bride on her wedding-day; so G 6, without explanation of the circumstances. In E 7–9, 12–15, he goes to the bridal-house, and sitting at a table vents words which the other guests cannot understand: there was a young man who loved a lass that to-day goes another man's bride, and plays her old love foul play; had *he* been so served, he would take the bride away. Upon this the English ask if he wishes a fight. There is something of this in B 7–10, F 13, 14, G 11–14.

The lover would wish to keep the strong body of men that he had brought with him quite in the background until their cue came. When, therefore, in I 8, 9, the bridegroom's friends ask him what was that troop of younkers they had seen, he puts them off with the phrase, It must have been the Fairy Court; so in L. In B 5, 6 (where a stanza, and more, has dropped out), when the bridegroom sees this troop from a high window, the bride (from incredulity, it must be, and not because she is in concert with her old lover) says he must have seen the Fairy Court. G 15, 16, where the phrase comes in again, seems to have suffered corruption; any way, the passage is not quite intelligible to me.

Katharine Jaffray (Jamphray, Janfarie) is the lass's name in A, C–G, K, L; Katharine Johnstone ‡ in J; in B, H, I, she is nameless.

The lover is Lochinvar in E, F, G, I, K, L (note); Lamington in D, H, J; Lauderdale in A, C; he has no name in B. The bridegroom is Lochinvar in D, H; Lamington in B, Lymington, K; Lauderdale in F, G; Lochinton A, Lamendall E, Limberdale I (obvious mixtures of the preceding); Faughanwood in C; in J he has no name. The bridegroom should be an Englishman, but Lochinvar, Lamington, and Lauderdale are all south-Scottish names. B puts a Scot from the North Country in place of the titular Englishman of the other copies, but this Norland man is laird of Lamington.

The place of the fight is Cadan bank and Cadan brae, C, D; Cowden bank (banks) and Cowden brae (braes), A, H, J, the variation being perhaps due to the very familiar Cowdenknows; Callien, Caylin, Caley bank (buss) and brae, in E, I, F; Foudlin dyke and Foudlin stane in K. No place is named in B, G §. In I, the lass lives in Bordershellin.

A copy from the recitation of a young

---

* This phrase, owing to the accidents of tradition, comes in without much pertinency in some places; as in A 11, K 22, where *she* gars the trumpet sound foul play (altered in J 17, 18, to 'a weel won play' and 'a' fair play ').

† And in A, as here printed; but in the MS., by misplacement of 3, 5, the *lover* is absurdly made to omit telling the lass till her wedding-day.

‡ Four-and-twenty bonnie boys of the bridegroom's party are in C 13 clad in 'the simple gray;' for which Scott reads 'Johnstone grey,' 'the livery of the ancient family of Johnstone.' This circumstance, says this editor, appears to support J, "which gives Katharine the surname of John-

stone." But the grey is the livery of Lord 'Faughanwood' in C, and the Johnstone seems to be a purely capricious venture of Scott's.

§ "Caddon bank," says W. Laidlaw in a letter to Scott, September 28, [1802], "is a very difficult pass on Tweedside opposite Innerliethen. The road is now formed through the plantation of firs. The bank is exceedingly steep, and I would not think it difficult even yet with ten clever fellows to give a hundred horsemen a vast of trouble." Letters addressed to Sir Walter Scott, I, No 74, Abbotsford. — Callien, etc., may be taken to be corruptions of Caden. Foudlin, in the northern K, might be Foudland, Aberdeenshire.

Irishwoman living in Taunton, Massachusetts (learned from print, I suppose, and in parts imperfectly remembered), puts the scene of the story at Edenborough town. A squire of high degree had courted a comely country girl. When her father came to hear of this, he was an angry man, and "requested of his daughter dear to suit his company," or to match within her degree. The only son of a farmer in the east had courted this girl until he thought he had won her, and had got the consent of her father and mother. The girl writes the squire a letter to tell him that she is to be married to the farmer's son. He writes in answer that she must dress in green at her wedding (a color which no Scots girl would wear, for ill luck), and he will wear a suit of the same, and wed her 'in spite of all that's there.' He mounts eight squire-men on milk-white steeds, and rides 'to the wedding-house, with the company dressed in green.' (See the note to L.)

'O welcome you, fair welcome!
   And where have you spent all day?
Or did you see those gentlemen
   That rode along this way?'

He looked at her and scoffed at her,
   He smiled and this did say,
'They might have been some fairy troops,
   That rode along this way.'

She fills him a glass of new port wine, which he drinks to all the company, saying, Happy is the man that is called the groom, but another may love her as well as he and take her from his side.

Up spoke the intended groom,
   And an angry man was he,
Saying, If it is to fight that you came here,
   I am the man for thee.

'It is not to fight that I came here,
   But friendship for to show;
So give me one kiss from your lovely bride,
   And away from you I'll go.'

He took her by the waist so small,
   And by the grass-green sleeve;
He took her out of the wedding-house,
   Of the company asked no leave.

The drums did beat and the trumpets sound,
   Most glorious to be seen,
And then away to Edenborough town,
   With the company dressed in green.

Scott's Lochinvar, in the fifth canto of Marmion, was modelled on 'Katharine Jaffray.'

Another ballad (but a much later and inferior) in which a lover carries off a bride on her wedding-day is 'Lord William,' otherwise 'Lord Lundy,' to be given further on.

A Norse ballad of the same description is 'Magnus Algotsøn,' Grundtvig, No 181, III, 734,* Syv, No 77, = 'Ungen Essendal,' Kristensen, Jydske Folkeminder, I, 104, No 41, 'Hr. Essendal,' X, 247, No 61, A, B. Syv's version is translated by Jamieson, Illustrations of Northern Antiquities, p. 335.

Scott's ballad is translated by Schubart, p. 198, Doenniges, p. 15. Knortz, Schottische Balladen, p. 65, translates Aytoun.

* The heroine of this ballad, an historical lady of high rank, was the third in a regular line to be forcibly carried off by a lover. The date is 1287. Her mother and her grandmother were taken by the strong hand out of a convent in 1245 and about 1210; these much against their will, the other not so reluctantly, according to ballads in which they are celebrated, for curiously enough each has her ballad. See Grundtvig, vol. iii, Nos 138, 155, and No. 181, as above, and his remarks, p. 234, third note, and p. 738 f.

A

a. Herd's MSS, I, 61, II, 56. b. The Aldine edition of Burns's Poems, by Sir Harris Nicolas, 1839, III, 181, from Burns's autograph.

1 THERE livd a lass in yonder dale,
    And doun in yonder glen, O
And Kathrine Jaffray was her name,
    Well known by many men. O

2 Out came the Laird of Lauderdale,
    Out frae the South Countrie,
All for to court this pretty maid,
    Her bridegroom for to be.

3 He has teld her father and mither baith,
    And a' the rest o her kin,
And has teld the lass hersell,
    And her consent has win.

4 Then came the Laird of Lochinton,
    Out frae the English border,
All for to court this pretty maid,
    Well mounted in good order.

5 He's teld her father and mither baith,
    As I hear sindry say,
But he has nae teld the lass her sell,
    Till on her wedding day.

6 When day was set, and friends were met,
    And married to be,
Lord Lauderdale came to the place,
    The bridal for to see.

7 'O are you came for sport, young man:
    Or are you come for play?
Or are you come for a sight o our bride,
    Just on her wedding day?'

8 'I'm nouther come for sport,' he says,
    'Nor am I come for play;
But if I had one sight o your bride,
    I'll mount and ride away.'

9 There was a glass of the red wine
    Filld up them atween,
And ay she drank to Lauderdale,
    Wha her true-love had been.

10 Then he took her by the milk-white hand,
    And by the grass-green sleeve,
And he mounted her high behind him there,
    At the bridegroom he askt nae leive.

11 Then the blude run down by the Cowden Banks,
    And down by Cowden Braes,
And ay she gard the trumpet sound,
    'O this is foul, foul play!'

12 Now a' ye that in England are,
    Or are in England born,
Come nere to Scotland to court a lass,
    Or else ye'l get the scorn.

13 They haik ye up and settle ye by,
    Till on your wedding day,
And gie ye frogs instead o fish,
    And play ye foul, foul play.

———

B

Herd's MSS, I, 164, II, 58.

1 THE gallant laird of Lamington
    Cam frae the North Countree
To court a gallant gay lady,
    And wi presents entered he.

2 He neither stood for gould nor gear —
    For she was a well-fared may —
And whan he got her friends' consent
    He set the wedding-day.

3 She's sent unto her first fere love,
    Gin he would come to see,

And he has sent word back again
    Weel answered should she be.

4 He has sent a messenger
    Right quietly throe the land,
Wi mony armed men,
    To be at his command.

5 The bridegroom looked out at a high window,
    Beheld baith dool and doon,
And there he spied her first fere love,
    Come riding to the toun.

6 She scoffed and she scorned him,
    Upo the wedding-day,

And said it had been the Fairy Court
   That he had seen in array.

7 But as he sat at yon table-head,
   Amo yon gentlemen,
And he began to speak some words
   That na ane there could ken.

8 'There is a lass into this town —
   She is a weel-far'd may —
She is another man's bride today,
   But she 'll play him foul play.'

9 Up did start the bonny bridegroom,
   His hat into his hand,
  . . . . . .
   . : . . .

10 'O cam you here, young man, to fight?
   Or came you here to flee?
Or cam you here to drink good wine,
   And be good company?'

11 They filled a cup o good red wine,
   Drunk out between them twa:
'For one dance wi your bonny bride,
   I shall gae hame my wa.'

12 He's taen her by the milk-white hand,
   And by the grass-green sleeve,

He's mounted her high behind himself,
   At her kin's speired nae leave.

13 Now .   .   .   .   .
   And swords flew in the skies,
And droop and drowsie was the blood
   Ran our yon lilly braes.

14 The blood ran our the lilly bank,
   And our the lilly brae,
And sighing said the bonny bride,
   'A, wae's me for foul play!'

15 'My blessing on your heart, sweet thing,
   Wae to your wilfu will!
So many a gallant gentleman's blood
   This day as ye 've garred spill.

16 'But a' you that is norland men,
   If you be norland born,
Come never south to wed a bryde,
   For they 'll play you the scorn.

17 'They will play you the scorn
   Upo your wedding-day,
And gie you frogs instead o fish,
   And do you foul, foul play.'

C

"Scotch Ballads, Materials for Border Minstrelsy,"
No 30, Abbotsford. Sent Scott by William Laidlaw, in
September, 1802; obtained by him from Jean Scott.

1 THERE leeft a may, an a weel-far'd may,
   High, high up in yon glen; O
Her name was Katarine Janfarie,
   She was courtit by monie men. O

2 Up then cam Lord Lauderdale,
   Up thrae the Lawland border,
And he has come to court this may,
   A' mountit in gude order.

3 He's telld her father, he's telld her mother,
   An a' the lave o her kin,
An he has telld the bonnie lass hersel,
   An has her favour win.

4 Out then cam Lord Faughanwood,
   Out frae the English border,
An for to court this well-far'd may,
   A' mountit in gude order.

5 He telld her father, he telld her mother,
   An a' the rest o her kin,
But he neer telld the bonnie lass hersell
   Till on her waddin-een.

6 When they war a' at denner set,
   Drinkin the bluid-red wine,
'T was up then cam Lord Lauderdale,
   The bridegroom soud hae been.

7 Up then spak Lord Faughanwood,
   An he spak very slee:
'O are ye come for sport?' he says,
   'Or are ye come for play?

Or are ye come for a kiss o our bride,
An the morn her waddin-day?'

8 'O I 'm no come for ought,' he says,
'But for some sport or play;
An ae word o yer bonnie bride,
Than I 'll horse an ride away.'

9 She filld a cup o the gude red wine,
She filld it to the ee:
'Here 's a health to you, Lord Lauderdale,
An a' your companie.'

10 She filld a cup o the gude red wine,
She filld it to the brim:
'Here 's a health to you, Lord Lauderdale,
My bridegroom should hae been.'

11 He 's taen her by the milk-white hand,
And by the gars-green sleeve,
An he has mountit her behind him,
O the bridegroom spierd nae leave.

12 'It '[s] now take yer bride, Lord Faughan-
wood,
Now take her an ye may;
But if ye take yer bride again
We will ca it foul play.'

13 There war four a twenty bonnie boys,
A' clad i the simple gray;
They said the wad take their bride again,
By the strang hand an the may.

14 Some o them were fu willin men,
But they war na willin a';
Sae four an twentie ladies gay
Bade them ride on their way.

15 The bluid ran down by the Cadan bank,
An in by the Cadan brae,
An ther the gard the piper play
It was a' for foul, foul play.

16 A' ye lords in fair England
That live by the English border,
Gang never to Scotland to seek a wife,
Or than ye 'll get the scorn.

17 They 'll keep ye up i temper guid
Untill yer wadin-day,
They 'll thraw ye frogs instead o fish,
An steal your bride away.

D

"Scotch Ballads, Materials for Border Minstrelsy," No.
3, Abbotsford. Sent Scott September 11, 1802, by William
Laidlaw; received by him from Mr Bartram of Biggar.

1 There lives a lass into yon bank,
She lives hersell alone,
Her name is Kathrine Jamphray,
Well known by many a one.

2 Than came the Laird of Lamington,
It 's frae the West Countrie,
And for to court this bonnie may,
Her bridegroom hopes to be.

3 He asked at her father, sae did he at her
mother,
And the chief of all her kin,
But still he askd the lass hersell,
Till he had her true love won.

4 At length the Laird of Lachenwar
Came from the English border,
And for to court this bonnie bride,
Was mounted in good order.

5 He asked at her father, sae did he at her
mother,
As I heard many say,
But he never loot the lassie wit
Till on her wedding-day.

6 She sent a spy into the west
Where Lamington might be,
That an he wad come and meet wi her
That she wad with him gae.

7 They taen her on to Lachenware,
As they have thought it meet;
They taen her on to Lachanware,
The wedding to compleat.

8 When they came to Lachanware,
    And near-han by the town,
There was a dinner-making,
    Wi great mirth and renown.

9 Lamington has mounted twenty-four wiel-wight
      men,
    Well mounted in array,
And he 's away to see his bonnie bride,
    Just on her wedding-day.

10 When she came out into the green,
    Amang her company,
Says, 'Lamington and Lachanware
    This day shall fight for me.'

11 When he came to Lachanware,
    And lighted on the green,
There was a cup of good red wine
    Was filled them between,
And ay she drank to Lamington,
    Her former love who 'd been.

12 It 's out and spake the bridegroom,
    And a angrie man was he:
'It 's wha is this, my bonnie bride,
    That ye loe better than me?

13 'It 's came you here for sport, young man?
    Or came you here for play?
Or came you for a sight of my bonnie bride,
    Upon her wedding-day?'

14 'I came not here for sport,' he says,
    'Nor came I here for play;

But an I had ae word of your bride,
    I 'll horse and gae my way.'

15 The first time that he calld on her,
    Her answer was him Nay;
But the next time that he calld on her,
    She was not slow to gae.

16 He took her by the milk-white hand,
    And by the grass-green sleeve,
He 's pulld her on behind him,
    At the bridegroom speard nae leave.

17 The blood ran up the Caden bank,
    And down the Caden brae,
And ay she bade the trumpet sound
    'It 's a' for foul, foul play.'

18 'I wonder o you English squires,
    That are in England born,
That ye come to court our Scots lasses,
    For fear ye get the scorn.

19 'For fear you get the scorn,' she says,
    'Upon your wedding-day;
They 'll gee you frogs instead of fish,
    And take your bride away.'

20 Fair fa the lads of Lamington,
    Has taen their bride away!
They 'll set them up in temper wood
    And scorn you all day.

E

Skene MS., p. 81; taken down in the north of Scotland,
1802–3.

1 BONNY Cathrin Jaffray,
    That proper maid sae fare,
She has loved young Lochinvar,
    She made him no compare.

2 He courted her the live-long winter-night,
    Sae has he the simmer's day;
He has courted her sae long
    Till he sta her heart away.

3 But the lusty laird of Lamendall
    Came frae the South Country,
An for to gain this lady's love
    In entreid he.

4 .   .   .   .   .   .

He has gained her friends' consent,
    An sett the wedding-day.

5 The wedding-day it being set,
    An a' man to it . . . ,
She sent for her first fair love,
    The wedding to come to.

6 His father an his mother came,
   .   .   .   .   .
  They came a', but he came no ;
    It was a foul play.

7 Lochinvar, as his comrads
   Sat drinkine at the wine,
  [' Fie] on you,' said his comrads,
   ' Tak yer bride for shame.

8 ' Had she been mine, as she was yours,
   An done as she has done to you,
  I wad tak her on her bridal-day,
   Fra a' her companie.

9 ' Fra a' her companie,
   Without any other stay ;
  I wad gie them frogs insted o fish,
   An tak their bride away.'

10 He gat fifty young men,
   They were gallant and gay,
  An fifty maidens,
   An left them on a lay.

11 Whan he cam in by Callien bank,
   An in by Callien brae,
  He left his company
   Dancing on a lay.

12 He cam to the bridal-house,
   An in entred he ;
   .   .   .   .   .

   .   .   .   .   .

13 ' There was a young man in this place
   Loved well a comly may,

But the day she gaes an ither man's bride,
   An played him foul play.

14 ' Had it been me as it was him,
   An don as she has don him tee,
  I wad ha geen them frogs instead o fish,
   An taen their bride away.'

15 The English spiered gin he wad fight ;
   It spak well in his mind ;
   .   .   .   .   .

   .   .   .   .   .

16 ' It was no for fightin I cam here,
   But to bear good fellowship ;
  Gae me a glass wi your bridegroom,
   An so I go my way.'

17 The glass was filled o guid red wine,
   . . . between them twa :
  ' Man, man I see yer bride,
   An so I gae my waa.'

18 He was on guid horseback,
   An whipt the bride him wi ;
  She grat an wrang her hands,
   An said, ' It is foul play.

19 .   .   .   .   .   .
   ' An this I dare well say,
  For this day I gaed anither man's bride,
   An it 's been foul play.'

20 But now sh 's Lochinvar's wife,
   .   .   .   .   .
  He gaed them frogs instead o fish,
   An tain their bride away.

F

Kinloch MSS, V, 315, in the handwriting of John Hill
Burton.

1 BONNY Catherine Janferry,
   The dainty dame so fair,
  She 's faun in love wi young Lochinvar,
   And she loved him without compare.

2 She loved him well, and wondrous well
   To change her mind away ;

But the day she goes another man's bride,
   And plays him foul play.

3 Home came the Laird o Lauderdale,
   A' from the South Countree,
  And a' to court this weel-fart may,
   And I wat good tent took he.

4 Gold nor gear he did no spare,
   She was so fair a may,
  And he agreed wi her friends all,
   And set the wedding-day.

5 She sent for her first true-love,
    Her wedding to come tee ;
His father and his mother both,
    They were to come him wi.

6 His father and his mother both,
    They were to come him wi ;
And they came both, and he came no,
    And this was foul play.

7 He 's sent a quiet messenger
    Now out thro a' the land,
To warn a hundred gentlemen,
    O gallant and good renown.

8 O gallant and good renown,
    And all o good aray,
And now he 's made his trumpet soun
    A voss o foul play.

9 As they came up by Caley buss,
    And in by Caley brae,
' Stay still, stay still, my merry young men,
    Stay still, if that you may.

10 ' Stay still, stay still, my merry young men,
    Stay still, if that you may ;
I 'll go to the bridal-house,
    And see what they will say.'

11 When he gaed to the bridal-house,
    And lighted and gaed in,
There were four and twenty English lords,
    O gallant and good renown.

12 O gallant and good renown,
    And all o good aray,
But aye he garred his trumpets soun
    A voss o foul play.

13 When he was at the table set,
    Amang these gentlemen,
He begoud to vent some words
    They couldna understan.

14 The English lords, they waxed wroth
    What could be in his mind ;
They stert to foot, on horseback lap,
    ' Come fecht ! what 's i your mind ? '

15 ' I came na here to feght,' he said,
    ' But for good sport and play ;

And one glass wi yer bonny bridegroom,
    And I 'll go boun away.'

16 The glass was filled o good reed wine,
    And drunken atween the twa ;
' And one glass wi your bonny bride,
    And I 'se go boun away.'

17 Her maiden she stood forbye,
    And quickly she said, ' Nay
I winna gee a word o her
    To none nor yet to thee.'

18 ' Oh, one word o yer bonny bride !
    Will ye refuse me one ?
Before her wedding-day was set,
    I would hae gotten ten.

19 ' Take here my promise, maiden,
    My promise and my hand,
Out oer her father's gates this day
    Wi me she shanna gang.'

20 He 's bent him oer his saddle-bow,
    To kiss her ere he gaed,
And he fastened his hand in her gown-breast,
    And tust her him behind.

21 He pat the spurs into his horse
    And fast rade out at the gate ;
Ye wouldna hae seen his yellow locks
    For the dust o his horse feet.

22 Fast has he ridden the wan water,
    And merrily taen the know,
And then the battle it began ;
    I 'me sure it was na mow.

23 Bridles brack, and weight horse lap,
    And blades flain in the skies,
And wan and drousie was the blood
    Gaed lapperin down the lays.

24 Now all ye English lords,
    In England where ye 'r borne,
Come never to Scotland to woo a bride,
    For they 'le gie you the scorn.

25 For they 'le gie you the scorn,
    The scorn, if that they may ;
They 'll gie you frogs instead of fish,
    And steal your bride away.

G

Maidment's North Countrie Garland, p. 34.

1 O BONNY Catharine Jaffery,
   That dainty maid so fair,
   Once lovd the laird of Lochinvar,
   Without any compare.

2 Long time she lood him very well,
   But they changed her mind away,
   And now she goes another's bride,
   And plays him foul play.

3 The bonny laird of Lauderdale
   Came from the South Countrie,
   And he has wooed the pretty maid,
   Thro presents entered he.

4 For tocher-gear he did not stand,
   She was a dainty may;
   He 'greed him with her friends all,
   And set the wedding-day.

5 When Lochinvar got word of this,
   He knew not what to do,
   For losing of a lady fair
   That he did love so true.

6 'But if I were young Lochinvar,
   I woud not care a fly
   To take her on her wedding-day
   From all her company.

7 'Get ye a quiet messenger,
   Send him thro all your land
   For a hundred and fifty brave young lads,
   To be at your command.

8 'To be all at your command,
   And your bidding to obey,
   Yet still cause you the trumpet sound
   The voice of foul play.'

9 He got a quiet messenger
   To send thro all his land,
   And full three hundred pretty lads
   Were all at his command.

10 Were all at his command,
   And his bidding did obey,
   Yet still he made the trumpet sound
   The voice of foul play.

11 Then he went to the bridal-house,
   Among the nobles a',
   And when he stepped upon the floor
   He gave a loud huzza.

12 'Huzza! huzza! you English men,
   Or borderers who were born,
   Neer come to Scotland for a maid,
   Or else they will you scorn.

13 'She 'll bring you on with tempting words,
   Aye till the wedding-day,
   Syne give you frogs instead of fish,
   And play you foul play.'

14 The gentlemen all wondered
   What could be in his mind,
   And asked if he 'd a mind to fight;
   Why spoke he so unkind?

15 Did he e'er see such pretty men
   As were there in array?
   'O yes,' said he, 'a Fairy Court
   Were leaping on the hay.

16 'As I came in by Hyland banks,
   And in by Hyland braes,
   There did I see a Fairy Court,
   All leaping on the leas.

17 'I came not here to fight,' he said,
   'But for good fellowship gay;
   I want to drink with your bridegroom,
   And then I 'll boun my way.'

18 The glass was filled with good red wine,
   And drunk between them twae:
   'Give me one shake of your bonny bride's hand,
   And then I 'll boun my way.'

19 He 's taen her by the milk-white hands,
   And by the grass-green sleeve,
   Pulld her on horseback him behind,
   At her friends askd nae leave.

20 Syne rode the water with great speed,
   And merrily the knows;
   There fifty from the bridal came —
   Indeed it was nae mows —

21 Thinking to take the bride again,
   Thro strength if that they may;
   But still he gart the trumpet sound
   The voice of foul play.

22 There were four and twenty ladies fair
    All walking on the lea;
  He gave to them the bonny bride,
    And bade them boun their way.

23 They splintered the spears in pieces now,
    And the blades flew in the sky,

But the bonny laird of Lochinvar
  Has gained the victory.

24 Many a wife- and widow's son
    Lay gasping on the ground,
  But the bonny laird of Lochinvar
    He has the victory won.

H

Kinloch MSS, V, 313.

1 THERE was a lady fair, fair,
    Lived low down in yon glen, O
  And she's been courted far an near
    By several gentlemen.   O

2 At length the laird of Lammington
    Came frae the West Country,
  All to court that pretty girl,
    And her bridegroom for to be.

3 He told her father, so did he her mother,
    And all the rest of her kin,
  And he has told the lass hersel,
    And her kind favour has won.

4 At length the laird of Laughenwaur
    Came frae the English border,
  And all to court that pretty girl,
    Well mounted in good order.

5 He told her father, so did he her mother,
    As I heard people say,
  But he ner told the lass hersel,
    Till on her wedding-day.

6 But when the wedding-day was fixed,
    And married for to be,
  Then Lamington came to the town,
    The bridegroom for to see.

7 'O are ye come for sport, sir?' he said,
    'Or are ye come for play?

Or are ye for a sight o my bonny bride,
  Upon her wedding-day?'

8 'A'm neither come for sport, sir,' he said,
    'Nor am I come for play,
  But if I had one word o the bride
    I'd mount and go away.'

9 There was a cup of the good red wine
    Was filled out them between,
  And aye she drank to Lammington,
    Who her true-love had been.

10 He's taen her by the milk-white hand,
    And by the grass-green sleeve;
  He's mounted her behind him then,
    At the bridegroom speered no leave.

11 The blood ran down by Cowden banks,
    And down by Cowden brae,
  And aye they gaured the piper play
    'It was a foul, foul play.'

12 Ye gentlemen of Lochenwaur,
    That's laigh in England born,
  Come ner to Scotland to court a wife,
    Or be sure ye'l get the scorn.

13 The'll keep ye up, and tamper ye at,
    Until yer wedding-day,
  And they'l gie ye frogs instead o fish,
    And they'll play ye a foul play.

I

Motherwell's MS., p. 327, "from the recitation of Robert Sim, weaver, in Paisley, 16 July, 1825. It was a song of his father's, a great reciter of heroick ballads."

1 In Bordershellin there did dwell
  A comely, handsome may,
And Lochinvar he courted her,
  And stole her heart away.

2 She loved him but owre weel,
  And his love drew away;
Another man then courted her,
  And set the wedding-day,

3 They set the wedding-day so plain,
  As plain as it might be;
She sent a letter to her former love,
  The wedding to come see.

4 When Lochinvar the letter read,
  He sent owre a' his land
For four and twenty beltit knichts,
  To come at his command.

5 They all came to his hand, I say,
  Upon that wedding-day;
He set them upon milk-white steeds,
  And put them in array.

6 He set them in array, I say,
  Most pleasant to be seen,
And he 's awa to the wedding-house,
  A single man his lane.

7 And when he was to the wedding-house come,
  They were all sitten down;
Baith gentlemen and knichts was there,
  And lords of high renown.

8 They saluted him, baith auld and young,
  Speired how he had spent the day,
And what young Lankashires was yon
  They saw all in array.

9 But he answerd them richt scornfullie,
  Upon their wedding-day;
He says, It 's been some Fairy Court
  Ye 've seen all in array.

10 Then rose up the young bridegroom,
  And an angry man was he:
'Lo, art thou come to fight, young man?
  Indeed I 'll fight wi thee.'

11 'O I am not come to fight,' he sayd,
  'But good fellowship to hae,
And for to drink the wine sae red,
  And then I 'll go away.'

12 Then they filld him up a brimming glass,
  And drank it between them twa:
'Now one word of your bonnie bride,
  And then I 'll go my wa.'

13 But some were friends, and some were faes,
  Yet nane o them was free
To let the bride on her wedding-day
  Gang out o their companie.

14 But he took her by the milk-white hand,
  And by the grass-green sleeve,
And set her on a milk-white steed,
  And at nane o them speerd he leave.

15 Then the blood ran down the Caylin bank,
  And owre the Caylin brae;
The auld folks knew something o the sport,
  Which gart them cry, Foul play!

16 Ye lusty lads of Limberdale,
  Tho ye be English born,
Come nae mair to Scotland to court a maid,
  For fear ye get the scorn.

17 For fear that ye do get the scorn
  Upon your wedding-day;
Least ye catch frogs instead of fish,
  And then ye 'll ca 't foul play.

J

Motherwell's MS., p. 75, from the recitation of Mrs Thomson, an old woman of Kilbarchan.

1 THERE was a lass, as I heard say,
    Lived low down in a glen;
Her name was Catharine Johnson,
    Weel known to many men.

2 Doun cam the laird o Lamingtoun,
    Doun frae the South Countrie,
And he is for this bonnie lass,
    Her bridegroom for to be.

3 He's askd her father and mother,
    The chief of a' her kin,
And then he askd the bonnie lass,
    And did her favour win.

4 Doun cam an English gentleman,
    Doun frae the English border;
He is for this bonnie lass,
    To keep his house in order.

5 He askd her father and mother,
    As I do hear them say,
But he never askd the lass hersell,
    Till on her wedding-day.

6 But she has wrote a lang letter,
    And sealed it wi her hand,
And sent it to Lord Lamington,
    To let him understand.

7 The first line o the letter he read,
    He was baith glad and fain;
But or he read the letter owre
    He was baith pale and wan.

8 Then he has sent a messenger,
    And out through all his land,
And four-and-twenty armed men
    Was all at his command.

9 But he has left his merry men,
    Left them on the lea;
And he's awa to the wedding-house,
    To see what he could see.

10 But when he came to the wedding-house,
    As I do understand,
There were four-and-twenty belted knights
    Sat at a table round.

11 They rose all for to honour him,
    For he was of high renown;
They rose all for to welcome him,
    And bade him to sit doun.

12 O meikle was the good red wine
    In silver cups did flow,
But aye she drank to Lamingtoun,
    For with him would she go.

13 O meikle was the good red wine
    In silver cups gaed round;
At length they began to whisper words,
    None could them understand.

14 'O came ye here for sport, young man?
    Or cam ye here for play?
Or cam ye for our bonnie bride,
    On this her wedding-day?'

15 'I came not here for sport,' he said,
    'Neither did I for play;
But for one word o your bonnie bride
    I'll mount and ride away.'

16 They set her maids behind her,
    To hear what they would say,
But the first question he askd at her
    Was always [answered] nay;
The next question he askd at her
    Was, 'Mount and come away.'

17 It's up the Couden bank,
    And doun the Couden brae;
And aye she made the trumpet sound,
    ''It's a weel won play.'

18 O meikle was the blood was shed
    Upon the Couden brae;
And aye she made the trumpet sound,
    'It's a' fair play.'

19 Come, all ye English gentlemen,
    That is of England born,
Come nae doun to Scotland,
    For fear ye get the scorn.

20 They'll feed ye up wi flattering words,
    And that's foul play;
And they'll dress ye frogs instead o fish,
    Just on your wedding-day.

K

Buchan's Gleanings of Scotch, English and Irish Scarce Old Ballads, 1825, pp. 74, 193; "taken down from oral tradition."

1 THERE lives a lass in yonder dale,
  In yon bonny borrows-town,
Her name it is Catherine Jeffrey,
  She is loved by mony a ane.

2 Lord Lochinvar has courted her
  These twelve months and a day;
With flattering words and fair speeches
  He has stown her heart away.

3 There came a knight from south sea-bank,
  From north England I mean,
He alighted at her father's yetts,
  His stile is Lord Lymington.

4 He has courted her father and moth
  Her kinsfolk ane and aye,
But he never told the lady hersell
  Till he set the wedding-day.

5 'Prepare, prepare, my daughter dear,
  Prepare, to you I say;
For the night it is good Wednesday night,
  And the morn is your wedding-day.'

6 'O tell to me, father,' she said,
  'O tell me who it is wi;
For I 'll never wed a man on earth
  Till I know what he be.'

7 'He 's come a knight from the south sea-bank,
  From north England I mean,
For when he lighted at my yetts,
  His stile is Lord Lymington.'

8 'O where will I get a bonny boy
  Will win baith meet and fee,
And will run on to Lochinvar
  And come again to me?'

9 'O here am I, a bonny boy
  That will win baith hose and sheen,
And will run on to Lochinvar,
  And come right seen again.'

10 'Where ye find the brigs broken,
  Bend your bow and swim;
Where ye find the grass growing,
  Slack your bow and run.

11 'When ye come on to Lochinvar,
  Byde not to chap nor ca,
But set your bent bow to your breast
  And lightly loup the wa.

12 'Bid him mind the words he last spake,
  When we sendered on the lee;
Bid him saddle and ride full fast,
  If he be set for me.'

13 Where he found the brigs broken,
  He bent his bow and swam;
Where he found the grass growing,
  He slackt his bow and ran.

14 When he came on to Lochinvar,
  He did not chap nor ca;
He set his bent bow till his breast
  And lightly leapt the wa.

15 'What news? what news, my bonny boy?
  What news have ye to me?'
'Bad news, bad news, my lord,' he said,
  'Your lady awa will be.

16 'You 'r bidden mind the words ye last spake,
  When we sendered on the lee;
You 'r bidden saddle and ride full fast,
  Gin ye set for her be.'

17 When he came to her father's yetts,
  There he alighted down;
The cups of gold of good red wine
  Were going roun and roun.

18 'Now came ye here for sport?' they said,
  'Or came ye here for play?
Or for a sight of our bonny bride,
  And then to boun your way?'

19 'I came not here for sport,' he says,
  'Nor came I here for play,
But if I had a sight of your bonny bride
  Then I will boun my way.'

20 When Lymington he called on her,
  She would not come at a',
But Lochinvar he called on her,
  And she was not sweer to draw.

21 He has taen her by the milk-white hand,
  And by her silken sleeve,
He has mounted her high him behind,
  He spiered nae mair their leave.

22 And aye she scoffed and scorned them,
    And aye she rode away,
  And aye she gart the trumpet sound
    The voice of foul play,
  To take the bride frae her bridegroom
    Upon her wedding-day.

23 As they came in by Foudlin dyke,
    And in by Foudlin stane,
  There were mony gallant Englishmen
    Lay gasping on the green.

24 Now a' you that are English lords,
    And are in England born,
  Come never here to court your brides,
    For fear ye get the scorn.

25 For aye they 'll scoff and scorn you,
    And aye they 'll ride away ;
  They 'll gie you frogs instead of fish,
    And call it foul play.

———◆———

L

Macmath MS., p. 72, communicated January 13, 1883, by Dr Robert Trotter, as remembered from the recitation of his father, Dr Robert Trotter, of Dalry, Kirkcudbrightshire.

1 THEY askëd him and speirëd him,
    And unto him did say,

' O saw ye ocht o an armed band,
    As ye cam on your way ? '

2 He jested them and jeerëd them,
    And thus to them did say,
' O I saw nocht but a fairy troop,
    As I rode on my way.'

———◆———

A. a. *The second copy has some different spellings, and drops the second* the *in* 11[1]. 3, 5 *are* 5, 3 *in both.* *Sense requires the change : cf. also* F 5, H 5, I 4.

  b. 1[4]. *to* many. 3 = *the MS.* 3. 4[4]. *All mounted.*

B. *The first copy is written in long lines (two to a stanza) ; neither is divided into stanzas. There are differences of spelling.* 3[1], 5[8], fere *seems to be meant for* fair *: cf.* C 5[8]. 4[4]. At her, *both : cf.* E 7, G 4, H 8. 5[2]. *Both copies have* doom. 5[2], 15[4]. *First,* behold, garned, *in my copy, probably by error.* *Second,* beheld, gard.

The second copy has these variations. 2[3]. got the. 3[1], 5[8]. fere *wanting.* 15[1]. thing *wanting.* 16[1]. that are.

The first edition of the ballad in Scott's Minstrelsy is made up as follows (it being remembered that the editor did not profess or practice a servile fidelity in the treatment of his materials) : B 1–6 ; B 10, A 7 ; A 8, B 11 ; A 9 ; B 12 ; B 13 (*but mostly Scott's*) ; A 11, B 14 ; B 15 ; B 16 ; A 13. 12 *of these* 15 *stanzas are repeated in the later edition ; the new stanzas in that copy* are 1–5, 14–16, 20. *These are substantially* C 1–5, 12–14, 16.

Some variations will be noticed under C.

C. O, *the tag to the second and fourth lines, is not written in* 2, 4, 16[2], 17[4].

  1[2]. into *written over* up.

  2[4]. Weel *in the margin against* A'.

  3[2]. rest *struck out before* lave.

  4[1]. Up *struck out before* Out. Faughan Wood, *here and* 7[1]; *in* 12[1], Faughan Wood.

  7[1]. Up the then.

  9[1]. gude *struck out before* red, *and* red *written over.*

  15[1]. *Originally* down by ; down *struck out.*

  15[2]. *Originally* in by ; in *struck out.* *These last two changes, and others, seem to be editorial.*

  1–5, 12–14, 16, *with variations, are* 1–5, 14–16, 20 *of the later edition of the ballad in Scott's Minstrelsy.* *Slight alterations, such as Scott was accustomed to make, do not require notice.*

Scott, 3[1,2]. He told na *in the Minstrelsy : almost certainly an arbitrary change, and not a good one, since it makes the hardship to Lauderdale the less.*

4[1]. Lochinvar (*also in* 14[1]) *for* Lord Faughan-wood; *introduced from* D.

15[2]. clad in the Johnstone grey: *for which no authority is known.*

16[3]. Leader lads *for* ladies gay: *probably a conjectural emendation.*

20[4]. For fear of sic disorder: *presumably a change for rhyme,* disorder *suggested by* 2[4].

D. 9[1]. 24. 12[1]. It 's *is of later insertion, perhaps editorial.*

14[1], I came not here: *obscured in the process of binding.*

20. *This must be a mixture of two stanzas. The third line has no sense, and is not much improved by reading* temper good, *as in* C 17[1].

E. *Written mostly in long lines, without separation of stanzas, sometimes without a proper separation of verses. The division here made is partly conjectural.*

2[1]. She courted him.

3[4]. entreid *or* entried: *indistinct.*

6, 7[1,2]. His father an his mother came they
     came a
         but he came no
     It was a foul play Lochinvar
     As his comrades sat drinkine at the
     wine

7[3]. . . . on.   13[2]. Lodged *for* Loved.

16[3]. Gae man glass me your.

17[2,3].   between them tva man
     Man I see, *etc.*

F. 23[1]. *We have had a similar verse in the north-Scottish version of* ' Hugh Spencer,' *No* 158, C 11: O bridles brak and great horse lap.

H. 11[4]. It was awful foul foul play. Awful *was probably a misunderstanding of* a foul.

I. 8[3]. Lank-a-Shires.   14[3]. He *is written over* And.

15[1]. bank, *the original reading, is changed to* heuch.

J. 12[1]. Oh.   15[4]. go *is written over* ride. *Motherwell made two slight changes in his printed copy.*

K. 1[4]. my mony.   2[1]. Loch-in-var; *and always.*

3[1]. South sea bank.   7[1]. the South sea bank.

10[3]. For *for* Where: *probably a misprint, perhaps a preservation of the northern* f *for* wh.

13[3]. the brigs broken, *wrongly repeated.*

16[2]. When we, *preserved from* 12[2].

23[3]. Englishman.

L. " The story of the ballad was that Lochinvar went to Netherby with a band of men dressed in green, whom he concealed near the tower, and with whose assistance he forcibly abducted the young lady."

222

BONNY BABY LIVINGSTON

A. 'Bonny Baby Livingston.'   a. Jamieson-Brown MS.   b. Jamieson's Popular Ballads, II, 135.

B. 'Barbara Livingston,' Buchan's MSS, I, 77.

C. Motherwell's MS., p. 375; 'Barbara Livingston,' Motherwell's Minstrelsy, p. 304.

D. 'Annie Livingston,' Campbell MSS, II, 254.

E. 'Baby Livingstone,' Kinloch MSS, V, 355.

Mrs Brown was not satisfied with A b, which Jamieson had taken down from her mouth, and after a short time she sent him A a. The verbal differences are considerable. We need not suppose that Mrs Brown had heard two "sets" or "ways," of which she blended the readings; the fact seems to be that, at the time when she recited to Jamieson, she was not in good condition to remember accurately.

A a. Glenlion carries off Barbara Livingston from Dundee and takes her to the Highlands. She is in a stupor of grief. Glenlion folds her in his arms, and says that he would give all his flocks and herds for a kind look. She tells him that he shall never get look or smile unless he takes her back to Dundee; and he her that she shall never see Dundee till he has married her. His brother John tries to dissuade him; he himself would scorn a hand without a heart; but Glenlion has long loved her, and is resolved to keep her, nevertheless. Glenlion's three sisters receive Baby kindly, and the youngest begs her to disclose the cause of her grief. Baby tells the sympathetic Jean that she has been stolen from her friends and from her lover, and obtains not only the means of writing a letter to Johny Hay, the lover, but a swift-footed boy to carry it to Dundee. Johny Hay, with a band of armed men, makes all speed to Glenlion's castle. He calls to Baby to jump, and he will catch her; she, more prudently, slips down on her sheets; her lover takes her on his horse and rides away. Glenlion hears the ring of a bridle and thinks it is the priest come to marry him. His brother corrects the mistake; there are armed men at the castle-gate, and it turns out that there are enough of them to deter Glenlion's Highlanders from an attack. So Johny Hay conveys Baby Livingstone safely back to Dundee.

The other versions give the story a tragical catastrophe. In B, Barbara is forced into Glenlion's bed. Afterwards she exclaims that if she had paper and pen she would write to her lover in Dundee. No difficulty seems to be made; she writes her letter, and sends it by the ever-ready boy. Geordie, lying in a window, sees the boy, asks for news, and is told that his love is stolen by Glenlion. He orders his horse, in fact three horses, and also

a mourning hat and cloak; but though he tires out all three horses, his love is dead before he reaches Glenlion. This copy is pieced out with all sorts of commonplaces from other ballads: see 9 (which is nonsense), 10, 13, 14, 19, 21, 23, 25, 27, 29, 30.

C is a briefer, that is, an unfarced, form of B. Glenlion is corrupted to Linlyon.

D has its commonplaces again. For Barbara we have Annie, and Glendinning for Glenlion, and a brother Jemmy instead of a lover. In E the ravisher is Lochell.

Dr Joseph Robertson in his Adversaria, MS., p. 87, gives these two lines of 'Baby Livingston:'

O bony Baby Livingston
Was playin at the ba.*

The kidnapping of women for a compulsory marriage was a practice which prevailed for hundreds of years, and down to a late date, and, of course, not only in Great Britain. The unprotected female, especially if she had any property, must have been in a state of miserable insecurity, and even a convent was far from furnishing her an asylum. See for England, in the first half of the fifteenth century, Beamont's Annals of the Lords of Warrington, pp. 256–61 and 265 f.; for Scotland, in the same century and the two following, Sharpe's Ballad Book, p. 99 ff., R. Chambers's Domestic Annals of Scotland, 1858, I, 223–5, 415 f.; for Ireland, Froude, The English in Ireland in the Eighteenth Century, 1872, I, 417 ff. Other Scottish ballads celebrating similar abductions are 'Eppie Morrie,' 'The Lady of Arngosk,' and 'Rob Roy,' which immediately follow. †

A b is translated by Grundtvig, Engelske og skotske Folkeviser, p. 126, No 18.

---

* At the end of the account of the parish of Livingstone, in The Statistical Account of Scotland, XX, 17, 1798, there is this paragraph: "It may also be expected that something should be said of the Bonny Lass of Livingstone, so famed in song; but although this ballad and the air to which it is sung seem to have as little claim to antiquity as they have to merit, yet we cannot give any satisfactory information upon the subject. All we can say is, that we have heard that she kept a public house at a place called the High House of Livingstone, about a mile west of the church; that she was esteemed handsome, and knew how to turn her charms to the best account." Dr Robertson, at the place above cited, treats this passage as pertaining to the ballad

before us. But the reference is certainly to a song known as the "Lass o Livingston," beginning, 'The bonie lass o Liviston;' concerning which see Cromek's Reliques of Robert Burns, p. 204 of the edition of 1817, and Johnson's Museum, IV, 18, 1853.

† I will add one more corn to a heap. "Mrs Wharton, who was lately stole, is returned home to her friends, having been married against her consent to Captain Campbell" (November, 1690). Luttrell's Relation, II, 130. There is partial comfort, but somewhat cold, in the fact that the ravisher was in many cases ultimately unsuccessful in his object, as he is in all the ballads here given.

A

a. Jamieson-Brown MS., Appendix, p. xii, sent by Mrs Brown to Jamieson, in a letter dated September 15, 1800.
b. Jamieson's Popular Ballads, II, 135, as taken from Mrs Brown's recitation a short time before a was written down.

1 O BONNY Baby Livingston
    Went forth to view the hay,
And by it came him Glenlion,
    Sta bonny Baby away.

2 O first he 's taen her silken coat,
    And neest her satten gown,
Syne rowd her in a tartan plaid,
    And hapd her round and rown.

3 He has set her upon his steed
    And roundly rode away,
And neer loot her look back again
    The live-long summer's day.

4 He 's carried her oer hills and muirs
    Till they came to a Highland glen,
And there he 's met his brother John,
    With twenty armed men.

5 O there were cows, and there were ewes,
    And lasses milking there,
But Baby neer anse lookd about,
    Her heart was filld wi care.

6 Glenlion took her in his arms,
    And kissd her, cheek and chin;
Says, I 'd gie a' these cows and ewes
    But ae kind look to win.

7 'O ae kind look ye neer shall get,
    Nor win a smile frae me,
Unless to me you 'll favour shew,
    And take me to Dundee.'

8 'Dundee, Baby? Dundee, Baby?
    Dundee you neer shall see
Till I 've carried you to Glenlion
    And have my bride made thee.

9 'We 'll stay a while at Auchingour,
    And get sweet milk and cheese,
And syne we 'll gang to Glenlion,
    And there live at our ease.'

10 'I winna stay at Auchingour,
    Nor eat sweet milk and cheese,
Nor go with thee to Glenlion,
    For there I 'll neer find ease.'

11 Than out it spake his brother John,
    'O were I in your place,
I 'd take that lady hame again,
    For a' her bonny face.

12 'Commend me to the lass that 's kind,
    Tho na so gently born;
And, gin her heart I coudna gain,
    To take her hand I 'd scorn.'

13 'O had your tongue now, John,' he says,
    'You wis na what you say;
For I 've lood that bonny face
    This twelve month and a day.

14 'And tho I 've lood her lang and sair
    A smile I neer coud win;
Yet what I 've got anse in my power
    To keep I think nae sin.'

15 When they came to Glenlion castle,
    They lighted at the yate,
And out it came his sisters three,
    Wha did them kindly greet.

16 O they 've taen Baby by the hands
    And led her oer the green,
And ilka lady spake a word,
    But bonny Baby spake nane.

17 Then out it spake her bonny Jean,
    The youngest o the three,
'O lady, dinna look sae sad,
    But tell your grief to me.'

18 'O wherefore should I tell my grief,
    Since lax I canna find?
I 'm stown frae a' my kin and friends,
    And my love I left behind.

19 'But had I paper, pen, and ink,
    Before that it were day,
I yet might get a letter sent
    In time to Johny Hay.'

20 O she 's got paper, pen, and ink,
    And candle that she might see,
And she has written a broad letter
    To Johny at Dundee.

21 And she has gotten a bonny boy,
   That was baith swift and strang,
Wi philabeg and bonnet blue,
   Her errand for to gang.

22 'O boy, gin ye 'd my blessing win
   And help me in my need,
Run wi this letter to my love,
   And bid him come wi speed.

23 'And here 's a chain of good red gowd,
   And gowdn guineas three,
And when you 've well your errand done,
   You 'll get them for your fee.'

24 The boy he ran oer hill and dale,
   Fast as a bird coud flee,
And eer the sun was twa hours height
   The boy was at Dundee.

25 And when he came to Johny's door
   He knocked loud and sair ;
Then Johny to the window came,
   And loudly cry'd, 'Wha 's there ?'

26 'O here 's a letter I have brought,
   Which ye maun quickly read,
And, gin ye woud your lady save,
   Gang back wi me wi speed.'

27 O when he had the letter read,
   An angry man was he ;
He says, Glenlion, thou shalt rue
   This deed of villany !

28 'O saddle to me the black, the black,
   O saddle to me the brown,
O saddle to me the swiftest steed
   That eer rade frae the town.

29 'And arm ye well, my merry men a',
   And follow me to the glen,
For I vow I 'll neither eat nor sleep
   Till I get my love again.'

30 He 's mounted on a milk-white steed,
   The boy upon a gray,
And they got to Glenlion's castle
   About the close of day.

31 As Baby at her window stood,
   The west wind saft did bla ;

She heard her Johny's well-kent voice
   Beneath the castle wa.

32 'O Baby, haste, the window jump !
   I 'll kep you in my arm ;
My merry men a' are at the yate,
   To rescue you frae harm.'

33 She to the window fixt her sheets
   And slipped safely down,
And Johny catchd her in his arms,
   Neer loot her touch the ground.

34 When mounted on her Johny's horse,
   Fou blithely did she say,
'Glenlion, you hae lost your bride !
   She 's aff wi Johny Hay.'

35 Glenlion and his brother John
   Were birling in the ha,
When they heard Johny's bridle ring,
   As first he rade awa.

36 'Rise, Jock, gang out and meet the priest,
   I hear his bridle ring ;
My Baby now shall be my wife
   Before the laverocks sing.'

37 'O brother, this is not the priest ;
   I fear he 'll come oer late ;
For armed men with shining brands
   Stand at the castle-yate.'

38 'Haste Donald, Duncan, Dugald, Hugh !
   Haste, take your sword and spier !
We 'll gar these traytors rue the hour
   That eer they ventured here.'

39 The Highland men drew their claymores,
   And gae a warlike shout,
But Johny's merry men kept the yate,
   Nae ane durst venture out.

40 The lovers rade the live-lang night,
   And safe gat on their way,
And bonny Baby Livingston
   Has gotten Johny Hay.

41 'Awa, Glenlion ! fy for shame !
   Gae hide ye in some den !
You 've lettn your bride be stown frae you,
   For a' your armed men.'

B

Buchan's MSS, I, 77.

1 BONNY Barbara Livingston
   Went out to take the air,
   When came the laird o Glenlyon
   And staw the maiden fair.

2 He staw her in her cloak, her cloak,
   He staw her in her gown;
   Before he let her look again,
   Was mony mile frae town.

3 So they rade over hills and dales,
   Through m[o]ny a wilsome way,
   Till they came to the head o yon hill,
   And showed her ewes and kye.

4 'O will ye stay with me, Barbara,
   And get good curds and whey?
   Or will ye go to Glenlyon,
   And be a lady gay?'

5 'The Highlands is nae for me, kind sir,
   The Highlands is nae for me,
   But, gin ye woud my favour win,
   Have me to bonny Dundee.'

6 'Dundee, Barbara? Dundee, Barbara?
   That town ye 'se never see;
   I 'll hae you to a finer place
   Than eer was in Dundee.'

7 But when she came to Glenlyon,
   And lighted on the green,
   Every lady spake Earse to her,
   But Barbara could speak nane.

8 When they were all at dinner set,
   And placed the table round,
   Every one took some of it,
   But Barbara took nane.

9 She put it to her cheek, her cheek,
   She put it to her chin,
   And put it to her rosey lips,
   But neer a bit gaed in.

10 When day was gone, and night was come,
   And a' man bound for bed,
   Glenlyon and that fair lady
   To one chamber were laid.

11 'O strip, O strip, my love,' he said,
   'O strip and lay you down;'
   'How can I strip? How can I strip,
   To bed wi an unco man?'

12 He 's taen out his little pen-knife,
   And he slit down her gown,
   And cut her stays behind her back,
   And forc'd her to lie down.

13 'O day, dear sir! O day, dear sir!
   O dear! if it were day,
   And me upon my father's steed,
   I soon shoud ride away.'

14 'Your father's steed is in my stable,
   Eating good corn and hay,
   And ye are in my arms twa;
   What needs you lang for day?'

15 'If I had paper, pens, and ink,
   And light that I may see,
   I woud write a broad, broad letter
   To my love in Dundee.'

16 They brought her paper, pen, and ink,
   And light that she might see,
   And she has written a broad letter
   To her love in Dundee.

17 And aye she wrote, and aye she grat,
   The saut tear blinded her ee;
   And aye at every verse's end,
   'Haste, my bonny love, to me!'

18 'If I had but a little wee boy,
   Would work for meat and fee,
   Would go and carry this letter
   To my love in Dundee!'

19 'O here am I, a little wee boy
   Will work for meat and fee,
   Will go and carry that letter
   To your love in Dundee.'

20 Upstarts the morn, the boy he ran
   Oer mony a hill and dale,
   And he wan on to bonny Dundee
   About the hour o twall.

21 There Geordy oer a window lay,
   Beholding dale and down;

And he beheld a little wee boy
    Come running to the town.

22 'What news? what news, my little wee boy,
    You run sae hastilie?'
'Your love is stown by Glenlyon,
    And langs your face to see.'

23 'Gae saddle to me the black, the black,
    Gae saddle to me the brown;
Gae saddle to me the swiftest steed
    Will hae me to the town.

24 'Get me my hat, dyed o the black,
    My mourning-mantle tee,
And I will on to Glenlyon,
    See my love ere she die.'

25 First he tired the black, the black,
    And then he tired the brown,
And next he tired the swiftest steed
    Ere he wan to the town.

26 But for as fast as her love rade,
    And as fast as he ran,

Before he wan to Glenlyon
    His love was dead and gane.

27 Then he has kissd her cheek, her cheek,
    And he has kissd her chin,
And he has kissd her comely mouth,
    But no life was therein.

28 'O wae mat worth you, Glenlyon,
    An ill death mat ye die!
Ye 've twind me and the fairest flower
    My eyes did ever see.

29 'But I will kiss your cheek, Barbara,
    And I will kiss your chin,
And I will kiss your comely mouth,
    But neer woman's again.

30 'Deal well, deal well at my love's lyke
    The beer but and the wine,
For ere the morn at this same time
    Ye 'll deal the same at mine.'

C

Motherwell's MS., p. 375, from the recitation of Agnes
Lyle of Kilbarchan.

1 FOUR-AND-TWENTY ladies fair
    Was playing at the ba,
And out cam Barbra Livingston,
    The flower amang them a'.

2 Out cam Barbra Livingston,
    The flower amang them a';
The lusty laird of Linlyon
    Has stown her clean awa.

3 'The Hielands is no for me, kind sir,
    The Hielands is no for me;
But, if you wud my favour win,
    You 'll tak me to Dundee.'

4 'The Hielands 'll be for thee, my dear,
    The Hielands will be for thee;
To the lusty laird o Linlyon
    A-married ye shall be.'

5 When they came to Linlyon's yetts,
    And lichted on the green,
Every ane spak Earse to her,
    The tears cam trinkling down.

6 When they went to bed at nicht,
    To Linlyon she did say,
'Och and alace, a weary nicht!
    Oh, but it 's lang till day!'

7 'Your father's steed in my stable,
    He 's eating corn and hay,
And you 're lying in my twa arms;
    What need you long for day?'

8 'If I had paper, pen, and ink,
    And candle for to see,
I wud write a lang letter
    To my love in Dundee.'

9 They brocht her paper, pen, and ink,
    And candle for to see,
And she did write a lang letter
    To her love in Dundee.

10 When he cam to Linlyon's yetts,
    And lichtit on the green,
    But lang or he wan up the stair
    His love was dead and gane.

11 'Woe be to thee, Linlyon,
    An ill death may thou die!
    Thou micht hae taen anither woman,
    And let my lady be.'

D

Campbell MSS, II, 254.

1 BONNIE Annie Livingstone
    Was walking out the way,
    By came the laird of Glendinning,
    And he's stolen her away.
      The Highlands are no for me, kind sir,
      The Highlands are no for me,
      And, if you wad my favour win,
      You'd take me to Dundee.

2 He mounted her on a milk-white steed,
    Himself upon a grey,
    He's taen her to the Highland hills,
    And stolen her quite away.

3 When they came to Glendinning gate,
    They lighted on the green;
    There many a Highland lord spoke free,
    But fair Annie she spake nane.

4 When bells were rung, and mass begun,
    And a' men bound for bed,
    Bonnie Annie Livingstone
    Was in her chamber laid.

5 'O gin it were but day, kind sir!
    O gin it were but day!
    O gin it were but day, kind sir,
    That I might win away!"

6 'Your steed stands in the stall, bonnie Ann,
    Eating corn and hay,

And you are in Glendinning's arms;
    What need ye long for day?'

7 'O fetch me paper, pen, and ink,
    A candle that I may see,
    And I will write a long letter
    To Jemmy at Dundee.'

8 When Jemmie looked the letter on,
    A loud laughter gave he;
    But eer he read the letter oer
    The tear blinded his ee.

9 'Gar saddle,' he cried, 'my war-horse fierce,
    Warn a' my trusty clan,
    And I'll away to Glendinning Castle
    And see my sister Ann.'

10 When he came to Glendinning yet,
    He lighted on the green,
    But ere that he wan up the stair
    Fair Annie she was gane.

11 'The Highlands were not for thee, bonnie
    Ann,
    The Highlands were not for thee,
    And they that would have thy favour won
    Should have brought you home to me.

12 'O I will kiss thy cherry cheeks,
    And I will kiss thy chin,
    And I will kiss thy rosy lips,
    For they will neer kiss mine.'

E

Kinloch MSS, V, 355, in the handwriting of John Hill Burton.

1 BONNY Baby Livingstone
   Went out to view the hay,
And by there came a Hieland lord,
   And he 's stown Baby away.

2 He 's stown her in her coat, her coat,
   And he 's stown her in her gown,
And he let not her look back again
   Ere she was many a mile from town.

3 He set her on a milk-white steed,
   Himself upon another,
And they are on to bonny Lochell,
   Like sister and like brother.

4 The bells were rung, the mass was sung,
   And all men bound to bed,
And Baby and her Hieland lord
   They were both in one chamber laid.

5 'Oh day, kind sir! Oh day, kind sir!
   Oh day fain would I see!
I would gie a' the lands o Livingstone
   For day-light, to lat me see.'

6 'Oh day, Baby? Oh day, Baby?
   What needs you long for day?
Your steed is in a good stable,
   And he 's eating baith corn and hay.

7 'Oh day, Baby? Oh day, Baby?
   What needs you long for day?
You 'r lying in a good knight's arms,
   What needs you long for day?'

8 'Ye 'll get me paper, pen, and ink,
   And light to let me see,
Till I write on a broad letter
   And send 't to Lord . . .'

*   *   *   *   *   *

———◆———

A. "On the other page you will find the whole ballad of Bonny Baby Livingston. I found
   upon recollection that I had the whole story
   in my memory, and thought it better to
   write it out entire, as what I repeated to
   you was, I think, more imperfect." *Mrs
   Brown, MS., Appendix, p. xv.*
   a. 35⁴. first *may be* fast, *as in* b.
   b. 1². gaed out. 2¹. And first. 2³. in his.
   3¹. He 's mounted her upon a.
   4¹. oer yon hich hich hill. 4². Intill a.
   4³. He met. 5¹. And there.
   5². And there were kids sae fair.
   5³. But sad and wae was bonny Baby.
   5⁴. was fu o.
   6¹. He 's taen her in his arms twa.
   6³. I wad gie a' my flocks and herds.
   6⁴. Ae smile frae thee to.
   7. A smile frae me ye 'se never win,
      I 'll neer look kind on thee;
   Ye 've stown me awa frae a' my kin,
      Frae a' that 's dear to me.

   Dundee, kind sir, Dundee, kind sir,
      Tak me to bonny Dundee!

For ye sall neer my favour win
   Till it ance mair I see.

8³. But I will carry you.
8⁴. Where you my bride shall be.
9¹. Or will ye stay at. 9². And get.
9³. Or gang wi me to. 9⁴. we 'll live.
10². I care neither for milk nor. 10³. gang.
11². If I were in. 11³. I'd send.
12³. coudna win.
13¹. tongue, my brother John. 13³. I hae.
13⁴. This mony a year and day.
14¹. I 've lued her lang and lued her weel.
14². But her love I.
14³. And what I canna fairly gain.
14⁴. To steal. 15³. they cam, his three sisters.
15⁴. Their brother for to greet.
16¹. And they have taen her bonny Baby.
17³. why look ye sae. 17⁴. Come tell.
18³. I 'm far frae. 19². Afore.
19³. letter wrate. 19⁴. And sent to.
After 19: And gin I had a bonny boy
         To help me in my need,
      That he might rin to bonny Dundee,
         And come again wi speed.

20. *Wanting.* 21¹. And they hae.
21². Their errand for to gang.
21³. And bade him run to bonny Dundee.
21⁴. And nae to tarry lang. 22, 23. *Wanting.*
24¹. oer muir. 24². As fast as he.
25, 26. *Wanting.*

27. Whan Johnie lookit the letter on,
    A hearty laugh leuch he ;
    But ere he read it till an end
    The tear blinded his ee.

    O wha is this, or what is that,
    Has stown my love frae me ?

Although he were my ae brither,
    An ill dead sall he die.

28¹. Gae saddle to me the black, he says.
28²,³. Gae. 29¹. He 's called upon his merry.
29². To follow him to.
29³. And he 's vowd he 'd neither.
29⁴. he got his. 30¹. him on.
30². And fast he rade away.
30³. And he 's come to Glenlyon's yett.
31². And the. 31⁴. Aneath.
32¹. window loup. 34. *Wanting.*
35⁴. As fast. 36⁴. laverock. 37¹. nae the.
B. 3⁴. ewes. *Indistinctly written.* 5². fore.

223

EPPIE MORRIE

'Eppie Morrie,' Maidment's North Countrie Garland, p. 40, 18

——•——

" THIS ballad," says Maidment, " is probably much more than a century old, though the circumstances which have given rise to it were unfortunately too common to preclude the possibility of its being of a later date." He does not tell us where the ballad came from, and no other editor seems to know of it. Two stanzas, 10, 11, occur in a copy of ' Rob Roy' (No 225, J) which had once been in Maidment's hands, and perhaps was obtained from the same region.

Four-and-twenty Highlanders, the leader of whom is one Willie, come to Strathdon from Carrie (Carvie ?) side to steal away Eppie Morrie, who has refused to marry Willie. They tie her on a horse and take her to a minister, whom Willie, putting a pistol to his breast, orders to marry them. The minister will not consent unless Eppie is willing, and she strenuously refuses; so they take her to

Carrie side and put her to bed. She defends herself successfully, and in the morning comes in her lover, Belbordlane, or John Forsyth, well armed, and we presume well supported, who carries her back to her mother, to be his bride.

Scott, Introduction to Rob Roy, Appendix, No V, cites two stanzas of a ballad derived from tradition which, if we had the whole, might possibly turn out to be the same story with different names.

Four-and-twenty Hieland men
    Came doun by Fiddoch side,
And they have sworn a deadly aith
    Jean Muir suld be a bride.

And they have sworn a deadly aith,
    Ilke man upon his durke,
That she should wed with Duncan Ger,
    Or they 'd make bloody worke.

1 FOUR-and-twenty Highland men
   Came a' from Carrie side
To steal awa Eppie Morrie,
   Cause she would not be a bride.

2 Out it 's came her mother,
   It was a moonlight night,
She could not see her daughter,
   Their swords they shin'd so bright.

3 'Haud far awa frae me, mother,
   Haud far awa frae me;
There 's not a man in a' Strathdon
   Shall wedded be with me.'

4 They have taken Eppie Morrie,
   And horse back bound her on,
And then awa to the minister,
   As fast as horse could gang.

5 He 's taken out a pistol,
   And set it to the minister's breast:
'Marry me, marry me, minister,
   Or else I 'll be your priest.'

6 'Haud far awa frae me, good sir,
   Haud far awa frae me;
For there 's not a man in all Strathdon
   That shall married be with me.'

7 'Haud far awa frae me, Willie,
   Haud far awa frae me;
For I darna avow to marry you,
   Except she 's as willing as ye.'

8 They have taken Eppie Morrie,
   Since better could nae be,
And they 're awa to Carrie side,
   As fast as horse could flee.

9 When mass was sung, and bells were rung,
   And all were bound for bed,
Then Willie an Eppie Morrie
   In one bed they were laid.

10 'Haud far awa frae me, Willie,
   Haud far awa frae me;
Before I 'll lose my maidenhead,
   I 'll try my strength with thee.'

11 She took the cap from off her head
   And threw it to the way;
Said, Ere I lose my maidenhead,
   I 'll fight with you till day.

12 Then early in the morning,
   Before her clothes were on,
In came the maiden of Scalletter,
   Gown and shirt alone.

13 'Get up, get up, young woman,
   And drink the wine wi me;'
'You might have called me maiden,
   I 'm sure as leal as thee.'

14 'Wally fa you, Willie,
   That ye could nae prove a man
And taen the lassie's maidenhead!
   She would have hired your han.'

15 'Haud far awa frae me, lady,
   Haud far awa frae me;
There 's not a man in a' Strathdon
   The day shall wed wi me.'

16 Soon in there came Belbordlane,
   With a pistol on every side:
'Come awa hame, Eppie Morrie,
   And there you 'll be my bride.'

17 'Go get to me a horse, Willie,
   And get it like a man,
And send me back to my mother
   A maiden as I cam.

18 'The sun shines oer the westlin hills;
   By the light lamp of the moon,
Just saddle your horse, young John Forsyth,
   And whistle, and I 'll come soon.'

———◆———

5¹. pistol, and.   5². Set.

16¹. their.

224

THE LADY OF ARNGOSK

Sharpe's Ballad Book, 1823, p. 99.

———◆———

"THE following fragment," says Sharpe in his preface (he had not then recovered the second stanza), "I cannot illustrate either from history or tradition." Very soon after the publication of the Ballad Book, full particulars of the carrying off of the Lady of Arngosk were procured for him by David Webster, the bookseller. Webster addressed himself to Mrs Isobell Dow, otherwise Mrs Mac Leish, of Newburgh, Fife, whose mother, he had learned, was waiting-maid to the lady at the time of the rape. "In my very early years," he wrote, July 4, 1823, "I have listened with great delight to my mother when she sung me a song the first stanza of which was this:

> The Highlandmen are a' cum down,
> They 're a' cum down almost,
> They 've stowen awa the bonny lass,
> The lady of Arngosk.

"Now Miss Finlay informs me that Isobel Stewart, your mother, was waiting-maid to the 'bonny lass' at the time she was 'stowen awa,' and that you are the most likely person now alive who will be able to recollect the song, or the particulars that gave rise to it. My reason for requesting this favour from a lady I have not the pleasure to know is, some gentlemen, my acquaintance, are making a collection of old Scots songs, which is printing, and they are anxious to have it as full as possible. We therefore wish a copy of the song entire, if you can recollect it, and the name of the lady who was the 'bonny lass,'" etc. Mrs Dow replied, July 8, through John Masterton, that she was "sorrow" to say that

she could not recollect more of the song than Webster was already in possession of, but the story she could never forget, having heard her mother repeat it so often: and this story Masterton proceeds to give in Mrs Dow's own words. Although Mrs Dow was liberal of details, Webster seems to have wanted to hear more, and accordingly Masterton writes at greater length July 30, repeating what had been said before, with "some particular incidents" omitted in the former letter, but nothing very material except that Miss Gibb was rich, and that Isobell Dow had "brought to her recolection another verse of the song" (st. 2). The earlier letter even is somewhat out of proportion to so meagre a relic of verse, an intolerable deal of bread to a half-penny worth of sack; but it is very readable, and has some value as a chapter from domestic life in Scotland in the first half of the last century.*

NEWBURGH, 8 *July*, 1823.

DEAR SIR. I am directed by Isobell Dow to acknowledge the receipt of your letter, and to write you an answer to your request respecting the stealing awa the Lady of Arngosk. She is sorrow to say she cannot recolect any more of the song than what you are in possession off already. As for the truth of the story, she can never forget, having heard her mother repeat it so often. I will therefore give you it in her own words.

Yours, &c., JN MASTERTON.

My mother was waiting-maid to the Lady of Arngask, whose name was Miss Margret Gibb, at which time two gentlemen paid addresses to her; the one a Mr Jamieson, a writer in Strathmiglo, the other a Mr Graham, of Bracko Castle, who was

---

* I owe the knowledge of these letters to Mr Macmath, who sent me a copy that he was allowed to make by the courtesy of the Messrs Brodie of Edinburgh, in whose possession they now are.

the subject of the story; but his love did not meet with a return suitable to his wishes; he therefore came to the strong resolution of taking her away by force. It will be proper to mention that he came two nights previous, when my mother was in the barn dighting corn, and accosted her thus: Tiby, I want to see Margret. She answerd: I doubt, Mr Graham, you canna see her the night, but I 'll gang an tell her. She went and was orderd to tell him that he could not see her; which put him in such a frenzy that he ran up and down the barn through chaff and corn up to the middle; however, he forced in to her company, but what passed betwixt them my mother did not know. But on the second night after, at midnight, when in bed (my mother alway sleeping with Miss Gibb),* a very sharp knock was heard at the door, which alarmd them very much, it being a lonely place. My mother went and called, who was there; she was answered, Open the door, Tiby, and see. She said: Keep me! Mr Graham, what way are you here at this time? Ye canna won in the night. She drew the bar, and was almost frighted out of her sences by the appearance of above thirty Hillandmen on horseback, all armed with swords and dirks, &c. She atempted to shut the door again, but Mr Graham pressed his knee in and forced his way. He went ben, and ordered them to put on their clothes an go along with him. Miss Gibb insisted on stoping ere daylight, and she would go with good will; but he would admit of no delay, but ordered her to dress herself imediately, otherwise he would do it by force. She then said she would not go unless Tiby acompanied her, which he said he intended to propose had she not mentioned it; but my mother would not go, she said, to ride behind none of these Hillandmen. Mr Graham then proposed to take her behind himself. They did then all mount; he at the same time used the precaution of placing sentries on the houses where the other servants lodged, to prevent them giving the alarm, and also three stout men at the bell of the church, to prevent it being rung. They kept their posts till they thought them a sufficient distance on the way, Mr Graham always joking to my mother about something or other, asuring her so soon as he had all over he would make her happy and comfortable all the days of her life. They rode on over hill and dale till within sight of Bracko Castle, when all of a sudden the Hillanmen dispersed, or deserted them, excepting his own imediate servants; which my

* "Being her guardian as well as waiting-maid, as appointed by old Mrs Gibb when on her death-bed, they being, as the saying is, cousins once removed." Letter of July 30.

mother thought was because he had deceived them, saying that the lady was willing to marry him but her friends would not alow, which by this time they must have found out. He told my mother that a minister was waiting them at Bracko, but he must have been disappointed, for the minister never appeared; else, she always thought, they would been married. Report said that Mr Jamieson had so contrived to stop his arrival. My mother and Miss Margret were then secured in an uper room in the castle till the next day, when there appeared mostly all the men of the parishes of Arngask and Strathmiglo, demanding their lady; my father among the rest, demanding my mother as his intended wife. It seemed so soon as the Hillan sentries were gone from the houses and church-bell of Arngask, that the servants ran to the bell, and rang such a peal as made all the Ochles resound wi the sad news that their lady was stowen awa by Graham an his clan. Mr Jamieson was no less busy in alarming and rousing the indignation of the good folk of Strathmiglo, who were much atached to her interest, so that both parishes rose to a man, and armed themselves with whatever came in the way, and marched in a body to make an attack on the castle, and rescue their much esteemed lady. But on their making their appearance before the castle in such formidable array, Mr Graham thought it prudent to surender rather than sustain the attack of such a body of desperate men. Mr Graham conducted them down stairs with his cap in hand (the gentlemen in those days wore velvet caps), and addressed her thus: I shall see you on your horse, Margret, for a' the ill you 've done me, and bade her a long and lasting farewell; at which she stamped with her foot and recommended him to the devil. They all came home in safety, and the bells, that so lately rang to alarm and spread the dismal news, were again rung to proclaim the happy return of the lady that was stowen awa. Bonefires were also erected on the highest of the Ochles. She was married that same year to Mr Jamieson, and I suppose some of their children are alive to this day. It was generaly reported that Mr Graham was so much affronted at the dissapointment that he left the country soon after.

Such, sir, is the story that gave rise to the song you are so much in request off, which I have gathered from Isobell Dow, and put in order according to my weak capacity, knowing it will fall into better and abler hands, and that, altho the song be a wanting, there is ample mater for composition.

I remain your most Obed^t H^{le} Servt,

JOHN MASTERTON, for ISOBELL DOW.

P. S.   I had almost forgot to mention as to the period of time when it happened, which cannot be less than 87 years, which Isobell makes out in the following maner; it being two years before her father and mother was married, and that they lived together fifty-one years, it being now thirty-four years since her mother died, which makes it to have been about the year 1736.

J. M.

—◆—

1 THE Highlandmen hae a' come down,
  They 've a' come down almost,
They 've stowen away the bonny lass,
  The Lady of Arngosk.

2 They hae put on her petticoat,
  Likewise her silken gown;

The Highland man he drew his sword,
  Said, Follow me ye 's come.

3 Behind her back they 've tied her hands,
  An then they set her on;
'I winna gang wi you,' she said,
  'Nor ony Highland loon.'

225

ROB ROY

A. Skene MS., p. 44.

B. 'Rob Roy,' Kinloch MSS, I, 343.

C. 'Rob Roy MacGregor,' Motherwell's MS., p. 93.

D. 'Rob Roy,' "Scotch Ballads, Materials for Border Minstrelsy," No 147, Abbotsford.

E. 'Rob Roy,' Piteairn's MSS, III, 41.

F. 'Rob Roy,' Campbell MSS, II, 229.

G. 'Rob Roy,' Cromek's Select Scotish Songs, 1810, II, 199.

H. Sir Walter Scott's Introduction to "Rob Roy," Appendix, No V.

I. 'Rob Roy,' Campbell's MSS, II, 58.

J. 'Rob Oig,' A Garland of Old Historical Ballads, p. 10, Aungervyle Society, 1881.

K. 'Rob Roy,' Laing's Thistle of Scotland, p. 93.

—◆—

THE hero of this ballad was the youngest of the five sons of the Rob Roy who has been immortalized by Sir Walter Scott, and was known as Robert Oig, young, or junior. When a mere boy (only twelve years old, it is said) he shot a man mortally whom he considered to have intruded on his mother's land, and for not appearing to underlie the law for this murder he was outlawed in 1736. He had fled to the continent, and there he enlisted in the British army, and was wounded and made prisoner at Fontenoy in 1745. He was exchanged, returned to Scotland and obtained a discharge from service, and, though still under ban, was able to effect a marriage with a woman of respectable family. She lived but a few years, and after her death, whether spontaneously or under the influence of his brother James, a man of extraordinary hardihood, Rob Oig formed a plan of bettering his own fortune, and incidentally that of his kin, by a marriage of the Sabine fashion with a woman of means. The person selected was Jean Key, who had been two months the widow of John Wright. She was but nineteen years of age, and was living with her mother at Edinbelly, in Stirlingshire, and her property is said to have been, not the twenty thousand pounds of some of the ballads, but some sixteen or eighteen thousand marks.

On the night of December 8, 1750, Rob Oig, accompanied by his brothers James and Duncan and others, first placing guards at the door and windows, to prevent escape from within and help from without, entered the house of Jean Key, and not finding her, because she had taken alarm and hidden herself in a closet, obliged the mother to produce her daughter, under threats " to murder every person in the family, or to burn the house and every person in it alive." Jean Key, on being brought out, was told by James MacGregor that the party had come to marry her to Robert, his brother. " Upon her desiring to be allowed till next morning, or some few hours, to deliberate upon the answer she was to give to so unexpected and sudden a proposal as a marriage betwixt her, then not two months a widow, and a man with whom she had no manner of acquaintance," after some little expostulation, they laid hands upon her, dragged her out of doors, tied her on the back of a horse, and carried her first to a house at Buchanan, six miles from Edinbelly, thence to Rowerdennan, " thence, by water, to some part of the Highlands about the upper part of Loch Lomond, out of the reach of her friends and relations, where she was detained in captivity and carried from place to place for upwards of three months." At Rowerdennan, or further north, a priest read the marriage-service while the resolute James held up the young woman before him, and declared Rob Oig and her to be man and wife.

The rest of the story does not come into the ballad, but it may be added that both the military and the civil power took the matter in hand ; that the MacGregors found it necessary to release their captive (who died, but not of the violence she had undergone, ten months after she was taken away) ; that James MacGregor was brought to trial in July, 1752, for hamesucken (invasion of a private house), forcible abduction of a woman, and constraining her to a marriage, was convicted of a part of the charge but not of the last count, and while the court had the verdict under consideration made his escape from Edinburgh castle ; that Rob Oig was apprehended the following year, tried and condemned to death, and was executed in February, 1754.*

We may easily believe that, as Scott says, the imagination of half-civilized Highlanders was not much shocked at the idea of winning a wife in a violent way. It had been common, and they may naturally have wondered why it should seem so particular in their instance. It is certain that Jean Key did not receive the sympathy of all of her own sex. A lady of much celebrity has told us that it is safest in matrimony to begin with a little aversion, and there were those in Jean Key's day, and after, who thought it mere silliness to make a coil about a little compulsion. " It is not a great many years," Sir Walter Scott testifies, "since a respectable woman, above the lower rank of life, expressed herself very warmly to the author on his taking the freedom to censure the behaviour of the MacGregors on the occasion in question. She said, ' that there was no use in giving a bride too much choice upon such occasions ; that the marriages were happiest lang syne which had been done off hand.' Finally, she averred that her ' own mother had never seen her father till the night he brought her up from

* The jury, in James's trial, brought in a special verdict with the intent to save his life, but no such effort was made in favor of Rob Oig, though there was a mitigating circumstance in his case. For Jean Key " had informed her friends that, on the night of her being carried off, Robin Oig, moved by her cries and tears, had partly consented to let her return, when James came up, with a pistol in his hand, and asking whether he was such a coward as to relinquish an enterprise in which he had risked everything to procure him a fortune, in a manner compelled his brother to persevere." It may be remarked, by the way, that Duncan MacGregor had his trial as well, but was found not guilty. (Scott, Introduction to " Rob Roy," which I have mostly followed, introducing passages from the indictment in James MacGregor's case when brevity would allow.)

the Lennox with ten head of black cattle, and there had not been a happier couple in the country.'"

The ballad adheres to fact rather closely; indeed a reasonably good "dittay" could be made out of it. The halt at Buchanan is mentioned B 8, C 10, K 14; the road would be through Drymen, as in C 10, K 13; and Balmaha, H 2, is a little beyond Buchanan. Ballyshine is substituted for Buchanan in E 6, J 4. At Buchanan, or Ballyshine ('as they came in by Drimmen town, and in by Edingarry,' K 13), a cloak and gown are bought (fetched) for the young woman to be married in, B 8, C 10, F 4. It is a cotton gown, E 6, coat and gown, A 8; in cotton gown she is married, J 4; meaning probably that she was married in a night-gown, having been roused from her bed. It is at Buchanan, or Ballyshine, that she is married. Four held her up to the priest, A, C, F (two, D, I, K, three, E, J, six, B), four laid her in bed, A, B, E, F, I, J, K (two, C, D).

Rob Roy is said to come from Drunkie (the home of his first wife), J 1; to come over the Loch of Lynn, G 2. Jean Key's abode seems to be called White House (Wright?) in A 2, but Blackhills, C 2, and in K 2 Jean Key is called Blackhill's daughter. Blackhill is apparently a corruption of Mitchell, Jean's mother's maiden name. The mother is called Jean Mitchell in J 2.

In A 8, Rob Roy's party are wrongly said to tarry at Stirling. In J 2, Glengyle is said to go with him to steal Jean Mitchell's daughter. Glengyle, Rob Oig's cousin, and chief of his immediate family was, for a MacGregor, an orderly man,* and did not countenance the proceeding. J 6, 7 belong to the ballad of 'Eppie Morrie,' No 223.

Rob Oig puts Jean Key's fortune at £20,000, A 13, C 19; 50,000 merks, D 14; 30,000, K 23; 20,000, which was not very far from right, E 10. The reading in B 15 is a manifest corruption of thirty thousand merks.

Old Rob Roy is in several copies spoken of as still alive. Though the time both of his birth and death is not accurately known, this was certainly not the case.

H is translated by Fiedler, Geschichte der schottischen Liederdichtung, I, 52.

A

Skene MS., p. 44; from recitation in the north of Scotland, 1802–3.

1 ROB ROY, frae the high Highlands,
    Came to the Lawlan border;
It was to steel a lady away,
    To keep his Highland house in order.

2 As he came in by White House,
    He sent nae ane before him;
She wad hae secured the house,
    For she did ay abhor him.

3 Twenty men surrount the house, an twenty
        they went in,
    They found her wi her mither;

Wi sighs an cries an watery eyes
    They parted frae ane anither.

4 'O will ye be my dear?' he says,
    'Or will ye be my honnie?
O will ye be my wedded wife?
    I lee you best of ony.'

5 'I winna be your dear,' [she says,]
    'Nor will I be your honnie,
Nor will I be your wedded wife;
    Ye lee me for my money.'

6 .   .   .   .   by the way,
    This lady aftimes fainted;
Says, Woe be to my cursed gold,
    This road for me 's invented!

* "Such, at least, was his general character; for when James Mohr [the Big], while perpetrating the violence at Edinbelly, called out, in order to overawe opposition, that Glengyle was lying in the moor with a hundred men to patronise his enterprise, Jean Key told him he lied, since she was confident Glengyle would never countenance so scoundrelly a business." Scott, Introduction to "Rob Roy," ed. 1846, p. c.

7 He gave her no time for to dress
   Like ladies when they 're ridin,
But set her on hie horseback,
   Himsel was ay beside her.

8 Whan they came to the Black House,
   And at Stirling tarried,
There he bought her coat an gown,
   But she would not [be] married.

9 Four men held her to the priest,
   An four they did her bed,
Wi sighs an cries an watery eyes
   Whan she by him was laid.

10 'Be content, be content,
   Be content wi me, lady;
Now ye are my wedded wife
   Untill the day ye die, lady.

11 'My father was a Highlan laird,
   McGrigor was his name, lady;
A' the country roun about
   They dreadit his great fame, lady.

12 'He kept a hedge about his lands,
   A prickle to his foes, lady,
An every ane that did him wrang,
   He took him by the nose, lady.

13 'My father he delights in nout and goats,
   An me in horse and sheep, lady;
You an twenty thousan pounds
   Makes me a man complete, lady.

14 'You 're welcome to this Highlan lan,
   It is my native plain, lady;
Think nae mair of gauin back,
   But tak it for your hame, lady.

15 'I 'm gauin, [I 'm gauin,]
   I 'm gauin to France, lady;
Whan I come back
   I 'll learn ye a dance, lady.

16 'Set your foot, [set your foot,]
   Set your foot to mine, lady;
Think nae mair of gauin back,
   But tak it for your hame, lady.'

B

Kinloch MSS, I, 343.

1 Rob Roy frae the Hielands cam
   Unto the Lawland border,
And he has stown a ladie fair,
   To haud his house in order.

2 He guarded the house round about,
   Himsel went in and found her out,
   She hung close by her mither;
Wi dolefu cries and watery eyes
   They parted frae each ither.

3 'Gang wi me, my dear,' he says,
   'Gang and be my honey;
Gang and be my wedded wife,
   I loe ye best o onie.'

4 'I winna gang wi you,' she says,
   'I winna be your honey;
I winna be your wedded wife;
   Ye loe me for my money.'

5 He gied na her na time to dress
   As ladies whan they 're brides,
But hurried her awa wi speed,
   And rowd her in his plaids.

6 He gat her up upon a horse,
   Himsel lap on ahind her;
And they 're awa to the Hieland hills;
   Her friends they canna find her.

7 As they gaed oure the Hieland hills,
   This lady aften fainted,
Saying, Wae be to my cursed gowd,
   This road to me invented!

8 As they gaed oure the Hieland hills,
   And at Buchanan tarried,
He bought to her baith cloak and goun,
   Yet she wadna be married.

9 Six held her up afore the priest,
   Four laid her in a bed, O;
Maist mournfully she wept and cried
   Whan she bye him was laid, O.

10 'O be content, be content,
    Be content to stay, ladie;
For now ye are my wedded wife
    Unto your dying day, ladie.

11 'Rob Roy was my father calld,
    M'Gregor was his name, ladie;
And in a' the country whare he dwalt
    He exceeded ae in fame, ladie.

12 'He was a hedge unto his friends,
    A heckle to his faes, ladie;
And ilka ane that did him wrang,
    He beat him on the neis, ladie.

13 'I 'm as bold, I am as bold
    As my father was afore, ladie;

Ilka ane that does me wrang
    Sall feel my gude claymore, ladie.

14 'There neer was frae Lochlomond west
    That eer I did him fear, ladie;
For, if his person did escape,
    I seizd upon his gear, ladie.

15 'My father delights in horse and kye,
    In sheep and goats and a', ladie,
And thee wi me and thirty merks
    Will mak me a man fu braw, ladie.

16 'I hae been in foreign lands,
    And servd the king o France, ladie;
We will get the bagpipes,
    And we 'll hae a dance, ladie.'

——◆——

C

Motherwell's MS., p. 93.

1 ROB ROY 's from the Hielands come
    Unto our Lowland border,
And he has stolen a lady away,
    To keep his house in order.

2 Rob Roy 's come to Blackhill's gate,
    Twenty men his arms did carry,
And he has stolen a lady away,
    On purpose her to marry.

3 None knew till he surrounded the house,
    No tidings came before him,
Or else she had been gone away,
    For she did still abhor him.

4 All doors and windows guarded were,
    None could the plot discover;
Himself went in and found her out,
    Professing how he loved her.

5 'Come go with me, my dear,' he said,
    'Come go with me, my honey,
And you shall be my wedded wife,
    I love you best of onie.'

6 'I will not go with you,' she said,
    'Nor will I be your honey;
I neer shall be your wedded wife,
    You love me for my money.'

7 But he her drew amongst his crew,
    She holding by her mother;
With mournful cries and watery eyes
    They parted from each other.

8 No time they gave her to be dressed
    As ladies when they 're brides, O,
But hurried her away in haste;
    They rowed her in their plaids, O.

9 As they went over hills and rocks,
    The lady often fainted;
Says, Wae may it be, my cursed money,
    This road to me invented!

10 They passed away by Drymen town,
    And at Buchanan tarried;
They bought to her a cloak and gown,
    Yet she would not be married.

11 But without consent they joined their hands;
    By law ought not to carry;
The priest his zeal it was so hot
    On her will he would not tarry.

12 Four held her up before the priest,
    Two laid her in the bed, O;
Och, mournfully she weeped and cried
    When she by him was laid, O.

13 'Now you 're come to the Highland hills,
    Out of your native clime, lady,

Never think of going back,
  But take this for your hame, lady.

14 'Be content, be content,
    Be content to stay, lady;
  Now ye are my wedded wife
    Unto your dying day, lady.

15 'O Rob Roy was my father called,
    But McGregor was his name, lady;
  In all the country far and near
    None did exceed his fame, lady.

16 'I 'm as bold, I 'm as bold,
    I 'm as bold as he, lady;
  In France and Ireland I 'll dance and fight,
    And from them take the gree, lady.

17 'He was a hedge about his friends,
    But a heckle to his faes, lady,
  And every one that did him wrong,
    He took them owre the nose, lady.

18 'I 'm as bold, I 'm as bold,
    I 'm as bold, and more, lady;
  Every one that does me wrong
    Shall feel my good claymore, lady.

19 'My father he has stots and ewes,
    And he has goats and sheep, lady,
  But you and twenty thousand punds
    Makes me a man complete, lady.'

———•———

D

"Scotch Ballads, Materials for Border Minstrelsy,"
No 147, Abbotsford; in a handwriting of the early part of
this century.

1 ROB ROY from the Highlands came
    Unto the Lowland border;
  It was to steal a ladie away,
    To keep his house in order.

2 He gae her nae time to dress herself
    Like a lady that was to be married,
  But he hoisd her out among his crew,
    And rowd her in his plaidie.

3 'Will ye go wi me, my dear?' he says,
    'Will ye go wi me, my honey?
  Will ye go wi me, my dear?' he says,
    'For I love you best of ony.'

4 'I winna be your dear,' she says,
    'Nor I 'll never be your honey;
  I 'll never be your wedded wife,
    For you love me but for my money.'

5 He hoisd her out among his crew,
    She holding by her mother;
  Wi watry eyes and mournfu cries
    They parted from each other.

6 As they gaed oer yon high hill,
    The ladie often fainted;

'Oh, wae be to my gold,' she said,
    'This road for me invented!'

7 Two held her up before the priest,
    And two put her to bed,
  Wi mournful cries and watry eyes
    As she lay by his side.

8 'Be content, be content,
    Be content wi me, ladie,
  For now you are my wedded wife
    Until the day ye die, ladie.

9 'Rob Roy was my father calld,
    McGrigor was his name, ladie,
  And a' the country round about
    Has heard of Roy's fame, ladie.

10 'You do not think yourself a match
    For such a one as I, ladie;
  But I been east and I been west,
    And saird the king of France, ladie.

11 'And now we hear the bag-pipe play,
    And we maun hae a dance, ladie,
  And a' the country round about
    Has heard of Roy's fame, ladie.

12 'Shake your foot, shake your foot,
    Shake your foot wi me, ladie,
  For now you are my wedded bride
    Until the day ye die, ladie.

13 'My father dealt in cows and ewes,
　　Likewise in goats and sheep, ladie,
And a' the country round about
　　Has heard of Roy's fame, ladie.

14 'And ye have fifty thousand marks,
　　Makes me a man compleat, ladie;

Why mayn't I maid
　　May I not ride in state, ladie?

15 'My father was a Highland laird,
　　Altho he be now dead, ladie,
And a' the country round about
　　Has heard of Roy's fame, ladie.'

E

Pitcairn's MSS, III, 41; "from tradition (Widow Stevenson)."

1 ROB ROY from the Highlands cam
　　Unto our Scottish border,
And he has stown a lady fair,
　　To haud his house in order.

2 And when he cam he surrounded the house;
　　Twenty men their arms did carry;
And he has stown this lady fair,
　　On purpose her for to marry.

3 And whan he cam he surrounded the house;
　　No tidings there cam before him,
Or else the lady would have been gone,
　　For still she did abhor him.

4 Wi murnfu cries and watery eyes,
　　Fast hauding by her mother,
Wi murnfu cries and watery eyes
　　They parted frae each other.

5 Nae time he gied her to be dressed
　　As ladys do when they 're bride, O,
But he hastened and hurried her awa,
　　And he rowd her in his plaid, O.

6 They rade till they cam to Ballyshine,
　　At Ballyshine they tarried;
He bought to her a cotton gown,
　　Yet would she never be married.

7 Three held her up before the priest,
　　Four carried her to bed, O,
Wi watery eyes and murnfu sighs
　　When she behind was laid, O.

8 'O be content, be content,
　　Be content to stay, lady,
For you are my wedded wife
　　Unto my dying day, lady.
　　　　　　　　Be content, *etc.*

9 'My father is Rob Roy called,
　　MacGregor is his name, lady;
In all the country whare he dwells,
　　He does succeed the fame, lady.
　　　　　　　　Be content, *etc.*

10 'My father he has cows and ewes,
　　And goats he has anew, lady,
And you and twenty thousand merks
　　Will mak me a man complete, lady.'
　　　　　　　　Be content, *etc.*

F

Campbell MSS, II, 229.

1 ROB ROY frae the Highlands came
　　Unto the Lawland border,
And he has stolen a lady away,
　　To haud his house in order.

2 He 's pu'd her out amang his men,
　　She holding by her mother;

With mournfu cries and watery eyes
　　They parted frae each other.

3 When they came to the heigh hill-gate,
　　O it 's aye this lady fainted:
'O wae! what has that cursed monie
　　That 's thrown to me invented?'

4 When they came to the heigh hill-gate,
　　And at Buchanan tarried,

They fetchd to her a cloak and gown,
   Yet wad she not be married.

5 Four held her up before the priest,
   Four laid her on her bed,
With mournfu cries and watery eyes
   When she by him was laid.

6 'I 'll be kind, I 'll be kind,
   I 'll be kind to thee, lady,
And all the country for thy sake
   Shall surely favoured be, lady.

7 'Be content, be content,
   Be content and stay, lady;
Now ye are my weded wife
   Until your dying-day, ladie.

8 'Rob Roy was my father called,
   McGregor was his name, lady;
In every country where he was,
   He did exceed the fame, lady.

9 'He was a hedge about his friends,
   A terror to his foes, lady,
And every one that did him wrong,
   He hit them oer the nose, lady.

10 'Be content, be content,
   Be content and stay, lady;
Now ye are my wedded wife
   Until your dying-day, lady.

11 'We will go, we will go,
   We will go to France, lady,
Where I before for safety fled,
   And there wee 'l get a dance, lady.

12 'Shake a fit, shake a fit,
   Shake a fit to me, lady;
Now ye are my wedded wife
   Until your dying-day, lady.

G

Cromek, Select Scotish Songs, 1810, II, 194, 199; sent by
Burns to William Tytler, in a letter.

1 ROB ROY from the Highlands cam
   Unto the Lawlan border,
To steal awa a gay ladie,
   To haud his house in order.

2 He cam owre the Lock o Lynn,
   Twenty men his arms did carry;
Himsel gaed in an fand her out,
   Protesting he would marry.

3 'O will ye gae wi me'? he says,
   'Or will ye be my honey?
Or will ye be my wedded wife?
   For I love you best of any.'

4 'I winna gae wi you,' she says,
   'Nor will I be your honey,
Nor will I be your wedded wife;
   You love me for my money.'

*   *   *   *   *   *

5 But he set her on a coal-black steed,
   Himsel lap on behind her,
An he 's awa to the Highland hills,
   Whare her friens they canna find her.

*   *   *   *   *   *   *

6 'Rob Roy was my father ca'd,
   MacGregor was his name, ladie;
He led a band o heroes bauld,
   An I am here the same, ladie.

7 'Be content, be content,
   Be content to stay, ladie;
For thou art my wedded wife
   Until thy dying day, ladie.

8 'He was a hedge unto his friens,
   A heckle to his foes, ladie,
Every one that durst him wrang,
   He took him by the nose, ladie.

9 'I 'm as bold, I 'm as bold,
   I 'm as bold, an more, ladie;
He that daurs dispute my word
   Shall feel my guid claymore, ladie.'

H

Sir Walter Scott's Introduction to his novel "Rob Roy," Appendix, No V, Waverley Novels, Cadell, 1846, VII, cxxxiii; "from memory."

1 ROB ROY is frae the Hielands come
    Down to the Lowland border,
And he has stolen that lady away,
    To haud his house in order.

2 He set her on a milk-white steed,
    Of none he stood in awe,
Untill they reached the Hieland hills,
    Aboon the Balmaha.

3 Saying, Be content, be content,
    Be content with me, lady ;
Where will ye find in Lennox land
    Sae braw a man as me, lady ?

4 'Rob Roy he was my father called,
    MacGregor was his name, lady ;
A' the country, far and near,
    Have heard MacGregor's fame, lady.

5 'He was a hedge about his friends,
    A heckle to his foes, lady ;
If any man did him gainsay,
    He felt his deadly blows, lady.

6 'I am as bold, I am as bold,
    I am as bold, and more, lady ;
Any man that doubts my word
    May try my gude claymore, lady.

7 'Then be content, be content,
    Be content with me, lady,
For now you are my wedded wife
    Until the day ye die, lady.'

I

Campbell MSS, II, 58.

1 ROB ROY is frae the Highlands come
    Unto the Scottish border,
And he has stolen a lady gay,
    To keep his house in order.

2 He and his crew surrounded the house ;
    No tidings came before him,
Cr else I'm sure she wad been gone,
    For she did still abhore him.

3 He drew her thro amang his crew,
    She holding by her mother ;
With watery eyes and mournfu cries
    They parted from each other.

4 He's set her on a milk-white steed,
    Himself jumped on behind her,
And he's awa to the Highland hills,
    And her friends they couldna find her.

5 'O be content, be content,
    O be content and stay, lady,
And never think of going back
    Until your dying day, lady.'

6 As they went over hills and dales,
    This lady oftimes fainted ;

Cries, Wae be to that cursed money
    This road to me invented !

7 'O dinna think, O dinna think,
    O dinna think to ly, lady ;
O think na ye yersell weel matchd
    On sic a lad as me, lady ?

8 'What think ye o my coal-black hair,
    But and my twinkling een, lady,
A little bonnet on my head,
    And cocket up aboon, lady ?

9 'O dinna think, O dinna think,
    O dinna think to ly, lady ;
O think nae ye yersell weel matchd
    On sic a lad as me, lady ?

10 'Rob Roy was my father calld,
    But Gregory was his name, lady ;
There was neither duke nor lord
    Could eer succeed his fame, lady.

11 'O may not I, may not I,
    May not I succeed, lady ?
My old father did so design ;
    O now but he is dead, lady.

12 'My father was a hedge about his friends,
    A heckle to his foes, lady,

And every one that did him wrang,
    He hit them oer the nose, lady.

13 'I ['m] as bold, I ['m] as bold,
    I ['m] as bold, and more, lady,
  And every one that does me wrong
    Shall feel my good claymore, lady.

14 'You need not fear our country cheer,
    Ye 'se hae good entertain, lady ;
  For ye shall hae a feather-bed,
    Both lang and broad and green, lady.

15 'Come, be content, come, be content,
    Come, be content and stay, lady,
  And never think of going back
    Until yer dying day, lady.'

16 Twa held her up before the priest,
    Four laid her in her bed,
  And sae mournfully she weeping cry'd
    When she by him was laid !

17 'Come, dinna think, come, dinna think,
    Come, dinna think to ly, lady ;
  You 'll surely think yersell weel matchd
    On sic a lad as me, lady.

18 'Come, be content, come, be content,
    Come, be content and stay, lady,
  And never think of going back
    Until your dying day, lady.'

———•———

J

A Garland of Old Historical Ballads, p. 10, Aungervyle Society, 1881, from a manuscript which had belonged to Maidment.

1 FROM Drunkie in the Highlands,
    With four and twenty men,
  Rob Oig is cam, a lady fair
    To carry from the plain.

2 Glengyle and James with him are cam,
    To steal Jean Mitchell's dauchter,
  And they have borne her far away,
    To haud his house in order.

3 And he has taen Jean Key's white hand,
    And torn her grass-green sleeve,
  And rudely tyed her on his horse,
    At her friends asked nae leave.

4 They rode till they cam to Ballyshine,
    At Ballyshine they tarried ;
  Nae time he gave her to be dressed,
    In cotton gown her married.

5 Three held her up before the priest,
    Four carried her to bed, O ;
  Wi watery eyes and mournfu sighs
    She in bed wi Rob was laid, O.

6 'Haud far awa from me, Rob Oig,
    Haud far awa from me !
  Before I lose my maidenhead,
    I 'll try my strength with thee.'

7 She 's torn the cap from off her head
    And thrown it to the way,
  But ere she lost her maidenhead
    She fought with him till day.

8 'Wae fa, Rob Oig, upon your head !
    For you have ravished me,
  And taen from me my maidenhead ;
    O would that I could dee !'

9 'My father he is Rob Roy called,
    And he has cows and ewes,
  And you are now my wedded wife,
    And can nae longer chuse.'

K

Laing's Thistle of Scotland, p. 93; compounded, with some alterations, from two copies, one from Miss Harper, Kildrummy, the other from the Rev. R. Scott, Glenbucket.

1 Rob Roy frae the Highlands came
  Doun to our Lowland border;
It was to steal a lady away,
  To haud his house in order.

2 With four-and-twenty Highland men,
  His arms for to carry,
He came to steal Blackhill's daughter,
  That lady for to marry.

3 Nae ane kend o his comming,
  Nae tiddings came before him,
Else the lady woud hae been away,
  For still she did abhore him.

4 They guarded doors and windows round,
  Nane coud their plot discover;
Rob Roy enterd then alane,
  Expressing how he lovd her.

5 'Come go with me, my dear,' he said,
  'Come go with me, my honey,
And ye shall be my wedded wife,
  For I love you best of any.'

6 'I will not go with you,' she said,
  'I'll never be your honey;
I will not be your wedded wife,
  Your love is for my money.'

7 They woud not stay till she was drest
  As ladies when thei 'r brides, O,
But hurried her awa in haste,
  And rowd her in their plaids, O.

8 He drew her out among his crew,
  She holding by her mother;
With mournful cries and watry eyes
  They parted from each other.

9 He placed her upon a steed,
  Then jumped on behind her,
And they are to the Highlands gone,
  Her friends they cannot find her.

10 With many a heavy sob and wail,
  They saw, as they stood by her,
She was so guarded round about
  Her friends could not come nigh her.

11 Her mournful cries were often heard,
  But no aid came unto her;
They guarded her on every side
  That they could not rescúe her.

12 Over rugged hills and dales
  They rode; the lady fainted;
Cried, Woe be to my cursed gold
  That has such roads invented!

13 As they came in by Drimmen town
  And in by Edingarry,
He bought to her both cloak and gown,
  Still thinking she would marry.

14 As they went down yon bonny burn-side,
  They at Buchanan tarried;
He clothed her there as a bride,
  Yet she would not be married.

15 Without consent they joind their hands,
  Which law ought not to carry;
His passion waxed now so hot
  He could no longer tarry.

16 Two held her up before the priest,
  Four laid her in the bed then,
With sighs and cries and watery eyes
  When she was laid beside him.

17 'Ye are come to our Highland hills,
  Far frae thy native clan, lady;
Never think of going back,
  But take it for thy home, lady.

18 'I'll be kind, I'll be kind,
  I'll be kind to thee, lady;
All the country, for thy sake,
  Shall surely favour be, lady.

19 'Rob Roy was my father calld,
  MacGregor was his name, lady,
And all the country where he dwelt
  He did exceed for fame, lady.

20 'Now or then, now or then,
  Now or then deny, lady;
Don't you think yourself well of
  With a pretty man like I, lady?

21 'He was a hedge about his friends,
  A heckle to his foes, lady,
And all that did him any wrong,
  He took them by the nose, lady.

22 'Don't think, don't think,
  Don't think I lie, lady,
Ye may know the truth by what
  Was done in your countrý, lady.

23 'My father delights in cows and horse,
  Likewise in goats and sheep, lady,
And you with thirty thousand marks
  Makes me a man complete, lady.

24 'Be content, be content,
    Be content and stay, lady;
Now ye are my wedded wife
    Untill your dying day, lady.

25 'Your friends will all seek after me,
    But I 'll give them the scorn, lady ;
Before dragoons come oer the Forth,
    We shall be doun by Lorn, lady.

26 'I am bold, I am bold,
    But bolder than before, lady;

Any one dare come this way
    Shall feel my good claymore, lady.

27 'We shall cross the raging seas,
    We shall go to France, lady ;
There we 'll gar the piper play,
    And then we 'll have a dance, lady.

28 'Shake a foot, shake a foot,
    Shake a foot wi me, lady,
And ye shall be my wedded wife
    Until the day ye die, lady.'

A. 6^{1,2}. *In one line:* By the way this lady aftimes fainted. *Cf.* B 7, C 9, *etc.*

    12^2. prickle: *a bad reading for* heckle.

    15, 16. *Each written in two lines in the MS.*

B. 15^3. wi me and thirty merks. *Corrupted from* wi, *or* and, thirty thousand merks: *cf.* K, 23^3.

C. "Tune, Gipsy Laddy," 1–12.

    13. "Tune changes to Haud awa fra me, Donald."

    14, 16, 18 *are written as a burden to the stanzas preceding* them.

    7^3. weepin *originally written for* watery, *and erased.*

    18^2. as bold I 'll roar: more *written over* roar.

D. *After* 7: Answer to Rob Roy. 8–15 *are written in four stanzas of long lines.*

    9^4. Rob *struck out before* Roy's.

E. "The first part [1–7] is sung to the air of Bonny House of Airly, and the last, Haud awa frae me, Donald."

    7^4. was laid behind, O: behind *wrongly for* by him. *Cf.* A 9^4, *etc.*

    9^4. succeed the fame. *So* I 10 *nearly:* F 8 did exceed the fame. *This line evidently troubled reciters. Another set, says Pit-*

cairn, *gives,* It did exceed the same. B 11, C 15, K 19 *have a reading which we may take to be near the original.*

F. 1^4. To keep (haud).

G. *In stanzas of eight lines.* "Tune, a rude set of Mill, Mill O." *After* 4: "The song went on to narrate the forcing her to bed ; when the tune changes to something like Jenny dang the weaver."

I. 12^4. *As a variation, but wrongly* (*see* 13^4), Did feel his good claymore, lady.

J. "I had the first copy from Miss Harper, Kildrummy ; but fearing imperfections, I made application, and by chance got another copy from the Rev. R. Scott, Glenbucket. These I blended together and formed a very good copy; but I have taken the liberty of altering the order of some of the stanzas, and in particular, taking out the ninth and making it the eleventh, and changing some of the words to make it more agreeable." p. 97. *Original readings in* 2^2, *specified by Laing, have been restored, and his* 11 *put back to* 9. *What follows* 16 *has the title,* Variation.

LIZIE LINDSAY

A. 'Lizie Lindsay.' **a.** Jamieson-Brown MS., Appendix, p. ii. **b.** Jamieson's Popular Ballads. II, 149.

B. 'Donald of the Isles,' Kinloch MSS, I, 237. Aytoun's Ballads of Scotland, 1859, I, 277.

C. 'Donald of the Isles,' Kinloch MSS, I, 253.

D. 'Lizzy Lindsay,' from a Note-Book of Dr Joseph Robertson, January, 1830, No 6.

E. 'Bonny Lizie Lindsay,' Buchan's Ballads of the North of Scotland, II, 102.

F. 'Lizzie Lindsay,' Whitelaw's Book of Scottish Ballads, p. 51.

G. 'Leezie Lindsay,' Notes and Queries, Third Series, I, 463.

OF **A** a Professor Robert Scott says, in the letter in which it was enclosed: "You will find above, all I have been able to procure in order to replace the lost fragment of 'Lizie Lindsay.' I believe it is not so correct or so complete as what was formerly sent, but there are materials enough to operate upon, and by forcing the memory of the recorder more harm than good might have been done." Jamieson says of **b**: "Transmitted to the editor by Professor Scott of Aberdeen, as it was taken down from the recitation of an old woman.* It is very popular in the northeast of Scotland, and was familiar to the editor in his early youth; and from the imperfect recollection which he still retains of it he has corrected the text in two or three unimportant passages."

There is nothing to show whether the lost copy was recovered, unless it be the fact that Jamieson prints about twice as many stanzas as there are in **a**. But Jamieson was not always precise in the account he gave of the changes he made in his texts.

In his preface to **B**, Kinloch remarks that the ballad is very popular in the North, "and few milk-maids in that quarter but can chaunt it, to a very pleasant tune. Lizie Lindsay," he adds, "according to the tradition of Mearnsshire, is said to have been a daughter

of Lindsay of Edzell; but I have searched in vain for genealogical confirmation of the tradition." Kinloch gave Aytoun a copy of this version, changing a few phrases, and inserting st. 20 of **C**.

The following stanza, printed as No 434 of the Musical Museum, was sent with the air to Johnson by Burns, who intended to communicate something more. (Museum, 1853, IV, 382):

> Will ye go to the Highlands, Leezie Lindsay?
>   Will ye go to the Highlands wi me?
> Will ye go to the Highlands, Leezie Lindsay,
>   My pride and my darling to be?

Robert Allan added three stanzas to this, Smith's Scotish Minstrel, II, 100, and again, p. 101 of the same, others (in which Lizie Lindsay is, without authority, made 'a puir lassie'). The second stanza of the second "set" is traditional (cf. B 8, C 6, D 6, E 8):

> To gang to the Hielands wi you, sir,
>   I dinna ken how that may be,
> For I ken nae the road I am gaeing,
>   Nor yet wha I 'm gaun wi.

Donald MacDonald, heir of Kingcausie, wishes to go to Edinburgh for a wife (or to get Lizie Lindsay for his wife). His mother

---

* "Leezie Lindsay from a maid-servant in Aberdeen, taken down by Professor Scott:" Jamieson to Scott, November, 1804, Letters addressed to Sir Walter Scott, I, No 117, Abbotsford.

consents, on condition that he shall use no flattery, and shall 'court her in great poverty' (policy, D). He sees many bonny young ladies at Edinburgh, but Lizie Lindsay is above compare with others. He presents himself to her in simple Highland garb; what he can offer is a diet of curds and whey and a bed of green rushes (bracken). Lizie would like to know where she would be going, and with whom. His father is an old shepherd (couper, souter), his mother an old dey, and his name is Donald MacDonald. Lizie's father and mother threaten to have him hanged, which daunts him not in the least. Her maid warmly seconds the suit. Lizie packs up her clothes and sets forth with Donald to foot the steep and dirty ways; she wishes herself back in Edinburgh. They come at last to a shieling, where a woman welcomes Sir Donald; he bids her call him Donald her son, and orders a supper of curds and whey, and a bed of green rushes. Lizie, 'weary with travel,' lies late in the morning, and is roused as if to help at the milking; this makes her repine again. But Donald takes her out of the hut and shows her Kingcausie, where she is to be lady.

Kingcausie is some seven miles from Aberdeen, on the south side of the Dee.

Ballads of this description are peculiarly liable to interpolation and debasement, and there are two passages, each occurring in several versions, which we may, without straining, set down to some plebeian improver.

In B 10, D 10, E 19, Lizie Lindsay, not quite ready to go with Donald, makes him an offer of five or ten guineas if he will stay long enough for her to take his picture, 'to keep her from thinking long.' In F 11 Donald makes the same offer for her picture. In E 10, F 6, Lizie tells Donald, who has asked where she lives, that if he will call at the Canongate Port, she will drink a bottle of sherry with him, and in the next stanza she is as good as her word. This convivial way of the young ladies of Edinburgh is, owing to an injury to the text, not perceptible in D 14, where Donald seems to be inviting Lizie's mother to bring a bottle of sherry with her in case she should call on him at the Canongate Port.

A b is translated by Grundtvig, Engelske og skotske Folkeviser, p. 122; by Rosa Warrens, Schottische Volkslieder der Vorzeit, p. 125, with deficient verses supplied from F. Knortz, Lieder u. Romanzen Alt-Englands, p. 158, translates Allingham's ballad.

A

a. Jamieson-Brown MS., Appendix, p. ii, as sent Jamieson by Professor Scott of Aberdeen, June 9, 1805. b. Jamieson's Popular Ballads, 1806, II, 149, "transmitted to the editor by Professor Scott of Aberdeen, as it was taken down from the recitation of an old woman," but "corrected" from Jamieson's recollection in two or three passages.

* * * * * * *

1 OUT it spake Lizee Linzee,
    The tear blinket in her ee;
How can I leave father and mother,
    Along with young Donald to gae!

2 Out spoke Lizee's young handmaid,
    A bonny young lassie was she;

Said, Were I heress to a kingdom,
    Along with young Donald I 'd ga.

3 'O say ye so to me, Nelly?
    O say ye so to me?
Must I leave Edinburgh city,
    To the high Highland to gae?'

4 Out spoke Lizie's own mother,
    A good old lady was she;
If you speak such a word to my dochter,
    I 'll gar hang [you] hi.

5 'Keep well your dochter from me, madam,
    Keep well your dochter fa me;
For I care as little for your dochter
    As ye can care for me.'

6 The road grew wetty and dubby,
    And Lizee began to think lang;
    Said, I wish had staid with my mother,
    And nae wi young Donald had gane.

7 'You'r welcome hame, Sir Donald,
    You'r thrice welcome to me;
    You'r welcome hame, Sir Donald,
    And your young lady you wi.'

8 . . . .
    . . . . .

'Ye call na me Sir Donald,
    But ca me Donald your son.'

9 'Rise up, Lizee Linzee,
    You [have] lain too long in the day;
    Ye might have helped my mother
    To milch her goats and her kie.'

10 Out it spake Lizee Linzee,
    The tear blinket in her eye;
    'The ladys of Edin*burgh* city,
    They neither milch goats nor kie.'

B

Kinloch MSS, I, 237, from Miss Catherine Beattie, Mearnsshire.

1 IT's of a young lord o the Hielands,
    A bonnie braw castle had he,
    And he says to his lady mither,
    'My boon ye will grant to me:
    Sall I gae to Edinbruch city,
    And fesh hame a lady wi me?'

2 'Ye may gae to Edinbruch city,
    And fesh hame a lady wi thee,
    But see that ye bring her but flattrie,
    And court her in grit povertie.'

3 'My coat, mither, sall be o the plaiden,
    A tartan kilt oure my knee,
    Wi hosens and brogues and the bonnet;
    I'll court her wi nae flattrie.'

4 Whan he cam to Edinbruch city,
    He playd at the ring and the ba,
    And saw monie a bonnie young ladie,
    But Lizie Lindsay was first o them a'.

5 Syne, dressd in his Hieland grey plaiden,
    His bonnet abune his ee-bree,
    He called on fair Lizie Lindsay;
    Says, Lizie, will ye fancy me?

6 'And gae to the Hielands, my lassie,
    And gae, gae wi me?
    O gae to the Hielands, Lizie Lindsay,
    I'll feed ye on curds and green whey.

7 'And ye'se get a bed o green bracken,
    My plaidie will hap thee and me;

Ye'se lie in my arms, bonnie Lizie,
    If ye'll gae to the Hielands wi me.'

8 'O how can I gae to the Hielands,
    Or how can I gae wi thee,
    Whan I dinna ken whare I'm gaing,
    Nor wha I hae to gae wi?'

9 'My father, he is an auld shepherd,
    My mither, she is an auld dey;
    My name it is Donald Macdonald,
    My name I'll never deny.'

10 'O Donald, I'll gie ye five guineas
    To sit ae hour in my room,
    Till I tak aff your ruddy picture;
    Whan I hae't, I'll never think lang.'

11 'I dinna care for your five guineas;
    It's ye that's the jewel to me;
    I've plenty o kye in the Hielands,
    To feed ye wi curds and green whey.

12 'And ye'se get a bonnie blue plaidie,
    Wi red and green strips thro it a';
    And I'll be the lord o your dwalling,
    And that's the best picture ava.

13 'And I am laird o a' my possessions;
    The king canna boast o na mair;
    And ye'se hae my true heart in keeping,
    There'll be na ither een hae a share.

14 'Sae gae to the Hielands, my lassie,
    O gae awa happy wi me;
    O gae to the Hielands, Lizie Lindsay,
    And hird the wee lammies wi me.'

15 'O how can I gae wi a stranger,
       Oure hills and oure glens frae my hame?'
   'I tell ye I am Donald Macdonald;
       I 'll ever be proud o my name.'

16 Doun cam Lizie Lindsay's ain father,
       A knicht o a noble degree;
   Says, If ye do steal my dear daughter,
       It 's hangit ye quickly sall be.

17 On his heel he turnd round wi a bouncie,
       And a licht lauch he did gie:
   'There 's nae law in Edinbruch city
       This day that can dare to hang me.'

18 Then up bespak Lizie's best woman,
       And a bonnie young lass was she;
   'Had I but a mark in my pouchie,
       It 's Donald that I wad gae wi.'

19 'O Helen, wad ye leave your coffer,
       And a' your silk kirtles sae braw,
   And gang wi a bare-houghd puir laddie,
       And leave father, mither, and a'?

20 'But I think he 's a witch or a warlock,
       Or something o that fell degree,
   For I 'll gae awa wi young Donald,
       Whatever my fortune may be.'

21 Then Lizie laid doun her silk mantle,
       And put on her waiting-maid's goun,
   And aff and awa to the Hielands
       She 's gane wi this young shepherd loun.

22 Thro glens and oure mountains they wanderd,
       Till Lizie had scantlie a shoe;

'Alas and ohone!' says fair Lizie,
       'Sad was the first day I saw you!
   I wish I war in Edinbruch city;
       Fu sair, sair this pastime I rue.'

23 'O haud your tongue now, bonnie Lizie,
       For yonder 's the shieling, my hame;
   And there 's my guid auld honest mither,
       That 's coming to meet ye her lane.'

24 'O ye 're welcome, ye 're welcome, Sir Donald,
       Ye 're welcome hame to your ain.'
   'O ca me na young Sir Donald,
       But ca me Donald my son;'
   And this they hae spoken in Erse,
       That Lizie micht not understand.

25 The day being weetie and daggie,
       They lay till 't was lang o the day:
   'Win up, win up, bonnie Lizie,
       And help at the milking the kye.'

26 O slowly raise up Lizie Lindsay,
       The saut tear blindit her ee:
   'O, war I in Edinbruch city,
       The Hielands shoud never see me!'

27 He led her up to a hie mountain
       And bade her look out far and wide:
   'I 'm lord o thae isles and thae mountains,
       And ye 're now my beautiful bride.

28 'Sae rue na ye 've come to the Hielands,
       Sae rue na ye 've come aff wi me,
   For ye 're great Macdonald's braw lady,
       And will be to the dav that ye dee.'

C

Kinloch MSS, I, 253; from the recitation of Mrs Bouchart,
of Dundee.

1 WHAT wad ye gie to me, mither,
       What wad ye gie to me,
   If I wad gae to Edinbruch city
       And bring hame Lizie Lindsey to thee?'

2 'Meikle wad I gie to thee, Donald,
       Meikle wad I gie to thee,
   If ye wad gang to Edinbruch city
       And court her as in povertie.'

3 Whan he cam to Edinbruch city,
       And there a while to resort,
   He called on fair Lizie Lindsey,
       Wha lived at the Canongate-Port.

4 'Will ye gang to the Hielands, Lizie Lindsey?
       Will ye gae to the Hielands wi me?
   And I will gie ye a cup o the curds,
       Likewise a cup of green whey.

5 'And I will gie ye a bed o green threshes,
       Likewise a happing o grey,

If ye will gae to the Hielands, Lizie Lindsey,
 If ye 'll gae to the Hielands wi me.'

6 'How can I gang?' says Lizie Lindsey,
 'How can I gang wi thee?
I dinna ken whare I am gaing,
 Nor wha I am gaing wi.'

7 'My father is a cowper o cattle,
 My mither is an auld dey;
My name is Donald Macdonald,
 My name I 'll never deny.'

8 Doun cam Lizie Lindsey's father,
 A revrend auld gentleman was he:
'If ye steal awa my dochter,
 Hie hanged ye sall be.'

9 He turned him round on his heel
 And [a] licht lauch gied he:
'There is na law in a' Edinbruch city
 This day that can hang me.'

10 It 's doun cam Lizie's hand-maid,
 A bonnie young lass was she:
'If I had ae crown in a' the warld,
 Awa wi that fellow I 'd gae.'

11 'Do ye say sae to me, Nelly?
 Do ye say sae to me?
Wad ye leave your father and mither,
 And awa wi that fellow wad gae?'

12 She has kilted her coats o green silk
 A little below her knee,
And she 's awa to the Hielands wi Donald,
 To bear him companie.

13 And whan they cam to the vallies
 The hie hills war coverd wi snow,
Which caused monie a saut tear
 From Lizie's een to flow.

14 'O, gin I war in Edinbruch city,
 And safe in my ain countrie,
O, gin I war in Edinbruch city,
 The Hielands shoud never see me.'

15 'O haud your tongue, Lizie Lindsey,
 Na mair o that let me see;
I 'll tak ye back to Edinbruch city,
 And safe to your ain countrie.'

16 'Though I war in Edinbruch city,
 And safe in my ain countrie,
Though I war in Edinbruch city,
 O wha wad care for me!'

17 Whan they cam to the shiels o Kilcushneuch,
 Out there cam an auld dey:
'Ye 're welcome here, Sir Donald,
 You and your lady gay.'

18 'Ca me na mair Sir Donald,
 But ca me Donald your son,
And I 'll ca ye my auld mither,
 Till the lang winter nicht is begun.'

19 'A' this was spoken in Erse,
 That Lizie micht na ken;
A' this was spoken in Erse,
 And syne the broad English began.

20 'Ye 'll gae and mak to our supper
 A cup o the curds and whey,
And ye 'll mak a bed o green threshes,
 Likewise a happing o grey.'

*   *   *   *   *   *

21 'Won up, won up, Lizie Lindsey,
 Ye 've lain oure lang in the day;
Ye micht hae been helping my mither
 To milk the ewes and the kye.'

22 Then up got Lizie Lindsey,
 And the tear blindit her ee:
'O, gin I war in Edinbruch city,
 The Hielands shoud never see me!'

23 'Won up, won up, Lizie Lindsey,
 A fairer sicht ye hae to see:
Do ye see yon bonnie braw castle?
 Lady o it ye will be.'

D

From a Note-Book of Joseph Robertson, January, 1830,
No. 6; derived from John Hill Burton.

1 THERE dwalt a lass in the South Countrie,
    Lizzy Lindsay called by name,
And many a laird and lord sought her,
    But nane o them a' could her gain.

2 Out spoke the heir o Kinkawsie,
    An down to his fader spoke he;
'Fat would ye think o me, fadther,
    Fat would ye think o me,
To go to Edinburgh city,
    Bring hame Lizzy Lindsay wi me?'

3 Out and spoke his auld modther,
    An auld revrend lady was she;
'Court her wi nae fause flatterie,
    But in great policie.'

4 He was nae in Edinbruch citie
    But a twalmont an a day,
When a' the young lairds an the ladies
    Went forth to sport an play:
There was nane like Lizzy Lindsay,
    She was baith gallan an gay.

5 'Will ye go to the Hielans, Lizzy Linsay?
    Will ye go to the Hielans wi me?
If ye'll go to the Hielans, Lizz[y] Linsay,
    I'll gar ye get crouds an green whey.'

6 'How can I go to the Hielans?
    Or hoo will I go with thee?
I dinna ken whaar I'm going,
    Or fa 't is I would go wi.'

7 'My fadther he is an auld couper,
    My modther a brave auld dey;
If ye'll go to the Hieland[s], Lizzy Linsay,
    I'll gar ye get cruds and green whey.'

8 Out it spoke Lizzy's best maiden,
    A wat a fine creature was she;
'Tho I were born heir till a crown,
    It's young Donald *that* I would go wi.'

9 'Oh say ye sae to me, Nelly?
    Oh say ye sae to me?
Will I cast off my fine gowns and laces,
    An gae to the Highlans him wi?'

10 She's putten her hand in her pocket,
    She's taen out ten guineas roun:
'And that wad I gie to thee, Donald,
    To stay but ae hour i my room,
Till I get your fair pictur painted,
    To haud me unthought lang.'

11 'I care as little for your guineas
    As you can care for mine;
But gin that ye like my fair face,
    Then gae wi me, if that ye incline.'

12 Out it spak Lizzy's auld mither,
    I wite a fine lady was she;
'Gin I hear you speak sae to my daughter,
    I vow I 'se cause them hang thee.'

13 He turned about on his heel,
    And a loud, loud laughter gae he:
'They are not in Edinburgh city,
    I trow, that dare hang me.

14 'But an ye come to the Canongate-Port —
    An there ye'll be sure to see me —
Bring wi ye a bottle of sherry,
    I'll bear you good company.'

15 They sought all Edinboro citie,
    They sought it roun an roun,
Thinkin to fin Lizzy Lindsay,
    But awa to the Highlans she's gane.

16 Whan they came to the shielin,
    Out bespoke the ould dye;
'You're welcome home, Sir Donald,
    Lang hae we been thinkin for thee.'

17 'Ye'll call me nae mair Sir Donald,
    Ye'll call me nae sic thing;
But ye 'se be my auld mither,
    And I 'se be Donald your sin.

18 'Ye'll mak for us a supper,
    A supper o cruds and green whey,
And likewise a bed o green rashes,
    For Lizzy and I to ly.'

19 She's made for them a supper,
    A supper o cruds and why,
And likewise a bed o green rashes,
    For Lizzy an him to ly.

20 But Donald rose up i the mornin,
    The rest o his glens to spy ;
    It was to look for his goats,
        His goats, his yows, an his kye.

21 But Lizzy, beein wearied wi travel,
    She lay till 't was lang i the day :
    'Get up, get up, Lizzy Linsay,
        What maks you sae lang for to ly ?
    You had better been helping my mither
        To milk her yews and her kye.'

22 But Lizzy drew till her her stockins,
    The tears fell down on her eye :
    'I wish I were at Edinboro city,
        I can neither milk yews nor kye.'

23 'Oh hold your tongue, Lizzy Linsay,
    Your weepin I mustna be wi ;
    I 'll sen you hame to your mither,
        In the greatest o safety.'

24 But he has tane her by the han,
    And has shewn her the straight way to go :
    'An dont you see bonny Kincawsie,
        Wher you and I is to ly ?'

25 Out then comes his old mither,
    An twenty brave knichts her wi :
    'Y 'er welcome home, Sir Donald,
        Lang hae we been thinkin for thee.'

26 Out then comes his old father,
    An twenty brave ladies him wi :
    'You 'r welcome home, Sir Donald,
        An that fair creature you wi.'

27 He 's taken her by the han,
    An he 's shewn her the straight way in :
    'An ye 'se be Lady Kincawsie,
        An ye 'se hae Donal, my sin.'

E

Buchan's Ballads of the North of Scotland, II, 102.

1 In Edinburgh lived a lady,
    Was ca'd Lizie Lindsay by name,
    Was courted by mony fine suitors,
    And mony rich person of fame :
    Tho lords o renown had her courted,
        Yet none her favour could gain.

2 Then spake the young laird o Kingcaussie,
    And a bonny young boy was he ;
    'Then let me a year to the city,
        I 'll come, and that lady wi me.'

3 Then spake the auld laird o Kingcaussie,
    A canty auld mannie was he ;
    'What think ye by our little Donald,
        Sae proudly and crously cracks he ?

4 'But he 's win a year to the city,
    If that I be a living man ;
    And what he can mak o this lady,
        We shall lat him do as he can.'

5 He 's stript aff his fine costly robes,
    And put on the single liverie ;

With no equipage nor attendance,
    To Edinburgh city went he.

6 Now there was a ball in the city,
    A ball o great mirth and great fame ;
    And fa danced wi Donald that day
    But bonny Lizie Lindsay on the green !

7 'Will ye gang to the Hielands, bonny Lizie ?
    Will ye gang to the Hielands wi me ?
    Will ye leave the South Country ladies,
        And gang to the Hielands wi me ?'

8 The lady she turned about,
    And answered him courteouslie ;
    'I 'd like to ken faer I am gaun first,
        And fa I am gaun to gang wi.'

9 'O Lizie, ae favour I 'll ask you,
    This favour I pray not deny ;
    Ye 'll tell me your place o abode,
        And your nearest o kindred do stay.'

10 'Ye 'll call at the Canogate-Port,
    At the Canogate-Port call ye ;
    I 'll gie you a bottle o wine,
        And I 'll bear you my companie.'

11 Syne he called at the Canogate-Port,
　　At the Canogate-Port calld he;
　She gae him a bottle o wine,
　　And she gae him her companie.

12 'Will ye gang to the Hielands, bonny Lizie?
　　Will ye gang to the Hielands wi me?
　Will ye leave the South Country ladies,
　　And gang to the Hielands wi me?'

13 Then out spake Lizie's auld mither,
　　For a very auld lady was she;
　'If ye cast ony creed on my dochter,
　　High hanged I 'll cause you to be.'

14 'O keep hame your dochter, auld woman,
　　And latna her gang wi me;
　I can cast nae mair creed on your dochter,
　　Nae mair than she can on me.'

15 'Now, young man, ae question I 'll ask you,
　　Sin ye mean to honour us sae;
　Ye 'll tell me how braid your lands lie,
　　Your name, and faer ye hae to gae.'

16 'My father he is an auld soutter,
　　My mither she is an auld dey,
　And I 'm but a puir broken trooper,
　　My kindred I winna deny.

17 'Yet I 'm nae a man o great honour,
　　Nor am I a man o great fame;
　My name it is Donald M'Donald,
　　I 'll tell it, and winna think shame.

18 'Will ye gang to the Hielands, bonny Lizie?
　　Will ye gang to the Hielands wi me?
　Will ye leave the South Country ladies,
　　And gang to the Hielands wi me?'

19 'O Donald, I 'll gie you ten guineas,
　　If ye woud but stay in my room
　Until that I draw your fair picture,
　　To look on it fan I think lang.'

20 'No, I carena mair for your guineas,
　　Nae mair than ye care for mine;
　But if that ye love my ain person,
　　Gae wi me, maid, if ye incline.'

21 Then out spake Lizie's bower-woman,
　　And a bonny young lassie was she;
　Tho I was born heir to a crown,
　　Young Donald, I woud gang him wi.

22 Up raise then the bonny young lady,
　　And drew till her stockings and sheen,
　And packd up her claise in fine bundles,
　　And awa wi young Donald she 's gane.

23 The roads they were rocky and knabby,
　　The mountains were baith strait and stay;
　When Lizie grew wearied wi travel,
　　For she 'd travelld a very lang way.

24 'O turn again, bonny Lizie Lindsay,
　　O turn again,' said he;
　'We 're but ae day's journey frae town,
　　O turn, and I 'll turn wi thee.'

25 Out speaks the bonny young lady,
　　Till the saut tear blinded her ee;
　Altho I 'd return to the city,
　　There 's nae person woud care for me.

26 When they came near the end o their journey,
　　To the house o their father's milk-dey,
　He said, Stay still there, Lizie Lindsay,
　　Till I tell my mither o thee.

27 When he came into the shielen,
　　She hailed him courteouslie;
　Said, Ye 're welcome hame, Sir Donald,
　　There 's been mony ane calling for thee.

28 'O ca me nae mair, Sir Donald,
　　But Donald M'Donald your son;
　We 'll carry the joke a bit farther,
　　There 's a bonny young lady to come.'

29 When Lizie came into the shielen,
　　She lookd as if she 'd been a feel;
　She sawna a seat to sit down on,
　　But only some sunks o green feall.

30 'Now make us a supper, dear mither,
　　The best o your cruds and green whey;
　And make us a bed o green rashes,
　　And covert wi huddins sae grey.'

31 But Lizie being wearied wi travel,
　　She lay till 't was up i the day:
　'Ye might hae been up an hour seener,
　　To milk baith the ewes and the kye.'

32 Out then speaks the bonny young lady,
　　Whan the saut tear drapt frae her eye;
　I wish that I had bidden at hame,
　　I can neither milk ewes nor kye.

33 'I wish that I had bidden at hame,
    The Hielands I never had seen,
    Altho I love Donald M'Donald,
    The laddie wi blythe blinking een.'

34 'Win up, win up, O bonny Lizie,
    And dress in the silks sae gay;
    I 'll show you the yetts o Kingcaussie,
    Whare I 've playd me mony a day.'

35 Up raise the bonny young lady,
    And drest in the silks sae fine,

And into young Donald's arms
    Awa to Kingcaussie she 's gane.

36 Forth came the auld laird o Kingcaussie,
    And hailed her courteouslie;
    Says, Ye 're welcome, bonny Lizie Lindsay,
    Ye 're welcome hame to me.

37 'Tho lords o renown hae you courted,
    Young Donald your favour has won;
    Ye 'se get a' the lands o Kingcaussie,
    And Donald M'Donald, my son.'

———————

F

Whitelaw's Book of Scottish Ballads, p. 51, "from the
recitation of a lady in Glasgow."

1 THERE was a braw ball in Edinburgh,
    And mony braw ladies were there,
    But nae ane at a' the assembly
    Could wi Lizzie Lindsay compare.

2 In cam the young laird o Kincassie,
    An a bonnie young laddie was he:
    'Will ye lea yere ain kintra, Lizzie,
    An gang to the Hielands wi me?'

3 She turned her roun on her heel,
    An a very loud laughter gaed she:
    'I wad like to ken whar I was ganging,
    And wha I was gaun to gang wi.'

4 'My name is young Donald M'Donald,
    My name I will never deny;
    My father he is an auld shepherd,
    Sae weel as he can herd the kye!

5 'My father he is an auld shepherd,
    My mother she is an auld dame;
    If ye 'll gang to the Hielands, bonnie Lizzie,
    Ye 's neither want curds nor cream.'

6 'If ye 'll call at the Canongate-Port,
    At the Canongate-Port call on me,
    I 'll give you a bottle o sherry,
    And bear you companie.'

7 He ca'd at the Canongate-Port,
    At the Canongate-Port called he;

She drank wi him a bottle o sherry,
    And bore him guid companie.

8 'Will ye go to the Hielands, bonnie Lizzie?
    Will ye go to the Hielands wi me?
    If ye 'll go to the Hielands, bonnie Lizzie,
    Ye shall not want curds nor green whey.'

9 In there cam her auld mither,
    A jolly auld lady was she:
    'I wad like to ken whar she was ganging,
    And wha she was gaun to gang wi.'

10 'My name is young Donald M'Donald,
    My name I will never deny;
    My father he is an auld shepherd,
    Sae weel as he can herd the kye!

11 'O but I would give you ten guineas
    To have her one hour in a room,
    To get her fair body a picture,
    To keep me from thinking long.'

12 'O I value not your ten guineas,
    As little as you value mine;
    But if that you covet my daughter,
    Take her with you, if you do incline.'

13 'Pack up my silks and my satins,
    And pack up my hose and my shoon,
    And likewise my clothes in small bundles,
    And away wi young Donald I 'll gang.'

14 They packd up her silks and her satins,
    They packd up her hose and her shoon,

And likewise her clothes in small bundles,
    And away with young Donald she 's gane.

15 When that they cam to the Hielands,
    The braes they were baith lang and stey ;
Bonnie Lizzie was wearied wi ganging,
    She had travelld a lang summer day.

16 'O are we near hame, Sir Donald?
    O are we near hame, I pray?'
'We 're no near hame, bonnie Lizzie,
    Nor yet the half o the way.'

17 They cam to a homely poor cottage,
    An auld man was standing by:
'Ye 're welcome hame, Sir Donald,
    Ye 've been sae lang away.'

18 'O call me no more Sir Donald,
    But call me young Donald your son,
For I have a bonnie young lady
    Behind me for to come in.'

19 'Come in, come in, bonnie Lizzie,
    Come in, come in,' said he ;
'Although that our cottage be little,
    Perhaps the better we 'll gree.

20 'O make us a supper, dear mother,
    And make it of curds an green whey ;

And make us a bed o green rushes,
    And cover it oer wi green hay.'

*   *   *   *   *   *

21 'Rise up, rise up, bonnie Lizzie,
    Why lie ye so long in the day?
Ye might hae been helping my mother
    To make the curds and green whey.'

22 'O haud your tongue, Sir Donald,
    O haud your tongue, I pray ;
I wish I had neer left my mother ;
    I can neither make curds nor whey.'

23 'Rise up, rise up, bonnie Lizzie,
    And put on your satins so fine,
For we maun to be at Kincassie
    Before that the clock strikes nine.'

24 But when they came to Kincassie
    The porter was standing by:
'Ye 're welcome home, Sir Donald,
    Ye 've been so long away.'

25 It 's down then came his auld mither,
    With all the keys in her hand,
Saying, Take you these, bonnie Lizzie,
    All under them 's at your command.

G

Notes and Queries, Third Series, I, 463; "from recitation, September, 1828."

1 'WILL you go to the Highlands wi me, Leezie?
    Will you go to the Highlands wi me?
Will you go to the Highlands wi me, Leezie?
    And you shall have curds and green whey.'

2 Then up spoke Leezie's mother,
    A gallant old lady was she;
'If you talk so to my daughter,
    High hanged I 'll gar you be.'

3 And then she changed her coaties,
    And then she changed them to green,
And then she changed her coaties,
    Young Donald to gang wi.

4 But the roads grew broad and broad,
    And the mountains grew high and high,
Which caused many a tear
    To fall from Leezie's eye.

5 But the roads grew broad and broad,
    And the mountains grew high and high,
Till they came to the glens of Glen Koustie,
    And out there came an old die.

6 'You 're welcome here, Sir Donald,
    And your fair ladie,
  . . . .
  . . . . . . ,'

7 'O call not me Sir Donald,
    But call me Donald your son,
And I will call you mother,
    Till this long night be done.'

8 These words were spoken in Gaelic,
    And Leezie did not them ken;
These words were spoken in Gaelic,
    And then plain English began.

9 'O make her a supper, mother,
    O make her a supper wi me;
O make her a supper, mother,
    Of curds and green whey.'

*   *   *   *   *   *

10 'You must get up, Leezie Lindsay,
    .   .   .   .   .   .

You must get up, Leezie Lindsay,
    For it is far in the day.'

11 And then they went out together,
    And a braw new bigging saw she,
And out cam Lord Macdonald,
    And his gay companie.

12 'You 're welcome here, Leezie Lindsay,
    The flower of a' your kin,
And you shall be Lady Macdonald,
    Since you have got Donald, my son.'

———◆———

A. a. *Written in stanzas of two long lines.*
    3^2. Oh.
  b. a *and* b *correspond nearly as follows:*
    a. 4, 5, 2, $3^{1,2}$, $8^{3,4}$, 7, $9^{1,2}$, $9^{3,4}$, 10.
    b. 2, 3, 4, $5^{1,2}$, $13^{3,4}$, 14, $16^{3,4}$, $17^{3,4}$, 18.

1 'Will ye go to the Highlands, Lizie Lindsay?
    Will ye go to the Highlands wi me?
Will ye go to the Highlands, Lizie Lindsay,
    And dine on fresh cruds and green whey?'

2 Then out spak Lizie's mother,
    A good old lady was she;
Gin ye say sic a word to my daughter,
    I 'll gar ye be hanged high.

3 'Keep weel your daughter frae me, madam;
    Keep weel your daughter frae me;
I care as little for your daughter
    As ye can care for me.'

4 Then out spak Lizie's ain maiden,
    A bonny young lassie was she;
Says, Were I the heir to a kingdom,
    Awa wi young Donald I 'd be.

5 'O say you sae to me, Nelly?
    And does my Nelly say sae?
Maun I leave my father and mother,
    Awa wi young Donald to gae?'

6 And Lizie 's taen till her her stockings,
    And Lizie 's taen till her her shoen,
And kilted up her green claithing,
    And awa wi young Donald she 's gane.

7 The road it was lang and weary;
    The braes they were ill to climb;
Bonny Lizie was weary wi travelling,
    And a fit furder coudna win.

8 And sair, O sair, did she sigh,
    And the saut tear blin'd her ee:
'Gin this be the pleasures o looing,
    They never will do wi me!'

9 'Now haud your tongue, bonny Lizie,
    Ye never shall rue for me;
Gie me but your love for my love,
    It is a' that your tocher will be.

10 'And haud your tongue, bonny Lizie,
    Altho that the gait seem lang,
And you 's hae the wale o good living
    Whan to Kincawsen we gang.

11 'There my father he is an auld cobler,
    My mother she is an auld dey,
And we 'll sleep on a bed o green rashes,
    And dine on fresh cruds and green whey.'

12 .   .   .   .   .   .
    .   .   .   .   .   .
    'You 're welcome hame, Sir Donald,
    You 're welcome hame to me.'

13 'O ca me nae mair Sir Donald;
    There 's a bonny young lady to come;
Sae ca me nae mair Sir Donald,
    But ae spring Donald your son.'

14 'Ye 're welcome hame, young Donald,
    Ye 're welcome hame to me ;
Ye 're welcome hame, young Donald,
    And your bonny young lady wi ye.'

15 She 's made them a bed of green rashes,
    Weel coverd wi hooding o grey ;
Bonny Lizie was weary wi travelling,
    And lay till 't was lang o the day.

16 'The sun looks in oer the hill-head,
    And the laverock is liltin gay ;
Get up, get up, bonny Lizie,
    You 've lain till it 's lang o the day.

17 'You might hae been out at the shealin,
    Instead o sae lang to lye,
And up and helping my mother
    To milk baith her gaits and kye.'

18 Then out spak Lizie Lindsay,
    The tear blindit her eye ;

'The ladies o Edinburgh city,
    They neither milk gaits nor kye.'

19 Then up spak young Sir Donald,
    .   .   .   .

20 'For I am the laird o Kincawsyn,
    And you are the lady free,
And   .   .   .   .   .
    .   .   .   .'

D. 9^1. nay (not) sae, not *struck out*. 25^4. wi.
E. 29. *In a much altered chap-book copy, printed
    by J. Morren, Edinburgh, we have :*

When they came to the braes o Kinkassie,
    Young Lizie began for to fail ;
There was not a seat in the house
    But what was made of the green fell.

F. 16^1, 22^1. *The* Sir *is an anticipation.*
G. 7^1, 9^{1-8}. Oh.

227

BONNY LIZIE BAILLIE

a. 'Bonny Lizie Balie, A New Song very much in Request,' Laing broadsides, No 46 ; no date or place. b. 'Bonny Lizzie Bailie,' Maidment's Scotish Ballads and Songs, 1859, p. 13. c. 'My bonny Lizzie Baillie,' Johnson's Museum, ed. 1853, IV, *451. d. 'Lizae Baillie,' Herd's MSS, I, 101, and, in part, II, 121. e. 'Lizie Baillie,' Campbell MSS, I, 98. f. 'Lizzie Bailie,' Smith's Scotish Minstrel, IV, 90. g. 'Lizie Baillie,' Buchan's Ballads of the North of Scotland, II, 173.

---

a, from the collection of broadsides made by David Laing, now in the possession of Lord Rosebery, may probably have been printed at the beginning of the last century, at Edinburgh. b was taken "from a tolerably old copy printed at Glasgow." Excepting the lack of two stanzas, the variations from a are mostly of slight consequence ; two or three are for the better. c (only the beginning, stanzas 1–4¹) was communicated by C. K. Sharpe, from a " MS. çopy of some antiquity." d–g are of no authority. d, e are fragmentary stanzas, misremembered if not corrupted. f has ten stanzas, eight of which (some with a word or two changed) are from d. g is a washy *rifacimento.*

d is printed in Herd's Ancient and Modern Scottish Songs, 1776, II, 3. The copy in Johnson's Museum, No 456, p. 469, is d without the first stanza.

Stanzas 19–21 of a, b, and their representatives in d, e, recall 'The Gypsy Laddie.'

Lizzie Baillie, of Castle Cary, Stirlingshire, while paying a visit to a sister at Gartartan, Perthshire, makes an excursion to Inchmahome, an island in Loch Menteith. Here she meets Duncan Graham, who, against the opposition of her parents, persuades her to prefer a Highland husband to any Lowland or English match.

"The heroine of this song," says Sharpe, "was a daughter of Baillie of Castle Carey, and sister, as it is said, to the wife of Macfarlane of Gartartan." The Baillies, as Maidment has shown, acquired Castle Cary "at a comparatively recent date," and that editor must be nearly, or quite, right in declaring the ballad to be not older than the commencement of the last century. Buchan has a bit of pseudo-history anent Lizie Baillie in his notes, at II, 326.

The story is told in a somewhat disorderly way even in a, and we may believe that we have not attained the original yet, though this copy is much older than any that has appeared in previous collections.

1 It fell about the Lambmass tide,
    When the leaves were fresh and green,
    Lizie Bailie is to Gartartain [gane],
    To see her sister Jean.

2 She had not been in Gartartain
    Even but a little while
    Till luck and fortune happend her,
    And she went to the Isle.

3 And when she went into the Isle
    She met with Duncan Grahame;
    So bravely as he courted her!
    And he convoyd her hame.

4 'My bonny Lizie Bailie,
    I'll row thee in my pladie,
    If thou will go along with me
    And be my Highland lady.'

5 'If I would go along with thee,
    I think I were not wise;
    For I cannot milk cow nor ewe,
    Nor yet can I speak Erse.'

6 'Hold thy tongue, bonny Lizie Bailie,
    And hold thy tongue,' said he;
    'For any thing that thou does lack,
    My dear, I'll learn thee.'

7 She would not have a Lowland laird,
    He wears the high-heeld shoes;
    She will marry Duncan Grahame,
    For Duncan wears his trews.

8 She would not have a gentleman,
    A farmer in Kilsyth,
    But she would have the Highland man,
    He lives into Monteith.

9 She would not have the Lowland man,
    Nor yet the English laddie,
    But she would have the Highland man,
    To row her in his pladie.

10 He took her by the milk-white hand,
    And he convoyed her hame,
    And still she thought, both night and day,
    On bonny Duncan Grahame.

11 'O bonny Duncan Grahame,
    Why should ye me miscarry?
    For, if you have a love for me,
    We'll meet a[t] Castle Carry.

12 'As I came in by Dennie bridge,
    And by the holland-bush,
    My mother took from me my cloaths,
    My rings, ay and my purse.

13 'Hold your tongue, my mother dear,
    For that I do not care;
    For I will go with Duncan Grahame
    Tho I should ner get mair.

14 'For first when I met Duncan Grahame
    I met with meikle joy,
    And many pretty Highland men
    Was there at my convoy.'

15 And now he is gone through the muir,
   And she is through the glen:
   'O bonny Lizie Bailie,
   When will we meet again!'

16 Shame light on these logerheads
   That lives in Castle Carry,
   That let away the bonny lass
   The Highland man to marry!

17 'O bonny Lizie, stay at home!
   Thy mother cannot want thee;
   For any thing that thou does lack,
   My dear, I 'll cause get thee.'

18 'I would not give my Duncan Grahame
   For all my father's land,
   Although he had three lairdships more,
   And all at my command.'

19 And she 's cast off her silken gowns,
   That she weard in the Lowland,
   And she 's up to the Highland hills,
   To wear [the] gowns of tartain.

20 And she 's cast off her high-heeld shoes,
   Was made of the gilded leather,
   And she 's up to Gillecrankie,
   To go among the heather.

21 And she 's cast off her high-heeld shoes,
   And put on a pair of laigh ones,
   And she 's away with Duncan Grahame,
   To go among the brachans.

22 'O my bonny Lizie Bailie,
   Thy mother cannot want thee;
   And if thou go with Duncan Grahame
   Thou 'll be a Gilliecrankie.'

23 'Hold your tongue, my mother dear,
   And folly let thee be;
   Should not I fancie Duncan Grahame
   When Duncan fancies me?

24 'Hold your tongue, my father dear,
   And folly let thee be;
   For I will go with Duncan Grahame
   Fore all the men I see.'

25 'Who is it that 's done this turn?
   Who has done this deed?'
   'A minister it 's, father,' she says,
   'Lives at the Rughburn bridge.'

26 'A minister, daughter?' he says,
   'A minister for mister!'
   'O hold your tongue, my father dear,
   He married first my sister.'

27 'O fare you well, my daughter dear,
   So dearly as I lovd thee!
   Since thou wilt go to Duncan Grahame,
   My bonny Lizie Bailie.'

28 'O fare you well, my father dear,
   Also my sister Betty;
   O fare you well, my mother dear,
   I leave you all compleatly.'

---

a. 3⁴. conveyd; cf. 10².
   17⁴. *Suspicious.* I 'll surely grant thee *in* b,
   which preserves the rhyme, and is otherwise
   preferable.
   20³, b *avoids* Gillecrankie *here by reading*
   to the Highland hills, *and lacks* 22.
   23², 24². *Hardly possible. In* 23² b *has,*
   With your folly let me be.
   27¹. fair ye: cf. 28¹,³.
b. 1¹. upon the. 1³. gane. 2¹. been long at.
   2³. to her. 3⁴. convoyd. 4³. wilt.
   5¹. I should: with you. 5². They 'd think.
   5³. can neither. 6³. dost. 6⁴. I will teach.
   7². That wears. 7³. But she would.

7⁴. he wears trews. 8³. have a.
8⁴. That lives. 11². you. 11⁴. at.
14³. mony a: Highlandman. 15¹. now she.
15². And he. 15³. O my. 17³. dost want.
17⁴. I 'll surely grant thee: better.
19¹. Now she 's: gown. 19². wore: Lowlands.
19⁴. the gowns. 20². oiled *for* the gilded.
20³. to the Highland hills. 20⁴, 21⁴. gang.
21². And *wanting.* 22. *Wanting.*
23². With your folly let me be.
23⁴. 'Fore all the men I see.
24 (*or,* 23⁴ 24¹⁻³). *Wanting.* 25¹. that has.
25². Or who hath. 25⁴. Red Burn.
27¹. So *for* O. 27². love. 27³. go with.

27⁴. Thou 'lt get no gear from me.
c. *Only* 1–4¹ *given.*
  1¹. It was in and about the Martinmass.
    *Absurd. Lammas, even, is late enough
    for leaves to be fresh and green; in fact
    both are verbiage.*
  1³. gane. 2¹. She was nae in.
  2². Even *wanting.* 2³. When luck.
  2⁴. she gaed.
  3¹. When she gaed to the bonny Isle.
d. 11 *stanzas:* 1³,⁴, 3²,⁴; 4; 5, *in two forms,
  one struck out;* 6 (?), 20, 19, 9, 11 (?),
  12, 18, 16.

  5. 'I am sure they wad nae ca me wise,
      Gin I wad gang wi you, sir,
    For I can neither card nor spin,
      Nor yet milk ewe nor cow, sir.'

  6. 'My bonie Liza Baillie,
      Let nane o these things daunt ye;
    Ye 'll hae nae need to card or spin,
      Your mither weel can want ye.'

  9. She wad nae hae a Lawland laird,
      Nor be an English ladie,
    But she wad gang wi Duncan Grame,
      And row her in his plaidie.

  11. (?) She was nae ten miles frae the town
      When she began to weary;
    She often looked back and said,
      'Farewell to Castlecarry!'

  12. The first place I saw my Duncan Grame
      Was near yon holland-bush;
    My father took frae me my rings,
      My rings but and my purse.

  19. And she 's cast aff her bonie goun,
      Made o the silk and sattin,
    And she 's put on a tartan plaid,
      To row amang the bracken. (21⁴.)

  20. Now she 's cast aff her bonie shoon,
      Made o the gilded leather,
    And she 's put on her Highland brogues,
      To skip amang the heather.

This is enough to show the quality of d. *It
has been extensively corrupted.* 11 *is out
of character, and suggested by* 'Lizie
Lindsay.'

e. *Stanzas* 4, 5, 17, 20, 19, 9, *only.*
  5. 'If I wad gang alang wi you
      They wadna ca me wise, sir;
    For I can neither card nor spin,
      Nor yet can I speak Erse, sir.'

  9. She wadna hae a Lawland laird,
      Nor be a English lady,
    But she 's awa wi Duncan Grahame
      He 's rowd her in his plaidy.

  17. 'My bonny Lizie Baillie,
      Your minny canna want you;
    Sae let the trooper gang his lane,
      And carry his ain portmanteau.'

  19. *Nearly as in* d. A' wrought wi gowd an
    satin: To sport amang.
  20. *Nearly as in* d. Spanish leather.

17³,⁴ *is not intelligible, and may have slipped
in from some* "*Trooper*" *ballad.*
f. 10 *stanzas, edited from some copy of* d. f
    3–9, 10 = d 2–8, 12, *nearly.*
  1¹. Lammas time. 1². trees were.
  1³. L. B. gaed to Garter town.

  2, 3. She 'd no been lang in Garter town
      Till she met wi Duncan Graham,
    Wha kindly there saluted her,
      And wad convoy her hame.

  4². Ye 's hae a tartan plaidie.
  9³. wad gang wi Duncan Graham.
  9⁴. And wear a tartan plaidie.
  19¹. her lowland braws.
  19³. put on the worset gown.
  19⁴. To skip amang the breckin.

g. 14 stanzas.
  2. She meant to go unto that place
      To stay a little while;
    But mark what fortune her befell
      When she went to the Isle.

    It fell out upon a day,
      Sheep-shearing at an end,
    Lizie Baillie she walkd out,
      To see a distant friend.

  3. But going down in a low glen
      She met wi Duncan Græme,

Who courted her along the way,
Likewise convoyed her hame.

*The whole ballad is treated with the like
freedom and feebleness.*

22. 'O stay at hame,' her father said,
'Your mither cannot want thee;

And gin ye gang awa this night
We 'll hae a Killycrankie.'

Killycrankie *for a* row : *a droll emendation of*
a, *and the only spirited line in the piece.*

228

GLASGOW PEGGIE

A. 'Glasgow Peggie,' Sharpe's Ballad Book, p. 40.

B. a. 'Glasgow Peggy,' Kinloch's Ancient Scottish Ballads, p. 174. **b.** Kinloch MSS, VII, 259. **c.** 'Glasgow Peggie,' Aytoun's Ballads of Scotland, 1859, II, 230.

C. a. 'Galla Water,' 'Bonny Peggy,' Motherwell's MS., p. 89. **b.** 'Glasgow Peggie,' "Scotch Ballads,

Materials for Border Minstrelsy," No 116, and Sharpe's Ballad Book, ed. 1880, p. 137, one stanza.

D. 'Donald of the Isles,' Buchan's Ballads of the North of Scotland, II, 155.

E. 'Glasgow Peggy,' Christie, Traditional Ballad Airs, I, 70.

F. 'The Young Maclean,' Alexander Laing's MS., p. 5.

"COMMON in stalls," says Motherwell, "under this title ['Glasgow Peggie'], or that of the 'Earl of Hume,' or 'The Banks of Omey:'" Minstrelsy, p. xciii, note 133. In his MS., p. 90, the stall-copy is said to be better than the imperfect C a.

A young Highlander comes to Glasgow and is smitten with bonnie Peggie. Her father says the Highlander may steal cow or ewe, but not Peggie; and her mother asks in disgust whether her daughter, so long the object of her care, would end with going off in such company. For all that, Peggie goes. The Earl of Argyle, or the Earl of Hume, or the young Earl of Hume, takes this much to heart. The pair ride to a low glen in the

north country, and lie down on the grass. The Lowland lass has some compunctions, stimulated by the lack of the good beds at home. The captivating Highlander reassures her. He has the same comforts which she misses; they are his, and will soon be hers. He points out a fine castle which is his too, and he himself is Donald, Earl of Skye, and she will be a lady. B and E, to make the contrast of her two homes the greater, maintain that, despite her regrets for the comforts of her father's mansion, all that Peggie left was a wee cot-house and a wee kail-yairdie.

In the fragment F, Maclean replaces Macdonald.

A

Sharpe's Ballad Book, No XV, p. 40.

1 'As I cam in by Glasgow town,
    The Highland troops were a' before me,
And the bonniest lass that eer I saw,
    She lives in Glasgow, they ca her Peggie.

2 'I wad gie my bonnie black horse,
    So wad I my gude grey naigie,
If I were twa hundred miles in the north,
    And nane wi me but my bonnie Peggie.'

3 Up then spak her father dear,
    Dear wow! but he was wondrous sorrie;
'Weel may ye steal a cow or a yowe,
    But ye dare nae steal my bonnie Peggie.'

4 Up then spak her mother dear,
    Dear wow! but she spak wondrous sorrie;
Now since I have brought ye up this length,
    Wad ye gang awa wi a Highland fellow?'

5 He set her on his bonnie black horse,
    He set himsel on his gude gray naigie,
And they have ridden oer hills and dales,
    And he's awa wi his bonnie Peggie.

6 They have ridden oer hills and dales,
    They have ridden oer mountains many,
Until they cam to a low, low glen,
    And there he's lain down wi his bonnie
      Peggie.

7 Up then spak the Earl of Argyle,
    Dear wow! but he spak wondrous sorrie;

'The bonniest lass in a' Scotland
    Is off and awa wi a Highland fellow!'

8 Their bed was of the bonnie green grass,
    Their blankets war o the hay sae bonnie;
He folded his philabeg below her head,
    And he's lain down wi his bonnie Peggie.

9 Up then spak the bonny Lowland lass,
    And wow! but she spak wondrous sorrie;
'I 'se warrant my mither wad hae a gay sair
      heart
    To see me lien here wi you, my Willie.'

10 'In my father's house there's feather-beds,
    Feather-beds, and blankets mony;
They 're a' mine, and they'll sune be thine,
    And what needs your mither be sae sorrie,
      Peggie?

11 'Dinna you see yon nine score o kye,
    Feeding on yon hill sae bonnie?
They 're a' mine, and they'll sune be thine,
    And what needs your mither be sorrie,
      Peggie?

12 'Dinna ye see yon nine score o sheep,
    Feeding on yon brae sae bonnie?
They 're a' mine, and they'll sune be thine,
    And what needs your mither be sorrie for
      ye?

13 'Dinna ye see yon bonnie white house,
    Shining on yon brae sae bonnie?
And I am the Earl of the Isle of Skye,
    And surely my Peggie will be ca'd a lady.'

B

a. Kinloch's Ancient Scottish Ballads, p. 174; from recitation.   b. Kinloch MSS, VII, 259; "from Mrs K.'s recitation."   c. Aytoun's Ballads of Scotland, 1859, II, 230.

1 THE Lawland lads think they are fine,
    But the Hieland lads are brisk and gaucy,
And they are awa, near Glasgow toun,
    To steal awa a bonnie lassie.

2 'I wad gie my gude brown steed,
    And sae wad I my gude grey naigie,

That I war fifty miles frae the toun,
    And nane wi me but my bonnie Peggy.'

3 But up then spak the auld gudman,
    And vow! but he spak wondrous saucie;
'Ye may steal awa our cows and ewes,
    But ye sanna get our bonnie lassie.'

4 'I have got cows and ewes anew,
    I 've got gowd and gear already;
Sae I dinna want your cows nor ewes,
    But I will hae your bonnie Peggy.'

5 'I'll follow you oure moss and muir,
    I'll follow you oure mountains many,
I'll follow you through frost and snaw,
    I'll stay na langer wi my daddie.'

6 He set her on a gude brown steed,
    Himself upon a gude grey naigie;
They're oure hills, and oure dales,
    And he's awa wi his bonnie Peggy.

7 As they rade out by Glasgow toun,
    And doun by the hills o Achildounie,
There they met the Earl of Hume,
    And his auld son, riding bonnie.

8 Out bespak the Earl of Hume,
    And O! but he spak wondrous sorry;
'The bonniest lass about a' Glasgow toun
    This day is awa wi a Hieland laddie!'

9 As they rade bye auld Drymen toun,
    The lasses leuch and lookit saucy,
That the bonniest lass they ever saw
    Sud be riding awa wi a Hieland laddie.

10 They rode on through moss and muir,
    And so did they owre mountains many,
Until that they cam to yonder glen,
    And she's lain doun wi her Hieland laddie.

11 Gude green hay was Peggy's bed,
    And brakens war her blankets bonnie,
Wi his tartan plaid aneath her head;
    And she's lain doun wi her Hieland laddie.

12 'There's beds and bowsters in my father's
        house,
    There's sheets and blankets, and a' thing
        ready,
And wadna they be angry wi me,
    To see me lie sae wi a Hieland laddie!'

13 'Tho there's beds and beddin in your father's
        house,
    Sheets and blankets, and a' made ready,
Yet why sud they be angry wi thee,
    Though I be but a Hieland laddie?

14 'It's I hae fifty acres of land,
    It's a' plowd and sawn already;
I am Donald, the Lord of Skye,
    And why sud na Peggy be calld a lady?

15 'I hae fifty gude milk kye,
    A' tied to the staws already;
I am Donald, the Lord of Skye,
    And why sud na Peggy be calld a lady?

16 'See ye no a' yon castles and towrs?
    The sun sheens owre them a sae bonnie;
I am Donald, the Lord of Skye,
    I think I'll mak ye as blythe as onie.'

17 A' that Peggy left behind
    Was a cot-house and a wee kail-yardie;
Now I think she is better by far
    Than tho she had got a Lawland lairdie.

———◦———

C

a. Motherwell's MS., p. 89; from recitation. b. "Scotch
Ballads, Materials for Border Minstrelsy," No 116, and
Sharpe's Ballad Book, ed. 1880, p. 137, the last stanza.

* * * * * * *

1 'HE set her on his bonnie black horse,
    He set himsel on his good gray naigie;
He has ridden over hills, he has ridden over
        dales,
    And he's quite awa wi my bonny Peggy.

2 'Her brow it is brent and her middle it is jimp,
    Her arms are long and her fingers slender;

One sight of her eyes makes my very heart
        rejoice,
    And wae's my heart that we should sun-
        der!'

3 His sheets were of the good green hay,
    His blankets were of the brackens bonnie;
He's laid his trews beneath her head,
    And she's lain down wi her Highland lad-
        die.

4 'I am my mother's ae daughter,
    And she had nae mair unto my daddie,

And this night she would have a sore, sore
heart
  For to see me lye down with a Highland
laddie.'

5 'Ye are your mother's ae daughter,
  And she had nae mae unto your daddie;
This night she need not have a sore, sore heart
  For to see you lie down with a Highland
laddie.

6 'I have four-and-twenty acres of land,
  It is ploughed, it is sown, and is always
ready,

And you shall have servants at your command;
  And why should you slight a Highland laddie?

7 'I have four-and-twenty good milk-kye,
  They are feeding on yon meadow bonnie;
Besides, I have both lambs and ewes,
  Going low in the haughs o Galla water.

8 'My house it stands on yon hill-side,
  My broadsword, durk, and bow is ready,
And you shall have servants at your command;
  And why may not Peggy be called a lady?'

D

Buchan's Ballads of the North of Scotland, II, 155.

1 A BONNY laddie brisk and gay,
  A handsome youth sae brisk and gaddie,
And he is on to Glasgow town,
  To steal awa his bonny Peggy.

2 When he came into Glasgow town,
  Upon her father's green sae steady,
'Come forth, come forth, old man,' he says,
  'For I am come for bonny Peggy.'

3 Out it spake her father then;
  'Begone from me, ye Highland laddie;
There's nane in a' the West Country
  Dare steal from me my bonny Peggy.'

4 'I've ten young men all at my back,
  That ance to me were baith true and steady;
If ance I call, they'll soon be nigh,
  And bring to me my bonny Peggy.'

5 Out it spake her mother then,
  Dear! but she spake wondrous saucy;
Says, Ye may steal my cow or ewe,
  But I'll keep sight o my ain lassie.

6 'Hold your tongue, old woman,' he says,
  'Ye think your wit it is fu ready;
For cow nor ewe I ever stole,
  But I will steal your bonny Peggy.'

7 Then all his men they boldly came,
  That was to him baith true and steady,

And thro the ha they quickly went,
  And forth they carried bonny Peggy.

8 Her father gae mony shout and cry,
  Her mother cursed the Highland laddie;
But he heard them as he heard them not,
  But fixd his eye on bonny Peggy.

9 He set her on his milk-white steed,
  And he himsell on his grey naigie;
Still along the way they rode,
  And he's awa wi bonny Peggy.

10 Says, I wad gie baith cow and ewe,
  And sae woud I this tartan plaidie,
That I was far into the north,
  And alang wi me my bonny Peggy.

11 As they rode down yon pleasant glen,
  For trees and brambles were right mony,
There they met the Earl o Hume,
  And his young son, were riding bonny.

12 Then out it spake the young Earl Hume,
  Dear! but he spake wondrous gaudie;
'I'm wae to see sae fair a dame
  Riding alang wi a Highland laddie.'

13 'Hold your tongue, ye young Earl Hume,
  O dear! but ye do speak right gaudie;
There's nae a lord in a' the south
  Dare eer compete wi a Highland laddie.'

14 Then he rade five miles thro the north,
  Thro mony hills sae rough and scroggie,

Till they came down to a low glen,
   And he lay down wi bonny Peggy.

15 Then he inclosed her in his arms,
   And rowd her in his tartan plaidie :
'There are blankets and sheets in my father's
      house,
   How have I lien down wi a Highland lad-
      die !'

16 Says he, There are sheep in my father's fauld,
   And every year their wool is ready ;
By the same our debts we pay,
   Altho I be but a Highland laddie.

17 'There are fifty cows in my father's byre,
   That all are tyed to the stakes and ready ;
Five thousand pounds I hae ilk year,
   Altho I be but a Highland laddie.

18 'My father has fifty well shod horse,
   Besides your steed and my grey naigie ;
I 'm Donald o the Isle o Sky,
   Why may not you be ca'd a lady ?

19 'See ye not yon fine castle,
   On yonder hill that stands sae gaudie ?
And there we 'll win this very night,
   Where ye 'll enjoy your Highland laddie.'

E

Christie, Traditional Ballad Airs, I, 70, as sung by an
old woman living near Keith, Banffshire.

1 THE Hielan lads sae brisk and braw,
   The Hielan lads sae brisk and gaudie,
Hae gane awa to Glasgow town,
   To steal awa the bonny Peggy.

2 As they cam on to Glasgow town,
   And passd the banks and braes sae bonny,
There they espied the weel-faurd may,
   And she said to them her name was Peggy.

3 Their chief did meet her father soon,
   And O! but he was wondrous angry ;
Says, Ye may steal my owsen and kye,
   But ye maunna steal my bonnie Peggy.

4 'O haud your tongue, ye gude auld man,
   For I 've got cows and ewes already ;
I come na to steal your owsen and kye,
   But I will steal your bonny Peggy.'

5 He set her on a milk-white steed,
   And he himsel rode a gude grey naigie,

And they are on mony miles to the north,
   And nane wi them but the bonny Peggy.

6 'I hae fifty acres o gude red lan,
   And a' weel ploughd and sawn already,
And why should your father be angry wi me,
   And ca me naething but a Hielan laddie ?

7 'I hae twenty weel mounted steeds,
   Black and brown and grey, already ;
And ilk ane o them is tended by a groom,
   Altho I be but a Hielan laddie.

8 'I hae now ten thousand sheep,
   A' feeding on yon braes sae bonny,
And ilka hundred a shepherd has,
   Altho I be but a Hielan laddie.

9 'I hae a castle on yonder hill,
   It 's a' set roun wi windows many ;
I 'm Lord M'Donald o the whole Isle of Skye ;
   And why shouldna Peggy be ca'd my Lady ?'

10 Now a' that Peggy had before
   Was a wee cot-house and a little kail-yairdie,
But now she is lady o the whole Isle of Skye,
   And now bonny Peggy is ca'd my Lady.

F

Alexander Laing's MS., 1829, p. 5.

1 THE young Maclean is brisk an bauld,
  The young Maclean is rash an ready,
  An he is to the Lowlands gane,
  To steal awa a bonnie ladye.

*   *   *   *   *   *   *

2 Out an spak her auld father,
  An O! but he spak wondrous angry;

'Ye may steal my cows an ewes,
  But ye shall not steal my dochter Peggie.'

3 'O haud your tongue, ye gude auld man,
  For I hae gear enough already;
  I cum na for your cows an ewes,
  But I cum for your dochter Peggie.'

4 He set her on a milk-white steed,
  Himsel upon a gude gray naggie,
  An they are to the Highlands gane,
  The young Maclean an his bonnie ladye.

———————

B. b. *Stanzas* 7, 3, 12², 6, 4.

  3. And then out and spak her father dear,
       And oh! but he was wondrous angrie:
     'It's ye may steal my cows and ews,
       But ye maunna steal my bonnie Peggy.'

  4. 'Hold your tongue, you silly auld man,
       For ye 've said eneuch already;
     I 'll neither steal your cows nor ews,
       But I wat I 'll steal your bonnie Peggy.'

  6¹. He 's mounted her on a milk-white.
  6³. are ouer hill and they 're ouer dale.
  6⁴. he 's clean awa.   7¹. As I cam in by.
  7³. I met.   7⁴. son, war.
  12². Feather beds and bowsters many.   (A,
       10.²)
  c. "I have carefully collated these [*Kinloch's*
     copy, B a, *and Sharpe's,* A] with another
     copy, giving, for the most part, the pref-
     erence to the version of Mr Kinloch."
     *Readings (quite unimportant) which do
     not occur in* B a, A:
  1³. they hae come doun to Glasgow toun.
  2¹. O I.   2³. were a hundred.   4³. or.
  After 4, *cf.* A 4¹,²:

  But up then spak the auld gudewife,
    And wow! but she lookd wondrous yellow.

5¹⁻³. follow him.   5⁴. I 'll bide.   7¹. out frae.
7². And by the side o Antermony.
7⁴. Wi him his.   8². sadly *for* sorry.
10¹. It 's they.   11⁴. wi the.
12¹. There 's mair than ae bed in.
16². on them.   16³. It 's I.
C. b. 8. *In a letter of John Hamilton's to Sir
     W. Scott, dated August* 17, 1803 *("Scotch
     Ballads," etc., No* 116), *this stanza is given
     thus:*

My palace stands on yon burn-brae,
  My bow is bent an arrows ready;
My name is Donald, in the Isle of Sky,
  Although I be but a Highland laddie.

*Scott probably trusted to his memory when
making the following note to* a, *printed in
Sharpe's Ballad Book, ed.* 1880:

'I have a dirk and a gude claymore,
  My bow is bent and my arrow ready;
My castle stands in the Isle of Skye,
  Although I am but a Highland laddie.'

"The above stanza, which I got from the late
  Mr Hamilton, music-seller in Edinburgh,
  seems to belong to 'Glasgow Peggie.'"

229

EARL CRAWFORD

A. a. 'Earl Crawford,' Christie's Traditional Ballad Airs, I, 290, from recitation. **b.** From recitation.

B. 'Earl Crawford,' Buchan's Ballads of the North of Scotland, I, 61. Abridged, in Christie's Traditional Ballad Airs, I, 68.

A. ONE of seven handsome sisters makes a great match with the Earl of Crawford. In a fit of jealousy at the fondness which he shows his young son, Ladie Lillie addresses to her husband a quip on that head, to which the earl replies in the same tone. But the matter does not end there. The earl sets his wife on a horse, with her son, and sends her home to her father at Stobhall, never to enter his gates again. Her father is surprised that she should come without notice or attendants; she tells him that a word from her merry mouth has parted her and her lord. The father offers to make a better match for her; she would not give a kiss of Crawford's for all her father's gold. She sends a messenger to the earl to see whether he retains affection for her; word is brought back that she is to stay with her father and never enter Crawford's gates again. Her heart breaks. Her father puts on black, rides to Crawford's, and finds the earl just setting forth with a party to bring Lady Lillie home. Upon learning that his wife is dead, the earl declares that the sun shall nevermore shine on him.

B. Lady Crawford rides to her husband's castle in person to see if the earl will pity her. He shuts his gates and steeks his doors, and will neither come down to speak with her himself nor send his man. She retires weeping. The earl in turn now goes to the castle where his lady is lying, to see if she will pity him. She shuts the gates and steeks the doors, and will neither come down to speak with him nor send her waiting-maid. Not the less she takes to her bed, both she and Crawford die before morning, and both are buried in one tomb.

The late Earl of Crawford recognized an agreement with fact in some of the details of this story: Christie, I, 289. David, eleventh earl of Crawford, who succeeded his father in 1574, married Lilias Drummond, daughter of David, second Lord Drummond, the Laird of Stobhall. This was considered so great a match for the lady that a tocher was given with her "far beyond what was customary in those times, to wit, ten thousand merks." Although the peerages mention no children by this marriage, there is evidence that Earl David had by Lilias "an only child, David, who died in infancy." "These collateral verities" seemed to Earl Crawford "to found a presumption in favor of the truth of the main incident of the ballad." Crawford did not live at Crawford Castle, as the ballad has it. "That place had ceased to be the family residence for a long while. Earl David lived at Finhaven Castle, in Angus; not too far from Stobhall to be in keeping with the riding to and fro recorded in the ballad."

The first lines of the ballad are probably borrowed from 'Gil Brenton:' see No 5, A 43, B 34, C 1, D 1, H 1, 2. A 11, 12, B 15, 16, is a common-place: see most of the versions of 'Jamie Douglas,' No 204, and of 'The Braes o Yarrow,' No 214, and 'Clerk Saunders,' No 69, E 15, G 27.

B is translated by Gerhard, p. 108.

A

a. Christie's Traditional Ballad Airs, I, 290, as taken down 1867–73, from the recitation of Mrs Mary Robertson, wife of James Robertson, shoemaker, Bogmoor, near Fochabers. b. Obtained by Mr Macmath, March 25, 1890, from the daughter of Mrs Robertson, Mrs Mary Thomson, wife of James Thomson, gardener at Gordon Castle gardens, Fochabers.

1 O WE were sisters, sisters seven,
　　We were a comely crew to see,
　And some got lairds, and some got lords,
　　And some got knichts o hie degree;
　And I mysel got the Earl o Crawford,
　　And wasna that a great match for me!

2 It was at fifteen that I was married,
　　And at sixteen I had a son;
　And wasna that an age ower tender
　　For a lady to hae her first-born!
　　And wasna, etc.

3 But it fell ance upon a day
　　I gaed into the garden green,
　And naebody was therein walking
　　But Earl Crawford and his young son.

4 'I wonder at you, ye Earl Crawford,
　　I wonder at you wi your young son;
　Ye daut your young son mair than your Lillie;
　　[I 'm sure you got na him your lane.']

5 [He turned about upon his heel,
　　I wite an angry man was he;
　Says, If I got nae my young son my lane,
　　Bring me here the one that helpet me.]

6 ['O hold your tongue, my Earl Crawford,
　　And a' my folly lat it be;
　There was nane at the gettin o oor son,
　　Nae body only but you and me.']

7 He set her on a milk-white steed,
　　Her little young son her before;
　Says, Ye maun gae to bonny Stobha,
　　For ye will enter my yates no more.

8 When she cam to her father's bowers,
　　She lichtit low down on the stane,
　And wha sae ready as her auld father
　　To welcome Lady Lillie in?

9 'O how 's a' wi you, my daughter Lillie,
　　That ye come here sae hastilie?
　And how 's a' wi' the Earl o Crawford,
　　That he didna send a boy wi thee?'

10 'O haud your tongue now, my old father,
　　And ye 'll lat a' your folly be;
　For ae word that my merry mou spak
　　Has parted my good lord and me.'

11 'O haud your tongue, my daughter Lillie,
　　And a' your follies lat them be;
　I 'll double your portion ten times ower,
　　And a better match I 'll get for thee.'

12 'O haud your tongue now, my old father,
　　And a' your folly lat it be;
　I wouldna gie ae kiss o Crawford
　　For a' the goud that ye can gie.

13 'Whare will I get a bonny boy,
　　That 's willin to win meat and fee,
　Wha will gae on to Earl Crawford
　　An see an 's heart be fawn to me?'

14 When he cam to the yates o Crawford,
　　They were a' sitting down to dine:
　'How comes it now, ye Earl Crawford,
　　Ye arena takin Lady Lillie hame?'

15 'Ye may gae tell her Lady Lillie,
　　And ye maun neither lee nor len,
　She may stay in her father's bowers,
　　For she 'll not enter my yates again.'

16 When he cam back to her father's yates,
　　He lichtit low down on his knee:
　'What news, what news, my bonny boy?
　　What news, what news hae ye to me?'

17 'I 'm bidden tell you, Lady Lillie —
　　I 'm bidden neither to lee nor len —
　She may stay in her father's bowers,
　　For she 'll not enter my yates again.'

18 She stretched out her lily hand,
　　Says, 'Adieu, adieu to ane and a'!
　Adieu, adieu to Earl Crawford!'
　　Wi that her sair heart brak in twa.

19 Then dowie, dowie her father raise up,
　　And dowie, dowie the black put on,

And dowie, dowie he mounted the brown,
    And dowie, dowie sat thereon.

20 And dowie rade to the yates o Crawford,
    And when to Crawford's yates he came,
    They were a' dressd in the robes o scarlet,
    Just gaun to tak Lady Lillie hame.

21 'Ye may cast aff your robes o scarlet —
    I wyte they set you wondrous weel —

And now put on the black sae dowie,
    And come and bury your Lady Lill.'

22 He took his hat into his hand,
    And laid it low down by his knee:
    'An it be true that Lillie's dead,
    The sun shall nae mair shine on me.'

B

Buchan's Ballads of the North of Scotland, I, 61.

1 O WE were seven bonny sisters,
    As fair women as fair could be,
    And some got lairds, and some got lords,
    And some got knights o high degree:
    When I was married to Earl Crawford,
    This was the fate befell to me.

2 When we had been married for some time,
    We walked in our garden green,
    And aye he clappd his young son's head,
    And aye he made sae much o him.

3 I turnd me right and round about,
    And aye the blythe blink in my ee:
    'Ye think as much o your young son
    As ye do o my fair body.

4 'What need ye clap your young son's head?
    What need ye make so much o him?
    What need ye clap your young son's head?
    I'm sure ye gotna him your lane.'

5 'O if I gotna him my lane,
    Show here the man that helpëd me;
    And for these words your ain mouth spoke
    Heir o my land he neer shall be.'

6 He calld upon his stable-groom
    To come to him right speedilie:
    'Gae saddle a steed to Lady Crawford,
    Be sure ye do it hastilie.

7 'His bridle gilt wi gude red gowd,
    That it may glitter in her ee;

And send her on to bonny Stobha,
    All her relations for to see.'

8 Her mother lay oer the castle wa,
    And she beheld baith dale and down,
    And she beheld her Lady Crawford,
    As she came riding to the town.

9 'Come here, come here, my husband dear,
    This day ye see not what I see;
    For here there comes her Lady Crawford,
    Riding alane upon the lee.'

10 When she came to her father's yates,
    She tirled gently at the pin:
    'If ye sleep, awake, my mother dear,
    Ye'll rise lat Lady Crawford in.'

11 'What news, what news, ye Lady Crawford,
    That ye come here so hastilie?'
    'Bad news, bad news, my mother dear,
    For my gude lord's forsaken me.'

12 'O wae's me for you, Lady Crawford,
    This is a dowie tale to me;
    Alas! you were too young married
    To thole sic cross and misery.'

13 'O had your tongue, my mother dear,
    And ye'll lat a' your folly be;
    It was a word my merry mouth spake
    That sinderd my gude lord and me.'

14 Out it spake her brither then,
    Aye as he stept ben the floor:
    'My sister Lillie was but eighteen years
    When Earl Crawford ca'ed her a whore.'

15 'But had your tongue, my sister dear,
  And ye 'll lat a' your mourning bee;
  I 'll wed you to as fine a knight,
  That is nine times as rich as hee.'

16 'O had your tongue, my brither dear,
  And ye 'll lat a' your folly bee;
  I 'd rather yae kiss o Crawford's mouth
  Than a' his gowd and white monie.

17 'But saddle to me my riding-steed,
  And see him saddled speedilie,
  And I will on to Earl Crawford's,
  And see if he will pity me.'

18 Earl Crawford lay o'er castle wa,
  And he beheld baith dale and down,
  And he beheld her Lady Crawford,
  As she came riding to the town.

19 He called ane o his livery men
  To come to him right speedilie:
  'Gae shut my yates, gae steek my doors,
  Keep Lady Crawford out frae me.'

20 When she came to Earl Crawford's yates,
  She tirled gently at the pin:
  'O sleep ye, wake ye, Earl Crawford,
  Ye 'll open, lat Lady Crawford in.

21 'Come down, come down, O Earl Crawford,
  And speak some comfort unto me;
  And if ye winna come yoursell,
  Ye 'll send your gentleman to me.'

22 'Indeed I winna come mysell,
  Nor send my gentleman to thee;
  For I tauld you when we did part
  Nae mair my spouse ye 'd ever bee.'

23 She laid her mouth then to the yates,
  And aye the tears drapt frae her ee;
  Says, Fare ye well, Earl Crawford's yates,
  You again I 'll nae mair see.

24 Earl Crawford calld on his stable-groom
  To come to him right speedilie,
  And sae did he his waiting-man,
  That did attend his fair bodie.

25 'Ye will gae saddle for me my steed,
  And see and saddle him speedilie,
  And I 'll gang to the Lady Crawford,
  And see if she will pity me.'

26 Lady Crawford lay oer castle-wa,
  And she beheld baith dale and down,
  And she beheld him Earl Crawford,
  As he came riding to the town.

27 Then she has calld ane o her maids
  To come to her right speedilie:
  'Gae shut my yates, gae steek my doors,
  Keep Earl Crawford out frae me.'

28 When he came to Lady Crawford's yates,
  He tirled gently at the pin:
  'Sleep ye, wake ye, Lady Crawford,
  Ye 'll rise and lat Earl Crawford in.

29 'Come down, come down, O Lady Crawford,
  Come down, come down, and speak wi me;
  And gin ye winna come yoursell,
  Ye 'll send your waiting-maid to me.'

30 'Indeed I winna come mysell,
  Nor send my waiting-maid to thee;
  Sae take your ain words hame again
  At Crawford castle ye tauld me.

31 'O mother dear, gae make my bed,
  And ye will make it saft and soun,
  And turn my face unto the west,
  That I nae mair may see the sun.'

32 Her mother she did make her bed,
  And she did make it saft and soun;
  True were the words fair Lillie spake,
  Her lovely eyes neer saw the sun.

33 The Earl Crawford mounted his steed,
  Wi sorrows great he did ride hame;
  But ere the morning sun appeard
  This fine lord was dead and gane.

34 Then on ae night this couple died,
  And baith were buried in ae tomb:
  Let this a warning be to all,
  Their pride may not bring them low down.

A. a. 4[4], 5, 6. *Omitted; supplied from* b. *Dean Christie notes that the lines omitted will be found in a copy which, with other things of the kind, he had destined for use in this collection. Unfortunately, and quite unaccountably, these pieces never came to hand.*

19[2]. put on the black.

b. *Of* b, *which was obtained some twenty years after* a *was written down, Mrs Thomson says:* Enclosed is the whole of the ballad, as I had it from my mother. . . . She never sang those two verses to us [5, 6]. She only repeated them to me when Dean Christie wanted the ballad. *We may, perhaps, infer from these last words that the ballad was originally taken down by the daughter from her mother's recitation, and not by Dean Christie. It is to be observed that the mother was still living in* 1890, *but when* b *was committed to paper is not said.*

a 8[3, 4], 9[1, 2], *are wanting in* b; b *has a stanza, an inevitable one, which* a *lacks, in answer to* 13.

1[1]. It 's we were sisters and.

1[3]. Some got dukes. 1[4]. got men.

1[5]. But I : Earl Crawford. 1[6]. a meet.

2[1]. Fifteen years that.

2[2]. And sixteen years I.

2[3]. that a tender age.

3[2]. We were walking in yon.

3[3]. There was nae body walking there.

3[4]. But the earl himself and. 4[1]. you, Earl.

4[2]. You mak sae much o your.

4[3]. I wonder at you, Earl Crawford.

4[4], 5, 6. *Inserted in* a.

7[2]. little son he set her.

7[3]. gee on to your father's bowers.

8[2]. down on her knee. 8[3, 4], 9[1, 2], *wanting.*

9[3]. Hoo 's a', hoo 's a. 9[4]. thee wi.

10[1]. now *wanting.* 10[2]. And a' my folly lat it.

10[3]. For one : mouth. 11[1]. my Lady.

11[2]. And I 'll lat a' your folly.

11[3]. portion oer again.

11[4]. I 'll provide for.

12[1]. now *wanting.*

12[2]. And speak nae mair o this to me.

12[3]. For I wad nae. 12[4]. ye could.

13[3]. That will : Crawford's.

13[4]. see gin 's hairt be faen tae.

After 13 :

'O here am I, a bonny boy,
  That 's willin to win meat and fee,
That will go on to Earl Crawford's,
  And see an 's hairt be faen to thee.'

14[1]. to Earl Crawford's gates.

14[2]. He lighted low down on a stane.

14[3]. Says, I wonder at you, E. C.

14[4]. You 'r nae gaun to tak.

15[1]. tell to Lady. 15[2]. Ye may neither.

15[3]. stay weel in. 15[4]. she 'll never.

16[1]. came to her father's bowers.

17[1]. tell to Lady.

17[3]. You 'r bidden stay well in your.

17[4]. For yu 'll never enter his. 18[1]. lily-white.

18[3]. to the Earl himsell.

18[4]. And wi that her bonny hairt did brack.

19[1]. Dowie, dowie raise up her father.

19[2]. And *wanting :* the black put on.

19[3]. And *wanting :* his steed he mounted.

20[1]. When he came to Earl Crawford's gates.

20[2]. They were all going to dine.

20[3]. And were all drest in robes of white.

21[1]. He says, You may put aff the robes o white.

21[3]. And ye 'll put on the dowie black.

22[1]. Earl Crawford took his hat in 's hand.

22[3]. Says, If this be true that L[ady] L[illie 's].

22[4]. sin shall never shine.

230

THE SLAUGHTER OF THE LAIRD OF MELLERSTAIN

In a folio volume with the title "Miscellanies," the last piece in the volume, Abbotsford.

BIRREL'S Diary has this entry under date of January 3, 1603: "The 3 of Januar Johne Hai[t]lie of Millstanes slaine at the Salt Tron be Williame Home hes guidfather. This William of Ball[int]a wes of the hous of Cowdenknowis." P. 57. In a proclamation of the Privy Council against reset of criminals, 20th January, 1603, the list of cases begins with "the reset of the persons who lately most shamefully and barbarously slew the Laird of Mellestanes." Register, VI, 525 f. There is nothing to show that these persons were ever brought to justice, and the efforts made by the public authorities to stop hostilities between the families concerned were, as usual, not readily successful. April 28, 1608, the parties to the "feud between James Haitlie, now of Mellirstanes [son of John], and Mr James Home of Eccles, on account of the slaughter of John Haitlie of Mellirstanes," are ordered to appear before the Council on the 12th of May following, to be reconciled and to chop hands together. Register, VIII, 81 f.

An entry of the 4th of December, 1599, censures Sir George Home, sheriff of Berwick, for not proceeding against "William Home, younger, called of Coldenknowis and now of Ballinta, who slew within the said shire Mr Alexander Dicksoun," and was denounced therefor 29th December, 1596. This William we may presume to have been the undegenerate son of the William whom Birrel calls Mellerstain's "guidfather." Register, VI, 57.

The lady of st. 1 was Marion Lumsden (otherwise Mariot, Margaret), "Lady Mellirstanes," "relicta Joannis Haitlie de Mellerstanes." Register P. C., VIII, 101; 366, Register of the Great Seal, VI, 722. Mellerstain stands on a rising ground near the right bank of the Eden, 1^2. Cowdenknows in 3^1 may have been Sir John Home of Cowdenknows, named as one of the curators of James Haitlie (a minor in 1607). Earlstoun is not determinate. Bemerside is an alternative reading for Earlstoun. The laird of Bemerside at the date of the slaughter was the turbulent James Haig. The lady in st. 4 is looking in several directions for the arrival of her husband's body. (I have not found Fieldiesha and Yirdandstane.) The Salt Tron is a locality of much note in the history of Edinburgh: see Wilson's Memorials, p. 249.

This fragment appears to have come into Sir Walter Scott's hands through Mr W. Yellowlees, who filled out two of the defective stanzas, and appended some remarks under the date of 29th October, 1828.*

---

1 .   .   .   .
  As they came in by the Eden side,
They heard a lady lamenting sair,
  Bewailing the time she was a bride.

2 .   .   .   .
  A stately youth of blude and lane,

John Hately, the laird of Mellerstain.

3 'Cowdenknows, had ye nae lack?
  And Earlstoun, had ye nae shame?

* It would have come in earlier (as No 195), had it been discovered in time.

Ye took him away beside my back,
  But ye never saw to bring him hame.'

4 And she has lookit to Fieldiesha,
  So has she through Yirdandstane ;
  She lookit to Earlstoun, and she saw the Fans,
  But he 's coming hame by West Gordon.

5 And she staggerd and she stood,

6 '. . . . . . .
  . . . . . wude ;
  How can I keep in my wits,
  When I look on my husband's blood ? '

7 'Had we been men as we are women,
  And been at his back when he was slain,
  It should a been tauld for mony a lang year,
  The slaughter o the laird of Mellerstain.'

2⁴. James John Hately. 3². Earlstoun Bemerside had.
Between 3 and 4 are two half stanzas which belong to ' James Hatley,' No. 241, *and are there given.*

4¹. Fieldies ha.
4². yird and stane.

231

THE EARL OF ERROL

A. a. 'Kate Carnegie,' Campbell MSS, II, 94. b. The Edinburgh Magazine, or Literary Miscellany, June, 1803, p. 458.

B. Skene MS., p. 113.

C. 'The Countess of Erroll,' Buchan's Ballads of the North of Scotland, II, 176.

D. a. 'Lord and Lady Errol,' Buchan's Gleanings, p. 158. b. 'Errol's Place,' Maidment's North Countrie Garland, p. 31. c. 'Earl of Errol,' Kinloch's Ballad Book, p. 31.

E. Letters from and to Charles Kirkpatrick Sharpe, edited by Alexander Allardyce, I, 180 ; Sharpe's Ballad Book, p. 89, No. 31.

F. 'The Earl of Erroll,' Kinloch MSS, III, 133.

SIR GILBERT HAY, tenth Earl of Errol, was married to Lady Catherine Carnegy. younger daughter of James, second Earl of Southesk, January 7, 1658, and had no children by her. He died in 1674. The ballad, says the person who communicated A b to the Edinburgh Miscellany, was " founded, it would seem, on some attempt to withhold from the Earl of Errol his consort's portion." It will be observed that the father proposes a beguil-ing to his daughter, and that she is ready to assent, in A, 12, 13.

It appears from a letter cited by Sharpe in his Ballad Book that the matters treated in the ballad were agitating, and had even " come to public hearing," in February, 1659.

Sir John Hay of Killour, as the nearest male heir, became the eleventh Earl of Errol. His wife was Lady Anne Drummond, only daughter of James, third Earl of Perth, so that the Earl of Perth might seem to have an interest in this affair of Errol's. She, however, was not born till January, 1656. Perth is actually made the other party in legal proceedings in **A a 1**, but in **A b** seems to espouse Errol's side.

Carnegy's other daughter, who in most of the versions censures her sister's conduct, is called Jean in **A 5, D a 7, F 10,** Anne in **D b c.** These are stock ballad-names, and we need not suppose that Anne comes from Lady Anne Drummond. The older daughter's name was Elizabeth.

Errol is in the Carse of Gowrie, a tract noted for its fertility ; which accounts for **B 2, D a 1, D c 1, F 2.**

E, F go the length of imputing to Lady Errol an attempt to poison her husband with wine which she offers him. A page, of Errol's kin, exposes her in **E** ; in **F** Errol gives the drink to a greyhound, and the dog bursts.

The last stanza of **A b, C, D c** has reference to "the ancient separate maintenance of a lady dissatisfied with or apart from her husband." (Edinburgh Magazine, as above.)

E is introduced in Sharpe's letter by some pages of mild pleasantry in the form of a preface to "a specimen of the fourth volume of the Border Minstrelsy, speedily to be published."

A

a. Campbell MSS., II, 94. b. The Edinburgh Magazine, or Literary Miscellany, June, 1803, p. 458.

1 THERE was a jury sat at Perth,
  In the merry month of May,
  Betwixt the noble Duke of Perth
  But and Sir Gilbert Hay.

2 My lord Kingside has two daughters,
  They are proper, straight and tall ;
  But my lord Carnegie he has two
  That far excells them all.

3 Then Errol he has dressd him,
  As very well he could ;
  I 'm sure there was not one cloth-yard
  But what was trimmd with gold.

4 'Ane asking, ane asking, my lord Carnegie,
  Ane asking I 've to thee ;
  I 'm come to court your daughter Jean,
  My wedded wife to be.'

5 'My daughter Jean was wed yestreen,
  To one of high degree,
  But where Jean got one guinea of gold
  With Kate I 'll give thee three.

6 'Full fifteen hundred pounds
  Had Jean Carnegie,
  But three fifteen hundred pounds
  With Kate I 'll gie to thee.'

7 Then Errol he has wed her,
  And fairly brought her hame ;
  There was nae peace between them twa
  Till they sundered oer again.

8 When bells were rung, and mess was sung,
  And a' man bound to bed,
  The Earl of Errol and his countess
  In one chamber was laid.

9 Early in the morning
  My lord Carnegie rose,
  The Earl of Errol and his countess,
  And they 've put on their clothes.

10 Up spake my lord Carnegie ;
  'Kate, is your toucher won ?'
  'Ye may ask the Earl of Errol,
  If he be your good-son.

11 'What need I wash my petticoat
  And hing it on a pin ?
  For I am as leal a maid yet
  As yestreen when I lay down.

12 'What need I wash my apron
  And hing it on the door ?
  It 's baith side and wide enough,
  Hangs even down before.'

13 Up spake my lord Carnegie ;
  'O Kate, what do ye think ?

We 'll beguile the Earl of Errol
    As lang as he 's in drink.'

14 'O what will ye beguile him wi ?
    Or what will ye do than ?
    I 'll swear before a justice-court
    That he 's no a sufficient man.'

15 Then Errol he cam down the stair,
    As bold as oney rae :
    'Go saddle to me my Irish coach,
    To Edinbro I 'll go.'

16 When he came to Edinbro,
    He lighted on the green ;
    There were four-and-twenty maidens
    A' dancing in a ring.

17 There were four-and-twenty maidens
    A' dancing in a row ;
    The fatest and the fairest
    To bed wi him must go.

18 He 's taen his Peggy by the hand,
    And he led her thro the green,
    And twenty times he kissd her there,
    Before his ain wife's een.

19 He 's taen his Peggy by the hand,
    And he 's led her thro the hall,
    And twenty times he 's kissd her there,
    Before his nobles all.

20 'Look up, look up, my Peggy lass,
    Look up, and think nae shame ;
    Ten hundred pounds I 'll gie to you
    To bear to me a son.'

21 He 's keepit his Peggy in his room
    Three quarter of a year,
    And just at the nine months' end
    She a son to him did bear.

22 'Now if ye be Kate Carnegie,
    And I Sir Gilbert Hay,
    I 'll make your father sell his lands
    Your toucher for to pay.'

23 'To make my father sell his lands,
    It wad be a great sin,
    To toucher oney John Sheephead
    That canna toucher win.'

24 'Now hold your tongue, ye whorish bitch,
    Sae loud as I hear ye lie !
    For yonder sits Lord Errol's son,
    Upon his mother's knee ;
    For yonder sits Lord Errol's son,
    Altho he 's no by thee.'

25 'You may take hame your daughter Kate,
    And set her on the glen ;
    For Errol canna please her,
    Nor nane o Errol's men ;
    For Errol canna please her,
    Nor twenty of his men.'

26 The ranting and the roving,
    The thing we a' do ken,
    The lady lost her right that night,
    The first night she lay down ;
    And the thing we ca the ranting o 't,
    The lady lies her lane.

B

Skene MS., p. 113 ; taken down from recitation in the
north of Scotland, 1802–3.

1 EARELL is a bonny place,
    It stands upon yon plain ;
    The greatest faut about the place
    Earell 's no a man.
        What ye ca the danting o 't,
        According as ye ken,
        For the pearting . . .
        Lady Earell lyes her lane.

2 Earell is a bonny place,
    It stands upon yon plain ;
    The roses they graw red an white,
    An apples they graw green.

3 'What need I my apron wash
    An hing upon yon pin ?
    For lang will I gae out an in
    Or I hear my bairnie's din.

4 'What need I my apron wash
    An hing upo yon door ?

For side and wide is my petticoat,
   An even down afore.

5 'But I will lace my stays again,
   My middle jimp an sma;
 I 'l gae a' my days a maiden,
   [Awa], Earell, awa!'

6 It fell ance upon a day Lord Earell
   Went to hunt him lane,

   .   .   .   .

     .   .   .   .

7 He was na a mile fra the town,
   Nor yet sae far awa,
 Till his lady is on to Edinburgh,
   To try hir all the law.

8 Little did Lord Earell think,
   Whan he sat down to dine,
 That his lady was on to Edinburgh,
   Nor what was in her mind.

9 Till his best servant came
   For to lat him ken

   .   .   .   .

     .   .   .   .

10 She was na in at the toun-end,
   Nor yet sae far awa,
 Till Earell was at her back,
   His gaudy locks to sha.

11 She was na in at the loan-head,
   Nor just at the end,
 Till Earell he was at her back,
   Her errand for to ken.

12 'As lang as they ca ye Kate Carnegie,
   An me Sir Gilbert Hay,
 I 's gar yer father sell Kinaird,
   Yer tocher for to pay.'

13 'For to gar my father sell Kinnaird,
   It wad be a sin,
 To gee it to ony naughty knight
   That a tocher canna win.'

14 Out spak the first lord,
   The best amang them a';
 'I never seed a lady come
   Wi sick matters to the law.'

15 Out spak the neest lord,
   The best o the town;
 'Ye get fifteen well-fared maids,
   An put them in a roun,
 An Earell in the midst o them,
   An lat him chuse out ane.'

16 They ha gotten fifteen well-fared maids,
   An pit them in a roun,
 An Earell in the mids o them,
   An bad him chuse out ane.

17 He viewed them a' intill a raw,
   Even up an down,
 An he has chosen a well-fared may,
   An Meggie was her name.

18 He took her by the hand,
   Afore the nobles a',
 An twenty times he kissed her mou,
   An led her thro the ha.

19 'Look up, Megie, look up, Megie,
   [Look up,] an think na shame;
 As lang as ye see my gaudy locks,
   Lady Earell 's be yer name.'

20 There were fifteen noblemen,
   An as mony ladies gay,
 To see Earell proven a man

   .   .   .   .

21 'Ye tak this well-fared may,
   And keep her three roun raiths o a year,
 An even at the three raiths' end
   I sall draw near.'

22 They hae taen that well-fared may,
   An keepd her three roun raiths o a year,
 And even at the three raiths' end
   Earell's son she bare.

23 The gentlemen they ga a shout,
   The ladies ga a caa,
 Fair mat fa him Earell!
   But ran to his lady.

24 He was na in at the town-head,
   Nor just at the end,
 Till the letters they were waiting him
   That Earell had a son.

25 'Look up, Meggie, look up, Meggie,
　　[Look up,] an think na shame;
　　As lang as ye see my bra black hat,
　　Lady Earell 's be yer name.

26 'I will gie my Meggie a mill,
　　But an a piece o land,
　　. 　. 　. 　. 　. 　. 　.
　　To foster my young son.

27 'Faur is a' my merry men a',
　　That I pay meat an gaire,
　　To convey my Meggy hame,
　　. 　. 　. 　. 　. 　.?'

28 . 　. 　. 　. 　. 　. 　.
　　. 　. 　. 　. 　. 　. 　.
　　Even in Lord Earell's coach
　　They conveyed the lassie hame.

29 'Take hame yer daughter, Lord Kinnaird,
　　An take her to the glen,
　　For Earell canna pleas her,
　　Earell nor a' his men.'

30 'Had I ben Lady Earell,
　　Of sic a bonny place,
　　I wad na gaen to Edinburgh
　　My husband to disgrace.'

———◆———

C

Buchan's Ballads of the North of Scotland, II, 176.

1 ERROLL it 's a bonny place,
　　It stands upon a plain;
　　A bad report this ladie 's raisd,
　　That Erroll is nae a man.

2 But it fell ance upon a day
　　Lord Erroll went frae hame,
　　And he is on to the hunting gane,
　　Single man alane.

3 But he hadna been frae the town
　　A mile but barely twa,
　　Till his lady is on to Edinburgh,
　　To gain him at the law.

4 O Erroll he kent little o that
　　Till he sat down to dine,
　　And as he was at dinner set
　　His servant loot him ken.

5 'Now saddle to me the black, the black,
　　Go saddle to me the brown,
　　And I will on to Edinburgh,
　　Her errands there to ken.'

6 She wasna well thro Aberdeen,
　　Nor passd the well o Spa,
　　Till Erroll he was after her,
　　The verity to shaw.

7 She wasna well in Edinburgh,
　　Nor even thro the town,
　　Till Erroll he was after her,
　　Her errands there to ken.

8 When he came to the court-house,
　　And lighted on the green,
　　This lord was there in time enough
　　To hear her thus compleen:

9 'What needs me wash my apron,
　　Or drie 't upon a door?
　　What needs I eek my petticoat,
　　Hings even down afore?

10 'What needs me wash my apron,
　　Or hing it upon a pin?
　　For lang will I gang but and ben
　　Or I hear my young son's din.'

11 'They ca you Kate Carnegie,' he says,
　　'And my name 's Gilbert Hay;
　　I 'll gar your father sell his land,
　　Your tocher down to pay.'

12 'To gar my father sell his land
　　For that would be a sin,
　　To such a noughtless heir as you,
　　That canno get a son.'

13 Then out it speaks him Lord Brechen,
　　The best an lord ava;
　　'I never saw a lady come
　　Wi sic matters to the law.'

14 Then out it speaks another lord,
　　The best in a' the town;

' Ye 'll wyle out fifeteen maidens bright
    Before Lord Erroll come : '
And he has chosen a tapster lass,
    And Meggie was her name.

15 They kept up this fair maiden
    Three quarters of a year,
And then at that three quarters' end
    A young son she did bear.

16 They hae gien to Meggie then
    Five ploughs but and a mill,
And they hae gien her five hundred pounds,
    For to bring up her chill.

17 There was no lord in Edinburgh
    But to Meggie gae a ring ;
And there was na a boy in a' the town
    But on Katie had a sang.

18 ' Kinnaird, take hame your daughter,
    And set her to the glen,
For Erroll canna pleasure her,
    Nor nane o Erroll's men.'

19 Seven years on Erroll's table
    There stand clean dish and speen,
And every day the bell is rung,
    Cries, Lady, come and dine.

D

a. Buchan's Gleanings, p. 158.   b. Maidment's North Countrie Garland, p. 31.   c. Kinloch's Ballad Book, p. 31.

1 O ERROL's place is a bonny place,
    It stands upon yon plain ;
The flowers on it grow red and white,
    The apples red and green.
      The ranting o 't and the danting o 't,
        According as ye ken,
      The thing they ca the danting o 't,
        Lady Errol lies her lane.

2 O Errol's place is a bonny place,
    It stands upon yon plain ;
But what 's the use of Errol's place ?
    He 's no like other men.

3 ' As I cam in by yon canal,
    And by yon bowling-green,
I might hae pleased the best Carnegy
    That ever bore that name.

4 ' As sure 's your name is Kate Carnegy,
    And mine is Gibbie Hay,
I 'll gar your father sell his land,
    Your tocher for to pay.'

5 ' To gar my father sell his land,
    Would it not be a sin,
To give it to a naughtless lord
    That couldna get a son ? '

6 Now she is on to Edinburgh,
    For to try the law,

And Errol he has followed her,
    His manhood for to shaw.

7 Then out it spake her sister,
    Whose name was Lady Jane ;
' Had I been Lady Errol,' she says,
    ' Or come of sic a clan,
I would not in this public way
    Have sham'd my own gudeman.'

8 But Errol got it in his will
    To choice a maid himsel,
And he has taen a country-girl,
    Came in her milk to sell.

9 He took her by the milk-white hand,
    And led her up the green,
And twenty times he kissd her there,
    Before his lady's een.

10 He took her by the milk-white hand,
    And led her up the stair ;
Says, Thrice three hundred pounds I 'll gie
    To you to bear an heir.

11 He kept her there into a room
    Three quarters of a year,
And when the three quarters were out
    A braw young son she bear.

12 ' Tak hame your daughter, Carnegy,
    And put her till a man,
For Errol he cannot please her,
    Nor any of his men.'

E

C. K. Sharpe's Letters, ed. Allardyce, I, 180 ff; written down from the recitation of Violet Roddick, a woman living near Hoddam Castle, 1803. Sharpe's Ballad Book, 1823, p. 89.

1   O ERROL it 's a bonny place,
    It stands in yonder glen;
The lady lost the rights of it
    The first night she gaed hame.
      A waly and a waly!
       According as ye ken,
    The thing we ca the ranting o 't,
    Our lady lies her lane, O.

2   'What need I wash my apron,
    Or hing it on yon door?
What need I truce my petticoat?
    It hangs even down before.'

3   Errol 's up to Edinburgh gaen,
    That bonny burrows-town;
He has chusit the barber's daughter,
    The top of a' that town.

4   He has taen her by the milk-white hand,
    He has led her through the room,
And twenty times he 's kisst her,
    Before his lady's een.

5   'Look up, look up now, Peggy,
    Look up, and think nae shame,
For I 'll gie thee five hundred pound,
    To buy to thee a gown.

6   'Look up, look up, now, Peggy,
    Look up, and think nae shame,
For I 'll gie thee five hundred pound
    To bear to me a son.

7   'As thou was Kate Carnegie,
    And I Sir Gilbert Hay,
I 'll gar your father sell his lands,
    Your tocher-gude to pay.

8   'Now he may take her back again,
    Do wi her what he can,
For Errol canna please her,
    Nor ane o a' his men.'

9   'Go fetch to me a pint of wine,
    Go fill it to the brim,
That I may drink my gude lord's health,
    Tho Errol be his name.'

10   She has taen the glass into her hand,
    She has putten poison in,
She has signd it to her dorty lips,
    But neer a drop went in.

11   Up then spake a little page,
    He was o Errol's kin;
'Now fie upon ye, lady gay,
    There 's poison there within.

12   'It 's hold your hand now, Kate,' he says,
    'Hold it back again,
For Errol winna drink on 't,
    Nor none o a' his men.'

13   She has taen the sheets into her arms,
    She has thrown them oer the wa:
'Since I maun gae maiden hame again,
    Awa, Errol, awa!'

14   She 's down the back o the garden,
    And O as she did murne!
'How can a workman crave his wage,
    When he never wrought a turn?'

———◆———

F

Kinloch MSS, III, 133.

1   O ERROLL is a bonny place,
    And stands upon yon plane,
But the lady lost the rights o it
    Yestreen or she came hame.

2   O Erroll is a bonny place,
    And lyes forenent the sun,
And the apples they grow red and white,
    And peers o bonny green.

3   'I nedna wash my apron,
    Nor hing it on the door;
But I may tuck my petticoat,
    Hangs even down before.

4   'Oh, Erroll, Erroll,
    Oh, Erroll if ye ken,

Why should I love Erroll,
  Or any of his men ? '

5 She 's turned her right and round about,
    Poured out a glass o wine ;
  Says, I will drink to my true love,
    He 'll drink to me again.

6 O Erroll stud into the fleer,
    He was an angry man :
  ' See here it is a good gray-hun,
    We 'll try what is the run.'

7 Then Erroll stud into the fleer,
    Steered neither ee nor bree,
  Till that he saw his good gray-hun
    Was burst and going free.

8 ' But ye are Kate Carnegie,' he said,
    ' And I am Sir Gilbert Hay ;
  I 'se gar your father sell Kinnaird,
    Your tocher-good to pay.'

9 Now she is on to Edinburgh,
    A' for to use the law,
  And brave Erroll has followed her,
    His yellow locks to sheu.

10 Out and spak her sister Jean,
    And an angry woman was she ;
  ' If I were lady of Erroll,
    And hed as fair a face,
  I would no go to Edinburgh,
    My good lord to disgrace.'

A. a. 23⁴. toucher one.
    26. *May have been a burden.*

  b. Ballad of Gilbert, Earl of Errol, and Lady Cath-
      erine Carnegie.

      .   .   .   .   °

13 Up spake Lord Carnegie,
    ' O Kate, what do you think ?
  We 'll beguile the Earl of Errol,
    As long as he 's in drink.'

14 ' O what need you beguile him?
    Or what would you do than?
  For I can easy vow and testify
    Lord Errol 's not a man.

12 ' You need not wash my petticoat
    And hang it at the door ;
  For it 's baith side and wide enough,
    And hangs even down before.

11 ' You need not wash my apron
    And hang it on a pin ;
  For I 'm as leil a maiden
    As first when I went in.'

15 Down came the Earl of Errol,
    As swift as any roe :
  ' Come harness me my Irish coach,
    To Edinburgh I go.'

16 And when he came to Edinburgh,
    A ganging through the green,
  Full four-and-twenty maidens
    A' dancing there were seen.

17 And there were fifteen maidens
    All dancing in a row,
  And the fairest and the fattest
    To prove that she must go.

18 He 's taen his Peggy by the hand,
    And led her through the green,
  And twenty times he 's kissed her,
    Before his lady's een.

19 He 's taen his Peggy by the hand,
    And led her through the hall,
  And twenty times he 's kissed her,
    Before the nobles all.

  He 's taen his Peggy by the hand,
    And led her to a room,
  And gave her a cup of claret wine,
    And syne a bed of down.

20¹,² ' Stand up, stand up, my Peggy,
    Stand up, and think na shame,
  Na hide your face within your hand,
    On me be all the blame.

  ' For you shall have a thousand pounds
    As soon as it is won,
20³,⁴ And you shall have ten thousand pounds
    If you bear to me a son.'

21 He kept his Peggy in a room
    Full nine months and a day,
  And at the very nine months' end
    She bore a son so gay.

As they were all at dinner sat,
　　And merrily went the can,
Up spake the noble Earl of Perth,
　　'Kate, what ails you at your man?'

'Oh, all the lands and earldom
　　Are now to ruin gone,
For I can easy vow and testify
　　He'll never get a son.'

24¹⁻⁴ 'Ye lie, ye lie, you filthy jade,
　　So loud I hear you lie!
For there sits Lord Errol's son,
　　Upon his mither's knee.'

22 'As you are Kate Carnegie
　　And I Sir Gilbert Hay,
I'll gar your father sell his land
　　Your tocher for to pay.'

23 'To gar my father sell his land
　　I'm sure would be a sin,
For to tocher any John Sheephead
　　Who could neer a tocher win.'

25¹⁻⁴ 'You may take hame your daughter Kate,
　　And set her in a glen,
For Lord Errol cannot please her,
　　Nor none of Errol's men.

'You may provide a knife and fork,
　　A trencher and a spoon,
A little boy to call her,
　　Come to your dinner, dame;
A little boy to call her
　　Till seven years are done.'

B. *Written in long lines, without division into stanzas ; carelessly and in a bad hand, like other transcripts by Skene. The frequent gaps (of which only one is indicated, 5⁴) make the division here adopted doubtful in some cases.*
The burden is given at the end only, and is badly corrupted. 1. the Darton all. 3. Pearting?
7⁴. hir all. *Corrupted?* hir, *or* him, *at?*
10¹. tour end : *see* 24¹,². 15³, 16³. Earl.
20². gay ladies.
23⁴. *Corrupted? some malediction on the lady?* 27². gaire *is, I suppose,* gear.
D. b. *Burden.* 1. The wally o't, the wally o't. 3. the ranting o't. 4. Our lady lies alane.
1³. at it. 3¹. It's I.
4¹ As sure as you're Jean. 4². And I am.
4³. I'll cause. 5¹. To cause.
5². I think would be.

5³. give to such a rogue as you.
5⁴. Who never could it win.
6¹. So he must go. 6². Amang the nobles a'.
6³. And there before good witnesses.
7². was called Miss Anne.
9³. she says *wanting.*

8–12 A servant girl there was found out,
　　On whom to show his skill ;
He gave to her a hundred pounds,
　　To purchase her good-will.

And still he cried, Look up, Peggy,
　　Look up, and think no shame,
And you shall have your hundred pounds
　　Before I lay you down.

Now he has lain him down wi her,
　　A hundred pounds in pawn,
And all the noblemen cried out
　　That Errol is a man.

'Tak hame your daughter,' Errol said,
　　'And tak her to a glen,
For Errol canna pleasure her,
　　Nor can no other man.'

c. *Burden.* 1. And the. 3. And the thing we.
4. Is, Errol's na a man.
1¹, 2¹. O Errol is.
1². Into the simmer time.
1³. The apples they grow.
1⁴. And the pears they grow green.
3⁴. bore the.
4¹. Tho your name be Dame Cathrine Carnegie. 4². mine Sir Gilbert.
4³. sell Kinnaird. 4⁴. tocher gude to.
5¹. If ye gar my father sell Kinnaird.
5². 'T will be a crying.
5³,⁴. To tocher onie weary dwrf, That canna tocher win. 6¹. The lady is. 6². A' for.
6⁴. His ainsell. 7¹. O up bespak.
7². Lady Ann. 7³. she says *wanting.*
After 7, two stanzas which are clearly a spurious interpolation.
8¹. Errol has got (But *wanting*).
8³. has chosen a weel-faurd may.
8⁴. Come. *After* 8 (= 10):

'Look up, look up, my weel-faurd may,
　　Look up, and think na shame ;
I'll gie to thee five hundred merk
　　To bear to me a son.'

9¹. He 's tane the lassie by the han.
9³. there *wanting*.   9⁴. Afore.
After 9:

> When they war laid in the proof-bed,
>   And a' the lords looking on,
> Then a' the fifteen vowd and swore
>   That Errol was a man.

11¹. But they hae keepit this lassie.
11³. And at the end o nine lang months.
11⁴. A son to him she bare.
After 11:

> And there was three thairbut, thairbut,
>   And there was three thairben,
> And three looking oure the window hie,
>   Crying, Errol 's provd a man!

> And whan the word gaed thro the toun,
>   The sentry gied a cry,
> 'O fair befa you, Errol, now!
>   For ye hae won the day.'

> 'O I 'll tak off my robes o silk,
>   And fling them oure the wa,
> And I 'll gae maiden hame again,
>   Awa, Errol, awa!'

12¹. Sir Carnegie.   12². till the glen.
12³, he *wanting*.   12⁴. nane o Errol's.
(12 *is found in Kinloch's MSS*, VII, 95,
  with Sir Carnegie *beginning the line*.)
After 12 :

> And ilka day her plate was laid,
>   Bot an a siller spune,
> And three times cried oure Errol's yett,
>   'Lady Errol, come and dine.'

Kinloch gives the following as a variant.   It
  is found in Kinloch's MSS, VII, 95 :

> Seven years the trencher sat,
>   And seven years the spune;
> Seven years the servant cried,
>   'Lady Errol, come and dine.'

Burden, at the end.   3. ye ca.
4. Lady Errol lies her leen.

E. *Sharpe made these changes in his Ballad*
  Book:
  3⁴. the toss.   4². He 's led her oer the green.
  4³. he kist.   7¹. Your name is.   7². And I 'm.
  12³. shall not.
F. 1¹, 2¹, 6¹. Oh.

232

RICHIE STORY

A. 'Ritchie Storie,' Motherwell's MS., p. 426.

B. Skene MS., p. 96.

C. a. 'Richie Story,' "Scotch Ballads, Materials for
Border Minstrelsy," No 65, MS. of Thomas Wilkie,
1813–15, p. 53, Abbotsford. **b.** 'Ritchie's Tory
Laddie,' Campbell MSS, II, 116.

D. 'Richy Story,' the late Mr Robert White's papers.

E. 'Richard Storie,' "Scotch Ballads, Materials for
Border Minstrelsy," No 76, Abbotsford.

F. a. 'Richie Storie,' Sharpe's Ballad Book, 1823, p.
95. **b.** 'Richie Storrie,' Nimmo, Songs and Ballads
of Clydesdale, 1882, p. 211.

G. a. 'Richard Storry,' Kinloch MSS, I, 203. **b.**
'Richie Tory,' Gibb MS., p. 77. **c.** 'Ritchie's
Lady,' Murison MS., p. 82. **d.** 'Richie's Lady,'
Christie's Traditional Ballad Airs, I, 72. **e.** Kin-
loch MSS, VII, 263, a fragment. **f.** 'The Earl of
Winton's Daughter,' Buchan's MSS, I, 87.

H. The Scots Magazine, 1803, LXV, 253, one stanza.

THE youngest (eldest, A) and fairest of the daughters of the Earl of Wigton, A, F (bonniest of his sisters, E), has fallen in love with her footman, Richie Story (Tory). Richie brings her a letter from a nobleman who desires to be her suitor ; the Earl of Hume, A, B, F, G a, d, e ; the Earl of Hume's son, D ; the Earl of Aboyne, E ; of Cumbernauld, G b ; of Mohun, G c ; of Wemyss, G f and a variant of E ; the Earls of Hume and Skimmerjim, Skimmerham (Kimmerghame), C. The lady has made a vow, and will keep it, to marry none but Richie. Richie deprecates ; he has nothing to maintain her with ; she is ready to descend to the lowest fortune. (In several versions she has enough of her own. Hunten Tour and Tillebarn and the House of Athol are hers, B ; Musselburgh, C ; the House of Athol and Taranadie, G d ; Blair-in-Athol and Dunkeld, H.) Asked by her sister, by Richie, or by some one else, whether she is not sorry to have left Cumbernauld (Castle Norry, G f) to follow a footman, she answers that there is no reason, she has her heart's desire and the lot that was ordained her. As she goes up the Parliament close, rides through Edinburgh town, Glasgow city (London city, C b, absurdly), she is greeted by many a lord, but few or none of them thought she was a footman's lady. Arrived at the domicile of the Storys, her good-mother bids her, gars her, kilt up her coats and muck the byres with Richie.

F, G, are not satisfied with this conclusion. The footman is really a lover in disguise, the Earl of Hume or of Cumbernauld, F, G a b. (G b 2 spoils the plot by making the Earl of Hume write to the lady that he will be her footman-laddie.) Four-and-twenty gentlemen welcome the bride at Ritchie's gates, or elsewhere, and she blesses the day that she was Richie's lady. This is incontestably a later invention.

G f, which is otherwise embellished, goes a good step beyond G a–e. Richie is an Englishman and takes the lady to London. ' Madam ' has left her kindred to gang with a servant ; he has ' left the sceptre and the crown ' her servant for to be ; little she knew that her waiting-man was England's royal king.

" Lillias Fleming, second daughter of John, Earl of Wigton by his wife Jane Drummond (a daughter of the Earl of Perth), did elope with and marry one of her father's servants, named Richard Storry. In 1673, she, with consent of her husband, resigned her portion, consisting of the five-merk land of Smythson, etc., in the barony of Lenzie, into the hands of her brother, Lieutenant-Colonel Fleming. The Fleming family afterwards procured for Richie a situation in the Custom-House." So Hunter, Biggar and the House of Fleming, p. 555, and, in part, Douglas's Peerage, where, however, Lady Lillias is said to have married Richard Storry, " Esq.: " ed. Wood, II, 616.

Douglas notes that " John, third Earl of Wigton, . . . had a charter of the lordship of Cumbernauld, 1st February, 1634." This place (Comarnad, Campernadie, etc., B, D, G a, c, d) is in Dumbartonshire. In F 11 it is attributed to the young Earl of Hume, and the disguised lover is the Earl of Cumbernauld in G b.

The lady, ready for any extremity, says in F 6 that she will lie ayont a dyke (on the other side of a wall), in E 6 sit below the dyke, in D 5 sit aneath the duke, and that she will be at Richie's command at all times. This matter was not understood by the reciter of B, and in B 7 the lady is made to say, We will go to sea, I 'll sit upon the *deck* (and be your servant, as in the other cases). In A the difficulty, such as it is, seems to have been evaded, and we read, 6, I 'll live whereer you please (and be ready at your call late or early).

For the relation of this ballad to 'Huntingtower' and 'The Duke of Athol,' see an appendix.

A

Motherwell's MS., p. 426 ; from the recitation of Mrs ——, of Kilbarchan, January 3, 1826.

1 THE Earl of Wigton had three daughters,
     Oh and a waly, but they were unco bonnie!
   The eldest of them had the far brawest house,
     But she's fallen in love with her footman-
        laddie.

2 As she was a walking doun by yon river-side,
     Oh and a wally, but she was unco bonnie!
   There she espied her own footman,
     With ribbons hanging over his shoulders sae
        bonnie.

3 'Here's a letter to you, madame,
     Here's a letter to you, madame ;
   The Earl of Hume is waiting on,
     And he has his service to you, madame.'

4 'I'll have none of his service,' says she,
   'I'll have none of his service,' says she,
   'For I've made a vow, and I'll keep it true,
     That I'll marry none but you, Ritchie.'

5 'O say not so again, madame,
     O say not so again, madame ;
   For I have neither lands nor rents
     For to keep you on, madam.'

6 'I'll live where eer you please, Ritchie,
     I'll live where eer you please, [Ritchie,]
   And I'll be ready at your ca',
     Either late or early, Ritchie.'

7 As they went in by Stirling toun,
     O and a wally, but she was unco bonnie!
   A' her silks were sailing on the ground,
     But few of them knew of Ritchie Story.

8 As they went in by the Parliament Close,
     O and a wally, but she was unco bonnie!
   All the nobles took her by the hand,
     But few of them knew she was Ritchie's lady.

9 As they came in by her goodmother's yetts,
     O and a wally, but she was unco bonnie!
   Her goodmother bade her kilt her coats,
     And muck the byre with Ritchie Storie.

10 'Oh, may not ye be sorry, madame,
      Oh, may not ye be sorry, madame,
    To leave a' your lands at bonnie Cumbernaud,
      And follow home your footman-laddie?'

11 'What need I be sorry?' says she,
      'What need I be sorry?' says she,
    'For I've gotten my lot and my heart's desire,
      And what Providence has ordered for me.'

B

Skene MS., p. 96 ; taken down in the north of Scotland, 1802–3.

1 COMARNAD is a very bonny place,
     And there is ladies three, madam,
   But the fairest and rairest o them a'
     Has married Richard Storry.

2 'O here is a letter to ye, madam,
     Here is a letter to ye, madam ;
   The Earle of Hume, that gallant knight,
     Has fallen in love wi ye, madam.'

3 'There is a letter to ye, madam,
     [There is a letter to ye, madam ;]
   That gallant knight, the Earl of Hume,
     Desires to be yer servan true, madam.

4 'I'll hae nane o his letters, Richard,
     I'll hae nane o his letters, [Richard ;]
   I hae voued, and will keep it true,
     I'll marry nane but ye, Richie.'

5 'Say ne sae to me, lady,
     Say ne sae to me, [lady,]
   For I hae neither lands nor rents
     To mentain ye, lady.'

6 'Hunten Tour and Tillebarn,
     The House o Athol is mine, Richie,
   An ye sal hae them a'
     Whan ere ye incline, Richie.

7 'For we will gae to sea, Richie,
     I'll sit upon the deck, Richie,
   And be your servant ere and late,
     At any hour ye like, [Richie.']

8 'O manna ye be sad, sister,
   An mann ye be sae sorry,
   To leave the house o bonny Comarnad,
   An follow Richard Storry?'

9 'O what neads I be sad, sister,
   An how can I be sorry?
   A bonny lad is my delit,
   And my lot has been laid afore me.'

10 As she went up the Parliament Close,
   Wi her laced shoon so fine,
   Many ane bad the lady good day,
   But few thought o Richard's lady.

11 As she gaed up the Parliament Close,
   Wi her laced shoon so fine,
   Mony ane hailed that gay lady,
   But few hailed Richard Storry.

———•———

C

a. "Scotch Ballads, Materials for Border Minstrelsy," No 65, MS. of Thomas Wilkie, 1813–15, p. 53, from the singing or recitation of Miss Euphemia Hislope. b. Campbell MSS, II, 116.

1 THERE are three white hens i the green, madam,
   There are three white hens i the green, madam,
   But Richie Story he's comd by,
   And he's stollen away the fairest of them.

2 'O are 'int ye now sad, sister,
   O are 'in[t] ye now sad, sister,
   To leave your bowers and your bony Skimmerknow,
   And follow the lad they call Richie Story?'

3 'O say not that again, sister,
   O say not that again, sister,
   For he is the lad that I love best,
   And he is the lot that has fallen to me.'

4 'O there's a letter to thee, madam,
   O there's a letter to thee, madam;
   The Earl of Hume and Skimmerjim,
   For to be sweethearts to thee, madam.'

5 'But I'll hae none of them, Richie,
   But I'll hae none of them, Richie,

For I have made a vow, and I'll keep it true,
   I'll have none but Ric[h]ie Story.'

6 'O say not that again, madam,
   O say not that again, madam,
   For the Earl of Hume and Skimmerjim,
   They are men of high renown.'

7 'Musslebury's mine, Richie,
   Musslebury's mine, Richie,
   And a' that's mine it shall be thine,
   If you will marry me, Richie.'

8 As she went up through Glasgow city,
   Her gold watch was shining pretty;
   Many [a] lord bade her good day,
   But none thought she was a footman's lady.

9 As she went up through London city,
   There she met her scolding minny:
   'Cast off your silks and kilt your coats,
   And muck the byre wi Richie Story.'

10 'Hold your tongue, my scolding minnie,
   Hold your tongue, my scolding minnie;
   For I'll cast of my silks and kilt my coats,
   And muck the byres wi Richie Story.'

———•———

D

The late Mr Robert White's papers.

1 As I came in by Thirlwirl Bridge,
   A coming frae the land of fair Camernadie,
   There I met my ain true love,
   Wi ribbons at her shoulders many.

2 'Here is a letter to you, madam;
   [Here is a letter to you, madam;]
   The Earl of Hume's eldest son
   Sent this letter to you, madam.

3 'I'll have none of his [letters], Richy,
   I'll have none of his letters, Richy;

I made a vow, and I'll keep it true,
    I'll wed wi nane but you, Richy.'

4 'Say not so again, madam,
    Say not so again, madam;
I have neither lands nor rents
    To maintain you on, madam.'

5 'I'll sit aneath the duke, Richy,
    I'll sit aneath the duke, Richy;
I'll sit on hand, at your command
    At ony time ye like, Richy.'

6 As they came in by Thirlewirle bridge,
    A coming frae fair Cummernadie,
She brak the ribbons that tied her shoon
    Wi following after the footman-laddie.

7 'O but ye be sad, sister,
    O but ye be sad and sorry,
To leave the lands o bonnie Cummernad,
    To gang alang wi a footman-laddie!'

8 'How can I be sad, sister?
    How can I be sad or sorry?
I have gotten my heart's delight;
    And what can ye get mair?' says she.

9 To the house-end Richy brought his lady,
    To the house-end Richy brought his lady;
Her mother-in-law gart her kilt her coats,
    And muck the byre wi Richy Story.

E

"Scotch Ballads, Materials for Border Minstrelsy," No 76, Abbotsford.

1 THE Earl of Wigton has seven sisters,
    And O but they be wondrous bonnie!
And the bonniest lass amang them a'
    Has fallen in love wi Richie Storie.

2 As I came down by yon river-side,
    And down by the banks of Eache bonnie,
There I met my own true-love,
    Wi ribbons on her shoulders bonnie.

3 'Here is a letter for you, madam,
    Here is a letter for you, madam;
The Earl of Aboyne has a noble design
    To be a suitor to you, madam.'

4 'I'll hae nane of his letters, Richie,
    I'll hae nane of his letters, Richie,
For I've made a vow, and I'll keep it true,
    That I'll hae nane but you, Richie.'

5 'Take your word again, madam,
    Take your word again, madam,
For I have neither land nor rents
    For to mentain you on, madam.'

6 'I'll sit below the dyke, Richie,
    I'll sit below the dyke, Richie,

And I will be at your command
    At ony time you like, Richie.

7 'Ribbons you shall wear, Richie,
    Ribbons you shall wear, Richie,
A cambric band about your neck,
    And vow but ye'll be braw, Richie!'

8 As they came in by the West Port,
    The naps of gold were bobbing bonnie;
Many a one bade this lady gude-day,
    But neer a one to Richie Storie.

9 As they came up the Parliament Close,
    Naps of gold were bobbing bonnie;
Many a gentleman lifted his cap,
    But few kennd she was Richie's lady.

10 .   .   .   .   .   .

    .   .   .   .   .   .
And ay methinks we'll drink the night
    In Cambernauld sae bonnie.

11 'It's are not you sick, sister,
    Are not you very sorrie,
To leave the lands of bonnie Cambernauld,
    And run awae wi Richie Storie?'

12 'Why should I be sick, sister,
    O why should I be any sorrie,
When I hae gotten my heart's delight?
    I hae gotten the lot was laid afore me.'

F

a. Sharpe's Ballad Book, p. 95, 1823. b. Nimmo, Songs and Ballads of Clydesdale, p. 211, 1882.

1 THE Erle o Wigton had three daughters,
  O braw wallie, but they were bonnie!
  The youngest o them, and the bonniest too,
  Has fallen in love wi Richie Storie.

2 'Here's a letter for ye, madame,
  Here's a letter for ye, madame;
  The Erle o Home wad fain presume
  To be a suitor to ye, madame.'

3 'I'l hae nane o your letters, Richie;
  I'l hae nane o your letters, Richie;
  For I've made a vow, and I'll keep it true,
  That I'l have none but you, Richie.'

4 'O do not say so, madame;
  O do not say so, madame;
  For I have neither land nor rent,
  For to maintain you o, madame.

5 'Ribands ye maun wear, madame,
  Ribands ye maun wear, madame;
  With the bands about your neck
  O the goud that shines sae clear, madame.'

6 'I'l lie ayont a dyke, Richie,
  I'l lie ayont a dyke, Richie;

  And I'l be aye at your command
  And bidding, whan ye like, Richie.'

7 O he's gane on the braid, braid road,
  And she's gane through the broom sae bon-
    nie,
  Her silken robes down to her heels,
  And she's awa wi Richie Storie.

8 This lady gade up the Parliament stair,
  Wi pendles in her lugs sae bonnie;
  Mony a lord lifted his hat,
  But little did they ken she was Richie's lady.

9 Up then spak the Erle o Home's lady;
  'Was na ye richt sorrie, Annie,
  To leave the lands o bonnie Cumbernauld
  And follow Richie Storie, Annie?'

10 'O what need I be sorrie, madame?
   O what need I be sorrie, madame?
   For I've got them that I like best,
   And war ordained for me, madame.'

11 'Cumbernauld is mine, Annie,
   Cumbernauld is mine, Annie;
   And a' that's mine, it shall be thine,
   As we sit at the wine, Annie.'

G

a. Kinloch MSS, I, 203, from Alexander Kinnear, of Stonehaven. b. Gibb MS., p. 77, from Mrs Gibb, senior. c. Murison MS., p. 82. d. Christie's Traditional Ballad Airs, I, 72, from the recitation of a native of Buchan. e. Kinloch MSS, VII, 263 (a fragment). f. Buchan's MSS, I, 87.

1 THERE were five ladies lived in a bouer,
  Lived in a bouer at Cumbernaldie;
  The fairest and youngest o them a'
  Has fa'n in love wi her footman-laddie.

2 'Here is a letter to you, ladye,
  Here is a letter to you, ladye;
  The Earl o Hume has written doun
  That he will be your footman-laddie.'

3 'I want nane o his service, Ritchie,
  I want nane o his service, Ritchie;

  For I've made a vow, and I'll keep it true,
  That I'll wed nane but thee, Ritchie.'

4 'O that canna be, ladye,
  O that canna be, ladye;
  For I've neither house nor land,
  Nor ought suiting ye, ladye.'

5 'Livd ye on yonder hill, Ritchie,
  Livd ye on yonder hill, Ritchie,
  There's my hand, I'm at your command,
  Marry me whan ye will, Ritchie!'

6 This boy he went to his bed,
  It was a' to try this fair ladye;
  But she went up the stair to him:
  'Ye maun leave your comrades, Ritchie.

7 'To the Borders we maun gang, Ritchie,
    To the Borders we maun gang, Ritchie,
For an my auld father he get word,
    It's you he will cause hang, Ritchie.'

8 'To the Borders we'll na gang, ladye,
    To the Borders we'll na gang, ladye;
For altho your auld father got word,
    It's me he dare na hang, ladye.'

9 As they passed by her mither's bouer,
    O but her sisters they were sorry!
They bade her tak aff the robes o silk,
    And muck the byres wi Ritchie Storry.

10 Whan they cam to yon hie hill,
    Dear vow, but the lady she was sorry!
She looked oure her left showther —
    'O an I war in bonny Cumbernaldie!'

11 'O are na ye sorry now, ladye,
    O are na ye sorry now, ladye,
For to forsake the Earl o Hume,
    And follow me, your footman-laddie?'

12 'How could I be sorry, Ritchie,
    How could I be sorry, Ritchie?

Such a gudely man as you,
    And the lot that lies afore me, Ritchie.'

13 As they rode up through Edinburgh toun,
    Her gowd watch hang doun sae gaudie;
Monie a lord made her a bow,
    But nane o them thoucht she was Ritchie's
    ladye.

14 Whan they cam to Ritchie's yetts,
    Dear vow, but the music playd bonnie!
There were four-and-twenty gay ladies
    To welcome hame Richard Storry's ladye.

15 He called for a priest wi speed,
    A priest wi speed was soon ready,
And she was na married to the Earl of Hume,
    But she blesses the day she got Richard
    Storry.

16 A coach and six they did prepare,
    A coach and six they did mak ready,
A coach and six they did prepare,
    And she blesses the day made her Ritchie's
    lady.

H

The Scots Magazine, LXV, 253, 1803, James Hogg.

Blair-in-Athol's mine, Ritchie,
    Blair-in-Athol's mine, Ritchie,
And bonny Dunkeld, where I do dwell,
    And these shall a' be thine, Ritchie.

A. 5¹. Oh. 7⁴. Ritchie's story.
B. 7⁴. ye lake, *or* take. 8². manna ye be sorry?
    9². An who.
C. a. *The air is said in the MS. to be beautiful
        and very plaintive.*
    5¹·². madam *instead of* Richie. *Richie in* b.
    6³. Skimmerjim *is glossed in the margin* Kim-
        merghame.
    8¹. *Written twice.* 8². hining. shining *in* b.
  b. 2¹·², 3¹·², 4¹·², 5¹·², 6¹·², *are written in one line.*

10². *is indicated by* &c. 1¹·². There's.
1³. And Richies tory he's come by.
2¹·². O care ye not sad. 2³. Skimmer knowes.
2⁴. And go wi the lad they ca Richies tory.
3¹·². not so again.
4¹·². O *wanting.* 4². madam *wanting.*
4³. For the: Skimmerham.
4⁴. They will be: to you.
5¹·². Richie, *for* madam *of* a.
5⁴. none but thee, Richie. 6. *Wanting.*

7². Richie *wanting*. 8¹. London city.

8². shining. 8³. Many a.

8⁴. But few thought her a.

9². mammy. 9⁴. Richies Torry.

10¹,². Now hold: mammy.

10³. and cast (*wrongly*).

10⁴. And I 'll muck the byre wi Richies Torry.

D. 1⁴. At his? *The ribbons seem more likely to belong to the footman: see* A 2, G f 1. *But compare* E 2, G d, *after* 1.

E. 1⁴. *Var.:* wi her brother's foot-boy.

2³. On his? 3³. *Var.:* Earl Wemyss.

11³. *Marginal note:* Lady Hume, whose son was suitor to the runaway lady.

F. b. *Evidently furbished, and therefore not collated. After* 6 *is inserted this stanza, corresponding to* 11:

Fair Powmoodie is mine, dear Richie,
  And goud and pearlins too;
Gin ye 'll consent to be mine, dear Richie,
  I will gie them a' to you.

G. *Trivial variations are not noticed.*

a, 15³,⁴. *It is certain from* 16 *and from other copies of* G *that she was married to the Earl of Hume, but I have let the text stand as delivered.*

b. *Stanzas* 1, 9³,⁴, 2, 7, 8, 10–14, 15³,⁴ (?), 16: *four marked as wanting.*

1¹,². Theres seven bonny ladies in yonder ha (*twice*).

1³. The youngest an bonniest amon.

2³,⁴. It 's from the Earl o Cumbernauld, An he is seekin you, lady.

7¹. we will go, Richie. 7². go, laddie.

9³. Ye 'll cast aff your gowns o silk.

9⁴. wi your Richie Tory.

10¹,². As they gaed down by yon bonny waterside, O but the sma birds they sang bonnie!

11². sorry, lassie.

11³. To leave the Earl o Cumbernauld.

12². sorry, laddie.

12³,⁴. The thing that 's afore us we maun endure, So what need I be sorry, laddie?

13¹,². As they gaed down by yon bonny waterside, O but her gold watch it hung bonny!

13³. a ane gaed her a low bow.

13⁴. But few kent she.

14¹,². As she gaed doun by yon bonny ha-house, Oh but the pibrochs they sang bonny!

14³. f. an t. belted knichts.

15³,⁴. Says, I 'm the Earl o Cumbernauld, That for your sake was a footman-laddie.

16³,⁴. Now she rides in her coach-an-six, An blesses the day she saw Richie Tory.

c. 11 *stanzas:* 1, 6–9, 13, 10, 14, 16, *and* 11, 12 *as a "chorus" to each of the others.*

1¹,². Seven sisters in yonder ha, Seven sisters in Campernadie.

6¹⁻³. Ritchie he went up the stair, Thinking for to meet his lady; But sae quick as she turnëd round.

7¹,². we will go. 8¹,². I 'll nae go.

9¹. they rode up by her sisters' bowers.

9³. Says, Ye mann tak aff the goons.

9⁴. byres, nor wi Ritchie tarry.

10². lady grew unco weary.

10⁴. were back at Campernadie.

11³. the yerl o Mohun.

11⁴. And wed wi me but.

12³,⁴. What is before me must nae I endure? An why should I be sorry, Ritchie?

13². O but her gowd it was shinin bonnie!

13³. Monie ane gae her a low bow.

13⁴. But few o.

14¹. As they rode doon by yonder glen.

14². the organs they.

14³,⁴. Four-an-twenty gentlemen Cam a'.

16³. An now she rides in her coach-an-six.

d. 16 *stanzas:* 1; *a stanza corresponding to* A 2, D 1, 2–9, 13, 10–12, 14, 16.

1¹,². There were ladies in yon ha, Seven ladies in Cumbernaudie. *After* 1: He gaed down the garden green, In amang the birks sae bonnie, And there he saw his lady gay, Wi ribbons on her shoulders mony.

2³,⁴. With Earl Hume's humble desire Your servant for to be.

3¹. I 'll hae nane o his letters.

3². Nane from Earl Hume.

3³,⁴. But I 'll hae him that I like best, And I 'll hae nane but you, Richie.

4¹,². Say na that to me. 4³. lands nor rents.

4⁴. For to maintain you wi.

5¹,². Say na that again, Richie.

5³,⁴. The House o Athole it is mine, Taranadie shall be thine, Richie.

6¹,². He gaed from the garden green, Thinking he would shun his lady.

6³. But quickly she followed after him.

7². I 'll gae to them wi thee, Richie.

8¹,². To the Borders we will gae, We will to them gang, lady.

9¹. rode by her sister's bowers.

9⁴. And gang and beg wi her Richard Storie: *editorial nicety.*

10². she grew wondrous weary.

12³,⁴. When I get him that I like best, And
what is laid before me, Richie.

13¹. rode thro yon burrow-town.

14¹. As they rode by yon bonny House.

14³,⁴. And four-and-twenty gallant knichts
Came.

16³. And now she rides in her coach-and-four.
Christie touched up his text here and there.

e. 11³,⁴, 12, 14, 16³,⁴. *Wanting.*

12⁴. What wad make me sorry?

14¹. yonder gates. 14². playd pretty.

14³. four-and-twenty noble knichts.

14⁴. welcome in Ritchie Torry's lady.

16³,⁴. Now she rides in her coach-and-six, She
blesses the day she got Ritchie Torry.

f. 18 *stanzas. Much manipulated, and not
entitled to confidence.*

1. As I came in yon bonny burn-side,
And down below the bloom sae bonny,

There I espied a handsome lad,
Wi ribbons on his shoulders mony.
(*Cf.* A 2.)

2³,⁴. Here 's a letter frae the Earl o Wemyss,
That he 's in suit o thee, madam.

11. Out it speaks her mother then;
O daughter, may not you be sorry
To gang alang wi a servant-man,
And lose the rights o Castle Norry?

12³,⁴. I'm sure I've chosen a bonny lad, The
lot has just been laid afore me.

14. When they gaed through the Parliament
Closs,
The silver loops hang down sae bonny;
Then four-and-twenty noble lords
Came hat in hand to Richard Storry.

APPENDIX

AYTOUN, II, 239, says of 'Richie Storie,' The
words, recast in a romantic form and applied to a
more interesting subject, have been set to music by
a noble lady, and are now very popular under the
title of 'Huntingtower.' The history of 'Huntingtower' is not so well known as might be expected.
I have not been able to ascertain the authorship or
the date of its first appearance (which was very
probably in society rather than in print). 'Richie
Storie' is not carried by our texts further back than
1802–3 (B, H). Kinloch published in 1827 a ballad from recitation, 'The Duke of Athol,' which is
'Huntingtower' passed through the popular mouth;
for 'Huntingtower' became, and has continued to
be, a favorite with the people. Christie, Traditional
Ballad Airs, I, 166, says that he had often heard
'The Duke of Athol' in his early years, and he
gives eight stanzas which do not differ remarkably
from Kinloch's ballad.

The marks of the derivation of 'Huntingtower'
are the terminations of lines 1, 2, 4 of each stanza,
and substantial agreements in the last two stanzas
with A, B, E, 5, D, F, G, 4, and with B 6, C 7,
H, respectively. The name Huntingtower occurs

only in B 6 of 'Richie Storie.' The author of
'Huntingtower' was no doubt possessed of a version of 'Richie Storie' which had its own peculiarities.

'Huntingtower' is too well known to require citing. It has been often printed; as, for example,
in Mr G. F. Graham's Popular Songs of Scotland,
revised by J. Muir Wood, Balmoral Edition, Glasgow, 1887, p. 152; The Songs of Scotland, the
words revised by Dr Charles Mackay, p. 5, London,
Boosey & Co. (Altered by the Baroness Nairne,
and very little left of it, Life and Songs of the Baroness Nairne, edited by the Rev. Charles Rogers,
1872, p. 177.) The pleasing air strongly resembles, says Mr Wood, one in D'Urfey's Pills to
Purge Melancholy, V, 42, ed. 1719.

'The Duke of Athol' may be given for the interest it has as a popular *rifacimento.*

THE DUKE OF ATHOL

"Taken down from the recitation of an idiot boy in Wi-
shaw;" Kinloch's Ancient Scottish Ballads, p. 170.

1 'I AM gaing awa, Jeanie,
I am gaing awa;
I am gaing ayont the saut seas,
I'm gaing sae far awa.'

2 'What will ye buy to me, Jamie?
    What will ye buy to me?'
'I 'll buy to you a silken plaid,
    And send it wi vanitie.'

3 'That 's na love at a', Jamie,
    That 's na love at a';
All I want is love for love,
    And that 's the best ava.

4 'Whan will ye marry me, Jamie?
    Whan will ye marry me?
Will ye tak me to your countrie,
    Or will ye marry me?'

5 'How can I marry thee, Jeanie?
    How can I marry thee,
Whan I 've a wife and bairns three?
    Twa wad na weill agree.'

6 'Wae be to your fause tongue, Jamie,
    Wae be to your fause tongue;
Ye promised for to marry me,
    And has a wife at hame!

7 'But if your wife wad dee, Jamie,
    And sae your bairns three,
Wad ye tak me to your countrie,
    Or wad ye marry me?

8 'But sin they 're all alive, Jamie,
    But sin they 're all alive,
We 'll tak a glass in ilka hand,
    And drink, Weill may they thrive!'

9 'If my wife wad dee, Jeanie,
    And sae my bairns three,
I wad tak ye to my ain countrie,
    And married we wad be.'

10 'O an your head war sair, Jamie,
    O an your head war sair,
I 'd tak the napkin frae my neck
    And tie doun your yellow hair.'

11 'I hae na wife at a', Jeanie,
    I hae na wife at a';
I hae neither wife nor bairns three;
    I said it to try thee.'

12 'Licht are ye to loup, Jamie,
    Licht are ye to loup;
Licht are ye to loup the dyke,
    Whan I maun wale a slap.'

13 'Licht am I to loup, Jeanie,
    Licht am I to loup;
But the hiest dyke that we come to
    I 'll turn and tak you up.

14 'Blair in Athol is mine, Jeanie,
    Blair in Athol is mine;
Bonnie Dunkel is whare I dwell,
    And the boats o Garry 's mine.

15 'Huntingtower is mine, Jeanie,
    Huntingtower is mine,
Huntingtower, and bonnie Belford,
    And a' Balquhither 's mine.'

233

ANDREW LAMMIE

A. 'The Trumpeter of Fyvie,' Jamieson's Popular Ballads, I, 126, 1806.

B. 'Tifty's Nanny,' Jamieson's Popular Ballads, II, 382, from a stall-copy.

C. a. 'Andrew Lammie,' Buchan's Gleanings, p. 98, 1825; Laing's Thistle of Scotland, p. 55, 1823.
b. Motherwell's Minstrelsy, p. 239.

JAMIESON, in his preface, 1806, says that this ballad was current in the Border counties within a few years, and that A was taken down by Leyden from the recitation of a young lady who learned it in Teviotdale. Writing to Scott, in November, 1804, of such ballads as he had already prepared for the press, he says, "Trumpeter of Fyvie, from tradition, furnished by Mr Leyden, and collated with a stall-copy" (probably B): Letters addressed to Sir Walter Scott, Abbotsford, I, No. 117.

Buchan, in the notes to his Gleanings, 1825,

p. 197, says of C a : " This is one of the greatest favorites of the people in Aberdeenshire that I know. I took it first down from the memory of a very old woman, and afterwards published thirty thousand copies of it. There are two versions, an old and a new ; but, although I have both, I prefer this one, the younger of the two, having been composed and acted in the year 1674." Laing, who reprints A in his Thistle of Scotland, p. 63, calls that the " old way of Andrew Lammie." Motherwell, 1827, reprints " a stall-copy published at Glasgow several years ago, collated with a recited copy which has furnished one or two verbal improvements: " C b. There are a great many variations from C a, of which precisely one or two are verbal improvements. But Motherwell also gives six stanzas which are not in a. His copy is repeated in The Ballad Minstrelsy of Scotland, Glasgow, 1871, and there the editor says that in a chap-book printed by J. and M. Robertson, Saltmarket, Glasgow, 1808, " Andrew Lammie is given with only a few slight verbal differences between it and the copy here printed." Such stall-copies as I have seen are late, and are reprints of C a or of C b. Motherwell assures us that the ballad as he has given it " agrees with any recited copy which the Editor has hitherto met with in the West Country."

A professed edition, " most carefully collated with all previous editions," was published at Peterhead, 1872 : " Mill o Tifty's Annie, A Buchan Ballad, with Introduction," etc. This is attributed to the Rev. Dr John Muir of Aberdeen. ' Mill o Tiftie's Annie ' in Christie, I, 48 " is epitomized from traditional copies ; " that is to say, it is taken from Motherwell, with a trifling change here and there. A copy given in Smith's New History of Aberdeenshire is compounded of A, B, and a couple of lines from C b.

Annie, daughter to a well-to-do miller, loses her heart to a handsome trumpeter in the service of Lord Fyvie. Her father will not hear of such a match. (Annie has five thousand marks, and the man not a penny, A 11.) The trumpeter is obliged to go to Edinburgh for a time, and Annie appoints him a tryst at a bridge. He will buy her her wedding-gear while he is away, and marry her when he comes back. Annie knows that she shall be dead ere he returns, and bids him an everlasting adieu.* The trumpeter goes to the top of the castle and blows a blast which is heard at his love's house. Her father beats her, her mother beats her ; her brother beats her and breaks her back. Lord Fyvie is passing on one of these occasions, comes in, and urges Mill of Tiftie to yield to his daughter's inclinations. The father is immovable ; she must marry higher than with a trumpeter. Annie is put to bed, with her face towards Fyvie, and dies of a broken heart and of the cruel treatment which she has undergone.

This is a homely ditty,† but the gentleness and fidelity of Annie under the brutal behavior of her family are genuinely pathetic, and justify the remarkable popularity which the ballad has enjoyed in the north of Scotland. In those parts the story has been played as well as sung. " The ballad used in former times to be presented in a dramatic shape at rustic meetings in Aberdeenshire," says Chambers (Scottish Ballads, p. 143) ; perhaps misinterpreting and expanding the enunciation made by Buchan and in the title of some stall-copies that " this tragedy was acted in the year 1674," which may rather refer to the date of the story. But however it may have been in former times, two rival companies in Aberdeenshire were performing plays founded on the ballad in 1887–8.‡

" Bonny Andrew Lammie " was a well-known personage at the beginning of the last century, for, as Jamieson has pointed out, he is mentioned in a way that implies this by Allan Ramsay, in the second of his two cantos in continuation of Christ's Kirk on the Green,

* " It is a received superstition in Scotland," says Motherwell, " that when friends or lovers part at a bridge they shall never again meet." Surely, lovers who were of this way of thinking would not appoint a bridge for a meeting.

† But not homely enough while C 2, 42 are retained. The mystical verses with which A and B begin are also not quite artless.

‡ The Scotsman newspaper, November 16, 1888.

written, as Ramsay says, in 1718. (Poems, London, 1731, I, 76, v. 70.)

Mill of Tiftie is, or was, a farm-house on the side of a glen about half a mile northeast of the castle of Fyvie, and in view of its turrets (on one of which there now stands a figure of the Trumpeter sounding towards Tiftie). The mill proper, now a ruin, was in the bottom of the glen, and gave its name to the house. The bridge of Sleugh, otherwise Skeugh, etc., was in the hollow between Tiftie and the castle.*

Annie was Agnes Smith, Nannie being among her people an affectionate form for Agnes. There is reason to believe that she may have been daughter of a William Smith who is known to have been a brother or near kinsman of the laird of Inveramsay, a person of some local consequence.† An inscription on her gravestone makes Agnes Smith to have died January 19, 1673.‡

"Some years subsequent to the melancholy fate of poor Tifty's Nanny," says Jamieson, II, 387, citing the current tradition of Fyvie, "her sad story being mentioned and the ballad sung in a company in Edinburgh when [Andrew Lammie] was present, he remained silent and motionless, till he was discovered by a groan suddenly bursting from him and *several of the buttons flying from his waist-*

coat." The peasants of Fyvie, Jamieson continues, "borrowed this striking characteristic of excessive grief" neither from the Laocoön group nor from Shakspere's King Lear, but from nature. The anecdote, and the comment too, is apt to be repeated by editors of 'Andrew Lammie.' That "affecting image of overpowering grief," as Chambers calls it, the flying off of the buttons (or the bursting of a waistcoat), we have had several times already, though in no ballad (or version) of much note: see II, 118, D 17, 186, C 15, 308, 4; IV, 101, I 15, 185, 11. It must be owned to be a stroke that does not well bear iteration. Mrs. Littlewit in 'Bartholomew Fair' has a tedious life with her Puritan, she says: "he breaks his buttons and cracks seams at every saying he sobs out." Ben Jonson has taken out one of the best things in our tragedy and put it into his comedy.

The air to which this ballad was usually, sung, Jamieson informs us, was "of that class which in Teviotdale they term a northern drawl; and a Perthshire set of it, but two notes lower than it is commonly sung, is to be found in Johnson's Scots Musical Museum [No. 175, p. 183], to the song 'How long and dreary is the night.'"

C b is translated by Wolff, Hausschatz, p. 199, Halle der Völker, I, 65.

A

Jamieson's Popular Ballads, I, 126; "taken down by Dr Leyden from the recitation of a young lady, Miss Robson, of Edinburgh, who learned it in Teviotdale."

1   'At Fyvie's yetts there grows a flower,
        It grows baith braid and bonny;
    There 's a daisie in the midst o it,
        And it 's ca'd by Andrew Lammie.

2   'O gin that flower war in my breast,
        For the love I bear the laddie!

I wad kiss it, and I wad clap it,
    And daut it for Andrew Lammie.

3 'The first time me and my love met
        Was in the woods of Fyvie;
    He kissed my lips five thousand times,
        And ay he ca'd me bonny,
    And a' the answer he gat frae me,
        Was, My bonny Andrew Lammie!'

4 'Love, I maun gang to Edinburgh;
        Love, I maun gang and leave thee!'

* Buchan, by the Rev. John B. Pratt, 3d ed., 1870, p. 324 f.
† An Aberdeen newspaper of April, 1885, from which I have a cutting.
‡ Buchan gives the year as 1631, and is followed by Chambers and Aytoun. The original tombstone having be-

come "decayed," Mr Gordon of Fyvie had it replaced in 1845 with "a fac-simile in every respect." A headstone in the form of a cross of polished granite was added in 1869, by public subscription. (New Statistical Account of Scotland, XII, 325; Mill o Tifty's Annie, Peterhead, 1872, p. 4.)

'I sighed right sair, and said nae mair
  But, O gin I were wi ye!'

5 'But true and trusty will I be,
  As I am Andrew Lammie;
  I'll never kiss a woman's mouth
  Till I come back and see thee.'

6 'And true and trusty will I be,
  As I am Tiftie's Annie;
  I'll never kiss a man again
  Till ye come back and see me.'

7 Syne he's come back frae Edinburgh
  To the bonny hows o Fyvie,
  And ay his face to the nor-east,
  To look for Tiftie's Annie.

8 'I hae a love in Edinburgh,
  Sae hae I intill Leith, man;
  I hae a love intill Montrose,
  Sae hae I in Dalkeith, man.

9 'And east and west, whereer I go,
  My love she's always wi me;
  For east and west, whereer I go,
  My love she dwells in Fyvie.

10 'My love possesses a' my heart,
  Nae pen can eer indite her;
  She's ay sae stately as she goes
  That I see nae mae like her.

11 'But Tiftie winna gie consent
  His dochter me to marry,
  Because she has five thousand marks,
  And I have not a penny.

12 'Love pines away, love dwines away,
  Love, love decays the body;
  For love o thee, oh I must die;
  Adieu, my bonny Annie!'

13 Her mither raise out o her bed,
  And ca'd on baith her women:
  'What ails ye, Annie, my dochter dear?
  O Annie, was ye dreamin?

14 'What dule disturbd my dochter's sleep?
  O tell to me, my Annie!'
  She sighed right sair, and said nae mair
  But, O for Andrew Lammie!

15 Her father beat her cruellie,
  Sae also did her mother;
  Her sisters sair did scoff at her;
  But wae betide her brother!

16 Her brother beat her cruellie,
  Till his straiks they werena canny;
  He brak her back, and he beat her sides,
  For the sake o Andrew Lammie.

17 'O fie, O fie, my brother dear!
  The gentlemen 'll shame ye;
  The Laird o Fyvie he's gaun by,
  And he'll come in and see me.

18 'And he'll kiss me, and he'll clap me,
  And he will speer what ails me;
  And I will answer him again,
  It's a' for Andrew Lammie.'

19 Her sisters they stood in the door,
  Sair grievd her wi their folly:
  'O sister dear, come to the door,
  Your cow is lowin on you.'

20 'O fie, O fie, my sister dear!
  Grieve me not wi your folly;
  I'd rather hear the trumpet sound
  Than a' the kye o Fyvie.

21 'Love pines away, love dwines away,
  Love, love decays the body;
  For love o thee now I maun die;
  Adieu to Andrew Lammie!'

22 But Tiftie's wrote a braid letter,
  And sent it into Fyvie,
  Saying his daughter was bewitchd
  By bonny Andrew Lammie.

23 'Now, Tiftie, ye maun gie consent,
  And lat the lassie marry;'
  'I'll never, never gie consent
  To the trumpeter of Fyvie.'

24 When Fyvie looked the letter on,
  He was baith sad and sorry:
  Says, The bonniest lass o the country-side
  Has died for Andrew Lammie.

25 O Andrew's gane to the house-top
  O the bonny house o Fyvie,

He 's blawn his horn baith loud and shill
　　Oer the lawland leas o Fyvie.

26 'Mony a time hae I walkd a' night,
　　And never yet was weary;
　But now I may walk wae my lane,
　　For I 'll never see my deary.

27 'Love pines away, love dwines away,
　　Love, love decays the body;
　For the love o thee now I maun die;
　　I come, my bonny Annie!'

———————

B

Jamieson's Popular Ballads, II, 382; "from a stall copy,
procured from Scotland."

1 'There springs a rose in Fyvie's yard,
　　And O but it springs bonny!
　There 's a daisy in the middle of it,
　　Its name is Andrew Lammie.

2 'I wish the rose were in my breast,
　　For the love I bear the daisy;
　So blyth and merry as I would be,
　　And kiss my Andrew Lammie.

3 'The first time I and my love met
　　Was in the wood of Fyvie;
　He kissèd and he dawted me,
　　Calld me his bonny Annie.

4 'Wi apples sweet he did me treat,
　　Which stole my heart so canny,
　And ay sinsyne himself was kind,
　　My bonny Andrew Lammie.'

5 'But I am going to Edinburgh,
　　My love, I 'm going to leave thee;'
　She sighd full sore, and said no more,
　　'I wish I were but wi you.'

6 'I will buy thee a wedding-gown,
　　My love, I 'll buy it bonny;'
　'But I 'll be dead or ye come back,
　　My bonny Andrew Lammie.'

7 'I will buy you brave bridal shoes,
　　My love, I 'll buy them bonny;'
　'But I 'll be dead or ye come back,
　　My bonny Andrew Lammie.'

8 'If you 'll be true and trusty too,
　　As I am Andrew Lammie,
　That you will neer kiss lad nor lown
　　Till I return to Fyvie.'

9 'I shall be true and trusty too,
　　As my name 's Tifty's Nanny,
　That I 'll kiss neither lad nor lown
　　Till you return to Fyvie.' —

10 'Love pines awa, love dwines awa,
　　Love pines awa my body;
　And love 's crept in at my bed-foot,
　　And taen possession o me.

11 'My father drags me by the hair,
　　My mother sore does scold me;
　And they would give one hundred merks
　　To any one to wed me.

12 'My sister stands at her bower-door,
　　And she full sore does mock me,
　And when she hears the trumpet sound, —
　　"Your cow is lowing, Nanny!"

13 'O be still, my sister Jane,
　　And leave off all your folly;
　For I 'd rather hear that cow low
　　Than all the kye in Fyvie.

14 'My father locks the door at night,
　　Lays up the keys fu canny,
　And when he hears the trumpet sound, —
　　"Your cow is lowing, Nanny!"

15 'O hold your tongue, my father dear,
　　And let be a' your folly;
　For I would rather hear that cow
　　Than all the kye in Fyvie.'

*　　*　　*　　*　　*　　*

16 'If you ding me, I will greet,
　　And gentlemen will hear me;
　Laird Fyvie will be coming by,
　　And he 'll come in and see me.'

17 'Yea, I will ding you though ye greet
　　And gentlemen should hear you;

Though Laird Fyvie were coming by,
    And did come in and see you.'

18 So they dang her, and she grat,
    And gentlemen did hear her,
And Fyvie he was coming by,
    And did come in to see her.

19 'Mill of Tifty, give consent,
    And let your daughter marry;
If she were full of as high blood
    As she is full of beauty,
I would take her to myself,
    And make her my own lady.'

20 'Fyvie lands ly broad and wide,
    And O but they ly bonny!
But I would not give my own true-love
    For all the lands in Fyvie.

21 'But make my bed, and lay me down,
    And turn my face to Fyvie,

That I may see before I die
    My bonny Andrew Lammie.'

22 They made her bed, and laid her down,
    And turnd her face to Fyvie;
She gave a groan, and died or morn,
    So neer saw Andrew Lammie.

23 Her father sorely did lament
    The loss of his dear Nannie,
And wishd that he had gien consent
    To wed with Andrew Lammie.

24 But ah! alas! it was too late,
    For he could not recall her;
Through time unhappy is his fate,
    Because he did controul her.

25 You parents grave who children have,
    In crushing them be canny,
Lest for their part they break their heart,
    As did young Tifty's Nanny.

C

a. Buchan's Gleanings, p. 98; taken down "from the memory of a very old woman" (p. 197). b. Motherwell's Minstrelsy, p. 239; a stall copy collated with a recited copy.

1 At Mill of Tifty lived a man,
    In the neighbourhood of Fyvie;
He had a luvely daughter fair,
    Was callëd bonny Annie.

2 Her bloom was like the springing flower
    That hails the rosy morning,
With innocence and graceful mein
    Her beautous form adorning.

3 Lord Fyvie had a trumpeter
    Whose name was Andrew Lammie;
He had the art to gain the heart
    Of Mill of Tifty's Annie.

4 Proper he was, both young and gay,
    His like was not in Fyvie,
Nor was ane there that could compare
    With this same Andrew Lammie.

5 Lord Fyvie he rode by the door
    Where livëd Tifty's Annie;

His trumpeter rode him before,
    Even this same Andrew Lammie.

6 Her mother called her to the door:
    'Come here to me, my Annie:
Did eer you see a prettier man
    Than the trumpeter of Fyvie?'

7 Nothing she said, but sighing sore,
    Alas for bonnie Annie!
She durst not own her heart was won
    By the trumpeter of Fyvie.

8 At night when all went to their bed,
    All slept full soon but Annie;
Love so oppresst her tender breast,
    Thinking on Andrew Lammie.

9 'Love comes in at my bed-side,
    And love lies down beyond me;
Love has possest my tender breast,
    And love will waste my body.

10 'The first time me and my love met
    Was in the woods of Fyvie;
His lovely form and speech so soft
    Soon gaind the heart of Annie.

11 ' He called me mistress ; I said, No,
    I 'm Tifty's bonny Annie ;
  With apples sweet he did me treat,
    And kisses soft and mony.

12 ' It 's up and down in Tifty's den,
    Where the burn runs clear and bonny,
  I 've often gane to meet my love,
    My bonny Andrew Lammie.'

13 But now alas ! her father heard
    That the trumpeter of Fyvie
  Had had the art to gain the heart
    Of Mill of Tifty's Annie.

14 Her father soon a letter wrote,
    And sent it on to Fyvie,
  To tell his daughter was bewitchd
    By his servant, Andrew Lammie.

15 Then up the stair his trumpeter
    He callëd soon and shortly :
  ' Pray tell me soon what 's this you 've done
    To Tifty's bonny Annie.'

16 ' Woe be to Mill of Tifty's pride,
    For it has ruined many ;
  They 'll not have 't said that she should wed
    The trumpeter of Fyvie.

17 ' In wicked art I had no part,
    Nor therein am I canny ;
  True love alone the heart has won
    Of Tifty's bonny Annie.

18 ' Where will I find a boy so kind
    That will carry a letter canny,
  Who will run to Tifty's town,
    Give it to my love Annie ?

19 ' Tifty he has daughters three
    Who all are wonderous bonny ;
  But ye 'll ken her oer a' the rest ;
    Give that to bonny Annie.

20 ' It 's up and down in Tifty's den,
    Where the burn runs clear and bonny,
  There wilt thou come and I 'll attend ;
    My love, I long to see thee.

21 ' Thou mayst come to the brig of Slugh,
    And there I 'll come and meet thee ;

It 's there we will renew our love,
    Before I go and leave you.

22 ' My love, I go to Edinburgh town,
    And for a while must leave thee ; '
  She sighëd sore, and said no more
    But ' I wish that I were with you ! '

23 ' I 'll buy to thee a bridal gown,
    My love, I 'll buy it bonny ; '
  ' But I 'll be dead ere ye come back
    To see your bonny Annie.'

24 ' If ye 'll be true and constant too,
    As I am Andrew Lammie,
  I shall thee wed when I come back
    To see the lands of Fyvie.'

25 ' I will be true and constant too
    To thee, my Andrew Lammie,
  But my bridal bed or then 'll be made
    In the green church-yard of Fyvie.'

26 ' The time is gone, and now comes on
    My dear, that I must leave thee ;
  If longer here I should appear,
    Mill of Tifty he would see me.'

27 ' I now for ever bid adieu
    To thee, my Andrew Lammie ;
  Or ye come back I will be laid
    In the green church-yard of Fyvie.'

28 He hied him to the head of the house,
    To the house-top of Fyvie,
  He blew his trumpet loud and shrill,
    It was heard at Mill of Tifty.

29 Her father lockd the door at night,
    Laid by the keys fu canny,
  And when he heard the trumpet sound
    Said, Your cow is lowing, Annie.

30 ' My father dear, I pray forbear,
    And reproach not your Annie ;
  I 'd rather hear that cow to low
    Than all the kye in Fyvie.

31 ' I would not for my braw new gown,
    And all your gifts so many,
  That it was told in Fyvie land
    How cruel ye are to Annie.

32 'But if ye strike me I will cry,
  And gentlemen will hear me;
Lord Fyvie will be riding by,
  And he 'll come in and see me.'

33 At the same time the lord came in;
  He said, What ails thee Annie?
'It's all for love now I must die,
  For bonny Andrew Lammie.'

34 'Pray, Mill of Tifty, give consent,
  And let your daughter marry;'
'It will be with some higher match
  Than the trumpeter of Fyvie.'

35 'If she were come of as high a kind
  As she's advanced in beauty,
I would take her unto myself,
  And make her my own lady.'

36 'Fyvie lands are far and wide,
  And they are wonderous bonny;
But I would not leave my own true-love
  For all the lands in Fyvie.'

37 Her father struck her wonderous sore,
  As also did her mother;
Her sisters also did her scorn,
  But woe be to her brother!

38 Her brother struck her wonderous sore,
  With cruel strokes and many;
He broke her back in the hall-door,
  For liking Andrew Lammie.

39 'Alas! my father and my mother dear,
  Why so cruel to your Annie?
My heart was broken first by love,
  My brother has broke my body.'

40 'O mother dear, make me my bed,
  And lay my face to Fyvie;
Thus will I lie, and thus will die
  For my dear Andrew Lammie.'

41 'Ye neighbours hear, baith far and near,
  And pity Tifty's Annie,
Who dies for love of one poor lad,
  For bonny Andrew Lammie.

42 'No kind of vice eer staind my life,
  Or hurt my virgin honour;
My youthful heart was won by love,
  But death will me exoner.'

43 Her mother than she made her bed,
  And laid her face to Fyvie;
Her tender heart it soon did break,
  And never saw Andrew Lammie.

44 Lord Fyvie he did wring his hands,
  Said, Alas for Tifty's Annie!
The fairest flower's cut down by love
  That ever sprang in Fyvie.

45 'Woe be to Mill of Tifty's pride!
  He might have let them marry;
I should have given them both to live
  Into the lands of Fyvie.'

46 Her father sorely now laments
  The loss of his dear Annie,
And wishes he had given consent
  To wed with Andrew Lammie.

47 When Andrew home frae Edinburgh came,
  With muckle grief and sorrow,
'My love is dead for me to-day,
  I'll die for her to-morrow.

48 'Now I will run to Tifty's den,
  Where the burn runs clear and bonny;
With tears I'll view the brig of Slugh,
  Where I parted from my Annie.

49 'Then will I speed to the green kirk-yard,
  To the green kirk-yard of Fyvie,
With tears I'll water my love's grave,
  Till I follow Tifty's Annie.'

* * *

C. a. 9³. Love so oppressd: b, has possessd.
  11⁴. mony: b, many.
  44³. flower: b, flower's.
  47¹. home: b, hame.

48². For *perhaps Aberdonian for* Where: b, Where.
b. *Insignificant variations will not be noted.*
  7¹. She sighed sore, but said no more.

8^2. Sound *for* soon (soun ?).
9^3. Love has possessd. 11^4. many.
13^4. Of Tiftie's bonny Annie. *After* 14 :

> When Lord Fyvie had this letter read,
>> O dear ! but he was sorry :
> 'The bonniest lass in Fyvie's land
>> Is bewitched by Andrew Lammie.'

16, 17 *are* 17, 16. 16^1. Woe betide Mill.
16^3. He 'll no hae 't. *After* 18 :

> ' Here you shall find a boy so kind
>> Who 'll carry a letter canny,
> Who will run on to Tiftie's town,
>> And gie 't to thy love Annie.'

19^3. a' the lave.
$20^{3,4}$. and meet thy love, Thy bonny Andrew
Lammie.

21. ' When wilt thou come, and I 'll attend?
>> My love, I long to see thee : '
> 'Thou mayst come to the bridge of Sleugh,
>> And there I 'll come and meet thee.'

24^2. As my name 's. 26^1. Our time.
28^3. schill. 30^4. Than hae a' the kine.

35^2. she 's adorned with. 36^1. are fair.
After 43 :

> But the word soon went up and down,
>> Through all the lands of Fyvie,
> That she was dead and buried,
>> Even Tiftie's bonny Annie.

44^3. flower 's. 45^1. O woe betide Mill.
After 46 :

> Her mother grieves both air and late,
>> Her sisters, cause they scornd her ;
> Surely her brother doth mourn and grieve
>> For the cruel usage he 'd givn her.

> But now alas ! it was too late,
>> For they could not recal her ;
> Through life unhappy is their fate
>> Because they did controul her.

47^1. hame. 47^3. love has died. 48^2. Where.
48^4. parted last with Annie. *After* 49 :

> Ye parents grave who children have,
>> In crushing them be canny,
> Lest when too late you do repent ;
>> Remember Tiftie's Annie.

234

CHARLIE MAC PHERSON

A. ' Charlie MacPherson,' Harris MS., fol. 23 b.

B. ' Charlie M'Pherson,' Buchan's Ballads of the North of Scotland, I, 85.

CHARLIE MACPHERSON comes to Kinaldie with a large party of men from the West Isle to take away Helen, whom he has long courted, A 1, 4. Helen's mother is obliged to admit them. When her daughter is asked for, MacPherson is told that she has gone to Whitehouse, to marry auld Gairn, A 5 (Dalgairn, B 12). The party go on to Whitehouse, where indeed they find Helen, and everybody there calling her bride. We expect a collision, and judging by A 8 there was one, with the bride wishing well to the assailants. But in B (where there is no hint that Helen favors her irregular suitor), MacPherson comports himself very mildly, and only wishes, as he goes off, that his heavy heart may light on Whitehouse of Cromar.

The ballad was known to Mrs Brown of

Falkland.* She gives it the title of 'The Carrying-off of the Heiress of Kinady,' from which it is warrantable to conclude that Mac-Pherson was so far successful.

There are several Kinaldies and more than one Whitehouse. The Kinaldie which we have to do with here is a small place in the parish of Logie-Coldstone, Cromar. Milton of Whitehouse is about a mile to the south of Kinaldie, and seems to be the place intended by Whitehouse o Cromar, B 18, 20. Braemar, A 7[1], should then be Cromar.

A

Harris MS., fol. 23 b; from Mrs Harris's singing.

1 CHARLIE MACPHERSON, that braw Hieland lad[die],
  On Valentine's even cam doun to Kinaltie,
  Courtit Burd Hellen, baith wakin an sleepin :
  'Oh, fair fa them has my love in keepin !'

2 Charlie MacPherson cam doun the dykeside,
  Baith Milton an Muirton an a' bein his guide;
  Baith Milton an Muirton an auld Water Nairn,
  A' gaed wi him, for to be his warn.

3 Whan he cam to the hoose o Kinaltie,
  'Open your yetts, mistress, an lat us come in !
  Open your yetts, mistress, an lat us come in !
  For here's a commission come frae your gude-son.

4 'Madam,' says Charlie, ' whare [i]s your dochter ?
  Mony time have I come to Kinatie an socht her ;

Noo maun she goe wi me mony a mile,
  Because I 've brocht mony men frae the West Isle.'

5 'As for my dochter, she has gane abroad,
  You 'll no get her for her tocher gude ;
  She 's on to Whitehouse, to marry auld Gairn :
  Oh, fair fa them that wait on my bairn !'

6 Charlie MacPherson gaed up the dykeside,
  Baith Muirtoun an Milton an a' bein his guide ;
  Baith Muirton an Milton an auld Water Nairn,
  A' gaed wi him, for to be his warn.

7 Whan he cam to the hoose in Braemar,
  Sae weel as he kent that his Nellie was there !
  An Nellie was sittin upon the bed-side,
  An every one there was ca'ing her, bride.

8 The canles gaed oot, they waurna weel licht,
  Swords an spears they glancet fou bricht ;
  Sae laith as she was her true-love to beguile,
  Because he brocht mony men frae the West Isle.

* * * * * * *

* "I have lately, by rummaging in a by-corner of my memory, found some Aberdeenshire ballads which totally escaped me before. They are of a different class from those I sent you, not near so ancient, but may be about a century ago. I cannot boast much of their poetical merits, but the family incidents upon which they are founded, the local allusions which they contain, may perhaps render them curious and not uninteresting to many people. They are as follows : 1st, ' The Baron of Braichly ' [No 203] ; 2d, ' The Lass of Philorth [No 239 ?] ; ' 3d, ' The Tryal of the Laird of Gycht ' [No 209] ; 4th, ' The Death of the Countess of Aboyne ' [No 235] ; 5th, ' The Carrying-off of the Heiress of Kinady.' All these I can recollect pretty exactly. I never saw any of them either in print or manuscript, but have kept them entirely from hearing them sung when a child." Letter to Alexander Fraser Tytler, December 23, 1800.

'Charlie MacPherson' should have been put with Nos 221-5.

B

Buchan's Ballads of the North of Scotland, I, 85.

1 CHARLIE M'PHERSON, that brisk Highland laddie,
At Valentine even he came to Kinadie:

2 To court her Burd Helen, baith waking and sleeping;
Joy be wi them that has her a keeping!

3 Auldtown and Muirtown, likewise Billy Beg,
All gaed wi Charlie, for to be his guide.

4 Jamie M'Robbie, likewise Wattie Nairn,
All gaed wi Charlie, for to be his warran.

5 When they came to Kinadie, they knockd at the door;
When nae ane woud answer, they gaed a loud roar.

6 'Ye'll open the door, mistress, and lat us come in;
For tidings we've brought frae your appearant guid-son.'

7 For to defend them, she was not able;
They bangd up the stair, sat down at the table.

8 'Ye'll eat and drink, gentlemen, and eat at your leisure;
Nae thing's disturb you, take what's your pleasure.'

9 'O madam,' said he, 'I'm come for your daughter;
Lang hae I come to Kinadie and there sought her.

10 'Now she's gae wi me for mony a mile,
Before that I return unto the West Isle.'

11 'My daughter's not at home, she is gone abroad;
Ye darena now steal her, her tocher is guid.

12 'My daughter's in Whitehouse, wi Mistress Dalgairn;
Joy be wi them that waits on my bairn!'

13 The swords an the targe that hang about Charlie,
They had sic a glitter, and set him sae rarelie!

14 They had sic a glitter, and kiest sic a glamour,
They showed mair light than they had in the chamour.

15 To Whitehouse he went, and when he came there
Right sair was his heart when he went up the stair.

16 Burd Helen was sitting by Thomas' bed-side,
And all in the house were addressing her, bride.

17 'O farewell now, Helen, I'll bid you adieu;
Is this a' the comfort I'm getting frae you?

18 'It was never my intention ye shoud be the waur;
My heavy heart light on Whitehouse o Cromar!

19 'For you I hae travelled full mony lang mile,
Awa to Kinadie, far frae the West Isle.

20 'But now ye are married, and I am the waur;
My heavy heart light on Whitehouse o Cromar!'

——◆——

A. *Air*, Whilk o ye lasses.

B. *Printed in stanzas of four short lines.*

235

THE EARL OF ABOYNE

A. 'The Earl of Aboyne,' Kinloch MSS, V, 351.

B. The Earl of Aboyne.' a. Buchan's Gleanings, p. 71. b. Gibb MS., p. 29, No 5.

C. Skene MS., p. 58.

D. 'The Earl o Boyn,' "Scotch Ballads, Materials for Border Minstrelsy," No 17, Abbotsford.

E. 'Earl of Aboyne,' Harris MS., fol. 21 b.

F. 'The Earl of Aboyne,' Motherwell's MS., p. 635.

G. Motherwell's MS., p. 131.

H. 'Bonny Peggy Irvine,' Campbell MSS, II, 105.

I. 'Earl of Aboyne,' or, 'Bonny Peggy Irvine,' Motherwell's MS., p. 128.

J. 'Earl of Aboyne,' or, 'Bonny Peggy Irvine,' Motherwell's MS., p. 135.

K. From the recitation of Miss Fanny Walker, two stanzas.

L. 'Earl of Aboyne,' Motherwell's Note-Book, p. 54, one stanza.

THE copy in The New Deeside Guide, by James Brown [Joseph Robertson], Aberdeen, 1832, p. 26, is B a with a few editorial changes. It is repeated in The Deeside Guide, Aberdeen, 1889, with slight variations. The copy in Christie's Traditional Ballad Airs, I, 22, is "given from the way the editor has heard it sung, assisted by Mr Buchan's copy in his Gleanings;" in fact, it is B a with unimportant variations, which must be treated as arbitrary. Smith's New History of Aberdeenshire, I, 207, repeats Aytoun, nearly, and Aytoun, II, 309, 1859, B a, nearly.

None of the versions here given go beyond 1800. Mrs Brown of Falkland, in an unprinted letter to Alexander Fraser Tytler, December 23, 1800, offers him 'The Death of the Countess of Aboyne,' which she had heard sung when a child: see p. 309, note.

A–I. The Earl of Aboyne (who is kind but careless, E) goes to London without his wife, and stays overlong. Information comes by letter that he has married there, B, or that he is in love with another woman, D. Word is brought that he is on his way home, and very near. His lady orders stable-grooms, minstrels, cooks, housemaids, to bestir themselves,

A–E, I, K, makes a handsome toilet, A, B, D, E, F, and calls for wine to drink his health, B, C, D, G. She comes down to the close to take him from his horse, B, C, D, F, and bids him thrice welcome. "Kiss me then for my coming," says the earl, and surprises his wife, and all of us, by adding that the morrow would have been his wedding-day, if he had stayed in London. The lady gives him an angry and disdainful answer. This he resents, and orders his men to mount again; he will go first to the Bog of Gight to see the Marquis of Huntly, and then return to London. The lady attempts, through a servant, to get permission to accompany him, but is repulsed, A, B, C, D (misplaced in G). According to A, C, D 24, F, the countess languished for about a twelvemonth, and then died of a broken heart; but D 25, G, H, make her death ensue before or shortly after the earl's arrival at the Bog o Gight. Aboyne is very much distressed at the tidings; he would rather have lost all his lands than Margaret Irvine, C, D, E, G, H. He goes to the burial with a train of gentlemen, all in black from the hose to the hat, A, C (horse to the hat, B, E, F).

J. No Earl of Aboyne ever married an Ir-

vine, and no Earl of Aboyne would have med-
itated open bigamy, and have informed his
wife while receiving her welcome home how
near he had come to perpetrating the same.
The historical difficulty and the practical absurdity are removed by assuming that J alone
has preserved (or restored) the true and original story, and that all the other copies, beginning with Mrs Brown's, which calls the
lady the Countess of Aboyne, have gone
wrong. In J, Peggy Irvine is only Aboyne's
love, 1^3, and Aboyne is her true lover, 8^3.
Aboyne was careless and kind, and kind to

every woman, and Aboyne staid over long in
London, A, and the ladies they did invite him,
H. Under these circumstances, some Aboyne
may have been on the brink of deserting a
Peggy Irvine to whom he was engaged.

Aboyne is Boyn, D, Boon, H; Irvine is
Harboun, Harvey, D, Ewan, E, K; Bog o
Gight is Bogs o the Geich, D, Bogs o the
Gay, G, Bughts o the Gight, H, Bog o Keith,
J. The Bog o Gight is made Aboyne's prop-
erty in D, G, H. The Marquis of Huntly is
blamed by Aboyne for inciting him to unkind-
ness, D 28, G 11.

A

Kinloch MSS, V, 351; in the handwriting of John Hill
Burton.

1 THE Earl of Aboyne he 's courteous and kind,
    He 's kind to every woman,
  And the Earl of Aboyne he 's courteous and
      kind,
    But he stays ower lang in London.

2 The ladie she stood on her stair-head,
    Beholding his grooms a coming;
  She knew by their livery and raiment so rare
    That their last voyage was from London.

3 'My groms all, ye 'll be well in call,
    Hold all the stables shining;
  With a bretther o degs ye 'll clear up my nags,
    Sin my gude Lord Aboyne is a coming.

4 'My minstrels all, be well in call,
    Hold all my galleries ringing;
  With music springs ye 'll try well your strings,
    Sin my gude lord 's a coming.

5 'My cooks all, be well in call,
    Wi pots and spits well ranked;
  And nothing shall ye want that ye call for,
    Sin my gude Lord Aboyne 's a coming.

6 'My chamber-maids, ye 'll dress up my beds,
    Hold all my rooms in shining;
  With Dantzic waters ye 'll sprinkle my walls,
    Sin my good lord 's a coming.'

7 Her shoes was of the small cordain,
    Her stockings silken twisting;
  Cambrick so clear was the pretty lady's smock,
    And her stays o the braided sattin.

8 Her coat was of the white sarsenent,
    Set out wi silver quiltin,
  And her gown was o the silk damask,
    Set about wi red gold walting.

9 Her hair was like the threads of gold,
    Wi the silk and sarsanet shining,
  Wi her fingers sae white, and the gold rings
      sae grite,
    To welcome her lord from London.

10 Sae stately she steppit down the stair,
    And walkit to meet him coming;
  Said, O ye 'r welcome, my bonny lord,
    Ye 'r thrice welcome home from London!

11 'If this be so that ye let me know,
    Ye 'll come kiss me for my coming,
  For the morn should hae been my bonny wed-
      ding-day
    Had I stayed the night in London.'

12 Then she turned her about wi an angry look,
    O for such an a sorry woman!
  'If this be so that ye let me know,
    Gang kiss your ladies in London.'

13 Then he looked ower his left shoulder
    To the worthie companie wi him;

Says he, Isna this an unworthy welcome
The we 've got, comin from London !

14 'Get yer horse in call, my nobles all,
   And I 'm sorry for yer coming,
   But we 'll horse, and awa to the bonny Bog o
     Gight,
   And then we 'll go on to London.'

15 'If this be Thomas, as they call you,
   You 'll see if he 'll hae me with him ;
   And nothing shall he be troubled with me
   But myself and my waiting-woman.'

16 'I 've asked it already, lady,' he says,
   'And your humble servant, madam ;
   But one single mile he winna lat you ride
   Wi his company and him to London.'

17 A year and mare she lived in care,
   And docters wi her dealin,

And with a crack her sweet heart brack,
And the letters is on to London.

18 When the letters he got, they were all sealed
     in black,
   And he fell in a grievous weeping ;
   He said, She is dead whom I loved best
   If I had but her heart in keepin.

19 Then fifteen o the finest lords
   That London could afford him,
   From their hose to their hat, they were all
     clad in black,
   For the sake of her corpse, Margaret Irvine.

20 The furder he gaed, the sorer he wept,
   Come keping her corpse, Margaret Irvine.
   Until that he came to the yetts of Aboyne,
   Where the corpse of his lady was lying.

B

a. Buchan's Gleanings, p. 71, 1825. b. Gibb MS., p. 29,
No 5, 1882, as learned by Mrs Gibb, senior, "fifty years
ago," in Strachan, Kincardineshire.

1 THE Earl o Aboyne to old England 's gone,
   An a his nobles wi him ;
   Sair was the heart his fair lady had
   Because she wanna wi him.

2 As she was a walking in her garden green,
   Amang her gentlewomen,
   Sad was the letter that came to her,
   Her lord was wed in Lunan.

3 'Is this true, my Jean,' she says,
   'My lord is wed in Lunan ?'
   'O no, O no, my lady gay,
   For the Lord o Aboyne is comin.'

4 When she was looking oer her castell-wa,
   She spied twa boys comin :
   'What news, what news, my bonny boys ?
   What news hae ye frae Lunan ?'

5 'Good news, good news, my lady gay,
   The Lord o Aboyne is comin ;
   He 's scarcely twa miles frae the place,
   Ye 'll hear his bridles ringin.'

6 'O my grooms all, be well on call,
   An hae your stables shinin ;
   Of corn an hay spare nane this day,
   Sin the Lord o Aboyne is comin.

7 'My minstrels all, be well on call,
   And set your harps a tunin,
   Wi the finest springs, spare not the strings,
   Sin the Lord o Aboyne is comin.

8 'My cooks all, be well on call,
   An had your spits a runnin,
   Wi the best o roast, an spare nae cost,
   Sin the Lord o Aboyne is comin.

9 'My maids all, be well on call,
   An hae your flours a shinin ;
   Cover oer the stair wi herbs sweet an fair,
   Cover the flours wi linen,
   An dress my bodie in the finest array,
   Sin the Lord o Aboyne is comin.'

10 Her gown was o the guid green silk,
   Fastned wi red silk trimmin ;
   Her apron was o the guid black gaze,
   Her hood o the finest linen.

11 Sae stately she stept down the stair,
   To look gin he was comin ;

She called on Kate, her chamer-maid,
  An Jean, her gentlewoman,
To bring her a bottle of the best wine,
  To drink his health that 's comin.

12 She 's gaen to the close, taen him frae 's horse,
  Says, You 'r thrice welcome fra Lunan !
'If I be as welcome hauf as ye say,
  Come kiss me for my comin,
For tomorrow should been my wedding-day
  Gin I 'de staid on langer in Lunan.'

13 She turned about wi a disdainful look
  To Jean, her gentlewoman :
'If tomorrow should been your wedding-day,
  Go kiss your whores in Lunan.'

14 'O my nobles all, now turn your steeds,
  I 'm sorry for my comin ;
For the night we 'll alight at the bonny Bog o
  Gight,
  Tomorrow tak horse for Lunan.'

15 'O Thomas, my man, gae after him,
  An spier gin I 'll win wi him ; '

'Yes, madam, I hae pleaded for thee,
  But a mile ye winna win wi him.'

16 Here and there she ran in care,
  An doctors wi her dealin ;
But in a crak her bonny heart brak,
  And letters gaed to Lunan.

17 When he saw the letter sealed wi black,
  He fell on 's horse a weeping :
'If she be dead that I love best,
  She has my heart a keepin.

18 'My nobles all, ye 'll turn your steeds,
  That comely face [I] may see then ;
Frae the horse to the hat, a' must be black,
  And mourn for bonny Peggy Irvine.'

19 When they came near to the place,
  They heard the dead-bell knellin,
And aye the turnin o the bell
  Said, Come bury bonny Peggy Irvine.

C

Skene MS., p. 58 ; taken down in the North of Scotland,
1802–3.

1 THE Earl of Aboyne he 's careless an kin,
  An he is new come frae London ;
He sent his man him before,
  To tell o his hame-comin.

2 First she called on her chamberline,
  Sin on Jeanie, her gentlewoman :
'Bring me a glass o the best claret win,
  To drink my good lord's well-hame-comin.

3 'My servants all, be ready at a call,
  .   .   .   .

  For the Lord of Aboyne is comin

4 'My cooks all, be ready at a call
  .   .   .   .

Wi the very best of meat,
  For the Lord of Aboyne is comin.

5 'My maids all, be ready at a call,
  .   .   .   .

The rooms I 've the best all to be dressd,
  For the Lord of Aboyn is comin.'

6 She did her to the closs to take him fra his
  horse,
  An she welcomed him frae London :
  .   .   .   .

  'Ye 'r welcome, my good lord, frae Lon-
    don ! '

7 'An I be sae welcome, he says,
  'Ye 'll kiss me for my comin,
For the morn sud hae bin my weddin-day
  Gif I had staid in London.'

8 She turned her about wi a disdainfull look,
  Dear, she was a pretty woman !
'Gif the morn shud hae bin yer weddin-day,
  Ye may kiss your whores in London.'

9 .   .   .   .
  .   .   .   .

'So I shall, madam, an ye 's hae na mare to
    sey,
  For I 'll dine wi the Marquis of Huntley.'

10 She did her to his servant-man,
     I wat they caed him Peter Gordon :
   ' Ye will ask my good lord if he will let me
     Wi him a single mile to ride [to London].'

11 ' Ye need not, madam,   .   .   .
     I have asked him already ;
   He will not let ye a single mile ride,
     For he is to dine with the Marquis o Huntly.'

12 She called on her chamber-maid,
     Sin on Jean, her gentlewoman :
   ' Ge make my bed, an tye up my head,
     Woe 's me for his hame-comin ! '

13 She lived a year and day, wi mickle grief and
     wae,
   The doctors were wi her dealin ;
   Within a crack, her heart it brack,
     An the letters they went to London.

14 He gae the table wi his foot,
     An koupd it wi his knee,
   Gared silver cup an easer dish
     In flinders flee.

15 .   .   .   .
      .   .   .   .
   ' I wad I had lost a' the lands o Aboyne
     Or I had lost bonny Margat Irvine.'

16 He called on his best serving-man,
     I wat the caed him Peter Gordon :
   ' Gae get our horses saddled wi speed,
     Woe 's me for our hame-comin !

17 .   .   .   .
      .   .   .   .
   ' For we will a' be in black, fra the hose to
     the hat,
   Woe 's me for bonny Margat Irvine !

18 ' We must to the North, to bury her corps,
     Alas for our hame-comin !
   I rather I had lost a' the lands o Aboyne
     Or I had lost bonny Margat Irvine.'

D

"Scotch Ballads, Materials for Border Minstrelsy," No
17 ; in the handwriting of Richard Heber.

1 THE guid Earl o Boyn 's awa to Lonon gone,
    An a' his gallan grooms wie him,
  But, for a' the ribbons that hing at her hat,
    He has left his fair lady behind him.

2 He had not been in London toun
    A month but barely one, O,
  Till the letters an the senes they came to her
    hand
  That he was in love with another woman.

3 ' O what think ye o this, my bonny boy ? ' she
    says,
  ' What think ye o my lord at London ?
  What think ye o this, my bonny boy ? ' she
    says,
  ' He 's in love wie another woman.'

4 That lady lookd out at her closet-window,
    An saw the gallan grooms coming ;

' What think ye o this, my bonny boy ? ' she
    says,
  ' For yonder the gallan grooms coming.'

5 Stately, stately steppit she doun
    To welcome the gallan grooms from London :
  ' Ye 're welcome, ye 're welcome, gallan grooms
    a' ;
  Is the guid Earl o Boyn a coming ?

6 ' What news, what news, my gallan grooms a' ?
    What news have ye from London ?
  What news, what news, my gallan grooms a' ?
    Is the guid Earl o Boyn a-coming ? '

7 ' No news, no news,' said they gallan grooms a',
    ' No news hae we from London ;
  No news, no news,' said the gallan grooms a',
    ' But the guid Earl o Boyn 's a coming,
  An he 's not two miles from the palace-gates,
    An he 's fast coming hame from London.'

8 ' Ye stable-grooms a', be ready at the ca,
    An have a' your stables in shening,

An sprinkle them over wie some costly water,
  Since the guid Earl o Boyn 's a coming.

9 'Ye pretty cooks a', be ready at the ca,
  An have a' your spits in turning,
An see that ye spare neither cost nor pains,
  Since the guid Earl o Boyn 's a coming.

10 'Ye servant-maids, ye 'll trim up the beds,
  An wipe a' the rooms oer wie linnen,
An put a double daisy at every stair-head,
  Since the guid Earl o Boyn 's a coming.

11 'Ye 'll call to me my chambermaid,
  An Jean, my gentlewoman,
An they 'll dress me in some fine array,
  Since the good Earl o Boyn 's a coming.'

12 Her stockens were o the good fine silk,
  An her shirt it was o the camric,
An her goun it was a' giltit oer,
  An she was a' hung oer wie rubbies.

13 That lady lookd out at her closet-window,
  An she thought she saw him coming:
'Go fetch to me some fine Spanish wine,
  That I may drink his health that 's a com-
    ing.'

14 Stately, stately steppit she doun
  To welcome her lord from London,
An as she walked through the close
  She 's peed him from his horse.

15 'Ye 're welcome, ye 're welcome, my dearest
    dear,
  Ye 're three times welcome from London!'
'If I be as welcome as ye say,
  Ye 'll kiss me for my coming;
Come kiss me, come kiss me, my dearest dear,
  Come kiss me, my bonny Peggy Harboun.'

16 O she threw her arms aroun his neck,
  To kiss him for his coming:
'If I had stayed another day,
  I 'd been in love wie another woman.'

17 She turned her about wie a very stingy look,
  She was as sorry as any woman;
She threw a napkin out-oure her face,
  Says, Gang kiss your whore at London.

18 'Ye 'll mount an go, my gallan grooms a',
  Ye 'll mount and back again to London;

Had I known this to be the answer my Meggy 's gein me,
  I had stayed some longer at London.'

19 'Go, Jack, my livery boy,' she says,
  'Go ask if he 'll take me wie him;
An he shall hae nae cumre o me
  But mysel an my waiting-woman.'

20 'O the laus o London the 're very severe,
  They are not for a woman;
An ye are too low in coach for to ride,
  I 'm your humble servant, madam.

21 'My friends they were a' angry at me
  For marrying ane o the house o Harvey;
And ye are too low in coach for to ride,
  I 'm your humble servant, lady.

22 'Go saddle for me my steeds,' he says,
  'Go saddle them soon and softly,
For I maun awa to the Bogs o the Geich,
  An speak wi the Marquess o Huntly.'

23 The guid Earl o Boyn 's awa to London gone,
  An a' his gallan gro[o]ms wie him;
But his lady fair he 's left behind
  Both a sick an a sorry woman.

24 O many were the letters she after him did
    send,
  A' the way back again to London,
An in less than a twelvemonth her heart it did
    break,
  For the loss o her lord at London.

25 He was not won well to the Bogs o the Geich,
  Nor his horses scarcely batit,
Till the letters and the senes they came to his
    hand
  That his lady was newly strickit.

26 'O is she dead? or is she sick?
  O woe 's me for my coming!
I 'd rather a lost a' the Bogs o the Geich
  Or I 'd lost my bonny Peggy Harboun.'

27 He took the table wi his foot,
  Made a' the room to tremble:
'I 'd rather a lost a' the Bogs o the Geich
  Or I 'd lost my bonny Peggy Harboun.

28 'Oh an alas! an O woe 's me!
  An wo to the Marquess o Huntly.

Wha causd the Earl o Boyn prove sae very
    unkin
To a true an a beautifu lady !'

29 There were fifteen o the bravest gentlemen,
    An the bravest o the lords o London,
They went a' to attend her burial-day,
    But the Earl o Boyn could not go wi them.

E

Harris MS., fol. 21 b ; from the recitation of Mrs Harris.

1 'My maidens fair, yoursels prepare.'

2 You may weel knaw by her hair, wi the dia-
    monds sae rare,
    That the Earl of Aboyne was comin.

3 'My minstrels all, be at my call,
    Haud a' your rooms a ringin,
. . . .
    For the Earl of Aboyne is comin.'

4 'Tomorrow soud hae been my bonnie waddin-
    day,
    If I had staid in London.'

5 She turned her aboot wi an angry look,
    An sic an angry woman !
'Gin tomorrow soud hae been your bonnie
    waddin-day,
    Gae back to your miss in Lunnon.'

6 For mony a day an year that lady lived in care,
    An doctors wi her dealin,
Till just in a crack her very heart did brak,
    An her letters went on to Lunnon.

7 There waur four-an-twenty o the noblest lords
    That Lonnon could aford him,
A' clead in black frae the saidle to the hat,
    To convey the corpse o Peggy Ewan.

8 'I 'd rather hae lost a' the lands o Aboyne
    Than lost my pretty Peggy Ewan.'

F

Motherwell's MS., p. 635 ; "from the recitation of Margaret Black, wife of Archie Black, sailor in Ayr, a native of
Aberdeenshire."

1 The Earl of Aboyne is to London gane,
    And a' his nobles with him ;
He 's left his lady him behin,
    He 's awa, to remain in Lundon.

2 She 's called upon her waiting-maid
    To busk her in her claithin ;
Her sark was o cambrick very fine,
    And her bodice was the red buckskin.

3 Her stockings were o silk sae fine,
    And her shoon o the fine cordan ;
Her coat was o the guid green silk,
    Turnit up wi a siller warden.

4 Her goun was also o the silk,
    Turned up wi a siller warden,

And stately tripped she doun the stair,
    As she saw her gude lord comin.

5 She gaed thro the close and grippit his horse,
    Saying, Ye 're welcome hame frae London !
'Gin that be true, come kiss me now,
    Come kiss me for my coming.

6 'For blythe and cantie may ye be,
    And thank me for my comin,
For the morn would hae been my wedding-day
    Had I remained in London.'

7 She turnd her richt and round about,
    She was a waefu woman :
'Gin the morn would hae been your weddin-day,
    Gae kiss your whores in London.'

8 He turned him richt and round about,
    He was sorry for his comin :
'Loup on your steeds, ye nobles a',
    The morn we 'll dine in London.'

9 She lived a year in meikle wae,
    And the doctors dealin wi her;
  At lang and last her heart it brast
    And the letters gade to London.

10 And when he saw the seals o black,
    He fell in a deadly weeping;
  He said, She 's dead whom I loed best,
    And she had my heart in keeping.

11 'Loup on your steeds, ye nobles a',
    I 'm sorry for our comin;
  Frae our horse to our hat, we 'll gae in black,
    And we 'll murn for Peggy Irwine.'

12 They rade on but stap or stay
    Till they came to her father's garden,
  Whare fifty o the bravest lords
    Were convoying Peggy Irwine.

G

Motherwell's MS., p. 131.

1 THE Earl Aboyne to London has gane,
    And all his nobles with him;
  For a' the braw ribbands he wore at his hat,
    He has left his lady behind him.

2 She 's called on her little foot-page,
    And Jean, her gentlewoman;
  Said, Fill to me a full pint of wine,
    And I 'll drink it at my lord's coming.

3 'You 're welcome, you 're welcome, you 're wel-
        come,' she says,
    'You 're welcome home from London!'
  'If I be welcome as you now say,
    Come kiss me, my bonnie Peggy Irvine.

4 'Come kiss me, come kiss me, my lady,' he
        says,
    'Come kiss me for my coming,
  For the morn should hae been my wedding-day,
    Had I staid any longer in London.'

5 She turned about with an angry look,
    Said, Woe 's me for your coming!
  If the morn should hae been your wedding-
        day,
    Go back to your whore in London.

6 He 's called on his little foot-page,
    Said, Saddle both sure and swiftly,
  And I 'l away to the Bogs o the Gay,
    And speak wi the Marquis o Huntly.

7 She has called on her little foot-page,
    Said, See if he 'll take me with him;
  And he shall hae nae mair cumber o me
    But nysell and my servant-woman.

8 'O London streets they are too strait,
    They are not for a woman,
  And it is too low to ride in coach wi me
    With your humble servant-woman.'

9 He had not been at the Bogs o the Gay,
    Nor yet his horse was baited,
  Till a boy with a letter came to his hand
    That his lady was lying streekit.

10 'O woe! O woe! O woe!' he says,
    'O woe 's me for my coming!
  I had rather lost the Bogs o the Gay
    Or I 'd lost my bonny Peggy Irvine.

11 'O woe! O woe! O woe!' he said,
    'O woe to the Marquis o Huntly,
  Gard the Earl of Aboyne prove very unkind
    To a good and a dutiful lady!'

H

Campbell MSS, II, 105.

1 THE Earl of Boon 's to London gone,
    And all his merry men with him;
  For a' the ribbonds hang at his horse's main,
    He has left his lady behind him.

2 He had not been a night in town,
    Nor a day into the city,

Until that the letters they came to him,
And the ladies they did invite him.

3 His lady has lookit oer her left shoulder,
To see if she saw him coming,
And then she saw her ain good lord,
Just newly come from London.

4 'Come kiss me, my dear, come kiss me,' he said,
'Come kiss me for my coming,
For if I had staid another day in town
Tomorrow I would hae been married in Lunnon.'

5 She turned about wi a very saucy look,
As saucy as eer did a woman;
Says, If a' be true that I 've heard of you,
You may go back and kiss your whores in Lunnon.

6 'Go call on Jack, my waiting-man,' he said,
'Go saddle and make him ready;
For I maun away to the Bughts o Gight,
To speak to the Marquess of Huntly.'

7 He had not been at the Bughts of the Gight,
Nor the horses yet weel bated,
Until that the letters came ta him
That his lady was newly streeket.

8 'Wae 's me, my dear! wae 's me!' he said,
'It waes me for my coming;
For I wad rather lost a' the Bughts o the Gight
Or I had lost my bonny Peggy Irvine.'

I

Motherwell's MS., p. 128.

1 THE Earl of Aboyne to London has gone,
And all his nobles with him;
For all the braw ribbands he wore at his hat,
He has left his lady behind him.

2 She has to her high castle gane,
To see if she saw him coming;
And who did she spy but her own servant Jack,
Coming riding home again from London.

3 'What news, what news, my own servant Jack?
What news have you got from London?'
'Good news, good news, my lady,' he says,
'For the Earl of Aboyne he is coming.'

4 She has to her kitchen-maid gane:
'Set your pots and your pans all a boiling;
Have every thing fine for gentry to dine,
For the Earl of Aboyne he is coming.

5 'Stable-grooms all, pray be well employed,
Set your stable-bells all a ringing;
Let your hecks be overlaid with the finest of good hay,
For the Earl of Aboyne he is coming.'

6 She has to her low gates gane,
To see if she saw him coming,
And long seven miles before they came to town
She heard their bridles ringing.

7 'Come kiss me, come kiss me, madam,' he says,
'Come kiss me for my coming,
For the morn should hae been my wedding-day
Had I staid any longer in London.'

8 She 's turned about with an angry look,
Says, Woe 's me for thy coming!
If the morn should hae been your wedding-day,
Go back and kiss your whores in London.

9 They 've turned their horses' heads around,
Their faces all for London;
With their hands to their hats they all rode off,
And they 're all away to London.

J

Motherwell's MS., p. 135; from the recitation of Widow Nicol, of Paisley.

1 THE Earl of Aboyne has up to London gone,
    And all his nobles with him,
  And three broad letters he sent into his love
    He would wed another woman in London.

2 She has turned the honey month about,
    To see if he was coming,
  And lang three miles ere he came to the town
    She heard his bridle ringing.

3 She's went down unto the close and she's taen
      him from his horse,
    Says, Ye're welcome home from London!
  'If I be as welcome, dear Peggy, as you say,
    Come kiss me for my coming.

4 'Come kiss me, come kiss me, dear Peggy,' he
      said,
    'Come kiss me for my coming,
  For tomorrow should have been my wedding-
      day
    Had I tarried any longer in London.'

5 She has turned herself round about,
    And she was an angry woman:
  'If tomorrow should have been your wedding-
      day,
    You may kiss with your sweethearts in Lon-
      don.'

6 'Go saddle me my steed,' he said,
    'Saddle and make him ready;

  For I must away to the bonny Bog of Keith,
    For to visit the Marquis of Huntley.'

7 'Go ask him, go ask, dear Thomas,' she said,
    'Go ask if he'll take me with him;'
  'I've asked him once, and I'll ask him no
      more,
    For ye'll never ride a mile in his company.'

8 'Go make to me my bed,' she said,
    'Make it soft and narrow;
  For since my true lover has slighted me so,
    I will die for him ere morrow.'

9 She has called her waiting-man,
    And Jean her gentlewoman:
  'Go bring to me a glass of red wine,
    For I'm as sick as any woman.'

10 The bed it was not made nor well laid down,
     Nor yet the curtains drawn on,
   Till stays and gown and all did burst,
     And it's alace for bonny Peggy Irvine!

11 The Earl of Aboyne was not at the Bog of
       Keith,
     Nor met wi the Marquis of Huntley,
   Till three broad letters were sent after him
     That his pretty Peggy Irvine had left him.

12 He gave such a rap on the table where he sat
     It made all the room for to tremble:
   'I would rather I had lost all the rents of
       Aboyne
     Than have lost my pretty Peggy Irvine.'

K

Communicated by Mr Alexander Laing; from the recitation of Miss Fanny Walker, of Mount Pleasant, near Newburgh-on-Tay.

1 THE Earl o Aboyne is awa to Lunnon gane,
    An he's taen Joannan wi him,
  An it ill be Yule ere he come again;
    But he micht hae taen his bonnie Peggie
      Ewan.

2 Cook-maidens all, be ready at my call,
    Hae a' your pats an pans a-reekin;
  For the finest o flowrs, gae through your
      bowrs,
    For the Earl o Aboyne's a comin.

L

Motherwell's Note-Book, p. 54. "An old woman (native of Banfshire) sings 'The Earl of Aboyne,' beginning:"

THE Lord Aboyn 's to London gone,
And his hail court wi him ;
Better he had staid at hame,
Or taen his lady wi him.

———•———

A. 3³. *Perhaps* bretlher a: *not understood by me in either case.* clear *may be* clean.
20². keping. *Glossed* "meeting" *in a note, but the line is not intelligible to me, and does not seem to be consistent with what follows.*
B. a. 9³. herbs sweet air. *Robertson, New Deeside Guide, prints* herbs sweet an fair.
12⁶. *Robertson prints* ony langer.

b. 1. The Earl o Aboyne he 's courteous an kind,
       He 's kind to every woman,
     An he has left the castle o Aboyne
       An gane to dwell in Lunan ;
     An sair was the heart his lady had,
       Because she wan na wi him.

   2. As she was walking in her garden green,
        Alang wi her gentlewoman,
      There was a letter brocht to her
        That her lord was wed in London.

3. *Wanting.* 4². saw twa bonny boys.
4⁴. bring ye. 5¹. ye lady.
5². For the Earl o. 5³,⁴. *Wanting.*
6¹. all *wanting.* 6⁴, 8⁴, 9⁶. Earl *for* Lord.
7, 8²,³, 9²⁻⁵, 10, 11¹,². *Wanting.*
9¹. maidens.
11⁵. Gae bring me a pint o the gude **red** wine.
12². Says, Ye 're welcome hame.
12³. welcome, he cried, as.

12⁵. wad hae been. 12⁶. only langer.
13¹. her about wi a scornfu.
13³. suld hae been his.
13⁴. He may kiss his miss in.
14¹. My merry men a'.
14². I 'm wae at heart for.
14³. The nicht we 'll licht.
14⁴. An the morn tak.
15, 16¹,², 17⁴, 18². *Wanting.*
18¹. My merry men a' now turn.
19¹. near to bonny Aboyne. 19³. the tollin.
a *may have been derived from a printed copy, and* b *learned from the same.*
C. *The latter half of the Skene MS. is very carelessly copied. Here, as in other places, stanzas are not separated, lines are improperly divided, and there are omissions which are in no way indicated.*
1³. man hin | Before to, *etc.*
D. 4⁴. yonder 's? *But* yonder *may* = yonder are.
14⁴. She speed.
G. 7, 8 *are* 2, 3 *in the* MS.
H. 7⁴. streeket. *MS., perhaps,* struket.
I. 1¹, 3⁴. of *is of later insertion.*
6³. came hame, *originally ;* hame *is erased and* to town *written above.*
J. 2¹. *I do not understand* turned the honey month.
3¹. taen from him.
3³. *as you say :* originally written *he says.*
7¹. him *struck out after the second* ask.

236

THE LAIRD O DRUM

A. a. Kinloch MSS, V, 9. **b.** 'Laird of Drum,' Kinloch's Ancient Scottish Ballads, p. 199.

B. 'The Laird of Doune' [miswritten for Drum], Skene MS., p. 78.

C. MS. copy formerly in the possession of Sir Walter Scott.

D. a. Buchan's Ballads of the North of Scotland, II, 194. **b.** 'The Laird of Drum,' Buchan's MSS, II,

101; Dixon, Scottish Traditional Versions of Ancient Ballads, p. 53, Percy Society, vol. xvii. **c.** The New Deeside Guide, by James Brown, [1832,] p. 11. **d.** Gibb MS., p. 21.

E. 'The Laird of Drum,' MS., inserted in Dr Joseph Robertson's interleaved copy of The New Deeside Guide, Aberdeen [1832].

F. a. 'The Ladye o the Drum,' Loudon MS., p. 7. **b.** 'The Laird o the Drum,' Macmath MS., p. 13.

FIRST taken into a collection by Kinloch, 1827, who remarks that the ballad had been printed as a broadside in the North, and was extremely popular. B, the oldest version that has been recovered, was written down in 1802–3. There are verbal agreements between B, especially, and a fragment in Herd's MSS (I, 55, II, 187, Herd's Scottish Songs, 1776, II, 6), and there has been borrowing from one side or the other. Herd's fragment belongs to a ballad of a shepherd's daughter and an earl which is preserved in two copies in Motherwell's MS. (I, 37, 252). No 397 of The Musical Museum, communicated to Johnson, says Stenhouse, by Burns, [1792,] and probably in a large measure his work, begins with stanzas which may have been suggested by the ballad before us or by the other. See an appendix.

The copy in Christie, I, 24, was epitomized from A b, with some alterations. That in The Deeside Guide, 1889, p. 17, is Aytoun's, compounded of A b and D a.

Alexander Irvine, the young laird of Drum, says Spalding, was married to the lady Mary

Gordon on December 7, 1643: Memorials of the Trubles in Scotland, etc., II, 296. Lady Mary Gordon was fourth daughter to George the second Marquis of Huntly, and niece to the Marquis of Argyll. The Laird of Drum suffered extremely in his worldly fortunes through his fidelity to the cause of the Stuarts. This would have been a natural reason for his declining a peerage offered him at the Restoration, and for his marrying, the second time, to win and not to spend. He took for his second wife Margaret Coutts (A 9), "a woman of inferior birth and manners, which step gave great offence to his relations." (Kinloch.) He died in 1687. After the death of Irvine of Drum, Margaret Coutts married Irvine of Cults. She died in 1710, at the age of only forty-five.*

Drum is ten miles west of Aberdeen.†

For the commonplace in A a 3, B 8, C 5, etc., see II, 181 b.

Knortz, Lieder und Romanzen Alt-Englands, No 29, p. 105, translates Allingham's ballad.

---

* Epitaphs and Inscriptions . . . in the North East of Scotland, by Andrew Jervise, 1875, I, 17. (W. Macmath.)

† The House of Drum is a well-known mansion in Liberton, near Edinburgh, and there is a note to **F a** importing (wrongly) that the ballad refers to this place.

A

a. Kinloch MSS, V, 9, in the handwriting of James Beattie. b. Kinloch's Ancient Scottish Ballads, p. 199; "from recitation."

1 O it fell out upon a day,
　　When Drums was going to ride, O
And there he met with a well-far'd may,
　　Keeping her flocks on yon side. O

2 'O fair may, O rare may,
　　Can not you fancy me?
Of a' the lasses here about
　　I like nane so well as thee.'

3 'Set your love on another, kind sir,
　　Set it not on me,
For I'm not fit to be your bride,
　　And your whore I'll never be.'

4 Drums is to her father gane,
　　Keeping his flocks on yon hill,
And he has gotten his consent,
　　And the maid was at his will.

5 'My daughter can neither read nor write,
　　She was neer brought up at school;
But well can she milk cow and ewe,
　　And make a kebbuck well.

6 'She'll winn in your barn at bear-seed time,
　　Cast out your muck at Yule;
She'll saddle your steed in time o need,
　　Draw aff your boots hersell.'

7 'Have not I no clergymen?
　　Pay I no clergy fee?
I'll school her as I think fit,
　　And as I think fit to be.'

8 Drums is to the Highlands gane
　　For to be made ready,
And a' the gentry thereabout
　　Says, Yonder comes Drums and his lady.

9 'Peggy Coutts is a very bonnie bride,
　　And Drums is a wealthy laddie;
But Drums might hae chosen a higher match
　　Than any shepherd's daughter.'

10 Then up bespake his brother John,
　　Says, Brother you've done us wrong;
You've married ane below our degree,
　　A stain to a' our kin.

11 'Hold your tongue, my brother John,
　　I have done you no wrong;
For I've married ane to wirk and win,
　　And ye've married ane to spend.

12 'The last time that I had a wife,
　　She was above my degree;
I durst not come in her presence
　　But with my hat on my knee.'

13 There was four-and-twenty gentlemen
　　Stood at the yetts o Drum;
There was na ane amang them a'
　　That welcomd his lady in.

14 He's taen her by the milk-white hand
　　And led her in himsell,
And in thro ha's and in thro bowers,
　　'And you're welcome, Lady o Drum.'

15 Thrice he kissd her cherry cheek,
　　And thrice her cherry chin,
And twenty times her comely mouth,
　　'And you're welcome, Lady o Drum.'

16 'Ye shall be cook in my kitchen,
　　Butler in my ha;
Ye shall be lady at my command
　　When I ride far awa.'

17 'But what will I do when auld Drum dies,
　　When auld Drum dies and leaves me?
Then I'll tak back my word again,
　　And the Coutts will come and see me.'

* 　 * 　 * 　 * 　 * 　 * 　 *

B

Skene MS., p. 78; taken down from recitation in the north of Scotland, 1802–3.

1 THERE was a knight, [an a gallant knight,]
 An a gallant knight was he,
 An he 's faen in love
  Wi his shepherd's daghterie.

2 . . . . . .
 He could neither gang nor ride,
 He fell so deep in her fancy,
  Till his nose began to bleed.

3 'Bonny may, an bra may,
 Canna ye on me rue?
 By a' the maid[s] I ever saw,
  There is nane I loo by you.'

4 'Ye 'r a shepherd's ae daghter,
 An I 'm a barron's son;
 An what pleasure I wad hae
  To see ye gae out an in!'

5 'I 'm a shepherd's ae dochter,
 An ye 'r a barron's son;
 An there is nae pleasure I could ha
  To see ye gae out or in.

6 . . . . . .
 . . . . . .
 'For I wadna gie the fancy of my bonny love
  For na love nor favour o you.'

7 'Bonny may, an bra may,
 Canna ye on me rue?
 By a' the maids I ever saw
  There is nane I loo by you.'

8 'Lay na yer fancy, sir, on me,' she says,
 'Lay na yer fancy on me;

For I 'm our low to be yer bride,
 An yer quine I 'll never be.

9 'For I will wear nane o yer silks,
 Nor nane o yer scarlet claes;
 For the hue o the whin shall be my gown,
  An I will gae as I pleas.'

10 . . . . . .
 . . . . . .
 'Ye 'r na our laigh to be my bride,
  An my quine ye 's never be.

11 'Bonny may, and bra may,
 Winna ye on me rue?
 By a' the maids I ever see,
  There 's nane I loo but you.'

12 'Gin ye ha faen so deep in my fancy
 Ye can neither gan[g] nor ride,
 Gae tak me to the middle o the ring,
  An bring me guid companie.'

13 He has taen her by the milk-white hand
 And led her thro haas an bowers:
 'Ye 'r the choice of my heart,
  An a' I hae is yours.'

14 He took her by the milk-white hand
 And led her out and in:
 'Ye 'r the choice o my heart,
  My dear, ye 'r welcome in.'

15 Out spake his brither John,
 'Brither, ye ha done great wrong;
 Ye hae married a wife this night
  Disdained by a' yer kin.'

16 'Hold yer tong, my brither John,
 For I hae don na wrong;
 For I ha married a wife to . . . ,
  An ye ha ane to spend.'

C

From a MS. copy formerly in possession of Sir Walter Scott; communicated by the Rev. W. Forbes-Leith, through Mr Macmath.

1 THERE was a shepherd's daughter
 Sheering at the bear,

And by cam the Laird o Drum,
 On an evening clear.

2 'O will ye fancy me, fair maid?
 O will ye fancy me?
 O will ye fancy me, fair maid,
  An lat the sheering be?'

3 'O say na sae again, kind sir,
　　O say na sae again;
　I 'm owr low to be your bride,
　　Ye 'r born owr high a man.'

4 Said, Fair maid, O rare maid,
　　Will ye on me rue?
　Amang a' the lasses o the land
　　I fancy nane but you.

5 'Lay your love on another,' she said,
　　'And lay it not on me,
　For I 'm owr low to be your bride,
　　Your miss I 'll never be.

6 'Yonder is my father dear,
　　Wi hogs upon yon hill;
　Gif ye get but his consent,
　　I shall be at your will.'

7 He 's taen him to her father dear,
　　Keeps hogs upon yon hill,
　An he has gotten his consent,
　　The may was at his will.

8 'My daughter canna read or write,
　　She never was at school;
　Weel can she milk cow and ewe,
　　An serve your house fu weel.

9 'Weel can she shack your barns
　　An gae to mill an kill,
　Saddle your steed in time o need,
　　And draw your boots hirsel.

10 'She canna wear your silk sae fine,
　　Nor yet your silver clear;

The hue o the ewe man be her weed,
　　Altho she was your dear.'

11 He 's wedded the shepherd's daughter,
　　An he has taen her hame;
　He 's wedded the shepherd's daughter,
　　An led her on to Drum.

12 There were four an twenty bold barons
　　Stood at the yet o Drum;
　There was na ane amang them a'
　　That welcomd his lady hame.

13 Out then spak his brother dear,
　　Says, Ye 'v done mickel wrong;
　Ye 'v wedded a mean woman,
　　The lack o a' our kin.

14 'I never did thee wrong, brother,
　　I never did thee wrong;
　I 've wedded a woman to work an win,
　　An ye hae ane to spen.

15 'The last woman I wedded
　　Was aboon my degree;
　I could na sit in her presence
　　But wi hat upon my knee.'

16 He 's taen her by the milk-white hand
　　An led her but an ben,
　An in the ha, amang them a',
　　He 's hailed her Lady Drum.

17 'Now I 've wedded the shepherd's daughter,
　　An I hae brought her hame,
　In the ha, amang ye a',
　　She is welcome hame to Drum.'

———————

D

a. Buchan's Ballads of the North of Scotland, II, 194.
b. Buchan's MSS, II, 101.　c. The New Deeside Guide, by
James Brown [Joseph Robertson], [1832], p. 11.　d. Gibb
MS., p. 21, No 4, from the recitation of a schoolfellow at
Auchinblae, Kincardineshire, about 1851.

1 THE laird o Drum is a hunting gane,
　　All in a morning early,
　And he did spy a well-far'd may,
　　Was shearing at her barley.

2 'O will ye fancy me, fair may,
　　And let your shearing be, O
　And gang and be the lady o Drum?
　　O will ye fancy me?' O

3 'I winna fancy you,' she says,
　　'Nor let my shearing be;
　For I 'm ower low to be Lady Drum,
　　And your miss I 'd scorn to be.'

4 'But ye 'll cast aff that gown o grey,
　　Put on the silk and scarlet;

I 'll make a vow, and keep it true,
  You 'll neither be miss nor harlot.'

5 'Then dee you to my father dear,
    Keeps sheep on yonder hill;
  To ony thing he bids me do
    I 'm always at his will.'

6 He has gane to her father dear,
    Keeps sheep on yonder hill:
  'I 'm come to marry your ae daughter,
    If ye 'll gie me your gude will.'

7 'She 'll shake your barn, and winna your corn,
    And gang to mill and kill;
  In time of need she 'll saddle your steed;
    And I 'll draw your boots mysell.'

8 'O wha will bake my bridal bread,
    And wha will brew my ale,
  And wha will welcome my lady hame,
    It 's mair than I can tell.'

9 Four an twenty gentle knights
    Gied in at the yetts o Drum;
  But nae a man lifted his hat
    Whan the lady o Drum came in.

10 But he has taen her by the hand,
     And led her but and ben;
   Says, You 'r welcome hame, my lady Drum,
     For this is your ain land.

11 For he has taen her by the hand,
     And led her thro the ha;
   Says, You 'r welcome hame, my lady Drum,
     To your bowers ane and a'.

12 Then he ['s] stript her o the robes o grey,
     Drest her in the robes o gold,
   And taen her father frae the sheep-keeping,
     Made him a bailie bold.

13 She wasna forty weeks his wife
     Till she brought hame a son;
   She was as well a loved lady
     As ever was in Drum.

14 Out it speaks his brother dear,
     Says, You 've dune us great wrang;
   You 've married a wife below your degree,
     She 's a mock to all our kin.

15 Out then spake the Laird of Drum,
     Says, I 've dune you nae wrang;
   I 've married a wife to win my bread,
     You 've married ane to spend.

16 'For the last time that I was married,
     She was far abeen my degree;
   She wadna gang to the bonny yetts o Drum
     But the pearlin abeen her ee,
   And I durstna gang in the room where she was
     But my hat below my knee.'

17 When they had eaten and well drunken,
     And all men bound for bed,
   The Laird o Drum and his lady gay
     In ae bed they were laid.

18 'Gin ye had been o high renown,
     As ye are o low degree,
   We might hae baith gane down the streets
     Amang gude companie.'

19 'I tauld you ere we were wed
     You were far abeen my degree;
   But now I 'm married, in your bed laid,
     And just as gude as ye.

20 'Gin ye were dead, and I were dead,
     And baith in grave had lain,
   Ere seven years were at an end,
     They 'd not ken your dust frae mine.'

———————

E

From Dr Joseph Robertson's interleaved and annotated
copy of The New Deeside Guide, [nominally] by James
Brown [but written by Joseph Robertson], Aberdeen [1832];
inserted at p. 12.

1 THE Laird of Drum is a wooing gane,
    All in a morning early,
  And there he spied a weel-far'd may,
    She was shearing at her barley.

2 'Will you fancy me, my bonny may,
    And will you fancy me? O
  And will you come and be Lady Drum,
    And let your shearing a be?' O

3 'It 's I winna fancy you, kind sir,
       I winna fancy thee ;
   For I 'm too low to be lady o Drum,
       And your whore I would scorn to be.'

4 'Ye 'll cast aff the robes of gray,
       And put on the silk and the scarlet,
   And here to you I 'll make a vow
       Ye 'se neither be whore nor harlot.'

5 'I winna cast aff the robes o gray,
       To put on the silk and the scarlet,
   But I 'll wear the colour of the ewe,
       For they set me better than a' that.

6 'But ye 'll do you doun to my father dear,
       Keeping sheep on yonder hill,
   And the first ae thing that he bids me I 'll do,
       For I wirk aye at his will.'

7 He 's done him doun to her father dear,
       Keeping sheep on yonder hill :
   'Ye hae a pretty creature for your daughter ;
       Dear me! but I like her well.'

8 'It 's she can neither read nor write,
       She was never brought up at the squeel ;
   She canna wash your china cups,
       Nor yet mak a dish o tea.

9 'But well can she do a' ither thing,
       For I learnt the girly mysell ;
   She 'll fill in your barn, and winnow your corn,
       She 'll gang to your kill and your mill,
   And, time o need, she 'll saddle your steed,
       And draw your boots hersell.'

10 'Wha will bake my bridal bread,
       And wha will brew my ale ?
   Wha will welcome my lady in ?
       For it 's more than I can tell.'

11 There was four-and-twenty gentlemen
       Stood a' in the yetts o Drum,
   But there was nane o them lifted their hats
       To welcome the young lady in.

12 But up spake his ae brither,
       Says, Brither, ye hae done wrang ;
   Ye have married a wife this day
       A lauch to a' our kin.

13 'I 've married ane to win my bread,
       But ye married ane to spend ;
   But as lang 's I 'm able to walk to the yetts o
           Drum
       On me she may depend.

14 'The last lady that I did wed
       Was far above my command ;
   I durst not enter the bower where she was
       But my hat low in my hand.'

15 When bells were rung, and mass was sung,
       And a' man bound for bed,
   The Laird o Drum and the shepherd's dother
       In one bed they were laid.

16 'If ye were come o noble bleed
       An were as high as me,
   We could gang to the yetts o Drum
       Amangst gueed companie.'

17 'I tald you ere we was wed
       I was oer low for thee,
   But now we are wedd and in ae bed laid,
       And you must be content wi me.

18 'For an ye were dead, an I were dead,
       And laid in the dust low down,
   When we were baith turnd up again
       Wha could ken your mould frae mine ?'

F

a. Manuscript of David Louden, Morham, Haddington, p. 7, 1873 ; from Mrs Dickson, Rentonhall, derived from her great-grandmother. b. Macmath MS., p. 13 ; from Mr William Traquair, S. S. C., Edinburgh, obtained originally in Perthshire.

1 'Oh, will ye fancy me, fair maid ?
       Oh, will ye fancy me ? O

   Or will ye go to be ladye o the Drum,
       An let a' your shearin abe ? O
           An let a' your shearin abe ? O
           An let a' your shearin abe ? ' O

2 'I can neither read nor write,
       Nor neer been brocht up at schule ;
   But I can do all other things,
       An keep a hoose richt weel.

3 'My faither he's a puir shepherd-man,
  Herds his hogs on yonder hill;
  Gin ye will go get his consent,
    Then I'll be at your call.'

4 He has gane to her father,
  That herds hogs on yonder hill;
  He said, 'You've got a pretty daughter,
    I'd fain tak her to my sel.'

5 'She can neither read nor write,
  Was neer brocht up at schule;
  But she can do all other things,
    An I learnt aye the lassie my sel.

6 'She'll milk your cows, she'll carry your corn,
  She'll gang to the mill or the kiln;
  She'll saddle your steed at any time of need,
    And she'll brush up your boots hersel.'

7 'It's who will bake my bridal bread?
  Or who will brew my ale?
  Or who will welcome this bonnie lassie in?
    For it's more than I can tell.'

8 There's four-and-twenty gentlemen
  Stand doun at the gate o the Drum;

Not one of them all would take off his hat
  For to welcome the bonnie lassie in.

9 .   .   .   .
  .   .   .   .
  'Oh, brother, you've married a wife this day
    A disgrace to all our kin.'

10 'Oh, brother, I've married a wife to win,
   And ye've got one to spen,
   And as long as the bonnie lassie walks out and
     in
   She shall aye be the ladye o the Drum.'

11 When all was done, and no bells rung,
   And all men bound for their bed,
   The laird and the shepherd's bonnie daughter
     In one bed they were laid.

12 'Though I'm not of as noble blood,
   Nor yet of as high degree,
   Now I lie locked in your arms two,
     And you must be contented wi me.

13 'If you were dead, and I were dead,
   And baith laid in one grave,
   If we were baith to be raised up again,
     Wha would ken your dust frae mine?

———◆———

A. a. 1³. wellfar'd May. 2¹. fair May: rare May.
    2⁴. as thee May.
    17. *This stanza looks like a spurious addition.*
  b. *Kinloch has taken fourteen of the seventeen
    stanzas of* a (*all but* 1, 2, 17) *into his
    printed copy, with a change of a word here
    and there* (*not here noticed*), *as was his
    way. The remaining ten stanzas must be
    from recitation, if Kinloch is to be under-
    stood strictly.*

  1. The laird o Drum is a-wooing gane;
       It was on a morning early;
     And he has fawn in wi a bonnie may,
       A-shearing at her barley.

  2. 'My bonnie may, my weel-faurd may,
       O will ye fancy me, O
     And gae and be the lady o Drum,
       And lat your shearing abee?' O

  3. 'It's I canna fancy thee, kind sir,
       I winna fancy thee;
     I winna gae and be lady o Drum,
       And lat my shearing abee.'

After 3. 'My father he is a shepherd mean,
       Keeps sheep on yonder hill,
     And ye may gae and spier at him,
       For I am at his will.

  4. Drum: *and always.*
After 7:

  'I'll learn your lassie to read and write,
     And I'll put her to the scheel;
   She'll neither need to saddle my steed,
     Nor draw aff my boots hersell.

  'But wha will bake my bridal bread,
     Or brew my bridal ale,

And wha will welcome my bonnie bride,
Is mair than I can tell.'

10⁴. lake *for* stain, *and so entered in pencil in
the MS.*
After 12 :

'The first wife that I did wed,
She was far abeen my degree ;
She wadna hae walkd to the yetts o Drum
But the pearls abeen her bree.

'But an she was adord for as much gold
As Peggie 's for beautie,
She micht walk to the yetts o Drum
Amang gueed companie.'

16³. in my command, *a plausible reading.*
After 16 :

'But I told ye afore we war wed
I was owre low for thee ;
But now we are wed, and in ae bed laid,
And ye maun be content wi me.

'For an I war dead, and ye war dead,
And baith in ae grave laid,
And ye and I war tane up again,
Wha could distan your mouls frae mine ?'

O *is added to the second and fourth lines except when the rhyme is in two syllables, as
in* 1.

B. *Title.* The Laird o Doune. *So written twice :
at p.* 75 *by anticipation, again at p.* 78.
1⁴. daighterie (i *undotted*) : daghter he ?
3¹. May : *and always.* 4⁴, 11⁴. May *added.
for singing.*
6⁴. Sir *added for singing.*
*No division into stanzas, and no indication of
gaps. The deficiency at the end of* 16³ *is
noted by* . . .
D. a. O *is added* (*for singing*) *to the second and
fourth verse of every stanza except* 1, 4,
which have two-syllable rhyme.
19 *is by mistake printed twice.*
b. O *added as in* a.
2¹. me, bonny lassie.
2³. O will ye fancy me, bonny lassie.
2⁴. And lat your shearing be.
3⁴, 4⁴. whore *for* miss. 4¹. ye cast.
7⁴. And *wanting.*
12, 13. *Wanting.*

16²,⁴, 19². above *for* abeen. 16⁵. durst not.
17². all man. 19. *Repeated, as in* a.
20². in your grave : lien.
Dixon made changes in printing this copy.
c. O *is not added as in* a. 1³. he has spied.
2¹. you. 3³. lady o. 5¹. go you.
7¹. winn. 7². mill or. 9⁴. Drum was come.
10⁴. is a' your ain. 12². in robes.
14⁴. all your.
19¹. you weel ere.

20. Gin we were dead, and in grave laid,
And then taen up again,
I doubt they would look wi a gay clear ee
That would ken your dust frae mine.

*In Robertson's annotated and interleaved copy,
besides some readings from* E, *there are
noted in the margin the following :*
7². to your mill and your kill.
9³. But there was nae ane did lift.
17³. and the herd's dochter.
19¹. you before that we. *This stanza twice,
as in* a.
20 *as in* a.
d. O *is not added as in* a, b. 1². Upon a.
1³. he has spied. 2². O will you fancy me.
2⁴. An let your shearin abee.
3¹. said. 3². abee.
3³. For *wanting.* I 'm far ower : lady o.
3⁴. your whore I winna. 4, 5. *Wanting.*
6¹. her auld faither. 6². Kept sheep upon the.
6³. *Wanting.*
6⁴. That the may was at his will.

7. But my daughter can neither read nor write,
She was never at the schule ;
But she 'll saddle your steed in time of need,
An draw aff your boots hersel.

8³. my bonny bride. 8⁴. Is more.
9¹. gentlemen. 9². Stood at.
9³. There was na ane that lifted.
9⁴. Drum was come. 10³. lady o.
10⁴. is a' your ain. 11–13. *Wanting.*
14¹. Out an spake his brither John.
14⁴. a' your. 15¹. Out an.
15³. to save my gear.
16¹. the first time I had a wife.
16³,⁴. I durstna, *etc.,* ⁵,⁶ *come before* ³,⁴.
17². to bed. 17³. an the weel-faured may.
19¹. afore we. 19³. we are : in ae.
19⁴. An I 'm : as thee. 20². in ae grave lain.

20³. were come an gane.
20⁴. Wha could ken your mools.
E. O *is appended, as in* D a, b, *except in* 1, 4, 5.
F. a. "Mrs Dickson says her mother used to say
    she has heard her (her mother's) grand-
    mother sing the following ballad with great
    glee. Air, Boyne Water."
9³,⁴, 10 *are given as one stanza, the last two
    lines* "instead of repeat."
    O *is appended throughout.*
b. *Variations given only in part.*
    O *is appended as in* D, E.
Begins :

The laird o the Drum a hunting went,
    One morning very early,
And there he spied a bonny, bonny may,
    A shearing at the barley.

1. 'And could ye fancy a gentleman?
    An wad ye married be? O
Or wad ye be the lady o the Drum?
    I pray ye tell to me.'

'I could, *etc.*
    And I wad, *etc.*
But for to be the lady o the Drum,
    It's by far too high for me.'

2. *Wanting.* 3², 4². Feeding sheep.
3⁴. I'm entirely at his will. (*Good prose :
    cf.* 5³.)
4³,⁴. It's I am in love wi your daughter, And
    I'll.
5³. But for all other things she'll do very well.
6¹,². *Wanting.* 7. *Wanting.*
8². Stood all at.
8³. And nane o them would put their hand to
    their hat.

9. 'O brother, you've married a wife the day,
    And you have done much ill ;
O brother you've married a wife today
    A scorn to a' your kin.'

10¹,². I've got a wife to win my bread, And
    you've got ane to spend it.
10³,⁴. *Wanting.*
After 10 :

The first wife that I married,
    She was far above my degree ;
I durst na enter the room she was in
    But wi hat below my knee.

11–13. *Wanting.*

APPENDIX

Herd's MSS, I, 55, II, 187 ; Herd's Scottish Songs, 1776, II, 6.

1 'O MY bonie, bonie may,
    Will ye not rue upon me?
A sound, sound sleep I'll never get
    Untill I lie ayon thee.

2 'I'll gie ye four-and-twenty good milk-kye,
    Wer a' caft in ae year, may,
And a bonie bull to gang them by,
    That blude red is his hair, may.'

3 'I hae nae houses, I hae nae land,
    I hae nae gowd or fee, sir ;
I am oer low to be your bryde,
    Your loon I'll never be, sir.'

*   *   *   *   *   *

Motherwell's MS., p. 37 ; from the recitation of Thomas
Risk, smith, learned by him in his youth at St Ninian's,
Stirlingshire.

1 MONTROSE he had a poor shepherd,
    And a poor shepherd was he ;
He had as fair a daughter
    As ever you could see,
And an earl has fallen in love wi her,
    And his bride now she must be.

2 The earl he came to the shepherd's door,
    And he tirled at the pin;
Slowly rose the fair maid
    For to let the earl in.

3 'Good day, good day, fair maid,' he says;
    'Good day, good day,' said she ;
'Good day unto thee, noble sir,
    What is thy will with me?'

4 'I'm so possessed with love to thee,
    That I cannot gang nor stand
Till you go unto yonder church,
    To give me thy right hand.'

5 'Oh, no, oh no,' the fair maid says,
  'Oh that can never be ;
For thou art a lord of good estate,
  And I but of mean degree.

6 'Oh no, oh no,' the fair maid says,
  'Thou 'rt rich and I am poor ;
And I am owre mean to be thy wife,
  Too good to be thy whore.

7 'I can shape, and I can sew,
  And cows and yowes can milk,
But I was neer brought up in a lady's room,
  To sew satin nor silk.

8 'And if you had your will of me
  Ye wud me soon forget;
Ye wad gar turn me doun your stairs
  And bar on me your yett.'

9 'Oh no, oh no,' the earl says,
  'For so shall never be ;
For this night or I eat or drink
  My honoured bride you shall be.'

10 'My father he 's a poor shepherd,
  He 's herding on yon hill ;
You may go to my old father,
  And ask at him his will.'

11 The earl he went to the poor shepherd,
  Who was herding on the lea ;
'Good day, good day, shepherd,' he says;
  'Good day, good day,' said he,
Good day unto your honour, sir ;
  What is your will with me ? '

12 'Oh you have a fair daughter ;
  Will ye give her to me,
Silk and satin she shall wear,
  And, shepherd, so shall ye.'

13 'It 's true I have a fair daughter,
  But I 'll not give her to thee ;
For thou art a lord of good estate,
  And she but of mean degree.

14 'The reason is, thou art too rich,
  And my daughter is too poor ;
She is ower mean to be thy wife,
  Too good to be thy whoore.

15 'She can shape, etc. (as verse 7).

16 'And if you had your will of her, etc. (8).

17 'Oh no, oh no,' the earl says, etc. (9).

18 The earl he to the fair maid again,
  Who was spinning at her wheel ;

She had but one petticoat on her,
  But oh she set it weel !

19 'Cast off, cast off that petticoat
  That you were wont to wear,
And put on a gown of the satin silk,
  With a garland in your hair.'

20 She cast off the petticoat
  That she was wont to wear,
And she put on a gown of the satin silk,
  With a garland in her hair.

21 Many, many was there that night
  To bear them company ;
And she is the earl's wife,
  She 's thrice fairer than he.

Motherwell's MS., p. 252; from the recitation of Mrs
Crum, Dumbarton, 7 April, 1825.

1 'O FAIR maid and true maid,
  Will ye not on me rue, maid?
Here 's my hand, my heart's command,
  I 'll come and go by you, maid.

2 'I 've four-and-twenty good milk-kye,
  A' calved in a[e] year, maid,
And a bonnie bill to eisin them,
  Just as red as your hair, maid.'

3 'Your kye go as far in my heart
  As they go in my heel, sir ;
And, altho I be but a shepherd's dochter,
  I love my body weel, sir.

4 'I love my body weel, sir,
  And my maidenhead far better ;
And I 'll keep it to marry me,
  Because I 'm scarse o tocher.'

5 This knicht he turned his bridle about,
  While the tear stood in his ee ;
And he 's awa to her father gane,
  As fast as he could dree.

6 'Gude een, gude een, you gude auld man,'
  'Gude een, you earl's knicht, sir;'
'But you have a fair dochter,' he says,
  'Will you grant her to me, sir?
O silks and satins she shall wear,
  Indeed and so shall ye, sir.'

7 'I have a fair dochter,' he says,
  'She 's fair of blood and bane, sir;
But an ye had your will o her
  Ye wud leave her alane, sir.'

8 'Ye would steek her not your chamber-doors,
  And bar her at your yett, sir ;

And an ye had your will o her
Ye wud her soon forget, sir.'

9 This knicht he turned his bridle about,
While the tear stood in his ee,
And he 's awa to this fair maid gane,
As fast as he could drie.

10 ' O fair maid and true maid,
Will ye not on me rue, maid ?
Here 's my hand, my heart's command,
I 'll come and go by you, maid.

11 ' Cast aff, cast aff your gay black gowns,
Put on your gowns of silk, maid ;
Cast aff, cast aff your gay black snoods,
Put the garlands on your hair, maid.'

12 ' It 's I can bake, and I can brew,
And good kye can I milk, sir ;
But I was neer born in the time o the year
To wear the gowns o silk, sir.

13 ' Yestreen I was a shepherd's dochter,
Whistling my hogs to the hill ;
But the nicht I am an earl's lady,
I may wear what I will.'

Johnson's Museum, No 397, p. 410.

As I went out ae May morning,
A May morning it chanc'd to be,
There I was aware of a weelfar'd maid,
Cam linkin oer the lea to me.

O but she was a weelfar'd maid,
The bonniest lass that 's under the sun ;
I spier'd gin she could fancy me,
But her answer was, I am too young.

' To be your bride I am too young,
To be your loun wad shame my kin ;
So therefore, pray, young man, begone,
For you never, never shall my favour win.'

237

THE DUKE OF GORDON'S DAUGHTER

a. ' The Duke of Gordon's Daughter,' The Duke of Gordon's Garland, Percy Papers, and another edition in a volume of garlands formerly in Heber's library. b. ' The Duke of Gordon's Daughters,' a stall-copy, printed for John Sinclair, Dumfries. c. ' The Duke of Gordon's Daughters,' Stirling, printed by M. Randall. d. ' The Duke of Gordon's Three Daughters,' Peterhead, printed by P. Buchan. e. ' The Duke of Gordon's Three Daughters,' Kinloch MSS, I, 125. f. ' The Duke o Gordon's Daughters,' Murison MS., p. 90, Aberdeenshire. g. ' The Duke o Gordon's Daughter,' Gibb MS., p. 13, No 3, from the recitation of Mrs Gibb, senior. h. ' The Duke of Gordon's Three Daughters,' Macmath MS., p. 31, a fragment recited by Mrs Macmath, senior, in 1874, and learned by her fifty years before.

A COPY of a was reprinted by Ritson, Scottish Songs, 1794, II, 169. (There are three slight variations in Ritson, two of which are misprints.) Fifteen stanzas are given from Ritson in Johnson's Musical Museum, ' The Duke of Gordon has three daughters,' No 419, p. 431, 1797 (with a single variation and the correction of a misprint). Smith's Scotish Minstrel, IV, 98, repeats the stanzas in the Museum, inserting a few words to fill out lines for singing. Christie, Traditional Ballad Airs, I, 2, has made up a ballad from three " traditional " copies. A fragment of four stanzas in Notes and Queries, Second Series, VII, 418, requires no notice.

Burns gave the first stanza as follows (Cromek's Reliques, p. 229, ed, 1817 ; Cromek's Select Scotish Songs, I, 86, 1810) :

The lord o Gordon had three dochters,
Mary, Marget, and Jean ;
They wad na stay at bonie Castle Gordon,
But awa to Aberdeen.

The first sister's name is given as Mary in e also.

It is very likely that the recited copies were

originally learned from print. e and g have two stanzas which do not appear in a–d, but these may occur in some other stall-copy, or have been borrowed from some other ballad.

Ritson pointed out that George Gordon, the fourth Earl of Huntly, killed at Corrichie in 1562, had three daughters, named Elizabeth, Margaret, and Jean, and that Jean, the youngest, married Alexander Ogilvie, Laird of Boyne. These facts, however, can have no relevancy to this ballad. Ogilvie was Lady Jean Gordon's third husband, and at the death of the second, in 1594, she was in her fiftieth year, or near to that. Her marriage with the Laird of Boyne was "for the utility and profit of her children," of which she had a full quiver.*

Jean, one of the three daughters of the Duke of Gordon (there was no Duke of Gordon before 1684, but that is early enough for our ballad), falls in love with Captain Ogilvie at Aberdeen. Her father threatens to have the captain hanged, and writes to the king to ask that favor. The king refuses to hang Ogilvie, but reduces him to the ranks, makes him a 'single' man. The pair lead a wandering life for three years, and are blessed with as many children. At the end of that time they journey afoot to the Highland hills, and present themselves at Castle Gordon in great destitution. Lady Jean is welcomed; the duke will have nothing to do with Ogilvie. Ogilvie goes over seas as a private soldier, but is soon after sent for as heir to the earldom of Northumberland. The duke is now eager to open Castle Gordon to the Captain. Ogilvie wants nothing there but Jean Gordon, whom, with her three children, he takes to Northumberland to enjoy his inheritance.

Nothing in the story of the ballad is known to have even a shadow of foundation in fact.

---

1 THE Duke of Gordon has three daughters,
    Elizabeth, Margaret, and Jean ;
They would not stay in bonny Castle Gordon,
    But they would go to bonny Aberdeen.

2 They had not been in Aberdeen
    A twelvemonth and a day
Till Lady Jean fell in love with Captain Ogilvie,
    And away with him she would gae.

3 Word came to the Duke of Gordon,
    In the chamber where he lay,
Lady Jean has fell in love with Captain Ogilvie,
    And away with him she would gae.

4 'Go saddle me the black horse,
    And you'll ride on the grey,
And I will ride to bonny Aberdeen,
    Where I have been many a day.'

5 They were not a mile from Aberdeen,
    A mile but only three,
Till he met with his two daughters walking,
    But away was Lady Jean.

6 'Where is your sister, maidens ?
    Where is your sister now ?
Where is your sister, maidens,
    That she is not walking with you ?'

7 'O pardon us, honoured father,
    O pardon us,' they did say ;
'Lady Jean is with Captain Ogilvie,
    And away with him she will gae.'

8 When he came to Aberdeen,
    And down upon the green,
There did he see Captain Ogilvie,
    Training up his men.

9 'O wo to you, Captain Ogilvie,
    And an ill death thou shalt die ;
For taking to thee my daughter,
    Hangèd thou shalt be.'

10 Duke Gordon has wrote a broad letter,
    And sent it to the king,
To cause hang Captain Ogilvie
    If ever he hanged a man.

* Lady Jean Gordon was divorced from the Earl of Bothwell in 1567, "being then twenty years of age," says Sir Robert Gordon. His continuator puts her death at 1629, in her eighty-fourth year. Genealogy of the Earls of Sutherland, pp. 143, 145, 169, 469.

11 'I will not hang Captain Ogilvie,
    For no lord that I see;
    But I 'll cause him to put off the lace and scarlet,
    And put on the single livery.'

12 Word came to Captain Ogilvie,
    In the chamber where he lay,
    To cast off the gold lace and scarlet,
    And put on the single livery.

13 'If this be for bonny Jeany Gordon,
    This pennance I 'll take wi;
    If this be for bonny Jeany Gordon,
    All this I will dree.'

14 Lady Jean had not been married,
    Not a year but three,
    Till she had a babe in every arm,
    Another upon her knee.

15 'O but I 'm weary of wandering!
    O but my fortune is bad!
    It sets not the Duke of Gordon's daughter
    To follow a soldier-lad.

16 'O but I 'm weary of wandering!
    O but I think lang!
    It sets not the Duke of Gordon's daughter
    To follow a single man.'

17 When they came to the Highland hills,
    Cold was the frost and snow;
    Lady Jean's shoes they were all torn,
    No farther could she go.

18 'O wo to the hills and the mountains!
    Wo to the wind and the rain!
    My feet is sore with going barefoot,
    No further am I able to gang.

19 'Wo to the hills and the mountains!
    Wo to the frost and the snow!
    My feet is sore with going barefoot,
    No farther am I able for to go.

20 'O if I were at the glens of Foudlen,
    Where hunting I have been,
    I would find the way to bonny Castle Gordon,
    Without either stockings or shoon.'

21 When she came to Castle Gordon,
    And down upon the green,

The porter gave out a loud shout,
    'O yonder comes Lady Jean!'

22 'O you are welcome, bonny Jeany Gordon,
    You are dear welcome to me;
    You are welcome, dear Jeany Gordon,
    But away with your Captain Ogilvie.'

23 Now over seas went the captain,
    As a soldier under command;
    A message soon followed after
    To come and heir his brother's land.

24 'Come home, you pretty Captain Ogilvie,
    And heir your brother's land;
    Come home, ye pretty Captain Ogilvie,
    Be Earl of Northumberland.'

25 'O what does this mean?' says the captain;
    'Where 's my brother's children three?'
    'They are dead and buried,
    And the lands they are ready for thee.'

26 'Then hoist up your sails, brave captain,
    Let 's be jovial and free;
    I 'll to Northumberland and heir my estate,
    Then my dear Jeany I 'll see.'

27 He soon came to Castle Gordon,
    And down upon the green;
    The porter gave out with a loud shout,
    'Here comes Captain Ogilvie!'

28 'You 're welcome, pretty Captain Ogilvie,
    Your fortune 's advanced I hear;
    No stranger can come unto my gates
    That I do love so dear.'

29 'Sir, the last time I was at your gates,
    You would not let me in;
    I 'm come for my wife and children,
    No friendship else I claim.'

30 'Come in, pretty Captain Ogilvie,
    And drink of the beer and the wine;
    And thou shalt have gold and silver
    To count till the clock strike nine.'

31 'I 'll have none of your gold or silver,
    Nor none of your white-money;
    But I 'll have bonny Jeany Gordon,
    And she shall go now with me.'

32 Then she came tripping down the stair,
  With the tear into her eye;
One babe was at her foot,
  Another upon her knee.

33 'You're welcome, bonny Jeany Gordon,
  With my young family;
Mount and go to Northumberland,
  There a countess thou shall be.'

———◆———

a. The Duke of Gordon's Garland, composed of several excellent New Songs. I. The Duke of Gordon's Daughter. II. A new song calld Newcastle Ale. Licensed and enterd according to order.

Heber's copy differs in a few places from Percy's, and generally for the worse.

4². on *wanting*. 7⁴. she woud.
10³. cause *wanting*. 13⁴. will not.
16². think it. 18². and rain. 24³. you.
24⁴. And be. 32². tears in her eyes.

Ritson's. 9³. *wants* thee. 13³. *wants* for. 31¹. gold and.

b. *Two copies, one in the British Museum,* 1078. i. 20 (7), Printed at the St. Michael Press, by C. M'Lachlan, Dumfries, *dated in the catalogue* 1785?

c. *British Museum,* 11621. b. 12 (28), *dated* 1810?

A beautiful old song, entitled the Duke of Gordon's three Daughters. To which is added The Challenge. Stirling: Printed by M. Randall.

d. *British Museum,* 1078. k. 4 (5), *dated* 1820? The Duke of Gordon's Three Daughters. To which is added Mrs Burns Lament for Burns. Peterhead: Printed by P. Buchan.

b, c, d. 1¹. had. 1³. stay at. 1⁴. they went to.
2¹. in bonny. 2³. Till Jean.
2⁴. b. him went she. c, d. And from him she would not stay.
3¹. come.
3³,⁴. How Lady Jean fell in love with a captain, And from him she would not stay.
4¹. to me: horse, he cry'd.
4². My servant shall ride on. 4³. will go.
4⁴. Forthwith to bring her away.
5². only one. 5³. walking *wanting*.
6¹,³. O where. 6⁴. c, d. not along with.
7¹. b. us, they did say.
7⁴. And from him she would (c, d, will) not stay.
8¹. to bonny.
8⁴. b. A training of. c, d. A training his gallant.

9¹. woe be to thee.
9⁴. High hanged. b. shalt thou.
10¹. b. The Duke he wrote. c, d. The D. of G. wrote a letter.
10². b. he sent. 10³. Desiring him to hang.
10⁴. b. eer he causd hang any. c, d. For marrying his daughter Jean.
11¹. b. O no I. c, d. Said the king, I'll not.
11². b. For any (c, d, all the) offence that.
11³. him put off the scarlet. 12¹. Now word.
12³. To strip off. 13¹,³. b. Jean.
13³. c, d. for my true-love.
13⁴. this and more I'll.
14². c, d. Not *wanting*. b, c, d. but only.
14⁴. And another.
15¹. b. weary, weary wandering. c, d. weary wandering.

16. O hold thy tongue, bonny Jean Gordon,
  O hold your tongue, my lamb!
                    (c, d. thy)
    For once I was a noble captain,
    Now for thy sake a single man.

17¹. b. O high is the hills and the mountains. c, d. high were: and mountains.
17². b. and the. 18, 19. *Wanting*.
20¹. b. was in. c, d. were in.
20³. I could go. b. Jean *for* Castle, *wrongly*.
19–21 *of* b *are displaced, and come after* b 26: *or,* 23–27 *of* a *follow* a 20, *and then come this stanza* (*not in* a) *and* a 21, 22.
After 20. b:

O hold thy tongue, bonny Jean (c, d. your) Gordon,
  O hold your tongue, my dow!
I've but one half-crown in the world,
  I'll buy hose and shoon (c, d. And I'll) to you.

21¹. b. Then, *wrongly*. b, c, d. to bonny.
21². And coming over the green.
21³. b. porter cried out with a cry. c, d. called out very loudly.

21⁴. b. O *wanting*.   b, c, d. comes our.
22¹. b. O *wanting*.   b, c, d. Jean.
22². b. dearly.   c, d. Her father he did say.
22³. Thou art: Jean.   22⁴. Captain *wanting*.
23¹. over the.   23³. But a messenger.
23⁴. Which caused a countermand.
24¹. b. home now pretty.   c, d. home now
    brave.   24². To enjoy your.
24³. b. home now pretty.   c, d. O come home
    gallant.
24⁴. You 'r the heir of.
25¹. c, d. O *wanting*.   25³. O they.   b. are all.
25⁴. The lands.   b. all ready.   26². And let 's.
26³. I 'll go home and have my.
26⁴. And then.   27¹. bonny Castle.
27². b. And then at the gate stood he.   c, d.
    he stood, *wrongly*.
27³. b. porter cry'd out.   c, d. cry'd with a
    loud voice.
27⁴. c, d. O here.   b. comes the.
28¹. c, d. O you 're welcome now, Captain.
28³. b. come to.   c, d. come within.
29¹. b. at *wrongly omitted*.   b, c, d. gate.
29³. c, d. Now I 'm.   30, 31. *Wanting*.
32¹. c, d. Then Jean came.
32². c, d. The salt tear in.
32³. babe she had at every foot.
32⁴. c, d. And one in her arms did ly.

33. b. You 're welcome, bonny Jean Gordon,
        You are dearly welcome to me ;
     You 're welcome, bonny Jeany Gordon,
        Countess of Cumberland to be.

c, d. The Captain took her straight in his arms,
        O a happy man was he !
     Saying, Welcome, *etc.*, *as in* b.

33⁴. c, d. Northumberland.   *After* 33. b.

So the captain came off (c, d. The captain)
    with his lady,
And also his sweet babes three ;
        (c, d. And his lovely babies three)
Saying, I 'm as good blood by descent,
    Tho the great Duke o Gordon you be.

e—h *are but partially collated*.
e. 1¹. had.   1². Lady Mary, Margret, and Jean.
1⁴. they wadna bide.
7⁴. From him she will not stay.
8. *Wanting*.   9⁴. Hie hangit shalt thou be.
10³ Desiring to hang.

10⁴. For marrying his dochter Jean.
11². For a' the offence I see.
11³. gar him throw aff his broad scarlet.
13⁴. A' this and mair I 'll dree.
14². A year but only three.
15¹. weary wandering.   16. *As in* b, c, d.
17¹. High war the hills and the mountains.
18, 19. *Wanting*.
20³. I could ga.   *After* 20:

'O an I war at bonnie Castle Gordon,
  .   .   .   .
O an I war at bonnie Castle Gordon,
    There I 'd get hose and sheen.'

'Though ye war at bonnie Castle Gordon,
    And standing on the green,
Your father is sae hard-hearted a man
    He wad na lat you in.'

'If I war at bonnie Castle Gordon,
    And standing on the green,
My mither 's a tender-hearted woman,
    She wad rise and lat me in.'

Then: O haud your tongue — I 'll buy hose
    and sheen to you, *as in* b, c, d.
22⁴. awa wi your Ogilvie.
23³. But a messenger.
23⁴. Which causd a countermand.
24⁴. Ye 're the heir of.
26³. I 'll gae hame and heir my estate.
After 26:

'Then hoist up your sail,' said the Captain,
  'And we 'll gae oure the sea,
And I 'll gae to bonnie Castle Gordon,
    There my dear Jeanie to see.'

27². And whan in sicht cam he.
Between 28, 29:

'The last time I cam to your yetts
    Ye wadna let me in,
But now I 'm again at your yetts,
    And in I will not gang.'

30, 31. *Wanting*.
32². Wi the saut tear in her ee.
32³. A babe she held in every arm.
32⁴. Anither gaun at her knee.
33. *As in* c, d, *and a concluding stanza as
    in* b, c, d.

f. 1[1]. had. 2[2]. Months but barely three.

2[4], 3[4], 7[4]. fae him she winna stay.

3[1]. Word 's come. 6[2]. sister Jean.

6[4]. ye are walkin alane. 9[4]. High hangëd.

10[4]. If ever he hangëd ane.

13[2,4]. A' this I 'll dee an mair.

14. *Wanting.* 15[1]. weary wanrin.

15[4]. a single sodger lad. 16. *As in* b, c, d.

18, 19. *Wanting.*

20[2]. Fa monie merry day I hae been.

After 20 a stanza as in b, c, d, *and then this silly one:*

'O they would be bad stockins,
O they would be worse sheen,
O they would be bad stockins
Ye 'd get for half a crown.'

21[1]. they cam to bonnie Aberdeen.

22[4]. awa wi your Ogilvie.

23[3]. But a messenger.

23[4]. Which proved a counterman.

24[4]. You 're the heir o. 26, 30, 31. *Wanting.*

32[2]. Wi the saut tear in her ee.

32[3]. She had a babe in ilka airm.

32[4]. An a third whar nane could see.

33[2]. Ye 're welcome, thrice welcome to me.

33[3,4]. Ye 're welcome, bonnie Jeannie Gordon,
Countess o Northumberlan to be.

g. 1[1]. had. 2[2]. A month but only one.

3[4]. from him she wald not stay.

4[2]. My servant shall ride on.

4[4]. An forthwith bring her away.

5[2]. only one. 6[4]. she 's not along with you.

7[4]. from him she will not stay.

8[4]. Training his gallant men.

9[4]. It 's high hangit ye sall.

10[3]. It was to hang.

10[4]. For marrying his daughter Jean.

11[2]. For all the offence I can see.

11[4]. 12[4]. Put on but the.

13. 'A' this I will do for your sake, Jeanie Gordon,
A' this I will do for thee;
I will cast aff the gold lace an scarlet,
Put on but the single livery.'

14[2]. Ae year but only three.

15[4]. a single soldier-lad.

16. 'O haud your tongue, Jeannie Gordon,
An dinna ye lichtlie me;

I was tane frae a captain's commission
An made low for lyin wi thee.'

(17 *as* 15.) 17[1]. High were the hills an the mountains.

18, 19. *Wanting.* *Before* 20:

'Haud your tongue, Jeannie Gordon,
Ye needna gloom on me;
I hae but ae half-crown in the warld,
I 'll buy stockings an shoon to thee.'

20[1]. If I were in the bonny glens o Ourdlie.

20[2]. Where mony bonny days I hae been.

After 20:

'If ye were at bonny Castle Gordon,
An lichtit on the green,
Your faither is a hard-hearted man,
He wald na let you in.'

'If I were at bonny Castle Gordon,
An lichtit on the green,
My mother 's a good-hearted woman,
She wald open an lat me in.'

22. The Duke o Gordon cam trippin doun stairs
Wi the saut tear in his ee: (*cf.* 32[2])
'Ye 're welcome here, Jeannie Gordon,
Wi a' your young family, (*cf.* 33[2])
Ye 're welcome here, Jeannie Gordon,
But awa wi your Ogilvie.'

23[1,2]. The Captain took ship an sailed, He sailed from the land.

23[3]. But a messenger.

23[4]. Which caused a countermand.

24[1,3]. Come back, come back, C. O.

24[4]. You are earl. 25. *Wanting.*

26[3]. I will gae hame an.

27[2]. An lichtit on the green.

27[4]. Says, Here 's Captain Ogilvie again.

After 27:

The Duke o Gordon cam trippin doun stairs,
Wi his hat into his hand:
'Ye 're welcome hame, Captain Ogilvie,
The heir o Northumberland.'

After 28:

'Put up your hat, Duke o Gordon,
An do not let it fa;

It never set the noble Duke o Gordon
To bow to a single soldier-lad.'

29⁴. No ither favour I claim.
30, 31. *Wanting.*
32². the saut tear in her ee.
32³·⁴. You're welcome hame, Captain Ogilvie,
You're dearly welcome to me.
33. *Wanting.   After* 33: The Captain went
aff with his lady, *nearly as in* b—e.
*The order of stanzas is deranged.   Some of
the variations are clearly misremembrances.*
h. *Nine stanzas only.   1¹.* had.
1⁴. wud awa.
2². A month but barely twa.
2⁴. from him she wudna stay.
3⁴. from him she will not stay.

11². For any offence that.
15¹. weary, weary wanderin.
After 15 : Had yer tongue — I 'll buy hose
and shoon for you, Had yer tongue — For
your sake I 'm a single man.
22⁴. awa wi your Ogilvie.
Christie's ballad has many of the readings of
a, *and a few of the editor's. Of* "two
verses, as sung in the counties of Banff and
Moray, hitherto unpublished," *one is in
all copies except* a; *the other is the inept
stanza* (*see* f) :

' Oh, coarse, coarse would be the stockings,
And coarser would be the shoon,
Oh, coarse, coarse would they baith be,
You would buy for ae siller crown.'

238

GLENLOGIE, OR, JEAN O BETHELNIE

A. Skene MS., p. 13.

B. 'Glenlogie,' Sharpe's Ballad Book, 1823, p. 37.

C. 'Glenlogie,' Gibb MS., No 6, p. 33.

D. 'There waur aucht an forty nobles,' Harris MS.,
fol. 17.

E. a. 'Jean o Bethelnie's Love for Sir G. Gordon,'
Buchan's Ballads of the North of Scotland, I, 188.
b. 'Bonnie Jean o Bethelnie,' Christie's Traditional
Ballad Airs, I, 54.

F. 'Jean o Bethelnie,' Percy Papers, communicated
by R. Lambe, 1768.

G. 'Glenlogie,' Alexander Laing's MS., p. 8.

H. 'Glenlogie,' Kinloch MSS, V, 431.

I. a. "Scotch Ballads, Materials for Border Minstrelsy," No 77, Abbotsford. b. 'Glenogie,' Smith's
Scotish Minstrel, IV, 78, 1822.

'GLENLOGIE,' in Chambers' Popular
Rhymes of Scotland, 1826, p. 200, is a repetition of B. F, the copy earliest taken down, is
not pure and unvarnished tradition. The re-
constructed copy in the Ballad Minstrelsy of
Scotland, Glasgow, 1871, p. 506, was " based
on a MS. version communicated to Mr
Buchan in a letter from Mr Alexander Laing,
dated Brechin, April 9th, 1829, and there
given by him as taken down from the recitation of the amiable daughter of a clergyman in the North." G, from Laing's MS.,

may be supposed to be the ballad sent to
Buchan by Laing. I b has been touched up
by one of " that parliament of gentle ladies,"
in Motherwell's phrase, who had charge
of the literary part of Smith's Scotish Minstrel.

Jean of Bethelnie, A, C, E, F, Jean Melville, B, D, G, of the age of fifteen or sixteen,
scarce seventeen, G, falls in love at sight with
Glenlogie (Earl Ogie, F, Glenogie, I b),
and opens her mind to him. Glenlogie,
though much flattered, is obliged to say that

he is already promised.* Jean takes to her bed, determined to die. Her father (mother, A†), as all too frequently happens at such conjunctures, proposes the miserable comfort of another and a better match, and, as usual, is told to hold his tongue. The chaplain of the family (the father himself is a king's chaplain in **F**) takes the business in hand, and writes a broad, long, and well-penned letter to Glenlogie, setting forth the desperate condition of the girl. Glenlogie is so much af-

fected that he rides to Bethelnie with all haste and presents himself to Jean as her bridegroom, although promised awa.

The young lady is Jean Gordon in **C**. **H** has changed Bethelnie to Belhelvie, another Aberdeenshire town. **I** has Glenfeldy for Bethelnie.

Gerhard, p. 103, has translated **E a**; Knortz, Schottische Balladen, p. 15, Aytoun's copy, that is, **B**.

A

Skene MS., p. 13; taken down from recitation in the north of Scotland, 1802–3.

1 FOUR an twenty noblemen they rode thro Banchory fair,
But bonnie Glenlogie was flower [of a'] that was there.

2 Four and twenty noblemen rode from Banchory ha,
But bonnie Glenlogie he was flower of them a'.

3 ' O bonnie Glenlogie, be constant and kind,
An, bonnie Glenlogie, I 'll tell you my mind.

4 .   .   .   .   so frank and so free,
.   .   .   and I get na Glenlogie, I 'll die.'

5 ' O bonnie Jeanie, your portion 's but sma
To lay your love on me, that 's promist awa.'

6 Her cherry cheeks grew pale an wan; with the tear in her ee,
' Gin I get na Glenlogie, I surely will die.'

7 Ben came her father, steps to her bowr:
' Dear Jeanie, you 'r acting the part of a [whore].

8 ' You 're seeking ane that cares na for thee;
Ye 's get Lord William, let Glenlogie be.'

9 ' O had you still, father, let your folly be;
Gin I get na Glenlogie, I surely will die.'

10 Ben came her mother, steps on the floor:
' Dear daughter Jeanie, you 're acting the [whore],

11 ' Seeking of ane that cares na for thee;
For ye 'll get Lord William, let Glenlogie be.'

12 ' O had your tongue, mother, and let me be;
An I get na Glenlogie, I surely will die.'

13 O ben came her father's chaplain, a man of great skill,
And he has written a broad letter, and he has pennd it well.

14 H 'as pennd it well, an sent it awa
To bonnie Glenlogie, the flower of them a'.

15 When he got the letter, his tears did down fa
' She 's laid her love on me, that was promist awa.'

16 He calld on his servant wi speed, and bade him saddle his horses, and bridle them a':
' For she has laid her love on me, altho I was promist awa.'

---

* There is, to tell the whole truth, an allusion in **A**, **H** to Jean's portion, or tocher, as not being sufficient to justify the breaking of a previous engagement. One would wish to think that ' portion ' in **A** 5 is a corruption of ' fortune,' and that what is meant is that her luck is hard. But tocher in **H** 3 is not easily disposed of.

† The gross and uncalled-for language of father and mother in **A** 7, 10, has slipped in by a mere trick of memory, I am convinced, from ' Lady Maisry,' No 65, **B**, **C**. See again the ballad which follows this.

17 The horses were saddled wi speed, but ere
    they came he was four mile awa,
    To Jean of Bethelny, the flowr of them a'.

18 But when he came to her bowr she was pale
    and wan,
    But she grew red and ruddy when Glenlogie
    came in.

19 'Cheer up, bonnie Jeannie, ye are flowr o
    them a';
    I have laid my love on you, altho I was prom-
    ist awa.'

20 Her beauty was charming, her tocher down
    tauld;
    Bonnie Jean of Bethelny was scarce fifteen
    year auld.

B

Sharpe's Ballad Book, p. 37, 1823.

1 Four and twenty nobles sits in the king's ha,
    Bonnie Glenlogie is the flower among them a'.

2 In came Lady Jean, skipping on the floor,
    And she has chosen Glenlogie 'mong a' that
    was there.

3 She turned to his footman, and thus she did
    say:
    Oh, what is his name? and where does he
    stay?

4 'His name is Glenlogie, when he is from
    home;
    He is of the gay Gordons, his name it is John.'

5 'Glenlogie, Glenlogie, an you will prove kind,
    My love is laid on you; I am telling my
    mind.'

6 He turned about lightly, as the Gordons does
    a':
    'I thank you, Lady Jean, my loves is promised
    awa.'

7 She called on her maidens her bed for to
    make,
    Her rings and her jewels all from her to take.

8 In came Jeanie's father, a wae man was he;
    Says, I 'll wed you to Drumfendrich, he has
    mair gold than he.

9 Her father's own chaplain, being a man of
    great skill,
    He wrote him a letter, and indited it well.

10 The first lines he looked at, a light laugh
    laughed he;
    But ere he read through it the tears blinded
    his ee.

11 Oh, pale and wan looked she when Glenlogie
    cam in,
    But even rosy grew she when Glenlogie sat
    down.

12 'Turn round, Jeanie Melville, turn round to
    this side,
    And I 'll be the bridegroom, and you 'll be the
    bride.'

13 Oh, 't was a merry wedding, and the portion
    down told,
    Of bonnie Jeanie Melville, who was scarce six-
    teen years old.

C

Gibb MS., No 6, p. 33, from the recitation of Mrs Gibb,
senior; traced to Mrs E. Lindsay, about 1800.

1 There was three score o nobles sat at the king's
    dine,
    An bonny Glenlogie was flower o thrice nine.

* * * * * * * *

2 .   .   .   .   cam trippin downstair,
    An she fancied Glenlogie ower a' that was
    there.

3 She called on the footman that ran by his side,
Says, What is that man's name, an where does he bide?

4 'His name is Glenlogie when he goes from home.
But he 's of the great Gordons, an his name is Lord John.'

5 'Glenlogie! Glenlogie! Glenlogie!' said she,
'An for bonnie Glenlogie I surely will die.'

6 She called on her maidens to make her her bed,

  .   .   .   .

*   *   *   *   *   *   *   *

7 When Glenlogie got the letter, amang noble-men,
'Dear me,' said Glenlogie, 'what does young women mean!'

8 Then up spake his father, Let it never be said
That such a fine lady should die for your sake.

9 'Go saddle my black horse, go saddle him soon,
Till I go to Bethelnie, to see Lady Jean.'

10 When he got to Bethelnie, there was naebody there
But was weeping an wailing an tearing their hair.

*   *   *   *   *   *   *   *

11 'Turn round, Jeanie Gordon, turn round to this side;
I 'll be the bridegroom, an ye 's be the bride.'

D

Harris MS., fol. 17; learned from Mrs Harris before 1832.

1 THERE waur aucht an forty nobles rade to the king's ha,
But bonnie Glenlogie was the flour o them a'.

2 There waur aucht an forty nobles rade to the king's dine,
But bonnie Glenlogie was the flour o thrice nine.

3 Bonnie Jeanie Melville cam trippin doun the stair,
An whan she saw Glenlogie her hairt it grew sair.

4 .   .   .   .
'He 's of the gay Gordons, his name it is John.'

5 'Oh, Logie! Oh, Logie! Oh, Logie!' said she,
'If I get na Glenlogie, I surely will dee.'

6 He turned him aboot, as the Gordons do a',
Says, I thank you, Lady Jeanie, but I 'm promised awa.

7 She called on her maidens her hands for to take,
An the rings from her fingers she did them a' break.

8 'Oh, what is my lineage, or what is my make.
That such a fine lady suld dee for my sake?'

9 Such a pretty wedding, as I have been told,
An bonnie Jeanie Melville was scarce sixteen years old.

E

a. Buchan's Ballads of the North of Scotland, I, 188.
b. Christie's Traditional Ballad Airs, I, 54.

1 THERE were four-and-twenty ladies dined i the
Queen's ha,
And Jean o Bethelnie was the flower o them a'.

2 Four-and-twenty gentlemen rode thro Banchory fair,
But bonny Glenlogie was the flower that was
there.

3 Young Jean at a window she chanced to sit
nigh,
And upon Glenlogie she fixed an eye.

4 She calld on his best man, unto him did say,
O what is that knight's name? or where does
he stay?

5 'He's of the noble Gordons, of great birth
and fame;
He stays at Glenlogie, Sir George is his name.'

6 Then she wrote a broad letter, and wrote it in
haste;
To send to Glenlogie, she thought it was best.

7 Says, O brave Glenlogie, unto me be kind;
I've laid my love on you, and told you my
mind.

8 Then reading the letter, as he stood on the
green,
Says, I leave you to judge, sirs; what does
women mean?

9 Then turnd about sprightly, as the Gordons
do a':
'Lay not your love on me, I'm promisd awa.'

10 When she heard this answer, her heart was
like to break,
That she laid her love on him, and him so
ungrate.

11 Then she calld on her maidens to lay her to bed,
And take her fine jewels and lay them aside.

12 'My seals and my signets, no more shall I
crave;
But linen and trappin, a chest and a grave.'

13 Her father stood by her, possessëd with fear
To see his dear daughter possessëd with care.

14 Says, Hold your tongue, Jeannie, let all your
folly be;
I'll wed you to Dumfedline, he is better than
he.

15 'O hold your tongue, father, and let me alane;
If I getna Glenlogie, I'll never have ane.

16 'His bonny jimp middle, his black rolling eye,
If I getna Glenlogie, I'm sure I shall die.'

17 But her father's old chaplain, a man of great
skill,
He wrote a broad letter, and pennëd it well.

18 Saying, O brave Glenlogie, why must it be
so?
A maid's love laid on you, shall she die in her
woe?

19 Then reading the letter, his heart was like to
break
That such a leal virgin should die for his
sake.

20 Then he calld on his footman, and likewise his
groom,
Says, Get my horse saddled and bridlëd soon.

21 Before the horse was saddled and brought to
the yate,
Bonnie Glenlogie was five miles on foot.

22 When he came to Bethelnie, he saw nothing
there
But weeping and wailing, vexation and care.

23 Then out spake her father, with the tear in his
ee,
You're welcome, Glenlogie, you're welcome
to me.

24 'If ye make me welcome, as welcome's ye
say,
Ye'll show me the chamber where Jeannie
does lay.'

25 Then one o her maidens took him by the hand,
To show him the chamber where Jeannie lay
in.

26 Before that she saw him, she was pale and
    wan ;
    But when she did see him, she grew ruddy
    again.

27 'O turn, bonny Jeannie, turn you to your side ;
    For I 'll be the bridegroom, and ye 'll be the
    bride.'

28 When Jeannie was married, her tocher down
    tauld,
    Bonny Jean o Bethelnie was fifteen years
    auld.

F

Communicated to Percy by Robert Lambe, of Norham,
August 17, 1768 ; dated April, 1768.

1 FOURSCORE nobles ride in the king's court,
    And bonny Earl Ogie 's the flower of the
    rout ;
    Fourscore lean oer the castle-wa,
    But Jean of Bethelnie 's the flower of em a'.

2 She writ a broad letter, and pennd it fou lang,
    And sent it Earl Ogie as fast as 't can gang:
    'Bonny Earl Ogie, be courteous and kind ;
    I 've laid my love on thee ; maun I die in my
    prime ? '

3 ' O pox on thee, Jenny, for being sae slaw !
    Bonny Earl Ogie is promisd awa : '
    This letter was like to mak her heart break,
    For revealing her mind to a man so ingrate.

4 ' Come here, all my handmaids, O do this with
    speed,
    Take my gowns and my passments, and lay
    me to bed ;
    Lay me to my bed, it is all that I crave ;
    Wi my sark in my coffin, lay me in my grave.'

5 Her father beheld her with heart full of grief,
    And spoke these words to her, to gi her relief :
    Hawd your tongue, Jenny, your mourning
    let be,
    You shall have Drumfinely, who 's as good as
    he.

6 ' Haud your tongue, father, your words make
    me sad ;
    If I get not Earl Ogie, I still shall be bad ;
    With his bonny streight body, and black roll-
    ing eee,
    If I get not Earl Ogie, for him I mun dee.'

7 Her father, king's chaplain, and one of great
    skill,
    Did write a broad letter, and pennd it fou weel ;
    He as writ a broad letter, and pennd it fou lang,
    And sent it Earl Ogie as fast as 't can gang.

8 ' Bonny Earl Ogie, be courteous and kind ;
    My daughter loves you ; must she die in her
    prime ? '
    When he read the first lines, a loud laugh gave
    he ;
    But or he redd the middle, the tear filld his ee.

9 ' Come here, all my footmen, and also my
    groom,
    Go saddle my horses, and saddle them soon : '
    They were not weel saddled and set on the
    green
    Or bonny Earl Ogie was twa mile his lain.

10 When he came to Bethelnie, he nothing saw
    there
    But mourning and weeping, lamentation and
    care :
    'O you that 's her handmaid, take me by the
    hand,
    Lead me to the chamber that Jenny lies in.'

11 When thither he came, she was pale and half
    dead ;
    As soon as she saw him, her cheeks they grew
    red :
    ' Come, turn thee, my Jenny, come, turn on
    thy side,
    I 'll be the bridegroom, you shall be the bride.'

12 Her spirit revived to hear him say sae,
    And thus ended luckily all her great wae ;
    Then streight were they married, with joy most
    profound,
    And Jean of Bethelnie was sav'd from the
    ground.

G

Alexander Laing's MS., "Ancient Ballads and Songs, etc., etc., from the Recitation of Old People," p. 8, 1829.

1 THERE was mony a braw noble cum to our
    king's ha,
But the bonnie Glenlogie was the flower o
    them a';
An the young ladye Jeanye, sae gude an sae
    fair,
She fancyd Glenlogie aboon a' that were there.

2 She speered at his footman that rode by his
    side
His name an his surname an whare he did
    bide :
'He bides a[t] Glenlogie whan he is at hame,
He is of the gay Gordons, an John is his name.'

3 'Oh, Logie, Glenlogie, I 'll tell you my mind ;
My luve is laid on you, O wad ye prove kind !'
He turned him about, as the Gordons do a',
'I thank [you], fair ladye, but I 'm promised
    awa.'

4 She called on her maidens her hands for to
    take,
An the rings on her fingers she did them a'
    break :
'Oh, Logie, Glenlogie ! Oh, Logie !' said she,
'Gin I get na Glenlogie, I 'm sure I will die.'

5 'O hold your tongue, daughter, an weep na sae
    sair,
For ye 'll get Drumfindlay, his father's young
    heir.'

'O hold your tongue, father, an let me alane,
Gin I get na Glenlogie, I winna hae ane.'

6 Her father wrote a broad letter wi speed,
And ordered his footman to run and ride ;
He wrote a broad letter, he wrote it wi skill,
An sent it to Glenlogie, who had dune her the
    ill.

7 The first line that he read, a light laugh gae he ;
The next line that he read, the tear filld his
    ee :
'O what a man am I, an hae I a maik,
That such a fine ladye shoud die for my sake ?

8 'Ye 'll saddle my horse, an ye 'll saddle him
    sune,
An, when he is saddled, bring him to the
    green : '
His horse was na saddled an brocht to the
    green,
When Glenlogie was on the road three miles
    his lane.

9 When he came to her father's, he saw naething
    there
But weeping an wailing an sobbing fu sair :
O pale an wan was she when Logie gaed in,
But red an ruddie grew she when Logie gaed
    ben.

10 'O turn, Ladye Jeany, turn ye to your side,
For I 'll be the bridegroom, an ye 'll be the
    bride : '
It was a blythe wedding as ever I 've seen,
An bonny Jeany Melville was scarce seven-
    teen.

----◆----

H

Kinloch MSS, V, 431 ; in Kinloch's hand.

1 SIX and six nobles gaed to Belhelvie fair,
But bonnie Glenlogie was flowr o a' there ;
Bonnie Jean o Behelvie gaed tripping doun
    the stair,
And fancied Glenlogie afore a' that was there.

2 She said to his serving-man, as he stood aside,
O what is that man's name, and whare does
    he bide ?

'They call him Glenlogie whan he goes frae
    home,
But he 's come o the grand Gordons, and [h]is
    name is Lord John.'

3 'Glenlogie, Glenlogie, be constant and kind ;
I 've laid my love on you, I 'll tell you my
    mind : '
'O wae 's me heart, Jeanie, your tocher 's oure
    sma ;
Lay na your love on me, for I 'm promised
    awa.'

4 She called for the servant to show her a room,
Likewise for a handmaid to mak her bed
doun;
Wi that Jeanie's father cam stepping on the
floor,
Says, What is the matter my dochter lies here?

5 'Forgie, honourd father, my folly,' said she,
'But for the sake o Glenlogie your dochter will
dee:'
'O cheer up, my dochter, for I'll gie ye my
hand
That ye'se get young Glenforbar, w' an earldom of land.

6 'O cheer up, my dochter, turn ance frae the
wa,
And ye'll get Glenforbar, the flowr o them a':'
'I wad rather tak Glenlogie wi his staff in his
hand
Afore I wad tak Glenforbar wi an earldom of
land.'

7 Jeanie's father was a scholar, and a man o
grit wit,
And he wrote him a letter, he thought it was
fit.

8 When Glenlogie gat the letter, he was amang
nobles a',
.   .   .   .   .   he lute his hat fa:
'I wonder i the warld what women see at
me,
For bonnie Jean o Belhelvie is a dying for
me:'

9 He calld for his servant to saddle his steed,
.   .   .   .   .   wi speed;
The horse was na saddled, but out on the
green,
Till bonnie Glenlogie was some miles him
leen.

10 Whan he cam to Belhelvie, he rade round
about,
And he saw Jeanie's father at a window look
out.

11 Bonnie Jean o Belhevie lay pale and wan,
But red and ruddy grew she when Glenlogie
cam in:
'Lie yont, bonnie Jeanie, and let me lie down,
For ye'se be bride, and I'se be bridegroom.'

I

a. "Scotch Ballads, Materials for Border-Minstrelsy,"
No. 77. Written down from the recitation of Mrs Graham,
of Inchbrakie, by Mrs Steuart, of Dalguise, and given, September, 1802, to Mr Robert Carlyle, by whom it was communicated to Sir Walter Scott. b. Smith's Scottish Minstrel, IV, 78 (of the second edition).

1 'THERE's fifty young nobles rides up the
king's hall
And bonny Glenlogie's the flower of them
all;
Wi his milk-white steed, and his black rolling ee,
If I get na Glenlogie, it's certain I'll die.

2 'Where will I get a bonny boy, to win hose
and shoon,
To go to Glenlogie and bid Logie come?'
'Here am I a pretty boy, to win baith hose
and shoon,
To go to Glenlogie and bid Logie come.'

3 When he came to Glenlogie, it was 'wash and
go dine:'
'Come in, my pretty boy, wash and go dine:'
'It was no my father's fashion, and I hope
it'll no be mine,
To run a lady's hasty errand, then to go dine.

4 'Here take this letter, Glenlogie,' said he.
The first ane line that he read, a low smile
gave he;
The next ane line that he read, the tear blinded
his ee;
But the next line that he read he garrd the
table flee.

5 'O saddle to me the black horse, saddle to me
the brown,
Saddle to me the swiftest horse that eer rode
frae the town:'
But lang or the horses could be brought to the
green
Bonie Glenlogie was twa mile his lean.

6 When he came to Glenfeldy's gates, little mirth
    was there,
Bonie Jean's mother was tearing her hair :
'You're welcome, Glenlogie, you're welcome
    to me,
You're welcome, Glenlogie, your Jeanie to see.'

7 O pale and wan was she when Logie came in,
But red and rosy grew she wheneer he sat
    down :
'O turn you, bonie Jeanie, O turn you to me,
For, if you'll be the bride, the bridegroom I
    will be.'

A. *Not divided into stanzas.*
    5¹. your portion's.   *Qy,* your fortune's?
        (*your luck is small*).
    5². I am promist awa, I'm promist awa, to
        lay your love on me that's promist awa.
    6². Gin I get na Glenlogie, I surely will die,
        I surely will die.
    7¹. fathers.
    9¹. your still, *which may possibly be meant.*
    10¹. mothers steps.

    19. Cheer up bonnie Jeannie
         I have laid my love on you
         Ye are flowr o them a'
         I have laid my love on you
         Altho I was promist awa.

C. *Written in stanzas of four short lines.*
D. *Written, as far as the imperfect text would
    allow, in stanzas of eight short lines.*
E. *In stanzas of four short lines.*
    b. "Epitomized from Buchan's Ballads, with a
        few alterations from the way the Editor has
        heard it sung."
    1². Bonnie Jean : was flower.
    2¹. There were four-and-twenty nobles.
    2². And bonnie : was flower o them there.
    3¹. Bonnie Jean.
    3². And on young G. : her eye.
    4¹. and to him.   6². for she.   7¹. And says.
    9¹. Then he.   10¹. heard his.   10². she'd.

28¹. and her tocher was tauld.
H. 7-11 *are in couplets in the MS.*
I. b. Glenogie *for* Glenlogie.
    1¹. Threescore o nobles rade.   1². But.
    1³. his bonny black.
    1⁴. Glenogie, dear mither, Glenogie for me !
    After 1 :

'O had your tongue, dochter, ye'll get better
    than he.'
'O say nae sae, mither, for that canna be ;
Tho Drumlie is richer, and greater than he,
Yet, if I maun tak him, I'll certainly dee.'

2²,⁴. Will gae : and cum shune again.
2³. O here : a bonny : win hose.   3¹. he gaed.
3². 'Twas wash ye, my.
3³. O 't was neer : and it neer shall.
3⁴. To gar : wait till I dine.
4¹. But there is, Glenogie, a letter to thee.
4². first line.   4³. next line.   4⁴. the last.
5¹. Gar saddle the : gae saddle the.
5². Gar saddle the swiftest steed eer rade frae a.
5³. ere the horse was drawn and brought.
5⁴. O bonny.   6¹. door *for* gates.
6³. (*end*) welcome, said she.
7¹. O *wanting :* Glenogie gaed ben.
7³,⁴. *An editorial improvement :*

She turned awa her head, but the smile was in
    her ee :
'O binna feared, mither, I'll may be no dee.'

239

LORD SALTOUN AND AUCHANACHIE

A. 'Lord Salton and Auchanachie.' **a.** Buchan's Ballads of the North of Scotland, II, 133. **b.** Maidment's North Countrie Garland, p. 10; Buchan's Gleanings, p. 161.

B. a. 'Young Annochie,' Murison MS., p. 76. **b.** 'Lord Saltoun and Annachie,' Christie's Traditional Ballad Airs, I, 10.

A. JEANIE GORDON loves Auchanachie, who is bonny and braw, but she is forced by her father to wed Saltoun, who is bowed in the back and thrawin in the knee; and all for Saltoun's lands. Jeanie refuses to be bedded; her maidens, at her father's order, loose off her gown (they cut her gown and stays); she falls in a swoon and dies. Auchanachie comes home from the sea the same day, learns what has happened, asks to be taken to the chamber where Jeanie lies, kisses her cold lips, and dies.

In **B** we have Gordon of Annachie in Buchan, instead of Gordon of Auchanachie in Strathbogie as in **A**. Christie, on very slight grounds, suggests that one Garden of Annachie was the proper hero: I, 287, 294.

There can hardly be a doubt that this ballad is Mrs Brown of Falkland's 'Lass o Philorth' (see note, p. 309). Philorth is the seat of the Frasers of Saltoun, near Fraserburgh, in the extreme northeast corner of Aberdeenshire.

As to **A** a $2^{1,2}$, b 1, **B** $2^{1,2}$, see note † to the preceding ballad, p. 339.

A

a. Buchan's Ballads of the North of Scotland, II, 133, 1828. b. Maidment's North Countrie Garland, p. 10, 1824; Buchan's Gleanings, p. 161, 1825.

1 'AUCHANACHIE GORDON is bonny and braw,
    He would tempt any woman that ever he saw;
    He would tempt any woman, so has he tempted me,
    And I 'll die if I getna my love Auchanachie.'

2 In came her father, tripping on the floor,
    Says, Jeanie, ye 're trying the tricks o a whore;
    Ye 're caring for them that cares little for thee;
    Ye must marry Salton, leave Auchanachie.

3 'Auchanachie Gordon, he is but a man;
    Altho he be pretty, where lies his free land?

Salton's lands they lie broad, his towers they stand hie,
    Ye must marry Salton, leave Auchanachie.

4 . . . .
    . . . .
    'Salton will gar you wear silk gowns fring'd to thy knee,
    But ye 'll never wear that wi your love Auchanachie.'

5 'Wi Auchanachie Gordon I would beg my bread
    Before that wi Salton I 'd wear gowd on my head,
    Wear gowd on my head, or gowns fring'd to the knee;
    And I 'll die if I getna my love Auchanachie.

6 'O Salton's [a] valley lies low by the sea,
   He's bowed on the back, and thrawin on the
      knee;'

. . . .

. . . .

7 'O Salton's a valley lies low by the sea;
   Though he's bowed on the back and thrawin
      on the knee,
   Though he's bowed on the back and thrawin
      on the knee,
   The bonny rigs of Salton they're nae thrawin
      tee.'

8 'O you that are my parents to church may me
      bring,
   But unto young Salton I'll never bear a son;
   For son or for daughter, I'll ne'er bow my
      knee,
   And I'll die if I getna my love Auchanachie.'

9 When Jeanie was married, from church was
      brought hame,
   When she wi her maidens sae merry shoud hae
      been,
   When she wi her maidens sae merry shoud hae
      been,
   She's called for a chamber, to weep there her
      lane.

10 'Come to your bed, Jeanie, my honey and my
      sweet,
   For to stile you mistress I do not think it
      meet:'
   'Mistress or Jeanie, it is a' ane to me,
   It's in your bed, Salton, I never will be.'

11 Then out spake her father, he spake wi re-
      nown;
   Some of you that are maidens, ye'll loose aff
      her gown;

Some of you that are maidens, ye'll loose aff
   her gown,
And I'll mend the marriage wi ten thousand
   crowns.

12 Then ane of her maidens they loosed aff her
      gown,
   But bonny Jeanie Gordon she fell in a swoon;
   She fell in a swoon low down by their knee;
   Says, Look on, I die for my love Auchana-
      chie!

13 That very same day Miss Jeanie did die,
   And hame came Auchanachie, hame frae the
      sea;
   Her father and mither welcomd him at the
      gate;
   He said, Where's Miss Jeanie, that she's nae
      here yet?

14 Then forth came her maidens, all wringing
      their hands,
   Saying, Alas for your staying sae lang frae the
      land!
   Sae lang frae the land, and sae lang on the
      fleed!
   They've wedded your Jeanie, and now she is
      dead.

15 'Some of you, her maidens, take me by the
      hand,
   And show me the chamber Miss Jeanie died
      in;'
   He kissd her cold lips, which were colder than
      stane,
   And he died in the chamber that Jeanie died
      in.

—————

B

a. Murison MS., p. 76.   b. Christie's Traditional Ballad
Airs, I, 10.

1 'BUCHAN, it's bonnie, an there lies my love,
   My heart is fixt on him, it winna remove;
   It winna remove for a' at I can dee,
   An I never will forsake him Young Annochie.'

2 Her father cam trippin, cam trippin ben the
      floor,
   Says, Jeannie, ye hae but the tricks o a whore;
   Ye care little for the man that cares muckle
      for thee,
   But I'll cause you marry Saltoun, let Annochie
      be.

3 'Ye may marry me to Saltoun before that I
   go home,
  But it is to Lord Saltoun I 'll never bear a
   son ;
  A son nor a daughter I 'll never bear to he,
  An I never will forsake him Young Annochie.'

4 'All you that is her maidens, ye 'll tak her by
   the han,
  An I will inheft her o five thousan poun ;
  She 'll wear silk to her heel and gowd to her
   knee,
  An I 'll cause her to forsake him Young Annochie.'

5 'All you that is my maidens winna tak me by
   the han,
  I winna be inhefted o five thousan poun ;
  I 'll nae wear silk to my heal nor wear gowd
   to my knee,
  An I never will forsake him Young Annochie.'

6 'All you that is her maidens, ye 'll show her
   to her bed ;
  The blankets they are ready, the sheets are
   comely spread ;
  She shall lie in my airms till twelve o the day,
  An I 'll cause her to forsake him Young Annochie.'

7 'All you that is my maidens winna show me
   to my bed,
  Tho the blankets they be ready, the sheets be
   comely spread ;
  I 'll nae lie in your airms till twelve o the day,
  An I never will forsake him Young Annochie.'

8 It 's that day they wedded her, an that day
   she died,
  An that day Young Annochie cam in on the
   tide ;
  .   .   .   .
  .   .   .   .

9 Her maidens did meet him, a' wringin their
   hans,
  Sayin, It 's a' for your stayin so long on the
   sans !
  They 've wedded your Jeannie, an now she is
   dead,
  An it 's a' for your stayin sae long on the
   fleed.

10 'All you that is her maidens ye 'll tak me by
   the han,
  Ye 'll show me the bower that Jeannie lies in : '
  He kissed her cold lips, they were both white
   an red,
  And for bonnie Jeannie Gordon Young Annochie died.

———◆———

A, a. 4–6 *are disarranged, and an attempt has
   been made at a better grouping.* $4^{3,4}$, $5^{1,2}$,
   are 4 ; $5^{3,4}$ *are* $5^{1,2}$; $6^{1,2}$ *are* $5^{3,4}$.
   14^{2}. *The reading of* b *is better :* on the sands.
   14^{3}. frae the fleed : b *reads, rightly,* on the
   flood (fleed).
 b. *Printed by Maidment in stanzas of four
   short lines ; by Buchan, in long lines, not
   properly grouped.*

1 Ben came her father, skipping on the floor,
  Said, Jeanie, you 're trying the tricks of a
   whore.

2 'You 're caring for him that cares not for
   thee ;
  And I pray you take Salton, let Auchanachie be.'

3 'I will not have Salton, it lies low by the
   sea ;
  He is bowed in the back, he 's thrawen in
   the knee ;
  And I 'll die if I get not my brave Auchanachie.'

4 'I am bowed in the back, lassie, as ye see,
  But the bonny lands of Salton are no crooked
   tee.'

5 And when she was married she would not
   lie down,
  But they took out a knife, and cuttit her
   gown.

6 Likewise of her stays the lacing in three ;
  And now she lies dead for her Auchanachie.

7 Out comes her bower-woman, wringing her
    hands,
  Says, Alas for the staying so long on the
    sands !

8 'Alas for the staying so long on the flood !
  For Jeanie was married, and now she is
    dead.'

B. a. 8, 9 *are written together.*
    9⁴, on the sans: *cf.* A a 14¹, b 8¹, B b.
  b. *Some trivial variations are not noticed.*
    Printed in six stanzas of eight long lines.
  1¹. lives.
  1⁴. Oh, never will I forget my love Annachie.
  After 1 :

  'For Annachie Gordon is bonnie and braw,
  He 'd entice any woman that ever him saw ;
  He 'd entice any woman, and sae he has done
    me,
  And I 'll die if I getna my love Annachie.'

  2¹,². *As in* A a. 2³. care meikle: cares little.
  2⁴. Saltoun and leave Annachie.
  After 2 :

  'For Annachie Gordon is nothing but a man ;
  Although he be brave, he has little free lan ;
  His towns a' lie waste, and his lands a' lie lea,
  And I 'll cause you marry Saltoun, let Anna-
    chie be.'

  3¹. wed me : before he goes home.
  3². neer hae.

  3³,⁴. 'A son or a daughter, it 's a' ane to me,
    For I 'll cause you marry Saltoun and
      leave Annachie.'

  After 3 :

  He wed her to Saltoun before he gaed home,
  But unto Lord Saltoun she neer had a son ;

For, instead of being merry her maidens
    among,
She gaed to her bower and wept there alone.

4¹. Some of you her.
4². infeft her in houses and land.
4³. shall wear silk and satin, wi red goud.
4⁴. to forget him the.

5¹,². Oh you, my maidens, you shall not take
    my hand,
  Nor will I be infefted in houses and land.

5³. Nor will I wear silk nor red goud.
5⁴. For never will I forget my love A.
After 5 :

'Wi Annachie Gordon I would beg my bread
Before wi Lord Saltoun I would wear goud
    red ;
For he 's bowd on the back and he 's thrawn
    in the knee : '
'But the bonnie rigs o Saltoun are nae thrawn
    tee.'

6, 7. *Wanting.*

8. The day she was married, that same day
    she died,
  While Annachie Gordon was waiting for
    the tide ;
  He waited for the tide to tak him oer the
    fleed,
  But he little thought his Jeanie Gordon was
    deed.

9¹. Then out cam her maidens.
9². Wae for : frae the. 9³. hae married.
9⁴. Oh, wae for : on the fleed.
10¹. Some of you her maidens : me ben.
10². the chamber where.
10³. were colder than clay.
10⁴. And he died in the chamber where his
    Jeanie lay.

240

THE RANTIN LADDIE

A. a. 'The Rantin Laddie,' Johnson's Museum, No
462, p. 474.   b. 'Lord Aboyne,' Buchan's Ballads of
the North of Scotland, II, 66.

B. 'The Rantin Laddie,' Skene MS., p. 55.

C. 'The Rantin Laddie,' Laing's Thistle of Scotland,
p. 7.

D. 'Bonnie Rantin Laddie,' Murison MS., p. 74.

'LORD ABOYNE,' in Smith's Scotish Minstrel, IV, 6, is mostly A a; a few verses are
from A b.

A young woman (Maggie in B) has played
cards and dice with a rantin laddie till she
has won a bastard baby.   Slighted now by all
her friends, she sends a letter to the rantin
laddie, who is the Earl of Aboyne, to inform

him of her uncomfortable circumstances. The
Earl of Aboyne, struck with pity and indignation, sets out at once with five hundred
men, A, C, or a select company of gentlemen
and ladies, B, D, and brings .her home as his
wife.

C 24 is perhaps derived from 'Geordie,'
but may be regarded as a commonplace.

A

a. Johnson's Musical Museum, No 462, p. 474, communicated by Robert Burns; 1797.   b. Buchan's Ballads of the
North of Scotland, II, 66, 1828.

1 'AFTEN hae I playd at the cards and the dice,
   For the love of a bonie rantin laddie,
   But now I maun sit in my father's kitchen-
     neuk
   And balow a bastard babie.

2 'For my father he will not me own,
   And my mother she neglects me,
   And a' my friends hae lightlyed me,
   And their servants they do slight me.

3 'But had I a servant at my command,
   As aft times I 've had many,
   That wad rin wi a letter to bonie Glenswood,
   Wi a letter to my rantin laddie!'

4 'O is he either a laird or a lord,
   Or is he but a cadie,
   That ye do him ca sae aften by name
   Your bonie, bonie rantin laddie?'

5 'Indeed he is baith a laird and a lord,
   And he never was a cadie,
   But he is the Earl o bonie Aboyne,
   And he is my rantin laddie.'

6 'O ye 'se get a servant at your command,
   As aft times ye 've had many,
   That sall rin wi a letter to bonie Glenswood,
   A letter to your rantin laddie.'

7 When Lord Aboyne did the letter get,
   O but he blinket bonie!
   But or he had read three lines of it
   I think his heart was sorry.

8 'O wha is [this] daur be sae bauld
   Sae cruelly to use my lassie?
   .   .   .   .
   .   .   .   .

9 'For her father he will not her know,
   And her mother she does slight her,
   And a' her friends hae lightlied her,
   And their servants they neglect her.

10 'Go raise to me my five hundred men,
    Make haste and make them ready,
    With a milk-white steed under every ane,
    For to bring hame my lady.'

11 As they cam in thro Buchanshire,
    They were a company bonie,
    With a gude claymor in every hand,
    And O but they shin'd bonie!

B

Skene MS., p. 55 ; taken down in the North of Scotland, 1802–3.

1 'Oft have I playd at the cards an the dyce,
    The war so very enticin ;
    But this is a sad an a sorrowfu seat,
    To see my apron risin.

2 'Oft hae I playd at the cards an the dice
    For love of my [rantin] laddie ;
    But now I man sit in my father's kitchie-nouk,
    A rokkin o my baby.

3 'But gin I had ane o my father's servans,
    For he has so mony,
    That wad gae to the wood o Glentanner,
    Wi a letter to the rantin laddie !'

4 'Here am I, ane o your father's servans,
    For he has sae mony,
    That will gae to the wood o Glentanner,
    Wi a letter to the rantin laddie.'

5 'Fan ye gae to Aboyne,
    To the woods o Glentanner sae bonny,
    Wi your hat in your hand gie a bow to the
        ground,
    In the presence o the rantin laddie.'

6 Fan he gaed to Aboyne,
    To the woods o Glentanner sae bonny,
    Wi his hat in his hand he gied a bow to the
        ground,
    In the presence of the rantin laddie.

7 Fan he looked the letter on
    Sae loud as he was laughin !
    But or he read it to an end
    The tears they cam down rappin.

8 'O fa is this or fa is that
    Has been so ill to my Maggie?
. . . .
    . . . .

9 'But ye gett four-and-twenty milk white steeds,
    Wi an car . . . . .
    An as mony gay ladies to ride them on,
    To gae an bring hame my Maggie.

10 'Ye get four-an-twenty bonny brown steeds,
    Wi an car o an ome,
    An as mony knights to ride them on,
    To gae an bring hame my Maggie.'

11 Ye lasses a', far ever ye be,
    An ye match wi ony o our Deeside laddies,
    Ye 'll happy be, ye 'l happy be,
    For they are frank an kind.

C

Laing's Thistle of Scotland, p. 7, 1823.

1 'Aft hae I playd at cards and dice
    For the love o a bonny rantin laddie,
    But now I maun sit i my father's kitchen-nook,
    And sing, Hush, balow, my baby.

2 'If I had been wise, and had taen advice,
    And dane as my bonny love bade me,

    I would hae been married at Martinmass,
    And been wi my rantin laddie.

3 'But I was na wise, I took nae advice,
    Did not as my bonny love bade me,
    And now I maun sit by mysel i the nook,
    And rock my bastard baby.

4 'If I had horse at my command,
    As often I had many,

I would ride on to the Castle o Aboyne,
    Wi a letter to my rantin laddie.'

5 Down the stair her father came,
    And lookëd proud and saucy:
  'Who is the man, and what is his name,
    That ye ca your rantin laddie?

6 'Is he a lord, or is he a laird?
    Or is he but a caddie?
  Or is it the young Earl o Aboyne
    That ye ca your rantin laddie?'

7 'He is a young and noble lord,
    He never was a caddie;
  It is the noble Earl o Aboyne
    That I ca my rantin laddie.'

8 'Ye shall hae a horse at your command,
    As ye had often many,
  To go to the Castle o Aboyne,
    Wi a letter to your rantin laddie.

9 'Where will I get a little page,
    Where will I get a caddie,
  That will run quick to bonny Aboyne,
    Wi this letter to my rantin laddie?'

10 Then out spoke the young scullion-boy,
    Said, Here am I, a caddie;
  I will run on to bonny Aboyne,
    Wi the letter to your rantin laddie.

11 'Now when ye come to bonny Deeside,
    Where woods are green and bonny,
  There will ye see the Earl o Aboyne,
    Among the bushes mony.

12 'And when ye come to the lands o Aboyne,
    Where all around is bonny,
  Ye 'll take your hat into your hand,
    Gie this letter to my rantin laddie.'

13 When he came near the banks of Dee,
    The birks were blooming bonny,
  And there he saw the Earl o Aboyne,
    Among the bushes mony.

14 'Where are ye going, my bonny boy?
    Where are ye going, my caddie?'
  'I am going to the Castle o Aboyne,
    Wi a letter to the rantin laddie.'

15 'See yonder is the castle then,
    My young and handsome caddie,
  And I myself am the Earl o Aboyne,
    Tho they ca me the rantin laddie.'

16 'O pardon, my lord, if I 've done wrong;
    Forgive a simple caddie;
  O pardon, pardon, Earl o Aboyne,
    I said but what she bade me.'

17 'Ye have done no wrong, my bonny boy,
    Ye 've done no wrong, my caddie;'
  Wi hat in hand he bowed low,
    Gave the letter to the rantin laddie.

18 When young Aboyne looked the letter on,
    O but he blinkit bonny!
  But ere he read four lines on end
    The tears came trickling mony.

19 'My father will no pity shew,
    My mother still does slight me,
  And a' my friends have turnd from me,
    And servants disrespect me.'

20 'Who are they dare be so bold
    To cruelly use my lassie?
  But I 'll take her to bonny Aboyne,
    Where oft she did caress me.

21 'Go raise to me five hundred men,
    Be quick and make them ready;
  Each on a steed, to haste their speed,
    To carry home my lady.'

22 As they rode on thro Buchanshire,
    The company were many,
  Wi a good claymore in every hand,
    That glancëd wondrous bonny.

23 When he came to her father's gate,
    He called for his lady:
  'Come down, come down, my bonny maid,
    And speak wi your rantin laddie.'

24 When she was set on high horseback,
    Rowd in the Highland plaidie,
  The bird i the bush sang not so sweet
    As sung this bonny lady.

25 As they rode on thro Buchanshire,
    He cried, Each Lowland lassie,

Lay your love on some lowland lown,
And soon will he prove fause t' ye.

26 'But take my advice, and make your choice
Of some young Highland laddie,
Wi bonnet and plaid, whose heart is staid,
And he will not beguile ye.'

27 As they rode on thro Garioch land,
He rode up in a fury,
And cried, Fall back, each saucy dame,
Let the Countess of Aboyne before ye.

D

Murison MS., p. 74; Aberdeenshire.

1 'Aft hae I played at the cards and the dice,
It was a' for the sake o my laddie,
But noo I sit i my father's kitchie-neuk,
Singing ba to a bonnie bastard babbie.

2 'Whar will I get a bonnie boy sae kin
As will carry a letter cannie,
That will rin on to the gates o the Boyne,
Gie the letter to my rantin laddie?'

3 'Here am I, a bonnie boy sae kin,
As will carry a letter cannie,
That will rin on to the gates o the Boyne,
Gie the letter to your rantin laddie.'

4 'When ye come to the gates o the Boyne,
An low doon on yon cassie,
Ye 'll tak aff your hat an ye 'll mak a low bow,
Gie the letter to my rantin laddie.'

5 'When ye come to the gates o the Boyne,
Ye 'll see lords an nobles monie;
But ye 'll ken him among them a',
He 's my bonnie, bonnie rantin laddie.'

6 'Is your bonnie love a laird or a lord,
Or is he a cadie,
That ye call him so very often by name
Your bonnie rantin laddie?'

7 'My love 's neither a laird nor a lord,
Nor is he a cadie,
But he is yerl o a' the Boyne,
An he is my bonnie rantin laddie.'

8 When he read a line or two,
He smiled eer sae bonnie;
But lang ere he cam to the end
The tears cam trinklin monie.

9 'Whar will I find fifty noble lords,
An as monie gay ladies,

*   *   *   *   *   *   *

A. a. 1⁴. below.   4¹. Oh.
8³,⁴. *The gap should be filled, says Stenhouse,
Musical Museum, IV, 405, with these lines:*

As to gar her sit in [her] father's kitchen-neuk
And balow a bastard babie.
b. 1, 2.

'Aft hae I played at the ring and the ba,
And lang was a rantin lassie,
But now my father does me forsake,
And my friends they all do neglect me.'

3¹. But gin I had servants.

3². As I hae had right mony.
3³. For to send awa to Glentanner's yetts.
4¹. O is your true-love a laird or lord.
4². he a Highland caddie.
4³. That ye sae aften call him by name.
5¹. My true-love he 's baith laird and lord.
5². Do ye think I hae married a caddie?
5³. O he is the noble earl o Aboyne.
5⁴. he 's my bonnie rantin.
6¹. ye 'se hae servants.
6². As ye hae had right mony.
6³. For to send awa to Glentanner's yetts.
6⁴. Wi a.   7¹. Aboyne the letter got.
7². Wow but.

7³. But ere three lines o it he read.

7⁴. O but his.

8¹,². His face it reddened like a flame, He grasped his sword sae massy.

8³ = 8¹. O wha is this, *etc.*

8⁴ = 8². Sae cruel to, *etc.*

9. *Wanting.*

10¹. Gae saddle to me five.

10². Gae saddle and.

10⁴. For I 'm gaing to.

11. And when they came to auld Fedderate
He found her waiting ready,

And he brought her to Castle Aboyne,
And now she 's his ain dear lady.

B. 9¹. he gett. 10¹. He gat.

D. *There is an initial stanza which, it seems to me, cannot have belonged originally to this ballad:*

' My father he feet me far, far away,
He feet me in Kirkcaldy ;
He feet me till an auld widow-wife,
But she had a bonnie rantin laddie.'

241

THE BARON O LEYS

A. Skene MS., p. 20.

B. 'Laird o Leys,' Kinloch's Ballad Book, p. 74.

C. 'The Baron o Leys,' Buchan's Ballads of the North of Scotland, II, 144.

' THE Baron o Leys,' in The New Deeside Guide by James Brown [= Joseph Robertson], Aberdeen [1832], p. 15, and The Deeside Guide, Aberdeen, 1889, p. 23, is **C**. **C** 4–11 seems to be an interpolation by a later hand.

"Part of this ballad," says Buchan, II, 322, "by ballad-mongers has been confused with the ballad of 'The Earl of Aboyne' [No 240, **A** b], called in some instances 'The Ranting Laddie.'" Laing, Thistle of Scotland, p. 11, appears to have confounded it with 'The Earl of Aboyne' proper. He gives this stanza :

' Some ca me that and some ca me this,
And The Baron o Leys they ca me,
But when I am on bonny Deeside
They ca me The Rantin Laddie.'

Herd's MSS, I, 233, II, fol. 71, give the two following stanzas under the title ' The Linkin Ladie : '

' Wae 's me that eer I made your bed !
Wae 's me that eer I saw ye !
For now I 've lost my maidenhead,
And I ken na how they ca ye.'

' My name is well kent in my ain country,
They ca me The Linking Ladie ;
If ye had not been as willing as I,
Shame fa them wad eer hae bade ye ! '

'The Linkin Ladie,' judging from this fragment (as it may be supposed to be), was much of a fashion with the ballad which we are engaged with, and may have been an earlier form of it. Sir Walter Scott, who cites these verses from memory (Sharpe's Ballad Book, ed. 1880, p. 162), says that the hero of them was a brother of the celebrated [Thomas] Boston, author of ' The Fourfold State.'

'The Baron o Leys' relates, or purports to relate, to an escapade of one of the Burnetts of Leys, Kincardineshire, Alexander, A, B, George, C. A woman who is with child by him gives him his choice of marriage, death, or the payment of ten thousand crowns. He

is a married man; his wife is ready to sell everything, to her silk gowns, to release her husband from his awkward position.

A

Skene MS., p. 20; taken down in the north of Scotland, 1802–3.

1 THE Laird of Leys is on to Edinbrugh,
　　To shaw a fit o his follie;
　He drest himsel in the crimson-brown,
　　An he provd a rantin laddie.

2 Ben came a weel-faird lass,
　　Says, Laddie, how do they ca ye?
　'They ca me this, an they ca me that,
　　Ye wudna ken fat they ca me;
　But whan I'm at home on bonnie Deeside
　　They ca me The Rantin Laddie.'

3 They sought her up, they sought her down,
　　They sought her in the parlour;
　She coudna be got but whar she was,
　　In the bed wi The Rantin Laddie.

4 'Tell me, tell me, Baron of Leys,
　　Ye tell me how they ca ye!
　Your gentle blood moves in my side,
　　An I dinna ken how they ca ye.'

5 'They ca me this, an they ca me that,
　　Ye couldna ken how they ca me;
　But whan I'm at home on bonnie Deeside
　　They ca me The Rantin Laddie.'

6 'Tell me, tell me, Baron of Leys,
　　Ye tell me how they ca ye!

　Your gentle blood moves in my side,
　　An I dinna ken how to ca ye.'

7 'Baron of Leys, it is my stile,
　　Alexander Burnett they ca me;
　Whan I'm at hame on bonnie Deeside
　　My name is The Rantin Laddie.'

8 'Gin your name be Alexander Burnett,
　　Alas that ever I saw ye!
　For ye hae a wife and bairns at hame,
　　An alas for lyin sae near ye!

9 'But I'se gar ye be headit or hangt,
　　Or marry me the morn,
　Or else pay down ten thousand crowns
　　For giein o me the scorn.'

10 'For my head, I canna want;
　　I love my lady dearly;
　But some o my lands I maun lose in the case,
　　Alas for lyin sae near ye!'

11 Word has gane to the Lady of Leys
　　That the laird he had a bairn;
　The warst word she said to that was,
　　'I wish I had it in my arms.

12 'For I will sell my jointure-lands —
　　I am broken an I'm sorry —
　An I'll sell a', to my silk gowns,
　　An get hame my rantin laddie.'

B

Kinloch's Ballad Book, p. 74, 1827.

1 THE Laird o Leys is to London gane;
　　He was baith full and gawdie;
　For he shod his steed wi siller guid,
　　And he's playd the ranting laddie.

2 He hadna been in fair London
　　A twalmonth and a quarter,
　Till he met wi a weel-faurd may,
　　Wha wishd to know how they ca'd him.

3 'They ca me this, and they ca me that,
　　And they're easy how they've ca'd me;

But whan I 'm at hame on bonnie Deeside
   They ca me The Ranting Laddie.'

4 'Awa wi your jesting, sir,' she said,
   'I trow you 're a ranting laddie;
But something swells atween my sides,
   And I maun ken how they ca thee.'

5 'They ca me this, and they ca me that,
   And they 're easy how they ca me;
The Baron o Leys my title is,
   And Sandy Burnet they ca me.'

6 'Tell down, tell down ten thousand crowns,
   Or ye maun marry me the morn;
Or headit or hangit ye sall be,
   For ye sanna gie me the scorn.'

7 'My head 's the thing I canna weel want;
   My lady she loves me dearlie;

Nor yet hae I means ye to maintain;
   Alas for the lying sae near thee!'

8 But word 's gane doun to the Lady o Leys
   That the Baron had got a babie:
'The waurst o news!' my lady she said,
   'I wish I had hame my laddie.

9 'But I 'll sell aff my jointure-house,
   Tho na mair I sud be a ladie;
I 'll sell a' to my silken goun,
   And bring hame my rantin laddie.'

10 So she is on to London gane,
   And she paid the money on the morn;
She paid it doun and brought him hame,
   And gien them a' the scorn.

C

Buchan's Ballads of the North of Scotland, II, 144.

1 THE Baron o Leys to France is gane,
   The fashion and tongue to learn,
But hadna been there a month or twa
   Till he gat a lady wi bairn.

2 But it fell ance upon a day
   The lady mournd fu sairlie;
Says, Who 's the man has me betrayed?
   It gars me wonder and fairlie.

3 Then to the fields to him she went,
   Saying, Tell me what they ca thee;
Or else I 'll mourn and rue the day,
   Crying, alas that ever I saw thee!

4 'Some ca's me this, some ca's me that,
   I carena fat befa me;
For when I 'm at the schools o France
   An awkward fellow they ca me.'

5 'Wae 's me now, ye awkward fellow,
   And alas that ever I saw thee!
Wi you I 'm in love, sick, sick in love,
   And I kenna well fat they ca thee.'

6 'Some ca's me this, some ca's me that,
   What name does best befa me;
For when I walk in Edinburgh streets
   The Curling Buckle they ca me.'

7 'O wae 's me now, O Curling Buckle,
   And alas that ever I saw thee!
For I 'm in love, sick, sick in love,
   And I kenna well fat they ca thee.'

8 'Some ca's me this, some ca's me that,
   Whatever name best befa's me;
But when I 'm in Scotland's king's high court
   Clatter the Speens they ca me.'

9 'O wae 's me now, O Clatter the Speens,
   And alas that ever I saw thee!
For I 'm in love, sick, sick in love,
   And I kenna well fat to ca thee.'

10 'Some ca's me this, some ca's me that,
   I carena what they ca me;
But when wi the Earl o Murray I ride
   It 's Scour the Brass they ca me.'

11 'O wae 's me now, O Scour the Brass,
   And alas that ever I saw thee!

For I 'm in love, sick, sick in love,
   And I kenna well fat to ca thee.'

12 'Some ca's me this, some ca's me that,
   Whatever name best befa's me;
But when I walk thro Saint Johnstone's town
   George Burnett they ca me.'

13 'O wae 's me, O wae 's me, George Burnett,
   And alas that ever I saw thee!
For I 'm in love, sick, sick in love,
   And I kenna well fat to ca thee.'

14 'Some ca's me this, some ca's me that,
   Whatever name best befa's me;
But when I am on bonny Dee side
   The Baron o Leys they ca me.'

15 'O weal is me now, O Baron o Leys,
   This day that ever I saw thee!
There 's gentle blood within my sides,
   And now [I] ken fat they ca thee.

16 'But ye 'll pay down ten thousand crowns,
   Or marry me the morn;
Else I 'll cause you be headed or hangd
   For gieing me the scorn.'

17 'My head is a thing I cannot well want;
   My lady loves me sae dearly;
But I 'll deal the gold right liberally
   For lying ae night sae near thee.'

18 When word had gane to the Lady o Leys
   The baron had gotten a bairn,
She clapped her hands, and this did say,
   'I wish he were in my arms!

19 'O weal is me now, O Baron o Leys,
   For ye hae pleased me sairly;
Frae our house is banishd the vile reproach
   That disturbed us late and early.'

20 When she looked ower her castle-wa,
   To view the woods sae rarely,
There she spied the Baron o Leys
   Ride on his steed sae rarely.

21 Then forth she went her baron to meet,
   Says, Ye 're welcome to me, fairly!
Ye 'se hae spice-cakes, and seed-cakes sweet,
   And claret to drink sae rarely.

———

C. 19[3,4]. Frae her house she banishd the vile re-
proach That disturbs us. *The Deeside
Guide has nearly the reading here substi-*
*tuted, and some correction is necessary.
The reference seems to be to childlessness.
In* A 8 *the baron is said to have bairns.*

———

242

THE COBLE O CARGILL

'The Coble o Cargill,' Motherwell's MS., p. 80; 'The
Weary Coble o Cargill,' Motherwell's Minstrelsy,
p. 230. Communicated to Motherwell by William
George, tenant in Cambus Michael, Perthshire, who
took it from the recitation of an old woman.

———

STOBHALL is on the left bank of the Tay,
eight miles above Perth, in Cargill parish, and
Cargill is a little further up. Balathy is opposite Cargill, and Kercock is higher up the
river on the right bank. The local tradition,
as given by Motherwell in his manuscript and
his book, is that the butler of Stobhall had a
leman both at Kercock and at Balathy. Upon

an occasion when the butler had gone to Kercock, the lass of Balathy scuttled the coble, which he had left below, " and waited his return, deeming that her suspicions of his infidelity would be well founded if he took the boat without visiting her in passing." The butler took the boat without stopping at Balathy, and in her sight the weary coble sank. Local tradition in such cases seldom means more than a theory which people have formed to explain a preëxisting ballad. The jealousy of the lass of Balathy has, in the ballad, passed the point at which confirmation would be waited for. She has many a time watched late for her chance to bore the coble, and she bores it ' wi gude will.'

St. 14 is a common-place which has been already several times noted.

The Rev. William Marshall's Historic Scenes in Perthshire, Edinburgh, 1879, p. 246, gives us a "modern" version of this ballad; that is, one written over in magazine style. This is repeated in Robert Ford's Auld Scots Ballants, 1889, p. 152. The Perthshire Antiquarian Miscellany, by Robert S. Fittis, Perth, 1875, p. 466, cites some stanzas from another ballad, composed by one James Beattie, journeyman-mason, but represented as having been taken down verbatim from the mouth of an old man. In these pieces the lass of Balathy has the name Jean, Jeanie Low (Low or Gow, according to Ford, p. 149).*

1 DAVID DRUMMOND'S destinie,
    Gude man o appearance o Cargill;
I wat his blude rins in the flude,
    Sae sair against his parents' will.

2 She was the lass o Balathy toun,
    And he the butler o Stobhall,
And mony a time she wauked late
    To bore the coble o Cargill.

3 His bed was made in Kercock ha,
    Of gude clean sheets and of [the] hay;
He wudna rest ae nicht therein,
    But on the prude waters he wud gae.

4 His bed was made in Balathy toun,
    Of the clean sheets and of the strae;
But I wat it was far better made
    Into the bottom o bonnie Tay.

5 She bored the coble in seven pairts,
    I wat her heart might hae been fu sair;
For there she got the bonnie lad lost
    Wi the curly locks and the yellow hair.

6 He put his foot into the boat,
    He little thocht o ony ill;
But before that he was mid-waters,
    The weary coble began to fill.

7 'Woe be to the lass o Balathy toun,
    I wat an ill death may she die!
For she bored the coble in seven pairts,
    And let the waters perish me.

8 'Oh, help, oh help, I can get nane,
    Nae help o man can to me come!'
This was about his dying words,
    When he was choaked up to the chin.

9 'Gae tell my father and my mother
    It was naebody did me this ill;
I was a-going my ain errands,
    Lost at the coble o bonnie Cargill.'

10 She bored the boat in seven pairts,
    I wat she bored it wi gude will;
And there they got the bonnie lad's corpse,
    In the kirk-shot o bonnie Cargill.

11 Oh a' the keys o bonnie Stobha
    I wat they at his belt did hing;
But a' the keys of bonnie Stobha
    They now ly low into the stream.

12 A braver page into his age
    Neer set a foot upon the plain;
His father to his mother said,
    'Oh, sae soon as we 've wanted him!

* I owe the knowledge of Marshall's and Fittis's publications to Mr Macmath.

13 'I wat they had mair luve than this
    When they were young and at the scule ;
But for his sake she wauked late,
    And bored the coble o bonnie Cargill.'

14 'There 's neer a clean sark gae on my back,
    Nor yet a kame gae in my hair ;
There 's neither coal nor candle-licht
    Shall shine in my bouir for evir mair.

15 'At kirk nor market I 'se neer be at,
    Nor yet a blythe blink in my ee ;
There 's neer a ane shall say to anither,
    That 's the lassie gard the young man die.

16 'Between the yates o bonnie Stobha
    And the kirk-style o bonnie Cargill,
There is mony a man and mother's son
    That was at my love's burial.'

14^2. Not yet.

243

JAMES HARRIS (THE DÆMON LOVER)

A. A Warning for Married Women, being an example of Mrs Jane Reynolds (a West-country woman), born near Plymouth, who, having plighted her troth to a Seaman, was afterwards married to a Carpenter, and at last carried away by a Spirit, the manner how shall presently be recited. To a West-country tune called 'The Fair Maid of Bristol,' 'Bateman,' or 'John True.' Pepys Ballads, IV, 101.

B. 'The Distressed Ship - Carpenter,' The Rambler's Garland, 1785 (?), British Museum, 11621, c. 4 (57).

C. 'James Herries,' Buchan's Ballads of the North of Scotland, I, 214.

D. 'The Carpenter's Wife,' Kinloch MSS, I, 297.

E. 'The Dæmon Lover,' Motherwell's MS., p. 97.

F. 'The Dæmon Lover,' Scott's Minstrelsy, II, 427, 1812.

G. 'The Dæmon Lover,' Motherwell's Minstrelsy, p. 93.

H. 'The Banks of Italy,' Christie, Traditional Ballad Airs, I, 138, two stanzas.

THE Pepys copy was printed for Thackeray and Passenger. Others are : Crawford, No 1114, Printed for A. M[ilbourne], W. O[nley], and T. Thackeray ; Ewing, 377, for Coles, Vere, and Gilbertson ; the same, 378, by and for W. O[nley]. No 71 in Thackeray's List, printed 1685. A later copy in the Douce ballads, II, fol. 249 b, Bodleian Library, printed by Thomas Norris at the Looking-Glass on London Bridge. Another, without publisher's name, in the Roxburghe collection, I, 502 ; Ballad Society, III, 200.

'The Dæmon Lover' was first published in Scott's Minstrelsy, 5th edition, 1812 (**F**). William Laidlaw, who furnished the copy, inserted four stanzas of his own (6, 12, 17, 18, here omitted).* Motherwell, in 1827, had not been able to get more than nine

* Carruthers, Abbotsford Notanda, appended to R. Chambers's Life of Scott, 1871, p. 122.
In the last edition of Sharpe's Ballad Book (1880), p.

158, we find this note by Scott: "I remember something of another ballad of diablerie. A man sells himself to the fause thief for a term of years, and the devil comes to claim

stanzas (G), but afterwards secured a version of twice as many (E).   Kinloch says of D, "My reciter, and others to whom I applied, assured me that they had never heard any more of it than what is given here."   Buchan, I, 313, referring to Motherwell's fragment (G), is "happy to say . . . there is still a perfect copy of this curious and scarce legend in existence, which is now for the first time given to the public " (C).

An Americanized version of this ballad was printed not very long ago at Philadelphia, under the title of 'The House-Carpenter.'   I have been able to secure only two stanzas, which were cited in Graham's Illustrated Magazine, September, 1858 :

'I might have married the king's daughter dear ; '
    'You might have married her,' cried she,
'For I am married to a house-carpenter,
    And a fine young man is he.'

'Oh dry up your tears, my own true love,
    And cease your weeping,' cried he,
'For soon you'll see your own happy home,
    On the banks of old Tennessee.'

B–H have for their basis the broadside A : the substance of the story is repeated, with traditional modifications.   Two or three stanzas of A are of the popular description, but it does not seem necessary to posit a tradition behind A.   The correspondences of the several versions are as follows :

A 18^{1,2}, C 2.
A 18^{3,4}, 19, B 1, D 1, E 1, 2^{1,2}, F 1.
A 20, C 3, D 2, E 2^{3,4}, F 2.
A 21, B 4^{1,2}, 3^{3,4}, C 6^1, 12^{3,4}, D 3.
A 22, B 2, C 4^{3,4}, 5^{1,2}, E 3, F 4.
A 23, C 7.
A 24, B 5, C 8, E 5^{1,2}, F 6.
A 25, B 6, C 9, F 7, G 1.
A 26, B 8, C 10, F 9^{3,4}.
A 28, B 11.
A 30, B 12.

B 3^{1,2}, E 4^{1,2}, F 5^{1,2}.
B 7, C 13, E 6^4, G 2, H 1.
B 9, 10, C 14, 17, D 5, E 12, 13, G 5.
B 12, C 23.
B 13, C 24.

C 3, D 2, E 2, F 2.
C 11, E 7, F 8, H 2.
C 16, D 6, E 16, F 12, G 6.
C 21, D 8.

D 1, E 1, F 1.
D 7, E 10, F 10, G 8.

E 11, F 11, G 7.
E 14, F 13.
E 15, F 14.
E 18, F 15.

F 9^2, G 4^{3,4}.

It will be observed that each of the versions B–F adds something which is taken up by a successor or successors.   The arrangement of E and F, of E especially, is objectionable.

A. Jane Reynolds and James Harris, a seaman, had exchanged vows of marriage.   The young man was pressed as a sailor, and after three years was reported as dead ; the young woman married a ship-carpenter, and they lived together happily for four years, and had children.   One night when the carpenter was absent from home, a spirit rapped at the window and announced himself as James Harris, come after an absence of seven years * to claim the woman for his wife.   She explained the state of things, but upon obtaining assurance that her long-lost lover had the means to support her — seven ships upon the sea — consented to go with him, for he was really *much* like unto a man.   'The woman-kind' was seen no more after that ; the carpenter hanged himself.

The carpenter is preserved in B–E, and

---

his forfeit.   He implores for mercy, or at least reprieve, and, if granted, promises this :

'And I will show how the lilies grow
    On the banks of Italy.'

Satan, being no horticulturist, pays no attention to this

proffer."   Scott's memory seems to have gone quite astray here.

* Why the ghost should wait four years, and what is meant in st. 18 by his travelling seven years, it is not easy to understand.   The author would probably take up the impregnable position that he was simply relating the facts as they occurred.

even his name in C. He swoons in B, and runs distracted in C, when he learns what has become of his wife; the other versions take no notice of him after the elopement. B–F all begin with the return of the long-absent lover. The ship (as it *is* to have in A 26) has silken sails and gold masts, or the like, C 10, F $9^{3,4}$ (*cf.* B 8, G 1); but there are no visible mariners, F $9^{1,2}$, G $4^{3,4}$. The pair have been only a short time afloat when the woman begins to weep for son, husband, or both, B 9, 10, C 14, D 5, E 12, 13, G 5. The seaman (as it will be convenient to call him) tells her to hold her tongue, he will show her how the lilies grow on the banks of Italy, C 16, D 6 (*cf.* E 16, 17), F 12, and, in a different connection, G 6. The seaman's countenance grows grim, and the sea gurly, D 7, E 10, F 10, G 8. He will let her see the fishes swim, where the lilies grow, in the bottom of the sea, C 21, D 8 (*cf.* E 16, 17). She discerns that the seaman has a cloven foot, E 11, F 11, G 7. She asks, What is yon bright hill? It is the hill of heaven, where she will never be. What is yon dark hill? It is the hill of hell, where they two shall be: E 14, 15, F 13, 14. The seaman reaches his hand to the topmast, strikes the sails, and the ship drowns, C 22; takes the woman up to the topmast and sinks the ship in a flash of fire, E 18; strikes the topmast with his hand, the foremast with his knee, and sinks the ship, F 15.

In E 9 he throws the woman into the main, and five-and-twenty hundred ships are wrecked; in G 9 the little ship runs round about and never is seen more.

In A the *revenant* is characterized as a spirit; in B, which is even tamer than A, he is called the mariner, and is drowned with the woman; in C he expressly says to the woman, I brought you away to punish you for breaking your vows to me. This explicitness may be prosaic, but it seems to me regrettable that the conception was not maintained. To explain the eery personality and proceedings of the ship-master, E–G, with a sort of vulgar rationalism, turn him into the devil, and as he is still represented in E, F (G being defective at the beginning) as returning to seek the fulfilment of old vows, he there figures as a "dæmon lover." D (probably by the fortunate accident of being a fragment) leaves us to put our own construction upon the weird seaman; and, though it retains the homely ship-carpenter, is on the whole the most satisfactory of all the versions.*

Scott's ballad is translated by Talvj, Versuch, etc., p. 558; by Gerhard, p. 84; and by Rosa Warrens, Schottische Volkslieder, No 14, p. 61 (after Aytoun, who repeats Scott, omitting one of Laidlaw's stanzas). Knortz, Lieder und Romanzen Alt-Englands, p. 192, translates Allingham's ballad.

A

Pepys Ballads, IV, 101; from a copy in Percy's papers.

1 THERE dwelt a fair maid in the West,
    Of worthy birth and fame,
  Neer unto Plimouth, stately town,
    Jane Reynolds was her name.

2 This damsel dearly was belovd
    By many a proper youth,
  And what of her is to be said
    Is known for very truth.

3 Among the rest a seaman brave
    Unto her a wooing came;
  A comely proper youth he was,
    James Harris calld by name.

4 The maid and young man was agreed,
    As time did them allow,
  And to each other secretly
    They made a solemn vow,

5 That they would ever faithfull be
    Whilst Heaven afforded life;
  He was to be her husband kind,
    And she his faithfull wife.

6 A day appointed was also
    When they was to be married;
  But before these things were brought to pass
    Matters were strangely carried.

* We must not be critical about copies which have been patched by tradition, but F 3 is singularly out of place for a "dæmon lover."

7 All you that faithfull lovers be
   Give ear and hearken well,
   And what of them became at last
   I will directly tell.

8 The young man he was prest to sea,
   And forcèd was to go;
   His sweet-heart she must stay behind,
   Whether she would or no.

9 And after he was from her gone
   She three years for him staid,
   Expecting of his comeing home,
   And kept herself a maid.

10 At last news came that he was dead
   Within a forraign land,
   And how that he was buried
   She well did understand,

11 For whose sweet sake the maiden she
   Lamented many a day,
   And never was she known at all
   The wanton for to play.

12 A carpenter that livd hard by,
   When he heard of the same,
   Like as the other had done before,
   To her a wooing came.

13 But when that he had gained her love
   They married were with speed,
   And four years space, being man and wife,
   They loveingly agreed.

14 Three pritty children in this time
   This loving couple had,
   Which made their father's heart rejoyce,
   And mother wondrous glad.

15 But as occasion servd, one time
   The good man took his way
   Some three days journey from his home,
   Intending not to stay.

16 But, whilst that he was gone away,
   A spirit in the night
   Came to the window of his wife,
   And did her sorely fright.

17 Which spirit spake like to a man,
   And unto her did say,
   'My dear and onely love,' quoth he,
   'Prepare and come away.

18 'James Harris is my name,' quoth he,
   'Whom thou didst love so dear,
   And I have traveld for thy sake
   At least this seven year.

19 'And now I am returnd again,
   To take thee to my wife,
   And thou with me shalt go to sea,
   To end all further strife.'

20 'O tempt me not, sweet James,' quoth she,
   'With thee away to go;
   If I should leave my children small,
   Alas! what would they do?

21 'My husband is a carpenter,
   A carpenter of great fame;
   I would not for five hundred pounds
   That he should know the same.'

22 'I might have had a king's daughter,
   And she would have married me;
   But I forsook her golden crown,
   And for the love of thee.

23 'Therefore, if thou 'lt thy husband forsake,
   And thy children three also,
   I will forgive the[e] what is past,
   If thou wilt with me go.'

24 'If I forsake my husband and
   My little children three,
   What means hast thou to bring me to,
   If I should go with thee?'

25 'I have seven ships upon the sea;
   When they are come to land,
   Both marriners and marchandize
   Shall be at thy command.

26 'The ship wherein my love shall sail
   Is glorious to behold;
   The sails shall be of finest silk,
   And the mast of shining gold.'

27 When he had told her these fair tales,
   To love him she began,
   Because he was in human shape,
   Much like unto a man.

28 And so together away they went
   From off the English shore,
   And since that time the woman-kind
   Was never seen no more.

29 But when her husband he come home
   And found his wife was gone,
   And left her three sweet pretty babes
   Within the house alone,

30 He beat his breast, he tore his hair,
   The tears fell from his eyes,
   And in the open streets he run
   With heavy doleful cries.

31 And in this sad distracted case
　　He hangd himself for woe
Upon a tree near to the place;
　　The truth of all is so.

32 The children now are fatherless,
　　And left without a guide,
But yet no doubt the heavenly powers
　　Will for them well provide.

———◆———

B

The Rambler's Garland, British Museum, 11621, c. 4
(57).　1785 (?)

1 'WELL met, well met, my own true love,
　　Long time I have been seeking thee;
I am lately come from the salt sea,
　　And all for the sake, love, of thee.

2 'I might have had a king's daughter,
　　And fain she would have married me;
But I 've forsaken all her crowns of gold,
　　And all for the sake, love, of thee.'

3 'If you might have had a king's daughter,
　　I think you much to blame;
I would not for five hundred pounds
　　That my husband should hear the same.

4 'For my husband is a carpenter,
　　And a young ship-carpenter is he,
And by him I have a little son,
　　Or else, love, I 'd go along with thee.

5 'But if I should leave my husband dear,
　　Likewise my little son also,
What have you to maintain me withal,
　　If I along with you should go?'

6 'I have seven ships upon the seas,
　　And one of them brought me to land,
And seventeen mariners to wait on thee,
　　For to be, love, at your command.

7 'A pair of slippers thou shalt have,
　　They shall be made of beaten gold,
Nay and be lin'd with velvet soft,
　　For to keep thy feet from cold.

8 'A gilded boat thou then shall have,
　　The oars shall gilded be also,
And mariners to row the[e] along,
　　For to keep thee from thy overthrow.'

9 They had not been long upon the sea
　　Before that she began to weep:
'What, weep you for my gold?' he said,
　　'Or do you weep for my fee?

10 'Or do you weep for some other young man
　　That you love much better than me?'
'No, I do weep for my little son,
　　That should have come along with me.'

11 She had not been upon the seas
　　Passing days three or four
But the mariner and she were drowned,
　　And never were heard of more.

12 When tidings to old England came
　　The ship-carpenter's wife was drownd,
He wrung his hands and tore his hair,
　　And grievously fell in a swoon.

13 'Oh cursed be those mariners!
　　For they do lead a wicked life;
They ruind me, a ship-carpenter,
　　By deluding away my wife.'

———◆———

C

Buchan's Ballads of the North of Scotland, I, 214.

1 'O ARE ye my father? Or are ye my mother?
　　Or are ye my brother John?
Or are ye James Herries, my first true-love,
　　Come back to Scotland again?'

2 'I am not your father, I am not your mother,
　　Nor am I your brother John;
But I 'm James Herries, your first true-love,
　　Come back to Scotland again.'

3 'Awa, awa, ye former lovers,
　　Had far awa frae me!

For now I am another man's wife
  Ye 'll neer see joy o me.'

4 'Had I kent that ere I came here,
  I neer had come to thee;·
For I might hae married the king's daughter,
  Sae fain she woud had me.

5 'I despised the crown o gold,
  The yellow silk also,
And I am come to my true-love,
  But with me she 'll not go.'

6 'My husband he is a carpenter,
  Makes his bread on dry land,
And I hae born him a young son;
  Wi you I will not gang.'

7 'You must forsake your dear husband,
  Your little young son also,
Wi me to sail the raging seas,
  Where the stormy winds do blow.'

8 'O what hae you to keep me wi,
  If I should with you go,
If I 'd forsake my dear husband,
  My little young son also?'

9 'See ye not yon seven pretty ships?
  The eighth brought me to land,
With merchandize and mariners,
  And wealth in every hand.'

10 She turnd her round upon the shore
  Her love's ships to behold;
Their topmasts and their mainyards
  Were coverd oer wi gold.

11 Then she 's gane to her little young son,
  And kissd him cheek and chin;
Sae has she to her sleeping husband,
  And dune the same to him.

12 'O sleep ye, wake ye, my husband?
  I wish ye wake in time!
I woudna for ten thousand pounds
  This night ye knew my mind.'

13 She 's drawn the slippers on her feet,
  Were coverd oer wi gold,
Well lined within wi velvet fine,
  To had her frae the cold.

14 She hadna sailed upon the sea
  A league but barely three
Till she minded on her dear husband,
  Her little young son tee.

15 'O gin I were at land again,
  At land where I woud be,
The woman neer shoud bear the son
  Shoud gar me sail the sea.'

16 'O hold your tongue, my sprightly flower,
  Let a' your mourning be;
I 'll show you how the lilies grow
  On the banks o Italy.'

17 She hadna sailed on the sea
  A day but barely ane
Till the thoughts o grief came in her mind,
  And she langd for to be hame.

18 'O gentle death, come cut my breath,
  I may be dead ere morn!
I may be buried in Scottish ground,
  Where I was bred and born!'

19 'O hold your tongue, my lily leesome thing,
  Let a' your mourning be;
But for a while we 'll stay at Rose Isle,
  Then see a far countrie.

20 'Ye 'se neer be buried in Scottish ground,
  Nor land ye 's nae mair see;
I brought you away to punish you
  For the breaking your vows to me.

21 'I said ye shoud see the lilies grow
  On the banks o Italy;
But I 'll let you see the fishes swim,
  In the bottom o the sea.'

22 He reached his hand to the topmast,
  Made a' the sails gae down,
And in the twinkling o an ee
  Baith ship and crew did drown.

23 The fatal flight o this wretched maid
  Did reach her ain countrie;
Her husband then distracted ran,
  And this lament made he:

24 'O wae be to the ship, the ship,
  And wae be to the sea,

And wae be to the mariners
Took Jeanie Douglas frae me!

25 'O bonny, bonny was my love,
  A pleasure to behold;
The very hair o my love's head
Was like the threads o gold.

26 'O bonny was her cheek, her cheek,
  And bonny was her chin,
And bonny was the bride she was,
  The day she was made mine!'

D

Kinloch MSS, I, 297; from the recitation of T. Kinnear, Stonehaven.

1 'O WHARE hae ye been, my dearest dear,
  These seven lang years and more?'
'O I am come to seek my former vows,
  That ye promisd me before.'

2 'Awa wi your former vows,' she says,
  'Or else ye will breed strife;
Awa wi your former vows,' she says,
  'For I 'm become a wife.

3 'I am married to a ship-carpenter,
  A ship-carpenter he 's bound;
I wadna he kend my mind this nicht
For twice five hundred pound.'

* * * * * * *

4 She has put her foot on gude ship-board,
  And on ship-board she 's gane,
And the veil that hung oure her face
Was a' wi gowd begane.

5 She had na sailed a league, a league,
  A league but barely twa,
Till she did mind on the husband she left,
  And her wee young son alsua.

6 'O haud your tongue, my dearest dear,
  Let all your follies abee;
I 'll show whare the white lillies grow,
  On the banks of Italie.'

7 She had na sailed a league, a league,
  A league but barely three,
Till grim, grim grew his countenance,
  And gurly grew the sea.

8 'O haud your tongue, my dearest dear,
  Let all your follies abee;
I 'll show whare the white lillies grow,
  In the bottom of the sea.'

9 He 's tane her by the milk-white hand,
  And he 's thrown her in the main;
And full five-and-twenty hundred ships
Perishd all on the coast of Spain.

E

Motherwell's MS., p. 97.

1 'WHERE have you been, my long lost lover,
  This seven long years and more?'
'I 've been seeking gold for thee, my love,
  And riches of great store.

2 'Now I 'm come for the vows you promised me,
  You promised me long ago;'
'My former vows you must forgive,
  For I 'm a wedded wife.'

3 'I might have been married to a king's daughter,
  Far, far ayont the sea;

But I refused the crown of gold,
  And it 's all for the love of thee.'

4 'If you might have married a king's daughter,
  Yourself you have to blame;
For I 'm married to a ship's-carpenter,
  And to him I have a son.

5 'Have you any place to put me in,
  If I with you should gang?'
'I 've seven brave ships upon the sea,
  All laden to the brim.

6 'I 'll build my love a bridge of steel,
  All for to help her oer;

Likewise webs of silk down by her side,
  To keep my love from the cold.'

7 She took her eldest son into her arms,
  And sweetly did him kiss:
'My blessing go with you, and your father too,
  For little does he know of this.'

8 As they were walking up the street,
  Most beautiful for to behold,
He cast a glamour oer her face,
  And it shone like the brightest gold.

9 As they were walking along the sea-side,
  Where his gallant ship lay in,
So ready was the chair of gold
  To welcome this lady in.

10 They had not sailed a league, a league,
  A league but scarsely three,
Till altered grew his countenance,
  And raging grew the sea.

11 When they came to yon sea-side,
  She set her down to rest;
It's then she spied his cloven foot,
  Most bitterly she wept.

12 'O is it for gold that you do weep?
  Or is it for fear?
Or is it for the man you left behind
  When that you did come here?'

13 'It is not for gold that I do weep,
  O no, nor yet for fear;
But it is for the man I left behind
  When that I did come here.

14 'O what a bright, bright hill is yon,
  That shines so clear to see?'
'O it is the hill of heaven,' he said,
  'Where you shall never be.'

15 'O what a black, dark hill is yon,
  That looks so dark to me?'
'O it is the hill of hell,' he said,
  'Where you and I shall be.

16 'Would you wish to see the fishes swim
  In the bottom of the sea,
Or wish to see the leaves grow green
  On the banks of Italy?'

17 'I hope I'll never see the fishes swim
  On the bottom of the sea,
But I hope to see the leaves grow green
  On the banks of Italy.'

18 He took her up to the topmast high,
  To see what she could see;
He sunk the ship in a flash of fire,
  To the bottom of the sea.

F

Minstrelsy of the Scottish Border, fifth edition, 1812, II,
427; taken down from the recitation of Walter Grieve by
William Laidlaw.

1 'O WHERE have you been, my long, long love,
  This long seven years and mair?'
'O I'm come to seek my former vows
  Ye granted me before.'

2 'O hold your tongue of your former vows,
  For they will breed sad strife;
O hold your tongue of your former vows,
  For I am become a wife.'

3 He turned him right and round about,
  And the tear blinded his ee:

'I wad never hae trodden on Irish ground,
  If it had not been for thee.

4 'I might hae had a king's daughter,
  Far, far beyond the sea;
I might have had a king's daughter,
  Had it not been for love o thee.'

5 'If ye might have had a king's daughter,
  Yer sel ye had to blame;
Ye might have taken the king's daughter,
  For ye kend that I was nane.

6 'If I was to leave my husband dear,
  And my two babes also,
O what have you to take me to,
  If with you I should go?'

7 'I hae seven ships upon the sea —
    The eighth brought me to land —
With four-and-twenty bold mariners,
    And music on every hand.'

8 She has taken up her two little babes,
    Kissd them baith cheek and chin:
'O fair ye weel, my ain two babes,
    For I 'll never see you again.'

9 She set her foot upon the ship,
    No mariners could she behold;
But the sails were o the taffetie,
    And the masts o the beaten gold.

10 She had not sailed a league, a league,
    A league but barely three,
When dismal grew his countenance,
    And drumlie grew his ee.

11 They had not saild a league, a league,
    A league but barely three,

Until she espied his cloven foot,
    And she wept right bitterlie.

12 'O hold your tongue of your weeping,' says he,
    'Of your weeping now let me be;
I will shew you how the lilies grow
    On the banks of Italy.'

13 'O what hills are yon, yon pleasant hills,
    That the sun shines sweetly on?'
'O yon are the hills of heaven,' he said,
    'Where you will never win.'

14 'O whaten a mountain is yon,' she said,
    'All so dreary wi frost and snow?'
'O yon is the mountain of hell,' he cried,
    'Where you and I will go.'

15 He strack the tap-mast wi his hand,
    The fore-mast wi his knee,
And he brake that gallant ship in twain,
    And sank her in the sea.

G

Motherwell's Minstrelsy, p. 93.

1 'I HAVE seven ships upon the sea,
    Laden with the finest gold,
And mariners to wait us upon;
    All these you may behold.

2 'And I have shoes for my love's feet,
    Beaten of the purest gold,
And linèd wi the velvet soft,
    To keep my love's feet from the cold.

3 'O how do you love the ship?' he said,
    'Or how do you love the sea?
And how do you love the bold mariners
    That wait upon thee and me?'

4 'O I do love the ship,' she said,
    'And I do love the sea;
But woe be to the dim mariners,
    That nowhere I can see!'

5 They had not sailed a mile awa,
    Never a mile but one,

When she began to weep and mourn,
    And to think on her little wee son.

6 'O hold your tongue, my dear,' he said,
    'And let all your weeping abee,
For I 'll soon show to you how the lilies grow
    On the banks of Italy.'

7 They had not sailed a mile awa,
    Never a mile but two,
Until she espied his cloven foot,
    From his gay robes sticking thro.

8 They had not sailed a mile awa,
    Never a mile but three,
When dark, dark, grew his eerie looks,
    And raging grew the sea.

9 They had not sailed a mile awa,
    Never a mile but four,
When the little wee ship ran round about,
    And never was seen more.

H

Christie, Traditional Ballad Airs, I, 138; taken down by the editor's father from the singing of an aged relative.

1 He 's given her a pair of shoes,
   To hold her frae the cold;
The one side of them was velvaret,
   And the other beaten gold.

2 Up she has taen her little wee son,
   And given him kisses three;
Says, Fare ye weel, my little wee son,
   I 'm gaun to sail the sea.

B. The Rambler's Garland, composed of some Delightful New Songs. *There are four: the
third is* The distressed Ship Carpenter.
"1785?"

  1¹. my my own.

E. 3². *Originally,* Had it not been for love of
thee.

  10³. *In the margin,* Till grim, grim grew.

  11⁴. Och hone *under the line.*

  14¹. *Altered to,* O whatena.

  15¹. *Altered to,* O whatena dark. (*The original readings are likely to have been the
traditional ones.*)

  17³. sea.

F. *In a letter to Scott, January 3, 1803, Laidlaw gives some account of the ballad sung
by Walter Grieve, and cites some verses
from recollection, which, not unnaturally,
differ from what he afterwards took down
in writing.*

  " He likewise sung part of a very beautiful ballad which I think you will not have seen. As
a punishment for her inconstancy, the Devil
is supposed to come and entice a young
woman from her husband, in the form of
her former lover. The tune is very solemn
and melancholy, and the effect is mixed with
a considerable proportion of horror. I remember but very few verses. He prevails
upon her to go abroad [aboard?] to hear his
musicians, after upbraiding her

  ' I might hae marrit a king's daughter, but
   I mindit my love for thee.'

" The description of her setting her child on
the nurse's knee and bidding him farewell
is waesome, but I have forgot it."

She set her foot into the ship, to hear the
   music play ;
The masts war o the beaten goud, and the
   sails o the silk sae gay.

They hadna saild a league thrae land, a
   league but barely three,
Till drearie grew his countenance, and drumlie grew his ee.

They hadna saild another league, another
   league but three,
Till she beheld his cloven fit, and she wept
   most bitterlie.

' O had yer tongue, my love,' he said, ' why
   weep ye sae mournfulie ?
We 're gaun to see how the lillies do grow
   on the banks o fair Italie.'

' What hills are yon, yon pleasant hills, where
   the sun shines [*a wafer here*]
' O yon 's the hills of heaven,' he said,
   ' where you will never win ! ' "

*Letters addressed to Sir Walter Scott, Vol.
I, No 78, Abbotsford.*

244

JAMES HATLEY

A. a. "Scotch Ballads, Materials for Border Minstrelsy," No 35, MS. of Thomas Wilkie, p. 6, Abbotsford. **b.** 'James Hatley,' Campbell MSS, II, 289. **c.** 'James Hatelie,' R. Chambers, The Romantic Scottish Ballads, their Epoch and Authorship, p. 37.

B. 'James Hately,' "Scotch Ballads, Materials for Border Minstrelsy," No 39, MS. of Thomas Wilkie, p. 18. The same, transcribed by Thomas Wilkie, "Scotch Ballads," etc., No 79, Abbotsford.

C. 'Jamie O'Lee,' Motherwell's MS., p. 654.

A. 'SIR FENWICK' steals the king's jewels and lays the blame on James Hatley, who is condemned to death. The king's daughter steals the prison-keys from under her father's head and pays a visit to Hatley, who assures her of his innocence, and tells her that Fenwick is the man. [b, the king is angry, and says that for stealing his jewels Hatley shall die 'over the barriers:' so B.] The princess goes to her father and begs the life of Hatley, and her boon is granted without demur. She asks one thing more, that Fenwick and Hatley may try their verity at the sword, and this is unhesitatingly conceded. Hatley is but fifteen years old (he is seventeen b, eighteen c, fifteen again C), and Fenwick is thirty-three; nevertheless, Fenwick gets three wounds. An English lord intermits: he would have given all his estates rather than Hatley should escape; a Scots lord replies that he would have fought to the knees in blood before Hatley should have been hanged. (The Scots lord is wanting in b; the passage is likely to be borrowed from 'Geordie,' No 209.) The king's eldest son asks Hatley to dine, and makes him his captain by land and sea;* the king's daughter invites him to dine, and announces that she has made a vow to marry no other man.

B. Hatley, accused of stealing the king's jewels, goes to the little prince and asks what he will do for his page; the prince goes to his father and asks what *he* will do for the page.

* Justifying Thackeray's 'Little Billee.'

The king says that Hatley has stolen his jewels, so a Norland lord has informed him, and Hatley must die 'over the barriers.' The prince offers to fight any man who lays the blame on Hatley. Fenwick maintains that Hatley is the thief. The prince gives Fenwick two or three mortal wounds; Fenwick hands him the key of his coffer, and in the coffer the jewels will be found. The king invests Hatley with Fenwick's lands.

C. A false knight, Phenix, steals the queen's jewels, and leaves the blame on Jamie O'Lee. The king sends for his son and tells him that Jamie has been accused of the theft by an English lord, and shall be banished from Scotland. The prince demands a man to fight with Jamie on this charge, and false Phenix offers himself. The prince at first objects, for Jamie is but fifteen years old, whereas Phenix is of course thirty-three; however, he tells Jamie that he must fight or be banished from *England* (8, compare 14). Jamie protests his innocence. He fights with Phenix and receives the first wound, then runs Phenix through the body; Phenix owns his guilt. The king tells Jamie to come home with him; every knight in the court shall be at his command. The queen bids Jamie come home with her; he shall have a new livery every month. The prince invites Jamie to come home with him; all his lands in Scotland shall be at Jamie's command. Jamie thanks king, queen, and nobility; he has been a prince's page all his life, and a prince's page he still will be.

Lines representing **B** 12³,⁴, **C** 17³,⁴, have been interpolated into the fragment of 'The Slaughter of the Laird of Mellerstain,' No 230 :

> They wad take the lands frae fause Fenwick,
>   And give them to James Hately.
>
> There is no a month in a' the year
>   But changëd should his claithing be.

———◆———

A

a. "Scotch Ballads, Materials for Border Minstrelsy," No 35, MS. of Thomas Wilkie, p. 6, Abbotsford ; "from Betty Hoyl, who learned it from her mother," Gattonside. **b.** Campbell MSS, II, 289. **c.** R. Chambers, The Romantic Scottish Ballads, etc., 1859, p. 37 ; "taken down many years ago from the singing of an old man in the south of Scotland."

1 It happened once upon a time,
     When the king he was from home,
   Sir Fenwick he has stolen his jewels,
     And laid the blame on James Hatley.

2 James Hatley was in prison strong,
     A wait he was condemned to die ;
   There was not one in all the court
     To speak one word for James Hatley.

3 No one but the king's daughter,
     A wait she loved him tenderlie ;
   She 's stolen the keys from her father's head,
     And gaed and conversed wi James Hatley.

4 'Come, tell to me now, James,' she said,
     'Come, tell to me if thou hast them stolen,
   And I 'll make a vow, and I 'll keep it true,
     Ye shall never be the worse of me.'

5 'I have not stolen them, lady,' he said,
     'Nor as little it was intended by me ;
   Sir Fenwick he has stolen them himself ;
     A wait he has laid the blame on me.'

6 'One asking, one asking, father dear,
     One asking, one asking grant to me,
   For I never asked one in my life ;
     I am sure you cannot but grant it to me.'

7 'Weel ask it, weel ask it, daughter dear,
     Ask it, and it granted shall be ;
   If it should be my hole estate,
     Naesaid, naesaid, it shall not be.'

8 'I want none of your gold, father,
     And I want none of your fee ;
   All that I ask, father dear,
     It is the life of James Hatley.'

9 'Weel ask it, weel ask it, daughter dear,
     Weel ask it, and it answerëd shall be ;
   For I 'll make a vow, and I 'll keep it true,
     James Hatley shall never hangëd be.'

10 'Another asking, father dear,
      Another asking grant to me ;
    Let Fenwick and Hatley go [to] the sword,
      And let them try their verity.'

11 ''T is weel askëd, daughter dear,
      'T is weel asked, and it granted shall be ;
    For eer the morn or twelve o'clock
      They both at the point of the sword shall be.'

12 James Hatley was fifteen years old,
      Sir Fenwick he was thirty three ;
    But James lap about, and he struck about,
      Till he 's gaen Sir Fenwick wounds three.

13 'Hold up, hold up, James Hatley,' he cry'd,
      'And let my breath go out and in ;
    For I have stolen them myself,
      More shame and disgrace it is to me.'

14 Up and spake an English lord,
      And O but he spake haughtily !
    'I would reather given my whole estates
      Before ye had not hanged James Hatley.'

15 But up and spake a Scottish lord,
      And O but he spake boldly !
    'I would reather hae foughten among blood to
        the knees
      Before ye had hanged James Hatley.'

16 Up and spake the king's eldest son,
　‘Come hame, James Hatley, and dine wi
　　me;
　For I 've made a vow, I 'll keep it true,
　　Ye 's be my captain by land and by sea.’

17 Up and spake the king's daughter,
　‘Come home, James Hatley, and dine wi
　　me;
　For I 've made a vow, I 'll keep it true,
　　I 'll never marry a man but thee.’

B

“ Scotch Ballads, Materials for Border Minstrelsy,” No
39, MS. of Thomas Wilkie, p. 18, “ as sung by Chirsty
Robertson, Dunse.” The same, transcribed by Thomas
Wilkie, “ Scotch Ballads,” etc., No 79. Abbotsford.

1 IT happened once upon a time,
　When the king he was from home,
　False Fennick he has stolen his jewels,
　And laid the blame on James Hately.

2 The day was sett 　.　.　.　.
　And the wind blew shill oer the lea;
　There was not one in all the court
　To speak a word for James Hately.

3 James is to the prince's chamber gone,
　And he 's bowd low down on his knee :
　‘What will ye do for me, my little pretty
　　prince?
　O what will ye do for your page, James
　　Hately?’

4 .　.　.　.　.　.　.　.
　‘And I will away to my father, the king,
　And see if your life can savëd be.’

5 The prince he 's to his father gone,
　And he 's bowed low down on his knee :
　‘What will ye do for me, my father?
　O what will ye do for my page, James
　　Hately?’

6 ‘James Hately has my jewels stolen,
　A Norland lord hath told it to me;

James Hately has my jewels stolen,
And oer the barras he maun die.’

7 The prince he drew his little brown sword —
　It was made of the metal so free —
　And he swore he would fight them man by
　　man
　That would lay the blame on James Hately.

8 Up then spoke the false Fennick,
　And an ill-spoken man was he;
　‘James Hately has the king's jewels stolen,
　.　.　.　.　.　.　.　.’

9 The prince he drew his little brown sword —
　It was made of the metal so free —
　And he 's thrust it in false Fennick's side,
　And given him death-wounds two or three.

10 ‘O hold your hand, my little pretty prince,
　And let my breath go out and in,
　For spilling of my noble blood
　And shaming of my noble kin.

11 ‘O hold your hand, my little pretty prince,
　And let my breath go out and in,
　And there 's the key of my coffer,
　And you 'll find the king's jewels lying
　　therein.’

12 ‘If this be true,’ the king he said,
　‘If this be true ye tell to me,
　I will take your lands, false Fennick,’ he said,
　‘And give them all to James Hately.’

C

Motherwell's MS., p. 654; "from the recitation of the wife of Charles Drain, sow-gelder, etc., Kilmarnock."

1 THERE was a fause knicht in the court,
    And he was fu o treacherie,
And he staw the queen's jewels in the nicht,
    And left the wyte on Jamie O'Lee.

2 The king he wrate a braid letter,
    And sealed it richt tenderlie,
And he sent it to his only son,
    To come and speak to him speedilie.

3 When he cam afore the king,
    He kneeled low down on his knee:
'What is your will, my sovereign leige?
    What is your will? cum tell to me.'

4 'Jamie O'Lee has my jewels stown,
    As the English lord tells unto me,
And out o Scotland he shall be sent,
    And sent awa to Germanie.'

5 'O no, O no,' then said the prince,
    'Sic things as that can never be;
But get me a man that will take on hand
    The morn to fecht young Jamie O'Lee.'

6 Syne out and spak the fause Phenix,
    And oh, he spak richt spitefullie;
'I am the man will tak on han
    To fecht and conquer Jamie O'Lee.'

7 'Oh no, oh no,' syne said the prince,
    'Sic things as that can never bee,
For Jamie O'Lee's no fifteen years auld,
    And ye, fause Phenix, are thretty three.'

8 The prince he mounted then wi speed,
    He's aff wi tidings to Jamie O'Lee,
Saying, The morn's morning ye maun fecht,
    Or out o England banisht bee.

9 When Jamie O'Lee the tidings heard,
    Fast the saut tear blindit his ee;
'I'm saikless o thae jewels,' he said,
    'As the bairn that sits on the nourice knee.'

10 Then Phenix munted a scaffold hie,
    A' for to shaw his veritie;

Whilk gart the nobles a' to cry
    'A dead man are ye, Jamie O'Lee!'

11 The first straik the fause Phenix gied,
    He gart the blude rin speedilie;
It gart the prince's heart to ache,
    And cry, Oh, alace for my Jamie O'Lee!

12 Jamie O'Lee he stepped back,
    Waiting for opportunitie,
And wi his sword baith lang and sharp
    He ran it thro Phenix fause bodie.

13 'O haud your hand, Jamie O'Lee,' he said,
    'And let the breath remain in me,
And skail nae mair o my noble blude,
    'T is a great disgrace to my loyaltie.'

14 'Confess, confess, ye fause Phenix,
    Confess your faults this day to me;
Were there nae mair men in a' England,
    My ain twa hands your death suld be.'

15 'Ye were sae great wi king and queen,
    I thocht I wuld hae banisht thee,
And I staw the queen's jewels in the nicht,
    And left the wyte on Jamie O'Lee.'

16 Syne out and spak the king himsell,
    Saying, Jamie O'Lee, come hame wi me,
And there's no a knicht in a' my court
    But what at your command sall be.

17 Syne out and spak the queen hersell,
    Saying, Jamie O'Lee, come hame wi me,
And there's no a month in a' the year
    But changed and brothered ye sall be.

18 Syne out and spak the prince himsell,
    Saying, Jamie O'Lee, come hame wi me;
I hae free lands in a' Scotland,
    And at your command they a' sall be.

19 'I thank ye, king, and I thank ye, queen,
    I thank ye a', nobilitie,
But a prince's page I was a' my life,
    And a prince's page I yet will be.'

20 The king gied him a silk waistcoat,
    And it was lined wi the taffetie,
Wi a band o gowd around his neck,
    And a prince's page he seems to be.

A. a. 1¹. day *written over* time.

1². from home was he?

2², 3², 5⁴. Await.

4². *The -ee rhyme may be restored by trans-posing* Come tell to me, *as in* c (*or adding* said she). 7⁴. Nae said, nae said.

13²–13³. *Two half-stanzas are wanting here: see* b, c. 16 *follows* 17, *but see* b, c.

b. 1². king was from home but lately.

1³. That Sir. 2¹. was laid. 2², 3², 5⁴. I wat.

2³. And there's not a man in.

2⁴. Wad speak. 3¹. king's fair.

3⁴. And went in and. 4². if you have.

4³. vow, I'll. 5². was it. 5⁴. And I wat he's.

After 5:

*   *   *   *   *   *

Up then spak the king himsel,
    And an angry man I wot was he:
'For stealin o my jewels rare,
    Hatlie shall oer the barriers die.'

6¹,². A boon, a boon, O.

6³. askit a boon before.

6⁴. And I'm sure that you will grant it me.

7¹. O ask it, ask it.

7³. And gin it be the half o my estate.

7⁴. Granted sal it be to thee.

8. 'O grant me this favour, father dear,
    O grant this favour unto me,
For I never askëd favour before;
    O spare the life of James Hatlie!'

9. *Wanting.*

10³. Let Hatley and Fenwick go to.

11¹. Well askëd, well askëd. 11². Well asked.

11³. Before the morn at.

12¹. he was seventeen.

12³. But *wanting*: strak. 12⁴. gien.

13¹. he said. *Between* 13² *and* 13³:

'For this is spillin of noble blude,
    And shamein of my noble kin.

'Hold up, hold up,' Sir Fenwick he said,
    'Hold up, and ye sal justified be;'

13³. stolen the jewels myself.

14¹. Up then spake a southern.

14³. rather have given the half o my land.

14⁴. Before James Hatlie should not hanged be. 15. *Wanting.*

16, 17. *The son speaks before the daughter.*

16¹, 17¹. Up then.

16³. For from this hour receive this dower.

16⁴. Ye sal be.

17³,⁴. For ere the sun gae down this night, O there's my hand, I'll marry thee.

c. 1¹. It fell upon a certain day.

1². from home he chanced to be.

1³. The king's jewels they were stolen all.

1⁴. And they.

2¹. And he is into prison cast.

2². And I wat he is.

2³. For there was not a man. 2⁴. speak a.

3. But the king's eldest daughter she loved him well,
    But known her love it might not be;
And she has stolen the prison-keys,
    And gane in and discoursed wi James Hatelie.

4¹. Oh, did you steal them, James.

4². Oh, did not you steal them? come tell to me.

4³. For I'll. 4⁴. You's.

5¹. I did not steal them, James.

5². And neither was it.

5³. For the English they stole them themselves.

5⁴. And I wat they've.

6¹,². Now she has hame to her father gane,
    And bowed her low down on her knee;
'I ask, I ask, I ask, father,' she said,
    'I ask, I ask a boon of thee.'

6³. For *wanting*.

6⁴. And one of them you must grant to me.

7¹,². Ask on, ask on, daughter, he said, And aye weel answered ye shall be.

7³. For if it were my whole.

7⁴. you shall.

8¹. I ask. 8². As little of your white monie.

8³. But all the asken that I do ask.

9¹. Ask on, ask on, daughter, he said.

9². And aye weel answered ye.

9³. and keep.

9⁴. shall not.

10¹. asken I ask, father: dear *wanting*.

10². asken I ask of thee. 10³. go to.

11¹,². Ask on, ask on, daughter, he said, And aye weel answered you shall be.

11³. For before the morn at.

12¹. eighteen years of age.

12². False F. was thirty years and three.
12³. He lap: strack.
12⁴. And he gave false F.
13¹. Oh, hold your hand, J. H., he said.
Between 13² *and* 13³:

'Were it not for the spilling of my noble
    blood,
And the shaming of my noble kin.

'Oh, hold your hand, James Hatelie,' he
    said,
'Oh, hold your hand, and let me be.'

13³. For I'm the man that stole the jewels.
13⁴. And a: it was.   14¹. Then up bespoke.
14². I wat but he.
14³. rather have lost all my lands.
14⁴. they had.
15¹. Then up bespoke a good Scotch.
15². I wat a good Scotch lord was he.
15³. to the knees in blood.   15⁴. Than they.

16, 17. *The son speaks before the daughter.*
16¹, 17¹. Then up bespoke.   16², 17². Come in.
16³, 17³. I'll make: and I'll.
16³. You'se: and sea.   17¹. king's eldest.
B. *The copy transcribed by Wilkie has been edited
    a little.* 2^{1,2}, *originally written in one line,
    are rightly divided as here;* 2^{3,4} *are made
    the concluding half of another stanza.*
2⁴. Would speak one.   3¹. James he.
3⁴. O *omitted.*   4³. And *omitted.*
5¹. prince is: father's chamber. 6². to *omitted.*
9². That hung low down by his knee.
9³. it *wanting.*   9⁴. Then gave him.
11 *is put before* 10, *and* 10^{1,2} *omitted.*
11⁴. king's laying (*careless copying*).
12³. false *omitted.*
Wilkie notes (No 39) that he had "heard this
sung also by a shepherd on Soltra hill," *but
it is not likely that these variations were derived from the shepherd.*
C. 9¹. When Johnie.   14³. War *for* Were *origi-
    nally.*   17⁴. brothered *in the MS.*

245

YOUNG ALLAN

A. Skene MS., p. 33.

B. 'Young Allan,' Buchan's MSS, II, 182.

C. 'Young Allan,' Buchan's Ballads of the North of
    Scotland, II, 11.

D. 'Young Allan,' Murison MS., p. 117.

E. 'Earl Patrick,' Kinloch MSS, V, 395.

THE copy in Christie's Traditional Ballad
Airs, I, 252, is abridged from C, with half a
dozen arbitrary and insignificant changes.

Skippers (lords) of Lothain, A, of Scarsburgh, C, of Aberdeen, D, are bragging over
their drink: some, absurdly enough, of their
hawks and hounds, A–C, some of their ladies,
young Allan of his ship, which will outsail all

others but three.* A boy in A, C, says that
his master has a boat (it is a coal-carrier in
C) which will take the wind from him. A
wager is laid, A, B, C. All the rest go to
drinking, 'to the tows,' but Allan to his pray-
ers, C 8. They sail; there is a terrible
storm, in the course of which the three com-
petitors are 'rent in nine,' A 9, or two of them

* Five are named in C 3, 4, but that is too many to allow.
Probably two versions may have been combined here. B
has only the three mentioned in C 4; the three of A 3 are
repeated in A 9; and there are three only in E 7–9. The
Black Burgess of C 3 occurs in A 3, and 'the smack
calld (caud) Twine' of C 3 looks like a corruption of 'the
small (sma') Cordvine.'

sink, and the topmast of the third 'gaes in nine,' E 7–9.

In A they have sailed only a few leagues, when Allan's ship is so racked by the storm that they see water through her sides. At this point, especially in A, Allan's seamanship appears to very little advantage; he is more of a fair-weather yachtsman than of a skeely skipper. If he could get a bonny boy to take the helm and bring the ship in safe, the boy should have a liberal share of his gold and land, and a daughter Ann besides, whom one is surprised that Young Allan should have to offer. In A and D the bonny boy evidently takes command of the ship, although in A 18 the sailors ascribe their safety, under God, to their good master. The ballad indeed suffers almost as grievously as the comely cog.

In B–E Allan calls for a bonny boy to take the helm while he goes to the masthead to look for land. In D he makes the same promises as in A, but the bonny boy cares only for Ann. In B, C the bonny boy suggests that Allan should waken his drunken men, for whom good thick shoes had been bought, though none had been given him. But in all the boy takes the helm, and in fact keeps it till the ship is in. Allan, at the masthead, can see neither day nor landmark; many feather-beds are floating on the water, B, C. The boy calls his master down; the sea can be seen through the ship's sides, B–E.

Orders are given, by the boy or by Allan (by the boy certainly in D, and by Allan in E), to take feather-beds and canvas and lay, busk, or wrap the ship round; pitch and tar are also recommended in B, C. This done, Allan addresses the ship: Spring up, and gold shall be your hire, A; Haste to dry land, and every nail that is in you shall be a gold pin, B; For every iron nail in you, of gold there shall be ten, C; in D, indirectly, Where she wants an iron nail drive in a silver pin, and where

she wants an oaken bolt beat in the gold, and the like in E. When the ship hears this, she springs from the water like sparks from the fire, A–C.

The first shore they come to is Troup, B, Howdoloot, C, Linn, D, E. The ship is kept off with cannon, B, C, with spears and bayonets, D; is towed in (wrongly), E. The next shore they come to is Lee, B, E, Howdilee, C, wanting in D; 'they bare her to the sea,' C, 'they turned their ship about,' D, the ship is towed in (wrongly), B, E. The third shore they come to is Lin, B, Howdilin, C, Aberdeen, D; the ship is towed in (welcomed), with drums beating and pipes playing, B, C, D.

Allan calls for the bonny boy that brought the ship safe in, that took the helm in hand, and offers him gold, land, and his daughter; the boy rejects gold and land, and takes the daughter, A, D; Allan makes over to the boy his comely cog and gives him his daughter, B; gives him his daughter, C.

Five-and-forty ships, A, three-and-fifty, C, one-and-twenty, E, went to sea, and only one came back.*

This ballad is mixed with that of 'Sir Patrick Spens,' No 58, II, 21 ff. E 1–6 belong entirely to No 58, and K 6–10, M 1, 3, of No 58 belong to 'Young Allan.' The bonny boy is found in 58, B, C, E, G, I, J; the floating feather-beds occur in E–H, J, O, R; the sea is seen through the ship in 58, C 15, I 21; cloth is wapped into the ship's side to keep out water, H 19, 20; feather-beds and canvas (and pitch) are used as here in I 22, 23.

By far the most interesting feature in this ballad is Allan's addressing his ship and the ship's intelligent behavior, A 16, 17, B 12–15, C 21–22. Friðþjóf's ship Elliða understood and obeyed the speech of its master: Fornaldar Sögur, II, 79, 443 (cited by Bugge). Ranild's ship came to him when he blew his

---

* In a note at the end of E (which he regarded as a variety of 'Sir Patrick Spens'), Burton says: "There appears to be still lurking in some.part of Aberdeenshire a totally different version of this ballad, connected with the localities of the North [that is, not with Dunfermline, with which 'Young Allan' has no concern, or with Linn or Lee, which are in Outopia]. A person who remembered having heard it said that it ends happily, with the mariners drinking the bluid-red wine at Aberdeen. It mentions Bennachie, or the Hill of Mist, a celebrated hill in Aberdeenshire, which is seen far out at sea, and seems to have guided the gallant mariner to the shore." All the copies "end happily" so far as Young Allan is concerned, and this is all that we are supposed to care for.

horn: 'Svend Ranild,' Grundtvig, No 28, I, 367 (translated by Prior, I, 286). In another Danish ballad, and one of the best, the Ox when sailed by St Olav, responds to his commands as if fully endowed with consciousness; he thwacks it in the side and over the eye, and it goes faster and faster; but it is animate only for the nonce: 'Hellig-Olavs Væddefart,' Grundtvig, No 50, II, 134, Prior, I, 356.

The Phæacian ships have neither helmsman nor helm, and know men's minds and the way to all cities: Odyssey, viii, 557 ff. There is a magical self-moving ship in Marie de France's Guigemar, and elsewhere.

A

Skene MS., p. 33; taken down in the north of Scotland, 1802-3.

1 A' THE skippers of bonny Lothain,
　As they sat at the wine,
　There fell a reesin them amang,
　An it was in unhappy time.

2 Some o them reesd their hawks,
　An some o them their hounds,
　An some o them their ladies gay,
　Trod neatly on the ground;
　Young Allan he reesd his comely cog,
　That lay upon the strand.

3 'I hae as good a ship this day
　As ever sailed our seas,
　Except it be the Burges Black,
　But an the Small Cordvine,
　The Comely Cog of Dornisdale;
　We's lay that three bye in time.'

4 Out spak there a little boy,
　Just at Young Allan's knee:
　'Ye lie, ye lie, Young Allan,
　Sae loud 's I hear ye lie.

5 'For my master has a little boat
　Will sail thrice as well as thine;
　For she 'll gang in at your foremast,
　An gae out your fore-lee,
　An nine times in a winter night
　She 'll tak the wind frae thee.'

6 'O what will ye wad, ye Young Allan?
　Or what will ye wad wi me?'
　'I 'll wad my head against your land
　Till I get more monnie.'

7 They had na saild a league,
　A league but barely three,

But through an thro the bonny ship
　They saw the green wall sea.

8 They had na saild a league,
　A league but barely five,
　But through an thro their bonny ship
　They saw the green well wave.

9 He gaed up to the topmast,
　To see what he coud see,
　And there he saw the Burgess Black,
　But an the Small Cordvine,
　The Comely Cog of Dornisdale;
　The three was rent in nine.

10 Young Allan grat an wrang his hands,
　An he kent na what to dee:
　'The win is loud, and the waves are proud,
　An we 'll a' sink in the sea.

11 'But gin I coud get a bonny boy
　Wad tak my helm in han,
　That would steer my bonny ship,
　An bring her safe to land,

12 'He shoud get the twa part o my goud,
　The third part o my land,
　An gin we win safe to shore
　He shoud get my dochter Ann.'

13 'O here am I, a bonny boy
　That will tak your helm in han,
　An will steer your bonny ship
　An bring her safe to lan.

14 'Ye tak four-an-twenty feather-beds
　An lay the bonny ship round,
　An as much of the good canvas
　As mak her hale an soun.'

15 They took four-an-twenty feather-beds
　An laid the bonny ship roun,

An as much o the good canvas
    As made her hale an soun.

16 'Spring up, spring up, my bonny ship,
    An goud sall be your hire!'
Whan the bonny ship heard o that,
    That goud shoud be her hire,
She sprang as fast frae the sat water
    As sparks do frae the fire.

17 'Spring up, spring up, my bonny ship,
    And goud sall be your fee!'
Whan the bonny ship heard o that,
    That goud shoud be her fee,
She sprang as fast frae the sat water
    As the leaf does frae the tree.

18 The sailors stan on the shore-side,
    Wi their auld baucheld sheen:
'Thanks to God an our guid master
    That ever we came safe to land!'

19 'Whar is the bonny boy
    That took my helm in han,

That steerd my bonny ship,
    An brought her safe to lan?

20 'He's get the twa part o my goud,
    The third part o my lan,
An, since we're come safe to shore,
    He's get my dochter Ann.'

21 'O here am I, the bonny boy
    That took your helm in han,
That steered your bonny ship,
    An brought her safe to lan.

22 'I winna hae the twa part o your goud,
    Nor the third part o your lan,
But, since we hae win safe to shore,
    I'll wed your dochter Ann.'

23 Forty ships went to the sea,
    Forty ships and five,
An there never came ane o a' back,
    But Young Allan, alive.

B

Buchan's MSS, II, 182.

1 THERE were four-an-twenty sailors bold
    Sat drinking at the wine;
There fell a rousing them among,
    In an unseally time.

2 Some there reasd their hawk, their hawk,
    And some there reasd their hound,
But Young Allan reasd his comely cog,
    As she floats on the feam.

3 'There's not a ship amang you a'
    Will sail alang wi me,
But the comely cog o Heckland Hawk,
    And Flower o Germanie,
And the Black Snake o Leve London;
    They are all gane frae me.'

4 The wager was a gude wager,
    Of fifty tuns of wine,
And as much o the gude black silk
    As cleathd their lemans fine.

5 At midnight dark the wind up stark,
    The seas began to rout;
Young Allan and his bonny new ship
    Gaed three times witherlins about.

6 'O faer will I get a bonny boy
    Will take my helm in hand
Ere I gang up to the tapmast-head
    To look for some dry land?'

7 'O waken, waken your drunken men,
    As they lie drunk wi wine;
For when ye came thro Edinburgh town
    Ye bought them shoes o ben.

8 'There was no shoe made for my feet,
    Nor gluve made for my hand;
But nevertheless, my dear master,
    I'll take your helm in hand
Till ye gae to the topmast head
    And look for some dry land.'

9 'I cannot see no day, no day,
    Nor no meathe can I ken;

But mony a bonny feather-bed
    Lies floating on the faem.'

10 'Come down, come down, my dear master,
    You see not what I see;
  Through an through your bonny new ship
    Comes in the green haw sea.'

11 'Take fifty ells o the canvas broad
    And wrap it in a' roun,
  And as much o good pich an tar
    Make her go hale an soun.

12 'Sail on, sail on, my bonny ship,
    And haste ye to dry lan,
  And every nail that is in you
    Shall be a gay gold pin.

13 'Sail on, sail on, my bonny ship,
    And hae me to some lan,
  And a firlot full o guineas red
    Will be dealt at the lan's end.'

14 The ship she hearkend to their voice
    And listend to their leed,
  And she gaed thro the green haw sea
    Like fire out o a gleed.

15 When the ship got word o that,
    Goud was to be her beat,

She's flowen thro the stormy seas
    Like sparks out o a weet.

16 The first an shore that they came till,
    It was the shore o Troup;
  Wi cannons an great shooting there,
    They held Young Allan out.

17 The next an shore that they came till,
    It was the shore o Lee;
  Wi piping an sweet singing there,
    They towed Young Allan tee.

18 The next an shore that they came till,
    It was the shore o Lin;
  Wi drums beating and pipers playing,
    They towed Young Allan in,
  And Allan's lady she was there,
    To welcome Allan hame.

19 'O faer is my little boy,' he said,
    'That I brought oer the sea?'
  'I'm coming, master, running, master,
    At your command shall be.'

20 'O take to you my comely cog,
    And wed my daughter free,
  And a' for this ae night's wark
    That ye did wake wi me.'

———————

C

Buchan's Ballads of the North of Scotland, II, 11.

1 ALL the skippers o Scarsburgh
    Sat drinking at the wine;
  There fell a rousing them amang,
    On an unsealy time.

2 Some there rousd their hawk, their hawk,
    And some there rousd their hound,
  But Young Allan rousd his comely cog,
    As she stood on dry ground.

3 'There's nae a ship in Scarsburgh
    Will sail the seas wi mine,
  Except it be the Burgess Black,
    Or than the smack calld Twine.

4 'There's nae a ship amang you a'
    Will sail alang wi me,
  But the comely cog o Hecklandhawk,
    And Flower o Yermanie,
  And the Black Snake o Leve London;
    They are a' gane frae me.'

5 Out it speaks a little wee boy
    Stood by Young Allan's knee;
  'My master has a coal-carrier
    Will take the wind frae thee.

6 'She will gae out under the leaf,
    Come in under the lee,
  And nine times in a winter night
    She'll turn the wind wi thee.'

7 When they had wagerd them amang
    Full fifty tuns o wine,
  Besides as mickle gude black silk
    As clathe their lemans fine,

8 When all the rest went to the tows,
    All the whole night to stay,
  Young Allan he went to his bower,
    There with his God to pray.

9 'There shall nae man gang to my ship
    Till I say mass and dine,
  And take my leave o my lady;
    Gae to my bonny ship syne.'

10 Then they saild east on Saturday,
    On Sunday sailëd west;
  Likewise they sailed on Mononday
    Till twelve, when they did rest.

11 At midnight dark the wind up stark,
    And seas began to rout,
  Till Allan and his bonny new ship
    Gaed three times witherlands about.

12 'O,' sighing says the Young Allan,
    'I fear a deadly storm;
  For mony a heaving sinking sea
    Strikes sair on my ship's stern.

13 'Where will I get a little wee boy
    Will take my helm in hand
  Till I gang up to my tapmast
    And see for some dry land?'

14 'O waken, waken your drunken men,
    As they lye drunk wi wine;
  For when ye came thro Edinbro town
    Ye bought them sheen o ben.

15 'There was nae shoe made for my foot,
    Nor gluve made for my hand;
  But nevertheless, my dear master,
    I'll take your helm in hand
  Till ye gang to the tall tapmast
    And look for some dry land.

16 'And here am I, a little wee boy
    Will take your helm in han
  Till ye gang up to your tapmast,
    But, master, stay not lang.'

17 'I cannot see nae day, nae day,
    Nor nae meathe can I ken;
  But mony a bonny feather-bed
    Lyes floating on the faem,
  And the comely cog o Normanshore,
    She never will gang hame.'

18 The comely cog o Nicklingame
    Came sailing by his hand;
  Says, Gae down, gae down, ye gude skipper,
    Your ship sails on the sand.

19 'Come down, come down, my gude master,
    Ye see not what I see;
  For thro and thro our comely cog
    I see the green haw sea.'

20 'Take fifty ells o gude canvas
    And wrap the ship a' round;
  And pick her weell, and spare her not,
    And make her hale and sound.

21 'If ye will sail, my bonny ship,
    Till we come to dry land,
  For ilka iron nail in you,
    Of gowd there shall be ten.'

22 The ship she listend all the while,
    And, hearing of her hire,
  She flew as swift threw the saut sea
    As sparks do frae the fire.

23 The first an shore that they came till,
    They ca'd it Howdoloot;
  Wi drums beating and cannons shouting,
    They held our gude ship out.

24 The next an shore that they came till,
    They ca'd it Howdilee;
  Wi drums beating and fifes playing,
    They bare her to the sea.

25 The third an shore that they came till,
    They ca'd it Howdilin;
  Wi drums beating and pipes playing,
    They towd our gude ship in.

26 The sailors walkd upon the shore,
    Wi their auld baucheld sheen,
  And thanked God and their Lady,
    That brought them safe again.

27 'For we went out o Scarsburgh
Wi fifty ships and three;
But nane o them came back again
But Young Allan, ye see.'

28 'Come down, come down, my little wee boy,
Till I pay you your fee;
I hae but only ae daughter,
And wedded to her ye 'se be.'

D

Murison MS., p. 117; learned by Mrs Murison from her
mother, Old Deer, Aberdeenshire.

1 THERE was three lords sat drinkin wine
In bonnie Aberdeen, [O]

. . . .

. . . . . .

2 Some o them talked o their merchandise,
An some o their ladies fine, [O]
But Young Allan he talked o his bonnie ship,
That cost him mony a poun.

* * * * * * *

3 'Whar will I get a bonnie wee boy
That 'll tak my helm in han, O
Till I gang up to my high topmast
An look oot for some dry lan?

4 'He 'll get half o my gowd, an half o my gear,
An the third pairt o my lan,
An gin he row me safe on shore
He shall hae my daughter Ann.'

5 'O here am I, a bonny wee boy
That 'll tak your helm in han
Till ye gang up to your high topmast
An look oot for some dry lan.

6 'I 'll nae seek your gowd, nor I 'll nae seek
your gear,
Nor the third pairt o your lan,
But gin I row you safe to shore
I shall hae your daughter Ann.

7 'Come doon, come doon, Young Allan,' he
cries,
'Ye see nae what I see;
For through an through your bonnie ship-side
An I see the open sea.

8 'Ye 'll tak twenty-four o your feather-beds,
Ye 'll busk your bonnie ship roon,

An as much o the guid canvas-claith
As gar her gang hale an soun.

9 'An whar ye want an iron bolt
Ye 'll ca a siller pin,
An whar ye want an oaken bolt
Ye 'll beat the yellow gold in.'

10 He 's taen twenty-four o his feather-beds
An buskit 's bonnie ship roon,
An as much o the guid canvas-claith
As gar her gang hale an soun.

11 An whar he 's wantit an iron bolt
He 's ca'd a siller pin,
An whar he 's wantit an oaken bolt
He 's beat the yellow gold in.

12 The firstan shore that they cam till,
It was the shore o Linn;
They held their spears an beenits oot,
An they wouldna lat Allan in.

13 The neistan shore that they cam till
It was the shore o . . .;

. . . .

An they turned their ship aboot.

14 But the neistan shore that they cam till,
'T was bonnie Aberdeen;
The fifes an drums they a' did play,
To welcome Allan in.

15 'O where is he, the bonnie wee boy
That took my helm in han
Till I gied up to my high topmast
An lookd oot for some dry lan?

16 'He 's get half o my gowd, an half o my
gear,
An the third pairt o my lan,
An since he 's rowt me safe to shore
He sall hae my daughter Ann.'

17 'O here am I, the bonnie wee boy
    That took your helm in han
    Till ye gied up to your high topmast
    An lookd oot for some dry lan.

18 'I 'll nae seek half o your good, nor half o your
       gear,
    Nor the third pairt o your lan,
    But since I 've rowt you safe to shore
    I sall hae your daughter Ann.'

E

Kinloch MSS, V, 395; in the handwriting of John Hill Burton, when a youth.

1 THE king he sits in Dumfermline,
    Birlin at the wine,
    And callin for the best skipper
    That ever sailed the faem.

2 Then out it spak a bonny boy,
    Sat at the king's right knee;
    'Earl Patrick is the best skipper
    That ever sailed the sea.'

3 The king he wrote a braed letter,
    And sealed it wi his ring,
    And sent it to Earl Patrick,
    .   .   .   .   .   .

4 'Oh wha is this, or wha is that,
    Has tald the king o me?
    For I was niver a gude mariner,
    And niver sailed the sea.

*   *   *   *   *   *   *

5 'Ye 'll eat and drink, my merry young men,
    The red wine you amang,
    For blaw it wind, or blaw it sleet,
    Our ship maun sail the morn.

6 'Late yestreen I saw the new meen
    Wi the auld meen in hir arm,'
    And sichand said him Earl Patrick,
    'I fear a deadly storm.'

7 They sailed up, sae did they down,
    Thro mony a stormy stream,
    Till they saw the Dam o Micklengaem,
    When she sank amang the faem.

8 They sailed up, sae did they down,
    Thro many a stormy stream,
    Till they saw the Duke o Normandy,
    And she sank among the faem.

9 They sailed up, sae did they down,
    Thro many a stormy stream,
    Till they saw the Black Shater o Leve London,
    And her topmast gaed in nine.

10 'Where will I get a bonny boy
    That will tack my helm in hand
    Till I gang up to my topmast,
    And spy for some dry land?'

11 'Now here am I, a bonny boy
    Will tack yer helm in hand
    Till ye go up to your topmast
    But I fear ye 'll never see land.'

12 'Cum down, cum down, my gude master,
    Ye see not what I see,
    For through and through yer bonny ship
    I see the raging sea.'

13 'Ye 'll tak four-and-twenty fether-beds
    And lay my bonny ship roun,
    And as muckle o the fine canvas
    As make her haill and soun.

14 'And where she wants an iron nail
    O silver she 's hae three,
    And where she wants a timmer-pin
    We 'll rap the red goud in.'

*   *   *   *   *   *   *

15 The firsten shore that they cam till,
    They cad it shore the Linn;
    Wi heart and hand and good command,
    They towed their bonny ship in.

16 The nexten shore that they came till,
    They caad it shore the Lee;
    With heart and hand and good command,
    They towed the bonny ship tee.

17 There was twenty ships gaed to the sea,
    Twenty ships and ane,
    And there was na ane came back again
    But Earl Patrick alane.

A. 18². ill buckled *corruptly for the* auld baucheld
   of C 26 (baucheld = down at the heels).

B. 2². hind.

   3⁵. snakes o Leveland den; *and* snakes o Levelanden, C 4⁵. *I have not found* snake, *for*
   ship, *in late English, but the A. S.* snacc =
   Icelandic snekkja, *a fast ship, may well*
   have come down. For Leve London *see*
   E 9³.

   11⁴. *We should perhaps read* As make; *cf.*
   A 14⁴, D 8⁴.

C. 4⁵. black snakes o Levelanden.

D. *After* 2. "A long, long gap, that I have got

nobody to fill up. I learned it from my
mother, but she has quite forgotten it."

9¹. whar he.

13³. *Remark:* "Not let land here either."

17³. to yon, *or* you.

O *is added at the end of every second line.*

E. 6³. sich and.

   9³. shater. Cf. B 3⁵, C 4⁵, *where the texts*
   have snakes (*corrected here to* snake). *The*
   writer of E *had begun the word with some-*
   thing different from sh, *but with what I*
   cannot make out.

11⁴. feear. 14¹. when *or* wher.

246

REDESDALE AND WISE WILLIAM

A. 'Reedisdale and Wise William,' Buchan's Ballads
of the North of Scotland, II, 70; Motherwell's MS.,
p. 452; Motherwell's Minstrelsy, p. 298.

B. 'Roudesdales,' Harris MS., fol. 14 b.

C. Kinloch MSS, V, 423, two stanzas.

REDESDALE boasts to William that he can
win any woman with a blink of his eye. William has a sister who, he maintains, is not to
be had so easily. A wager is laid, William's
head against Redesdale's lands. William is
shut up to prevent his warning his sister, but
sends her a letter by a carrier-bird. Redesdale
rides to the maiden's bower, and, seeing her
at the window, tries to induce her to come
down by a series of offers of silk-gowns, jewels, etc. His offers proving bootless, he threat-

ens to fire the house, and does so. The maid
and her women don wet mantles and pass the
reek and flame unhurt. She sends word to
her brother, who claims Redesdale's lands.

A 1, 2, 5 are substantially a repetition of
No 245, A 1, 2¹·⁴, 6, etc. The sharp shower
in B 16–18, which puts out, and does not put
out, the fire, is an inept interpolation.

This ballad may be an offshoot from a
widely spread story which is tediously told
further on in 'Twa Knights.'

A

Buchan's Ballads of the North of Scotland, II, 70; written down from memory by Mr Nicol, Strichen, as learned
in his earlier years from old people.

1 WHEN Reedisdale and Wise William
   Were drinking at the wine,
There fell a roosing them amang,
   On an unruly time.

2 For some o them hae roosd their hawks,
   And other some their hounds,
   And other some their ladies fair,
   And their bowers whare they walkd in.

3 When out it spake him Reedisdale,
   And a rash word spake he;
   Says, There is not a lady fair,
   In bower wherever she be,
   But I could aye her favour win
   Wi ae blink o my ee.

4 Then out it spake him Wise William,
   And a rash word spake he;
   Says, I have a sister of my own,
   In bower where ever she be,
   And ye will not her favour win
   With three blinks of your ee.

5 'What will ye wager, Wise William?
   My lands I 'll wad with thee;'
   'I 'll wad my head against your land,
   Till I get more monie.'

6 Then Reedisdale took Wise William,
   Laid him in prison strang,
   That he might neither gang nor ride,
   Nor ae word to her send.

7 But he has written a braid letter,
   Between the night and day,
   And sent it to his own sister
   By dun feather and gray.

8 When she had read Wise William's letter,
   She smilëd and she leugh;
   Said, Very well, my dear brother,
   Of this I have eneuch.

9 She looked out at her west window
   To see what she could see,
   And there she spied him Reedisdale
   Come riding ower the lea.

10 Says, Come to me, my maidens all,
   Come hitherward to me;
   For here it comes him Reedisdale,
   Who comes a-courting me.

11 'Come down, come down, my lady fair,
   A sight of you give me;'
   'Go from my yetts now, Reedisdale,
   For me you will not see.'

12 'Come down, come down, my lady fair,
   A sight of you give me;
   And bonny are the gowns of silk
   That I will give to thee.'

13 'If you have bonny gowns of silk,
   O mine is bonny tee;
   Go from my yetts now, Reedisdale,
   For me you shall not see.'

14 'Come down, come down, my lady fair,
   A sight of you I 'll see;
   And bonny jewels, brooches and rings
   I will give unto thee.'

15 'If you have bonny brooches and rings,
   O mine are bonny tee;
   Go from my yetts now, Reedisdale,
   For me you shall not see.'

16 'Come down, come down, my lady fair,
   One sight of you I 'll see;
   And bonny are the ha's and bowers
   That I will give to thee.'

17 'If you have bonny ha's and bowers,
   O mine are bonny tee;
   Go from my yetts now, Reedisdale,
   For me you shall not see.'

18 'Come down, come down, my lady fair,
   A sight of you I 'll see;
   And bonny are my lands so broad
   That I will give to thee.'

19 'If you have bonny lands so broad,
   O mine are bonny tee;
   Go from my yetts now, Reedisdale,
   For me ye will not see.'

20 'Come down, come down, my lady fair,
   A sight of you I 'll see;
   And bonny are the bags of gold
   That I will give to thee.'

21 'If you have bonny bags of gold,
   I have bags of the same;
   Go from my yetts now, Reedisdale,
   For down I will not come.'

22 'Come down, come down, my lady fair,
   One sight of you I 'll see;

Or else I 'll set your house on fire,
    If better cannot be.'

23 Then he has set the house on fire,
    And all the rest it tuke;
He turned his wight horse head about,
    Said, Alas, they 'll ne'er get out!

24 'Look out, look out, my maidens fair,
    And see what I do see,
How Reedisdale has fired our house,
    And now rides oer the lea.

25 'Come hitherwards, my maidens fair,
    Come hither unto me;
For thro this reek, and thro this smeek,
    O thro it we must be!'

26 They took wet mantles them about,
    Their coffers by the band,
And thro the reek, and thro the flame,
    Alive they all have wan.

27 When they had got out thro the fire,
    And able all to stand,
She sent a maid to Wise William,
    To bruik Reedisdale's land.

28 'Your lands is mine now, Reedisdale,
    For I have won them free;'
'If there is a gude woman in the world,
    Your one sister is she.'

B

Harris MS., fol. 14 b; from Mrs Harris.

1 ROUDESDALES an Clerk William
    Sat birlin at the wine,
An a' the talk was them atween
    Was aboot the ladies fine, fine,
    Was aboot the ladies fine.

2 Says Roudesdales to Clerk William,
    I 'll wad my lands wi thee,
I 'll wad my lands against thy head,
    An that is what I 'll dee,

3 'That there 's no a leddy in a' the land,
    That 's fair, baith ee an bree,
That I winna wed withoot courtin,
    Wi ae blink o my ee.'

4 Says William, I 've an ae sister,
    She 's fair, baith ee an bree;
An you 'll no wed her withoot courtin,
    Wi ae blink o your ee.'

5 He has wrote a broad letter,
    Between the nicht an the day,
An sent it to his ae sister
    Wi the white feather an the gray.

6 The firsten line she luekit on,
    A licht lauchter gae she;

But eer she read it to the end
    The tear blindit her ee.

7 'Oh wae betide my ae brither,
    Wald wad his head for me,

  · · · · · ·

  · · · · · ·'

8 Roudesdales to her bour has gane,
    An rade it round aboot,
An there he saw that fair ladie,
    At a window lookin oot.

9 'Come doon, come doon, you fair ladie,
    Ae sicht o you to see;
For the rings are o the goud sae ried
    That I will gie to thee.'

10 'If yours are o the goud sae ried,
    Mine 's o the silver clear;
So get you gone, you Roudesdales,
    For you sall no be here.'

11 'Come doon, come doon, you lady fair,
    Ae sicht o you to see;
For the gouns are o the silk sae fine
    That I will gie to thee.'

12 'If yours are o the silk sae fine,
    Mine 's o the bonnie broun;

Sa get you gone, you Roudesdales,
   For I will no come doon.'

13 'Come doon, come doon, you ladie fair,
      Ae sicht o you to see ;
   For the steeds are o the milk sae white
      That I will gie to thee.'

14 'If yours are o the milk sae white,
      Mine 's o the bonnie broun ;
   Sae get you gone, you Roudesdales,
      For I will no come doon.'

15 'Come doon, come doon, you ladie fair,
      Ae sicht o you to see ;
   Or I will set your bour on fire
      Atween your nurse an thee.'

16 'You may set my bowr on fire,
      As I doubt na you will dee,

But there 'll come a sharp shour frae the
      wast
   Will slocken 't speedilie.'

17 He has set her bour on fire,
      An quickly it did flame ;
   But there cam a sharp shour frae the wast
      That put it oot again.

18 Oot amang the fire an smoke
      That bonnie lady cam,
   Wi as muckle goud aboon her bree
      As wald bocht an earldom.

19 'Oh wae betide you, ill woman,
      An ill, ill died may you dee !
   For ye hae won your brither's head,
      An I go landless free.'

C

Kinloch MSS, V, 423.

1 REDESDALE and Clerk William
   Sat drinking at the wine ;
They hae fawn a wagering them atween
   At a wanhappy time.

2 'What will ye wad,' says Redesdale,
      'O what will ye wad wi me
   That there 's na a lady in a' the land
      But I wad win wi ae blink o my ee ? '

A. *There are some very trivial variations from
   Buchan's text in Motherwell's copies ;
   mostly* is, *with a plural subject, Scottice,
   for* are. *Motherwell received the ballad
   from Buchan, and was much in the way
   of making small betterments.*
B. *Air*, 'Johnnie Brod.' 4⁴. o her.
   5². *Perhaps* necht.   6². *Perhaps* leiht.

247
LADY ELSPAT

'Lady Elspat.' **a.** Jamieson-Brown MS., p. 19. Printed in Jamieson's Popular Ballads, II, 191. **b.** "Scottish Songs," MS., fol. 30, Abbotsford Library, N. 3, in the handwriting of Walter Scott, about 1795.

THIS ballad was No 10 of the fifteen of Mrs Brown's which were obtained by William Tytler from Professor Thomas Gordon in 1783: Anderson to Percy, December 29, 1800, in Nichols's Illustrations, VII, 177, where the first stanza (of twelve) is cited. These transcripts were accompanied with the airs. In b, which is now ascertained to be in the handwriting of Walter Scott,* there is a mawkish stanza after 4, and another after 9, which do not occur in a, and many verbal variations. These two stanzas are not likely to have been inserted by Scott, for, so far as we know, the ballad has been preserved only by Mrs Brown. As for the other variations, we are not in a condition to say which are Mrs Brown's, which Scott's.

An appointment for an elopement made by Lady Elspat with Sweet William is revealed to her mother by an eavesdropping page. William is bound with his own bow-string and brought before the Lord Justice. The mother accuses him of stealing her jewels; Lady Elspat denies this, and says that his only crime is too small an estate. The judge sees no fault in the young man (whom he discovers to be his sister's son!), hands him over to Lady Elspat, and promises the pair as much land as a valuable horse of his can ride about in a summer's day.

Truly not impressive in story or style, and very fit to have been forgotten by Mrs Brown.

Translated from Jamieson by Grundtvig, Engelske og skotske Folkeviser, p. 196, No 30; by Rosa Warrens, Schottische Volkslieder, p. 118, No 26; by Loève-Veimars, p. 337.

---

1 'How brent's your brow, my Lady Elspat!
   How golden yellow is your hair!
Of all the maids of fair Scotland,
   There's nane like Lady Elspat fair.'

2 'Perform your vows, Sweet William,' she says,
   'The vows which ye ha made to me,
An at the back o my mother's castle
   This night I'll surely meet wi thee.'

3 But wae be to her brother's page,
   Who heard the words this twa did say!
He's told them to her lady mother,
   Who wrought Sweet William mieckle wae.

4 For she has taen him Sweet William,
   An she's gard bind him wi his bow-string
Till the red bluide o his fair body
   Frae ilka nail o his hand did spring.

---

* Mr Macmath informs me that all the traditional pieces in "Scottish Songs" are in the hand of Scott, of about 1795. At folio 11 (the top part of which has been torn away), Scott says: "These ballads are all in the Northern dialect, but I recollect several of them as recited in the south of Scotland divested of their Norlandisms, and also varying considerably in other respects. In a few instances where my memory served me, I have adopted either additional verses or better readings than those in Mr Tytler's collection. Such variations can excite no reasonable surprise in any species of composition which owes preservation to oral tradition only."

5   O it fell once upon a time
      That the Lord Justice came to town;
    Out has she taen him Sweet William,
      Brought him before Lord Justice boun.

6   'An what is the crime, now, madame,' he says,
      'Has been committed by this young man?'
    'O he has broken my bonny castel,
      That was well biggit wi lime an stane.

7   'An he has broken my bonny coffers,
      That was well banded wi aiken ban,
    An he has stoln my rich jewels;
      I wot he has them every one.'

8   Then out it spake her Lady Elspat,
      As she sat by Lord Justice knee;
    'Now ye hae taul your tale, mother,
      I pray, Lord Justice, you'l now hear me.

9   'He has na broken her bonny castel,
      That was well biggit wi lime an stane,

    Nor has he stoln her rich jewels,
      For I wot she has them every one.

10 'But tho he was my first true love,
      An tho I had sworn to be his bride,
    Cause he had not a great estate,
      She would this way our loves divide.'

11 An out it spake the Lord Justice,
      I wot the tear was in his ee;
    'I see nae fault in this young man,
      Sae loose his bans, an set him free.

12 'Take back your love, now, Lady Elspat,
      An my best blessing you baith upon!
    For gin he be your first true love,
      He is my eldest sister's son.

13 'There is a steed in my stable
      Cost me baith gold and white money;
    Ye's get as mieckle o my free lan
      As he'll ride about in a summer's day.'

———◆———

a. 3¹. to our.   5³. has he.
b. 1³. maids in.   2¹. said.
   3¹,². And this beheard her mother's foot-page,
   Who listed the words thae twa.
   3³. He tauld them ower to.
   4². Gart bind: his ain.   4⁴. hands.
   After 4:

    They threw him into dungeon-keep;
      Full little he reckd the pain;
    But sair he mournd each springing hope
      That was blasted a' sae sune.

5¹. fell out.   5². That *wanting.*
5³. And they hae.
5⁴. him to thole a deadly doom.
6³,⁴. For gin I judge frae his gentle look I
   think he is where he should na stand.

7. 'Yet has he broken my highest towr,
     Was bigged strong wi stane and lime,
   And stolen forth my rich jewels
     Frae my coffer bound wi aiken beam.'

8¹. out and spak sweet.
8². sat near hir mother's.
8³. hae ye tauld.
8⁴. Justice, hear you.
9¹,². has not broken her highest towr, Was
   bigged strong wi stane and lime.
9⁴. ane.   *After* 9:

   'Yet has he stolen a dearer pledge,
     Not frae my mother, but frae me;
   For he has stolen a virgin's heart
     Should have waited for ane o high degree.'

10¹. first fair.
11¹. Then out and spake the good.
11³. nae harm.
11⁴. his hands.
12¹. love, sweet Lady.
12³. first fair.
13. *Wanting, and probably also in W. Tytler's copy.*

248

THE GREY COCK, OR, SAW YOU MY FATHER?

a. 'The Grey Cock,' Herd's Ancient and Modern Scots Songs, 1769, p. 324; Herd's MSS, I, 4; Herd's Ancient and Modern Scottish Songs, 1776, II, 208. b.

'Saw you my father?' Chappell's Popular Music, p. 731.

———

STANZAS 1, 4, 6, 7, are printed in Herd, 1769; the three others are among the "Additions to songs in the former volume" [of 1769], at the beginning of the first volume of the MS.; the whole is given in Herd, 1776.

Repeated from Herd, 1776 (with a change or two) in Pinkerton's Select Scotish Ballads II, 155, 1783, and in Johnson's Museum, p. 77, No 76, 1787, 'O saw ye my father?' Stenhouse had not found the verses in any collection prior to that of Herd, but asserts that the song had been "a great favorite in Scotland for a long time past" (1820, Museum, ed. 1853, IV, 81).

"This song," says Chappell, "is printed on broadsides, with the tune, and in Vocal Music, or the Songster's Companion, II, 36, second edition, 1772. This collection was printed by Robert Horsfield, in Ludgate Street, and probably the words and music will also be found in the first edition, which I have not seen." The words, he adds, are in several "Songsters."

Three stanzas from recitation, wrongly attached to 'The Broomfield Hill,' No 43, E, have been given at p. 399 of the first volume of this collection. Much of the ballad has been adopted into 'Willie's Fatal Visit,' Buchan's Ballads of the North of Scotland, II, 259, the two concluding stanzas with little change. These two stanzas are given by a correspondent * of Notes and Queries, First Series, XII, 227, as heard by him in the nursery about 1787. They have been made the kernel

of a song by Allan Cunningham, impudently put forward as "the precious relique of the original," Cromek, Remains of Nithsdale and Galloway Song, 1810, p. 72.

The injunction to the cock is found in 'The Swain's Resolve,' Lyle's Ancient Ballads and Songs, 1827, p. 142:

She cries to the cock, saying, Thou must not crow
  Until that the day be worn,
And thy wings shall be made of the silvery gray,
  And thy voice of the silver horn.

It is also cited in Graves's Irish Songs and Ballads, London, 1882, p. 249, No 50, as occurring "in a ballad descriptive of the visit of a lover's ghost to his betrothed," in which the woman, to protract the interview, says:

'O my pretty cock, O my handsome cock,
  I pray you do not crow before day,
And your comb shall be made of the very beaten
    gold,
  And your wings of the silver so gray.'

The cock is remiss or unfaithful, again, in a little ballad picked up by Burns in Nithsdale, 'A Waukrife Minnie,' Cromek, Select Scotish Songs, 1810, II, 116 (of which another version is furnished by Lyle, p. 155, 'The Wakerife Mammy'):

O weary fa the waukrife cock,
  And the foumart lay his crawin!
He waukend the auld wife frae her sleep
  A wee blink or the dawin.

---

* 'C,' safely to be identified with John Wilson Croker, says Colonel W. F. Prideaux, who, in Notes and Queries, VI, xii, 223, has brought together most of the matter pertaining

to this ballad. If Colonel Prideaux's supposition is well founded, 'The Grey Cock' was known in Ireland in the last century.

The first stanza of 'The Grey Cock' seems to have been suggested by 'Sweet William's Ghost' (of which the Irish ballad noted by Graves may have been a variety), as again is the case in Buchan's 'James Herries.' The fantastic reward promised the cock in stanza 6 is an imitation, or a corruption, of the bribe to the parrot in No 4, D 23, E 15, F 10, or in No 68, A 10, B 13, C 14, etc.

Of the same general description is 'Le Chant de l'Alouette,' Victor Smith, Chansons de Velay, etc., Romania, VII, 56 (see further note 6 of Smith); 'Le Rendez-vous,' Mélusine, I, 285 ff., Rolland, Recueil, etc., IV, 43,

No 196. Again, 'La Rondinella,' Kopisch, Agrumi, p. 80, 1837; 'La Visita,' Wolf, Volkslieder aus Venetien, p. 8; 'La Rondine importuna,' Ferraro, C. p. monferrini, p. 75, No 54; 'Il Furto amoroso' Gianandrea, C. p. marchigiani, p. 274; 'La Rondinella,' Archivio, VII, 401, No 6. The treacherous or troublesome bird is in French the lark, in one case the cock; in Italian the swallow.

This piece is a variety of the *aube* (concerning which species see Jeanroy, Les Origines de la Poésie lyrique en France, the third chapter), but is none the less quite modern.

———————

1 'O SAW ye my father? or saw ye my mother?
   Or saw ye my true-love John?'
'I saw not your father, I saw not your mother,
   But I saw your true-love John.

2 'It's now ten at night, and the stars gie nae light,
   And the bells they ring ding, dang;
He's met wi some delay that causeth him to stay,
   But he will be here ere lang.'

3 The surly auld carl did naething but snarl,
   And Johny's face it grew red;
Yet, tho he often sighd, he neer a word replied
   Till all were asleep in bed.

4 Up Johny rose, and to the door he goes,
   And gently tirlèd the pin;

The lassie taking tent unto the door she went,
   And she opend and let him in.

5 'And are ye come at last? and do I hold ye fast?
   And is my Johny true?'
'I hae nae time to tell, but sae lang's I like myself
   Sae lang will I love you.'

6 'Flee, flee up, my bonny grey cock,
   And craw whan it is day;
Your neck shall be like the bonny beaten gold,
   And your wings of the silver grey.'

7 The cock prov'd false, and untrue he was,
   For he crew an hour oer soon;
The lassie thought it day when she sent her love away,
   And it was but a blink of the moon

———————

a. 4¹. *MS.* Then up. 5⁴. *Ed.* 1776, sall I.
b. 1¹. Saw you my father? Saw you my mother.
   1². Saw you.
   1³,⁴. He told his only dear that he soon would be here, But he to another is gone.
   2¹,² = 1³,⁴.
   2³. has met with . . . which has caused.
   2⁴. here anon. 3. *Wanting.*
   4¹. Then John he up arose.
   4². And he twirld, he twirld at.

   4³. lassie took the hint and to the.
   4⁴. she let her true love in. 5. *Wanting.*
   6¹. Fly up, fly up.
   6³. Your breast shall be of the beaming gold.
   7¹. cock he. 7². crowd an hour too soon.
   7³. day, so she. 7⁴. it prov'd but the.
   Notes and Queries, I, xii, 227: 6². But crow not until it be day.
   6³. And your breast shall be made of the burnishd gold.

249
AULD MATRONS

'Auld Matrons,' Buchan's Ballads of the North of Scotland, II, 238 ; Motherwell's MS., p. 585, with the title
'Love Annie.'

WILLIE tirls at Annie's bower-door and is admitted. After the exchange of familiar formulas, Willie expresses apprehension of "Matrons," an old woman who is sitting by the kitchen-fire. Annie says there is no occasion to mind the old woman ; she has not walked for seven years. But while the lovers are occupied with endearments the old woman makes speed to the sheriff, and informs him that Willie is with his daughter. The sheriff, guided by Matrons, goes to the bower, with men in mail. Annie hears the bridles ring, and wakens Willie. There is shooting of arrows and fire is set to the bower (cf. st. 17 and st. 33 of No 116). Willie maintains himself with spirit, but is so hard pressed that he is fain to blow his horn for his brother John, who is lying in Ringlewood. John wounds fifty and fifteen with his first shot, and with the next strikes out the sheriff's eyes. The sheriff or-

ders a retreat, and threatens, very illogically, to burn the old woman.

This piece was made by some one who had acquaintance with the first fit of 'Adam Bell.' The anonymous 'old wife' becomes 'auld Matrons;' Inglewood, Ringlewood. The conclusion is in imitation of the rescues in Robin Hood ballads. Stanzas 2–5 are hacknied commonplaces.

It is not considerate of Willie to take a foot-groom with him when he goes to pass a night at the bower of an unprovided seamstress, though the seamstress be a gentlewoman and the daughter of a sheriff. William of Cloudesly did not so. That the sheriff's unmarried daughter should be living apart from her father is unusual, but a separate establishment was probably a necessity in Kelso for a gentlewoman who had 'her living by the seam.'

1 My love she is a gentlewoman,
    Has her living by the seam ;
 I kenna how she is provided
    This night for me and my foot-groom.

2 He is gane to Annie's bower-door,
    And gently tirled at the pin :
 'Ye sleep, ye wake, my love Annie,
    Ye 'll rise and lat your true-love in.'

3 Wi her white fingers lang and sma
    She gently lifted up the pin ;
 Wi her arms lang and bent
    She kindly caught sweet Willie in.

4 'O will ye go to cards or dice ?
    Or will ye go to play ?
 Or will ye go to a well made bed,
    And sleep a while till day ?'

5 'I winna gang to cards nor dice,
    Nor yet will I to play ;
 But I will gang to a well made bed,
    And sleep a while till day.

6 'My love Annie, my dear Annie,
    I would be at your desire ;
 But wae mat fa the auld Matrons,
    As she sits by the kitchen fire !'

7 ' Keep up your heart, Willie,' she said,
   ' Keep up your heart, dinna fear ;
It 's seven years, and some guid mair,
   Sin her foot did file the flear.'

8 They hadna kissd nor love clapped,
   As lovers when they meet,
Till up it raise the auld Matrons,
   Sae well 's she spread her feet.

9 O wae mat fa the auld Matrons,
   Sae clever 's she took the gate !
And she 's gaen ower yon lang, lang hill,
   Knockd at the sheriff's yate.

10 ' Ye sleep, ye wake, my lord ? ' she said ;
   ' Are ye not your bower within ?
There 's a knight in bed wi your daughter,
   I fear she 's gotten wrang.'

11 ' Ye 'll do ye down thro Kelso town,
   Waken my wall-wight men ;
And gin ye hae your wark well dune
   I 'll be there at command.'

12 She 's done her down thro Kelso town,
   Wakend his wall-wight men ;
But gin she had her wark well done
   He was there at command.

13 He had his horse wi corn fodderd,
   His men armd in mail ;
He gae the Matrons half a merk
   To show them ower the hill.

14 Willie sleepd, but Annie waked
   Till she heard their bridles ring ;

Then tapped on her love's shoulder,
   And said, Ye 've sleepit lang.

15 ' O save me, save me, my blessd lady,
   Till I 've on my shooting-gear ;
I dinna fear the king himsell,
   Tho he an 's men were here.'

16 Then they shot in, and Willie out,
   The arrows graz'd his brow ;
The maid she wept and tore her hair,
   Says, This can never do.

17 Then they shot in, and he shot out,
   The bow brunt Willie's hand ;
But aye he kissd her ruby lips,
   Said, My dear, thinkna lang.

18 He set his horn to his mouth,
   And has blawn loud and shrill,
And he 's calld on his brother John,
   In Ringlewood he lay still.

19 The first an shot that Lord John shot,
   He wound fifty and fifteen ;
The next an shot that Lord John shot,
   He ca'd out the sheriff's een.

20 ' O some o you lend me an arm,
   Some o you lend me twa ;
And they that came for strife this day,
   Take horse, ride fast awa.

21 ' But wae mat fa yon, auld Matrons,
   An ill death mat ye die !
I 'll burn you on yon high hill-head,
   Blaw your ashes in the sea.'

———•———

2^8. Ye sleep ye, wake ye: *cf.* 10^1.
21^2. All ill.

21^8. And burn. *Motherwell*, I 'll.

250

HENRY MARTYN

A. a, b. 'Henry Martyn;' taken down from recitation, by the Rev. S. Baring-Gould.

B. a. A broadside, Catnach, Seven Dials. **b.** 'Henry Martin,' Kidson, Traditional Tunes, p. 31. **c.** The same, p. 30.

C. 'Robin Hood,' Motherwell's MS., p. 660.

D. ['Andrew Bodee'], from New Hampshire, U. S. A., communicated by Mr George M. Richardson; two stanzas.

A COPY edited from A, B a, with the addition of one stanza for a "snapper," is printed in Baring-Gould and Sheppard's Songs and Ballads of the West, No 53. Four traditional versions were obtained by Mr Baring-Gould.

Three brothers in Scotland cast lots to determine which of them shall rob on the sea to maintain them. The lot falls on the youngest, Henry Martyn, A, B; Robin Hood, C; Andrew Bodee, D. The pirate meets and stops an English ship the very first day (third, A b; fifth, B, C). There is a brisk fight, and the English ship is sunk by shot, A, B. She is plundered and then scuttled, C. In A a, Henry Martyn gets a deep wound and falls by the mast.

The ballad must have sprung from the ashes of 'Andrew Barton,' of which name Henry Martyn would be no extraordinary corruption. Only one copy, A a, preserves the trait of Barton's death, an incident not quite in keeping with the rest of the story of the new ballad.

Robin Hood, C, is always at the service of any ballad-monger who wants a name for his hero. But it will be remembered that he is credited with taking a French ship in 'The Noble Fisherman,' No 148, and that is enough to explain his appearance here. 'Andrew Bodee' may just conceivably be a corruption of Andrew Wood, who displaces Patrick Spens in two versions of No 58 (A b, D). Motherwell knew of a copy in which the hero was called Roberton: MS., p. 660.

A

Taken down by the Rev. S. Baring-Gould. **a.** From Matthew Baker, an old cripple, Lew Down, Devon. **b.** From Roger Luxton, an old man at Halwell, North Devon.

1 In merry Scotland, in merry Scotland
   There lived brothers three;
   They all did cast lots which of them should go
   A robbing upon the salt sea,

2 The lot it fell on Henry Martyn,
   The youngest of the three;
   That he should go rob on the salt, salt sea,
   To maintain his brothers and he.

3 He had not a sailed a long winter's night,
   Nor yet a short winter's day,
   Before that he met with a lofty old ship,
   Come sailing along that way.

4 O when she came by Henry Martyn,
   'I prithee now, let us go!'
   'O no! God wot, that, that will I not,
   O that will I never do.

5 'Stand off! stand off!' said Henry Martyn,
   'For you shall not pass by me;
   For I am a robber all on the salt seas,
   To maintain us brothers three.

6 'How far, how far,' cries Henry Martyn,
   'How far do you make it?' said he;
'For I am a robber all on the salt seas,
   To maintain us brothers three.'

7 For three long hours they merrily fought,
   For hours they fought full three;
At last a deep wound got Henry Martyn,
   And down by the mast fell he.

8 'T was broadside to a broadside then,
   And a rain and hail of blows,

But the salt sea ran in, ran in, ran in,
   To the bottom then she goes.

9 Bad news, bad news for old England,
   Bad news has come to the town,
For a rich merchant's vessel is cast away,
   And all her brave seamen drown.

10 Bad news, bad news through London street,
   Bad news has come to the king,
For all the brave lives of the mariners lost,
   That are sunk in the watery main.

B

a. A broadside, Catnach, Seven Dials. b. Kidson, Traditional Tunes, p. 31, 1891; from fishermen at Flamborough, Yorkshire. c. Kidson, etc., p. 30; "sung by a very old woman . . . about ninety years ago."

1 THERE was three brothers in merry Scotland,
   In merry Scotland there were three,
And each of these brothers they did cast lots,
   To see which should rob the salt sea.

2 Then this lot did fall on young Henry Martyn,
   The youngest of these brothers three,
So now he's turnd robber all on the salt seas,
   To maintain his two brothers and he.

3 He had not saild one long winter's night,
   One cold winter's night before day,
Before he espied a rich merchant-ship,
   Come bearing straight down that way.

4 'Who are you? Who are you?' said Henry
   Martyn,
   'Or how durst thou come so nigh?'

'I'm a rich merchant-ship for old England
   bound,
   If you please, will you let me pass by.'

5 'O no! O no!' cried Henry Martyn,
   'O no! that never can be,
Since I have turnd robber all on the salt seas,
   To maintain my two brothers and me.

6 'Now lower your topsails, you alderman bold,
   Come lower them under my lee;'
Saying, 'I am resolved to pirate you here,
   To maintain my two brothers and me.'

7 Then broadside to broadside to battle they
   went
   For two or three hours or more;
At last Henry Martyn gave her a death-wound,
   And down to the bottom went she.

8 Bad news, bad news to England has come,
   Bad news I will tell to you all,
'T was a rich merchant-ship to England was
   bound,
   And most of her merry men drownd.

C

Motherwell's MS., p. 660; from the recitation of Alexander Macdonald, coal-heaver, Barkip, parish of Dalry, Ayr; a song of his mother's, a native of Ireland.

1 THERE were three brothers in bonnie Scotland,
   In bonnie Scotland lived they,

And they cuist kevels themsells amang,
   Wha sould gae rob upon the salt sea.

2 The lot it fell upon bold Robin Hood,
   The youngest brither of the hale three:
'O, I sall gae rob upon the salt sea,
   And it's all to mauntain my two brothers
   and me.'

3 They hadna sailed a lang winter night,
   A lang winter night scarselie,
Till they were aware of a tall, tall ship,
   Coming sailin down under the lee.

4 'O where are you bound for, my bonnie ship?'
   Bold Robin Hood he did cry;
'O I'm a bold merchantman, for London
   bound,
   And I pray you, good sir, let us by.'

5 'O no! O no!' said bold Robin Hood,
   'O no such thing may be;

For I will gae in and plunder your ship,
   And your fair bodies I'll drown in the sea.'

6 O he has gone in and plundered their ship,
   And holes in her bottom bored three;
The water came in so thick and so fast
   That down, down to the bottom gade she.

7 Bad news, bad news to old England is gone,
   Bad news to our king, old Henrie,
That his merchant-goods were taken on board,
   And thirty-five seamen drownd in the sea.

———————

D

Communicated by Mr George M. Richardson, as learned
by a lady in northern New Hampshire more than fifty years
ago from an aged aunt.

1 THREE loving brothers in Scotland dwelt,
   Three loving brothers were they,
And they cast lots to see which of the three

Should go robbing all oer the salt sea, salt
   sea,
   Should go robbing all oer the salt sea.

2 The lot it fell to Andrew Bodee,
   The youngest of the three,
That he should leave the other two,
   And go robbing all oer the salt sea.

———————

A. b. 3¹. a sailed three winter's nights.
   3². When a little before the day.
   3³. He spied the king his gay gallant ship.
   4. *Wanting*.

   5. 'Stand off! Stand off!' the captain he
      cried,
      'The life-guards they are aboard;
   My cannons are loaden with powder and
      shot,
      And every man hath a sword.'

   7. They merrily fought for three long hours,
      They fought for hours full three,
   And many a blow dealt many a wound,
      As they fought on the salt, salt sea.

   8. 'T was a broadside to a broadside then,
      And at it the which should win;
   A shot in the gallant ship bored a hole,
      And then did the water rush in.

   9, *Wanting*.   10³. of the life-guards.
   10⁴. O the tidings be sad that I bring.

B. b.

1 In Scotland there lived three brothers of
   late,
   In Scotland there lived brothers three;
Now the youngest cast lots with the other
   two,
   Which should go rob on the salt sea.

2 The lot it did fall to bold Henry Martin,
   The youngest of all the three,
And he had to turn robber all on the salt
   seas,
   To maintain his two brothers and he.

3 He had not been sailing past a long winter's
   night,
   Past a long winter's night before day,
Before he espied a lofty fine ship
   Come sailing all on the salt sea.

4 'O where are you bound for?' cried Henry
   Martin,
   'O where are you bound for?' cried he;

' I 'm a rich-loaded ship bound for fair Eng-
    land,
    I pray you to let me pass free.'

5 ' O no ! O no ! ' cried Henry Martin,
    ' O no ! that can never be,
    Since I have turned robber all on the salt
        sea,
    To maintain my two brothers and me.

6 ' Heave down your main tack, likewise your
    main tie,
    And lig yourself under my lee ;
    For your rich glowing gold I will take it
        away,
    And your fair bodies drown in the salt
        sea.'

7 Then broadside to broadside they merrily
    fought,
    For fully two hours or three,
    When by chance Henry Martin gave her a
        broadside,
    And right down to the bottom went she.

8 Bad news, bad news unto old England,
    Bad news I tell unto thee ;
    For your rich glowing gold is all wasted
        away,
    And your mariners are drownd in the
        salt sea.

c. 1 There lived three brothers in merry Scot-
    land,
    In merry Scotland lived brothers three,
    And they did cast lots which should rob on
        the sea,
    To maintain his two brothers and he.

2 And the lot it did light on Henry Martin,
    The youngest of all the brothers three,
    And he went a roaming on the salt sea,
    To maintain his two brothers and he.

3 And when they had sailëd five days and
    more
    On a rich merchant-ship coming down they
        then bore,
    As he went a roaming on the salt sea,
    To maintain his two brothers and he.

4 The rich merchant-ship got wounded by he,
    And right down to the bottom of the salt sea
        went she,
    As he went a roaming on the salt sea,
    To maintain his two brothers and he.

B. c. 1^2. three brothers.
C. 1^4. sould *may possibly be* wuld.
    2^3, 4^1, 6^1. Oh.

251

LANG JOHNNY MORE

' Lang Johnny Moir,' Buchan's Ballads of the North of Scotland, I, 248.

—◆—

' LANG JOHNNY MORE,' Christie's Traditional Ballad Airs, I, 44, is epitomized from
Buchan, " with a few alterations from the way
the editor has heard it sung." The variations
are absolutely of no account, as in other cases
in which Christie has used this phrase.

Johnny More, a youth fourteen feet tall
and three yards round the waist, goes to London to bear the king's banner. He falls in
love with the king's daughter, and she with
him, and the king locks the lady up in her
chamber and swears that he will hang the
Scot. Johnny laughs at the hanging ; but
the English give him laudanum, and when he
wakes he finds his jaws and hands in iron
bands and his feet in fetters. He sends a boy

with a letter asking his uncle to come to his aid, and to bring with him Jock o Noth. These champions, 'twa grizly ghosts to see,' have three feet between their brows and three yards between their shoulders. Coming to London they find the gates locked, because, as they learn from a keeper, a Scot is to be hanged that morn. The keeper declining to open the gates, Jock o Noth drives in three yards of the wall with his foot. Johnny More is standing with the rope round his neck, ready to be turned off. Though the portentous pair have a giant's strength, they are quite too superior to use it like a giant; they tell Johnny that there is no help for him if he has been guilty of a heinous crime. Learning that his only crime is loving a gay lady, they require that his sword shall be given back to him, then go before the king and demand the lady; they have come to her wedding. Take her, says the king. I never thought to see such men. Jock of Noth could have brought a man thrice three times bigger, if he had supposed that his own size would cause such astonishment. Any way, says the craven king, the boy that took the message shall be hanged. In that case, replies Jock, we shall attend the burial and see that you get your reward. The king yields everything. Johnny More calls for a priest to join him and his love; the king for a clerk to seal the tocher. Johnny is rich, and spurns tocher. Auld Johnny More, Young Johnny More, Jock o Noth and the boy go off with the lady.

This ballad has been referred to under No 99, II, 378, as perhaps an imitation, and in fact almost a parody, of 'Johnie Scot.' In No 99

John is the little Scot; here he is the muckle Scot, stanza 6 (Gaelic mor = big), and his helpmates, as well as he, are of gigantic size. Excepting in this and one other particular, the stories are materially the same. In both Johnie goes to England to bear the king's banner; a love-affair ensues between him and the king's daughter; the king puts his daughter into confinement, and threatens to hang Johnie, but in the end is constrained to give him his daughter; Johnie calls for a priest to marry him and the princess, the king calls for a clerk to arrange the tocher; Johnie refuses tocher, and goes off with his love or bride.

In No 99 Johnie, who has escaped, comes to the rescue of the princess with a redoubtable force; in this ballad Johnie is made prisoner, and sends for his uncle and another giant to come to his help. Their monstrous dimensions make them, for ballad-purposes, fairly equivalent to the five hundred men who accompany Johnie in No 99.

Some versions of No 99, as already remarked, have borrowed features from this ballad. Auld Johnie and Jock o Noth are presented here, stanza 21, as twa grizly ghosts to see, and their brows are three feet apart, their shoulders three yards; and so with the champion in A, H, L, of No 99.

Quite curiously, the hero of the Breton ballad which resembles 'Johnie Scot' is described as a giant (we must suppose on traditionary authority) in the title of two copies.

Auchindoir and Rhynie (parishes) are in the west of Aberdeenshire, north of the Don. Noth is a considerable hill in the latter.

---

1 THERE lives a man in Rynie's land,
　Anither in Auchindore,
The bravest lad amo them a'
　Was lang Johnny Moir.

2 Young Johnny was an airy blade,
　Fu sturdy, stout, and strang;
The sword that hang by Johnny's side
　Was just full ten feet lang.

3 Young Johnny was a clever youth,
　Fu sturdy, stout, and wight,
Just full three yards around the waist,
　And fourteen feet in hight.

4 But if a' be true they tell me now,
　And a' be true I hear,
Young Johnny 's on to Lundan gane,
　The king's banner to bear.

5 He hadna been in fair Lundan
   But twalmonths twa or three
Till the fairest lady in a' Lundan
   Fell in love wi young Johnny.

6 This news did sound thro Lundan town,
   Till it came to the king
That the muckle Scot had fa'in in love
   Wi his daughter, Lady Jean.

7 Whan the king got word o that,
   A solemn oath sware he,
This weighty Scot sall strait a rope,
   And hanged he shall be.

8 When Johnny heard the sentence past,
   A light laugh then gae he:
'While I hae strength to wield my blade,
   Ye darena a' hang me.'

9 The English dogs were cunning rogues;
   About him they did creep,
And gae him draps o lodomy
   That laid him fast asleep.

10 Whan Johnny wakend frae his sleep
   A sorry heart had he;
His jaws and hands in iron bands,
   His feet in fetters three.

11 'O whar will I get a little wee boy
   Will work for meat and fee,
That will rin on to my uncle,
   At the foot of Benachie?'

12 'Here am I, a little wee boy
   Will work for meat and fee,
That will rin on to your uncle,
   At the foot of Benachie.'

13 'Whan ye come whar grass grows green,
   Slack your shoes and rin;
And whan ye come whar water 's strong,
   Ye 'll bend your bow and swim.

14 'And whan ye come to Benachie
   Ye 'll neither chap nor ca;
Sae well 's ye 'll ken auld Johnny there,
   Three feet abeen them a'.

15 'Ye 'll gie to him this braid letter,
   Seald wi my faith and troth,
And ye 'll bid him bring alang wi him
   The body Jock o Noth.'

16 Whan he came whar grass grew green,
   He slackt his shoes and ran;
And whan he came whar water 's strong
   He bent his bow and swam.

17 And whan he came to Benachie
   Did neither chap nor ca;
Sae well 's he kent auld Johnny there,
   Three feet abeen them a'.

18 'What news, what news, my little wee boy?
   Ye never were here before;'
'Nae news, nae news, but a letter from
   Your nephew, Johnny Moir.

19 'Ye 'll take here this braid letter,
   Seald wi his faith and troth,
And ye 're bidden bring alang wi you
   The body Jock o Noth.'

20 Benachie lyes very low,
   The tap o Noth lyes high;
For a' the distance that 's between,
   He heard auld Johnny cry.

21 Whan on the plain these champions met,
   Twa grizly ghosts to see,
There were three feet between their brows,
   And shoulders were yards three.

22 These men they ran ower hills and dales,
   And ower mountains high,
Till they came on to Lundan town,
   At the dawn o the third day.

23 And whan they came to Lundan town
   The yetts were lockit wi bands,
And wha were there but a trumpeter,
   Wi trumpet in his hands?

24 'What is the matter, ye keepers all?
   Or what 's the matter within
That the drums do beat and bells do ring,
   And make sic dolefu din?'

25 'There 's naething the matter,' the keeper said,
   'There 's naething the matter to thee,
But a weighty Scot to strait the rope,
   And the morn he maun die.'

26 'O open the yetts, ye proud keepers,
   Ye 'll open without delay;'
The trembling keeper, smiling, said,
   'O I hae not the key.'

27 'Ye 'll open the yetts, ye proud keepers,
  Ye 'll open without delay,
Or here is a body at my back
  Frae Scotland has brought the key.'

28 'Ye 'll open the yetts,' says Jock o Noth,
  'Ye 'll open them at my call;'
Then wi his foot he has drove in
  Three yards braid o the wall.

29 As they gaed in by Drury Lane,
  And down by the town's hall,
And there they saw young Johnny Moir
  Stand on their English wall.

30 'Ye 're welcome here, my uncle dear,
  Ye 're welcome unto me;
Ye 'll loose the knot, and slack the rope,
  And set me frae the tree.'

31 'Is it for murder, or for theft?
  Or is it for robberie?
If it is for ony heinous crime,
  There 's nae remeid for thee.'

32 'It 's nae for murder, nor for theft,
  Nor yet for robberie;
A' is for the loving a gay lady
  They 're gaun to gar me die.'

33 'O whar 's thy sword,' says Jock o Noth,
  'Ye brought frae Scotland wi thee?
I never saw a Scotsman yet
  But coud wield a sword or tree.'

34 'A pox upo their lodomy,
  On me had sic a sway
Four o their men, the bravest four,
  They bore my blade away.'

35 'Bring back his blade,' says Jock o Noth,
  'And freely to him it gie,
Or I hae sworn a black Scot's oath
  I 'll gar five million die.'

36 'Now whar 's the lady?' says Jock o Noth,
  'Sae fain I woud her see;'
'She 's lockd up in her ain chamber,
  The king he keeps the key.'

37 So they hae gane before the king,
  With courage bauld and free;

Their armour bright cast sic a light
  That almost dim'd his ee.

38 'O whar 's the lady?' says Jock o Noth,
  'Sae fain as I woud her see;
For we are come to her wedding,
  Frae the foot o Benachie.'

39 'O take the lady,' said the king,
  'Ye welcome are for me;
I never thought to see sic men,
  Frae the foot o Benachie.'

40 'If I had kend,' said Jock o Noth,
  'Ye 'd wonderd sae muckle at me,
I woud hae brought ane larger far
  By sizes three times three.'

41 'Likewise if I had thought I 'd been
  Sic a great fright to thee,
I 'd brought Sir John o Erskine Park;
  He 's thretty feet and three.'

42 'Wae to the little boy,' said the king,
  'Brought tidings unto thee!
Let all England say what they will,
  High hangèd shall he be.'

43 'O if ye hang the little wee boy
  Brought tidings unto me,
We shall attend his burial,
  And rewarded ye shall be.'

44 'O take the lady,' said the king,
  'And the boy shall be free;'
'A priest, a priest,' then Johnny cried,
  'To join my love and me.'

45 'A clerk, a clerk,' the king replied,
  'To seal her tocher wi thee;'
Out it speaks auld Johnny then,
  These words pronounced he:

46 'I want nae lands and rents at hame,
  I 'll ask nae gowd frae thee;
I am possessd o riches great,
  Hae fifty ploughs and three;
Likewise fa's heir to ane estate
  At the foot o Benachie.

47 'Hae ye ony masons in this place,
  Or ony at your call,

That ye may now send some o them
  To build your broken wall?'

48 'Yes, there are masons in this place,
  And plenty at my call;
  But ye may gang frae whence ye came,
  Never mind my broken wall.'

49 They 've taen the lady by the hand
  And set her prison-free;

Wi drums beating, and fifes playing,
  They spent the night wi glee.

50 Now auld Johnny Moir, and young Johnny
  Moir,
  And Jock o Noth, a' three,
  The English lady, and little wee boy,
  Went a' to Benachie.

27⁴. hae.

252

THE KITCHIE-BOY

A. Skene MS., p. 89.

B. 'Earl Richard's Daughter,' Buchan's Ballads of
the North of Scotland, I, 145.

C. 'Bonny Foot-Boy,' Alexander Fraser Tytler's
Brown MS., No 7.

D. 'The Kitchie-Boy,' Harris MS., fol. 21.

E. 'Willie, the Kitchie-Boy,' Joseph Robertson's Note-
Book, 'Adversaria,' p. 88.

A LADY of birth falls in love with her father's kitchen-boy (foot-boy, C). She makes her passion known to him. He begs for secrecy, for her father would hang him; this is quite too likely, and she would be sent to a nunnery. The danger quickens her wits: she will send him off in a fine ship, and he can come back 'like some earl or baron's son' and marry her (C). Being well provided with gold, her mother's legacy, she has no difficulty in carrying out her plan; a very noble ship is provided, and she gives Willie (B, C, E) a ring to mind him of her. She warns him, C 8, E 13, that there are pressing reasons why he should not stay away very long. After a voyage of from three weeks to twelve months, Willie lands at London, A, E; in Spain, B, C, D. A lady, looking over her castle-wall, sees the ship coming in, and goes down to the shore with her maries to invite the master to dine. The master excuses himself; she asks him if he can fancy her; the woman he loves is far over the sea; the fairest woman in Scotland would break her heart if he should not return to her. The Spanish (or English) lady offers him a rich ring, to wear for her sake; he has a ring on his finger which is far dearer than any she could give him. He sails homeward; the lady's father sees the ship coming in, and is as much impressed as his daughter could desire; he thinks some man of mark must be aboard, and tells his daughter to busk herself, for he means to ask the squire or lord to dine; he would give all his rents to have this same marry his daughter. Willie blackens or paints or masks or veils his face, and goes with the father to the castle. He asks the lady if she can fancy him; her father asks her if she will marry this lord, C. The man is far over sea that shall have her love, she replies. Willie hands her the ring which she had given him. Gat ye that by sea? or gat ye that by land? or gat ye it on the Spanish coast upon a dead man's hand? He gat it on a drowned man's hand. Alas! she cries, my true-love Willie! Upon this, Willie reveals himself. The father calls for a priest, little knowing that this lord was his own kitchen-boy.

The ballad is a modern " adaptation " of 'King Horn,' No 17, from which A 33, 34, B 47, D 7, 8, are taken outright. In the particular of the hero's having his choice of two women it is more like the *gest* of 'King Horn,' or 'Horn Childe and Maiden Rimnild;' but an independent invention of the Spanish lady is not beyond the humble ability of the composer of 'The Kitchie-Boy.'

***

A

Skene MS., p. 89; taken down in the north of Scotland, 1802–3.

1 THERE was a lady fair,
    An een a lady of birth an fame,
  She eyed her father's kitchen-boy,
    The greater was her shame.

2 She could never her love reveal,
    Nor to him talk,
  But in the forest wide an brade,
    Where they were wont to walk.

3 It fell ance upon a day
    Her father gaed frae home,
  And she sent for the kitchen-boy
    To her own room.

4 'Canna ye fancy me, Willie?
    Canna ye fancy me?
  By a' the lords I ever saw
    There is nane I loo but ye.'

5 'O latna this be kent, lady,
    O latna this be . . . ,
  For gin yer father got word of this
    I vou he 'd gar me die.'

6 'Yer life shall no be taen, Willie,
    Yer life sal na be taen ;
  I wad er loss my ain heart's blood
    Or thy body gat wrang.'

7 Wi her monny fair speeches
    She made the boy bold,
  Till he began to kiss an clap,
    An on her sine lay hold.

8 They hadna kissed an love claped,
    As lovers whan they meet,
. . . .
. . . .

9 'The master-cook he will on me call,
    An answered he man be ;
  An it wer kent I war in bower wi thee,
    I fear they wad gar me die.'

10 'The master-cook may on ye call,
    But answerd he will never be,
. . . .
. . . .

11 'For I hae three coffers fu o goud,
    Yer eyen did never see,
  An I will build a bonny ship for my love,
    An set her to the sea,
  And sail she east or sail she wast
    The ship sal be fair to see.'

12 She has built a bonny ship,
    And set her to the sea ;
  The topmasts war o the red goud,
    The sails of tafetie.

13 She gae him a gay goud ring,
. . . .
  To mind him on a gay lady
    That ance bear love to him.

14 The day was fair, the ship was rare,
    Whan that swain set to sea ;
  Whan that day twal-moth came and gaed,
    At London landed he.

15 A lady looked our the castle-wa,
   Beheld the day gae down,
And she beheld that bonny ship
   Come hailing to the town.

16 'Come here, come here, my maries a',
   Ye see na what I see ;
The bonniest ship is come to land
   Yer eyes did ever see.

17 'Gae busk ye, busk ye, my maries a',
   Busk ye unco fine,
Till I gae down to yon shore-side,
   To invite yon squar to dine.

18 'O ye come up, gay young squar,
   An take wi me a dine ;
Ye sal eat o the guid white loaf,
   An drink the claret wine.'

19 'I thank ye for yer bread,
   I thank ye for yer wine,
I thank ye for yer courticie,
   But indeed I hanna time.'

20 'Canna ye fancy me ? ' she says,
   ' Canna ye fancy me ?
O a' the lords an lairds I see
   There 's nane I fancy but ye.'

21 ' The 'r far awa fra me,' he says,
   ' The 'r clean ayont the sea,
That has my heart in hand,
   An my love ae sal be.'

22 ' Here is a guid goud ring,
   .   .   .   .   .
It will mind ye on a gay lady
   That ance bare love to ye.'

23 'I ha a ring on my finger
   I loe thrice as well as thine,
Tho yours were o the guid red goud
   An mine but simple tin.'

24 The day was fair, the ship was rare,
   Whan that squar set to sea ;
Whan that day twal-month came an gaed,
   At hame again landed he.

25 The lady's father looked our castle-wa,
   To see the day gae down,

An he beheld that bonny ship
   Come hailing to the town.

26 ' Come here, my daughter,
   Ye see na what I see ;
The bonniest ship is come to land
   My eyes did ever see.

27 ' Gae busk ye, my dochter,
   G[a]e busk ye unco fine,
An I 'll gae down to yon shore-side,
   To invite the squar to dine ;
I wad gie a' my rents
   To hae ye married to him.'

28 ' The 'r far awa frae me,' she says,
   ' Far ayont the sea,
That has my heart in hand
   An my love ai sal be.'

29 ' O will ye come, ye gay hine squar,
   An take wi me a dine ?
Ye sal eat o the guid white bread,
   And drink the claret wine.'

30 'I thank ye for yer bread,
   I thank ye for yer wine,
I thank ye for yer courticie,
   For indeed I hanna grait time.

31 ' O canna ye fancy me ? ' he says,
   ' O canna ye fancy me ?
O a' the ladys I eer did see
   There 's nane I loo by ye.'

32 ' They are far awa fra me,' she says,
   ' The 'r far ayont the sea,
That has my heart in hand,
   An my love ay sall be.'

33 ' Here it is, a gay goud ring,
   .   .   .   .   .
It will mind ye on a gay hin chil
   That ance bare love to ye.'

34 ' O gat ye that ring on the sea sailing ?
   Or gat ye it on the land ?
O gat ye it on the shore laying,
   On a drowned man's hand ? '

35 'I got na it on the sea sailing,
   I got na it on the land,

But I got it on the shore lying,
   On a drowned man's hand.

36 'O bonny was his cheek,
   An lovely was his face!'
'Allas!' says she, 'it is my true-love Willie,'
.   .   .   .   .   .

37 He turned him round about,
   An sweetly could he smile;
She turned her round, says, My love Willie,
   How could ye me beguile?

38 'A priest! a priest!' the old man cries,
   'An lat this twa married be:'
Little did the old man kin
   It was his ain kitchen-boy.

——————

B

Buchan's Ballads of the North of Scotland, I, 145.

1 EARL RICHARD had but ae daughter,
   A maid o birth and fame;
She loved her father's kitchen-boy,
   The greater was her shame.

2 But she could neer her true-love see,
   Nor with him could she talk,
In towns where she had wont to go,
   Nor fields where she could walk.

3 But it fell ance upon a day
   Her father went from home;
She's calld upon the kitchen boy
   To come and clean her room.

4 'Come sit ye down by me, Willie,
   Come sit ye down by me;
There's nae a lord in a' the north
   That I can love but thee.'

5 'Let never the like be heard, lady,
   Nor let it ever be;
For if your father get word o this
   He will gar hang me hie.'

6 'O ye shall neer be hangd, Willie,
   Your blude shall neer be drawn;
I'll lay my life in pledge o thine
   Your body's neer get wrang.'

7 'Excuse me now, my comely dame,
   No langer here I'll stay;
You know my time is near expir'd,
   And now I must away.

8 'The master-cook will on me call,
   And answered he must be;
If I am found in bower with thee,
   Great anger will there be.'

9 'The master-cook will on you call,
   But shall not answerd be;

I'll put you in a higher place
   Than any cook's degree.

10 'I have a coffer full of gold,
   Another of white monie,
And I will build a bonny ship,
   And set my love to sea.

11 'Silk shall be your sailing-clothes,
   Gold yellow is your hair,
As white like milk are your twa hands,
   Your body neat and fair.'

12 This lady, with her fair speeches,
   She made the boy grow bold,
And he began to kiss and clap,
   And on his love lay hold.

13 And she has built a bonny ship,
   Set her love to the sea,
Seven score o brisk young men
   To bear him companie.

14 Then she's taen out a gay gold ring,
   To him she did it gie:
'This will mind you on the ladie, Willie,
   That's laid her love on thee.'

15 Then he's taen out a piece of gold,
   And he brake it in two:
'All I have in the world, my dame,
   For love I give to you.'

16 Now he is to his bonny ship,
   And merrily taen the sea;
The lady lay oer castle-wa,
   The tear blinded her ee.

17 They had not saild upon the sea
   A week but barely three
When came a prosperous gale of wind,
   On Spain's coast landed he.

18 A lady lay oer castle-wa,
   Beholding dale and down,

And she beheld the bonny ship
   Come sailing to the town.

19 'Come here, come here, my maries a',
   Ye see not what I see ;
For here I see the bonniest ship
   That ever saild the sea.

20 'In her there is the bravest squire
   That eer my eyes did see ;
All clad in silk and rich attire,
   And comely, comely 's he.

21 'O busk, O busk, my maries all,
   O busk and make ye fine ;
And we will on to yon shore-side,
   Invite yon squire to dine.

22 'Will ye come up to my castle
   Wi me and take your dine ?
And ye shall eat the gude white bread,
   And drink the claret wine.'

23 'I thank you for your bread, lady,
   I thank you for your wine ;
I thank you for your kind offer,
   But now I have not time.'

24 'I would gie all my land,' she says,
   'Your gay bride were I she ;
And then to live on a small portion
   Contented I would be.'

25 'She 's far awa frae me, lady,
   She 's far awa frae me
That has my heart a-keeping fast,
   And my love still she 'll be.'

26 'But ladies they are unconstant,
   When their loves go to sea,
And she 'll be wed ere ye gae back ;
   My love, pray stay wi me.'

27 'If she be wed ere I go back,
   And prove sae false to me,
I shall live single all my life;
   I 'll neer wed one but she.'

28 Then she 's taen out a gay gold ring,
   And gae him presentlie :
''T will mind you on the lady, young man,
   That laid her love on thee.'

29 'The ring that 's on my mid-finger
   Is far dearer to me,
Tho yours were o the gude red gold,
   And mine the metal free.'

30 He viewd them all, baith neat and small,
   As they stood on the shore,

Then hoist the mainsail to the wind,
   Adieu, for evermore !

31 He had not saild upon the sea
   A week but barely three
Until there came a prosperous gale,
   In Scotland landed he.

32 But he put paint upon his face,
   And oil upon his hair,
Likewise a mask above his brow,
   Which did disguise him sair.

33 Earl Richard lay oer castle-wa,
   Beholding dale and down,
And he beheld the bonny ship
   Come sailing to the town.

34 'Come here, come here, my daughter dear,
   Ye see not what I see ;
For here I see the bonniest ship
   That ever saild the sea.

35 'In her there is the bravest squire
   That eer my eyes did see ;
O busk, O busk, my daughter dear,
   Come here, come here, to me.

36 'O busk, O busk, my daughter dear,
   O busk, and make ye fine,
And we will on to the shore-side,
   Invite yon squire to dine.'

37 'He 's far awa frae me, father,
   He 's far awa frae me
Who has the keeping o my heart,
   And I 'll wed nane but he.'

38 'Whoever has your heart in hand,
   Yon lad 's the match for thee,
And he shall come to my castle
   This day and dine wi me.

39 'Will ye come up to my castle
   With me and take your dine?
And ye shall eat the gude white bread,
   And drink the claret wine.'

40 'Yes, I 'll come up to your castle
   With you and take my dine,
For I would give my bonny ship
   Were your fair daughter mine.'

41 'I would give all my lands,' he said,
   'That your bride she would be ;
Then to live on a small portion
   Contented would I be.'

42 As they gaed up from yon sea-strand
   And down the bowling-green,

He drew the mask out-oer his face,
  For fear he should be seen.

43 He 's done him down from bower to bower,
  Likewise from bower to ha,
  And there he saw that lady gay,
  The flower out-oer them a'.

44 He 's taen her in his arms twa,
  And haild her courteouslie :
  ' Excuse me, sir, there 's no strange man
  Such freedom use with me.'

45 Her father turnd him round about,
  A light laugh then gave he :
  ' Stay, I 'll retire a little while,
  Perhaps you may agree.'

46 Now Willie 's taen a gay gold ring,
  And gave her presentlie ;
  Says, Take ye that, ye lady fair,
  A love-token from me.

47 ' O got ye 't on the sea sailing?
  Or got ye 't on the sand?
  Or got ye 't on the coast of Spain,
  Upon a dead man's hand? '

48 ' Fine silk it was his sailing-clothes,
  Gold yellow was his hair ;
  It would hae made a hale heart bleed
  To see him lying there.

49 ' He was not dead as I passd by,
  But no remeid could be ;

50 ' And by the marks he has descryvd
  I 'm sure that you are she ;
  So take this token of free will,
  For him you 'll never see.'

51 In sorrow she tore her mantle,
  With care she tore her hair :
  ' Now since I 've lost my own true-love,
  I 'll neer love young men mair.'

52 He drew the mask from off his face,
  The lady sweetly smiled :
  ' Awa, awa, ye fause Willie !
  How have you me beguiled? '

53 Earl Richard he went thro the ha,
  The wine-glass in his hand,
  But little thought his kitchen-boy
  Was heir oer a' his land.

54 But this she kept within her heart,
  And never told to one
  Until nine months they were expir'd,
  That her young son came home.

55 She told it to her father dear ;
  He said, Daughter, well won ;
  You 've married for love, not for gold,
  Your joys will neer be done.

He gave me this token to bear
  Unto a fair ladie.

C

Alexander Fraser Tytler's Brown MS., No 7.

1 O THERE was a ladie, a noble ladie,
  She was a ladie of birth and fame,
  But she fell in love wi her father's foot-boy,
  I wis she was the mair to blame.

2 A word of him she neer could get
  Till her father was a hunting gone ;
  Then she calld on the bonny foot-boy
  To speak wi her in her bower alone.

3 Says, Ye ken you are my love, Willie,
  And that I am a ladie free,
  And there 's naething ye can ask, Willie,
  But at your bidding I maun be.

4 O the loving looks that ladie gave
  Soon made the bonny boy grow bold,

And the loving words that ladie spake
  As soon on them he did lay hold.

5 She has taen a ring frae her white finger,
  And unto him she did it gie ;
  Says, Wear this token for my sake,
  And keep it till the day you die.

6 ' But shoud my father get word of this
  I fear we baith will have cause to rue,
  For to some nunnery I shoud be sent,
  And I fear, my love, he would ruin you.

7 ' But here is a coffer of the good red gowd,
  I wot my mother left it to me ;
  And wi it you 'll buy a bonny ship,
  And ye maun sail the raging sea ;
  Then like some earl or baron's son
  You can come back and marrie me.

8 'But stay not lang awa, Willie,
   O stay not lang across the fame,
For fear your ladie shoud lighter be,
   Or your young son shoud want a name.'

9 He had not been o the sea sailling
   But till three months were come and gane,
Till he has landed his bonny ship;
   It was upon the coast of Spain.

10 There was a ladie of high degree
   That saw him walking up and down;
She fell in love wi sweet Willie,
   But she wist no how to make it known.

11 She has calld up her maries a',
   Says, Hearken well to what I say;
There is a young man in yon ship
   That has been my love this many a day.

12 'Now bear a hand, my maries a',
   And busk me brave and make me fine,
And go wi me to yon shore-side
   To invite that noble youth to dine.'

13 O they have buskit that ladie gay
   In velvet pall and jewels rare;
A poor man might have been made rich
   Wi half the pearles they pat in her hair.

14 Her mantle was of gowd sae red,
   It glaned as far as ane coud see;
Sweet Willie thought she had been the queen,
   And bowd full low and bent his knee.

15 She 's gard her maries step aside,
   And on sweet Willie sae did smile;
She thought that man was not on earth
   But of his heart she could beguile.

16 Says, Ye maun leave your bonny ship
   And go this day wi me and dine,
And you shall eat the baken meat,
   And you shall drink the Spanish wine.

17 'I canna leave my bonny ship,
   Nor go this day to dine wi thee,
For a' my sails are ready bent
   To bear me back to my ain countrie.'

18 'O gin you 'd forsake your bonny ship
   And wed a ladie of this countrie,
I would make you lord of a' this town,
   And towns and castles twa or three.'

19 'Should I wed a ladie of this countrie,
   In sooth I woud be sair to blame,
For the fairest ladie in fair Scotland
   Woud break her heart gin I gaed na hame.'

20 'That ladie may choose another lord,
   And you another love may choose;
There is not a lord in this countrie
   That such a proffer could refuse.'

21 'O ladie, shoud I your proffer take,
   You 'd soon yoursell have cause to rue,
For the man that his first love forsakes
   Woud to a seccond neer prove true.'

22 She has taen a ring frae her white finger,
   It might have been a prince's fee;
Says, Wear this token for my sake,
   And give me that which now I see.

23 'Take back your token, ye ladie fair;
   This ring you see on my right hand
Was gien me by my ain true-love,
   Before I left my native land.

24 'And tho yours woud buy it nine times oer
   I far more dearly prize my ain;
Nor woud I make the niffer,' he says,
   'For a' the gowd that is in Spain.'

25 The ladie turnd her head away
   To dry the sat tears frae her eyne;
She naething more to him did say
   But, I wish your face I neer had seen!

26 He has set his foot on good ship-board,
   The ladie waved her milk-white hand,
The wind sprang up and filld his sails,
   And he quickly left the Spanish land.

27 He soon came back to his native strand,
   He langd his ain true-love to see;
Her father saw him come to land,
   And took him some great lord to be.

28 Says, Will ye leave your bonny ship
   And come wi me this day to dine?
And you shall eat the baken meat,
   And you shall drink the claret wine.

29 'O I will leave my bonny ship,
   And gladly go wi you to dine,
And I woud gie thrice three thousand pounds
   That your fair daughter were but mine.'

30 'O gin ye will part wi your bonny ship
   And wed a ladie of this countrie,
I will gie you my ae daughter,
   Gin she 'll consent your bride to be.'

31 O he has blaket his bonny face
   And closs tuckd up his yellow hair;
His true-love met them at the yate,
   But she little thought her love was there.

32 'O will you marrie this lord, daughter,
    That I 've brought hame to dine wi me?
    You shall be heir of a' my lands,
    Gin you 'll consent his bride to be.'

33 She looked oer her left shoulder,
    I wot the tears stood in her eye ;
    Says, The man is on the sea sailling
    That fair wedding shall get of me.

34 Then Willie has washd his bonny face,
    And he 's kaimd down his yellow hair ;
    He took his true-love in his arms,
    And kindly has he kissd her there.

35 She 's looked in his bonny face,
    And thro her tears did sweetly smile,
    Then sayd, Awa, awa, Willie !
    How could you thus your love beguile ?

36 She kept the secret in her breast,
    Full seven years she 's kept the same,
    Till it fell out at a christning-feast,
    And then of it she made good game.

37 And her father laughd aboon the rest,
    And said, My daughter, you 'r nae to blame ;
    For you 've married for love, and no for land,
    So a' my gowd is yours to claim.

D

Harris MS., fol. 21 ; from the recitation of Mrs Harris and others.

1 THERE lived a lady in the north
    O muckle birth an fame ;
    She 's faun in love wi her kitchie-boy,
    The greater was her shame.

* * * * * * *

2 ' Maister cook, he will cry oot,
    An answered he maun be ; '
.   .   .   .

3 ' I hae a coffer o ried gowd
    My mither left to me,
    An I will build a bonnie ship,
    And send her ower the sea,
    An you 'll come hame like lord or squire,
    An answered you maun be.'

4 She has biggit a bonnie ship,
    Sent her across the main,
    An in less than sax months an a day
    That ship cam back again.

5 ' Go dress, go dress, my dochter Janet,
    Go dress, an mak you fine,

An we 'll go doun to yon shore-side
    An bid yon lords to dine.'

6 He 's pued the black mask ower his face,
    Kaimed doun his yellow hair,
    A' no to lat her father ken
    That ere he had been there.

* * * * * * *

7 ' Oh, got you that by sea sailin ?
    Or got you that by land ?
    Or got you that on Spanish coast,
    Upon a died man's hand ? '

8 ' I got na that by sea sailin,
    I got na that by land ;
    But I got that on Spanish coast,
    Upon a died man's hand.'

9 He 's pued the black mask aff his face,
    Threw back his yellow hair,
.   .   .   .

10 ' A priest, a priest,' the lady she cried,
    ' To marry my love an me ; '
    ' A clerk, a clerk,' her father cried,
    ' To sign her tocher free.'

E

Joseph Robertson's Note-Book " Adversaria," p. 88 ; from tradition.

* * * * * * *

1 AND she has built a lofty ship,
    And set her to the main ;
    The masts o her were o gude reed gowd,
    And the sails o silver clear.

2 ' Ye winna bide three months awa
    When ye 'll return again,
  In case your lady lichter be,
    And your baby want the name.'

3 But the wind blew high,
    The mariners they did land at Lundin soon.

4 A lady sat on the castell-wa,
    Beheld baith dale and down,
  And there she saw this lofty ship,
    Comin sailin in the Downs.

5 ' Look out, look out, my maidens a',
    Ye seena what I see ;
  For I do see as bonny a ship
    As ever sailed the sea,
  And the master o her 's the bonniest boy
    That ever my eyes did see.'

6 She 's taen her mantell her about,
    Her cane intill her han,
  And she 's away to the shore-side,
    Till invite the square to dine.

7 ' O will ye come to our castell ?
    Or will ye sup or dine ? '
  ' O excuse me, madam,' he said,
    ' For I hae but little time.'

   *   *   *   *   *   *   *

8 The wind blew high,
    The mariners they did land at home again.

9 The old man sat in the castell-wa,
    Beholding dale and down,
  And there he spied this goodly ship
    Come sailin to the town.

10 ' Look out, look out, my dauchter dear,
    Ye see not what I see ;
  For I do see as bonny a ship
    As ever sailed the sea.

11 ' And the master o her 's the bonniest boy
    That my eyes did ever see,
  And if I were a woman as I 'm a man
    My husband he should be.'

12 ' Haud far awa frae me, fader,
    Haud far awa frae me,
  For I never had a lad but ane,
    And he 's far awa at sea.

13 ' There is a love-token atween us twa,
    It 'll be mair ere it be less,
  An aye the langer he bides awa
    It will the mair encreass.'

14 He 's taen his mantell him about,
    His cane intil his hand,
  And he 's awa to the shore-side,
    To invite the square to dine.

15 ' O will ye come to our castle ?
    Or will ye sup or dine ? '
  ' Indeed I will, kind sir,' he said,
    ' Tho I 've but little time.'

16 The lady sat on castle-wa,
    Beholding dale and down,
  But he 's put his veil upon his face,
    That she might not him ken.

   *   *   *   *   *   *   *

———◆———

A. *Written in long couplets.* 8^1. hadne.
   22^4, 32^4. ance hane ? *Cf.* 3^4.
   23^2. I lee. 35^2. got no.
B. 11^2. yellow in.
C. 14^2. glaned. Glant, glent *is probably intended.*
   Glancd *is less likely.*
   20^4. could. *MS. possibly* would.
E. *Before* 1 : " A lady falls in love with her father's kitchie-boy when her father is absent,
and to conceal him from him procures a
ship and puts him to sea. Her father thinks
he has run away."
   After 7 : She kills herself.
   After 16 : Continued on page   : *but not continued.*

253

THOMAS O YONDERDALE

a. Buchan's Ballads of the North of Scotland, I, 221.　　b. Christie's Traditional Ballad Airs, I, 96.

---

b is epitomized from a, with a few variations, mostly very trifling, as Christie had heard the ballad sung.

Thomas of Yonderdale gains Lady Maisry's love and has a son by her. Overhearing some reproachful words one day as he passes her bower, he is touched, and promises to marry her after returning from a voyage, but while he is in a strange country wooes another woman. He dreams that Maisry stands by his bed upbraiding him for his inconstancy, and sends a boy to her to bring her to his wedding. Maisry comes, arrayed, as she had been directed, in noble style. The bride asks the boy who she may be, and is told that she is Thomas's first love. Maisry asks Thomas why she was sent for: she is to be his wife. The nominal bride asks his will: she is to go home, with the comfort of being sent back in a coach, whereas she came on a hired horse! This ill-used, but not diffident, young woman proposes that Thomas shall give two thirds of his lands to his brother and make him marry her. Thomas refuses to divide his lands for any woman, and has no power over his brother. According to b, the discarded bride asks only a modest third of Thomas's lands for the brother; Thomas promises to give a third to *her*, but disclaims, as in a, his competency to arrange a marriage for his brother.

This looks like a recent piece, fabricated, with a certain amount of cheap mortar, from recollections of 'Fair Annie,' No 62, 'Lord Thomas and Fair Annet,' No 73, and 'Young Beichan,' No 53.

1　Lady Maisry lives intill a bower,
　　She never wore but what she would;
　Her gowns were o the silks sae fine,
　　Her coats stood up wi bolts o gold.

2　Mony a knight there courted her,
　　And gentlemen o high degree,
　But it was Thomas o Yonderdale
　　That gaind the love o this ladie.

3　Now he has hunted her till her bower,
　　Baith late at night and the mid day,
　But when he stole her virgin rose
　　Nae mair this maid he would come nigh.

4　But it fell ance upon a time
　　Thomas her bower he walkëd by;

There he saw her Lady Maisry,
　　Nursing her young son on her knee.

5　'O seal on you, my bonny babe,
　　And lang may ye my comfort be!
　Your father passes by our bower,
　　And now minds neither you nor me.'

6　Now when Thomas heard her speak,
　　The saut tear trinkled frae his ee;
　To Lady Maisry's bower he went,
　　Says, Now I'm come to comfort thee.

7　'Is this the promise ye did make
　　Last when I was in your companie?
　You said before nine months were gane
　　Your wedded wife that I should be.'

8 'If Saturday be a bonny day,
   Then, my love, I maun sail the sea;
But if I live for to return,
   O then, my love, I 'll marry thee.'

9 'I wish Saturday a stormy day,
   High and stormy be the sea,
Ships may not sail, nor boats row,
   But gar true Thomas stay wi me.'

10 Saturday was a bonny day,
   Fair and leesome blew the wind;
Ships did sail, and boats did row,
   Which had true Thomas to unco ground.

11 He hadna been on unco ground
   A month, a month but barely three,
Till he has courted anither maid,
   And quite forgotten Lady Maisry.

12 Ae night as he lay on his bed,
   In a dreary dream dreamed he
That Maisry stood by his bedside,
   Upbraiding him for 's inconstancie.

13 He 's calld upon his little boy,
   Says, Bring me candle, that I see;
And ye maun gang this night, [my] boy,
   Wi a letter to a gay ladie.

14 'It is my duty you to serve,
   And bring you coal and candle-light,
And I would rin your errand, master,
   If 't were to Lady Maisry bright.

15 'Tho my legs were sair I coudna gang,
   Tho the night were dark I coudna see,
Tho I should creep on hands and feet,
   I woud gae to Lady Maisry.'

16 'Win up, win up, my bonny boy,
   And at my bidding for to be;
For ye maun quickly my errand rin,
   For it is to Lady Maisry.

17 'Ye 'll bid her dress in the gowns o silk,
   Likewise in the coats o cramasie;
Ye 'll bid her come alang wi you,
   True Thomas's wedding for to see.

18 'Ye 'll bid her shoe her steed before,
   And a' gowd graithing him behind;
On ilka tip o her horse mane,
   Twa bonny bells to loudly ring.

19 'And on the tor o her saddle
   A courtly bird to sweetly sing;
Her bridle-reins o silver fine,
   And stirrups by her side to hing.'

20 She dressd her in the finest silk,
   Her coats were o the cramasie,
And she 's awa to unco land,
   True Thomas's wedding for to see.

21 At ilka tippet o her horse mane,
   Twa bonny bells did loudly ring,
And on the tor o her saddle
   A courtly bird did sweetly sing.

22 The bells they rang, the bird he sang,
   As they rode in yon pleasant plain;
Then soon she met true Thomas's bride,
   Wi a' her maidens and young men.

23 The bride she garned round about,
   'I wonder,' said she, 'who this may be?
It surely is our Scottish queen,
   Come here our wedding for to see.'

24 Out it speaks true Thomas's boy,
   'She maunna lift her head sae hie;
But it 's true Thomas's first love,
   Come here your wedding for to see.'

25 Then out bespake true Thomas's bride,
   I wyte the tear did blind her ee;
If this be Thomas's first true-love,
   I 'm sair afraid he 'll neer hae me.

26 Then in it came her Lady Maisry,
   And aye as she trips in the fleer,
'What is your will, Thomas?' she said,
   'This day, ye know, ye calld me here.'

27 'Come hither by me, ye lily flower,
   Come hither and set ye down by me,
For ye 're the ane I 've call'd upon,
   And ye my wedded wife maun be.'

28 Then in it came true Thomas's bride,
   And aye as she trippd on the stane,
'What is your will, Thomas?' she said,
   'This day, ye know, ye calld me hame.'

29 'Ye hae come on hired horseback,
   But ye 'se gae hame in coach sae free;
For here 's the flower into my bower
   I mean my wedded wife shall be.'

30 'O ye will break your lands, Thomas,
　　And part them in divisions three;
　　Gie twa o them to your ae brother,
　　And cause your brother marry me.'

31 'I winna break my lands,' he said,
　　'For ony woman that I see;
　　My brother 's a knight o wealth and might,
　　He 'll wed nane but he will for me.'

———◆———

b. 1⁴. And a' stood. 2¹. And mony knight.
2⁴. this gay. 8³. return again.
10¹. And Saturday. 10⁴. took true.
13². I may see. 13³. my boy.
16². ye maun be. 24³. ain first.
30³. Gie ane.

31. 'O I will break my lands,' he said,
　　'And ae third will I gie to thee;
　　But my brother 's ane o wealth and might,
　　And he 'll wed nane but he will for me.'

———————

254

LORD WILLIAM, OR, LORD LUNDY

A. Motherwell's MS., p. 361.　Sweet William,'
Motherwell's Minstrelsy, p. 307.

B. 'Lord Lundy,' Buchan's Ballads of the North of
Scotland, II, 57.

C. 'Lord William,' Buchan's MSS, II, 126; Dixon,
Scottish Traditional Versions of Ancient Ballads,
p. 57, Percy Society, vol. xvii.

———◆———

SWEET WILLIAM (Lord William's son, or Lord William) and the Baillie's daughter (Lord Lundy's daughter) have been lovers: they have in fact been over-sea together, learning "some unco lair." The young woman's father recalls her from her studies abroad, and requires her to marry a Southland lord (the young prince of England). She will submit to her father's will, though she had rather die. In A she sends a letter to William by a bird. The minister has begun the marriage-service, when the lover enters the church with a party of armed men and bids the bridegroom stand back; the bride shall join with him. The father fumes; would shoot William if he had a pistol, A; will give his daughter no dowry, B. William of course cares not the least for dowry; he has what he wants. He tells his 'foremost man' to lift his bride on her horse, and sends commendations to her mother.

A 4, B 10, 11, C 6, 7, may be borrowed from 'Fair Janet,' No 64, G 1, 2, II, 110.

———◆———

A

Motherwell's MS., p. 361; from the recitation of Agnes Lyle, an old woman of Kilbarchan.

1 SWEET WILLIAM 's gone over seas,
　　Some unco lair to learn,

And our gude Bailie's ae dochter
Is awa to learn the same.

2 In one broad buke they learned baith,
　　In one broad bed they lay;

But when her father came to know
  He gart her come away.

3 'It 's you must marry that Southland lord,
  His lady for to be;
It 's ye maun marry that Southland lord,
  Or nocht ye 'll get frae me.'

4 'I must marry that Southland lord,
  Father, an it be your will;
But I rather it were my burial-day,
  My grave for to fill.'

5 She walked up, she walked down,
  Had none to make her moan,
Nothing but the pretty bird
  Sat on the causey-stone.

6 'If thou could speak, wee bird,' she says,
  'As weell as thou can flee,
I would write a long letter
  To Will ayont the sea.'

7 'What thou wants wi Will,' it says,
  'Thou 'll seal it with thy ring,
Tak a thread o silk and anither o twine,
  About my neck will hing.'

8 What she wanted wi Willie
  She sealed it wi a ring,
Took a thread of silk, another o twine,
  About its neck did hing.

9 This bird flew high, this bird flew low,
  This bird flew owre the sea,
Until it entered the same room
  Wherein was Sweet Willie.

10 This bird flew high, this bird flew low,
  Poor bird, it was mistaen!
It let the letter fa on Baldie's breist,
  Instead of Sweet William.

11 'Here 's a letter, William,' he says,
  'I 'm sure it 's not to me;

And gin the morn gin twelve o'clock
  Your love shall married be.'

12 'Come saddle to me my horse,' he said,
  'The brown and a' that 's speedie,
And I 'll awa to Old England,
  To bring home my ladie.'

13 Awa he gaed, awa he rade,
  Awa wi mickle speed;
He lichtit at every twa miles' end,
  Lichtit and changed his steed.

14 When she entered the church-style,
  The tear was in her ee;
But when she entered the church-door
  A blythe sicht did she see.

15 'O hold your hand, you minister,
  Hold it a little wee,
Till I speak wi the bonnie bride,
  For she 's a friend to me.

16 'Stand off, stand off, you braw bridegroom,
  Stand off a little wee;
Stand off, stand off, you braw bridegroom,
  For the bride shall join wi me.'

17 Up and spak the bride's father,
  And an angry man was he;
'If I had pistol, powther and lead,
  And all at my command,
I would shoot thee stiff and dead
  In the place where thou dost stand.'

18 Up and spoke then Sweet William,
  And a blithe blink from his ee;
'If ye neer be shot till I shoot you,
  Ye 'se neer be shot for me.

19 'Come out, come out, my foremost man,
  And lift my lady on;
Commend me all to my good-mother,
  At night when ye gang home.'

B

Buchan's Ballads of the North of Scotland, II, 57.

1 LORD WILLIAM has but ae dear son,
  In this world had nae mair;

  Lord Lundie had but ae daughter,
    And he will hae nane but her.

2 They dressed up in maids' array,
  And passd for sisters fair;

With ae consent gaed ower the sea,
 For to seek after lear.

3 They baith did eat at ae braid board,
 In ae bed baith did lye;
When Lord Lundie got word o that,
 He 's taen her soon away.

4 When Lord Lundie got word of that,
 An angry man was he;
He wrote his daughter on great haste
 To return right speedilie.

5 When she looked the letter upon,
 A light laugh then gae she;
But ere she read it till an end
 The tear blinded her ee.

6 'Bad news, bad news, my love Willie,
 Bad news is come to me;
My father 's written a braid letter,
 Bids me gae speedilie.

7 'Set trysts, set trysts, my love Willie,
 Set trysts, I pray, wi me;
Set trysts, set trysts, my love Willie,
 When will our wedding be.'

8 'On Wednesday, on Wednesday,
 The first that ever ye see;
On Wednesday at twelve o'clock,
 My dear, I 'll meet wi thee.'

9 When she came to her father's ha,
 He hailed her courteouslie;
Says, I 'll forgie offences past,
 If now ye 'll answer me.

10 'Will ye marry yon young prince,
 Queen of England to be?
Or will you marry Lord William's son,
 Be loved by nane but he?'

11 'I will marry yon young prince,
 Father, if it be your will;
But I woud rather I were dead and gane,
 My grave I woud win till.'

12 When she was in her saddle set,
 She skyred like the fire,
To go her bridegroom for to meet,
 For whom she 'd nae desire.

13 On every tippet o her horse mane
 There hang a siller bell,
And whether the wind blew east or west
 They gae a sundry knell.

14 And when she came to Mary's kirk
 She skyred like the fire;
There her young bridegroom she did meet,
 For whom she 'd nae desire.

15 She looked ower her left shoulder,
 The tear blinded her ee;
But looking ower her right shoulder,
 A blythe sight then saw she.

16 There she saw Lord William's son,
 And mony a man him wi,
Wi targes braid and glittering spears
 All marching ower the lee.

17 The minister looked on a book
 Her marriage to begin:
'If there is naething to be said,
 These two may join in ane.'

18 'O huly, huly, sir,' she said,
 'O stay a little wee;
I hae a friend to welcome yet
 That 's been a dear friend to me.'

19 O then the parson he spake out,
 A wise word then spake he;
'You might hae had your friends welcomd
 Before ye 'd come to me.'

20 Then in it came the bride's first love,
 And mony a man him wi:
'Stand back, stand back, ye jelly bridegroom,
 Bride, ye maun join wi me.'

21 Then out it speaks him Lord Lundie,
 An angry man was he;
'Lord William's son will hae my daughter
 Without leave askd of me.

22 'But since it 's sae that she will gang,
 And proved sae fause to thee,
I 'll make a vow, and keep it true,
 Nae portion shall I gie.'

23 Then out it speaks the bride's first love,
 And [a] light laugh then gae he;

'I've got the best portion now, my lord,
  That ye can gie to me.

24 'Your gude red gold I value not,
    Nor yet your white monie;
  I hae her by the hand this day
    That's far dearer to me.

25 'So gie the prince a coffer o gold
    When he gaes to his bed,
  And bid him clap his coffer o gold,
    And I'll clap my bonny bride.'

C

Buchan's MSS, II, 126.

1 LORD WILLIAM has gane oer the sea
    For to seek after lear;
  Lord Lundie had but ae daughter,
    And he'd wed nane but her.

2 Upon a book they both did read,
    And in ae bed did ly:
  'But if my father get word of this,
    I'll soon be taen away.'

3 'Your father's gotten word of this,
    Soon married then ye'll be;
  Set trysts, set trysts wi me, Janet,
    Set trysts, set trysts wi me.

4 'Set trysts, set trysts wi me, Janet,
    When your wedding-day's to be;
  'On Saturday, the first that comes,
    Must be my wedding-day.'

5 'Bad news, bad news is come, Janet,
    Bad news is come to me;
  Your father's gotten word of this,
    Soon married then ye'll be.'

6 'O will ye marry the young prince, daughter,
    The queen of England to be?
  Or will ye marry Lord William,
    And die immediately?'

7 'O I will marry the young prince, father,
    Because it is your will;
  But I wish it was my burial-day,
    For my grave I could gang till.'

8 When they gaed in into the kirk,
    And ae seat they sat in,

The minister took up the book,
  The marriage to begin.

9 'Lay down the book, O dear, kind sir,
    And wait a little wee;
  I have a lady to welcome yet,
    She's been a good friend to me.'

10 Out then spake the minister,
    An angry man was he;
  'You might have had your ladies welcomd
    Before ye came to me.'

11 She looked oer her left shoulder,
    And tears did blind her ee;
  But she looked oer her right shoulder,
    And a blythe sight saw she,
  For in there came him Lord William,
    And his valiant company.

12 And in there came him Lord William,
    His armour shining clear,
  And in it came him Lord William,
    And many glittering spear.

13 'Stand by, stand by, ye bonny bridegroom,
    Stand by, stand by,' said he;
  'Stand by, stand by, ye bonny bridegroom,
    Bride, ye maun join wi me.

14 'Let the young prince clap his coffer of gold
    When he gangs to his bed;
  Let the young prince clap his coffer of gold,
    But I'll clap my bonny bride.'

15 Out it spake him Lord Lundie,
    And an angry man was he;
  'My daughter will marry him Lord William,
    It seems, in spite of me.'

A, C. *Motherwell and Dixon have made a few slight changes.*

255

WILLIE'S FATAL VISIT

Buchan's Ballads of the North of Scotland, II, 259.

A MAID, Meggie, inquires after her lover, Willie, and is told that he will be with her at night. Willie tirls the pin and is admitted. He is given the option of cards, wine, or bed, and chooses the bed, a too familiar commonplace in Buchan's ballads. Meggie charges the cock not to crow till day, but the cock crows an hour too soon. Willie dons his clothes, and in a dowie den encounters a grievous ghost, which, wan and weary though it be, smiles upon him; smiles, we may suppose, to have caught him. Willie has travelled this road often, and never uttered a prayer for safety; but he will never travel that road again. The ghost tears him to pieces, and hangs a bit 'on every seat' of Mary's kirk, the head right over Meggie's pew! Meggie rives her yellow hair.

The first half of this piece is a medley of 'Sweet William's Ghost,' 'Clerk Saunders,' and 'The Grey Cock.' For 1$^{3-6}$, 2, compare No 77, A, E, 2, 3, No 248, 1; for 5–8, No 69, F 3–6, No 70, B 2, 4; for 9, 10, No 248, 6, 7. 13 is caught, or taken, from 'Clyde's Water,' No 216, A 7.

Stanzas 15–17, wherever they came from, are too good for the setting: nothing so spirited, word or deed, could have been looked for from a ghost wan, weary, and smiling.

---

1 'TWAS on an evening fair I went to take the air,
  I heard a maid making her moan;
Said, Saw ye my father? Or saw ye my mother?
  Or saw ye my brother John?
Or saw ye the lad that I love best,
  And his name it is Sweet William?

2 'I saw not your father, I saw not your mother,
  Nor saw I your brother John;
But I saw the lad that ye love best,
  And his name it is Sweet William.'

3 'O was my love riding? or was he running?
  Or was he walking alone?
Or says he that he will be here this night?
  O dear, but he tarries long!'

4 'Your love was not riding, nor yet was he running,
  But fast was he walking alone;

He says that he will be here this night to thee,
  And forbids you to think long.'

5 Then Willie he has gane to his love's door,
  And gently tirled the pin:
'O sleep ye, wake ye, my bonny Meggie,
  Ye 'll rise, lat your true love in.'

6 The lassie being swack ran to the door fu snack,
  And gently she lifted the pin,
Then into her arms sae large and sae lang
  She embraced her bonny love in.

7 'O will ye gang to the cards or the dice,
  Or to a table o wine?
Or will ye gang to a well-made bed,
  Well coverd wi blankets fine?'

8 'O I winna gang to the cards nor the dice,
  Nor yet to a table o wine;

But I 'll rather gang to a well-made bed,
   Well coverd wi blankets fine.'

9 'My braw little cock, sits on the house tap,
   Ye 'll craw not till it be day,
And your kame shall be o the gude red gowd,
   And your wings o the siller grey.'

10 The cock being fause untrue he was,
   And he crew an hour ower seen;
They thought it was the gude day-light,
   But it was but the light o the meen.

11 'Ohon, alas!' says bonny Meggie then,
   'This night we hae sleeped ower lang!'
'O what is the matter?' then Willie replied,
   'The faster then I must gang.'

12 Then Sweet Willie raise, and put on his claise,
   And drew till him stockings and sheen,
And took by his side his berry-brown sword,
   And ower yon lang hill he 's gane.

13 As he gaed ower yon high, high hill,
   And down yon dowie den,
Great and grievous was the ghost he saw,
   Would fear ten thousand men.

14 As he gaed in by Mary kirk,
   And in by Mary stile,
Wan and weary was the ghost
   Upon sweet Willie did smile.

15 'Aft hae ye travelld this road, Willie,
   Aft hae ye travelld in sin;
Ye neer said sae muckle for your saul
   As My Maker bring me hame!

16 'Aft hae ye travelld this road, Willie,
   Your bonny love to see;
But ye 'll never travel this road again
   Till ye leave a token wi me.'

17 Then she has taen him Sweet Willie,
   Riven him frae gair to gair,
And on ilka seat o Mary's kirk
   O Willie she hang a share;
Even abeen his love Meggie's dice,
   Hang 's head and yellow hair.

18 His father made moan, his mother made moan,
   But Meggie made muckle mair;
His father made moan, his mother made moan,
   But Meggie reave her yellow hair.

256

ALISON AND WILLIE

A. 'My luve she lives in Lincolnshire,' Harris MS., fol. 18 b; Mrs Harris. b. 'Alison' Buchan's MSS., I, 231.

ALISON gaily invites Willie to her wedding; he will not come unless to be the bridegroom, with her for bride. That day you will never see, says Alison; once on your horse, you will have no more mind of me than if I were dead. Willie rides slowly away, and his heart breaks with the pains of love; he dies by the way, and is left to the birds. A letter stops the wedding, and breaks Alison's heart.

Stanza 7 must be left to those who can interpret Thomas of Erceldoune's prophecies.

1 'My luve she lives in Lincolnshire,
   I wat she 's neither black nor broun,
But her hair is like the thread o gowd,
   Aye an it waur weel kaimëd doun.'

2 She 's pued the black mask owre her face,
   An blinkit gaily wi her ee:
'O will you to my weddin come,
   An will you bear me gude companie?'

3 'I winna to your weddin come,
    Nor [will] I bear you gude companie,
Unless you be the bride yoursell,
    An me the bridegroom to be.'

4 'For me to be the bride mysel,
    An you the bonnie bridegroom to be —
Cheer up your heart, Sweet Willie,' she said,
    'For that 's the day you 'll never see.

5 'Gin you waur on your saiddle set,
    An gaily ridin on the way,
You 'll hae nae mair mind o Alison
    Than she waur dead an laid in clay.'

6 When he was on his saiddle set,
    An slowly ridin on the way,
He had mair mind o Alison
    Than he had o the licht o day.

7 He saw a hart draw near a hare,
    An aye that hare drew near a toun,
An that same hart did get a hare,
    But the gentle knicht got neer a toun.

8 He leant him owre his saiddle-bow,
    An his heart did brak in pieces three ;
Wi sighen said him Sweet Willie,
    'The pains o luve hae taen hald o me.'

9 .   .   .   .
    .   .   .   .
There cam a white horse an a letter,
    That stopped the weddin speidilie.

10 She leant her back on her bed-side,
    An her heart did brak in pieces three ;
She was buried an bemoaned,
    But the birds waur Willie's companie.

———◆———

a. 2³. Oh.   10³. He was.
b. But *wanting :* threads.
    2¹. She pu'd : mask aff.   2². blinked blythely.
    2³. Says, Will ye.   2⁴. Or : gude *wanting.*
    3². Nor will ; gude *wanting.*
    3⁴. the bonny bridegroom be.
    4². to *wanting.*   4³. Sweet *wanting.*
    5². And merry.   5³. Ye 'll mind nae mair o.
    5⁴. When.   6². An weary.
    7¹. He spied : draw till.   7². aye the.

7³. An *wanting.*   8¹. leand his back to his.
8³. said that sweet.   8⁴. luve 's taen.
9¹·². Their wedding-day it was well set, And a'
    their friends invited there.   9³. While came.
9⁴. wedding in prepare.
Before 10¹ : She said, If Willie he be dead, A
    wedded wife I 'll never be.
10¹. Then leand her back to her bed-stock.
10². Her heart in pieces broke in three.
10³. then was.

———————

257

BURD ISABEL AND EARL PATRICK

A. 'Burd Bell,' Kinloch MSS, I, 211.

B. 'Burd Isbel and Sir Patrick,' Buchan's Ballads of the North of Scotland, I, 76.

C. 'Earl Patrick and Burd Isabel,' Motherwell's MS., p. 440.

———◆———

CHRISTIE, Traditional Ballad Airs, II, 34, I, 42, says that an old woman in Buckie, Enzie, Banff, who died in 1866 at the age of nearly eighty, and whose father was a noted ballad-singer, sang him words which, so far as he could remember, were like those of **B.**

A. Unmarried Burd Isabel bears a son to Earl Patrick. He has passed his word to make her his wife in case the expected bairn should be a boy, but his mother objects. He now promises to bring her home after the demise of his parents, and in the mean while builds her a gold and silver bower (which for a reason inscrutable is 'strawn round wi sand'). Father and mother die; Patrick takes no step to fulfil his engagement, and Isabel asks why. Patrick wishes that a hundred evils may enter him, and he 'fa oure the brim,' if ever he marries another; nevertheless he weds a duke's daughter. His bride has a fancy to see his son, and Patrick sends his aunt (or his grand-aunt, or his great-grand-aunt) to fetch the boy. Isabel dares any woman to take the bairn away. Patrick comes in person. Isabel repeats the words she had used to his aunt, and reminds him of the curse which he had conditionally wished himself at their last interview. The perjured man turns to go away, the hundred evils enter him, and he falls 'oure the brim.'

B has nearly the same story with additional circumstances. Patrick wishes that eleven devils may attend his last day should he wed another woman. When he goes to inquire how Isabel came to refuse the request he had made through his aunt, he takes the opportunity to make over to her child the third part of his land. She has two clerks, her cousins, at her call, who see to the legal formalities pertaining to this transfer; she commits the boy to one of these, and herself goes to an unco land to drive love out of her mind. We hear of nothing worse happening to Earl Patrick for selling his precious soul than his never getting further ben the church than the door.

C is a variety of B, but not half so long. Whether B has added or C omitted, no reader will much concern himself to know.

St. 7 (nearly) occurs in No 92, B 17, II, 313, and something similar in various ballads.

A

Kinloch MSS, I, 211; "obtained in the North Country, from the recitation of Mrs Charles."

1 THERE is a stane in yon water,
   It's lang or it grow green;
  It's a maid that maks her ain fortune,
   It'll never end its leen.

2 Burd Bell was na full fyfteen
   Till to service she did gae;
  Burd Bell was na full sixteen
   Till big wi bairn was scho.

*   *   *   *   *   *

3 'Burd Bell she is a gude woman,
   She bides at hame wi me;
  She never seeks to gang to church,
   But bides at hame wi me.'

4 It fell ance upon a day
   She fell in travail-pain;

He is gane to the stair-head
   Some ladies to call in.

5 'O gin ye hae a lass-bairn, Burd Bell,
   A lass-bairn though it be,
  Twenty ploughs bot and a mill
   Will mak ye lady free.

6 'But gin ye hae a son, Burd Bell,
   Ye'se be my wedded wife,

 .   .   .   .   .   .

  .   .   .   .   .   .'

7 The knichts they knack their white fingers,
   The ladies sat and sang,
  T was a' to cheer bonnie Burd Bell,
   She was far sunk in pain.

*   *   *   *   *   *   *

8 Earl Patrick is to his mither gane,
   As fast as he could hie:
  'An askin, an askin, dear mither,
   An askin I want frae thee.

9 'Burd Bell has born to me a son;
　　What sall I do her wi?'
　'Gie her what ye like, Patrick,
　　Mak na her your ladie.'

10 He has gane to bonnie Burd Bell,
　　Hir heart was pressd wi care :
　．　　．　　．　　．　　．　　．　　．

11 'My father will dee, bonnie Burd Bell,
　　My mither will do the same,
　And whan ye hear that they are gane
　　It 's then I 'll bring ye hame.'

12 Earl Patrick 's bigget to her a bour,
　　And strawn it round wi sand;
　He coverd it wi silver on the outside,
　　Wi the red gowd within.

13 It happened ance upon a day
　　She was kaiming his yellow hair,
　．　　．　　．　　．　　．　　．　　．

14 'Your father is dead, Earl Patrick,
　　Your mither is the same;
　And what is the reason, Earl Patrick,
　　Ye winna tak me hame?'

15 'I 've bigget to you a bonnie bour,
　　I 've strawn it round wi sand;
　I 've coverd it wi silver on the outside,
　　Wi gude red gowd within.

16 'If eer I marry anither woman,
　　Or bring anither hame,
　I wish a hundred evils may enter me,
　　And may I fa oure the brim!'

17 It was na very lang after this
　　That a duke's dochter he 's wed,
　Wi a waggon fu of gowd
　．　　．　　．　　．　　．　　．　　．

18 Burd Bell lookit oure her castle-wa,
　　And spied baith dale and down,

And there she saw Earl Patrick's aunt
　　Come riding to the town.

19 'What want ye here, Earl Patrick's aunt?
　　What want ye here wi me?'
　'I want Earl Patrick's bonnie young son;
　　His bride fain wad him see.'

20 'I wad like to see that woman or man,
　　Of high or low degree,
　That wad tak the bairn frae my foot
　　That I ance for bowd my knee.'

＊　＊　＊　＊　＊　＊　＊

21 'Burd Bell, she 's the bauldest woman
　　That ever I did see:'
　'It 's I 'll gang to bonnie Burd Bell,
　　She was never bauld to me.'

22 Burd Bell lookit oure her castle-wa,
　　Behauding brave dale and down,
　And there she spied him Earl Patrick
　　Slowly riding to the town.

23 'What said ye to my great-grand-aunt
　．　　．　　．　　．　　．　　．
　．　　．　　．　　．　　．　　．'

24 'I said nathing to your great-grand-aunt
　　But I will say to thee:
　I wad like to see the woman or man,
　　Of high or low degree,
　That wad tak the bairn frae my foot
　　I ance for bowd my knee.

25 'O dinna ye mind, Earl Patrick,
　　The vows ye made to me,
　That a hundred evils wad enter you
　　If ye provd fause to me?'

26 He 's turnd him richt and round about,
　　His horse head to the wind,
　The hundred evils enterd him,
　　And he fell oure the brim.

B

Buchan's Ballads of the North of Scotland, I, 76.

1 TAKE warning, a' ye young women,
    Of low station or hie,
Lay never your love upon a man
    Above your ain degree.

2 Thus I speak by Burd Isbel;
    She was a maid sae fair,
She laid her love on Sir Patrick,
    She 'll rue it for evermair.

3 And likewise, a' ye sprightly youths,
    Of low station or hie,
Lay never your love upon a maid
    Below your ain degree.

4 And thus I speak by Sir Patrick,
    Who was a knight sae rare;
He 's laid his love on Burd Isbel,
    He 'll rue it for evermair.

5 Burd Isbel was but ten years auld,
    To service she has gane;
And Burd Isbel was but fifteen
    Whan her young son came hame.

6 It fell ance upon a day
    Strong travelling took she;
None there was her bower within
    But Sir Patrick and she.

7 'This is a wark now, Sir Patrick,
    That we twa neer will end;
Ye 'll do you to the outer court
    And call some women in.'

8 He 's done him to the outer court,
    And stately there did stand;
Eleven ladies he 's calld in,
    Wi ae shake o his hand.

9 'Be favourable to Burd Isbel,
    Deal favourable if ye may;
Her kirking and her fair wedding
    Shall baith stand on ae day.

10 'Deal favourable to Burd Isbel,
    Whom I love as my life;
Ere this day month be come and gane,
    She 's be my wedded wife.'

11 Then he is on to his father,
    Fell low down on his knee;
Says, Will I marry Burd Isbel?
    She 's born a son to me.

12 'O marry, marry Burd Isbel,
    Or use her as ye like;
Ye 'll gar her wear the silks sae red
    And sae may ye the white.
O woud ye marry Burd Isbel,
    Make her your heart's delight?

13 'You want not lands nor rents, Patrick,
    You know your fortune 's free;
But ere you 'd marry Burd Isbel
    I 'd rather bury thee.

14 'Ye 'll build a bower for Burd Isbel,
    And set it round wi sand;
Make as much mirth in Isbel's bower
    As ony in a' the land.'

15 Then he is to his mother gane,
    Fell low down on his knee:
'O shall I marry Burd Isbel?
    She 's born a son to me.'

16 'O marry, marry Burd Isbel,
    Or use her as ye like;
Ye 'll gar her wear the silks sae red,
    And sae may ye the white.
O would ye marry Burd Isbel,
    Make her wi me alike?

17 'You want not lands and rents, Patrick,
    You know your fortune 's free;
But ere you marry Burd Isbel
    I 'd rather bury thee.

18 'Ye 'll build a bower to Burd Isbel,
    And set it round wi glass;
Make as much mirth in Isbel's bower
    As ony in a' the place.'

19 He 's done him down thro ha, thro ha,
    Sae has he in thro bower;
The tears ran frae his twa grey eyes,
    And loot them fast down pour.

20 'My father and my mother baith
    To age are coming on;
When they are dead and buried baith,
    Burd Isbel I 'll bring home.'

21 The words that passd atween these twa
 Ought never to be spoken;
 The vows that passd atween these twa
 Ought never to be broken.

22 Says he, If I another court,
 Or wed another wife,
 May eleven devils me attend
 At the end-day o my life.

23 But his father he soon did die,
 His mother nae lang behind;
 But Sir Patrick of Burd Isbel
 He now had little mind.

24 It fell ance upon a day,
 As she went out to walk,
 And there she saw him Sir Patrick,
 Going wi his hound and hawk.

25 'Stay still, stay still, now Sir Patrick,
 O stay a little wee,
 And think upon the fair promise
 Last year ye made to me.

26 'Now your father's dead, kind sir,
 And your mother the same;
 Yet nevertheless now, Sir Patrick,
 Ye're nae bringing me hame.'

27 'If the morn be a pleasant day,
 I mean to sail the sea,
 To spend my time in fair England,
 All for a month or three.'

28 He hadna been in fair England
 A month but barely ane
 Till he forgot her Burd Isbel,
 The mother of his son.

29 Some time he spent in fair England,
 And when returnd again
 He laid his love on a duke's daughter,
 And he has brought her hame.

30 Now he's forgot his first true love
 He ance lovd ower them a';
 But now the devil did begin
 To work between them twa.

31 When Sir Patrick he was wed,
 And all set down to dine,

Upon his first love, Burd Isbel,
 A thought ran in his mind.

32 He calld upon his gude grand-aunt
 To come right speedilie;
 Says, Ye'll gae on to Burd Isbel,
 Bring my young son to me.

33 She's taen her mantle her about,
 Wi gowd gloves on her hand,
 And she is on to Burd Isbel,
 As fast as she coud gang.

34 She haild her high, she haild her low,
 With stile in great degree:
 'O busk, O busk your little young son,
 For he maun gang wi me.'

35 'I woud fain see the one,' she said,
 'O low station or hie,
 Woud take the bairn frae my foot,
 For him I bowed my knee.

36 'I woud fain see the one,' she said,
 'O low station or mean,
 Woud take the bairn frae my foot
 Whom I own to be mine.'

37 Then she has done her hame again,
 As fast as gang coud she;
 'Present,' said he, 'my little young son,
 For him I wish to see.'

38 'Burd Isbel's a bauld woman,' she said,
 'As eer I yet spake wi;'
 But sighing said him Sir Patrick,
 She ne'er was bauld to me.

39 But he's dressd in his best array,
 His gowd rod in his hand,
 And he is to Burd Isbel's bower,
 As fast as he coud gang.

40 'O how is this, Burd Isbel,' he said,
 'So ill ye've used me?
 What gart you anger my gude grand-aunt,
 That I did send to thee?'

41 'If I hae angerd your gude grand-aunt,
 O then sae lat it be;
 I said naething to your gude grand-aunt
 But what I'll say to thee.

42 ' Iwoud fain see the one, I said,
   O low station or hie,
Wha woud take this bairn frae my foot,
   For him I bowed the knee.

43 ' I woud fain see the one, I said,
   O low station or mean,
Woud take this bairn frae my foot
   Whom I own to be mine.'

44 ' O if I had some counsellers here,
   And clerks to seal the band,
I woud infeft your son this day
   In third part o my land.'

45 ' I hae two couzins, Scottish clerks,
   Wi bills into their hand,
An ye 'll infeft my son this day
   In third part o your land.'

46 Then he calld in her Scottish clerks,
   Wi bills into their hand,

And he 's infeft his son that day
   The third part o his land.

47 To ane o these young clerks she spoke,
   Clerk John it was his name ;
Says, Of my son I gie you charge
   Till I return again.

48 ' Ye 'll take here my son, clerk John,
   Learn him to dance and sing,
And I will to some unco land,
   Drive love out of my mind.

49 ' And ye 'll take here my son, clerk John,
   Learn him to hunt the roe,
And I will to some unco land ;
   Now lat Sir Patrick go.

50 ' But I 'll cause this knight at church-door stand,
   For a' his noble train ;
For selling o his precious soul
   Dare never come farther ben.'

C

Motherwell's MS., p. 440.

1 ALL young maidens fair and gay,
   Whatever your station be,
Never lay your love upon a man
   Above your own degree.

2 I speak it all by Bird Isabel ;
   She was her father's dear,
She laid her love on Earl Patrick,
   Which she rues ever mair.

3 ' Oh, we began a wark, Patrick,
   That we two cannot end ;
Go you unto the outer stair
   And call some women in.'

4 He 's gone unto the outer stair,
   And up in it did stand,
And did bring in eleven ladies,
   With one sign of his hand.

5 He did him to the doctor's shop,
   As fast as he could gang,
But ere the doctor could get there
   Bird Isabel bore a son.

6 But he has courted a duke's daughter,
   Lived far beyont the sea ;
Burd Isabel's parents were but mean,
   They had not gear to gie.

7 He has courted a duke's daughter,
   Lived far beyond the foam ;
Burd Isabel was a mean woman,
   And tocher she had none.

8 Now it fell once upon a day
   His wedding day was come ;
He 's hied him to his great-grand-aunt,
   As fast as he could gang.

9 Says, Will you go this errand, aunt?
   Go you this errand for me,
And if I live and bruick my life
   I will go as far for thee.

10 ' Go and bring me Bird Isbel's son,
   Dressed in silks so fine,
And if he live to be a man
   He shall heir all my land.'

11 Now she went hailing to the door,
   And hailing ben the floor,

And Isabel styled her madame,
And she, her Isabel dear.

12 'I came to take Earl Patrick's son,
To dress in silks so fine;
For if he live to be a man
He is to heir his land.'

13 'Oh is there ever a woman,' she said,
'Of high station or mean,
Daur take this bairn from my knee?
For he is called mine.

14 'Oh is there ever a woman,' she said,
'Of mean station or hie,
Daur tak this bairn frae my foot?
For him I bowed my knee.'

15 His aunt went hailing to his door,
And hailing ben the floor,
And she has styled him, Patrick,
And [he] her, aunty dear.

16 She says, I have been east and west,
And far beyond the sea,
But Isabel is the boldest woman
That ever my eyes did see.

17 'You surely dream, my aunty dear,
For that can never be;

Burd Isabel 's not a bold woman,
She never was bold to me.'

18 Now he went hailing to her door,
And hailing ben the floor,
And she has styled him, Patrick,
And he her, Isabel dear.

19 'O ye have angered my great-grand-aunt;
You know she 's a lady free;'
'I said naught to your great-grand-aunt
But what I 'll say to thee.

20 'Oh is there ever a woman, I said,
Of high station or mean,
Daur tak this bairn from my knee?
For he is called mine.

21 'Oh is there ever a woman, I said,
Of mean station or hie,
Daur tak this bairn from my foot?
For him I bowed my knee.

22 'But I 'll cause you stand at good church-door,
For all your noble train;
For selling of your precious soul,
You shall not get further ben.'

258

BROUGHTY WA'S

a. 'Helen,' Buchan's MSS, I, 233.

b. 'Burd Hellen,' or, 'Browghty Wa's,' Harris MS., fol. 17 b; from Mrs Harris.

A YOUNG woman is carried off from Broughty Castle, near Dundee, by a body of armed Highlanders. Her lover, who is making her a visit at the time, is either taken along with her — an unnecessary incumbrance, one would think — or follows her. The pair go out to take the air; she throws herself into a river; her lover leaps in after her and is drowned. She kilts up her clothes and makes her way to Dundee, congratulating herself that she had learned to swim for liberty.

Stanza 9, as it runs in b, is a reminiscence of 'Bonny Baby Livingston,' and 13 recalls 'Child Waters,' or 'The Knight and the Shepherd's Daughter.'

1 BURD HELEN was her mother's dear,
    Her father's heir to be;
He was the laird of Broughty Walls,
    And the provost o Dundee.

2 Burd Helen she was much admired
    By all that were round about;
Unto Hazelan she was betrothed,
    Her virgin days were out.

3 Glenhazlen was a comely youth,
    And virtuous were his friends;
He left the schools o bonny Dundee
    And on to Aberdeen.

4 It fell upon a Christmas Day
    Burd Helen was left alone
For to keep her father's towers;
    They stand two miles from town.

5 Glenhazlen's on to Broughty Walls,
    Was thinking to win in;
But the wind it blew, and the rain dang on
    And wat him to the skin.

6 He was very well entertaind,
    Baith for his bed and board,
Till a band o men surrounded them,
    Well armd wi spear and sword.

7 They hurried her along wi them,
    Lockd up her maids behind;

They threw the keys out-ower the walls,
    That none the plot might find.

8 They hurried her along wi them,
    Ower mony a rock and glen,
But, all that they could say or do.
    From weeping would not refrain.

9 'The Hiland hills are hie, hie hills,
    The Hiland hills are hie;
They are no like the banks o Tay,
    Or bonny town o Dundee.'

10 It fell out ance upon a day
    They went to take the air;
She threw hersell upon the stream,
    Against wind and despair.

11 It was sae deep he coudna wide,
    Boats werna to be found,
But he leapt in after himself,
    And sunk down like a stone.

12 She kilted up her green claiding
    A little below her knee,
And never rest nor was undrest
    Till she reachd again Dundee.

13 'I learned this at Broughty Walls,
    At Broughty near Dundee,
That if water were my prison strong
    I would swim for libertie.'

---

a. 7^2. Tuckd.
b. 1^4. the *wanting*. 2^8. But to Hunglen.
   3^2. were *wanting*.
   4^1. fell oot once upon a time. 4^3. All for.
   4^4. stand ten.
   5^1. Glenhazlen he cam ridin bye.
   5^2. An thinkin to get in.
   $7^1, 8^1$. They hiesed.
   7^2. Locked up.
   7^8. An flang. 8^4. To weep she wald.
   $9^{3,4}$. An if you wald my favour gain, Oh, tak
     me to Dundee!
   10^1. once upon a time.

10^2. went oot to.
10^8. into the. 10^4. Between.
11^1. The stream was deep.
11^2. So he: after her himsell.
After 11:

   'The Highland hills are high, high hills,
     The Highland hills are hie;
   They 're no like the pleasant banks o Tay,
     Nor the bonnie town o Dundee'.

13^8. water waur my prison-walls.
13^4. I could.

259

LORD THOMAS STUART

Maidment's North Countrie Garland, p. 1.

———•———

LORD THOMAS STUART has married a young countess, and has given her Strathbogie and Aboyne for a morning-gift. The lady has a desire to see these places. As they are on their way thither (from Edinburgh), her husband is attacked with a pain which obliges him to turn back; he tells her to ride on, and she seems so to do. The pain proves to be beyond the skill of leeches. Lord Thomas begs his father to see that his wife gets what he has given her. He dies; the horses turn wild in the stables, the hounds howl on the leash. Lady Stuart has the usual dream (No 74, A 8, B 11, etc.). She comes back wringing her hands; she knows by the horses that are standing about the house that the burial is preparing.

———•———

1 THOMAS STUART was a lord,
    A lord of mickle land;
  He used to wear a coat of gold,
    But now his grave is green.

2 Now he has wooed the young countess,
    The Countess of Balquhin,
  An given her for a morning-gift
    Strathboggie and Aboyne.

3 But women's wit is aye willful,
    Alas that ever it was sae!
  She longed to see the morning-gift
    That her gude lord to her gae.

4 When steeds were saddled an weel bridled,
    An ready for to ride,
  There came a pain on that gude lord,
    His back, likewise his side.

5 He said, Ride on, my lady fair,
    May goodness be your guide!
  For I'm sae sick an weary that
    No farther can I ride.

6 Now ben did come his father dear,
    Wearing a golden band;
  Says, Is there nae leech in Edinburgh
    Can cure my son from wrang?

7 'O leech is come, an leech is gane,
    Yet, father, I'm aye waur;
  There's not a leech in Edinbro
    Can death from me debar.

8 'But be a friend to my wife, father,
    Restore to her her own;
  Restore to her my morning-gift,
    Strathboggie and Aboyne.

9 'It had been gude for my wife, father,
    To me she'd born a son;
  He would have got my land an rents,
    Where they lie out an in.

10 'It had been gude for my wife, father,
    To me she'd born an heir;
  He would have got my land an rents,
    Where they lie fine an fair.'

11 The steeds they strave into their stables,
    The boys could'nt get them bound ;
    The hounds lay howling on the leech,
    Cause their master was behind.

12 ' I dreamed a dream since late yestreen,
    I wish it may be good,
    That our chamber was full of swine,
    An our bed full of blood.'

13 I saw a woman come from the West,
    Full sore wringing her hands,

    And aye she cried, Ohon, alas !
    My good lord 's broken bands.

14 As she came by my good lord's bower,
    Saw mony black steeds an brown :
    ' I 'm feared it be mony unco lords
    Havin my love from town ! '

15 As she came by my gude lord's bower,
    Saw mony black steeds an grey :
    ' I 'm feared it 's mony unco lords
    Havin my love to the clay ! '

260

LORD THOMAS AND LADY MARGARET

A. a. ' Lord Thomas,' Motherwell's MS., p. 407. b.
' Lord Thomas and Lady Margaret,' the same, p. 71.

B. ' Clerk Tamas,' Buchan's Ballads of the North of
Scotland, I, 43.

CHRISTIE, who gives B, " epitomized and slightly changed," under the title ' Clerk Tamas and Fair Annie,' Traditional Ballad Airs, II, 12, says that he can trace the ballad, traditionally, far into the last century.

A. Lord Thomas goes a-hunting, and Lady Margaret rides after him ; when he sees her following, he orders his servants to hunt her far from him, and they hunt her high and low. She comes upon a tall young man, and begs ' relief ' from him for a lady wronged in love and chased from her ' country.' No relief is to be had from him unless she will renounce all other men and be his wife. After a time, Lady Margaret, sewing at her window, observes a vagrant body, who turns out to be Lord Thomas, reduced to beggary ; he has been banished from his own country, and asks relief. No relief from her ; she would hang him were he within her bower. Not so, says Lord Thomas ; rather he would kill her lord with his broadsword and carry her off. Not so, says Lady Margaret, but you must come in and drink with me. She poisons three bottles of wine, and pretends

to be his taster. Lord Thomas drinks away merrily, but soon feels the poison. I am wearied with this drinking, he says. And so was I when you set your hounds at me, she replies ; but you shall be buried as if you were one of my own.

B has Clerk Tamas for Lord Thomas, and Fair Annie for Lady Margaret. Tamas has loved Annie devotedly, but now hates her and the lands she lives in. Annie goes to ask him to pity her ; he sees her coming, as he lies ' over his shot-window,' and orders his men to hunt her to the sea. A captain, lying ' over his ship - window,' sees Annie driven from the town, and offers to take her in if she will forsake friends and lands for him. The story goes on much as in A.

A 8 is borrowed from ' The Douglas Tragedy,' see No 7, C 9. B $14^{3,4}$ is a commonplace, which, in inferior traditional ballads, is often, as here, an out-of-place. B 15, 16 is another commonplace, of the silly sort : see No 87, B 3, 4, D 4, 5, and Buchan's ' Lady Isabel,' 20, 21.

A

a. Motherwell's MS., p. 407; from the recitation of Mrs Parkhill, Maxweltown, 28 September, 1825 (with variations, furnished by another person of the same neighborhood, interlined). b. Motherwell's MS., p. 71; from Miss ——, Glasgow.

1 LORD THOMAS is to the hunting gone,
    To hunt the fallow deer;
  Lady Margaret's to the greenwood shaw,
    To see her lover hunt there.

2 He has looked over his left shoulder,
    To see what might be seen,
  And there he saw Lady Margaret,
    As she was riding her lane.

3 He called on his servants all,
    By one, by two, by three:
  'Go hunt, go hunt that wild woman,
    Go hunt her far from me!'

4 They hunted her high, they hunted her low,
    They hunted her over the plain,
  And the red scarlet robes Lady Margaret had on
    Would never be mended again.

5 They hunted her high, they hunted her low,
    They hunted her over the plain,
  Till at last she spy'd a tall young man,
    As he was riding alane.

6 'Some relief, some relief, thou tall young man!
    Some relief I pray thee grant me!
  For I am a lady deep wronged in love,
    And chased from my own countrie.'

7 'No relief, no relief, thou lady fair,
    No relief will I grant unto thee
  Till once thou renounce all the men in the world
    My wedded wife for to be.'

8 Then he set her on a milk-white steed,
    Himself upon a gray,
  And he has drawn his hat over his face,
    And chearfully they rode away.

9 Lady Margaret was at her bower-window,
    Sewing her silken seam,
  And there she spy'd, like a wandering bodie,
    Lord Thomas begging alane.

10 'Some relief, some relief, thou lady fair!
    Some relief, I pray thee grant me!
  For I am a puir auld doited carle,
    And banishd from my ain countrie.'

11 'No relief, no relief, thou perjured man,
    No relief will I grant unto thee;
  For oh, if I had thee within my bower,
    There hanged dead thou would be.'

12 'No such thing, Lady Margaret,' he said,
    'Such a thing would never be;
  For with my broadsword I would kill thy wedded lord,
    And carry thee far off with me.'

13 'Oh no, no! Lord Thomas,' she said,
    'Oh, no such things must be;
  For I have wine in my cellars,
    And you must drink with me.'

14 Lady Margaret then called her servants all,
    By one, by two, by three:
  'Go fetch me the bottles of blude-red wine,
    That Lord Thomas may drink with me.'

15 They brought her the bottles of blude-red wine,
    By one, by two, by three,
  And with her fingers long and small
    She poisond them all three.

16 She took the cup in her lilly-white hand,
    Betwixt her finger and her thumb,
  She put it to her red rosy lips,
    But never a drop went down.

17 Then he took the cup in his manly hand,
    Betwixt his finger and his thumb,
  He put it to his red rosy lips,
    And so merrily it ran down.

18 'Oh, I am wearied drinking with thee, Margaret!
    I am wearied drinking with thee!'
  'And so was I,' Lady Margaret said,
    'When thou hunted thy hounds after me.'

19 'But I will bury thee, Lord Thomas,' she said,
    'Just as if thou wert one of my own;
  And when that my good lord comes home
    I will say thou's my sister's son.'

B

Buchan's Ballads of the North of Scotland, I, 43.

1 CLERK TAMAS lovd her fair Annie
    As well as Mary lovd her son;
But now he hates her fair Annie,
    And hates the lands that she lives in.

2 'Ohon, alas!' said fair Annie,
    'Alas! this day I fear I 'll die;
But I will on to sweet Tamas,
    And see gin he will pity me.'

3 As Tamas lay ower his shott-window,
    Just as the sun was gaen down,
There he beheld her fair Annie,
    As she came walking to the town.

4 'O where are a' my well-wight men,
    I wat, that I pay meat and fee,
For to lat a' my hounds gang loose
    To hunt this vile whore to the sea.'

5 The hounds they knew the lady well,
    And nane o them they woud her bite,
Save ane that is ca'd Gaudywhere,
    I wat he did the lady smite.

6 'O wae mat worth ye, Gaudywhere!
    An ill reward this is to me;
For ae bit that I gae the lave,
    I 'm very sure I 've gien you three.

7 'For me, alas! there 's nae remeid,
    Here comes the day that I maun die;
I ken ye lovd your master well,
    And sae, alas for me! did I.'

8 A captain lay ower his ship-window,
    Just as the sun was gaen down;
There he beheld her fair Annie,
    As she was hunted frae the town.

9 'Gin ye 'll forsake father and mither,
    And sae will ye your friends and kin,
Gin ye 'll forsake your lands sae broad,
    Then come and I will take you in.'

10 'Yes, I 'll forsake baith father and mither,
    And sae will I my friends and kin;
Yes, I 'll forsake my lands sae broad,
    And come, gin ye will take me in.'

11 Then a' thing gaed frae fause Tamas,
    And there was naething byde him wi;
Then he thought lang for Arrandella,
    It was fair Annie for to see.

12 'How do ye now, ye sweet Tamas?
    And how gaes a' in your countrie?'
'I 'll do better to you than ever I 've done,
    Fair Annie, gin ye 'll come an see.'

13 'O Guid forbid,' said fair Annie,
    'That e'er the like fa in my hand!
Woud I forsake my ain gude lord
    And follow you, a gae-through-land?

14 'Yet nevertheless now, sweet Tamas,
    Ye 'll drink a cup o wine wi me,
And nine times in the live lang day
    Your fair claithing shall changed be.'

15 Fair Annie pat it till her cheek,
    Sae did she till her milk-white chin,
Sae did she till her flattering lips,
    But never a drap o wine gaed in.

16 Tamas pat it till his cheek,
    Sae did he till his dimpled chin;
He pat it till his rosy lips,
    And then the well o wine gaed in.

17 'These pains,' said he, 'are ill to bide;
    Here is the day that I maun die;
O take this cup frae me, Annie,
    For o the same I am weary.'

18 'And sae was I o you, Tamas,
    When I was hunted to the sea;
But I 'se gar bury you in state,
    Which is mair than ye 'd done to me.'

————◆————

A. a. 12¹. (no such thing) *a second time; inserted apparently by Motherwell.*

Interlineations: 2². what he might spy.
    2⁴. riding by.

8³. his broadsword from his side.

8⁴. And slowly.

9². To see what she might spy.

9³. spy'd Lord Thomas.

9⁴. A begging along the highway.

10³. puir oppressed man.

15¹. They glowred, but they brought the blude-red wine.

b. 1¹. is a. 1². the green wood oer.

1³. Lady Margaret has followed him.

1⁴. To seek her own true-love. 2. *Wanting.*

3¹. He has called up his merrie men all.

3³. Hunt away, hunt away this.

3⁴. her away from. 4¹, 5¹. and they.

4², 5². Till she ran quite over.

4³. The scarlet robes. 4⁴. They can never.

5³. And there she spied. 5⁴. Just as.

6². Some relief, some relief grant me.

6³. lady that is deep, deep in.

6⁴. And I am banished from. 7¹. fair ladie.

7². No relief, no relief I 'll grant thee.

7³. Unless you forsake : in this.

7⁴. And my : you will be.

8¹. He has mounted her.

8². And himself on a dapple.

8³. The buglet horn hung done by there side.

8⁴. And so slowly as they both.

9¹. One day L. M. at her castle-window.

9². Was sewing. 9³. espied L. T.

9⁴. A begging all. 10¹. fair ladie.

10². Some relief, some relief grant me.

10³,⁴, 11. No relief, no relief, Lord Thomas, she said, But hanged thou shalt be.

12¹. O no, O no, Lady.

12². For no such things must be.

12³. But with : I will.

12⁴. And I 'll ride far off with thee.

13¹. O no, O no. 13². O no : must not.

14¹. She has called up her.

14², 15². and by.

14³. Go bring to me a bottle of wine.

15¹. her up a bottle of wine.

15³. so long. 15⁴. The rank poison in put she.

16, 17. *Wanting.*

18¹. I 'm wearied, I 'm wearied, Lady Margaret, he said.

18². O I 'm : talking to.

18³. I, Lord Thomas, she.

18⁴. you hounded your dogs.

19¹. bury you as one of my own.

19². And all in my own ground.

19⁴. say you 're.

261

LADY ISABEL

'Lady Isabel,' Buchan's Ballads of the North of Scotland, **I, 129.**

LADY ISABEL'S step-mother accuses her of being her father's leman; he gives her finer gowns than he gives his wife. Isabel replies that, in the first place, she is young, which is reason enough why her gowns should be fairer; but that, as a matter of fact, a lover of hers over seas sends her ten gowns to one that her father buys her. The step-mother invites Isabel to take wine with her. Isabel wishes first to go to a church. At this church she sees her own mother, and asks whether she shall flee the country or drink what has been prepared for her. Her mother enjoins her to drink the dowie drink; before she is cold she will be in a better place. Upon returning, Isabel is again pressed to take wine, and again begs to be excused for the moment; she wishes to see her maids in the garden. She gives her maids ring and brooch. A third time the step-mother proposes that they shall take wine together; the daughter, with due courtesy, begs the elder to begin. The step-mother goes through certain motions customary in ballads of this description, and swallows not a drop; Isabel duly repeats the mummery, but drinks. She has time to tell this wicked dame that their beds will be made very far apart. The step-mother goes mad.

Stanzas 20, 21, as has already been intimated, are a commonplace, and a foolish one. Stanza 24, in various forms, not always well adapted to the particular circumstances, ends several ballads: as No 64, F; No 65, H; No 66, A 28, 29, B 20, 21; No 67, B; No 70, B.

Translated by Gerhard, p. 161.

———

1   'T was early on a May morning
    Lady Isabel combd her hair;
  But little kent she, or the morn
    She woud never comb it mair.

2   'T was early on a May morning
    Lady Isabel rang the keys;
  But little kent she, or the morn
    A fey woman she was.

3   Ben it came her step-mother,
    As white 's the lily flower:
  'It 's tauld me this day, Isabel,
    You are your father's whore.'

4   'O them that tauld you that, mother,
    I wish they neer drink wine;
  For if I be the same woman
    My ain sell drees the pine.

5   'And them that 's tauld you that, mother,
    I wish they neer drink ale;
  For if I be the same woman
    My ain sell drees the dail.'

6   'It may be very well seen, Isabel,
    It may be very well seen;
  He buys to you the damask gowns,
    To me the dowie green.'

7   'Ye are of age and I am young,
    And young amo my flowers;
  The fairer that my claithing be,
    The mair honour is yours.

8   'I hae a love beyond the sea,
    And far ayont the faem;
  For ilka gown my father buys me,
    My ain luve sends me ten.'

9   'Come ben, come ben now, Lady Isabel,
    And drink the wine wi me;
  I hae twa jewels in ae coffer,
    And ane o them I 'll gie [ye].'

10   'Stay still, stay still, my mother dear,
    Stay still a little while,
  Till I gang into Marykirk;
    It 's but a little mile.'

11   When she gaed on to Marykirk,
    And into Mary's quire,
  There she saw her ain mother
    Sit in a gowden chair.

12   'O will I leave the lands, mother?
    Or shall I sail the sea?
  Or shall I drink this dowie drink
    That is prepar'd for me?'

13   'Ye winna leave the lands, daughter,
    Nor will ye sail the sea,
  But ye will drink this dowie drink
    This woman 's prepar'd for thee.

14   'Your bed is made in a better place
    Than ever hers will be,
  And ere ye 're cauld into the room
    Ye will be there wi me.'

15   'Come in, come in now, Lady Isabel,
    And drink the wine wi me;
  I hae twa jewels in ae coffer,
    And ane o them I 'll gie [ye].'

16   'Stay still, stay still, my mother dear,
    Stay still a little wee,
  Till I gang to yon garden green,
    My Maries a' to see.'

17 To some she gae the broach, the broach,
   To some she gae a ring;
   But wae befa her step-mother!
   To her she gae nae thing.

18 'Come in, come in now, Lady Isabel,
   And drink the wine wi me;
   I hae twa jewels in ae coffer,
   And ane o them I 'll gie [ye].'

19 Slowly to the bower she came,
   And slowly enterd in,
   And being full o courtesie,
   Says, Begin, mother, begin.

20 She put it till her cheek, her cheek,
   Sae did she till her chin,
   Sae did she till her fu fause lips,
   But never a drap gaed in.

21 Lady Isabel put it till her cheek,
   Sae did she till her chin,
   Sae did she till her rosy lips,
   And the rank poison gaed in.

22 'O take this cup frae me, mother,
   O take this cup frae me;
   My bed is made in a better place
   Than ever yours will be.

23 'My bed is in the heavens high,
   Amang the angels fine;
   But yours is in the lowest hell,
   To drie torment and pine.'

24 Nae moan was made for Lady Isabel
   In bower where she lay dead,
   But a' was for that ill woman,
   In the fields mad she gaed.

262

LORD LIVINGSTON

"Lord Livingston,' Buchan's Ballads of the North of Scotland, II, 39.

As far as can be made out, Livingston and Seaton engage themselves to play against one another at some game, the victor expecting to stand the better in the eyes of a lady. They then proceed to Edinburgh castle, where a lady, whose 'gowns seem like green,' marshals the company in pairs, and chooses Livingston for her own partner. This preference enrages Seaton, who challenges Livingston to fight with him the next day. Up to this point the pairing may have been for a dance, or what not, but now we are told that Livingston and the fair dame are laid in the same bed, and further on that they were wedded that same night. In the morning Livingston arms himself for his fight; he declines to let his lady dress herself in man's clothes and fight in his stead. On his way 'to plain fields' a witch warns him that she has had the dream which Sweet William dreams in No 74, and others elsewhere. Livingston is 'slain,' but for all that stands presently bleeding by his lady's knee: see No 73, B 34, D 17. She begs him to hold out but half an hour, and every leech in Edinburgh shall come to him: see No 88, A 12, etc. He orders his lands to be dealt to the auld that may not, the young that cannot, etc.: see No 92, A 10, B 15. The lady declares that it was known from her birth that she was to marry a knight and lose him the next day. She will now do for his sake what other ladies would not be equal to (and which nevertheless many other ballad-ladies have undertaken, as in No 69 and else-

where). When seven years are near an end
her heart breaks.

This ballad, or something like it, was
known at the end of the last century. The
story has a faint resemblance to that of ' Armstrong and Musgrave,' a broadside printed in
the last quarter of the seventeenth century:
Crawford Ballads, No 123, Old Ballads, 1723,
I, 175; Evans, Old Ballads, 1777, II, 70.

Pinkerton acknowledges that he composed the
' Lord Livingston' of his Tragic Ballads,
1781, p. 69, but he says that he had " small
lines from tradition." (Ancient Scotish Poems, 1786, I, cxxxi.) Pinkerton's ballad
is the one which Buchan refers to, II, 308.
It is translated by Grundtvig, Engelske og
skotske Folkeviser, p. 139, No 21.

1 IT fell about the Lammas time,
    When wightsmen won their hay,
  A' the squires in merry Linkum
    Went a' forth till a play.

2 They playd until the evening tide,
    The sun was gaeing down;
  A lady thro plain fields was bound,
    A lily leesome thing.

3 Two squires that for this lady pledged,
    In hopes for a renown,
  The one was calld the proud Seaton,
    The other Livingston.

4 ' When will ye, Michaell o Livingston,
    Wad for this lady gay?'
  ' To-morrow, to-morrow,' said Livingston,
    ' To-morrow, if you may.'

5 Then they hae wadded their wagers,
    And laid their pledges down;
  To the high castle o Edinbro
    They made them ready boun.

6 The chamber that they did gang in,
    There it was daily dight;
  The kipples were like the gude red gowd,
    As they stood up in hight,
  And the roof-tree like the siller white,
    And shin'd like candles bright.

7 The lady fair into that ha
    Was comely to be seen;
  Her kirtle was made o the pa,
    Her gowns seemd o the green.

8 Her gowns seemd like green, like green,
    Her kirtle o the pa;

  A siller wand intill her hand,
    She marshalld ower them a'.

9 She gae every knight a lady bright,
    And every squire a may;
  Her own sell chose him Livingston,
    They were a comely tway.

10 Then Seaton started till his foot,
    The fierce flame in his ee:
  ' On the next day, wi sword in hand,
    On plain fields meet ye me.'

11 When bells were rung, and mass was sung,
    And a' man bound for bed,
  Lord Livingston and his fair dame
    In bed were sweetly laid.

12 The bed, the bed where they lay in
    Was coverd wi the pa;
  A covering o the gude red gowd
    Lay nightly ower the twa.

13 So they lay there, till on the morn
    The sun shone on their feet;
  Then up it raise him Livingston
    To draw to him a weed.

14 The first an weed that he drew on
    Was o the linen clear;
  The next an weed that he drew on,
    It was a weed o weir.

15 The niest an weed that he drew on
    Was gude iron and steel;
  Twa gloves o plate, a gowden helmet,
    Became that hind chiel weel.

16 Then out it speaks that lady gay —
    A little forbye stood she —
'I 'll dress mysell in men's array,
    Gae to the fields for thee.'

17 'O God forbid,' said Livingston,
    'That eer I dree the shame;
My lady slain in plain fields,
    And I coward knight at hame!'

18 He scarcely travelled frae the town
    A mile but barely twa
Till he met wi a witch-woman,
    I pray to send her wae!

19 'This is too gude a day, my lord,
    To gang sae far frae town;
This is too gude a day, my lord,
    On field to make you boun.

20 'I dreamd a dream concerning thee,
    O read ill dreams to guid!
Your bower was full o milk-white swans,
    Your bride's bed full o bluid.'

21 'O bluid is gude,' said Livingston,
    'To bide it whoso may;
If I be frae yon plain fields,
    Nane knew the plight I lay.'

22 Then he rade on to plain fields
    As swift 's his horse coud hie,
And there he met the proud Seaton,
    Come boldly ower the lee.

23 'Come on to me now, Livingston,
    Or then take foot and flee;
This is the day that we must try
    Who gains the victorie.'

24 Then they fought with sword in hand
    Till they were bluidy men;
But on the point o Seaton's sword
    Brave Livingston was slain.

25 His lady lay ower castle-wa,
    Beholding dale and down,

When Blenchant brave, his gallant steed,
    Came prancing to the town.

26 'O where is now my ain gude lord
    He stays sae far frae me?'
'O dinna ye see your ain gude lord
    Stand bleeding by your knee?'

27 'O live, O live, Lord Livingston,
    The space o ae half hour,
There 's nae a leech in Edinbro town
    But I 'll bring to your door.'

28 'Awa wi your leeches, lady,' he said,
    'Of them I 'll be the waur;
There 's nae a leech in Edinbro town
    That can strong death debar.

29 'Ye 'll take the lands o Livingston
    And deal them liberallie,
To the auld that may not, the young that can-
    not,
    And blind that does na see,
And help young maidens' marriages,
    That has nae gear to gie.'

30 'My mother got it in a book,
    The first night I was born,
I woud be wedded till a knight,
    And him slain on the morn.

31 'But I will do for my love's sake
    What ladies woudna thole;
Ere seven years shall hae an end,
    Nae shoe 's gang on my sole.

32 'There 's never lint gang on my head,
    Nor kame gang in my hair,
Nor ever coal nor candle-light
    Shine in my bower mair.'

33 When seven years were near an end,
    The lady she thought lang,
And wi a crack her heart did brake,
    And sae this ends my sang.

263

THE NEW–SLAIN KNIGHT

'The New-Slain Knight,' Buchan's Ballads of the North of Scotland, I, 197.

———◆———

A KNIGHT (who twaddles in the first person at the beginning) finds a maid sleeping under a hedge, wakes her, and tells her that he has seen a dead man in her father's garden. She asks about the dead man's hawk, hound, sword. His hawk and hound were gone, his horse was tied to a tree, a bloody sword lay under his head. She asks about his clothes, and receives a description, with the addition that his hair was bonny and new combed. 'I combed it late yesterday!' says the lady. 'Who now will shoe my foot, and glove my hand, and father my bairn?' The knight offers himself for all these, but the lady will commit herself only to Heaven. The knight, after knacking his fingers quite superfluously, unmasks; he has only been making a trial of her truth.

A large part of this piece is imitated or taken outright from very well known ballads (as has already been pointed out by the editor of the Ballad Minstrelsy of Scotland, 1871, p. 345): 5–8 from 'Young Johnstone,' No 88; 10, 11 from 'The Lass of Roch Royal,' No 76 (see particularly E 1–4, and compare No 66, A 24, etc.); for $13^{1,2}$ see No 91, B 5^1, 6^1, 7^1, D $7^{1,2}$, No 257, A 7.

Grundtvig notes that this piece is of the same description as the Danish 'Troskabspröven,' Danmarks gamle Folkeviser, IV, 553, No 252, one version of which is translated by Prior, III, 289, No 146. Naturally, the fidelity of maid or wife is celebrated in the ballads of every tongue and people. This particular ballad, so far as it is original, is of very ordinary quality. The ninth stanza is pretty, but not quite artless.

Translated by Grundtvig, Engelske og skotske Folkeviser, p. 294, No 46.

———◆———

1 MY heart is lighter than the poll;
   My folly made me glad,
As on my rambles I went out,
   Near by a garden-side.

2 I walked on, and farther on,
   Love did my heart engage;
There I spied a well-faird maid,
   Lay sleeping near a hedge.

3 Then I kissd her with my lips
   And stroked her with my hand:
'Win up, win up, ye well-faird maid,
   This day ye sleep oer lang.

4 'This dreary sight that I hae seen
   Unto my heart gives pain;

At the south side o your father's garden,
   I see a knight lies slain.'

5 'O what like was his hawk, his hawk?
   Or what like was his hound?
And what like was the trusty brand
   This new-slain knight had on?'

6 'His hawk and hound were from him gone,
   His steed tied to a tree;
A bloody brand beneath his head,
   And on the ground lies he.'

7 'O what like was his hose, his hose?
   And what like were his shoon?
And what like was the gay clothing
   This new-slain knight had on?'

8 'His coat was of the red scarlet,
  His waistcoat of the same ;
His hose were of the bonny black,
  And shoon laced with cordin.

9 'Bonny was his yellow hair,
  For it was new combd down ; '
Then, sighing sair, said the lady fair,
  'I combd it late yestreen.

10 ' O wha will shoe my fu fair foot ?
  Or wha will glove my hand ?
Or wha will father my dear bairn,
  Since my love 's dead and gane ? '

11 ' O I will shoe your fu fair foot,
  And I will glove your hand ;

And I 'll be father to your bairn,
  Since your love 's dead and gane.'

12 'I winna father my bairn,' she said,
  'Upon an unkent man ;
I 'll father it on the King of Heaven,
  Since my love 's dead and gane.'

13 The knight he knackd his white fingers,
  The lady tore her hair ;
He 's drawn the mask from off his face,
  Says, Lady, mourn nae mair.

14 'For ye are mine, and I am thine,
  I see your love is true ;
And if I live and brook my life
  Ye 'se never hae cause to rue.'

10¹, 11¹. fair fu.

264

THE WHITE FISHER

'The White Fisher,' Buchan's Ballads of the North of Scotland, I, 200.

A YOUNG lord, Willie, asks his 'gay lady' whose the child is that she is going with. She owns that a priest is the father, which does not appear to disconcert Willie. A boy is born, and the mother charges Willie to throw him into the sea, 'never to return till white fish he bring hame.' Willie takes the boy (now called his son) to his mother, and tells her that his 'bride' is a king's daughter ; upon which his mother, who had had an ill opinion of the lady, promises to do as well by Willie's son as she had done by Willie. Returning to his wife, he finds her weeping and repining for the 'white fisher' that she had 'sent to the sea.' Willie offers her a cordial ; she says that the man who could have drowned her son would be capable of poison-ing her. Willie then tells her that his mother has the boy in charge ; she is consoled, and declares that if he had not been the father she should not have been the mother.

To make this story hang together at all, we must suppose that the third and fourth stanzas are tropical, and that Willie was the priest ; or else that they are sarcastic, and are uttered in bitter resentment of Willie's suspicion, or affected suspicion. But we need not trouble ourselves much to make these counterfeits reasonable. Those who utter them rely confidently upon our taking folly and jargon as the marks of genuineness. The white fisher is a trumpery fancy ; 2, 7, 8, 12 are frippery commonplaces.

1 'IT is a month, and isna mair,
   Love, sin I was at thee,
But find a stirring in your side ;
   Who may the father be ?

2 'Is it to a lord of might,
   Or baron of high degree?
Or is it to the little wee page
   That rode along wi me?'

3 'It is not to a man of might,
   Nor baron of high degree,
But it is to a popish priest ;
   My lord, I winna lie.

4 'He got me in my bower alone,
   As I sat pensively ;
He vowed he would forgive my sins,
   If I would him obey.'

5 Now it fell ance upon a day
   This young lord went from home,
And great and heavy were the pains
   That came this lady on.

6 Then word has gane to her gude lord,
   As he sat at the wine,
And when the tidings he did hear
   Then he came singing hame.

7 When he came to his own bower-door,
   He tirled at the pin :
'Sleep ye, wake ye, my gay lady,
   Ye 'll let your gude lord in.'

8 Huly, huly raise she up,
   And slowly put she on,
And slowly came she to the door ;
   She was a weary woman.

9 'Ye 'll take up my son, Willie,
   That ye see here wi me,
And hae him down to yon shore-side,
   And throw him in the sea.

10 'Gin he sink, ye 'll let him sink,
    Gin he swim, ye 'll let him swim ;
And never let him return again
    Till white fish he bring hame.'

11 Then he 's taen up his little young son,
    And rowd him in a band,
And he is on to his mother,
    As fast as he could gang.

12 'Ye 'll open the door, my mother dear,
    Ye 'll open, let me come in ;

My young son is in my arms twa,
    And shivering at the chin.'

13 'I tauld you true, my son Willie,
    When ye was gaun to ride,
That lady was an ill woman
    That ye chose for your bride.'

14 'O hold your tongue, my mother dear,
    Let a' your folly be ;
I wat she is a king's daughter
    That 's sent this son to thee.

15 'I wat she was a king's daughter
    I loved beyond the sea,
And if my lady hear of this
    Right angry will she be.'

16 'If that be true, my son Willie —
    Your ain tongue winna lie —
Nae waur to your son will be done
    Than what was done to thee.'

17 He 's gane hame to his lady,
    And sair mourning was she :
'What ails you now, my lady gay,
    Ye weep sa bitterlie ?'

18 'O bonny was the white fisher
    That I sent to the sea ;
But lang, lang will I look for fish
    Ere white fish he bring me !

19 'O bonny was the white fisher
    That ye kiest in the faem ;
But lang, lang will I look for fish
    Ere white fish he fetch hame !

20 'I fell a slumbering on my bed
    That time ye went frae me,
And dreamd my young son filld my arms,
    But when waked, he 's in the sea.'

21 'O hold your tongue, my gay lady,
    Let a' your mourning be,
And I 'll gie you some fine cordial,
    My love, to comfort thee.'

22 'I value not your fine cordial,
    Nor aught that ye can gie ;
Who could hae drownd my bonny young son
    Could as well poison me.'

23 'Cheer up your heart, my lily flower,
    Think nae sic ill o me ;
Your young son 's in my mother's bower,
    Set on the nourice knee.

24 'Now, if ye 'll be a gude woman,
    I 'll neer mind this to thee ;
  Nae waur is done to your young son
    Than what was done to me.'

25 'Well fell 's me now, my ain gude lord ;
    These words do cherish me ;
  If it hadna come o yoursell, my lord,
    'T would neer hae come o me.'

7^8. Ye sleep ye, wake ye.

265

THE KNIGHT'S GHOST

'The Knight's Ghost,' Buchan's Ballads of the North of Scotland, I, 227.

A LADY who is expecting the return of her lord from sea goes down to the strand to meet him. The ship comes in, but the sailors tell her that she will never see her husband ; he has been slain. She invites the men to drink with her, takes them down to the cellar, makes them drunk, locks the door, and bids them lie there for the bad news they have told ; then she throws the keys into the sea, to lie there till her lord returns. After these efforts she falls asleep in her own room, and her dead lord starts up at her feet ; he brings the keys with him, and charges her to release his men, who had done their best for him and were not to blame for his death. The lady, to turn this visit to the more account, asks to be informed what day she is to die, and what day to be buried. The knight is not empowered to answer, but, come to heaven when she will, he will be her porter. He sees no objection to telling her that she will be married again and have nine children, six ladies free and three bold young men.

The piece has not a perceptible globule of old blood in it, yet it has had the distinction of being more than once translated as a specimen of Scottish popular ballads. 'Monie' in 2^2 may be plausibly read, or understood, 'menie,' retinue ; still the antecedent presumption in favor of nonsense in ballads of this class makes one hesitate. $7^{3,4}$ is unnatural ; no dissembling would be required to induce the young men to drink. In 8^3, 'birled them wi the beer' is what we should expect, not 'birled wi them.'

Translated by Rosa Warrens, Schottische Volkslieder der Vorzeit, p. 57, No 13 ; by Gerhard, p. 154.

1 'THERE is a fashion in this land,
    And even come to this country,
  That every lady should meet her lord
    When he is newly come frae sea :

2 'Some wi hawks, and some wi hounds,
    And other some wi gay monie ;
  But I will gae myself alone,
    And set his young son on his knee.'

3 She 's taen her young son in her arms,
    And nimbly walkd by yon sea-strand,
  And there she spy'd her father's ship,
    As she was sailing to dry land.

4 'Where hae ye put my ain gude lord,
    This day he stays sae far frae me ? '
  'If ye be wanting your ain gude lord,
    A sight o him ye 'll never see.'

5 'Was he brunt? or was he shot?
  Or was he drowned in the sea?
Or what 's become o my ain gude lord,
  That he will neer appear to me?'

6 'He wasna brunt, nor was he shot,
  Nor was he drowned in the sea;
He was slain in Dumfermling,
  A fatal day to you and me.'

7 'Come in, come in, my merry young men,
  Come in and drink the wine wi me;
And a' the better ye shall fare
  For this gude news ye tell to me.'

8 She 's brought them down to yon cellar,
  She brought them fifty steps and three;
She birled wi them the beer and wine,
  Till they were as drunk as drunk could be.

9 Then she has lockd her cellar-door,
  For there were fifty steps and three:
'Lie there, wi my sad malison,
  For this bad news ye 've tauld to me.'

10 She 's taen the keys intill her hand
  And threw them deep, deep in the sea :
'Lie there, wi my sad malison,
  Till my gude lord return to me.'

11 Then she sat down in her own room,
  And sorrow lulld her fast asleep,

And up it starts her own gude lord,
  And even at that lady's feet.

12 'Take here the keys, Janet,' he says,
  'That ye threw deep, deep in the sea;
And ye 'll relieve my merry young men,
  For they 've nane o the swick o me.

13 'They shot the shot, and drew the stroke,
  And wad in red bluid to the knee ;
Nae sailors mair for their lord coud do
  Nor my young men they did for me.'

14 'I hae a question at you to ask,
  Before that ye depart frae me ;
You 'll tell to me what day I 'll die,
  And what day will my burial be?'

15 'I hae nae mair o God's power
  Than he has granted unto me ;
But come to heaven when ye will,
  There porter to you I will be.

16 'But ye 'll be wed to a finer knight
  Than ever was in my degree ;
Unto him ye 'll hae children nine,
  And six o them will be ladies free.

17 'The other three will be bold young men,
  To fight for king and countrie ;
The ane a duke, the second a knight,
  And third a laird o lands sae free.'

ADDITIONS AND CORRECTIONS

VOL. I.

1. Riddles Wisely Expounded.

Pp. 1–3, 484 ; II, 495 a. **Little-Russian.** Three lads give a girl riddles. 'If you guess right, shall you be ours ? ' Golovatsky, II, 83, 19. Two other pieces in the same, III, 180, 55. (W. W.)

A king's daughter, or other maid, makes the reading of her riddles a condition of marriage in several Polish tales ; it may be further stipulated that a riddle shall be also given which the woman cannot guess, or that those who fail shall forfeit their life. Karłowicz in Wisła, III, 258, 270, where are cited, besides a MS. communication, Zbiór wiadomości do antropologii krajowej, V, 194, VII, 12 ; Gliński, Bajarz Polski, III, No 1; Kolberg, Krakowskie, IV, 204.

2. The Elfin Knight.

P. 7 a. The last two stanzas of **F** are also in Kinloch MSS, V, 275, with one trivial variation, and the burden, ' And then, etc.'

Sir Walter Scott had a copy beginning, ' There lived a wife in the wilds of Kent :' Sharpe's Ballad Book, 1880, p. 147 f.

7 b, 484 a. Add: **P, Q,** Hruschka u. Toischer, Deutsche Volkslieder aus Böhmen, p. 171, No 124, a, b.

7 b, III, 496 a. ' Store Fordringer,' Kristensen, Jyske Folkeminder, X, 342, No 85 (with the stupid painted roses).

7 f, 484 a, II, 495 a, III, 496 a. Add : ' I tre Tamburi,' Ferraro, C. P. del Basso Monferrato, p. 52 ; ' Il Compito,' Romaic, Tommaseo, III, 13 (already cited by Nigra).

8 a, II, 495 a. Tasks. **Servian** ballads. Karadžić, Sr. n. pj., I, 164, No 240, ' The Spinster and the Tsar ;' I, 165, No 242, ' The Spinster and the Goldsmith.' Cf. I, 166, No 243. Also, Karadžić, Sr. n. pj. iz Herz., p. 217, No 191 ; Petranović, I, 13, No 16 (where the girl's father sets the tasks), and p. 218, No 238 ; Rajković, p. 209, No 237. **Bulgarian.** Collection of the Bulgarian Ministry of Public Instruction, II, 31, 3 ; III, 28, 4. Cf. Verković, p. 52, 43 ; Bezsonov, II, 74, 105 ; Miladinof, p. 471, 536. **Russian.** An episode in the old Russian legend of Prince Peter of Murom and his wife Fevronija, three versions : Kuśelev-Bezborodko, Monuments of Old Russian Literature, I, 29 ff. (W. W.)

Wit-contests in verse, the motive of love or marriage having probably dropped out. Polish. Five examples are cited by Karłowicz, Wisła, III, 267 ff. : Kolberg, Krakowskie, II, 149, and Mazowsze, II, 149, No 332, Zbiór wiad. do antrop., X, 297, No 217, and two not before printed. Moravian examples from Sušil, p. 692 f., No 809, p. 701 ff., No 815 : make me a shirt without needle or thread, twist me silk out of oaten straw ; count me the stars, build me a ladder to go up to them ; drain the Red Sea, make me a bucket that will hold it ; etc. Zapolski, White Russian Weddings and Wedding-Songs, p. 35, No 19. Wisła, as before, III, 532 ff.

Polish tales of The Clever Wench are numerous : Wisła, III, 270 ff.

13 b. A fragment of a riddle given by a wise man to the gods is preserved in a cuneiform inscription : [What is that] which is in the house ? which roars like a bull ? which growls like a bear ? which enters into the heart of a man ? etc. The answer is evidently air, wind. George Smith, The Chaldean Account of Genesis, 1876, p. 156 : cited by J. Karłowicz, Wisła, III, 273.

15–20, 484 f., II, 495 f. Communicated by the Rev. S. Baring-Gould. " From the north of Cornwall, near Camelford. This used to be sung as a sort of game in farm-houses, between a young man who went outside the room and a girl who sat on the settle or a chair, and a sort of chorus of farm lads and lasses. Now quite discontinued." The dead lover represents the auld man in **I.**

1 A fair pretty maiden she sat on her bed,
    The wind is blowing in forest and town
  She sighed and she said, O my love he is dead !
    And the wind it shaketh the acorns down

2 The maiden she sighed ; ' I would,' said she,
  ' That again my lover might be with me ! '

3 Before ever a word the maid she spake,
  But she for fear did shiver and shake.

4 There stood at her side her lover dead ;
  ' Take me by the hand, sweet love,' he said.

5 .   .   .   .
   .   .   .   .

6 ' Thou must buy me, my lady, a cambrick shirt,
    Whilst every grove rings with a merry antine

And stitch it without any needle-work.

O and thus shalt thou be a true love of mine

7 'And thou must wash it in yonder well,
Whilst, etc.

Where never a drop of water in fell.

O and thus, etc.

8 'And thou must hang it upon a white thorn
That never has blossomed since Adam was
born.

9 'And when that these tasks are finished and
done

I 'll take thee and marry thee under the sun.'

10 'Before ever I do these two and three,
I will set of tasks as many to thee.

11 'Thou must buy for me an acre of land
Between the salt ocean and the yellow sand.

12 'Thou must plough it oer with a horse's horn,
And sow it over with one peppercorn.

13 'Thou must reap it too with a piece of leather,
And bind it up with a peacock's feather.

14 'And when that these tasks are finished and
done,

O then will I marry thee under the sun.'

15 'Now thou hast answered me well,' he said,
The wind, etc.

'Or thou must have gone away with the dead.'
And the wind, etc.

16 .   .   .   .
.   .   .   .

Mr Frank Kidsen has given a copy of ' Scarborough
Fair,' with some better readings, as sung " in Whitby
streets twenty or thirty years ago," in Traditional
Tunes, p. 43, 1891.

1–4, *second line of burden*, true love.

2^2. Without any seam or needlework.

3^1. yonder dry well. 3^2. no water sprung.

4^1. Tell her to dry it on yonder thorn.

4^2. Which never bore blossom since.

5, 6. *Wanting*. 7^1. O will you find me.

7^2. Between the sea-foam [and] the sea-sand. Or
never be a true lover of mine.

8^1. O will you plough. 9^1. O will you reap it.

9^2. And tie it all up.

10^1. And when you have done and finished your
work.

10^2. You may come to me for your. And then
you shall be a. *At p. 172, the first stanza of
another version is given, with* Rue, parsley, rosemary and thyme *for the first line of the burden.*

3. The Fause Knight upon the Road.

Pp. 20, 485 (also, 14 a, 484 a), III, 496 a. Foiling
mischievous sprites and ghosts by getting the last word,
or prolonging talk till the time when they must go,
especially the noon-sprite : Wisła, III, 275 f., and notes
44–6 ; also, 269 f. The Wends have the proverbial
phrase, to ask as many questions as a noon-sprite.
The Poles have many stories of beings that take service without wages, on condition of no fault being found,
and make off instantly upon the terms being broken.

20, III, 496 a. The last verses of ' Tsanno d'Oymé,'
Daymard, Vieux Chants pop. recueillis en Quercy, p.
70, are after the fashion of this ballad.

'Tsano d'Oymé, atal fuessés négado !'
'Lou fil del rey, et bous né fuessés l'aygo !'

'Tsano d'Oymé, atal fuessés brullado !'
'Lou fil del rey, et bous fuessés las clappos !'

4. Lady Isabel and the Elf-Knight.

P. 24 a. A copy in Christie's Traditional Ballad
Airs, II, 236, ' May Colvine and Fause Sir John ' (of
which no account is given), is a free compilation from
D b, D a, and **C c.**

The Gaelic tale referred to by Jamieson may be seen,
as Mr Macmath has pointed out to me, in Rev. Alexander Stewart's 'Twixt Ben Nevis and Glencoe, Edinburgh, 1885, p. 205 ff. Dr Stewart gives nine stanzas
of a Gaelic ballad, and furnishes an English render-
ing. The story has no connection with that of No 4.

25 b, note. ' Halewyn en het kleyne Kind,' in the
first volume of the MS. Poésies pop. de la France, was
communicated by Crussemaker, and is the same piece
that he printed. Other copies in Lootens et Feys, No
45, p. 85 (see p. 296) ; Volkskunde, II, 194, ' Van Mijn-
heerken van Bruindergestem.'

27 a, note †. Add : Mac Inness, Folk and Hero Tales
[Gaelic], p. 301, a Highland St George: see I, 487, note.

27 f. Professor Bugge, Arkiv för nordisk Filologi,
VII, 120–36, 1891, points out that a Swedish ballad
given in Grundtvig, D. g. F. IV, 813 f., **F,** and here referred to under ' Hind Etin,' I, 364 b, as Swedish **C,**
has resemblances with ' Kvindemorderen.' Fru Malin
is combing her hair *al fresco,* when a suitor enters her
premises ; he remarks that a crown would sit well on
her head. The lady skips off to her chamber, and exclaims, Christ grant he may wish to be mine ! The

suitor follows her, and asks, Where is the fair dame who wishes to be mine? But when Fru Malin comes to table she is in trouble, and the suitor puts her several leading questions. She is sad, not for any of several reasons suggested, but for the bridge under which her seven sisters (syskon) lie. 'Sorrow not,' he says, 'we shall build the bridge so broad and long that four-and-twenty horses may go over at a time.' They pass through a wood; on the bridge her horse stumbles, and she is thrown into the water. She cries for help; she will give him her gold crown. He cares nothing for the crown, and never will help her out. Bugge maintains that this ballad is not, as Grundtvig considered it, a compound of 'Nökkens Svig' and 'Harpens Kraft,' but an independent ballad, 'The Bride Drowned,' of a set to which belong 'Der Wasserman,' Haupt and Schmaler, I, 62, No 34, and many German ballads: see Grundtvig, IV, 810 f, and here I, 365 f., 38.

29-37, 486 a. Add: E E, Hruschka u. Toischer, Deutsche Volkslieder aus Böhmen, p. 126, No 35. Like Q, p. 35.

39 ff. The Polish ballad 'Jás i Kasia.' Mr John Karłowicz has given, in Wisła, IV, 393-424, the results of a study of this ballad, and they are here briefly summarized.

Ten unprinted versions are there added to the large number already published, making about ninety copies, if fragments are counted. Copies not noted at I, 39, 486, are, besides these ten, the following. Kolberg, Krakowskie, II, 111, 168, Nos 208, 336; Kieleckie, II, 148, No 453; Lęczychie, p. 131, No 223; Lubelskie, I, 289 ff., Nos 473, 474; Poznańskie, IV, 63, No 131; Mazowsze, III, 274, No 386, IV, 320, No 346. Zbiór wiadomości do antropologii krajowej, II, 78, Nos 89, 90; IV, 129; X, 123. Wisła, II, 132, 159. Prace filologiczne, II, 568. Kętrzyński, O Mazurach, p. 35, No 1. Zawiliński, Z powieści i pieśni górali beskidowych, p. 88, No 66. Wasilewski, Jagodne, etc., No 120. Federowski, Lud okolic Żarek, etc., p. 102, No 49.

Most of the ten versions printed in Wisła agree with others previously published; in some there are novel details. In No 3, p. 398, Kasia, thrown into the water by her lover, is rescued by her brother. In No 10, p. 404, Jás, when drowning the girl, tells her that he has drowned four already, and she shall be the fifth; her brother comes sliding down a silken rope; fishermen take the girl out dead. There are still only two of all the Polish versions in which Catharine kills John, A a, b. The name Ligar, in the latter, points clearly, Mr Karłowicz remarks, to the U-linger, Ad-elger, Ollegehr of the German versions, and he is convinced that the ballad came into Poland from Germany, although the girl is not drowned in the German ballad, as in the Polish, English, and French.

John, who is commonly the hero in the Polish ballad, is at the beginning of many copies declared to have sung, and the words have no apparent sense. But we observe that in the versions of western Europe the hero plays on the horn, sings a seductive song, promises

to teach the girl to sing, etc.; the unmeaning Polish phrase is therefore a survival.

In many of the German versions a bird warns the maid of her danger. This feature is found once only in Polish: in Zawiliński (No 69 A of Karłowicz).

At p. 777 of Sušil's Moravian Songs there are two other versions which I have not noticed, the second of them manifestly derived from Poland.

There is a Little-Russian ballad which begins like the Polish 'Jás i Kasia,' but ends with the girl being tied to a tree and burned, instead of being drowned: Wisła, IV, 423, from Zbiór wiadom. do antrop., III, 150, No 17. Traces of the incident of the burning are also found in Polish and Moravian songs: Wisła, pp. 418-22. It is probable that there were two independent ballads, and that these have been confounded.

42 a, III, 497 a. A. Add: 'Renaud et ses Femmes,' Revue des Traditions Populaires, VI, 34.

43 a. 'Lou Cros dé Proucinello,' Daymard, Vieux Chants p. recueillis en Quercy, p. 130, has at the end two traits of this ballad. A young man carries off a girl whom he has been in love with seven years; he throws her into a ravine; as she falls, she catches at a tree; he cuts it away; she cries, What shall I do with my pretty gowns? and is answered, Give them to me for another mistress. Cf. also Daymard, p. 128.

43 b, III, 497 a. 'La Fille de Saint-Martin.' Add: 'Le Mari Assassin,' Chanson du pays de Caux, Revue des Traditions Populaires, IV, 133.

43 f., 488 a, III, 497. Italian. The ballad in Nannarelli (488 a) I have seen: it is like 'La Monferrina incontaminata.' Add: 'La bella Inglese,' Salvadori, in Giornale di Filologia Romanza, II, 201; 'Un' eroina,' A. Giannini, Canzoni del Contado di Massa Lunense, No 1, Archivio, VIII, 273; ['Montiglia'], ['Inglesa'], Bolognini, Annuario degli Alpinisti Tridentini, XIII, Usi e Costumi del Trentino, 1888, p. 37 f.

44 b. 'La Princesa Isabel,' Pidal, Romancero Asturiano, p. 350 (sung by children as an accompaniment to a game), is a variety of 'Rico Franco.'

45 a, 488 a. Another Portuguese version, 'O caso de D. Ignez,' Braga, Ampliações ao Romanceiro das Ilhas dos Açores, Revista Lusitana, I, 103.

45 b. Breton, 5. Marivonnic also in Quellien, Chansons et Danses des Bretons, 1889, p. 99.

50 b, note ‖. As to this use of blood, cf. H. von Wlisłocki, Volksthümliches zum Armen Heinrich, Ztschr. f. deutsche Philologie, 1890, XXIII, 217 ff; Notes and Queries, 7th Series, VIII, 363. (G. L. K.)

55. B. A copy in Walks near Edinburgh, by Margaret Warrender, 1890, p. 104, differs from B b in only a few words, as any ordinary recollection would. As:

4^8, 6^3, 8^3. my guid steed.

9^4. It will gar our loves to twine.

10^4. An I 'll ring for you the bell.

11^3. Grant me ae kiss o your fause, fause mouth (*improbable reading*).

14^2. she won. 14^8. most heartily.

56 ff., 488 f., II, 497 f.

The copy of 'May Collin' which follows is quite the best of the series **C–G**. It is written on the same sheet of paper as the "copy of some antiquity" used by Scott in making up his 'Gay Goss Hawk' (ed. 1802, II, 7). The sheet is perhaps as old as any in the volume in which it occurs, but may possibly not be the original. 'May Collin' is not in the same hand as the other ballad.

According to the preface to a stall-copy spoken of by Motherwell, Minstrelsy, p. lxx, 24, "the treacherous and murder-minting lover was an ecclesiastic of the monastery of Maybole," and the preface to **D d** (see I, 488) makes him a Dominican friar. So, if we were to accept these guides, the 'Sir' would be the old ecclesiastical title and equivalent to the 'Mess' of the copy now to be given.

'May Collin,' "Scotch Ballads, Materials for Border Minstrelsy," No 146, Abbotsford.

1 May Collin . . . . . .
        .   .   .   was her father's heir,
    And she fell in love with a falsh priest,
    And she rued it ever mair.

2 He followd her butt, he followd her benn,
        He followd her through the hall,
    Till she had neither tongue nor teeth
        Nor lips to say him naw.

3 'We 'll take the steed out where he is,
        The gold where eer it be,
    And we 'll away to some unco land,
        And married we shall be.'

4 They had not riden a mile, a mile,
        A mile but barely three,
    Till they came to a rank river,
        Was raging like the sea.

5 'Light off, light off now, May Collin,
        It 's here that you must die ;
    Here I have drownd seven king's daughters,
        The eight now you must be.

6 'Cast off, cast off now, May Collin,
        Your gown that 's of the green ;
    For it 's oer good and oer costly
        To rot in the sea-stream.

7 'Cast off, cast off now, May Collin,
        Your coat that 's of the black ;
    For it 's oer good and oer costly
        To rot in the sea-wreck.

8 'Cast off, cast off now, May Collin,
        Your stays that are well laced ;
    For thei 'r oer good and costly
        In the sea 's ground to waste.

9 'Cast [off, cast off now, May Collin,]
        Your sark that 's of the holland ;
    For [it 's oer good and oer costly]
        To rot in the sea-bottom.'

10 'Turn you about now, falsh Mess John,
        To the green leaf of the tree ;
    It does not fit a mansworn man
        A naked woman to see.'

11 He turnd him quickly round about,
        To the green leaf of the tree ;
    She took him hastly in her arms
        And flung him in the sea.

12 'Now lye you there, you falsh Mess John,
        My mallasin go with thee !
    You thought to drown me naked and bare,
        But take your cloaths with thee,
    And if there be seven king's daughters there
        Bear you them company.'

13 She lap on her milk steed
        And fast she bent the way,
    And she was at her father's yate
        Three long hours or day.

14 Up and speaks the wylie parrot,
        So wylily and slee :
    'Where is the man now, May Collin,
        That gaed away wie thee ?'

15 'Hold your tongue, my wylie parrot,
        And tell no tales of me,
    And where I gave a pickle befor
        It 's now I 'll give you three.'

1¹·². *One line*: May Collin was her father's heir.
7⁴. on the.   8⁴. ina? *indistinct*.   12⁵. 7.

5. Gil Brenton.

P. 63 b. **Swedish**. 'Riddar Olof,' Lagus, Nyländska Folkvisor, I, 63, No 16, *a, b*, imperfect copies.

64 b. **Danish**. 'Den rette Brudgom' (Samson and Vendelru), Kristensen, Jyske Folkeminder, X, 363, No 97.

65 b. 'Herr Peders Hustru,' the same, p. 365, = Grundtvig, No 278.

70. **B.** The three stanzas which follow were communicated to Scott by Major Henry Hutton, Royal Artillery, 24th December, 1802 (Letters, I, No 77), as recollected by his father and the family. " Scotch Ballads, Materials for Border Minstrelsy,'' No 18. Instead of 3, 4 :

There 's five o them with meal and malt,
And other five wi beef and salt ;
There 's five o them wi well-bak'd bread,
And other five wi goud so red.

There 's five o them wi the ladies bright,
There 's other five o belted knights ;
There 's five o them wi a good black neat,
And other five wi bleating sheep.

" And before the two last stanzas, introduce "

O there was seald on his breast-bane,
' Cospatric is his father's name ; '
O there was seald on his right hand
He should inherit his father's land.

so *is written over the second* and *in* 1^2.

7. Earl Brand.

P. 88. 'Ribold og Guldborg :' Kristensen, Jyske Folkeminder, X, 33, ' Nævnet til døde,' No 15, **A–I.**

91 b. **Swedish.** ' Kung Valdemo,' ' Ellibrand och Fröken Gyllenborg,' Lagus, Nyländska Folkvisor, I, 1, No 1, *a, b.* (" Name not my name," *a* 20, *b* 12.)

95 b, 489 b ; III, 498 a. For the whole subject, see K. Nyrop. Navnets Magt, 1887, and especially sections 4, 5, pp. 46–70. As to reluctance to have one's name known, and the advantage such knowledge gives an adversary, see E. Clodd, in The Folk Lore Journal, VII, 154 ff., and, in continuation, Folk-Lore, I, 272.

The berserkr Glammaðr could pick off any man with his pike, if only he knew his name. Saga Egils ok Ásmundar, Rafn, Fornaldar Sögur, III, 387, Ásmundarson, F. s. Norðrlanda, III, 292. (G. L. K.)

The demonic Gelô informs certain saints who force her " to tell them how other people's children [may] be defended from her attacks," that if they " can write her twelve names and a half she shall never be able to come within seventy-five stadia and a half : '' Thomas Wright, Essays on Subjects connected with the Literature, etc., of the Middle Ages, 1846, I, 294 (referring to Leo Allatius, De Græcorum hodie quorundam opinationibus). The passage in question is to be found at p. 127 of Leo Allatius, De templis Græcorum recentioribus, ad Ioannem Morinum ; De Narthece ecclesiæ veteris ; nec non De Græcorum hodie quorundam opinationibus, ad Paullum Zacchiam. Coloniæ Agrippinæ, 1645. (G. L. K.)

96 b. **Swedish.** Two copies of ' Rosen lilla ' in Lagus, Nyländska Folkvisor, I, 37, No 10.

Danish. Kristensen, Jyske Folkeminder, X, 215, No 52, **C** 9, two lilies ; p. 318, No 78, 9, 10, graves south and north, two lilies.

97 b. **French.** 'Les deux Amoureux,' Daymard, Vieux Chants p. rec. en Quercy, p. 122, lavender and tree.

97 b, 489 b, II, 498 a, III, 498 b. **Slavic.** (1.) White-Russian : he buried in church, she in ditch ; plane and linden (planted) ; plane embraces linden. MS. (2.) Little-Russian : buried apart ; plane grows over his grave, two birches over hers ; branches do *not* interlace. Kolberg, Pokucie, p. 41. (3.) White-Russian : he in church, she near church ; oak, birch (planted) ; trees touch. Zbiór wiado. do antropol., XIII, 102 f. (4.) Little-Russian : burial apart in a church ; rosemary and lily from graves. Var.: rose and sage, rosemary ; flowers interlace. Holovatzky, III, 254. (J. Karłowicz, in Mélusine, V, 39 ff.)

Bulgarian. A poplar from the maid's grave, a pine from her lover's : Collection of the Bulgarian Ministry of Instruction, I, 35. (W. W.)

97 b, 490 a, III, 498 b. **Breton.** Luzel, Soniou, I, 272–3 : a tree from the young man's grave, a rose from the maid's.

99 ff., 490 ff. ' The Earl o Bran,' " Scotch Ballads, Materials for Border Minstrelsy," No 22 b, Abbotsford ; in the handwriting of Richard Heber.

1 Did ye ever hear o guid Earl o Bran
  An the queen's daughter o the south-lan ?

2 She was na fifteen years o age
  Till she came to the Earl's bed-side.

3 ' O guid Earl o Bran, I fain wad see
  My grey hounds run over the lea.'

4 ' O kind lady, I have no steeds but one,
  But ye shall ride, an I shall run.'

5 ' O guid Earl o Bran, but I have tua,
  An ye shall hae yere wael o those.'

6 The 're ovr moss an the 're over muir,
  An they saw neither rich nor poor.

7 Till they came to ald Carl Hood,
  He 's ay for ill, but he 's never for good.

8 ' O guid Earl o Bran, if ye loe me,
  Kill Carl Hood an gar him die.'

9 ' O kind lady, we had better spare ;
  I never killd ane that wore grey hair.

10 'We 'll gie him a penny-fie an let him gae,
   An then he 'll carry nae tiddings away.'

11 'Where hae been riding this lang simmer-day ?
   Or where hae stolen this lady away ? '

12 'O I hae not riden this lang simmer-day,
   Nor hae I stolen this lady away.

13 'For she is my sick sister
   I got at the Wamshester.'

14 'If she were sick an like to die,
   She wad na be wearing the gold sae high.'

15 Ald Carl Hood is over the know,
   Where they rode one mile, he ran four.

16 Till he came to her mother's yetts,
   An I wat he rapped rudely at.

17 'Where is the lady o this ha ? '
   'She 's out wie her maidens, playing at
   the ba.'

18 'O na ! fy na !
   For I met her fifteen miles awa.

19 'She 's over moss, an she 's over muir,
   An a' to be the Earl o Bran's whore.'

20 Some rode wie sticks, an some wie rungs,
   An a' to get the Earl o Bran slain.

21 That lady lookd over her left shoudder-bane :
   'O guid Earl o Bran, we 'll a' be taen !
   For yond 'r a' my father's men.

22 'But if ye 'll take my claiths, I 'll take thine,
   An I 'll fight a' my father's men.'

23 'It 's no the custom in our land
   For ladies to fight an knights to stand.

24 'If they come on me ane by ane,
   I 'll smash them a' doun bane by bane.

25 'If they come on me ane and a',
   Ye soon will see my body fa.'

26 He has luppen from his steed,
   An he has gein her that to had.

27 An bad her never change her cheer
   Untill she saw his body bleed.

28 They came on him ane by ane,
   An he smashed them doun a' bane by bane.

29 He sat him doun on the green grass,
   For I wat a wearit man he was.

30 But ald Carl Hood came him behind,
   An I wat he gae him a deadly wound.

31 He 's awa to his lady then,
   He kissed her, an set her on her steed again.

32 He rode whistlin out the way,
   An a' to hearten his lady gay.

33 'Till he came to the water-flood :
   'O guid Earl o Bran, I see blood ! '

34 'O it is but my scarlet hood,
   That shines upon the water-flood.'

35 They came on 'till his mother's yett,
   An I wat he rappit poorly at.

36 His mother she 's come to the door :
   'O son, ye 've gotten yere dead wie an English whore ! '

37 'She was never a whore to me ;
   Sae let my brother her husband be.'

38 Sae ald Carl Hood was not the dead o ane,
   But he was the dead o hale seeventeen.

   Note at the end : I have not written the chorus, but
   Mr Leyden, having it by him, knows how to insert it.

"Scotch Ballads, Materials for Border Minstrelsy," No
22 d. In the handwriting of William Laidlaw. Scott has
written at the head, Earl Bran, another copy.

1 Earl Bran 's a wooing gane ;
      Ae lalie, O lilly lalie
   He woo'd a lady, an was bringing her hame.
      O the gae knights o Airly

2 .   .   .   .
   They met neither wi rich nor poor.

3 Till they met wi an auld palmer Hood,
  Was ay for ill, an never for good.

4 'O yonder is an auld palmer Heed:
  Tak your sword an kill him dead.'

5 'Gude forbid, O ladie fair,
  That I kill an auld man an grey hair.

6 'We 'll gie him a   an forbid him to tell ; '
  The gae him a   an forbad him to tell.

7 The auld man than he 's away hame,
  He telld o Jane whan he gaed hame.

8 'I thought I saw her on yon moss,
  Riding on a milk-white horse.

9 'I thought I saw her on yon muir ;
  By this time she 's Earl Bran's wh*o*re.'

10 Her father he 's ca'd on his men :
   'Gae follow, an fetch her again.'

11 She 's lookit oer her left shoulder :
   'O yonder is my father's men !

12 'O yonder is my father's men :
   Take my cleadin, an I 'll take thine.'

13 'O that was never law in land,
   For a ladie to feiht an a knight to stand.

14 'But if yer father's men come ane an ane,
   Stand ye by, an ye 'll see them slain.

15 'If they come twae an twae,
   Stand ye by, an ye 'll see them gae.

16 'And if they come three an three,
   Stand ye by, an ye 'll see them die.'

17 Her father's men came ane an ane,
   She stood by .   .   .   .

18 Than they cam by twae an twae,
   .   .   .   .   .   .

19 Than they cam by three an three,
   .   .   .   .   .   .

20 But ahint him cam the auld palmer Hood,
   An ran him outthro the heart's blood.

21 'I think I see your heart's blood : '
   'It 's but the glistering o your scarlet hood.'

*   *   *   *   *   *   *   *

7[1]. *MS.*, he 's *, *and, in the margin,* * away has been gane. *Over* away hame *is written* thre them (= thrae, frae, them), *or, perhaps,* thre than. 20[1]. *MS.*, palmer weed : *cf.* 3[1], 4[1]. 20[2]. outr thro.

P. 100, **B** ; 489 b, 492, **I.** The printed copy used by Scott was 'Lord Douglas' Tragedy,' the first of four pieces in a stall - pamphlet, "licensed and entered, 1792 : " "Scotch Ballads, Materials for Border Minstrelsy," No 1. **I** is another edition of the same. The variations from **I** are as follows :

1[1]. says. 2[2]. your arms. 3[4]. father who.
4[3]. seven *wanting.* 4[4]. just now.
5[1]. better *for* (*the obvious misprint*) bitter.
5[3]. once that. 6[1]. Hold your hand. 7[2]. wounds.
7[4]. forkd in the. 8[1]. Lady Margret.
9[3], 13[3]. blue gilded, *as in* **I,** *for* bugelet : hanging down. 9[4], 13[4]. slowly they both.
10[3]. yon clear river-side. 11[3]. his pretty.
12[3]. 'T is nothing. 15[2]. soft. 16[2]. long ere day.
16[4]. died *wanting.* 17[1]. St *for* Lady.
17[3]. sprung. 18[2]. be near. 18[3]. ye : weil.

8. Erlinton.

P. 107. The two copies from which (with some editorial garnish and filling out) **A** was compounded were : a. "Scotch Ballads, Materials for Border Minstrelsy," No 20, obtained from Nelly Laidlaw, and in the handwriting of William Laidlaw ; b. 'Earlington's Daughter,' the same collection, No 11, in the handwriting of James Hogg. The differences are purely verbal, and both copies may probably have been derived from the same reciter ; still, since only seven or eight verses in sixty-eight agree, both will be given entire, instead of a list of the variations.

a. 1 Lord Erlinton had ae daughter,
     I trow he 's weird her a grit sin ;
   For he has bugn a bigly bower,
     An a' to pit his ae daughter in.
       An he has buggin, etc.

2 An he has warn her sisters six,
    Her sisters six an her brethren se'en,
  Thei 'r either to watch her a' the night,
    Or than to gang i the mornin soon.

3 She had na been i that bigly bower
    Not ae night but only ane
  Untill that Willie, her true-love,
    Chappit at the bower-door, no at the gin.

ADDITIONS AND CORRECTIONS

4 'Whae 's this, whae 's this chaps at my bower-
    door,
  At my bower-door, no at the gin?'
'O it is Willie, thy ain true-love;
  O will ye rise an let me in?'

5 'In my bower, Willie, there is a wane,
  An in the wane there is a wake;
But I will come to the green woods
  The morn, for my ain true-love's sake.'

6 This lady she 's lain down again,
  An she has lain till the cock crew thrice;
She said unto her sisters baith,
  Lasses, it 's time at we soud rise.

7 She 's putten on her breast a silver tee,
  An on her back a silken gown;
She 's taen a sister in ilka hand,
  An away to the bonnie green wood she 's
    gane.

8 They hadna gane a mile in that bonnie green
    wood,
  They had na gane a mile but only ane,
Till they met wi Willie, her ain true-love,
  An thrae her sisters he has her taen.

9 He 's taen her sisters ilk by the hand,
  He 's kissd them baith, an he 's sent them
    hame;
He 's muntit his ladie him high behind,
  An thro the bonnie green wood thei 'r gane.

10 They 'd ridden a mile i that bonnie green wood,
  They hadna ridden but only ane,
When there cam fifteen o the baldest knights
  That ever boor flesh, bluid an bane.

11 Than up bespak the foremost knight,
  He woor the gray hair on his chin;
'Yield me yer life or your lady fair,
  An ye sal walk the green woods within.'

12 'For to gie my wife to thee,
  I wad be very laith,' said he;
'For than the folk wad think I was gane mad,
  Or that the senses war taen frae me.'

13 Up than bespak the niest foremost knight,
  I trow he spak right boustrouslie;
'Yield me yer life or your ladie fair,
  An ye sall walk the green woods wi me.'

14 'My wife, she is my warld's meed,
  My life, it lyes me very near;
But if ye be man o your manhood
  I serve will while my days are near.'

15 He 's luppen off his milk-white steed,
  He 's gien his lady him by the head:
'See that ye never change yer cheer
  Till ance ye see my body bleed.'

16 An he 's killd a' the fifteen knights,
  He 's killed them a' but only ane;
A' but the auld grey-headed knight,
  He bade him carry the tiddins hame.

17 He 's gane to his lady again,
  I trow he 's kissd her, baith cheek an chin;
'Now ye 'r my ain, I have ye win,
  An we will walk the green woods within.'

2³. Their *struck out.*
9³. muntit *struck out, and set written above.*
12³. than *struck out.*
14⁴. while, are, *struck out, and* till, be, *written above.*
16⁴. tiddins : *one* d *struck out. These changes
would seem to be somebody's editorial improvements.*
Wi me *in* 13⁴ *sacrifices sense to rhyme. We are to
understand in* 11³˙⁴, 13³˙⁴ *that Willie is to die if
he will not give up the lady, but if he will resign
her he may live, and walk the wood at his pleasure.*
14⁴ *is corrupt in both texts.*

b. 1 O Earlington, he has ae daughter,
  And I wot he has ward her in a great sin;
He has buggin to her a bigly bowr,
  And a' to put his daughter in.

2 O he has warnd her sisters six,
  Her sisters six and her brethren seven,
Either to watch her a' the night,
  Or else to search her soon at morn.

3 They had na been a night in that bigly bowr,
  'T is not a night but barely ane,
Till there was Willie, her ain true-love,
  Rappd at the door, and knew not the gin.

4 'Whoe 's this, whoe 's this raps at my bowr-
    door,
  Raps at my bowr-door, and knows not the
    gin?'
'O it is Willie, thy ain true-love;
  I pray thee rise and let me in.'

5 'O in my bower, Willie, there is a wake,
    And in the wake there is a wan;
But I 'll come to the green wood the morn,
    To the green wood for thy name's sake.'

6 O she has gaen to her bed again,
    And a wait she has lain till the cock crew
        thrice;
Then she said to her sisters baith,
    Lasses, 't is time for us to rise.

7 She 's puten on her back a silken gown,
    And on her breast a silver tie;
She 's taen a sister in ilka hand,
    And thro the green wood they are gane.

8 They had na walkt a mile in that good green
        wood,
    'T is not a mile but barely ane,
Till there was Willie, her ain true-love,
    And from her sisters he has her taen.

9 He 's taen her sisters by the hand,
    He kist them baith, he sent them hame;
He 's taen his lady him behind,
    And thro the green wood they are gane.

10 They had na ridden a mile in the good green
        wood,
    'T is not a mile but barely ane,
Till there was fifteen of the boldest knights
    That ever bore flesh, blood or bane.

11 The foremost of them was an aged knight,
    He wore the gray hair on his chin:
'Yield me thy life or thy lady bright,
    And thou shalt walk these woods within.'

12 ''T is for to give my lady fair
    To such an aged knight as thee,
People wad think I were gane mad,
    Or else the senses taen frae me.'

13 Up then spake the second of them,
    And he spake ay right bousterously;
'Yield me thy life or thy lady bright,
    And thou shalt walk these woods within.'

14 'My wife, she is my warld's meed,
    My life it lies me very near;
But if you 'll be man of your manheed,
    I 'll serve you till my days be near.'

15 He 's lighted of his milk-white steed,
    He 's given his lady him by the head:
'And see ye dinna change your cheer
    Till you do see my body bleed.'

16 O he has killd these fifteen lords,
    And he has killd them a' but ane,
And he has left that old aged knight,
    And a' to carry the tidings hame.

17 O he 's gane to his lady again,
    And a wait he has kist her, baith cheek and
        chin:
'Thou art my ain love, I have thee bought,
    And thou shalt walk these woods within.'

5. wake *should be* wane *and* wan wake, *as in* **A.**

10. The Twa Sisters.

P. 119 a. **Danish.** 'De talende Strenge,' Kristensen, Jyske Folkeminder, X, 68, 375, No 19, **A–E.**

119 b. **Swedish.** 'De två systrarna,' Lagus, Nyländska Folkvisor, I, 27, No 7, *a, b;* the latter imperfect.

124 b. Bohemian, Waldau, Böhmische Granaten, II, 97, No 137 (with the usual variations).

125 b, 493 b; II, 498 b; III, 499 a. Add: 'Les roseaux qui chantent,' Revue des Traditions Populaires, IV, 463, V, 178; 'La rose de Pimperlé,' Meyrac, Traditions, etc., des Ardennes, p. 486 ff.; 'L'os qui chante,' seven Walloon versions, E. Monseur, Bulletin de Folklore Wallon, I, 39 ff.

128. **C.** 'The Cruel Sister,' "Scotch Ballads, Materials for Border Minstrelsy," No 16; communicated to Scott by Major Henry Hutton, Royal Artillery, December 24, 1802 (Letters, I, No 77), as recollected by his father " and the family."

1 There were twa sisters in a bowr,
        Binnorie, O Binnorie
    The eldest was black and the youngest fair.
        By the bonny milldams o Binnorie

After 13 (or as 14):
    Your rosie cheeks and white hause-bane
    Garrd me bide lang maiden at hame.

After 15:
    The miller's daughter went out wi speed
    To fetch some water to make her bread.

After 17:
    He coud not see her fingers sma,
    For the goud rings they glistend a'.

He coud na see her yellow hair
For pearlin and jewels that were so rare.

And when he saw her white hause-bane
Round it hung a gouden chain.

He stretched her owt-our the bra
And moanëd her wi mekle wa.

" Then, at the end, introduce the following " (which,
however, are not traditional).

The last tune the harp did sing,
'And yonder stands my false sister Alison.

' Ó listen, listen, all my kin,
'T was she wha drownd me in the lin.'

And when the harp this song had done
It brast a' o pieces oer the stane.

" Alison.　The writer of these additional stanzas un-
derstands the name was Alison, and not Helen."　Alison occurs in **D, K.**

Pp. 133, 139.　**L.** Anna Seward to Walter Scott, April
25–29, 1802 : Letters addressed to Sir Walter Scott,
I, No 54, Abbotsford.　" The Binnorie of endless repetition has nothing truly pathetic, and the ludicrous use
made of the drowned sister's body is well burlesqued
in a ridiculous ballad, which I first heard sung, with
farcial grimace, in my infancy [born 1747], thus : "

1 And O was it a pheasant cock,
　　Or eke a pheasant hen ?
　Or was it and a gay lady,
　　Came swimming down the stream ?

2 O it was not a pheasant cock,
　　Or eke a pheasant hen,
　But it was and a gay lady,
　　Came swimming down the stream.

3 And when she came to the mill-dam
　　The miller he took her body,
　And with it he made him a fiddling thing,
　　To make him sweet melody.

4 And what did he do with her fingers small ?
　He made of them pegs to his vial.

5 And what did he do with her nose-ridge ?
　Why to his fiddle he made it a bridge.
　　Sing, O the damnd mill-dam, O

6 And what did he do with her veins so blue ?
　Why he made him strings his fiddle unto.

7 And what did he do with her two shins ?
　Why to his vial they dancd Moll Sims.

8 And what did he do with her two sides ?
　Why he made of them sides to his fiddle be-
　　sides.

9 And what did he do with her great toes ?
　Why what he did with them that nobody
　　knows.
　　Sing, O the damnd mill-dam, O

For 4, 5, 6, 7, see **A** 8, 9, 10, 13.

P. 137.　MS. of Thomas Wilkie, p. 1, in " Scotch Ballads, Materials for Border Minstrelsy," No 32; taken
down " from a Miss Nancy Brockie, Bemerside." 1813.

1 There were twa sisters sat in a bower,
　　　By Nera and by Nora
　　The youngest was the fairest flower.
　　　Of all the mill-dams of Bennora

2 It happened upon a bonnie summer's day
　　The eldest to the youngest did say :
　　　In the bonnie mill-dams of Bennora

3 ' We must go and we shall go
　　To see our brother's ships come to land.'
　　　In, etc. (*and throughout*).

4 ' I winna go and I downa go,
　　For weeting the corks o my coal-black shoes.'

5 She set her foot into a rash-bush,
　　To see how tightly she was dressd.

6 But the youngest sat upon a stone,
　　But the eldest threw the youngest in.

7 ' O sister, oh sister, come lend me your hand,
　　And draw my life into dry land ! '

8 ' You shall not have one bit o my hand ;
　　Nor will I draw you to dry land.'

9 ' O sister, O sister, come lend me your hand,
　　And you shall have Sir John and all his
　　　land.'

10 ' You shall not have one bit o my hand,
　　And I 'll have Sir John and all his land.

11 The miller's daughter, clad in red,
Came for some water to bake her bread.

12 'O father, O father, go fish your mill-dams,
For there either a swan or a drownd woman.'

13 You wad not have seen one bit o her waist,
The body was swelld, and the stays strait
laced.

14 You wad not have seen one bit o her neck,
The chains of gold they hang so thick.

15 He has taen a tait of her bonnie yellow hair,
He's tied it to his fiddle-strings there.

16 The verry first spring that that fiddle playd
Was, Blest be [the] queen, my mother! [it]
has said.

17 The verry next spring that that fiddle playd
Was, Blest be Sir John, my own true-love!

18 The very next spring that that fiddle playd
Was, Burn my sister for her sins!

4². *Written at first* my black heeld shoes.
12². swain. 17². thy own.

11. The Cruel Brother.

P. 142 b, 496 a, III, 499 a. **B** was repeated by Salvadori in Giornale di Filologia Romanza, II, 197 ; and
E was first published by Mazzatinti in IV, 69, of the
same.

142 f. A variety of 'Graf Friedrich' in Hruschka
u. Toischer, Deutsche Volkslieder aus Böhmen, p. 101,
No 25.

143 b. III, 499. Testament. 'Hr. Adelbrand.' Kristensen, Jyske Folkeminder, X, 227, 232, No 54, **A**,
20 ff., **F**, 10 ff. = 'Herr Radibrand och lilla Lena,'
'Skön Helena och riddaren Hildebrand,' Lagus, Nyländska Folkvisor, I, 89, No 25, *a*, *b*.

'Adelbrand' is No 311 of Danmarks gamle Folkeviser, V, II, 297, ed. Olrik, of which the versions that
have been cited in this book are **B**, **K** e, **G** e, **F**,
K b, **I**. There is a testament in other copies of the
same. Also in No 320, not yet published.

145 ff. "Scotch Ballads, Materials for Border Minstrelsy," No 22 a. In the handwriting of William
Laidlaw ; "from Jean Scott."

There was three ladies playd at the ba,
With a hey hey an a lilly gay

Bye cam three lords an woo'd them a'.
Whan the roses smelld sae sweetly

The first o them was clad in yellow :
'O fair may, will ye be my marrow?'
Whan the roses smell, etc.

The niest o them was clad i ried :
'O fair may, will ye be my bride?'

The thrid o them was clad i green :
He said, O fair may, will ye be my queen?

12. Lord Randal.

Pp. 152 b, 498 b, III, 499 b. **Italian.** Add **L**, ''U
Cavalieru Traditu ;' communicated to La Calabria, October 15, 1888, p. 5, 'Storie popolari Acresi,' by Antonio Julia.

154 a. **Danish.** 'Den forgivne Søster' (with testament), Kristensen, Jyske Folkeminder, X, 358, No
92.

156 b. Vuk, I, No 302, is translated by Bowring, p.
143.

157 ff., 499 ff. "Scotch Ballads, Materials for Border Minstrelsy," No 22 g, in the handwriting of William Laidlaw.

1 'Where ha ye been, Lord Randal, my son?'
'I been at the huntin, mother, mak my bed
soon ;
I'm weariet wi huntin, I fain wad lie down.'

2 'What gat ye to yer supper, Lord Randal,
my son?'
'An eel boild i broo, mother, mak my bed
soon ;
I'm,' etc.

3 'What gat yer dogs, Earl Randal, my son?'
'The broo o the eel, mother,' etc.

4 'What leave [ye] yer false love, Lord Ran-
dal, my son?'
'My goud silken garters, to hang hersel on ;
I'm,' etc.

4¹. leave year.

U

Letters addressed to Sir Walter Scott, XX, No 77, Abbotsford ; from Joseph Jamieson Archibald, Largs, 18th
February, 1830.

"By the bye! How does your copy of 'Willie Doo' go? Or is it the same as our 'Auld Nursery Lilt,' better known by the name of 'My Wee Croodling Doo'? To give you every justice, I shall copy a stanza or two."

1 'Whare were ye the lea lang day,
  My wee crooding doo, doo?'
 'I hae been at my step-dame's;
  Mammy, mak my bed noo, noo!'

2 'Whare gat she the wee, wee fish?'
 'She gat it neist the edder-flowe.'

3 'What did she wi the fishie's banes?'
 'The wee black dog gat them to eat.'

4 'What did the wee black doggie then?'
 'He shot out his fittie an deed;
  An sae maun I now too, too.' Etc.

"The wee crooding doo next received a fatal drink, and syne a lullaby, when his bed was made 'baith saft an fine,' while his lang fareweel and dying lamentation was certainly both trying and afflicting to the loving parents." *The drink after the fish was a senseless interpolation; the 'lang fareweel' was probably the testament of the longer ballad.*

500. The title of **Q** in the MS. is 'Lord Randal;' of **R**, 'Little wee toorin dow.'

14. Babylon, or, The Bonnie Banks o Fordie.

P. 171 a. **Danish.** 'Herr Tures Døtre,' Kristensen, Jyske Folkeminder, X, 294, No 72.

15. Leesome Brand.

P. 178 a. 'Jomfru i Hindeham,' D. g. F. No 58, Kristensen, Jyske Folkeminder, X, 14, No 7.

179 a, III, 500 b. **Danish**, II, 'Barnefødsel i Lunden,' six copies and a fragment, in Kristensen's Skattegraveren, X, 145 ff., Nos 416–22, 1888. ('Sadlen for trang, vejen for lang,' 416, 17, 20; man's help, 416, 419; children buried alive, 417, 18, 22; sister and brother, 418; lilies from grave, 416, 17.) 'Skjøn Medler,' Kristensen, Jyske Folkeminder, X, 182, No 46, **A–H**. (Saddle, way, **A**; man's help, **A, B, E, F, H**; children buried alive, **A, B, C, E, F**.)
Swedish. 'Herr Riddervall,' Lagus, Nyländska Folkvisor, I, 75, No 20.

16. Sheath and Knife.

P. 186. **D** is in or from T. Lyle's Ancient Ballads and Songs, 1827, p. 241. Scott, as Lyle says, has nearly the same burden in a stanza (of his own?) which he makes E. Deans sing, in The Heart of Mid-Lothian.

17. Hind Horn.

P. 193 b (2). 'Hr. Lovmand,' Kristensen, Jyske Folkeminder, X, 252, No 62, **A–D**.
194 ff., 502 f.; II, 499 b; III, 501 b. Ring stories. Cf. MacInnes, Folk and Hero Tales (Argyllshire), 1890, p. 157. (G. L. K.)
Bulgarian ballad. — Stojan is married on Sunday; on Monday he is ordered to join the army. His wife gives him a posy, which will remain fresh until she marries another man. He serves nine years; the tenth the queen discovers from his talk that he has a wife, and gives him permission to go home. He arrives the very day on which his wife is to be remarried, goes to the wedding, and asks her to kiss his hand and accept a gift from him. She recognizes him by the ring on his hand, sends off the guests, and goes home with him. Collection of the Ministry of Instruction, I, 39. In a variant, Verković, p. 329, No 301, the man is gone three years, and arrives just as the wedding procession comes for the bride. (W. W.)
198 b. 'Le Retour du Mari.' 'Un Retour de Guerre' (cards), Daymard, pp. 203, 4.
202 a, III, 501 b. For more of these curiosities (in Salman u. Morolf, Orendel, Virginal, Laurin, etc.), see Vogt's note, p. 181 (248 ff.), to Salman u. Morolf.
206. **H.** I have received from Mr Walker, of Aberdeen, author of 'The Bards of Bonaccord,' a copy of 'Hind Horn' which was taken down by a correspondent of his on lower Deeside about 1880. It closely resembles **G** and **H**. Collated with **H**, the more noteworthy variations are as follows:

1¹. Hey how, bound, lovie, hey how, free.
6². An the glintin o 't was aboon.
10. An when he looked the ring upon, O but it was pale an wan!
13². What news, what news is in this lan?
19. Ye 'll ging up to yon high hill,
   An ye 'll blaw yer trumpet loud an shrill.
20. Doun at yon gate ye will enter in,
   And at yon stair ye will stan still.
21. Ye 'll seek meat frae ane, ye 'll seek meat frae twa,
   Ye 'll seek meat fra the highest to the lowest o them a'.
22. But it 's out o their hans an ye will tak nane
   Till it comes out o the bride's ain han.
26². Wi the links o the yellow gowd in her hair.
After 27: An when she looked the ring upon, O but she grew pale an wan!
After 28: Or got ye it frae ane that is far, far away, To gie unto me upon my weddin-day?
30. But I got it frae you when I gaed away, To gie unto you on your weddin-day.

32. It 's I 'll gang wi you for evermore, An beg my bread frae door to door.

502 a.   There can hardly be a doubt that the two stanzas cited belonged to 'The Kitchie-Boy,' 'Bonny Foot-Boy,' No 252. Cf. **A** 34, 35, **B** 47, **D** 7, 8, of that ballad.

18. Sir Lionel.

P. 209 b.   'Blow thy horne, hunter.' Found, with slight variations, in Add. MS. 31922, British Museum, 39, b (Henry VIII) : Ewald, in Anglia, XII, 238.

19. King Orfeo.

P. 215.   The relations of the Danish 'Harpens Kraft,' and incidentally those of this ballad, to the English romance are discussed, with his usual acuteness, by Professor Sophus Bugge in Arkiv för nordisk Filologi, VII, 97 ff., 1891. See II, 137, of this collection.

20. The Cruel Mother.

P. 218 b, III, 502 a.   'Barnemordersken,' Kristensen, Jyske Folkeminder, X, 356, No 90, **A**, **B**.

219 b, 504 a, II, 500 a, III, 502 b.   Add : **Q**, **R**, Hruschka u. Toischer, Deutsche Volkslieder aus Böhmen, p. 129, No 40 a, b.

220 ff.   **a.** MS. of Thomas Wilkie, p. 4, in "Scotch Ballads, Materials for Border Minstrelsy," No 33. "Taken down from Mrs Hislope, Gattonside. The air is plaintive and very wild." 1813. **b.** "Scotch Ballads, Materials," etc., No 113 ; in the hand of T. Wilkie.

1 As I looked over my father's castle-wa,
    All alone and alone, O
  I saw two pretty babes playing at the ba.
  Down by yone greenwood side, O

2 'O pretty babes, if ye were mine,'
    All alone, etc.,
  'I would clead you o the silk so fine.'
  Alone by the, etc.

3 'O mother dear, when we were thine,
  Ye houket a hole fornent the sun,'
  And laid yer two babes in, O

4 'O pretty babes, if ye were mine,
  I would feed you wi the morning's milk.'
  Alone by, etc.

5 'O mother dear, when we were thine,
  Ye houket a hole fornent the sun.
  And laid yer two babes in, O.

6 'But we are in the heavens high,
    And ye hae the pains of hell to dri.'
    Alone by, etc.

7 'O pretty babes, pray weel for me !'
  'Aye, mother, as ye did for we.'
    Down by, etc.

a. 3¹. when that ye had done *is written above* we were thine.
b. 1. *Burden, second line*, by the.   2². with the. *After* 2 :

    ' O mother dear, when we were thine,
    Ye stabd us wi your little penknife.'
      Down by the, etc.

3¹. when that ye had done.   4, 5. *Wanting.*
6. *Burden, second line*, Down by the, etc.

The copy at II, 500 b (Pepys, V, 4, No 2), is also in the Crawford collection, No 1127, and in that from the Osterley Park library, British Museum, C. 39. k. 6 (60). It is dated 1688–95 in the Crawford catalogue, and 1690 ? in the Museum catalogue.

The text printed II, 500 is here corrected according to the Museum copy.

2¹. lovd.   3². for her heaviness.   6². pritty.
8¹. long and sharp.   12². other as naked as.
13². would.   14². dress us.
21¹, 22¹. O mother, O mother.
23¹. Alass ! said.   *After* 10, *etc.:* hair and.
Title: Infants whom.
Imprint: London : Printed, *etc.:* Guiltspur.
(9², 19². *have* into, *wrongly.*)

21. The Maid and the Palmer.

P. 228, III, 502.   'Synderinden,' Kristensen, Jyske Folkeminder, X, 71, No 20.

Swedish **K** is repeated in Lagus, Nyländska Folkvisor, I, 105, No 32.

230 b. A Bohemian ballad, to the same effect, in Waldau's Böhmische Granaten, II, 210, No 299.

231, III, 502 b.   **French.** **A** has been printed by Rolland, Chansons Populaires, VI, 22, *o* (it is folio 60 of the MS.). Two other before unprinted versions *p*, *q*, at pp. 25, 26, of Rolland.

232, 504 b.   'Maria Maddalena,' three stanzas only, Archivio, VIII, 323, Canti Parmigiani, No 2.

22. St Stephen and Herod.

P. 236 a.   **French.** 'Trois Pelerins de Dieu,' Meyrac, Traditions, etc., des Ardennes, p. 280.

240 f., 505 f., II, 501 b.   Add :

Cantou il gatsu:
¡ Cristu naciú!
Dixu il buey:
¿ Agú?
Dixu la ubecha:
¡ En Bilén!
Dixu la cabra:
¡ Catsa, cascarra,
Que nació en Grenada!

Munthe, Folkpoesi från Asturien, III, No 24, cited by Pitrè in Archivio, VIII, 141.
"Quando Christo nasceu, disse o gallo : Jesus-Christo é ná . . . á . . . á . . . do." Leite de Vasconcellos, Tradições pop. de Portugal, p. 148, No 285 b.
241. Greek ballad, The Taking of Constantinople. There is a Bulgarian version. A roasted cock crows, fried fish come to life : Sbornik of the Ministry of Public Instruction, II, 82. In other ballads the same incident is transferred to the downfall of Bulgaria: Kačanofskij, p. 235, No 116 ; Sbornik, II, 129, 2, and II, 131, 2. (W. W.)

24. Bonnie Annie.

P. 245 ff. The Rev. S. Baring-Gould has recently found this ballad in South Devon.
a. Taken down from a man of above eighty years at Bradstone. b. From a young man at Dartmoor. c. From an old man at Holne.

1 'T was of a sea-captain came oer the salt billow,
He courted a maiden down by the green willow:
'O take of your father his gold and his treasure,
O take of your mother her fee without measure.'

2 'I'll take of my father his gold and his treasure,
I'll take of my mother her fee without measure:'
She has come with the captain unto the seaside, O,
'We'll sail to lands foreign upon the blue tide, O!'

3 And when she had sailed today and tomorrow,
She was beating her hands, she was crying in sorrow;
And when she had sailed the days were not many,
The sails were outspread, but of miles made not any.

4 And when she had sailed today and tomorrow,
She was beating her hands, she was crying in sorrow;
And when she had sailed not many a mile, O,
The maid was delivered of a beautiful child, O.

5 . . . .

6 'O take a white napkin, about my head bind it!
O take a white napkin, about my feet wind it!
Alack! I must sink, both me and my baby,
Alack! I must sink in the deep salten water.

7 'O captain, O captain, here's fifty gold crown, O,
I pray thee to bear me and turn the ship round, O;
O captain, O captain, here's fifty gold pound, O,
If thou wilt but set me upon the green ground, O.'

8 'O never, O never! the wind it blows stronger,
O never, O never! the time it grows longer;
And better it were that thy baby and thou, O,
Should drown than the crew of the vessel, I vow, O.'

9 'O get me a boat that is narrow and thin, O,
And set me and my little baby therein, O:'
'O no, it were better that thy baby and thou, O,
Should drown than the crew of the vessel, I vow, O.'

10 They got a white napkin, about her head bound it,
They got a white napkin, about her feet wound it;
They cast her then overboard, baby and she, O,
Together to sink in the cruel salt sea, O.

11 The moon it was shining, the tide it was running;
O what in the wake of the vessel was swimming?
'O see, boys! O see how she floats on the water!
O see, boys! O see! the undutiful daughter!

12 'Why swim in the moonlight, upon the sea swaying?
O what art thou seeking? for what art thou praying?'

'O captain, O captain, I float on the water;
For the sea giveth up the undutiful daughter.

13 'O take of my father the gold and the trea-
sure,
O take of my mother her fee without measure;
O make me a coffin of gold that is yellow,
And bury me under the banks of green willow!'

14 'I will make thee a coffin of gold that is yel-
low,
I 'll bury thee under the banks of green willow;
I 'll bury thee there as becometh a lady,
I 'll bury thee there, both thou and thy baby.'

15 The sails they were spread, and the wind it
was blowing,
The sea was so salt, and the tide it was flow-
ing;
They steered for the land, and they reachd the
shore, O,
But the corpse of the maiden had reachd there
before, O.

b. 1¹,². There was a sea-captain came to the sea-
side, O,
He courted a damsel and got her in trouble.
13³. coffin of the deepest stoll yellow.
15⁴. But the mother and baby had got there before, O.

c. 1 'T is of a sea-captain, down by the green willow,
He courted a damsel and brought her in trouble;
When gone her mother's good will and all her
father's money,
She fled across the wide sea along with her
Johnny.

2 They had not been sailing the miles they were
many
Before she was delivered of a beautiful baby:
'O tie up my head! O and tie it up easy,
And throw me overboard, both me and my
baby!'

3 She floated on the waves, and she floated so
easy,
That they took her on board again, both she
and her baby.
(*The rest forgotten.*)

25. Willie's Lyke-Wake.

Pp. 247 ff., 506. 'The Blue Flowers and the Yellow,' Greenock, printed by W. Scott [1810].

1 'This seven long years I 've courted a maid,'
As the sun shines over the valley
'And she neer would consent for to be my
bride.'
Among the blue flowers and the yellow

2 'O Jamie, O Jamie, I 'll learn you the way
How your innocent love you 'll betray.'

3 'If you will give to the bell-man a groat,
And he 'll toll you down a merry night-wake.'

4 Now he has given the bell-man a groat,
And he has tolld him down a merry night-
wake.

5 'It 's I must go to my true-love's wake,
For late last night I heard he was dead.'

6 'Take with you your horse and boy,
And give your true lover his last convoy.'

7 'I 'll have neither horse nor boy,
But I 'll go alone, and I 'll mourn and cry.'

8 When that she came to her true-love's hall,
Then the tears they did down fall.

9 She lifted up the sheets so small,
He took her in his arms and he threw her to
the wa.

10 'It 's let me go a maid, young Jamie,' she said,
'And I will be your bride, and to-morrow we 'll
be wed.'

11 'If all your friends were in this bower,
You should not be a maid one quarter of an
hour.'

12 'You came here a maid meek and mild,
But you shall go home both marryd and with
child.'

13 He gave to her a gay gold ring,
And the next day they had a gay wedding.

The unfortunate Weaver. To which are added The
Farmer's Daughter and The Blue Flowers and the
Yellow. Greenock. Printed by W. Scott. [1810.]
British Museum, 11621. b. 7 (43).

248 a (C), III, 503 a. 'Hr. Mortens Klosterrov,'
Kristensen, Jyske Folkeminder, X, 264, No 64.

249 b, 506 a, III, 503 a. **Swedish.** 'Herr Karl,'
Lagus, Nyländska Folkvisor, I, 51, No 12.

26. The Three Ravens.

P. 253.   J. Haslewood made an entry in his copy of Ritson's Scotish Song of a MS. Lute-Book (presented to Dr C. Burney by Dr Skene, of Marischal College, in 1781), which contained airs "noted and collected by Robert Gordon, at Aberdeen, in the year of our Lord 1627." Among some ninety titles of tunes mentioned, there occur 'Ther wer three ravens,' and 'God be with the, Geordie.' (W. Macmath.)

"The song of 'The Twa Corbies' was given to me by Miss Erskine of Alva (now Mrs Kerr), who, I think, said that she had written it down from the recitation of an old woman at Alva." C. K. Sharpe to Scott, August 8, 1802, Letters, I, 70, Abbotsford; printed in Sharpe's Letters, ed. Allardyce, I, 136.

29. The Boy and the Mantle.

P. 268 a.   **Flowers.** 2. A garland, Kathá Sarit Ságara, Tawney's translation, II, 601.

269 b.   The chaste Sítá clears herself of unjust suspicion by passing safely over a certain lake: Kathá Sarit Ságara, Tawney's translation, I, 486 f.

A chessboard that can be "mated" only by one that has never been false in love: English Prose Merlin, ed. Wheatley, ch. 21, vol. i, part II, p. 363. (G. L. K.)

31. The Marriage of Sir Gawain.

P. 289, II, 502 b.   On the loathly damsel in the Perceval of Chrestien de Troyes, see The Academy, October 19, 1889, p. 255. (G. L. K.)

290, note †.   One shape by day, another by night: Curtin, Myths and Folk-Lore of Ireland, 1890, pp. 51, 68, 69, 71, 136.

32. King Henry.

P. 298 b.   Second paragraph. Prince as lindworm restored by maid's lying in bed with him one night: 'Lindormen,' Kristensen, Jyske Folkeminder, X, 20, No 9, Lagus, Nyländske Folkvisor, I, 97, No 29, a, b. (Lindworm asks for a kiss in a 4, b 2.)

34. Kemp Owyne.

P. 307 b.   Second paragraph. 'Jomfruen i Linden,' Kristensen, Jyske Folkeminder, X, 22, No 10.

37. Thomas Rymer.

P. 323 ff.   "Thomas the Rhymer. Variations. J. Ormiston, Kelso." "Scotch Ballads, Materials for Border Minstrelsy," No 96, Abbotsford; in the handwriting of John Leyden.

Her horse was o the dapple-gray,
  And in her hands she held bells nine:
'Harp and carp, Thomas,' she said,
  'For a' thae bonny bells shall be thine.'

It was a night without delight,

And they rade on and on, I wiss,   (amiss)
  Till they came to a garden green;
He reached his hand to pu an apple,
  For lack o fruit he was like to tyne.

'Now had your hand, Thomas,' she said,
  'Had your hand, and go wi me;
That is the evil fruit o hell,
  Beguiled man and women in your countrie.

'O see you not that road, Thomas,
  That lies down by that little hill?
Curst is the man has that road to gang,
  For it takes him to the lowest hell.

'O see you not that road, Thomas,
  That lies across yon lily lea?
Blest is the man has that road to gang,
  For it takes him to the heavens hie.

'When ye come to my father's ha,
  To see what a learned man you be
They will you question, one and a',
  But you must answer none but me,
And I will answer them again
  I gat you at the Eildon tree.'

And when, etc.
  He answered none but that gay ladie.

'Harp and carp, gin ye gang wi me,
It shall be seven year and day
  Or ye return to your countrie.

'Wherever ye gang, or wherever ye be,
  Ye 'se bear the tongue that can never lie.

'Gin ere ye want to see me again,
  Gang to the bonny banks o Farnalie.'

'Thomas the Rhymer,' "Scotch Ballads, Materials for Border Minstrelsy," No 97, Abbotsford; communicated to Sir Walter Scott by Mrs Christiana Greenwood, London, May 27, 1806 (Letters, I, 189), from the recitation of her mother and of her aunt, both then above sixty, who learned it in their childhood from Kirstan Scot, a very old woman, at Longnewton, near Jedburgh.

1 Thomas lay on the Huntlie bank,
 A spying ferlies wi his eee,
And he did spy a lady gay,
 Come riding down by the lang lee.

2 Her steed was o the dapple grey,
 And at its mane there hung bells nine;
He thought he heard that lady say,
 'They gowden bells sall a' be thine.'

3 Her mantle was o velvet green,
 And a' set round wi jewels fine;
Her hawk and hounds were at her side,
 And her bugle-horn in gowd did shine.

4 Thomas took aff baith cloak and cap,
 For to salute this gay lady:
'O save ye, save ye, fair Queen o Heavn,
 And ay weel met ye save and see!'

5 'I 'm no the Queen o Heavn, Thomas;
 I never carried my head sae hee;
For I am but a lady gay,
 Come out to hunt in my follee.

6 'Now gin ye kiss my mouth, Thomas,
 Ye mauna miss my fair bodee;
Then ye may een gang hame and tell
 That ye 've lain wi a gay ladee.'

7 'O gin I loe a lady fair,
 Nae ill tales o her wad I tell,
And it 's wi thee I fain wad gae,
 Tho it were een to heavn or hell.'

8 'Then harp and carp, Thomas,' she said,
 'Then harp and carp alang wi me;
But it will be seven years and a day
 Till ye win back to yere ain countrie.'

9 The lady rade, True Thomas ran,
 Untill they cam to a water wan;
O it was night, and nae delight,
 And Thomas wade aboon the knee.

10 It was dark night, and nae starn-light,
 And on they waded lang days three,
And they heard the roaring o a flood,
 And Thomas a waefou man was he.

11 Then they rade on, and farther on,
 Untill they came to a garden green;
To pu an apple he put up his hand,
 For the lack o food he was like to tyne.

12 'O haud yere hand, Thomas,' she cried,
 'And let that green flourishing be;
For it 's the very fruit o hell,
 Beguiles baith man and woman o yere coun-
 trie.

13 'But look afore ye, True Thomas,
 And I shall show ye ferlies three;
Yon is the gate leads to our land,
 Where thou and I sae soon shall be.

14 'And dinna ye see yon road, Thomas,
 That lies out-owr yon lilly lee?
Weel is the man yon gate may gang,
 For it leads him straight to the heavens hie.

15 'But do you see yon road, Thomas,
 That lies out-owr yon frosty fell?
Ill is the man yon gate may gang,
 For it leads him straight to the pit o hell.

16 'Now when ye come to our court, Thomas,
 See that a weel-learnd man ye be;
For they will ask ye, one and all,
 But ye maun answer nane but me.

17 'And when nae answer they obtain,
 Then will they come and question me,
And I will answer them again
 That I gat yere aith at the Eildon tree.

* * * * * * *

18 'Ilka seven years, Thomas,
 We pay our teindings unto hell,
And ye 're sae leesome and sae strang
 That I fear, Thomas, it will be yeresell.'

1⁴. the Lang-lee. 12². flour is hing.

39. Tam Lin.

P. 335. **D a**, excepting the title and the first stanza, is in a hand not Motherwell's.

I a first appeared in the second edition of the Minstrelsy, 1803, II, 245. The "gentleman residing near Langholm," from whom Scott derived the stanzas of a modern cast, was a Mr Beattie, of Meikledale, and Scott suspected that they might be the work of some poetical clergyman or schoolmaster: letter to W. Laidlaw, January 21, 1803, cited by Carruthers, Abbotsford Notanda, appended to R. Chambers's Life of Scott, 1871, p. 121 f.

336 b. 'Den förtrollade prinsessan,' Lagus, Nyländska Folkvisor, I, 67, No 17.

356 b. Add: **D c**, 12². aft.

340 a, II, 505 b, III, 505 b. Sleeping under an

apple-tree. See also st. 14 of the version immediately following.

So Lancelot goes to sleep about noon under an apple-tree, and is enchanted by Morgan the Fay. Malory's Morte Darthur, bk. vi, ch. 1, ch. 3, ed. Sommer, I, 183, 186. (G. L. K.)

K

Communicated to Scott November 11, 1812, by Hugh Irvine, Drum, Aberdeenshire, as procured from the recitation of an old woman in Buchan: Letters, V, No 137, Abbotsford. (Not in Irvine's hand.)

1 Leady Margat stands in her boor-door,
   Clead in the robs of green ;
   She longed to go to Charters Woods,
   To pull the flowers her lean.

2 She had not puld a rose, a rose,
   O not a rose but one,
   Till up it starts True Thomas,
   Said, Leady, let alone.

3 'Why pull ye the rose, Marget?
   Or why break ye the tree?
   Or why come ye to Charters Woods
   Without the leave of me?'

4 'I will pull the rose,' she said,
   'And I will break the tree,
   For Charters Woods is all my own,
   And I 'l ask no leave of the.'

5 He 's tean her by the milk-white hand,
   And by the grass-green sleeve,
   And laid her lo at the foot of the tree,
   At her he askt no leave.

6 It fell once upon a day
   They wer a pleaying at the ba,
   And every one was reed and whyte,
   Leady Marget's culler was all awa.

7 Out it speaks an elder man,
   As he stood in the gate,
   'Our king's daughter she gos we bern,
   And we will get the wait.'

8 'If I be we bern,' she said,
   ' My own self beer the blame!
   There is not a man in my father's court
   Will get my bern's name.'

9 'There grows a flower in Charters Woods,
   It grows on gravel greay,
   It ould destroy the boney young bern
   That ye got in your pley.'

10 She 's tean her mantle her about,
    Her green glove on her hand,
    And she 's awa to Charters Woods,
    As fest as she could gang.

11 She had no puld a pile, a pile,
    O not a pile but one,
    Up it startid True Thomas,
    Said, Leady, lat alean.

12 'Why pull ye the pile, Marget,
    That grows on gravel green,
    For to destroy the boney young bern
    That we got us between?'

13 'If it were to an earthly man,
    As [it is] to an elphan knight,
    I ould walk for my true-love's sake
    All the long winter's night.'

14 'When I was a boy of eleven years old,
    And much was made of me,
    I went out to my father's garden,
    Fell asleep at yon aple tree :
    The queen of Elphan [she] came by,
    And laid on her hands on me.

15 'Elphan it 's a boney place,
    In it fain wid I dwall ;
    But ey at every seven years end
    We pay the teene to hell :
    I 'm so full of flesh and blood
    I 'm sear feart for mysel.

16 'The morn 's Hallow Even's night,
    When a' our courts do ride,
    Through England and through Irland,
    Through a' the world wide :
    And she that would her true-love borrow
    At Miles Corse she may bide.

17 'The first an court that ye come till,
    Ye let them a' pass by ;
    The next an court that ye come till,
    Ye hile them reverendly.

18 'The next an court that ye come till,
    An therein rides the queen,

Me upon a milk-whyte steed,
   And a gold star in my croun;
Because I am a erle's soon,
   I get that for my renoun.

19 'Ye take me in your armes,
   Give me a right sear fa;
The queen of Elphan she 'l cry out,
   True Thomas is awa!

20 'First I 'l be in your armes
   The fire burning so bold;
Ye hold me fast, let me no pass
   Till I be like iron cold.

21 'Next I 'l be in your armes
   The fire burning so wild;
Ye hold me fast, let me no pass,
   I 'm the father of your child.'

22 The first court that came her till,
   She let them a' pass by;
The nex an court that came her till,
   She helt them reverendly.

23 The nex an court that came her till,
   And therein read the queen,
True Thomas on a milk-whyte steed,
   A gold star in his croun;
Because he was a earl's soon,
   He got that for his renoun.

24 She 's tean him in her arms,
   Geen him a right sore fa;
The queen of Elphan she cried out,
   True Thomas is awa!

25 He was into her arms
   The fire burning so bold;
She held him fast, let him no pass
   Till he was like iron cold.

26 He was into her arms
   The fire burning so wild;
She held him fast, let him no pass,
   He was the father of her child.

27 The queen of Elphan she cried out,
   An angry woman was she,
'Let Leady Marget an her true-love be,
   She 's bought him dearer than me.'

3². breat. 15⁴. tune (?). 16¹. Thee.
27². woman *is struck out.*

The following fragment does not appear to have been among the "several recitals from tradition" used by Scott in making up his ballad. Some lines which it might be supposed to have furnished occur in the edition of 1802, issued before Scott's acquaintance with Laidlaw began.

L

"Scotch Ballads, Materials for Border Minstrelsy," No 27, Abbotsford; in the handwriting of William Laidlaw.

1 I charge ye, a' ye ladies fair,
   That wear goud in your hair,
To come an gang bye Carterhaugh,
   For young Tam Lien is there.

   *   *   *   *   *   *   *

2 Then Janet kiltit her green cleadin
   A wee aboon her knee,
An she 's gane away to Carterhaugh,
   As fast as she can dree.

3 When Janet cam to Carterhaugh,
   Tam Lien was at the wall,
An there he left his steed stannin,
   But away he gaed his sell.

4 She had na pu'd a red, red rose,
   A rose but only thre,
Till up then startit young Tam Lien,
   Just at young Jenet's knee.

5 'What gars ye pu the rose, Janet,
   Briek branches frae the tree,
An come an gang by Carterhaugh,
   An speir nae leave of me?'

6 'What need I speir leave o thee, Tam?
   What need I speir leave o thee,
When Carterhaugh is a' mine ain,
   My father gae it me?'

   *   *   *   *   *   *   *

7 She 's kiltit up her green cleadin
   A wee aboon her knee,
An she 's away to her ain bower-door,
   As fast as she can dree.

   *   *   *   *   *   *   *

8 There war four-an-twentie fair ladies
   A' dancin in a chess,

An some war blue an some war green,
    But Janet was like the gress.

9 There war four-an-twentie fair ladies
    A' playin at the ba,
An some war red an som wer white,
    But Jennet was like the snaw.

1³. To *is doubtful; almost bound in.*
6⁴. gae *written over* left *struck out.*
8², 9². A' *in the MS.*

M

" Scotch Ballads, Materials for Border Minstrelsy," No
15. Communicated to Scott by Major Henry Hutton, Royal
Artillery, 24th December, 1802, as recollected by his father
" and the family:" Letters I, No 77. Major Hutton intimates that stanzas 46–49 of the first edition of ' Tamlane '
(' Roxburgh was my grandfather,' ff., corresponding to **I**
28–32) should be struck out, and his verses inserted. But
4–12 of Hutton's stanzas belong to ' Thomas Rymer.'

1 My father was a noble knight,
    And was much gi'n to play,
And I myself a bonny boy,
    And followed him away.

2 He rowd me in his hunting-coat
    And layd me down to sleep,
And by the queen of fairies came,
    And took me up to keep.

3 She set me on a milk-white steed;
    'T was o the elfin kind;
His feet were shot wi beaten goud,
    And fleeter than the wind.

4 Then we raid on and on'ard mair,
    Oer mountain, hill and lee,
Till we came to a hie, hie wa,
    Upon a mountain's bree.

5 The apples hung like stars of goud
    Out-our that wa sa fine;
I put my hand to pu down ane,
    For want of food I thought to tine.

6 ' O had your hand, Tamas ! ' she said,
    ' O let that evil fruit now be !
It was that apple ye see there
    Beguil'd man and woman in your country.

7 ' O dinna ye see yon road, Tamas,
    Down by yon lilie lee ?

Blessd is the man who yon gate gaes,
    It leads him to the heavens hie.

8 ' And dinna ye see yon road, Tamas,
    Down by yon frosty fell ?
Curst is the man that yon gate gaes,
    For it leads to the gates of hell.

9 ' O dinna ye see yon castle, Tamas,
    That 's biggit between the twa,
And theekit wi the beaten goud ?
    O that 's the fairies' ha.

10 ' O when ye come to the ha, Tamas,
    See that a weel-learnd boy ye be;
They 'll ask ye questions ane and a',
    But see ye answer nane but me.

11 ' If ye speak to ain but me, Tamas,
    A fairie ye maun ever bide;
But if ye speak to nane but me, Tamas,
    Ye may come to be your country's pride.'

12 And when he came to Fairie Ha,
    I wot a weel-learnd boy was he;
They askd him questions ane and a',
    But he answerd nane but his ladie.

13 There was four-and-twenty gude knights'-
        sons
    In fairie land obliged to bide,
And of a' the pages that were there
    Fair Tamas was his ladie's pride.

14 There was four-and-twenty earthly boys,
    Wha all played at the ba,
But Tamas was the bonniest boy,
    And playd the best amang them a'.

15 There was four-and-twenty earthly maids,
    Wha a' playd at the chess,
Their colour rosy-red and white,
    Their gowns were green as grass.

16 ' And pleasant are our fairie sports,
    We flie o'er hill and dale;
But at the end of seven years
    They pay the teen to hell.

17 ' And now 's the time, at Hallowmess,
    Late on the morrow's even,
And if ye miss me then, Janet,
    I 'm lost for yearis seven.'

N

'Tamlane,' "Scotch Ballads, Materials for Border Minstrelsy," No 96 a; in the handwriting of John Leyden.

'Gowd rings I can buy, Thomas,
 Green mantles I can spin,
But gin ye take my maidenheid
 I 'll neer get that again.'

Out and spak the queen o fairies,
 Out o a shot o wheat,
'She that has gotten young Tamlane
 Has gotten my heart's delight.'

40. The Queen of Elfan's Nourice.

P. 358, II, 505 b, III, 505 b. More cases in 'Fairy Births and Human Midwives,' E. S. Hartland, The Archæological Review, IV, 328 ff.

The elf-woman's daughter has lain on the floor nineteen days in travail, for she cannot be delivered unless a mortal man lay hands upon her. Hrólfr is lured to the elf-woman's hall for this purpose. Göngu-Hrólfs Saga, c. 15, Rafn, Fornaldar Sögur, III, 276, Ásmundarson, Fornaldarsögur Norðrlanda, III, 174, 175. (G. L. K.)

41. Hind Etin.

P. 361 b, III, 506 a. Danish. X, 'Agnete i Bjærget,' Kristensen, Jyske Folkeminder, X, 3, No 2.

364 a, III, 506 a. Danish. M–O, 'Agnete i Havet,' Kristensen, Jyske Folkeminder, X, 6, No 3, A–C.

365 a, II, 506 a. German. J. 'Die schöne Dorothea,' Gadde-Gloddow, V. l. aus Hinterpommern, Zeitschrift für Volkskunde, III, 227.

42. Clerk Colvill.

P. 374 b. Danish. 'Elvedansen,' Kristensen, Jyske Folkeminder, X, 10, 372, No 5, A, B, C.

380, II, 506 a, III, 506 a. PP, QQ, 'Arnaud,' Quercy, Daymard, p. 167 f., 34 verses, 26 verses. RR, 'Lou Counte Arnaud,' Bas-Quercy, Soleville, Chants p. du Bas-Quercy, 1889, p. 13, 10 stanzas. SS, version limousine, La Tradition, V, 184.

384, III, 506 a. Spanish. 'Don Pedro,' El Folk-Lore Frexnense y Bético–Extremeño, Fregenal, 1883–84; (1) p. 129 (and 180), Zafra, Badajoz, D. Sergio Hernandez ; (2) p. 182, Badajoz ; (3) p. 183, Montanchez, provincia de Cácares ; (4) Constantina, provincia de Sevilla, D. Antonio Machado y Alvarez.

386 a. Bohemian. A a also = Wenzig, Slawische V. l., 1830, p. 47.

43. The Broomfield Hill.

P. 392 b, III, 506. Sleep-thorn, sleep-pin. Add : Curtin, Myths and Folk-Lore of Ireland, 1890, pp. 40,

130 ff., 200 ; Hyde, Beside the Fire, Irish-Gaelic Folk-Stories, p. 43 ; MacInnes, Folk and Hero Tales, 1890, p. 141 (cf. p. 459).

Sleep-pin, Wlisłocki, M. u. S. der transylvanischen Zigeuner, p. 46. Compare the wand in J. H. Knowles's Folk-Tales of Kashmir, p. 199. (G. L. K.)

393, III, 506 b. Italian. 'La bella Brunetta,' Ferrari, C. p. in San Pietro Capofiume ; 'La Bevanda sonnifera,' Giannini, Canzoni del Contado di Massa Lunense, Archivio, VII, 109, No 11, 279, No 7.

44. The Twa Magicians.

P. 400 a, II, 506 b, III, 506 b. French. W, 'J'ai fait une maîtresse,' Daymard, p. 51, Quercy. X, 'Margarideto,' Soleville, Chants p. du Bas-Quercy, p. 94.

Italian. Add to Tigri's *rispetto* : Vigo, Canti p. siciliani, 1870–74, No 1711, Pitrè, Studj di Poesia pop., p. 76 ; Casetti e Imbriani, C. p. delle Provincie meridionali, p. 187 : all cited by d'Ancona, Poesia pop., p. 341.

400 b. Bohemian. Waldau, Böhmische Granaten, II, 75, No 107, dove, gun ; fish, hook ; hare, dog.

401 b. Tale in Curtin's Myths and Folk-Lore of Ireland, pp. 152–6.

Cf. also Notes and Queries, 7th Series, IX, 101, 295 ; Clouston, Popular Tales and Fictions, I, 413 ff. (G. L K.)

45. King John and the Bishop.

P. 403 f. Roxburghe, III, 883, is B. Roxburghe, III, 494 was printed and sold by John White, Newcastle-upon-Tyne, " circa 1777 : " Ebsworth, Roxburghe Ballads, VI, 749. 'The King and the Bishop,' Roxburghe, III, 170, is printed in the same volume, p. 751, and ' The Old Abbot and King Olfrey,' Pepys, II, 127, at p. 753.

405 b, II, 507. An Armenian, a Slovak, and a Hungarian version, by H. v. Wlisłocki, Zs. f. vergleichende Litteraturgeschichte, u. s. w., N. F., IV, 106 ff., 1891.

404 b, 2d paragraph. Of this kind is the Russian tale, How Fraud made entrance into Russia. Ivan the Terrible demands tribute of neighboring princes. They propose to him three riddles : if he guesses them, they are to pay twelve casks of gold and tribute ; if he fails, they take his kingdom. A marvellous old man helps the Tsar out. He has been promised a cask of gold, but the Tsar fills one of the casks two thirds with sand, and offers that. The old man tells him that he, the Tsar, has brought Fraud into the land, never to be eradicated. Ivan begs him to take one of the other casks, but in vain. The old man vanishes ; it was God. Rybnikof, II, 232, No 39. (W. W.)

46. Captain Wedderburn's Courtship.

P. 417 a, II, 507 b, III, 507 a. Heads on spikes ; only one spike without a head : Curtin, Myths and Folk-Lore of Ireland, 1890, pp. 37, 114 f, 193 ; Mac Innes, Folk and Hero Tales, Folk-Lore Society, 1890, pp. 79, 453.

47. Proud Lady Margaret.

P. 426. **A.** Two stanzas (6, 9) and a line were wanting in the copy supplied by Hamilton. March 23, 1803, Hamilton sent to Scott the following verses, "to come in at the first break." There were still four lines, which should come before these, that Hamilton could not recollect. "Scotch Ballads, Materials for Border Minstrelsy," No 117. See **B** 17, **C** 11, where also there is defect, and **D** 6, 7.

'O wherein leems the beer?' she said,
  'Or wherein leems the wine?
O wherein leems the gold?' she said,
  'Or wherein leems the twine?'

'The beer is put in a drinking-horn,
  The wine in glasses fine,
There's gold in store between two kings,
  When they are fighting keen,
And the twine is between a lady's two hands
  When they are washen clean.'

49. The Twa Brothers.

P. 436, II, 14, III, 381 b. 'Tell my mother I am married,' etc.: so in the beautiful Roumanian 'Miorita,' Alecsandri, p. 3.
438. **A b.** 'The Two Brothers,' Walks near Edinburgh, by Margaret Warrender, 1890, p. 60. Given to Lady John Scott many years ago by Campbell Riddell, brother of Sir James Riddell of Ardnamurchan.

1 There were two brothers in the north,
    Lord William and Lord John,
  And they would try a wrestling match,
    So to the fields they've gone, gone, gone,
    So to the fields they've gone.

2 They wrestled up, they wrestled down,
    Till Lord John fell on the ground.
  And a knife into Lord William's pocket
    Gave him a deadly wound.

3 'Oh take me on your back, dear William,' he said,
  'And carry me to the burnie clear,
  And wash my wound sae deep and dark,
    Maybe 't will bleed nae mair.'

4 He took him up upon his back,
    An carried him to the burnie clear,
  But aye the mair he washed his wound
    It aye did bleed the mair.

5 'Oh take me on your back, dear William,' he said,
  'And carry me to the kirkyard fair,
  And dig a grave sae deep and dark,
    And lay my body there.'

6 'But what shall I say to my father dear
    When he says, Willie, what's become of John?'
  'Oh tell him I am gone to Greenock town,
    To buy him a puncheon of rum.'

7 'And what shall I say to my sister dear
    When she says, Willie, what's become of John?'
  'Oh tell her I've gone to London town
    To buy her a marriage-gown.'

8 'But what shall I say to my grandmother dear
    When she says, Willie, what's become of John?'
  'Oh tell her I'm in the kirkyard dark,
    And that I'm dead and gone.'

53. Young Beichan.

P. 459 a. **Danish.** 'Ellen henter sin Fæstemand,' Kristensen, Jyske Folkeminder, X, 125, No 34, **A, B.**
462 a, III, 507 b. 'Gerineldo,' again, in Munthe, Folkpoesie från Asturien, No 2, second part, p. 112 b (Upsala Universitets Årsskrift); but imperfect.
462 b, 463 a, II, 508 a. Another version of the French ballad ('Tout au milieu de Paris') in Meyrac, Traditions, etc., des Ardennes, p. 238.
463 ff. 'Earl Bichet,' "Scotch Ballads, Materials for Border Minstrelsy," No 83, Abbotsford. Communicated to Scott by Mrs Christiana Greenwood, London, May 27, 1806 (Letters, I, No 189), as heard by her in her youth at Longnewton, near Jedburgh, "where most of the old women could sing it."

1 Earl Bichet's sworn a mighty aith,
    And a solemn vow made he,
  That he wad to the Holy Land,
    To the Holy Land wad he gae.

2 When he came to the Holy Land,
    Amang the Infidels sae black,
  They hae consulted them amang
    The Earl Bichet for to take.

3 And when they basely him betrayd
    They put him into fetters strang,
  And threw him in a dungeon dark,
    To spend the weary night sae lang.

4 Then in ilka shoulder they bored a hole,
   In his right shoulder they bored three,
And they gard him draw the coops o wine,
   Till he was sick and like to dee.

5 Then they took him out o their carts and wains,
   And put him in a castle of stone;
When the stars shone bright, and the moon
     gave light,
   The sad Earl Bichet he saw none.

6 The king had only ae daughter,
   And it was orderd sae to be
That, as she walked up and down,
   By the strong-prison-door cam she.

7 Then she heard Earl Bichet sad
   Making his pityful mane,
In doolfu sounds and moving sighs
   Wad melt a heart o stane.

8 'When I was in my ain countrie,
   I drank the wine sae clear;
But now I canna get bare bread;
   O I wis I had neer come here!

9 'When I was in my ain countrie,
   I drank the wine sae red;
But now I canna get a bite o bare bread;
   O I wis that I were dead!'

*   *   *   *   *   *   *

10 'Gae bring to me the good leaven [bread],
   To eat when I do need;
Gae bring to me the good red wine,
   To drink when I do dread.'

11 'Gae ask my father for his leave
   To bring them unto me,
And for the keys o the prison-door,
   To set Earl Bichet free.'

*   *   *   *   *   *   *

12 Then she went into her ain chamber
   And prayd most heartilie,
And when that she rose up again
   The keys fell at her knee.

*   *   *   *   *   *   *

13 Then they hae made a solemn vow
   Between themselves alone,

That he was to marry no other woman,
   And she no other man.

14 And Earl Bichet's to sail to fair Scotland,
   Far oer the roaring faem,
And till seven years were past and gone
   This vow was to remain.

15 Then she built him a stately ship,
   And set it on the sea,
Wi four-and-twenty mariners,
   To bear him companie.

16 'My blessing gae wi ye, Earl Bichet,
   My blessing gae wi thee;
My blessing be wi a' the mariners
   That are to sail wi thee.'

17 Then they saild east, and they saild wast,
   Till they saild to Earl Bichet's yett,
When nane was sae ready as his mother
     dear
   To welcome her ain son back.

18 'Ye're welcome, welcome, Earl Bichet,
   Ye're dearly welcome hame to me!
And ye're as welcome to Lady Jean,
   For she has lang looked for thee.'

19 'What haste, what haste, O mother dear,
   To wale a wife for me?
For what will I do wi the bonny bride
   That I hae left ayont the sea?'

20 When seven years were past and gone,
   Seven years but and a day,
The Saracen lady took a crying in her sleep,
   And she has cried sair till day.

21 'O daughter, is it for a man o might?
   Or is it for a man o mine?'
'It's neither for a man o might,
   Nor is it for a man o thine.

22 'Bat if ye'll build me a ship, father,
   And set it on the sea,
I will away to some other land,
   To seek a true-love free.'

23 Then he built her a gallant ship,
   And set it on the sea,
Wi a hunder and fifty mariners,
   To bear her companie.

24 At every corner o the ship
   A siller bell did hing,
And at ilka jawing o the faem
   The siller bells did ring.

25 Then they saild east, and they saild wast,
   Till they cam to Earl Bichet's yett;
Nane was sae ready as the porter
   To open and let her in thereat.

26 'O is this Earl Bichet's castle-yett?
   Or is that noble knight within?
For I am weary, sad and wet,
   And far I 've come ayont the faem.'

27 'He 's up the stair at supper set,
   And mony a noble knight wi him;
He 's up the stair wi his bonny bride,
   And mony a lady gay wi them.'

28 She 's put her hand into her purse
   And taen out fifty merks and three:
'If this be the Earl Bichet's castle,
   Tell him to speak three words wi me.

29 'Tell him to send me a bit o his bread
   But an a bottle o his wine,
And no forget the lady's love
   That freed him out o prison strong.'

30 The porter he gaed up the stair,
   And mony bow and binge gae he;
'What means, what means,' cried Earl Bichet,
   'O what means a' this courtesie?'

31 'O I hae been porter at yere yett
   These four-and-twenty years and three;
But the fairest lady now stands thereat
   That ever my two eyes did see.

32 'She has a ring on her foremost finger,
   And on her middle-finger three;
She has as much gowd about her waist
   As wad buy earldoms o land for thee.

33 'She wants to speak three words wi thee,
   And a little o yere bread and wine,
And not to forget the lady's love
   That freed ye out o prison strong.'

34 'I 'll lay my life,' cried Earl Bichet,
   'It 's my true love come oer the sea!'

Then up and spake the bride's mother,
   'It 's a bonny time to speak wi thee!'

35 'O your doughter came here on a horse's back,
   But I 'll set her hame in a chariot free;
For, except a kiss o her bonny mouth,
   Of her fair body I am free.'

36 There war thirty cups on the table set,
   He gard them a' in flinders flee;
There war thirty steps into the stair,
   And he has louped them a' but three.

37 Then he took her saftly in his arms,
   And kissed her right tenderlie:
'Ye 're welcome here, my ain true love,
   Sae dearly welcome ye 're to me!'

*   *   *   *   *   *   *

7³. doolfu: l *struck out.*
At the end: "Some verses are wanting at the conclusion."

The following stanza, entered by Scott in the quarto volume "Scottish Songs," 1795, fol. 29 back, Abbotsford library, N. 3, is much too good to be lost ·.

Young Bechin was in Scotland born,
   He longed far countries for to see,
And he bound himself to a savage Moor,
   Who used him but indifferently.

———◆———

VOL. II.

55. The Carnal and the Crane.

P. 7, 509 b, III, 507 b. The Sower. Add: Legeay, Noëls Anciens, Première Série, 1875, 'Saint Joseph avec Marie,' No 34, p. 68; Daymard, Vieux Chants p. rec. en Quercy, 'La Fuite en Egypte,' p. 333; Soleville, Ch. p. du Bas-Quercy, 'Lou Bouiaje,' p. 126; La Tradition, IV, 139.

56. Dives and Lazarus.

P. 10, III, 507 b. 'Le mauvais riche,' Daymard, Vieux Chants p. rec. en Quercy, p. 282.

57. Brown Robyn's Confession.

P. 13. **Swedish.** 'Herr Päders Sjöresa,' Lagus, Nyländska Folkvisor, I, 56, No 14, a, b.

Danish. 'Jon Rimaardsens Sejlads,' Kristensen, Jyske Folkeminder, X, 296, No 73, **A–D.**

13 ff., II, 510, also No 20, I, 244. While Prince Lundarasena is on a voyage, a great hurricane arises. An offering of jewels is made to the sea, but does not quiet it. Lundarasena says : " It is through my demerits in former births that this day of doom has suddenly come upon you." He flings himself into the water ; the wind falls immediately and the sea becomes calm. (He is not drowned.) Kathá Sarit Ságara, Tawney's translation, II, 375.

A ship stopped. Cf. the story told by Henry of Huntingdon, viii, 22, of one Reiner, a follower of Geoffrey Mandeville (Gaufridus de Magna Villa).

" Princeps autem peditum suorum, Reinerus nomine, cujus officium fuerat ecclesias frangere vel incendere, dum mare cum uxore sua transiret, ut multi perhibuerunt, navis immobilis facta est. Quod monstrum nautis stupentibus, sorte data rei causam inquirentibus, sors cecidit super Reinerum. Quod cum ille nimirum totis contradiceret nisibus, secundo et tertio sors jacta in eum devenit. Positus igitur in scapha est, et uxor ejus, et pecunia scelestissime adquisita, et statim navis cursu velocissimo ut prius fecerat pelagus sulcat, scapha vero cum nequissimis subita voragine circumducta in æternum absorpta est." This was in the year 1144. Henrici Archidiaconi Huntendunensis Historia Anglorum, ed. Arnold, Rolls Series, 1879, p. 278. (G. L. K.)

" Audivi a fratre Galtero de Leus quod, cum quedam mulier, mare transiens, pulcritudine sua omnes qui erant in navi ita attraxisset ut omnes qui erant ibi fere cum ea peccassent vel per actum aut consensum, et non evitaret patrem aut filium, sed indifferenter omnibus, licet occulte, se exponeret, facta in mari tempestate et navi periclitante, cepit clamare coram omnibus omnia peccata sua et confiteri ea, credens quod alii propter ea deberent periclitari. Tunc, aliis confitentibus, cessavit mare a furore suo. Facta tranquillitate, nullus potuit scire que esset illa mulier aut cognoscere eam." Anecdotes historiques, Légendes et Apologues tirés du Recueil inédit d'Étienne de Bourbon, ed. Lecoy de la Marche, 1877, p. 160. (G. L. K.)

A merchant is making a voyage to Mount Athos with a cargo of wax and incense. St Nicolas freezes the ship in, and will not thaw it out until the master makes a vow to present the cargo to the monastery there. **Bulgarian,** Miladinof, p. 56, No 50. A ship in which Milica is captive is stopped by her tears and plaints until she and her brother are released. **Servian,** Karadžić, I, 556, No 729. (W. W.)

16. 'Captain Glen.' Christie's Traditional Ballad Airs, I, 241, from recitation. As Christie remarks, some verses of the ballad are introduced into Scott's Pirate, ch. 36.

59. Sir Aldingar.

P. 33 f. The child champion in **A.** (Compare also the notes to No 90, II, 513 b, III, 515 b.) Children who distinguish themselves by valorous exploits, and even get the better of heroes, are especially common in Bulgarian epos. A child of three days kills a monster that stops the way of a marriage-train, and then requires the guests to come to its baptism : Miladinof, p. 79, No 59. Marko Kraljević is vanquished by one of these, seven years old : Miladinof, p. 173, No 121 ; Kačanofskij, pp. 341–55, Nos 151–55. In Kačanofskij, p. 355, No 156, the child is but seven months old. More of this extravagance in Miladinof, p. 266, No 173 ; Sbornik of the Ministry of Instruction, I, 59, No 4. (W. W.)

35, note. In The Order of Combats for Life in Scotland, Spalding Club Misc., II, 387 (of uncertain date), the second oath to be proposed to the parties is, that they have not brought into the lists other armor or weapons than was allowed, neither any engine, charm, herb, or enchantment, etc.

60. King Estmere.

P. 50 b, the last paragraph. It might have been remarked that ' King Estmere ' resembles in a general way a series of German poems of adventure, in which a young king (or his guardians) is nice about a wife, and the princess proposed to him is won only with great difficulty: König Rother (ed. Rückert, v. 13 ff.) ; Ortnit (Ortnit und die Wolfdietriche, ed. Amelung und Jänicke, I, 4, st. 8 ff.) ; Hugdietrich (the same, p. 168, st. 9 ff.) ; Oswald (Sant Oswaldes Leben, ed. Ettmüller, p. 6, v. 140 ff) ; Orendel (ed. Berger, p. 8, v. 192 ff.) ; Dietwart (Dietrichs Flucht, ed. Martin, Heldenbuch, IIʳ Teil, p. 68, v. 785 ff.). To which may be added Fore, in Salman und Marolf (ed. Vogt, p. 5, str. 24 ff.), and Tsar Vasily, in Russian *byliny* (see Vogt, p. XLII).

61. Sir Cawline.

P. 60, III, 508 b. Cucúlin pulls liver and lights out of the throats of two lions : Curtin, Myths and Folk-Lore of Ireland, p. 317.

62. Fair Annie.

P. 65 a. **Swedish.** ' Skön Anna,' ' Skön Anna och Herr Peder,' Lagus, Nyländska Folkvisor, I, 13, No 4, *a*, *b*. The bride throws down one half of a gold ring, Fair Annie the other ; the parts run together: *a* 23, *b* 16.

67. The romance of Galerent follows the story of Marie's *lai*, and is thought to be founded on it : Le Roman de Galerent, Comte de Bretagne, par le trouvère Renaut, A. Boucherie, 1888. (G. L. K.)

68, note. The story is in Coryat's Crudities, 1611, p. 646 f. ; III, 81 f., of the ed. of 1776. (G. L. K.)

63. Child Waters.

P. 84 b, III, 508 b. Add : Skattegraveren, 1888, II, 135, Nos 408–11.

64. Fair Janet.

P. 101 b. **Danish.** 'Kong Valdemar og hans Søster,' Kristensen, Jyske Folkeminder, X, 75, 378, No 23.

102 b. **Breton** ballad. After Luzel, II, 6–15, add 558, the page of the third ballad.

Quellien, Chansons et Danses des Bretons, p. 73, is a fourth version. This ballad, says Quellien, is widely spread, and has various titles, one of which is 'Le Comte de Poitou.'

103 ff. "Scotch Ballads, Materials for Border Minstrelsy," Abbotsford, No 25. In the handwriting of William Laidlaw; "from Jean Scott."

1 Young Janet sits in her garden,
      Makin a heavie maen,
   Whan by cam her father dear,
      Walkin himself alane.

2 'It 's telld me in my bower, Janet,
      It 's telld me in my bed,
   That ye 're in love wi Sweet Willie;
      But a French lord ye maun wed.'

3 'In it be telld ye in yer bower, father,
      In it be telld ye in your bed,
   That me an Willie bears a love,
      Yet a French lord I maun wed,
   But here I mak a leel, leel vow
      He 's neer come in my bed.

4 'An for to please my father dear
      A French lord I will wed;
   But I hae sworn a solemn oth
      He 's neer come in my bed.'

5 Young Janet 's away to her bower-door,
      As fast as she can hie,
   An Willie he has followd her,
      He 's followd speedilie.

6 An whan he cam to her bowr-door
      He tirlt at the pin:
   'O open, open, Janet love,
      Open an let me in.'

7 'It was never my mother's custm, Willie,
      It never sal be mine,
   For a man to come the bower within
      When a woman 's travelin.

8 'Gae yer ways to my sisters' bower,
      Crie, Meg, Marion an Jean,

   Ye maun come to yer sister Janet,
      For fear that she be gane.'

9 Sae he gaed to her sisters' bower,
      Cry'd, Meg, Marion an Jean,
   Ye maun come to yer sister Janet,
      For fear that she be gane.

10 Some drew to their silk stokins,
       An some drew to their shoon,
    An some drew to their silk cleadin,
       For fear she had been gane.

11 When they cam to her bower-door
       They tirlt at the pin;
    For as sick a woman as she was,
       She raise an loot them in.

12 They had na the babie weel buskit,
       Nor her laid in her bed,
    Untill her cruel father cam,
       Cried, Fye, gar busk the bride!

13 'There a sair pain in my back, father,
       There a sair pain in my head,
    An sair, sair is my sidies to;
       This day I downa ride.'

14 'But I hae sorn a solemn oath,
       Afore a companie,
    That ye sal ride this day, Janet,
       This day an ye soud die.

15 'Whae 'll horse ye to the kirk, Janet?
       An whae will horse ye best?'
    'Whae but Willie, my true-love?
       He kens my mister best.'

16 'Whae 'll horse ye to the kirk, Janet?
       An whae will horse ye there?'
    'Whae but Willie, my true-love?
       He neer will doo 'd nae maer.

17 'Ye may saddle a steed, Willie,
       An see that ye saddle 't soft;
    Ye may saddle a steed, Willie,
       For ye winna saddle 't oft.

18 'Ye may saddle a steed, Willie,
       An see that ye saddle 't side;
    Ye may saddle a steed, Willie;
       But I thought to have been yer bride.'

19 When they war a' on horse-back set,
    On horse-back set sae hie,
    Then up spak the bold bridegroom,
    An he spak boustresslie.

20 Up then spak the bold bridegroom,
    An he spak loud an thrawn;
    'I think the bride she be wi bairn,
    She looks sae pale an wan.'

21 Then she took out her bible-book,
    Swoor by her fingers five
    That she was neither wi lad nor lass
    To no man was alive.

22 Then she took out her bible-book,
    Swoor by her fingers ten
    An ever she had born a bairn in her days
    She had born 'd sin yestreen :
    Then a' the ladies round about
    Said, That 's a loud leesin.

23 Atween the kitchin an the kirk
    It was a weel-met mile;
    It was a stra'd i the red roses,
    But than the camomile.

24 When the war a' at dener set,
    Drinkin at the wine,
    Janet could neither eat nor drink
    But the water that ran so fine.

25 Up spak the bride's father,
    Said, Bride, will ye dance wi me ?
    'Away, away, my cruel father !
    There nae dancin wi me.'

26 Up then spak the bride's mother,
    Said, Bride, will ye dance wi me ?
    'Away, away, my mother dear !
    There nae dancin wi me.'

27 Up then spak the bride's sisters, etc.

28 Up then spak the bride's brother, etc.

29 Then up spak the bold bridegroom, [etc.]

30 Up then spak the Sweet Willie,
    An he spak wi a vance;
    'An ye 'll draw of my boots, Janet,
    I 'll gie a' yer lassies a dance.'

31 'I seen 't other ways, Willie,
    An sae has mae than me,
    When ye wad hae danced wi my fair body,
    An leten a' my maidens be.'

32 He took her by the milk-white hand,
    An led her wi mickle care,
    But she drapit down just at his feet,
    And word spak little mair.

33 'Ye may gae hire a nurse, Willie,
    An take yer young son hame;
    Ye may gae hire a nurse, Willie,
    For bairn's nurse I 'll be nane.'

34 She 's pu'd out the keys o her coffer,
    Hung leugh down by her gair;
    She said, Gie thae to my young son,
    Thrae me he 'll neer get mair.'

35 Up then spak the bold bridegroom,
    An he spak bousterouslie;
    'I 've gien you the skaeth, Willie,
    But ye 've gien me the scorn;
    Sae there 's no a bell i St Mary's kirk
    Sall ring for her the morn.'

36 'Ye 've gien me the skaeth, bridegroom,
    But I 'll gee you the scorn;
    For there 's no a bell i St Marie's kirk
    But sal ring for her the morn.

37 'Gar deal, gar deal at my love's burial
    The wheat-bread an the wine,
    For or the morn at ten o clock
    Ye 'll deal 'd as fast at mine.'

38 Then he 's drawn out a nut-brown sword,
    Hang leugh down by his gair,
    He 's thrust it in just at his heart,
    An word spak never mair.

39 The taen was buried i St Mary's kirk,
    The tother i St Mary's queer,
    An throw the taen there sprang a birk,
    Throw the tother a bonnie brier.

40 Thae twae met, an thae twae plaet,
    An ay they knitit near,
    An ilka ane that cam thereby
    Said, There lies twa lovers dear.

41 Till by there came an ill French lord,
    An ill death may he die !
  For he pu'd up the bonnie brier,

   .   .   .   .

  5[1]. Away *struck out, and* on *written over.*
  9[1]. An *at the beginning struck out.*
  10[1,2,3]. drew to them their ? Cf. **A** 10.
  11[4]. *The fourth verse is written as the second* (it *for*
    in), *but struck out.* 12[1]. bukit.
  13[3]. *Changed, by striking out, to* An sair, sair my
    side. An sair, sair is my side *should probably be*
    the second line.
    Cf. **A** 17, **C** 12. 15[2]. An whae l will.
  16[4]. He 'll neer will.
  18[4]. But *struck out.* 23[4]. But an ?
  30[1]. he Sweet Willie ? 34[2]. Hang ? Cf. 38[2].
  39[2]. *MS.* queer   Choir. 40[4]. twa *struck out.*

65. Lady Maisry.

P. 112 b. **I.** "Mrs Baird says that this ballad was
printed in the Saltmarket [Glasgow] by the Robertsons
about seventy years ago." Note by Motherwell in a
copy of his Minstrelsy.
113, note §. 'Galancina' also in Munthe, Folkpoesi från Asturien, No 3, Upsala Universitets Årsskrift,
1887.

J

'Lady Margery,' "Scotch Ballads, Materials for Border
Minstrelsy," No 71, MS. of Thomas Wilkie, p. 71, Abbotsford. "From the recitation of Janet Scott, Bowden, who
sung a dysmal air, as she called it, to the words."
  This version resembles **D.** 12, 13, may be caught from
'Lord Derwentwater:' see No 208, **E** 8, 9, **F** 9, 10. Omens
are not in place after the positive information given in 11.

1 Lady Margery was the king's ae daughter,
    But an the prince's heir ; O
  She 's away to Strawberry Castle,
    To learn some English lair. O

2 She had not been in Strawberry Castle
    A twelvemonth and a day
  Till she 's even as big wi child
    As ever a lady could gae.

3 Her father 's to the cutting o the birks,
    Her mother to the broom,
  And a' for to get a bundle o sticks
    To burn that fair lady in.

4 'O hold your hand now, father dear,
    O hold a little while,
  For if my true-love be yet alive
    I 'll hear his bridle ring.

5 'Where will I get a bonny boy,
    That will win hoes and shoon,
  That will run to Strawberry Castle
    And tell my love to come ?'

6 She 's called on her waiting-maid
    To bring out bread and wine :
  'Now eat and drink, my bonny boy,
    Ye 'll neer eat mair o mine.'

7 Away that bonny boy he 's gaen,
    As fast as he could rin ;
  When he cam where grass grew green
    Set down his feet and ran.

8 And when he cam where brigs were broken
    He bent his bow and swam ;

   .   .   .   .

   .   .   .   .

9 When he came to Strawberry Castle,
    He lighted on the green ;
  Who was so ready as the noble lord
    To rise and let the boy in !

10 'What news ? what news, my pretty page ?
    What tydings do ye bring ?
  Is my lady lighter yet
    Of a daughter or a son ?'

11 'Bad news, bad news, my noble lord,
    Bad tydings have I brung ;
  The fairest lady in a' Scotland
    This day for you does burn.'

12 He has mounted a stately steed
    And he was bound to ride ;
  The silver buttons flew off his coat
    And his nose began to bleed.

13 The second steed that lord mounted
    Stumbled at a stone ;
  'Alass ! alass !' he cried with grief,
    'My lady will be gone.'

14 When he came from Strawberry Castle
    He lighted boots and a' ;
  He thought to have goten a kiss from her,
    But her body fell in twa.

15 For the sake o Lady Margery
    He 's cursed her father and mother,
  For the sake o Lady Margery
    He 's cursed her sister and brother.

16 And for the sake o Lady Margery
    He 's cursed all her kin;
He cried, Scotland is the ae warst place
    That ever my fit was in!

O, *added in singing to the second and fourth lines of
each stanza, is sometimes not written in the* M S.
9 *is written as the third and fourth lines of* 8.
15 *and* 16 *are written as one stanza of four long
lines.*

K

"Scotch Ballads, Materials for Border Minstrelsy," No
22 f; in the handwriting of William Laidlaw. "From Jean
Scott." This version resembles **E**.

1 Marjorie was her father's dear,
    Her mother's only heir,
An she 's away to Strawberry Castle,
    To learn some unco lear.

2 She had na been i Strawberry Castle
    A year but barely three
Till Marjorie turnd big wi child,
    As big as big could be.

* * * * * *

3 'Will ye hae that old, old man
    To be yer daily mate,
Or will ye burn in fire strong
    For your true lover's sake?'

4 'I winna marry that old, old man
    To be my daily mate;
I 'll rather burn i fire strong
    For my true lover's sake.

* * * * * *

5 'O where will I get a bonnie boy
    That will win hose an shoon
An will gae rin to Strawberry Castle,
    To gar my good lord come soon?'

6 'Here am I, a bonnie boy
    That will win hose an shoon,
An I 'll gae rin to Strawberry Castle,
    And gar your lord come soon.'

7 'Should ye come to a brocken brig,
    Than bend your bow an swim;

An whan ye com to garse growin
    Set down yer feet an rin.'

8 When eer he came to brigs broken,
    He bent his bow an swam,
And whan he cam to grass growin
    He set down his feet an ran.

7 When eer he cam to Strawberry Castle
    He tirlt at the pin;
There was nane sae ready as that young lord
    To open an let him in.

8 'Is there ony o my brigs broken?
    Or ony o my castles win?
Or is my lady brought to bed
    Of a daughter or a son?'

9 'There 's nane o a' yer brigs broken,
    Ther 's nane of your castles win;
But the fairest lady in a' your land
    This day for you will burn.'

10 'Gar saddle me the black, black horse,
    Gar saddle me the brown,
Gar saddle me the swiftest stead
    That eer carried man to town.'

11 He 's burstit the black unto the slack,
    The grey unto the brae,
An ay the page that ran afore
    Cried, Ride, sir, an ye may.

12 Her father kindlet the bale-fire,
    Her brother set the stake,
Her mother sat an saw her burn,
    An never cried Alack!

13 'Beet on, beet [on], my cruel father,
    For you I cound nae friend;
But for fifteen well mete mile
    I 'll hear my love's bridle ring.'

14 When he cam to the bonnie Dundee,
    He lightit wi a glent;
Wi jet-black boots an glittrin spurs
    Through that bale-fire he went.

15 He thought his love wad hae datit him,
    But she was dead an gane;
He was na sae wae for that lady
    As he was for her yong son.

16 'But I 'll gar burn for you, Marjorie,
    Yer father an yer mother,
    An I 'll gar burn for you, Marjorie,
    Your sister an your brother.

17 'An I will burn for you, Marjorie,
    The town that ye 'r brunt in,
    An monie ane 's be fatherless
    That has but little sin.'

4³. But *at the beginning struck out.*
10. grey *is written over* brown *in the second line*
(*perhaps because of* grey *in* 11²), *and* to town *is
struck out* **in the fourth line,** *but nothing supplied.*

67. Glasgerion.

P. 136. " Glen Kindy, or rather Glen Skeeny, I have
heard, and there is a ballad in Percy's collection that
is very much the same." Mrs Brown, in a letter to
Jamieson, June 18, 1801, Jamieson-Brown MS., Appendix, p. x.
137 a, second paragraph. 'Riddaren och torpar-
drängen,' Lagus, Nyländska Folkvisor, I, 133, No 43.

68. Young Hunting.

P. 142 b. The four additional stanzas in **J** first appeared in the second edition of the Minstrelsy, 1803,
II, 44.
143 b, 512 a, III, 509 a. Discovery of drowned bodies. Add : La Tradition, IV, 236.
143 b, second paragraph. Many cases in Pitcairn's
Criminal Trials, III, 182–99.

69. Clerk Saunders.

P. 157 f. Scandinavian ballads. See Danmarks gamle
Folkeviser, now edited by Axel Olrik, V, II, 210, No
304, 'De hurtige Svar.' There are two Färöe versions,
A a, A b, B, now No 124 of the MS. Føroyjakvæði.
Hammershaimb's ballad is a compound of A a, B. There
is a Norwegian copy, which I failed to note, in Danske
Viser, IV, 363 f, and there are others in the hands of
Professor Bugge. There are two Swedish unprinted
copies in Arwidsson's collection, and others are referred
to by Afzelius. **Danish,** A–D : A a and B c are the
copies referred to at p. 158, C, D were published in
1889, in Kristensen's Jyske Folkeminder, X, 210 ff.,
No 51. For the Icelandic ballads see Olrik, No 294,
p. 69 ff. A tendency to the comic is to be remarked in
the Swedish and Danish group, in which (with one exception) a brother takes the place of the father.
158 a, III, 509 a. **Spanish,** add : 'Mañanita, mañanita,' El Folk-Lore Frexnense y Bético-Extremeño,
Fregenal, 1883–84, p. 171.

158 ff. 'Clerk Sandy,' " Scotch Ballads, Materials
for Border Minstrelsy," No 22 c ; in the handwriting of
Richard Heber.

1 Clerk Sandy an his true-love
    Came oer the bent so brown ,
    There was never sic a word between them tua
    Till the bells rang in the toun.

2 'Ye maun take out your pocket-napkin
    An put it on my een,
    That safely I may say the morn
    I saw na yow yestreen.

3 'Take me on your back, lady,
    An carry me to your bed,
    That safely I may say the morn
    Yere bouer's floor I never tread.'

4 She 's taen him in her armeys tua,
    An carried him to her bed,
    That safely he may say the morn
    Her bouer's floor he never tread.

5 'I have seven brethren,' she says,
    'An bold young men they be ;
    If they see me an you thegether,
    Yere butcher they will be.'

6 They had na sutten as lang, as lang
    As other lovers when they meet,
    Till Clerk Sandy an his true-love
    They fell baith sound asleep.

7 In an came her seven brethren,
    An bold young men they 've been :
    'We have only ae sister in a' the world,
    An wi Clerk Sandy she 's lein.'

8 Out an spake her second brother :
    'I 'm sure it 's nae injury ;
    If there was na another man in a' the world,
    His butcher I will be.'

9 He 's taen out a little pen-knife,
    Hang low doun by his gaer,
    An thro an thro Clerk Sandy's middle ;
    A word spake he never mair.

10 They lay lang, an lang they lay,
    Till the bird in its cage did sing ;
    She softly unto him did say,
    I wonder ye sleep sae soun.

11 They lay lang, an lang they lay,
  Till the sun shane on their feet;
  She softly unto him did say,
  Ye ly too sound asleep.

12 She softly turnd her round about,
  An wondred he slept sae soun;
  An she lookd ovr her left shoulder,
  An the blood about them ran.

1². bents o Broun.

71. The Bent Sae Brown.

P. 170 a, III, 509 a, IV, 164 b. **Danish.** 'Jom-
fruens Brødre,' 'Hr. Hjælm,' Kristensen, Jyske Folkeminder, X, 266, 269, No 65, **A, B,** No 66.

72. The Clerk's Twa Sons o Owsenford.

P. 174, 512 a, III, 509 a. M. Gaston Paris has made
it strongly probable that Pontoise, and not Toulouse,
was originally the scene of the French-Catalan-Italian
ballad. Three students had inadvertently trespassed
on the hunting-grounds of Enguerrand de Couci; the
baron had them arrested by his foresters and hanged
from the battlements of his castle; for which St Louis
made him pay a heavy fine, and with the money founded
a hospital at Pontoise. Journal des Savants, Sept.–
Nov., 1889, p. 614.

73. Lord Thomas and Fair Annet.

P. 180. Norse (1). 'Peder och liten Stina,' Lagus,
Nyländska Folkvisor, I, 18, No 5. Stina hangs herself
in the orchard. Peder runs on his spear.
181, III, 510 b. French ballads. 'La Délaissée,'
Daymard, Vieux Chants p. rec. en Quercy, p. 50. 'Le
Rossignolet,' Revue des Traditions pop., V, 144, 205.

I

P. 182 f. "Scotch Ballads, Materials for Border
Minstrelsy," No 22 h; in the handwriting of William
Laidlaw. From Jean Scott.

1 Fair Annie an Sweet Willie
  Sat a' day on yon hill;
  Whan day was gane an night was comd,
  They hadna said their fill.

2 Willie spak but ae wrang word,
  An Annie took it ill:
  'I 'll never marry a fair woman
  Against my friends's will.'

3 Annie spak but ae wrang word,
  An Willy lookit down:

'If I binna gude eneugh for yer wife,
  I 'm our-gude for yer loun.'

4 Willie 's turnd his horse's head about,
  He 's turnd it to the broom,
  An he 's away to his father's bower,
  I the ae light o the moon.

5 Whan he cam to his father's bower,
  [He tirlt at the pin;
  Nane was sae ready as his father
  To rise an let him in.]

6 'An askin, an askin, dear father,
  An askin I 'll ask thee;'
  'Say on, say on, my son Willie,
  Whatever your askin be.'

7 'O sall I marry the nit-brown bride,
  Has corn, caitle an kye,
  Or sall I marry Fair Annie,
  Has nought but fair beauty?'

8 'Ye ma sit a gude sate, Willy,
  Wi corn, caitle an kye;
  But ye 'll but sit a silly sate
  Wi nought but fair beauty.'

9 Up than spak his sister's son,
  Sat on the nurse's knee,
  Sun-bruist in his mother's wame,
  Sun-brunt on his nurse's knee:

10 'O yer hogs will die out i the field,
  Yer kye ill die i the byre;
  An than, whan a' yer gear is gane,
  A fusom fag by yer fire!
  But a' will thrive at is wi you
  An ye get yer heart's desire.'

11 Willie 's turnd his horse's head about,
  He 's away to his mother's bour, etc.

12 'O my hogs ill die out i the field,
  My kye die i the byre,
  An than, whan a' my gear is gane,
  A fusom fag bi my fire!
  But a' will thrive at is wi me
  Gin I get my heart's desire.'

13 Willie 's, etc.,
  He 's awae to his brother's bower, etc.

14 "   "   "   " sister's bower, etc.

15 Than Willie has set his wadin-day
    Within thirty days an three,
An he has sent to Fair Annie
    His waddin to come an see.

16 The man that gade to Fair Annie
    Sae weel his errant coud tell :
'The morn it 's Willie's wadin-day,
    Ye maun be there yer sell.'

17 'T was up an spak her aged father,
    He spak wi muckle care ;
'An the morn be Willie's wadin-day,
    I wate she maun be there.

18 'Gar take a steed to the smiddie,
    Caw on o it four shoon ;
Gar take her to a merchant's shop,
    Cut off for her a gown.'

19 She wadna ha 't o the red sae red,
    Nor yet o the grey sae grey,
But she wad ha 't o the sky couler
    That she woor ilka day.

*   *   *   *   *   *   *

20 There war four-an-twontie gray goss-hawks
    A flaffin their wings sae wide,
To flaff the stour thra off the road
    That Fair Annie did ride.

21 The[re] war four-a-twontie milk-white dows
    A fleein aboon her head,
An four-an-twontie milk-white swans
    Her out the gate to lead.

22 Whan she cam to St Marie's kirk,
    She lightit on a stane ;
The beauty o that fair creature
    Shone oer mony ane.

23 'T was than out cam the nit-brown bride,
    She spak wi muckle spite ;
'O where gat ye the water, Annie,
    That washes you sae white ? '

24 'I gat my beauty
    Where ye was no to see ;
I gat it i my father's garden,
    Aneath an apple tree.

25 'Ye ma wash i dubs,' she said,
    'An ye ma wash i syke,

But an ye wad wash till doomsday
    Ye neer will be as white.

26 'Ye ma wash i dubs,' she said,
    'An ye ma wash i the sea,
But an ye soud wash till doomsday
    Ye 'll neer be as white as me.

27 'For I gat a' this fair beauty
    Where ye gat never none,
For I gat a' this fair beauty
    Or ever I was born.'

28 It was than out cam Willie,
    Wi hats o silks and flowers ;
He said, Keep ye thae, my Fair Annie,
    An brook them weel for yours.'

29 'Na, keep ye thae, Willie,' she said,
    'Gie them to yer nit-brown bride ;
Bid her wear them wi mukle care,
    For woman has na born a son
    Sal mak my heart as sair.'

30 Annie 's luppen on her steed
    An she has ridden hame,
Than Annie 's luppen of her steed
    An her bed she has taen.

31 When mass was sung, an bells war rung,
    An a' man bound to bed,
An Willie an his nit-brown bride
    I their chamber war laid.

32 They war na weel laid in their bed,
    Nor yet weel faen asleep,
Till up an startit Fair Annie,
    Just up at Willie's feet.

33 'How like ye yer bed, Willie ?
    An how like ye yer sheets ?
An how like ye yer nut-brown bride,
    Lies in yer arms an sleeps ? '

34 'Weel eneugh I like my bed, Annie,
    Weel eneugh I like my sheets ;
But wae be to the nit-brown bride
    Lies in my arms an sleeps ! '

35 Willie 's ca'd on his merry men a'
    To rise an pit on their shoon ;
'An we 'll awae to Annie's bower,
    Wi the ae light o the moon.'

36 An whan he cam to Annie's bower,
  He tirlt at the pin;
  Nane was sae ready as her father
   To rise an let him in.

37 There was her father a[n] her se'en brethren
  A makin to her a bier,
  Wi ae stamp o the melten goud,
   Another o siller clear.

38 When he cam to the chamber-door
  Where that the dead lay in,
  There was her mother an six sisters
  A makin to her a sheet,
  Wi ae drap o . . . .
   Another o silk sae white.

39 'Stand by, stand by now, ladies a',
  Let me look on the dead;
  The last time that I kiss[t] her lips
   They war mair bonny red.'

40 'Stand by, stand by now, Willie,' they said,
  'An let ye her alane;
  Gin ye had done as ye soud done,
   She wad na there ha lien.'

41 'Gar deal, gar deal at Annie's burrial
  The wheat bread an the wine,
  For or the morn at ten o clock
   Ye 's deal'd as fast at mine.'

5. Whan he cam to his father's bower, etc. *Completed from* 36.

7². caitle *written under* cattle.

8⁴. Annie *written over* nought.

11. 4–8 *are intended to be repeated, with* mother *substituted for* father.

13, 14. 4–8, 12, *are intended to be repeated, with the proper substitutions for* brother, sister.

After 19 : Something about her sadle and steed.

20², 37², 38⁴. A'; *which may be intended.*

29. *Compare* E 30 : *but I am unable to suggest a satisfactory restoration of the stanza.*

After 41 : etc. See Sweet Willie an Janet. *What should follow is probably,* Sweet Willie was buried, *etc.*

There are six stanzas of 'Lord Thomas and Fair Elenor,' from Mrs Gammell's recitation, in Pitcairn's MSS, III, 35. They are of no value.

75. Lord Lovel.

P. 204 f., note †, 512 b. Add: Hruschka u. Toischer, Deutsche V. l. aus Böhmen, p. 108, No 20, a–f.

205 a, note, III, 510 b. For 'Stolten Hellelille, see Danmarks gamle Folkeviser, V, II, 352, No 312, 'Gøde og Hillelille.' Add : 'Greven og lille Lise,' Kristensen, Jyske Folkeminder, X, 319, No 79, A–E.

205 b, III, 510 b. 'Den elskedes Død :' the same volume of Kristensen, 'Herr Peders Kjæreste,' p. 327, No 80.

206, 512 b, III, 510 b. 'Lou Fil del Rey et sa Mio morto,' Daymard, Vieux Chants p. rec. en Quercy, p. 82.

There is a similar ballad, ending with admonition from the dead mistress, in Luzel, Soniou, I, 324, 25, 'Cloaregic ar Stanc.'

76. The Lass of Roch Royal.

213 a. Title of **B**. Not Lochroyan in Herd, I, 144, but, both in title and text, Lochvoyan. In Herd, II, 60, the title has Lochroyan ; the word does not occur in so much of the text as remains. Printed Lochroyan by Herd, and probably Lochroyan was intended in I, 144, as the alternative, though the last letter but one is indistinctly written, and may be read *e*. **B** came to Herd "by post from a lady in Ayrshire (?), name unknown." Also, No 38, **A** a, No 51, **A** a ; No 161, **B** a ; No 220, **A**. Note (in pencil, and indistinct as to the place), Herd's MSS, I, 143.

215 a. A part of this ballad is introduced into two versions of 'The Mother's Malison,' No 216 ; see IV, 186. See also 'Fair Janet,' No 64, **A** 13, **D** 5, **G** 5.

217. **B**. Lochvoyan everywhere, not Lochroyan.

221. **E** 2². Finlay, in a letter to Scott, March 27, 1803 (Letters, I, No 87), says, "in a copy which I have seen, with the music, it is a birchen, instead of a silver, kame."

'The Lass of Lochroyan,' "Scotch Ballads, Materials for Border Minstrelsy," No 82, Abbotsford. Communicated to Scott by Major Henry Hutton, Royal Artillery, 24th December, 1802 (Letters I, No 77), as recollected by his father and the family.

Some ten stanzas of this version (16–19, 25–27, 30, 32, 34) appear to have been used by Scott in compiling the copy printed in his Minstrelsy, **E** b. (The note on **E** b, p. 226, requires correction.) There is much in common with **B**, **E** a, **F**.

1 'O wha will shoe my bonny foot?
  And wha will glove my hand?
  And wha will bind my middle jimp
   Wi a lang, lang linen band?

2 'O wha will kame my yellow hair,
  With a haw bayberry kame?
  And wha will be my babe's father
   Till Gregory come hame?'

3 'Thy father, he will shoe thy foot,
    Thy brother will glove thy hand,
  Thy mither will bind thy middle jimp
    Wi a lang, lang linen band.

4 'Thy sister will kame thy yellow hair,
    Wi a haw bayberry kame;
  The Almighty will be thy babe's father
    Till Gregory come hame.'

5 'And wha will build a bonny ship,
    And set it on the sea?
  For I will go to seek my love,
    My ain love Gregory.'

6 Up then spak her father dear,
    A wafu man was he;
  'And I will build a bonny ship,
    And set her on the sea.

7 'And I will build a bonny ship,
    And set her on the sea,
  And ye sal gae and seek your love,
    Your ain love Gregory.'

8 Then he's gard build a bonny ship,
    And set it on the sea,
  Wi four-and-twenty mariners,
    To bear her company.

9 O he's gart build a bonny ship,
    To sail on the salt sea;
  The mast was o the beaten gold,
    The sails [o] cramoisie.

10 The sides were o the gude stout aik,
    The deck o mountain pine,
  The anchor o the silver shene,
    The ropes o silken twine.

11 She had na saild but twenty leagues,
    But twenty leagues and three,
  When she met wi a rank rever,
    And a' his companie.

12 'Now are ye queen of heaven hie,
    Come to pardon a' our sin?
  Or are ye Mary Magdalane,
    Was born at Bethlam?'

13 'I'm no the queen of heaven hie,
    Come to pardon ye your sin,
  Nor am I Mary Magdalane,
    Was born in Bethlam.

14 'But I'm the lass of Lochroyan,
    That's sailing on the sea
  To see if I can find my love,
    My ain love Gregory.'

15 'O see na ye yon bonny bower?
    It's a' covered oer wi tin;
  When thou hast saild it round about,
    Lord Gregory is within.'

16 And when she saw the stately tower,
    Shining both clear and bright,
  Whilk stood aboon the jawing wave,
    Built on a rock of height,

17 Says, Row the boat, my mariners,
    And bring me to the land,
  For yonder I see my love's castle,
    Close by the salt sea strand.

18 She saild it round, and saild it round,
    And loud and loud cried she
  'Now break, now break your fairy charms,
    And set my true-love free.'

19 She's taen her young son in her arms
    And to the door she's gane,
  And long she knockd, and sair she ca'd,
    But answer got she nane.

20 'O open, open, Gregory!
    O open! if ye be within;
  For here's the lass of Lochroyan,
    Come far fra kith and kin.

21 'O open the door, Lord Gregory!
    O open and let me in!
  The wind blows loud and cauld, Gregory,
    The rain drops fra my chin.

22 'The shoe is frozen to my foot,
    The glove unto my hand,
  The wet drops fra my yellow hair,
    Na langer dow I stand.'

23 O up then spak his ill mither,
    An ill death may she die!
  'Y're no the lass of Lochroyan,
    She's far out-our the sea.

24 'Awa, awa, ye ill woman,
    Ye're no come here for gude;
  Ye're but some witch or wil warlock,
    Or mermaid o the flood.'

25 'I am neither witch nor wil warlock,
　　Nor mermaid o the sea,
　But I am Annie of Lochroyan,
　　O open the door to me!'

26 'Gin ye be Annie of Lochroyan,
　　As I trow thou binna she,
　Now tell me of some love-tokens
　　That past tween thee and me.'

27 'O dinna ye mind, love Gregory,
　　As we sat at the wine,
　We chang'd the rings frae our fingers?
　　And I can shew thee thine.

28 'O yours was gude, and gude enough,
　　But ay the best was mine,
　For yours was o the gude red gowd,
　　But mine o the diamond fine.

29 'Yours was o the gude red gowd,
　　Mine o the diamond fine;
　Mine was o the purest troth,
　　But thine was false within.'

30 'If ye be the lass of Lochroyan,
　　As I kenna thou be,
　Tell me some mair o the love-tokens
　　Past between thee and me.'

31 'And dinna ye mind, love Gregory,
　　As we sat on the hill,
　Thou twin'd me o my maidenheid,
　　Right sair against my will?

32 'Now open the door, love Gregory!
　　Open the door! I pray;
　For thy young son is in my arms,
　　And will be dead ere day.'

33 'Ye lie, ye lie, ye ill woman,
　　So loud I hear ye lie;
　For Annie of the Lochroyan
　　Is far out-our the sea.'

34 Fair Annie turnd her round about:
　　'Weel, sine that it be sae,
　May neer woman that has borne a son
　　Hae a heart sae fu o wae!

35 'Take down, take down that mast o gowd,
　　Set up a mast of tree;
　It disna become a forsaken lady
　　To sail sae royallie.'

36 When the cock had crawn, and the day did
　　　dawn,
　　And the sun began to peep,
　Up then raise Lord Gregory,
　　And sair, sair did he weep.

37 'O I hae dreamd a dream, mither,
　　I wish it may bring good!
　That the bonny lass of Lochroyan
　　At my bower-window stood.

38 'O I hae dreamd a dream, mither,
　　The thought o 't gars me greet!
　That fair Annie of Lochroyan
　　Lay dead at my bed-feet.'

39 'Gin it be for Annie of Lochroyan
　　That ye make a' this main,
　She stood last night at your bower-door,
　　But I hae sent her hame.'

40 'O wae betide ye, ill woman,
　　An ill death may ye die!
　That wadna open the door yoursell
　　Nor yet wad waken me.'

41 O he's gane down to yon shore-side,
　　As fast as he coud dree,
　And there he saw fair Annie's bark
　　A rowing our the sea.

42 'O Annie, Annie,' loud he cried,
　　'O Annie, O Annie, bide!'
　But ay the mair he cried Annie
　　The braider grew the tide.

43 'O Annie, Annie, dear Annie,
　　Dear Annie, speak to me!'
　But ay the louder he gan call
　　The louder roard the sea.

44 The wind blew loud, the waves rose hie
　　And dashd the boat on shore;
　Fair Annie's corpse was in the feume,
　　The babe rose never more.

45 Lord Gregory tore his gowden locks
　　And made a wafu moan;
　Fair Annie's corpse lay at his feet,
　　His bonny son was gone.

46 'O cherry, cherry was her cheek,
　　And gowden was her hair,

And coral, coral was her lips,
    Nane might with her compare.'

47 Then first he kissd her pale, pale cheek,
    And syne he kissd her chin,
And syne he kissd her wane, wane lips,
    There was na breath within.

48 'O wae betide my ill mither,
    An ill death may she die!
She turnd my true-love frae my door,
    Who came so far to me.

49 'O wae betide my ill mither,
    An ill death may she die!
She has no been the deid o ane,
    But she's been the deid of three.'

50 Then he's taen out a little dart,
    Hung low down by his gore,
He thrust it through and through his heart,
    And words spak never more.

1[1], 43[1]. Oh.

77. Sweet William's Ghost.

P. 233. **G.** These three stanzas, which Scott annexed to 'Clerk Saunders' in the second edition of the Minstrelsy, 1803, II, 41, were contributed by the Ettrick Shepherd, who writes, not quite lucidly: " Altho this ballad [Clerk Saunders] is mixed with another, according to my mother's edition, in favour of whose originality I am strongly prepossessed, yet, as the one does in no sense disgrace the other in their present form, according to her it ends thus."

" Scotch Ballads, Materials for Border Minstrelsy," No 141, Abbotsford ; in the handwriting of James Hogg.

1 'But plett a wand o bonnie birk
    An lay it on my breast,
An drap a tear upon my grave,
    An wiss my saul gude rest.

2 'But fair Marget, an rare Marget,
    An Marget, o verity,
If eer ye loe another man,
    Neer loe him as ye did me.'

3 But up then crew the milk-white cock,
    An up then crew the grey ;
Her lover vanishd in the air,
    An she gaed weepin away.

78. The Unquiet Grave.

P. 236 b.   Add : Waldau's Böhmische Granaten, II, 121, No 176.

236 f., III, 512 f. The Rev. S. Baring-Gould has recovered several copies of 'The Unquiet Grave' in the West Country. It will be observed that the variations in this ballad do not take a wide range. The verses are not always sung in the same order ; there is not story enough to keep them in place. Mr Baring-Gould informs me that there is a Devon popular tale which is very similar (possibly a prose version of the ballad). In this, a bramble-leaf comes between the lips of the maiden and her dead lover, and her life is saved thereby. This tale is utilized in the ballad as printed in Songs of the West, No 6, 'Cold blows the wind, sweetheart !'

H

a. Sent Rev. S. Baring-Gould by Mrs Gibbons, daughter of the late Sir W. L. Trelawney, as she remembered it sung by her nurse, Elizabeth Doidge, a woman of the neighborhood of Brentor, about 1828. **b.** Obtained by the same from John Woodrich, blacksmith, parish of Thrustleton, as heard from his grandmother about 1848. **c.** By the same, from Anne Roberts, Scobbeter.

1 'Cold blows the wind tonight, sweet-heart,
    Cold are the drops of rain ;
The very first love that ever I had
    In greenwood he was slain.

2 'I'll do as much for my sweet-heart
    As any young woman may ;
I'll sit and mourn on his grave-side
    A twelve-month and a day.'

3 A twelve-month and a day being up,
    The ghost began to speak :
'Why sit you here by my grave-side
    And will not let me sleep ?

4 'What is it that you want of me,
    Or what of me would have ?'
'A kiss from off your lily-white lips,
    And that is all I crave !'

5 'Cold are my lips in death, sweet-heart,
    My breath is earthy strong ;
To gain a kiss of my cold lips,
    Your time would not be long.

6 'If you were not my own sweet-heart,
    As now I know you be,
I'd tear you as the withered leaves
    That grew on yonder tree.'

7 'O don't you mind the garden, love,
    Where you and I did walk?
  The fairest flower that blossomd there
    Is withered on the stalk.

*   *   *   *   *   *   *

8 'And now I 've mourned upon his grave
    A twelvemonth and a day,
  We 'll set our sails before the wind
    And so we 'll sail away.'

b. 1 Cold blows the wind to-night, my love,
    Cold are the drops of rain;
  The very first love that ever I had
    In greenwood he was slain.

2 'I 'll do as much for my true-love
    As any young woman may;
  I 'll sit and mourn upon his grave
    A twelve-month and a day.'

3 When a twelve-month and a day were up,
    His body straight arose:
  'What brings you weeping oer my grave
    That I get no repose?'

4 'O think upon the garden, love,
    Where you and I did walk;
  The fairest flower that blossomd there
    Is withered on the stalk.

5 'The stalk will bear no leaves, sweet-heart,
    The flower will neer return,
  And my true-love is dead, is dead,
    And I do naught but mourn.'

6 'What is it that you want of me
    And will not let me sleep?
  Your salten tears they trickle down
    And wet my winding-sheet.'

7 'What is it that I want of thee,
    O what of thee in grave?
  A kiss from off your lily-white lips,
    And that is all I crave.'

8 'Cold are my lips in death, sweet-heart,
    My breath is earthy strong;
  If you do touch my clay-cold lips,
    Your time will not be long.'

9 'Cold though your lips in death, sweet-heart,
    One kiss is all I crave;
  I care not, if I kiss but thee,
    That I should share thy grave.'

10 'Go fetch me a light from dungeon deep,
    Wring water from a stone,
  And likewise milk from a maiden's breast
    That never maid hath none. (*Read* babe had.)

*   *   *   *   *   *   *

11 'Now if you were not true in word,
    As now I know you be,
  I 'd tear you as the withered leaves
    Are torn from off the tree.'

c. 1 'It 's for to meet the falling drops,
    Cold fall the drops of rain;
  The last true-love, *etc.*

2 'I 'll do as much for my fair love
    As any,' *etc.*
  The rest " almost exactly "as b.

'Charles Graeme,' Buchan's Ballads of the North of Scotland, I, 89, Motherwell's MS., p. 624, begins with stanzas which belong to this ballad. What follows after the third, or just possibly the sixth, stanza reads as if some contributor had been diverting himself with an imposition on the editor's simplicity. Buchan himself remarks in a note, p. 299: "There seems to be a very great inconsistency manifested throughout the whole of this ballad in the lady's behavior towards the ghost of her departed lover. Perhaps she wished to sit and sigh alone, undisturbed with visits from the inhabitants of the grave." (Translated by Gerhard, p. 63.)

1 'Cauld, cauld blaws the winter night,
    Sair beats the heavy rain;
  Young Charles Graeme 's the lad I love,
    In greenwood he lies slain.

2 'But I will do for Charles Graeme
    What other maidens may;
  I 'll sit and harp upon his grave
    A twelvemonth and a day.'

3 She harped a' the live-lang night,
    The saut tears she did weep,
  Till at the hour o one o'clock
    His ghost began to peep.

4 Pale and deadly was his cheek,
    And pale, pale was his chin;

And how and hollow were his een,
No light appeard therein.

5 ' Why sit ye here, ye maiden fair,
To mourn sae sair for me?'
' I am sae sick, and very love-sick,
Aye foot I cannot jee.

6 ' Sae well 's I loved young Charles Graeme,
I kent he loved me ;
My very heart 's now like to break
For his sweet companie.'

7 ' Will ye hae an apple, lady,
And I will sheave it sma ?'
' I am sae sick, and very love-sick,
I cannot eat at a'.'

8 ' Will ye hae the wine, lady,
And I will drain it sma ?'
' I am sae sick, and very love-sick,
I cannot drink at a'.

9 ' See ye not my father's castle,
Well covered ower wi tin ?
There 's nane has sic an anxious wish
As I hae to be in.'

10 ' O hame, fair maid, ye 'se quickly won,
But this request grant me ;
When ye are safe in downbed laid,
That I may sleep wi thee.'

11 ' If hame again, sir, I could win,
I 'll this request grant thee ;
When I am safe in downbed laid,
This night ye 'se sleep wi me.'

12 Then he poud up a birken bow,
Pat it in her right han,
And they are to yon castle fair,
As fast as they coud gang.

13 When they came to yon castle fair,
It was piled round about ;
She slipped in and bolted the yetts,
Says, Ghaists may stand thereout.

14 Then he vanishd frae her sight
In the twinkling o an ee ;
Says, Let never ane a woman trust
Sae much as I 've done thee.

80. Old Robin of Portingale.

P. 240, 513 a, III, 514. Mabillon cites Balderic's
history of the first crusade, whose words are : " Multi
etiam de gente plebeia crucem sibi divinitus innatam

jactando ostentabant, quod et idem quædam ex mu-
lierculis præsumpserunt ; hoc enim falsum deprehen-
sum est omnino. Multi vero ferrum callidum instar
crucis sibi adhibuerunt, vel peste jactantiæ, vel bonæ
suæ voluntatis ostentatione." Migne, Patrologiæ Curs.
Compl., tom. clxvi, col. 1070.

A man who is looking forward to a pilgrimage to the
Holy Land wishes to have the cross burned into his
right shoulder, since then, though he should be stript
of his clothes, the cross would remain : Miracula S.
Thomæ, Auctore Benedicto, Robertson, Materials for
the History of Thomas Becket, II, 175. The brand-
ing of the cross in the flesh must have become common,
since it was forbidden by the canon law. In some editions of the Sarum Missal, a warning is inserted in the
Servitium Peregrinorum : " Combustio crucis in carne
peregrinis euntibus Hierusalem prohibitum est in lege,
secundum jura canonica, sub pœna excommunicationis
majoris." Sarum Missal, Burntisland, 1867, col. 856 *.
(Cited by Cutts, Scenes and Characters of the Middle
Ages, p. 167.)

81. Little Musgrave and Lady Barnard.

P. 242 ff. **F**, which Jamieson says he received from
Scotland, happens to have been preserved at Abbotsford. Since Jamieson made a considerable number of
small changes, the original text is now given here.

" Scotch Ballads, Materials for Border Minstrelsy,"
No 133 c, Abbotsford ; in the handwriting of James
Hogg.

1 ' I have a towr in Dalesberry,
Whilk now is dearly dight,
And I will gie it to young Musgrave,
To lodge wi me a night.'

2 ' To lodge wi thee a night, fair lady,
Wad breed baith sorrow and strife ;
For I see by the rings on your fingers
Ye 're good Lord Barnaby's wife.'

3 ' Lord Barnaby's wife although I be,
Yet what is that to thee ?
For we 'l beguile him for this ae night ;
He 's on to fair Dundee.

4 ' Come here, come here, my little foot-page,
This guinea I will give thee,
If ye will keep thir secrets closs
Tween young Musgrave an me.

5 ' But here hae I a little pen-knife,
Hings low down by my gare ;
If ye dinna keep thir secrets closs,
Ye 'l find it wonder sair.'

6 Then she 's taen him to her chamber,
An down in her arms lay he ;

The boy koost off his hose an shoon
An ran for fair Dundee.

7 When he came to the wan water,
He slackd his bow an swam,
An when he wan to growan gress
Set down his feet an ran.

8 And whan he came to fair Dundee,
Could nouther rap nor ca,
But set his braid bow to his breast
An merrily jumpd the wa.

9 'O waken ye, waken ye, my good lord,
Waken, an come away !'
'What ails, what ails my wee foot-page
He cry's sae lang or day ?

10 'O is my towers burnt, my boy ?
Or is my castle won ?
Or has the lady that I loe best
Brought me a daughter or son ? '

11 'Your halls are safe, your towers are safe
An free frae all alarms ;
But oh, the lady that ye loe best
Lyes sound i Musgrave's arms.'

12 'Gae saddle me the black,' he cry'd,
'Gae saddle me the gray ;
Gae saddle me the milk-white steed,
To hie me out the way.'

13 'O lady, I heard a wee horn tout,
An it blew wonder clear,
An ay the turnin o the note
Was, Barnaby will be here !

14 'I thought I heard a wee horn blaw,
An it blew loud an hie,
An ay at ilka turn it said,
Away, Musgrave, away !'

15 'Lye still, my dear, lye still, my dear,
Ye keep me frae the cold !
For it is but my father's shepherds,
Drivin there flocks to the fold.'

16 Up they lookit, an down they lay,
An they 're fa'n sound asleep ;
Till up start good Lord Barnaby,
Just closs at their bed-feet.

17 'How do ye like my bed, Musgrave ?
An how like ye my sheets ?
An how like ye my fair lady,
Lyes in your arms an sleeps? '

18 'Weel I like your bed, my lord,
An weel I like your sheets ;

But ill like I your fair lady,
Lyes in my arms an sleeps.

19 'You got your wale o se'en sisters,
An I got mine o five ;
So take ye mine, an I 's take thine,
An we nae mair shall strive.'

20 'O my woman 's the best woman
That ever brake world's bread,
But your woman 's the worst woman
That ever drew coat oer head.

21 'I have two swords in my scabbart,
They are baith sharp an clear ;
Take ye the best, and I the worst,
An we 'l end the matter here.

22 'But up an arm thee, young Musgrave,
We 'l try it hand to hand ;
It 's neer be said o Lord Barnaby
He struck at a naked man.'

23 The first stroke that young Musgrave got,
It was baith deep an sair,
An down he fell at Barnaby's feet,
An word spak never mair.

24 'A grave ! a grave !' Lord Barnaby cry'd,
'A grave to lay them in !
My lady shall lye on the sunny side,
Because of her noble kin.'

25 But O how sorry was that good lord,
For a' his angry mood,
When he espy'd his ain young son
All weltering in his blood !

The following copy was kindly communicated to me
by Mr David MacRitchie, Honorary Secretary of the
Gypsy Lore Society, in advance of its publication in
the Journal of the society. While it preserves the
framework of the story, it differs very considerably in
details from all the printed copies. It is evidently of
the same origin as some of the Scottish versions (all
of which seem to derive from print), though it has no
marked resemblance to the actual form of any particular one of these. Some peculiarities are plausibly
attributable to dim or imperfect recollection. Thus,
the ball-play of **D, E,** etc., is turned into a ball. Lord
Barnard is made a king, and the page the king's brother
(neither of which changes is an improvement). We
may observe that in **J** Lord Barnabas is at the king's
court, and in **I** Sir Grove is Lord Bengwill's brother ;
but these points are not decisive, and the changes may
be purely arbitrary. 4 shows traces of **E** 5 and **F** 3 ;
8 may have been suggested by something like **G** 4 ;
and the last line of 14 looks like a corruption of **G** 29.
This involves the supposition that the source of the
ballad was a version somewhat different from any hith-

erto recovered ; but 'Little Musgrave' is one of the best known of all ballads, and the variants must have been innumerable. On the whole, 1–8, 14, present a free treatment of ill-remembered matter ; 9–13 are fairly well preserved ; compare **E** 13–17.

O

'Moss Groves,' taken down in 1891 by Mr John Sampson, Liverpool, from Philip Murray, an old tinker, who learned the ballad in his boyhood from an old gypsy named Amos Rice.

1 There was four-and-twenty ladies
    Assembled at a ball,
And who being there but the king's wife,
    The fairest of them all.

2 She put her eye on the Moss Groves,
    Moss Groves put his eye upon she :
'How would you like, my little Moss Groves,
    One night to tarry with me ? '

3 'To sleep one night with you, fair lady,
    It would cause a wonderful sight ;
For I know by the ring upon your hand
    You are the king's wife.'

4 'If I am the king's wife,
    I mean him to beguile ;
For he has gone on a long distance,
    And won't be back for a while.'

5 Up spoke his brother,
    An angry man was he ;
' Another night I'll not stop in the castle
    Till my brother I'll go see.'

6 When he come to his brother,
    He was in a hell of a fright :
'Get up, get up, brother dear !
    There's a man in bed with your wife.'

7 'If it's true you tell unto me,
    A man I'll make of thee ;
If it's a lie you tell unto me,
    It's slain thou shalt be.'

8 When he came to his hall,
    The bells begun to ring,
And all the birds upon the bush
    They begun to sing.

9 'How do you like my covering-cloths ?
    And how do you like my sheets ?
How do you like my lady fair,
    All night in her arms to sleep ? '

10 'Your covering-cloths I like right well,
    Far better than your sheets ;

Far better than all your lady fair,
    All night in her arms to sleep.'

11 'Get up, get up now, little Moss Groves,
    Your clothing do put on ;
It shall never be said in all England
    That I drew on a naked man.

12 'There is two swords all in the castle
    That cost me very dear ;
You take the best, and I the worst,
    And let's decide it here.'

13 The very first blow Moss Groves he gave,
    He wounded the king most sore ;
The very first blow the king gave him,
    Moss Groves he struck no more.

14 She lifted up his dying head
    And kissed his cheek and chin :
'I'd sooner have you now, little Moss Groves,
    Than all their castles or kings.'

259 a. Insert under **C : d.** Printed and sold in Aldermary Church-yard, Bow Lane, London.

83. Child Maurice.

P. 266. **B.** Motherwell sent 'Child Noryce' to Sir Walter Scott in a letter dated 28 April, 1825 (Letters, XIV, No 94, Abbotsford). He changed several readings (as, orders to errand, in 6⁴), and in three cases went back to original readings which he has altered in his manuscript. I am now convinced that the alterations made in the manuscript are not in general, if ever, corrections derived from the reciters, but Motherwell's own improvements, and that the original readings should be adhered to.

86. Young Benjie.

P. 281. "From Jean Scott." In the handwriting of William Laidlaw. "Scotch Ballads, Materials for Border Minstrelsy," No 29, Abbotsford.
Excepting the first stanza, the whole of this fragment (with slight changes) is found in the ballad in Scott's Minstrelsy. That ballad has about twice as many verses, and the other half might easily have been supplied by the editor.

1 Fair Marjorie sat i her bower-door,
    Sewin her silken seam,
When by then cam her false true-love,
    Gard a' his bridles ring.

2 'Open, open, my true-love,
    Open an let me in ; '
' I dare na, I dare na, my true-love,
    My brethren are within.'

3 'Ye lee, ye lee, my ain true-love,
    Sae loud I hear ye lee!
For or I cam thrae Lothian banks
    They took fare-weel o me.'

4 The wind was loud, that maid was proud,
    An leath, leath to be dung,
But or she wan the Lothian banks
    Her fair coulour was gane.

5 He took her up in his armis,
    An threw her in the lynn.

6 Up then spak her eldest brother,
    Said, What is yon I see?
Sure, youn is either a drowned ladie
    Or my sister Marjorie.

7 Up then spak her second brother,
    Said, How will wi her ken?
Up then spak her . . . brother,
    There a hinnie-mark on her chin.

8 About the midle o the night
    The cock began to craw;
About the middle o the night
    The corpse began to thraw.

9 'O whae has doon ye wrang, sister?
    O whae has doon ye wrang?'

10 'Young Boonjie was the ae first man
    I laid my love upon;
He was sae proud an hardie
    He threw me oer the lynne.'

11 'O shall we Boŏnjie head, sister?
    Or shall we Boonjie hang?
Or shall we pyke out his twa grey eyes,
    An punish him or he gang?'

12 'O ye sanna Boŏnjie head, brother,
    Ye sana Boŏnjie hang;
But ye maun pyke out his twa grey eyes,
    An punish him or he gang.'

13 'The ae best man about your house
    Maun wait young Boonjie on.'

3⁸. *thare.* 4 *should probably follow* 5.
6⁸. either a *substituted for* some.
7⁸. her second : second *struck out.* youngest?
8². The corpse : corpse *struck out.*

89. Fause Foodrage.

P. 297. **Danish.** Now printed as No 298 of Danmarks gamle Folkeviser, by Axel Olrik, the continuator of that noble collection, with the title 'Svend af Vollersløv.' There are fifteen old versions besides Tragica 18 (which is a compounded and partly ungenuine text) and the one recently printed by Kristensen, the basis of which is the copy in Tragica. 'Ung Villum' is Tragica 18 with two stanzas omitted.

298, III, 515 b. 'Liden Engel' is No 297 of Danmarks gamle Folkeviser. There are eight old copies, and Kristensen has added five from recent tradition : the two here noted and three in Jyske Folkeminder, No 49, **A–C,** 201 ff. There is also a Swedish copy of 1693, printed in Dybeck's Runa, 1844, p. 93, which I had not observed.

90. Jellon Grame.

P. 303 b, 513 b, III, 515 b. Robert le Diable in Luzel's ballad, II, 24 f, when one year old, was as big as a child of five.

At the age of five, Cuchulinn sets out for his uncle's court, where he performs prodigies of strength. In his seventh year he is received among the heroes, etc.: Zimmer, Göttingische Gelehrte Anzeigen, 1890, pp. 519–20. Merlin, when two years old, "speaks and goes," and defends his mother before the justice: Arthour and Merlin, vv. 1069–70, ed. Turnbull for the Abbotsford Club, p. 41. Ögmundr when seven years old was as strong as a full-grown man : Örvar-Odds Saga, c. 19, Rafn, Fornaldar Sögur, II, 241. The three-nights-old son of Thórr and Járnsaxa removes the foot of Hrungnir from the neck of his father when all the gods have tried in vain. He also speaks. Skáldskaparmál, c. 17. "The Shee an Gannon was born in the morning, named at noon, and went in the evening to ask his daughter of the king of Erin :" Curtin, Myths and Folk-Lore of Ireland, p. 114. Cf. p. 223, where a champion jumps out of the cradle. (G. L. K.)

91. Fair Mary of Wallington.

P. 309. **B.** "The ballad about Lady Livingston appears to be founded on a truth ; her fate is mentioned by Sir R. Gordon. Only her mother, Lady Huntley, is made a queen ; which it was natural enough in a Highland poet to do." Charles Kirkpatrick Sharpe to Sir Walter Scott, Letters, XV, No 231, Abbotsford, 1825 or 26.

What Sir Robert Gordon says is: "In July 1616 yeirs, Elizabeth Gordoun, Ladie of Livingstoun (wyff to the Lord Livingstoun, now Earle of Lithgow), daughter to the Marquis of Huntly, died in chyld-bed, at Edinburgh, of a son called George, who is now Lord Livingstoun.'' (Genealogy of the Earls of Sutherland, p. 335.) The characteristic particulars are wanting.

D is also in Kinloch MSS, V, 363, in the youthful handwriting of J. H. Burton, and is probably the original copy. The differences from the text of D, p. 314, except spellings, are these:
1¹. it was. 1³. and me.

93. Lamkin.

P. 321, note *. See further in Notes and Queries, First Series, II, 519 ; V, 32, 112, 184, 355.
321 ff., 513.

X

'Lamkin,' "Scotch Ballads, Materials for Border Minstrelsy," No 133, Abbotsford ; in the handwriting of James Hogg.

1 Lamkin was as good a mason
    As ever liftit stane ;
  He built to the laird o Lariston,
    But payment gat he nane.

2 Oft he came, an ay he came,
    To that good lord's yett,
  But neither at dor nor window
    Ony entrance could get.

3 Till ae wae an weary day
    Early he came,
  An it fell out on that day
    That good lord was frae hame.

4 He bade steek dor an window,
    An prick them to the gin,
  Nor leave a little wee hole,
    Else Lamkin wad be in.

5 Noorice steekit dor an window,
    She steekit them to the gin ;
  But she left a little wee hole
    That Lamkin might win in.

6 'O where 's the lady o this house ?'
    Said cruel Lamkin ;
  'She 's up the stair sleepin,'
    Said fause noorice then.

7 'How will we get her down the stair ?'
    Said cruel Lamkin ;
  'We 'l stogg the baby i the cradle,'
    Said fause noorice then.

8 He stoggit, and she rockit,
    Till a' the floor swam,

An a' the tors o the cradle
    Red wi blude ran.

9 'O still my son, noorise,
    O still him wi the kane ;'
  'He winna still, madam,
    Till Lariston come hame.'

10 'O still my son, noorice,
    O still him wi the knife ;'
  'I canna still him, madam,
    If ye sude tak my life.'

11 'O still my soon, noorice,
    O still him wi the bell ;'
  'He winna still, madam,
    Come see him yoursel.'

12 Wae an weary rase she up,
    Slowly pat her on
  Her green claethin o the silk,
    An slowly came she down.

13 The first step she steppit,
    It was on a stone ;
  The first body she saw
    Was cruel Lamkin.

14 'O pity, pity, Lamkin,
    Hae pity on me!'
  'Just as meikle pity, madam,
    As ye paid me o my fee.'

15 'I 'll g' ye a peck o good red goud,
    Streekit wi the wand ;
  An if that winna please ye,
    I 'll heap it wi my hand.

16 'An if that winna please ye,
    O goud an o fee,
  I 'll g' ye my eldest daughter,
    Your wedded wife to be.'

17 'Gae wash the bason, lady,
    Gae wash 't an mak it clean,
  To kep your mother's heart's-blude,
    For she 's of noble kin.'

18 'To kep my mother's heart's-blude
    I wad be right wae ;
  O tak mysel, Lamkin,
    An let my mother gae.'

19 'Gae wash the bason, noorice,
   Gae wash 't an mak it clean,
To kep your lady's heart's-blude,
   For she 's o noble kin.'

20 'To wash the bason, Lamkin,
   I will be right glad,
For mony, mony bursen day
   About her house I 've had.'

21 But oh, what dule an sorrow
   Was about that lord's ha,
When he fand his lady lyin
   As white as driven snaw!

22 O what dule an sorrow
   Whan that good lord cam in,
An fand his young son murderd,
   I the chimley lyin!

   9². kane. kame, **B** 13². *But cf.* wand, **A** 16²
   J 10², **M** 3².

95. The Maid freed from the Gallows.

P. 346, III, 516 a. Add 'Leggenda Napitina' (still sung by the sailors of Pizzo); communicated to La Calabria, June 15, 1889, p. 74, by Salvatore Mele; Canto Marinaresco di Nicotera, the same, September 15, 1890. A wife is rescued by her husband.

347 b. **Swedish.** 'Den bortsålda,' Lagus, Nyländska Folkvisor, I, 22, No 6, *a, b, c.*

349 b, 514 a, III, 516 b, and especially 517 a. A wounded soldier calls to mother, sister, father, brother for a drink of water, and gets none; calls to his love, and she brings it: Waldau, Böhmische Granaten, II, 57, No 81.

I

"Scotch Ballads, Materials for Border Minstrelsy," No 127, Abbotsford. Sent to John Leyden, by whom and when does not appear.

1 'Hold your tongue, Lord Judge,' she says,
   'Yet hold it a little while;
Methinks I see my ain dear father
   Coming wandering many a mile.

2 'O have you brought me gold, father?
   Or have you brought me fee?
Or are you come to save my life
   From off this gallows-tree?'

3 'I have not brought you gold, daughter,
   Nor have I brought you fee,

But I am come to see you hangd,
   As you this day shall be.'

["The verses run thus untill she has seen her mother, her brother, and her sister likewise arrive, and then

Methinks I see my ain dear lover, etc."]

4 'I have not brought you gold, true-love,
   Nor yet have I brought fee,
But I am come to save thy life
   From off this gallows-tree.'

5 'Gae hame, gae hame, father,' she says,
   'Gae hame and saw yer seed;
And I wish not a pickle of it may grow up,
   But the thistle and the weed.

6 'Gae hame, gae hame, gae hame, mother,
   Gae hame and brew yer yill;
And I wish the girds may a' loup off,
   And the Deil spill a' yer yill.

7 'Gae hame, gae hame, gae hame, brother,
   Gae hame and lie with yer wife;
And I wish that the first news I may hear
   That she has tane your life.

8 'Gae hame, gae hame, sister,' she says,
   'Gae hame and sew yer seam;
I wish that the needle-point may break,
   And the craws pyke out yer een.'

J

Communicated by Dr George Birkbeck Hill, May 10, 1890, as learned forty years before from a schoolfellow, who came from the north of Somersetshire and sang it in the dialect of that region. Given from memory.

1 'Hold up, hold up your hands so high!
   Hold up your hands so high!
For I think I see my own father
   Coming over yonder stile to me.

2 'Oh father, have you got any gold for me?
   Any money for to pay me free?
To keep my body from the cold clay ground,
   And my neck from the gallows-tree?'

3 'Oh no, I 've got no gold for thee,
   No money for to pay thee free,
For I 've come to see thee hangd this day,
   And hangëd thou shalt be.'

4 'Oh the briers, prickly briers,
   Come prick my heart so sore;
   If ever I get from the gallows-tree,
   I'll never get there any more.'

["The same verses are repeated, with mother, brother,
and sister substituted for father. At last the sweet-
heart comes. The two first verses are the same, and
the third and fourth as follows."]

5 'Oh yes, I've got some gold for thee,
   Some money for to pay thee free;
   I'll save thy body from the cold clay ground,
   And thy neck from the gallows-tree.'

6 'Oh the briers, prickly briers,
   Don't prick my heart any more;
   For now I've got from the gallows-tree
   I'll never get there any more.'

["I do not know any title to this song except 'Hold
up, hold up your hands so high!' It was by that title
that we called for it."]

Julius Krohn has lately made an important contribution to our knowledge of this ballad in an article in
Virittäjä, II, 36–50, translated into German under the
title 'Das Lied vom Mädchen welches erlöst werden
soll,' Helsingfors, 1891. Professor Estlander had previously discussed the ballad in Finsk Tidskrift, X, 1881
(which I have not yet seen), and had sought to show
that it was of Finnish origin, a view which Krohn
disputes and refutes. There are nearly fifty Finnish
versions. The curse with which I ends, and which is
noted as occurring in Swedish C (compare also the
Sicilian ballad), is never wanting in the Finnish, and
is found also in the Esthonian copies.

96. The Gay Goshawk.

P. 356 a, III, 517 a. Add: (18) 'La Fille dans la
Tour,' Daymard, Vieux Chants p. rec. en Quercy, p.
174; (19) 'La belle dans la Tour,' Pas de Calais, communicated by M. G. Doncieux to Revue des Traditions
populaires, VI, 603; (20) 'Belle Idoine,' Questionnaire
de Folklore, publié par la Société du Folklore Wallon,
p. 79.

M. Doucieux has attempted a reconstruction of the
text in Mélusine, V, 265 ff. He cites M. Gaston Paris
as having lately pointed out a striking similitude between the first half of the French popular ballad and
that of a little romance of Bele Ydoine composed in the
twelfth century by Audefrois le Bastars (Bartsch, Alt-
französische Romanzen und Pastourellen, p. 59, No 57).
This resemblance has, I suppose, occasioned the title of
'Belle Idoine' to be given editorially to No 20 above,
for the name does not occur in the ballad.

356 b, III, 517 a. Add: 'Au Jardin des Olives,'

Guillon, p. 83, 'Dessous le Rosier blanc,' Daymard, p.
171 (Les trois Capitaines). A girl feigns death to
avoid becoming a king's mistress, 'Hertig Henrik och
Konungen,' Lagus, Nyländska Folkvisor, I, 117, No 37.

363. E. The following is the MS. copy, "of some
antiquity," from which E was in part constructed.
(Whether it be the original or a transcript cannot be
determined, but Mr Macmath informs me that the paper on which it is written "seems about the oldest sheet
in the volume.") The text was freely handled. 'Lord
William' does not occur in it, but the name is found in
another version which follows this.

"Scotch Ballads, Materials for Border Minstrelsy," No
146 a, Abbotsford.

1 'O waly, waly, my gay goss-hawk,
   Gin your feathering be sheen!'
  'O waly, waly, my master dear,
   Gin ye look pale and lean!

2 'Whether is it for the gold sae rid,
   Or is it for the silver clear?
   Or is it for the lass in southen land,
   That she cannot win here.'

3 'It is not for the gold sae rid,
   Nor is it for the silver clear,
   But it is for the lass in southen land,
   That she cannot win her[e].'

4 'Sit down, sit down, my master dear,
   Write a love-letter hastily,
   And put it in under my feathern gray,
   And I'll away to southen land as fast as I
     can flee.

5 'But how shall I your true-love ken?
   Or how shall I her know?
   I bear the tongue never wi her spake,
   The eye that never her saw.'

6 'The red that is in my love's cheek
   Is like blood spilt amang the snaw;
   The white that is on her breast-bone
   Is like the down on the white sea-maw.

7 'There's one that stands at my love's gate
   And opens the silver pin,
   And there ye may safely set ye on
   And sing a lovely song.

8 'First ye may sing it loud, loud, loud,
   And then ye may sing it clear,
   And ay the oerword of the tune
   Is, Your love cannot win here.'

9 He has written a love-letter,
　　Put it under his feathern gray,
　And he 's awa to southen land,
　　As fast as ever he may.

10 When he came to the lady's gate,
　　There he lighted down,
　And there he sat him on the pin
　　And sang a lovely song.

11 First he sang it loud, loud, loud,
　　And then he sang it clear,
　And ay the oerword of the tune
　　Was, Your love cannot win here.

12 'Hold your tongues, my merry maids all,
　　And hold them a little while;
　I hear some word from my true-love,
　　That lives in Scotland's isle.'

13 Up she rose, to the door she goes,
　　To hear what the bird woud say,
　And he 's let the love-letter fall
　　From under his feathern gray.

14 When she looked the letter on,
　　The tear blinded her eye,
　And when she read it oer and oer
　　A loud laughter took she.

15 'Go hame, go hame, my bonny bird,
　　And to your master tell,
　If I be nae wi him at Martinmass,
　　I shall be wi him at Yule.'

16 The lady 's to her chamber gane,
　　And a sick woman grew she;
　The lady 's taen a sudden brash,
　　And nathing she 'll do but die.

17 'An asking, an asking, my father dear,
　　An asking grant to me!
　If that I die in southen land,
　　In Scotland bury me.'

18 'Ask on, ask on, my daughter dear,
　　That asking is granted thee;
　If that you die in southen land,
　　In Scotland I 'll bury thee.'

19 'Gar call to me my seven bretheren,
　　To hew to me my bier,
　The one half of the beaten gold,
　　The other of the silver clear.

20 'Go call to me my seven sisters,
　　To sew to me my caul;
　Every needle-steik that they put in
　　Put by a silver bell.'

21 The first Scots kirk that they came to,
　　They heard the mavis sing;
　The next Scots kirk that they came to,
　　They heard the dead-bell ring.

22 The next Scots kirk that they came to,
　　They were playing at the foot-ball,
　And her true-love was them among,
　　The chieftian amangst them all.

23 'Set down, set down these corps,' said he,
　　'Let me look them upon;'
　As soon as he lookd the lady on,
　　The blood sprang in her chin.

24 'One bite of your bread, my love,
　　And one glass of your wine!
　For I have fasted these five long days,
　　All for your sake and mine.

25 'Go hame, go hame, my seven brothers,
　　Go hame and blaw your horn,
　And ye may tell thro southen land
　　How I playd you the scorn.'

26 'Woe to you, my sister dear,
　　And ane ill death may you die!
　For we left father and mother at hame
　　Breaking their heart for thee.'

The Ettrick Shepherd sent Scott the following stanzas to be inserted in the first edition at places indicated. Most of them are either absolutely base metal or very much worn by circulation. The clever contrivance for breathing (found also in **G** 39, **H** 19) and the bribing of the surgeon provoke scorn and resentment.

'Gay Gos Hawk,' " Scotch Ballads, Materials for Border Minstrelsy," No 143, No 133 a, Abbotsford; in the handwriting of James Hogg.

After 12 of ed. 1802 (**E** 13):
　He happit off the flowry birk,
　　Sat down on the yett-pin,
　And sang sae sweet the notes o love
　　Till a' was coush within.

After 15 (**E** 16):
　'O ye maun send your love a kiss,
　　For he has sent you three;

O ye maun send your love a kiss,
  And ye maun send it wi me.'

'He has the rings off my fingers,
  The garland off my hair;
He has the heart out o my bouk,
  What can I send him mair?'

After 22:
'The third Scotts kirk that ye gang to
  Ye's gar them blaw the horn,
That a' the lords o fair Scotland
  May hear afore the morn.'

After 23:
She wyld a wright to bore her chest,
  For caller air she'd need;
She brib'd her surgeon wi the goud
  To say that she was dead.

After 25:
'What ails, what ails my daughter dear
  Her colour bides sae fine?'
The surgeon-lad reply'd again,
  She's nouther pin'd nor lien.

After 30:
The third Scotts kirk that they cam to,
  Sae loud they blew the horn,
An a' the lads on yon water
  Was warnd afore the morn.

After 31:
'Set down, set down the bier,' he said,
  'These comely corps I'll see;'
'Away, away,' her brothers said,
  'For nae sick thing shall be.

'Her een are sunk, her lips are cold,
  Her rosy colour gane;
'T is nine lang nights an nine lang days
  Sin she deceasd at hame.'

'Wer't nine times nine an nine times nine,
  My true-love's face I'll see;
Set down the bier, or here I swear
  My prisners you shall be.'

He drew the nails frae the coffin,
  An liftit up the cone,
An for a' sae lang as she'd been dead
  She smil'd her love upon.

After 35:
'And tell my father he sent me
  To rot in Scotland's clay;
But he sent me to my Willie,
  To be his lady gay.'

H

"Scotch Ballads, Materials for Border Minstrelsy," No
28 b, Abbotsford; in the handwriting of William Laidlaw.

1 Lord William was walkin i the garden green,
    Viewin the roses red,
  An there he spyed his bonnie spier-hawk,
    Was fleein aboon his head.

2 'O could ye speak, my bonnie spier-hawk,
    As ye hae wings to flee,
  Then ye wad carry a luve-letter
    Atween my love an me.'

3 'But how can I your true-love ken?
    Or how can I her know?
  Or how can I your true-love ken,
    The face I never saw?'

4 'Ye may esily my love ken
    Amang them ye never saw;
  The red that's on o my love's cheek
    Is like bluid drapt on the snaw.'

*   *   *   *   *   *   *

5 'O what will be my meat, master?
    An what'll be my fee?
  An what will be the love-tokens
    That ye will send wi me?'

6 'Ye may tell my love I'll send her a kiss,
    A kiss, aye, will I three;
  If ever she come [to] fair Scotland,
    My wedded wife she's be.

7 'Ye may tell my love I'll send her a kiss,
    A kiss, aye, will I twae;
  An ever she come to fair Scotland,
    I the red gold she sall gae.'

*   *   *   *   *   *   *

8 The hawk flew high, an she flew leugh,
    An south aneath the sun,
  Untill it cam, etc.

9 'Sit still, sit still, my six sisters,
  An sew your silken seam,
Till I gae to my bower-window
  An hear yon Scottish bird sing.'

10 Than she flew high, an she flew leugh,
  An' far aboon the wa;
She drapit to that ladie's side,
  An loot the letter fa.

11 'What news, what news, my bonnie burd?
  An what word carry ye?
An what are a' the love-tokens
  My love has sent to me?'

12 'O ye may send your love a kiss,
  For he has sent ye three;
Ye hae the heart within his buik,
  What mair can he send thee?'

13 'O I will send my love a kiss,
  A kiss, I, will I three;
If I can win to fair Scotland,
  His wedded wife I'll be.

14 'O I will send my love a kiss,
  An the caim out o my hair;
He has the heart that's in my buik,
  What can I send him mair?

15 'An gae yer ways, my bonnie burd,
  An tell my love frae me,
If [I] be na there gin Martinmas,
  Gin Yool I there will be.'

*   *   *   *   *   *   *

16 'T was up an spak her ill step-minnie,
  An ill deed may she die!
'Yer daughter Janet's taen her bed,
  An she'll do nought but die.'

17 'An askin, an askin, dear father,
  An askin I crave o thee;
If I should die just at this time,
  In Scotland burry me.'

18 'There's room eneugh in wide England
  To burry thee an me;
But sould ye die, my dear daughter,
  I Scotland I'll burry thee.'

19 She's warnd the wrights in lilly Londeen,
  She's warnd them ane an a',

To mak a kist wi three windows,
  The cauler air to blaw.

20 'O will ye gae, my six sisters,
  An sew to me a sheet,
The tae half o the silk sae fine,
  The tother o cambric white.'

21 Then they hae askit the surgeon at, etc.

22 Then said her cruel step-minnie,
  Take ye the boilin lead
An some o't drap on her bosom;
  We'll see gif she be dead.

23 Then boilin lead than they hae taen
  An drappit on her breast;
'Alas! alas!' than her father he cried,
  'For she's dead without the priest!'

24 She neither chatterd in her teeth
  Nor shivert wi her chin;
'Alas! alas!' her father cried,
  'For there nae life within!'

*   *   *   *   *   *   *

25 'It's nine lang days, an nine lang nights,
  She's wantit meat for me;
But for nine days, nine langer nights,
  Her face ye salna see.'

26 He's taen the coffin wi his fit,
  Gard it in flinders flie, etc.

27 'Fetch me,' she said, 'a cake o yer bread
  An a wi drap o your wine,
For luve o you an for your sake
  I've fastit lang nights nine.'

28 'T was up then spak an eldrin knight,
  A grey-haird knight was he;
'Now ye hae left yer auld father,
  For you he's like to die.

29 'An ye hae left yer sax sisters
  Lamentin a' for you;
I wiss that this, my dear ladie,
  Ye near may hae to rue.'

30 'Commend me to my auld father,
  If eer ye come him niest;
But nought say to my ill step-minnie.
  Gard burn me on the breist.

31 'Commend me to my six sisters,
  If ye gang bak again;
But nought say to my ill step-minnie,
  Gard burn me on the chin.

32 'Commend me to my brethren bald,
  An ever ye them see;
If ever they come to fair Scotland
  They's fare nae war than me.

33 'For I cam na to fair Scotland
  To lie amang the dead,
But I cam down to fair Scotland
  To wear goud on my head.

34 'Nor did I come to fair Scotland
  To rot amang the clay,
But I cam to fair Scotland
  To wear goud ilka day.'

10^2. *Var.* aboon them a'.

367 b. The second edition of the Minstrelsy, 1803,
II, 6, inserted 13, from Hogg's communication, substituted 22, 23, 24 of Laidlaw's (**H**) for 27, 28, introduced
30 of Laidlaw after 36 (all with changes), and made
the consequently necessary alteration in 37.

99. Johnie Scot.

P. 378 b. Another copy of the Breton ballad, 'Lézo-
bré,' in Quellien, Chansons et Danses des Bretons, 1889,
p. 65.
379 ff.

Q

"Scotch Ballads, Materials for Border Minstrelsy," No
4 a, Abbotsford; in the handwriting of William Laidlaw.

1 Young Johnie's up to England gane
  Three quarters of a year;
Young Johnie's up to England gane,
  The king's banner for to bear.

2 But he had not in England been
  The one half of the time
Till the fairest laidy in all the court
  Was going with child to him.

3 Word unto the kitchen's gane,
  And word's to the hall,
And word unto the court has gane,
  Among the nobles all.

4 And word unto the chamber's gane,
  The place where the king sat,
That his only daughter is with child
  To Johnie, the little Scott.

5 'If this be true,' then sais the king,
  'As I true well it be,
I'll put hir in a strong castle,
  And hungre hir till she dee.'

6 Hir breast-plate was made of iron,
  In place of the beaten gold,
A belt of steel about hir waist,
  And O but she was cold!

7 'O where will I get a pritty little boy,
  That will win hoes and shoon,
That will go doun to yonder lee
  And tell my Johnie to come?'

8 'Here am I, a pritty little boy,
  That will win hoes and shoon,
And I'll go doun to yonder lee
  And tell young Johnie to come.'

9 She has wrote a brod letter,
  And seald it tenderly,
And she has sent it to Johnie the Scott,
  That lay on yonder lee.

10 When Johnie first the letter got,
  A blith, blith man was he;
But or he read the half of it
  The salt teer blind Johnie's ee.

11 'I will go to fair England,' says he,
  'What ever may betide,
For to releave that gay laidy
  Who last lay by my side.'

12 Up then spoke his old mother,
  A sorrifull woman was she;
'If you go to England, John,
  I'll never see you mare.'

13 Up then spoke Johnie's father,
  His head was growing gray;
'If you go to England, John,
  O fair you well for me!'

14 Up then spoke Johnie's uncle,
  Our Scottish king was he;

'Five hundred of my merry men
Shall bear you company.'

15 When Johnie was mounted on his steed
He looked wondorous bold,
The hair that oer his shouldiers hang
Like threeds of yellow gold.

16 'Now come along with me, my men,
O come along with me,
We 'l blow thier castles in the air,
And set free my gay laidy.'

17 The first gay town that they came to,
Made mass for to be sung;
The nixt gay town that they came to,
Made bells for to be rung.

18 But when they came to London town,
They made the drums beat round,
Who made the king and all his court
To wonder at the sound.

19 'Is this the Duke of Mulberry,
Or James the Scottish king?
Or is it a young gentleman
To England new come home?'

20 'It is not the Duke of Mulberry,
Nor James the Scottish [king];
But it is a young gentleman,
MacNaughten is his name.'

21 'If MacNaughten be your name,' says the king,
'As I true well it be,
Before the morn at eight o clock
Dead hanged you shall be.'

22 Up bespoke one of Johnie's little boys,
And a well-spoke boy was he;
'Before we see our master hangd,
We 'l all fight till we dee.'

23 'Well spoke, well spoke, my little boy,
That is well spoke of thee;
But I have a champian in my bower
That will fight you three by three.'

24 Up then spoke Johnie himself,
And he spoke manfully;
'If it please your Majesty,
May I this champian see?'

25 The king and all his nobles then
Rode down unto the plain,
The queen and all [her] gay marries,
To see young Johnie slain.

26 When the champian came out of the bower,
He looked at Johnie with disdain;
But upon the tope of Johnie's brodsword
This champian soon was slain.

27 He fought on, and Johnie fought on,
With swords of tempered steel,
And ay the blood like dropes of rain
Came trinkling down thier hiel.

28 The very nixt stroke that Johnie gave,
He brought him till his knee;
The nixt stroke that Johnie gave,
He clove his head in twa.

29 He swapt his sword on every side,
And turned him on the plain:
'Have you any more of your English dogs
That wants for to be slain?'

30 'A clerk, a clerk!' the king he crys,
'I 'll seal her taucher free;'
'A priest, a priest!' the queen she crys,
'For weded they shall be.'

31 'I 'll have none of your [gold],' say[s] he,
'Nor any of your white money;
But I will have my ain true-love;
This day she has cost me dear.'

27⁴. hill. 29⁴. two.

R

"Scotch Ballads, Materials for Border Minstrelsy," No
37, Abbotsford, MS. of Thomas Wilkie, p. 11; from Miss
Nancy Brockie, Bemerside. Another copy, "Scotch Ballads," etc., No 139, in the handwriting of T. Wilkie, and
somewhat retouched by him.

1 Lord Jonnie 's up to England gone
Three quarters of an year;
Lord Jonnie 's up to England gone,
The king's banner to bear.

2 He had not been in fair England,
Three quarters he was not,

Till the king's eldest daughter
    Goes with child to Lord Jonnie Scott.

3 Word is to the kitchen gone,
    And word 's gone to the hall,
    And word 's gone to the high, high room,
    Among the nobles all.

4 Word 's gone to the king himsel,
    In the chamber where he sat,
    That his eldest daughter goes with child
    To Lord Jonnie Scott.

5 'If that be true,' the king replied,
    'As I suppose it be,
    I 'll put her in a prison strong,
    And starve her till she die.'

6 'O where will I get a little boy,
    That has baith hose and shoon,
    That will run into fair Scotland,
    And tell my love to come?'

7 'O here is a shirt, little boy,
    Her own hand sewed the sleeve;
    Tell her to come to good greenwood,
    Not ask her father's leave.'

3 'What news, what news, my little boy?
    What news have ye brought to me?'
    'No news, no news, my master dear,
    But what I will tell thee.

9 'O here is a shirt, madam,
    Your awn hand sewed the sleeve;
    You must gang to good greenwood,
    Not ask your parents' leave.'

10 'My doors they are all shut, little boy,
    My windows round about;
    My feet is in the fetters strong,
    And I cannot get out.

11 'My garters are of the black, black iron,
    And O but they are cold!
    My breast-plate 's o the strong, strong steel,
    Instead of beaten gold.

12 'But tell him for to bide away,
    And not come near to me,
    For there 's a champion in my father's ha
    Will fight him till he dee.'

13 'What news, what news, my little boy?
    What news have ye to me?'
    'No news, no news, my master dear,
    But what I will tell thee.

14 'Her doors they are all shut, kind sir,
    Her windows round about;
    Her feet are in the fetters strong,
    And she cannot get out.

15 'Her garters are of the black, black iron,
    And O but they are cold!
    Her breast-plate 's of the strong, strong steel,
    Instead of beaten gold.

16 'She bids you for to bide away,
    And not go near to see,
    For there 's a champion in her father's house
    Will fight you till you die.'

17 Then up and spoke Lord Jonnie's mother,
    But she spoke out of time;
    'O if you go to fair England
    I fear you will be slain.'

18 But up and spoke a little boy,
    Just at Lord Jonnie's knee,
    'Before you lose your ain true-love,
    We 'll a' fight till we die.'

19 The first church-town that they came to,
    They made the bells be rung;
    The next church-town that they came to,
    The[y] gard the mass be sung.

20 The next church-town that they came to,
    They made the drums go through;
    The king and all his nobles stood
    Amazing for to view.

21 'Is this any English gentleman,
    Or James our Scottish king?
    Or is it a Scottish gentleman,
    To England new come in?'

22 'No, 't is no English gentleman,
    Nor James the Scottish king;
    But it is a Scottish gentleman,
    Lord Jonnie is my name.'

23 'If Lord Jonnie be your name,
    As I suppose it be,

I have a champion in my hall
  Will fight you till you die.'

24 'O go fetch out that gurrley fellow,
  Go fetch him out to me;
  Before I lose my ain true-love,
  We 'll all fight till we die.'

25 Then out and came that gurrly fellow,
  A gurrly fellow was he,
  With twa lang sclasps between his eyes,
  His shoulders there were three.

26 The king and all his nobles stood
  To see the battle gained;
  The queen and all her maries stood
  To see Lord Jonnie slain.

27 The first stroke that Lord Jonnie gave,
  He wounded very sore;
  The next stroke that Lord Jonnie gave,
  The champion could fight no more.

28 He 's taen a whistle out from his side,
  He 's blawn a blast loud and shill:
  'Is there any more of your English dogs
  To come here and be killed?'

29 'A clerk, a clerk!' the king did say,
  'To cry her toucher free;'
  'A priest, a priest!' Lord Jonnie [did] cry
  'To wed my love and me.

30 ''T was for none of your monnie I fought,
  Nor for none of your world's gear;
  But it was for my own true-love;
  I think I 've bought her dear.'

"This song (L. Jonnie) I took down from the same girl who sung Hughie Graeme."

5². supose.
8³. no news *thrice*: master *wrongly, in anticipation of* 13³.
In No 139.
4³,⁴. That the king's eldest daughter Goes with child to.
7¹. There is a shift, little boy. 7⁴. parents leave.
8². ye to. 16¹. But she. 16³. father's hall.
19². They gard. 19⁴. They made.
22². James our. 23¹. name, kind sir. 25¹. out soon.
28². blown it baith loud. 29¹. did cry.
29². tocher fee. 29³. Jonnie cri's.
30¹. our. 30². Nor none.

S

"Scotch Ballads, Materials for Border Minstrelsy," No 140, Abbotsford; in the handwriting of James Hogg, who remarks at the end: "The repeater of the above song called the hero once or twice Johny Scott, which I ommitted in the MS., seeing it contradicted in the 22 verse. I thought it best to apprise you of this, in case you might find any tract of its being founded on fact, because, if it is not, it hath little else to reccomend it."

1 O Johny 's up thro England gane
  Three quarters of a year,
  An Johny 's up thro England gane,
  The king's banner to bear.

2 He had not been in London town
  But a very little while
  Till the fairest lady in the court
  By Johny gaes wi child.

3 But word is to the kitchin gane,
  An word 's gane to the ha,
  An word 's gane to yon high, high court,
  Amang our nobles a'.

4 An when the king got wit o that
  An angry man was he:
  'On the highest tree in a' the wood
  High hangit shall he be!

5 'An for the lady, if it 's true,
  As I do fear it be,
  I 'll put her in yon castle strong,
  An starve her till she die.'

6 But Johny had a clever boy,
  A clever boy was he,
  O Johny had a clever boy,
  His name was Gregory.

7 'O run, my boy, to yon castle,
  All windows round about,
  An there you 'l see a fair lady,
  At a window looking out.

8 'Ye maun bid her take this silken sark —
  Her ain hand sewd the gare —
  An bid her come to the green wood,
  For Johny waits her there.'

9 Away he ran to yon castle,
  All windows round about,
  Where he espy'd a lady fair,
  At a window looking out.

10 'O madam, there's a silken sark —
   Your ain hand sewd the gare —
   An haste ye to the good green wood,
   For Johny waits you there.'

11 'O I'm confin'd in this castle,
   Though lighted round about;
   My feet are bound with fetters strong,
   That I cannot win out.

12 'My gartens are of stubborn ern,
   Alas! baith stiff and cold;
   My breastplate of the sturdy steel,
   Instead of beaten gold.

13 'Instead of silken stays, my boy,
   With steel I'm lac'd about;
   My feet are bound with fetters strong,
   And how can I get out?

14 'But tell him he must stay at home,
   Nor venture here for me;
   Else an Italian in our court
   Must fight him till he die.'

15 When Johny he got wit o that,
   An angry man was he:
   'But I will gae wi a' my men
   My dearest dear to see.'

16 But up then spake a noble lord,
   A noble lord was he;
   'The best of a' my merry men
   Shall bear you company.'

17 But up then spake his auld mother,
   I wat wi meikle pain;
   'If ye will gae to London, son,
   Ye'l neer come back again.'

18 But Johny turnd him round about,
   I wat wi meikle pride:
   'But I will gae to London town,
   Whatever may betide.'

19 When they were a' on horseback set,
   How comely to behold!
   For a' the hairs o Johny's head
   Did shine like threads o gold.

20 The first ae town that they gaed through,
   They gart the bells be rung,
   But the neist town that they gaed through
   They gart the mass be sung.

21 But when they gaed to London town
   The trumpets loud were blown,
   Which made the king and a' his court
   To marvel at the sound.

22 'Is this the Duke of Morebattle?
   Or James the Scottish king?'
   'No, sire, I'm a Scottish lord,
   McNaughten is my name.'

23 'If you be that young Scottish lord,
   As I believe you be,
   The fairest lady in my court
   She gaes wi child by thee.'

24 'And if she be with child by me,
   As I think sae may be,
   It shall be heir of a' my land,
   And she my gay lady.'

25 'O no, O no,' the king reply'd,
   'That thing can never be,
   For ere the morn at ten o clock
   I'll slay thy men an thee.

26 'A bold Italian in my court
   Has vanquishd Scotchmen three,
   And ere the morn at ten o clock
   I'm sure he will slay thee.'

27 But up then spake young Johny's boy,
   A clever boy was he;
   'O master, ere that you be slain,
   There's mae be slain than thee.'

28 The king and all his court appeard
   Neist morning on the plain,
   The queen and all her ladies came
   To see youn[g] Johny slain.

29 Out then stepd the Italian bold,
   And they met on the green;
   Between his shoulders was an ell,
   A span between his een.

30 When Johny in the list appeard,
   Sae young and fair to see,
   A prayer staw frae ilka heart,
   A tear frae ilka ee.

31 And lang they fought, and sair they fought,
   Wi swords o temperd steel,
   Until the blood like draps o rain
   Came trickling to their heal.

32 But Johny was a wannle youth,
    And that he weel did show;
    For wi a stroke o his broad sword
    He clove his head in two.

33 'A priest, a priest!' then Johny cry'd,
    'To wed my love and me;'
    'A clerk, a clerk!' the king reply'd,
    'To write her tocher free.'

T

'John, the little Scot;' in the youthful handwriting of Sir Walter Scott, inserted, as No 4, at the beginning of a MS. volume, in small folio, containing a number of prose pieces, etc., Abbotsford Library, L. 2.

1 Johnny's gane up to fair England
    Three quarters of a year,
    And Johny's gane up to fair England,
    The king's broad banner to bear.

2 He had not been in fair England,
    Even but a little while,
    When that the king's ae dochter
    To Johnny gaes wi child.

3 And word is gane to the kitchen,
    And word's gane to the ha,
    And word's gane to the high, high court,
    Amang the nobles a'.

4 And word is gane unto the king,
    In the chair where he sat,
    That his ae dochter's wi bairn
    To John the little Scott.

5 'If that I thought she is wi bairn,
    As I true weell she be,
    I'll put her up in high prison,
    And hunger her till she die.'

6 'There is a silken sark, Johnny,
    My ain sell sewed the gare,
    And if ye come to tak me hence
    Ye need nae taken mare.

7 'For I am up in high prison,
    And O but it is cold!
    My garters are o the cold, cold iron,
    In place o the beaten gold.'

8 'Is this the Duke o York?' they said,
    'Or James the Scottish king?
    Or is it John the little Scott,
    Frae Scotland new come hame?'

9 'I have an Italian in my bower,
    This day he has eaten three;
    Before I either eat or sleep
    The fourth man ye shall be.'

10 .   .   .   .   .
    .   .   .   .   .
    Between his een there was two spans,
    His shoulders ells were three.

11 Johnny drew forth his good braid glaive
    And slate it on the plain:
    'Is there any more of your Italian dogs
    That wanteth to be slain?'

12 'A clerk, a clerk!' her father cry'd
    'To register this deed;'
    'A priest, a priest!' her mother cry'd,
    'To marry them wi speed.'

1¹. gane *struck out.* 1⁴. broad *struck out.*
8¹. king o Scots, *originally, for* Duke o York.
9¹. n Italian *struck out, and* Lion *written above.*

100. Willie o Winsbury.

P. 399 ff. MS. of Thomas Wilkie, p. 5, in "Scotch Ballads, Materials for Border Minstrelsy," No 34. From Mrs Hislope, Gattonside. 1813.

1 The king calld on his merry men all,
    By one, by two, and by three;
    Lord Thomas should been the foremost man,
    But the hindmost man was he.

2 As he came tripping down the stairs,
    His stockings were of the silk,
    His face was like the morning sun,
    And his hand as white as milk.

3 'No wonder, no wonder, Lord Thomas,' he said,
    'Then my daughter she loved thee;
    For, if I had been a woman as I am a man,
    Tom, I would hae loved thee.'

106. The Famous Flower of Serving-Men.

P. 429. The fragment printed by Scott was given him by the Ettrick Shepherd. It was printed with no important change except in the last stanza, all of which is the editor's but the second line. The two lines of stanza 7 are scored through in the MS.

"Scotch Ballads, Materials for Border Minstrelsy," No 133 b, Abbotsford; in the handwriting of James Hogg.

1 My love he built me a bonny bowr,
   An cled it a' wi lily-flowr;
   A brawer bowr ye neer did see
   Than my true-love he built to me.

2 There came a man by middle day,
   He spy'd his sport an went away,
   An brought the king that very night,
   Who brak my bowr, an slew my knight.

3 He slew my knight, to me sae dear;
   He slew my knight, an poind his gear;
   My servants all for life did flee,
   An left me in extremity.

4 I sewd his sheet, making my moan;
   I watchd the corpse, mysel alone;
   I watchd his body night and day;
   No living creature came that way.

5 I took the corpse then on my back,
   And whiles I gaed, and whiles I sat;
   I digd a grave, and laid him in,
   And hapd him wi the sod sae green.

6 But thinkna ye my heart was sair
   When I laid the mool on his yellow hair?
   O thinkna ye my heart was wae
   When I turnd about, away to gae?

7 Nae langer there I could remain
   Since that my lovely knight was slain;
   .   .   .   .
   .   .   .   .

110. The Knight and the Shepherd's Daughter.

P. 457 a, 476 f. **A.** **b** is printed in the Ballad Society's ed. of the Roxburghe Ballads, III, 449. It is in the Crawford collection, No 1142. There are four copies in the Douce collection: I, 11 b, 14, 21 b, IV, 33, two of Charles II.'s time, two of no account (Chappell).

458 b. The Danish ballad is now No 314 of Danmarks gamle Folkeviser, continued by Axel Olrik, V, II, 377, 'Ebbe Galt — Hr. Tidemand.' There are four Danish versions, **A–D,** some of the sixteenth century; a Färöe version in five copies, 'Ebbin kall,' Føroyja-kvæði, as elaborated by Grundtvig and Bloch, No 123, D. g. F., **E** ; an Icelandic version, 'Símonar kvæði,' Íslenzk Fornkvæði, I, 224, No 26. Danish **C,** Vedel, III, No 17, is compounded of **B** and a lost version which must have resembled **A.** The copy in Danske Viser, Abrahamson, No 63, is recompounded from **C** and one of the varieties of **D.** Herr Tidemand is the offending knight in **A, C**; Ebbe Galt in **B, D** and the Färöe **E**; Kóng Símon in the Icelandic version. **A** has fifteen stanzas, **B** only eleven ; the story is extended to sixty-seven in **D.** **A** begins directly with a complaint on the part of the injured husband before the King's Bench ; the husband in this version is of a higher class than in the others, — Herr Peder, and not a peasant. The forcing is done at the woman's house in **A** and the Icelandic version ; in **B–E** in a wood. In all, the ravisher is capitally punished.

Hr. Olrik is disposed to think 'The Knight and the Shepherd's Daughter' a not very happy patching together of 'Ebbe Galt,' a lost ballad, and 'Tærning-spillet,' D. g. F., No 248, by a minstrel who may perhaps have had Chaucer's story in mind. I am not prepared to go further than to admit that there is a gross inconsistency, even absurdity, in the English ballad ; the shepherd's daughter of the beginning could not possibly turn out a duke's, an earl's, or a king's daughter in the conclusion.

'Malfred og Sallemand,' p. 458, note §, which has many verses in common with 'Ebbe Galt,' is now No 313 of Danmarks gamle Folkeviser, V, II, 367.

M

'Earl Richmond,' "Scotch Ballads, Materials for Border Minstrelsy," No 81, Abbotsford; in the handwriting of James Skene of Rubislaw.

1 There was a shepherd's daughter
   Kept hogs upo yon hill,
   By cam her a gentle knight,
   And he would hae his will.

2 Whan his will o her he had,
   [His will] as he had taen,
   'Kind sir, for yer courtesy,
   Will ye tell me yer name?'

3 'Some they ca me Jock,' he says,
   'And some they ca me John ;
   But whan 'm in our king's court
   Hitchcock is my name.'

4 The lady being well book-read,
  She spelt it oer again :
'Hitchcock in our king's court
  Is Earl Richard at hame.'

5 He pat his leg out-oer his steed
  And to the get he 's gane ;
She keltit up her green clothing,
  And fast, fast followed him.

6 'Turn back, turn back, ye carl's daughter,
  And dinna follow me ;
It sets na carl's daughters
  Kings' courts for to see.'

7 'Perhaps I am a cerl's daughter,
  Perhaps I am nane,
But whan ye gat me in free forest
  Ye might ha latten 's alane.'

8 Whan they cam to yon wan water
  That a' man does call Clyde,
He looket oer his left shuder,
  Says, Fair may, will ye ride ?

9 'I learnt it in my mother's bowr,
  I wis I had learnt it better,
Whan I cam to wan water
  To soom as does the otter.'

10 Or the knight was i the middle o the water,
  The lady she was oer ;
She took out a came o gold,
  To came down her yellow hair.

11 'Whar gat ye that, ye cerl's daughter ?
  I pray ye tell to me : '
'I got it fra my mither,' she says,
  'To beguil sick chaps as thee.'

12 Whan they cam to our king's court,
  He rade it round about,
And he gade in at a shot-window,
  And left the lady without.

13 She gade to our king hersel,
  She fell low down upon her knee :
'There is a knight into your court
  This day has robbed me.'

14 'Has he robbd ye o your goud ?
  Or o yer well-won fee ?
Or o yer maidenhead,
  The flower o yer body ? '

15 'He has na robbd me o my goud,
  For I ha nane to gee ;
But he has robbd me o my maidenhead,
  The flower o my body.'

16 'O wud ye ken the knight,' he says,
  'If that ye did him see ? '
'I wud him ken by his well-fared face
  And the blyth blink o his ee.'

17 'An he be a married man,
  High hanged sall he be,
And an he be a free man,
  Well wedded to him ye 's be,
Altho it be my brother Richie,
  And I wiss it be no he.'

18 The king called on his merry young men,
  By ane, by twa, by three ;
Earl Richmond had used to be the first,
  But the hindmost was he.

19 By that ye mith ha well kent
  That the guilty man was he ;
She took him by the milk-white hand,
  Says, This same ane is he.

20 There was a brand laid down to her,
  A brand but an a ring,
Three times she minted to the brand,
  But she took up the ring ;
A' that was in our king's court
  Countet her a wise woman.

21 'I 'll gi ye five hundred pounds,
  To mak yer marriage we,
An ye 'l turn back, ye cerl's daughter,
  And fash nae mere wi me.'

22 'Gae keep yer five hundred pounds
  To mak yer merriage we,
For I 'll hae nathing but yersel
  The king he promised me.'

23 'I 'll gae ye one thousand pounds
  To mak yer marriage we,
An ye 'l turn back, ye cerl's daughter,
  And fash nae mere wi me.'

24 'Gae keep yer one thousand pounds,
  To mak yer merriage we,
For I 'll hae nathing but yersel
  The king he promised me.'

25 He took her down to yon garden,
    And clothed her in the green;
  Whan she cam up again,
      Sh[e] was fairer than the queen.

26 They gad on to Mary kirk, and on to Mary
        quire,
    The nettles they grew by the dyke:
  'O, an my mither wer her[e],
      So clean as she wud them pick!'

27 'I wiss I had druken water,' he says,
    'Whan I drank the ale,
  That ony cerl's daughter
      Sud tell me sick a tale.'

28 'Perhaps I am a cerl's daughter,
    Perhaps I am nane;
  But whan ye gat me in free forest
      Ye might ha latten 's alane.

29 'Well mat this mill be,
    And well mat the gae!
  Mony a day they ha filled me pock
      O the white meal and the gray.'

30 'I wiss I had druken water,' he says,
    'When I drank the ale,
  That ony cerl's daughter
      Sud tell me sick a tale.'

31 'Perhaps I am a cerl's daughter,
    Perhaps I am nane;
  But whan ye gat me in free forest
      Ye might ha latten 's alane.

32 'Tak awa yer siller spoons,
    Tak awa fra me,
  An gae me the gude horn spoons,
      It 's what I 'm used tee.

33 'O an my mukle dish wer here,
    And sine we hit were fu,
  I wud sup file I am saerd,
      And sine lay down me head and sleep wi
        ony sow.'

34 'I wiss I had druken water,' he says,
    'Whan I drank the ale,
  That any cerl's daughter
      Sud tell me sick a tale.'

35 'Perhaps I am a cerl's daughter,
    Perhaps I am nane,

  But whan ye gat me in free forest,
      Ye might ha latten 's alane.'

36 He took his hat in oer his face,
    The tear blindit his ee;
  She threw back her yellow locks,
      And a light laughter leugh she.

37 'Bot an ye be a beggar geet,
    As I trust well ye be,
  Whar gat ye their fine clothing
      Yer body was covered we?'

38 'My mother was an ill woman,
    And an ill woman was she;
  She gat them .   .   .   .
      Fra sic chaps as thee.'

39 Whan bells were rung, and mess was sung,
    And aa man bound to bed,
  Earl Richard and the carl's daughter
      In a chamer were laid.

40 'Lie yont, lie yont, ye carl's daughter,
    Yer hot skin burns me;
  It sets na carl's daughters
      In earls' beds to be.'

41 'Perhaps I am a carl's daughter,
    Perhaps I am nane;
  But whan ye gat me in free forest
      Ye might ha latten 's alane.'

42 Up it starts the Belly Blin,
    Just at their bed-feet.

43 'I think it is a meet marrige
    Atween the taen and the tither,
  The Earl of Hertford's ae daughter
      And the Queen of England's brither.'

44 'An this be the Earl of Hertford's ae daugh-
        ter,
    As I trust well it be,
  Mony a gude horse ha I ridden
      For the love o thee.'

1–34. *Written as far as 36 in long lines, two to a
    stanza: there is no division of stanzas.*
23, 24, 28, 30, 31, 34, 35, 41, *are not fully written
    out.*
29². *Possibly* mat she gae, *but observe the plural in
    the next line.*

112. The Baffled Knight.

P. 480 a. There is another variety of **D** in The Calleen Fuine, to which are added The Shepherd's Boy, etc. Limerick, Printed by W. Goggin, corner of Bridge - Street. British Museum, 11621. e. 14 (16). Dated 1810 ? in the catalogue.
This begins :

> There was a shepherd's boy,
>   He kept sheep upon a hill,
> And he went out upon a morning
>   To see what he could kill.
>   It 's blow away the morning dew,
>   It 's blow, you winds, hi ho !
>   You stole away my morning blush,
>   And blow a little, blow.

481 a. 'Lou Cabalier discret' ('Je vous passerai le bois '), Daymard, Vieux Chants p. rec. en Quercy, p. 126.

481 b, III, 518 a. Dans le bois elle s'est mise à pleurer : Revue des Traditions Populaires, IV, 514 ; 'J'ai fini ma journée,' Gothier, Recueil de Crâmignons, p. 5, 'Youp ta deritou la la,' Terry et Chaumont, Recueil d'Airs de Crâmignons, etc., p. 66, No 34 ; 'Après ma journée faite,' Meyrac, Traditions, etc., des Ardennes, pp. 277, 279.

Varieties : 'Lou Pastour brégountsous (trop discret),' Daymard, p. 124 ; 'A la ronde, mesdames,' Terry et Chaumont, p. 22, No 13 ; 'La belle et l'ermite,' 'La jeune couturière,' La Tradition, IV, 346, 348, Chansons populaires de la Picardie (half-popular).

482 a. **A Breton** song gives the essence of the story in seven couplets : Quellien, Chansons et Danses des Bretons, p. 156.

Danish. 'Den dyre Kaabe,' Kristensen, Jyske Folkeminder, X, 142, No 38.

482 b, third paragraph. The incident of the boots in Hazlitt, Jest-Books, II, 241 (Tarlton's Jests, 1611, but printed before 1600).

113. The Great Silkie of Sule Skerry.

P. 494, III, 518. See David MacRitchie, The Finn-Men of Britain, in The Archæological Review, IV, 1–26, 107–129, 190 ff., and Alfred Nutt, p. 232.

A husband who is a man by day, but at night a seal : Curtin, Myths and Folk-Lore of Ireland, p. 51. (G. L. K.)

— — — —

VOL. III.

114. Johnie Cock.

P. 1. There is a ballad of 'Bertram, the Bauld Archer' in Pitcairn's MSS, III, 51; printed in Maidment's Scotish Ballads and Songs, 1859, p. 46. Pitcairn derived it from Mrs McCorquodale, Stirling, a farmer's wife, who remembered it "to have been sung by her grandmother, a woman above eighty years old, who stated that she had it from an old woman, her aunt." The reciter herself was above sixty-five, and had "first heard it when a little girl." Nevertheless, Bertram is fustian, of a sort all too familiar in the last century. The story, excepting perhaps the first stanza, is put into the mouth of Bertram's mistress, à la Gilderoy. The bauld archer has gone to the forest for to mak a robberie. The king has made proclamation that he will give five hunder merk for Bertram's life. John o Shoumacnair (Stronmaknair, Maidment) proposes to his billies to kill Bertram and get the money. They busk themselves in hodden gray, 'like to friers o low degree,' present themselves to Bertram and ask a boon of him, which Bertram grants without inquiry. While they are parleying, Shoumacnair drives his dirk into Bertram's back. But, though he swirls wi the straik, Bertram draws his awsome bran, kills ane, wounds twa, and then his stalwart, gallant soul takes its flight to heaven.

2 b. Braid. "This version [' Johnie of Braidisbank,' I] was taken down by Motherwell and me from the recitation of Mr James Knox, land-surveyor at Tipperlinne, near Edinburgh, in the month of May, 1824, when we met him in the good town of Paisley. At 17 a tradition is mentioned which assigns Braid to have been the scene of this woeful hunting. Mr Knox is the authority for this tradition. Braid is in the neighborhood of Tipperlinne." Note by Mr P. A. Ramsay in a copy of the Minstrelsy which had belonged to Motherwell. (W. Macmath.)

Wolves in Scotland. "It is usually said that the species was extirpated about 1680 by Sir Ewen Cameron of Lochiel, but the tradition to that effect appears to be true only of Sir Ewen's own district of western Invernessshire." The *very* last wolf may have been killed in 1743. R. Chambers, Domestic Annals of Scotland, III, 690.

7. **F** was made up from several copies, one of which was the following, 'John o Cockielaw,' in Scott's youthful handwriting, inserted, as No 3, at the beginning of a MS. volume, in small folio, containing a number of prose pieces, and beginning with excerpts from Law's Memorials. Abbotsford Library, L. 2.

> 1 Johnny got up in a May morning,
>   Calld for water to wash his hands :
> 'Gar louse to me my good gray dogs
>   That are tied with iron bands.'

> 2 When Johnny's mother got word o that,
>   For grief she has lain down :
> 'O Johnny, for my benison,
>   I red you bide at hame !'

> 3 He 's putten on his black velvet,
>   Likewise his London brown,

And he 's awa to Durrisdeer,
    To hunt the dun deer down.

4 Johnny shot, and the dun deer lap,
    And he wounded her on the side ;
Between the water and the brae,
    There he laid her pride.

5 He 's taken out the liver o her,
    And likewise sae the lungs,
And he has made a' his dogs to feast
    As they had been earl's sons.

6 They eat sae much o the venison,
    And drank sae much of the blood,
That they a' then lay down and slept,
    And slept as they had been dead.

7 And bye there cam a silly ald man,
    And an ill death might he die !
And he 's awa to the seven forresters,
    As fast as he can drie.

8 'As I cam down by Merriemas,
    And down aboon the scroggs,
The bonniest boy that ever I saw
    Lay sleeping amang his doggs.

9 'The shirt that was upon his back
    Was of the holland fine,
The cravat that was about his neck
    Was of the cambrick lawn.

10 'The coat that was upon his back
    Was of the London brown,
The doublet   .   .   .   .
    Was of the Lincome twine.'

11 Out and spak the first forrester,
    That was a forrester our them a' ;
If this be John o Cockielaw,
    Nae nearer him we 'll draw.

12 Then out and spak the sixth,
    That was .   forrester amang them a' ;
If this is John o Cockielaw,
    Nearer to him we 'll draw.

13 Johnny shot six of the forresters,
    And wounded the seventh, we say,
And set him on a milk-white steed
    To carry tidings away.

4⁴. Wi He there he (he *written in place of another word*). Wi He *struck out*.
6⁸. *Originally*, That they lay a' them down.
7². *Originally*, And a silly ald man was he.
11². was hed. hed *struck out*.

116. Adam Bell, etc.

P. 18. The Tell story in The Braemar Highlands, by Elizabeth Taylor, Edinburgh, 1869, pp. 99–103, is a transparent plagiarism, as indeed the author of the book seems to be aware.

117. A Gest of Robyn Hode.

P. 40 ff. Thomas Robinhood is one of six witnesses to a grant in the 4th of Richard II. (June 22, 1380– June 21, 1381). See Historical MSS Commission, Fifth Report, Appendix, p. 511, col. 2. The pronunciation, Robinhood (p. 41 a, note †), is clearly seen in the jingle quoted by Nash, Strange Newes, 1593, Works, ed. Grosart, II, 230 : " Ah, neighbourhood, neighbourhood, Dead and buried art thou with Robinhood."

Among the disbursements of John Lord Howard, afterwards Duke of Norfolk, occurs the following : " And the same day, my Lord paide to Robard Hoode for viij. shafftys xvj. d." (This is Friday, Sept. 26, 1483.) Household Books of John Duke of Norfolk and Thomas Earl of Surrey, temp. 1481–1490, ed. by J. P. Collier, 1844, Roxburghe Club, p. 464. Collier, p. 525, remarks that " the coincidence that the duke bought them of a person of the name of Robin Hood is singular."

The Crosscombe Church-Wardens' Accounts (in Church-Wardens' Accounts of Croscombe, Pilton, Yatton, etc., ranging from 1349 to 1560, ed. by Right Rev. Bishop Hobhouse, Somerset Record Soc. Publications, IV, 1890) :

" Comes Thomas Blower and John Hille, and presents in xl *s.* of Roben Hod's recones." 147$\frac{5}{7}$ (accounts for 147$\frac{5}{7}$), p. 4.

" Comys Robin Hode and presents in xxxiij *s.* iv *d.*" 148$\frac{2}{3}$ (for 148$\frac{1}{2}$), p. 10.

" Ric. Willes was Roben Hode, and presents in for yere past xxiij *s.*" 148$\frac{3}{4}$ (for 148$\frac{3}{4}$), p. 11.

" Comys Robyn Hode, Wyllyam Wyndylsor, and presents in for the yere paste iij *l.* vj *s.* viij *d.* ob." 148$\frac{5}{6}$ (for 148$\frac{5}{6}$), p. 14.

" Robyn Hode presents in xlvj *s.* viij. *d.*" 149$\frac{1}{5}$ (for 149$\frac{3}{4}$), p. 20.

And so of later years.

A pasture called Robynhode Closse is mentioned in the Chamberlains' Accounts of the town of Nottingham in 1485, 1486, and 1500 : Records of the Borough of Nottingham, III, 64, 230, 254. A Robynhode Well near the same town is mentioned in a presentment at the sessions of July 20, 1500 (III, 74), and again in

1548 as Robyn's Wood Well (IV, 441). Robin Hood's Acre is mentioned in 1624 (IV, 441). Robbin-hoodes Wele is mentioned in Jack of Dover, his Quest of Inquirie, 1604, Hazlitt, Jest-Books, II, 315. (The above by G. L. K.)

49 b. Italian robber-songs. " Sulle piazze romane e napoletane ognuno ha potuto sentire ripetere i canti epici che celebrano le imprese di famosi banditi o prepotenti, Meo Pataca, Mastrilli, Frà Diavolo : " Cantù, Documenti alla Storia universale (1858), V, 891.

53 a. Note on 243–47. The same incident in The Jests of Scogin, Hazlitt's Jest-Books, II, 151. (G. L. K.)

53 f., 519 a. See also the traditional story how Bishop Forbes, of Corse, lent his brother a thousand marks on the security of God Almighty, in The Scotsman's Library, by James Mitchell, 1825, p. 576. (W. Macmath.)

121. Robin Hood and the Potter.

P. 108 a. Compare the Great-Russian bylinas about Il'ja of Murom and his son (daughter). Il'ja is captain of the march-keepers, Dobrynja second in command. No man, on foot or on horse, no bird or beast, undertakes to pass. But one day a young hero crosses, neither greeting nor paying toll. One of the guards, commonly Dobrynja, is sent after him, but comes back in a fright. Il'ja takes the matter in hand, has a fight with the young man, is worsted at first, but afterwards gets the better of him. Wollner, Volksepik der Grossrussen, p. 115. (W. W.)

141. Robin Hood rescuing Will Stutly.

P. 186. Stanzas 19, 20. The boon of being allowed to fight at odds, rather than be judicially executed, is of very common occurrence in South-Slavic songs, generally with the *nuance* that the hero asks to have the worst horse and the worst weapon. A well-known instance is the Servian song of Jurišić Janko, Karadžić, II, 319, No 52, and the older Croat song of Svilojević (treating the same matter), Bogišić, p. 120 No 46. (W. W.)

155. Sir Hugh, or, The Jew's Daughter.

P. 241. For the subject in general, and particularly ' el santo niño de la Guardia,' see further H. C. Lea, in The English Historical Review, IV, 229, 1889.

242 b, fourth paragraph. See J. Loeb, Un mémoire de Laurent Ganganelli sur la calomnie du meurtre rituel, in Revue des Etudes juives, XVIII, 179 ff., 1889. (G. L. K.) For the other side : Il sangue cristiano nei riti ebraici della moderna sinagoga. Versione dal greco del Professore N. F. S. Prato, 1883. Henri Desportes, Le mystère du sang chez les Juifs de tous les temps. Paris, 1889.

246 b. E 5. The following stanza was inserted by Motherwell as a variation in a copy of his Minstrelsy afterwards acquired by Mr P. A. Ramsay :

She went down to the Jew's garden,
  Where the grass grows lang and green,
She pulled an apple aff the tree,
  Wi a red cheek and a green,
She hung it on a gouden chain,
  To wile that bonnie babe in.

249 ff. A version resembling **H–M, O** has been kindly communicated by Mr P. Z. Round.

S

Written down April, 1891, by Mrs W. H. Gill, of Sidcup, Kent, as recited to her in childhood by a maidservant in London.

1 It rained so high, it rained so low,

  .   .   .   .

  In the Jew's garden all below.

2 Out came a Jew,
    All clothèd in green,
  Saying, Come hither, come hither, my sweet
      little boy,
  And fetch your ball again.

3 ' I won't come hither, I shan't come hither,
    Without my school-fellows all ;
  My mother would beat me, my father would
      kill me,
  And cause my blood to pour.

4 ' He showed me an apple as green as grass,
    He showed me a gay gold ring,
  He showed me a cherry as red as blood,
    And that enticed me in.

5 ' He enticed me into the parlour,
    He enticed me into the kitchen,
  And there I saw my own dear sister,
    A picking of a chicken.

6 ' He set me in a golden chair
    And gave me sugar sweet ;
  He laid me on a dresser-board,
    And stabbed me like a sheep.

7 ' With a Bible at my head,
    A Testament at my feet,

A prayer-book at the side of me,
   And a penknife in so deep.

8 'If my mother should enquire for me,
      Tell her I 'm asleep;
   Tell her I 'm at heaven's gate,
      Where her and I shall meet.'

156. Queen Eleanor's Confession.

Pp. 258 ff.

G

'Earl Marshall,' "Scotch Ballads, Materials for Border
Minstrelsy," No 4 b, Abbotsford; in the handwriting of
William Laidlaw.

1 The queen of England she is seek,
      And seek and like to dee;
   She has sent for friers out of France,
      To bespeek hir speed[i]ly.

2 The king has cald on his merrymen,
      By thirtys and by threes;
   Earl Marshall should have been the formest
      man,
   But the very last man was he.

3 'The queen of England s[h]e is seek,
      And seek and like to dee,
   And she has sent for friers out of France,
      To bespeek hir speedyly.

4 'But I will put on a frier's weeg,
      And ye 'l put on another,
   And we 'll away to Queen Helen gaits,
      Like friers both together.'

5 'O no, no,' says Earl Marshall,
      'For this it must not be;
   For if the queen get word of that,
      High hanged I will be.'

6 'But I will swear by my septer and crown,
      And by the seas so free,
   I will swear by my septer and crown,
      Earl Marshall, thow 's no dee.'

7 So he has put on a frier's wig,
      And the king has put on another,
   And they are away to Queen Helen gaits,
      Like friers both together.

8 When they came to Queen Helen gaits,
      They tirled at the pin;
   There was non so ready as the queene herself
      To open and let them in.

9 'O are you two Scottish dogs?—
      And hanged you shall be—
   Or are [you] friers come out of France,
      To bespeek me speedily?'

10 'We are not two Scottish dogs,
      Nor hanged we shall be;
   For we have not spoken a wrong word
      Since we came over the sea.'

11 'Well then, the very first that ever I sind
      I freely confess to thee;
   Earl Marshall took my maidenhead
      Below yon greenwood tree.'

12 'That is a sin, and very great sin,
      But the Pope will pardon thee;'
   'Amene, Amene,' says Earl Marshall,
      But a feert, feert heart had he.

13 'The very next sin that ever I sind
      I freely confess to thee;
   I had [poisen] seven years in my breast
      To poisen King Hendry.'

14 'That is a sin, and very great sin,
      But the Pope forgiveth thee;'
   'Amene, Amene,' says Earl Marshall,
      But a feert, feert heart had he.

15 'The very next sin that ever I sind
      I freely confess to thee;
   I poisoned one of my court's ladies,
      Was far more fairer than me.'

16 'That is a sin, and a very great sin,
      But the Pope forgiveth thee;'
   'Amene, Amene,' says Earl Marshall,
      But a feert, feert heart had he.

17 'Do you see yon bony boys,
      Playing at the baw?
   The oldest of them is Earl Marshall's,
      And I like him best of all.'

18 'That is a sin, and very great sin,
      But the Pope forgiveth thee;'

'Amene, Amene,' says Earl Marshall,
But a feert, feert heart had he.

19 'Do ye see two bony [boys],
Playing at the baw?
The youngest of them is King Hendry's,
And I like him worst of all.

20 'Because he is headed like a bull,
And his nose is like a boar;'
'What is the matter?' says King Henry,
'For he shall be my heir.'

21 Now he put off his frier's wig
And drest himself [in] red;
She wrung hir hands, and tore hir hair,
And s[w]ore she was betraid.

22 'Had I not sworn by my septer and crown,
And by the seas so free,
Had I not sworn by my septer and crown,
Earl Marshall, thowst have died.'

4². yet. 4³. will. 14². they.
19². is Earl Marshall's.

158. Hugh Spencer's Feats in France.

III, 276, note †. I had remarked that this ballad was after the fashion of Russian bylinas. Professor Wollner indicates especially the bylina of Dobrynja and Vasilij Kazimirović, which in a general way is singularly like 'Hugh Spencer.' In this very fine ballad, Vladimir is in arrears with his tribute to a Saracen king, and appoints Vasilij his envoy, to make payment. Vasilij asks that he may have Dobrynja go with him, and Dobrynja asks for Ivanuška's company. (Compare **B**.) Dobrynja beats the king at chess and at the bow (which corresponds to the justing in the English ballad); then follows a great fight, the result of which is that the Saracen king is fain to pay tribute himself. Wollner, Volksepik der Grossrussen, pp. 123–125.

Other examples of difficult feats done in foreign lands, commonly by comrades of the hero, in Karadžić, II, 445, 465, Nos 75, 79; also II, 132, No 29; and the Bulgarian Sbornik, II, 130, 1, 132, 3. (W. W.)

161. The Battle of Otterburn.

Pp. 294, 520. St George Our Lady's Knight. 'Swete Sainct George, our ladies knyght,' Skelton, 'Against the Scottes,' v. 141, Dyce, I, 186; 'Thankyd be Saynte Gorge our ladyes knythe,' in the 'Ballade of the Scottysche Kynge,' p. 95 of the fac-simile edition by J. Ash-

ton, 1882 (where the passage is somewhat different). In his note, II, 220, to the poem 'Against the Scottes,' Dyce remarks that St George is called Our Lady's Knight "in a song written about the same time as the present poem, Cott. MS. Domit. A. xviii. fol. 248." This appears to be the song quoted from the same MS. by Sir H. Ellis, Original Letters, First Series, I, 79:

'Swet Sent Jorge, our Ladyes knyte,
Save Kyng Hary bothe be day and ny3th.'

In his Chorus de Dis, super triumphali victoria contra Gallos, etc., Skelton speaks of St George as Gloria Cappadocis divæ milesque Mariæ, v. 13; Dyce, I, 191. See also John Anstis, The Register of the Most Noble Order of the Garter, London, 1724, I, 122; II, 27, 48 f. (G. L. K.)

299. **C**. First published in the second edition of the Minstrelsy, 1803, I, 27. 1³,⁴ there read The doughty earl of Douglas rode Into England, to catch a prey; 31¹, Yield thee, O yield thee, etc., and 31³, Whom to shall I yield, said, etc.

For his later edition of 'The Battle of Otterburn,' Scott says he used "two copies . . . obtained from the recitation of old persons residing at the head of Ettrick Forest." James Hogg sent Scott, in a letter dated September 10 (1802?), twenty-nine stanzas "collected from two different people, a crazy old man and a woman deranged in her mind," and subsequently recovered, by "pumping" his "old friends' memory," other lines and half lines out of which (using the necessary cement, and not a little) he built up eleven stanzas more, and these he seems to have forwarded·in the same letter. These two communications are what is described by Scott as two copies. They will be combined here according to Hogg's directions, and the second set of verses bracketed for distinction.

The materials out of which **C** was constructed can now easily be separated. We must bear in mind that Scott allowed himself a liberty of alteration; this he did not, however, carry very far in the present instance. 1–13, 15–19, 23 are taken, with slight change or none, from Hogg's first "copy" of verses; 24, 26–29 from the second; 30–35 are repeated from Scott's first edition. 14 is altered from **A** 16; 20 = Hogg 21¹,² + Scott; 21 = Hogg 22¹ + Hogg 35²⁻⁴; 22 = Hogg 23¹,³ + Scott; 25 = Hogg 28¹ + **B** 8²⁻⁴. Scott did well to drop Hogg 9, and ought to have dropped Hogg 8.

"Scotch Ballads, Materials for Border Minstrelsy," No 132, Abbotsford, stanzas 1–24, 35–38, 40; the same, No 5, stanzas 25–34, 39. Communicated to Scott, in a letter, by James Hogg.

1 It fell about the Lammas time,
When the muir-men won their hay,
That the doughty Earl Douglas went
Into England to catch a prey.

2 He chose the Gordons and the Graemes,
    With the Lindsays light and gay ;
  But the Jardines wadna wi him ride,
    And they rued it to this day.

3 And he has burnt the dales o Tine
    And part of Almonshire,
  And three good towers on Roxburgh fells
    He left them all on fire.

4 Then he marchd up to Newcastle,
    And rode it round about :
  ' O whae 's the lord of this castle,
    Or whae 's the lady o 't ? '

5 But up spake proud Lord Piercy then,
    And O but he spak hie !
  I am the lord of this castle,
    And my wife 's the lady gaye.'

6 ' If you are lord of this castle,
    Sae weel it pleases me ;
  For ere I cross the border again
    The ane of us shall die.'

7 He took a lang speir in his hand,
    Was made of the metal free,
  And for to meet the Douglas then
    He rode most furiously.

8 But O how pale his lady lookd,
    Frae off the castle wa,
  When down before the Scottish spear
    She saw brave Piercy fa !

9 How pale and wan his lady lookd,
    Frae off the castle hieght,
  When she beheld her Piercy yield
    To doughty Douglas' might !

10 ' Had we twa been upon the green,
    And never an eye to see,
  I should have had ye flesh and fell ;
    But your sword shall gae wi me.'

11 ' But gae you up to Otterburn,
    And there wait dayes three,
  And if I come not ere three days' end
    A fause lord ca ye me.'

12 ' The Otterburn 's a bonny burn,
    'T is pleasant there to be,

But there is naught at Otterburn
    To feed my men and me.

13 ' The deer rins wild owr hill and dale,
    The birds fly wild frae tree to tree,
  And there is neither bread nor kale
    To fend my men and me.

14 ' But I will stay at Otterburn,
    Where you shall welcome be ;
  And if ye come not ere three days' end
    A coward I 'll ca thee.'

15 ' Then gae your ways to Otterburn,
    And there wait dayes three ;
  And if I come not ere three days' end
    A coward ye 's ca me.'

16 They lighted high on Otterburn,
    Upon the bent so brown,
  They lighted high on Otterburn,
    And threw their pallions down.

17 And he that had a bonny boy
    Sent his horses to grass,
  And he that had not a bonny boy
    His ain servant he was.

18 But up then spak a little page,
    Before the peep of the dawn ;
  ' O waken ye, waken ye, my good lord,
    For Piercy 's hard at hand ! '

19 ' Ye lie, ye lie, ye loud liar,
    Sae loud I hear ye lie !
  The Piercy hadna men yestreen
    To dight my men and me.

20 ' But I have seen a dreary dream,
    Beyond the isle o Sky ;
  I saw a dead man won the fight,
    And I think that man was I.'

21 He belted on his good broad-sword
    And to the field he ran,
  Where he met wi the proud Piercy,
    And a' his goodly train.

22 When Piercy wi the Douglas met,
    I wat he was right keen ;
  They swakked their swords till sair they swat,
    And the blood ran them between.

23 But Piercy wi his good broad-sword,
   Was made o the metal free,
   Has wounded Douglas on the brow
   Till backward he did flee.

24 Then he calld on his little page,
   And said, Run speedily,
   And bring my ain dear sister's son,
   Sir Hugh Montgomery.

25 [Who, when he saw the Douglas bleed,
   His heart was wonder wae:
   'Now, by my sword, that haughty lord
   Shall rue before he gae.'

26 'My nephew bauld,' the Douglas said,
   'What boots the death of ane?
   Last night I dreamd a dreary dream,
   And I ken the day's thy ain.

27 'I dreamd I saw a battle fought
   Beyond the isle o Sky,
   When lo, a dead man wan the field,
   And I thought that man was I.

28 'My wound is deep, I fain wad sleep,
   Nae mair I 'll fighting see;
   Gae lay me in the breaken bush
   That grows on yonder lee.

29 'But tell na ane of my brave men
   That I lye bleeding wan,
   But let the name of Douglas still
   Be shouted in the van.

30 'And bury me here on this lee,
   Beneath the blooming brier,
   And never let a mortal ken
   A kindly Scot lyes here.'

31 He liftit up that noble lord,
   Wi the saut tear in his ee,
   And hid him in the breaken bush,
   On yonder lily lee.

32 The moon was clear, the day drew near,
   The spears in flinters flew,
   But mony gallant Englishman
   Ere day the Scotsmen slew.

33 Sir Hugh Montgomery he rode
   Thro all the field in sight,

And loud the name of Douglas still
He urgd wi a' his might.

34 The Gordons good, in English blood
   They steepd their hose and shoon,
   The Lindsays flew like fire about,
   Till a' the fray was doon.]

35 When stout Sir Hugh wi Piercy met,
   I wat he was right fain;
   They swakked their swords till sair they swat,
   And the blood ran down like rain.

36 'O yield thee, Piercy,' said Sir Hugh,
   'O yield, or ye shall die!'
   'Fain wad I yield,' proud Piercy said,
   'But neer to loun like thee.'

37 'Thou shalt not yield to knave nor loun,
   Nor shalt thou yield to me;
   But yield thee to the breaken bush
   That grows on yonder lee.'

38 'I will not yield to bush or brier,
   Nor will I yield to thee;
   But I will yield to Lord Douglas,
   Or Sir Hugh Montgomery.'

39 [When Piercy knew it was Sir Hugh,
   He fell low on his knee,
   But soon he raisd him up again,
   Wi mickle courtesy.]

40 He left not an Englishman on the field

   .   .   .   .

   That he hadna either killd or taen
   Ere his heart's blood was cauld.

35^3. swords still.

Hogg writes:
"As for the scraps of Otterburn which I have got,
they seem to have been some confused jumble, made by
some person who had learned both the songs which you
have, and in time had been straitened to make one out of
them both. But you shall have it as I had it, saving that,
as usual, I have sometimes helped the measure, without
altering one original word."
After 24: "This ballad, which I have collected from
two different people, a crazy old man and a woman deranged in her mind, seems hitherto considerably entire;
but now, when it becomes most interesting, they have

both failed me, and I have been obliged to take much of it in plain prose. However, as none of them seemed to know anything of the history save what they had learned from the song, I took it the more kindly. Any few verses which follow are to me unintelligible.

"He told Sir Hugh that he was dying, and ordered him to conceal his body, and neither let his own men nor Piercy's know ; which he did, and the battle went on headed by Sir Hugh Montgomery, and at length " (35, etc.).

After 38 : " Piercy seems to have been fighting devilishly in the dark; indeed, my relaters added no more, but told me that Sir Hugh died on the field, but that " (40).

In the postscript, Hogg writes :

" Not being able to get the letter away to the post, I have taken the opportunity of again pumping my old friends' memory, and have recovered some more lines and half lines of Otterburn, of which I am become somewhat enamourd. These I have been obliged to arrange somewhat myself, as you will see below; but so mixed are they with original lines and sentences that I think, if you pleased, they might pass without any acknowledgment. Sure no man will like an old song the worse of being somewhat harmonious. After [24] you may read [25–34]. Then after [38] read [39]."

Of Almonshire [3²] Hogg writes : "Almon shire may probably be a corruption of Banburgh shire, but as both my relaters called it so, I thought proper to preserve it."

Andrew Livingston writes to Scott, Airds by Castle Douglas, 28th April, 1806, Letters, I, No 183 : " My mother recollects seven or eight verses of the ballad of 'The Battle of Otterburn' different from any I have seen either in the first and second editions of the Minstrelsy or in Percy's Reliques. . . . In several parts they bear a great resemblance to the copy in the first edition of the Minstrelsy."

162. The Hunting of the Cheviot.

P. 306. Fighting on or with stumps, etc.

Ketilbjörn's foot is cut off at the ankle-joint. He does not fall, but hobbles against his enemies and kills two of them before his strength gives out : Gull-þóris Saga, c. 18, ed. Maurer, p. 75. Gnúpr fought on his knees after his foot was off : Vemundar Saga ok Víga-skútu, c. 13, Rafn, Íslendinga Sögur, II, 266. Sörli kills eleven men with his club, hobbling round on one foot and one stump (apparently, though Sörli and Hárr are perhaps confused in the narrative): Göngu-Hrólfs Saga, c. 31, Rafn, Fornaldar Sögur, III, 329, Ásmundarson, III, 214 (wrongly, 114). Már fights when both his hands are off : Gull-þóris Saga, c. 10, Maurer, p. 59. Compare the exploits of Sölvi after both his hands have been cut off : Göngu-Hrólfs Saga, c. 31,

Rafn, F. S., III, 331, Ásmundarson, III, 215 (wrongly 115) ; and Röndólfr's performances after one of his hands has been cut off and all the toes of one foot, in the same saga, c. 30, Rafn, p. 324 f., Ásmundarson, p. 211 (111) ; and Göngu-Hrólfr's, who has had both feet cut off while he slept, the same saga, c. 25, Rafn, pp. 307–9, Ásmundarson, 197 f. The Highlander at the battle of Gasklune had his predecessor in Ali, in the same saga, c. 30, Rafn, p. 324, Ásmundarson, p. 210 (110). (G. L. K.)

167. Sir Andrew Barton.

P. 338 b. Gold to bury body. So in the story of Buridan and the Queen of France, Haupt's Zeitschrift II, 364. (G. L. K.)

In Apollonius of Tyre : puellam in loculo conposuit . . . et uiginti sestertios ad caput ipsius posuit, et scripturam sic continentem : Quicumque corpus istud inuenerit et humo tradiderit medios sibi teneat, medios pro funere expendat ; et misit in mare. C. 25, ed. Riese, p. 29. Cf. Jourdains de Blaivies, 2222–33, K. Hofmann, Amis et Amiles und Jourdains de Blaivies, 1882, p. 168 f. (P. Z. Round.)

'The Sonnge of Sir Andraye Barton, Knight,' English Miscellanies, edited by James Raine, Surtees Society, vol. lxxxv, p. 64, 1890 ; from a MS. in a hand of the sixteenth century now in York Minster Library.

This very interesting version of Sir Andrew Barton, the editor informs us, was originally No 25 of a ballad-book in small quarto. It came recently " into the possession of the Dean and Chapter of York with a number of papers which belonged in the seventeenth century to the episcopal families of Lamplugh and Davenant." If, as is altogether probable, there were copies of other ballads in the same book in quality as good as this, and if, as is equally probable, no more of the book can be recovered, our only comfort is the cold one of having had losses. In several details this copy differs from that of the Percy MS., but not more than would be expected. The English sail out of the Thames on the morrow after midsummer month, July 1, and come back the night before St Maudlen's eve, or the night of July 20, stanzas 17, 74. In stanza 42 Barton boasts that he had once sent thirty Portingail heads home salted — 'to eat with bread ' ! We read in Lesley's History that the Hollanders had taken and spoiled divers Scots ships, and had cruelly murdered and cast overboard the merchants and passengers ; in revenge for which Andrew Barton took many ships of that country, and filled certain pipes with the heads of the Hollanders and sent them to the Scottish king. (Ed. 1830, p. 74 ; ed. 1578, p. 329.) The eating is a ferocious addition of the ballad. Several passages of this copy are corrupted. A throws light upon some of these places, but others remain to me unamendable.

1 It fell against a midsomer moneth,
  When birds soonge well in every tree,
Our worthë prence, Kinge Henrye,
  He roode untoe a chelvellrye.

2 And allsoe toe a forrest soe faire,
  Wher his Grace wente toe tak the ayre;
And twentye marchantes of London citie
  Then on there knees they kneelled there.

3 'Ye are welcome home, my rich merchants,
  The best salers in Christentie!'
'We thanke yowe; by the rood, we are salers
  good,
But rich merchantes we cannot be.

4 'To France nor Flanders we der not goe,
  Nor a Burgesse voy[a]ge we der not fare,
For a robber that lyes abrod on the sea,
  And robs us of oure merchantes-ware.'

5 King Henry was stout, and turnd hime
  about;
He sware by the lord that was mickell of
  might,
'Is ther any rober in the world soe stoute
  Der worke toe England that unrighte?'

6 The merchantes answered, soore they sight,
  With a woefull harte to the kinge againe,
'He is one that robes us of our right,
  Were we twentie shippes and he but one.'

7 King Henrye lookte over his shoulder agayne,
  Amongst his lordes of hye degree:
'Have I not a lord in all my land soe stoute
  Der take yon robber upon the sea?'

8 'Yes,' then did answeer my lord Charls How-
  warde,
Neare the kinge's grace that he did stande;
He saide, If your Grace will give me leave,
  My selfe will be the onlie man,

9 'That will goe beat Sir Andrewe Barton
  Upon the seas, if he be there;
I 'le ether bringe hime and his shippe toe this
  lande,
Ore I 'le come in England never more.'

10 'Yow shall have five hundrethe men,' saide
  Kinge Henrye,
'Chuse them within my realme soe free,

Beside all other merriners and boys,
  Toe gide the great shippe on the sea.'

11 The first of all the lord up cald,
  A noble gunner he was one;
This man was thre score yeares and ten,
  And Petter Symond height his name.

12 'Petter,' quoeth he, 'I must saill the sea,
  Toe looke an enemye, God be my speede!
As thowe arte ould, I have chossen the
  Of a hundreth gunners to be the headde.'

13 He said, If your Honor have chossen me
  Of a hundreth gunners to be the headd,
On your mayn-mast-tre let me be hangd,
  If I miss thre mille a pennye breed.

14 Then next of all my lord up cald,
  A noble boweman he was ane;
In Yorkeshier was this gentleman borne,
  And William Horsley height his name.

15 'Horsley,' saide he, 'I must saill the sea,
  To meete an enemee, thow must knowe;
I have oft [been] told of thy artillorye,
  But of thy shootinge I never sawe.

16 'Yet fore thye drawght that thowe dost drawe,
  Of a hundreth bowemen to be the heade;'
Said Horsley then, Let me be hang[d]e,
  If I mis twelve score a twelt penc[e]
  breed.

17 Yea, pickmen more, and bowmen both,
  This worthë Howward tooke to the sea;
On the morowe after midsomer moneth
  Out of Temes mouth saillëd he.

18 Hee had not sailled one daie but three,
  After his Honor tooke to the sea,
When he mette with one Harrie Huntte,
  In Newcastell ther dwelte hee.

19 When he sawe the lion of England out blaisse,
  The streemers and the roose about his eye,
Full soonne he let his toppe-saill fall;
  That was a tooken of curtissie.

20 My lord he cald of Henry Huntte,
  Bad Harry Hunt both stay and stande;
Saies, Tell me where thy dwellinge is,
  And whome unto thye shippe belonnges.

21 Henrye Hunt he answered, sore he sight,
    With a woefull hart and a sorrowefull
        minde,
'I and this shippe doth both belonge
Unto the Newe Castell that stands upon
    Tyne.'

22 'But haist thowe harde,' said my lord Charles
        Hawward,
    'Wher thowe haist travelled, by daie or by
        night,
Of a robber that lies abroode on the sea,
    They call him Sir Andrewe Barton, knight?'

23 'Yes,' Harye answered, sore he sight,
    With a woefull hart thus did he saye;
'Mary, overwell I knowe that wight,
    I was his pressoner yesterdaie.

24 'Toe frome home, my lord, that I was boune,
    A Burgess voyage was boune so faire,
Sir Andrewe Barton met with me,
    And robd me of mye merchantes-waire.

25 'And I ame a man in mickle debte,
    And everye one craves his owne of mee;
And I am boune to London, my lorde,
    Fore toe comepleanne to good King Henrye.'

26 'But even I pray the,' saies Lord Charlles
        Howeerd,
    'Henrye, let me that robber see,
Where that Scott hath teyne from the a
        grootte,
I 'le paye the back a shillinge,' said hee.

27 'Nay, God forbid! yea, noble lord,
    I heare your Honor speake amisse;
Christ keepe yowe out of his companye!
    Ye wott not what kine a man he is.

28 'He is brase within and steelle without,
    He beares beames in his topcastle hye,
He hath threscore peece on ether side,
    Besides, my lorde, well mande is he.

29 'He hath a pennis is dearelye deighte,
    She is dearelye deighte and of mickell pried;
His pennis hath ninescorre men and more,
    And thirtene peece on ethere side.

30 'Were yowe twentie shippes, my lorde,
    As your Honor is but one,

Ethere bye lerbord or by lowe
    That Scootte would overcome yowe, everye
        one.'

31 'Marye, that 's ill hartinge,' saies my lord
        Charlls Howeward,
    'Harye, to welcome a stranger to the sea;
I 'le ether bringe thatt Scootte and his shippe
        toe England,
Or into Scootteland hee ['s] carrye me.'

32 'Well, since the matter is soe flatte,
    Take heed, I 'le tell yowe this before;
If yowe Sir Andrewe chance toe borde,
    Let noe man toe his topcastle goe.

33 'Excepte yowe have a gunner goode
    That can well marke with his eye;
First seeke to gette his pennis sunk,
    The soonner overcome his selfe may bee.

34 'Yesterdaie I was Sir Andrewe's pressonner,
    And ther he tooke me sworne,' saide hee;
'Before I 'le leave off my serving God,
    My wild-maide oeth may brooken be.

35 'Will yowe lend me sexe peece of ordenance,
        my lord,
    To carye into my shippe with mee?
Toe morrowe by seven a clocke, and souner,
    In the morne yowe shall Sir Andrewe see.

36 'Fore I will set yowe a glasse, my lord,
    That yowe shall saille forth all this night;
Toe morrowe be seven a clocke, and souner,
    Yow 's se Sir Andrewe Barton, knight.'

37 Nowe will we leave talkinge of Harry Hunt;
    The worthye Howwarde tooke to the sea;
By the morne, by seven a clocke, and souner,
    My lord hee did Sir Andrewe see.

38 A larborde, wher Sir Andrewe laye,
    They saide he tould his gold in the light;
'Nowe, by my faith,' saide my lord Charlles
        Howwarde,
    'I se yonne Scootte, a worthë wight!

39 'All our greatt ordienance wee 'll take in;
    Fetch downe my streemers,' then saide hee,
'And hange me forth a white willowe-wande,
    As a marchante-man that sailles by the
        sea.'

40 By Sir Andrewe then mye lord he past,
  And noe topsaille let fall would hee :
'What meanes yonne English dogg?' he saies,
'Dogs doe knowe noe curtissie.

41 'For I have staid heare in this place
  Admirall more then years three ;
Yet was not ther Englisheman or Portingaill
  Could passe by me with his liffe,' saide he.

42 'Once I met with the Portingaills,
  Yea, I met with them, ye, I indeed ;
I salted thirtie of ther heades,
  And sent them home to eate with breade.

43 'Nowe by me is yoen pedler past;
  It greves me at the hart,' said hee ;
'Fetch me yoen English dogs,' he saide,
  'I 'le hange them al on my mayn-mast-
    tree.'

44 Then his pennis shotte of a peec[e] of orde-
    nance ;
  The shootte my lord might verye well ken,
Fore he shootte downe his missonne-mast,
  And kild fifteen of my lordë's men.

45 'Come hether, Peter Simond,' said my lord
    Charles Howward,
  'Letes se thi word standis in steede ;
On my mayn-mast-tre thowe must be hunge,
  If thowe misse three mill a penney breed.'

46 Petter was ould, his hart was bould ;
  He tooke a peece frome hie and laid hir be-
    loue ;
He put in a chean of yeard[ë]s nine,
  Besides all other greate shoote and smalle.

47 And as he maide that gune to goe,
  And verye well he marke[d] with his eie,
The first sight that Sir Andrewe sawe,
  He sawe his penis sunke in the sea.

48 When Sir Andrewe sawe his pennis sunke,
  That man in his hart was no thinge well :
'Cut me my cabells! let me be lousse !
  I 'le fetch yoen English dogges me selne.'

49 When my lord sawe Sir Andrewe from his an-
    ker loouse,
  Nay, Lord! a mighty man was hee :

'Let my drumes strike up and my trumpetes
    sound,
  And blaise my banners vailliantlie.'

50 Peter Simon's sonne shoote of a gune ;
  That Sir Andrewe might very well ken ;
Fore he shoott throughe his over-decke,
  And kild fifttie of Sir Andrewe's men.

51 'Ever alack !' said Sir Andrewe Barton,
  'I like not of this geare,' saide hee ;
'I doubt this is some English lorde
  That 's comed to taik me on the sea.'

52 Harrye Hunt came in on the other side ;
  The shoote Sir Andrewe might very well ken ;
Fore he shoote downe his misson-mast,
  And kild other fortye of his men.

53 'Ever alacke !' said Sir Andrewe Barton,
  'What maye a trewe man thinke or saye ?
He is becomed my greatest enymye
  That was my pressonner yesterdaie.

54 'Yet feare no English dogges,' said Sir Andrew
    Barton,
  'Nor fore ther forse stand ye [in] no awe ;
My hands shall hange them all my selfe,
  Froe once I let my beames downe fawe.

55 'Come hether quick, thou Girdon goode,
  And come thou hether at my call,
Fore heare I may noe longer staye ;
  Goe up and let my beames down fall.'

56 Then he swarmd up the maine-mast-tree,
  With mickell might and all his maine ;
Then Horsley with a broode-headed arrowe
  Stroke then Girdon throughe the weame.

57 And he fell backe to the hatches againe,
  And in that wound full sore did bleed ;
The blood that ran soe fast from hime,
  They said it was the Girdon's deed.

58 'Come hether, thow James Hamelton,
  Thowe my sister's sonne, I have noe moe ;
I 'le give the five hundreth pound,' he saide,
  'Ife thowe wilt toe the top[ca]saille goe.'

59 Then he swarmd up the mayn-mast-tree,
  With mickell might and all his mayne ;

Then Horsley with a broode-arrowe-head
  Tooke hime in at the buttuke of the utuer
    beame.

60 Yet frome the tre he would not parte,
  But up in haist he did prossed;
Then Horsley with anotheir arrowe
  Strooke then Hamelton throughe the heade.

61 When Sir Andrewe sawe his sister's sonne
    slayne,
  That man in his heart was nothinge well:
'Fight, maisters!' said Sir Andrewe Barton,
  'It 's time I 'le to the top myselne.'

62 Then he put on the armere of prooffe,
  And it was guilt with gold full cleare:
'My brother John of Barton,' he saide,
  'Full longe against Portingaill he it weare.'

63 When he had on that armore of prooffe,
  Yea, on his bodye he had that on,
Marry, they that sawe Sir Andrewe Barton
  Said arrowes nor guns he feared none.

64 Yet Horsley drewe a broode-headed arrowe,
  With mickell might and all his mayne;
That shaft against Sir Andrewe's brest
  Came back to my lord Howwarde's shippe
    agayne.

65 When my lord he sawe that arrowe comme,
  My lord he was a woefull wight;
'Marke well thine ame, Horsley,' he saide,
  'Fore that same shoote I 'le make the
    knight.'

66 'Ever alacke!' said Horsley then,
  'For howe soe ever this geare doth goe,
If I for my service louse my heade,
  I have in this shippe but arrowe[s] towe.'

67 Yet he mar[k]t hime with the one of them,
  In a previe place and a secrete pert;
He shoote hime in at the left oxtere,
  The arrowe quiett throughe [the] harte.

68 'Feight, maisters!' said Sir Andrewe Bar-
    ton,
  'I 'se a lettle hurt, but I ame not slayne;
I 'le lie me downe and bleede a whill,
  I 'le risse and feight with yowe agayne.

69 'Yet feare noe English dogges,' said Sir An-
    drewe Barton,
  'Nore fore there force stand ye [in] noe
    awe;
Stick stifeley to Sir Andrewe Barton,
  Feight till ye heare my whisstill blowe.'

70 The could noe skill of the whisstill heare;
  Quoeth Hary Hunt, I der lay my heade,
My lord, yowe maye take the shippe when
    yowe will,
  I se Sir Andrewe Barton ['s] deade.

71 And then they borded that noble shippe,
  On both the sides, with all ther men;
Ther was eighten [score] Scootes a live,
  Besides all other was hurte and slayne.

72 Then up my lord tooke Sir Andrewe Barton,
  And of he cutt the dead man's head:
'I would forsweare England for twenty years,
  Toe have the quicke as thowe art deade.

73 But of he cut the dead man's heade,
  And bounde his bodye toe borden tre,
And tiede five hundreth angels about his midle,
  That was toe cause hime buried toe bee.

74 Then they sailled toe Ingland agayne,
  With mickle merienes, as I weane;
They entred Englishe land agayn
  On the night before Ste Maudlen even.

75 Toe mete my lord came the kinge an quen,
  And many nobles of hie degree;
They came fore noe kind of thinge
  But Sir Andrewe Barton they would see.

76 Quoth my lord, Yowe may thanke Allmighty
    God,
  And foure men in the shippe with mee,
That ever we scaipt Sir Andrewe['s] hands;
  England had never such an enniemie.

77 'That 's Henrye Hunt and Petter Symon,
  William Horsley and Petter Symon['s]
    sonne;
Reward all thoesse fore there paynes,
  They did good service att that time.'

78 'Henry Hunt shall have his whistle and chean,
  A noble a daie I 'le give him,' quoeth hee,

'And his coustome betwexte Trent tid and
    Tyne,
    Soe longe as he doth use the sea.

79 'Petter Symon shall have a crowne a daie,
    Halfe a crowne I 'le give his sonne;
    That was fore a shoott he sente
    Sir Andrew Barton with his gune.

80 'Horsley, right I 'le make the a knight,
    In Yorkshiere shall thy dwellinge be;
    My lord Charlles Howwarde shall be an earle,
    And soe was never Howward before,' quoth
    he.

81 'Everye Englishe man shall have eightten pens
    a daie
    That did mainetayne [t]his feight soe free,
    And everye Scotchman a shillinge a daie
    Till they come atte my brother Jamie.'

In eight-line stanzas.
1⁴. chelvellrye. chevachie? *or some sort of* vallie?
3¹. Yea. 4². farre. 10³. and blause.
10⁴. give the the. 14⁴. height: was *interlined.*
16². thou 's be? 19². sterne. *For* streemers, *see*
    39², *and* B 33². 23⁸. weight.
28⁸. threscoore. 29⁴. sidde.
30¹. Were yare. *Perhaps* thare.
30⁸. by lowe. *Cf.* A 29² :=hull? 32⁸. you and.
38⁴, 65². weight. 44⁴. xv^th. 45². the word.
46⁸. ninee. 47⁸. sawee. 52¹. sidde. 54². yea no.
55¹. hether, drinke. 58². noe more.
58⁴, 66². goee. 59⁸. *Probably* broode - headed ar-
    rowe, *as in* 56⁸, 64¹.
59⁴. utuer = outer? bane? *But I do not under-*
    stand.
62⁴. Portingaill they weare: *cf.* A 59⁴. 72⁸. xx^th.
73⁸. 5: angles. 75¹. Toe might. 78². An noble.
79⁴. gunee. 81⁴. Jamie, Jamiee.

168. Flodden Field.

P, 351 b, 12. See an account of the exhumation of
a corpse wrapped in a hide without a covering of lead,
in Archæologia, I, 34. (G. L. K.)

169. Johnie Armstrong.

P. 367, note †. A new-born child thrown into the
water by its mother tells her that she has lost Paradise :
'L'Enfant noyé,' La Tradition, V, 116.

172. Musselburgh Field.

P. 378. Is this the song quoted by Sir Toby in
Twelfth Night, II, 3 (and hitherto unidentified), "O,
the twelfth day of December"? (G. L. K.)

173. Mary Hamilton.

Pp. 379-97. I a was first printed in the second edition of the Minstrelsy, 1803, II, 163. (Read in 1², on
her; in 3², hand.) The copy principally used was one
furnished by Sharpe, which was not A a, and has not
so far been recovered. Besides this, "copies from various quarters" were resorted to. (Half a dozen stanzas are found in G, but G itself is very likely a compilation). Eight copies from Abbotsford are now printed
for the first time. Two of these may have been in
Scott's hands in time to be used, two were certainly
not, and for the others we have no date.

There is only one novel feature in all these copies:
in U 13 Mary's paramour is a pottinger. The remark
that there is no trace of an admixture of the Russian
story with that of the apothecary, page 383, must therefore be withdrawn.* Mary in this version, as in E, F,
Q, T, U, V, Y, is daughter of the Duke of York.

X, like E, F, has borrowed from No 95: see 13-15.

S

Finlay sent Scott, March 27, 1803, the following copy
of 'The Queen's Marie,' as he "had written it down
from memory:" Letters addressed to Sir Walter Scott,
I, No 87, Abbotsford. Stanzas 10, 9, 12 appear in the
second volume of the Minstrelsy, 1802, p. 154, with the
variation of a couple of words, as 'The Lament of the
Queen's Marie' (here I b). Perhaps Finlay adopted
these three stanzas into his copy. Stanzas 1, 3, 6, 8,
with very slight variations, were printed by Finlay in
the preface to his Scottish Ballads, 1808 (O).

1 There lived a lord into the South,
    An he had daughters three ;
    The youngest o them 's gaen to the king's
        court,
    To learn some courtesie.

2 She had na been in the king's court
    A twelvemonth an a day,
    When word is thro the kitchen gaen,
    An likewise thro the ha,
    That Mary Moil was gane wi child
    To the highest steward of a'.

* Scott suggested that the passage in Knox was the
foundation of the ballad, January, 1802, in the first edition
of his Minstrelsy, where only three stanzas were given.
The Rev. Mr Paxton, however, first saw Scott's fragment
not long before 1804, and then in the second number of the
Edinburgh Review, where there is no mention of the apothecary. Thereupon, he says, I "instantly" wrote the enclosed
piece from the mouth of my aged mother. There is no
room, consequently, for the supposition that either mother
or son might have taken a hint from Knox, and put in the
pottinger.

3 She rowd it into a basket
    An flang 't into the sea,
Saying, Sink ye soon, my bonny babe,
    Ye 'se neer get mair o me.

4 She rowd it into a basket
    An flang 't into the faem,
Saying, Sink ye soon, my bonny babe,
    I 'se gang a maiden hame.

5 O whan the news cam to the king
    An angry man was he ;
He has taen the table wi his foot,
    An in flinders gart it flie.

6 'O woe be to you, ye ill woman,
    An ill death may ye die !
Gin ye had spared the sweet baby's life,
    It might have been an honour to thee.

7 'O busk ye, busk ye, Mary Moil,
    O busk, an gang wi me,
For agen the morn at ten o clock
    A rare sight ye sall see.'

8 She wadna put on her gown o black,
    Nor yet wad she o brown,
But she wad put on her gown o gowd,
    To glance thro Embro town.

9 O whan she cam to the Netherbow Port
    She gied loud laughters three,
But whan she cam to the gallows-foot
    The tear blinded her ee.

10 Saying, O ye mariners, mariners,
    That sail upon the sea,
Let not my father nor mother to wit
    The death that I maun die.

11 'For little did father or mother wit,
    The day they cradled me,
What foreign lands I should travel in,
    Or what death I should die.

12 'Yestreen the Queen had four Maries,
    The night she 'll hae but three ;
There was Mary Seton, an Mary Beaton,
    An Mary Carmichael, an me.'

3³, 4³. *We should read* Sink ye, soom ye, *as in*
A 3³, **U** 14³, **X** 4³, *and other copies.*

T

Communicated to Sir Walter Scott by Mrs Christiana
Greenwood, London, 21st February and 27th May, 1806,
from the recitation of her mother and her aunt, who learned
the ballad above fifty years before from Kirstan Scot, then
an old woman, at Longnewton, near Jedburgh : Letters at
Abbotsford, I, Nos 173, 189.

1 There was a duke, and he dwelt in York,
    And he had daughters three ;
One of them was an hostler-wife,
    And two were gay ladies.

2 O word 's gane to Queen Mary's court,
    As fast as it coud gee,
That Mary Hamilton 's born a bairn,
    And the baby they coud na see.

3 Then came the queen and a' her maids,
    Swift tripping down the stair :
'Where is the baby, Mary,
    That we heard weep sae sair ? '

4 'O say not so, Queen Mary,
    Nor bear ill tales o me,
For this is but a sore sickness
    That oft times troubles me.'

5 They sought it up, they sought it down,
    They sought it below the bed,
And there the[y] saw the bonny wee babe,
    Lying wallowing in its bluid.

6 'Now busk ye, busk ye, Mary Hamilton,
    Busk ye and gang wi me,
For I maun away to Edinbro town,
    A rich wedding to see.'

7 Mary wad na put on the black velvet,
    Nor yet wad put on the brown,
But she 's put on the red velvet,
    To shine thro Edinbro town.

8 When she came unto the town,
    And near the Tolbooth stair,
There stood many a lady gay,
    Weeping for Mary fair.

9 'O haud yeer tongue[s], ye ladys a',
    And weep na mair for me !
O haud yeer tongues, ye ladys a',
    For it 's for my fault I dee.

10 'The king he took me on his knee
    And he gae three drinks to me,
And a' to put the babie back,
    But it wad na gang back for me.

11 'O ye mariners, ye mariners a',
    That sail out-owr the sea,
Let neither my father nor mother get wit
    What has become o me!

12 'Let neither my father nor mother ken,
    Nor my bauld brethren three,
For muckle wad be the gude red bluid
    That wad be shed for me.

13 'Aft hae I laced Queen Mary's back,
    Aft hae I kaimed her hair,
And a' the reward she 's gein to me 's
    The gallows to be my heir.

14 'Yestreen the queen had four Marys,
    The night she 'l hae but three;
There was Mary Seatoun, and Mary Beatoun,
    An Mary Carmichal, an me.'

U

'Lament of the Queen's Marie,' "Scotch Ballads, Materials for Border Minstrelsy," No 92, Abbotsford. Communicated to Scott, 7th January, 1804, by Rev. George Paxton,
Kilmaurs, near Kilmarnock, Ayrshire (afterwards professor
of divinity at Edinburgh); from the mouth of Jean Milne,
his "aged mother, formerly an unwearied singer of Scotish songs."

1 'My father was the Duke of York,
    My mother a gay ladye,
And I myself a daintie dame;
    The queen she sent for me.

2 'But the queen's meat it was sae sweet,
    And her clothing was sae rare,
It made me long for a young man's bed,
    And I rued it evermair.'

3 But word is up, and word is down,
    Amang the ladyes a',
That Marie 's born a babe sin yestreen,
    That babe it is awa.

4 But the queen she gat wit of this,
    She calld for a berry-brown gown,
And she 's awa to Marie's bower,
    The bower that Marie lay in.

5 'Open your door, my Marie,' she says,
    'My bonny and fair Marie;
They say you have born a babe sin yestreen,
    That babe I fain wad see.'

6 'It is not sae wi me, madam,
    It is not sae wi me;
It is but a fit of my sair sickness,
    That oft times troubles me.'

7 'Get up, get up, my Marie,' she says,
    'My bonny and fair Marie,
And we 'll away to Edinburgh town,
    And try the verity.'

8 Slowly, slowly, gat she up,
    And slowly pat she on,
And slowly went she to that milk-steed,
    To ride to Edinburgh town.

9 But when they cam to Edinburgh,
    And in by the Towbooth stair,
There was mony a virtuous ladye
    Letting the tears fa there.

10 'Why weep ye sae for me, madams?
    Why weep ye sae for me?
For sin ye brought me to this town
    This death ye gar me die.'

11 When she cam to the Netherbow Port,
    She gae loud laughters three;
But when she cam to the gallows-foot
    The tear blinded her ee.

12 'Yestreen the queen had four Maries,
    The night she 'll hae but three;
There was Marie Seton, and Marie Bea-
        toun,
    And Marie Carmichael, and me.

13 'My love he was a pottinger,
    Mony drink he gae me,
And a' to put back that bonnie babe,
    But alas! it wad na do.

14 'I pat that bonny babe in a box,
    And set it on the sea;
O sink ye, swim ye, bonny babe!
    Ye 's neer get mair o me.

15 'O all ye jolly sailors,
    That sail upon the sea,

Let neither my father nor mother ken
The death that I maun die.

16 'But if my father and mother kend
The death that I maun die,
O mony wad be the good red guineas
That wad be gien for me.'

V

"Scotch Ballads, Materials for Border Minstrelsy," No 9,
Abbotsford; in the handwriting of William Laidlaw.

1 'My father was the Duke of York,
My mother the gay ladie,
An I myself a maiden bright,
An the queen desired me.'

2 But there word gane to the kitchen,
There 's word gane to the ha,
That Mary mild she gangs wi child
To the uppermost stewart of a'.

3 Than they sought but, and they sou[ght] ben,
They sought aneath the bed,
An there the fand the bonnie lad-bairn,
Lyin lappin in his blood.

4 'Gae buss ye, Marie Hamilton,
Gae buss ye, buss ye bra,
For ye maun away to Edin[brough] town,
The queen's birthday . . . '

5 She wadna put on her black, bla[ck] silk,
Nor wad she put on the brown,
But she pat on the glisterin stufs,
To glister in Edinbrough town.

6 An whan she cam to the water-gate
Loud laughters gae she three,
But whan she cam to the Netherbow Port
The tear blinded Marie's ee.

7 'T was up than spak Queen Marie's nurse,
An a sorry woman was she :
'Whae sae clever o fit and ready o wit
Has telld sic news o thee!'

8 'Oft have I   Queen Marie's head
Oft have I caimd her hair,
An a' the thanks I 've gotten for that
Is the gallows to be my heir!

9 'Oft have I dressd Queen Marie's head,
An laid her in her bed,
An a' the thanks I 've gotten for that
Is the green gallows-tree to tread !

10 'O spare, O spare, O judge,' she cried,
' O spair a day for me ! '
' There is nae law in our land, ladie,
To let a murderer be.'

11 ' Yestreen the queen had four Maries,
The night she 'll hae but three ;
There was Marie Seaton, and Ma[rie] Bea-
[ton],
An Marie Carmichael, an me.

12 'O if my father now but kend
The death that I 'm to die,
O muckle, muckle wad be the red gowd
That he wad gie for me.

13 'An if my brothers kend the death
That I am now to die,
O muckle, muckle wad be the red blood
That wad be shed for me.'

$2^{3,4}$. Or :

That Mary Hamilton 's born a bairn
An murderd it at the wa.

3^1, 11^3. *Edge bound in.*
8^1. caimd *written, but struck out.* 8^3. & I the.

W

"Scotch Ballads, Materials for Border Minstrelsy," No
85, Abbotsford.

1 There lived a man in the North Countree
And he had doghters three ;
The youngest o them 's to Edinbourgh gaen,
Ane o the queen's Marys to be.

2 Queen Mary's bread it was sae white,
And her wine it ran sae clear,
It shewed her the way to the butler's bed,
And I wait she 's bought dear.

3 For Mary 's to the garden gaen,
To eat o the saven tree,
And a' 's to pit her young son back,
But back he wad na be.

4 So Mary 's to her chamber gaen,

. . . .

. . . .

5 Queen Mary she came down the stair,
   And a' her maids afore her :
'Oh, Mary Miles, where is the child
   That I have heard greet sae sore O?'

6 'There is no child with me, madam,
   There is no child with me ;
It was only a bit of a cholick I took,
   And I thought I was gawen to dee.'

7 So they looked up, and they looked down,
   And they looked beneath the bed-foot,
And there they saw a bonnie boy,
   Lying weltering in his blood.

8 . . . .

   . . . .
'Since that you have killed your own dear child,
   The same death you shall dee.'

9 When Mary came afore the court,
   A loud laugh laughed she ;
But when she came to the [gallows-]fit
   The tear blinded her ee.

* * * * * * *

10 'O wha will comb Queen Mary's heed ?
   Or wha will brade her hair ?
And wha will lace her middle sae jimp
   Whan [I] am nae langer there ?

11 'Yestreen the queen [had] four Maries,
   The night she 'll hae but three ;
There was Mary Seaten, and Mary Beaten,
   And Mary Carmichal, and me.

* * * * * * *

12 'I 'll not put on my robes of black,
   Nor yet my robes of brown,
But I 'll put on a shining braw garb,
   That will shine thro Edinbourgh town.'

* * * * * * *

13 Oh, whan she came to the Cannongate,
   The Cannongate sae hee,

There mony a lord and belted knight
   Was grieved for her beautee.

* * * * * * *

14 And whan she came to [the] Hee Town,
   The Hee Town sae hee,

* * * * * * *

10[1]. Oh. 11[1,2]. *Added in a different hand.*
12[3]. shinning.

X

'The Queen's Maries,' "Scotch Ballads, Materials for Border Minstrelsy," No 91, Abbotsford.

1 There livd a lord in the West Country,
   And he had daughters three ;
The youngest o them 's to the queen's court,
   To learn some courtesy.

2 She hadna been at the queen's court
   A year but and a day
Till she has fa'n as big wi child,
   As big as she coud gae.

3 She 's gane into the garden
   To pu thè sycamore tree,
And taen the bony bairn in her arms
   And thrown it in the sea.

4 She rowd it in her apron
   And threw it in the sea :
'Gae sink or soom, my bony sweet babe,
   Ye 'll never get mair o me.'

5 Then in an came Queen Mary,
   Wi gowd rings on her hair :
'O Mary mild, where is the child
   That I heard greet sae sair ?'

6 'It wasna a babe, my royal liege,
   Last night that troubled me,
But it was a fit o sair sickness,
   And I was lyken to dee.'

7 'O hold yere tongue, Mary Hamilton,
   Sae loud as I hear ye lee !
For I 'll send you to Enbro town,
   The verity to see.'

8 She wadna put on the ribbons o black,
   Nor yet wad she the brown,
   But she wad put on the ribbons o gowd,
   To gae glittring through Enbro town.

9 As she rade up the Sands o Leith,
   Riding on a white horse,
   O little did she think that day
   To die at Enbro Corss !

10 As she rade up the Cannongate,
   She leugh loud laughters three,
   And mony a lord and lady said,
   ' Alas for that lady ! '

11 ' Ye needna say Oh, ye needna cry Eh,
   Alas for that lady !
   Ye 'll neer see grace in a graceless face,
   As little ye 'll see in me.'

12 When she came to the Netherbow Port,
   She leugh loud laughters three,
   But ere she came to the gallows-foot
   The tear blinded her eie ;
   Saying, Tye a white napkin owr my face,
   For that gibbet I downa see.

13 ' O hold yere hand, Lord Justice !
   O hold it a little while !
   I think I see my ain true-love
   Come wandring mony a mile.

14 ' O have ye brought me ony o my gowd ?
   Or ony o my weel-won fee ?
   Or are ye come to see me hangd,
   Upon this gallows-tree ? '

15 ' O I hae brought ye nane o yere gowd,
   Nor nane o yere weel-won fee,
   But I am come to see ye hangd,
   And hangit ye shall be.'

16 ' O all ye men and mariners,
   That sail for wealth or fame,
   Let never my father or mother get wit
   But what I 'm coming hame.

17 ' O all ye men and mariners,
   That sail upon the sea,
   Let never my father or mother get wit
   The death that I maun dee.

18 ' Yestreen the queen had four Maries,
   The night she 'll hae but three ;
   There was Mary Seaton, and Mary Beaton,
   And Mary Carmichael, and me.'

Y

'The Queen's Marys,' "Scotch Ballads, Materials for Border Minstrelsy," No 144, Abbotsford.

1 ' Yestreen the queen had four Marys,
   The night she 'll hae but three ;
   She had Mary Beaton, and Mary Seaton,
   And Mary Carmichael, and me.

2 ' My feather was the Duke of York,
   My mother a gay lady,
   And I mysell a bonnie young may,
   And the king fell in love we me.

3 ' The king's kisses they were so sweet,
   And his wine it was so strong,
   That I became a mother
   Before fifteen years old.'

4 ' O tell the truth now, Mary,
   And sett this matter right ;
   What hae ye made o the babey
   Was greeting yesternight ? '

5 ' O I will tell you, madam the queen,
   I winna tell a lie ;
   I put it in a bottomless boat
   And bad it sail the sea.'

6 ' Ye lie, ye lie now, Mary,
   Sae loud 's I hear you lie !
   You wasnae out o the palace,
   So that coud never be.'

7 ' Weel I will tell you, madam,
   Though it should gar me weep ;
   I stabbd it we my little pen-knife,
   And bad it take a sleep.'

8 When she came up the Netherbow,
   She geed loud laughters three ;
   But when she came out o the Parliament Close
   The tear blinded her ee.

9 ' O little does my feather ken
   The death I am to die,
   Or muckel wad be the red, red gould
   Wad be payed doun for me.

10 'O little does my mother think
    The death that I am to die,
Or monie wad be the saut, saut tears
    That she wad shed for me.

11 'O never lett my brothers ken
    The death that I am to die,
For muckel wad be the red, red blood
    That wad be shed for me.

12 'Aft hae I washd the king's bonnie face,
    Kaimd doun his yellow hair,
And this is a' the reward he 's geen me,
    The gallows to be my share.'

Z

'The Queen's Marie,' "Scotch Ballads, Materials for Border Minstrelsy," No 90 a, Abbotsford; in the handwriting of John Leyden.

1 'Buss ye, bonny Marie Hamilton,
    Buss and gae wi me,
For ye maun gae to Edinborough,
    A great wedding to see.'

2 'Ride hooly, hooly, gentlemen,
    Ride hooly now wi me,
For never, I'm sure, a wearier bride
    Rode in your cumpany.'

3 Little wist Marie Hamilton,
    When she rode on the brown,
That she was gawn to Edinborough,
    And a' to be put down.

4 When she came to the Council stairs,
    She ga loud laughters three;
But or that she came down again
    She was condemmd to dee.

5 'O ye mariners, mariners, mariners,
    When ye sail oer the faem,
Let never my father nor mother to wit
    But I 'm just coming hame.

6 'Let never my father nor mother to wit,
    Nor my bauld brether[en] three,
Or meckle wad be the red, red gowd
    This day be gien for me.

7 'Let never my father or mother to wit,
    Nor my bauld brethren three,

Or meckle war the red, red blude
    This day wad fa for me.'

AA

"Scotch Ballads, Materials for Border Minstrelsy," No 142, Abbotsford; in the handwriting of James Hogg.

'Oft hae I kaimd Queen Mary's head,
    An oft hae I curld her hair,
An now I hae gotten for my reward
    A gallows to be heir.'

178. Captain Car, or, Edom o Gordon.

P. 426, note *. This history borrows from Sir Robert Gordon. See what he says, p. 166 f., and also previously, p. 164 ff.

428 a. F, G. "I have a manuscript where the whole scene is transferred to Ayrshire, and the incendiary is called Johnnie Faa." Note of Sir W. Scott in Sharpe's Ballad Book, ed. 1880, p. 142.

This copy has not as yet been recovered, but there is another at Abbotsford, a fine fragment, in which Lady Campbell is the heroine. As to Adam McGordon, the c of Mac is often dropped, so that Adam MaGordon and Adam o Gordon are of pretty much the same sound (a remark of Mr Macmath). The Andrew Watty of 13[3] is noted on the last page of the MS. to be "a riding man."

H

"Scotch Ballads, Materials for Border Minstrelsy," No 75, Abbotsford. Communicated to Scott November 6, 1803, by Bruce Campbell, Sornbeg, Galston, Ayrshire, through David Boyle, Advocate, afterwards Lord Justice General of Scotland.

1 It fell about the Martinmass time,
    When the wind blew shill and cald,
That Adam McGordon said to his men,
    Where will we get a hall?

2 'There is a hall here near by,
    Well built with lime and stone;
There is a lady there within
    As white as the . . bone.'

3 'Seven year and more this lord and I
    Has had a deadly feud,
And now, since her good lord's frae hame,
    His place to me she 'll yield.'

4 She looked oer her castle-wall,
    And so she looked down,

And saw Adam McGordon and his men
Approaching the wood-end.

5 'Steik up, steik up my yett,' she says,
'And let my draw-bridge fall ;
There is meickle treachery
Walking about my wall.'

6 She had not the sentence past,
Nor yet the word well said,
When Adam McGordon and his men
About the walls were laid.

7 She looked out at her window,
And then she looked down,
And then she saw Jack, her own man,
Lifting the pavement-stane.

8 'Awa, awa, Jack my man !
Seven year I paid you meat and fee,
And now you lift the pavement-stane
To let in the low to me.'

9 'I yield, I yield, O lady fair,
Seven year ye paid me meat and fee ;
But now I am Adam McGordon's man,
I must either do or die.'

10 'If ye be Adam McGordon's man,
As I true well ye be,
Prove true unto your own master,
And work your will to me.'

11 'Come down, come down, my lady Camp-
bell,
Come down into my hand ;
Ye shall lye all night by my side,
And the morn at my command.'

12 'I winna come down,' this lady says,
'For neither laird nor lown,
Nor to no bloody butcher's son,
The Laird of Auchindown.

13 'I wald give all my kine,' she says,
'So wald I fifty pound,
That Andrew Watty he were here ;
He would charge me my gun.

14 'He would charge me my gun,
And put in bullets three,
That I might shoot that cruel traitor
That works his wills on me.'

15 He shot in, and [s]he shot out,
The value of an hour,
Until the hall Craigie North
Was like to be blawn in the air.

16 He fired in, and she fired out,
The value of houris three,
Until the hall Craigie North
The reik went to the sea.

17 'O the frost, and ae the frost,
The frost that freezes fell !
I cannot stay within my bower,
The powder it blaws sae bald.'

18 But then spake her oldest son,
He was both white and red ;
'O mither dear, yield up your house !
We 'll all be burnt to deed.'

19 Out then spake the second son,
He was both red and fair ;
'O brother dear, would you yield up your
house,
And you your father's heir ! '

20 Out then spake the little babe,
Stood at the nurse's knee ;
'O mither dear, yield up your house !
The reik will worry me.'

21 Out then speaks the little nurse,
The babe upon her knee ;
'O lady, take from me your child !
I 'll never crave my fee.'

22 'Hold thy tongue, thou little nurse,
Of thy prating let me bee ;
For be it death or be it life,
Thou shall take share with me.

23 'I wald give a' my sheep,' she says,
'T[hat] . . yon . . s[ha],
I had a drink of that wan water
That runs down by my wa.'

2¹. hall there.
2⁴. *An illegible word ending seemingly in* hie.
3¹. this lord and I *begins the second line.*
3³. has good : has *caught from the line above.*
3⁴. shall *altered to* she 'll ; *but* she shall *is clearly
meant.*
7⁴, 11⁴, 15⁴, 16³, 21¹. y^e. 14¹. would : wald, *perhaps.*

16². valuue, *or*, valaue, *or*, valuae.

16³. *A preposition seems to be wanting. Hall here and in* 15³ *is troublesome. Perhaps the reading should be in* 15³ *that all, in* 16³ *that through all.*

23². *The paper is folded here, and the line has been so much rubbed as to be illegible.*

"An old ballad upon the burning of an old castle of Loudoun by the Kennedys of Auchruglan." Bruce Campbell.

181. The Bonny Earl of Murray.

P. 447. Add to the citation from Spottiswood : History of the Church of Scotland, 1655, p. 387.

182. The Laird o Logie.

P. 449. **A** was first published in the second edition of Scott's Minstrelsy, 1803, I, 243.

B was repeated in the first edition of Scott's Minstrelsy, I, 220, 1802, 'The Laird of Ochiltree.'

452. The following is the original, unimproved copy of **A**. There is a transcript of this, in William Laidlaw's hand, "Scotch Ballads," etc., No 23, which is somewhat retouched, but by no means with the freedom exercised by the editor of the Minstrelsy. Some of Laidlaw's changes were adopted by Scott.

A

'The Laird of Logie,' "Scotch Ballads, Materials for Border Minstrelsy," No 3 a, Abbotsford. Sent Scott September 11, 1802, by William Laidlaw; received by him from Mr Bartram of Biggar.

1 I will sing, if ye will harken,
  An ye wad listen unto me ;
I 'll tell ye of a merry passage
  Of the wanton laird of Young Logie.

2 Young Logie 's laid in Edin*borough* chapel,
  Carmichaell 's keeper of the key ;
I heard a may lamenting sair,
  All for the laird of Young Logie.

3 'Lament, lament na, May Margret,
  And o your weeping let me be ;
For ye maun to the king *your* sell,
  And ask the life of Young Logie.'

4 May Margaret has kilted her green cleeding,
  And she 's currld back her yellow hair,
And she 's away to the king hersell,
  And adieu to Scotland for ever mair !

5 When she came before the king,
  She fell low down on her knee :
' It 's what 's your will wi me, May Margret,
  And what makes all this courtesey ? '
' Naething, naething, my sovreign liege,
  But grant me the life of Young Logie.'

6 ' O no, O no, May Margret,
  No, in sooth it maun na be ;
For the morn, or I taste meat or drink,
  Hee hanged shall Young Logie be.'

7 She has stolen the king's reeding-comb,
  But an the queen her wedding-knife,
And she has sent it to Carmichaell,
  To cause Young Logie come by life.

8 She sent him a purse of the red gold,
  Another of the white money,
And sent him a pistol into each hand,
  And bade him shoot when he got fra.

9 When he came to the Tolbooth stair,
  There he loot his volley flee,
Wh*ich* made the king in his chamber start,
  Even in the chamber where he lay.

10 ' Gae out, gae out, my merrie men,
  And gar Carmichael come speake wi me,
For I 'll lay my life the pledge of that,
  That yon 's the volley of Young Logie.'

11 When Carmichael came before the king,
  He fell low down on his knee ;
The very first word that the king spake,
  ' How dois the laird o Young Logie ? '

12 Carmichael turnd him round about,
  A wait the salt tear blint his eye :
' There came a tacken frae the king
  Has tean the laird awa frae me.'

13 ' Hast thou playd me that, Carmichael ?
  Hast thou playd me that ? ' quo he ;
' The morn the Justice Court 's to stand,
  And Logie's place ye maun supply.'

14 Carmichal 's awa to May Margr[e]t's bower,
  Een as fast as he may dree :
' It 's if Young Logie be within,
  Tell him to come speak to me.'

15 May Margret 's turnd her round about,
  A wait a loud laughter gae she :

'The egg is cheeped and the bird is flown,
    And seek ye the laird of Young Logie.'

16 The one is sheppd at the pier o Leith,
    The other at the Queen's Ferry,
    And she has gotten a father to her bairn,
    The wanton laird of Young [Logie].

4². yer *for* her.
6⁴. Yea *for* Hee. Hie *in Laidlaw's transcript.
    Taking into account the apparent* yer *for* her *in
    4², it looks as if* hea, her *were intended.* 8⁴. free?
12². blint *may be* blent.

453. **B.** 'The Winsome Laird of Young Logie,'
"Scotch Ballads, Materials for Border Minstrelsy," No
137 a, " sung by Lady A. Lindsay," closely resembles
Herd's version, but in one passage approaches **C,** and
Young Logie displaces Ochiltrie. This copy will be
treated as **B b.**

b. 1¹. O *wanting.* 1². To the tale I tell.
1³. How the.
1⁴. The winsom laird of Young Logie.
2¹. Whan the queen did hear the same.
2³. Alas for poor Lady Margaret.
3², 8². as *wanting.* 3⁴. Or never kend.
4¹. Fye, oh no, said : that maunna be *wanting.*
4². Fy, O no, thus (*partly altered to* this).
4³. find out some cunning way.
4⁴. To loose and let Young Logie free.

Between 5² and 5³:
The king he's risen and taen her up,
    Says, What means a' this curtesy. (*As* 5³·⁴.)

When you took me to be your queen,
    You promisd me favours twa or three. (*As* 6¹·².)*

5³·⁴ :
The first ane that I ask of yow
    Is to loose and let Young Logie free. (*As* 6³·⁴.)

6¹. O *wanting :* of me. 6². would hae granted.
6⁴, 7⁴. Winna save. 7¹. queen than she came.
7². And she came down.

8³·⁴ :
I wish that I had neer been born,
    Or never kend Young Logie's name. (*As in* 3.)

9¹. Fye, oh no, said. 9². Fye, O no, this maun ne.
9³. I'll find out some other.
9⁴. To save the life o. 10¹. she triped.
11¹. She gae to. 11³. And twa.
11⁴. And bade him shoot as he gaed by.

* Compare here 'Adam Bell,' V, 28, stanzas 125, 128.

12¹. And *wanting.* 12³. O peace : our gudely.
13¹. O *wanting.* 14¹. Gae bring to.
14². Gae bring them. 14³. Before the : by ten.
14⁴. they each ane. 15. *Wanting.*
16¹. Fye, O no, said.
16². Fye, O no, this maun ne. 16³. hang at a'.
17¹. Lady Marg' took shiping.
17². Young Logie at. 17³. the lass : her lad.
Tune of Logan Water.

183. Willie Macintosh.

P. 456. The account in 'The History of the Feuds'
is taken from Sir Robert Gordon's History of Sutherland, p. 217.

Jamieson, writing to Scott, in November, 1804, says :
" I have heard a scrap of the rude ballad on the burning
of Achindoun, 'Bonny Willie Mackintosh — You've
tint a feather frae your cap — By the day dawing,' etc.,
or something of this kind, from the Revᵈ John Grant
of Elgin. The Duchess of Gordon applied to him
about it some years ago, but he could never recover it."
(Letters addressed to Sir W. Scott, I, No 117, Abbotsford.)

186. Kinmont Willie.

P. 470 b, at the end of the first paragraph. Strike
out 1639. Spottiswood's account begins at the same
page, 413, in the edition of 1655.

188. Archie o Cawfield.

P. 484. **B b** was first printed in the second edition
of the Minstrelsy, 1803, I, 195.

The following is the copy from which Scott derived
the stanzas introduced into this later edition of the ballad. It will be observed that 'luve of Teviotdale' is
the reading of 4², and not a correction of Scott's, as suggested at 486 b.

'Archie o Ca'field, Variations,' "Scotch Ballads, Materials for Border Minstrelsy," No 90, Abbotsford; in the
handwriting of John Leyden.

1 The one unto the other did say,
    ' Blythe and merry how can we be,
When the night is billie Archie's lyke-wake,
    The morn the day that he maun die?'

2 'An ye wad be blythe an ye wad be sad,
    What better wad billie Archie be,
Unless I had thirty men to mysell,
    And a' to ride in our companie?

3 'Ten to had the horses' heads,
    And other ten to walk alee,
And ten to break up the strang prisoun
    Where billie Archie he does lie.'

4 Up bespak him mettled John Hall,
    The luve o Teviotdale ay was he ;
  ' An I had eleven men to mysell,
    It 's ay the twalt man I wad be.'

5 Up bespak him coarse Ca'field,
    I wat and little gude worth was he ;
  ' Thirty men is few enow,
    And a' to ride in our cumpanie.'

6 Then a' the night thae twal men rade,
    And ay untill they were a' wearie,
  Till they came to the strang prisoun
    Where billie Archie he did lie.

7 ' Sleeps thou, wakes thou, billie ? ' he said,
    ' Or did ye hear whan I did cry ?
  The night it is your lyke-wake night,
    The morn it is your day to die.'

8 .   .   .   .   .   .
  .   .   .   .   .   .
  ' Work ye within and I without,
    And soon a loose man shall you be.'

9 Dickie pu'd the prisoner on o his back,
    And down the stair cam merrilie ;
  ' Now by my sooth,' quo mettled John Hall,
    ' Ye may let a leg o him lean to me.'

10 ' I have my billie upon my back,
     I count him lighter than a flee ;
   Gin I were at my little black mare,
     At Ca'field soon I trust to be.'

11 Then a' the night these twelve men rade,
     And aye untill they were a' wearie,
   Untill they came to the wan water,
     And it was gawn like ony see.

12 ' There lives a smith on the water-side,
     Sae has he done thirty years and three :
   .   .   .   .   .   .
   .   .   .   .   .   .

13 ' O I have a crown in my pocket,
     And I 'll give it every groat to thee
   .   .   .   .   .   .
     Gin thou shoe my little black mare for me.'

14 ' The night is mirk, and vera pit-mirk,
     And wi candle-light I canna weel see ;

The night it is mirk, and vera pit-mirk,
  And there 'll never a nail ca right for me.'

15 ' Shame fa you and your trade baith,
     Canna beet a gude fallow by your mysterie !
   But lees me on thee, my little black mare,
     Thou 's worth thy weight o gowd to me.'

16 Then thay lay down to take a sleep,
     But ay on fit stood noble Dickie,
   And he 's looked oer his left shoulder,
     And a' to see what he could see.

17 ' Get up, get up, ye drowsy sleepers !
     Ye dinna see what I do see ;
   For yonder comes the land-lieutenant,
     Two hunder men in his cumpanie.

18 ' This night an they lay hands on us,
     This night, as I think weel it will be,
   This night sall be our lyke-wake night,
     The morn like as mony dogs we 'll die.'

19 ' My mare is young, and vera young,
     And in o the weel she will drown me ; '
   ' But ye 'll take mine, and I 'll take thine,
     And soon thro the water we sall be.'

20 Then up bespak him coarse Ca'field,
     I wate and little gude worth was he ;
   ' We had better lose ane than lose a' the lave,
     We 'll leave the prisoner, we 'll gae free.'

21 ' Shame fa you and your lands baith,
     Wad ye een your lands to your born billie ?
   But hey ! bear up, my little black mare,
     And yet thro the water we sall be.'

*   *   *   *   *   *   *   *

22 ' Come thro, come thro now,' Dickie he said,
     ' Come thro, come thro and drink wi me ;
   There 's no be a Saturday in a' the year
     But changed sall your garments be.

*   *   *   *   *   *   *   *

23 .   .   .   .   .   .
   .   .   .   .   .   .
   While a bit o your iron hads thegether,
     Barefit sall she never be.'

12¹. *Var.* other side o the water.
12, 13 *are written as one stanza.*

VOL. IV.

190. Jamie Telfer of the Fair Dodhead.

P. 4 a. James Hogg, writing to Scott, June 30, [1802 ?] says : " I am surprised to find that the songs in your collection differ so widely from my mother's. . . . ' Jamie Telfer ' differs in many particulars." (Letters, I, No. 44.) Scott's remarks should have been cited from the edition of 1802, I, 91.

5. Mr Andrew Lang has obligingly called my attention to difficulties which attend the assumption that the Dodhead of the ballad is the place of that name in Selkirkshire. Jamie Telfer, st. 7, runs ten miles between Dodhead and Stobs, and this is far enough if help is to be timely ; but he would have to run thirty if his Dodhead were in Selkirkshire. With succor not nearer than that, Telfer would soon have been harried out of existence. The distances are too great both for the English and the Scots. But there is a Dod south of the Teviot, not far from Skelfhill, which is some seven miles only from Stobs. (Dodhead is not entered here on the Ordnance map, " but Dodburn is just under Dodrig, and where there is a Dodburn there is ' tied ' to be a Dodhead in this country.") Turning from Stobs to Teviot, Telfer would come in due order to Coltherdscleugh, Branxholm, and Borthwick Water, without the loss of time which he would, on the other supposition, incur in passing and returning. (See a note, by Mr Lang, in Mrs G. R. Tomson's Ballads of the North Countrie, 1888, p. 435.)

Several other matters are not quite clear. Catslockhill, for instance, seems to be misplaced. Mr Lang, a native of Ettrick valley, knows of no Catslack but that in Yarrow. Of this, Mr T. Craig-Brown (Selkirkshire, I, 21), who accepts Scott's Dodhead, says, " A long ride, if Catslack is in Yarrow."

191. Hughie Grame.

P. 8. **C.** Substitute for Scott's Minstrelsy, etc., " Scotch Ballads, Materials for Border Minstrelsy," No 87, Abbotsford. Add : **H.** 'Hughie Grame,' " Scotch Ballads, Materials for Border Minstrelsy," No 4. **I.** ' Hughie Græme,' Wilkie's MS., in " Scotch Ballads, Materials for Border Minstrelsy," No 36.

P. 10 ff. For **C** substitute this, the original copy, as procured for Scott by William Laidlaw.

" Scotch Ballads, Materials for Border Minstrelsy," No 87, Abbotsford ; in the handwriting of William Laidlaw. " From Robert Laidlaw."

1 Gude Lord Scroop's to the huntin gane ;
　　He 's ridden oer monie a moss an muir,
　An he has grippit Hughie the Græme,
　　For stealin o the bishop's mare.

2 An they hae grippit Hughie the Græme,
　　An brought him up thro Carlisle town ;
　The lasses an lads they stood by the wa's,
　　Cryin, Hughie the Græme, thou 's no gae down !

3 They ha chosen a jury o men,
　　The best that were i Coventry,
　An fifteen o them out a' at anse,
　　' Hughie the Græme, thou art guiltie.'

4 Than up bespak him gude Lord Hume,
　　As he sat at the judge's knee ;
　' Twentie white ousen, my gude lord,
　　If ye 'll grant Hughie the Græme to me.'

5 ' O no, no, no, my gude Lord Hume,
　　For sooth an so it mauna be ;
　For war there but twae Græms o the name,
　　They sould be hangit a' for me.'

6 ' T was up than spak her gude Lady Hume,
　　As she sat by the judge's knee ;
　' A peck o white pennies, my gude lord,
　　If ye 'll grant Hughie the Greame to me.'

7 ' O no, O no, my gude Lady Hume,
　　For sooth an so it sal na be ;
　For war there but twae Greames of the name,
　　They soud be hangit a' for me.'

8 ' If I be guilty,' said Hughie the Greame,
　　' Of me my friends sal hae nae lack ; '
　An he has luppen fifteen feet an three,
　　An his hands they war tyed ahint his back.

9 He 's lookit oer his left shouther,
　　To see what he coud see,
　An there he saw his auld father commin,
　　An he was weepin bitterlie.

10 ' O had yer tongue, my father,' he says,
　　' An see that ye dinna weep for me,
　For they may ravish me o my life,
　　But they canna banish me thrae the heavens hie.

11 ' Fare ye weel, Maggie, my wife ;
　　The last time I came oer the muir,
　It was you berievt me o my life,
　　An wi the bishop playd the w[hore].'

H

"Scotch Ballads, Materials for Border Minstrelsy," No 4, Abbotsford; in the handwriting of William Laidlaw.

1 Lairds and lords a hounting gane,
Out-over hills and valleys clear,
And there they met Hughie Grame,
Was riding on the bishop's mare.

2 And they have tied him hand and foot,
And they have carried him to Stirling town;
The lads and lasses there about
Crys, Hughie Grame, you are a lown!

3 'If I be a lown,' says he,
'I am sure my friends has had bad luck;'
We that he jumpted fifteen foot,
With his hands tied behind his back.

4 Out and spoke Laidy Whiteford,
As she sat by the bishop's knee;
'Four-and-twenty milk-kie I 'll give to thee,
If Hughie Grame you will let free.'

5 'Hold your tongue, my laidy Whiteford,
And of your pleading now lay by;
If fifty Grames were in his coat,
Upon my honour he shall die.'

6 Out and spoke Lord Whiteford,
As he sat by the bishop's knee;
'Four-and-twenty stots I 'll give thee,
If Hughie Grame you will let free.'

7 'Hold your tongue, my lord Whiteford,
And of your pleading now lay by;
If twenty Grames were in his coat,
Upon my honour he shall die.'

8 'You may tell to Meg, my wife,
The first time she comes through the mu[ir],
She was the causer of my death,
For with the bishop [she] plaid the whore.

9 'You may tell to Meg, my wife,
The first time she comes through the town,
She was the causer of my death,
For with the bishop [she] plaid the lown.'

10 He looked oer his left shoulder,
To see what he could spy or see,

And there he spied his old father,
Was weeping bitterly.

11 'Hold your tongue, my dear father,
And of your weeping now lay by;
They may rub me of my sweet life,
But not from me the heavence high.

12 'You may give my brother John
The sword that 's of the mettle clear,
That he may come the morn at four o clock
To see me pay the bishop's mare.

13 'You may give my brother James
The sword that 's of the mettle brown;
Tell him to come the morn at four o clock
To see his brother Hugh cut down.'

14 Up and spoke his oldest son,
As he sat by his nurse's knee;
'If ere I come to be a man,
Revenged for my father['s] death I 'll be.'

I

"Scotch Ballads, Materials for Border Minstrelsy," No 36, Abbotsford, MS. of Thomas Wilkie, 1813–15, p. 9; "from a young girl, a Miss Nancy Brockie, Bemerside, who learned it from an old woman called Maron Miller, Threepwood." Another copy, in Wilkie's hand, No 86 of the same.

1 Ye dukes and lords that hunt and go
Out-over moors and mountains clear,
And they have taen up poor Hughie Græme,
For stealing of the bishope's mare.
Fall all the day, fall all the daudy,
Fall all the day, fall the daudy O.

2 They hae tied him hand and foot,
They hae led him thro the town;
The lads and lassies they all met,
Cried, Hughie Græme, ye 've playd the loon!

3 'O if that I had playd the loon,
My friends of me they hae bad luck;'
With that he jumped fifteen feet,
Wi his hands tied fast behind his back.

4 Up then spoke my lady Whiteford,
As she sat by the bishope's knee;
'Five hundred white pence I 'll give thee,
If you let Hughie Græme go free.'

5 'I 'll hae nane of your hundred pense,
   And your presents you may lay by;
For if Græme was ten times in his coat,
   By my honour, Hugh shall die.'

6 Up then spoke my lord Whiteford,
   As he sat by the bishope's knee;
' Five score of good stotts I 'll thee give,
   If you 'll sett Hughie Græme but free.'

7 'I 'll have none of your hundred stotts,
   And all your presents you may keep to your-
    sell;
' For if Græme was ten times in his coat
   Hugh shall die, and die he shall.'

8 Then they hae tied him hand and foot,
   And they hae led [him] to the gallows high;
The lads and lassies they all met,
   Cried, Hughie Græme, thou art to die !

9 Now 's he looked oer his left shoulder,
   All for to see what he could spy,
And there he saw his father dear,
   Stood weeping there most bitterlie.

10 'O hold your tongue now, father,' he said,
   ' And of your weeping lai'd now by;
For they can rob me of my life,
   But they cannot rob me of the heavens high.

11 ' But you must give to my brother John
   The sword that 's bent in the middle clear,
And tell him to come at twelve o clock
   And see me pay the bishope's mare.

12 'And you may give to my brother James
   The sword that 's bent in the middle brown,
And tell him to come at four o clock
   And see his brother Hugh cut down.

13 'And you may tell to Meg, my wife,
   The first time she comes thro the town,
She was the occasion of my death
   And wi the bishope playd the loon.

14 'And you may tell to Meg, my wife,
   The first time she comes thro the fair,
She was the occasion of my death,
   And from the bishope stole the mare.'

A. *A copy in* The Northern Garland, Newcastle Garlands, No 1, Bell Ballads, Abbotsford Library,

P. 5, *has these readings, some of which appear to
be editorial:*
2^2. after him for some time. 4^4. shall soon.
11^3. my fault. 16^2. down low.
22^3. cause and the loss.

H. 8^3, 9^3. the casurer, the casure. *Perhaps we should
read* occasion : *cf.* **I** 13^3, 14^3. 9^4. plaid the
whore ; *but cf.* **E** 13^4, **I** 13^4.

I. 2^3. they (all met) ran in flocks : *cf.* 8^3. 3^1. Of that :
see No 86, *below.* 5^3. in = his coat = ocent (*sic*).
10^2. (laid = lay it.)
No 86, *the other copy of* **I**, *has variations which seem
to be mostly, if not wholly, editorial.*
1^3. taken Hughie Græme. 2^3. lassies ran in flocks.
3^1. O if. 3^2. has had. 3^4. And his.
4^3. I will give. 4^4. ye 'll let. 5^2. And of your.
6^2. at the. 6^4. ye 'll let : go free.
7^1. *Above* hundred *is written* five score.
7^2. And of your presents ye may lay by.
7^4. By my honour, Hugh shall die, *bracketed with
the reading in the text.*
8^2. And led him to. 9^1. Now he 's. 9^3. he spied.
10^1. now, father dear : he said *wanting.*
10^2. laid. 11^1. may give my.
12^1. give my. 13^3, 14^3. That she 's.

193. The Death of Parcy Reed.

P. 24 a. **B.** Telfer sent "the real verses" to Sir
Walter Scott. It appears, as might be surmised, that
one half of **B** is of his own making. 1–3 = **B** 4, 5, 7;
4, 5 = **A** 4, 18; 6 = **B** 14; 7 = **B** 15, **A** 6; 8 = **A** 7,
B 16; 9–14 = **B** 18–23; 15 = **A** 15; 16 = **B** 25;
17–20 = **B** 38, 39, 33, 41.

B

Letters addressed to Sir Walter Scott, XIII, No 73, Abbotsford. "Parcy Reed, exactly as it is sung by an old
woman of the name of Cathrine Hall, living at Fairloans,
in the remotest corner of Oxnam parish :" James Telfer,
Browndeanlaws, May 18, 1824.

1 O Parcy Reed has Crozer taen,
   And has deliverd him to the law;
But Crozer says he 'll do warse than that,
   For he 'll gar the tower of the Troughend fa.

2 And Crozer says he will do warse,
   He will do warse, if warse can be;
For he 'll make the bairns a' fatherless,
   And then the land it may lie lea.

3 O Parcy Reed has ridden a raid,
   But he had better have staid at hame;
For the three fause Ha's of Girsenfield
   Alang with him he has them taen.

4 He 's hunted up, and he 's hunted down,
 He 's hunted a' the water of Reed,
Till wearydness has on him taen,
 I the Baitinghope he 's faen asleep.

5 . . . .
 . . . .
And the fause, fause Ha's o Girsenfield,
 They 'll never be trowed nor trusted again.

6 They 've taen frae him his powther-bag,
 And they 've put water i his lang gun;
They 've put the sword into the sheathe
 That out again it 'll never come.

7 'Awaken ye, awaken ye, Parcy Reed,
 For I do fear ye 've slept owre lang;
For yonder are the five Crozers,
 A coming owre by the hinging-stane.'

8 'If they be five and we be four,
 If that ye will stand true to me,
If every man ye will take one,
 Ye surely will leave two to me.

9 'O turn, O turn, O Johny Ha,
 O turn now, man, and fight wi me;
If ever ye come to Troughend again,
 A good black nag I will gie to thee;
He cost me twenty pounds o gowd
 Atween my brother John and me.'

10 'I winna turn, I canna turn;
 I darena turn and fight wi thee;
For they will find out Parcy Reed,
 And then they 'll kill baith thee and me.'

11 'O turn, O turn now, Willie Ha,
 O turn, O man, and fight wi me,
And if ever ye come to the Troughend again
 A yoke of owsen I will gie thee.'

12 'I winna turn, I canna turn;
 I darena turn and fight wi thee;
For they will find out Parcy Reed,
 And they will kill baith thee and me.'

13 'O turn, O turn, O Thommy Ha,
 O turn now, man, and fight wi me;
If ever ye come to the Troughend again,
 My daughter Jean I 'll gie to thee.'

14 'I winna turn, I darena turn;
 I winna turn and fight with thee;

For they will find out Parcy Reed,
 And then they 'll kill baith thee and me.'

15 'O woe be to ye, traitors a'!
 I wish England ye may never win;
Ye 've left me in the field to stand,
 And in my hand an uncharged gun.

16 'Ye 've taen frae me my powther-bag,
 And ye 've put water i my lang gun;
Ye 've put the sword into the sheath
 That out again it 'll never come.

17 'O fare ye weel, my married wife!
 And fare ye weel, my brother John!
That sits into the Troughend ha
 With heart as black as any stone.

18 'O fare ye weel, my married wife!
 And fare ye weel now, my sons five!
For had ye been wi me this day
 I surely had been man alive.

19 'O fare ye weel, my married wife!
 And fare ye weel now, my sons five!
And fare ye weel, my daughter Jean!
 I loved ye best ye were born alive.

20 'O some do ca me Parcy Reed,
 And some do ca me Laird Troughend,
But it 's nae matter what they ca me,
 My faes have made me ill to ken.

21 'The laird o Clennel wears my bow,
 The laird o Brandon wears my brand;
Whae ever rides i the Border side
 Will mind the laird o the Troughend.'

9². wi me. along with *in the margin.* 13³. ever I.
"There is," says Telfer in his letter, "a place
in Reed water called Deadwood Haughs, where
the country-people still point out a stone where
the unshriven soul of Parcy used to frequent
in the shape of a blue hawk, and it is only a few
years since he disappeared. . . . The ballad of
Parcy Reed has a tune of its own. . . . It is a
very mournfull air."

196. The Fire of Frendraught.

P. 39. Miscellanea Curiosa, MS., vol. vi, Abbotsford Library, A. 3, has for its last piece 'The Burning of the Tower of Frendraught, an Historical Ballad," in forty-eight stanzas. It begins:

O passd ye by the Bog of Gicht?
　　Heard ye the cry of grief and care?
Or in the bowers of Rothymay
　　Saw ye the lady tear her hair?

" A Satyre against Frendraught, in which ware
burned the Vicount of Melgum, Laird of Rothiemay,
and sundrie other gentlemen, in anno 1630," 218 lines,
MS. in a seventeenth-century hand, is No 1 in a volume with the title Scottish Tracts, Abbotsford Library,
B. 7. Mr. Macmath suggests that this may be the
" flyte" which Sharpe and Sir W. Scott thought of
printing.

200. The Gypsy Laddie.

IV, 61 b. 'Johnnie Faa' in [Wm Chambers's] Exploits . . . of the most remarkable Scottish Gypsies
or Tinklers, 3d ed., 1823, p. 17, is **B a**. The ballad
is not in the second edition, 1821, reprinted in 1886.
(W. Macmath.)

201. Bessy Bell and Mary Gray.

P. 75 b., first line. Say: **c**. Scott's Minstrelsy, 1830,
XI, 39, 1833, etc.

203. The Baron of Brackley.

P. 83, note †.
I prefer to say, two or more events. The citations
already given in this work may possibly cover four distinct tragedies, and William Anderson, in his Genealogy and Surnames, 1865, p. 104, tells us (but without
stating his authority) there was " a line of nine barons,
all of whom, in the unruly times in which they lived,
died violent deaths." The ballad may have com-
menced originally: " Inverawe (= Inner-Aw) cam
doun Deeside." (W. Macmath.)

208. Lord Derwentwater.

P. 117 b. The omen of nose-bleed occurs in the
Breton ballad 'Ervoan Camus,' Luzel, Soniou, I, 216.

211. Bewick and Graham.

P. 144 a. Scott's improved copy first appeared in
the third edition of the Minstrelsy, 1806, II, 277.

214. The Braes o Yarrow.

Q

P. 164 ff. 'The Dowie Dens of Yarrow,' Kidson's
Traditional Tunes, etc., 1891, p. 21. From Mrs Calvert,

of Gilnockie, Eskdale; obtained by her on the braes of
Yarrow from her grandmother, Tibbie Stuel. (Compare, especially, **J–L.**)

1 There lived a lady in the West,
　　I neer could find her marrow;
　She was courted by nine gentlemen,
　　And a ploughboy-lad in Yarrow.

2 These nine sat drinking at the wine,
　　Sat drinking wine in Yarrow;
　They made a vow among themselves
　　To fight for her in Yarrow.

3 She washed his face, she kaimed his hair,
　　As oft she'd done before, O,
　She made him like a knight sae bright,
　　To fight for her in Yarrow.

4 As he walked up yon high, high hill,
　　And down by the holmes of Yarrow,
　There he saw nine armëd men,
　　Come to fight with him in Yarrow.

5 'There's nine of you, there's one of me,
　　It's an unequal marrow;
　But I'll fight you all one by one,
　　On the dowie dens of Yarrow.'

6 Three he slew, and three they flew,
　　And three he wounded sorely,
　Till her brother John he came in beyond,
　　And pierced his heart most foully.

7 'Go home, go home, thou false young man,
　　And tell thy sister Sarah
　That her true-love John lies dead and gone
　　On the dowie dens of Yarrow.'

8 'O father dear, I dreamed a dream,
　　I'm afraid it will bring sorrow;
　I dreamed I was pulling the heather-bell
　　In the dowie dens of Yarrow.'

9 'O daughter dear, I read your dream,
　　I doubt it will prove sorrow;
　For your true-love John lies dead and gone
　　On the dowie dens of Yarrow.'

10 As she walked up yon high, high hill,
　　And down by the holmes of Yarrow,
　There she saw her true-love John,
　　Lying pale and dead on Yarrow.

11 Her hair it being three quarters long —
    The colour it was yellow —
    She wrapped it round his middle sma,
    And carried him hame to Yarrow.

12 'O father dear, you 've seven sons,
    You may wed them a' tomorrow,
    But a fairer flower I never saw
    Than the lad I loved in Yarrow.'

13 The fair maid being great with child,
    It filled her heart with sorrow;
    She died within her lover's arms,
    Between that day and morrow.

$6^{1.2}$. Three *misprinted* there.
8^1, 9^1, 12^1. Oh.

R

Macmath MS. p. 91. Inserted in a copy of The Scottish Ballads . . . by Robert Chambers, 1829, p. 145, latterly belonging to Rev. Dr James C. Burns, Free Church, Kirkliston.

1 There were three lords drinking at the wine
    In the Leader Haughs of Yarrow:
    'Shall we go play at cards and dice,
    As we have done before, O?
    Or shall we go play at the single sword,
    In the Leader Haughs of Yarrow?'

*   *   *   *   *   *   *

2 Three he wounded, and five he slew,
    As he had [done] before, O,
    But an English lord lap from a bush,
    And he proved all the sorrow;
    He had a spear three quarters long,
    And he thrust his body thorogh.

*   *   *   *   *   *   *

3 'I dreamed   .   .   .   .
    I wis it prove nae sorrow!
    I dreamed I was puing the apples green
    In the dowie howms o Yarrow.'

4 'O sister, sister, I 'll read your dream,
    And I 'll read it in sorrow;
    Ye may gae bring hame your ain true-love,
    For he 's sleepin sound in Yarrow.'

5 She sought him east, she sought him west,
    She sought him all the forest thorogh;
    She found him asleep at the middle yett,
    In the dowie howms o Yarrow.

6 Her hair it was three quarters lang,
    And the colour of it was yellow;
    She 's bound it round his middle waist,
    And borne him hame from Yarrow.

$1^{2.6}$. Leader Haughs. "Obviously nonsense, but so my minstreless sung it."
3^1. *The rest torn away.*
3^3. apples *substituted for* heather *struck out.*

217. The Broom of Cowdenknows.

P. 192. Mrs Greenwood, of London, had heard (presumably at Longnewton, near Jedburgh) "the old Cowdenknows, where, instead of the Laird of the Oakland hills, it is the Laird of the Hawthorn-wide." Letters addressed to Sir W. Scott, I, No 189, May 27, [1806.]

221. Katharine Jaffray.

P. 216 a. Scott's 'Katherine Janfarie' was printed in the second edition of the Minstrelsy, 1803, I, 238.

222. Bonny Baby Livingston.

P. 231 f. "I can get a copy of a ballad the repeating verse of which is:

    The Highlands are no for me,
        The Highlands are no for me;
    But gin ye wad my favour win
        Than carry me to Dundee.

His name is sometimes called Glendinnin, and his residence the same: however, I think it is a Highland ballad, from other circumstances." W. Laidlaw to Sir W. Scott, September 11, 1802: Letters, I, No 73. Compare D.

225. Rob Roy.

P. 243. The Harris MS. has one stanza, fol. 27 b, from Mrs Isdale, Dron, 'Robin Oigg's Elopement.'

    An they hae brocht her to a bed,
        An they hae laid her doun,
    An they 've taen aff her petticoat,
        An stript her o her goun.

226. Lizie Lindsay.

P. 255. Communicated by Mr Walker, of Aberdeen, as procured October 5, 1891, from George Nutchell, Ground Officer at Edzell Castle, who derived it from his step-grandmother Mrs Lamond (Nelly Low), fifty-eight years ago, she being at the time eighty years old.

1 'Will ye gang to the Highlands, Lizzie Lindsay?
    Will ye gang to the Highlands wi me?
Will ye gang to the Highlands, Lizzie Lindsay,
    My bride an my darling to be?'

2 She turned her round on her heel,
    And a very loud laugh gaed she:
'I'd like to ken whaur I'm ganging,
    An wha I am gaun to gang wi.'

3 'My name is Donald Macdonald,
    I'll never think shame nor deny;
My father he is an old shepherd,
    My mither she is an old dey.

4 'Will ye gang to the Highlands, bonnie Lizzie?
    Will ye gang to the Highlands wi me?
For ye shall get a bed o green rashes,
    A pillow an a covering o grey.'

5 Upraise then the bonny young lady,
    An drew till her stockings an sheen,
An packd up her claise in fine bundles,
    An away wi young Donald she's gaen.

6 When they cam near the end o their journey,
    To the house o his father's milk-dey,
He said, Stay still there, Lizzie Lindsay,
    Till I tell my mither o thee.

7 'Now mak us a supper, dear mither,
    The best o yer curds an green whey,
An mak up a bed o green rashes,
    A pillow an covering o grey.

8 'Rise up, rise up, Lizzie Lindsay,
    Ye have lain oer lang i the day;
Ye should hae been helping my mither
    To milk her ewes an her kye.'

9 Out then spak the bonnie young lady,
    As the saut tears drapt frae her ee,
'I wish I had bidden at hame;
    I can neither milk ewes or kye.'

10 'Rise up, rise up, Lizzie Lindsay,
    There is mair ferlies to spy;
For yonder's the castle o Kingussie,
    An it stands high an dry.'

11 'Ye are welcome here, Lizzie Lindsay,
    The flower o all your kin,
For ye shall be lady o Kingussie,
    An ye shall get Donald my son.'

243. James Harris.

P. 360 a. **B.** There is another, and perhaps slightly earlier, copy of The Rambler's Garland, British Museum, 11621, c. 2 (64), with a few trifling differences, for better or worse.

251. Lang Johnny More.

P. 396. 'Bennachie,' by Alex. Inkson McConnochie, Aberdeen, 1890, has a copy of this ballad, p. 66, longer by a few verses and with some verbal differences. But as this copy has been edited, though "without violence having been done," the variations, in themselves quite immaterial, do not demand registration.

To be Corrected in the Print.

I, 135 b, **P** 13². *Read* There's.
  188 b, line 15. *Read* 207.
  200 b, line 6. *Read* Vidyádharí.
  401 b, fourth paragraph, line 3 f. *Read* No 68, III, 117.
II, 10 a, eighth line from below. *Read* **B** *for* **C.**
  26 b 13¹. *Read* moon.
  84 b, last line of third paragraph. *Read* **G** 21.
  266, **B** 5³. *Read* you.
  428 b, **e.** *Read* 3⁴ *for* 3¹.
  482 b, third paragraph, last line. *Read* V, 101.
  507 a, Josefs Gedicht. Eighth line, *read* Den . . . in queme. First line of answer, *read* De; third, deme; seventh, konde.
III, 41 b, third paragraph, second line. *Read* MS. *for* Mr.
  264 a, 17⁴. *Read* hee.
  b 23². *Read* soe.
  276 a, line 7. *Read* queen's own son.
  281 a, 5². *Read* new.
  288 a, line 4 of the first paragraph. *Read* William Lord Douglas.
  b, line 16. *Read* wail.
  306 a, note *, fourth line. *Read* Minstrelsy, II, 325, ed. 1802.
  348 b [**A** 12¹]. *Read* sais. 15². *Read* mirrie.
  376 b, **G** 2¹. *Read* great.

379 a, 173, **A a**, first line. *Read* Sharpe's.

383 a, line 32. *Read* pavlovsk.

384 a, 5¹. *Read* was never.

397, **P** 1¹. *Read* father is.

435 a, **E** 5². *Read* loon.

448 a, **A**, heading. *Read* 1750.

459 a, 7¹. *Read* Buss. 10². *Read* o the Dun.

463 a, first line of citation from Maitland. *Read* spuilzie.

473 b, 24⁴. *Read* never.

475 b, citation from Maitland, line 5. *Read* ane guyd.

477 b, third paragraph, line 2. *Read* moss-trooper.

485 b, first paragraph, line 9 from the end. *Read* would.

489 b, **B** 9¹. *Read*, There (= There are) six.

499 a, **9**, line 8 f. *Read* Vuk, II, 376, No 64.

504 a, third line from the bottom. *Read* **O** *for* **J**.

504 b, third line. *Read* Rae.

505 a, 13⁴. *Read* And aye. 18¹. *Read* o the.

510 b. The note to p. 215 belongs under No 76.

IV, 6 a, 8¹. *Read* whan. (10¹. Gar seek in the early editions, Gae in ed. 1833.)

7 b, 41¹. *Read* thy kye.

8 a, 46³. *Read* dare.

18 a, 10³. *Read* Then. 12⁴. *Read* [to]. b, 19². *Read* Whan.

21 b, 17⁸. *Read* grey.

23 a, **A a**, fourth line. *Read* former [**B**].

28 a. Title of 194 **B**, Laird o Waristoun, in the MS. copy; Laird of Wariestoun, in the printed.

34 b, **B**. Lord Maxwell's Goodnight is the title in Scott's Minstrelsy. It is Lord Maxwell's Farewell in the Table of Contents of Glenriddell.

36 a, preface, last line but two, and b, line 3. *Read* Lord Maxwell *for* Lord John.

38 a, 11². *Read*, *perhaps*, fathers' : cf. their, in line 3.

45 b, **B** 7¹. *Read* he 's.

47 b, 18¹. *Read* Lady.

54 a, No 199, **B**. *Insert the title :* 'Bonny House of Airly.'

66 a, **B** 5¹. *Read* Gar . . . manteel.

68 a, **D**, third line. *Read* Corse *for* Cragievar.

69 a, 6⁸. *Read* Stincher. 8³. *Read* kill.

75 a, ninth line of preface. *Read* in his Poems.

76 a, fifth line. *Read* Beauchie.

81 b, seventeenth and twenty-fourth lines. *Read* Abergeldy.

82 b, note, first line. *Read* Brachally in Dee Water Side.

90 a, **E**. *Insert* 'Laird of Blackwood,' as the title of the printed copy.

91 a, tenth line of the second paragraph. *Read* after the birth of his son *for* after that event. note *. *Read* IV, 277 f, II, 449 f.

92 a, second line. *Read* **A, C**.

93 b, **A** 2¹. *Read* cam.

94 a, **B**, 1⁴. *Read* wont.

95 b, **B** 12⁸. *Read* I 'me. **C** 6⁴. *Read* country. 8¹˒². *Read* well.

96 a, **D** 3⁸. *Read* fire-boams.

105 a, sixth line of Appendix. *Read* Broadside.

110 b, No 207, **D**, third line. *Read* p. 135.

123 b, **I** b. *Strike out* (Lord ?) **K**. *Read* p. 370.

124 b, fifth paragraph, last line but four. *Read* Pitbagnet's.

129 a, 23³. *Read* feght. b, 28³. *Read* burd. **C** b. *Read* in Wilkie's hand, *dropping what follows.*

138 b, **C b** 12¹˒². *Read* Wanting, *for* A man spoke loud.

139 a, **I** b 3⁴, 4¹. *Read* Pitbagnet's.

152 b, 10³. *Read* showd.

153 b, 9². *Read* was.

155 a, second line after title. *After* library, *insert* P. 6.

157 a, 2². *Read* nourice.

168 a, 7². *Read* doon.

201 b, 26³. *Read* kye.

202 a, **K** 2². *Read* It is.

207 a, 20². *Read* them a' out.

212 a, 4³. *Read* sallads.

221 b, 13². *Read* grey.

224 b, 22¹. *Read* hes he.

226 a, 6³. *Read* Lammington.

248 a, 2². *Read* ladie.

A CATALOGUE OF SELECTED DOVER BOOKS
IN ALL FIELDS OF INTEREST

ALPHABETS AND ORNAMENTS, Ernst Lehner. Well-known pictorial source for decorative alphabets, script examples, cartouches, frames, decorative title pages, calligraphic initials, borders, similar material. 14th to 19th century, mostly European. Useful in almost any graphic arts designing, varied styles. 750 illustrations. 256pp. 7 x 10. 21905-4 Paperbound $4.00

PAINTING: A CREATIVE APPROACH, Norman Colquhoun. For the beginner simple guide provides an instructive approach to painting: major stumbling blocks for beginner; overcoming them, technical points; paints and pigments; oil painting; watercolor and other media and color. New section on "plastic" paints. Glossary. Formerly *Paint Your Own Pictures*. 221pp. 22000-1 Paperbound $1.75

THE ENJOYMENT AND USE OF COLOR, Walter Sargent. Explanation of the relations between colors themselves and between colors in nature and art, including hundreds of little-known facts about color values, intensities, effects of high and low illumination, complementary colors. Many practical hints for painters, references to great masters. 7 color plates, 29 illustrations. x + 274pp. 20944-X Paperbound $3.00

THE NOTEBOOKS OF LEONARDO DA VINCI, compiled and edited by Jean Paul Richter. 1566 extracts from original manuscripts reveal the full range of Leonardo's versatile genius: all his writings on painting, sculpture, architecture, anatomy, astronomy, geography, topography, physiology, mining, music, etc., in both Italian and English, with 186 plates of manuscript pages and more than 500 additional drawings. Includes studies for the Last Supper, the lost Sforza monument, and other works. Total of xlvii + 866pp. 7⅞ x 10¾. 22572-0, 22573-9 Two volumes, Paperbound $12.00

MONTGOMERY WARD CATALOGUE OF 1895. Tea gowns, yards of flannel and pillow-case lace, stereoscopes, books of gospel hymns, the New Improved Singer Sewing Machine, side saddles, milk skimmers, straight-edged razors, high-button shoes, spittoons, and on and on . . . listing some 25,000 items, practically all illustrated. Essential to the shoppers of the 1890's, it is our truest record of the spirit of the period. Unaltered reprint of Issue No. 57, Spring and Summer 1895. Introduction by Boris Emmet. Innumerable illustrations. xiii + 624pp. 8½ x 11⅝. 22377-9 Paperbound $8.50

THE CRYSTAL PALACE EXHIBITION ILLUSTRATED CATALOGUE (LONDON, 1851). One of the wonders of the modern world—the Crystal Palace Exhibition in which all the nations of the civilized world exhibited their achievements in the arts and sciences—presented in an equally important illustrated catalogue. More than 1700 items pictured with accompanying text—ceramics, textiles, cast-iron work, carpets, pianos, sleds, razors, wall-papers, billiard tables, beehives, silverware and hundreds of other artifacts—represent the focal point of Victorian culture in the Western World. Probably the largest collection of Victorian decorative art ever assembled—indispensable for antiquarians and designers. Unabridged republication of the Art-Journal Catalogue of the Great Exhibition of 1851, with all terminal essays. New introduction by John Gloag, F.S.A. xxxiv + 426pp. 9 x 12. 22503-8 Paperbound $5.00

A HISTORY OF COSTUME, Carl Köhler. Definitive history, based on surviving pieces of clothing primarily, and paintings, statues, etc. secondarily. Highly readable text, supplemented by 594 illustrations of costumes of the ancient Mediterranean peoples, Greece and Rome, the Teutonic prehistoric period; costumes of the Middle Ages, Renaissance, Baroque, 18th and 19th centuries. Clear, measured patterns are provided for many clothing articles. Approach is practical throughout. Enlarged by Emma von Sichart. 464pp. 21030-8 Paperbound $3.50

ORIENTAL RUGS, ANTIQUE AND MODERN, Walter A. Hawley. A complete and authoritative treatise on the Oriental rug—where they are made, by whom and how, designs and symbols, characteristics in detail of the six major groups, how to distinguish them and how to buy them. Detailed technical data is provided on periods, weaves, warps, wefts, textures, sides, ends and knots, although no technical background is required for an understanding. 11 color plates, 80 halftones, 4 maps. vi + 320pp. 6⅛ x 9⅛. 22366-3 Paperbound $5.00

TEN BOOKS ON ARCHITECTURE, Vitruvius. By any standards the most important book on architecture ever written. Early Roman discussion of aesthetics of building, construction methods, orders, sites, and every other aspect of architecture has inspired, instructed architecture for about 2,000 years. Stands behind Palladio, Michelangelo, Bramante, Wren, countless others. Definitive Morris H. Morgan translation. 68 illustrations. xii + 331pp. 20645-9 Paperbound $3.00

THE FOUR BOOKS OF ARCHITECTURE, Andrea Palladio. Translated into every major Western European language in the two centuries following its publication in 1570, this has been one of the most influential books in the history of architecture. Complete reprint of the 1738 Isaac Ware edition. New introduction by Adolf Placzek, Columbia Univ. 216 plates. xxii + 110pp. of text. 9½ x 12¾. 21308-0 Clothbound $12.50

STICKS AND STONES: A STUDY OF AMERICAN ARCHITECTURE AND CIVILIZATION, Lewis Mumford. One of the great classics of American cultural history. American architecture from the medieval-inspired earliest forms to the early 20th century; evolution of structure and style, and reciprocal influences on environment. 21 photographic illustrations. 238pp. 20202-X Paperbound $2.00

THE AMERICAN BUILDER'S COMPANION, Asher Benjamin. The most widely used early 19th century architectural style and source book, for colonial up into Greek Revival periods. Extensive development of geometry of carpentering, construction of sashes, frames, doors, stairs; plans and elevations of domestic and other buildings. Hundreds of thousands of houses were built according to this book, now invaluable to historians, architects, restorers, etc. 1827 edition. 59 plates. 114pp. 7⅞ x 10¾. 22236-5 Paperbound $4.00

DUTCH HOUSES IN THE HUDSON VALLEY BEFORE 1776, Helen Wilkinson Reynolds. The standard survey of the Dutch colonial house and outbuildings, with constructional features, decoration, and local history associated with individual homesteads. Introduction by Franklin D. Roosevelt. Map. 150 illustrations. 469pp. 6⅝ x 9¼. 21469-9 Paperbound $5.00

THE ARCHITECTURE OF COUNTRY HOUSES, Andrew J. Downing. Together with Vaux's *Villas and Cottages* this is the basic book for Hudson River Gothic architecture of the middle Victorian period. Full, sound discussions of general aspects of housing, architecture, style, decoration, furnishing, together with scores of detailed house plans, illustrations of specific buildings, accompanied by full text. Perhaps the most influential single American architectural book. 1850 edition. Introduction by J. Stewart Johnson. 321 figures, 34 architectural designs. xvi + 560pp.
22003-6 Paperbound $5.00

LOST EXAMPLES OF COLONIAL ARCHITECTURE, John Mead Howells. Full-page photographs of buildings that have disappeared or been so altered as to be denatured, including many designed by major early American architects. 245 plates. xvii + 248pp. 7⅞ x 10¾.
21143-6 Paperbound $3.50

DOMESTIC ARCHITECTURE OF THE AMERICAN COLONIES AND OF THE EARLY REPUBLIC, Fiske Kimball. Foremost architect and restorer of Williamsburg and Monticello covers nearly 200 homes between 1620-1825. Architectural details, construction, style features, special fixtures, floor plans, etc. Generally considered finest work in its area. 219 illustrations of houses, doorways, windows, capital mantels. xx + 314pp. 7⅞ x 10¾.
21743-4 Paperbound $4.00

EARLY AMERICAN ROOMS: 1650-1858, edited by Russell Hawes Kettell. Tour of 12 rooms, each representative of a different era in American history and each furnished, decorated, designed and occupied in the style of the era. 72 plans and elevations, 8-page color section, etc., show fabrics, wall papers, arrangements, etc. Full descriptive text. xvii + 200pp. of text. 8⅜ x 11¼.
21633-0 Paperbound $5.00

THE FITZWILLIAM VIRGINAL BOOK, edited by J. Fuller Maitland and W. B. Squire. Full modern printing of famous early 17th-century ms. volume of 300 works by Morley, Byrd, Bull, Gibbons, etc. For piano or other modern keyboard instrument; easy to read format. xxxvi + 938pp. 8⅜ x 11.
21068-5, 21069-3 Two volumes, Paperbound $12.00

KEYBOARD MUSIC, Johann Sebastian Bach. Bach Gesellschaft edition. A rich selection of Bach's masterpieces for the harpsichord: the six English Suites, six French Suites, the six Partitas (Clavierübung part I), the Goldberg Variations (Clavierübung part IV), the fifteen Two-Part Inventions and the fifteen Three-Part Sinfonias. Clearly reproduced on large sheets with ample margins; eminently playable. vi + 312pp. 8⅛ x 11.
22360-4 Paperbound $5.00

THE MUSIC OF BACH: AN INTRODUCTION, Charles Sanford Terry. A fine, nontechnical introduction to Bach's music, both instrumental and vocal. Covers organ music, chamber music, passion music, other types. Analyzes themes, developments, innovations. x + 114pp.
21075-8 Paperbound $1.95

BEETHOVEN AND HIS NINE SYMPHONIES, Sir George Grove. Noted British musicologist provides best history, analysis, commentary on symphonies. Very thorough, rigorously accurate; necessary to both advanced student and amateur music lover. 436 musical passages. vii + 407 pp.
20334-4 Paperbound $4.00

MATHEMATICAL PUZZLES FOR BEGINNERS AND ENTHUSIASTS, Geoffrey Mott-Smith. 189 puzzles from easy to difficult—involving arithmetic, logic, algebra, properties of digits, probability, etc.—for enjoyment and mental stimulus. Explanation of mathematical principles behind the puzzles. 135 illustrations. viii + 248pp.
20198-8 Paperbound $2.00

PAPER FOLDING FOR BEGINNERS, William D. Murray and Francis J. Rigney. Easiest book on the market, clearest instructions on making interesting, beautiful origami. Sail boats, cups, roosters, frogs that move legs, bonbon boxes, standing birds, etc. 40 projects; more than 275 diagrams and photographs. 94pp.
20713-7 Paperbound $1.00

TRICKS AND GAMES ON THE POOL TABLE, Fred Herrmann. 79 tricks and games— some solitaires, some for two or more players, some competitive games—to entertain you between formal games. Mystifying shots and throws, unusual caroms, tricks involving such props as cork, coins, a hat, etc. Formerly *Fun on the Pool Table*. 77 figures. 95pp.
21814-7 Paperbound $1.25

HAND SHADOWS TO BE THROWN UPON THE WALL: A SERIES OF NOVEL AND AMUSING FIGURES FORMED BY THE HAND, Henry Bursill. Delightful picturebook from great-grandfather's day shows how to make 18 different hand shadows: a bird that flies, duck that quacks, dog that wags his tail, camel, goose, deer, boy, turtle, etc. Only book of its sort. vi + 33pp. $6\frac{1}{2}$ x $9\frac{1}{4}$. 21779-5 Paperbound $1.00

WHITTLING AND WOODCARVING, E. J. Tangerman. 18th printing of best book on market. "If you can cut a potato you can carve" toys and puzzles, chains, chessmen, caricatures, masks, frames, woodcut blocks, surface patterns, much more. Information on tools, woods, techniques. Also goes into serious wood sculpture from Middle Ages to present, East and West. 464 photos, figures. x + 293pp.
20965-2 Paperbound $2.50

HISTORY OF PHILOSOPHY, Julián Marias. Possibly the clearest, most easily followed, best planned, most useful one-volume history of philosophy on the market; neither skimpy nor overfull. Full details on system of every major philosopher and dozens of less important thinkers from pre-Socratics up to Existentialism and later. Strong on many European figures usually omitted. Has gone through dozens of editions in Europe. 1966 edition, translated by Stanley Appelbaum and Clarence Strowbridge. xviii + 505pp.
21739-6 Paperbound $3.50

YOGA: A SCIENTIFIC EVALUATION, Kovoor T. Behanan. Scientific but non-technical study of physiological results of yoga exercises; done under auspices of Yale U. Relations to Indian thought, to psychoanalysis, etc. 16 photos. xxiii + 270pp.
20505-3 Paperbound $2.50